Lecture Notes in Computer Science 3687

Commenced Publication in 1973
Founding and Former Series Editors:
Gerhard Goos, Juris Hartmanis, and Jan van Leeuwen

Editorial Board

David Hutchison
   Lancaster University, UK
Takeo Kanade
   Carnegie Mellon University, Pittsburgh, PA, USA
Josef Kittler
   University of Surrey, Guildford, UK
Jon M. Kleinberg
   Cornell University, Ithaca, NY, USA
Friedemann Mattern
   ETH Zurich, Switzerland
John C. Mitchell
   Stanford University, CA, USA
Moni Naor
   Weizmann Institute of Science, Rehovot, Israel
Oscar Nierstrasz
   University of Bern, Switzerland
C. Pandu Rangan
   Indian Institute of Technology, Madras, India
Bernhard Steffen
   University of Dortmund, Germany
Madhu Sudan
   Massachusetts Institute of Technology, MA, USA
Demetri Terzopoulos
   New York University, NY, USA
Doug Tygar
   University of California, Berkeley, CA, USA
Moshe Y. Vardi
   Rice University, Houston, TX, USA
Gerhard Weikum
   Max-Planck Institute of Computer Science, Saarbruecken, Germany

Sameer Singh   Maneesha Singh
Chid Apte   Petra Perner (Eds.)

Pattern Recognition and Image Analysis

Third International Conference on
Advances in Pattern Recognition, ICAPR 2005
Bath, UK, August 22-25, 2005
Proceedings, Part II

 Springer

Volume Editors

Sameer Singh
Maneesha Singh
Loughborough University
Research School of Informatics
Loughborough LE11 3TU, UK
E-mail: {s.singh/m.singh}@lboro.ac.uk

Chid Apte
IBM Corporation
1133 Westchester Avenue, White Plains, New York 10604, US
E-mail: apte@us.ibm.com

Petra Perner
Institute of Computer Vision and Applied Computer Sciences, IBaI
Körnerstr 10, 04107 Leipzig, Germany
E-mail: ibaiperner@aol.com

Library of Congress Control Number: Applied for

CR Subject Classification (1998): I.5, I.4, H.2.8, I.2.6-7, I.3.5, I.7.5, F.2.2, K.5

ISSN   0302-9743
ISBN-10   3-540-28833-3 Springer Berlin Heidelberg New York
ISBN-13   978-3-540-28833-6 Springer Berlin Heidelberg New York

This work is subject to copyright. All rights are reserved, whether the whole or part of the material is concerned, specifically the rights of translation, reprinting, re-use of illustrations, recitation, broadcasting, reproduction on microfilms or in any other way, and storage in data banks. Duplication of this publication or parts thereof is permitted only under the provisions of the German Copyright Law of September 9, 1965, in its current version, and permission for use must always be obtained from Springer. Violations are liable to prosecution under the German Copyright Law.

Springer is a part of Springer Science+Business Media

springeronline.com

© Springer-Verlag Berlin Heidelberg 2005
Printed in Germany

Typesetting: Camera-ready by author, data conversion by Scientific Publishing Services, Chennai, India
Printed on acid-free paper   SPIN: 11552499   06/3142   5 4 3 2 1 0

Preface

This LNCS volume contains the papers presented at the 3rd International Conference on Advances in Pattern Recognition (ICAPR 2005) organized in August, 2005 in the beautiful city of Bath, UK. The conference was first organized in November 1998 in Plymouth, UK and subsequently in March 2001 in Rio de Janeiro, Brazil. The conference encouraged papers that made significant theoretical and application-based contributions in pattern recognition. The emphasis was on an open exchange of ideas and shared learning. The papers submitted to ICAPR 2005 were thoroughly reviewed by up to three referees per paper and less than 40% of the submitted papers were accepted. The papers have been finally published as two volumes of LNCS and these are organized under the themes of Pattern Recognition and Data Mining (which included papers from the tracks on Pattern Recognition Methods, Knowledge and Learning, and Data Mining), and Pattern Recognition and Image Analysis (which included papers from the Applications track). From the conference technical programme point of view, the first volume contains papers on pattern recognition, data mining, signal processing and OCR/document analysis. The second volume contains papers from the Workshop on Pattern Recognition for Crime Prevention, Security and Surveillance, Biometrics, Image Processing and Medical Imaging.

ICAPR 2005 was run in parallel with the International Workshop on Pattern Recognition for Crime Prevention, Security and Surveillance that was organized on the 22nd of August, 2005. This workshop brought together a number of excellent papers that focussed on how pattern recognition techniques can be used to develop systems that help with crime prevention and detection. On the same day, a number of tutorials were also organized. Each tutorial focussed on a specific research area and gave an exhaustive overview of the scientific tools and state-of-the-art research in that area. The tutorials organized dealt with the topics of Computational Face Recognition (given by Dr. Babback Moghaddam, MERL, USA), 2-D and 3-D Level Set Applications for Medical Imagery (given by Dr. Jasjit Suri, Biomedical Technologies, USA; Dr. Gilson Antonio Giraldi, National Laboratory of Computer Science, Brazil; Prof. Sameer Singh, Loughborough University, UK; and Prof. Swamy Laxminarayan, Idaho State University, USA), Geometric Graphs for Instance-Based Learning (given by Prof. Godfried Toussaint, McGill University, Canada), and Dissimilarity Representations in Pattern Recognition (given by Prof. Bob Duin and Elzbieta Pekalska, Delft University of Technology, The Netherlands).

The conference also had three plenary speeches that were much appreciated by the audience. On the first day of the conference, Prof. David Hogg from the University of Leeds, UK gave an excellent speech on learning from objects and activities. On the second day of the conference Prof. Ingemar Cox from University College London, UK gave the second plenary speech. On the final day of the conference Prof. John Oommen from Carlton University, Canada gave a plenary speech on the general problem of syntactic pattern recognition and string processing.

ICAPR was a fully reviewed and well-run conference. We would like to thank a number of people for their contribution to the review process, especially the Program Chairs, Tutorial Chair Dr. Majid Mirmehdi and Workshops Chair Prof. Marco Gori. The members of the Program Committee did an excellent job with reviewing most of the papers. Some papers were also reviewed by academics who were not in the committee and we thank them for their efforts. We would also like to thank the local arrangements committee and University of Bath Conference Office for their efforts in ensuring that the conference ran smoothly. In particular, our thanks are due to Dr. Maneesha Singh, Organizing Chair and Mr. Harish Bhaskar, Organizing Manager who both worked tirelessly. The conference was supported by the British Computer Society and a number of local companies within the UK. We would like to thank Springer in extending their support to publish the proceedings as LNCS volumes. Finally, we thank all the delegates who attended the conference and made it a success.

August 2005

Sameer Singh
Maneesha Singh
Chid Apte
Petra Perner

Organization

Executive Committee

Conference Chair	Sameer Singh (Loughborough University, UK)
Program Chairs	Chid Apte (IBM, New York, USA)
	Petra Perner (University of Leipzig, Germany)
Organizing Chair	Sameer Singh (Loughborough University, UK)
	Maneesha Singh (Loughborough University, UK)
Organizing Manager	Harish Bhaskar (Loughborough University, UK)
Tutorials and Demonstrations	Majid Mirmehdi (University of Bristol, UK)
Workshops	Marco Gori (University of Siena, Italy)

Program Committee

Edward J. Delp
Purdue University, USA

Christophe Garcia
France Télécom R&D, France

Mohamed Cheriet
University of Quebec, Canada

J. Ross Beveridge
Colorado State University, USA

Horst Haussecker
Intel, USA

Roger Boyle
University of Leeds, UK

Nozha Boujemaa
INRIA, France

Xiang "Sean" Zhou
Siemens Corporate Research Inc., USA

Hassan Foroosh
University of Central Florida, USA

Venu Govindaraju
State University of New York, Buffalo, USA

Mubarak Shah
University of Central Florida, USA

B.B. Chaudhuri
Indian Statistical Institute, India

Horst Bischof
Technical University Graz, Austria

Edwin Hancock
University of York, UK

Andrew Calway
University of Bristol, UK

Terry Caelli
ANU, Australia

Fionn Murtagh
Royal Holloway, UK

Filiberto Pla
Universitat Jaume I, Spain

Andreas Dengel
German Research Center for Artificial Intelligence, Germany

Isabelle Bloch
Telecom Paris, France

Zhengyou Zhang
Microsoft Research, USA

Daming Shi
Nanyang Technological University, Singapore

Miroslaw Pawlak
University of Manitoba, Canada

Jasjit Suri
Biomedical Technologies, USA

Peter Meer
Rutgers University, USA

Rae-Hong Park
Sogang University, Korea

Ajay Divakaran
MERL, USA

Bob Duin
Technical University Delft, Netherlands

Ludmila Kuncheva
University of Wales, Bangor, UK

Godfried Toussaint
McGill University, Canada

Daniel Lopresti
Lehigh University, USA

Vittorio Murino
University of Verona, Italy

Geoff West
Curtin University, Australia

Alberto del Bimbo
University of Florence, Italy

Jesse Jin
University of Newcastle, Australia

Louisa Lam
Hong Kong Institute of Education, China

Adnan Amin
University of New South Wales,
Australia

Kobus Barnard
University of Arizona at Tucson, USA

Hans Burkhardt
University of Freiburg, Germany

Witold Pedrycz
University of Alberta, Canada

Patrick Bouthemy
IRISA, France

Xiaoyi Jiang
University of Munster, Germany

XiaoHui Liu
Brunel University, UK

David Maltoni
University of Bologna, Italy

Sudeep Sarkar
University of South Florida, USA

Mayer Aladjem
Ben-Gurion University, Israel

Jan Flusser
Academy of Sciences of the
Czech Republic, Czech Republic

Vladimir Pavlovic
Rutgers University, USA

Jean-Michel Jolion
INSA, France

Ingemar Cox
University College London, UK

Michal Haindl
Academy of Sciences of the
Czech Republic, Czech Republic

Luigi Cordella
University of Napoli, Italy

Ales Leonardis
University of Ljubljana, Slovenia

Ata Kaban
University of Birmingham, UK

Mike Fairhurst
University of Kent, UK

Sven Loncaric
University of Zagreb, Croatia

Boaz Lerner
Ben-Gurion University, Israel

Mohamed Kamel
University of Waterloo, Canada

Peter Tino
University of Birmingham, UK

Richard Everson
University of Exeter, UK

Hiromichi Fujisawa
Central Research Laboratory, Hitachi,
Japan

Ian Nabney
Aston University, UK

Wojtek Krzanowski
University of Exeter, UK

Andrew Martin
University College London, UK

Steve Oliver
University of Manchester, UK

David Hoyle
University of Exeter, UK

Malcolm Strens
QinetiQ, UK

John McCall
Robert Gordon University, UK

Rachel Martin
Shimadzu-Biotech, UK

Herv Bourlard
Swiss Federal Institute of Technology, Switzerland

Mario Figueiredo
Inst. for Telecommunication, Portugal

Matthew Turk
University of California, USA

Nicu Sebe
University of Amsterdam, Netherlands

Ana Fred
Inst. of Telecommunication, Portugal

Mario Vento
University of Salerno, Italy

Fabio Roli
University of Cagliari, Italy

B.S. Manjunath
University of California, USA

Edoardo Ardizzone
University of Palermo, Italy

David Parry-Smith
Purely Proteins, UK

Gerhard Rigoll
Munich University of Technology, UK

Mark Last
Ben-Gurion University, Israel

Theo Gevers
University of Amsterdam, Netherlands

Mads Nielsen
University of Copenhagen, Denmark

Mohamed Kamel
University of Waterloo, Canada

Jonathan Hull
Ricoh Innovations Inc., USA

Paulo Lisboa
Liverpool John Moores University, UK

Steve Maybank
Birkbeck College, UK

Andrew Webb
QinetiQ, UK

John McCall
Robert Gordon University, UK

Heinrich Niemann
Universitaet Erlangen-Nuernberg, Germany

Table of Contents – Part II

International Workshop on Pattern Recognition for Crime Prevention, Security and Surveillance

Image Enhancement Optimization for Hand-Luggage Screening at Airports
  Maneesha Singh, Sameer Singh 1

Parameter Optimization for Image Segmentation Algorithms: A Systematic Approach
  Maneesha Singh, Sameer Singh, Derek Partridge 11

Fingerprint Image Enhancement Using STFT Analysis
  Sharat Chikkerur, Venu Govindaraju, Alexander N. Cartwright 20

Symmetric Hash Functions for Fingerprint Minutiae
  Sergey Tulyakov, Faisal Farooq, Venu Govindaraju 30

A Digital Rights Management Approach for Gray-Level Images
  Shu-Fen Tu, Ching-Sheng Hsu 39

Millimetre-Wave Personnel Scanners for Automated Weapon Detection
  *Beatriz Grafulla-González, Christopher D. Haworth,
  Andrew R. Harvey, Katia Lebart, Yvan R. Petillot,
  Yves de Saint-Pern, Mathilde Tomsin, Emanuele Trucco* 48

A Thermal Hand Vein Pattern Verification System
  Lingyu Wang, Graham Leedham 58

Illumination Tolerant Face Recognition Using Phase-Only Support Vector Machines in the Frequency Domain
  Jingu Heo, Marios Savvides, B.V.K. Vijayakumar 66

Regional and Online Learnable Fields
  Rolf Schatten, Nils Goerke, Rolf Eckmiller 74

Spatial Feature Based Recognition of Human Dynamics in Video Sequences
  Jessica JunLin Wang, Sameer Singh 84

Using Behavior Knowledge Space and Temporal Information for
Detecting Intrusions in Computer Networks
L.P. Cordella, I. Finizio, C. Mazzariello, C. Sansone 94

Biometrics

View Independent Video-Based Face Recognition Using Posterior
Probability in Kernel Fisher Discriminant Space
Kazuhiro Hotta 103

Attention Based Facial Symmetry Detection
Fred Stentiford 112

An Efficient Iris Segmentation Method for Recognition
XiaoFu He, PengFei Shi 120

Multi-scale Palmprint Recognition Using Registration Information and
2D Gabor Feature
Liang Li, Jie Tian, Yuliang Hi, Xin Yang 127

Effects of JPEG and JPEG2000 Compression on Face Recognition
Kresimir Delac, Mislav Grgic, Sonja Grgic 136

3D Action Modeling and Reconstruction for 2D Human Body Tracking
Ignasi Rius, Daniel Rowe, Jordi González, F. Xavier Roca 146

A Non-parametric Dimensionality Reduction Technique Using Gradient
Descent of Misclassification Rate
S. Redmond, C. Heneghan 155

On the Automatic 2D Retinal Vessel Extraction
C. Alonso-Montes, D.L. Vilariño, M.G. Penedo 165

Modeling Phase Spectra Using Gaussian Mixture Models for Human
Face Identification
Sinjini Mitra, Marios Savvides, Anthony Brockwell 174

Belief Theory Applied to Facial Expressions Classification
Zakia Hammal, A. Caplier, M. Rombaut 183

Face Recognition Using Uncorrelated, Weighted Linear Discriminant
Analysis
Yixiong Liang, Weiguo Gong, Yingjun Pan, Weihong Li 192

Face Recognition Using Heteroscedastic Weighted Kernel Discriminant
Analysis
    Yixiong Liang, Weiguo Gong, Weihong Li, Yingjun Pan 199

Class-Specific Discriminant Non-negative Matrix Factorization for
Frontal Face Verification
    Stefanos Zafeiriou, Anastasios Tefas, Ioan Buciu, Ioannis Pitas 206

Partial Relevance in Interactive Facial Image Retrieval
    Zhirong Yang, Jorma Laaksonen 216

An Integration of Biometrics and Mobile Computing for Personal
Identification
    J. You, K.H. Cheung, Q. Li, P. Bhattacharya 226

Eyes Segmentation Applied to Gaze Direction and Vigilance Estimation
    Zakia Hammal, Corentin Massot, Guillermo Bedoya, Alice Caplier ... 236

Bilinear Discriminant Analysis for Face Recognition
    Muriel Visani, Christophe Garcia, Jean-Michel Jolion 247

Adaptive Object Recognition Using Context-Aware Genetic Algorithm
Under Dynamic Environment
    Mi Young Nam, Phill Kyu Rhee 257

A Multi-scale and Multi-pose Face Detection System
    Mi-Young Nam, Phill-Kyu Rhee 268

Conditionally Dependent Classifier Fusion Using AND Rule for
Improved Biometric Verification
    Krithika Venkataramani, B.V.K. Vijaya Kumar 277

Measurement of Face Recognizability for Visual Surveillance
    Hsi-Jian Lee, Yu-Cheng Tsao 287

A Fingerprint Authentication Mobile Phone Based on Sweep Sensor
    Qi Su, Jie Tian, Xinjian Chen, Xin Yang 295

A Robust and Efficient Algorithm for Eye Detection on Gray Intensity
Face
    Kun Peng, Liming Chen, Su Ruan, Georgy Kukharev 302

Silhouette Spatio-temporal Spectrum (SStS) for Gait-Based Human
Recognition
    Toby H.W. Lam, Tony W.H. Ao Ieong, Raymond S.T. Lee 309

Adaptive Estimation of Human Posture Using a Component-Based Model
Kyoung-Mi Lee 316

Fusion of Locally Linear Embedding and Principal Component Analysis for Face Recognition (FLLEPCA)
Eimad Eldin Abusham, David Ngo, Andrew Teoh 326

Proposal of Novel Histogram Features for Face Detection
Haijing Wang, Student Member (IEEE), Peihua Li, Tianwen Zhang 334

Feature Selection Based on KPCA, SVM and GSFS for Face Recognition
Weihong Li, Weiguo Gong, Yixiong Liang, Weiming Chen 344

Eigen and Fisher-Fourier Spectra for Shift Invariant Pose-Tolerant Face Recognition
Ramamurthy Bhagavatula, Marios Savvides 351

Image Processing

Q-Gram Statistics Descriptor in 3D Shape Classification
Evgeny Ivanko, Denis Perevalov 360

A New Inpainting Method for Highlights Elimination by Colour Morphology
Francisco Ortiz, Fernando Torres 368

Clustering of Objects in 3D Electron Tomography Reconstructions of Protein Solutions Based on Shape Measurements
Magnus Gedda 377

Improving Tracking by Handling Occlusions
Daniel Rowe, Ignasi Rius, Jordi Gonzàlez, Juan J. Villanueva 384

Image Reconstruction with Polar Zernike Moments
Yongqing Xin, Miroslaw Pawlak, Simon Liao 394

Texture Exemplars for Defect Detection on Random Textures
Xianghua Xie, Majid Mirmehdi 404

Semantic-Based Cross-Media Image Retrieval
Ahmed Id Oumohmed, Max Mignotte, Jian-Yun Nie 414

Texture Image Retrieval: A Feature-Based Correspondence Method in
Fourier Spectrum
  *Celia A. Zorzo Barcelos, Márcio J.R. Ferreira,
  Mylene L. Rodrigues* 424

Surface Reconstruction from Stereo Data Using Three-Dimensional
Markov Random Field Model
  Hotaka Takizawa, Shinji Yamamoto 434

Unsupervised Markovian Segmentation on Graphics Hardware
  Pierre-Marc Jodoin, Jean-François St-Amour, Max Mignotte 444

Texture Detection for Image Analysis
  Sébastien Chabrier, Bruno Emile, Christophe Rosenberger 455

Evaluation of the Quality of Ultrasound Image Compression by Fusion
of Criteria with a Genetic Algorithm
  C. Delgorge, C. Rosenberger, G. Poisson, P. Vieyres 464

3D Model Retrieval Based on Adaptive Views Clustering
  Tarik Filali Ansary, Mohamed Daoudi, Jean-Phillipe Vandeborre 473

Colour Texture Segmentation Using Modelling Approach
  Michal Haindl, Stanislav Mikeš 484

Human-Centered Object-Based Image Retrieval
  Egon L. van den Broek, Eva M. van Rikxoort, Theo E. Schouten 492

Multi-scale Midline Extraction Using Creaseness
  Kai Rothaus, Xiaoyi Jiang 502

Automatic Indexing of News Videos Through Text Classification
Techniques
  G. Percannella, D. Sorrentino, M. Vento 512

Weighted Adaptive Neighborhood Hypergraph Partitioning for Image
Segmentation
  Soufiane Rital, Hocine Cherifi, Serge Miguet 522

Parallel-Sequential Texture Analysis
  Egon L. van den Broek, Eva M. van Rikxoort 532

Region Growing with Automatic Seeding for Semantic Video Object
Segmentation
  Yue Feng, Hui Fang, Jianmin Jiang 542

Object Coding for Real Time Image Processing Applications
  Asif Masood, Shaiq A. Haq 550

Designing a Fast Convolution Under the LIP Paradigm Applied to
Edge Detection
  José M. Palomares, Jesús González, Eduardo Ros 560

Local Feature Saliency for Texture Representation
  M.K. Bashar, N. Ohnishi, K. Agusa 570

A Segmentation Algorithm for Rock Fracture Detection
  Weixing Wang, Eva Hakami 580

ELIS: An Efficient Leaf Image Retrieval System
  Yunyoung Nam, Eenjun Hwang, Kwangjun Byeon 589

Mosaicing and Restoration from Blurred Image Sequence Taken with
Moving Camera
  Midori Onogi, Hideo Saito 598

Finding People in Video Streams by Statistical Modeling
  S. Harasse, L. Bonnaud, M. Desvignes 608

Camera Motion Estimation by Image Feature Analysis
  Thitiporn Lertrusdachakul, Terumasa Aoki, Hiroshi Yasuda 618

Shape Retrieval by Principal Components Descriptor
  Binhai Wang, Andrew J. Bangham, Yanong Zhu 626

Automatic Monitoring of Forbidden Areas to Prevent Illegal Accesses
  *M. Leo, T. D'Orazio, A. Caroppo, T. Martiriggiano,
  P. Spagnolo* 635

Dynamic Time Warping of Cyclic Strings for Shape Matching
  Andrés Marzal, Vicente Palazón 644

Meeting the Application Requirements of Intelligent Video Surveillance
Systems in Moving Object Detection
  *Donatello Conte, Pasquale Foggia, Michele Petretta,
  Francesco Tufano, Mario Vento* 653

Classification Using Scale and Rotation Tolerant Shape Signatures
from Convex Hulls
  Muhammad Zaheer Aziz, Baerbel Mertsching, Asim Munir 663

On the Filter Combination for Efficient Image Preprocessing Under Uneven Illumination
    Mi Young Nam, Phill Kyu Rhee 673

Image Merging Based on Perceptual Information
    Mohd. Shahid, Sumana Gupta 683

An Automated Video Annotation System
    Wei Ren, Sameer Singh 693

Tracking by Cluster Analysis of Feature Points and Multiple Particle Filters
    Wei Du, Justus Piater 701

Medical Imaging

A Benchmark for Indoor/Outdoor Scene Classification
    Andrew Payne, Sameer Singh 711

Spinal Deformity Detection Employing Back Propagation on Neural Network
    Hyoungseop Kim, Joo kooi Tan, Seiji Ishikawa, Marzuki Khalid, Max Viergever, Yoshinori Otsuka, Takashi Shinomiya 719

Bone Segmentation in Metacarpophalangeal MR Data
    Olga Kubassova, Roger D. Boyle, Mike Pyatnizkiy 726

Lung Field Segmentation in Digital Postero-Anterior Chest Radiographs
    Paola Campadelli, Elena Casiraghi 736

Relationship Between the Stroma Edge and Skin-Air Boundary for Generating a Dependency Approach to Skin-Line Estimation in Screening Mammograms
    Yajie Sun, Jasjit Suri, Rangaraj Rangayyan, Roman Janer 746

Segmentation of Erythema from Skin Photographs for Assisted Diagnosis in Allergology
    Elodie Roullot, Jean-Eric Autegarden, Patrick Devriendt, Francisque Leynadier 754

Learning Histopathological Microscopy
    James Shuttleworth, Alison Todman, Mark Norrish, Mark Bennett ... 764

An Adaptive Rule Based Automatic Lung Nodule Detection System
    Maciej Dajnowiec, Javad Alirezaie, Paul Babyn 773

Experiments with SVM and Stratified Sampling with an Imbalanced
Problem: Detection of Intestinal Contractions
*Fernando Vilariño, Panagiota Spyridonos, Petia Radeva,
Jordi Vitrià* 783

Multiple Particle Tracking for Live Cell Imaging with Green Fluorescent
Protein (GFP) Tagged Videos
Sameer Singh, Harish Bhaskar, Jeremy Tavare, Gavin Welsh 792

Author Index 805

Table of Contents – Part I

Pattern Recognition and Data Mining

Enhancing Trie-Based Syntactic Pattern Recognition Using AI Heuristic Search Strategies
  Ghada Badr, B. John Oommen 1

Mathematical Features for Recognizing Preference in Sub-saharan African Traditional Rhythm Timelines
  Godfried Toussaint 18

Empirical Bounds on Error Differences When Using Naive Bayes
  Zoë Hoare 28

Effective Probability Forecasting for Time Series Data Using Standard Machine Learning Techniques
  David Lindsay, Siân Cox 35

A Continuous Weighted Low-Rank Approximation for Collaborative Filtering Problems
  Nicoletta Del Buono, Tiziano Politi 45

GP Ensemble for Distributed Intrusion Detection Systems
  Gianluigi Folino, Clara Pizzuti, Giandomenico Spezzano 54

Clustered Trie Structures for Approximate Search in Hierarchical Objects Collections
  R. Giugno, A. Pulvirenti, D. Reforgiato Recupero 63

On Adaptive Confidences for Critic-Driven Classifier Combining
  Matti Aksela, Jorma Laaksonen 71

The RW2 Algorithm for Exact Graph Matching
  Marco Gori, Marco Maggini, Lorenzo Sarti 81

Making Use of Unelaborated Advice to Improve Reinforcement Learning: A Mobile Robotics Approach
  David L. Moreno, Carlos V. Regueiro, Roberto Iglesias, Senén Barro 89

Consolidated Trees: Classifiers with Stable Explanation. A Model to Achieve the Desired Stability in Explanation
Jesús M. Pérez, Javier Muguerza, Olatz Arbelaitz, Ibai Gurrutxaga, José I. Martín 99

Discovering Predictive Variables When Evolving Cognitive Models
Peter C.R. Lane, Fernand Gobet 108

Mathematical Morphology and Binary Geodesy for Robot Navigation Planning
F. Ortiz, S. Puente, F. Torres 118

Neural Network Classification: Maximizing Zero-Error Density
Luís M. Silva, Luís A. Alexandre, J. Marques de Sá 127

Taxonomy of Classifiers Based on Dissimilarity Features
Sarunas Raudys 136

Combination of Boosted Classifiers Using Bounded Weights
Hakan Altınçay, Ali Tüzel 146

Prediction of Commodity Prices in Rapidly Changing Environments
Sarunas Raudys, Indre Zliobaite 154

Develop Multi-hierarchy Classification Model: Rough Set Based Feature Decomposition Method
Qingdong Wang, Huaping Dai, Youxian Sun 164

On Fitting Finite Dirichlet Mixture Using ECM and MML
Nizar Bouguila, Djemel Ziou 172

Disease Classification from Capillary Electrophoresis: Mass Spectrometry
Simon Rogers, Mark Girolami, Ronald Krebs, Harald Mischak 183

Analyzing Large Image Databases with the Evolving Tree
Jussi Pakkanen, Jukka Iivarinen 192

A Sequence Labeling Method Using Syntactical and Textual Patterns for Record Linkage
Atsuhiro Takasu 199

Recognition Tasks Are Imitation Games
Richard Zanibbi, Dorothea Blostein, James R. Cordy 209

Use of Input Deformations with Brownian Motion Filters for
Discontinuous Regression
    Ramūnas Girdziušas, Jorma Laaksonen 219

Hierarchical Clustering of Dynamical Systems Based on Eigenvalue
Constraints
    Hiroaki Kawashima, Takashi Matsuyama 229

An Optimally Weighted Fuzzy k-NN Algorithm
    Tuan D. Pham 239

A Tabu Search Based Method for Minimum Sum of Squares Clustering
    Yongguo Liu, Libin Wang, Kefei Chen 248

Approximation of Digital Circles by Regular Polygons
    Partha Bhowmick, Bhargab B. Bhattacharya 257

A Novel Feature Fusion Method Based on Partial Least Squares
Regression
    Quan-Sen Sun, Zhong Jin, Pheng-Ann Heng, De-Shen Xia 268

Combining Text and Link Analysis for Focused Crawling
    George Almpanidis, Constantine Kotropoulos 278

A Weighting Initialization Strategy for Weighted Support Vector
Machines
    Kuo-Ping Wu, Sheng-De Wang 288

Configuration of Neural Networks for the Analysis of Seasonal Time
Series
    T. Taskaya-Temizel, M.C. Casey 297

Boosting Feature Selection
    D.B. Redpath, K. Lebart 305

Similarity Searching in Image Retrieval with Statistical Distance
Measures and Supervised Learning
    Md. Mahmudur Rahman, Prabir Bhattacharya, Bipin C. Desai 315

Using Patterns to Generate Prime Numbers
    Udayan Khurana, Anirudh Koul 325

Empirical Study on Weighted Voting Multiple Classifiers
    Yanmin Sun, Mohamed S. Kamel, Andrew K.C. Wong 335

Spectral Clustering for Time Series
  Fei Wang, Changshui Zhang 345

A New EM Algorithm for Resource Allocation Network
  Kyoung-Mi Lee 355

A Biased Support Vector Machine Approach to Web Filtering
  A-Ning Du, Bin-Xing Fang, Bin Li 363

A New Approach to Generate Frequent Patterns from Enterprise
Databases
  Yu-Chin Liu, Ping-Yu Hsu 371

Consolidated Tree Classifier Learning in a Car Insurance Fraud
Detection Domain with Class Imbalance
  *Jesús M. Pérez, Javier Muguerza, Olatz Arbelaitz, Ibai Gurrutxaga,
  José I. Martín* 381

Missing Data Estimation Using Polynomial Kernels
  *Maxime Berar, Michel Desvignes, Gérard Bailly, Yohan Payan,
  Barbara Romaniuk* 390

Predictive Model for Protein Function Using Modular Neural Approach
  *Doosung Hwang, Ungmo Kim, Jaehun Choi, Jeho Park,
  Janghee Yoo* 400

Using kNN Model for Automatic Feature Selection
  Gongde Guo, Daniel Neagu, Mark T.D. Cronin 410

Multi-view EM Algorithm for Finite Mixture Models
  Xing Yi, Yunpeng Xu, Changshui Zhang 420

Segmentation Evaluation Using a Support Vector Machine
  *Sébastien Chabrier, Christophe Rosenberger, Hélène Laurent,
  Alain Rakotomamonjy* 426

Detection of Spots in 2-D Electrophoresis Gels by Symmetry Features
  Martin Persson, Josef Bigun 436

Analysis of MHC-Peptide Binding Using Amino Acid Property-Based
Decision Rules
  Jochen Supper, Pierre Dönnes, Oliver Kohlbacher 446

Accuracy of String Kernels for Protein Sequence Classification
  J. Dylan Spalding, David C. Hoyle 454

An Efficient Feature Selection Method for Object Detection
  Duy-Dinh Le, Shin'ichi Satoh 461

Multi-SOMs: A New Approach to Self Organised Classification
  Nils Goerke, Florian Kintzler, Rolf Eckmiller 469

Selection of Classifiers Using Information-Theoretic Criteria
  Hee-Joong Kang 478

ICA and GA Feature Extraction and Selection for Cloud Classification
  *Miguel Macías-Macías, Carlos J. García-Orellana,
  Horacio González-Velasco, Ramón Gallardo-Caballero* 488

Signal Processing

A Study on Robustness of Large Vocabulary Mandarin Chinese Continuous Speech Recognition System Based on Wavelet Analysis
  Long Yan, Gang Liu, Jun Guo 497

Recognition of Insect Emissions Applying the Discrete Wavelet Transform
  *Carlos García Puntonet, Juan-José González de-la-Rosa,
  Isidro Lloret Galiana, Juan Manuel Górriz* 505

On the Performance of Hurst-Vectors for Speaker Identification Systems
  R. Sant'Ana, R. Coelho, A. Alcaim 514

Transformations of LPC and LSF Parameters to Speech Recognition Features
  Vladimir Fabregas Surigué de Alencar, Abraham Alcaim 522

Redshift Determination for Quasar Based on Similarity Measure
  Fuqing Duan, Fuchao Wu 529

Learning with Segment Boundaries for Hierarchical HMMs
  Naoto Gotou, Akira Hayashi, Nobuo Suematu 538

A Bayesian Method for High-Frequency Restoration of Low Sample-Rate Speech
  Yunpeng Xu, Changshui Zhang, Naijiang Lu 544

Probabilistic Tangent Subspace Method for Multiuser Detection
  Jing Yang, Yunpeng Xu, Hongxing Zou 553

OCR/Document Analysis

Feature Extraction for Handwritten Chinese Character by Weighted Dynamic Mesh Based on Nonlinear Normalization
Guang Chen, Hong-Gang Zhang, Jun Guo 560

Post Processing of Handwritten Phonetic Pitman's Shorthand Using a Bayesian Network Built on Geometric Attributes
Swe Myo Htwe, Colin Higgins, Graham Leedham, Ma Yang 569

Ancient Printed Documents Indexation: A New Approach
Nicholas Journet, Rémy Mullot, Jean-Yves Ramel, Veronique Eglin 580

Applying Software Analysis Technology to Lightweight Semantic Markup of Document Text
Nadzeya Kiyavitskaya, Nicola Zeni, James R. Cordy, Luisa Mich, John Mylopoulos 590

Noisy Digit Classification with Multiple Specialist
Andoni Cortes, Fernando Boto, Clemente Rodriguez 601

Automatic Table Detection in Document Images
Basilios Gatos, Dimitrios Danatsas, Ioannis Pratikakis, Stavros J. Perantonis 609

High Performance Classifiers Combination for Handwritten Digit Recognition
Hubert Cecotti, Szilárd Vajda, Abdel Belaïd 619

A Novel Approach for Text Detection in Images Using Structural Features
H. Tran, A. Lux, H.L. Nguyen T, A. Boucher 627

Optical Flow-Based Segmentation of Containers for Automatic Code Recognition
Vicente Atienza, Ángel Rodas, Gabriela Andreu, Alberto Pérez 636

Hybrid OCR Combination for Ancient Documents
Hubert Cecotti, Abdel Belaïd 646

New Holistic Handwritten Word Recognition and Its Application to French Legal Amount
Abderrahmane Namane, Abderrezak Guessoum, Patrick Meyrueis 654

Handwriting Documents Denoising and Indexing Using Hermite Transform
Stéphane Bres, Véronique Eglin, Carlos Rivero 664

Evaluation of Commercial OCR: A New Goal Directed Methodology for Video Documents
Rémi Landais, Laurent Vinet, Jean-Michel Jolion 674

Author Index 685

Image Enhancement Optimization for Hand-Luggage Screening at Airports

Maneesha Singh and Sameer Singh

ATR Lab, Research School of Informatics,
University of Loughborough, Loughborough, UK

Abstract. Image enhancement is very important for increasing the sensitivity of screening luggage performance at airports. On the basis of 11 statistical measures of image viewability we propose a novel approach to optimizing the choice of image enhancement tools. We propose a neural network predictor that can be used for predicting, on a given test image, the best image enhancement algorithm for it. The network is trained using a number of image examples. The input to the neural network is a set of viewability measures and its output is the choice of enhancement algorithm for that image. On a number of test images we show that such a predictive system is highly capable in forecasting the correct choice of enhancement algorithms (as judged by human experts). We compare our predictive system against a baseline approach that uses a fixed enhancement algorithm for all batch test images, and find the proposed model to be substantially superior.

Keywords: Aviation Security, Enhancement, Viewability.

1 Introduction

The current set-up of screening operations at airports uses only three main enhancement techniques, which we refer to in this paper as techniques DB (Deep Boost), HE (Histogram Equalization) and CC (Crystal Clear). It is well understood from our research with airport screening staff that these techniques only provide a marginal advantage over the original images of airport luggage and in some case their application even deteriorates the image quality. In the context of improving image quality for the detection of explosives, it is important to note the following issues (Singh and Singh, 2003, Singh 2004):

a) The images of the airport luggage are in colour, but each colour is related to the atomic number of the material being imaged (Krug and Stein, 1991; Michette and Buckley, 1993). The image contains three colours: orange (organic), blue (inorganic) and green (mixed). Where the x-ray fails to penetrate the regions are nearly black. Figure 1 shows two example image.

b) The baggage x-ray systems come with many image manipulation options and some screeners are not conversant enough in the intricacies of their functionality to allow them to pick the best one or the best combination for a particular image with high speed.

c) It turns out to be the case that human judgment of security images across different operators is not uniform. Two experts' performance could match well in terms of their ability to pick out dangerous objects, but not in terms of grading image quality. For this reason, designing viewability measures that are quantitative depend on image alone, and yet correlate well with the visual perception of different human experts remains a challenging task.

d) In general practice, most operators simply enhance the image once using technique CC and work with it. Since each operator must decide on each bag within a 6 second window, most functions on the console never get used.

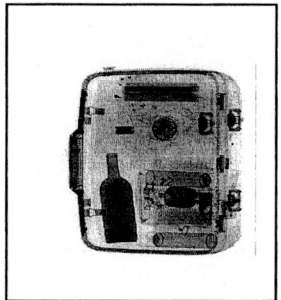 

Fig. 1. Example images containing explosives

2 Enhancement Techniques

In this study we use several state-of-the-art enhancement techniques from the literature to develop our predictive system. The enhancement techniques compared include: Low pass and High Boost filter (Gonzalez and Woods, 1993), Unsharp masking (Cheikh and Gabbouj, 1998; 2000), Adpative unsharp masking (Polesel *et al.*, 2000), Cubic Unsharp masking (Ramponi, 1998), Product of linear operators (Ramponi, 1999), Adaptive contrast enhancement (Rangayyan et al., 1997), Adaptive contrast enhancement based on local entropy (Singh, and Singh 2001), Fuzzy enhancement (Singh and Al-Mansoori, 2000; Zadeh, 1965), Extreme value sharpening and Local adaptive scaling (Klette and Zamperoni, 1996); Potential functions (Fotopoulos et al., 1997; Sindoukas et al., 1997).

3 Viewability Measures

In order to develop a predictive system, we must have some measurement of image viewability before and after enhancement. Such a measurement forms the input to a predictor whose output is the recommended choice of enhancement algorithm. During the course of our research we have found that no single measurement is sufficient and a range of measurements is needed. We briefly summarize here the viewability measures that can be computed on a single image.

1) *Cumulative edge strength* - Cumulative edge strength is the average edge strength per pixel of the whole image.

   For a colour image, its gradient can be computed in different channels as follows:

$$g_{xx} = \left(\frac{\partial R}{\partial x}\right)^2 + \left(\frac{\partial G}{\partial x}\right)^2 + \left(\frac{\partial B}{\partial x}\right)^2 \qquad (1)$$

$$g_{yy} = \left(\frac{\partial R}{\partial y}\right)^2 + \left(\frac{\partial G}{\partial y}\right)^2 + \left(\frac{\partial B}{\partial y}\right)^2 \qquad (2)$$

$$g_{xy} = \left(\frac{\partial R}{\partial x}\right)\left(\frac{\partial R}{\partial y}\right) + \left(\frac{\partial G}{\partial x}\right)\left(\frac{\partial G}{\partial y}\right) + \left(\frac{\partial B}{\partial x}\right)\left(\frac{\partial B}{\partial y}\right) \qquad (3)$$

$$|\vec{\nabla}C| = \left[\frac{1}{2}\left\{g_{xx} + g_{yy} + \sqrt{(g_{xx} - g_{yy})^2 + 4g_{xy}^2}\right\}\right]^{\frac{1}{2}} \qquad (4)$$

   Edge strength is given by the magnitude of vector C. Cumulative edge strength is the average edge strength per pixel of the whole image which is represented by $|\vec{\nabla}C|$.

2) *Number of edge pixels* - This measure computes the proportion of edge pixels in the image above a certain threshold.
3) *Histogram Area* - This measure can be calculated as follows: The edge-strength values of a particular image are distributed in bins (of size 10). Then the frequency of existence of a particular bin is plotted against the edge-strength in the form of a histogram. The area under the curve is then computed which serves as a measure of viewability.
4) *Edge Contrast* - A contrast edge in a photo is the boundary between areas of different brightness or colour. So we will be measuring the distance between edges. All the edge pixels are first computed using edge detection operators. For each pixel we find the edge pixels in its 'neighbourhood'. We average the Euclidean distance between the pixel and these neighbours, which gives the contrast value for the pixel. Contrast of the image is computed by averaging the 'contrast matrix'.
5) *Proportion of Very dark pixels* - Very dark pixels are the pixels that are almost black in the scale image. The proportion of very dark pixels in the image is computed by counting the number of pixels with the RGB values less than 100.
6) *Uniformity of texture in the edge removed image* - This is computed by taking into account the non-edge pixels and computing the texture variability in a neighbourhood around it. The neighbourhood considered in this case is 3x3.
7) *Difference in the neighbourhood pixels* - The average difference between the neighbourhood edge pixels and non-edge pixels is computed and is used as a viewability measure.
8) *Mean of Pixel Intensity*.

9) *Standard Deviation of Pixel Intensity.*
10) *Skewness of Pixel Intensity.*
11) *Kurtosis of Pixel Intensity.*

4 Enhancement Predictor

The proposed predictive system uses a neural network for mapping viewability measure to human ranking. We have used a feed-forward multilayer perceptron neural network using SNNS package (SNNS- http://www-ra.informatik.uni-tuebingen.de/SNNS/) with back-propagation with momentum training method. In order to find the true generalisation error, ten fold cross-validation is used. The main objective is to use ten different training and test sets, such that training and test sets are disjoint, and results are averaged across the ten trials. For each trial, the number of network inputs and outputs remain fixed, however, a number of training parameters need to be determined. These include: (a) number of hidden nodes, (b) learning rate η, and (c) momentum μ. For all of our experiments we use $\eta = .1$ $\mu = .9$. The number of hidden nodes however needs to be empirically determined. Using less than required number of hidden nodes leads to under-generalisation, whereas using too many hidden nodes leads to over-generalisation. It is not possible to optimise the number of hidden nodes on test data since in practice this should be determined prior to using it on test data. Hence, we divide our data into three sets: training set (70% data), validation set (20%), and test set (10%). For our experiments, we have a total of 273 samples from the same number of *x*-ray images of luggage, of which we use 22 in testing, 44 in validation set and 207 in training. The number of hidden nodes to be used is optimised on the basis of the validation set.

The inputs to the predictive system are the measures of image viewability that are mapped to the enhancement algorithm. In order words, the mapping problem can be stated as follows: "*Given*: An image X with its viewability defined by a vector of measurements $(v_1, v_2, ..., v_n)$; and a binary vector defining the suitability of enhancement algorithms denoted as $(r_1, r_2, ..., r_m)$: where $r_i = 1$, for $1 \leq i \leq m$, only when the human expert judges the algorithm to be suitable, otherwise $r_i = 0$. *Aim*: To map the vector $(v_1, v_2, ..., v_n)$ to vector $(r_1, r_2, ..., r_m)$".

The ground-truth was generated where screening experts assigned a rank between 1 and 6 (1 is the best) when presented with six images (original and five enhanced images). The original image was included in this set to determine whether the enhancement methods did make the image better than the original or otherwise. These experiments were conducted on a set of 273 original images and their five enhanced versions per image. Six monitors of same specifications were used to present the images at the same time. The images presented were on screens similar to those used by screening operators at the airports. All monitors had the same settings to ensure that there was no brightness/contrast difference. Also, the experiments were conducted under the same lighting conditions in which the operators normally work at the airports. A total of two experts from a UK airport participated in this task. Both experts were asked to make judgements individually.

5 Experimental Details

We have a total of 273 images belonging to 17 known classes. Each class represents a unique choice of algorithms. Given that we might prefer the original image (un-enhanced), or one or more of its enhanced versions, the vector $\{r_1, r_2, ..., r_6\}$ represents the options possible. Hence a vector $\{0\ 0\ 0\ 0\ 1\ 1\}$ suggests that the human experts chose algorithms r_5 or r_6. We first generate a total of ten folds of training, validation and test sets. The training data is used to train a neural network. As a first step, ten disjoint partitions of training and testing data are created. Each time training data partition has 90% of data and the test data partition has remaining 10% of the data. As such we conduct 10 separate training/testing trials. All classes represented in the test data set are also represented in the training data set. From the training data, 20% of data is randomly picked to create a validation set that is used to determine the optimal number of hidden nodes. In this process, different neural networks with varying number of hidden nodes (5-30) are trained, and for each trained network generalisation error using the validation set is computed. The network which gives the least generalisation error is selected for use on the test set. During the test phase, the ground truth labelling is used only to compare the predicted network value and calculate classification error.

6 Results

Neural networks are ideally suited for function mapping tasks with small amounts of data. The knowledge in the network is stored finally as the resultant weights on links. The cost of training neural networks could be high however they are very cheap to operate when testing. For developing a commercial system, they will need to be trained with a larger data set, and must be optimised for parameters such as the number of hidden nodes. Our primary criterion for success is the ability to correctly select the enhancement algorithm for a given image. A further step of analysis can be integrated that matches the viewability of images before and after enhancement and generates an alarm if the image is by mistake made less viewable.

We show our results in Figure 4 on a ten fold cross-validation task using classification rates. Each graph plots the generalisation error on the validation set by varying the neural network architecture (increasing the number of hidden nodes). Our primary criterion for success is the ability to correctly select the enhancement algorithm for a given image. A further step of analysis can be integrated that matches the viewability of images before and after enhancement and generates an alarm if the image is by mistake made less viewable. The chosen architecture is highlighted, e.g in Figure 4 (a), the least generalisation error is observed on the validation set with 20 hidden nodes. The test results obtained by using the selected network on test data are quoted below the graph, e.g. in Figure 4 (a) we get 88.18% accuracy on the test set.

We can observe the following points from Figure 4

a) The performance across different folds of analysis is moderately variable. At worst, we are 68.17% correct and at best we are 98.00% correct. Overall, the results are very good.

b) Better performances can be obtained if the network is trained on good quality data. This can be observed from the results of Fold3 (for Fold3 we get the best training and validation performance).
c) The quality of training and network convergence is good as shown by low validation set errors.

In addition, we perform an analysis to find out the proportion of images on which the predicted enhancement method improves the viewability of the image by at least 1 point (one a scale of [1,10]). Remembering that human expert rankings lie between [1,6] range, a change of 0.5 improvement on this scale is roughly equivalent to a shift of 1 on a [1,10] scale. The analysis can be phrased as follows: "If the original image had a viewability rank of x (given by an expert), on how many images did the enhanced version of the same image that is predicted optimal by our system, have a rank y (given by an expert), where $(y-x) > 0.5$ assuming that higher rank suggests improvement in visual quality?" It should be noted that the prediction itself is based on the knowledge-based framework without any information on the ground-truth on test image enhancements. In our analysis we used 273 images, out of which 254 showed a positive movement (93.04%), 17 showed no change (6.22%), and 2 showed negative change (.73%). It is for those cases that show negative change that we propose an alarm system that will block any such 'negative' image enhancement.

Computational Time Analysis of the Proposed Approach
One of the key considerations is the actual time taken to process images. This is particularly important since the screening operator has less than 6 seconds for each image. It is desirable that most of the computation should take place less than half that time, or even less than 1 second. Total system execution time is composed of the following four processes:

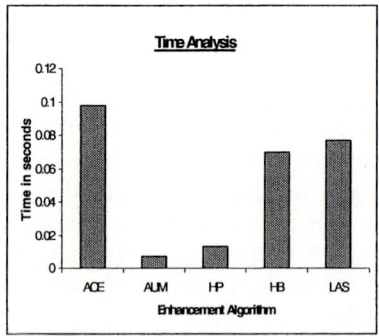

Fig. 2. Time taken in seconds by the 5 image enhancement methods on a 2.7 GHz machine for a single image

a) *Enhancement algorithms*: In Figure 2 we plot the time taken on a single image by an enhancement algorithm written in C and executed in Linux operating environment. Since at a given time, only one algorithm is executed, at worst it takes 0.098 seconds, and at best 0.007 seconds.

b) *Viewability measures computation*: This takes a total of 0.085 seconds per image with Intel 2.7 GHz processor. The computation takes the same time for all the images because all images are of the same size

c) *Training a MLP*: This is an off-line process and it could take from a few minutes to a few hours. This process does not affect the time to view online images.

d) *Selecting an enhanced algorithm with MLP:* This takes a total of 0.0002 seconds per image with Intel 2.7 GHz processor.

Hence, the total time by adding the above per image with Intel 2.7 GHz processor, lies between the range [0.0922, 0.1832] seconds. This meets our requirement of processing information in less than 1 second.

7 Baseline Comparison

In this section we present the results of comparison of our predictive system with the baseline approach. The baseline approach is based on the principle of using a given image enhancement algorithm on all images (without any optimisation). In our experiments, we set each of the five enhancement methods used, as baseline methods in turn and compare the results with the machine learning approach. The comparison is based on the following:

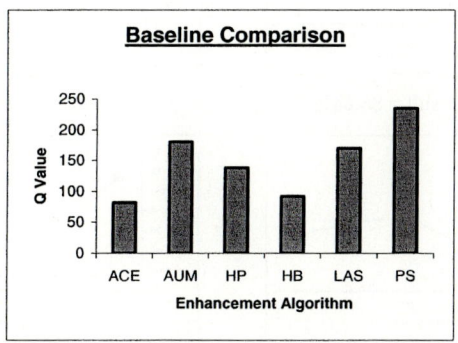

Fig. 3. The graph showing the baseline comparison

a) Given a total of N images $(I_1,...,I_N)$. For each image I_j, the output image after the application enhancement algorithm is also known and ground-truthed in terms of its visual quality. The ground-truth is a quality index for this image given as $R(I_j)$, $1 \leq j \leq N$, where $R(I_j) = 0$ for poor quality image enhancement and $R(I_j) = 1$ for good quality enhancement. If a total of five image enhancement algorithms $(e_1, e_2,..., e_5)$ are used, then the quality achieved with enhancement algorithm e_i, $1 \leq i \leq 5$, is given as $R(I_{ij})$, which again is 0 or 1.

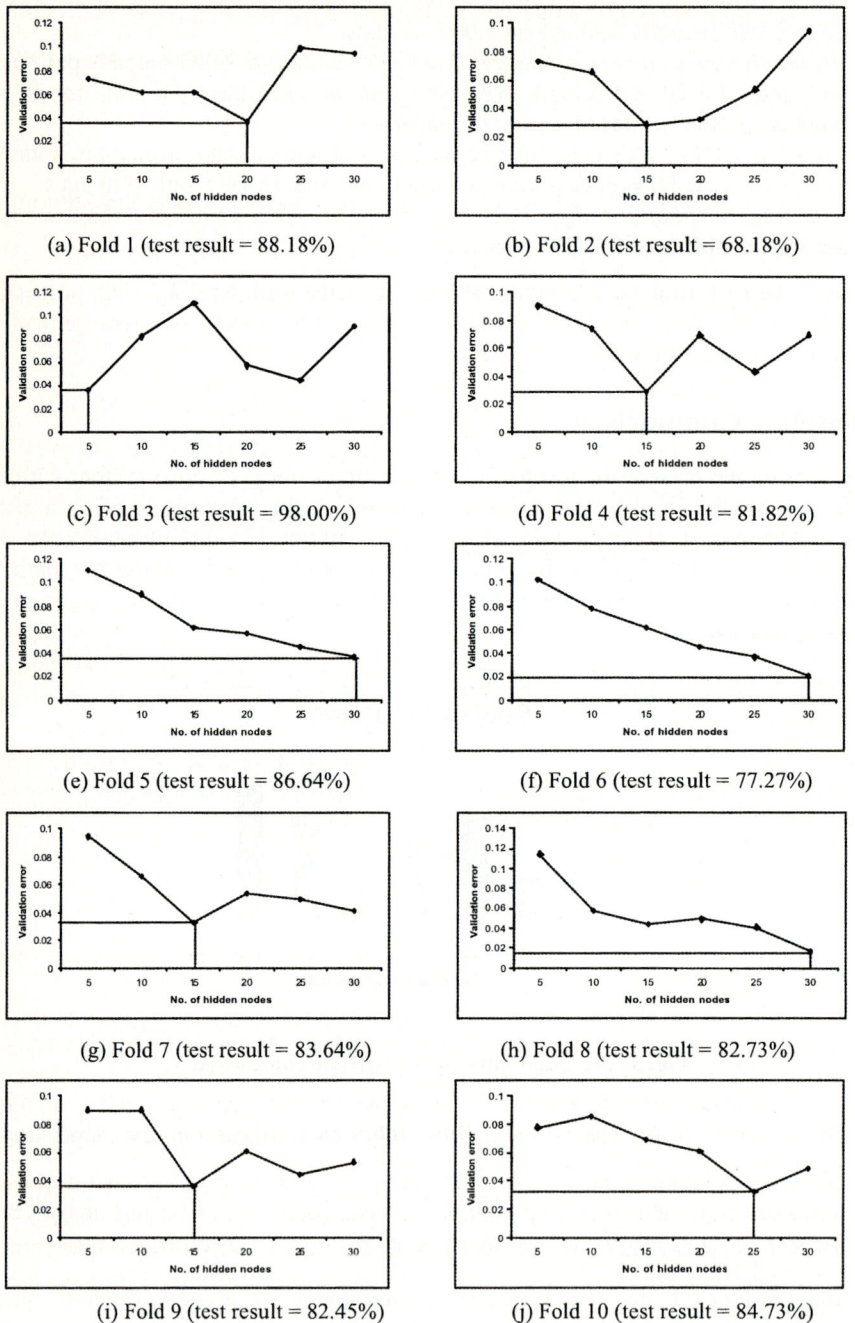

Fig. 4. The test set performance of MLP with varying number of hidden nodes for the validation set on ten folds

b) If we fix the use of algorithm e_i for application on all N images $(I_1,...,I_N)$, then the overall success in terms of the ability of e_i to lead to a good image enhancement is given by $Q_i = \sum_{j=1}^{N} R(I_{ij})$.

c) If we use the predictive system, then for a given image I_j, the algorithm to be applied on it is predicted as $e_{predicted}$, and the ground-truth of this is given by $R(I_{predicted}, j)$. Hence the overall quality index is given as

$$Q_{predicted} = \sum_{j=1}^{N} R(I_{predicted}, j).$$

d) In Figure 3 the values of Q_{ACE}, Q_{HP}, Q_{HB}, Q_{AUM}, Q_{LAS}, $Q_{predicted}$ are plotted as the six values. It is easy to see the $Q_{predicted}$ turns out to be the best.

8 Conclusions

This paper presented the results of a prediction system for choosing appropriate image enhancement technique(s) for a given image. The results show extremely good predictive ability of the system in selecting good enhancement algorithms from a database of algorithms. The computational time analysis of the algorithms was also studied and found to meet the requirements of a real system.

References

[1] I.E. Abdou, W.K. Pratt, "Qualitative design and evaluation of enhancement/thresholding edge detector", *Proceedings of IEEE*, vol. 67, no. 5, May 1979, pp. 753-763.

[2] F. A. Cheikh and M. Gabbouj, "Directional unsharp masking-based approach for color image enhancement", Proceedings of the Noblesse Workshop on non-linear model based image analysis (NMBIA), pp. 173-178, Glasgow, UK, July 1-3, 1998.

[3] F. A. Cheikh and M. Gabbouj, "Directional-rational approach for color image enhancement", Proceedings of the IEEE International Symposium on Circuits and Systems, Geneva, Switzerland, May 28-31, 2000.

[4] S.Fotopoulos, D. Sindoukas, N. Laskaris and G. Economou, "Image enhancement using color and spatial information", IEEE International conference on Acoustics, Speech, and Signal Processing, Vol. 4, pp. 2581-2584, April 1997.

[5] R.C. Gonzalez and R.E. Woods, "Digital Image Processing", Addison-Wesley publishing company, 1993.

[6] R. Klette and P. Zamperoni, "Handbook of Image Processing Operators", John Wiley and Sons, 1996.(Extreme value sharpening and LAS)

[7] K.D. Krug and J.A. Stein, Advanced dual energy x-ray for explosives detection, Proc. of 1st International Symposium on Explosive Detection Technology, 1991, pp. 282-284.

[8] A.G. Michette and C.J. Buckley, X-ray science and technology, Institute of Physics Publishing, Bristol, 1993, pp. 1-44.
[9] A. Polesel, G. Ramponi and V.J. Mathews, "Image enhancement via adaptive unsharp masking", *IEEE Transactions on Image Processing*, Vol. 9, Issue 3, 2000.
[10] G. Ramponi, "Contrast enhancement in images via the Product of Linear filters", *Signal Processing*, Vol. 77, Issue 3, pp. 349-353, 1999.
[11] G. Ramponi, "A cubic unsharp masking technique for contrast enhancement", *Signal Processing*, Vol. 67, Issue 2, pp. 211-222, 1998.
[12] M.R. Rangayyan et al. "Improvement of sensitivity of breast cancer diagnosis with adaptive neighbourhood enhancement of mammograms", *IEEE Transactions on IT in Biomedicine*, vol. 1, issue 3, pp. 161-169, 1997.
[13] D. Sindoukas, N. Laskaris and S. Fotopoulos, "Algorithms for color image edge enhancement using potential functions", *IEEE Signal Processing Letters*, Vol. 4, Issue 9, pp. 269-272, 1997.
[14] S. Singh and K.J. Bovis, "Digital Mammography Segmentation", in Advanced Algorithmic Approach to Medical Image Segmentation: State-of-the-Art Application in Cardiology, Neurology, Mammography and Pathology, J. Suri, S.K. Setarehdan and S. Singh (Ed.), Springer-Verlag Ltd., pp. 440-540, 2001.
[15] M. Singh, " A machine learning approach for image enhancement and segmentation for Aviation Security", PhD Thesis, 2004.
[16] S. Singh and R. Al-Mansoori, "Identification of region of interest in digital mammograms", *Journal of Intelligent Systems*, Vol. 10, Issue 2, pp. 183-210, 2000.
[17] S. Singh and M. Singh, "Explosives Detection Systems (EDS) for aviation security: a review", *Signal Processing*, vol. 83, issue 1, pp. 31-55, 2003.
[18] SNNS, http://www-ra.informatik.uni-tuebingen.de/SNNS.
[19] L. A. Zadeh, Fuzzy logic and its applications, 1965.

Parameter Optimization for Image Segmentation Algorithms: A Systematic Approach

Maneesha Singh[1], Sameer Singh[1], and Derek Partridge[2]

[1] ATR Lab, Research School of Informatics, University of Loughborough,
Loughborough, UK
[2] Department of Computer Science, University of Exeter, Exeter, UK

Abstract. Image segmentation is one of the most fundamental steps of image analysis. Almost all image segmentation algorithms have their parameters that need to be optimally set for a good segmentation. The problem of automatically setting algorithm parameters on a per image basis has been largely ignored in the vision community. In this paper we present a novel solution to this problem based on classification complexity and image edge analysis.

1 Introduction

Image segmentation is often considered to be the most important bottleneck in most computer vision tasks [6]. Over the last few decades, several image segmentation algorithms have appeared [3,7,8,9,15,17]. None of these algorithms have established themselves as the definitive image segmentation method and their performance is often dependent on the skill of the user who applies them. In addition, different algorithms perform better or worse on different images (principle of selective ability). There are four open research issues related to the performance evaluation of image enhancement algorithms. *(a)* Exhaustive comparison of image segmentation algorithms on a range of benchmarks; *(b)* Generating ground-truth data for such benchmarks (synthetic or natural); *(c)* Optimising algorithm parameters automatically, and *(d)* Developing machine learning systems that map the properties of images to optimal algorithms to predict which algorithm will work best on test images.

Several studies have tackled the issue of comparative analysis of segmentation algorithms [11,23]. A crucial but related issue is how to compare algorithms. Human judgment alone is not sufficient and also impossible on large data sets. Quantitative evaluation requires that each pixel in the image is ground-truthed (allocated to its true class) so that segmentation error can be calculated. This is a nearly impossible task for most images and for this reason alone most comparisons have been based on artificial data sets for which ground-truth is easy to establish [2,19,20,22]. The only disheartening but important finding of comparative studies has been that no single algorithm is a clear winner. On different data sets, different algorithms have turned out to be the best.

In light of these findings, the holy grail of image segmentation research is to develop a machine learning approach that can, on a per image basis, select the optimal image segmentation algorithm with its associated parameters. In this process, we no longer view it important to prove which algorithm is better than another, but it simply becomes a matter choice for a given image. Some previous effort in this area for developing an expert or rule based system for image segmentation includes [12,13,14,16].

In this paper we propose a novel technique for automatic selection of image segmentation algorithm parameter setting. If an image x is segmented as m outputs $(x_1, x_2, ..., x_m)$ by the same algorithm with m different parameter settings, then our propose method automatically picks out the best segmentation without any human intervention. In addition, the strength of the algorithm lies in the fact that no ground-truth is needed for the original image. This makes the technique extremely powerful since it can be robustly applied to any image. In this paper, we only use ground-truth to verify that our proposed technique generates valid results.

The proposed technique is not bound to any specific application. In this paper we have used a number of x-ray colour coded images of airport luggage. The aim of segmenting such images is to develop an automatic system for threat detection for which image segmentation is needed to separate out objects of interest. Further analysis on the shape and colour of objects can be used to give a rough estimate of the identity of the object. Any suspicious objects are then hand-checked by the airport staff. The main reason for choosing such images is that they are extremely hard to segment. Image regions are extremely edgy and there is significant colour feature variation even within the same region. Hence, this represents a significant challenge for any segmentation algorithm.

Our paper is laid out as follows. First, in section 2 we introduce three image segmentation methods that we have used, namely fuzzy c-means clustering, self-organising maps and Gaussian mixture models. We show example segmented images using these three methods. In section 3, we detail our methodology for automatic image segmentation parameter selection. This methodology is based on classification complexity and image edge analysis. In section 4, we show our results on a number of images, and conclude the paper in section 5.

2 Image Segmentation Algorithms

We have used three image segmentation algorithms that are diverse in terms of how they operate. These include fuzzy c-means clustering (based on region growing with clustering concept), self-organising maps (a clustering approach using unsupervised neural networks), and Gaussian mixture model (a statistical approach based on modelling pixel probabilities). A brief description of these segmentation algorithms and their associated parameters is given below.

Fuzzy c-Means Clustering: Fuzzy c-means clustering [1] is a method of data clustering based on the similarity in value between a data feature point and a cluster of data. In our experiments we fixed two of its parameters as follows. First, the number of iterations used (each iteration leads to an update in cluster membership of the data points) is fixed to 10. Second, the termination threshold is fixed at 0.25. We vary a single variable, $\aleph$, which is the number of clusters required. We vary this parameter between $\aleph = 2$, and $\aleph = 9$.

Self-organising Maps: A self-organising map [10] is a unsupervised scheme which finds the best set of weights for hard clusters in an iterative, sequential manner. The application of self-organising maps to image segmentation process is well-established. The segmentation process can be treated as a feature vector quantisation problem. It can be interpreted as a mapping from the pixels in the input image $\{z = f(x, y)\}$ of size N_x by N_y to a set of M regions $R = \{R_i, 1 \leq i \leq M\}$. Self-organising map can be used to learn this mapping. Only feature vectors consisting of position and intensity of pixels can be used as input. For SOM, we need to define a parameter that specifies the maximum number of clusters, which is set equal to 2 and 5 for two runs.

Gaussian Mixture Models: A Gaussian Mixture Model (GMM) [5] uses information of the likelihood of different pixel values occurring for image segmentation. A grey-scale image is represented as a one dimensional array $X = \{x_1, x_2, ..., x_N\}$, where x_n is an input feature for pixel n and N is the total number of pixels in the image. The input feature vector x_n may be a D dimensional vector or simply the grey-scale value of the pixel n. Let the underlying true segmentation of the image be denoted as $Y = \{y_1, y_2, ..., y_N\}$. It is assumed that the number of classes is predetermined as a set of known class labels ω_l, where $l \in \{1, ..., L\}$ and therefore the class label of pixel n is indicated as $y_n \in \{\omega_l\}_{l=1}^{L}$. A common assumption in modelling a density with a GMM for image segmentation is that each component m $m \in \{1, ..., M\}$ will model the *pdf* of each class $M = L$. Using the labelled training data, a Maximum Likelihood (ML) estimate of all component parameters and mixing coefficients can be found. In our study, the only parameter we vary is M, the number of components used. We have used 1 and 2 Gaussian components for segmentation.

At this stage, it is worth making an important point of observation before we proceed. The segmentation algorithms and their parameters are by no means exhaustive. The choice of segmentation algorithms and their associated parameters is based on our experience and the methodology we present next is generic, which would work equally well on a much larger choice of algorithms and their parameters. We now proceed to discuss our measure of segmentation quality that can be used to rank the output images obtained by varying algorithm parameters.

3 Measuring Image Segmentation Quality

Evaluating the quality of image segmentation without ground-truth is a difficult task. As we mentioned earlier, for real images obtaining ground-truth pixel by pixel is nearly an impossible task. Once the image is segmented into different regions, a key question is how valid these regions are. A good segmentation algorithm will create the correct number of regions as well as correct region boundaries. In our approach, we define the following measures of image segmentation quality.

3.1 Classification Complexity Estimate Using Davies Bouldin Index DB_{index}

A measure of classification complexity is based on how separable image regions are. From each image region, we can calculate a set of colour features from each pixel, and determine how separable these features from different regions are. In our research we have used a total of 41 colour features based on different colour spaces which are computed for each pixel. A simple measure of classification complexity is based on inter- intra cluster separability. Davies Bouldin index [4] is widely used to measure this. It is defined as follows:

Consider a total of C clusters. We can define inter-cluster distance $S(Q_k)$ and between cluster distances $d(Q_k, Q_l)$. Now considering the fact that samples $x_i, x_{i'} \in Q_k$, $i \neq i'$, $x_j \in Q_l$, $k \neq l$, and N_k is the number of samples in cluster Q_k, the cluster centroids are defined as: $c_k = 1/N_k \sum_{x_i \in Q_k} x_i$. The inter-cluster distance is given by $S_c = \dfrac{\sum_i \| x_i - c_k \|}{N_k}$, and the between cluster distance is given by: $d_{ce} = \| c_k - c_l \|$. Davies Bouldin index aims to minimise the following function:

$$\frac{1}{C} \sum_{k=1}^{C} \max_{l \neq k} \left\{ \frac{S_c(Q_k) + S_c(Q_l)}{d_{ce}(Q_k, Q_l)} \right\}.$$

3.2 Average Edge Gradient μ_{aeg}

The magnitude of edge strength for each image in the pixel can be computed using a number of different image operators. Since we are dealing with colour images, we calculate edge strength for each colour channel separately that is then combined to give an overall edge strength per pixel.

In an ideal image, each distinct region will have a high degree of colour uniformity. However, in our application images, the regions themselves are edgy, and thresholding edge strength is necessary to distinguish between pixels within a region that have a slight degree of noise content, from those that truly lie on the image boundary or represent high noise content within the region. We therefore first compute for a given region, the average edge gradient [17] of all pixels that lie within it. Let this be denoted as $\mu_{aeg}(region)$. The edge gradients of all pixels that is above this average within that region is now summed and averaged to obtain the revised estimate of μ_{aeg}. It is expected that we now include mostly those pixels in the computation that represent high level of noise or lie on the true boundary. For a perfect segmentation, this value will be low. On the other hand, for poor segmentation, e.g. if it over-segments and the region now contains another region boundary, then the value will be high. The aim is to minimise μ_{aeg} for the whole image (the values obtained from the different regions can now be averaged to give an overall estimate for an image).

3.3 Algorithm Colour Purity *CDS*

We use the "Cluster Dominance and Separation" (CDS) [17, 18] measure to define the colour purity of the segmented region. The main objective is to make this estimate sensitive to the number of clusters found within a histogram, the proportion of elements within these clusters and the relative separation between clusters. The measure can be used on any histogram (raw pixel values or features computed from these). The following algorithm defines the pseudo code for this novel measure.

1. For an image *I* of size *M X N*, assume that the pixel values for the red, green and blue channels are given by *r(x,y), g(x,y) and b(x,y)* respectively where $0 \leq x \leq M-1$ and $0 \leq y \leq N-1$.
2. Segment the image *I* using *Fuzzy-c-means algorithm* (Bezdek et al., 1984) into *n* regions, and create a map-file *Map* of size *M x N* where each region is uniquely labelled $1 \leq region \leq n$. Colour purity is now computed on a per region basis. The following steps operate on a given region *R*.
3. For each pixel in region *R* compute two colour histograms. The joint probability histogram of the three channels for each region *H1* and a histogram of the saturation information *H2*. The steps 4 to 9 are followed for each histogram separately.
4. Cluster the histogram information using a simple method that generates narrow peaks and wide valleys into *m+1* clusters.
5. Find the most dominant cluster *C* (the cluster with the highest proportion of pixels) in the histogram, and the other clusters $(c_1, c_2..c_m)$.
6. Each other cluster is assigned a weight. Find weights of $(c_1, c_2..c_m)$ as $(w_1, w_2..w_m)$ as the proportion of number of pixels contained within the cluster compared to the total number of pixels.
7. Compute α as the number of pixels from region *R* not present in the dominant cluster *C*.
8. For every cluster in $(c_1, c_2..c_m)$, compute the distances $(d_1, d_2..d_m)$ between the mode values of these clusters and the mode value of the dominant cluster *C*. This is simply the spatial distance between colour values on a histogram. If a 3D histogram was plotted in 2D, where each unique RGB combination was indexed as a separate colour and linearly ordered, then the distance would simply be the difference in colour indices along the *x*-axis of the histogram.
9. Compute the colour purity measure as: $CDS = \alpha + w_1 d_1, w_2 d_2 + ..w_m d_m$.

The *CDS* measure is computed on the histograms *H1* and *H2* separately. The unique features of the above algorithm include: (a) The measurement gives larger weights to bigger clusters (i.e. with more pixels) and hence the effect of pixels with incoherent colours is minimised; (b) The measurement centres around the most dominant colour within the histogram and measures the distance between this and other clusters; (c) The measurement is contained within the [0,1] range and should be minimised for maximum colour purity; and (d) It is based on histogram information that is readily available.

Since the three measures DB_{index}, μ_{aeg} and CDS lie on different scales, therefore it is not possible to combine them directly. However, combining ranked images is relatively straightforward. This is done as follows

Given: An original image I, which is segmented using a segmentation algorithm with m different parameters giving the following m images: $(I_1, ..., I_m)$.

Method: Compute the values of the three measures as follows: $(DB_1, ..., DB_m)$, $(\mu_{avg1}, ..., \mu_{avgm})$ and $(CDS_1, ..., CDS_m)$. The aim is to minimise all three measures. In descending order, each vector value can be converted into a rank as follows: $(rDB_1, ..., rDB_m)$, $(r\mu_{avg1}, ..., r\mu_{avgm})$ and $(rCDS_1, ..., rCDS_m)$. The average rank of image I_j is given as: $(rDB_j + r\mu_{avgj} + CDS_j)/3$. So in case all three measures do not agree, we take the case where at least two of the measures have lower values.

In this manner we can rank different image segmentation parameters without the need of ground-truth data to calculate any segmentation error. By preferring a particular image, we prefer the segmentation parameter that was used for it.

4 Results

We have used a total of 75 images of colour coded *x*-ray images. These real images were obtained using dual-energy *x*-ray machine when monitoring checked in luggage at a UK airport. The images are colour coded on the basis of the atomic number of objects scanned. There are three main colours and their shades: orange (organic matter), blue (inorganic matter), and green (mixed organic and inorganic). The images have a high level of noise and their segmentation is quite difficult. Each image contains at least one illicit or explosive object within it. A good segmentation method should show a good segmentation of this object.

We applied FCM with its 8 different parameter values giving us 8 images for each of the 75 images. Similarly we obtained 2 images per 75 images for both self-organising maps and Gaussian mixture models. These images are ground truthed by a screening expert in terms of the quality of segmentation. Figure 1 shows an example result of our analysis using different parameters. We next find the best parameter choice as suggested by DB_{index}, μ_{aeg} and *CDS* and analyse whether they agree with themselves or not, and whether their combined ranking agrees with our ground-truth or not.

We can summarise the important conclusions as follows:

a) For FCM segmentation, DB_{index}, μ_{aeg} and *CDS* rankings are in agreement most of the time (96% of the time), which was the same as the ground-truth 97.2% of the time (i.e. 576 times out of 600 all three measures were in agreement and 560 times out of 576 the values matched the ground-truth).

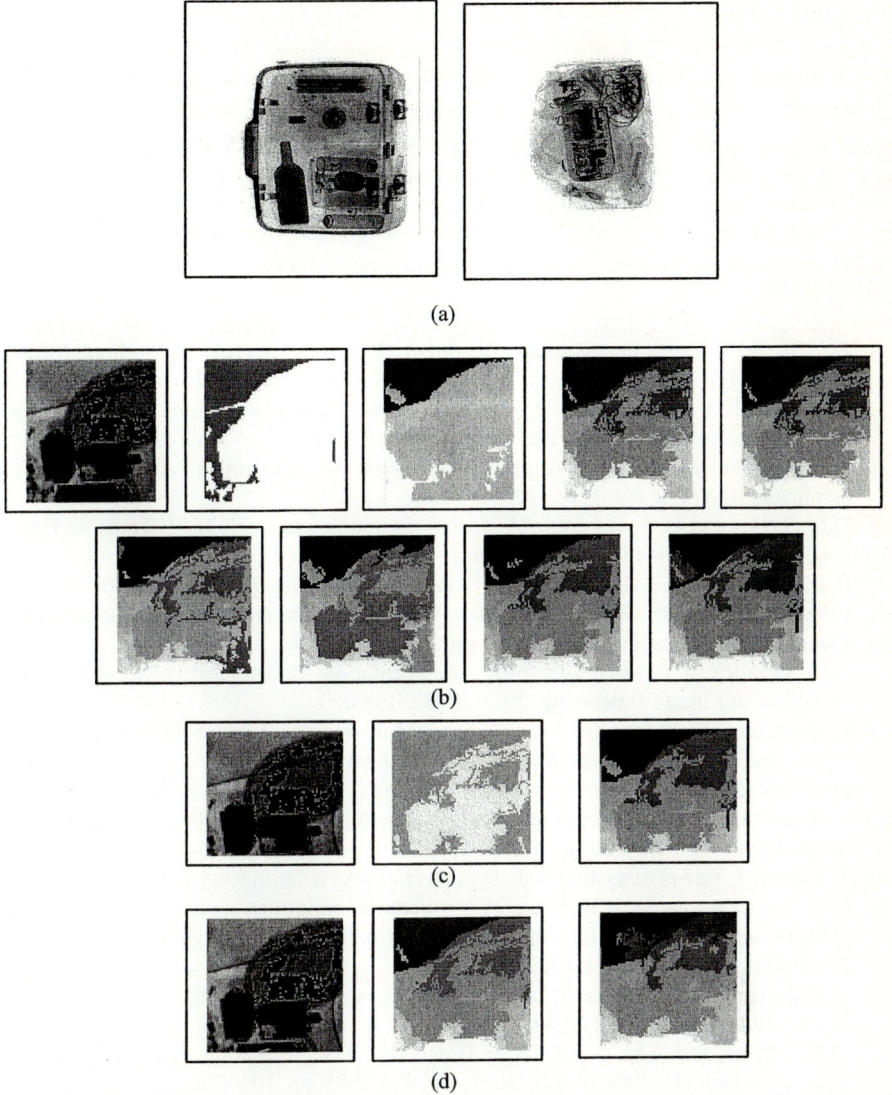

Fig. 1. (a) Two example images of luggage containing explosives; (b) original image and 8 segmented FCM images; (c) original image and 2 segmented GMM images; and (d) original image and 2 segmented SOM images.

b) For GMM segmentation, DB_{index}, μ_{aeg} and CDS rankings are in agreement most of the time (94% of the time), and the resultant ranking matched with ground-truth for 100% of the images.

c) For SOM segmentation, DB_{index}, μ_{aeg} and CDS rankings are in agreement most of the time (97.3% of the time), and the resultant ranking matched with ground-truth for 98.63% of the images.

5 Conclusions

In this paper we introduced a novel approach to the measurement of image segmentation quality. This approach was based on estimating classification complexity using Davies Bouldin Index, use of edge strength and a novel measure of colour purity. This work has laid the basic principles on the basis of which segmentation algorithm parameters can be selected.

References

[1] J.C. Bezdek, Pattern Recognition with Fuzzy Objective Function Algorithms, Plenum, New York, 1981.
[2] M. Borsotti, P. Campadelli, R. Schettini, "Quantitative evaluation of color image segmentation results", Pattern Recognition Letters, Vol. 19, pp. 741.747, 1998.
[3] Carvalho, Gau and Herman, "Algorithms for Fuzzy Segmentation", Pattern Analysis and Applications, Vol. 2, No. 1, pp. 73-81, 1999.
[4] D.L. Davies and D.W. Bouldin, "A cluster separation measure", IEEE Trans on Pattern Analysis and Machine Intelligence, vol. 1, no. 2, 1979.
[5] R.O. Duda, P.E. Hart and D.G. Stork, *Pattern classification*, John Wiley, 2001.
[6] E.M. Gurari, and H. Wechsler, "On the Difficulties Involved in the Segmentation of Pictures", PAMI(4), No. 3, May 1982, pp. 304-306.
[7] R.H. Haralick, L.G. Shapiro, "Image Segmentation Techniques", Computer Vision, Graphics, and Image Processing, 29, 100-132, 1985.
[8] Hauta-Kasari, Parkkinen and Jaaskelainen, "Multi-spectral Texture Segmentation Based on the Spectral Cooccurrence Matrix", Pattern Analysis and Applications, Vol. 2, No. 4, pp. 275-284, 1999.
[9] Kampke and Kober, "Non Parametric Image Segmentation", Pattern Analysis and Applications, Vol. 1, No. 3, pp. 145-154, 1998.
[10] T. Kohonen, Self-organisation and associative memory, Springer, 1988.
[11] S.U. Lee, S.Y. Chung, R.H. Park, "A comparative performance study of several global thresholding techniques for segmentation", Computer Vision Graphics and Image Processing, vol. 52, pp. 171-190, 1990.
[12] M.D. Levine, and A.M. Nazif, "An Optimal Set of Image Segmentation Rules", Pattern Recognition Letters, vol. 2, 1984, pp. 243-248.
[13] M.D. Levine, and A.M. Nazif, "Rule-Based Image Segmentation: A Dynamic Control Strategy Approach", CVGIP(32), No. 1, October 1985, pp. 104-126.
[14] A.M. Nazif, and M.D. Levine, "Low Level Image Segmentation: An Expert System", IEEE PAMI(6), No. 5, September 1984, pp. 555-577.
[15] N.R.Pal and S.K. Pal, "A Review on Image Segmentation Techniques", Pattern Recognition, vol. 26, issue 9, pp. 1277-1294, 1994.
[16] T. Pavlidis, "Low Level Image Segmentation: An Expert System", Pattern Analysis and Machine Intelligence, Vol. 8, No. 5, 1986, pp. 675-676.
[17] M. Singh, "A Machine Learning Approach for Image Enhancement and Segmentation for Aviation Security", PhD Thesis, University of Exeter, 2004.
[18] S. Singh and M. Singh, "A novel measure of estimating colour purity of image regions", IEEE International Conference on Computational Intelligence for Homeland Security and Personal Safety, Venice, Italy, 21-22 July, 2004.

[19] J.S. Weszka, A. Rosenfeld, "Threshold evaluation techniques", IEEE Transactions on Systems, Man and Cybernetics, vol. 8, pp. 622-629, 1978.
[20] W.A. Yasnoff, W.A. Mui, and J.W. Bacus, "Error Measures in Scene Segmentation", Pattern Recognition, vol. 9, No. 4, 1977, pp. 217-231.
[21] Yuan, Goldman and Moghaddamzadeh, "Segmentation of Colour Images with Highlights and Shadows sing Fuzzy-like Reasoning", Pattern Analysis and Applications, Vol. 4, No. 4, pp. 272-282, 2001.
[22] Y.J. Zhang, "A Survey on Evaluation Methods for Image Segmentation", Pattern Recognition, vol. 29, No. 8, August 1996, pp. 1335-1346.
[23] http://www.dcs.ex.ac.uk/research/pann/pecva/segment/surveys.htm

Fingerprint Image Enhancement Using STFT Analysis

Sharat Chikkerur*, Venu Govindaraju, and Alexander N. Cartwright

Center for Unified Biometrics and Sensors, University at Buffalo, NY, USA
ssc5@eng.buffalo.edu

Abstract. Contrary to popular belief, despite decades of research in fingerprints, reliable fingerprint recognition is still an open problem. Extracting features out of poor quality prints is the most challenging problem faced in this area. This paper introduces a new approach for fingerprint enhancement based on Short Time Fourier Transform(STFT) Analysis. STFT is a well known technique in signal processing to analyze non-stationary signals. Here we extend its application to 2D fingerprint images.The algorithm simultaneously estimates all the intrinsic properties of the fingerprints such as the foreground region mask, local ridge orientation and local frequency orientation. We have evaluated the algorithm over a set of 800 images from FVC2002 DB3 database and obtained a 17% relative improvement in the recognition rate.

1 Introduction

The performance of a fingerprint feature extraction and matching algorithm depends critically upon the quality of the input fingerprint image. While the 'quality' of a fingerprint image cannot be objectively measured, it roughly corresponds to the the clarity of the ridge structure in the fingerprint image. Where as a 'good' quality fingerprint image has high contrast and well defined ridges and valleys, a 'poor' quality fingerprint is marked by low contrast and ill-defined boundaries between the ridges. There are several reasons that may degrade the quality of a fingerprint image.

1. Presence of creases, bruises or wounds may cause ridge discontinuities.
2. Excessively dry fingers lead to fragmented and low contrast ridges.
3. Sweat on fingerprints leads to smudge marks and connects parallel ridges.

While most algorithms are designed to operate on well defined ridge structures, the quality of fingerprint encountered during verification varies over a wide range as shown in Fig. 1. It is estimated that roughly 10% of the fingerprint encountered during verification can be classified as 'poor' [1]. The robustness of the fingerprint recognition system can be improved by incorporating an enhancement stage prior to feature extraction. Due to the non-stationary nature of the fingerprint image, general-purpose image processing algorithms are not very useful in this regard but only serve as a preprocessing step in the overall enhancement scheme. The majority the existing techniques are based on the use of *contextual* filters whose parameters depend on the properties of the local neighborhood. The filters themselves may be defined in spatial or in the Fourier domain.

---

* Corresponding author.

Fig. 1. Fingerprint images of different quality. The quality decreases from left to right. (a) Good quality image with high contrast between the ridges and valleys (b) Insufficient distinction between ridges and valleys in the center of the image (c) Dry print.

1.1 Prior Related Work

O'Gorman et al. [2] proposed the use of contextual filters for fingerprint image enhancement for the first time. They used an anisotropic smoothening kernel whose major axis is oriented parallel to the ridges. For efficiency, they precompute the filter in 16 directions. The net result of the filter is that it increases contrast in a direction perpendicular to the ridges while performing smoothening in the direction of the ridges. Recently, Greenberg et al. [3] proposed the use of an anisotropic filter that is based on structure adaptive filtering [4]. Another approach based on directional filtering kernel was given by Hong et al. [5]. The algorithm uses a properly oriented Gabor kernel for performing the enhancement. Gabor filters have important properties from a signal processing perspective such as optimal joint space frequency resolution [6]. Gabor elementary functions form a very intuitive representation of fingerprint images since they capture the periodic,yet non-stationary nature of the fingerprint regions. This is by far, the most popular approach for fingerprint image enhancement.

Sherlock and Monro [7] perform contextual filtering completely in the Fourier Domain. Here, each image is convolved with precomputed filters of the same size as the image. The contextual filtering is actually accomplished by a 'selector' that uses the local orientation information to combine the results of the filter bank using appropriate weights for each output. The algorithm also accounts for the curvature of the ridges. In regions of high curvature, having a fixed angular bandwidth leads to processing artifacts and subsequently spurious minutiae.

1.2 Intrinsic Images

The *intrinsic images* represent the important properties of the fingerprint image as a pixel map. These include the ridge orientation image, the ridge frequency image and the region mask. The computation of the intrinsic images forms a very critical step in the feature extraction and in the matching process. Applications that require a reliable orientation image include enhancement [5,7,2,8], singular point detection [9,10,11] and segmentation [12] and most importantly fingerprint classification [13,14,15,16,17]. The region mask is used to eliminate spurious fingerprint features [8,5].

Orientation Image. The orientation image **O** represents the instantaneous ridge orientation at every point in the fingerprint image. There have been several approaches to estimate the orientation image of a fingerprint image. Here we discuss some popular approaches for computing the orientation image.

Except in the region of singularities such as core and delta, the ridge orientation varies very slowly across the image. Therefore, the orientation image is seldom computed at full-resolution. Instead each non-overlapping block of size $W \times W$ of the image is assigned a single orientation that corresponds to the most probable or *dominant* orientation of the block. The horizontal and vertical gradients $G_x(x,y)$ and $G_y(x,y)$ respectively, are computed using simple gradient operators such as a Sobel mask [18]. The block orientation θ is given by $\theta = \frac{1}{2}\tan^{-1}\frac{G_{yy}}{G_{xx}}$, where

$$G_{xy} = \sum_{u \in W}\sum_{v \in W} 2G_x(u,v)G_y(u,v) \qquad (1)$$

$$G_{xx} = \sum_{u \in W}\sum_{v \in W} G_x^2(u,v) - G_y^2(u,v) \qquad (2)$$

A rigorous derivation of the above relation is provided in [19]. The dominant orientation so obtained still contains inconsistencies caused by creases and ridge breaks. Utilizing the regularity property of the fingerprint, the orientation image is smoothened by vector averaging.

Frequency Image. The ridge frequency is another intrinsic property of the fingerprint image. It is also a slowly varying property and hence is computed only once for each non-overlapping block of the image. It indicates the average inter-ridge distance within a block and is estimated based on the projection sum taken along a line oriented orthogonal to the ridges [5], or based on the variation of gray levels in a window oriented orthogonal to the ridge flow [20]. These methods depend upon the reliable extraction of the local ridge orientation. The projection sum forms a sinusoidal signal and the distance between any two peaks provides the inter-ridge distance. The frequency image so obtained may be further filtered to remove the outliers.

Region Mask. The region mask indicates the parts of the image where ridge structures are present. It is also known as the foreground mask and is used to eliminate spurious features that may occur outside the fingerprint area.

2 Proposed Approach: STFT Analysis

We present a new fingerprint image enhancement algorithm based on contextual filtering in the Fourier domain. The fingerprint image may be thought of as a system of oriented texture with non-stationary properties. Therefore, traditional Fourier analysis is not adequate to analyze the image completely. We need to resolve the properties of the image both in space and also in frequency. We can extend the traditional one dimensional time-frequency analysis to two dimensional image signals to perform short (time/space)-frequency analysis. In this section, we recapitulate some of the principles

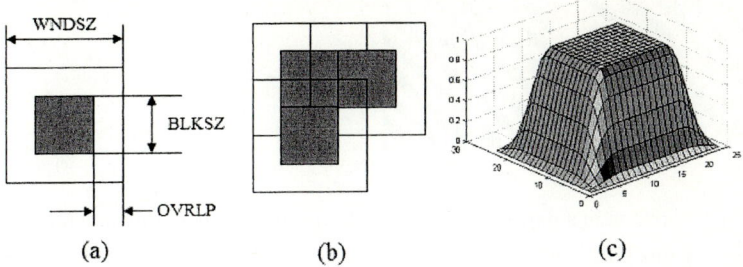

Fig. 2. (a) Overlapping window parameters used in the STFT analysis (b) Illustration of how analysis windows are moved during analysis (c) Spectral window used in STFT analysis.

---

of 1D STFT analysis and show how it is extended to two dimensions for the sake of analyzing the fingerprint.

When analyzing a non-stationary 1D signal $x(t)$ it is assumed that it is approximately stationary in the span of a temporal window $w(t)$ with finite support. The STFT of $x(t)$ of such a signal is represented by time frequency *atoms* $X(\tau, \omega)$ [21] and is given by

$$X(\tau, \omega) = \int_{-\infty}^{\infty} x(t) \omega^*(t - \tau) e^{-j\omega t} dt \qquad (3)$$

In the case of 2D signals such as a fingerprint image, the space-frequency *atoms* is given by

$$X(\tau_1, \tau_2, \omega_1, \omega_2) = \int_{-\infty}^{\infty} \int_{-\infty}^{\infty} I(x, y) W^*(x - \tau_1, y - \tau_2) e^{-j(\omega_1 x + \omega_2 y)} dx dy \qquad (4)$$

Here τ_1, τ_2 represent the spatial position of the two dimensional window W(x,y). ω_1, ω_2 represents the spatial frequency parameters. Figure 2 illustrates how the spectral window is parameterized. At each position of the window, it overlaps OVRLP pixels with the previous position. This preserves the ridge continuity and eliminates 'block' effects common with other block processing image operations. Each such analysis frame yields a single value of the dominant orientation and frequency in the region centered around (τ_1, τ_2). However, unlike regular Fourier transform, the result of the STFT is dependent on the choice of the window $w(t)$. For the sake of analysis, any smooth spectral window such as hanning, hamming or even a gaussian [22] window may be utilized. However, since we are also interested in enhancing and reconstructing the fingerprint image directly from the Fourier domain, our choice of window is fairly restricted. We chose a 12×12 window since it provides a good trade-off between local stationarity and processing complexity. Larger windows are unsuitable since the image will no longer be stationary within it. In order to provide suitable reconstruction during enhancement, we utilize a raised cosine window that tapers smoothly near the border and is unity at the center of the window. The raised cosine spectral window is obtained using

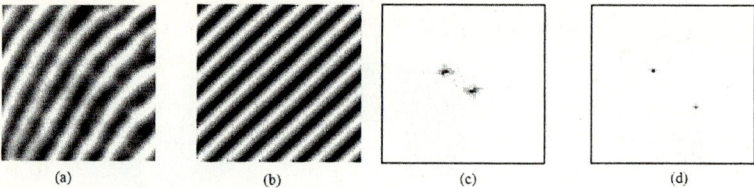

(a) (b) (c) (d)

Fig. 3. (a) Local region in a fingerprint image (b) Surface wave approximation (c,d) Fourier spectrum of the real fingerprint and the surface wave. The symmetric nature of the Fourier spectrum arrives from the properties of the Fourier transform for real signals [18].

$$W(x,y) = \begin{Bmatrix} 1 \text{ if}(|x|,|y|) < \text{BLKSZ}/2 \\ \frac{1}{2}(1 + cos(\frac{\pi x}{OVRLP})) \text{ otherwise} \end{Bmatrix} (x,y) \in [-WNDSZ/2, WNDSZ/2) \quad (5)$$

With the exception of the singularities such as core and delta any local region in the fingerprint image has a consistent orientation and frequency. Therefore, the local region can be modeled as a surface wave that is characterized completely by its orientation θ and frequency f (See Fig. 3). It is these parameters that we hope to infer by performing STFT analysis. This approximation model does not account for the presence of local discontinuities but is useful enough for our purpose. A local region of the image can be modeled as a surface wave according to $I(x,y) = A\{2\pi f \cos(x\cos(\theta) + y\sin(\theta))\}$.

The parameters of the surface wave (f, θ) may be easily obtained from its Fourier spectrum that consists of two impulses, whose distance from the origin indicates the frequency and angular location indicates the orientation of the wave. However, this straight forward approach is not very useful since the maximum response is prone to errors. Creases running across the fingerprint can easily put off such maximal response estimators. Instead, we propose a probabilistic approximation of the dominant ridge orientation and frequency. Representing the Fourier spectrum in polar form as $F(r, \theta)$, we can define a probability density function $p(r, \theta)$ and the marginal density functions $p(\theta), p(r)$ as

$$p(r,\theta) = \frac{|F(r,\theta)|^2}{\int_r \int_\theta |F(r,\theta)|^2} \quad (6)$$

$$p(r) = \int_\theta p(r,\theta)d\theta, p(\theta) = \int_r p(r,\theta)dr. \quad (7)$$

2.1 Ridge Orientation Image

To compute the ridge orientation image, we assume that the orientation θ is a random variable that has the probability density function $p(\theta)$. The expected value of the orientation may then be obtained by performing a vector averaging according to 8. The terms $\sin(2\theta)$ and $\cos(2\theta)$ are used to resolve the orientation ambiguity between orientations $\pm 180°$

$$E\{\theta\} = \frac{1}{2}tan^{-1}\left\{\frac{\int_\theta p(\theta)\sin(2\theta)d\theta}{\int_\theta p(\theta)\cos(2\theta)d\theta}\right\} \quad (8)$$

However, if there is a crease in the fingerprints that spans several analysis frames, the orientation estimation will still be wrong. The estimate will also be inaccurate when the frame consists entirely of unrecoverable regions with poor ridge structure or poor ridge contrast. In such instances, we can estimate the ridge orientation by considering the orientation of its immediate neighborhood. The resulting orientation image $O(x,y)$ is further smoothened using vectorial averaging. The smoothened image $O'(x,y)$ is obtained using

$$O'(x,y) = \frac{1}{2}\left\{tan^{-1}\frac{\sin(2O(x,y))*W(x,y)}{\cos(2O(x,y)*W(x,y)}\right\} \quad (9)$$

Here $W(x,y)$ represent a gaussian smoothening kernel. It has been our experience that a smoothening kernel of size 3x3 applied repeatedly provides a better smoothening result than using a larger kernel of size 5x5 or 7x7.

2.2 Ridge Frequency Image

The average ridge frequency is estimated in a manner similar to the ridge orientation. We can assume the ridge frequency to be a random variable with the probability density function $p(r)$ as in Eq 7. The expected value of the ridge frequency is given by $E\{r\} = \int_r p(r)rdr$.

The frequency map so obtained is smoothened by process of isotropic diffusion. Simple smoothening cannot be applied since the ridge frequency is not defined in the background regions. The smoothened is obtained by the following.

$$F'(x,y) = \frac{\sum_{u=x-1}^{x+1}\sum_{v=y-1}^{y+1}F(u,v)W(u,v)I(u,v)}{\sum_{v=y-1}^{y+1}W(u,v)I(u,v)} \quad (10)$$

This is similar to the approach proposed in [5]. Here H,W represent the height and width of the frequency image. $W(x,y)$ represents a gaussian smoothening kernel of size 3x3. The indicator variable $I(x,y)$ ensures that only valid ridge frequencies are considered during the smoothening process. $I(x,y)$ is non zero only if the ridge frequency is within the valid range (3-25 pixels per ridge [5]).

2.3 Region Mask

The fingerprint image may be easily segmented based on the observation that the surface wave model does not hold in regions where ridges do not exist. In the areas of background and noisy regions, there is very little energy content in the Fourier spectrum. We define an energy image $E(x,y)$, where each value indicates the energy content of the corresponding block. The fingerprint region may be differentiated from the background by thresholding the energy image. We take the logarithm values of the energy to compress the large dynamic range to a linear scale.

$$E(x,y) = \log\left\{\int_r\int_\theta |F(r,\theta)|^2\right\} \quad (11)$$

The resulting binary image is processed further to retain the largest connected component and binary morphological processing [23].

Coherence Image. Enhancement is especially problematic in regions of high curvature close to the core and deltas that have more than one dominant direction. Excessively narrow angular bandwidth causes spurious artifacts and ridge discontinuities in the reconstructed image. Sherlock and Monro [7] used a piece wise linear dependence between the angular bandwidth of their filter and the ridge curvature. However, this requires a reasonable estimation of the singular point location. Most algorithms for singular point location [9,10] are not reliable in noisy and poor quality images. Therefore we rely on a flow-orientation/angular coherence measure [24] that is more robust than singular point detection. The coherence is related to dispersion measure of circular data and is given by

$$C(x_0, y_0) = \frac{\sum_{(i,j) \in W} |\cos(\theta(x_0, y_0) - \theta(x_i, y_i))|}{W \times W} \quad (12)$$

The coherence is high when the orientation of the central block $\theta(x_0, y_0)$ is similar to each of its neighbors $\theta(x_i, x_j)$. In a fingerprint image, the coherence is expected to be low closer to regions of high curvature. We therefore utilize this coherence measure to adapt the angular bandwidth of the directional filter.

2.4 Enhancement

The algorithm consists of two stages. The first stage consists of STFT analysis outlined before and is responsible for computing all the intrinsic images of the fingerprint. The image is divided into overlapping windows as shown in Fig˙ 2. It is assumed that the image is stationary within this small window and can be modeled approximately as a surface wave. The fourier spectrum of this small region is analyzed and probabilistic estimates of the ridge frequency and ridge orientation are obtained as outlined before. In each window we apply a filter that is tuned to the radial frequency and aligned with the dominant ridge direction. The filter itself is separable in angle and frequency and is identical to the filters mentioned in [7] and is given by

$$H(\rho, \phi) = H_\rho(\rho) H_\phi(\phi) \quad (13)$$

$$H_\rho(\rho) = \sqrt{\left[\frac{(\rho \rho_{BW})^{2n}}{(\rho \rho_{BW})^{2n} + (\rho^2 - \rho_0^2)^{2n}}\right]} \quad (14)$$

$$H_\phi(\phi) = \begin{cases} \cos^2 \frac{\pi}{2} \frac{(\phi - \phi_c)}{\phi_{BW}} & \text{if } |\phi| < \phi_{BW} \\ 0 & \text{otherwise} \end{cases} \quad (15)$$

Here $H_\rho(\rho)$ is a band-pass butterworth filter with center defined by ρ_0 and bandwidth ρ_{BW}. ρ_0 is derived from the intrinsic orientation image while the bandwidth ρ_{BW} is chosen to be inversely proportional to the angular coherence measure. The angular filter is a raised cosine filter in the angular domain with support ϕ_{BW} and center ϕ_c. The enhanced image is reconstructed by tiling the results of enhancement of each local window. Figure 5 shows the results of enhancement on some sample images.

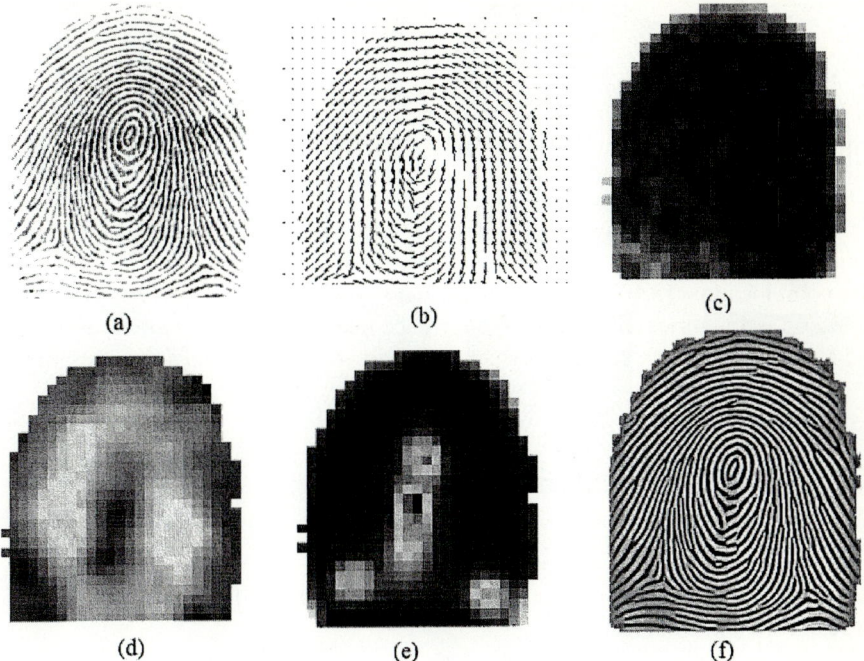

Fig. 4. (a) Original Image (b) Orientation Image (c) Energy Image (d) Ridge Frequency Image (e) Angular Coherence Image (f) Enhanced Image.

3 Experimental Evaluation

While the effect of the enhancement algorithm may be guaged visually, the final objective of the enhancement process is to increase the accuracy of the recognition system. We evaluated the effect of our enhancement on a set of 800 images (100 users, 8 images each) derived from FVC2002 [25] DB3 database. In order to obtain the performance characteristics such as EER (Equal Error Rate) we perform a total of 2800 genuine (each instance of a finger is compared with the rest of the instances resulting in (8x7)/2 tests per finger) comparison and 4950 impostor comparisons (the first instance of each finger is compared against the first instance of all other fingers resulting in a total of (100x99)/2 tests for the entire database). We used NIST's NFIS2 open source software (http://fingerprint.nist.gov) for feature extraction and matching. The summary of the results is provided in Table 1.

4 Summary

The performance of a fingerprint feature extraction and matching algorithms depend critically upon the quality of the input fingerprint image. We presented a new fingerprint image enhancement algorithm based on STFT analysis and contextual/non-stationary

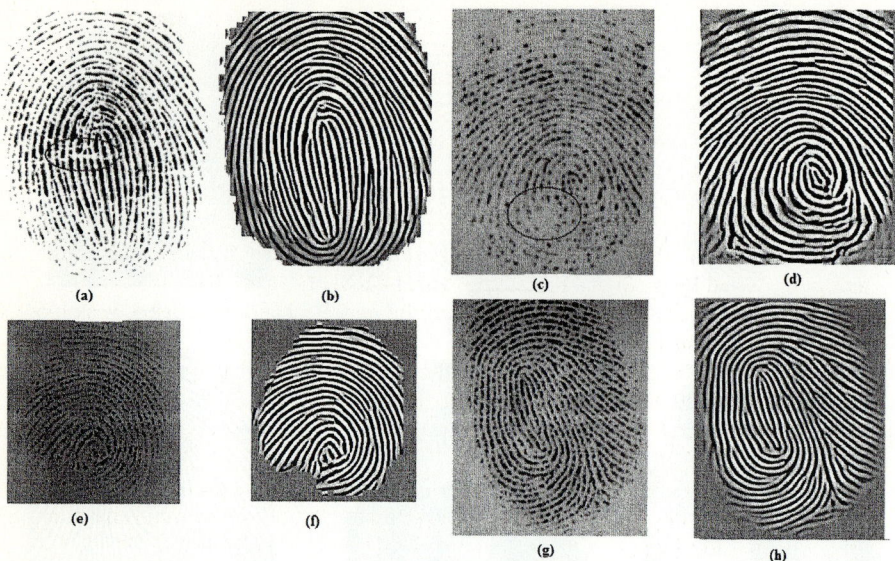

Fig. 5. Original and enhanced images (Samples from FVC2002 [25] database): (a,b) DB1 database,(c,d) DB2 (e,f) DB3, (g,h) DB4.

Table 1. Effect on enhancement on the final recognition accuracy

DB3 Results	Equal Error Rate
Without Enhancement	10.35%
With Enhancement	8.5%
Improvement	17%

filtering in the Fourier domain to address this problem. The proposed approach obviates the need for multiple algorithms to compute the intrinsic images and replaces it with a single unified approach. The algorithm utilized complete contextual information including instantaneous frequency, orientation and even orientation coherence/reliability. We performed an objective evaluation of the enhancement algorithm by considering the improvement in matching accuracy for poor quality fingerprints and showed that it results in net improvement in recognition rate. (The matlab code for the enhancement is available for download at http://www.cubs.buffalo.edu).

References

1. Maio, D., Maltoni, D., Jain, A.K., Prabhakar, S.: Handbook of Fingerprint Recognition. Springer Verlag (2003)
2. O'Gormann, L., J.V.Nickerson: An approach to fingerprint filter design. Pattern Recognition **22** (1989) 29–38

3. S., G., M., A., D., K., I., D.: Fingerprint image enhancement using filtering techniques. In: International Conference on Pattern Recognition. Volume 3. (2000) 326–329
4. Yang, G.Z., Burger, P., Firmin, D.N., Underwood, S.R.: Structure adaptive anisotropic image filtering. Image and Vision Computing **14** (1996) 135–145
5. Hong, L., Wang, Y., Jain, A.K.: Fingerprint image enhancement: Algorithm and performance evaluation. Transactions on PAMI **21** (1998) 777–789
6. Qian, S., Chen, D.: Joint Time-Frequency Analysis, Methods and Applications. Prentice Hall (1996)
7. B.G.Sherlock, D.M.Monro, K.Millard: Fingerprint enhancement by directional fourier filtering. In: Visual Image Signal Processing. Volume 141. (1994) 87–94
8. Connell, J., Ratha, N.K., Bolle, R.M.: Fingerprint image enhancement using weak models. In: IEEE International Conference on Image Processing. (2002)
9. Srinivasan, V.S., Murthy, N.N.: Detection of singular points in fingerprint images. Pattern Recognition **25** (1992) 139–153
10. Bazen, A.M., Gerez, S.: Extraction of singular points from directional fields of fingerprints. (2001)
11. Kawagoe, Tojo: Fingerprint pattern classification. Pattern Recogntion **17** (1987) 295–303
12. Mehtre, B.M., Murthy, N.N., Kapoor, S., Chatterjee, B.: Segmentation of fingerprint images using the directional image. Pattern Recognition **20** (1987) 429–425
13. Cappelli, R., Lumini, A., Maio, D., Maltoni, D.: Fingerprint classification by directional image partitioning. IEEE Transactions on Pattern Analysis and Machine Intelligence **21** (1999)
14. Candela, G.T., Grother, P.J., Watson, C.I., Wilkinson, R.A., Wilson, C.L.: Pcasys - a pattern-level classification automation system for fingerprints (1995)
15. Karu, K., Jain, A.: Fingerprint classification (1996)
16. Rao, K., Balck, K.: Type classification of fingerprints: A syntactic approach. IEEE Transactions on Pattern Analysis and Machine Intelligence **2** (1980) 223–231
17. Jain, A.K., Prabhakar, S., Hong, L.: A multichannel approach to fingerprint classification. IEEE Transactions on Pattern Analysis and Machine Intelligence **21** (1999) 348–359
18. Gonzalez, Woods, Eddins: Digital Image Processing. Prentice Hall (2004)
19. Kaas, M., Witkin, A.: Analyzing oriented patterns. Computer Vision Graphics Image Processing **37** (1987) 362–385
20. D., M., D., M.: Neural network based minutiae filtering in fingerprint images. In: 14th International Conference on Pattern Recognition. (1998) 1654–1658
21. Haykin, S., Veen, B.V.: Signals and Systems. John Wiley and Sons (1999)
22. Rabiner, Schafer: Digital Processing of Speech Signals. Prentice Hall International (1978)
23. Sonka, Hlavac, Boyle: Image Processing, Analysis and Machine Vision, second edition. Thomson Asia (2004)
24. Rao, A.R.: A Taxonomy of Texture Descriptions. (Springer Verlag)
25. : (Fingerprint verification competition) http://bias.csr.unibo.it/fvc2002/.

Symmetric Hash Functions for Fingerprint Minutiae

Sergey Tulyakov, Faisal Farooq, and Venu Govindaraju

Center for Unified Biometrics and Sensors, SUNY at Buffalo, NY 14228, USA

Abstract. The possibility that a biometric database is compromised is one of the main concerns in implementing biometric identification systems. The compromise of a biometric renders it permanently useless. In this paper we present a method of hashing fingerprint minutia information and performing fingerprint identification in a new space. Only hashed data is transmitted and stored in the server database, and it is not possible to restore fingerprint minutia locations using hashed data. We also present a performance analysis of the proposed algorithm.

1 Introduction

The problem we are dealing with is well described in section 9.7 of Handbook of Fingerprint recognition[1]. Plaintext passwords can be hashed, and only hash values are stored in the database and transmitted across networks. Password authentication requires comparison of the hashed values and not original passwords. If database with hash values is ever compromised, subjects can be re-enrolled using different passwords or different hash functions.

The situation is different when using biometric data for person authentication. Due to the difficulty of devising hash functions for biometric data, the biometric templates are often stored unprotected in a central database. Even if stored templates are encrypted, matching is still performed using decrypted templates, and decryption process can be compromised as well. If the biometric database is compromised and an intruder obtains a person's biometric template, using this biometric will be impossible for the rest of person's life.

In this work we want to devise a method for biometric data, in particular fingerprint data, to be hashed, and the biometric identification to be performed using hashed biometric data. Hashing functions can be one-way functions, and given such hash values it is impossible to reconstruct original template. Only the hash values are transmitted over the network and stored in the biometric database. In case the hash values are compromised, person will be re-enrolled using new hash functions. The original biometric(e.g. fingerprint) is safe and never compromised.

Figure 1 presents the architecture of a system using proposed hashing algorithm. Fingerprints are obtained by the scanner, minutia locations are found and hashes of minutia subsets are constructed. Finding minutiae and hashes can be incorporated into scanner. Only hashes are transmitted and stored in the

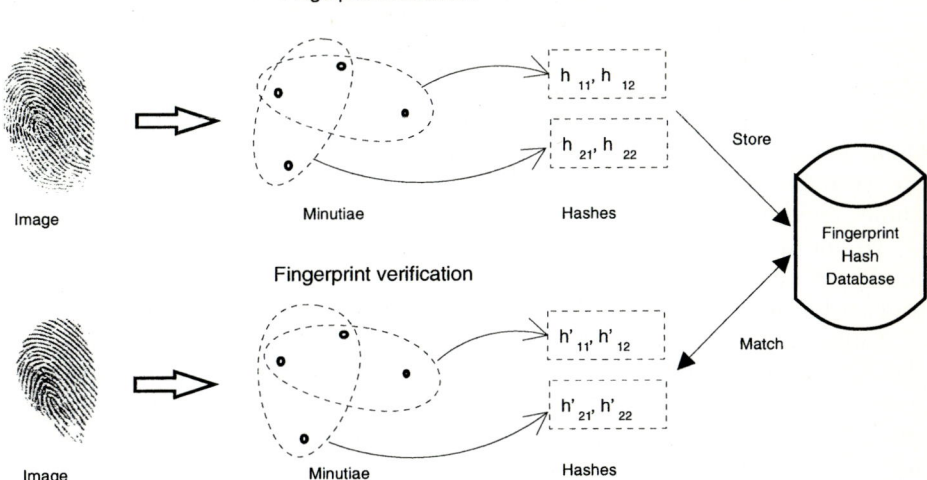

Fig. 1. Architecture of the proposed hashing algorithm

database. During the verification, new hash values are produced by the scanner and are matched with those stored in the database. Matching can be performed either on the client or on the server.

2 Related Work

The hashing functions for text passwords usually change hash values completely, even if a single character in a password is changed. Is it possible to construct a person authentication algorithm if we allow the password to change slightly? Error correcting codes [2] are designed to deal with such situations of recovering changed data and their use might be appropriate here. Indeed, Davida et al.[3] presented an authentication algorithm based on error correcting codes. In this algorithm, error-correcting digits are generated from the biometric data and some other verifying data, and stored in the database. During authenticating stage, possibly changed biometric data is combined with stored error-correcting digits and error correction is performed. The amount of correction required serves as a measure of the authentication success. This algorithm was later modified as fuzzy commitment scheme in the work of Juels and Wattenberg[4] and some of its properties were derived.

Fingerprint data with minutia positions as features presents additional challenges for designing hashes. Minutia sets of two fingerprints usually do not coincide, it is nearly impossible to introduce some order in minutia set, and global transformation parameters are usually present between corresponding minutiae. A fuzzy vault algorithm (Juels and Sudan [5]) improves upon fuzzy commitment scheme in trying to solve first two challenges and also uses error-correcting codes. The security of the algorithm relies on the addition of chaff points, or, in the case of fingerprint vault, false minutia points. The attacker would try to find a subset of points well intersecting with non-chaff point set. Thus more chaff points provides better security, but arguably worse vault unlocking performance. The application of fuzzy vault to fingerprint identification appeared in the work of Clancy et al.[6]. That paper showed realistic expectations on the numbers of chaff points and associated attack complexity. The algorithm used the assumption that fingerprints are aligned, and corresponding minutiae had similar coordinates.

To address the frequent impossibility to properly align fingerprint images, Uludag and Jain [7] proposed to use features independent of global rotation and translation. It is still unclear if this approach will work.

Soutar et al. [8] took another approach to secure fingerprint biometrics. The algorithm operates on images by constructing special filter in Fourier space encoding key data. The data can be retrieved only by presenting similar fingerprint image to the decoder. The matching procedure is correlation based, thus translations of images are possible but not rotations.

In our work we use ideas similar to [9] to combine results of localized matchings into the whole fingerprint recognition algorithm. In that work localized matching consists in matching minutia triplets using such features as angles and lengths between minutia points. For each minutia feature vector of length 3 (x,y,θ) and its two nearest neighbors, a secondary feature vector of length 5 is generated which is based on the Euclidean distances and orientation difference between the central minutia and its nearest neighbors. Matching is performed on these secondary features. In contrast, for localized matchings in this work we keep only limited information about matched neighborhoods, so that minutia positions can not be restored. Global matching is essentially finding a cluster of localized matchings with similar rotation(r) and transformation(t) parameters. It seems that proposed algorithm of Uludag and Jain[7] might also use this 2-stage technique. Unlike fingerprint vault algorithm[6] our algorithm performs hashing of not only enrolled fingerprint, but of test fingerprint also. Thus hashing can be incorporated into scanner, and original fingerprint data will never be transmitted nor stored in the database.

3 Hash Functions of Minutia Points

The main difficulty in producing hash functions for fingerprint minutiae is the inability to somehow normalize fingerprint data, for example, by finding specific fingerprint orientation and center. If fingerprint data is not normalized, then the values of any hashing functions are destined to be orientation/position- dependent. The way to overcome this difficulty is to have hash functions as well as matching algorithm deal with transformations of fingerprint data.

We represent minutia points as complex numbers $\{c_i\}$. We assume that two fingerprints of the same finger can have different position, rotation and scale, coming from possibly different scanners and different ways to put the finger on scanner. Thus the transformation of one fingerprint to the other can be described by the complex function $f(z) = rz + t$. In our approach we construct hash functions and corresponding matching algorithm, so that this transformation function is taken into account. Additionally we cannot set specific order of minutiae, so we want our hash functions be independent of this order. Thus we consider symmetric complex functions as our hash functions.

Specifically, given n minutia points $\{c_1, c_2, \ldots, c_n\}$ we construct following m symmetric hash functions

$$
\begin{aligned}
h_1(c_1, c_2, \ldots, c_n) &= c_1 + c_2 + \cdots + c_n \\
h_2(c_1, c_2, \ldots, c_n) &= c_1^2 + c_2^2 + \cdots + c_n^2 \\
&\cdots \\
h_m(c_1, c_2, \ldots, c_n) &= c_1^m + c_2^m + \cdots + c_n^m
\end{aligned}
\tag{1}
$$

Suppose that the another image of the fingerprint is obtained through above described transformation $f(z) = rz + t$, thus locations of corresponding minutia points are $c'_i = f(c_i) = rc_i + t$. Hash functions of the transformed minutiae can be rewritten as

$$
\begin{aligned}
h_1(c'_1, c'_2, \ldots, c'_n) &= c'_1 + c'_2 + \cdots + c'_n \\
&= (rc_1 + t) + (rc_2 + t) + \cdots + (rc_n + t) \\
&= r(c_1 + c_2 + \cdots + c_n) + nt = rh_1(c_1, c_2, \ldots, c_n) + nt \\
h_2(c'_1, c'_2, \ldots, c'_n) &= c'^2_1 + c'^2_2 + \cdots + c'^2_n \\
&= (rc_1 + t)^2 + (rc_2 + t)^2 + \cdots + (rc_n + t)^2 \\
&= r^2(c_1^2 + c_2^2 + \cdots + c_n^2) + 2rt(c_1 + c_2 + \cdots + c_n) + nt^2 \\
&= r^2 h_2(c_1, c_2, \ldots, c_n) + 2rh_1(c_1, c_2, \ldots, c_n) + nt^2 \\
&\cdots
\end{aligned}
\tag{2}
$$

Let us denote the hash values of the minutia set of one fingerprint as $h_i = h_i(c_1, c_2, \ldots, c_n)$ and hash values of corresponding minutia set of another fingerprint as $h'_i = h_i(c'_1, c'_2, \ldots, c'_n)$. Equations 2 now become

$$
\begin{aligned}
h'_1 &= rh_1 + nt \\
h'_2 &= r^2 h_2 + 2rth_1 + nt^2 \\
h'_3 &= r^3 h_3 + 3r^2 th_2 + 3rt^2 h_1 + nt^3 \\
&\cdots
\end{aligned}
\tag{3}
$$

Equations 3 have two unknown variables r and t. If we take into account errors introduced during fingerprint scanning and minutia search, the relation between hash values of enrolled fingerprint $\{h_1, \ldots, h_m\}$ and hash values of test fingerprint $\{h'_1, \ldots, h'_m\}$ can be represented as

$$
h_i = f_i(r, t, h_1, \ldots, h_n) + \epsilon_i
\tag{4}
$$

The matching between hash values of enrolled fingerprint $\{h_1, \ldots, h_m\}$ and hash values of test fingerprint $\{h'_1, \ldots, h'_m\}$ consists in finding r and t that minimize errors ϵ_i. During algorithm implementation we considered minimization of error functions $\epsilon = \sum \alpha_i |\epsilon_i|$, where weights α_i were chosen empirically.

4 Global Fingerprint Matching Using Hash Functions

It turns out that trying to use hash functions with respect to the minutia set of whole fingerprint is impractical. Even the small difference in minutia sets of two prints of the same finger will produce significant difference in hash values. Additionally, the higher order hash values tend to change greatly with the small change in positions of minutia points.

To overcome these difficulties we considered using hash functions for matching localized sets of minutia, and global matching of two fingerprints as a collection of localized matchings with similar transformation parameters r and t. As in base fingerprint matcher[9] the localized set is determined by a particular minutia and few of its neighbors. The hashes are calculated for each localized set. Total hash data extracted from fingerprint is a set of hashes $\{h_{i,1}, \ldots, h_{i,m}\}$, $i = 1, \ldots, k$, where k is the total number of localized minutia sets.

During matching of two hash sets we first perform a match of all localized sets in one fingerprint to all localized sets in another fingerprint. The matches with highest confidences are retained. Then, assuming in turn that a particular match is a correct match, we find how many other matches have similar transformation parameters. The match score is composed from the number of close matches and confidences of those matches.

5 Experiments

We carried out experiments with different configurations, using different number of minutia points(n) and hashing functions(m). We tried out the configurations as follows

1. $n = 2$, $m = 1$. For each minutia point we find its nearest neighbor, and the hash function $h(c_1, c_2) = \frac{c_1+c_2}{2}$
2. $n = 3$, $m = 1$. For each minutia point we find two nearest neighbors and the hash function $h(c_1, c_2, c_3) = \frac{c_1+c_2+c_3}{3}$
3. $n = 3$, $m = 2$: for each minutia point find three nearest neighbors, and for each minutia triplet including original minutia point construct two hash functions using the formula $h_m(c_1, c_2, \ldots, c_n) = c_1^m + c_2^m + \cdots + c_n^m$ where $m = 1, 2$.

We use similar formulae for directions.

We compared performance with fingerprint matching algorithm developed in [9] and using same set of fingerprints with identically extracted minutiae points. Also, since in configurations 1 and 2 we simply get another set of minutia points, we used matching algorithm of [9] to perform matching. We tested our system on $FVC2002$'s DB1 database. The dataset consists of 110 different fingers and

8 impressions for each finger. There are a total of 880 fingerprints(388 pixels by 374 pixels) at 500 dpi with various image quality. We followed the protocols of FVC2002 to evaluate the FAR(False Accept Rate) and FRR(False Reject Rate). For FRR the total number of genuine tests is $\frac{(8*7)}{2}*100 = 2800$. For FAR the total number of impostor tests is $\frac{(100*99)}{2} = 4950$. Currently achieved equal error rate(EER) of proposed algorithm is $\sim 3\%$. The EER for plain matching is $\sim 1.7\%$. The ROC characteristics of the baseline system and the different configurations of our system are shown in figure 2.

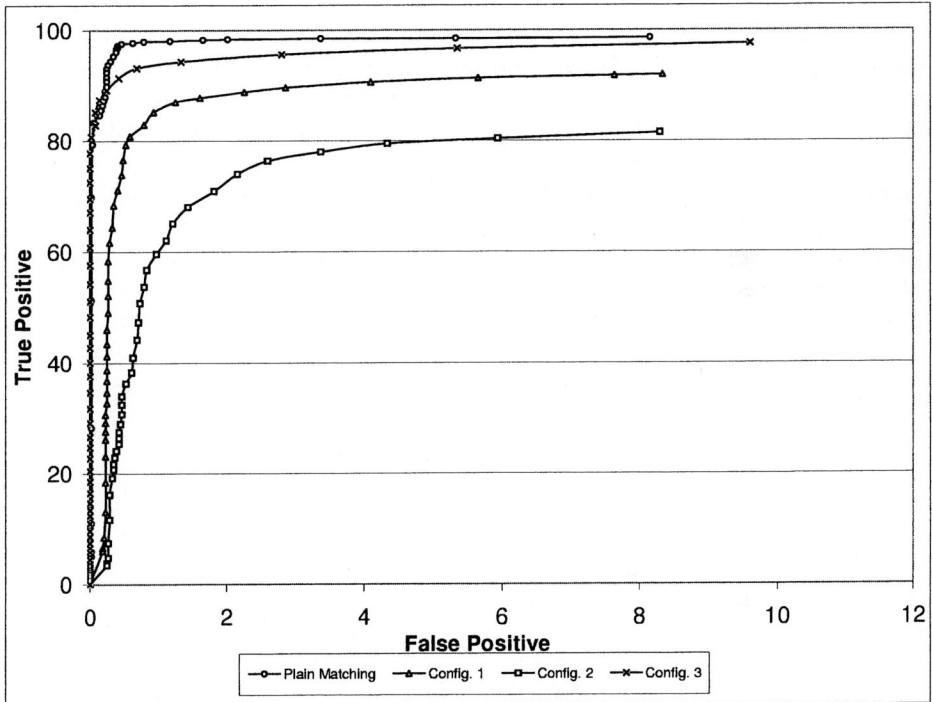

Fig. 2. ROC Curves for the baseline system[9] and the different experimental configurations

The decrease in the accuracy might be caused by the loss in information when keeping reduced number of variables based on minutia triplets. For every three neighboring minutia points we have reduced the number of variables to 4 (2 complex numbers) instead of original 6. It should be also noted that the total number of hashed values is not reduced in the same proportion since the same minutia can participate in the production of more than one triplet as described in figure 3. Thus the total size of stored hash values can be even bigger than the size of original fingerprint template. There can be additional reasons for observed performance hit, such as difficulty in matching localized hashed values and reduced number of matched localized neighborhoods. Determining exact cause of performance loss and correcting it is one of the future research topics.

Nevertheless, the benefits of securing fingerprint data can easily outweigh the performance loss in many applications. Performance loss would mean stricter decisions on matching, and more frequent repeat matching attempts. Arguably many people will trade off the assurance on their fingerprint template privacy for the inconvenience of performing repeat fingerprint scan.

6 Security of Proposed Algorithm

The main purpose of the proposed algorithm is to conceal original fingerprint and minutiae locations from an attacker. Is it possible to reconstruct minutia positions given stored hash values? Since the number of hash values for each local minutia set is less than number of these minutiae, it is not possible to get locations using only information of one local set. On the other hand, it seems possible to construct a big system of equations involving all hashes (hashes of only first order might be considered for linearity). The biggest problem in constructing such system is that it is not known which minutia participated in the creation of particular hash value.

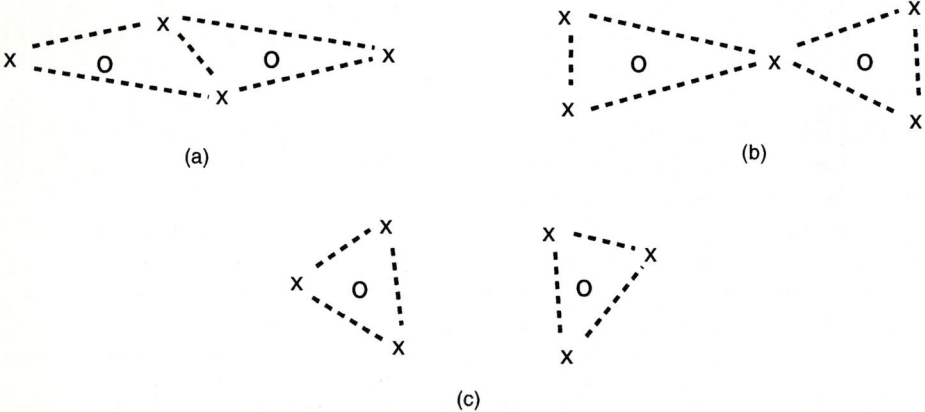

Fig. 3. Different number of minutiae(crosses) can participate in the creation of two triplet centers(circles)

The problem is illustrated in figure 3. Two triplet centers are formed from 4, 5 and 6 minutia points. Thus during constructing an equation system for finding minutia positions, we have a problem of deciding how many minutiae should be, in addition to matching minutia to triplet centers.

Hill-climbing type attacks[10] will probably have more difficult time to make a match since varying minutia position might have effect on few triplets, thus influencing matching score in a more complex way. Also, we think, that even if attack succeeded and match is found, the resulting minutiae locations will be different from original. In this situation, change of hashing algorithm will make reconstructed fingerprint unmatchable.

7 Future Work

In this paper we presented one method of constructing hash functions. To achieve a cancellable biometric algorithm we need to provide a way to automatically construct and use randomly generated hash functions. Presented set of hash functions is an algebraic basis in the set of polynomial symmetric functions. Thus, we were able to express hash functions of transformed minutia set through original set of symmetric functions. This is a clue to constructing other similar hash functions. Essentially we can take arbitrary algebraic basis of symmetric polynomials of degree less than or equal to m, $\{s_1, \ldots, s_m\}$ as our hash functions. Then the hash functions of the transformed minutiae, $s_i(rc_1 + t, \ldots, rc_n + t)$, will still be symmetric functions of the same degree with respect to variables $c_1, \ldots, c_n$. Thus, hashes of transformed minutia could be expressed using original hashes, $s'_i = s_i(rc_1 + t, \ldots, rc_n + t) = F_i(r, t, s_1, \ldots, s_m)$ for some polynomial functions F_i. These equations will allow matching localized minutia sets, and finding corresponding transformation parameters.

In presented algorithm global matching relies heavily on first order hash functions, basically centers of minutia triplets. If we want to use arbitrary symmetric hash functions, then the global matching algorithm should be modified.

The ROC curves in figure 2 suggest that the algorithm has slightly lesser accuracy than the baseline system which could be attributed to the fact that by considering centers of minutia triplets as the features to match, we might lose some information that the original minutia possess. Currently we are working on improving the accuracy of the system by possibly learning the parameters automatically and also trying to possibly use different scoring techniques.

Additional possible area of research is the use of scalar functions. For example, it is easy to construct minutia triplet features which are rotation and translation invariant. But, since algorithm requires estimation of rotation and translation, these features will not suffice.

References

1. Maltoni, D., Maio, D., Jain, A.K., Prabhakar, S.: Handbook of Fingerprint Recognition. Springer, New York, (2003)
2. Peterson, W., Weldon, E.: Error-Correcting Codes. 2nd edn. MIT Press, Cambridge, USA (1972)
3. Davida, G., Frankel, Y., Matt, B.: On enabling secure applications through on-line biometric identification. In: Proc. of the IEEE 1998 Symp. on Security and Privacy, Oakland, Ca. (1998)
4. Juels, A., Wattenberg, M.: A fuzzy commitment scheme. In: ACM Conference on Computer and Communications Security. (1999) 28–36

5. Juels, A., Sudan, M.: A fuzzy vault scheme. In: IEEE International Symposium on Information Theory. (2002)
6. Clancy, T., Lin, D., Kiyavash, N.: Secure smartcard-based fingerprint authentication. In: ACM Workshop on Biometric Methods and Applications (WBMA 2003). (2003)
7. Uludag, U., Jain, A.: Fuzzy fingerprint vault. In: Proc. Workshop: Biometrics: Challenges Arising from Theory to Practice. (2004) 13–16
8. Soutar, C., Roberge, D., Stoianov, A., Gilroy, R., Kumar, V.: Biometric encryption. In Nichols, R., ed.: ICSA Guide to Cryptography. McGraw-Hill (1999)
9. Jea, T.Y., Chavan, V.S., Govindaraju, V., Schneider, J.K.: Security and matching of partial fingerprint recognition systems. In: SPIE Defense and Security Symposium. (2004)
10. Uludag, U., Jain, A.: Attacks on biometric systems: a case study in fingerprints. In: SPIE-EI 2004, Security, Seganography and Watermarking of Multimedia Contents VI. (2004)

A Digital Rights Management Approach for Gray-Level Images

Shu-Fen Tu[1] and Ching-Sheng Hsu[2]

[1] Department of Information Management, Chinese Culture University,
No.55, Huagang Rd., Shihlin District, Taipei City 11114, Taiwan, R.O.C
`dsf3@faculty.pccu.edu.tw`
[2] Institute of Information Management, Ming Chuan University,
No.5, Deming Rd., Gueishan Township, Taoyuan County 33348, Taiwan, R.O.C
`cshsu@alumni.nccu.edu.tw`

Abstract. This paper presents a digital rights management approach for gray-level images. The ownership of the original image is identified with an ownership statement, which is a gray-level image as well. The proposed scheme utilizes block truncation coding (BTC) to create a master share, which is then used to produce an ownership share against the ownership statement. When in doubt about the property of an image, the author should address his/her ownership share to reveal the ownership statement to claim the ownership. Since our method does not embed the ownership statement into the host image, we can register more than one ownership statements for a single image without destroying the former ownership statements. Besides, the original image does not need to involve in the process of identifying the ownership. Finally, experimental results will show the robustness of our scheme against several common attacks.

1 Introduction

Digital watermarking is a kind of techniques for protecting the intellectual property right of digital images. A meaningful signature, called a watermark, is embedded into a digital image, called a host, to register the ownership and can be detected when the ownership of the image needs to be identified. Most related techniques have to alter the original image to embed the information of the digital watermark [1–4]. Although some methods can embed multiple watermarks in a single image, the damage to the former watermark caused by the later one is inevitable. Recently, Chang et al. [5] proposed a new copyright protection scheme with a four-color signature. Their method transforms the host image and the signature into two binary images using discrete cosine transform (DCT) and visual cryptography (VC), respectively. Then, the two binary images are used to create an ownership share, which can be a key to reveal the signature to identify the ownership. Since the signature is not embedded into the host image, multiple ownership can be registered without destroying each other. However, their method can use four-color images as signatures only. Generally speaking, a meaningful chromatic image usually has more than four colors. Hence their method becomes impracticable when one needs to use a meaningful chromatic image to be the signature. Besides, their method spends 12×12 pixels to carry one pixel of the signature. Therefore, when the number of colors of the signature increases, the size of the watermark has to be much smaller than that of the host image. Moreover, a transformation of the host image from the spatial domain to the frequency domain must be preformed so that the binary image can be constructed.

In consideration of facilitating using more meaningful images as signatures, we propose another copyright protection method for gray-level digital images, where a gray-level image is used as an ownership statement. Our scheme has two phases: one is the ownership share generation phase; the other is the ownership identification phase. In the ownership share generation phase, we utilize block truncation coding (BTC) [6–7] to transform the original image into a binary image, called a master share, which represents the features of the original image. Then, an ownership share is produced in the light of the master share and the ownership statement. For the sake of security, we will disarrange the pixels of the original image using a pseudo random number generator before producing the master share. The ownership share is the key to reveal the ownership statement in the future, so it has to be sent to a trusted third party for authentication to show good faith to everyone. In the ownership identification phase, the test image is transformed to a master share by means of BTC firstly. Then, the ownership statement can be revealed according to the master share and the ownership share held by the author.

Our method has several advantages. Firstly, we don't need to alter the host image; hence the image quality won't be decreased. Secondly, our method can identify the ownership without resorting to the original image. Only the ownership share needs to be addressed to identify the ownership when the dispute about the property of an image is happened. Thirdly, multiple ownership can be registered for a single image without interfering with each other. Fourthly, our method can attain the requirement of robustness for the ownership statement as shown in the experimental results. Finally, and most importantly, the ownership statement is not restricted to be binary images only or to be images with limit colors. We can handle gray-level signatures; therefore, our method has more applications than copyright protection. For example, our method can be used to cover the transmission of confidential images.

The rest of this paper is organized as follows. In Sect. 2, we will explain the proposed copyright protection scheme for gray-level images in detail. Then, the experimental results and some discussions are presented in Sect. 3. And finally, we will give some conclusions in Sect. 4.

2 The Proposed Scheme

2.1 Ownership Share Generation

Assume that an ownership statement W is a gray-level image of $N \times M$ pixels and the original image H is a gray-level image of $3N \times 3M$ pixels. Before the process starts, H has to be permuted using a pseudo-random number generator seeded by a key *key* to enhance the robustness of the scheme. Then we perform the block truncation coding (BTC) to encode the permuted image H' into a binary master share of $3N \times 3M$ pixels. The image H' is divided into blocks of 3×3 pixels firstly. Then, for each block, we compute a mean value μ of all pixels, and for each pixel in a block, we set it to '1' if its value is greater than or equal to μ; otherwise, we set it to '0'. Hereafter, BTC is completed, and the master share is produced. Next, each pixel s of the ownership statement is converted into an 8-bit binary string, i.e. $(s_1s_2s_3s_4s_5s_6s_7s_8)_2$. Each binary string is arranged as a block of 3×3 pixels from top-left to bottom-right. Since the number of pixels of a block is more than the length of the binary string by one, the most bottom-right pixel of the block is left unused and marked with bit '0'. By doing so, we can transform each pixel of the ownership statement into a binary block. Finally, all of the blocks are collectively formed as a binary image of $3N \times 3M$ pixels. From now on, we can produce our ownership share O by performing the logic XOR operation on the binary image and the master share. Fig. 1 depicts the whole process of ownership share generation, and the algorithm is shown below.

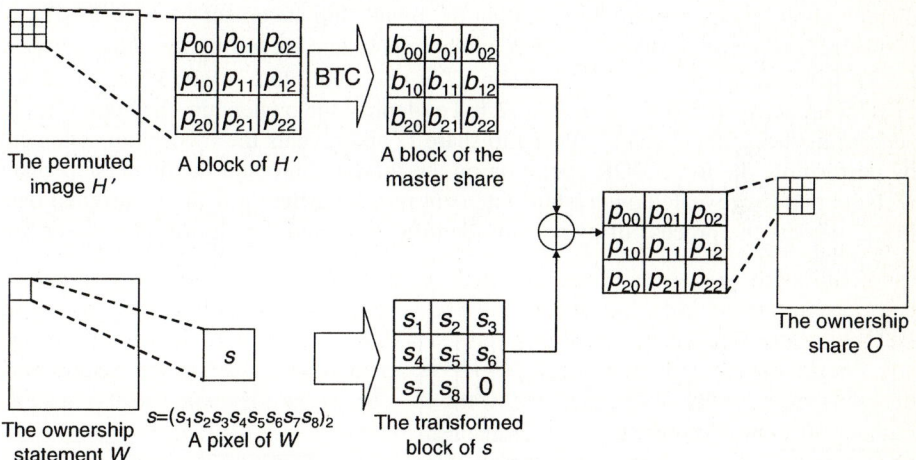

Fig. 1. Illustration of ownership share generation

Algorithm. *Ownership Share Generation*
Input: A gray-level ownership statement W of $N \times M$ pixels
A gray-level host image H of $3N \times 3M$ pixels
A seed *key* of the pseudo random number generator
Output: An ownership share O of $3N \times 3M$ pixels
Step 1. Permute H using pseudo-random number generator seeded by *key*. Denote the permuted image as H'.
Step 2. Divide H' into equal-size block of 3×3 pixels to derive a set of blocks $\{H'_{ij}\}$, where $i = 0..(N-1)$ and $j = 0..(M-1)$. Each pixel of H'_{ij} is denoted as p^{ij}_{mn}, where $m = 0..2$ and $n = 0..2$, and p^{ij}_{00} is located at the position $(3i, 3j)$ of H'.
Step 3. For the block H'_{ij} of H', calculate the mean value μ_{ij} of the pixels. Set p^{ij}_{mn} to '1' if its value greater than or equal to μ_{ij}; otherwise, set it to '0', where $m = 0..2$ and $n = 0..2$.

Step 4. Convert the pixel w_{ij} of W to an 8-bit binary number s^{ij}, where $i = 0..(N-1)$ and $j = 0..(M-1)$. Append bit 0 to s^{ij}, and denote each bit of s^{ij} as s_t^{ij}, where $t = 1..9$.

Step 5. Generate the pixel q_{uv} of O through logic XOR; i.e. $q_{uv} = p_{mn}^{ij} \oplus s_{3m+n+1}^{ij}$, where $u = 3i + m$, $v = 3j + m$, $m = 0..2$ and $n = 0..2$.

Step 6. Repeat Step 3 to 5 until all blocks of H' are processed.

2.2 Ownership Identification

If a gray-level image G is suspected to be a piracy copy, the author can resolve the dispute about the ownership by revealing the ownership statement from G. Firstly, G is disarranged using a pseudo-random number generator seeded by the same key *key*. Let G' denote the permuted image. Then, G' is encoded into a master share by means of BTC as we have described in Sect. 2.1. To identify the ownership, the author has to address his/her authenticated ownership share O and reveals the ownership statement by performing the logic XOR operation on the master share and the ownership share O. Note that the revealed ownership statement may be different from the original one. Fig. 2 depicts the process of ownership identification, and the algorithm is described as follows.

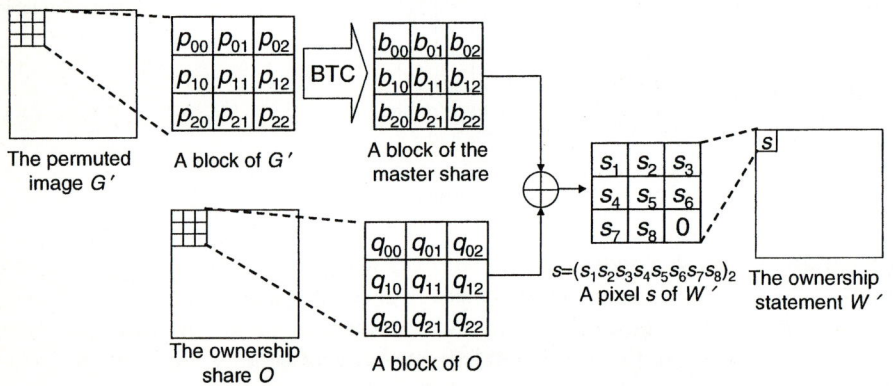

Fig. 2. Illustration of ownership identification

Algorithm. *Ownership Identification*
Input: A gray-level test image G of $3N \times 3M$ pixels
An ownership share O of $3N \times 3M$ pixels
A seed *key* of the pseudo random number generator
Output: An ownership statement W of $N \times M$ pixels
Step 1. Permute G using a pseudo-random number generator seeded by *key*. Denote the permuted image as G'.

Step 2. Divide G' into equal-size blocks of 3×3 pixels to derive a set of blocks $\{G'_{ij}\}$, where $i = 0..(N - 1)$ and $j = 0..(M - 1)$. Each pixels of G'_{ij} are denoted as p^{ij}_{mn}, where $m = 0..2$ and $n = 0..2$, and p^{ij}_{00} is located at $(3i, 3j)$ of G'.

Step 3. Divide O into equal-size blocks of 3×3 pixels to derive a set of blocks $\{O_{ij}\}$, where $i = 0..(N - 1)$ and $j = 0..(M - 1)$. Each pixels of O_{ij} are denoted as q^{ij}_{mn}, where $m = 0..2$ and $n = 0..2$, and q^{ij}_{00} is located at the position $(3i, 3j)$ of G'.

Step 4. For the block G'_{ij} of G', calculate the mean value μ_{ij} of the pixels. Set p^{ij}_{mn} to 1 if its value greater than or equal to μ_{ij}; otherwise, set it to 0, where $m = 0..2$ and $n = 0..2$.

Step 5. Generate a 9-bit binary string $(s_1s_2s_3s_4s_5s_6s_7s_8s_9)_2$ through performing logic XOR on p^{ij}_{mn} and q^{ij}_{mn}, i.e. $s_{3m+n} = p^{ij}_{mn} \oplus q^{ij}_{mn}$, where $m = 0..2$ and $n = 0..2$.

Step 6. Set the value of pixel w_{ij} of W according to the following equation:

$$w_{ij} = \sum_{k=1}^{8}\left(s_k \times 2^{8-k}\right). \tag{1}$$

Step 7. Repeat Step 4 to 6 until all blocks of G' are processed.

3 Results and Discussions

In this section, several experiments are performed to demonstrate the robustness of the proposed scheme against several common attacks, including darkening, lightening, rescaling, blurring, sharpening, noising, geometric distortion, cropping, and JPEG lossy compression attacks. The above attacks are done by Adobe Photoshop version 7.0, and the related parameters of each attack are listed in Table 1. The gray-level host image of 540×540 pixels and the gray-level ownership statement of 180×180 pixels are shown in Fig. 3(a) and Fig. 3(b), respectively. Besides, we use the peak signal-to-noise ratio (PSNR) to measure the similarity between two gray-level images. The similarity measurement PSNR is defined as follows:

$$PSNR = 10 \times \log \frac{255^2}{MSE}. \tag{2}$$

For gray-level images, MSE can be defined as

$$MSE_{gray} = \frac{1}{M_1 \times M_2}\sum_{i=1}^{M_1}\sum_{j=1}^{M_2}(c_{i,j} - c'_{i,j})^2, \tag{3}$$

Table 1. Parameters of attacks

Attacks	Parameters (Adobe Photoshop version 7.0)
Darkening	Brightness: −30
Lightening	Brightness: +30
Rescaling	Downscaling the image by a factor of 2 in each direction and then upscaling the downscaled image to the original size
Blurring	Blur more
Sharpening	Sharpen more
Noising	Add noise: amount = 10%, distribution = uniform
Geometric distortion	Ripple: amount = 100%, size = medium
Cropping	Erasing about 20% area of the image
JPEG	Quality = 5, format option = baseline optimized

(a) (b)

Fig. 3. (a) The gray-level host image (540 × 540 pixels, 300 dpi); (b) The gray-level ownership statement (180 × 180 pixels, 150 dpi).

where $c_{i,j}$ denotes a gray-level of the original image, $c'_{i,j}$ denotes a gray-level of the attacked image, and $M_1 \times M_2$ is the image size.

In Fig. 4, we illustrate the attacked images and their corresponding recovered gray-level ownership statements upon different image processing operations. Note that $PSNR_w$ denotes the *PSNR* between the recovered ownership statement and the original one, and $PSNR_a$ denotes the *PSNR* between the original image and the attacked image. As shown in the experimental results, we could conclude that the proposed scheme can resist several common attacks. Especially, we found that our method can effectively resist the lightening and darkening image processing operations. However, we also found that the proposed scheme appears weak against the cropping attack with more than 25% area copped.

In case an adversary knows our scheme, he may try to alter the host image so that the ownership statement may not be successfully revealed. One possible way to achieve his purpose is to disturb the pattern of the master share. We make a reasonable assumption that the adversary does not know the seed of the pseudo-random number generator; therefore, he may directly divide the host image into 3×3

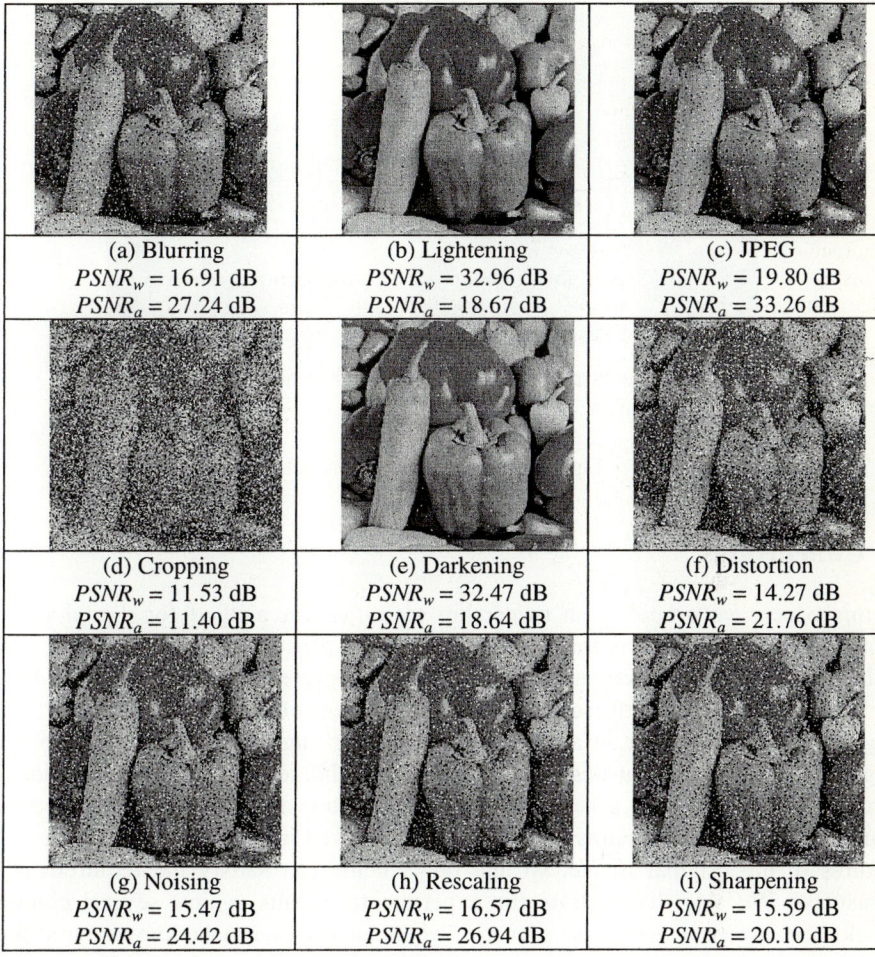

Fig. 4. The experimental results of gray-level ownership statements

blocks without disarranging it. Then, for each block, the adversary can interchange pixels whose values are greater than or equal to the mean value with other pixels whose values are less than the mean value. By doing so, the binary blocks of the master share may be largely different from the original one, and thus the revealed gray-level ownership statement cannot be identified. Such scenario can be represented by the experiment shown in Fig. 5. Fig. 5(a) is the attacked result ($PSNR_a$ = 17.35 dB), and Fig. 5(b) is the corresponding revealed ownership statement ($PSNR_w$ = 11.99 dB). According to the low $PSNR$ value of Fig. 5(a), we can know that the host image is seriously damaged. Nevertheless, we still can identify the content of the revealed ownership statement with eyes. Therefore, even though an adversary knows our scheme and attempts to destroy the host image, the revealed ownership statement is still robust enough to be identified.

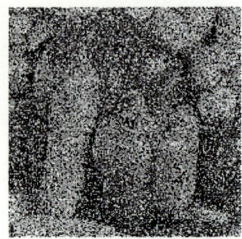

(a) The attacked result
$PSNR_a = 17.35$ dB

(b) Known-Scheme attack
$PSNR_w = 11.99$ dB

Fig. 5. The known-scheme attack

4 Conclusions

In this paper, we proposed an ownership identification method for digital images using a gray-level image as an ownership statement. Since the scheme dose not really embed the ownership statement into the image to be protected, the host image will not be altered, and the rightful ownership can be identified without resorting to the original image. Moreover, it also allows registering more than one ownership for a single host image without destroying each other. Unlike many transformed-domain approaches, the proposed scheme does not need to transform the image between the spatial and frequency domains. Instead, BTC is utilized in our scheme to preserve the features of the original image, so that our scheme can satisfy the requirement of robustness. We also demonstrate the experimental results against several common attacks and discuss a worst-case scenario, where an adversary who knows our scheme may attempt to attack the host image. In the future, we will extend our scheme to 256-color and true-color ownership statements.

References

1. Cox, I.J., Kilian, J., Leighton, T., and Shamoon, T.: Secure Spread Spectrum Watermarking for Multimedia. IEEE Trans. Image Processing 6 (12) (1997) 1673–1687
2. Low, S. and Maxemchuk, N.: Performance Comparison of Two Text Marking Methods. IEEE J. Selected Areas in Commun. 16 (4) (1998) 561–572
3. Matsui, K., Ohnishi, J., and Nakamura, Y.: Embedding a Signature to Pictures under Wavelet Transform. IEICE Trans. J79-D-II (6) (1996) 1017–1024
4. Ohbuchi, R., Masuda, H., and Aono, M.: Watermarking Three-Dimensional Polygonal Models through Geometric and Topological Modifications. IEEE J. Selected Areas in Commun. 16 (4) (1998) 551–560

5. Chang, C.C., Hsiao, J.Y., and Yeh, J.C.: A Colour Image Copyright Protection Scheme Based on Visual Cryptography and Discrete Cosine Transform. Imaging Science J. 50 (2002) 133–140
6. Delp, E.J. and Mitchell, O.R.: Image Compression Using Block Truncation Coding. IEEE Trans. Commun. COM-27 (1979) 1335–1342
7. Fränti, P., Nevalatinen, O., and Kaukoranta, T.: Compression of Digital Images by Block Truncation Coding: A Survey. The Computer J. 37 (4) (1994) 308–332

Millimetre-Wave Personnel Scanners for Automated Weapon Detection

Beatriz Grafulla-González, Christopher D. Haworth, Andrew R. Harvey,
Katia Lebart, Yvan R. Petillot, Yves de Saint-Pern,
Mathilde Tomsin, and Emanuele Trucco

Electrical, Electronic and Computer Engineering Department,
School of Engineering and Physical Sciences,
Heriot-Watt University, EH14 4AS, Edinburgh, United Kingdom
{bg5, C.D.Haworth}@hw.ac.uk

Abstract. The ATRIUM project aims to the automatic detection of threats hidden under clothes using millimetre-wave imaging. We describe a simulator of realistic millimetre-wave images and a system for detecting metallic weapons automatically. The latter employs two stages, detection and tracking. We present a detector for metallic objects based on mixture models, and a target tracker based on particle filtering. We show convincing, simulated millimetre-wave images of the human body with and without hidden threats, including a comparison with real images, and very good detection and tracking performance with eight real sequences. (International Workshop on Pattern Recognition for Crime Prevention, Security and Surveillance)

1 Introduction

The ATRIUM project (Automatic Threat Recognition and Identification Using Millimetre-waves) emerges from the necessity to protect public environments such as airports, train stations and other public buildings. The project investigates the use of a millimetre-wave (henceforth MMW) imaging sensor combined with image processing techniques for detecting threats hidden under clothes.

We present our current work and results on two image processing approaches: an *image-based strand*, whereby image intensities are analysed without reference to the physics of image formation; and a *physics-based strand*, whereby the image is analysed on the basis of a physical model of MMW image formation.

Specifically, we report a system for the automatic detection and tracking of metallic objects concealed on moving people in sequences of MMW images (image-based strand), and a complete model for the formation and simulation of MMW images (physics-based strand).

We adopt QinetiQ's recently demonstrated, proof-of-concept sensor, providing video-frame sequences with near-CIF resolution (320 × 240 pixels). It can image through clothing, plastics and fabrics. Together, through-clothes imaging and current video sequence analysis offer huge potential for automatic, covert detection of weapons concealed under clothes.

Existing MMW simulation packages, e.g., PMWCM or Speos, are not designed for indoors scenes and do not model specular reflections or bulk emission, which makes them unsuitable for ATRIUM. We have therefore developed a novel simulator combining a ray-tracer (Zemax) and low-level Matlab modules to process ray-tracing data. The system models both the geometry *and* the physical parameters of the scene objects, allowing full simulation of MMW images and sequences of indoors scenes.

To our best knowledge, very little work has been reported on the automatic analysis of MMW sequences or images. Most authors focus on very basic segmentation [1] or image fusion. In a related application, shape identification on segmented images [1] has been investigated and suitable shape descriptors proposed. More recently, basic work on object detection has appeared [2]. The main contribution of our work is therefore to apply advanced image processing techniques to a new video imaging technology of high potential for public security.

This paper is divided into three parts: first, an introduction to MMW images focusing on image formation and simulation; second, a description of our metallic-threat detection algorithm; third, experimental results for both simulation and detection.

2 Millimetre-Wave Images

2.1 Formation of Millimetre-Wave Images

Two different phenomena influence the formation of MMW images; (1) the combination of signal power from various components of the scene and (2) the modification of the recorded signal by the instrument response, including the impulse response of the imaging sensor and noise artifacts such as, for instance, those due to scanning and interpolation.

The radiation frequency used is $f = 35$ GHz or equivalently $\lambda \approx 9$ mm in wavelength. The focal length of the imager is 0.8 m resulting in a diffraction-limited spot-size of ~ 2 cm. We consider only short-range indoor scenes with mostly incoherent illumination [3].

The temperature of the objects in the scene is above absolute zero, so that scene objects radiate power in the MMW range with an emissivity ϵ compared to the radiation of an ideal black body. Since the surfaces of body and threats are flat at the scale of the illumination wavelength, reflections are considered specular [4]. This implies that scattering effects are small and light propagation within the scene obeys ray optics approximations. The intensity of MMW radiation at each pixel is determined by three different contributions: self-emission by scene components, reflections from illumination source and background radiation. We consider illumination as ambient background black body radiation with temperature around 290 K and by extended diffuse sources with high equivalent temperatures of, typically, 800 K. The reflectivity, R, the emissivity, ϵ, and the transmissivity t are related through Equation (1) [5].

$$R + \epsilon + t = 1 \qquad (1)$$

These three coefficients depend on the physical characteristics of materials and geometrical aspects of the scene defined via the dielectric constant ε, the permeability μ, the angle of incidence θ_i, the angle between the electric field and the plane of incidence α, and the polarization p (horizontal or vertical). Note that these coefficients can be expressed as a sum of their "projections" on the horizontal and vertical polarization planes, as described in Equation (2) for the power reflectivity [6]:

$$R(\varepsilon, \mu, \theta, \alpha) = R_p(\varepsilon, \mu, \theta) \cos^2 \alpha + R_s(\varepsilon, \mu, \theta) \sin^2 \alpha, \qquad (2)$$

where $R_p(\varepsilon, \mu, \theta)$ is the power reflectivity in P-polarisation and $R_s(\varepsilon, \mu, \theta)$ the power reflectivity in S-polarisation. Similar equations can be obtained for transmissivity and emissivity.

Since the source is incoherent, the three intensity coefficients in Equation (1) are added (Fig. 1), obtaining Equation (3). This describes the temperature received by the sensor [4]:

$$T_{rec}(\varepsilon, \mu, \theta, \alpha) = R\, T_{ill} + \epsilon\, T_{obj} + t\, T_{back}, \qquad (3)$$

where $T_{rec}(\varepsilon, \mu, \theta, \alpha)$ is the received temperature, T_{ill} the temperature of the illumination, T_{obj} the temperature of the object and T_{back} the temperature of the background. T_{ill}, T_{obj} and T_{back} are constant values.

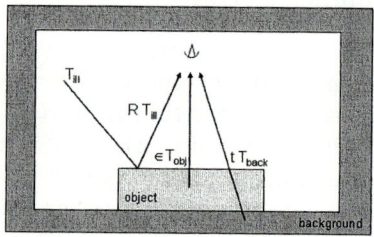

Fig. 1. Illustration of the combination of power from various scene components

Finally, we assume a highly incoherent illumination source to allow Equation (3). However, it is important to remark that the source has some residual spatial and temporal coherence, resulting in low-level speckle noise (see Subsection 4.1).

2.2 Simulation of Millimetre-Wave Images

As we consider indoors scenes with incoherent illumination, MMW image formation is modelled as superposition of the components in Equation (3). To generate synthetic MMW images we must model these components as well as relevant sensor effects.

In envisaged security applications, the scene is composed by a person possibly carrying one or several threats (weapons, knives, explosives, etc). The relevant physical characteristics of scene objects are the dielectric constant ε_{obj}, the permeability μ_{obj} (which is unity for non-magnetic materials) and the physical temperature T_{obj}. The value of the dielectric constant depends on the type of material: for instance, flesh is well approximated by salty water with a dielectric constant of $\varepsilon_{body} \approx 28 + i\,34$. The body geometry is modelled by a triangular mesh, and threats as metallic or dielectric patches located on the body. Table 1 shows the reference dimensions of a typical scene.

Table 1. Dimensions of the scene

Description	Length (m)
Range object - closest part of the imager	1.6
Range object - apeture	2.9
Focal length	0.8
Lens diameter	1.6
Height of the body	1.8
Dimensions of the threat	0.075×0.075

The MMW-image simulator is composed of two parts. A ray-tracing programme, *Zemax*, is used to propagate rays back from each detector pixel via reflections from scene components to the source (either hot or background). All reflections within the scene are characterised using *Zemax* and the history of every ray is stored as a text file. By repeated application of Equation (3) at each intercept of a ray with a scene component, we can calculate the intensity of MMW radiation incident on each pixel detector. This component is executed by MATLAB code reading the *Zemax* output text file. The code calculates the equivalent temperatures at each pixel. Convolution of these images with the imager's point spread function (Airy disk) and the addition of random, low-level speckle noise to images yields the final, simulated MMW image.

The ray-optics model used here is strictly valid only for large scene dimensions compared to the wavelength (a few centimetres); more accurate models are required otherwise, e.g., electromagnetic methods used with unbounded problems such as the Boundary Element Method. When imaging people, the ray-optics model will provide accurate results for large body parts with large radii of curvature, but some inaccuracies might be expected for smaller features such as fingers and details of the face. Although these inaccuracies may become noticeable with future improvements in detector technology, they are currently unobservable due to noise levels and discrepancies between model parameters and real values. The salient advantage of the ray optics model is computation speed, crucial when simulating the large numbers of video sequences required for training automated detection algorithms.

2.3 Mixture Models for MMW Images

MMW images offer good data for material discrimination as different materials yield, generally speaking, different image properties. In analysing the image statistics it would be desirable to have an understanding of the physical process which could be incorporated in a model for the MMW image formation process. However, given the complexity of the MMW imager and the extensive amount of hardware calibration, software equalisation and interpolation undertaken to produce a MMW image, this is a non-trivial task.

In this paper we adopt an approach modelling the differences in image properties statistically, using a weighted mixture model in which each pdf, f_i, is associated to a specific material:

$$f_{mix} = \sum_{i=1}^{N} \alpha_i f_i(\boldsymbol{\theta}) \qquad (4)$$

where α_i is a weight and $\boldsymbol{\theta}$ a vector of parameters.

To identify the best-fitting pdf for each material (incl. background, i.e., non-figure pixels), we built a number of mixture models made by combinations of standard distributions (e.g. Gaussian, Rayleigh, Laplacian), optimised the parameters with a standard Maximum Likelihood (ML) algorithm and picked the best fitting combination for the observed image histograms using a Chi-Square test. We started with background-only sequences (no subject) to identify the background distribution. We then moved to sequences of scenes with a subject but no threats, then with a subject carrying threats (metallic objects). The final result is a best-fitting mixture model for each material (types of component distributions, and parameters). As an example, Figure 2 shows histograms and results of the ML distribution fit for a scene.

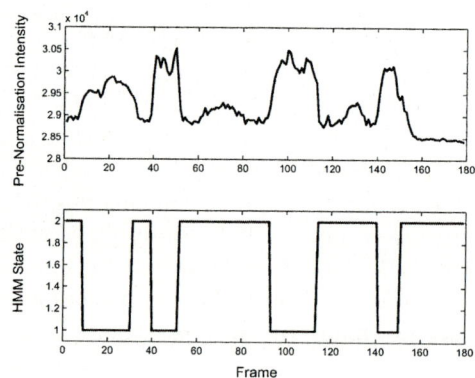

Fig. 2. An example of the HMM model being applied to a sequence of 180 frames. In the top row the maximum image intensity is shown for each frame in the sequence. In the bottom row the HMM state (1=object present, 2=no object) is shown across the sequence.

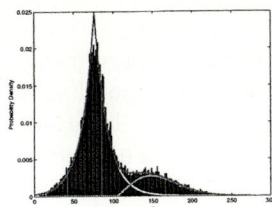 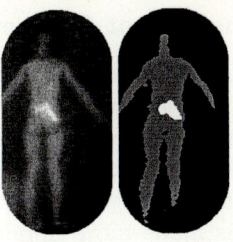

Fig. 3. Example of threat location showing an example PDF classification (left) with a MMW image containing a potential target (centre) and the Expectation-Maximisation classification (right).

3 Automatic Detection of Metallic Objects

3.1 Identifying Sequences Containing Threats

The presence of metallic objects changes the maximum temperature recorded significantly, providing a good criterion to identify frames containing threats. Within a sequence, the range of variation of the maximum image temperature provides a reliable measure of the presence of a threat when compared to a normalised threshold. However, detecting which frames in the sequence contain objects is more difficult.

3.2 Identifying Frames Containing Threats

To solve the problem of identifying individual frames containing metallic objects we trained a standard Hidden Markov Model (HMM) to detect significant changes in maximum temperatures (i.e., image intensities). The data is first quantised into 10 levels and the hidden field is composed of 2 states (threat, no threat). A Baum-Welch algorithm [7] is used for parameter estimation, and a Viterbi algorithm to determine the optimal state sequence. As an example, Figure 3 shows the maximum temperature signal for a sequence of 180 frames, and the corresponding frame classification.

3.3 Locating Threat Regions Within Frames

In frames classified as containing threats, we use Expectation-Maximisation (EM) [8] to perform the necessary unsupervised clustering. The EM algorithm uses ML to recompute the pdf parameters until a convergence criterion is met. We initialise the mixture model to the one containing the optimal distributions for the background-body-metal case (as defined in Subsection 2.3) with default parameters. Although not strictly necessary, this improves the convergence speed significantly. An example of threat location is shown in Fig. 3, with an example PDF classification (left), original image (centre) and classified image (right).

3.4 Tracking Threat Regions

The previous classification stage yields two results: a set of frames showing metal threats, plus, in each such frame, the regions corresponding to threats. Such regions are characterised by frame number, centroid location, and area. The problem is now to track such regions throughout a sequence for as long as the region remains visible, with frequent births, deaths and temporary occlusions. The problem is made more difficult by the noisy nature of the MMW images, making accurate segmentation difficult.

Tracking objects in visible-wavelength sequences is a well-studied problem in image processing and computer vision [9]. Particle Filters (PF) [10] are a powerful class of algorithms removing the Gaussian constraint typical of Kalman filters. They also provide robustness against clutter, a significant problem in MMW images. Common to PF is the *degeneracy problem* whereby all but a few particles have negligible weights after several iterations. For this reason we employ a Regularised PF (RPF) [10] which has an improved re-sampling stage, helping to avoid the degeneracy problem.

To start we define the tracking as an inference problem on a dynamic system, with a *system model* defining the evolution of the state with time and a *measurement model* which relates the measurements to the state. Let $x_{0..t}$ be the state sequence (x_t is a random vector representing the target state at time t) and $z_{1..t}$ be the sequence of measurements obtained. The tracking problem is governed by two functions:

$$x_t = F_t(x_{t-1}, v_{t-1}) \tag{5}$$
$$z_t = H_t(x_t, n_t) \tag{6}$$

where $v_{1..t}$ is the process noise sequence from the system model and $n_{1..t}$ is the measurement noise sequence. A detailed derivation of the inference problem for the PF can be found in [10].

The state vector employed is a 5D vector containing the position, velocity and area of the target: $(x, \dot{x}, y, \dot{y}, \phi)^T$. A constant velocity model for target position and a constant area model for target area are assumed, giving the following models for the functions F_t and H_t respectively:

$$x_t = \begin{pmatrix} 1 & 1 & 0 & 0 & 0 \\ 0 & 1 & 0 & 0 & 0 \\ 0 & 0 & 1 & 1 & 0 \\ 0 & 0 & 0 & 1 & 0 \\ 0 & 0 & 0 & 0 & 1 \end{pmatrix} x_{t-1} + \begin{pmatrix} 0.5 & 0 & 0 \\ 1 & 0 & 0 \\ 0 & 0.5 & 0 \\ 0 & 1 & 0 \\ 0 & 0 & 1 \end{pmatrix} v_{t-1} \tag{7}$$

$$z_t = \begin{pmatrix} 1 & 0 & 0 & 0 & 0 \\ 0 & 0 & 1 & 0 & 0 \\ 0 & 0 & 0 & 0 & 1 \end{pmatrix} x_t + n_t \tag{8}$$

Suitable values for the prediction (C_{vt}) and observation (C_{nt}) noise covariance matrices were determined experimentally. Due to the nature of the segmentation, it is necessary to allow greater variance within the area measurements than for the position estimate.

4 Results

4.1 Simulation of MMW Images

Fig. 4 presents the images generated by the MMW simulator. As can be observed, the differences in terms of grey levels range between synthetic and real images are minimal except for specific situations. For instance, the man in Fig. 4(a) carries three different objects: one below the chest, one on the abdomen and one on the (left) knee. These objects are not represented in the simulated scene and therefore no shading areas appear in the synthetic image.

In the case of the woman in Fig. 4(b), no big difference can be appreciated in terms of grey level range and shape, even if the mesh model does not fit perfectly the real body. However, as can be seen, images are not exactly the same. This is due to imperfections in the real sensor, the simulator and the illumination which is slightly different in real (highly incoherent) and synthetic (completely incoherent) scenes. But the noticeable difference is noise as it has not been included in the simulator yet. The study of noise distributions in real images as well as its addition into synthetic images remain as a future task.

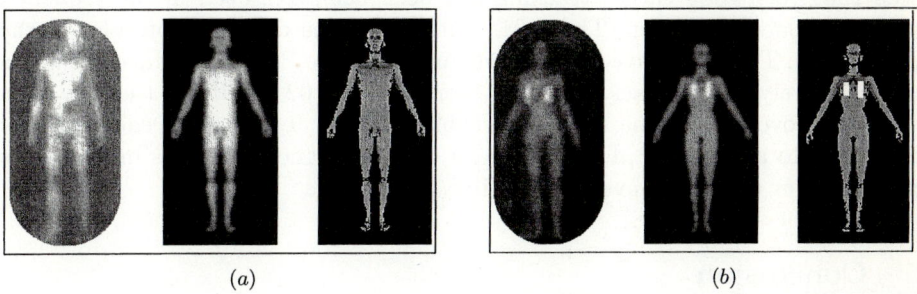

Fig. 4. Real and synthetic images: (a) man carrying three objects; (b) woman carrying two metal patches. For each box: (left) real image, (middle) simulated image including convolution with point spread function and (right) intensity image (power distribution of the scene, i.e. the received temperature at the input of the sensor for each pixel).

4.2 Automatic Detection of Metallic Objects

We tested our system with eight real sequences, four with subjects without a threat and four with subjects carrying a threat, giving a total of 1629 frames of which 137 frames where a threat was visible (see summary in Table 2, columns 1-3).

Table 2 (columns 4-6) shows the results of the sequence and frame threat identification described in Section 3, giving percentage error in classified frames ($Error$) with a breakdown of target frames missed (E_{miss}) compared to false alarms (E_{false}). The results clearly show that both stages of the threat identification perform very effectively. Missed target frames occurred primarily when targets were identified through shape rather than intensity. The false alarms seen in Threat03 are due to particularly strong reflections from the subjects scapula

Table 2. Threat Identification & Target tracking

Sequence	Frames	Threat?	Error	E_{false}	E_{miss}	Average Targets	RMSE
Plain01	211	No	—	—	—	—	—
Plain02	252	No	—	—	—	—	—
Plain03	218	No	—	—	—	—	—
Plain04	236	No	—	—	—	—	—
Threat01	242	Yes	8%	0%	100%	2.4	8.1
Threat02	155	Yes	3%	0%	100%	2.1	11.6
Threat03	179	Yes	5%	22%	78%	1.3	5.1
Threat04	136	Yes	8%	0%	100%	1.1	5.5

(shoulder blades). The effect is inherent within this sensor and is similar to the bright spot (specular reflection) seen in visual images.

Table 2 (columns 7 & 8) shows results for EM classification and RPF target tracking, giving the average number of targets (true target + clutter) per frame for the sequence and RMSE of the tracked position. The ground truth for the target position was established manually and is accurate to ±2 pixels. It can be seen that very good target tracking has been achieved, even in the sequences with considerable clutter (Threat01, Threat02). The classification false alarms produced in Threat03 have no negative impact on the PF tracking accuracy. The comparatively poorer tracking results seen in Threat02 are due to the very short time span over which the threat is visible (approx. 9 frames on each occasion compared to an average of 15 frames for other sequences). In this instance, the particle filter does not have enough time to converge.

5 Conclusion

We have described the formation and simulation of MMW images as well as an automatic system to detect and track metallic threats concealed on people. Initial results show that the geometric and physical models deployed yield good-quality MMW sequences compared to real ones. We have also demonstrated an automatic system for metallic threat detection, showing good performance with eight real sequences in field conditions. Key future work will address the inclusion of low-level speckle noise, non-uniform sampling and post-processing of images for the simulator, and of a wider range of materials, more complex tracking scenarios, and human body models for tracking. Further work will concern 3-D visualisation techniques preserving privacy.

Acknowledgements

The authors would like to acknowledge the support of QinetiQ. Beatriz Grafulla-González and Christopher D. Haworth are supported by EPSRC Research Grant GRS/68088 "ATRIUM" under the Think Crime programme.

References

1. Slamani, M.A., Varshney, P.K., Ferris, D.D.: Survey of image processing techniques applied to the enhancement and detection of weapons in mmw data. In: Passive Millimeter-Wave Imaging Technology VI. Volume 4719B., SPIE (2002) 296–305
2. Haworth, C.D., González, B.G., Tomsin, M., Appleby, R., Coward, P., Harvey, A., Lebart, K., Petillot, Y., Trucco, E.: Image analysis for object detection in millimetre-wave images. In Appleby, R., Chamberlain, J.M., Krapels, K.A., eds.: Passive Millimetre-wave and Terahertz Imaging and Technology. Volume 5619., SPIE (2004) 117–129
3. Coward, P., Appleby, R.: Development of an illumination chamber for indoor millimetre-wave imaging. In: SPIE Proceedings, Passive Millimeter-Wave Imaging Technology VI and Radar Sensor Technology VII. Volume 5077. (2003) 54–61
4. Sinclair, G.N., Appleby, R., Coward, P., Price, S.: Passive millimetre wave imaging in security scanning. In: SPIE Proceedings, Passive Millimeter-Wave Imaging Technology IV. Volume 4032. (2000) 40–45
5. Salmon, N.A., Appleby, R., Price, S.: Scene simulation of passive millimetre wave images of plastic and metal objects. SPIE Passive Millimetre Wave Imaging Technology VI (2002)
6. Born, M., Wolf, E.: Principles of Optics. Sixth edn. Pergamon Press (1987)
7. Rabiner, L.R.: A tutorial on hidden markov models and selected applications in speech recognition. Proceedings of the IEEE **77** (1989) 257–285
8. Choi, K.N., Carcassoni, M., Hancock, E.R.: Recovering facial pose with the em algorithm. Pattern Recognition **35** (2002) 2073–2093
9. Trucco, E., Plakas, K.: Video tracking: a concise survey. IEEE Journal of Oceanic Engineering **30** (2005)
10. Arulampalam, M.S., Maskell, S., Gordon, N., Clapp, T.: A tutorial on particle filters for online nonlinear/non-gaussian bayesian tracking. IEEE Transactions on Signal Processing **50** (2001) 174–188

A Thermal Hand Vein Pattern Verification System

Lingyu Wang and Graham Leedham

School of Computer Engineering, Nanyang Technological University,
N4-#2A-32 Nanyang Avenue, Singapore 639798
{wa0001yu, asgleedham}@ntu.edu.sg

Abstract. Many biometrics, such as face, fingerprint and iris images, have been studied extensively for personal verification purposes in the past few decades. However, verification using vein patterns is less developed compared to other human traits. A new personal verification system using the thermal-imaged vein pattern in the back of the hand is presented in the paper. The system consists of five individual steps: *Data Acquisition, Image Enhancement, Vein Pattern Segmentation, Skeletonization and Matching*. Unlike most biometric systems that carry out comparisons based on a pre-selected feature set, this system directly recognizes the shapes of the vein pattern by measuring their Line-Segment Hausdorff Distance. Preliminary testing on a database containing 108 different images has been carried out and all the images are correctly recognized.

1 Introduction

Public awareness of security issues has been greatly heightened since September 2001. This has led to a massive rise in demand for the personal identification systems. Traditional methods make use of smart cards or Personal Identification Numbers (PIN) etc to identify a person. However, these methods only offer limited security and are usually unreliable. Over the past few years, various biometric systems have been developed to overcome these disadvantages.

Biometrics is the science of identifying a person using its physiological or behavioral features [1]. These features range from physical traits like fingerprints, faces, retina etc. to personal behaviors (such as signatures). Compared to traditional methods, biometric features are much harder for intruders to copy or forge, and it is very rare for them to be lost. Hence, for identification systems making use of biometric features, they offer a much more secure and reliable performance.

During the past few decades, many researchers have carried out extensive studies on utilizing various biometric features (both physiological and behavioral) for personal verification. Amongst those biometric features, the most popular ones are fingerprints, faces, and iris scans for physiological biometrics, as well as signatures for behavioral one. Each of these biometric features has its

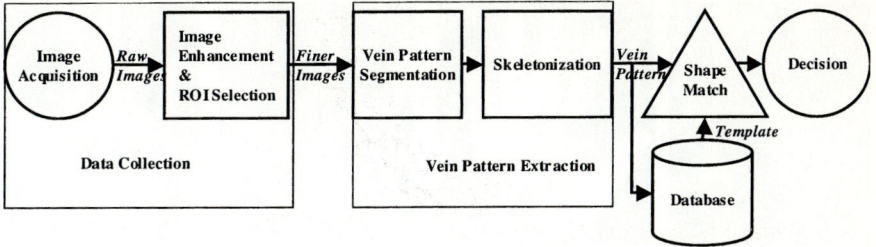

Fig. 1. Hand vein pattern verification system model

strengths and weaknesses [2]. Recently, hand vein pattern biometrics has attracted increasing interest from both research communities [3,4,5] and industries [6]. Anatomically, aside from surgical intervention, the shape of vascular patterns in the back of the hand is distinct from each other [7], and it remains stable over a long period. In addition, as the blood vessels are hidden underneath the skin and are invisible to the human eye, vein patterns are much harder for intruders to copy as compared to other biometric features. All these special properties of hand vein patterns make it a potentially good biometrics to offer more secure and reliable features for personal verification.

In this paper, a new personal verification system using vein patterns in the back of the hand is proposed. The system consists of five individual processing stages: *Hand Image Acquisition, Image Enhancement, Vein Pattern Segmentation, Skeletonization and Matching*, as shown in Figure 1. The system captures the vein pattern images using a thermal camera. Unlike other vein pattern verification systems that compare the vein patterns based on a predefined set of features extracted using techniques like Multiresolution analysis [5], the proposed system recognizes the shapes of the preprocessed vein patterns by calculating their line segment Hausdorff distances.

2 Data Collection

2.1 Image Acquisition

Veins are hidden underneath the skin, and are generally invisible to the naked eye and other visual inspection systems. However, human superficial veins have higher temperature than the surrounding tissue. Based on this fact, the vein pattern in the back of the hand can be captured using a thermal camera. In this work, an NEC Thermal Tracer is utilized to acquire thermal images of the back of the hand. Figure 2 shows some of the images collected from different people in a normal office environment $(20-25°C)$, and it can be seen that the veins appear to be brighter in the images and are now visually distinguishable. A rectangular region in the hand images can be defined as the region of interest (ROI). The technique of locating the ROI is similar to the one proposed by Lin and Fan [5], where the landmarks of the hand such as finger tips and valleys between the

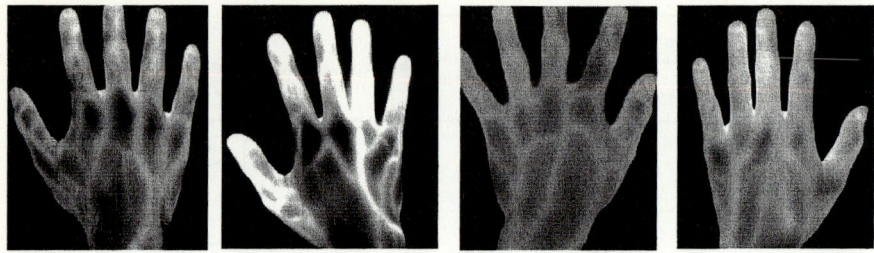

Fig. 2. Thermal images of the back of the hands in normal office environment

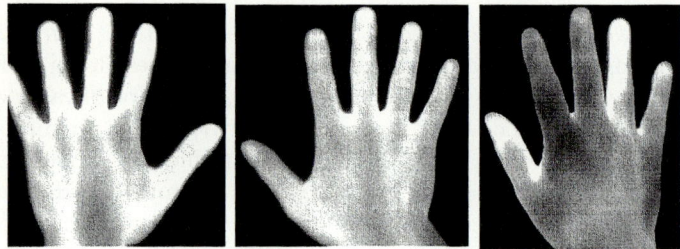

Fig. 3. Thermal images of the back of the hands in an outdoor environment

fingers are first located, then a fixed size rectangular region is defined as the ROI based on the location of these landmark points. The image on the left of Figure 4 shows the result of the extracted ROI.

The images in Figure 2 were captured in a normal office environment, where the temperature and humidity are lower than outside. Figure 3 shows another set of images captured in a tropical outside environment ($30 - 34°C$ and $> 80\%$ humidity). It can be seen that the ambient temperature and humidity have a negative impact on the image quality, and the vein patterns in these images are now not easily visually distinguishable. Therefore, in our work, we use the image data collected in a normal office environment instead of an outside environment for better system performance.

2.2 Image Enhancement

The clearness of the vein pattern in the extracted ROI varies from image to image, therefore, the quality of these images need to be enhanced before further processing. A 5x5 Median Filter was used to remove the speckling noise in the images. Then, a 2-D Gaussian low pass filter $H(u,v) = e^{-D^2(u,v)/2\sigma^2}$ with standard deviation $\sigma = 0.8$ was applied to the vein pattern images to suppress the effect of high frequency noise.

After removing the speckling and other high frequency noise, the vein pattern images are normalized to have pre-specified mean and variance values. The normalization process is to reduce the possible imperfections in the image due to the sensor noise and other effects. The method for normalization employed in this work is similar to the one suggested by Hong et al [8]. Let $I(x,y)$ denote the intensity value at position (x,y) in a vein pattern image. The mean and variance of image are denoted as μ and σ^2 respectively. For an image sized $N \times M$, they are computed using Equation 1 and 2.

$$\mu = \frac{1}{N \times M} \sum_{x=0}^{N-1} \sum_{y=0}^{M-1} I(x,y) \ . \tag{1}$$

$$\sigma^2 = \frac{1}{N \times M} \sum_{x=0}^{N-1} \sum_{y=0}^{M-1} (I(x,y) - \mu)^2 \ . \tag{2}$$

Then the normalized image $I'(x,y)$ is given by the pixel-wise operations in Equation 3, where μ_d and σ_d^2 are the desired values for mean and variance respectively.

$$I'(x,y) = \begin{cases} \mu_d + \sqrt{\frac{\sigma_d^2 \cdot (I(x,y) - \mu)^2}{\sigma^2}}, & I(x,y) > \mu \\ \mu_d - \sqrt{\frac{\sigma_d^2 \cdot (I(x,y) - \mu)^2}{\sigma^2}}, & \text{Otherwise} \end{cases} \ . \tag{3}$$

Figure 4 shows the vein pattern image after normalization. It can be seen that the quality of the image has been improved significantly

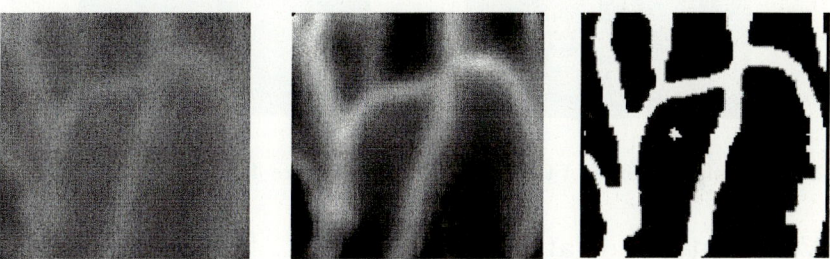

Fig. 4. Left: Region of interest; Center: After normalization; Right: After local threholding.

3 Vein Pattern Extraction

3.1 Local Thresholding

After noise reduction and normalization, the quality of the image improves. However, the vein pattern is still surrounded by many faint white regions. To obtain a better representation of the shape of the vein pattern, it is necessary to separate the vein pattern from the image background. Due to the fact that the gray-level intensity values of the vein vary at different locations in the image, global threholding techniques do not provide satisfactory results. Hence, a locally adaptive thresholding algorithm was utilized to segment the vein patterns from the background. The algorithm chooses different threhold values for every pixel in the image based on the analysis of its surrounding neighbors. For every pixel in the image, its threshold value is set as the mean value of its 13×13 neighborhood. The binary image on the right side of Figure 4 shows the vein pattern has been successfully segmented from the original image after applying the local threholding algorithm.

3.2 Skeletonization

As the size of veins grow as human beings grow, only the shape of the vein pattern is used as the sole feature to recognize each individual. A good representation of the pattern's shape is via extracting its skeleton. Figure 5 shows the skeleton of the vein pattern after applying the thinning algorithm proposed by Zhang and Suen [9]. It can be seen that after the pruning process, the skeletons of the vein pattern are successfully extracted and the shape of the vein pattern is well preserved.

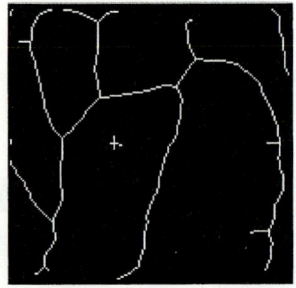
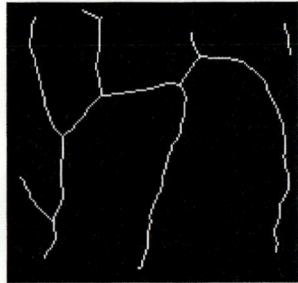

Fig. 5. Left: Skeleton of the vein pattern in Figure 4; Right: After pruning.

4 Vein Pattern Matching

Vein pattern matching is done by measuring the line segment Hausdorff distance between a pair of vein patterns. Hausdorff distance is a natural measure for comparing similarity of shapes. It is a distance measure between two point sets, and Equation 4 and 5 give the definition for a modified version of Hausdorff distance.

$$H(M^p, T^p) = \max\left(h(M^p, T^p), h(T^p, M^p)\right). \quad (4)$$

$$h(M^p, T^p) = \frac{1}{N_m^p} \sum_{m_i^p \in M^p} \min_{t_j^p \in T^p} \| m_i^p - t_j^p \|. \quad (5)$$

Hausdorff distance uses the spatial information of an image, but lacks local structure representation such as orientation when it comes to comparing the shapes of curves. To overcome this weakness, in this paper, the line segment Hausdorff distance (LHD) is calculated to match the shapes of vein patterns.

Line segment Hausdorff distance was proposed by Gao and Leung [10] for a face matching application. It incorporates the structural information of line segment orientation and line-point association, and hence is effective to compare two shapes made up of a number of curve segments.

Given two finite line segment sets $M^l = \{m_1^l, m_2^l, ..., m_p^l\}$ and $T^l = \{t_1^l, t_2^l, ..., t_p^l\}$, LHD is built on the vector $\vec{d}(m_i^l, t_j^l)$ representing the distance between the two line segment sets, and the vector is defined as

$$\vec{d}(m_i^l, t_j^l) = [d_\theta(m_i^l, t_j^l), \quad d_\parallel(m_i^l, t_j^l), \quad d_\perp(m_i^l, t_j^l)]^T \quad (6)$$

where $d_\theta(m_i^l, t_j^l)$, $d_\parallel(m_i^l, t_j^l)$ and $d_\perp(m_i^l, t_j^l)$ are the *angle distance, parallel distance and perpendicular distance* respectively. The numerical value of the distance is given by equation 7. The directed and undirected LHDs are defined in equation 8 and 9, where $l_{m_i^l}$ is the length of line segment m_i^l.

$$d(m_i^l, t_j^l) = \sqrt{(W_a \cdot d_\theta(m_i^l, t_j^l))^2 + d_\parallel^2(m_i^l, t_j^l) + d_\perp^2(m_i^l, t_j^l)} \quad (7)$$

$$h_l(M^l, T^l) = \frac{1}{\sum_{m_i^l \in M^l} l_{m_i^l}} \sum_{m_i^l \in M^l} l_{m_i^l} \cdot \min_{t_j^l \in T^l} d(m_i^l, t_j^l) \quad (8)$$

$$H_l(M^l, T^l) = \max(h_l(M^l, T^l), h_l(T^l, M^l)) \quad (9)$$

In this application, the vein patterns are divided into a number of curve segments. For each individual curve segment, a few points are sampled to represent the curve segment. Using these sample points as the end points, a set of line segments representing the shape of the vein pattern are obtained. By this means, the undirected LHD can then be calculated to measure the similarity of two vein patterns.

5 Testing Results

Testing was carried out on a vein pattern image database consisting of 108 images from 12 people (9 from each person). Prior to testing, three images for each person were selected randomly to form the class templates for that person. During the verification stage, three undirected LHDs (H_1, H_2, H_3) are computed between the incoming vein pattern image and the three template images. The average value H' of H_1, H_2 and H_3 is then calculated, which is the similarity measure between the incoming vein pattern and the target class. Figure 6 shows the distribution of the genuine and intruder accesses against the value H'. It can be easily seen from the figure that the smaller H' is, the higher the probability the vein pattern belonging to the genuine class. By choosing 9.0 to be the threshold value, the system achieves 0% false acceptance rate (FAR) and 0% false rejection rate (FRR) for all the 108 images in both the testing set (containing 72 images) and the template set (containing 36 images).

The results of the experiment are encouraging. However, the images in the current database are taken in a more controlled manner, where the participants

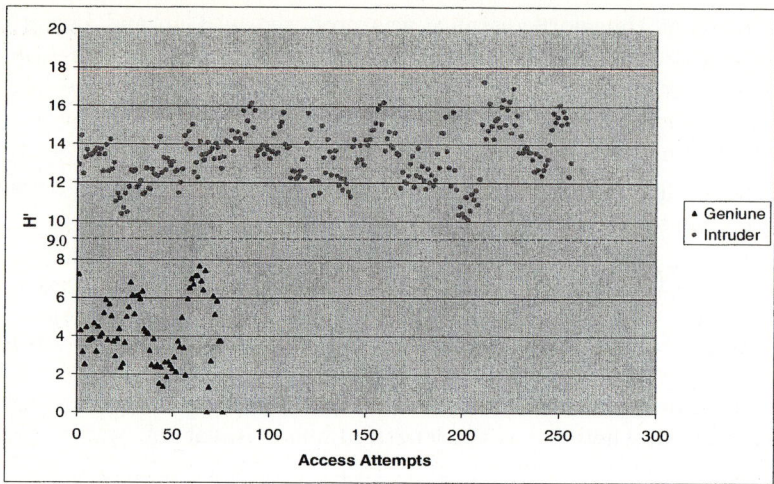

Fig. 6. Distribution of genuine and intruder accesses against similarity measure H'

are fully cooperative and the image acquisition is carried out in a normal office environment with ambient temperature around $20°C$ and humidity of $< 50\%$. For a real life application, the surrounding conditions are unknown. Therefore the quality of the vein pattern images may reduce, and as a result, a decrease of verification accuracy can be expected.

6 Conclusions

This paper presents a biometric system that recognizes the shapes of the vein pattern in the back of the human hands captured using a thermal camera. Unlike other approaches, the system directly recognizes the shapes of the vein pattern using line segment Hausdorff distance. Preliminary testing results show that all the vein pattern images in the database have been correctly recognized, and it demonstrates the potential usefulness of such a system. Nevertheless, a number of research issues need to be addressed in the future. First of all, the clearness of the vein pattern in the image is affected by a number of factors such as ambient temperature, nearness of the vein to the skin etc. An investigation is needed into the impact of these factors on the quality of the vein pattern image. Secondly, more experiments need to be carried out using a larger image database for a thorough evaluation on the efficacy of hand vein pattern biometrics. Lastly, it is likely that the vein patterns will be used in conjunction with other biometrics in a multi-modal system.

References

1. N.K. Ratha, A. Senior, and R.M. Bolle, "Tutorial on Automated Biometrics" in Proceedings of International Conference on Advances in Pattern Recognition. March 2001. Rio de Janeiro, Brazil

2. J.O. Kim, W. Lee, J. Hwang, K.S. Baik, and C.H. Chung, "Lip Print Recognition for Security Systems by Multi-resolution Architecture". Future Generation Computer Systems. 20 (2004) 295-301
3. J.M. Cross and C.L. Smith. "Thermographic Imaging of Subcutaneous Vascular Network Of The Back Of The Hand For Biometric Identification". in Proceedings of IEEE 29th International Carnahan Conference on Security Technology. October 1995. Sanderstead, Surrey, England
4. S.-K. Im, H.-M. Park, S.-W. Kim, C.-K. Chung, and H.-S. Choi, "Improved Vein Pattern Extracting Algorithm And Its Implementation". in Digest of technical papers of International Conference on Consumer Electronics. June 2000
5. C.-L Lin and K.-C. Fan, "Biometric Verification Using Thermal Images Of Palm-dorsa Vein Patterns". IEEE Trans. Circuits and Systems for Video Technology, 2004. 14(2): p. 199-213
6. Fujitsu-Laboratories-Ltd, "Fujitsu Laboratories Develops Technology For World's First Contactless Palm Vein Pattern Biometric Authentication System". March 31, 2003, "http://pr.fujitsu.com/en/news/2003/03/31.html"
7. A. Jain, R.M. Bolle, and S. Pankanti, Biometrics: Personal Identification In Networked Society. 1999, Dordrecht: Kluwer Academic Publishers
8. L. Hong, Y. Wan, and A. Jain, "Fingerprint Image Enhancement: Algorithm And Performance Evaluation". IEEE Trans. Pattern Analysis and Machine Intelligence, 1998. 20(8): p. 777-789
9. C.Y. Suen and T.Y. Zhang, "A Fast Parallel Algorithm for Thinning Digital Patterns". Communications of the ACM 27 (3). March 1984
10. Y. Gao and M.K.H. Leung, "Line Segment Hausdorff Distance on Face Matching". Pattern Recognition. 35 (2002) 361-371

Illumination Tolerant Face Recognition Using Phase-Only Support Vector Machines in the Frequency Domain

Jingu Heo, Marios Savvides, and B.V.K. Vijayakumar

Department of Electrical and Computer Engineering,
Carnegie Mellon University, U.S.A.
jheo@cmu.edu, msavvid@ri.cmu.edu, kumar@ece.cmu.edu

Abstract. This paper presents a robust method for recognizing human faces under varying illuminations. Unlike conventional approaches for recognizing faces in the spatial domain, we model the phase information of face images in the frequency domain and use them as features to represent faces. Then, Support Vector Machines (SVM) are applied to claim an identity using different kernel methods. Due to large variations of the face images, algorithms which perform in the space domain need more training images to achieve reasonable performance. On the other hand, the SVM combined with the phase-only representation of faces performs well even with small number of training images. Principal Component Analysis (PCA), Linear Discriminant Analysis (LDA), and 3D Linear Subspace (3DLS) are included in the experiment changing the size of images and the number of training images in order to find the best parameters associated with each method. The illumination subset of the CMU-PIE database is used for the performance evaluation.

1 Introduction

Recognizing faces under different illumination conditions is an essential part of face recognition systems. Since a face is essentially a 3D object, lighting sources from different directions may dramatically change visual appearances due to self-shadowing and specular reflections. Currently there are many algorithms that have been developed with the aim of handling visual face recognition in the presence of illumination variations. Most algorithms developed for face recognition perform in the spatial domain by reducing the dimensionality of the face spaces. Such subspace analysis methods include PCA (Eigenfaces) [1], LDA (Fisherfaces) [2], 3DLS, Local Feature Analysis (LFA) [3], and Independent Component Analysis (ICA) [4] and those are still active research fields due to the unsatisfactory performance in practical applications [5][6].

In this paper, we present a robust method for dealing with illumination tolerant face recognition utilizing the phase information in the frequency domain. Although the importance of the phase information has been addressed by several researchers [7][8], the effectiveness of the phase spectrum has not been explored extensively in the face recognition area. We also argue that current unsatisfactory performance of face recognition results from the fact that the number of training images or gallery images per individuals is limited therefore a face image cannot represent the identity of a person efficiently because of large variations in facial images caused by lighting changes, expressions, poses, makeup, aging, and eyeglasses. Therefore, algorithms typically need multiple training images such as Individual PCA (IPCA), 3D Linear Subspace [9], LDA, Neural Networks (NN), and SVM can be employed in real applications by representing an identity in a compact way or by finding an optimal decision boundary among individuals. In this experiment we seek the best performance of each algorithm and claim that each algorithm can produce reasonable performance depending on the number of gallery images per individuals. On the other hand, the SVM combined with the phase information performs well even with small number of training images.

2 Background

As suggested by researchers, the phase spectrum contains the structural information of the images and is less prone to the effects of lighting variations. Figure 1 shows a representation of the phase spectrum by applying the inverse Fourier transform of the phase-only spectrums. As shown in Figure 1, the phase spectrum of the faces looks like containing structural information of the faces thus can provide an alternative face representation that is more tolerant to illumination variations.

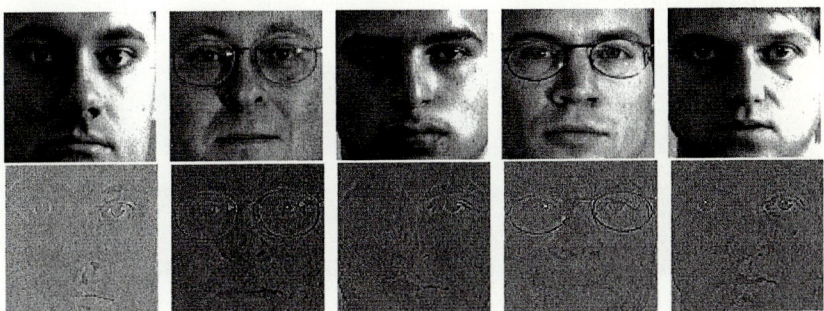

Fig. 1. Examples of the images used in the experiment (top) and the inverse Fourier transform of the phase spectrum with unit magnitude respectively (bottom)

We utilize the phase information with and without performing PCA using the SVM. Support Vector Machines [10][11][12] have been successfully applied in the field of object recognition utilizing the reduced features sets and mapping data into higher-dimensional feature spaces using the kernel trick. The SVM finds the optimal separating hyperplane that maximizes the margin of separation in order to minimize the risk of misclassification not only for the training samples, but also in hopes of generalizing to the unseen data in the test set. Although it is not so obvious that the SVM can produce better classification performance over other classifiers, an appropriate choice of kernels and feature sets leads to maximize the performance of the SVM. In this paper, we apply linear machines as well as different kernel methods such as Radial Basis Functions (RBF) and Polynomial Kernels in order to find the best separating vectors varying parameters associated with each kernel method.

3 Experiments

In this experiment, we selected different sets of training images which were constant for experiment across different pattern recognition methods. Table 1 shows the test database used in the experiment. We divided into two groups of the database depending on the light conditions such as the dataset which contains ambient background lighting (room lights on) and the second dataset with no ambient background lighting (room lights off). Each database contains 65 individuals with 21 different images under different illumination variations. Figure 2 shows examples of the images used in the experiment and Figure 3 shows 21 different illumination conditions in the dataset 2. We also experimented with the number of training images used (first 5 labeled images in Figure 3) and varying the resolution of these images to examine the actual dimensionality of the face spaces.

Table 1. Subset of the PIE illumination database

	Gallery (65 individuals)	Probe (65 individuals)
Dataset 1 (Room lights on)	1~5 images/person	16 images /person
Dataset 2 (Room lights off)	1~5 images/person	16 images / person

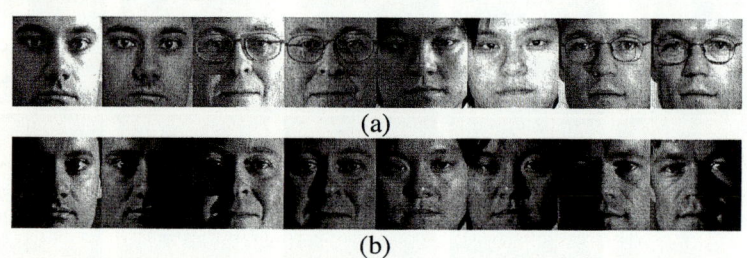

Fig. 2. Examples of the images used in the experiment, (a) from dataset 1(room lights on), and (b) from dataset 2(room lights off)

The face images were cropped and normalized for scale using the eye-locations provided. In some experiments we also performance histogram equalization to compensate for illumination variations. In case of the PCA, after computing the eigenface subspace, the images are projected on this basis and the resulting projection coefficients are stored for matching between gallery images and probe images. We normalized these coefficients by making them zero-mean and unit-variance as an improvement in performance which was observed by doing so. Such a preprocessing is an important step to improve the performance not only for the PCA and other algorithms. Since dataset 1 contains simple illumination sets, we achieve relatively high performance even with a single training image from each class for training as shown in Figure 4. The performance of Eigenphases outperform over Eigenfaces and Fisherfaces. The classifiers used here is nearest neighbor rule. One thing we notice here is that large normalized faces do not necessarily guarantee better performance since large portions of the face images are filled with redundant information.

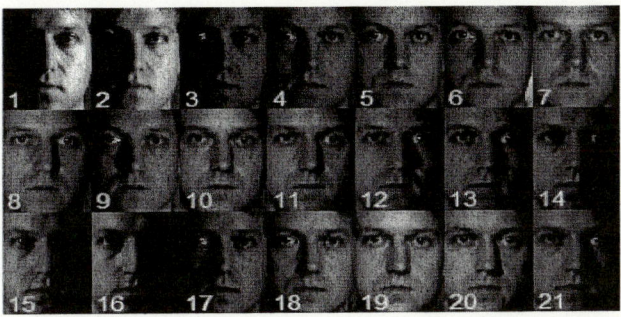

Fig. 3. 21 labeled images from a subject in the PIE database illumination subset captured with no background lighting (dataset 2)

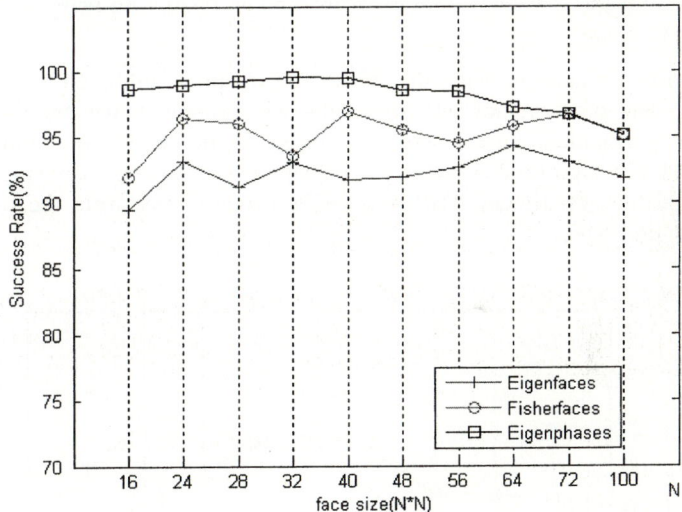

Fig. 4. Performance comparison with Eigenfaces, Fisherfaces and Eigenphases from dataset 1 varying the size of the normalized faces

Throughout the analysis of the dataset 1, we assume each algorithm is somewhat optimized and produces reasonable performance in case of small illumination variations. On the other hand, we evaluate the performance on the harder illumination set (dataset 2) as shown in Figure 3. In order to find out the best feature representation in the SVM, we apply kernel methods such as RBF, and Polynomial kernels as well as Linear SVM as shown in Figure 5. We achieve the best performance using the Linear SVM after cross validation, therefore the Linear SVM used instead of mapping onto higher dimensional space. This process also gives an intuition about the database whether it can be linearly separable or not.

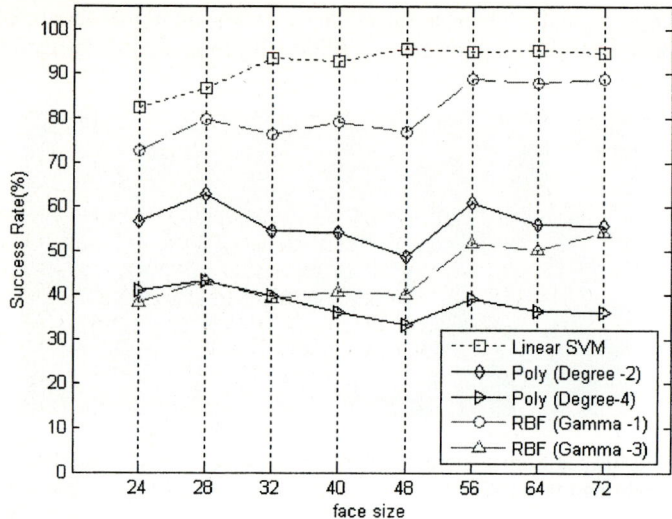

Fig. 5. Evaluation of kernel methods for the SVM using dataset 2

As shown in Figure 6, with the phase information combined with the SVM produces the best performance although only one training image per individuals is used in the experiment. Figure 7 shows the effect of the number of training images. Regardless of the algorithms, better performance is achieved than single training image used in the experiment. Still best performance comes from the utilizing the Phase-Only with SVM.

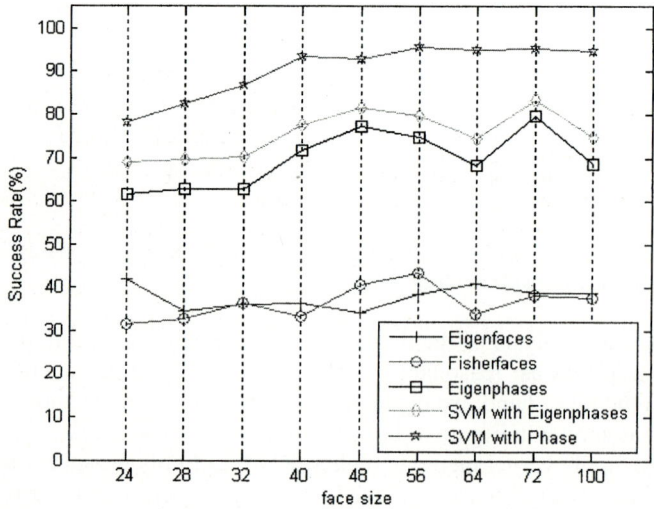

Fig. 6. Performance comparison using dataset 2 varying the size of the normalized faces with 1 training image per individuals

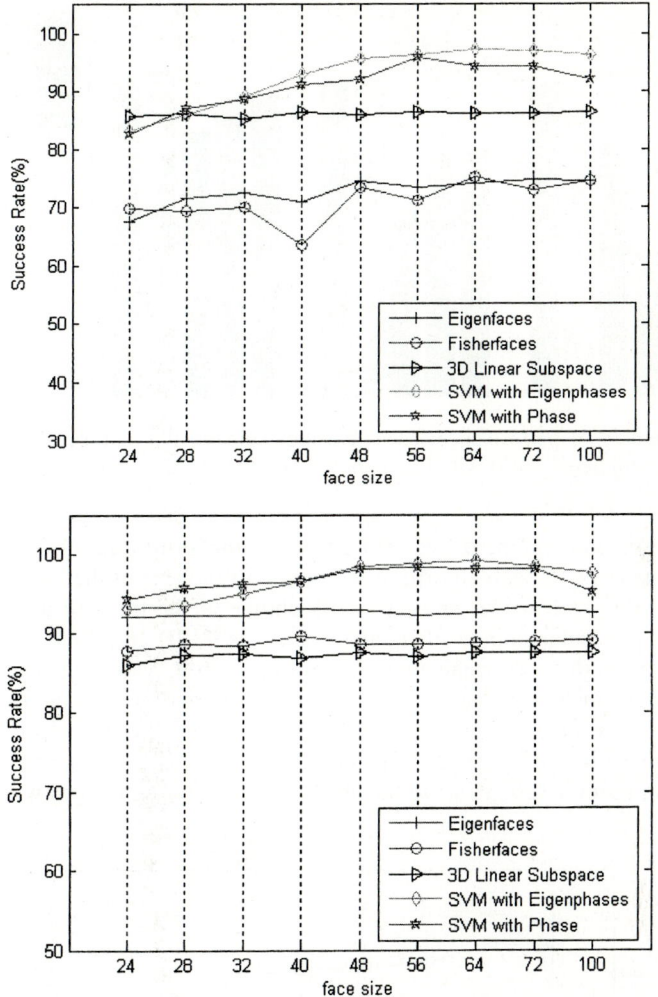

Fig. 7. Performance comparison using dataset 2(room lights off) varying the size of the normalized faces with 3(top graph) and 5(bottom graph) training images per individuals

Regarding the features and classifiers used in the experiment, only holistic features are applied without performing any local feature extraction methods. In case of Eigenfaces and Eigenphases, the number of eigenvectors is defined up to 95% of the reconstruction rate regardless of the number of the training images. Fisherfaces uses c-1 projection vectors where c is the number of classes. The nearest neighbor classifier is used commonly for Eigenfaces, Fisherfaces, and Eigenphases. In stead of using Eigenphases with the nearest neighbor classifier, we apply SVM with Eigenphases. On the other hand, the Phase-Only SVM does not involve with any dimensionality reduction schemes. Figure 8 shows the summary of the overall

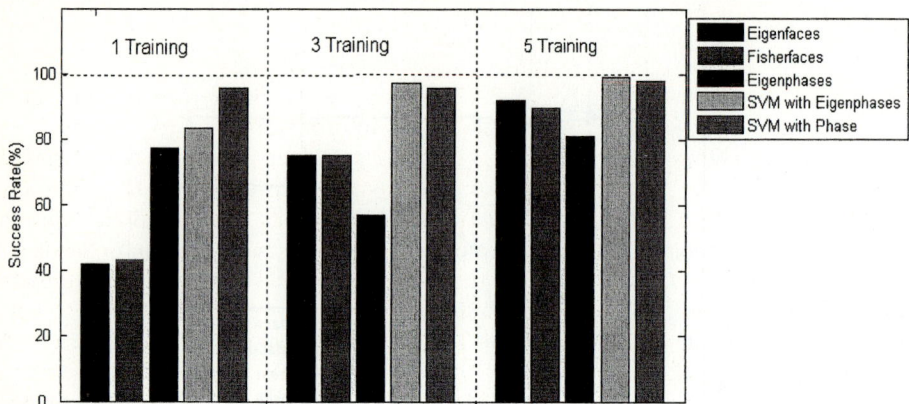

Fig. 8. A summary of performance; each five bar indicates the performance of Eigenfaces, Fisherfaces, Eigenphases, SVM with Eigenphases, and Phase Only SVM (from left to right).

performance evaluated in the paper with different number of training images. We seek the best performance of each algorithm regardless of the size of the faces.

So far we do not consider any particular choice of the training images. It can be shown that a particular choice of database such as 7, 10 and 19 labeled images in Figure 3 enhances the performance as shown in Figure 9. Most Eigen-based methods give better performance instead of using first 5 illumination sets as training images (Figure 3). On the other hand, the SVM methods give almost perfect classification results with these training images. This can be interpreted as the performance of the SVM schemes seem to less prone to the choice of the training images while others do.

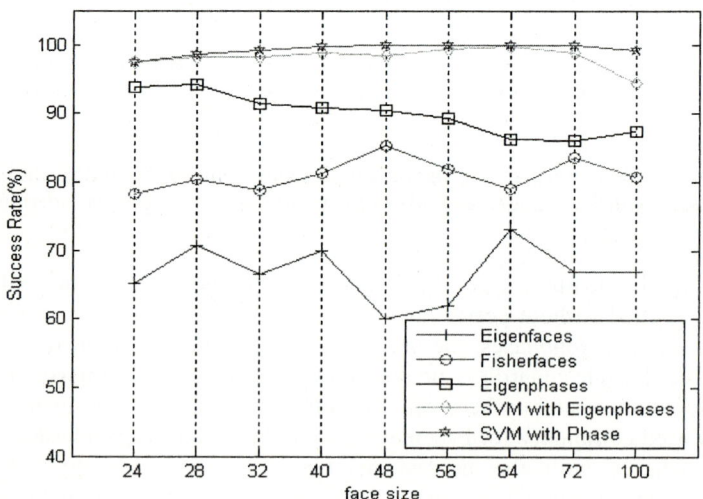

Fig. 9. Performance comparison with particular training images (7, 10 and 19 labeled images used in the training -dataset 2)

4 Discussion

Unlike conventional approaches for recognizing faces that typically work in the spatial image domain, we model the phase information of face images in the frequency domain and try to find optimal hyperplane decision boundaries for classifying each class using the phase-only representation. We show that Phase-Only SVM performs extremely well in the presence of illumination variations even with small number of training images compared to traditional spatial domain methods such as Eigenfaces, Fisherfaces, 3D-Linear subspace method and even previously proposed Eigen*phases* method. Most Eigen-based methods give better performance with a proper choice of the training images. This can be interpreted as there is a strong correlation among classifiers in terms of making mistakes due to large variations between the test and training images. On the other hand, the performance of the SVM scheme seems to less prone to the choice of the training images. Our results on the CMU-PIE database show that our proposed method outperforms previous methods for achieving illumination tolerant face recognition.

References

[1] M. Turk and A. Pentland, "Eigenfaces for Recognition," Journal of *Cognitive Neuroscience*, Vol. 3, pp.72-86, 1991.
[2] P.Belhumeur, J. Hespanha, and D. Kriegman, "Eigenfaces vs Fisherfaces: Recognition Using Class Specific Linear Projection," *IEEE Trans. PAMI,* Vol. 19, No. 7, pp. 711-720. 1997.
[3] P. S. Penev, "Local Feature Analysis: A Statistical Theory for Information Representation and Transmission," *Ph.D. Thesis, The Rockefeller University*, 1998.
[4] M.S.Bartlett, J.R.. Movellan, and T.J. Sejnowski, "Face recognition by independent component analysis," *IEEE Trans. on Neural Networks.* Vol 13, No. 6 pp. 1450-1464, 2002.
[5] S. G. Kong, J. Heo, B. Abidi, J. Paik, and M. Abidi, "Recent Advances in Visual and Infrared Face Recognition - A Review," *Computer Vision and Image Understanding*, Vol. 97, No. 1, pp.103-135, 2005.
[6] P. J. Phillips, P. Grother, R. J. Micheals, D. M. Blackburn, E. Tabassi, and M. Bone, "Face Recognition Vendor Test 2002," *Evaluation Report, National Institute of Standards and Technology*, pp.1-56, 2003.
[7] A. V. Oppenheim and J. S. Lim, "The Importance of phase in signals," *Proc. IEEE*. Vol. 69, No.5, pp. 529-541, May 1981
[8] M. Savvides, B.V.K. Vijaya Kumar and P.K. Khosla, "Eigenphases vs. Eigenfaces," *Proceeding of the ICPR*, 2004.
[9] P.Belhumeur and D.Kriegman, "What is the Set of Images of an Object under All Possible Illumination Conditions," *Int. J. Computer Vision*, Vol.28, No.3, pp.245-260, 1998.
[10] V. N. Vapnik, *The Nature of Statistical Learning Theory*, New York: Springer-Verlag, 1995.
[11] B. Schölkopf, *Support Vector Learning*, Munich, Germany: Oldenbourg-Verlag, 1997.
[12] P. J. Phillips, "Support vector machines applied to face recognition," *Advances in Neural Information Processing Systems 11*, M. S. Kearns, S. A. Solla, and D. A. Cohn, eds., 1998.

Regional and Online Learnable Fields

Rolf Schatten, Nils Goerke, and Rolf Eckmiller

University of Bonn, D-53117 Bonn, Germany
{schatten, goerke, eckmiller}@nero.uni-bonn.de
http://www.nero.uni-bonn.de

Abstract. Within this paper a new data clustering algorithm is proposed based on classical clustering algorithms. Here k-means neurons are used as substitute for the original data points. These neurons are online adaptable extending the standard k-means clustering algorithm. They are equipped with perceptive fields to identify if a presented data pattern fits within its area it is responsible for.

In order to find clusters within the input data an extension of the ε-nearest neighbouring algorithm is used to find connected groups within the set of k-means neurons.

Most of the information the clustering algorithm needs are taken directly from the input data. Thus only a small number of parameters have to be adjusted.

The clustering abilities of the presented algorithm are shown using data sets from two different kind of applications.

1 Introduction

To find clusters within given input data using an unsupervised clustering algorithm the k-means clustering or the k-nearest neighbouring may be used. k-means clustering uses k representatives each of them standing for one cluster centre. Since an input pattern is assigned to the closest of the k cluster centres it is not possible to cluster e.g. two concentric circles. The k-nearest neighbouring algorithm builds a neighbourhood graph using all of the input data and therefore may be used to cluster input data from any kind of shape. Since all data points are used to build the neighbourhood this clustering algorithm needs a lot of memory. The presented algorithm doesn't store any data patterns but only stores representative neurons and thereby reduces the necessary memory.

Furthermore, both clustering algorithms are not online adaptable. The here presented clustering algorithm is online adaptable, it adapts after each presented pattern. Therefore while learning no additional temporal memory is needed. When presenting patterns in the recall phase both algorithms always return the centre or the area with the shortest distance to the presented pattern. Thus both algorithms are not able to detect new input patterns appertaining new clusters.

The clustering algorithm presented within this paper combines the advantages of both clustering algorithms and introduces some improvements:

- Representatives are used to reduce memory
  The learnt neurons represent the input data. Only the neurons are stored, not the original input data.

- Contiguous areas are detected
  Since the clustering algorithm detects contiguous areas within the input space, it is useful to detect partitions, well separated clusters, within the input space.
- Online adaptable
  The net learns while presenting pattern by pattern.
- Perceptive fields detect new input patterns
  The algorithm is capable to detect patterns belonging to new clusters.

1.1 Neural Structure

The presented algorithm uses special artificial neurons that have a perceptive area. As illustrated in fig. 1 each neuron is defined by its position or centre c and by its width σ. During the learning phase the centre c adapts towards the mean of the input data covered by the perceptive area while σ adapts towards the standard deviation.

To calculate each neuron's perceptive area the parameter ρ is used. ρ depends on the probability distribution of the input data and defines the accepting area of the neurons. ρ is constant. The radius r of the active area is defined as

$$r = \rho \cdot \sigma.$$

Since each neuron is equipped with a perceptive area it is able to decide whether it accepts a presented input pattern or not. Input patterns are accepted by a neuron if the pattern is positioned within the perceptive area of the neuron. Otherwise the neuron will not accept the provided input pattern.

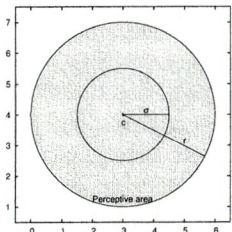

Fig. 1. Neuron with perceptive area: The figure illustrates the structure of the neurons. Each neuron is defined by its position c, here $c = (3 : 4)$ in the n dimensional input space (here: 2) and by its width σ (here: 1.5). The radius r of the perceptive area is $r = \rho \cdot \sigma$. With $\rho = 2.0$ the neuron in the figure has a perceptive area with radius $r = 3.0$.

1.2 Initial Values

The presented algorithm has only a few initial values to be set. For equally distributed input data $\rho = 2.0$ showed good results since this neuron covers mean$\pm 2.0 \cdot \sigma$. For Gaussian distributed input data ρ should be about 3.0 to cover the input data. η_σ and η_c are the learning rates of the net. The smaller they are the longer it takes the net to learn a good representation of the input data. σ_{init} is the most influential initial value. It appoints the size of the perceptive areas. The value should be selected big enough to cover the structure of the input data and it should be small enough to enable the separation of the clusters.

1.3 Learning Algorithm

Two different parts of the learning algorithm have to be contemplated: the learning algorithm of a single neuron and the learning algorithm of the whole net. A single neuron learns by providing input patterns. The neuron only learns, if it accepts the presented input pattern. It learns by adapting c and σ. The whole net learns by adapting the winning neuron if it accepts the input pattern. It creates a new neuron if no accepting neuron exists. When the learning phase is completed the net builds a neighbourhood graph to detect contiguous areas.

Online Adaptation of Neurons. Every neuron is defined by the two parameters c and σ. In an n dimensional data space c as an n dimensional vector represents the centre or the position of the neuron. σ is the width of the neuron representing the mean distance of the input data patterns within its perceptive field and thereby σ is scalar.

Adapting c. The centre c of a neuron will be adapted by presenting a pattern with position p to the net. Thereby the current position of the centre at time t, $c(t)$ will be adapted towards the position p of the pattern. Thus a new position $c(t+1)$ will be calculated:

$$c(t+1) = c(t) + \eta_c \cdot (p - c(t))$$

This calculation rule is equivalent to the instruction for adapting the winning neuron in a self-organised map as described in [1]. η_c is the learning rate used for adapting centres. The instruction considers no neighbourhood of the neurons at all. Thus the here presented algorithm only adapts the winning neuron.

Adapting σ. Independent from the dimensionality of the input data σ is always scalar. σ will be adapted towards the distance $d = \|c - p\|$. η_σ is the learning rate used for adapting σ. Thus σ adapts towards the mean distance between the accepted patterns and the centre of the neuron.

$$\sigma(t+1) = \sigma(t) + \eta_\sigma \cdot (d - \sigma(t)) \quad \text{with} \quad d = \|c(t) - p\|$$

Learning Algorithm of the Neural Net. The classification algorithm is designed for online learning. Thus the training patterns are normally presented only once and not stored. After learning phase has finished the space covered by the input data should be completely represented by the neurons and their perceptive areas. Since the neurons have a perceptive area (see fig. 1) two possibilities arise while presenting training patterns: a) an accepting neuron may exist which has to be adapted or b) no accepting neurons exist and a new neuron has to be created.

If there are accepting neurons, the closest accepting neuron will be adapted. Its centre moves towards the pattern and its σ moves towards the distance between the centre and the pattern. If no accepting neuron exists, a new neuron will be created. Therefore the centre of this new neuron is set to the position of the presented pattern. σ may be set to one of the following strategies:

– Init-σ: Use an initial value σ_{init} for σ
– Minimum-σ: Use the minimum value of all σ

- Maximum-σ: Use the maximum value of all σ
- Mean-σ: Use the mean value of all σ

Since the parameters of the classification algorithm should arise from the presented data we propose the mean-σ as favourite strategy. After adding a new neuron re-clustering of the patterns is not necessary since the algorithm is designed for online learning. Therefore input patterns do not have to be stored. The learning algorithm of the neural net can be described in meta language:

```
for each PATTERN with position p
    if exists accepting NEURON
        get closest accepting NEURON
        adapt c and σ of this NEURON
    elseif
        create new NEURON
        set c = p
        set σ
```

Building Neighbourhood. After the training phase has finished the neighbourhood will be built to find contiguous areas. Since the neurons still have perceptive areas the network is able to detect novel patterns and may build new neurons.

During the training phase no neighbourhood between the neurons is calculated or used to adapt the neurons. Only the accepting and winning neuron will be adapted. The winning neuron is the neuron with the shortest distance to the currently provided input pattern.

Before starting the recall phase a neighbourhood graph is created using an algorithm we call the σ nearest neighbouring algorithm. This algorithm is a modification of the ε nearest neighbouring algorithm. Within the ε nearest neighbouring a fixed boundary around each neuron is used to compute connections between two neurons with centres c_1 and c_2. The σ nearest neighbouring uses the perceptive area around each neuron to compute these connections. Two neurons with centres c_1 and c_2 will be connected with an edge if the perceptive areas of the two neurons overlap. Therefore the distance d between c_1 and c_2 is calculated:

$$d = \|c_1 - c_2\|$$

The neurons with centres c_1 and c_2 are connected with an edge if:

$$d \leq (\sigma(c_1) + \sigma(c_2)) \cdot \rho$$

After building edges between neurons with overlapping perceptive areas it is possible to find connected groups of neurons which belong to the same cluster.

2 Main Results

Within this section the clustering abilities of the presented algorithm are shown. First a two dimensional input consisting of two concentric circles and another two dimensional input consisting of several rectangles are used to show the functionality of the approach and to show how the neighbourhood between the neurons is built. Then high dimensional input patterns are used to show that the presented algorithm can cope with high dimensional data. These input patterns are 720 dimensional and extracted from audio data.

2.1 Two Concentric Circles

The algorithm is designed for clustering input data and for self-detecting the number of clusters covered by the input data. A standard k-means clustering fails to cluster two concentric rings as shown in figure 2(a). Since the shown data is divided into two rings the parameter k should be 2. Hence the rings are concentric both clusters have the same centre and the k-means clustering is not able to discern the two clusters or the two rings respectively.

To show the abilities of the presented algorithm input data as shown in figure 2(a) are used. The input data comprise 20000 two-dimensional data points with approximately 10% of these data points in the outer ring. Thus, 1866 data points are in the outer and 18134 data points are in the inner ring.

Training Phase. All 20000 data points are presented once to the algorithm. The following parameters are used: ρ: 2.0 η_c: 0.01 η_σ: 0.01 σ_{init}: 0.4, mean-σ strategy.

After all 20000 patterns have been presented, the algorithm created 76 neurons with mean σ=0.335. Two connected groups within these neurons are found as shown in fig. 2(b).

During the 20000 learning steps the number of neurons increases while the number of classes decreases. The development of these numbers during the training phase is shown in figures 3(a) and 3(b).

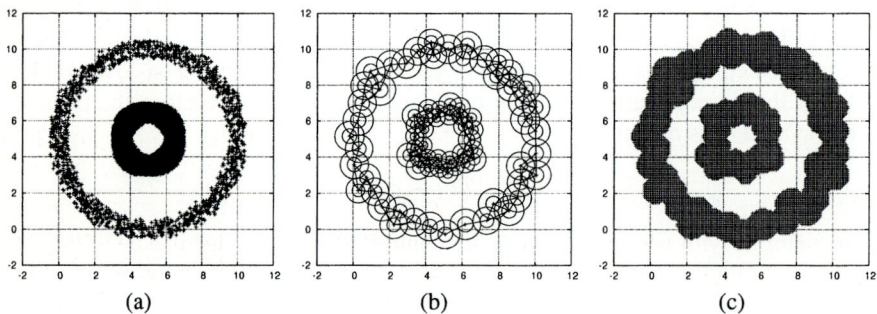

Fig. 2. To show the abilities of the algorithm and to test it two 2D concentric rings as shown in the figure are used. (a) shows the input data comprising of 20000 data points with approximately 10% of these data points (1866) in the outer ring. (b) shows the training results after 20000 input patterns. Parameters: ρ: 2.0, η_c: 0.01, η_σ: 0.01, σ_{init}: 0.4, mean-σ strategy. 76 neurons were created with mean σ=0.335. 2 connected groups were detected. (c) shows the input space divided into patterns which are accepted by the network and patterns which are not accepted by the network. 19881 data points were presented to the algorithm starting with -2.0 up to 12.0, step size 0.1.

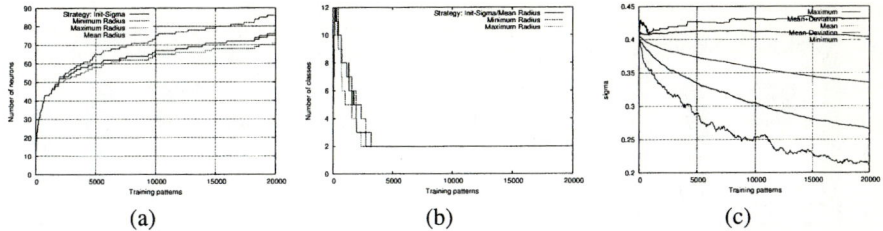

Fig. 3. The figure shows the development of internal parameters during the training phase. The parameters are the same as used in fig. 2(b) except the σ strategy. (a) shows the development of the number of the neurons for all four mentioned strategies. (b) shows the development of the number of connections between the neurons, the number of clusters. (c) shows the development of σ of the neurons. The minimum, maximum, and mean σ are shown. Also mean ± standard deviation is shown.

Not only the number of neurons or classes develop during the training phase but also the size of the neurons. The development of σ is shown in fig. 3(c). It can be seen that the neurons shrink with parameter $\rho = 2.0$ and therefore the number of neurons must increase to cover the input data. With $\rho = 3.0$ the neurons tend to grow and therefore the number of neurons is limited. 23 to 25 neurons are created depending on the strategy used to initialise σ. Nevertheless, the algorithm is still able to separate the two rings but since the perceptive area of the neurons is larger, a larger part of the free space outlying the two rings will be assigned to one of the rings.

Recall Phase. To verify the algorithm's functionality it is useful to cluster the input data again after the algorithm has been trained. The results of this recall phase are shown in table 1(a). The input data comprise of two clusters, the outer and the inner ring. When presenting a pattern to the algorithm it returns the label of the cluster the algorithm has built. We have chosen numbers as labels. If no neuron accepts the input pattern the algorithm returns -1.

Table 1(a) shows, that one input pattern taken from the outer ring is marked "-1" which means that the algorithm didn't find any accepting neuron. 19 neurons taken from the inner ring are marked as "-1". Hence 20 out of 20000 patterns (only 0.1%!) were unclassified, the algorithm didn't find any matching neuron. The algorithm did no misclassification, it only said "unknown" pattern.

Another possibility to verify the results of the algorithm is to present patterns equally distributed within the input space. Thereby you get a "map" of the input space showing areas where the algorithm accepts patterns as shown in fig. 2(c).

2.2 Rectangles

The two concentric rings shown in fig. 2(a) could be easier classified using polar coordination. But therefore a priori knowledge would be necessary. In the general case no coordinate transformation will be available.

The input data shown in figure 4(a) could not be classified using transformations into polar coordination. The input data comprise 50000 two-dimensional data points with approximately $\frac{2}{3}$ of these data points on the outer square.

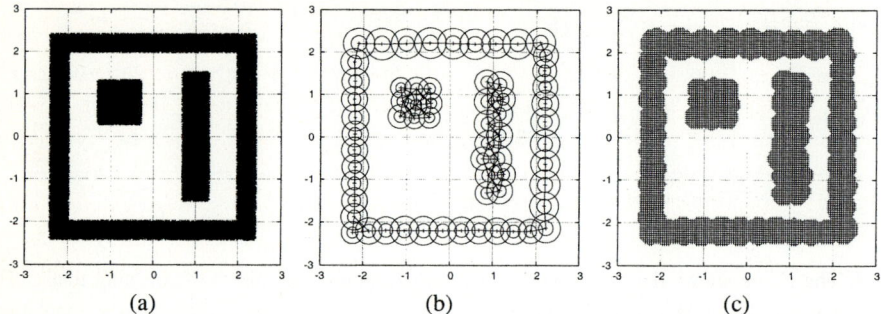

Fig. 4. To show the abilities of the algorithm and to test it some rectangles as shown in the figure are used. (a) shows the input data comprising of 50000 data points with approximately $\frac{2}{3}$ of these data points (33295) on the outer square. (b) shows the training results after 50000 input patterns. Parameters: ρ: 2.0, η_c: 0.01, η_σ: 0.01, σ_{init}: 0.2, mean-σ strategy. 63 neurons were created with mean σ=0.153454. 3 connected groups were detected. (c) show the input space divided into patterns which are accepted by the algorithm and patterns which are not accepted by the algorithm. 14641 data points were presented to the algorithm starting with -3.0 up to 3.0, step size 0.05.

Table 1. Recall results

(a) Two concentric rings			(b) Rectangles			
	outer ring	inner ring		inner square	inner rectangle	outer square
-1	1	19	-1	0	3	0
0	0	18115	0	8302	0	0
1	1865	0	1	0	0	33295
			2	0	8400	0

Training Phase. All 50000 data points are presented once to the algorithm. The following parameters are used: ρ: 2.0 η_c: 0.01 η_σ: 0.01 σ_{init}: 0.2, mean-σ strategy.

After all 50000 patterns have been presented, the algorithm created 63 neurons with mean σ=0.153454. Three connected groups within these neurons are found as shown in fig. 4(b).

Recall Phase. The results of the recall phase are shown in table 1(b). The input data comprise of three clusters, the outer and two inner rectangles.

Table 1(b) shows, that three input pattern taken from the inner rectangle are labelled "-1" which means that the algorithm didn't find any accepting neuron. Hence 3 out of 50000 patterns (only 0.006%!) were unclassified, the algorithm didn't find any matching neuron. But the algorithm didn't classify these 3 patterns wrong, it only said "unknown" pattern.

As before patterns equally distributed within the input space are provided to the network to evaluate the clustering capabilities. The resulting "map" is shown in fig. 4(c).

2.3 Audio Data

To check if the developed algorithm is really capable to find an adequate clustering, 7 auditory patterns spoken by a human were presented. The patterns were the 7 words "Start", "Stop", "Go", "Kurt", "Left", "Right", and "Back" each repeated 35 times by one speaker and recorded with a microphone with a sample frequency of 8 kHz.

An implementation for audio signal processing is described in [2] and in [3]. There the k-means clustering algorithm is used to distinguish between these seven words. The silhouette coefficient as described in [4] is used to rate a clustering and to determine the parameter k. Many initialisations with different k have to be run in parallel.

The approach presented in this paper detects groups within the input data by itself and therefore it should be able to find a good clustering with only one initialisation.

To get input data for the clustering algorithm the raw audio data is divided into windows each containing 512 audio points. These windows are weighted using the Blackman window function and Fourier transformed. To increase the temporal resolution these windows are shifted by 256 points. To transform the data routines available on [5] will be used. Binaries for MS Windows are available on [6].

To reduce the data 24 linear critical bands are used. To enhance the clustering results it could be useful to use nonlinear critical bands. E. Zwicker described in [7] the division of human sensible frequencies in critical bands. These critical bands may be rationed linearly or geometrically (logarithmically).

The patterns in this experiments contain 30 time slices and therefore they are 960 ms long. Thus we get 720-dimensional input patterns for the clustering algorithm.

Training Phase. The 245 preprocessed audio patterns are presented once to the clustering algorithm. The following parameters are used: ρ: 2.0 η_c: 0.01 η_σ: 0.01 σ_{init}: 1.49, mean-σ strategy.

After all input patterns have been presented to the algorithm 245 neurons were created, one for each pattern. The connected neurons build 11 clusters.

Recall Phase. Presenting again all patterns to the algorithm and comparing these patterns to the 11 clusters the system computed it can be seen that the algorithm was able to distinguish the seven spoken words. Just 4 patterns (1.63%) were not clustered correctly. A closer look at the patterns revealed that these 4 were spoken unclear. The algorithm managed to find these patterns on its own. The results are shown in table 2(a).

If σ_{init} is set to 1.5 the system returns in the recall phase table 2(b). The table shows, that the system is not able to distinguish between the commands "Left" and "Back".

3 Further Work

The presented neural network showed its clustering abilities with three input data examples. It managed to cluster the input data unsupervised into the estimated clusters.

While clustering input data it could be expected, that the neurons behave almost similar. The centres c of the neurons should be equally distributed within the input data space and the σ should be alike.

Table 2. Recall results: Audio Data

(a) σ_{init}: 1.49, mean-σ strategy

	Start	Stop	Go	Kurt	Left	Right	Back
0	35						
1		35					
2			35				
3				34			
4					32		
5					*1*		
6						35	
7							35
8				*1*			
9				*1*			
10				*1*			

(b) σ_{init}: 1.50, mean-σ strategy

	Start	Stop	Go	Kurt	Left	Right	Back
0	35						
1		35					
2			35				
3				34			
4					*32*		35
5					*1*		
6						35	
7						*1*	
8						*1*	
9				*1*			

Figure 2(b) shows that the centres c are distributed very well within the input data space but figure 3(c) shows that the standard deviation of the σ grows. If the neurons belonging to the same cluster would be equally sized the standard deviation of σ should shrink, not grow. Therefore it could be useful to adapt also the neurons within the calculated neighbourhood similar to the neurons of a self-organised map.

4 Conclusions

Within this paper an unsupervised clustering algorithm is presented. The algorithm combines two standard clustering algorithms, the k-means clustering and the ε nearest neighbour clustering.

Adaptation rules known from self-organising maps are transferred to the k-means clustering algorithm to make it online-adaptable. The perceptive area of the neurons serves as a novelty detector for patterns. Thus the net is able to grow and to build representatives to reduce the input data for the ε nearest neighbour.

After the k-means clustering has computed the perceptive neurons, a variation of the ε nearest neighbour is used to build a neighbourhood between these neurons to detect contiguous areas.

Since the perceptive area of the neurons is still enabled after learning it is possible to detect new incoming data not covered by the neurons so far and to create new neurons with new contiguous areas.

The functionality and the structure of the presented neural algorithm is shown with two concentric rings and with rectangles in 2D. Moreover audio data in 720 dimensional input space was clustered. The algorithm detected the contiguous areas correctly and showed its high reliability in the recall phase. Moreover the combination of the k-means clustering and the ε nearest neighbour clustering managed to separate clusters with the same cluster centre as show for the two concentric rings example.

Acknowledgement

Part of this work is supported by the European Commission's Information Society Technologies Programme, project SIGNAL, IST-2000-29225. Partners in this project are Napier University, National Research Council Genoa, Austrian Research Institute OFAI, and the University of Bonn.

References

1. Kohonen, T.: Self-Oranizing Maps. Springer Series in Information Sciences (1995)
2. Schatten, R.: Entwicklung einer aufwachsenden Struktur zum Erlernen einer einfachen Sprache mit Hilfe neuronaler Netze. Master's thesis, Universität Bonn, Institut für Informatik VI, Neuroinformatik (2002)
3. Schatten, R.: Systemic architecture for audio signal processing. In: Proceedings of the European Conference on Advances in Artificial Life (ECAL'2003) Dortmund. LNAI 2801, Springer (2003) 491–498
4. Berkhin, P.: Survey of clustering data mining techniques. Technical report, Accrue Software, San Jose, CA (2002)
5. Frigo, M., Johnson, S.G.: Fastest Fourier Transform in the West. http://www.fftw.org/ (1999)
6. Sterian, A.: FFTW for Win32. http://claymore.engineer.gvsu.edu/~steriana/software.html (1999)
7. Zwicker, E.: Subdivision of the Audible Frequency Range into Critical Bands (Frequenzgruppen). JASA **33(2)** (1961) 248

Spatial Feature Based Recognition of Human Dynamics in Video Sequences

Jessica JunLin Wang and Sameer Singh

Research School of Informatics, Loughborough University,
Loughborough LW11 3TU, United Kingdom

Abstract. The reliable identification of human activities in video, for example whether a person is walking, clapping, waving, etc. is extremely important for video interpretations. Since different people could perform the same action across different number of frames, matching two different sequences of the same actions is not a trivial task. In this paper we discuss a new technique for video sequence matching where the matched sequences are of different sizes. The proposed technique is based on frequency domain analysis of feature data. The experiments are shown to achieve high recognition accuracy of 95.4% on recognizing 8 different human actions, and out-perform two baseline methods of comparison.

1 Introduction

Human activity recognition from video streams has a wide range of applications such as human-machine interaction, surveillance, choreography, content-based image/video retrieval, biometric applications, etc. [17,19]. In our work, we distinguish between two main categories of actions: *passive actions* e.g. sit and do nothing, thinking, turning the head to follow someone across the room (watch the world go by), etc.; and *active actions* e.g. waving, clapping, lifting objects, reading (some of these actions are repetitive, and others are non-repetitive), etc. These actions can be performed with the person sitting or standing. Our aim is to develop a machine learning system that uses training data of different actions (performed by a number of subjects) to automatically classify (identify) actions in test videos.

The main problem with matching training and test video shots (a shot is a sequence of video frames) is that each shot is of a different length and exact matching is impossible. For example, consider two people waving in two different videos. This action in the first video v_1, say, takes $L1$ frames and this action in the second video v_2 takes $L2$ frames. In addition, these actions would most likely start at different times in their corresponding videos. The matching problem can be defined as follows:

Given: Videos v_1 and v_2 that contain shots: $v_1 = (a_1, a_2, ..., a_n)$ and $v_2 = (b_1, b_2, ..., b_n)$. The video v_1 is training video, with shot a_i ground truthed as class c_k, "e.g. c_k =waving" and v_2 is test video.

Problem: Match all shots of v_2 with a_i to confirm if any of them are "waving". This will be based on a measure of similarity. The problem of speed variation makes the matching process difficult. In most real cases, the same activity is usually performed with different speed and acceleration by different people. The solution to such a problem requires a complex search for the optimum match with various sequence lengths and phase shifts.

The problem of video shot matching has been tackled in the past with a view to video retrieval. For this purpose, only key frames rather than all frames are mostly used for matching. Such methods have achieved limited success by matching a set of key frames that are assumed to be unique for actions. There are four mentionable solutions to the problem of matching two video sequences containing human activities. These approaches are based on either matching a set of key frames or a continuous set of frames, and are described in the works of Kim and Park [8], Ben-Arie *et al.* [3], Duda and Hart [5] and Tsai *et al.*[17].

In Kim and Park's [8] approach for matching video sequences, they extract the key frames and these key frames are matched for similarity using modified Hausdorff distance. In Ben-Arie *et al.*'s [3] approach, they describe human activity as a temporal sequence of pose vectors that represent sampled poses of body parts. Multi-dimensional indexing is used to represent angles and angular velocities of each body part. For the 9 body parts considered, votes are accumulated and the voting is done only on a few representative frames which are sparsely sampled from the test video sequence. It is also possible to use edit-distances [5] for matching video sequences. A number of statistical features can be extracted from each video frame that are then recoded as discrete alphabets, where each alphabet represents an interval within the overall min-max range of that feature. A video sequence can be represented as a one dimensional vector of multidimensional vectors (string of strings). The process of matching is now based on calculating the cost of transforming one string into another and the best match is based on the least cost. Finally, correlation techniques can be used to detect cycles in 2D trajectories created by points on a moving object [17]. The trajectories are represented as two 1D trajectories, namely speed and direction, and the cyclic motions (e.g. walking motions) are detected by finding cycles in the curvature of the spatio-temporal curve. The detected cycles are then applied to a method proposed by Rangarajan *et al.* [13] for matching pairs of single trajectories.

There are two major limitations of the above approaches: (a) A number of methods are based on sparse matching of frames, e.g. matching key frames alone, which fails to consider the temporal aspect of activity recognition. It is possible for similar actions to have different temporal information across frames but still have similar key frames; and (b) Approaches based on cyclic actions can be applied only to a limited number of actions where the action primitives repeat themselves.

Apart from these main approaches in human dynamics, there have been other approaches proposed in other fields of research related to time series analysis aimed at solving the problem of matching two time indexed data sequences of different lengths. The approaches used can be divided into two main categories: *sub-sequence matching* and *energies transform based matching*.

The idea behind sub-sequence matching is that: Given a collection of N sequences of varying length, $S_1, S_2, \ldots, S_N$, the user specifies a query subsequence Q of variable length *Len(Q)* and tolerance ε (maximum acceptable dissimilarity or distance). The aim is then to find all sequences $S_i : (1 \leq i \leq N)$, along with correct offsets k, such $S_i[k:k+Len(Q)-1]$ that matches the query subsequence Q, such that the distance D is less than the threshold, i.e. $D(Q, S_i[k:k+Len(Q)-1]) \leq \varepsilon$. Faloutsos et al. [6] proposed a method of mapping each data sequence into a small set of multidimensional rectangles in feature space which are indexed using spatial access methods such as R^* trees [2]. Moon et al. [9,10] proposed a Dual Match method that uses the Faloutsos et al. [6]'s approach in constructing windows, where the data sequence is divided into disjoint windows and a query sequence is divided into sliding windows. Whereas Faloutsos's method could lead to several false alarms by only storing the minimum bounding rectangles rather than individual data points, Moon's Dual Match approach is able to store individual points in the index. Savnik et al. [14] uses matching algorithm to extract all possible windows of length ω from the input sequence s_u.

Energy transform approaches either use wavelet transform [4] or Fourier transform [1,11,12]. Chan and Fu [4] used Discrete Wavelet Transform (DWT) to accommodate vertical shift of time series which leads to an efficient k-nearest neighbour query in time series databases. Agrawal et al. [1] introduced a solution where each data sequence of length n is transformed into the frequency domain by using Discrete Fourier Transform (DFT), and the first $f (\leq n)$ features are extracted for matching. Rafiei and Mendelzon [11,12] studied a set of linear transformations on Fourier series representation of a sequence which is used as the basis for similarity queries on time-series data.

Unfortunately, most of the above approaches proposed to solve the problem of time series data matching assume that either there is no speed variation, i.e. the strings that matched are of the same length in terms of number of frames, or if they assume that there is speed variation (and hence we have different length sequences), then data is interpolated to make the sequences matched to be of the same length. The sub-sequence matching approaches are limited to using small window sizes that limits the query length, and increases false alarms. In energy transform approaches, a high number of false positives are observed because only the first f energy features are used. In our previous work [19] we proposed a frequency based analysis solution to overcome these limitations for human activity recognition. A modified WFT (Windowed Fourier Transform) approach was used to extract features from each sequence and these features were used to calculate a dissimilarity measure that assigns the sequence to the least dissimilar action type. We experimented on synthetic data (simulating real life actions) and real data. Result showed that our approach not only overcomes the limitations of the previous approaches mentioned above, but it also shows that using Fourier features improves the classification accuracy considerably compared to using raw features. The recognition accuracy in [19] ranged between 56.1% (7 classes) to 83.6% (2 classes).

In this paper we present a novel technique for recognising human activities in video. As shown later, this method outperforms our previous efforts [19] significantly and takes the temporal information of human actions into full consideration when extracting features. The paper is organised as follows. In section 2, we detail our methodology along with the set of features used. The experimental details with data description are presented in section 3. Section 3 also presents the results of our proposed method, comparisons with a baseline results from [19] and recognition results using Ben-Arie's method in [3]. Some key conclusions are drawn in section 4.

2 Methodology

The recognition of human activities in video requires a range of image processing operations coupled with sophisticated pattern recognition techniques. The main steps involve image pre-processing, image co-registration, video capturing, skin detection, region identification, ellipse fitting, feature extractions, and classification (see Fig. 1). In this section we describe briefly the feature extraction and feature selection steps.

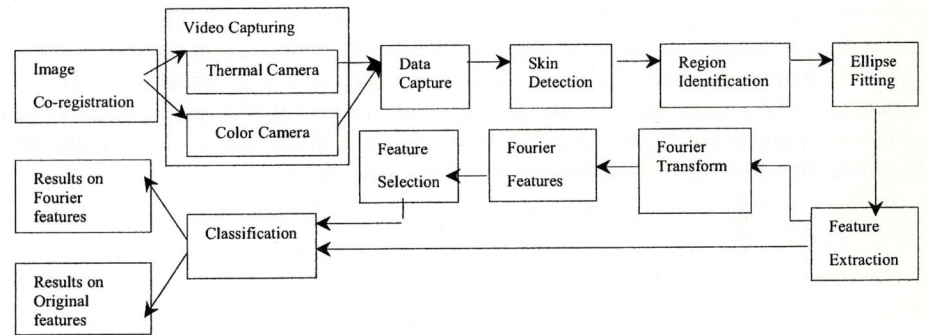

Fig. 1. Flowchart for recognising human dynamics in video sequences

2.1 Feature Extraction

The classification accuracy depends on the quality of features used. We generate features at two levels. Firstly, features $(f_1,...,f_p)$ are computed directly from the hand and face region location information. For a video sequence V consisting of N frames, we get a set of features per frame. Secondly, these features are processed in the frequency domain to generate a new set of features $(g_1,...,g_q)$ that define the overall video sequence V. In the following description we first define the features $(f_1,...,f_{41})$ that can be computed from the output of hand/face localisation step.

Features (f_1, f_2, f_3, f_4) are type of triangles formed with head, left and right arm regions; feature f_5 is used to determine whether the area of triangle formed changes significantly or not; features (f_6, f_7) denote the direction of change, i.e. area increases or decreases; features $(f_8,...,f_{34})$ are calculated to find the spatial relationships between head, left arm and right arm regions. The spatial relationships can be computed based on determining the 3 sets of sub-features: sub-features (sf_1, sf_2, sf_3) determine the spatial proximity of left arm and the head regions; sub-features (sf_4, sf_5, sf_6) determine the spatial proximity of right arm and the head regions and sub-features (sf_7, sf_8, sf_9) determine the spatial proximity of left and the right arm regions. Features (f_{35}, f_{36}, f_{37}) determine the movement and direction of left arm oscillation when moving in horizontal directions (left and right); feature (f_{38}, f_{39}, f_{40}) determine the amount and direction of right arm oscillation when moving in horizontal plane (left and right); and feature (f_{41}) determine whether the area of the head region changes significantly across two frames which indicates head movement.

2.2 Feature Selection

For each video sequence we extract the above described 41 features. Each feature contains a binary vector of size N, $(b_1,...,b_N)$, for a total of N frames. From the above set of features, we generate a new set of Fourier features that separate the high and low frequency components in our data. The temporal information is best preserved using Fourier analysis and the speed of movement of body parts is encoded within the frequency data. We use 1D Discrete Fourier Transform for further analysis. The basic algorithm of feature extraction is described below.

Algorithm Fourier Feature Selection :

Given: A video containing N frames, from which 41 features $(f_1,...,f_{41})$ have been extracted. Each feature can be represented as a vector of binary numbers, i.e. $f_i = (b_{i1},...,b_{iN})$.

Step 1: Discrete Fourier transform is applied on a given feature which generates a Fourier representation $\Im(f_i) = (u_{i1},...,u_{iN})$, where u_i is a complex number, and its magnitude can be used for further analysis.

Step 2: Compute the mean μ_i and standard deviation σ_i of the Fourier magnitudes of u_i.

Step 3: The final 82 Fourier features used for classification are now given as $(\mu_1, \sigma_1,...\mu_{41}, \sigma_{41})$. This can now be represented as the new feature set $(g_1,...g_{82})$.

3 Experimental Details and Results

A total of 22 subjects were asked to perform the 8 actions of 1) sitting and do nothing; 2) turning the head; 3) thinking1 (with one of the hands under the chin), 4) clapping; 5) waving; 6) drinking; 7) reading; and 8) thinking2 (with both hands under the chin).

The classification performance of our proposed technique can be discussed under 4 separate sections: (a) classification using all of the 82 Fourier features (section 3.1); (b) classification after some basic feature selection (section 3.2); (c) comparison with baseline results published in [19] (section 3.3); and d) comparison with Ben-Arie's method in [3] (section 3.4).

3.1 Classification with Complete Feature Set

We use a k-nearest classifier to generate 4-fold cross-validation results. The results are shown in Table 1. Table 1 shows the classification results of data with classes ranging from 2 to 8.

Table 1. Overall classification accuracy using Fourier features on data ranging from 2 to 8 classes

No. of Classes	2	3	4	5	6	7	8
Fold1 Classification %	100.0	100.0	100.0	100.0	100.0	100.0	100.0
Fold2 Classification %	100.0	100.0	100.0	100.0	97.6	96.3	95.3
Fold3 Classification %	100.0	100.0	100.0	100.0	97.6	96.3	95.3
Fold4 Classification %	100.0	100.0	100.0	100.0	100.0	98.6	97.6
Ave. Classification %	100.0	100.0	100.0	100.0	98.8	97.7	97.1

3.2 Classification with Reduced Feature Set

Not all of the features used necessarily distinguish between the different actions we are interested in. On the training data we calculate correlation coefficients between the features $(g_1,...g_{82})$ and the class label for all actions. Out of 82 features, only 42 showed correlation > 0.03, and these are shown in Fig. 2 (dark colour represents high correlation with the class label).

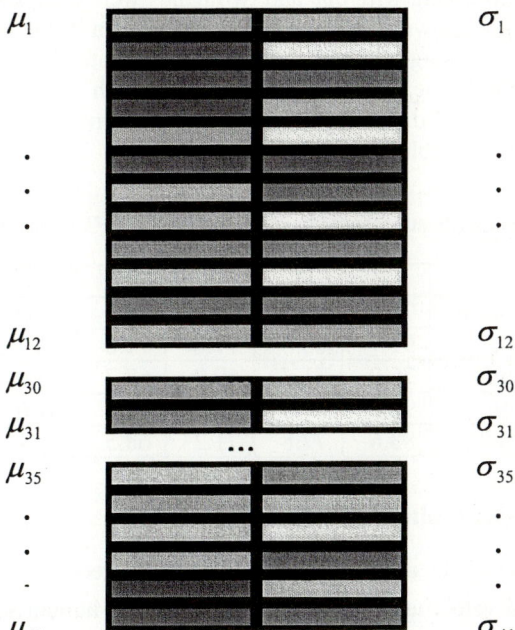

Fig. 2. Correlation of each feature to the classes

The k-nearest neighbour classifier is used as before for 4-fold cross-validation. The results are shown in Table 2. The results show that the reduced feature set is adequate for recognition since the recognition accuracy only drops by 1.1% even though 40 features have been removed from the data set. These removed features could be useful if we have more actions, and therefore it is recommended that for any problem with a given set of actions, feature reduction should be performed first to find which features are discriminatory for that problem.

Table 2. Overall classification accuracy using reduced Fourier features using data ranging from 2 to 8 classes

No. of Classes	2	3	4	5	6	7	8
Fold1 Classification %	100.0	100.0	100.0	100.0	100.0	100.0	100.0
Fold2 Classification %	100.0	100.0	100.0	96.3	96.6	94.3	95.0
Fold3 Classification %	100.0	100.0	100.0	100.0	96.6	94.3	95.0
Fold4 Classification %	100.0	100.0	100.0	100.0	100.0	97.1	97.6
Ave. Classification %	100.0	100.0	100.0	99.1	98.3	96.4	96.9

3.3 Comparison with Baseline Approaches

In our previous study [19] we used modified Windowed Fourier Transform on the same video data considered in this paper. In total 55 features were used – these were based on the difference in angles of the major axis of the fitted ellipse around hand and face regions, and change in centroid positions of each region. In our previous study, the actions of thinking with one and two hands were analysed as a single class. The results of [19] are shown as a baseline comparison in Table 3, which shows the results of classifying varying number of classes ($\neg C$ denotes the classes not included in classification) using a k nearest neighbour classifier with 4 fold cross-validation.

The results below showed that the classification performance is quite poor for real data in comparison with Table 2.

Table 3. The classification result based on modified WFT from approach [18]

No. of Classes	2	3	4	5	6	7	8
Fold1 Classification %	75.0	75.0	69.2	71.0	63.9	56.1	49.2
Fold2 Classification %	91.7	83.3	77.0	71.0	66.7	63.4	59.1
Fold3 Classification %	76.9	71.4	69.2	67.7	63.9	56.1	52.7
Fold4 Classification %	90.9	81.3	69.6	64.3	57.6	48.8	41.3
Ave. Classification %	83.6	77.8	71.2	68.5	63.1	56.1	50.6

3.4 Comparison with Multidimensional-Indexing

The principle of Ben-Arie et al.'s [3] approach is to recognize activity based on angular poses θ and velocities $\dot{\theta}$ of 9 body parts, where human activity is describes as a temporal sequence of pose vectors that represent sampled poses of these body parts. Our activities only involves upper body movement, therefore in our implementation only 5 body parts are used, namely the torso, the upper left arm, the lower left arm, the upper right arm and the lower right arm. All sequences are interpolated into the same length, by inserting between frames.

For training, three hash tables are built, h_1 for the torso, h_2 for upper and lower left arm and h_3 for upper and lower right arm. The indices in these hash tables are the poses of the corresponding body parts and the contents of these hash tables are the identities of the activities and their time labels.

The recognition consist of three stages: 1) voting for individual body parts; 2) combining the votes of all body parts for each test frame; and 3) integrating the votes of all frames in a test sequence.

The vote for each frame k, an activity type m at frame number t, in hash table h_i is denoted as $V_{mk}^{hi}(t)$. When voting for the torso, it is calculated as $V_{mk}^{h1}(t) = f(|q_1^k - q_1'|, |q_2^k - q_2'|)$, where q_1^k denotes the bin of the angular pose of the torso in test frame k, q_2^k denotes the bin of the angular velocity of the torso in test frame k, q_1' and q_2' denote 1 of the neighbouring bins and the mapping function f is a logarithm of a 2D Gaussian $f(a,b) = \log[e^{\frac{-1}{2}[(\frac{a-a_0}{\sigma_a})^2 + (\frac{b-b_0}{\sigma_b})^2]}]$, where σ_a and σ_b denotes the scale of the Gaussian along the respective axes, and a_0 and b_0 represent the center of the function.

The votes are calculated for each activity type of each body part, and for each activity type, votes are accumulated from all body parts of the frame, then votes of each frame are integrated for the whole sequence to get the final vote for each activity type. The test sequence is recognized as the activity type that returns the maximum final vote.

The experiment is performed using 4-fold cross-validation and the results are shown in Table 4.

Table 4. Recognition result using Ben-Arie's method on 4-fold cross-validation from 2 classes to 8 classes

No. of Classes	2	3	4	5	6	7	8
Fold1 Classification %	80.0	60.0	42.9	29.6	27.6	20.0	17.5
Fold2 Classification %	60.0	53.3	38.1	44.4	41.4	34.3	30.0
Fold3 Classification %	70.0	66.7	47.6	37.0	34.5	25.7	22.5
Fold4 Classification %	80.0	73.3	52.4	44.4	41.4	31.4	27.5
Ave. Classification %	72.5	63.3	45.2	38.9	36.2	27.9	24.4

The comparison shows that our new features can out perform the comparison method by significant margin. Even on comparison with our previous approach, which uses angular features as well, the result shows better improvement then the comparison method, proving that our energy-based approach are better at recognizing complicated activities and giving the right features can correctly recognize a large number of activities.

4 Conclusion

One of the major difficulties in analysing human dynamics data is the fact that each person performs the same action at different speeds with large variation in terms of the movement of their body parts. This makes the process of matching action sequences of different lengths difficult. Several approaches have been attempted to solve these problems, however, most of these have been successful only in tackling the time shift problem and not speed variations. Our approach shows that robust features can be extracted from human dynamics video data with adequate image analysis for skin identification, and hand/face detection. Our scheme of using Fourier based features generates feature sequences used in classification to be of the same length irrespective of the length of video clips. The results generated on real data in this paper are very promising at 95.4%. We expect that similar performances can be achieved on a larger number of classes with adequate feature extraction and temporal feature analysis using our Fourier method. It is however important to remember that high quality features can only be extracted subsequent to robust image analysis, which requires substantial work before real systems can be built.

References

1. R. Agrawal, C. Faloutsos and A. Swami, "Efficient Similarity Search In Sequence Databases", Proceedings of the 4th International Conference of Foundations of Data Organization and Algorithms (FODO), Chicago, pp. 69-84, October 1993.
2. N. Beckmann, H-P. Kriegel, R. Schneider and B. Seeger, "The R^* -tree: An Efficient and Robust Access Method for Points and Rectangles", In Proc. Int'l Conf. On Management of Data, ACM SIGMOD, Atlantic City, New Jersey, pp. 322-331, May 1990.
3. J. Ben-Arie, Z. Wang, P. Pandit and S. Rajaram, "Human Activity Recognition Using Multidimensional Indexing", IEEE Transactions on Pattern Analysis and Machine Intelligence, Vol. 24, No. 8, pp. 1091-1104, August 2002.
4. K-P. Chan and A. W-C. Fu, "Efficient Time Series Matching by Wavelets", 15th IEEE International Conference on Data Engineering, Sydney, Australia, pp. 126-133, March 1999.
5. R. Duda, P.E. Hart and D. Stork, "Pattern Classification", 2nd ed., New York: John Wiley and Sons, 2001.
6. C. Faloutsos, M. Ranganathan and Y. Manolopoulos, "Fast subsequence matching in Time-series Databases", Proceedings 1994 ACM SIGMOD Conference, Minneapolis, MN, pp. 419-429, 1994.
7. T. Horprasert, D. Harwood and L. S. Davis, "A statistical App. roach for Real-time Robust Background Subtraction and Shadow Detection", Proceeding of IEEE ICCV'99, pp. 1-19, 1999.

8. S. H. Kim and R-H. Park, "An Efficient Algorithm For Video Sequence Matching Using The Modified Hausdorff Distance and the Directed Divergence", IEEE Transactions on Circuits and Systems for Video Technology, Vol. 12, No. 7, pp. 592-296, July 2002.
9. Y-S. Moon, K-Y. Whang and W-K Loh, "Efficient Time-Series Subsequence Matching using Duality in Constructing Windows", Information Systems, vol. 26, no. 4, pp. 279-293, June 2001.
10. Y-S. Moon, K-Y Whang and W-K Loh, "Dual Match: Duality-Based Subsequence Matching in Time-series Databases", Proceedings of the 17th International Conference on Data Engineering, pp. 263272, April 2001.
11. D. Rafiei and A. Mendelzon, "Similarity-based Queries for Time series Data", In Proc. Int'l Conf. On Management of Data, ACM SIGMOD, Tucson, Arizona, pp. 13-25, May 1997.
12. D. Rafiei, "On similarity-based queries for time series data", In Proc. The 15th Int'l Conf. On Data Engineering, Sydney, Australia, pp. 410-417, February 1999.
13. K. Rangarajan, B. Allen and M. Shah, "Matching Motion Trajectories", Pattern Recognition, Vol.26, No. 4, pp. 595-610, July 1993.
14. I. Savnik, G. Lausen, H-P. Kahle, H. Spiecker and S. Hein, "Algorithm for Matching Sets of Time Series", Principles of Data Mining and Knowledge Discovery, Lyon, France, pp. 277-288, September 2000.
15. M. Sonka, V. Hlavac and R. Boyle, "Image Processing, Analysis and Machine Vision" Brooks/Cole Publishing, Chapter6, 1999.
16. A. Tolba, "Arabic Glove Talk: A Communication Aid for Vocally Impaired", Pattern Analysis and Applications, vol. 1, issue 4, pp. 218-230, 1998.
17. P-S. Tsai, M. Shah, K. Keiter and T. Kasparis, "Cyclic Motion Detection", Department of Computer Science Technical Report, University of Central Florida, Orlando, 1993.
18. J. Wang and S. Singh, "Video Based Human Dynamics: A Review", Real Time Imaging, vol. 9, no.5, pp. 321-346, 2003.
19. J. Wang and S. Singh, "Video Based Human Behavior Identification using Frequency Domain Analysis", IDEAL Conference, Exeter, LNCS, Springer, pp. 218-224, August 2004.

Using Behavior Knowledge Space and Temporal Information for Detecting Intrusions in Computer Networks[*]

L.P. Cordella, I. Finizio, C. Mazzariello, and C. Sansone

Dipartimento di Informatica e Sistemistica, Università di Napoli "Federico II",
Via Claudio, 21 I-80125 Napoli, Italy
{cordel, ifinizio, cmazzari, carlosan}@unina.it

Abstract. Pattern Recognition (PR) techniques have proven their ability for detecting malicious activities within network traffic. Systems based on multiple classifiers can further enforce detection capabilities by combining and correlating the results obtained by different sources.

An aspect often disregarded in PR approaches dealing with the intrusion detection problem is the use of temporal information. Indeed, an attack is typically carried out along a set of consecutive network packets; therefore, a PR system could improve its reliability by examining sequences of network connections before expressing a decision.

In this paper we present a system that uses a multiple classifier approach together with temporal information about the network packets to be classified. In order to improve classification reliability, we introduce the concept of rejection: instead of emitting an unreliable verdict, an ambiguously classified packet can be logged for further analysis.

The proposed system has been tested on a wide database made up of real network traffic traces.

1 Introduction

The most common and best known tools used to ensure security of companies, campuses and, more in general, of any network, are Firewalls and Antiviruses. Though famous and well known, such tools alone are not enough to protect a system from malicious activities. Based on such assumption, many researchers started to develop systems able to successfully detect intrusions and, in some cases, trace the path leading to the attack source.

On the basis of the information sources analyzed to detect an intrusive activity, the Intrusion Detection Systems (IDS) can be grouped into different categories. In the following, we will concentrate our attention on Network-based IDS (N-IDS) [1]. On the other hand, depending on the detection technique employed, they can be roughly classified as belonging to two main groups as well [2]. The first one, that exploits

---

[*] This work has been partially supported by the Ministero dell'Istruzione, dell'Università e della Ricerca (MIUR) in the framework of the FIRB Project "Middleware for advanced services over large-scale, wired-wireless distributed systems (WEB-MINDS)".

signatures of known attacks for detecting when an attack occurs, is known as *misuse* (or *signature*) *detection* based. IDS's that fall in this category are based on a model of all the possible misuses of the network resources. The completeness request is actually their major limit [3].

A dual approach tries to characterize the normal usage of the resources under monitoring. An intrusion is then suspected when a significant difference from the resource's normal usage is revealed. IDS's following this approach, known as *anomaly detection* based, seem to be more promising because of their potential ability to detect unknown intrusions (the so-called zero-day attacks). However, there is also a major challenge, because of the need to acquire a model of the normal resources usage which is general enough to allow authorized users to work without raising false alarms, but specific enough to recognize unauthorized usages [4,5].

The network intrusion detection problem can also be formulated as a binary classification problem: once the information about network connections between pairs of hosts is given, the task is to assign each connection to one out of two classes, which represent normal traffic conditions or an attack. Here the term *connection* refers to a sequence of data packets sharing some properties. In this framework, several proposals have been made in order to extract high-level features from data packets [6,7]. Each network connection can be then described by a "pattern" to be classified, and a pattern recognition (PR) approach can be followed.

PR systems typically follow the misuse detection approach. Their main advantage is the ability to generalize. They are able to detect some novel attacks, since different variants of the same attack will be typically described by very similar patterns. Moreover, the high-level features extracted from connections relative to a totally new attack should exhibit a behavior quite different from those extracted from normal connections.

Summarizing, these PR systems don't need a complete description of all the possible attack signatures. This overcomes one of the main drawbacks of the misuse detection approach. Signature based systems, in fact, may fail in detecting attacks undergone to even slight modifications from a known pattern.

Different misuse-based PR systems have been reported in the recent past for realizing an IDS, mainly based on neural network architectures [8,9]. In order to improve the detection performance, approaches based on multi-expert architectures have been also proposed [10,11,12].

Indeed, also anomaly-based systems have been considered in the PR field. Here, they can be ascribed to the more general category of approaches based on the novelty detection, i.e. the identification of new or unknown data or signal that a system is not aware of during training [13]. Examples of neural-based systems that follow the anomaly detection approach can be found in [14,15].

However, one of the main drawbacks occurring when using PR techniques in real environments is the high false alarm rate they often produce [10]. This is a very critical point, as pointed out in [16].

An information source that is commonly disregarded in PR systems is the temporal sequence of the traffic network patterns. According to our opinion, however, this kind of information can be profitably used for augmenting the reliability of the attack detection. An attack is, in fact, typically spread along several network packets close to each other. Even though high level features are extracted from the traffic, it is quite unusual for an attack to spread over a single connection pattern isolated within a sequence of normal connections. A PR system could then improve its performance by examining sequences of network connections.

In order to realize an IDS that is capable of detecting intrusion by keeping the number of false alarms as low as possible, in this paper we propose a multiple classifier system that combines the behavior knowledge space with temporal information coming from a real-time analysis of the network traffic.

In particular, starting from the proposal made in [6], a framework for extracting features from real traffic is adopted [7]. Then the collected data are fed to a multiple classifier system that employs the Behavior Knowledge Space rule for combining the output of the composing classifiers. The standard BKS rule is here generalized for coping with the temporal information of a connection pattern sequence. In order to maximize the complementariness of the decisions to be combined, a rule-based classifier [17] and a neural network are employed as base classifiers.

The organization of the paper is as follows: in Section 2 the proposed approach is presented, while in Section 3 the database obtained form real network traffic is described. Tests of the proposed IDS are reported in Section 4; finally, some conclusions are drawn in Section 5.

2 A Behavior-Knowledge Space Combining Rule Using Temporal Information Algorithm

In [18], Huang and Suen proposed a combining rule that does not require the independence assumption of the base classifiers. It derives the information needed to combine a set of classifiers from a knowledge space, which can concurrently record the decision of all the classifiers on a suitable set of samples. This means that such a space records the behavior of all the classifiers on this set, and thus it is called the Behavior Knowledge Space. The combining rule that uses it is called the Behavior-Knowledge Space (BKS) rule.

More in details, a Behavior-Knowledge Space is a K-dimensional space where each dimension corresponds to the decision of a classifier. Given a pattern x to be assigned to one out of M possible classes, the ensemble of classifiers can in theory provide M^K different decisions. Each one of these decisions $(D_1(x), D_2(x), \ldots, D_K(x))$ - where $D_j(x)$ represent the guess class supplied by the j-th classifier - constitutes one *unit* of the BKS. In our case M is equal to 2, so the number of units is 2^K.

The BKS combining rule operates in two phases: a learning phase for knowledge modeling and an operating phase for decision-making.

In the learning phase the BKS look-up table is built-up: each BKS unit U can record M different values e_i, one for each class. Given a suitably chosen training set, each pattern x_{tr} of this set is classified by all the classifiers and the unit (called *focal unit*) that corresponds to the particular decision of the ensemble of classifiers $(D_1(x_{tr}), D_2(x_{tr}), \ldots, D_K(x_{tr}))$ is activated. Let us denote this unit with $FU(x_{tr})$. It records the actual class $C(x_{tr})$ of x_{tr}, say j, by adding one to the value of e_j.

At the end of this phase, each unit can calculate the best representative class associated to it, say $C(U)$, defined as the class that exhibits the highest value of e_i, i.e.:

$$C(U) = j \quad \text{where } j = \underset{i}{\operatorname{argmax}} \, e_i \tag{1}$$

In other words, this class corresponds to the most likely class, given a classifiers' decision that activates that unit.

In the operating mode, for each pattern x_{test} to be classified, the decisions ($D_1(x_{test})$, $D_2(x_{test})$, ... , $D_K(x_{test})$) of the classifiers are collected and the corresponding focal unit $FU(x_{test})$ is selected. Then the class attributed to x_{test} is the best representative class associated to that focal unit, i.e.:

$$C(x_{test}) = C(U) \quad \text{where } U = FU(x_{test}) \tag{2}$$

Since in our case the temporal sequence of the patterns to be classified assumes a particular significance, the BKS can be augmented with a temporal dimension. In this case, the number of units becomes $2^{K \cdot t}$, where t is the size of the considered temporal window. Each unit, in fact, has to record a sequence of t values for each of the K classifiers, so the new behavior knowledge space assumes a dimensionality equal to $K \cdot t$.

In operating mode, t successive decisions for each classifier (relative to a sequence of t consecutive patterns) need to be collected. Then, these $K \cdot t$ values will select a focal unit whose best representative class will be associated to the last pattern of the sequence. The next pattern will be classified by shifting the temporal window one pattern forward, so individuating a (possibly) different focal unit.

The sequence of decisions relative to a temporal window can also be used for evaluating the reliability of each classification act. A reliability $R(U)$ can be in fact associated to each unit, as specified in the following. In operating mode, all the times a focal unit is selected, its reliability will be the reliability of the performed classification.

We have chosen to evaluate $R(U)$ in the following way:

$$R(U) = \begin{cases} e_j / e_k & \text{if } e_j > 0 \\ 0 & \text{if } e_j = 0 \end{cases} \quad \text{where } e_j = \max_i e_i \text{ and } e_k = \max_{i \neq j} e_i \tag{3}$$

In other words, $R(U)$ is the ratio between the values associated to the first and the second most representative class of this unit. If the value associated to the most representative class of a unit is zero (i.e., the considered unit was never activated by the patterns belonging to the training set), the reliability of this unit is set to zero.

The value of $R(U)$ can be profitably used for choosing to reject a pattern instead of running the risk of misclassifying it. Rejection, in this context, implies that the data about a 'rejected' connection are only logged for further processing, without raising an alert for the system manager [12].

In order to make a rejection, a suitably chosen threshold has to be fixed. This could be done, by using the method proposed in [19], in an adaptive way with respect to the requirements of the application at hand. This notwithstanding, in Sect. 4 results with a reliability threshold value fixed to 0.6 will be reported.

Finally, in order to choose the optimal value of the temporal window, an analysis of the performance of the proposed approach on a suitable set of data can be performed as a function of the value of t. Then, the value of t that allows us to obtain the best trade-off between reject and error rate can be selected. If the chosen set is sufficiently representative of the target domain this should guarantee the best performance also in the operating mode.

3 A Real Network Traffic Database

One of the main issues related to PR in intrusion detection is the use of a proper database. Two main approaches are possible: the former relies on simulating a real-world network scenario; the latter builds the data set using actual network traffic.

The first approach has been usually adopted. The most well-known dataset is the so-called KDD Cup 1999 Data[1], which was created for the Third International Knowledge Discovery and Data Mining Tools Competition, held within KDD-99, The Fifth International Conference on Knowledge Discovery and Data Mining. It was created by the Lincoln Laboratory at MIT in order to conduct a comparative evaluation of intrusion detection systems, developed under DARPA (Defense Advanced Research Projects Agency) and AFRL (Air Force Research Laboratory) sponsorship[2]. This set was created in order to evaluate the ability of data mining and PR algorithms to build predictive models able to distinguish between a normal and a malicious behaviour. The KDD Cup 1999 Data contain a set of connection records coming out from a pre-processing of raw *TCPdump* data. Each connection is labelled as either *normal* or *attack*. The connection records are built from a set of higher-level connection features, defined by Lee and Stolfo [6], that are able to tell apart normal activities from illegal network activities. Although it is widely employed [9,10,12,20], some criticisms have been raised against such database [21].

Indeed, numerous research works analyze the difficulties arising when trying to reproduce actual network traffic patterns by means of simulation [22]. Actually, the major issue resides in the effectiveness of reproducing the behaviour of network traffic sources. On the basis of the above considerations, we have concluded that the KDD Cup 1999 Data can just be used to make a first evaluation of the effectiveness of the PR algorithms under study, rather than providing useful indications for a real application of intrusion detection systems.

On the other hand, collecting real traffic can be considered as a viable alternative approach for the construction of a traffic data set [23]. Although it can prove effective in real-time intrusion detection, it still presents some concerns. In particular, the collection of a real traffic data set needs a data pre-classification process for packet labelling. Indeed, no information is available in the real traffic to distinguish the normal activities from the malicious ones in order to label the data set. Last but not least, the issue of privacy of the information contained in the real network data has to be considered: payload anonymizers and IP address spoofing tools are needed in order to preserve sensitive information.

This notwithstanding, we decided to collect real traffic traces. We deem that such an approach represents an enforced solution in case the computed patterns have to be

---

[1] http://kdd.ics.uci.edu/databases/kddcup99/kddcup99.html
[2] http://www.ll.mit.edu/IST/ideval

applied in a system that must exploit temporal information. Our data set has been built by collecting real traffic on the local network at Genova National Research Council (CNR).

The *raw traffic* data set contains about one million packets, equivalent to 1*GByte* of data. The network traffic has been captured by means of the *TCPdump* tool and logged to a file. In order to solve the pre-classification problem (which, as already stated, requires labelling the items in the data set), we have used a previous work of Genova's research team. By using different intrusion detection systems, researchers in Genova have analyzed the generated alert files and manually identified, in the logged traffic, a set of known intrusions. We have leveraged the results of this research in order to extract the connection features record and properly label it with either a *normal* or an *attack* tag. The number of attack packets in the whole data set is about 3,500; both Denial of Service and Probing attacks have been found in the traffic data.

As regards the considered connection features, starting form the Lee and Stolfo work [6], we extracted 26 features for each network connection. More details about the feature extraction process – that can be carried out in real time - can be found in [7].

4 Experimental Results

As stated before, we defined 26 features starting from the 41 proposed by Lee and Stolfo in [6]. Such a high number of features, indeed, may result in redundancy in the information provided about each traffic pattern to be analyzed; furthermore, not all the features are necessary to detect the presence of a particular attack type. Regarding the particular attack distribution and normal traffic characteristics of the analysed network scenario, it is desirable to reduce the feature space dimensionality by preserving most of the information. Thus, we applied a feature selection process to the above described database, by adopting a Sequential Forward Selection strategy, with the Minimum Estimated Probability classification criterion. Though Best Feature Selection would probably lead to slightly better results, its heavy computation load and the huge amount of data to be analyzed led us to choose the quoted technique. At the end of the feature selection process, each network connection was represented by a feature vector of 8 components.

The whole database was then split into three disjoint sets: a training set (in the following TRS) used for training the base classifiers and for calculating the BKS look-up tables, a validation set (in the following VS) used for stopping the learning process so as to avoid a possible overtraining and for choosing the optimal value of t, and a test set (TS).

In particular 30% of the data (about 300,000 patterns) was used as TRS, 30% as VS (about 300,000 patterns) and the remaining 40% as TS (about 400,000 patterns).

As base classifiers, we employed a neural network, namely a LVQ classifier - with 10 prototypes for the attack class and 50 prototypes for the normal class - and a rule-based learning system –SLIPPER - that creates a rule set by iteratively boosting a greedy rule-builder [17]. In Table 1 the results of these classifiers, in terms of the overall error rate on TRS, VS and TS, are shown.

Table 1. Results obtained by the base classifiers on the three considered data sets

Classifier	Data Set	Error rate
LVQ	TRS	0.265 %
	VS	0.456 %
	TS	1.004 %
SLIPPER	TRS	0.204 %
	VS	0.223 %
	TS	0.261 %

As it is evident from Table 1, the performance of the base classifiers is certainly good. Nevertheless, the best result on the TS, obtained by SLIPPER, indicates that there is still a thousand of connection records that are misclassified.

In order to choose a value for t by following the approach described in Sect. 2, Table 2 reports the results obtained by the proposed system on the VS, for different values of the temporal window t. From this table it is evident that the optimal value of t can be fixed to 4, even if also values of t equal to 3 and 5 give rise to good results.

Table 2. Results obtained by the proposed system on the VS as the value of t varies. The reliability threshold was fixed to 0.6. The optimal value of t is reported in bold.

t	Error rate	Reject rate
1	0.198 %	0.216 %
2	0.191 %	0.153 %
3	0.189 %	0.165 %
4	**0.187 %**	**0.179 %**
5	0.187 %	0.202 %
6	0.294 %	0.118 %
7	0.289 %	0.153 %

In order to verify the exactness of this choice, Table 3 reports the results obtained on the TS as a function of t.

In this case, indeed, the best results were obtained for a slightly different value of t (i.e., 3 instead of 4). However, also the results obtained for the selected value of t are very significant. In particular, the proposed system is able to reduce the number of errors, which are about halved with respect to the best base classifier.

The use of the temporal window allows us to have a slight improvement in terms of error rate with respect to the case $t = 1$ (i.e., when the standard BKS rule is used). But the temporal information improves the reliability of the system: the adoption of a value of t equal to 4 instead of using the standard BKS rule implies that the reject rate decreases from 0.922% to 0.735%. Since the error rate remains practically the same, this means that about eight hundred patterns are now correctly classified and no more rejected.

Table 3. Results obtained by the proposed system on the TS as the value of t varies. The reliability threshold was fixed to 0.6.

t	Error rate	Reject rate
1	0.163 %	0.922 %
2	0.162 %	0.666 %
3	0.162 %	0.656 %
4	0.162 %	0.735 %
5	0.162 %	0.861 %
6	0.536 %	0.522 %
7	0.522 %	0.688 %

5 Conclusions

In this paper we proposed a multiple classifier approach to the problem of detecting intrusions in computer networks. It makes an explicit use of temporal information for improving the reliability of the detection.

The approach has been tested on a wide database of patterns extracted from real traffic network traces. It demonstrated to be able to improve the classification capability of the base classifiers, as well as the reliability of the performed detection, by suitably exploiting the temporal information.

As a future development of the proposed multi classifier approach, we have planned to address the problem of automatically selecting the optimal reject threshold value. Moreover, we will work on the analysis of the rejected packets with slower but more accurate algorithms, in order to further improve the detection capability of the proposed approach.

References

1. G. Vigna, R. Kemmerer, "Netstat: a network based intrusion detection system", Journal of Computer Security, vol. 7, no. 1, 1999.
2. S. Axelsson, Research in Intrusion Detection Systems: A Survey, TR 98-17, Chalmers University of Technology, 1999.
3. R. Kumar, E.H. Spafford, "A Software Architecture to Support Misuse Intrusion Detection", in Proceedings of the 18th National Information Security Conference, pp. 194-204, 1995.
4. A.K. Ghosh, A. Schwartzbard, "A Study in Using Neural Networks for Anomaly and Misuse Detection", Proc. 8'th USENIX Security Symposium, Aug. 26-29 1999, Washington DC.
5. T. Lane, C.E. Brodley, "Temporal Sequence learning and data reduction for anomaly detection", ACM Trans. on Inform. and System Security, vol. 2, no. 3, pp. 295-261, 1999.
6. W. Lee, S.J. Stolfo, "A framework for constructing features and models for intrusion detection systems", ACM Transactions on Inform. System Security, vol. 3, no. 4, pp. 227-261, 2000.

7. M. Esposito, C. Mazzariello, F. Oliviero, S.P. Romano, C. Sansone, "Real Time Detection of Novel Attacks by Means of Data Mining Techniques", Proceedings of the 7th International Conference on Enterprise Information Systems, Miami (USA), May 24-28, pp. 120-127, 2005.
8. S. C. Lee, D.V. Heinbuch, "Training a neural Network based intrusion detector to recognize novel attack", IEEE Trans. Syst, Man., and Cybernetic, Part-A, vol. 31, pp. 294-299, 2001.
9. M. Fugate, J.R. Gattiker, "Computer Intrusion Detection with Classification and Anomaly Detection, using SVMs", International Journal of Pattern Recognition and Artificial Intelligence, vol. 17, no. 3, pp. 441-458, 2003.
10. G. Giacinto, F. Roli, L. Didaci, "Fusion of multiple classifiers for intrusion detection in computer networks", Pattern Recognition Letters, vol. 24, pp. 1795-1803, 2003.
11. G. Giacinto, F. Roli, L. Didaci, "A Modular Multiple Classifier System for the Detection of Intrusions", Lecture Notes in Computer Science vol. 2709, pp. 346-355, 2003.
12. L. P. Cordella, A. Limongiello, C. Sansone, "Network Intrusion Detection by a Multi Stage Classification System", Lecture Notes in Computer Science vol. 3077, Springer, Berlin, pp. 324-333, 2004.
13. S. Singh, M. Markou, Novelty detection: a review - part 2: neural network based approaches, Signal Processing, vol. 83, no. 12, pp. 2499-2521, 2003.
14. J. Ryan, M.J. Lin, R. Miikkulainen, Intrusion detection with neural networks, in Advances in Neural Information Processing Systems 10, M. Jordan et al., Eds., Cambridge, MA: MIT Press, pp. 943-949, 1998.
15. K. Labib and R. Vemuri. NSOM: A real-time network-based intrusion detection system using self-organizing maps. Technical report, Dept. of Applied Science, University of California, Davis, 2002.
16. S. Axelsson, "The Base-Rate Fallacy and the Difficulty of Intrusion Detection", ACM Trans. on Information and System Security, vol. 3, no.3, pp. 186-205, 2000.
17. W.W. Cohen, Y. Singer, "Simple, Fast, and Effective Rule Learner" in Proc. of the Sixteenth National Conference on Artificial Intelligence and Eleventh Conference on Innovative Applications of Artificial Intelligence, July 18-22, Orlando, Florida, USA, pp. 335-342, 1999.
18. Y. S. Huang, C. Y. Suen, "A Method of Combining Multiple Experts for the Recognition of Unconstrained Handwritten Numerals", IEEE Transactions on Pattern Analysis and Machine Intelligence, vol. 17, no. 1, pp. 90-94, 1995.
19. L.P. Cordella, C. Sansone, F. Tortorella, M. Vento, C. De Stefano, "Neural Network Classification Reliability: Problems and Applications", in Image Processing and Pattern Recognition, vol. 5 of Neural Network Systems Techniques and Applications, Academic Press, San Diego, CA, pp. 161-200, 1998.
20. Y. Liu, K. Chen, X. Liao, W. Zhang, "A genetic clustering method for intrusion detection", Pattern Recognition vol. 37, 2004.
21. J. McHugh, "Testing Intrusion Detection Systems: A Critique of the 1998 and 1999 DARPA Intrusion Detection System Evaluations as Performed by Lincoln Laboratory", ACM Transactions on Information and System Security, vol. 3, no. 4, pp. 262-294, 2000.
22. V. Paxson, S. Floyd, "Difficulties in simulating the internet", IEEE/ACM Transactions on Networking, vol. 9, no. 4, pp. 392–403, 2001.
23. M. Mahoney, A Machine Learning Approach to Detecting Attacks by Identifying Anomalies in Network Traffic, PhD thesis, Florida Institute of Technology, 2003.

View Independent Video-Based Face Recognition Using Posterior Probability in Kernel Fisher Discriminant Space

Kazuhiro Hotta

The University of Electro-Communications,
1-5-1 Chofugaoka, Chofu-shi, Tokyo 182-8585, Japan
hotta@ice.uec.ac.jp

Abstract. This paper presents a view independent video-based face recognition method using posterior probability in Kernel Fisher Discriminant (KFD) space. In practical environment, the view of faces changes dynamically. The robustness to view changes is required for video-based face recognition in practical environment. Since the view changes induces large non-linear variation, kernel-based methods are appropriate. We use KFD analysis to cope with non-linear variation. To classify image sequence, the posterior probability in KFD space is used. KFD analysis assumes that the distribution of each class in high dimensional space is Gaussian. This makes the computation of posterior probability in KFD space easy. The effectiveness of the proposed method is shown by the comparison with the other feature spaces and classification methods.

1 Introduction

Face recognition has many potential applications such as security system, man-machine interface, and the search from video databases or WWW. Therefore, many researchers work actively and many still image based face recognition methods have been proposed [1,2]. In recent years, some video-based face recognition methods which use the temporal information are proposed [3,4,5,6,7]. It is reported that the recognition rate is improved by using temporal information.

In practical environment, the view of faces changes dynamically. Therefore, the robustness to view changes is necessary for video-based face recognition in practical environment. Since the view changes of faces induce large non-linear variation in feature space [8,9], almost of conventional video-based face recognition methods can not cope with view changes. However, if non-linear variation induced by view changes are treated well, it is not so difficult to realize the view independent recognition. For example, Aggarwal et al. [7] propose a view independent video-based face recognition method. They use autoregressive and moving average model to cope with the view changes. Lee et al. [4] cope with the view changes by using view dependent manifolds. In that method, the transition probabilities between manifolds are trained, and classification is done by the posterior probability. Namely, they use the piecewise linear discriminant to cope with non-linear variation induced by view changes. In this paper, non-linear variation is treated by simpler way. If we construct the new feature space which can represent non-linear variation well, it is expected that view independent video-based face recognition is realized easily without special processing.

In recent years, the effectiveness of kernel based methods is reported [10,11,12]. Kernel based methods can treat non-linear variation easily. We can use kernel based method to represent non-linear variation. However, only the representation may be insufficient for accurate recognition. The difference between subjects should be emphasized. For this purpose, Kernel Fisher Discriminant (KFD) analysis [13] is appropriate. If KFD analysis is used to construct the feature space by using the face images with different views, it is expected that the influence of view changes of each subject is minimized and the difference between subjects is maximized. Although some face recognition methods based on KFD analysis are proposed [12,14,15], conventional methods do not use KFD analysis to cope with view changes. To classify the input sequence, the posterior probability of image sequence can be used [4]. KFD analysis assumes that the distribution of each class in high dimensional space is Gaussian. This makes the computation of posterior probability in KFD space easy. By using posterior probability in KFD space, view independent video-based face recognition is realized.

The performance of the proposed method is evaluated by using 100 subjects with 9 views obtained from HOIP (Human and Object Interaction Processing) face database [16]. The face images with 5 views are used as the image sequence for training. The rest untrained 4 views of each subject are used as the test image sequence. The effectiveness of KFD space is demonstrated by the comparison with linear discriminant space and original feature space. In addition, in order to investigate the effectiveness of posterior probability of image sequence, the proposed method is compared with simple voting and still image based recognition. The effectiveness of proposed method is confirmed. Furthermore, the proposed method is evaluated by using UMIST (University of Manchester Institute of Science and Technology) face database [17] which captured as image sequence. We show that the proposed method can recognize all test sequences correctly.

In section 2, we explain a video-based face recognition method based on posterior probability in KFD space. Section 3 shows the effectiveness of the proposed method by using HOIP and UMIST face databases. Conclusion and future works are described in section 4.

2   View Independent Video-Based Recognition

In section 2.1, KFD analysis is explained. The kernel function used in the following experiments is also described. How to compute the posterior probability of face image sequence in KFD space is explained in section 2.2.

2.1   Kernel Fisher Discriminant Analysis

First, we explain KFD analysis [10,13] briefly. When training data $\{x_1, \ldots, x_l\}$ are given, all training data are mapped into high dimensional space by $\Phi(x)$. By applying standard linear discriminant analysis in high dimensional space, KFD analysis can be done. KFD analysis determines the weight vector w which maximizes the following criterion.

$$J(w) = \frac{w^T S_B^\Phi w}{w^T S_W^\Phi w}, \quad (1)$$

where S_B^Φ and S_W^Φ are the between-class and within-class covariance matrices in high dimensional space. These are defined by

$$S_B^\Phi = \frac{1}{C} \sum_k^C (m_k^\Phi - m_T^\Phi)(m_k^\Phi - m_T^\Phi)^T,$$

$$S_W^\Phi = \frac{1}{l} \sum_k^C \sum_i^{l_k} (\Phi(x_i^k) - m_k^\Phi)(\Phi(x_i^k) - m_k^\Phi)^T, \quad (2)$$

where C is the number of classes, l_k is the number of samples of class k, $m_k^\Phi = \frac{1}{l_k} \sum_i^{l_k} \Phi(x_i^k)$ is the mean vector of class k in high dimensional space, and $m_T^\Phi = \frac{1}{l} \sum_i^l \Phi(x_i)$ is the mean vector of all samples in high dimensional space.

The weight vector w lies in the span of $\Phi(x_1), \ldots, \Phi(x_l)$. Therefore, the weight vector are represented by $w = \sum_i^l \alpha_i \Phi(x_i)$ where α_i is the coefficient. By substituting this in equation (1), the discriminant criterion can be written as

$$J(\alpha) = \frac{\alpha^T M \alpha}{\alpha^T N \alpha},$$

$$M = \frac{1}{C} \sum_k^C (M_k - M_T)(M_k - M_T)^T,$$

$$N = \frac{1}{l} \sum_k^C K_k (I - \mathbf{1}_{l_k}) K_k^T, \quad (3)$$

where $(M_k)_i = \frac{1}{l_k} \sum_j^{l_k} K(x_i, x_j^k)$, $(M_T)_i = \frac{1}{l} \sum_j^l K(x_i, x_j)$, K_k is a $l \times l_k$ matrix with $(K_k)_{nm} = K(x_n, x_m^k) = \Phi(x_n)^T \Phi(x_m^k)$, I is the identity matrix, and $\mathbf{1}_{l_k}$ is the matrix that all entries are $1/l_k$. The optimal α is obtained by finding the eigenvector of $N^{-1} M$. An input vector x is mapped into discriminant space by

$$w^T \Phi(x) = \sum_i^N \alpha_i K(x_i, x). \quad (4)$$

Next, we consider the type of kernel function. Gaussian kernel gives good performance when the optimal value of variance is used. However, the optimal parameter selection is difficult. It is reported that normalized polynomial kernel gives the comparable performance with Gaussian kernel [18]. In addition, the parameter dependency of normalized polynomial kernel is low. Therefore, we use normalized polynomial kernel as the kernel function. Normalized polynomial kernel is defined as

$$K(x, y) = \frac{(1 + x^T y)^d}{\sqrt{(1 + x^T x)^d (1 + y^T y)^d}}. \quad (5)$$

In the following experiments, parameter d is set to 15 by preliminary experiment.

2.2 Posterior Probability of Image Sequence

In this paper, the posterior probability in KFD space is used for video-based face recognition. To classify the image sequence, we compute the posterior probability $p(C|x_1, \ldots, x_t)$ when from 1st frame to t-th frame in sequence are observed. In the following, $x_1, \ldots, x_t$ is noted as $x_{1:t}$. We assume that x_t is independent of $x_{1:t-1}$ and $p(C_k|x_0)$ is $P(C_k)$. Then the posterior probability is defined as

$$\begin{aligned}p(C_k|x_{1:t}) &= \alpha\, p(x_t|C_k, x_{1:t-1})\, p(C_k|x_{1:t-1}) \\ &= \alpha\, p(x_t|C_k)\, p(C_k|x_{1:t-1}) \\ &= \alpha \prod_i^t p(x_i|C_k)\, p(C_k), \end{aligned} \qquad (6)$$

where $*_k$ represents the class k and α is a normalization term. From this equation, we understand that the posterior probability is computed recursively.

To compute posterior probability, we have to compute $p(x_i|C_k)$. KFD assumes that the distribution of each class in high dimensional space is Gaussian. Therefore, $p(x_i|C_k)$ in KFD space is defined as Gaussian. In the following experiment, log likelihood of posterior probability is used. The log likelihood is computed by

$$L(C_k|x_{1:t}) = \sum_{i=1}^{t} \left(-\frac{D}{2}\log(2\pi) - \frac{1}{2}\log(|\Sigma_k|) - \frac{1}{2}(x_i - \mu_k)^T \Sigma_k^{-1}(x_i - \mu_k)\right) + \log P(C_k), (7)$$

where μ_k is the mean vector of class k in KFD space, Σ_k^{-1} is the inverse of covariance matrix, $|\Sigma_k|$ is the determinant of covariance matrix, and D is the dimension of KFD space. The mean vector and covariance matrix of each class are estimated from training samples. In the following experiments, $P(C_k)$ is set to $1/K$.

To classify the input image sequence, log likelihoods of all classes are computed. The input sequence is classified to the class given highest likelihood.

3 Experiments

The proposed method is evaluated by using two databases. First, we use HOIP face database which includes view changes. To show the robustness to view changes, face images with untrained views are used as the test image sequence. The effectiveness of posterior probability in KFD space is shown by the comparison with the still image based classification and temporal voting. These results are shown in section 3.1. After that, the proposed method is evaluated by using UMIST face database captured as image sequence. The experimental result using UMIST database is shown in section 3.2.

3.1 Effectiveness of the Proposed Method

First, the image database is explained. We use the face images of 100 subjects with 9 views obtained from HOIP database[1]. The face regions of 30×30 pixels are cropped

---

[1] The facial data in this paper are used by permission of Softpia Japan, Research and Development Division, HOIP Laboratory. It is strictly prohibited to copy, use, or distribute the facial data without permission.

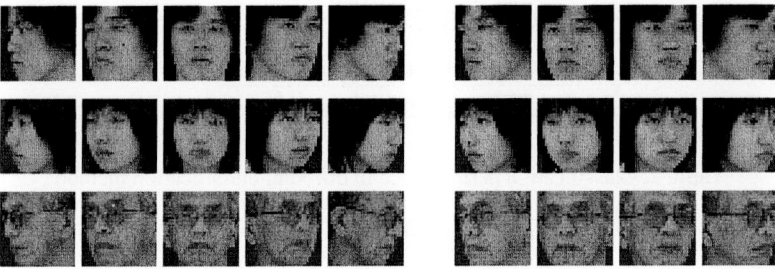

Fig. 1. Examples of HOIP face images

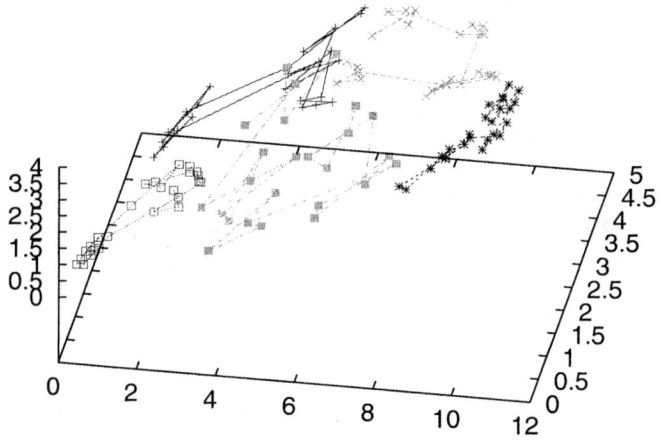

Fig. 2. KFD space obtained from HOIP face images

by using the positions of eyes, nose, and mouth. Examples of face images are shown in Figure 1. In this experiment, left 5 views shown in Figure 1 are used as the image sequence for training. The face images with untrained 4 views shown in right side of Figure 1 are used as the test image sequence. Each class has one training and test sequence. Since 5 images per person are too small to represent each class, the original face images are shifted 1 pixel horizontally and vertically [19]. By shifting the original images, the number of face images is increased 5 times by this processing.

KFD space is constructed by using the raster scanned 900 dimensional intensity features of training sequences. In this experiment, the dimension of KFD space is set to 91 that the cumulative contribution rate is 0.85. Example in KFD space is shown in Figure 2. Figure 2 shows only 6 subjects in 100 subjects. Each class corresponds to the training sequence of each subject. We understand that the influence of view changes is reduced and the distribution of each subject is like a Gaussian. Therefore, it is expected that the proposed method works well. The performance is evaluated by using the log likelihood of image sequence in KFD space. Table 1 shows the performance of the proposed method. Although the image sequence of untrained views are used for test, the high recognition rate is obtained. This result shows that the proposed method can recognize face image sequence under view changes.

Table 1. Classification performance in different feature space

KFD space	LD space	Original space
0.97	0.68	0.55

Table 2. Classification performance in different classification method

Posterior probability	Still image	Temporal voting
0.97	0.72	0.94

To show the effectiveness of KFD space, the proposed method is compared with other feature space. In this experiment, Linear Discriminant (LD) space and original intensity feature space are used in comparison. The training images and classification method are same as the proposed method. The probability distribution of each class is represented by Gaussian in each space, and log likelihood of posterior probability shown in equation (7) is used for classification. In the case of LD space, the performance is evaluated while changing the dimension of LD space. Table 1 shows the performance of LD space. When LD analysis is used to construct the discriminant space, the best recognition rate is 68%. Since LD analysis can not represent non-linear variation induced by view changes well, the performance becomes low. The performance of original intensity feature space is also shown in Table 1. The performance of original intensity feature is very low by the influence of view changes. These results show the effectiveness of KFD analysis. Since KFD analysis can represent non-linear variation, the high recognition rate is obtained.

Next, the effectiveness of temporal information in probabilistic formulation is investigated when feature space is fixed to KFD space. First, the proposed method is compared with still image based classification. Still image based method classifies every image in input sequence independently by using Mahalanobis distance in KFD space. Namely, 400 images (= 100 subjects × 4 images in test sequence) are classified independently. The performance is shown in Table 2. The performance becomes low without temporal information. This results shows the effectiveness of temporal information. Second, in order to show the effectiveness of temporal information in probabilistic formulation, the performance is compared with temporal voting of image sequence. Each image in test sequence is classified by using Mahalanobis distance in KFD space, and voting is performed to the class which gives the minimum distance. After all images in sequence are classified, the input sequence is classified to the class which has the maximum number of votes. The performance of temporal voting is also shown in Table 2. We understand that the performance is improved by using temporal information in probabilistic formulation.

These experimental results demonstrate the effectiveness of the posterior probability in KFD space.

3.2 Evaluation Using UMIST Face Database

In this section, the proposed method is evaluated by using UMIST face database [17]. UMIST database includes the image sequences of 20 subjects with view changes. In

 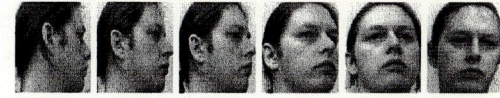

Fig. 3. Examples of UMIST face images

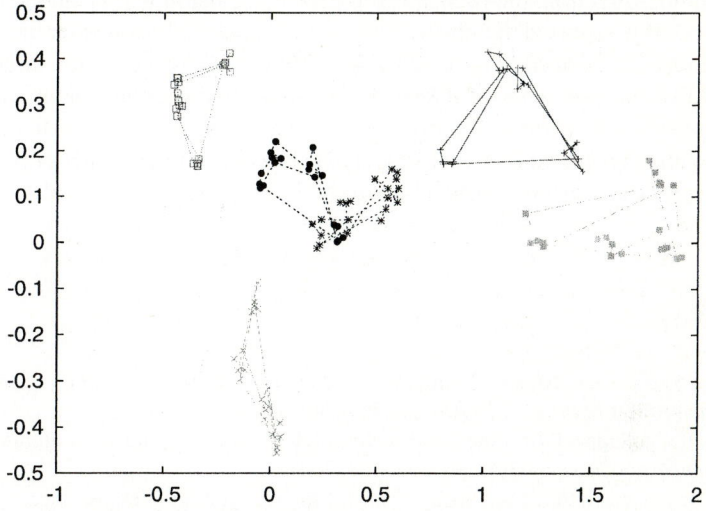

Fig. 4. KFD space obtained from UMIST face images

training phase, the typical views of each subject are needed to reduce the influence of view changes. Therefore, 4 face images with about 0, 30, 60, and 90 degrees are selected manually from video sequence of each subject. The face images shifted 1 pixel horizontally and vertically are also used in training. The rest images of each subjects are used as test sequences. The length of test sequence is different between subjects. The maximum number of frames in test sequence is 44 and the minimum is 15. In this experiment, the training and test sequence are fixed. Examples of training and test sequences are shown in Figure 3. The size of face images is set to 56×46 pixels. The left 4 images and right 6 images in Figure 3 show the training sequence and some images in test sequence. KFD space is constructed by using the training sequences of 20 subjects. The dimension of KFD space is set to 30 that the cumulative contribution rate is 1.05. Example in KFD space is shown in Figure 4. Only 7 subjects in 20 subjects are shown. Each subject constructs a cluster in KFD space, and the variation between subjects are large. Therefore, in this experiment, all 20 test sequences are classified correctly. This result shows that the proposed method can recognize image sequence including view changes.

4 Conclusion

For video-based face recognition in practical environment, the robustness to view changes is required. In this paper, the robustness of view changes is realized by using KFD analysis. KFD analysis assumes that the distribution of each subject in high dimensional space is Gaussian. This makes the computation of posterior probability easy. The combination of KFD analysis and posterior probability of image sequence are the main contribution of this paper. The effectiveness of the proposed method is demonstrated by the comparison with other feature spaces and classification methods.

As the future direction, the robustness to partial occlusion will be added to the proposed method. It is reported that the robustness to partial occlusion is realized by using the summation of local kernels arranged at local regions of a recognition target [20,21]. If we use KFD analysis with local kernels, it is expected that the robust video-based face recognition under view and partial occlusion will be realized. Furthermore, new KFD algorithm is proposed in recent years [22]. That method gives better performance in face recognition than normal KFD analysis. The use of that method is one of the future works.

References

1. R.Chellappa, C.L.Wilson, and S.Sirohey, "Human and machine recognition of faces: A survey," *Proceedings of the IEEE* **83**(5), pp. 705–740, 1995.
2. W.Zhao, R.Chellappa, P.J.Phillips, and A.Rosenfeld, "Face recognition: A literature survey," *ACM Computing Surveys* **35**(4), pp. 399–458, 2003.
3. S.Zhou, V.Krueger, and R.Chellappa, "Probabilistic recognition of human faces from video," *Computer Vision and Image Understanding* **91**, pp. 214–245, 2003.
4. K.-C.Lee, J.Ho, M.-H.Yang, and D.Kriegman, "Video-based face recognition using probabilistic appearance manifolds," in *Proc. IEEE Computer Society Conerence on Computer Vision and Pattern Recognition*, pp. 313–320, 2003.
5. X.Liu and T.Chen, "Video-based face recognition using adaptive hidden markov models," in *Proc. IEEE Computer Society Conerence on Computer Vision and Pattern Recognition*, pp. 340–345, 2003.
6. A.Hadid and M.Pietikäinen, "From still image to vide-based face recognition: An experimental aanlysis," in *Proc. Sixth IEEE International Conference on Automatic Face and Gesture Recognition*, pp. 813–818, 2004.
7. G.Aggarwal, A.K.R.Chowdhury, and R.Chellappa, "A system identification approach for video-based face recognition," in *Proc. 17th International Conference on Pattern Recognition*, pp. 175–178, 2004.
8. H.Murase and S.K.Nayar, "Visual learning and recognition of 3d objects from appearance," *International Journal of Computer Vision* **14**(1), pp. 5–24, 1995.
9. T.Kurita and T.Takahashi, "Viewpoint independent face recognition by competition of viewpoint dependent classifiers," *Neurocomputing* **51**, pp. 181–195, 2003.
10. K.-R.Müller, S.Mika, G.Rätsch, K.Tsuda, and B.Schölkopf, "An introduction to kernel-based learning algorithms," *IEEE Trans. Neural Networks* **12**(2), pp. 181–201, 2001.
11. J.Shawe-Taylor and N.Cristianini, *Kernel Methods for Pattern Analysis*, Cambridge University Press, 2004.
12. M.-H.Yang, "Face recognition using kernel methods," in *Advances in Neural Information Processing Systems 14*, pp. 215–220, 2002.
13. S.Mika, G.Rätsch, J.Weston, B.Schölkopf, and K.-R.Müller, "Fisher discriminant analysis with kernels," in *Proc. IEEE International Workshop on Neural Networks for Signal Processing*, pp. 41–48, 1999.

14. T.Kurita and T.Taguchi, "A modification of kernel-based fisher discriminant analysis for face detection," in *Proc. fifth IEEE International Conference on Automatic Face and Gesture Recognition*, pp. 300–305, 2002.
15. Y.Feng and P.Shi, "Face detection based on kernel fisher discriminant analysis," in *Proc. sixth IEEE International Conference on Automatic Face and Gesture Recognition*, pp. 381–384, 2004.
16. *HOIP face database*. http://www.hoip.jp/web_catalog/top.html.
17. D.B.Graham and N.M.Allinson, "Characterizing virtual eigensignatures for general purpose face recognition," *Face Recognition: From Theory to Applications, NATO ASI Series F, Computer and Systems Science, Vol.163, H.Wechsler, P.J.Pillips, V.Bruce, F.Fogelman-Soulie and T.S.Huang (eds.)*, pp. 446–456, 1998.
18. R.Debnath and H.Takahashi, "Kernel selection for the support vector machine," *IEICE Trans. Info. & Syst.* **E87-D**(12), pp. 2903–2904, 2004.
19. H.A.Rowley, S.Baluja, and T.Kanade, "Neural network-based face detection," *IEEE Trans. Pattern Analysis and Machine Intelligence* **20**(1), pp. 23–38, 1998.
20. K.Hotta, "Support vector machine with local summation kernel for robust face recognition," in *Proc. 17th International Conference on Pattern Recognition*, pp. 482–485, 2004.
21. K.Hotta, "A robust face detector under partial occlusion," in *Proc. IEEE International Conference on Image Processing*, pp. 597–600, 2004.
22. J.Yang, A.F.Frangi, and J-Y.Yang, "A new kernel fisher discriminant algorithm with application to face recogntion," *Neurocomputing* **56**(1), pp. 415–421, 2004.

Attention Based Facial Symmetry Detection

Fred Stentiford

UCL Adastral Park Campus, Martlesham Heath, Ipswich, UK
f.stentiford@adastral.ucl.ac.uk

Abstract. Symmetry is a fundamental structure that is found to some extent in all images. It is thought to be an important factor in the human visual system for obtaining understanding and extracting semantics from visual material. This paper describes a method of detecting axes of reflective symmetry in faces that does not require prior assumptions about the image being analysed. The approach is derived from earlier work on visual attention that identifies salient regions and translational symmetries.

1 Introduction

Symmetries abound both in man made objects and in the structures to be found in nature itself. Symmetry is an important feature in natural scenes that attracts our attention and seems to guide the process of recognition. This has motivated many studies of symmetry and associated techniques that might be applied to image processing.

Symmetry analysis compares image regions and their transforms through translation, rotation and reflection in order to detect relevant structure. Most approaches avoid exhaustive search and reduce the enormous computational requirements by measuring intuitive features that characterise the presence of symmetrical structures. Marola [1] describes a method that can only be applied to shapes that are almost symmetric and requires the computation of the centre of mass. Sun et al [2] also make the assumption that the image is symmetric and measure the correlation between orientation histograms to detect planes of symmetry. Loy et al [3] use gradients to detect points of radial symmetry, but encounter problems of noise which are offset to some extent through the introduction of thresholds. Gradients and edges are also used by Reisfeld et al [4] who requires that symmetry transforms are local. Autocorrelation peaks are employed to determine the presence of symmetry in research by Liu et al. [5]. It was observed in this approach that significant parts of the image were overwhelmed by large expanses of background and that geometric distortions affected the results. Kiryati et al [6] develop a measure of local symmetry which is optimised using a probabilistic genetic algorithm. In the context of faces Mitra et al. [7] require an initial manual indication of the axis of symmetry, and Wu et al [8] need an alignment stage between the original and a reflected version. Symmeter [9] are able to measure the level of symmetry in faces but only if the axis is provided.

The approach taken in this paper is based upon a model of human visual attention [10] that identifies what is important in a scene. The next sections briefly outline this model and how it is modified to extract reflection symmetries. Some illustrative results on human faces are provided.

2 Visual Attention

Salient regions in images may be detected through a process that compares small regions with others within the image. A region that does not match most other regions in the image is very likely to be anomalous and will stand out as foreground material. For example, the edges of large objects and the whole of small objects normally attract high attention scores mainly because of colour adjacencies or textures that only occur rarely in the image. Repetitive backgrounds that display a translational symmetry are assigned low attention scores. No weight is given to the presence or otherwise of reflection or rotation symmetries.

Region matching requires a few pixels (a fork) within that region to match in a translated position in another region. If the difference in colour of one pixel pair exceeds a certain threshold a mismatch is counted and the attention score is incremented.

Let a pixel x in an image correspond to a measurement a where

$$x = (x_1, x_2) \text{ and } a = (a_1, a_2, a_3)$$

Define a function F such that $a = F(x)$.
Consider a neighbourhood N of x with radius r where

$$\{x' \in N \text{ iff } |x_i - x'_i| < r_i \, \forall \, i\}$$

Select a fork of m random points S_x in N where

$$S_x = \{x'_1, x'_2, x'_3, ..., x'_m\}$$

Shift S_x by a displacement δ in the image to become S_y where

$$S_y = \{x'_1 + \delta, x'_2 + \delta, ..., x'_m + \delta\} \text{ and } y = x + \delta$$

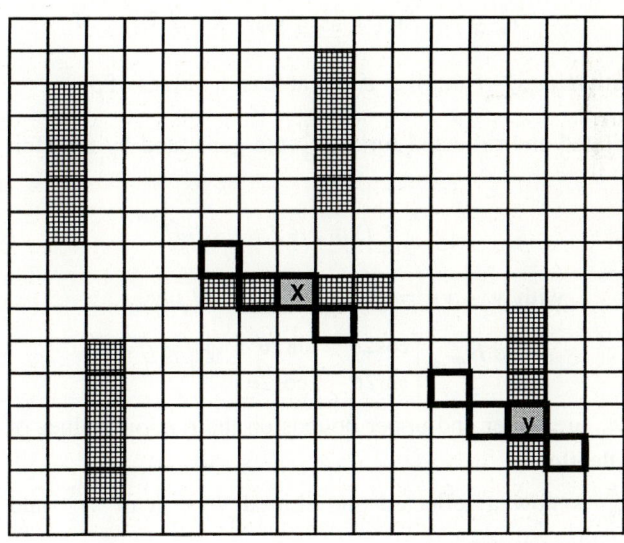

Fig. 1. Fork at y mismatching at y with $\delta = (6,4)$

The fork S_x matches S_y if

$$|F_j(x'_i) - F_j(x'_i + \delta_i)| < \varepsilon_j \ \forall \ i,j.$$

In Fig. 1 a fork of $m = 4$ pixels x' is selected in the neighbourhood of a pixel x and is shown mismatching in the neighbourhood of pixel y. The neighbourhood of the second pixel y matches the first if the colour intensities of the corresponding pixels all have values within ε of each other. The attention score $V(x)$ for each pixel x is incremented each time a mismatch occurs in the fork comparisons with a sequence of pixels y. A location x will be worthy of attention if a sequence of t forks matches only a few other neighbourhoods in the space. Pixels x that achieve high mismatching scores over a range of t forks S_x and pixels y are thereby assigned a high estimate of visual attention. An application to image compression is described in [11].

3 Symmetry Detection

In this paper symmetries are detected using the same mechanism for measuring attention, but transforming forks through reflections *before* translation and testing for a match. Peaks in the distributions of reflection axis angles at which matches are found indicate the locations and strengths of the symmetries present in the image. Forks must include some (h) pixels that mismatch each other otherwise large background tracts of self-matching sky, for example, would appear to exhibit trivial symmetries.

A fork of m random pixels S_x is defined as a set of pixel positions where

$$S_x = \{x_1, x_2, x_3, ..., x_m\}.$$

A series of M such forks is given by

$$S_x^k = \{x_{1k}, x_{2k}, x_{3k}, ..., x_{mk}\} \quad k = 1, 2, ..., M$$

with $|F_j(x_{pk}) - F_j(x_{qk})| > \varepsilon_j$ for at least h values of p. (1)

Randomly translated and reflected forks S_y^k are generated by transforming the S_x^k as follows

$$S_y^k = \{y_{1k}, y_{2k}, y_{3k}, ..., y_{mk}\}$$

with $y_{ik} - y_{1k} = R_\theta [x_{ik} - x_{1k}] \quad \forall \ i,k$ (2)

and $R_\theta = \begin{bmatrix} \cos 2\theta & \sin 2\theta \\ \sin 2\theta & -\cos 2\theta \end{bmatrix}$, $\alpha_1 \leq \theta \leq \alpha_2$

where α_1 and α_2 are lower and upper bounds on the random values of θ, the angle of the axis of reflection.

The fork S_y^k is now a reflected and shifted version of S_x^k and matches S_x^k indicating a possible symmetry if

$$|F_j(x_{ik}) - F_j(y_{ik})| < \varepsilon_j \ \forall \ i,j.$$

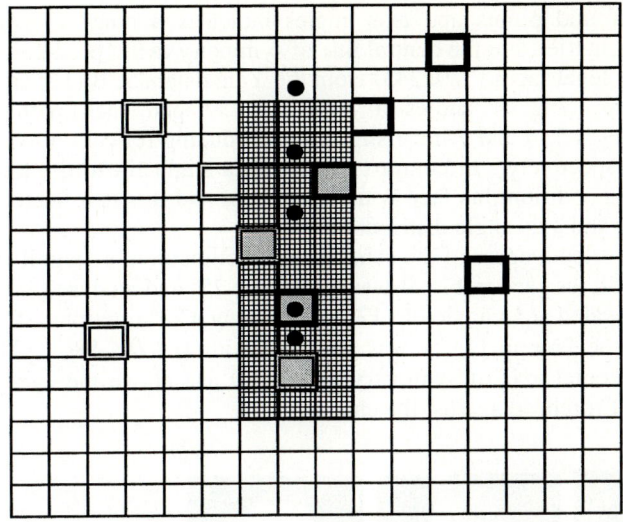

Fig. 2. Symmetric forks matching pattern with $\theta = \pi/2$

Fig. 2 shows a 5 pixel fork and its reflection about an axis at 90° with both forks fitting a vertically symmetric pattern. The mid points of lines joining corresponding fork pixels lie along the axis of symmetry of the shape as indicated by the dots. In this case reflected versions of all white or all black pixel forks would trivially match the background or totally within the shape and are excluded by (1).

Distributions of reflection or rotation symmetries are described in the following steps:

1. Set histogram of reflection axis angles to zero.
2. Generate a fork S_x^k with h pixels mismatching remaining *(m-h)* pixels
3. Reflect S_x^k about an axis at a random angle θ and apply a random shift.
4. If no match is found loop to step 3, P times else increment histogram bin at θ following a match.
5. Loop to step 2, $k = M$ times.

4 Results

Parameter values used to generate forks and symmetry distributions reported here are $m = 12, h = 3, M = 10000, P = 100, \alpha_1 = 45°, \alpha_2 = 135°, \varepsilon = 80$. The location of axes of reflection can be revealed by plotting pixels at the mid points of corresponding pixels in matching forks. The mid points will lie on the axis that was used to generate the reflected fork and a concentration of plotted points will indicate the presence of an axis of reflective symmetry. Fig. 3 shows a grey level face image (276x245) together with a display of the mid points in matching forks, a display of the optimum axis of reflection, and the distribution of reflection axis angles for matching forks. The distributions of mid points and axis angles indicates a range of spurious or less significant symmetries, but the central line of symmetry at 90° predominates.

Some grey level faces (320x243) from the Yale database B [12] are analysed in a similar fashion. Fig. 4 shows a more oval shaped face with more peaked distributions. Figs 5, 6 and 7 have slight tilts producing reflection axis peaks at 86°, 87° and 86°, respectively. In contrast Fig. 8 has a slight tilt to the left with an axis angle of 91°. In addition this face is much rounder and this is reflected in the spread of the midpoint and axis angle distributions.

To test the effectiveness of the symmetry detection on more significant deviations from the vertical, the face in Fig. 4 was rotated by 25° and analysed in the same way. The axis was located at an angle of 112° representing a 23° rotation in Fig. 9.

In addition the face in Fig. 1 was analysed with $0 \leq \theta \leq 180$. This revealed a secondary horizontal axis of symmetry in Fig. 10 just above the eyes that seems to balance areas of forehead against the cheeks.

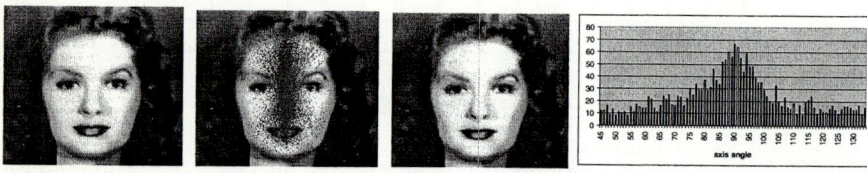

Fig. 3. Original, fork pixel midpoint locations, axis display, and axis angle distribution

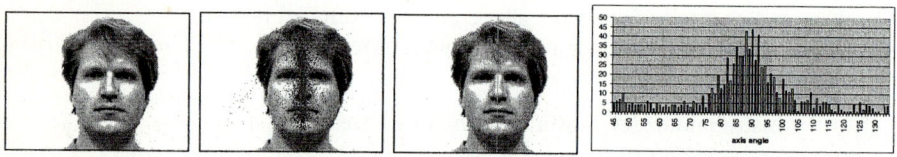

Fig. 4. Original, fork pixel midpoint locations, axis display, and axis angle distribution

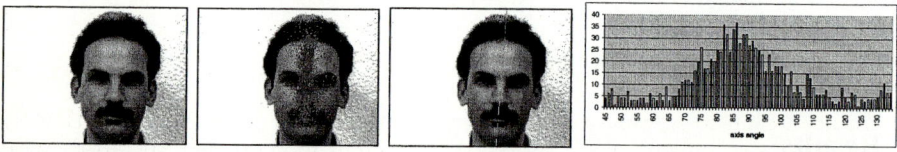

Fig. 5. Original, fork pixel midpoint locations, axis display, and axis angle distribution

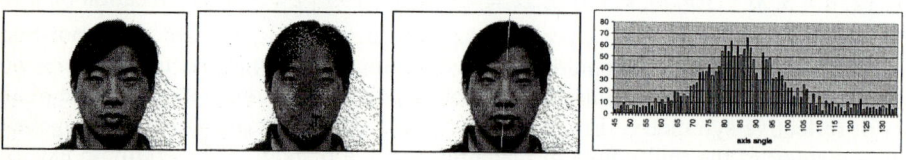

Fig. 6. Original, fork pixel midpoint locations, axis display, and axis angle distribution

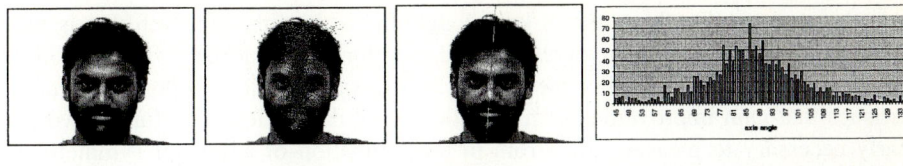

Fig. 7. Original, fork pixel midpoint locations, axis display, and axis angle distribution

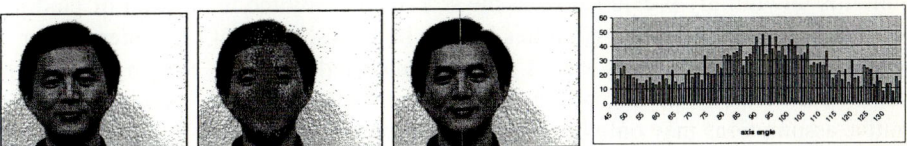

Fig. 8. Original, fork pixel midpoint locations, axis display, and axis angle distribution

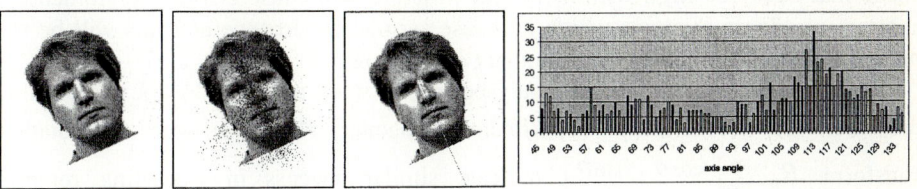

Fig. 9. Original, fork pixel midpoint locations, axis display, and axis angle distribution

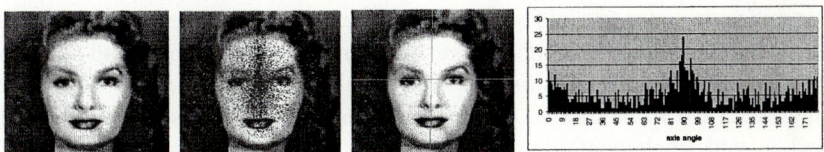

Fig. 10. Original, fork pixel midpoint locations, axis display, and axis angle distribution

5 Discussion

The results presented here only refer to grey level images, but the mechanisms apply equally to colour images. Pixel matching for colour requires that all three colour components independently have values within ε_j of each other. Preliminary experiments indicate that the choice of colour space makes little difference, but that thresholds tailored to specific images yield more informative results.

Key advantages in this approach over other techniques include the absence of any need for the specification of any a priori features that might characterise aspects of symmetrical structures. In addition no restrictions are placed on the minimum strength of any symmetry that must be present in the data for the algorithm to function effectively. Finally there is no manual intervention necessary to either initialise or guide the process. To the author's knowledge this is the first approach that is fully independent of any human involvement and therefore it would be difficult to make any fair comparisons with other methods as it is always possible to provide intuitive heuristics that gain improvements on specific sets of data. However, further work is clearly necessary to measure the errors in the estimation of angles of symmetry on much larger sets of data.

It is worth stressing that the random generation of pixel forks ensures that no solution is unwittingly precluded from the search space by the imposition of guiding heuristics. The universe of possibilities is huge but this should not be a deterrent for a simple trial and error process that is scalable and yields results. Nothing is known with logical certainty about natural image search spaces and we believe that any intuitive assumptions may only have short term benefits.

The method is not specific to the analysis of facial images but can be applied to any pattern. This necessarily means that any symmetrical form appearing in the image that does not align with the facial structure will cause errors. Asymmetrical lighting introduces shadows which do cause serious disturbance and this will be the subject of some future work on illuminant correction.

Rotation symmetries are not analysed in this work as faces do not possess this structure. However, initial experiments replacing R_θ in (2) with the rotation transform $R_\theta = \begin{bmatrix} \cos\theta & \sin\theta \\ -\sin\theta & \cos\theta \end{bmatrix}$ indicate similar success in extracting rotation symmetries when they are present.

The results reported in this paper have been produced with 10000 iterations of fork generation in order to yield accuracies of the order of one degree. Although the computational steps are very simple there are a large number of them and a symmetry analysis takes about 10 seconds on a 1.8GHz machine running in C++. However, the matching of forks can be carried out in parallel as each match is independent of the next and related implementations on the Texas Instruments DM642 DSP platform indicate that processing can take place at video speeds.

6 Conclusions

This paper has described a technique for extracting symmetries from 2D facial images that does not require manual intervention or the prior specification of features that characterise those symmetries. The features or forks are produced through a modified attention focussing mechanism that selects the best combination of positional and reflection transforms that maximises the matching of forks. Future work will be directed at natural colour images and illuminant correction where the objective will be to extract image relationships that can be used in Content Based Image Retrieval applications.

This research has been conducted with the support of BT and within the framework of the European Commission funded Network of Excellence "Multimedia Understanding through Semantics, Computation and Learning" (MUSCLE) [13].

References

1. Marola, G.: On the detection of the axes of symmetry of symmetric and almost symmetric planar images. IEEE Trans on PAMI. Vol. 11. (1989) 104-108
2. Sun, C., Sherrah, J.: 3D symmetry detection using the extended Gaussian image. IEEE Trans. on PAMI. Vol. 19, no. 2. (1997) 164-168
3. Loy, G., Zelinsky, A.: Fast radial symmetry for detecting points of interest. IEEE Trans. on PAMI. Vol. 25. no. 8. (2003) 959-973.
4. Reisfeld, D., Yeshurun, H.W.Y.: Context free attentional operators: the generalised symmetry transform. Int. J. Comp. Vis. Vol. 14. (1995) 119-130
5. Liu, Y., Collins, R.T.: A computational model for periodic pattern perception based on frieze and wallpaper groups. Trans. on PAMI. Vol. 26. no. 3. (2004) 354-371
6. Kiryati, N., Gofman, Y.: Detecting symmetry in grey level images: the global optimization approach. Int. J. Comp. Vis. Vol. 29. (1998) 29-45
7. Mitra, S., Liu, Y.: Local facial asymmetry for expression classification. Proc. CVPR. (2004)
8. Wu, Y., Pan, G., Wu, Z.: Face authentication based on multiple profiles extracted from range data. 4th Int. Conf. on Audio and Video based Biometric Person Authentication. Univ. Surrey, June 9-11, (2003)
9. Symmeter, http://www.symmeter.com/concept.htm
10. Stentiford, F.W.M.: Automatic identification of regions of interest with application to the quantification of DNA damage in cells. Proc. SPIE. Vol. 4662. (2002) 244-253
11. Stentiford, F.W.M.: An estimator for visual attention through competitive novelty with application to image compression. Picture Coding Symposium. (2001) Seoul
12. Georghiades, A.S., Belhumeur, P.N., Kriegman, D.J.: From few to many: illumination cone models for face recognition under variable lighting and pose. Trans. on PAMI. Vol. 23. no. 6. (2001) 643-660
13. Multimedia Understanding through Semantics, Computation and Learning, Network of Excellence. EC 6th Framework Programme. FP6-507752. http://www.muscle-noe.org/

An Efficient Iris Segmentation Method for Recognition

XiaoFu He and PengFei Shi

Institute of Image Processing and Pattern Recognition,
Shanghai Jiaotong University, Shanghai 200030, China
{xfhe, pfshi}@sjtu.edu.cn

Abstract. In this paper, an efficient iris segmentation method for recognition is described. The method is based on crossed chord theorem and zigzag collarette area. We select the zigzag collarette region as personal identification pattern, which can remove unnecessary areas and get good recognition rate. Zigzag collarette area is one of the most important parts of iris complex pattern. It is insensitive to the pupil dilation and not affected by the eyelid or eyelash since it is closed with the pupil. In our algorithm, we could avoid procedure for eyelid detection and searching the radius and the center position of the outer boundary between the iris and the sclera, which is difficult to locate when there is little contrast between iris and sclera regions. The method was implemented and tested using two iris database sets, i.e CASIA and SJTU-IDB, with different contrast quality. The experimental results show that the performance of the proposed method is encouraging and comparable to the traditional method.

1 Introduction

In recent years, the increasing security requirement has led to a rapid development of personal identification systems based on biometrics. Iris recognition is one of the most reliable biometric technologies, the most important part for an iris recognition system is the iris segmentation. The goal of iris segmentation is to separate the iris from the surrounding noises, such noises include the pupil, the sclera, the eyelids, the eyelashes, the eyebrows, the reflections and the surrounding skin. Isolating such noises is of great importance for iris recognition system performance.

However, it is difficult to separate the iris from the surrounding noises. The main reason is that the eyelid or eyelashes usually occlude the iris and the incorrect outer boundary detection between the iris and sclera, especially when there is little contrast between iris and sclera regions. In previous segmentation methods, most of which are based on Hough transform or integrodifferential operator. John G. Daugman [1][2][3] proposed an integrodifferential operator for localizing iris regions along with removing the possible eyelid noises. Wildes [4] processed iris segmentation through filtering and histogram operations. Eyelid edges were detected when edge detectors were processed with horizontal and then modeled as parabolas. Ma et al. [5][6] processed iris segmentation by edge detection and Hough Transform. Huang et al. [7] proposes a new noise-removing approach based on the fusion of edge and region information. Edge information extraction was based on phase congruency. The iris is segmented using edge detection and Hough transform. There are some disadvantages in conventional Hough transform algorithm, such as the huge computation and time consumption. Space and time complexities are the main concerns in the application of Hough transform for detecting circles. Direct application of the Hough transform for detecting circles and eyelid in images is not practical due to the expensive requirements of 3-dimensional parameter spaces. Moreover, if boundaries of iris pupil and sclera were clearly distinguished, most the automatic segmentation methods will be proved to be successful. However, in practical application, it is very difficult to locate the boundary between the iris and the sclera. Difficulties arise from the fact that edge detection will fail to find the edges of the iris border.

In this paper, we proposed a new iris segmentation method based on crossed chord theorem and zigzag collarette area. Zigzag collarette area is one of the most important parts of iris complex pattern. It is insensitive to the pupil dilation and not affected by the eyelid or eyelashes since it is closed with the pupil. In our algorithm, we could avoid procedure for eyelid detection and searching the radius and the center position of the outer boundary between the iris and the sclera. So, it can reduce computational cost and the circle can be located through the crossed chord method which parameters can be calculated by triple-points method.

The remainder of this paper is organized as follows: Section 2 provides a description of the proposed method for iris segmentation. Section 3 introduces the zigzag collarette area and localization. Normalization is also given in this section. Section 4 simply describes the feature extraction and recognition method. Section 5 reports experiments and results. Section 6 concludes this paper.

2 Iris Segmentation

The iris is an annular part between the pupil (inner boundary) and the sclera (outer boundary). Both of them can approximately be taken as circles. Using the iris prior-knowledge, we first roughly determine the iris region in the original image and use intensity threshold to binarize the iris together with morphological operations. Then use the geometrical method to exactly calculate the parameters of the inner circle in the determined region after edge detection.

2.1 Rough Localization

To capture the rich details of iris patterns, an imaging system should resolve a minimum of 70 pixels in iris radius [3]. In most deployments of these algorithms to date, the resolved iris radius has typically been 80 to 130 pixels, though some companies have minute differences. So we can use the prior-knowledge to roughly locate the iris region. This will reduce the region for subsequent processing, which results in lower computational cost. Then we use intensity threshold to binarize the iris.

2.2 Edge Detection

From the above processing, we usually get a noised binary image, especially the eyelashes, since the intensity of the eyelash is similar to the pupil. All these may affect the subsequent processing, so we use morphological operations to exclude unnecessary regions in order to get a connected adjacent region. Then we use Sobel operator to extract the edges. In order to evaluate our algorithm, we applied the 4-directional Sobel operator to segment the iris region.

2.3 Pupillary Localization

We use the crossed chord theorem to locate the pupil. From crossed chord theorem, we can see that if two chords of a circle AB and CD intersect at the point P, as shown in the diagram in Fig.1(a), then get the equation: PA×PB=PC×PD. In order to simplify the problem, we use two perpendicular chords AB and CD intersect at P. IF the four points (A, B, C, D) satisfy the crossed chord theorem, then use three of the four points to calculate the radius and the center coordinates of the circle, since three points which are not on the same line can determine a circumcircle.

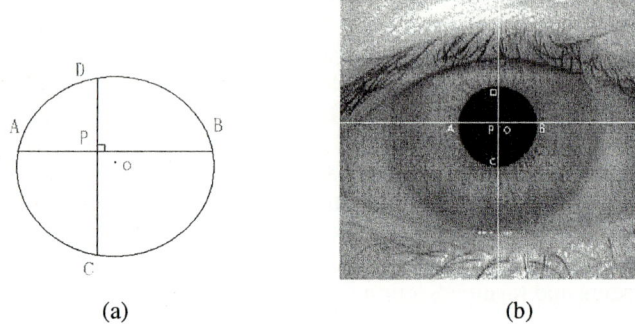

Fig. 1. Circle localization. (a) Diagram. (b) Perpendicular chords overlaid on iris image.

We project the binary image in the vertical and horizontal direction to approximately estimate the centroid $P(x_p, y_p)$, which is usually not the center of the pupil. But at least we can see that $P(x_p, y_p)$ is the inner of the pupil since the pupil is usually darker than other areas. We draw two perpendicular chords AB and CD through the inner point $P(x_p, y_p)$, shown in Fig.1 (b). If the four points (A, B, C, D) satisfy the crossed chord theorem, then use three of the four points to calculate the radius and the center of the circle, else rotate a certainty degree along the anticlockwise direction until find the satisfactory points. The result of the pupil localization can be seen in Fig.2.

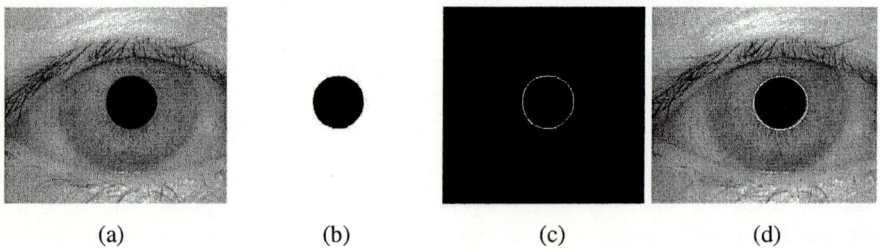

Fig. 2. Pupil localization. (a) Original image. (b) Binary image. (c) Edge image. (d) Localized image.

3 Zigzag Collarette Detection

Iris complex pattern contains many distinctive features such as arching ligaments, furrows, ridges, crypts, rings, corona, freckles, and a zigzag collarette area [2][3]. Zigzag collarette area is one of the most important parts of iris complex pattern. It is insensitive to the pupil dilation and not affected by the eyelid or eyelash unless the pupil is partly not visible since it is closed with the pupil. We have found empirically that zigzag collarette area is usually concentric with the pupil and the radius of the zigzag collarette areas is restricted in a certain range. Some samples are shown in Fig. 3. So we can get the zigzag collarette area easily through the center of the pupil.

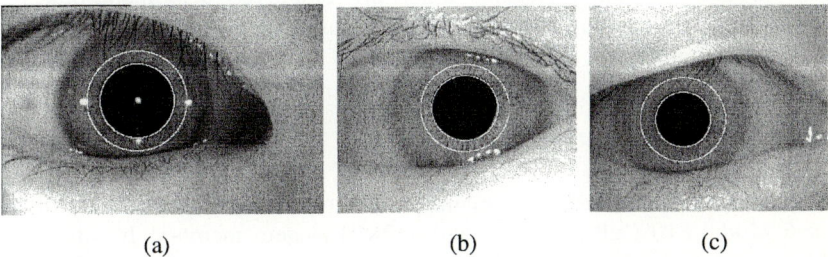

(a)   (b)   (c)

Fig. 3. Zigzag collarette area localization. (a) From SJTU-IDB. (b) and (c) From CASIA iris database.

Because we only use zigzag collarette area for iris recognition, so it is unnecessary to detect eyelid since zigzag collarette area is not occluded by the eyelid in most cases. We use intensity threshold to denoise the eyelashes and reflection. In order to achieve invariance to translation and scale, the annular iris region is further normalized to a rectangular block of a fixed size using Daugman's Rubber Sheet model [1], shown in Fig.4.

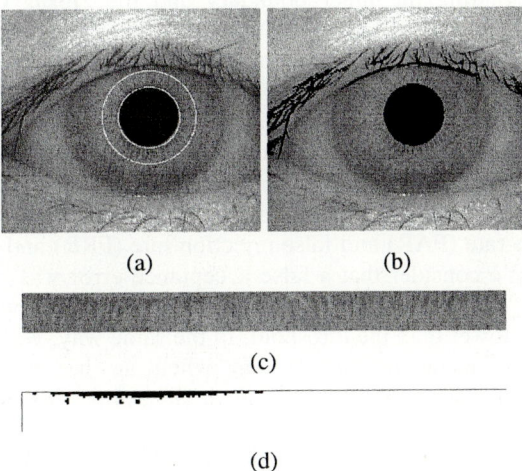

Fig. 4. Normalization. (a) Localized iris. (b) Noise detection overlaid on iris image. (c) Normalized image. (d) The detected noise.

4 Feature Extraction and Recognition

In this work, feature encoding was implemented by convolving the normalized iris pattern with Log-Gabor wavelets and use phase-quadrant demodulation coding method, which is proposed by John G. Daugman. Log Gabor filters allow arbitrarily large bandwidth filters to be constructed while still maintaining a zero DC component in the even-symmetric filter. (A zero DC value cannot be maintained in Gabor functions for bandwidths over one octave.) [8].

Hamming Distance is widely used as the measure of the dissimilarity between any two irises [1]. At matching stage, we select the Hamming distance as a metric for recognition. The Hamming distance algorithm employed also incorporates noise masking, so that only significant bits are used in calculating the Hamming distance between two iris templates.

5 Experimental Results

The proposed methods have been implemented using Matlab 6.5 on a PC with an X86 Family 6 Model 810 Dell processor and 512MB system memory. In this work, we exploited two iris database sets. The first database (DB1) has been realized in our Institute, i.e Iris DataBase of Shanghai Jiao Tong University (SJTU-IDB). The SJTU-IDB contains 400 grayscale eye images collected from 100 persons (100 classes) and 4 different images of each person. The size of eye images in this database is 372×245.

The second database (DB2) comes from the National Laboratory of Pattern Recognition (NLPR) in China, that is the CASIA Iris Database [9] collected by the Institute of Automation of the Chinese Academy of Science, which contains 756 grayscale eye images with 108 unique eyes or classes and 7 different images of each unique eye, captured in 2 sessions. The size of eye images in this database is 320×280.

We evaluated the success rate for the proposed methods using above two iris database sets for finding the inner boundary and the zigzag collarette area. The success rate was 100% both at DB1 and DB2. Also, we evaluated the recognition rate using the zigzag collarette area for recognition. In DB1, one iris is chosen to build the template and the rest for testing. For each iris pattern in DB2, three irises which are collected in the first session are chosen to build the template and the rest for testing. We evaluated recognition in two methods. In the case of using the whole iris information between the pupil boundary and the sclera boundary, we called traditional method. Another method is using the zigzag collarette area. Results are given in terms of false acceptance rate (FAR) and false rejection rate (FRR) and also represented by the ROC curves. We consider that a false acceptance error was made by the system when an iris code and a template corresponding to two different persons lead to a Hamming distance lower than the threshold. In the same way, we consider that a false rejection error was made by the system when an iris code and a template corresponding to the same person lead to a Hamming distance higher than the threshold.

Figure 5 represents the comparison of the ROC results. In the case of that eyelid and eyelashes occlude iris or when there is little contrast between iris and sclera regions which results in the failure detection of the outer boundary, the traditional approach performs poorly both on DB1 and DB2. In this case, the proposed method is more robust because the zigzag collarette does not be affected by the eyelid and eyelashes noise. Also, In the case of that eyelid and eyelashes occlude iris badly so that the pupil is partly invisible, our proposed method leads to false rejections since in this case the zigzag collarette area contains too much noise.

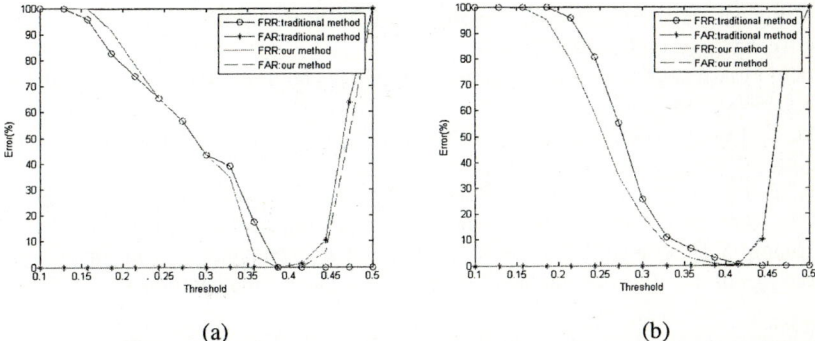

Fig. 5. ROC curves comparing the traditional method and our method on DB1 and DB2, (a) ROC curve on DB1. (b) ROC curve on DB2.

In general, under the same conditions and using the same iris database, the localized zigzag collarette area of the proposed method contains abundant information for personal identification. In the case of that iris is occluded by eyelid and eyelashes or when there is little contrast between iris and sclera regions, our method seems to be more advantageous than the traditional method.

6 Conclusion

In this paper, we have presented an efficient iris segmentation method based on crossed chord theorem and zigzag collarette area, which is insensitive to glasses reflection, rotation invariant, eyelashes and eyelid occlude. Though zigzag collarette area seems contain less information than the previous method, it can also be used for personal identification since zigzag collarette has enough discriminating features. We evaluated recognition rates in two iris database sets. Experimental results have illustrated the encouraging performance of the current method in accuracy.

In the future work, we will conduct experiments on a large number of iris databases in various environments for the proposed method to be more stable and reliable.

Acknowledgements

This work is funded by NNSF (No.60427002). Portions of the research in this paper use the CASIA iris image database collected by Institute of Automation, Chinese Academy of Sciences.

References

1. J. G. Daugman. High Confidence Visual Recognition of persons by a Test of Statistical Independence, IEEE Transaction on Pattern Analysis and Machine Intelligence, 15(11),(1993) 1148-1160
2. J.G. Daugman. The importance of being random: Statistical principles of iris recognition. Pattern Recognition,36(2), (2003) 279–291
3. J. G. Daugman. How iris recognition works. IEEE Transactions on Circuits and Systems for Video Technology,14(1),(2004) 21-30
4. R.Wildes. Iris recognition: An emerging biometric technology. Proceedings of the IEEE, 85(9), (1997) 1348–1363
5. L. Ma, T. Tan, Y. Wang, D. Zhang. Efficient iris recognition by characterizing key local variations. IEEE Transactions on Image Processing,13(6),(2004) 739-750
6. L. Ma, T. Tan, Y. Wang, D. Zhang. Personal Recognition Based on Iris Texture Analysis. IEEE Transaction on Pattern Analysis and Machine Intelligence,25(12),(2003) 1519–1533
7. J.Z. Huang, Y.H. Wang, T. Tan, et al. A new iris segmentation method for recognition. Proceedings of the 17th International Conference on Pattern Recognition.Vol.3,(2004) 554-557
8. Peter Kovesi. Image Features From Phase Congruency. Videre: A Journal of Computer Vision Research. MIT Press. 1(3), Summer, (1999)
9. CASIA Iris Image Database, http://www.sinobiometrics.com

Multi-scale Palmprint Recognition Using Registration Information and 2D Gabor Feature[*]

Liang Li, Jie Tian[**], Yuliang Hi, and Xin Yang

Center for Biometrics and Security Research,
Key Laboratory of Complex Systems and Intelligence Science, Institute of Automation,
Chinese Academy of Sciences, Graduate School of the Chinese Academy of Science,
P.O.Box 2728, Beijing 100080, China
tian@doctor.com
http://www.fingerpass.net

Abstract. This paper describes a novel method for palmprint recognition based on registration information and 2D Gabor features. After preprocessing, a unified coordinate system is constructed for each palmprint image and used to guide ROI extraction. A multi-scale matching strategy is employed to match registration information and 2D Gabor features. In the first two levels, registration information is extracted and used to measure the global similarity between two palmprint patterns. In the third level, two palmprints are aligned with their registration information and then are matched using their corresponding Gabor features. The experimental results demonstrate the effectiveness of the method.

1 Introduction

In information and vastly interconnected society, biometric technologies have been paid more attention in personal authentication since they are more convenient, reliable and stable. Different techniques have been developed and applied in many fields. From all these techniques, palmprint is considered as a relatively new biometric feature for personal verification and have several advantages: stability and uniqueness; medium cost as it only needs a platform and a low/medium resolution CCD camera or scanner; it is very difficult to be mimicked; high user acceptance. It is for these reasons that palmprint recognition has attracted more interests from researchers.

There are many features in a palmprint image that can be extracted for authentication. Principal lines, wrinkles, ridges, minutiae points, singular points, and textures are regarded as useful features for palmprint pattern representation[1]. For palmprint, though, there is no universal method of feature extraction and recognition. In existing research, the majority focused on: points and lines[2][3][4][5]; texture analysis[6][7][8]; statistic features[9][10] and hybrid of different types of features[11].

---

[*] This paper is supported by the Project of National Science Fund for Distinguished Young Scholars of China under Grant No. 60225008, the Key Project of National Natural Science Foundation of China under Grant No. 60332010, the Project for Young Scientists' Fund of National Natural Science Foundation of China under Grant No.60303022, and the Project of Natural Science Foundation of Beijing under Grant No.4052026.

[**] Corresponding author. Telephone: 8610-62532105; Fax: 8610-62527995.

In this paper we investigate a novel palmprint recognition method which uses multi-scale verification strategy based on registration information and 2D Gabor features. In Level-1 stage we register two ROI images and extract their registration information using Fourier-Mellin Transformation (FMT) and phase correlation technique. In Level-2 stage, each ROI image is divided into 2×2 blocks and each pair of corresponding blocks is registered to obtain more detailed registration information. Registration information describes global similarity between two palmprint patterns at coarse level. In Level-3 stage each pair of blocks is firstly aligned with their registration information previously extracted, then a Gabor feature based image matching is performed in the superposition area of two blocks at fine level for the final confirmation. Our method is focusing on palmprint verification and is different with the method proposed in [12], which adopted multiple features and matching criteria and mainly used for palmprint identification in a large database.

The rest of this paper is organized as follows. In the Section 2 is the preprocessing stage. Section 3 presents palmprint registration with FMT and Section 4 is devoted to multi-scale palmprint verification strategy. Experimental results are listed in Section 5. At last, we discuss our algorithm and future work in Section 6.

2 Preprocessing

Our work is carried on the PolyU Palmprint Database[13]. The images of this database contain the whole palmprint and other parts of a palm and background. Therefore a preprocessing step is needed to extract the ROI. The detailed information about preprocessing steps can be referred [14]. Fig.1 shows these steps and ROI image after preprocessing.

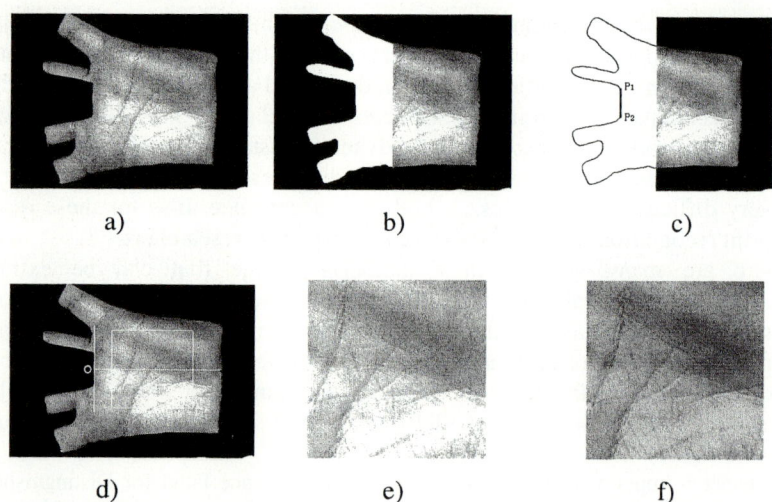

Fig. 1. The main steps of preprocessing. (a)Original database image, (b)Binarizing half of image, (c)Tracking boundary and searching line segment, (d)Building coordinate system, (e)Extracting ROI, (f)Normalizing ROI.

3 Palmprint Registration Using FMT

The Fourier-Mellin Transformation is a useful mathematical tool for the recognition of images because its resulting spectrum is invariant in rotation, translation and scale. The Fourier Transformation itself is invariant in translation in Cartesian coordinate system and in rotation by converting the Cartesian coordinate system to Polar coordinate system; the Mellin Transformation provides the invariant results for scales[15].

Here we use FMT for automatic image registration. We make a hypothesis that one palmprint image is a translated, rotated and scaled replica of another one with translation (T_x, T_y), rotation θ and uniform scale factor σ. From this point of view, the amounts of translation, rotation, and scale in constant time irrespective of the type of images can be computed by phase correlation technique based on their FMT features. Fig. 2 shows a registration example of genuine match and imposter match. The second row of the images in Fig.2 is FMT spectra derived by the FFT of the Log-Polar transformation.

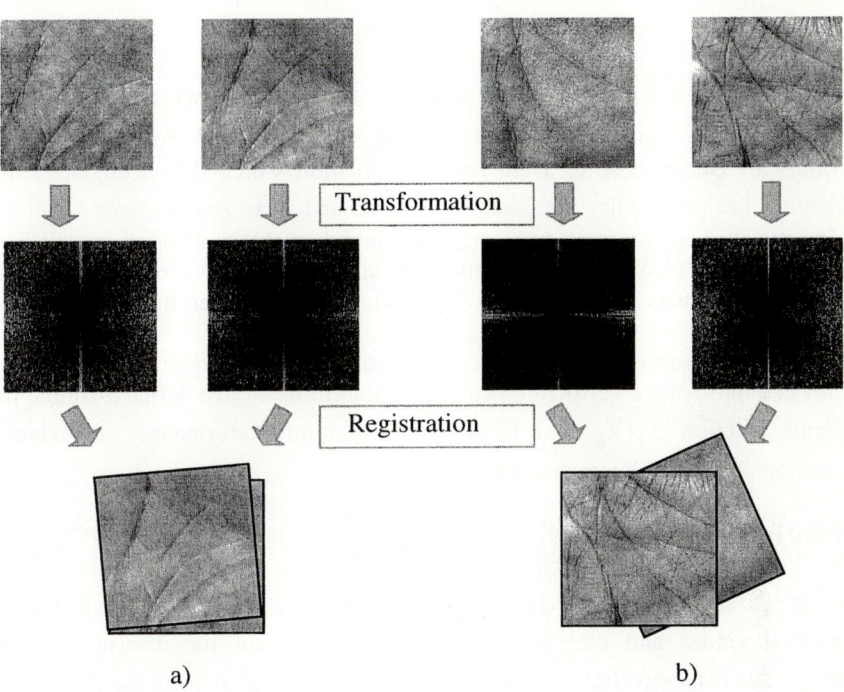

Fig. 2. Example of palmprint registration. a) Genuine registration, b) Imposter registration

4 Multi-scale Palmprint Recognition

In complex classification tasks it is widely used the approach which adopts multi-scale or hierarchical matching strategy in order to find the right trade-off between accuracy and speed. Specifically for palmprint recognition, we study a system where two palmprint images are firstly classified by a 2-scale classifier based on FMT features. Only patterns not rejected by the 2-scale classifier are forwarded to a fine classifier based on 2D Gabor features. This method combines multi-scale features and multi-stage verification strategy and it is possible to reach the trade-off between error and response time.

4.1 Level-1 Stage

Firstly, each ROI image is transformed to frequency domain by using FMT as described above. Before being mapped to log-polar plane, the FMT spectra need to be multiplied with a highpass filter to reduce the effect of discretization and logarithm resampling. Secondly, we use FMT-based registration technique to obtain the translation, rotation and scaling information of each pair of images. The vector that describes the similarity of two images is given by

$$V_{level-1} = (d, \theta, \sigma) \quad (1)$$

where $d, \theta (0° \leq \theta \leq 180°)$ and σ are the translation distance and rotation angle and scaling factor respectively. Ideally the values of d and θ are near to zero, and the values of σ are near to 1. In realistic situation where displacements exist in acquisition, the probability that the value of d and θ is zero is very small when genuine match, because even two images captured in the same session will have a amount of offsets in translation, rotation and scale. However the amount of registration parameters when imposter match is much larger than the one when genuine match.

The main purpose of this paper is to investigate the effectiveness of multi-scale features and multi-stage verification strategy, therefore, we just define a simple linear similarity function $S_1(V_{level-1})$ to test classification performance of registration information. This function is given by

$$S_1(d,\theta,\sigma) = \alpha \exp(-\sqrt{(\frac{d-d_{max}}{u_d})^2}) + \beta \exp(-\sqrt{(\frac{\theta-\theta_{max}}{u_\theta})^2}) + \gamma \exp(-\sqrt{(\frac{\sigma-\sigma_{max}}{u_\sigma})^2}) \quad (2)$$

where α, β and γ are the weight factor and $\alpha + \beta + \gamma = 1$. α, β and γ are the experiential values and their values are set in terms of the discriminability of d, θ and σ, respectively. d_{max}, θ_{max}, σ_{max}, u_d, u_θ and u_σ will be found out in training stage in terms of the sample distribution of d, θ and σ, respectively, see in Section 5.2. $S_1(V_{level-1})$ will give the similarity score which is between 0 and 1. If this score is smaller than a threshold τ_1, 2 ROI images are verified as imposter match, otherwise, 2 images will be matched in Level-2 stage.

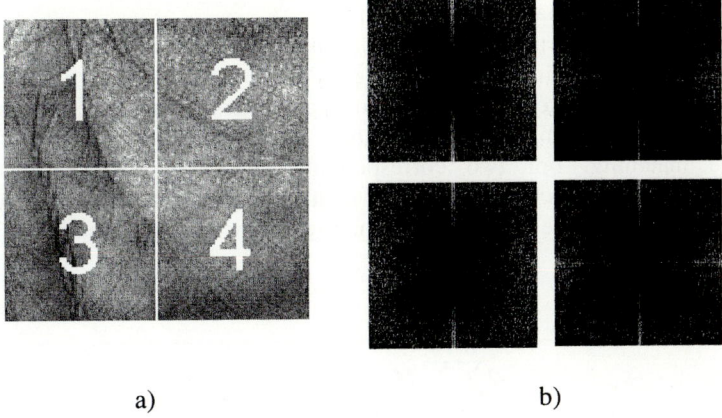

Fig. 3. a) Divided ROI, b) FMT feature images of blocks.

4.2 Level-2 Stage

In this stage, ROI images are divided equally into 2×2 blocks and extracted their FMT features of each block if they are not rejected by Level-1 classifier, as shown in Fig.3. Each pair of corresponding block of two images is registered in a similar way described in Section 4.1. By dividing the ROI, more detailed registration information will be extracted. A feature vector is computed as

$$V_{level-2} = (d_1, d_2, d_3, d_4, \theta_1, \theta_2, \theta_3, \theta_4, \sigma_1, \sigma_2, \sigma_3, \sigma_4) \qquad (3)$$

Also, a similarity function $S_2(V_{level-2})$ is employed to give the similarity score in terms of $V_{level-2}$, and a threshold τ_2 is used to make classification decision in this stage. If this score is higher than a threshold τ_2, two palmprints will be matched in Level-3 stage.

Registration information describes the global similarity between two palmprints at coarse level. Moreover, registration information can be used to register two palmprint images and we can match them at fine level after alignment, see in Section 4.3. τ_1 and τ_2 can be considered as a relaxing factor that controls the speed of recognition algorithm and the value of FAR in some specific occasions when necessary. The response time for the classifier at the first two levels can be reduced by using relatively large values for both τ_1 and τ_2.

4.3 Level-3 Stage

In order to improve the robustness of recognition algorithm, a fine verification stage was needed in Level-3 stage especially for genuine match. The circular Gabor filter is an effective tool for texture analysis and has been proved its efficiency for palmprint recognition and iris recognition[7][16]. We adopt 2D Gabor phase coding scheme for palmprint representation and hamming distance for feature matching. It's noted that we also adopt the optimized parameters used in [7].

Since the amount of vertical and horizontal translation, rotation angle and scaling factor have been obtained in previous stage, it's very convenient to align two palmprint blocks according to their registration parameters. Alignment process can counteract the displacement in acquisition to some extent and, therefore, is useful for Gabor feature matching. For two corresponding blocks of ROI images, the superposition area of two blocks and a mask which encloses the superposition area is generated after alignment. The normalized hamming distance is described as

$$D_1 = \frac{\sum_{i=1}^{M}\sum_{j=1}^{N} M(i,j) \cap (P_R(i,j) \otimes Q_R(i,j)) + M(i,j) \cap (P_I(i,j) \otimes Q_I(i,j))}{2\sum_{i=1}^{M}\sum_{j=1}^{N} M(i,j)} \quad (4)$$

where $P_R(Q_R), P_I(Q_I),$ '$\otimes$', and '$\cup$' have the same meanings as in [7]. The size of the mask is $M \times N$.

Then we compute the distance by

$$D_0 = 1 - \frac{1}{4}\sum_{i=1}^{4} D_i \quad (5)$$

Obviously D_0 is between 0 and 1. For the best matching, D_0 should be 1.

5 Experimental Results

5.1 Palmprint Image Database

The PolyU Palmprint Database is so far the first and the largest open palmprint database, which contains 600 grayscale images corresponding to 100 different palms in BMP image format. These images were captured from above 300 different palms and each palm was captured 10 images. Factors such as population coverage and capturing time interval had been considered when constructing database. Six samples were selected from 10 images of each of these palms were collected from the same person in two sessions, where 3 samples were captured in the first session and the other 3 in the second session. The average interval between the first and the second collection was two months.

5.2 Training Stage

In our experiment, we divide the Database into 2 subsets. The first subset includes total 300 images of the first 50 palms and is used to train the parameters of $S_1(V_{level-1})$ and $S_2(V_{level-2})$, e.g. d_{max}, θ_{max}, σ_{max}, u_d, u_θ and u_σ etc. The

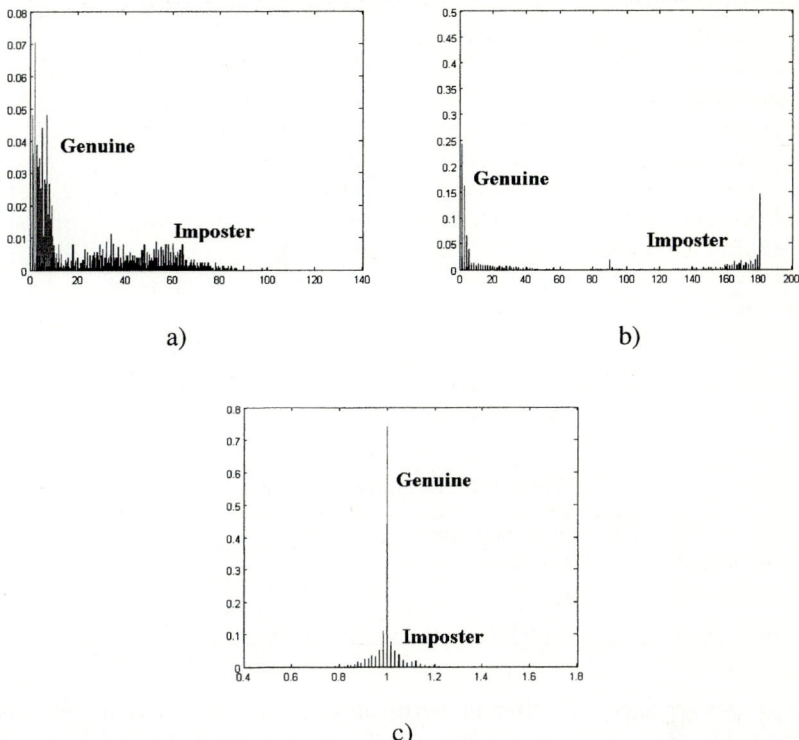

Fig. 4. Distribution of training samples. a) Distribution of d, b) Distribution of θ, c) Distribution of σ.

second one includes the rest of images and is used to test the recognition performance. The training subset and test subset were from different palms. This kind of partition can be helpful to test the generality of recognition algorithm.

According to the distribution of training samples when genuine match, we can train the parameters of $S_1(V_{level-1})$ and $S_2(V_{level-2})$, which will be used to compute similarity score. The distribution of d, θ and σ obtained in Level-1 stage can be seen in Fig.5. As it is clearly seen, d and θ have a strong discriminability in distribution while the discriminability of σ is weaker.

5.3 Test Stage

In this stage, each sample in test subset is matched against the remaining samples of the same palm to compute the False Rejection Rate (FRR). The first sample of each palm in the test subset is matched against the first sample of the remaining palms in this subset to compute the False Acceptance Rate(FAR).

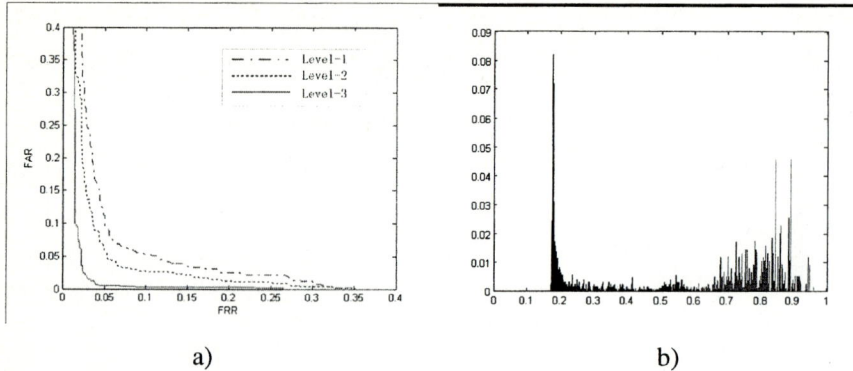

Fig. 5. a) Receiver operating curve for Level-1, Level-2 and Level-3 matching scheme, b) Genuine and imposter match score distributions in Level-3.

Table 1. Performance Evaluation

Matching Scheme	EER(%)
Level-1	6.83
Level-2	5.32
Level-3	2.42

To test performance of different verification levels, we carried out totally 6 verification for imposter and genuine match and for Level-1,Level-2 and Level-3,respectively. It is noted that Level-2 and Level-3 are combining classifiers. The performance of different levels on test subset is presented by Receiver Operating Characteristic (ROC) curves. Fig.5(a) illustrates the ROC curves for 3 levels and Table 1 shows the performance evaluation in terms of EER. Note that Level-3 matching scheme achieves better performance than Level-2, while Level-2 better than Level-1, the experimental results reveals the efficiency of combining levels matching scheme compared to both Level-1 and Level-2 in the verification task, this also can be seen from the Table 1. The normalized score of genuine match and imposter match in Level-3 is illustrated in Fig.5(b).

6 Clusions and Future Work

A novel method to palmprint feature matching strategy is proposed in this paper. A multi-scale verification strategy is employed to match registration information and 2D Gabor feature. Registration information is extracted to describe the global similarity and make classification at coarse level and 2D Gabor feature is extracted to verify two palmprints at fine level. The experimental results show that this strategy achieves good performance for palmprint recognition and still have potential to improve. In the future work, we will investigate the fusion of registration information with the other features. The design of compact classifier will be investigated as well.

References

1. Shu, W., Zhang, D. :Automated Personal Identification by Palmprint, Optical Eng.,Vol.37.1998(2659-2362).
2. Zhang, D., Shu, W. :Two novel characteristics in palmprint verification: Datum point invariance and line feature matching. Pattern Recognition,Vol.32,1999(691-702).
3. Duta, N., Jain, A.K., Mardia, K.V. :Matching of Palmprints, Pattern Recognition Letters, Vol.23.2001(477-485).
4. Wu, X., Wang, K., Zhang, D. :HMMs Based Palmprint Identification, 1st International Conference on Biometric Authentication, Springer Lecture Notes in Computer Science, Vol. 3072. Springer-Verlag, Berlin Heidelberg New York (2004)775–781.
5. Wu, X., Wang, K., Zhang, D. : An Approach to Line Feature Representation and Matching for Palmprint Recognition, Journal of Software, Vol.15.2004(869-880).
6. Kong, W., Zhang, D. :Palmprint feature extraction using 2-D Gabor filters, Pattern Recogntion, Vol.36.2003(2339-2347).
7. Zhang, D., Kong, W., You, J., Wong, M. :Online Palmprint identification, IEEE Trans. on Pattern Analysis and Machine Intelligence, Vol.25.2003(1041-1050).
8. Li, W., Zhang, D., Xu, Z. :Palmprint identification by Fourier Transform. Int.J.Pattern Recognit. Artificial Intell., Vol.16.2002(417-432).
9. Lu, G., Zhang, D., Wang, W. :Palmprint recognition using eigenpalms features,Pattern Recognition Letters, Vol.24.2003(1463-1467).
10. Connie, T., Teoh, A., Goh, M., Ngo, D. :Palmprint Recognition with PCA and ICA, Conference of Image and Vision Computing New Zealand 2003 (IVCNZ'03), pp 227-232, November 26th 2003, Massey University, Palmerstone North, New Zealand.
11. You, J., Li, W., Zhang, D. :Hierarchical palmprint identification via multiple feature extraction, Pattern Recognition, Vol.35.2002(847-850).
12. You, J., Kong, W., Zhang, D. : On Hierarchical Palmprint Coding With Multiple Features for Personal Identification in Large Databases, IEEE Trans. on Pattern Analysis and Machine Intelligence, Vol.14.2004(234-243).
13. PolyU Palmprint Palmprint Database, http://www.comp.polyu.edu.hk/~biometrics/
14. Li, L., Tian, J. He, Y., Yang, X. : Palmprint Recognition Using Fourier-Mellin Transformation based Registration Method, Audio- and Vedio-based Biometric Person Authentication 2005, accepted.
15. Reddy, B.S., Chatterji, B.N. :An FFT-based Technique for Translation, Rotation and Scale-Invariant Image Registration, IEEE Transactions on Image Processing, Vol5.1996(1266-1271).
16. Daugman, J.G. :High Confidence Visual Recognition of Persons by a Test of Statistical Independence, IEEE Trans. on Pattern Analysis and Machine Intelligence, Vol.15.1993(1148-1161).

Effects of JPEG and JPEG2000 Compression on Face Recognition

Kresimir Delac, Mislav Grgic, and Sonja Grgic

University of Zagreb, FER, Unska 3/XII, Zagreb, Croatia
kdelac@ieee.org

Abstract. In this paper we analyse the effects that JPEG and JPEG2000 compression have on subspace appearance-based face recognition algorithms. This is the first comprehensive study of standard JPEG2000 compression effects on face recognition, as well as an extension of existing experiments for JPEG compression. A wide range of bitrates (compression ratios) was used on probe images and results are reported for 12 different subspace face recognition algorithms. Effects of image compression on recognition performance are of interest in applications where image storage space and image transmission time are of critical importance. It will be shown that not only that compression does not deteriorate performance but it, in some cases, even improves it slightly. Some unexpected effects will be presented (like the ability of JPEG2000 to capture the information essential for recognizing changes caused by images taken later in time) and lines of further research suggested.

1 Introduction

With the growing number of face recognition applications in everyday life, image- and video-based recognition methods are becoming more and more important research topic [1]. Effects of pose, illumination and expression are issues most studied in face recognition so far. Very little has been done to investigate the effects of compression on face recognition. Still-to-still image experimental setups are often researched but only in uncompressed image formats. Still-to-video research mostly deals with issues of tracking and recognizing faces in a sense that still uncompressed images are used as a gallery and compressed video segments are probes. Effects of compression are rarely discussed in such papers and rarely researched in general because there is a general belief that the effect of compression in machine vision applications is deleterious. The compression is, therefore, often avoided. Since surveillance cameras and other image acquisition equipment often give their output in a compressed format, exploring compression effects on known face recognition algorithms seems like a reasonable line of research and that is the one we will pursue in this paper. Another important issue would be ability to store compressed face images (without performance degradation when subject to recognition) on a low-capacity chips and smart cards. This would be a great advantage and would contribute to faster implementation of biometrics in every day life (a good example is the *e-passport*).

In this paper we will compare different face recognition algorithms' behaviour in a still-to-still setup with uncompressed training and gallery images and probe images compressed with various compression ratios. This setup mimics the expected real-life circumstances where the image captured by a surveillance camera is probed to existing high-quality gallery images. Algorithms tested in this paper are well-established subspace face recognition projection methods: Principal Component Analysis (PCA) [2], Independent Component Analysis (ICA) [3] and Linear Discriminant Analysis (LDA) [4], combined with common distance metrics (L1, L2 and cosine) in a nearest-neighbour matching system. Bits per pixel (bpp) will be a measure of compression for both tested compression algorithms: JPEG [5] and JPEG2000 [6]. It will be shown that compression does not significantly affect performance even at 0.2 bpp (a 40:1 compression). Actually, in many cases the performance goes slightly up for some compression ratios.

The rest of this paper is organized as follows: Section 2 gives an overview of previous work, Section 3 describes experimental setup used in our research, Section 4 reports results and analyses them and Section 5 concludes the paper.

2 Previous Work

FRVT 2000 [7] tried to estimate the effects of lossy image compression on the performance of face recognition algorithms by minimising a situation in which the gallery images were obtained under favourable, uncompressed circumstances, but the probe sets were obtained in a less favourable environment in which compression was applied. They used JPEG compression and tested algorithms with *dup1* probe set with images in it compressed to 0.8, 0.4, 0.25 and 0.2 bpp. With this setup, they concluded that compression does not adversely affect performance and that the performance of algorithms drops significantly only with images compressed below 0.2 bpp. In their experiment the recognition rate goes up slightly for compression ratios of 10:1 (0.8 bpp) and 20:1 (0.4 bpp). In conclusion, they recommend that additional studies on the effect of compression be conducted as their results are aggregated and only consider JPEG compression. This paper was the main motivation for our research.

Wat & Srinivasan [8] explored the effects of JPEG compression on PCA and LDA with the same setup as in FRVT 2000 (compressed probes, uncompressed gallery). Results were presented as a function of JPEG quality factor and are therefore very hard to interpret (the same quality factor will result in a different compression ratios for different images, dependent on the given image's statistical properties). By using two different histogram equalization techniques they claim that there is a slight increase in performance with the increase in compression ratio for LDA in the illumination task (*fc* probe set). For all other combinations the results remain the same or decrease with higher compressions. This is in slight contradiction with results obtained in FRVT 2000.

Moon & Phillips [9] examined the effects of both JPEG and wavelet compression (no details on wavelet compression were given). The original images were compressed and then uncompressed prior to being processed by the normalization step. For both compression methods, the images were compressed to 0.5 bpp. The standard PCA+L1 algorithm was tested with eigenvectors derived using uncompressed images. Results show no degradation of performance for JPEG and a slight (questionably significant) increase in performance for wavelet compression (for *dup1* and *fb* sets).

As can be seen, none of the above papers used standard JPEG2000 compression and none gives a comprehensive study across various probe sets and for a larger number of algorithms. By experimenting with standard JPEG and JPEG2000 compression techniques over a wide range of compression ratios, we will give the first comprehensive comparison of the influence of those two techniques on recognition performance, across 12 different subspace face recognition algorithms.

3 Experimental Setup

Our experiment was performed on a standard grey FERET data set [10], consisting of images of 1196 individuals taken under various conditions and at various points in time. Also, to achieve highly reproducible results, standard test sets were used, i.e. *fb* (different expression test), *fc* (different illumination), *dup1* (images taken anywhere between one minute and 1,031 days after the gallery image) and *dup2* (images taken at least 18 months after the gallery image was taken). By using all four sets, our results will present a substantial expansion of FRVT 2000 compression experiment.

All images in these subsets were compressed using JPEG and JPEG2000 compression techniques, with various compression ratios (bitrate, bpp): 0.1, 0.2, ... , 1.0 bpp. To compress images using JPEG, the Independent JPEG Group's JPEG software packet (JPEG6b32) [11] was used. To yield various bitrates, quality parameter was iteratively set until the desired bitrate was achieved. Due to the relative simplicity of face images in FERET database, it was impossible to compress some of the images to exactly 0.1 bpp. In those cases, the lowest possible bitrate was used. The bitrates thus varied from 0.1 to about 0.15 in some cases. For the sake of clarity we will refer to all those bitrates as 0.1 bpp in further text. To compress images using JPEG2000 standard, a Kakadu V4.2 (up to date with Part 1 of the JPEG2000 standard) [12] was used with the switch "-rate" set to a required bitrate value. For JPEG2000 there was no trouble achieving the exact predefined bitrates.

Compression was done on original images of size of 256 × 384 pixels. After compression, all images (compressed and uncompressed) were rotated (using affine transformations with bilinear interpolation) to align the eyes at a fixed location across all images, cropped to the size of 128 × 128 pixels and histogram equalized to values 0 to 255 (see Figure 1). It is important to mention that all compressed images were uncompressed prior to recognition stage, thus, the recognition was done in pixel domain.

Algorithms were trained using uncompressed images of 225 individuals for which there were exactly 3 images per person in the data set. Thus, the training set consists of 675 images. This set of images overlaps with the query sets in the following manner: 224 images are in the gallery (*fa* set), another 224 images are in the *fb* set and of the same subject as the ones taken from the gallery. Further 3 images are from the *dup1* set and the rest 224 images are not in any set used in the recognition stage. After training, a 270-dimensional subspace (224-dimensional for LDA) was derived retaining more than 95% of the original information. Recognition was done in those subspaces by standard nearest neighbour matching with L1, L2 and cosine (COS) metrics.

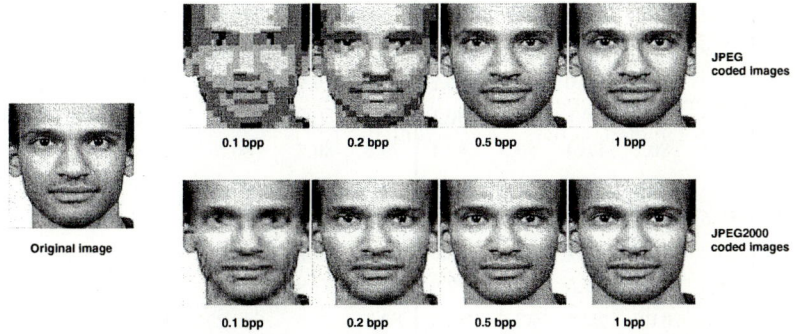

Fig. 1. Example of image degradation when subject to compression

4 Results and Analysis

We tested all 12 algorithms with compressed probe images in four standard test sets against uncompressed gallery images. As can be seen, results obtained using compressed probe images (Tables 1-4) are comparable to the ones obtained using uncompressed probe images (the rightmost column in all tables). The values in tables present rank 1 recognition percentage. The conclusion of FRVT 2000 that performance goes slightly up for compression ratios of 10:1 (0.8 bpp) and 20:1 (0.4 bpp) is confirmed in our experiment. Actually, we also show that in many other cases performance goes slightly up for compressions between 0.2 and 0.8 bpp. These cases are bolded in all tables. Our results are in some disagreement with Wat & Srinivasan because we found that the performance goes up with compression in quite a few cases and not just for LDA. Moon & Phillips' results are confirmed here also. All this gives us the reason to believe that our conducted experiments are consistent with previous studies so we can give a relevant contribution for a wide range of bitrates. Some recognition performance results obtained by other authors with JPEG compression will be confirmed and expanded. In addition, new results using JPEG2000 will be reported, making this paper a first comprehensive study of the effect of JPEG2000 compression on face recognition.

If you take a closer look at the results shown in tables, you will observe that in 36 out of possible 48 cases, the performance goes up for one or more compression ratios and compression techniques tested. Even though the difference is often not statistically significant (we proved this by using McNemar's hypothesis test - details given in Appendix) we believe that this is an important result as it encourages further research into the theoretical properties of both compression and recognition algorithms that led to this performance improvement.

Table 1. Rank 1 recognition percentage for the *fb* probe set

Algorithm	JPEG coded images - bitrate [bpp]					JPEG2000 coded images - bitrate [bpp]					Original images
	0.1	0.2	0.5	0.8	1	0.1	0.2	0.5	0.8	1	
PCA+L1	76.2	80.0	80.7	**81.0**	80.9	80.5	80.6	**81.0**	**81.0**	80.8	80.9
PCA+L2	78.7	80.1	81.1	**81.3**	**81.3**	81.0	81.4	81.1	81.2	81.1	81.4
PCA+cos	76.9	80.1	**80.5**	**80.5**	**80.5**	**80.5**	**80.5**	80.6	80.6	80.5	80.4
ICA1+L1	76.9	79.8	80.0	80.0	**80.2**	80.0	79.9	80.0	80.0	80.0	80.1
ICA1+L2	77.5	79.9	**80.1**	**80.2**	**80.1**	79.9	80.0	80.0	**80.2**	**80.3**	80.1
ICA1+cos	76.1	**80.2**	80.4	80.3	80.1	79.8	**80.5**	80.3	80.3	**80.4**	80.1
ICA2+L1	51.2	62.0	65.1	64.8	65.0	64.0	64.6	65.0	**65.3**	65.0	65.3
ICA2+L2	58.6	70.7	73.3	73.6	73.5	71.8	73.1	**73.8**	73.5	73.4	73.5
ICA2+cos	75.2	80.7	**82.7**	82.3	**82.6**	82.1	**82.9**	82.7	82.8	**82.6**	82.3
LDA+L1	75.0	77.4	77.6	77.8	**77.9**	77.7	77.8	**80.0**	**77.9**	77.8	77.8
LDA+L2	79.6	81.0	**82.4**	**82.5**	**82.4**	82.2	82.0	82.2	82.3	82.3	82.3
LDA+cos	77.0	80.5	81.0	**81.1**	81.0	81.0	**81.3**	**81.4**	**81.2**	**81.2**	81.0

Table 2. Rank 1 recognition percentage for the *fc* probe set

Algorithm	JPEG coded images - bitrate [bpp]					JPEG2000 coded images - bitrate [bpp]					Original images
	0.1	0.2	0.5	0.8	1	0.1	0.2	0.5	0.8	1	
PCA+L1	33.5	47.4	**50.1**	49.4	49.4	46.9	48.9	49.4	49.4	**50.0**	49.4
PCA+L2	21.6	24.2	23.7	24.2	24.2	23.7	24.2	24.2	24.2	24.2	24.2
PCA+cos	13.4	18.0	**18.5**	18.0	18.0	18.0	18.0	18.0	18.0	18.0	18.0
ICA1+L1	18.0	22.1	**23.2**	**23.2**	22.6	22.1	22.6	22.1	22.6	22.6	22.6
ICA1+L2	19.0	21.6	21.6	**22.1**	21.6	21.6	21.6	21.6	**22.1**	**22.1**	21.6
ICA1+cos	12.3	**17.5**	**17.5**	16.4	16.4	**17.0**	**17.0**	16.4	16.4	16.4	16.4
ICA2+L1	12.3	16.4	15.9	16.4	17.5	15.9	15.9	16.4	17.5	17.0	17.5
ICA2+L2	22.6	39.1	40.7	41.7	41.7	39.1	40.2	41.7	41.7	41.7	41.7
ICA2+cos	42.2	64.4	64.4	64.4	64.4	62.8	**64.9**	63.9	64.4	63.9	64.4
LDA+L1	17.5	22.1	21.6	22.1	22.1	19.5	20.6	22.1	22.1	22.1	22.1
LDA+L2	22.1	25.7	26.2	26.2	26.2	25.2	25.7	26.2	**26.8**	**26.8**	26.2
LDA+cos	14.4	19.0	19.5	19.5	19.0	18.5	19.0	19.5	19.5	19.5	19.5

Many cases where performance goes up with compression are observed for the *fb* probe set (Table 1). For more difficult tasks, the improvement with compression in less often. For the *dup1* set (Table 3) with images compressed using JPEG2000 at 0.2 bpp there is an improvement in almost all algorithms. The trend continues for *dup2* set (Table 4), but is not so emphasized. The fact that performance, almost persistently, goes up with JPEG2000 compression for *dup1* and *dup2* set indicates that JPEG2000 compression is able to efficiently eliminate the differences between original images and the ones taken later in time. Besides, our results show that this effect is consistent

Table 3. Rank 1 recognition percentage for the *dup1* probe set

Algorithm	JPEG coded images - bitrate [bpp]					JPEG2000 coded images - bitrate [bpp]					Original images
	0.1	0.2	0.5	0.8	1	0.1	0.2	0.5	0.8	1	
PCA+L1	33.5	36.0	36.9	36.9	36.9	36.7	**37.4**	**37.4**	36.9	37.1	37.1
PCA+L2	32.8	33.1	33.8	**33.9**	**33.8**	33.2	**33.9**	**33.9**	33.8	33.8	33.8
PCA+cos	31.3	33.3	33.2	**33.5**	**33.5**	33.3	**33.9**	33.5	33.5	33.5	33.3
ICA1+L1	31.5	**32.5**	**32.5**	32.4	32.4	32.5	**32.5**	32.4	32.2	32.2	32.4
ICA1+L2	31.4	32.5	32.8	32.6	32.9	32.9	32.8	32.8	32.8	32.9	32.9
ICA1+cos	30.8	**33.9**	33.8	33.6	33.8	33.9	**34.0**	33.8	33.6	33.6	33.8
ICA2+L1	19.8	26.5	29.7	29.7	29.9	28.3	**30.1**	29.9	29.9	**30.0**	29.9
ICA2+L2	22.3	29.2	32.1	32.2	32.4	30.1	32.2	32.4	31.9	32.1	32.5
ICA2+cos	34.0	39.2	43.0	42.5	42.8	40.5	42.5	42.2	**43.0**	**43.0**	42.8
LDA+L1	31.8	32.8	**33.5**	**33.5**	**33.5**	34.3	**33.6**	33.5	33.6	33.3	33.3
LDA+L2	33.1	32.9	33.2	33.2	33.2	32.6	**33.3**	**33.3**	33.2	33.2	33.2
LDA+cos	31.1	33.2	33.2	33.3	33.3	**33.5**	**33.5**	33.3	33.3	33.3	33.3

Table 4. Rank 1 recognition percentage for the *dup2* probe set

Algorithm	JPEG coded images - bitrate [bpp]					JPEG2000 coded images - bitrate [bpp]					Original images
	0.1	0.2	0.5	0.8	1	0.1	0.2	0.5	0.8	1	
PCA+L1	14.1	17.5	17.9	17.9	17.5	17.1	**18.3**	**18.3**	17.5	17.9	17.9
PCA+L2	9.8	9.8	10.2	10.2	10.2	8.5	10.2	10.2	10.2	10.2	10.2
PCA+cos	10.2	11.1	10.6	11.1	11.1	10.6	11.1	11.1	11.1	11.1	11.1
ICA1+L1	10.6	**11.9**	11.1	11.1	11.1	10.6	11.1	11.1	11.1	11.1	11.1
ICA1+L2	10.2	10.6	11.1	10.6	11.1	10.2	10.6	10.6	11.1	11.1	11.1
ICA1+cos	10.2	11.9	12.3	12.3	12.3	11.5	11.9	12.3	12.3	12.3	12.3
ICA2+L1	12.3	14.5	**16.6**	16.2	16.2	16.2	**18.3**	16.6	16.6	16.6	16.2
ICA2+L2	14.1	17.5	18.8	19.2	18.8	17.9	**19.6**	18.8	18.8	18.8	19.2
ICA2+cos	21.3	25.2	26.9	26.9	27.7	23.5	26.9	26.5	**27.7**	26.9	27.3
LDA+L1	12.3	**14.1**	14.5	13.6	13.2	**14.1**	14.5	14.5	13.2	13.2	13.2
LDA+L2	**10.2**	9.8	9.4	9.4	9.4	8.9	**10.2**	9.8	9.4	9.4	9.4
LDA+cos	9.4	10.6	10.2	**10.6**	10.2	**10.6**	10.2	**10.6**	**10.6**	**10.6**	10.2

across almost all algorithms, and it indicates that the information eliminated is not algorithm specific but is a property of compression of those images. The *fc* test (Table 2) turns out to be the most difficult one regarding performance improvement with compressed images. Obviously, both JPEG and JPEG2000 compression techniques eliminate the important information for illumination changes less efficiently than for changes induced by images taken later in time. We can make an *ad hoc* assumption as to why is this so by looking at the images in Figure 1. Obviously, when the original image is compressed, the minor differences caused by different expression and/or temporal changes are reduced. For example, the images compressed using

JPEG2000 look a bit "smeared". The fact that both JPEG and JPEG2000 are low-pass filters in some sense could explain the improvements in *fb*, *dup1* and *dup2* tests. Situation with illumination changes is a bit different because the differences in images that arise from different illuminations are larger and affect the whole image. Thus, the low-pass filtering in most cases does not improve performance. In overall, JPEG2000 seems superior in all tests and should be considered as a standard for storing and transmission of face images for biometric purposes.

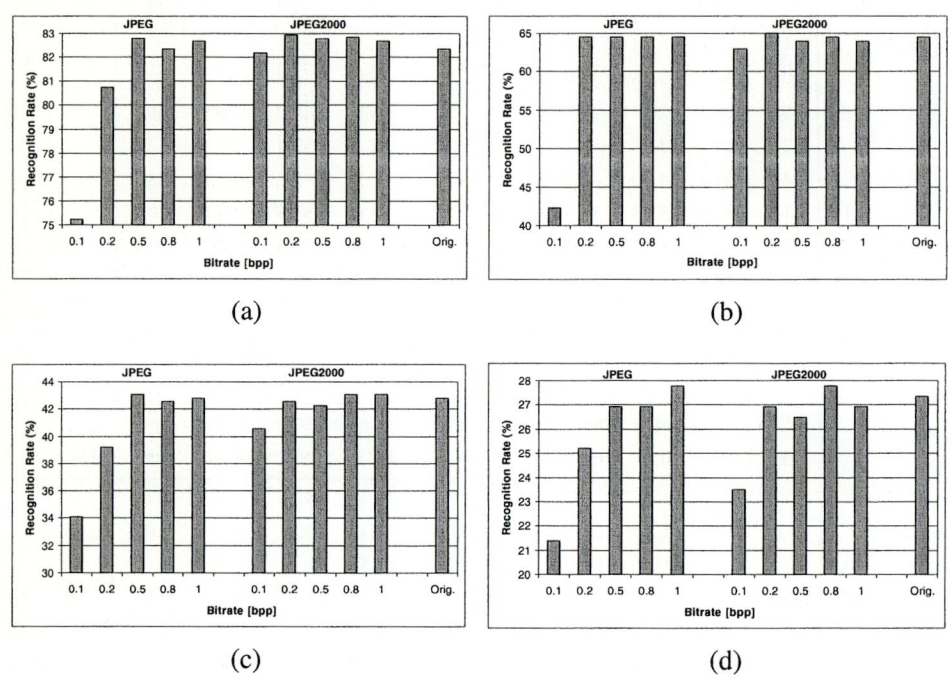

Fig. 2. ICA2+COS performance as a function of bpp: (a) *fb* probe set, (b) *fc* probe set, (c) *dup1* probe set, (d) *dup2* probe set.

Illustrated by the ICA2+COS algorithm (the best algorithm for all tasks in our experiments) in Figure 2, a significant superiority of JPEG2000 over JPEG on high compression ratios can be seen. For example, if we look at Figure 2(b), we can see that performance for compression ratio of 80:1 (0.1 bpp) using JPEG2000 is only slightly (statistically insignificant difference) lower than with original images. Using JPEG compression for that same case deteriorates performance for more than 20%. Again, this trend is persistent throughout all cases and is therefore a rule in our experiments. All the conclusions brought in the previous text are also clearly illustrated by Figure 2(a)-2(d).

And finally, a word about metrics. Our results show that cosine (angle) metric takes the most advantage out of compression across all algorithms (you can easily confirm this by looking at the bolded values in Table 1). The reason for this behaviour stays unclear.

5   Conclusions and Further Work

In this paper we explored the effects of JPEG and JPEG2000 compression techniques on face recognition algorithm performance. This is the first comprehensive study of standard JPEG2000 compression effects on face recognition, as well as an extension of existing experiments for JPEG compression. A wide range of bitrates (compression ratios) was used on probe images and results are reported for 12 different subspace face recognition algorithms. We found that not only that compression does not deteriorate performance but it, in some cases, even improves it slightly. We believe that this is more than enough reason to further explore the theoretical effects of compression on face recognition and eventually to use some compression scheme for storing and transmission of face images used as a biometric (JPEG2000 seems like a reasonable choice by our experiments).

The future perspectives of using standard surveillance equipment as input into superior performance recognition systems are becoming a reality. Storing compressed face images on low-capacity chips, ID and smart cards are a reality also. A general belief that the effect of compression in machine vision applications is deleterious is proven to be questionable by this study.

Our further research will focus on explaining the noticed unexpected effects, like the effect that JPEG2000 is able to efficiently capture information essential for recognizing changes caused by differences between images taken later in time or that cosine metric seems to take the most advantage of compression. Quantifying image quality (for compressed and uncompressed images) prior to using it as input to recognition systems, in a way that the best image be chosen as input, is another subject worth researching.

Acknowledgment

Portions of the research in this paper use the Color FERET database of facial images collected under the FERET program.

References

1. W. Zhao, R. Chellappa, J. Phillips, and A. Rosenfeld, "Face Recognition in Still and Video Images: A Literature Survey", ACM Computing Surveys, Vol. 35, Dec. 2003, pp. 399-458
2. M. Turk, A. Pentland, "Eigenfaces for Recognition", Journal of Cognitive Neuroscience, Vol. 3, No. 1, 1991, pp. 71-86
3. M.S. Bartlett, J.R. Movellan, T.J. Sejnowski, "Face Recognition by Independent Component Analysis", IEEE Trans. on Neural Networks, Vol. 13, No. 6, November 2002, pp. 1450-1464
4. P. Belhumeur, J. Hespanha, D. Kriegman, "Eigenfaces vs. Fisherfaces: Recognition Using Class Specific Linear Projection", Proc. of the Fourth European Conference on Computer Vision, ECCV'96, Vol. 1, 15-18 April 1996, Cambridge, UK, pp. 45-58
5. G. Wallace, "The JPEG Still-picture Compression Standard", Communications of the ACM Vol. 34, No. 4, 1991, pp. 31-44

6. C. Chistopoulos, A. Skodras, T. Ebrahimi, "The JPEG2000 Still Image Coding System: An Overview", IEEE Trans. on Consumer Electronics, Vol. 46, November 2000, pp. 1103-1127
7. D.M. Blackburn, J.M. Bone, P.J. Phillips, "FRVT 2000 Evaluation Report", February 2001, Available: http://www.frvt.org/FRVT2000/documents.htm
8. K. Wat, S.H. Srinivasan, "Effect of Compression on Face Recognition", Proc. of the 5th International Workshop on Image Analysis for Multimedia Interactive Services, WIAMIS 2004, 21-23 April 2004, Lisboa, Portugal
9. H. Moon, P.J. Phillips, "Computational and Performance Aspects of PCA-based Face-recognition Algorithms", Perception, Vol. 30, 2001, pp. 303-321
10. P.J. Phillips, H. Moon, S.A. Rizvi, P.J. Rauss, The FERET Evaluation Methodology for Face Recognition Algorithms, IEEE Trans. on Pattern Analysis and Machine Intelligence, Vol. 22, No. 10, October 2000, pp. 1090-1104
11. Independent JPEG Group's JPEG software packet, Available: ftp://ftp.uu.net/graphics/jpeg/jpegsrc.v6b.tar.gz
12. Kakadu JPEG2000 software, Available:http://www.kakadusoftware.com/win32_executables.zip

Appendix

Hypothesis testing using McNemar's test on results of comparisons in Tables 1 - 4. Here we report p-values for performance of a given algorithm on original images and the best case for compressed images (p-1) and between performance on original images and the worst case for compressed images (p-2). Table 5 gives results for JPEG compression and Table 6 for JPEG2000. When p-value is higher than 0.05 (standard cut-off) the difference in performance is statistically insignificant.

Table 5. p-values obtained by McNemar's test for results with JPEG compression

Algorithm	*fb* probe set		*fc* probe set		*dup1* probe set		*dup2* probe set	
	p-1	p-2	p-1	p-2	p-1	p-2	p-1	p-2
PCA+L1	0.50	10^{-12}	0.50	10^{-10}	0.50	10^{-4}	1.00	0.03
PCA+L2	0.50	10^{-5}	0.75	0.15	0.50	0.13	1.00	0.50
PCA+cos	0.25	10^{-7}	0.50	0.02	0.50	10^{-3}	0.50	0.31
ICA1+L1	0.25	10^{-7}	0.50	0.01	0.50	0.19	0.25	0.50
ICA1+L2	0.31	10^{-5}	0.50	0.13	1.00	0.03	1.00	0.36
ICA1+cos	0.12	10^{-10}	0.25	0.01	0.50	10^{-4}	1.00	0.03
ICA2+L1	0.37	10^{-39}	1.00	0.02	0.68	10^{-17}	0.50	10^{-3}
ICA2+L2	0.50	10^{-44}	1.00	10^{-11}	0.50	10^{-18}	1.00	10^{-4}
ICA2+cos	0.08	10^{-15}	1.00	10^{-12}	0.36	10^{-12}	0.50	10^{-3}
LDA+L1	0.50	10^{-5}	0.75	0.03	0.50	0.02	0.12	0.36
LDA+L2	0.12	10^{-5}	0.50	0.03	1.00	0.50	0.50	0.34
LDA+cos	0.50	10^{-10}	1.00	10^{-3}	1.00	10^{-3}	0.50	0.34

Table 6. *p*-values obtained by McNemar's test for results with JPEG2000 compression

Algorithm	*fb* probe set		*fc* probe set		*dup1* probe set		*dup2* probe set	
	p-1	p-2	p-1	p-2	p-1	p-2	p-1	p-2
PCA+L1	0.50	0.21	0.50	1.00	0.36	0.31	0.50	0.31
PCA+L2	0.62	0.25	1.00	1.00	0.50	0.19	1.00	0.06
PCA+cos	0.12	0.50	1.00	1.00	0.06	0.62	1.00	0.50
ICA1+L1	0.68	0.38	1.00	0.50	0.50	0.50	1.00	0.50
ICA1+L2	0.25	0.40	0.50	1.00	0.60	0.50	1.00	0.25
ICA1+cos	0.12	0.26	0.50	1.00	0.31	0.50	1.00	0.25
ICA2+L1	0.65	0.02	0.75	0.22	0.40	0.02	0.03	0.65
ICA2+L2	0.22	10^{-3}	1.00	0.06	0.50	10^{-3}	0.50	0.18
ICA2+cos	0.11	0.44	0.20	0.22	0.31	10^{-3}	0.50	0.01
LDA+L1	0.31	0.50	1.00	0.03	0.25	0.07	0.18	1.00
LDA+L2	1.00	0.50	0.50	0.25	0.19	0.19	0.25	0.50
LDA+cos	0.06	0.61	1.00	0.25	0.50	0.50	0.50	1.00

3D Action Modeling and Reconstruction for 2D Human Body Tracking

Ignasi Rius, Daniel Rowe, Jordi González, and F. Xavier Roca

Centre de Visió per Computador/Department of Computer Science,
Universitat Autònoma de Barcelona, 08193 Bellaterra, Barcelona, Spain
irius@cvc.uab.es

Abstract. In this paper we present a technique for predicting the 2D human body joints and limbs position in monocular image sequences, and reconstructing its corresponding 3D postures using information provided by a 3D action model. This method is used in a framework based on particle filtering, for the automatic tracking and reconstruction of the 3D human body postures. A set of the reconstructed postures up to time t are projected on the action space defined in this work, which is learnt from Motion Capture data, and provides us a principled way to establish similarity between body postures, natural occlusion handling, invariance to viewpoint, robustness, and is able to handle different people and different speeds while performing an action. Results on manually selected joint positions on real image sequences are shown in order to prove the correctness of this approach.

1 Introduction

Human motion analysis is a very challenging and active domain. It is a fact that it has become one of the most interesting and intensive study areas by many researchers all over the world. The motivations for this increasing interest are, on one hand, the non-stopping advancements in computing power which has turned cheap computers into machines able to deal with big amounts of data in nearly real-time, thus making the analysis of video sequences an achievable task by desktop computers. On the other hand, visual human analysis brings a wide range of promising applications which are especially in touch with today's needs, i.e. automatic video surveillance, advanced interfaces, augmented reality applications, sports performance analysis and motion synthesis among others.

These applications strongly demand the reconstruction and analysis of underlying 3D information of the human body from 2D images [10,2,5]. Towards this end, there have been many approaches for reconstructing the 3D full-body motion from 2D image sequences. For example, Wachter and Nagel [9] use an iterated extended Kalman filter (IEKF) to propagate a 3D model of the body joints over time. They assume a constant velocity dynamic model and use region and edge information in order to match the model to the data, thus recovering the 3D body configuration from monocular image sequences. Bregler and Malik [1] aim to track 3D motion at the level of joints by integrating twists and products of exponential maps into region based motion estimation, thus obtaining both image motion and kinematic chain parameters at the same time. Alternatively, other approaches make use of particle filtering techniques [4] to incorporate a priori knowledge about the non-linear human dynamics [8] into the tracking.

Likewise our strategy relies on successfully tracking the 2D body joints positions on monocular video sequences by means of a 3D model of human dynamics embedded into a particle filtering framework, thus reconstructing the 3D body positions using the information provided by our action model.

In this paper, we first present a procedure derived from [6] to recover the 3D model configuration of the human body from monocular video sequences. The method is based on assuming an orthographic projection camera model, and known topological restrictions of the human body. Afterwards, we present the 3D action model, which is built using prerecorded 3D motion patterns acquired with a commercial Motion Capture System. Such a model provides us a framework for comparing 3D human body postures and developing a dynamic model for predicting postures over time. We use a Bayesian filtering technique implemented as a particle filter derived from [4] which will track the model parameters over time within such space. The use of a particle filter provides us a principled way to incorporate *a priori* knowledge about human motion dynamics by means of our 3D action model.

In order to evaluate our method, we manually introduce the 2D body joints positions of a video sequence, reconstruct its 3D structure, and define a fitness function of the estimated 3D body position to the 2D image. This *likelihood* or prediction evaluation function is defined as a Mahalanobis distance between the manually reconstructed sequence and the estimated one from the particle filter.

The reminder of this paper is organized as follows: section 2 explains the 3D recovering algorithm used in this work. Section 3 describes the basis of the 3D action model, and states some properties of the action space developed to represent the human postures. Section 4 focuses on the probabilistic framework used to face the tracking problem, and the probabilistic match between actions. Section 5 shows experimental results on real image data, and section 6 concludes this paper.

2 The 3D Reconstruction Algorithm

We aim to recover the 3D positions of the human body from monocular image sequence data. However, algorithms for the accurate 3D reconstruction of any object in a scene rely on the collinearity equations, which demand having two images from different viewpoints of the object to be reconstructed. Thus, a point in the object space must have at least one corresponding point on each image which must be estimated accurately for the algorithm to work properly. Unfortunately, this is a too-strong requirement for many applications of visual human analysis, where recovering a very accurate 3D model might not be as important as recovering qualitative 3D information which permits us to make complex reasoning about the scene.

Our reconstruction algorithm is based on the method presented by Remondino in [6], and performs a reliable and accurate enough reconstruction of the 3D human postures from monocular image sequences. By simplifying the collinearity equations, we obtain the perspective projection equations:

$$x = -c \cdot \frac{X}{Z},$$
$$y = -c \cdot \frac{Y}{Z}, \qquad (1)$$

which relate the (x,y) image coordinates of each point to its corresponding (X,Y,Z) scene coordinates only by the camera constant c. By making some more assumptions on the scene and the involved points, Eq.(1) can be further simplified, thus deriving the orthographic projection equations scaled by a factor $s = -c/Z$:

$$x = s \cdot X,$$
$$y = s \cdot Y. \qquad (2)$$

The use of an orthographic projection model implies a planar approximation to the 3D scene. Therefore, this assumption holds when the relative depths between the implied points, i.e. the object points to be reconstructed, are much smaller than their distance to the camera. Hence, the scale factor s will remain almost constant in Eq. (2) for all the involved points.

However, this scale factor cannot be determined only by Eq. (2), since this is an under-determined system, so more constraints need to be introduced. Fortunately, our aim is to reconstruct human body postures rather than any generic object. Thus, we can introduce more constraints to the system by means of topological restrictions of the bodies to be recovered. Hence, our algorithm needs to be initialized by a calibration process that extracts the relative proportions of the limbs for each subject to be reconstructed.

Given that the already-known limb length between joint i and joint j is the relative length between 2 adjacent points in the space, we can compute such a length as $L_{ij}^2 = (X_i - X_j)^2 + (Y_i - Y_j)^2 + (Z_i - Z_j)^2$. By combining it with Eq. (2), the relative depth between two adjacent joints can be expressed as:

$$(Z_i - Z_j)^2 \simeq L_{ij}^2 - [(x_i - x_j)^2 + (y_i - y_j)^2]/s^2. \qquad (3)$$

Notice that in order to compute the relative depth from Eq. (3) we need to find a suitable scale factor s for a particular configuration of 2D image points. In order to have a real solution, we must find an s that satisfies $s \geq [\sqrt{(x_i - x_j)^2 + (y_i - y_j)^2}]/L_{ij}$ for each limb of the human model.

Once an appropriate s is estimated, we must set an arbitrary depth for the first joint, and use Eq. (3) to calculate the relative depth of the rest of the joints. We might use the 3D human model and the history of reconstructed postures in order to decide which of the two possible solutions of Eq. (3) is the appropriate one for each point, depending on which joint is closer to the camera.

Finally, in order to deal with 2D joint position estimation errors, the results are improved by some additional constraints, such as imposing the parallelism conditions for two limbs in some known cases, or forcing that a predefined set of joints must lie in the same plane.

Summarizing, this procedure allows us to recover the 3D configuration of the human body from monocular video sequences. Within this work, such a reconstruction will be used for the initialization step of the tracking process, and for defining a fitness function of predicted postures within a particle filtering framework. The particle filter will propagate the parameters of a human body model within an action eigenspace, as described next.

3 The 3D Action Model

We acquired by means of a commercial Motion Capture system, several sequences of 3D postures performed by several actors for several actions in order to compile a database of human motion. In this work we use the human action model and the human action space defined in [3], called *p-action* and *aSpace* respectively. We use this action model to develop a dynamic model suitable to be used for human posture prediction, which focuses and restricts the search space to those postures that will have higher likelihoods in factored sampling techniques.

An action $\boldsymbol{A}_i$ is represented as a sequence of f_i postures, each posture ψ_j defined by means of a 37 dimensional body model. The body model employed is composed of twelve rigid body parts (hip, torso, shoulder, neck, two thighs, two legs, two arms and two forearms) and fifteen joints. These joints are structured in a hierarchical manner, where the root is located at the hip. Subsequently, we represent the human postures by describing the relative elevation and orientation of each limb using three different angles which are natural to be used for limb movement description. As a result, each human body posture ψ_j is defined by thirty-six relative joint angles, and the height of the hip at each posture. See [3] for further details.

As a result, we define the complete set of human postures for an action $\boldsymbol{A}_i$ as $\boldsymbol{A}_i = \{\psi_1, \psi_2, ..., \psi_{f_i}\}$. Then, we perform a Principal Component Analysis (PCA) on the training set $\boldsymbol{A}_i$ to build the lower dimensional space called *aSpace*. The use of the *aSpace* provides us a natural approach for identifying the main modes of variation of human gait, as well as a principled way to define distances between human postures: close points within the *aSpace* correspond to similar human postures. We project the set $\boldsymbol{A}_i$ of 3D postures in this space, thus obtaining a lower dimensional representation of the postures, i.e. $\hat{\boldsymbol{A}}_i = \{\hat{\psi}_1, \hat{\psi}_2, ..., \hat{\psi}_{f_i}\}$. Thus, the Mahalanobis distance between two points $\hat{\psi}_k, \hat{\psi}_l$ in the *aSpace* can be considered as a measure of similarity between postures.

4 Probabilistic Tracking Framework

The objective of visual tracking is to estimate the parameters of a model over time. In this paper, we estimate ϕ_t at time t given the sequence of images $\boldsymbol{I}_t$ up to that moment. In other words, we need to compute the *posterior* probability density function (pdf) $p(\phi_t|\mathbf{I_t})$ over the parameters ϕ_t of the model to be tracked at time t. Thus, using the Bayes' rule, we formulate the computation of our model parameters over time as:

$$p(\phi_t|\mathbf{I_t}) = k\, p(I_t|\phi_t) \int p(\phi_t|\phi_{t-1})\, p(\phi_{t-1}|\mathbf{I_{t-1}})\, dt, \qquad (4)$$

where ϕ_t represents the estimated 3D pose of the human body at time t, $\mathbf{I}_t$ is the image sequence up to time t, k is a normalizing factor, $p(I_t|\phi_t)$ is the *likelihood* of observing the image I_t given the parametrization ϕ_t of our body model at time t, and finally $p(\phi_t|\phi_{t-1})$ is the transition model, or *dynamic model* in this paper.

The recursive Bayesian filter provides the theoretical optimal solution. Unfortunately, Eq.(4) relies on an integral which cannot be analytically calculated unless strong assumptions about Gaussianity and linearity on the involved distributions are made. Instead, we can approximate the true posterior distribution $p(\phi_t|\mathbf{I_t})$ by means of a particle filter [4].

Each particle ϕ_t^s represents a particular body posture, and has its own probability of being propagated over time, depending on how likely is the body posture that it represents to be found on the image I_t. The method works as follows: the posterior pdf at time $t-1$ is represented by a weighted set of samples, $\{\phi_{t-1}^s, \overline{\pi}_{t-1}^s; s = 1 : N\}$. The temporal prior $\{\phi_t^s\}$ is obtained by applying the dynamic model $p(\phi_t|\phi_{t-1})$ to each sample. The likelihood $p(I_t|\phi_t)$ is represented by weights π_t^s. The set is re-sampled using normalized weights $\overline{\pi}_t^s$ as probabilities. This sample set represents the posterior pdf at time t, i.e. $p(\phi_t|\mathbf{I_t})$. The final estimated body posture at time t is calculated as follows:

$$\phi_t = \sum_{s=1}^{N} \overline{\pi}_t^s \phi_t^s \qquad (5)$$

This Bayesian model-based tracking approach brings us a principled way for considering multiple hypotheses about the human body posture, and allows us to integrate prior knowledge about the non-linear human dynamics into the tracking, thereby making it more robust and efficient.

On the other hand, a proper dynamic model should capture the behaviour of human motion accurate enough to predict only new feasible postures, but generic enough to be able to track different actors and human motions. Actually, the *aSpace* learns the implicit probabilistic model of 3D human motion by using an example-based approach. Consequently, the dynamic model will use the database of learnt performances of an action $\hat{A}_i$ in order to predict the most suitable future body poses. Subsequently, we will perform a probabilistic search within the *aSpace* between the last estimated subsequence of d postures $\Phi_t = [\phi_t^T, ..., \phi_{t-d}^T]^T$ and all the subsequences of d postures from the *aSpace*, i.e. $\hat{\Psi}_i = [\hat{\psi}_i^T, ..., \hat{\psi}_{i-d}^T]^T$. Following the approach described by Sidenbladh in [8], our dynamic model can be defined as :

$$p(\phi_t|\phi_{t-1}) = p(\phi_t|\hat{\Psi}_{i-1}) p(\hat{\Psi}_{i-1}|\Phi_{t-1}), \qquad (6)$$

where $p(\phi_t|\hat{\Psi}_{i-1})$ is defined as 1 if $\phi_t = \hat{\psi}_i$, or 0 otherwise. Assuming that subsequences Φ_t of estimated postures follow a Gaussian distribution around matching subsequences $\hat{\Psi}_i$ on the *aSpace* , $p(\hat{\Psi}_i|\Phi_t)$ is defined as :

$$p(\hat{\Psi}_i|\Phi_t) = k\, e^{-\frac{1}{2}(\hat{\Psi}_i - \Phi_t)^T \Delta_d^{-1} (\hat{\Psi}_i - \Phi_t)}, \qquad (7)$$

where k is a normalizing factor, Δ_d is a covariance matrix defined by calculating the covariance Δ of the *aSpace*, and storing d copies of Δ along the diagonal of the covariance matrix Δ_d. By doing this, we give the same importance to each posture when matching the sequences. Thus, new predicted postures ϕ_t will be the immediately following postures of the recognized subsequence $\hat{\Psi}_{t-1}$ from the database plus some Gaussian noise empirically determined. Details on the probabilistic matching process and posture sampling technique can be found in [7].

5 Experimental Results

In order to evaluate the correctness of this approach, we have tested this framework with a real image sequence of an actor performing a bending action. The motion presented in the image sequence has been reconstructed from 2D sequences by hand. Fig. 1 shows the manually introduced 2D stick figure, and the resulting 3D reconstructed posture using the technique described in section 2. On the other hand, the dynamic model has been trained with a set $A_1 = \{\psi_1, \psi_2, ..., \psi_{f_1}\}$ of 49 different performances of a bending action executed by 8 different actors, resulting in a total of $f_1 = 3258$ 3D body postures for this action. Subsequently, we have calculated its corresponding *aSpace* as defined in Section 3.

The first 10 reconstructed postures are used to initialize the particle filter as the first 10 estimated postures, i.e. $\Phi_1 = [\phi_1^T, ..., \phi_{10}^T]^T$. Hereafter, the last $d = 10$

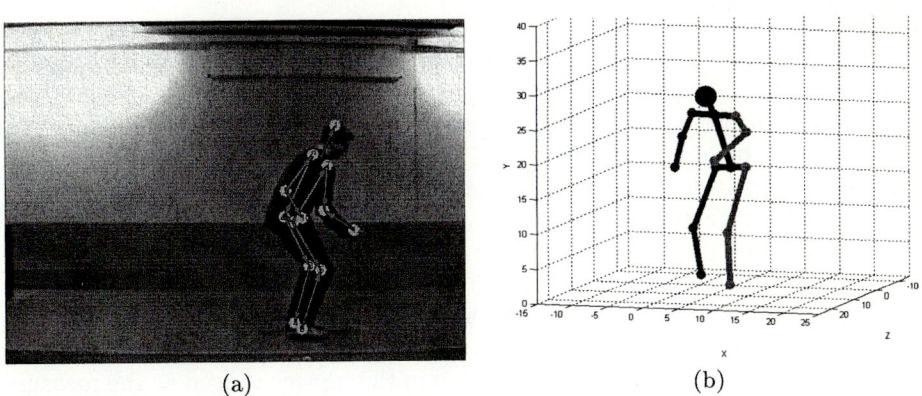

Fig. 1. (a) 2D stick figure of the manually entered joints on a frame of the sequence. (b) Recovered 3D posture from it.

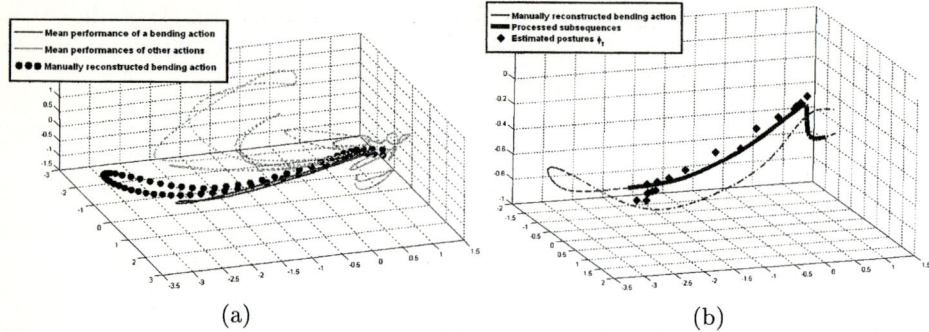

Fig. 2. (a) Manually recovered 3D postures (big dots) projected in the action space with 9 different types of actions. (b) Estimated postures from the dynamic model at each time step (big dots).

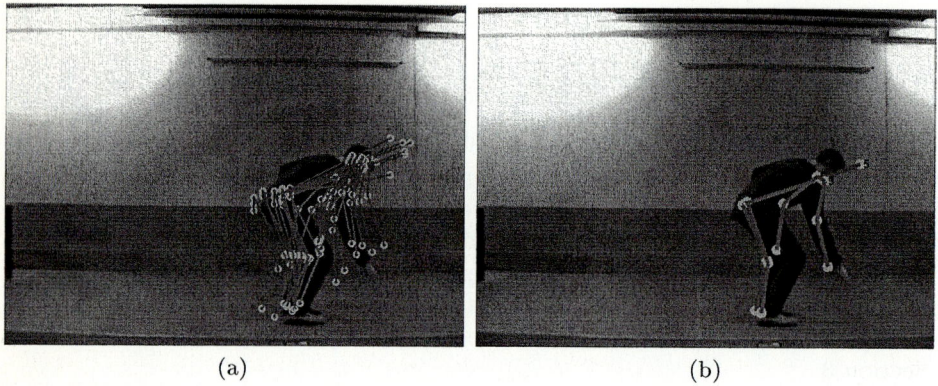

Fig. 3. (a) Randomly selected set of predicted postures $\{\phi^s_t\}$ projected in the image 2D space. (b) 2D projection of the final estimated posture ϕ_t for a particular frame.

estimated postures at time t, are projected in the *aSpace* in order to perform the probabilistic match described in section 4.

In Fig. 2.(a) it is shown the projection in the *aSpace* of the manually reconstructed 3D performance (big dots) which lies in the same portion of the space than the mean bending performance of the dynamic model's training set (solid line). This action space has been built in the same fashion than the *aSpace* for the single bending action, but including 9 different types of actions. Dashed lines correspond to the projections $\hat{\Psi}_j$ of the mean performances for each action.

Subsequently, we sample new $N = 500$ predicted postures at time $t + 1$, i.e. $\{\phi^s_{t+1}\}$. In order to assign weights to each sample, we use the manually recovered 3D performance to determine how well each predicted sample ϕ^s_{t+1} fits to real data. The Mahalanobis distance in the *aSpace* is used as the measure of similarity between human postures: Consequently, we use this distance as a fitness function of the predictions ϕ^s_{t+1}. According to the weights assigned to each particle, a mean weighted posture ϕ_{t+1} is finally calculated.

Fig. 2.(b) shows a run of the particle filter, where big dots correspond to the estimated postures at each time step, i.e. $[\phi_1, \phi_2, ..., \phi_t]$. The manually reconstructed 3D performance is represented by the dashed line, although, for visualization purposes, we have only processed half of the performance (thick solid line).

Fig. 3.(a) shows a frame of the sequence with a randomly selected set of predicted postures $\{\phi_t^s\}$ projected over it. In Fig. 3.(b) we can observe the same frame with the projection of the final estimated posture ϕ_t.

6 Conclusions and Future Work

This paper introduces a framework for human action tracking and reconstruction from monocular 2D video sequences based on a particle filtering technique and a 3D action model. The particle filter provides us a principled way for introducing a priori knowledge about human motion when performing the tracking task, by means of a dynamical model derived from a database of 3D actions acquired with a commercial Motion Capture System. The use of a 3D human body model allows the handling of self-occlusions and view-point independence of the approach. Moreover, a technique for reconstructing the 3D human postures from 2D joints position is presented, which is used to reconstruct the 3D human postures of a real image sequence.

Subsequently, we built an action model called *aSpace* and trained with 3D data from several performances of an action, and a dynamic model for the particle filter which predicts the most feasible postures given a reduced set of the previous estimated postures. Besides, the action space brings us a natural similarity measure between human postures by means of Mahalanobis distance, since each dimension of the *aSpace* represents a particular mode of variation of human motion. Such a similarity is used as the likelihood function in the particle filter.

In order to result in a complete automatic tracking algorithm, future work relies on developing appropriate likelihood functions which make use of the information obtained automatically from 2D image sequences in order to evaluate the predictions of the dynamic model. In this work we used an ideally perfect likelihood in order to prove the correctness of the prediction process. Regardless, the 3D reconstruction technique presented here can be used for the initialization of the algorithm and for failure recovery.

Further work needs to be done to improve the probabilistic matching technique between human postures, which will lead to a more refined action model. Furthermore, the action model should be extended in order to represent more human actions: this approach is naturally extensible to a bigger set of actions by only considering more training actions for the *aSpace*. Another open issue is the high computational cost of the probabilistic search, which could be addressed by efficient indexing the motion database.

Acknowledgments. This work has been supported by the Spanish CYCIT TIC2003-08865 and Generalitat de Catalunya Research Department (DURSI).

References

1. C. Bregler, J. Malik, and K. Pullen. Twist based acquisition and tracking of animal and human kinematics. *International Journal of Computer Vision*, 56(3):179–194, May 2004.
2. D. M. Gavrila. The visual analysis of human movement: A survey. *Computer Vision and Image Understanding: CVIU*, 73(1):82–98, 1999.
3. Jordi Gonzàlez, Javier Varona, , F.Xavier Roca, and Juan J. Villanueva. Automatic keyframing of human actions for computer animation. In *1st IbPRIA, Port d'Andratx, Spain*, June 2003.
4. M. Isard and A. Blake. Condensation – conditional density propagation for visual tracking. *International Journal of Computer Vision*, 29(1):5–28, 1998.
5. Thomas B. Moeslund and Erik Granum. A survey of computer vision-based human motion capture. *Computer Vision and Image Understanding: CVIU*, 81(3):231–268, 2001.
6. Fabio Remondino and Andreas Roditakis. 3d reconstruction of human skeleton from single images or monocular video sequences. *25th Pattern Recognition Symposium, Lecture Notes in Computer Science, DAGM 03*, pages 100–107.
7. Ignasi Rius, Daniel Rowe, Jordi Gonzàlez, and F.Xavier Roca. A 3d dynamic model of human actions for probabilistic image tracking. In *2nd IbPRIA, Estoril, Portugal*, June 2005.
8. Hedvig Sidenbladh, Michael J. Black, and Leonid Sigal. Implicit probabilistic models of human motion for synthesis and tracking. In *ECCV (1)*, pages 784–800, 2002.
9. S. Wachter and H. H. Nagel. Tracking persons in monocular image sequences. *Computer Vision and Image Understanding*, 74(3):174–192, June 1999.
10. L. Wang, W. Hu, and T. Tan. Recent developments in human motion analysis. *Pattern Recognition*, 36:585–601, 2003.

A Non-parametric Dimensionality Reduction Technique Using Gradient Descent of Misclassification Rate

S. Redmond and C. Heneghan

Department of Electronic Engineering, University College Dublin, Ireland
`Stephen.Redmond@ee.ucd.ie, Conor.Heneghan@ucd.ie`

Abstract. We present a technique for dimension reduction. The technique uses a gradient descent approach to attempt to sequentially find orthogonal vectors such that when the data is projected onto each vector the classification error is minimised. We make no assumptions about the structure of the data and the technique is independent of the classifier model used. Our approach has advantages over other dimensionality reduction techniques, such as Linear Discriminant Analysis (LDA), which assumes unimodal gaussian distributions, and Principal Component Analysis (PCA) which is ignorant of class labels. In this paper we present the results of a comparison of our technique with PCA and LDA when applied to various 2-dimensional distributions and the two class cancer diagnosis task from the Wisconsin Diagnostic Breast Cancer Database, which contains 30 features.

1 Originality and Contribution

At the time of submission we were not aware that this concept has been previously presented in a more general form in [1, 2]. However, the work we present here was arrived at independently and does contain subtle differences. Nonetheless, we hope the reader finds the examples in this paper illustrative of the basic concept described in [1] and [2].

In a typical pattern recognition problem, we are usually faced with large sets of features which may have utility in providing reliable classification. In practice however many of these features may be strongly correlated with one another, or may not contribute to classification in any way. Accordingly, we may wish to perform dimensionality reduction on our data for various reasons: the dimension of the data is too large to handle from a memory or computational point of view, or the in the case of classification, the removal of features containing no information can improve classification results. Projection Pursuit is a popular technique for reducing the dimension of large data set in which we seek a projection of the higher dimensional data onto lower dimensions. However many projection pursuit techniques attempt to maximise, or minimise, some objective function which inherently makes assumptions about the structure of the data. For Linear Discriminant Analysis (LDA) the assumption is that each class distribution is unimodal gaussian, and that the class separation information is contained in the difference of the means of each class distribution as much as it is contained in the variance. Principal Component Analysis (PCA) assumes that the class separation information is contained in the direction of maximum variance of the data. We shall present a technique which attempts to converge on a projection which will minimise the classification error of the chosen classifier instead of imposing a structure on the data by maximising an objective function.

2 Introduction

Dimensionality reduction can also be thought of as a feature selection process. In feature selection, we generally retain the minimum (and best set) of features for a classification. Feature selection is therefore a special case of dimensionality reduction, but where the basis is an exact subset of the feature basis. A feature selection algorithm is a vital building block of any pattern recognition system. Feature selection, the rejection of null features, those that contain no information, can greatly improve recognition results. In theory when using features that contain little or no relevant information in the classification process the performance of the ideal classifier will not degrade. One could simply include all features in the classification process and features containing no information will be ignored by the classifier. In practice this is rarely true - null features add noise to the system, and the removal of these redundant features can greatly improve results. For example Witten [3] notes experiments with a decision tree classifier which show that adding a binary random variable to the feature set can deteriorate performance by 5-10%.

Here we will present a dimensionality reduction technique which sequentially chooses the vectors of an orthogonal basis with a lower dimension than the data so that when the data is projected onto this basis, the classifier error will be minimised.

In Section 3 we will give a brief overview of some existing techniques used for dimensionality reduction, and their shortcomings to motivate our new technique. In Section 4 we will give a detailed description of our technique. Section 5 outlines the data sets, the classifier model, and the experimental procedure used in comparing our method with LDA and PCA as a dimensionality reduction technique. Finally, in Sections 6 and 7 we summarise the comparative results and draw our conclusions.

3 Review of Existing Techniques

Firstly, we will review some methods of dimensionality reduction. In general, these techniques try to choose a projection which preserves the class separation information of the data but suppresses some of the noisy or null features. An intuitive example of dimensionality reduction would be projecting 3-dimensional data onto a 2-dimensional plane. Some techniques for doing this are Principal Component Analysis (PCA) [4], Linear Discriminant Analysis (LDA) [5], and Orthogonal LDA (OLDA) [6]. We will now briefly describe these algorithms in more detail.

PCA finds the directions of maximum variance of all the data by finding the eigenvectors of the covariance matrix of all data, irrespective of class. A lower dimension representation of the data may then be found by projecting onto the first m eigenvectors corresponding to largest m eigenvalues. However, PCA is ignorant of the class labels attached to the data so a good class separation in the lower dimension data is not guaranteed.

LDA attempts to find projections which maximise the separation between the means of the classes while simultaneously trying to minimise the variance of each class about its mean. LDA implicitly assumes each class belongs to a single gaussian distribution. We will not present the mathematics of the LDA technique here, however for a C class problem LDA will return $C-1$ eigenvectors corresponding to the $C-1$ non-zero eigenvalues. The magnitude of the eigenvectors correspond to how well the objective function was maximised. A shortcoming of LDA is that the objective function accounts for Euclidean distance or Mahalonobis distance, but not classification error.

OLDA simply expands the concept of LDA to choose various orthogonal projections. For example if we use LDA and choose the eigenvector, corresponding to the maximum eigenvalue, to project onto in 3-dimensional space and we then create a 2-d basis (plane) orthogonal to that vector and project the data onto the 2-d basis, we then perform the LDA analysis on the 2-d data to obtain the second projection vector, orthogonal to the first. Again, in general this technique does not directly optimise with respect to classification accuracy.

As mentioned in Section 2, a more general version of this work has been explored independently in [1, 2]. We point the interested reader here.

4 Proposed Method

Let $\mathbf{X}$ be an n x d matrix of features, where n represents the number of instances, and d denotes the number of dimensions the features space spans. In general $\mathbf{X}$ is drawn from 2 or more classes which we wish to distinguish. We wish to choose a projection of the d dimensional data, $\mathbf{X}$, onto m orthogonal vectors ($m \leq d$) such that the classification error is a minimum for whatever classifier is chosen. The projection should also be robust when we move to independent test data.

We use a gradient descent method. We choose an initial d x 1 vector at random, $\mathbf{w}$, and project the data, X onto it:

$$\mathbf{p} = \mathbf{X}\mathbf{w} \qquad (1)$$

We pass the vector $\mathbf{p}$ to the classifier as both the training and test data. Hence, here we are training and testing using the same data. In practice, of course, this would not be the case. But, we do it here to illustrate the mechanisms of the algorithm rather than worrying about training bias. In practice a transformation matrix is found using the training data. Once the dimensionality reduction transformation matrix is found it can be applied to any new data.

For the data vector $\mathbf{p}$, we identify which instances have been erroneously classified in $\mathbf{p}$, using our classifier of choice. For example, Figure 1 (a)(i) shows two gaussian distributions in a 2-dimensional feature space. Instances from class 1 are marked with an 'x' and those from class 2 with a '+'. The initial vector $\mathbf{w}$ is shown starting at the origin and pointing southeast. Figure 1 (a)(ii) shows a histogram of $\mathbf{p}$ separated by class. The dashed vertical line shows were the classifier placed the decision boundary of the classifier which minimises misclassification. The solid histogram values to the left of the decision boundary and the dashed histogram values to the right of the boundary represent histograms of the wrongly classified instances. To improve our classification, we wish to adjust **w** so that the errors on the right of the decision boundary move toward the left and those on the left move toward the right. In Figure 1 (a)(i) we have marked the misclassified instances we wish to move to the right with a '▽' and those we wish to move to the left with an 'o'. We now compute the mean of the instances marked '▽' and denote that vector **a**, and we also compute the mean of the instances marked 'o' and denote that vector **b**. The direction we wish **w** to move is hence **v** = **b** − **a**. The vector **v** is shown in Figure 1 (a)(i). We only want to move **w** a small increment in that direction, so our update equation for **w** is:

$$\mathbf{w}_{new} = \mathbf{w}_{old} + \epsilon.\mathbf{v} \tag{2}$$

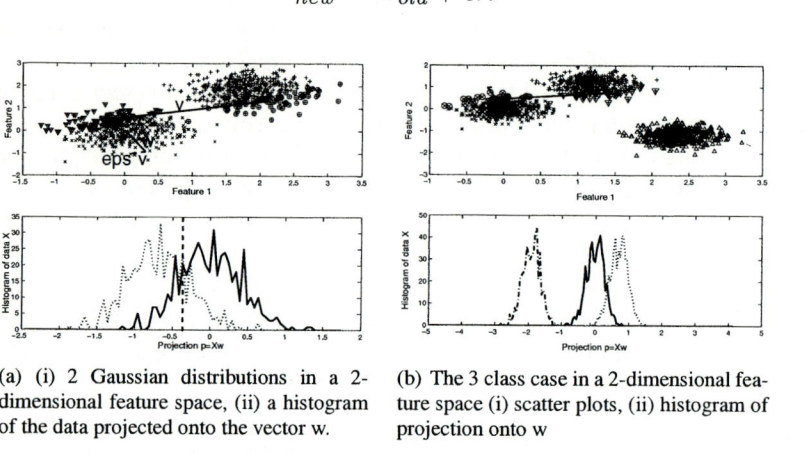

(a) (i) 2 Gaussian distributions in a 2-dimensional feature space, (ii) a histogram of the data projected onto the vector w.

(b) The 3 class case in a 2-dimensional feature space (i) scatter plots, (ii) histogram of projection onto w

Fig. 1. Plots of 2 different distributions

Here ϵ is some small step size. We then compute the new value of **p** with $\mathbf{w}_{new}$, classify again and re-adjust **w** until convergence is reached. This idea generalises easily to multiple classes. In the multi-class case, the direction in which we choose to move the misclassified instances (left or right along **w**) is determined by the direction along **w** in which the nearest correct classification of that class is located. What we are trying to do is choose the next projection $\mathbf{p}_{new} = \mathbf{X}\mathbf{w}_{new}$ so that on average the misclassifications of $\mathbf{p}_{new}$ are moved closer to the correct classifications of the same class and hence encourage those misclassifications to be turned into correct classifications. An example of a 3 class problem is shown in Figure 1 (b), in which the class instances are marked with '+', 'x', and '△'. Again, right moving instances are marked '▽' and left moving 'o'. **w** is shown starting at the origin and pointing northwest.

Since we are using a gradient descent method it is possible to converge upon a locally minimal solution, which is not necessarily globally optimal. To help overcome this and find a global minimum we search for **w** from various different initial vectors. These could be chosen using LDA or PCA, but in our case we chose them to be a set of random but orthogonal vectors. We then choose the **w** which has converged upon the *best* projection (the lowest classification error).

Once **w** has been found we can then create an orthonormal basis, which is orthogonal to **w** but which will be of dimension $d-1$, and we then project data onto this basis to create a new data set, with the information contained in the direction of **w** removed. This orthonormal basis is easily created using a QR decomposition of a $d \times d$ matrix which has **w** as its first column and $d-1$ other random columns, the basis is formed using the last $d-1$ columns of the Q matrix. Once we have transformed the data, **X**, to a new $(d-1)$-dimensional dataset we start the procedure of finding a **w** for this reduced dimension data set. The sequence of finding **w** and reducing the dimension of the data set can continue until we have found m different **w** vectors.

As we have already stated, we are passing both the training and test data to the classifier so as to keep the concept simple and illustrate the algorithm. In practice we may not have much training data and hence cross-fold validation will be used to obtain a reliable estimate of classification error. This algorithm may be applied in this case to minimise misclassification rate. If we were using 5-fold cross validation, for example, we would have 5 test-training data pairs. For one test-training data pair we train the classifier (given a projection, $\mathbf{p_{train}}$, of the training data onto **w**) and test with a projection, $\mathbf{p_{test}}$, of the test data, onto **w**. We then decide whether the points in the test data are left moving or right moving (as above). This is done for all 5 sets of test data, using there corresponding training sets to train. Then the vectors **a**, **b**, **v** are calculated and **w** is updated.

5 Data and Experimental Design

5.1 Data Sets

5.1.1 Synthetic Data – 2 Dimensions

To illustrate the utility of our technique, we provide examples of the simplest possible dimensionality reduction task, from two dimensions to one. We constructed 6 different data sets all 2-dimensional which we considered interesting, i.e. LDA and PCA may find it difficult to choose a single projection to discriminate the class information. Plots of the data sets are shown in Figure 2. We will briefly describe each different data set.

Data set (a) consists of 2 classes. Instances of class 1 are marked with '+' and class 2 with 'x'. Class 1 comprises of 3 gaussian distributions centred at (0, 1), (1.5, 0) and (0, -1). Class 2 comprises 3 gaussian distributions centred at (0, 0), (0, 2) and (-1.5, 1). All gaussian distributions had covariance matrices $\Sigma_n = \begin{bmatrix} 0.05 & 0 \\ 0 & 0.05 \end{bmatrix}$. Data set (b) consists of 6 classes. Each class distribution is gaussian, with covariance, Σ_n. Data set (c) consists of 2 classes. Each class distribution is a mixture of two gaussian distributions with different means. Class 1 is marked with a '+' and the gaussian means are (0, 2) and (2, 0). Class 2 is marked

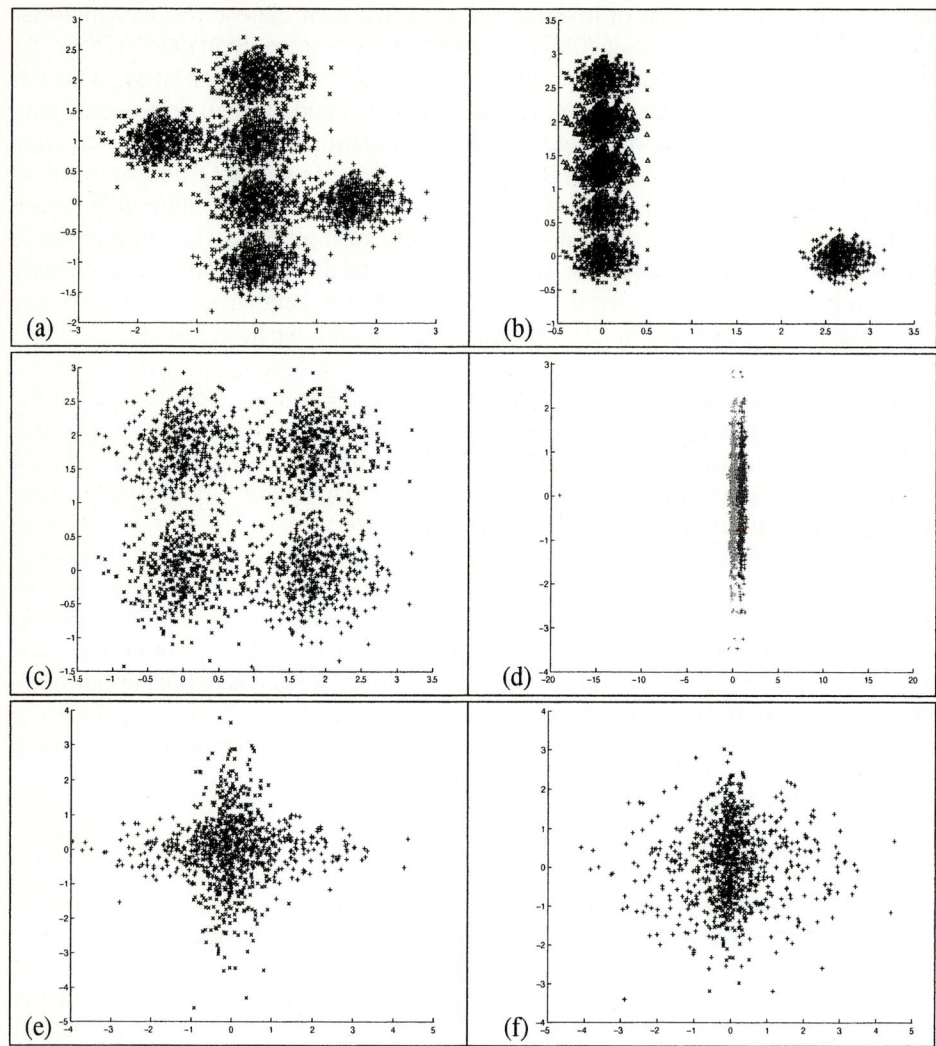

Fig. 2. Data sets

with an 'x' and the gaussian means are (0, 0) and (2, 2). All gaussians has covariance, Σ_n. Data set (d) comprises 2 classes. Class 1, marked 'x', is constructed of 500 instances drawn from a gaussian distribution centred at (0 ,0) with covariance, Σ_n, and 1 instance at (20, 0). Class 2, marked '+', is constructed of 500 instances drawn from a gaussian distribution with covariance, Σ_n, centred at (1 ,0) and 1 instance at (-19, 0). Data set (e) contains 2 classes. Class 1 marked '+' is drawn from a gaussian distribution with mean (0, 0) and covariance $\Sigma = \begin{bmatrix} 0.45 & 0 \\ 0 & 0.05 \end{bmatrix}$, and so is scaled along the x-ordinate. Class 2 marked 'x' is drawn from a gaussian distribution which also mean (0, 0) but has covariance $\Sigma = \begin{bmatrix} 0.05 & 0 \\ 0 & 0.45 \end{bmatrix}$, and thus is scaled along the y-ordinate. Finally, data set (f) contains 2 classes. Class 1 marked '+' is drawn from a gaussian distribution with mean (0, 0) and covariance $\Sigma = \begin{bmatrix} 0.45 & 0 \\ 0 & 0.05 \end{bmatrix}$, and hence scaled along the x-ordinate. Class 2 marked 'x' is drawn from a gaussian distribution of mean (0, 0.1) which was not scaled in any direction and has covariance matrix Σ_n.

5.1.2 Wisconsin Diagnostic Breast Cancer Database – 30 Dimensions

The Wisconsin Diagnostic Breast Cancer Database is a database of 30 features from 569 patients tested for breast cancer. There are two classes, Benign and Malignant. The features are computed from a digitized image of a fine needle aspirate (FNA) of a breast mass. They describe characteristics of the cell nuclei present in the image. The database is available from the UCI Machine Learning Repository: http://www.ics.uci.edu/~mlearn/MLRepository.html.

5.2 Classifier Design

The tool that we will use for classification is a quadratic discriminant classifier (QDC), based on Bayes rule. A quadratic discriminant classifier is derived as follows. Let ω_i signify the ith class. Let $\mathbf{x}$ denote the feature vector corresponding to a certain instance of the data, $\mathbf{X}$, i.e. $\mathbf{x}$ is a row of $\mathbf{X}$. Using Bayes rule we wish to find the class i which will maximise the posterior probability:

$$p(\omega_i|\mathbf{x}) = \frac{p(\mathbf{x}|\omega_i)P(\omega_i)}{p(\mathbf{x})}.$$

Maximising the $p(\omega_i|\mathbf{x})$ is equivalent to maximising its logarithm. Therefore, assuming a normal distribution for the feature vector, $p(\mathbf{x}|\omega_i)$ becomes:

$$p(\mathbf{x}|\omega_i) = \left\{ (2\pi)^{-\frac{d}{2}} |\mathbf{\Sigma}_i|^{-\frac{1}{2}} \right\} exp\left[-\tfrac{1}{2}(\mathbf{x}-\mu_i)^T \mathbf{\Sigma}_i^{-1} (\mathbf{x}-\mu_i)\right],$$

where $\mathbf{\Sigma}_i$ is the covariance matrix of the ith class, and μ_i is the mean vector of the ith class. Substituting $p(\mathbf{x}|\omega_i)$ into the natural logarithm of $p(\omega_i|\mathbf{x})$, our problem is transformed into finding the class i which maximises the discriminant value $g_i(\mathbf{x})$ for a given test feature vector $\mathbf{x}$:

$$g_i(\mathbf{x}) = \mathbf{x}^T \mathbf{H}_i \mathbf{x} + \mathbf{h}_i x + k_i,$$

where $H_i = -\tfrac{1}{2}\Sigma_i^{-1}$, $h_i = \Sigma_i^{-1}\mu_i$, and $k_i = -\tfrac{1}{2}\mu_i^T \Sigma_i^{-1} \mu_i - \tfrac{1}{2}ln|\Sigma_i| + ln(P(\omega_i))$. The class with the highest discriminant value is chosen as the assigned class for that feature vector. To construct the quadratic discriminant classifier, therefore, we must estimate the covariance matrix and mean for the features corresponding to each class, and also the prior probability of the class occurring.

5.3 Experimental Design

We present each of our 6 synthetic data sets and the Breast Cancer data to the three techniques under comparison; (1) Our Gradient Descent method, (2) PCA, and (3) LDA. The PCA projection is chosen as the eigenvector corresponding to the maximum eigenvalue after performing an eigenvalue decomposition on the covariance matrix of X. The LDA projection we choose corresponds to the maximum eigenvector returned when maximising the objective function:

$$J(\mathbf{w}) = |\mathbf{w}^T \mathbf{S}_B \mathbf{w}| / |\mathbf{w}^T \mathbf{S}_W \mathbf{w}|,$$

where $\mathbf{S}_B$ is matrix representing the scatter of the class means about the overall mean, and $\mathbf{S}_W$ is a matrix describing the scatter of instances about each class mean (see [6] for a detailed description of the scatter matrices), where $||$ denotes the determinant. The eigenvectors are those of the matrix $\mathbf{S}_W^{-1} \mathbf{S}_B$. Each method will return a 1-dimensional projection of the initial multi-dimensional data. This projection will be used to train and test the QDC described in Section 5.2. We will use classification error as a measure of performance.

6 Results

6.1 Results – Synthetic Data

We see that the gradient descent technique outperforms or equals performance of PCA and LDA on all 6 datasets. The data sets where PCA performed worse were simply those where the class information was not in the direction of maximum variance. We will briefly interpret the results for each data set and explain why LDA failed to perform as well. The multi-modal gaussian structure of the class distribution violated the assumptions LDA is based on. In data set (b) when LDA attempted to maximise the variance of the class means about the overall mean it chose a projection which maximised the LDA objective function but obscured the

Table 1. Results: synthetic data

	Gradient Descent Classification Error	Projection Chosen	PCA Classification Error	Projection Chosen	LDA Classification Error	Projection Chosen
Data set (a)	26%	(-0.91, 0.42)	33%	(-0.1, 0.98)	62%	(-0.82, -0.58)
Data set (b)	3%	(-0.44, 0.9)	17%	(0.01, 0.99)	23%	(-0.6, -0.8)
Data set (c)	8%	(0.7, -0.72)	10%	(0.72, 0.68)	49%	(0, -1)
Data set (d)	1.6%	(-1, 0)	1.6%	(1, 0)	48%	(0, -1)
Data set (e)	24%	(0, 1)	39%	(0.89, 0.45)	39%	(0.5, 0.87)
Data set (f)	19%	(1, 0)	19%	(1, 0)	45%	(0, -1)

outlying class at (2.7, 0). In data set (c) the assumptions of LDA are again violated with two bimodal class distributions. Also, since the class means are approximately equal, no separating information is contained in the means, which is what LDA depends upon. In data set (d) the two outlying points at (-19, 0) and (20 , 0) cause the distributions to appear to be skewed along the x-axis hence the LDA technique attempts to minimise the variance about the class means and chooses to project onto the y-axis, which is a projection containing no class separability information. In data set (e) both classes have the same mean and hence the projection LDA chooses is essentially random; dependent on the variances of the distributions. In data set (f) the means of the class distributions are offset along the y-axis, but the information is contained along the x-axis. LDA ignores the variance and maximises the distance between the means.

6.2 Results – Wisconsin Diagnostic Breast Cancer Data

We see that LDA performs the worst on this dataset. This most likely due to the data being skewed and non-gaussian. PCA performs reasonably well because it is only two class problem and the direction of maximum variance is very likely to be along the vector between the means of each class. In fact the data set is linearly separable, but our choice of classifier, which assumes that the class distributions are gaussian when projected onto $\mathbf{w}$, caused some errors because the distributions are not gaussian. Plots of the histograms of the final projections, $\mathbf{p}$, are shown in Figure 3.

Table 2. Results: Breast Cancer data

	Gradient Descent Classification Error	PCA Classification Error	LDA classification error
Breast cancer data	1.4%	9.1%	37.6%

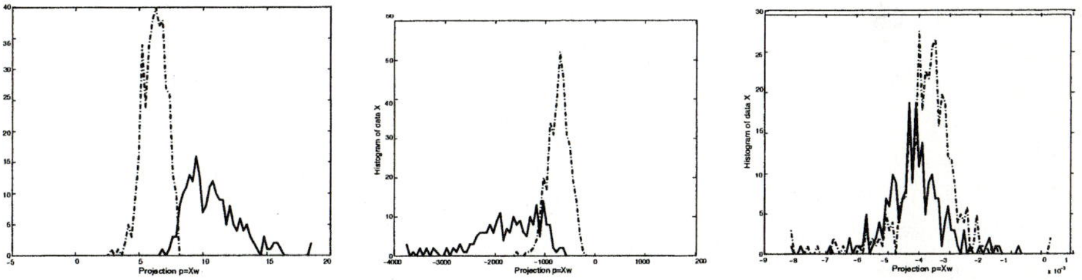

(a) Gradient Descent	(b) PCA	(c) LDA

Fig. 3. Histograms of final projections, p, for Breast Cancer data

7 Conclusions

We have described a gradient descent method for dimensionality reduction which makes no assumptions about the structure of the data and can use an arbitrary classifier. While the system we describe here assumes that the same data is used for testing and training, this is only for illustration purposes. In reality the gradient descent process would operate on the classification results from several cross-fold validation runs. We have compared our systems performance with PCA and LDA, both standard techniques for dimension reduction, and found it to be superior, or at least equal, for all data sets.

References

[1] B. H. Juang and S. Katagiri, "Discriminative learning for minimum error classification [pattern recognition]," *Signal Processing, IEEE Transactions on [see also Acoustics, Speech, and Signal Processing, IEEE Transactions on]*, vol. 40, no. 12, pp. 3043–3054, 1992.

[2] X. Wang and K. K. Paliwal, "Using minimum classification error training in dimensionality reduction," vol. 1, pp. 338–345, 2000.

[3] I. H. Witten and E. Frank, *Data Mining: Practical Machine Learning tools and techniques with Java Implementations*. Morgan Kaufman, 1999.

[4] I. T. Jolliffe, *Principal Component Analysis*. New York: Springer, 2002.

[5] R. A. Fisher, "The use of multiple measurements in taxonomic problems, " *Annu. Eugenics*, vol. 7, pp. 179188, 1936.

[6] T. Okada and S. Tomita, "An optimal orthonormal system for discriminant analysis," *Pattern Recognition*, vol. 18, no. 2, pp. 139–144, 1985.

On the Automatic 2D Retinal Vessel Extraction

C. Alonso-Montes[1], D.L. Vilariño[2], and M.G. Penedo[1]

[1] Department of Computer Science, University of Coruña, Spain
{carmen, cipenedo}@dc.fi.udc.es
[2] Department of Electronics and Computer Science,
University of Santiago de Compostela, Spain
dlv@dec.usc.es

Abstract. Retinal vessel extraction has become an important task of medical image processing applications in order to diagnose ocular diseases. In this paper, a novel methodology is proposed to extract vessels automatically from retinal angiographies. The proposed methodology has been implemented by means of Cellular Neural Networks techniques to take advantage of their capabilities of massively parallel processing reducing computation time required.

1 Introduction

The study of vessel extraction techniques in medical images has become an important aspect related with a variety of applications in order to diagnose ocular diseases. Considerable research has been devoted to develop automatic extraction algorithms [1] specially regarding on the accuracy of the obtained results. In this sense, strategies based on active contour [2] have been used in medical images due to their robustness against noise. The main disadvantages of these techniques are both their high computational cost and the initialisation which usually requires user interaction. In this sense, some research has focused on improving computational cost required for active contour techniques [3, 4].

The aim of this paper is to propose a novel methodology to extract the edge vessel contour automatically from retinal angiographies by means of a active contour technique. The proposed methodology has been tackled by means of Cellular Neural Networks [5] (CNNs) techniques instead of classical image processing techniques [6], in order to take advantage of their suitability for hardware implementation on a chip-set architecture based on the CNN Universal Machine (CN-NUM) paradigm [7]. One advantage of using CNN-based techniques [8] is that image processing applications with either high computational cost or real-time requirements could be addressed properly since they allows a massively parallel processing reducing computational time required [9]. A further argument is that hardware integration with any kind of input devices, such as cameras or sensors can be made.

This paper is structured as follows: in *Section 2* the proposed methodology is discussed, in *Section 3* the main results are shown and, finally, *Section 4* presents the conclusions.

2 Automatic Vessel Extraction Methodology

In this section the proposed methodology in order to deal with the vessel extraction is explained (Fig. 1). The main goal of this methodology is to fit the vessel edges by means of an active contour technique providing an automatic way of obtaining both the initial and the external potential images needed. Several stages has been defined (Fig. 1): *Vessel Segmentation, Initial Contour and External Potential Estimation* and *Vessel Extraction*. Each stage of the methodology has been applied to 128x128 windows obtained from angiographies (Fig. 2).

Firstly, vessels are segmented from the background of the image in order to identify the regions between the vessels. During the second stage, both the initial contour and the external potential images needed by the active contours are estimated automatically using the the images previously obtained. During the last stage, the active contours achieve and fit the vessel edges, extracting the vessel structure which is the initial point for several applications, like vessel measurement.

Every stage of the proposed methodology is compounded by different process or steps (Fig. 1) in order to be implemented by means of CNN-based techniques. Although these steps can be implemented by means of classical image processing techniques [10, 11, 12, 13, 14], the use of CNN-based techniques is proposed in

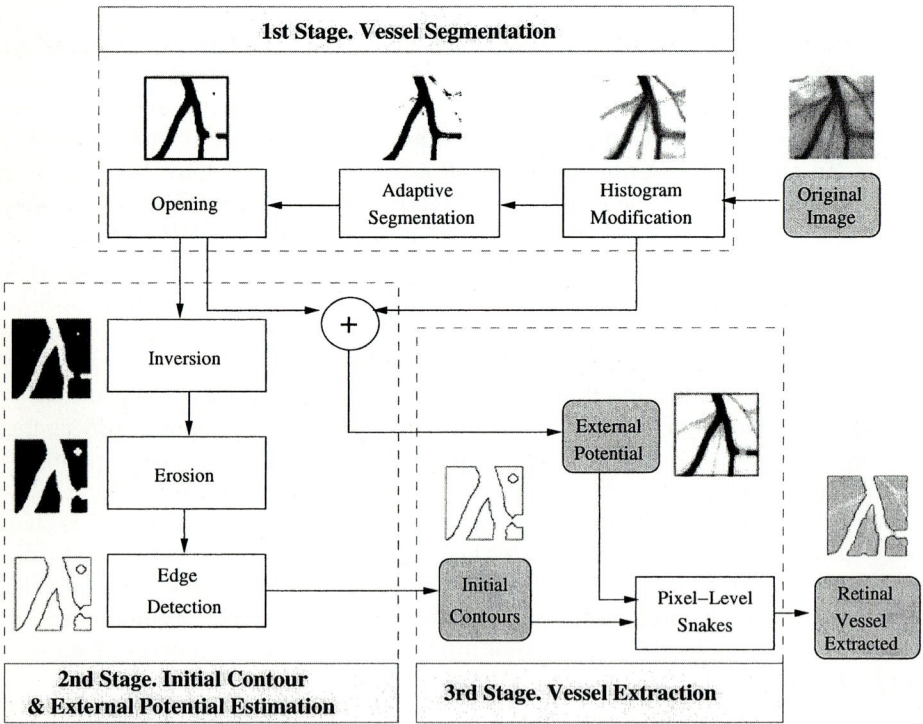

Fig. 1. Automatic Vessel Extraction Methodology: Stages and Steps

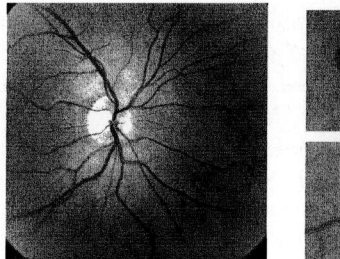

Fig. 2. Left: Angiography image example, **right:** 128x128 windows obtained from the image on the left.

order to take advantage of the computation time reduction provided by the massive parallel processing.

2.1 Vessel Segmentation

The main issue of this stage is to segment vessels from the image background removing noisy points as much as possible. This stage has been split into several steps (Fig. 1): *Histogram Modification*, *Adaptive Segmentation* and, finally, an *Opening* step.

Firstly, an histogram modification algorithm is used to improve image contrast in order to enhance vessels in low contrast images. For this step, we have made use of the CNN-based histogram equalisation algorithm addressed in [15].

Then, during the adaptive segmentation step an optimal and suitable threshold value is needed in order to segment properly the vessels. The approach used in this paper is based on that addressed in [16], where a local threshold estimation is proposed in order to determine the space-variant threshold level (T_{est}) computed from local statistics of the image

$$T_{est} = \alpha E_m + \beta E_v + thres, \quad \alpha \in [0,1], \beta \in [-1,0] \qquad (1)$$

where E_m and E_v are the mean and the variance estimations of the considered image, respectively, whose CNN implementation is explained in [16]; *thres* is a constant threshold value which depends on the gray-level of the considered image and α and β are scale factors, whose values are heuristically estimated. The motivation behind the above formulation (Eq. 1) is to obtain the optimal threshold estimation for each pixel in order to describe the object boundaries. Since the variance in the boundaries is higher than in homogeneous regions, the combination of both the mean and the variance estimations allows us to obtain a suitable T_{est} improving the segmentation results. Taking into account the retinal images used in this paper, we propose to compute the *thres* value as follows

$$thres = \max\left[\frac{\sum_{i=1}^{N} I_{i1}}{N}, \frac{\sum_{i=1}^{N} I_{i2}}{N}, \ldots, \frac{\sum_{i=1}^{N} I_{iM}}{N}\right] \qquad (2)$$

where I_{ij} is the gray-level value in the i-row and j-column in the NxM input image and $(\sum_{i=1}^{N} I_{ij})/N$ is the mean value of the j-column. It has been experimentally checked that the selection of the maximum mean value improves the segmentation results in images whose gray-level values have less differences between them. After this step, noise and vessel discontinuities could appear. Vessel discontinuities cannot be avoided in some images because of the non uniformity of the gray level values in the vessels. The opening step tries to remove noise maintaining at the same time the vessels. Noisy isolated points are easily removed by means of the opening process. However, noisy regions cannot be removed during this step. Both the noisy regions and the vessel discontinuities can be solved during the following stages of the methodology.

2.2 Initial Contour and External Potential Estimation

The active contour technique used in this paper need two main input images, an initial contour image and an external potential image. The external potential image guides the active contours towards the object boundaries. The main issue of this stage is to get automatically an initialisation for the active contours and an estimation of the external potential image.

The initial contour image is obtained after several steps (Fig. 1): *inversion*, *erosion* and *edge detection*. The aim of these steps is to minimise the discontinuities appeared during the previous stage in order to get a suitable initial contour image. First, the segmented vessel image, obtained during the first stage, is inverted in order to obtain the regions which are between the vessels. These regions are eroded several times, during the erosion step, in order to avoid the vessel discontinuities which have appeared in the previous stage. Finally, an edge detection is made over these eroded regions in order to obtain the initial contour image.

The external potential image is proposed to be computed as follows

$$I_{ext} = \rho I_{eq} + \delta I_{op}, \quad \rho, \delta \in [0,1] \tag{3}$$

where both I_{eq} and I_{op} images are obtained during the first stage of the methodology (Fig. 1), I_{eq} is the equalised image and I_{op} is the image with the segmented vessels; ρ and δ are scale factors, which are empirically estimated. I_{op} image contains the segmented vessels, whereas I_{eq} gives additional vessel continuity information lost in I_{op}, which help the active contours to fit properly the vessels. An appropriate scale factor is needed in order to weight properly the significance of both images (I_{eq} and I_{op}) since I_{op} can contain noisy regions which have been segmented during the first stage. The motivation behind this formulation (Eq. 3) is that I_{eq} image should have the enough significance in order to allow active contours to remove noisy regions and to maintain vessel continuity at the same time.

2.3 Vessel Extraction

The aim of this stage is to extract the vessel edges using a CNN-based active contour technique, the so-called pixel-level snakes (PLS) [17]. The main input images needed by PLS have been estimated during the previous stage. The PLS technique can handle several snakes or contours at the same time and manage the required changes in topology in a simple way. This kind of technique is more dependent on the initialisation, so a suitable initial contour image is needed.

The better control of the contour deformation makes this parametric model suitable for tasks with a previous knowledge of the application domain and the approximate shape of the objects into the scene.

The PLS represent a topographic iterative active contour technique where the contours, explicitly represented, evolve guided by local information. All of the contour points influence the contour evolution. Therefore it could be considered as a continuous treatment of the contour, given that its discretization is of the same order as the spatial variable in the images to be treated (pixel-level discretization). The main advantage of using PLS is that high computational requirement applications can be properly addressed. A further argument is that PLS can merge and split contours, being suitable to deal with segmentation problems where object number and location are not known a priori. In this sense, the noisy regions appeared during the previous stage can be easily removed. The PLS contour evolution is guided by forces derived from the potential fields $P(x,y)$ defined in the image space

$$\boldsymbol{F} = -\nabla P(x,y) = -\frac{\partial P}{\partial x}\boldsymbol{i} - \frac{\partial P}{\partial y}\boldsymbol{j} = F_x\boldsymbol{i} + F_y\boldsymbol{j} \tag{4}$$

The PLS potential field is defined as follows

$$P(x,y) = k_{int}P_{int}(x,y) + k_{ext}P_{ext}(x,y) + k_{inf}P_{inf}(x,y) \tag{5}$$

where P_{int} and P_{ext} are the internal and external potential, respectively; P_{inf} is the balloon potential and k_{int}, k_{ext} and k_{inf} are scale factors, where $k_{int}, k_{ext} \in [-1,0]$ and $k_{inf} \in [0,1]$. According to the formulation of Eq. 5 the contour evolution is controlled by the forces derived by the global potential field. The external potential guides the PLS towards the boundaries of interest. The internal potential controls the smoothing effect of the snake giving more robustness to the model against noise. The external potential should have higher influence since it contains the main information of the image. The balloon forces control the inflation or deflation tendency respect to the external forces and they are usually required to guide the contour evolution when the external potential is too weak. There is not an exact rule to determine the influence of each kind of potential fields (P_{int}, P_{ext}, P_{inf}) which clearly depends on the definition of the external potential image and the previous knowledge of the structures to be segmented (shape, location, ...). The influence of each potential is weighted by the k_{int}, k_{ext} and k_{inf} values, respectively and, like in classical active contour techniques these scale factors must be determined heuristically. For further details about the PLS performance see [17].

3 Results

The algorithm has been simulated in MATCNN [18] environment, using 128x128 windows obtained from 1024x1024 retinal angiographies (Fig. 3). A number of 20 angiographies has been selected obtaining 64 windows from each angiography. The 128x128 windows size has been selected in order to fit the current implementations on chip of the CNN machine [17].

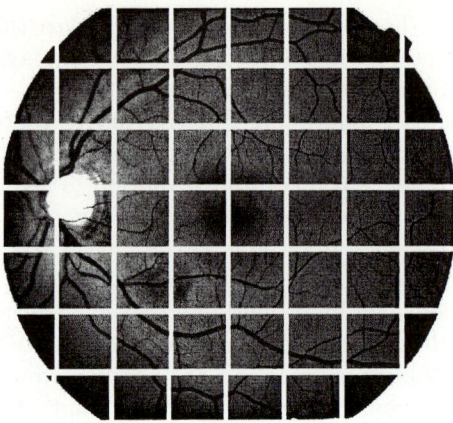

Fig. 3. 128x128 windows obtained from an angiography

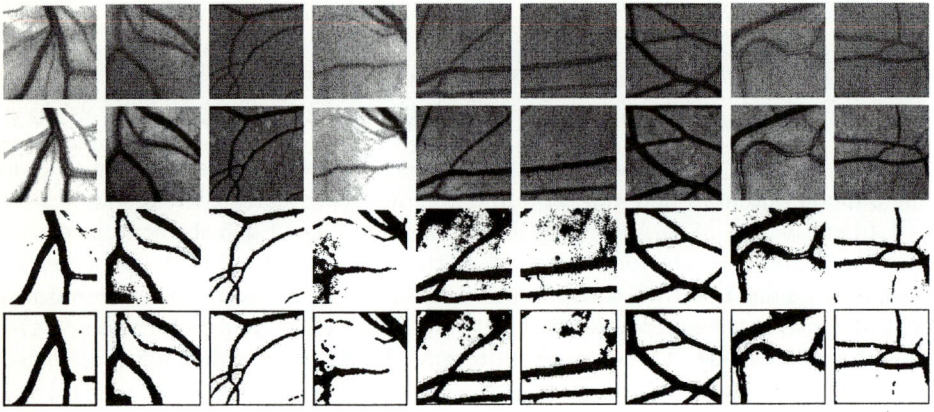

Fig. 4. *Vessel Segmentation Stage* **1st row** Original Image, **2nd row** Histogram Equalisation Step, **3rd row** Adaptive Segmentation Step and **4th row** Opening Step.

The original images (1st row Fig. 4) are processed following the methodology steps proposed for the vessel segmentation stage. Firstly, the histogram equalisation step has improved particularly low-contrast images (2nd row Fig. 4). Then, vessels have been segmented during the adaptive segmentation step (3rd row Fig. 4). It has been experimentally checked that $\alpha = 0.1$ and $\beta = -0.9$ of Eq. 1 optimise the obtained results. During this step, noisy points appeared and they were removed by the opening step (4th row Fig. 4). Vessels were properly segmented during this first stage, see 4th row in Fig. 4. A suitable vessel segmentation is needed in order to improve the image results during the following stages.

In the second stage, both the initial contour and the external potential images are estimated. The image containing the segmented vessels (4th row Fig. 4) is inverted to obtain the regions which are between the vessels. Then, these regions are eroded 5 times in order to avoid vessel discontinuities, it has been

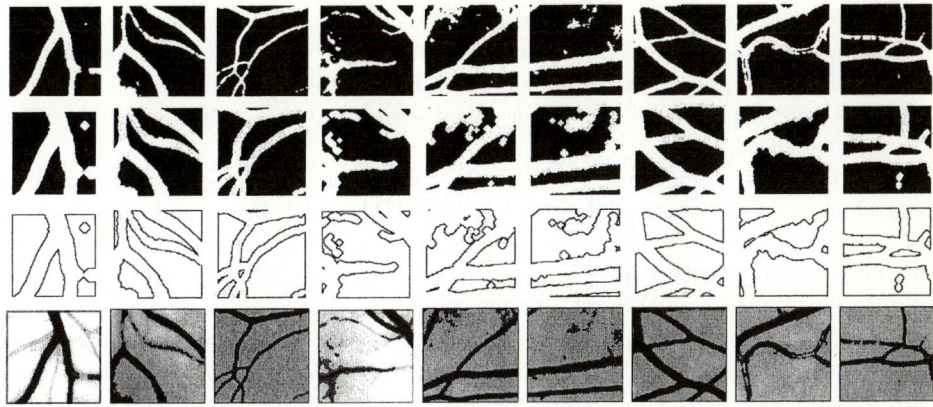

Fig. 5. *Initial Contour and External Potential Estimation Stage*: **1st row** Inversion, **2nd row** Erosion, and **3rd row** Edge Detection which gets the Initial Contour Image; and, finally, **4th row** External Potential Image.

Fig. 6. *Vessel Extraction Stage*: PLS shown in black over the vessels in white

experimentally checked that this is the minimum number of erosion operations in order to obtain a suitable initial contours avoiding discontinuities. Finally, the edge contour step has obtained a suitable initial contour image (see 1st, 2nd and 3rd rows Fig. 5). The estimation of the external potential image is computed by means of equation 3, using $\rho = \delta = 0.5$, which have been empirically estimated. Note that the equalised image (I_{eq}) contains additional vessel continuity information which has been lost in the I_{op} image, compare 2nd row and 4th row Fig. 4 with the external potential image computed (last row in Fig. 5). In this sense, vessel continuity information is maintained whereas vessel points have more significance. Note that noise from the first stage has less influence than points belonging to vessel regions.

Both images previously obtained, the initial contour and the external potential images, were used by the PLS in the vessel extraction stage. The main parameters of Eq. 5, $k_{ext} = -0.4$, $k_{int} = -0.005$ and $k_{inf} = 0.2$, have been empirically estimated. PLS are guided by P_{ext}, whereas P_{int} smooths the snake surface. Due to the type of images used for this evaluation, an inflation potential is established in order to achieve the vessels. The vessels extracted by PLS are shown in Fig. 6. PLS deal properly with noisy points and regions, using their capability of merging and splitting contours (see 4th, 5th and 6th columns Fig. 6). The external potential image has helped PLS in order to maintain vessel continuity (1st, 2nd and 3rd columns Fig. 6).

Accurate results have been obtained regardless of image complexity (Fig. 6). An accurate result has been obtained in a 95 % of the windows processed by means of the proposed methodology, since PLS using their pixel-level discretisation feature can achieve the vessel edges with an accuracy of a pixel far from the real vessel edge.

The simulation made in the MATCNN environment allows us to check the performance of the methodology for a CNNUM architecture and this feature give us the possibility of a future implementation of the proposed methodology in a chip-set architecture achieving real-time requirements. The processing time required in a hardware chip-set implementation cannot be established from the simulation made in MATCNN since it depends on the integration capacity of the processing elements of the specific chip, nevertheless in [19] gives an approximation of the times handled in different hardware architectures. In this sense, the simulation made for this methodology takes minutes of software time processing but in a hardware architecture this time can be reduced to milliseconds or μ-seconds, depending on the specific hardware implementation.

4 Conclusions

The proposed methodology deals properly with the automatic retinal vessel extraction. Accurate results have been obtained from different retinal images regardless of the image complexity. In this sense, due to its simplicity and general nature, this methodology is expected to be applicable to a variety of other tasks, like vessel measurement or personal identification systems. The different stages have been implemented by means of CNN-based techniques in order to take advantage of the massively parallel processing. Taking into account this feature, real-time applications can be properly addressed. Furthermore, the PLS capability of merging and splitting contours allows us to avoid noisy regions and to fit the vessels accurately.

In conclusion, it can be said that using the methodology characterised in this paper vessels are extracted suitability and accurately especially regarding on computational time improvement.

Acknowledgements

This work has been partly supported by Xunta de Galicia (PGIDIT03TIC10-503PR and PGIDT04PXIC10501PN).

References

1. Gang, L., Chutatape, O., Krishnan, S.M.: Detection and Measurement of Retinal Vessels in Fundus Images using Amplitude Modified Second-Order Gaussian Filter. IEEE Trans. Biomed. Eng. **49** (2002) 168–172

2. Valverde, F., Guil, N., Munoz, J., Li, Q., Aoyama, M., Doi, K.: A deformable model for image segmentation in noisy medical images. In: Proc. Int. IEEE Conf. Image Processing. Volume 3. (2001) 82–85
3. Caselles, V., Kimmel, R., Sapiro, G.: Geodesic Active Contours. International Journal of Computer Vision **22** (1997) 61–79
4. Goldenberg, R., Kimmel, R., Rivlin, E., Rudzdky, M.: Fast geodesic active contours. IEEE Trans. Image Processing **10** (2001) 1467–1475
5. Chua, L.O., Yang, L.: Cellular Neural Networks: Theory. IEEE Trans. Circuits Syst. **35** (1988) 1257–1272
6. Chaudhuri, S., Chatterjee, S., Katz, N., Nelson, M., M.Goldbaum: Detection of Blood Vessels in Retinal Images using Two-Dimensional Matched Filters. IEEE Trans. Med. Imag. **8** (1989)
7. Roska, T., Chua, L.O.: The CNN Universal Machine: An Analogic Array Comuter. IEEE Trans. Circuits Syst. II **40** (1993) 163–173
8. Vilariño, D., Cabello, D., Pardo, X., Brea, V.M.: Cellular neural networks and active contours: a tool for image segmentation. Image and Vision Computing **21** (2004) 189–204
9. Chua, L., Roska, T.: The CNN paradigm. IEEE Trans. Circuits Syst. **40** (1993) 147–156
10. Eviatar, H., Somorjai, R.L.: A fast, simple active contour algorithm for biomedical images. Pattern Recogn. Lett. **17** (1996) 969–974
11. Miles, F., Nuttall, A.: Matched filter estimation of serial blood vessel diameters from video images. IEEE Trans. Med. Imag. **12** (1993) 147–152
12. Sonka, M., Winninford, M.D., Collins, S.M.: Robust Simultaneous Detection of Coronary Borders in Complex Images. IEEE Trans. Med. Imag. **14** (1995) 151–161
13. Thackray, B.D., Nelson, A.C.: Semi-Automatic Segmentation of Vascular Network Images Using a Rotating Structuring Element (ROSE) with Mathematical Morphology and Dual Feature Thresholding. IEEE Trans. Med. Imag. **12** (1993) 385–392
14. Figueiredo, M.A.T., Leitão, J.M.N.: A nonsmoothing approach to the estimation of vessel contours in angiograms. IEEE Trans. Med. Imag. **14** (1995) 162–172
15. Cserey, G., Rekeczky, C., Foldesy, P.: PDE Based Histogram Modification with Embedded Morphological Processing of the Level-sets. In: Proc. 7th IEEE Int. Workshop CNNs and their Applications. (2002) 315–322
16. Rekeczky, C., Schultz, A., Szatmari, I., Roska, T., Chua, L.O.: Image Segmentation and Edge Detection via Constrained Diffusion and Adaptive Morphology: a CNN approach to Bubble/debris Image Enhancement. In: Proc. 6th Int. Symp. Nonlinear Theory and its Applications (NOLTA '97). (1997) 209–212
17. Vilariño, D., Rekeczky, C.: Pixel-Level Snakes on the CNNUM: Algorithm Design, On-Chip Implementation and Applications. International Journal of Circuit Theory and Applications **33** (2005) 17–51
18. Rekeczky, C.: MATCNN - Analogic Simulation Toolbox for Matlab. Technical report, Analogic Neural Computing Lab., Hungarian Academy of Sciences (1997)
19. Kozek, T., Wu, C.W., Zarandy, A., Chen, H., Roska, T., Kunt, M., Chua, L.: New results and measurements related to some tasks in object-oriented dynamic image coding using CNN universal chips. IEEE Trans. Circuits Syst. Video Technol. **7** (1997) 606–614

Modeling Phase Spectra Using Gaussian Mixture Models for Human Face Identification

Sinjini Mitra[1], Marios Savvides[2], and Anthony Brockwell[3],*

[1] Department of Statistics, Carnegie Mellon University,
Pittsburgh, PA 15213
smitra@stat.cmu.edu
[2] Electrical and Computer Engineering Department,
Carnegie Mellon University, Pittsburgh, PA 15213
msavvid@cs.cmu.edu
[3] Department of Statistics, Carnegie Mellon University,
Pittsburgh, PA 15213
abrock@stat.cmu.edu

Abstract. It has been established that information distinguishing one human face from another is contained to a large extent in the Fourier domain phase component of the facial image. However, to date, formal statistical models for this component have not been deployed in face recognition tasks. In this paper we introduce a model-based approach using Gaussian mixture models (GMM) for the phase component for performing human identification. Classification and verification are performed using a MAP estimate and we show that we are able to achieve identification error rates as low as 2% and verification error rates as low as 0.3% on a database with 65 individuals with extreme illumination variations. The proposed method is easily able to deal with other distortions such as expressions and poses, and hence this establishes its robustness to intra-personal variations. A potential use of the method in illumination normalization is also discussed.

1 Introduction

Automated tools for face recognition are in ever increasing demand today, partly as a result of efforts to improve security in various walks of the society today. The recently adopted practice of recording photographs and fingerprints of foreign passengers at U.S. airports provides evidence of the increased importance of biometrics today. Facial recognition is generally preferred to classification based on other biometric traits since it is difficult to falsify and the method of acquiring face images is non-intrusive and widely acceptable. However, while facial recognition is trivial for humans (an infant can discriminate his or her mother's face from a stranger's at the age of 45 hours ([17])), it is an extremely challenging task to automate the process. Other applications of face identification include criminal identification in law enforcement, searching for missing people, national ID cards, physical access to buildings, ATMs, etc.

---

* The authors wish to thank CyLab and Technical Support Working Group (TSWG).

The growing importance of face recognition has led to a substantial amount of research in computer vision over the past few decades, with applications ranging from still, controlled mug-shot verification to dynamic and uncontrolled face identification in a cluttered background. Faces are rich in information about individual identity, mood and mental state, and position relationships between face parts, such as eyes, nose, mouth and chin, as well as their shapes and sizes are widely used as discriminative features for identification. Some well-known methods for face identification and verification include Support Vector Machines ([6]), Linear Discriminant Analysis ([7]), Independent Component Analysis ([4]) and Neural Networks ([11]).

Most of the face recognition systems that are available today use a spatial domain approach based directly on the image intensities. Recently, much research effort has focused on the frequency domain as well, which possesses useful properties that have been successfully exploited in many signal processing applications ([10]). The frequency domain representation of an image (the spectrum) consists of two components, the *magnitude* and *phase*. In 2D images particularly, the phase captures more of the image intelligibility than magnitude and hence is very significant for performing image reconstruction ([5]). [14] showed that correlation filters built in the frequency domain can be used for efficient face verification. Recently, the significance of phase has been utilized in identification problems also. [12] proposed correlation filters based only on phase, which performed as well as the original filters, and [13] demonstrated that performing PCA in the frequency domain using only the phase spectrum not only outperforms spatial domain PCA, but also has attractive features like illumination and occlusion tolerance. All these results suggest that classification methods in the frequency domain, especially based on phase, may yield potentially good results.

Model-based approaches include use of Gaussian models ([16]), deformable models ([18]), and inhomogeneous Gibbs models ([8]), which are good at capturing local details of a face using a minimax entropy principle proposed in [19]. Model-based identification methods are usually more rigorous than feature-based methods as they are more capable of capturing the inherent variability in the data and have greater statistical validity. One class of flexible statistical models is the family of *mixture models* ([9]). Such models can represent complex distributions through an appropriate choice of its components to represent accurately the local areas of support of the true distribution. Apart from statistical applications, Gaussian mixture models (GMM), the most popular of the mixture models, have also been used in computer vision. [19] used GMM for modeling the shape and texture of face images. However, no work has been done, as to the authors' knowledge, on developing model-based face identification systems in the frequency domain.

The rest of the paper is organized as follows. Section 2 provides a brief description of the database used. Section 3 presents our GMM approach, along with parameter estimation techniques and classification scheme, and Section 4 contains the results. Finally, additional discussion appears in Section 5.

2 Data

The dataset used for developing our technique for facial identification is a subset of the publicly available "CMU-PIE Database" ([15]) which contains frontal images of 65 people under 21 different illumination conditions ranging from shadows to balanced and overall dark. A small sample of images of 6 people under 3 different lighting effects is shown in Figure 1.

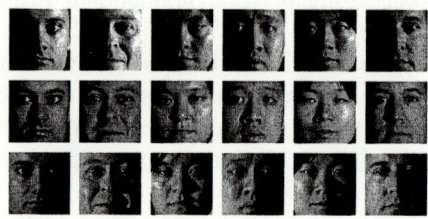

Fig. 1. Sample images from the CMU-PIE database

3 Gaussian Mixture Models

The usefulness of mixture distributions in the modeling of heterogeneity in a cluster analysis context is obvious. But as any continuous distribution can be approximated arbitrarily well by a finite mixture of Gaussian densities with common variance, mixture models provide a convenient semiparametric framework in which to model unknown distributional shapes. It can handle situations where a single parametric family is unable to provide a satisfactory model for local variations in the observed data. The model framework is briefly described below.

Let $(\mathbf{Y_1}, \ldots, \mathbf{Y_n})$ be a random sample of size n where $\mathbf{Y_j}$ is a p-dimensional random vector with probability distribution $f(\mathbf{y_j})$ on $\mathcal{R}^p$. Also, let $\boldsymbol{\theta}$ denote a vector of the model parameters to be estimated. A g-component mixture model can be written in parametric form as:

$$f(\mathbf{y_j}; \boldsymbol{\Psi}) = \sum_{i=1}^{g} \pi_i f_i(\mathbf{y_j}, \boldsymbol{\theta}_i), \qquad (1)$$

where the vector $\boldsymbol{\Psi}$ containing all the unknown parameters in the mixture model is written as $\boldsymbol{\Psi} = (\pi_1, \ldots, \pi_{g-1}, \boldsymbol{\xi}^T)^T$, and $\boldsymbol{\xi}$ is the vector containing all the parameters in $\boldsymbol{\theta}_1, \ldots, \boldsymbol{\theta}_g$ known *a priori* to be distinct. Here, $\boldsymbol{\theta}_i$ represents the model parameters for the ith mixture component and $\boldsymbol{\pi} = (\pi_1, \ldots, \pi_g)^T$ is the vector of the mixing proportions with $\sum_{i=1}^{g} \pi_i = 1$.

Over the years several methods have been used to estimate mixture distributions. They include graphical models, method of moments, minimum-distance methods, maximum likelihood (ML) and Bayesian approaches ([9]). But the most popular one is by using ML estimation via the EM algorithm. However, with the advent of computational power, estimation in a Bayesian framework is now feasible and practical using posterior simulation via Markov Chain Monte Carlo (MCMC) methods such as the Gibbs sampler. We use the Bayesian estimation method since it yields a nice framework for performing statistical inference based on the posterior distributions of the parameters which is not provided by EM. According to [2], the EM-type approximation is not really an adequate substitute for the more refined numerical approximation provided by the Gibbs sampler.

The Gibbs sampler yields a Markov chain $\{\boldsymbol{\Psi}^{(k)}, k = 1, 2, \ldots\}$ whose distribution converges to the true posterior distribution of the parameters. For our parameter estimates, we use the posterior mean, which could be estimated by the average of the first N values of the Markov chain. However, to reduce error associated with the fact that the chain takes time to converge to the correct distribution, we discard the first N_1 samples as *burn-in*. Thus our parameter estimates are

$$E\{\widehat{\boldsymbol{\Psi}}|\mathbf{y}\} = \sum_{k=N_1+1}^{N} \frac{\boldsymbol{\Psi}^{(k)}}{(N-N_1)}. \qquad (2)$$

The parameter N_1 is chosen by inspection of plots of the components of the Markov chain. In particular, we choose it to be 2000 out of a total of $N = 5000$ iterations, since after this many iterations, visual inspection indicates that the chain has "settled down" into its steady-state behaviour.

3.1 The Phase Model

Despite the well-established significance of phase in face identification tasks, modeling the phase angle poses several difficulties such as, the "wrapping around" property (it lies between $-\pi$ and π) and its sensitivity to distortions such as illuminations and expressions. This prompted us to choose an alternative representation of phase for modeling purposes.

To this end, we constructed the "phase-only" images by removing the magnitude component from the frequency spectrum of the images. The resultant spectrum thus represents only the image phase (and is of unit magnitude). Since magnitude does not play as active a role in face identification, this is expected not to affect the system. We then use the real and imaginary parts of these phase-only frequencies for modeling purposes. This is a simple and effective way of modeling phase, as it provides an adequate representation and at the same time does not suffer from most of the difficulties associated with direct phase modeling mentioned above.

Let $R_{s,t}^{k,j}$ and $I_{s,t}^{k,j}$ respectively denote the real and the imaginary part at the $(s,t)^{th}$ frequency of the phase spectrum of the jth image from the kth person, $s,t = 1,2,\ldots,100$, $k = 1,\ldots,65$, $j = 1,\ldots,21$. We will model $(R_{s,t}^{k,j}, I_{s,t}^{k,j})$, $j = 1,\ldots,21$ as a mixture of bivariate normal distributions. Notationally,

$$\begin{pmatrix} R_{s,t}^{k,j} \\ I_{s,t}^{k,j} \end{pmatrix} \sim N\left(\begin{pmatrix} \mu_{s,t}^k \\ \nu_{s,t}^k \end{pmatrix}, \begin{pmatrix} (\sigma_{s,t}^k)^2 & \rho_{s,t}^k \sigma_{s,t}^k \eta_{s,t}^k \\ \rho_{s,t}^k \sigma_{s,t}^k \eta_{s,t}^k & (\eta_{s,t}^k)^2 \end{pmatrix} \right), \qquad (3)$$

where μ and ν are respectively the frequency-wise means, σ^2 and η^2 the frequency-wise variances and ρ is the correlation coefficient between the real and the imaginary parts. We model only the low frequencies within a 50 × 50 grid around the origin of the spectral plane since only a few frequencies contain all the identifiability of any image ([10]). This succeeds in reducing the dimensionality of the problem to a considerable extent. We fit a model to every frequency and for each person.

In the the mixture model notation, for each frequency (s,t) and each person k, $\mathbf{Y_j} = (R^j, I^j)^T$. The density $f(\cdot)$ then represents bivariate Gaussian, and hence each mixture component is given by:

$$f(\mathbf{y_j}; \boldsymbol{\theta}_i) = \phi(\mathbf{y_j}; \boldsymbol{\mu}_i, \boldsymbol{\Sigma}_i), \quad \text{where}$$

$$\phi(\mathbf{y_j}; \boldsymbol{\mu}_i, \boldsymbol{\Sigma}_i) = (2\pi)^{-1}|\boldsymbol{\Sigma}_i|^{-\frac{1}{2}}\exp\{-\frac{1}{2}(\mathbf{y_j} - \boldsymbol{\mu}_i)^T \boldsymbol{\Sigma}_i^{-1}(\mathbf{y_j} - \boldsymbol{\mu}_i)\} \quad (4)$$

where ϕ denotes the bivariate Gaussian density with mean vector $\boldsymbol{\mu}_i$ and covariance matrix $\boldsymbol{\Sigma}_i$, $i = 1, \ldots, g$, their components being specified in eqn. (3). They form the unknown parameters of $\boldsymbol{\Psi}$, so that $\boldsymbol{\Psi} = (\pi_i, \mu_i, \nu_i, \sigma_i^2, \eta_i^2, \rho_i,$ $i = 1, \ldots, g$. The mixture model now has the form:

$$f(\mathbf{y_j}; \boldsymbol{\Psi}) = \sum_{i=1}^{g} \pi_i \phi(\mathbf{y_j}; \boldsymbol{\mu}_i, \boldsymbol{\Sigma}_i). \quad (5)$$

3.2 Classification Scheme

The ultimate goal of our approach is to use our model-based system to classify a new test image. This can be done with the help of a MAP (maximum a *posteriori*) estimate based on the posterior likelihood of the data. For a new observation $Y_j = (R^j, I^j)$ extracted from the phase spectrum of a test image, if $f(\mathbf{y_j}; \boldsymbol{\Psi})$ denotes its mixture density for each pixel (s,t) of each person k, the observed likelihood of the new image given under the model for person k is obtained by multiplying the GMM likelihood at each frequency (assuming independence among frequencies) as:

$$g(R, I|k) = \Pi_{\text{all freq.}} f(\mathbf{y_j}; \boldsymbol{\Psi}), \quad k = 1, \ldots, 65, \quad (6)$$

where $f(\cdot)$ is the GMM given by eqn. (5). The convention is to use log-likelihoods for computational convenience. The posterior likelihood of the observed data belonging to a specific person is then given by:

$$f(k|R, I) \propto f(R, I|k)p(k), \quad (7)$$

where $p(k)$ denotes the prior probability for each person which can be safely assumed to be uniform over all the possible people in the database. A particular image will then be assigned to class C if:

$$C = \arg\max_k f(k|L, P). \quad (8)$$

4 Classification Results

We started with a two-component mixture model ($g = 2$), the mixtures representing the illumination variations in the images of a person. A key step in the Bayesian estimation method consists of the specification of suitable priors for all the unknown parameters in Ψ. We chose our priors in the same way as was done in [1], which were conjugate in nature and simplified computations significantly.

Table 1 shows the classification results using different number of training images and different number of subjects. The latter helps to study the how performance changes as the database is gradually scaled up to include more and more people. The training set in each case (except the last) was randomly selected and the rest used for testing. This selection of training set in all the cases, is repeated 20 times (in order to remove selection bias) and the final errors are obtained by averaging over those from the 20 iterations. The results

Table 1. Error rates for GMM using different training and different number of people. The standard deviations are computed over the 20 repetitions in each case.

# of Training images	# of test images	# of Subjects	Error Rate	Standard Deviation
15	6	20	0.00%	0.00%
		65	1.25%	0.69%
10	11	20	0.00%	0.00%
		65	2.25%	1.12%
6	15	20	1.53%	1.41%
		65	9.67%	2.89%
Frontal	Shadows &	20	0.00%	-
	overall dark	65	12.83%	-

are indeed impressive even with a large number of people, especially when we compare this to results obtained using a PCA classifier for phase which yielded error rates close to those from random guessing ($> 90\%$). This shows that the GMM was able to capture the phase variation suitably. This is imperative since even the slightest loss of phase information can lead to drastic results as was in the case of the PCA models. Even when training only on images with frontal illumination, results are satisfactory which aptly established the robustness of our approach. However, we notice that an adequate number of training images are required to be able to estimate all the parameters of the mixture models in a reliable manner; in our case 10 is an optimal number of training images required for this method. The associated standard errors in each case also show that performance is not very sensitive to training set selection.

Often model fitting (and hence classification results) can be improved upon by increasing the number of mixture components in a GMM. The classification results with $g = 3$ and $g = 4$ were respectively 2.19 and 2.08 when using 10 training images and all the 65 people. Clearly, these results are not significantly better than those from using $g=2$ (hypothesis tests yielded p-values of nearly 1). Moreover, using more components increases the complexity of the model considerably in terms of computing time and power, by introducing many additional parameters. We thus conclude that a GMM with 2 components represents the best parsimonious model. This is further corroborated by rigorous statistical model selection methods like Bayesian Information Criterion or BIC ([3]) which suggested that $g = 2$ provides the best fit from the standpoint of accuracy and model complexity.

4.1 Verification

The problem of verification involves confirming whether a person's claimed identity is correct or incorrect. Verification of a test image requires only one matching operation as opposed to the N operations required to perform identification (for a database with N people). In our case, this amounts to computing the posterior likelihood of a test image only for the particular person which is the claimed identity. Then based on a certain chosen threshold, a decision is made as to whether the test image indeed belongs to that person or not.

Figure 2(a) shows the ROC curve obtained by plotting the false alarm rates (False Acceptance Rate (FAR) and False Rejection Rates (FRR)) with varying threshold on the posterior likelihood. We use the optimal GMM with $g = 2$ and 10 training images for all 65 people and an uniform threshold for all the people. Very impressive authentication results are achieved, in particular, the FAR never exceeds 3% for all the thresholds and the Equal Error Rate (EER) is approximately 0.3% at a threshold log-likelihood value of -1700. This is significantly better than the authentication EER value of 0.9% yielded by the MACE filter system ([14]) on the PIE database. As expected, verification is an easier task than identification involving fewer comparisons.

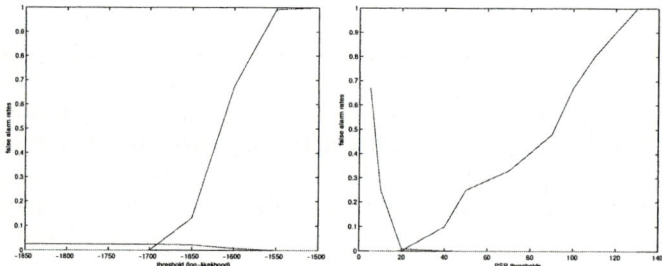

Fig. 2. ROC curve for authentication based on GMM (left) and MACE (right). The lower curve is the FAR in each case. The point of intersection of the FAR and the FRR curves gives the EER.

5 Discussion

This paper introduced a novel face identification and verification scheme based on phase and GMM. Although the importance of phase is well-known, this fact had not been utilized in building model-based classification techniques. This is partially because modeling phase requires an appropriate representation of its variability across different images of a person which is indeed a challenging task and our experiments show convincingly that our proposed models are able to handle it perfectly. Not only this, we have demonstrated that our approach is tolerant to illuminations; in fact, we believe that owing to its general framework, it should be easily be used to model any kind of distortion, such as, expression, noise, pose, by assigning different types of images to different components of mixture distributions. This proves the tremendous practical utility of this method for handling real life databases that are often subject to extraneous variations. Very good classification rates are obtained and the results scale up well with increasing number of individuals, an attractive property for any pattern recognition system. Moreover, the model also yields a very efficient verification tool which extends its domain of application to authentication at places like the airport, casinos, banks and other security-enabled places. In conclusion, both GMM and phase have enormous potential in computer vision, and harnessing this combined strength has indeed proved to be a grand success.

Our immediate future direction of work consists of assessing the performance of our GMM model on databases with expression and pose variations. One natural extension of this model for our present database will be toward classifying the illumination level in an image. Knowing this, one can easily remove this illumination effect using a normalization procedure and the resultant reconstructed images with no or reduced illumination will pose less of a threat to the ability of many existing face identification systems.

References

1. Bensmail, H., Celeux, G., Raftery, A., and Robert, C.P. Inference in model-based cluster analysis. *Statistics and Computing*, 7:1–10, 1997.
2. Gelfand, A.E., Hills, S.E., Racine-Poon, A., and Smith,A.F.M. Illustration of bayesian inference in normal data models using gibbs sampling. *Journal of the American Statistical Association*, 85(412):972–985, 1990.
3. Gelman, A., Carlin, J.B., Stern, H.S., and Rubin, D.B. *Bayesian Data Analysis*. Chapman and Hall, 1995.
4. Havran, C., Hupet, L., Czyz, J., Lee, J., Vandendorpe, L., and Verleysen, M. Independent component analysis for face authentication. *KES 2002 proceedings - Knowledge-Based Intelligent Information and Engineering Systems, Crema (Italy)*, 2002.
5. Hayes, M.H. The reconstruction of a multidimensional sequence from the phase or magnitude of its fourier transform. *ASSP*, 30(2):140–154, 1982.
6. Jonsson, K., Kittler, J., Li, Y.P., and Matas, J. (1999). Support vector machines for face authentication. *Proceedings of BMVC99*, 1999.

7. Li, Y., Kittler, J., and Matas, J. Effective implementation of Linear Discriminant Analysis for face recognition and verification. In *8th International Conference on Computer Analysis and Patterns*, Berlin, 1999.
8. Liu, C., Zhu, S.C., and Shum, H.Y. Learning inhomogeneous gibbs model of faces by minimax entropy. In *The IEEE International Conference on Computer Vision (ICCV)*, pages 281–287, 2001.
9. McLachlan, G. and Peel, D. *Finite Mixture Models*. John Wiley and Sons, 2000.
10. Oppenheim, A.V. and Schafer, R.W. *Discrete-time Signal Processing*. Prentice Hall, NJ, 1989.
11. Palanivel, S., Venkatesh, B.S., and Yegnanarayana, B. Real time face authentication system using autoassociative neutral network models. *In Proceedings of IEEE International Conference on Multimedia and Expo, Baltimore.*, 2003.
12. Savvides, M. and Kumar, B.V.K. Eigenphases vs.eigenfaces. *ICPR*, 2004.
13. Savvides, M., Kumar, B.V.K., and Khosla, P.K. Corefaces - robust shift invariant PCA based correlation filter for illumination tolerant face recognition. *CVPR*, 2004.
14. Savvides, M., Vijaya Kumar, B.V.K., and Khosla, P. Face verification using correlation filters. In *3rd IEEE Automatic Identification Advanced Technologies*, pages 56–61, Tarrytown, NY, 2002.
15. Sim, T., Baker, S., and Bsat, M. The CMU pose, illumination, and expression (PIE) database. In *Proceedings of the 5th International Conference on Automatic Face and Gesture Recognition*, 2002.
16. Turk, M.A. and Pentland, A.P. Face recognition using eigenfaces. *In Proceedings of CVPR*, 1991.
17. Voth, D. In the news: face recognition technology. IEEE magazine on intelligent systems, May-June 2003. Vol. 18, Issue 3, pp. 4-7.
18. Yuille, A. (1991). Deformable templates for face recognition. *Journal of Cognitive Neuroscience*, 3(1), 1991.
19. Zhu, S., Wu, Y., and Mumford, D. Minimax entropy principle and its application to texture modeling. *Neural Computation*, 9(8), 1997.

Belief Theory Applied to Facial Expressions Classification

Z. Hammal, A. Caplier, and M. Rombaut

Laboratory of Images and Signals,
46 Avenue Felix Viallet, Grenoble, France
zakia_hammal@yahoo.fr, firstname.name@lis.inpg.fr

Abstract. A novel and efficient approach to facial expression classification based on the belief theory and data fusion is presented and discussed. The considered expressions correspond to three (*joy, surprise, disgust*) of the six universal emotions as well as the *neutral* expression. A robust contour segmentation technique is used to generate an expression skeleton with facial permanent features (mouth, eyes and eyebrows). This skeleton is used to determine the facial features deformations occurring when an expression is present on the face defining a set of characteristic distances. In order to be able to recognize "pure" as well as "mixtures" of facial expressions, a belief-theory based fusion process is proposed. The performances and the limits of the proposed recognition method are highlighted thanks to the analysis of a great number of results on three different test databases: the Hammal-Caplier database, the Cohn-Kanade database and the Cottrel database. Preliminary results demonstrate the interest of the proposed approach, as well as its ability to recognize non separable facial expressions.

1 Introduction

In recent years, the user interfaces for computer systems have been producing a growing interest. The key idea for those systems is to make the communication/ interaction with machines more intuitive using the human behavior, especially facial expressions, like in a face-to-face human interaction.

Facial expression classification methods can be divided into three categories: statistical methods [1] that use characteristic points or characteristic blocks in the face; template based methods [2] using models of facial features or models of facial motion and rule-based methods [3].

In this paper, we propose a new method for facial expressions classification. Firstly, this method allows the classification of different expressive states like "pure" expression or mixture of expressions. Considering that "binary" or "pure" facial expressions are rarely produced (people show a mixture of facial expressions), the classification of any facial expression into a single emotion category is not realistic. Secondly the proposed method can deal with different expressions intensities and allows to determine the "*unknown*" expressions corresponding to all facial deformations that can not be categorized into one of the predefined facial expressions. Here, due to the difficulty for non actor to simulate all the six universal emotions, we only consider the following expressions: *joy, disgust, surprise, neutral* and, additionally, the *unknown* expression. The originality of our work consists in supposing that all information necessary to the recognition of a given facial expression is included in the deformations of some facial permanent features (eyes, mouth and eyebrows) and to propose a fusion architecture based on the belief theory. This approach is proved to be very well suited to the problem of facial expression classification because it is possible to deal with possible imprecise data (which could be the case with data coming from a video based segmentation algorithm), and it is possible take into account intrinsic doubt of emotion in the recognition process.

2 Facial Expressions Characterisation

Eyes, lips and brows contours are automatically extracted by using the algorithms described in [4, 5]. The considered approaches use parametric models, which allows to obtain very realistic contours of eyes, eyebrows and mouth (Fig. 1.a). The segmentation leads to the skeleton of an expression (Fig. 1.b).

Five distances are defined on these skeletons: D_1: eye opening, D_2: distance between the interior corner of the eye and the interior corner of the eyebrow, D_3: mouth opening in width, D_4: mouth opening in height, D_5: distance between each corner of the mouth and the external corner of the corresponding eye (Fig. 1.b).

In order to cope with doubt between several expressions, a post processing stage based on the analysis of transient wrinkles in the nasal root and based on the analysis of the mouth shape is added. Since these two features are not present in all the expressions and in order to use the same information for the classification system whatever the considered expression, they are not directly used for the transferable belief model but to solve the doubt between two expressions.

The presence or absence of wrinkles in the nasal root (Fig. 1.c) is detected by using a Canny edge detector. We compare the number of detected edge points in a frame with a *neutral* expression (i.e. without any wrinkles in the nasal root) with the number of edge points in the current frame. If there is almost twice more edge points in the nasal root of the current frame than in the nasal root of the frame with the *neutral* expression, the presence of transient wrinkles is validated.

In addition to wrinkles information, mouth shape can be used (Fig. 1.d, 1.e). According to the expression, the ratio between length and width of the mouth is larger or smaller than its corresponding value for the *neutral* expression.

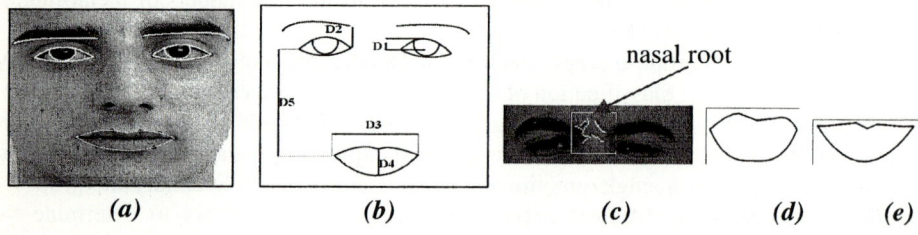

(a)   *(b)*   *(c)*   *(d)*   *(e)*

Fig. 1. (a) facial features segmentation; (b) facial skeleton and distances D_i, (c) wrinkles in the nasal root, examples of mouth shapes in case of : (d) *joy*, (e) *disgust*.

We suppose that facial features deformations characterized by the five distances defined on Fig. 1.b, mouth shape information and transient wrinkles information are sufficient to recognize each of the four considered expressions. This particular assumption has been validated by a rate of 60% of good recognition obtained by a psycho-experimental test, where 60 judge subjects (30 males and 30 females) had to recognize an expression by only viewing the facial skeletons.

3 Belief Theory

Initially introduced by Dempster, the belief theory was taken again by Shafer [6]. Based on this work, Smets has enriched this theory and called it TBM (Transferable Belief Model) [7]. This theory can be seen as a generalization of the theory of probabilities. It requires the definition of a set Ω made up of N exclusive and exhaustive assumptions E_i.

Considering this theory, the reasoning relates to the framework of understanding 2^Ω which is the whole set of 2^N subsets A of Ω. For each element A of 2^Ω, we associate an elementary piece of evidence $m(A)$ which indicates all confidence that one can have in this proposal without favouring any class. The function m is defined by:

$$m: \quad 2^\Omega \to [0,1] \tag{1}$$
$$A \mapsto m(A)$$

With:
$$\sum_{A \subseteq \Omega} m(A)$$

In our application, the assumptions E_i correspond to the four facial expressions : *joy* (E_1), *surprise* (E_2), *disgust* (E_3), *neutral* (E_4); 2^Ω corresponds to the subsets of expressions or combination of expressions $\{E_1, E_2, E_3, ..., E_1 E_2, E_2 E_3, ...\}$ and A is one of its element.

3.1 Definition of the Symbolic States Associated to the Measures

The analysis of the numerical values of all the distances D_i for the four expressions contained in the expertise database [8] shows that, for each of the four facial expressions, each D_i can be either higher, either lower or equal to its corresponding distance for the *neutral* expression. We associate to each distance D_i one of the three possible symbolic states:

- The *neutral* state S: if its current value is close to its value for the *neutral* expression;
- The C^+ state: if its current value is significantly higher than its value for the *neutral* expression;
- The C^- state: if its current value is significantly lower than its value for the *neutral* expression.

This yields to three symbolic states $\{C^+, C^-, S\}$ to be identified for each distance D_i for all the expressions.

The analysis of the evolution of the D_i curves on the frames of an expertise database shows that a similar evolution can be associated to each distance D_i for a given emotion whatever the subject.

3.2 Modeling

We are concerned with the computation of the state to be associated to each distance D_i and to its piece of evidence. We define a basic belief assignment (BBA) by:

$$m_{Di} : \quad 2^{\Omega'} \to [0,1] \qquad (2)$$

With $\Omega' = \{C^+, C^-, S\}$, $2^{\Omega'} = \{C^+, C^- B \to m_{Di}(B), S, SC^+, SC^-\}$ (the remaining states C^+SC^- and C^+C^- are considered impossible), where $S \cup C^+$ (noted SC^+) states the doubt between S and C^+, $S \cup C^-$ (noted SC^-) states the doubt between S and C^- and $m_{Di}(B)$ is the piece of evidence (PE) of each state B. A numerical/symbolic conversion is carried out, which associates one of the symbols of $2^{\Omega'}$ to each value of Di. To carry out this conversion, we define a model for each distance using the states of $2^{\Omega'}$ (Fig. 2).

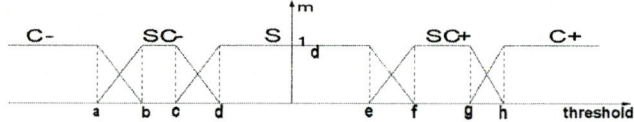

Fig. 2. Model

m is the PE associated to each possible state in $2^{\Omega'}$ and the thresholds *(a... h)* are the limit values of D_i corresponding to each state or subset of states.

3.3 Thresholds for the States (C^+, C^-, S, SC^+, SC^-)

For each distance D_i, the threshold **h** (resp. **a**) of the state C^+ (resp. C^-) corresponds to the average of the maximum (resp. minimal) values of D_i for all the subjects and all the expressions of the expertise database. The thresholds **d** and **e** of the state S are defined in the same way.

The states SC^+ and SC^- are associated to the states of doubt when the value of D_i is higher than the value corresponding to the *neutral* state S but is not high enough to be in the state C^+ nor small enough to be in the state C^-.

The median of the maximum values of each distance for all the subjects and all the expressions of the expertise database is computed. The thresholds **f**, **b** (resp. **c**, **g**) of the intermediate states are defined by mean+median (resp. mean-median) of each state (C^+, C^-, S).

4 Recognition of Expressions

4.1 Analysis

The analysis of the states for the five distances associated to each of the four expressions *(joy, surprise, disgust* and *neutral)* allows us to exhibit a specific combination of these states for each expression. Table 1 left shows the resulting combinations of states. For example, in case of *joy* (E_1), the mouth is opening (C^+ state for D_3 and D_4), the corners of the mouth are going back toward the tears (C^- state for D_5) and the eyebrows are slackened (S state for D_2). The distance between the interior corner of the eye and the interior corner of the eyebrow decreases (C^- state for D_2) and the eyes become slightly closed (C^- state for D_1).

In some cases, two different states are possible for a given distance (see D_2 for *joy* for example). This could produce a total doubt between two expressions as a result of the classification process. For example, the classifier is not always able to distinguish *disgust* and *joy* because both expressions could be described by the same combination of states in some cases.

The proposed combinations of symbolic states associated to each D_i for the four expressions (*joy, surprise, disgust and neutral*) are compared to the MPEG-4 description of the deformations of facial features for such expressions [9]. As a result, the proposed combinations are compliant with MPEG-4 description and give even some extensions.

The expression E_5 is added as the *unknown* expression or class of reject. It represents all the expressions which do not correspond to any of the descriptions of Table1 left.

Table 1. left: Theoretical table of D_i states for each expression; right: example of combination of PEs of two distances. $\emptyset$ is the empty set.

	D_1	D_2	D_3	D_4	D_5	D_1/D_2	E_1	E_2	$E_1 \cup E_3$
Joy E_1	C^-	S/C^-	C^+	C^+	C^-	$E_2 \cup E_3$	$\emptyset$	E_2	E_3
Surprise E_2	C^+	C^+	C^-	C^+	C^+	E_1	E_1	$\emptyset$	E_1
Disgust E_3	C^-	C^-	S/C^+	C^+	S/C^-	E_2	$\emptyset$	E_2	$\emptyset$
Neutral E_4	S	S	S	S	S				

4.2 Combination and Decision

We have several sources of information (D_i) to which we associate PEs. Our goal is to obtain a PE which takes into account all the available information. The BBA is obtained using the rule of conjunctive combination or orthogonal sum. In the case of two distances D_1 and D_2, the orthogonal sum is defined in the following way:

$$m = m_{D_1} \oplus m_{D_2} \qquad (3)$$

$$m(A) = \sum_{B \cap C = A} m_{D1}(B) m_{D2}(C)$$

where A, B and C are expressions or subsets of expressions. This leads to have propositions whose number of elements are lower than the initial ones and to associate them a piece of evidence. The final PE is thus more accurate. In a more explicit way, if one takes two basic belief assignments:

$m_{D1}(E_1 \cup E_3)$ $m_{D1}(E_1)$ $m_{D1}(E_2)$,
$m_{D2}(E_1)$ $m_{D2}(E_2)$ $m_{D2}(E_1 \cup E_2)$,
their combination gives the results of Table 1 right.

The piece of evidence of each expression by the combination of results of the two distances is calculated by:

$m_{D12}(E_1) = m_{D1}(E_1) \cdot m_{D2}(E_1) + m_{D1}(E_1) \, m_{D2}(E_1 \cup E_3)$.
$m_{D12}(E_2) = m_{D1}(E_2 \cup E_3) \cdot m_{D2}(E_2) + m_{D1}(E_2) \cdot m_{D2}(E_2)$.
$m_{D12}(E_3) = m_{D1}(E_2 \cup E_3) \cdot m_{D2}(E_1 \cup E_3)$.
$m_{D12}(\emptyset) = m_{D1}(E_2 \cup E_3) \cdot m_{D2}(E_1) + m_{D1}(E_1) \cdot m_{D2}(E_2) + m_{D1}(E_2) \cdot m_{D2}(E_1) + m_{D1}(E_2) \cdot m_{D2}(E_1 \cup E_3)$.

However, conflicts can appear in the case of incoherence sources noted $\emptyset$. Considering the theoretical context of the presented application, the conflict corresponds to a configuration of distance states which does not appear in Table 1 left. This is due to the fact that Ω is not exhaustive. The added expression *unknown* or class of reject E_5 includes all these conflict states (Table 1 right).

The decision is the ultimate step of the classification process. We have to choose between various assumptions E_i and their possible combinations. Making a choice means taking a risk, except if the result of the combination is perfectly reliable: $m(E_i)=1$. Here the accepted proposal is the one with maximum value of PE.

5 Experimental Results

The performances of the classification system are evaluated for the four expressions (*joy, surprise, disgust, neutral*). For the expertise step, 1170 frames from the Hammal-Caplier database (13 subjects and 4 expressions) have been considered (Fig. 3). All the frames of our expertise database are segmented and the five distances defined on Fig. 1.b are computed and used in order to define the thresholds of §3.3 and to establish Table 1 left.

In order to evaluate the robustness to different variations (gender, ethnicity, difference of expressions…), the system is tested on three test databases: the last part of our database (630 frames for 7 subjects and 4 expressions), the Cohn-Kanade database (122 frames, 4 expressions) [10] and the Cottrel database (24 frames, 4 expressions) [11]. In the two last databases we only have two images for each expression: the *neutral* state and the caricatured expression itself.

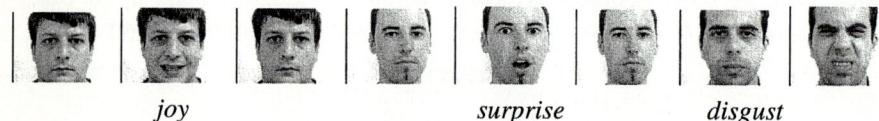

joy   surprise   disgust

Fig. 3. Examples of the Hammal-Caplier database. Each record starts and finishes by a neutral state. The sequences have been acquired during 5 seconds at 25 images/second.

Table 2 presents the classification rates for the frames of our test database. The right expressions are given in column and the expressions recognized by the system correspond to the lines. Expressions E_1 (*joy*) and E_4 (*neutral*) yield good classification rates. On the contrary, the classification rate E_3 (*disgust*) is lower. This is due to individual variability (Fig. 4.a) and to the difficulty for a non actor to simulate this expression (Fig. 4.b). For E_1, there is a high rate of total doubt between E_1 and E_3: the system is sure that it is one of the two expressions but is not able to know which one. This has to be related to the definition of Table 1 left with two possible different states for a given distance. In our database, the *unknown* state often appears for intermediate frames where the person is neither in a *neutral* state, nor in a particular expression (Fig. 4.c).

In order to be able to choose between *joy* and *disgust* in case of doubt, we add a post-processing step which takes into account information about transient features and mouth shape (§2). Nasal root wrinkles (Fig. 1.c) are characteristic for *disgust*. This is used to solve the problem of doubt between *joy* and *disgust*. In the case of absence of transient features, we use the ratio between length and width of the mouth (Fig. 1.d, 1.e). Our analysis shows that this ratio is larger than its value for the *neutral* expression in the case of *joy* and lower in the case of *disgust*. With the proposed post-processing step to make a distinction between *joy* and *disgust* in case of doubt, the recognition rate for E_1 (*joy*) increases by 15% and $E_1 \cup E_3$ (*joy-disgust*) decreases by 17% (2% of false detection of *disgust*). We increase by 19% for E_3 (*disgust*) and $E_1 \cup E_3$ (*joy-disgust*) decreases by 11% (5% of false detection of *joy*).

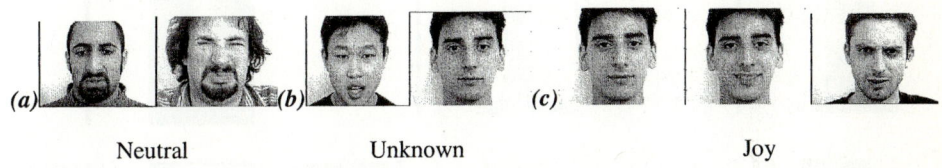

(a)   (b)   (c)

Neutral   Unknown   Joy

Fig. 4. Examples of *disgust* expressions. (a): individual variability; (b): poor simulations; (c): example of *unknown* state: 3 consecutive frames from *neutral* to *joy* during a sequence of a simulated *joy*.

Given the fact that the state of doubt *joy-disgust* is related to the rules defined in the Table1 left, it is not due to classification errors of the proposed system. It is thus possible to consider them as a good classification and to associate them to the corresponding expression which allows us to add their respecting rates leading to the results of the last row of Table 2 and Table 3.

Table 3 (on the left of E_4 column) presents the results obtained on the Cohn-Kanade database. 30 frames have been chosen for *joy*, 25 for *surprise* and 17 for *disgust*. The classification rates for this database are comparable with those of Table 2. In Table 3 right (on the right of E_4 column) are presented the classification rates obtained on the Cottrel database. In the same way, associating the expression and the corresponding mixture of expressions, the system gives good classification rates.

Table 2. Classification rates on the Hammal-Caplier database

Syst\Exp	E_1	E_2	E_3	E_4
E_1 joy	76.36%	0	9.48	3%
E_2 surprise	0	84.44%	0	0
E_3 disgust	0	0	43.10%	2%
$E_1 \cup E_3$	10.90%	0	8.62%	0
E_4 neutral	6.66%	0.78%	15.51%	88%
E_5 unknown	6.06%	11.8%	12.06%	7%
Total	**87.26%**	**84.44%**	**51.72%**	**88%**

Table 3. Classification rates: on the left of E_4, classification rates for the Cohn-Kanade database, on the right of E_4, classification rates for the Cottrel database. The column E_4 is the same for both databases.

Syst\Exp	E_1	E_2	E_3	E_4	E_1	E_2	E_3
E_1joy	64.51%	0	0	0	62.50	0	0
E_2surprise	0	100%	0	0	0	100%	0
E_3disgust	0	0	52.94	0	0	0	75%
$E_1 \cup E_3$	32.25%	0	47.05	0	37.50	0	0
E_4neutral	0	0	0	100%	0	0	0
E_5unknonw	3.22%	0	0	0	0	0	25%
Total	96.76%	100%	99.99	100%	100%	100%	75%

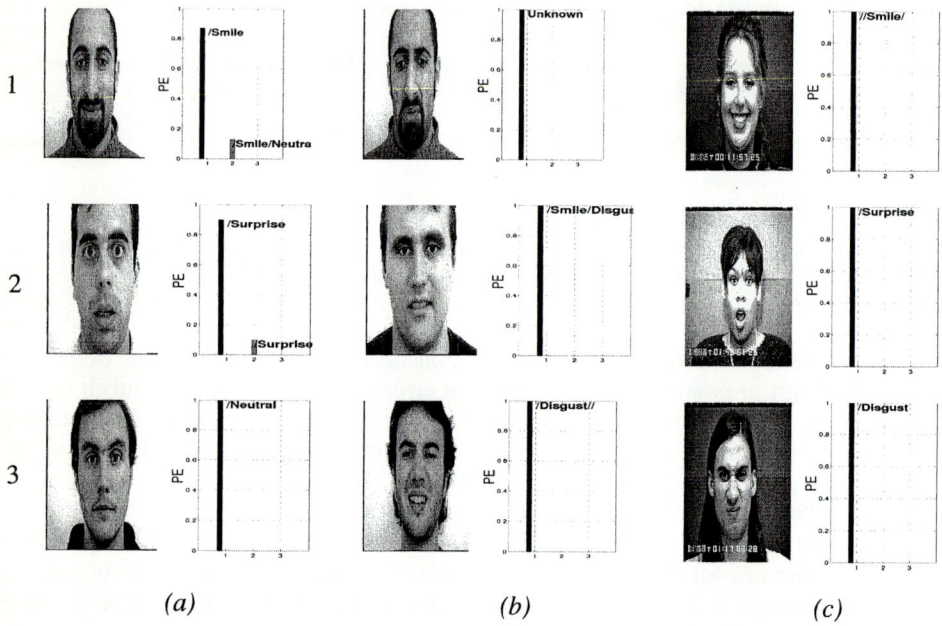

(a) (b) (c)

Fig. 5. Examples of expressions classification: first and second columns, images of Hammal-Caplier database, third column, images from Cohn-Kanade database. The bar graph presents the recognized expression and its associated piece of evidence.

Fig. 5 shows some examples of classification of the four facial expressions. We observe very good results for the *neutral* and the *apex* states of each facial expression (Fig. 5 a.3, b.3, c). The proposed method is able to recognize different intensities of one expression (Fig. 5 a.1, a.2), to recognize the intermediate state between two expressions as *unknown* (*neutral-disgust*) expression (Fig. 5 b.1) and to recognize the mixed expressions (Fig. 5 b.2).

6 Conclusion

We presented a novel method for classification of facial expressions based on the analysis of characteristic distances computed on facial skeletons of expression. The belief theory formalism used in the presented rule-based method is proved to be well suited to the problem of facial expression classification. It can deal with the mixtures of expressions and allows to recognize the *unknown* expressions. To improve these results, we can increase the number and the quality of measurements, by taking into account the explicit shape of the facial features contours and by taking into account the temporal evolution of the measurements.

References

1. Shinza, Y., Saito, Y., Kenmochi, Y., Kotani, K.: Facial Expression Analysis by Integrating Information of Feature-Point Positions and Gray Levels of Facial Images. IEEE Proc. ICIP, Vancover Canada (2000).
2. Tian, Y., Kanade, T., Cohn, J.: Recognition Actions Units for Facial Expression Analysis". IEEE Trans. PAMI, Vol. 23. N. 2. (2001) 97–115.
3. Pantic, M., Rothkrantz, L.J.M.: Expert System for Automatic Analysis of Facial Expressions. ELSIVIER Trans. IVC, Vol. 18. (2000) 881–905.
4. Eveno, N., Caplier, A., Coulon, P.Y.: Automatic and Accurate Lip Tracking. IEEE Trans. CSVT, Vol. 14. (2004) 706–715.
5. Hammal, Z., Caplier, A.: Eye and Eyebrow Parametric Models for Automatic Segmentation. IEEE Proc. SSIAI, Lake Tahoe Nevada (2004).
6. Shafer, G.: A Mathematical Theory of Evidence. Princeton University Press, Princeton and London (1976).
7. Smets, PH.: Data Fusion in the Transferable Belief Model. Proc. ISIF, Paris France (2000) 21–33.
8. http://www.lis.inpg.fr/pages_perso/hammal/index.htm.
9. Malciu, M., Preteux, F.: MPEG-4 Compliant Tracking of Facial Features in Video Sequences. Proc. EUROIMAGE, ICAV3D, Greece (2001) 108–111.
10. http://www-2.cs.cmu.edu/~face.
11. Dailey, M., Cottrell, G.W., Reilly, J.: California Facial Expressions, CAFE, unpublished digital images, Computer Science and Engineering Department, UCSD (2001).

Face Recognition Using Uncorrelated, Weighted Linear Discriminant Analysis

Yixiong Liang, Weiguo Gong, Yingjun Pan, and Weihong Li

Key Lab of Optoelectronic Technology & Systems of Education Ministry of China,
Chongqing University, Chongqing 400044, China
{yxliang, wggong, pyj, weihongli}@cqu.edu.cn

Abstract. In this paper, we propose an uncorrelated, weighted LDA (UWLDA) technique for face recognition. The UWLDA extends the uncorrelated LDA (ULDA) technique by integrating the weighted pairwise Fisher criterion and nullspace LDA (NLDA), while retaining all merits of ULDA. Experiments compare the proposed algorithm to other face recognition methods that employ linear dimensionality reduction such as Eigenfaces, Fisherfaces, DLDA and NLDA on the AR face database. The results demonstrate the efficiency and superiority of our method.

1 Introduction

Face recognition has a wide range of applications, such as face-based video indexing and browsing engines, biometric identity authentication, human-computer interaction, and multimedia monitorring/surveillance. Within the last decades, numerous novel FR algorithms have been proposed [1]. A central issue to this approaches is the feature exaction. The most well-known technique for linear feature extraction is the linear discriminant analysis (LDA). Its basic idea is to seek an optimal set of discriminant vectors $\mathbf{W} = [\mathbf{w}_1, \ldots, \mathbf{w}_l]$ by maximizing the Fisher criterion

$$J_F(\mathbf{W}) = tr[(\mathbf{W}^T \mathbf{S}_w \mathbf{W})^{-1}(\mathbf{W}^T \mathbf{S}_b \mathbf{W})] \ , \tag{1}$$

where, $\mathbf{S}_b = \sum_{i=1}^{c} p_i (\mathbf{m}_i - \mathbf{m})(\mathbf{m}_i - \mathbf{m})^T$ and $\mathbf{S}_w = \sum_{i=1}^{c} p_i \mathbf{S}_i$ are the between- and within-class scatter matrices, respectively; $\mathbf{m}$ is the mean of all samples and $\mathbf{m}_i$ is the mean of class i with prior probability p_i; $\mathbf{S}_i$ is the covariance matrices of class i. Uncorrelated features are usually desirable in pattern recognition because an uncorrelated feature set is likely to contain more discriminatory information than a correlated one. Recently, Jin et al. [2] proposed the uncorrelated LDA technique (ULDA), which tries to find the optimal discriminant vectors by maximizing the Fisher criterion under the conjugated orthogonal constrains: $\mathbf{w}_j^T \mathbf{S}_t \mathbf{w}_i = 0, (i \neq j)$, where $\mathbf{S}_t = \sum_{i=1}^{n} (\mathbf{x}_i - \mathbf{m})(\mathbf{x}_i - \mathbf{m})^T$ denotes total scatter matrix. Therefore, ULDA can extract a set of statistically uncorrelated discriminant features with better discriminant power as shown experimentally in Ref. [2].

However, the ULDA technique still has some deficiencies as follows: first, it still suffers from the so-called *small sample size problem* (SSSP) which is often encountered in face recognition; second, the Fisher criterion that ULDA maximized isn't optimal for a c-class ($c > 2$) classification problem in that it overemphasizes the larger distance between classes and causes large overlaps of neighboring classes. In this paper, we propose an uncorrelated, weighted linear LDA (UWLDA) technique to solve the above problems. The reminder of this paper is organized as follows. The related work on LDA is described in section 2. Then our UWLDA is presented in section 3. Experiments are reported in section 4 and finally section 5 concludes this paper.

2 Related Work

2.1 ULDA

Suppose that $\mathbf{S}_b$ is a positive semi-definite matrix and $\mathbf{S}_w$ is a positive definite matrix. The first ULDA discriminant vector, denoted by $\mathbf{w}_1$, is calculated as the first eigenvector corresponding to the maximal eigenvalue of the generalized eigenequation $\mathbf{S}_b\mathbf{w} = \lambda\mathbf{S}_w\mathbf{w}$. Suppose that r ULDA discriminant vectors $\mathbf{W}_r = [\mathbf{w}_1, \ldots, \mathbf{w}_r]$ have been obtained. Then the $(r+1)$th discriminant vector $\mathbf{w}_{r+1}$ can be taken as the eigenvector corresponding to maximum eigenvalues of the generalized eigenequation: $\mathbf{MS}_b\mathbf{w} = \lambda\mathbf{S}_w\mathbf{w}$, where $\mathbf{M} = \mathbf{I} - \mathbf{S}_t\mathbf{W}_r(\mathbf{W}_r^T\mathbf{S}_t\mathbf{S}_w^{-1}\mathbf{S}_t\mathbf{W}_r)^{-1}\mathbf{W}_r^T\mathbf{S}_t\mathbf{S}_w^{-1}$.

2.2 NLDA

In many practical face recognition tasks, there are not enough samples to make $\mathbf{S}_w$ nonsingular and then both LDA and ULDA suffer from the well-known SSSP which arises whenever the number of available samples is smaller than the dimensionality of the samples [3]. The traditional solutions to this problem is to project all samples onto a subspace, as it was done for example in Fisherfaces [4], where the resulting within-class scatter matrix is no longer singular. However, Chen et al. [3] proved that the nullspace of $\mathbf{S}_w$, denoted by $\mathcal{N}(\mathbf{S}_w)$, contains the most discriminant information when a SSSP takes place. Based this finding, they proposed an enhanced LDA that we refer to as NLDA, to extract the most discriminant information for recognition. Intrinsically, NLDA tries to find a transform $\mathbf{W}$ who satisfies

$$\mathbf{W}^T\mathbf{S}_w\mathbf{W} = 0, \mathbf{W}^T\mathbf{S}_b\mathbf{W} = \mathbf{\Lambda} \ . \tag{2}$$

2.3 WLDA

In Fisher criterion, as discussed in [5] and [6], all class pairs have the same weights irrespective of their separability in the original space and the resulting transformation will preserve the distances of already well-separated classes, causing a large overlap of neighboring classes. Two similarly motivated solutions to this problem have been proposed: weighted pairwise Fisher criteria [5] and fractional-step LDA [6]. Although quite effective [6], the fractional-step LDA is iterative and very time-consuming. The other solution, weighted pairwise Fisher criteria, is more easily to implement and we refer the resulting algorithm as weighted LDA or WLDA. In WLDA, the between-class scatter matrix $\mathbf{S}_b$ in Fisher criterion is replaced by the following weighted between-class scatter matrix

$$\hat{\mathbf{S}}_b = \sum_{i=1}^{c-1} \sum_{j=i+1}^{c} p_i p_j w(d_{ij}) (\mathbf{m}_i - \mathbf{m}_j)(\mathbf{m}_i - \mathbf{m}_j)^T , \qquad (3)$$

where $w(d_{ij}) = \frac{1}{2d_{ij}^2} erf(\frac{d_{ij}}{2\sqrt{2}})$ is the weighting function that depends on the Mahanalobis distance d_{ij} between the classes i and j.

3 UWLDA

From the discussion in the previous section, it would certainly be desirable to exploit the benefits of ULDA, NLDA and WLDA. There are, however, a potential contradiction: the primary motivation for NLDA is the preservation of the $\mathcal{N}(\mathbf{S}_w)$, while in $\mathcal{N}(\mathbf{S}_w)$ both ULDA and WLDA will break down. In the remainder of this paper, we intend to solve this problem and propose a new combining algorithm. To begin, as suggested in Ref. [7], we project all samples onto the subspace Ω adopted in NLDA where the resulting between-class scatter matrix $\bar{\mathbf{S}}_b$ is full rank while the resulting within-class scatter matrix $\bar{\mathbf{S}}_w$ is zero. This subspace can be easily determined by removing the nullspace of $\mathbf{S}_t$ first and then extracting the nullspace of the intermediate within-scatter matrix. Notice that in Ω the Mahanalobis distance d_{ij} between the classes i and j is undefined and then the calculation of weighted between-class scatter matrix $\hat{\mathbf{S}}_b$ is intractable. As our solutions to this question, we first alter d_{ij} so that it is equal to Euclidean distance because in Ω the distribution of each class is exactly a point and the similarity between classes can be easily measured by Euclidean distance. Then we simply set the weighting function

$$w(d_{ij}) = (d_{ij})^{-k}, \ k > 0 , \qquad (4)$$

where k is the parameter. The rationale behind this is that classes which are closer together are more likely to have more confusion and should therefore be more heavily weighted.

Now we turn our attention to combine the WLDA and ULDA in the subspace Ω. Notice that in Ω the Fisher criterion or weighted pairwise Fisher criterion is not longer in effect for giving an arbitrary vector $\mathbf{w} \in \Omega$, the Fisher criterion will definitely reach infinite. Motivated by NLDA and WLDA, we introduce a new criterion

$$J(\mathbf{w}) = \mathbf{w}^T \hat{\mathbf{S}}_b \mathbf{w}, \ \mathbf{w} \in \Omega . \qquad (5)$$

Moreover, as the total scatter matrix in Ω is definitely equal to $\bar{\mathbf{S}}_b$, then the conjugated orthogonal constraint is equal to

$$\mathbf{w}_j^T \bar{\mathbf{S}}_b \mathbf{w}_i = 0 \ (i \neq j) . \qquad (6)$$

By maximizing (5) under the constrain (6), we derive a novel UWLDA technique. Likewise, in UWLDA the first optimal discriminant vector $\mathbf{w}_1$ is the eigenvector corresponding to the largest eigenvalues of $\hat{\mathbf{S}}_b$. In order to obtain the other directions, we introduce the following theorem.

Theorem 1. *The $(r+1)$th desired optimal discriminant vector $\mathbf{w}_{r+1}$ is the eigenvector corresponding to maximum eigenvalues of the following eigenequation:*

$$\mathbf{M}\hat{\mathbf{S}}_b \mathbf{w} = \lambda \mathbf{w} , \qquad (7)$$

where

$$\mathbf{M} = \mathbf{I} - \bar{\mathbf{S}}_b \mathbf{W}_r (\mathbf{W}_r^T \bar{\mathbf{S}}_b \bar{\mathbf{S}}_b \mathbf{W}_r)^{-1} \mathbf{W}_r^T \bar{\mathbf{S}}_b , \qquad (8)$$

$$\mathbf{W}_r = [\mathbf{w}_1, \cdots, \mathbf{w}_r] . \qquad (9)$$

Proof. It is noted that besides the constraints (6), $\mathbf{w}_{r+1}$ should be normalized, i.e.

$$\mathbf{w}_{r+1}^T \mathbf{w}_{r+1} = 1 . \qquad (10)$$

Therefore, the Lagrange function can be expressed as

$$L(\mathbf{w}_{r+1}) = \mathbf{w}_{r+1}^T \hat{\mathbf{S}}_b \mathbf{w}_{r+1} - \lambda(\mathbf{w}_{r+1}^T \mathbf{w}_{r+1} - 1) - \mathbf{w}_{r+1}^T \bar{\mathbf{S}}_b \mathbf{W}_r \mathbf{U} , \qquad (11)$$

where $\mathbf{U} = [u_1, \cdots, u_r]^T$. Set the derivative of $L(\mathbf{w}_{r+1})$ with respect to $\mathbf{w}_{r+1}$ equal to zero, namely

$$2\hat{\mathbf{S}}_b \mathbf{w}_{r+1} - 2\lambda \mathbf{w}_{r+1} - \bar{\mathbf{S}}_b \mathbf{W}_r \mathbf{U} = 0 . \qquad (12)$$

Multiplying the left-hand side of the above equation by $\mathbf{W}_r^T \bar{\mathbf{S}}_b$, we obtain

$$2\mathbf{W}_r^T \bar{\mathbf{S}}_b \hat{\mathbf{S}}_b \mathbf{w}_{r+1} - \mathbf{W}_r^T \bar{\mathbf{S}}_b \bar{\mathbf{S}}_b \mathbf{W}_r^T \mathbf{U} = 0 , \qquad (13)$$

Thus we have

$$\mathbf{U} = 2(\mathbf{W}_r^T \bar{\mathbf{S}}_b \bar{\mathbf{S}}_b W_r)^{-1} W_r^T \bar{\mathbf{S}}_b \hat{\mathbf{S}}_b \mathbf{w}_{r+1} . \qquad (14)$$

Substituting Eq. (14) into Eq. (12), we will obtain

$$(I - \bar{\mathbf{S}}_b \mathbf{W}_r (\mathbf{W}_r^T \bar{\mathbf{S}}_b \bar{\mathbf{S}}_b \mathbf{W}_r)^{-1} \mathbf{W}_r^T \bar{\mathbf{S}}_b) \hat{\mathbf{S}}_b \mathbf{w}_{r+1} = \lambda \mathbf{w}_{r+1} . \qquad (15)$$

Therefore, Eq. (7) is obtained.

It is worth noting that in our UWLDA, if we substitute $\hat{\mathbf{S}}_b$ with the unweighted one, the resulting method is the generalization of ULDA to the SSSP cases. Moreover, one can easily prove that the resulting method is definitely equal to the original NLDA because the optimal discriminant vectors derived from NLDA can satisfied the conjugated orthogonal constraint (6). However, in our UWLDA, due to integrating the weighted pairwise Fisher criterion to replace the original Fisher criterion, i.e. we change $\bar{\mathbf{S}}_b$ into another matrix $\hat{\mathbf{S}}_b$. Therefore, the traditional NLDA solution based on the weighted pairwise Fisher criterion cannot guarantee the derived discriminant features are statistically uncorrelated, whereas the proposed UWLDA technique that combines the ULDA, NLDA and the weighted pairwise Fisher criterion can obtain the statistically uncorrelated features.

4 Experimental Results

In this section, we present experimental results on a subset of AR face database [8] using our method and comparing with the performance of several popular subspaces projection-based schemes such as Eigenfaces [9], Fisherfaces [4], DLDA [10] and NLDA [3]. This subset contains 1652 non-occluded images corresponding to 118 persons with changes in facial expression and illumination conditions, and images taken in two sessions two weeks apart. For illustration, some available images for one subject are shown in Fig.1.

To begin, we convert the RGB images to gray scale ones by adding all three-color channels. Later, each image is scaled, translated, rotated and cropped to a size of 53 × 56 to obtain a "face" which includes only the middle portion of the face images. We also apply the histogram matching technology to images as photometric normalization. Subsequently we smooth them with a Gaussian filter (3 by 3 with sigma 1) for noise reduction and globally normalize them to have zero mean and unit standard deviation. As the regions on the two sides of the chin are usually not important but the magnitude of the summation vectors there may be large, we removed these regions by an elliptical mask. The preprocessed images of one person are shown in Fig.2. In our experiments, the simple nearest center classifier (NCC) is adopted to recognize the unknown face images by using L2 norm as the distance measurement.

In our UWLDA technique, the optimal parameter k_{opt} can be found by searching highest accuracy over the variation of k. We randomly select 5 images per subject for training and the remains for testing. The results of different k within the range from 1 to 10 are shown in Table 1, from which $k_{opt} = 4$ is obtained for the following comparative experiments.

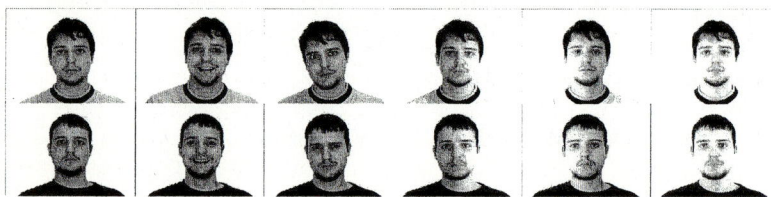

Fig. 1. Some face samples of one subject from the AR database

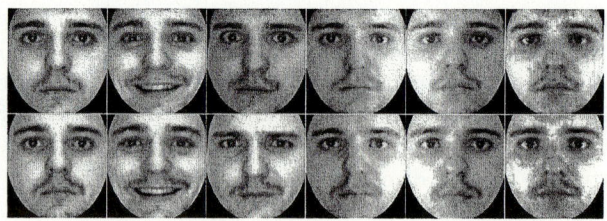

Fig. 2. The preprocessed images

Table 1. Recognition accuracy corresponding to different k in UWLDA (%)

k	1	2	3	4	5	6	7	8	9	10
Accuracy	93.34	93.83	94.03	**94.88**	93.29	92.31	91.42	89.09	85.41	81.14

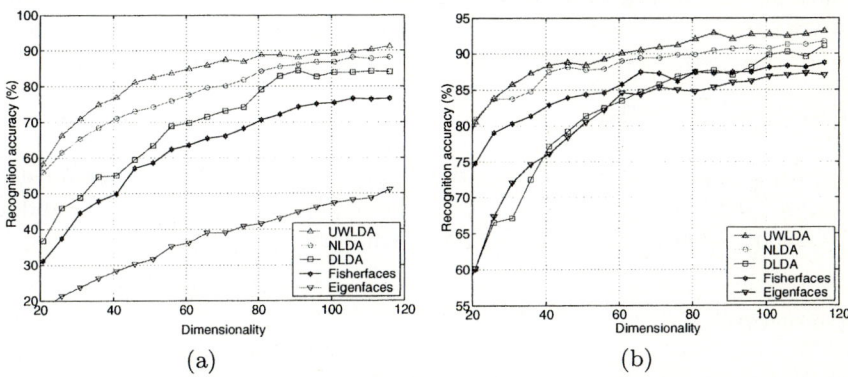

Fig. 3. Comparative recognition performance. (a) Under the condition of variations in illuminance. (b) Under the condition of variations in facial expression.

In the next experiment, our aim is to compare Eigenfaces, Fisherfaces, DLDA, NLDA and the proposed UWLDA under varying illumination conditions. For each subject, we select two images with normal lighting condition corresponding to the first column in Fig.2 for training and 6 images with varying light conditions corresponding to the rightmost 3 columns in Fig.2 for testing. In total, we have 236 training samples and 708 testing samples. Fig. 3(a) shows the recognition accuracy under a varying number of selected features. This figure indicates that the performance of those LDA-based methods (Fisherfaces, DLDA, NLDA and UWLDA) is much better than PCA-based Eigenfaces under conditions where lighting is varied. In general, UWLDA performs better than the other methods. The last experiment is performed to evaluate the performance of different methods under the condition of variations in expression. As in the previous experiment, we still select two neutral images per subject for training. The probe set comprises 4 images for each person which involve variations in facial expressions (smile and angry). Thus, the total number of training samples is 236 and the number of testing samples is 472. The experiment results are shown in Fig.3(b), with the recognition accuracy against number of selected features. Again, the proposed UWLDA obtains the best performance when more than 28 features are used.

5 Conclusions

In this short paper, we present a novel LDA-based subspace projection method for face recognition that unifies nullspace LDA (NLDA), uncorrelated LDA

(ULDA) and weighted pairwise Fisher criteria (WLDA) in a single algorithm we refer to as uncorrelated, weighted LDA (UWLDA). This approach can extract the most discriminatory features which are statistically uncorrelated. Experimental results indicate that under the conditions of varying in illuminance and facial expressions, UWLDA performs better than other state-of-the-art methods such as Eigenfaces, Fisherfaces, NLDA and DLDA in terms of classification accuracy.

Acknowledgements

This work is supported by the Scientific Technology Key Project of Ministry of Education (02057) and Key Project of Chongqing Natural Science Foundation (CSTC2005BA2002, CSTC2005BB2181), China.

References

1. Zhao, W., Chellappa, R.,Rosenfeld A., Phillips P. J.: Face Recognition: A Literature Survey. ACM Computing Survey. **35** (2003) 399–458
2. Jin, Z., Yang, J. Y., Hu, Z. S., Lou, Z.: Face Recognition Based on the Uncorrelated Discriminant Transformation. Pattern Recognition. **34** (2001) 1405–1416
3. Chen, L. F., Liao, H. Y., Lin, J. C., Ko, M. T., Yu, G. J.: A New LDA-based Face Recognition System Which Can Solve the Small Sample Size Problem. Pattern Recognition. **33** (2000) 1713–1726
4. Belhumeur, P. N., Hespanha, J. P., Kriegman, D. J.: Eigenfaces vs. Fisherfaces: Recognitin Using Class Specific Linear Projection. IEEE Trans. Pattern Anal. Machine Intell. **9** (1997) 711–720
5. Loog, M., Duin, R. P. W., Haeb-Umbach, R.: Multiclass Linear Simension Reduction by Weighted Pairwise Fisher Criteria. IEEE Trans. Pattern Anal. Mach. Intell. **23** (2001) 762–766
6. Lotlikar, R., Kothari, R.: Fractional-Step Dimensionality Reduction. IEEE Trans. Pattern Anal. Mach. Intell. **22** (2000) 623–627
7. Huang, R., Liu, Q. S., Lu, H. Q., Ma, S. D.: Solving the Small Smaple Size Problem of LDA. In: Proceedings of the 16th International Conference on Pattern Recognition. **3** (2002) 29–32
8. Martinez, A. M., Benavente, R.: The AR face database. CVC Tech. Report. **34** (1998)
9. Turk, M., Pentland, A. Eigenfaces for Recognition. Journal of Cognitive Neuroscience. **3** (1991) 72–86.
10. Yu, H., Yang, J.: A Direct LDA Algorithm for High-dimensional Data – with Application to Face Recognition. Pattern Recognition. **34** (2001) 2067–2070

Face Recognition Using Heteroscedastic Weighted Kernel Discriminant Analysis

Yixiong Liang, Weiguo Gong, Weihong Li, and Yingjun Pan

Key Lab of Optoelectronic Technology & Systems of Education Ministry of China,
Chongqing University, Chongqing 400044, China
{yxliang, wggong, weihongli, pyj}@cqu.edu.cn

Abstract. In this paper, we propose a novel heteroscedastic weighted kernel discriminant analysis (HW-KDA) method that extends the linear discriminant analysis (LDA) to deal explicitly with heteroscedasticity and nonlinearity of the face pattern's distribution by integrating the weighted pairwise Chernoff criterion and Kernel trick. The proposed algorithm has been tested, in terms of classification rate performance, on the multiview UMIST face database. Results indicate that the HW-KDA methodology is able to achieve excellent performance with only a very small set of features and outperforms other two popular kernel face recognition methods, the kernel PCA (KPCA) and generalized discriminant analysis (GDA).

1 Introduction

Within the last decades, face recognition has received extensive attention due to its wide range of application from identity authentication, access control and surveillance to human-computer interaction. As a result, numerous novel FR algorithms have been proposed [1]. A successful face recognition scheme should consider how to find low-dimensional feature representation from high-dimensional facial images with enhanced discriminatory power. Principle component analysis (PCA) and linear discriminant analysis (LDA) are two classic techniques widely used in face recognition for dimensionality reduction and feature extraction. It is generally believed that when it comes to solving problems of face recognition, LDA-based algorithms always outperform PCA-based ones because, as intuition would suggest, the former deals directly with discrimination between classes, whereas the latter deals with the data in its entirety for the PCA without paying any particular attention to the underlying class structure. However, LDA does not guarantee to find the optimal directions when the so-called *outlier class* is dominant in estimating the scatter matrices [2]. Moreover, it is incapable of dealing with heteroscedastic data in a proper way due to the implicit assumption that the covariance matrices for all classes are equal [3]. The traditional solution to these problems is to employ iterative optimization procedures. Recently, more effective non-iterative solution, we refer to as heteroscedastic weighted LDA (HW-LDA), has been proposed [4]. Although successful in many cases, linear method fails to deliver good performance when face patterns are subject to large variations in viewpoints, which results in a highly non-convex and complex distribution. Intuitively, it's reasonable to assume that a better solution to this inherent nonlinear problem could be achieved using nonlinear techniques, such as the kernel trick.

In this paper, prompted by the success of support vector machines (SVMs)[5], kernel PCA (KPCA) [6] and generalized discriminant analysis (GDA) [7], we propose a novel kernel discriminant analysis technique we refer to as heteroscedastic weighted kernel discriminant analysis or HW-KDA for face recognition. The proposed HW-KDA can simultaneously provide the advantages of HW-LDA and GDA while overcoming many of their shortcomings.

2 Heteroscedastic Weighted KDA Technique

2.1 LDA

LDA is concerned with the search for a linear transformation $\mathbf{W} = [\mathbf{w}_1, \ldots, \mathbf{w}_l]$ from a h-dimensional data space to a l-dimensional feature space ($l < h$) that maximizes the so-called Fisher criterion J_F

$$J_F(\mathbf{W}) = tr[(\mathbf{W}^T \mathbf{S}_w \mathbf{W})^{-1} (\mathbf{W}^T \mathbf{S}_b \mathbf{W})] \ . \tag{1}$$

Here $\mathbf{S}_b = \sum_{i=1}^{c} p_i (\mathbf{m}_i - \mathbf{m})(\mathbf{m}_i - \mathbf{m})^T$ and $\mathbf{S}_w = \sum_{i=1}^{c} p_i \mathbf{S}_i$ are the the between-class scatter (BCS) matrix and within-class scatter (WCS) matrix, respectively; c represents the total number of pattern classes; $\mathbf{m}_i$ denotes the centroid of class i with prior probability p_i and $\mathbf{m}$ is the global centroid; $\mathbf{S}_i$ is the covariance matrix of class i. Optimizing (1) comes down to determining an eigenvalue decomposition of $\mathbf{S}_w^{-1} \mathbf{S}_b$ and taking the columns of $\mathbf{W}$ to equal the eigenvectors corresponding to the l largest eigenvalues.

2.2 HW-LDA

In Fisher criterion (1), as discussed in [2], all class pairs have the same weights irrespective of their separability in the original space and the resulting transformation will preserve the distances of already well-separated classes while causing unnecessarily overlap of neighboring classes. Moreover, the Fisher criterion (1) does not take the heteroscedasticity of data into account and consequently fail to extract the discriminatory information present in the differences between the per class covariance matrices [3]. Recently, a set of modified versions of the Fisher criterion were proposed to avoid these shortcomings. To restrain the negative influence of the *outlier class*, Loog et al. [2] proposed an extended criterion named approximate pairwise accuracy criterion (aPAC) by rewriting the BCS matrix $\mathbf{S}_b$ as

$$\mathbf{S}_b = \sum_{i=1}^{c-1} \sum_{j=i+1}^{c} p_i p_j \omega(d_{ij}) (\mathbf{m}_i - \mathbf{m}_j)(\mathbf{m}_i - \mathbf{m}_j)^T \ , \tag{2}$$

here $\omega(d_{ij}) = \frac{1}{2d_{ij}^2} erf(\frac{d_{ij}}{2\sqrt{2}})$ is the weighting function and d_{ij}'s are the Mahanalobis distance between the classes i and j in the original space. Considering the heteroscedasticity of the data, Loog et al. [3] proposed a heteroscedastic extension of Fisher criterion, called Chernoff Criterion, by replacing $\mathbf{S}_b$ used in Fisher criterion with the following multi-class direct distance matrix $\mathbf{S}_c$

$$\mathbf{S}_c = \sum_{i=1}^{c-1} \sum_{j=i+1}^{c} p_i p_j \mathbf{S}_c^{ij} \qquad (3)$$

$$= \sum_{i=1}^{c-1} \sum_{j=i+1}^{c} p_i p_j \mathbf{S}_w^{1/2} ((\mathbf{S}_w^{-1/2} \mathbf{S}_{ij} \mathbf{S}_w^{-1/2})^{-1/2} \mathbf{S}_w^{-1/2} (\mathbf{m}_i - \mathbf{m}_j)(\mathbf{m}_i - \mathbf{m}_j)^T$$

$$\times \mathbf{S}_w^{-1/2} (\mathbf{S}_w^{-1/2} \mathbf{S}_{ij} \mathbf{S}_w^{-1/2})^{-1/2} + \frac{1}{\pi_i \pi_j} \log(\mathbf{S}_w^{-1/2} \mathbf{S}_{ij} \mathbf{S}_w^{-1/2})$$

$$- \pi_i \log(\mathbf{S}_w^{-1/2} \mathbf{S}_i \mathbf{S}_w^{-1/2}) - \pi_j \log(\mathbf{S}_w^{-1/2} \mathbf{S}_j \mathbf{S}_w^{-1/2})) \mathbf{S}_w^{1/2} \;,$$

where $\pi_i = p_i/(p_i + p_j)$ and $\pi_j = p_j/(p_i + p_j)$ are the relative a priori taking into two classes that define the particular pairwise term; $\mathbf{S}_c^{ij}$ and $\mathbf{S}_{ij}$ are the pairwise directed distance matrix between classes i and j and the average pairwise within-class scatter matrix defined as $\pi_i \mathbf{S}_i + \pi_j \mathbf{S}_j$. Based on aPAC and Chernoff criterion, Qin et al. [4] proposed a named weighted Chernoff criterion by substituting $\mathbf{S}_c$ with the following the weighted multi-class direct distance matrix

$$\hat{\mathbf{S}}_c = \sum_{i=1}^{c-1} \sum_{j=i+1}^{c} p_i p_j \omega(d_{ij}^c) \mathbf{S}_c^{ij} \;, \qquad (4)$$

where d_{ij}^c's are the pairwise Chernoff distance measure. The resulting LDA is referred to as HW-LDA.

2.3 HW-KDA

Although the efficiency of HW-LDA has been experimentally demonstrated, it is still a linear technique in nature and so it is inadequate to describe the complexity of real face images because of pose variations. Here, we introduce the kernel trick into the weighted Chernoff criterion, which is demonstrated to be able to efficiently represent complicated nonlinear relation of input data [5], [6], [7]. The critical idea behind kernel trick is to map the input data into an implicit feature space $\mathcal{F}$, $\phi : \mathbf{x} \in \mathcal{R}^h \to \phi(\mathbf{x}) \in \mathcal{F}$, with a nonlinear dot product kernel function $k(\mathbf{x}, \mathbf{y}) = (\phi(\mathbf{x}) \cdot \phi(\mathbf{y}))$, where the distribution of face patterns is supposed to be linearized and simplified. Thus, the incorporation of the weighted Chernoff criterion and kernel trick can not only deal with the nonlinear cases but also extract the discriminatory information in both class means differences and the class covariance matrices' differences.

However, in practice, it is very difficult or even impossible to formalize the weighted Chernoff criterion-based KDA directly. Fortunately, it is recently proved that the GDA is equivalent to KPCA plus LDA [8]. Prompted by that, we adopt the two-stage strategy, as it was done for example in Fisherfaces [9], to implement the combining method: first projecting original samples onto the KPCA-transformed space and then performing HW-LDA in this subspace for further feature extraction. Considering the training set $\mathbf{X} = (\mathbf{x}_1, \ldots, \mathbf{x}_n)$, the centered kernel matrix $\mathbf{K}$ is given by

$$\mathbf{K} = \hat{\mathbf{K}} - \mathbf{1}_n \hat{\mathbf{K}} - \hat{\mathbf{K}} \mathbf{1}_n + \mathbf{1}_n \hat{\mathbf{K}} \mathbf{1}_n , \qquad (5)$$

where $\hat{\mathbf{K}}$ is a $n \times n$ matrix whose elements are determined by $\hat{\mathbf{K}}_{ij} = k(\mathbf{x}_i, \mathbf{x}_j)$; $\mathbf{1}_n = (1/n)_{n \times n}$. Then the KPCA transform matrix $\mathbf{U} = [\mathbf{u}_1, \ldots, \mathbf{u}_p]$ can be achieved by performing eigen-decomposition on $\mathbf{K}/n$ and selecting eigenvectors corresponding to p largest eigenvalues $\mathbf{\Lambda} = [\lambda_1, \ldots, \lambda_p]$. By virtue of $\mathbf{U}$, $\mathbf{K}$ and $\mathbf{\Lambda}$, the projection of $\mathbf{X}$ can be calculated by $\mathbf{Y} = (\mathbf{K}\mathbf{U}\mathbf{\Lambda}^{-1/2})^T$. Using the projection $\mathbf{Y}$ instead of $\mathbf{X}$ to calculate the scatter matrices and following the same steps as HW-LDA to generate discriminant vectors, we derived a novel HW-KDA technique. Being linear in the feature space $\mathcal{F}$, but nonlinear in the input space, HW-KDA thus is capable of deriving low-dimensional features that incorporate nonlinear discriminant information. Moreover, the computational cost is reduced greatly because in the high-dimensional input space $\mathcal{R}^h$, the size of scatter matrices is $h \times h$ while $p \times p$ in the KPCA-transformed space ($p \ll h$). For example, the size of $\hat{\mathbf{S}}_c$ in HW-LDA amounts to 10304×10304 for face images of size 112×92 such as those used in our experiments while 100×100 in HW-KDA if $p = 100$.

Although the proposed HW-KDA has demonstrated promising characteristics, it still suffers from the instability problem in the implementation. In face recognition tasks, the classwise covariance matrix $\mathbf{S}_i$'s are always singular and then $\hat{\mathbf{S}}_c$ is undefined. Similar to Qin's solution [4], here we still employ the named maximum entropy covariance selection (MECS) method [10] to estimate $\mathbf{S}_i$. However, MECS requires the WCS matrix $\mathbf{S}_w$ be full rank, which is seldom satisfied in face recognition. In HW-KDA, the singularity of $\mathbf{S}_w$ can be avoided by selecting $p \leq rank(\mathbf{S}_w)$.

3 Experimental Results

In order to establish the performance of HW-KDA, we carried out a set of experiments on the multiview UMIST face database [11] which consists of 575 gray-scale images of 20 subjects, each covering a wide range of poses from profile to frontal views as well as race, gender and appearance. Each image is cropped to 112×92 and then the resulting input vectors are of dimensionality $h = 10304$. For illustration, some sample images of a typical subject in the UMIST database are shown in Fig.1. In our experiments, all images are normalized to have zero mean and unit standard deviation. We select two state-of-the-art kernel methods for comparison: KPCA as a benchmark and GDA. For each subject, six images are randomly selected as training samples and the remaining are used for testing. Thus, we have 120 samples for training while 455 samples for testing. The nearest center classifier is adopted due to the simplicity. Recognition accuracies are estimated by using a ten-run average. During the recognition stage, we first

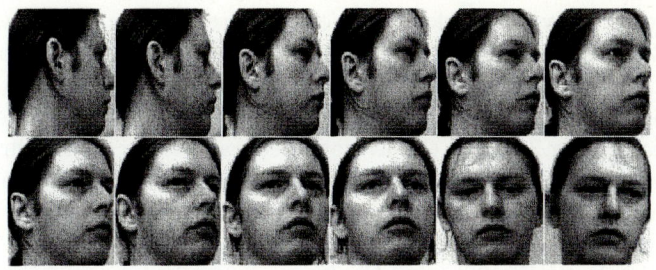

Fig. 1. Some face samples of one subject from the UMIST face database

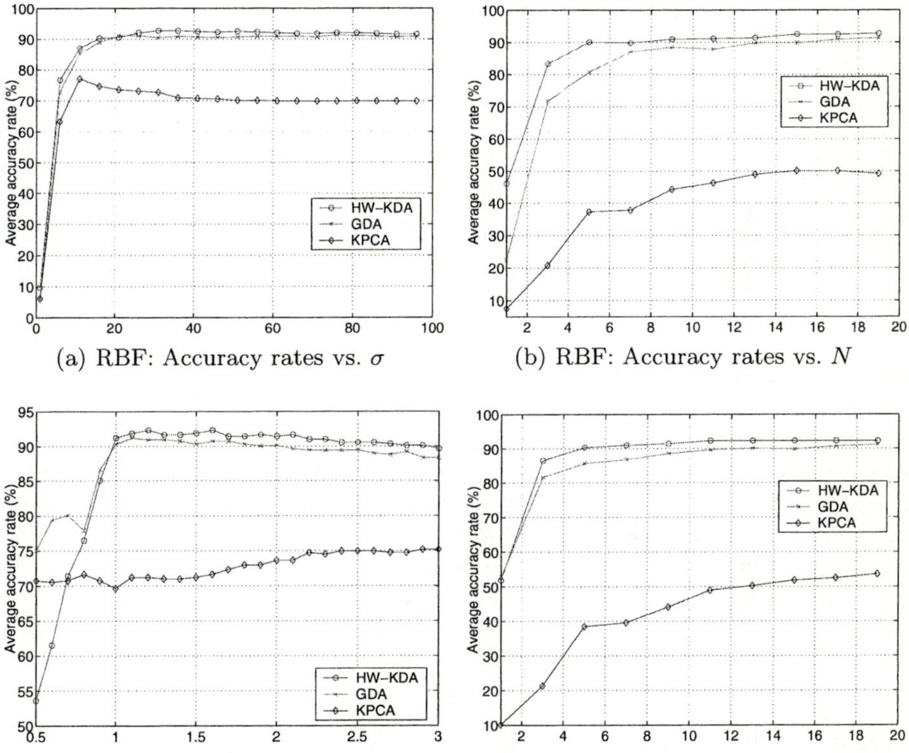

(a) RBF: Accuracy rates vs. σ

(b) RBF: Accuracy rates vs. N

(c) polynomial: Accuracy rates vs. d

(d) polynomial: Accuracy rates vs. N

Fig. 2. Comparative recognition performance

project the testing sample vector $\mathbf{x}^{(t)}$ onto the KPCA-transformed space and then perform the HW-LDA method to extract its feature. The projection $\mathbf{y}^{(t)}$ can be determined by $\mathbf{y}^{(t)} = (\mathbf{K}^{(t)}\mathbf{U}\mathbf{\Lambda}^{-1/2})^T$, here

$$\mathbf{K}^{(t)} = \hat{\mathbf{K}}^{(t)} - \mathbf{1}_n'\hat{\mathbf{K}} - \hat{\mathbf{K}}^{(t)}\mathbf{1}_n + \mathbf{1}_n'\hat{\mathbf{K}}\mathbf{1}_n , \qquad (6)$$

where $\hat{\mathbf{K}}^{(t)}$ is a $1 \times n$ matrix whose elements $\hat{\mathbf{K}}^{(t)}_{1j} = k(\mathbf{x}^{(t)}, \mathbf{x}_j)$ and $\mathbf{1}_n' = (1/n)_{1 \times n}$.

To evaluate the overall performance of the three methods, two typical kernel functions, RBF kernel $k(\mathbf{x},\mathbf{y}) = exp(-\|\mathbf{x}-\mathbf{y}\|^2/2\sigma^2)$ and polynomial kernel $k(\mathbf{x},\mathbf{y}) = (\mathbf{x}\cdot\mathbf{y}+1)^d$, and a wide range of parameter values are tested. Sensitivity analysis is performed with respect to the kernel parameters and the number of used features N. Fig.2 shows the average accuracy rates of the three methods compared when RBF and polynomial kernels are used. Fig.2(a) and Fig.2(c) depict the accuracy rates as functions of kernel parameter σ and d respectively with a predefined $N = N_p$. For KPCA, $N_p = 100$ while for GDA and HW-KDA, $N_p = 19$. From Fig.2(a) and Fig.2(c), we obtain $\sigma_{opt} = 11$, $d_{opt} = 2.9$ for KPCA, $\sigma_{opt} = 76$, $d_{opt} = 1.1$ for GDA and $\sigma_{opt} = 31$, $d_{opt} = 1.2$ for HW-KDA. Then we fix the optimal kernel parameters and vary the number of features N from 1 to 19. The experimental results are shown in Fig.2(b) and Fig.2(d). It is easy to conclude that in our experiments, those methods based on discriminant analysis (GDA and HW-KDA) also perform better than the KPCA method. Moreover, compared with KPCA and GDA, the proposed HW-KDA can extract more powerful discriminatory information present in the differences between per class means and the differences between per class covariance matrices, thereby achieves the best performance only using a small set of features. It should be also noted that Fig.2(c) reveals the numerical stability problems existing in practical implementation of GDA. Comparing the GDA performance to that of HW-KDA we can easily see that the latter is more stable and predictable.

4 Conclusion

We have developed a novel HW-KDA method for face recognition that combines kernel-based methodologies with a heteroscedastic LDA technique. The KPCA technique is first utilized to map the original face patterns to an implicit feature space, where the highly non-convex and complex distribution of face patterns is linearized and simplified. Then the heteroscedastic LDA is performed in this space to extract the nonlinear discriminant features with respect to original input space. Experimental results indicate that the performance of the HW-KDA method is overall superior to KPCA and GDA approaches.

Acknowledgements

This work is supported by the Scientific Technology Key Project of Ministry of Education and Key Project of Chongqing Natural Science Foundation, China.

References

1. Zhao, W., Chellappa, R.,Rosenfeld A., Phillips P. J.: Face Recognition: A Literature Survey. ACM Computing Survey. **35** (2003) 399–458
2. Loog, M., Duin, R. P. W., Haeb-Umbach, R.: Multiclass Linear Simension Reduction by Weighted Pairwise Fisher Criteria. IEEE Trans. Pattern Anal. Mach. Intell. **23** (2001) 762–766

3. Loog, M., Duin, R. P. W.: Linear Dimensionality Reduction via a Heteroscedastic Extension of LDA: The Chernoff Criterion. IEEE Trans. Pattern Anal. Mach. Intell. **26** (2004) 732–739
4. Qin, A. K., Suganthan, P. N., Loog, M.: Uncorrelated Heterosecdastic LDA Based on the Weighted Pairwise Chernoff Criterion. Pattern Recogniton. **38** (2005) 613–616
5. Vapnik, V.N.: Statistical Learning Theory. John Wiley and Sons, New York (1998)
6. Scholkopf, B., Smola, A., Muller, K.R.: Nonlinear Component Analysis as a Kernel Eigenvalue Problem. Neural Computation. **10** (1998) 1299–1319
7. Baudatg, G., Anouar, F.: Generalized Discriminant Analysis Using a Kernel Approach. Neural Computation. **12** (2000) 2385–2404
8. Yang, J., Jin, Z., Yang, J. Y., Zhang, D., Frangi, A. F.: Essence of Kernel Fisher Discriminant: KPCA Plus LDA. Pattern Recognition. **37** (2004) 2097–2100
9. Belhumeur, P. N., Hespanha, J. P., Kriegman, D. J.: Eigenfaces vs. Fisherfaces: Recognitin Using Class Specific Linear Projection. IEEE Trans. Pattern Anal. Machine Intell. **9** (1997) 711–720
10. Thomaz, C. E., Gillies, D. F., Feitosa, R. Q.: A New Covariance Estimate for Bayesian Classifier in Biometric Recognition. IEEE Trans. Circuit Syst. Video Technol. **14** (2004) 214–223
11. Graham, D. B., Allinson, N. M.: Characterizing Virtual Eigensignatures for General Purpose Face Recognition. In: Wechsler, H., Phillips, P. J., Bruce, V., Soulie, F. F., Huang, T. S. (eds.): Face Recognition: From Theory to Applications. NATO ASI Series F, Computer and Systems Sciences, Vol. 163. Springer-Verlag, Berlin Heidelberg New York (1998) 446–456

Class-Specific Discriminant Non-negative Matrix Factorization for Frontal Face Verification

Stefanos Zafeiriou, Anastasios Tefas, Ioan Buciu, and Ioannis Pitas

Aristotle University of Thessaloniki, Department of Informatics 54124,
Thessaloniki, Greece
{dralbert, tefas, nelu, Pitas}@aiia.csd.auth.gr

Abstract. In this paper, a supervised feature extraction method having both non-negative bases and weights is proposed. The idea is to extend the *Non-negative Matrix Factorization* (NMF) algorithm in order to extract features that enforce not only the spatial locality, but also the separability between classes in a discriminant manner. The proposed method incorporates discriminant constraints inside the NMF decomposition in a class specific manner. Thus, a decomposition of a face to its discriminant parts is obtained and new update rules for both the weights and the basis images are derived. The introduced methods have been applied to the problem of frontal face verification using the well known XM2VTS database. The proposed algorithm greatly enhance the performance of NMF for frontal face verification.

1 Introduction

Face recognition/verification has attracted the attention of researchers for more than two decades and is among the most popular research areas in the field of computer vision and pattern recognition. The most popular among the techniques used for frontal face recognition/verification are the subspace methods. The subspace algorithms consider the entire image as a feature vector and their aim is to find projections (bases) that optimize some criterion defined over the feature vectors that correspond to different classes. Then the original high dimensional image space is projected into a low dimensional one. The classification is usually performed according to a simple distance measure in the final multidimensional space.

Various criteria have been employed in order to find the bases of the low dimensional spaces. Some of them have been defined in order to find projections that best express the population (e.g. *Principal Component Analysis* (PCA) [1], NMF [2], *Local Non-negative Matrix Factorization* (LNMF) [3]) without using the information of how the data are separated to different classes. Another class of criteria is the one that deals directly with discrimination between classes (e.g. *Linear Discriminant Analysis* (LDA) [4]).

A subspace method that aims at finding a face representation by using basis images without using class information is NMF [2]. The NMF algorithm, like PCA, represents a face as a linear combination of bases. The difference with PCA is that it does not allow negative elements in both the basis vectors and the weights of the linear combination. This constraint results to radically different bases than PCA. On one hand the bases of

PCA are eigenfaces, some of which resemble distorted versions of the entire face. On the other hand the bases of NMF are localized features that correspond better to the intuitive notions of face parts [2]. An extension of NMF that gives even more localized bases by imposing additional locality constraints is the so-called LNMF [3].

NMF variants for object recognition have been proposed in [5,6]. Various distance metrics suitable to NMF representation space have been proposed in [7]. Methods for initializing the weights and the bases of the NMF decomposition have been proposed in [8]. Theoretical aspects regarding why NMF gives a unique decomposition of an object into its parts are provided in [9].

In the proposed technique we incorporate discriminant constraints inside the NMF decomposition and that way a part based decomposition with enhanced discriminant power is taken. The introduced method results to a class specific decomposition that is unique for each facial (person) class. The intuitive motivation behind the class-specific methods is to find for every face a unique decomposition into its own discriminant parts. Class- specific discriminant transforms have been also used for discriminant dimensionality reduction in the feature vectors of the elastic grids and for discriminant weighting of their nodes [10,11,12,13]. The introduced algorithm is applied to the frontal face verification problem using the XM2VTS database.

2 Frontal Face Verification and Subspace Techniques

Let $\mathcal{U}$ be a facial image database. Each facial image $\mathbf{x} \in \mathcal{U}$ is supposed to belong to one of the K facial (person) classes $\{\mathcal{U}_1, \mathcal{U}_2, \ldots, \mathcal{U}_K\}$ with $\mathcal{U} = \bigcup_{i=1}^{K} \mathcal{U}_i$. For a face verification system that uses the database $\mathcal{U}$, a genuine (or client) claim is performed when a person t provides its facial image $\mathbf{x}$, claiming that $\mathbf{x} \in \mathcal{U}_r$ and $t = r$. When a person t provides its facial image $\mathbf{x}$ and claims that $\mathbf{x} \in \mathcal{U}_r$, with $t \neq r$, an impostor claim occurs. The scope of a face verification system is to handle properly these claims by accepting the genuine claims and rejecting the impostor ones.

Let the facial image database $\mathcal{U}$ be comprised by L facial images $\mathbf{x}_j \in \Re_+^F$, where $\Re_+ = [0, +\infty)$ and let the cardinality of each facial class $\mathcal{U}_r$ to be N_r. A linear subspace transformation of the original F-dimensional space onto a M-dimensional subspace (usually $M \ll F$) is a matrix $\mathbf{W} \in \Re^{M \times F}$ estimated using the database $\mathcal{U}$. The new feature vector $\acute{\mathbf{x}} \in \Re^M$ is given by:

$$\acute{\mathbf{x}} = \mathbf{W}\mathbf{x}. \qquad (1)$$

The rows of the matrix $\mathbf{W}$ contain the bases of the lower dimension feature space. The bases matrix $\mathbf{W}$ could be the same for all facial classes of the database or could be unique for each facial class. In case of class-specific image bases, for the reference person r, the set $\mathcal{I}_r = \mathcal{U} - \mathcal{U}_r$, that corresponds to impostor images is used in order to construct the two-class problem (genuine versus impostor class) [11].

After the projection given by (1), a distance metric is chosen in order to measure the similarity of a test facial image to a certain class. This similarity measure can be the L_1 norm, the L_2 norm, the normalized correlation or the Mahalanobis distance. In case of face verification, the algorithm should also learn a threshold on the similarity measure in order to accept or reject a client/impostor claim.

3 The NMF Algorithm

In order to apply NMF, the matrix $\mathbf{X} \in \Re_+^{F \times L} = [x_{i,j}]$ should be constructed, where $x_{i,j}$ is the i-th element of the j-th image. In other words the j-th column of $\mathbf{X}$ is the $\mathbf{u}_j$ facial image. NMF aims to find two matrices $\mathbf{Z} \in \Re_+^{F \times M} = [z_{i,k}]$ and $\mathbf{H} \in \Re_+^{M \times L} = [h_{k,j}]$ such that,

$$\mathbf{X} \approx \mathbf{ZH}. \qquad (2)$$

The facial image $\mathbf{x}_j$ after the NMF decomposition can be written as $\mathbf{x}_j \approx \mathbf{Zh}_j$, where $\mathbf{h}_j$ is the j-th column of $\mathbf{H}$. Thus, the lines of the matrix $\mathbf{Z}$ can be considered as bases images and the $\mathbf{h}_j$ as the weight vector. The $\mathbf{h}_j$ vectors can also be considered as the projected vectors of a lower dimensional feature space.

The NMF imposes non-negative constraints in both the elements of $z_{i,k}$ and of $h_{k,j}$. Thus, only non-subtractive combinations are allowed. This is believed to correspond better to the intuitive notion of combining parts of face in order to create a whole one.

One of the algorithms initially proposed for finding the matrices $\mathbf{Z}$ and $\mathbf{H}$ used the Kullback-Leibler divergence [14]:

$$D_N(\mathbf{X}||\mathbf{ZH}) = \sum_{i,j}(x_{i,j}\ln(\frac{x_{i,j}}{\sum_k z_{i,k}h_{k,j}}) + \sum_k z_{i,k}h_{k,j} - x_{i,j}) \qquad (3)$$

as the measure of the cost for factoring $\mathbf{X}$ into $\mathbf{ZH}$ [14]. The NMF factorization is the outcome of the optimization:

$$\min_{\mathbf{Z},\mathbf{H}} D_N(\mathbf{X}||\mathbf{ZH}) \text{ subject to} \qquad (4)$$

$$z_{i,k} \geq 0, \ h_{k,j} \geq 0, \ \sum_i z_{i,j} = 1, \ \forall j.$$

By using an auxiliary function and the Expectation Maximization (EM) algorithm [14], the following update rules for $h_{k,j}$ and $z_{i,k}$ guarantee a non increasing behavior of (3). The update rule for the t-th iteration for $h_{k,j}$ is given by:

$$h_{k,j}^{(t)} = h_{k,j}^{(t-1)} \frac{\sum_i z_{i,k}^{(t-1)} \frac{x_{i,j}}{\sum_l z_{i,l}^{(t-1)} h_{l,j}^{(t-1)}}}{\sum_i z_{i,k}^{(t-1)}} \qquad (5)$$

whereas, for the $z_{i,k}$, the update rule is given by:

$$z_{i,k}^{(t)} = z_{i,k}^{(t-1)} \frac{\sum_j h_{k,j}^{(t)} \frac{x_{i,j}}{\sum_l z_{i,l}^{(t-1)} h_{l,j}^{(t)}}}{\sum_j h_{k,j}^{(t)}}. \qquad (6)$$

Since $\mathbf{x}_j \approx \mathbf{Zh}_j$, a natural way to compute the projection of $\mathbf{x}_j$ to a lower dimensional feature space using NMF is $\hat{\mathbf{x}}_j = \mathbf{Z}^\dagger \mathbf{x}_j$. The pseudo-inverse $\mathbf{Z}^\dagger$ can be calculated using singular value decomposition methods [15]. In any case, we can not use the coefficient matrix $\mathbf{H}$ computed directly from the update rules (which gives us its values in the training phase), since we do not have any expression for calculating this representation for the test images.

4 The LNMF Algorithm

The idea of NMF decomposition was further extended to the LNMF [3] where additional constraints concerning the spatial locality of the bases were employed in the optimization problem defined in (4).

Let $\mathbf{U} = [u_{i,j}] = \mathbf{Z}^T\mathbf{Z}$, $\mathbf{V} = [v_{i,j}] = \mathbf{HH}^T$, both being $M \times M$, LNMF aims at learning local features by imposing the following three additional locality constraints on the NMF. The first constraint is to create bases that cannot be further decomposed into more components [3]. This is accomplished by making the bases as sparse as possible by imposing $\sum_i u_{i,i}$ to be minimal [3].

Another constraint is to make the bases to be as orthogonal as possible, so as to minimize the redundancy between different bases. This can be imposed by requiring $\sum_{i \neq j} u_{i,j}$ to be minimal. Another employed constraint, requires that $\sum_i v_{i,i}$ is maximized [3].

When the above constraints are incorporated in (3), a new cost function is created as:

$$D_L(\mathbf{X}||\mathbf{ZH}) = D_N(\mathbf{X}||\mathbf{ZH}) + \alpha \sum_{i,j} u_{i,j} - \beta \sum_i v_{i,i} \tag{7}$$

where $\alpha, \beta > 0$ are constants. A solution for the minimization of the cost given in (7) subject to non-negative constraints, can be found in [3]. In order to ensure that the cost function (7) is nonincreasing, the following update rules for $z_{i,k}$ and $h_{k,j}$ are employed:

$$h_{k,j}^{(t)} = \sqrt{h_{k,j}^{(t-1)} \sum_i z_{i,k}^{(t-1)} \frac{x_{i,j}}{\sum_l z_{i,l}^{(t-1)} h_{l,j}^{(t-1)}}} \tag{8}$$

$$\acute{z}_{i,k}^{(t)} = z_{i,k}^{(t-1)} \frac{\sum_j h_{k,j}^{(t)} \frac{x_{i,j}}{\sum_l z_{i,l}^{(t-1)} h_{l,j}^{(t)}}}{\sum_j h_{k,j}^{(t)}} \tag{9}$$

$$z_{i,k}^{(t)} = \frac{\acute{z}_{i,k}^{(t)}}{\sum_l \acute{z}_{l,k}^{(t)}}. \tag{10}$$

5 The CSDNMF Algorithm

In this Section discriminant constraints are integrated inside the cost function (3). The minimization procedure of the new cost function yields a *Class-Specific Discriminant Non-negative Matrix Factorization* (CSDNMF) method. In order to formulate the CSDNMF decomposition, the facial image vectors of the genuine claims to the reference person r are in the first $N_r = N_G$ columns of the matrix $\mathbf{X}$. Then, the columns from $N_r + 1$ to L correspond to impostor claims. The total number of impostor claims is $N_I = L - N_r$. The coefficient vector $\mathbf{h}_j$ of the image $\mathbf{x}_j$ that corresponds to the ρ-th image of the genuine class will be denoted as $\eta_\rho^{(G)}$. If the facial vector $\mathbf{x}_j$ is the ρ-th image of the impostor class then the corresponding coefficient vector $\mathbf{h}_j$ will be denoted as $\eta_\rho^{(I)}$.

Let a distance metric (e.g. the L_2 norm) be used in order to quantify the similarity of a test facial image vector $\mathbf{x}_j$ to a given facial class. It sounds reasonable to require that the feature vectors corresponding to the genuine class, should have great similarity (small distance metric value), while the feature vectors of the impostor class should have small similarity (large distance metric value).

In order to define the similarity of the projection $\mathbf{h}_j$ of the facial image $\mathbf{x}_j$ to a given class r in the feature space of the coefficients, the L_2 norm can be used as:

$$d_r(\mathbf{h}_j) = ||\mathbf{h}_j - \boldsymbol{\mu}^{(G)}||^2 \tag{11}$$

where $\boldsymbol{\mu}^{(G)}$ is the mean vector of the vectors $\boldsymbol{\eta}_\rho^{(G)}$. In the reduced feature space of the vectors $\mathbf{h}_j$ we demand that the similarity measures $d_r(\boldsymbol{\eta}_\rho^{(I)})$ (impostor similarity measures) to be maximized while minimizing the similarity measures $d_r(\boldsymbol{\eta}_\rho^{(G)})$ (genuine similarity measures). Then the optimization problem for the class r is the maximization of:

$$\frac{1}{N_I} \sum_{\mathbf{x}_j \in \mathcal{I}_r} d_r(\mathbf{h}_j) = \frac{1}{N_I} \sum_{\rho=1}^{N_I} ||\boldsymbol{\eta}_\rho^{(I)} - \boldsymbol{\mu}^{(G)}||^2 = \mathrm{tr}[\mathbf{W}_r], \tag{12}$$

where $\mathbf{W}_r = \frac{1}{N_I} \sum_{\rho=1}^{N_I} (\boldsymbol{\eta}_\rho^{(I)} - \boldsymbol{\mu}^{(G)})(\boldsymbol{\eta}_\rho^{(I)} - \boldsymbol{\mu}^{(G)})^T$. The second optimization problem is the minimization of:

$$\frac{1}{N_G} \sum_{\mathbf{x}_j \in \mathcal{U}_r} d_r(\mathbf{h}_j) = \frac{1}{N_G} \sum_{\rho=1}^{N_G} ||\boldsymbol{\eta}_\rho^{(G)} - \boldsymbol{\mu}^{(G)}||^2 = \mathrm{tr}[\mathbf{B}_r], \tag{13}$$

where $\mathbf{B}_r = \frac{1}{N_G} \sum_{\rho=1}^{N_G} (\boldsymbol{\eta}_\rho^{(G)} - \boldsymbol{\mu}^{(G)})(\boldsymbol{\eta}_\rho^{(G)} - \boldsymbol{\mu}^{(G)})^T$. We impose these two additional constraints in the cost function given in (4) as:

$$D_c(\mathbf{X}||\mathbf{Z}_r\mathbf{H}_r) = D_N(\mathbf{X}||\mathbf{Z}_r\mathbf{H}_r) + \zeta\mathrm{tr}[\mathbf{B}_r] - \theta\mathrm{tr}[\mathbf{W}_r] \tag{14}$$

where $\zeta, \theta > 0$ are constants. The minimization of (14) gives a person specific decomposition (different bases $\mathbf{Z}_r$ for each reference face class r).

In order to derive the coefficients of CSDNMF we have used an auxiliary function similar to those used in the EM algorithm in [14]. Let G be an auxiliary function for $Y(\mathbf{F})$ if $G(\mathbf{F}, \mathbf{F}^{(t-1)}) \geq Y(\mathbf{F})$ and $G(\mathbf{F}, \mathbf{F}) = \mathbf{F}$. If G is an auxiliary function of Y, then Y is nonincreasing under the update $\mathbf{F}^t = \arg\min_\mathbf{F} G(\mathbf{F}, \mathbf{F}^{(t-1)})$. Let r be the reference facial class, we can prove that $\mathbf{G}_c(\mathbf{H}, \mathbf{H}^{(t-1)})$ is an auxiliary function of $Y_c(\mathbf{H}) = D_c(\mathbf{X}||\mathbf{Z}_r\mathbf{H}_r)$, where $\mathbf{G}_c(\mathbf{H}, \mathbf{H}^{(t-1)})$ is given by:

$$\begin{aligned}\mathbf{G}_c(\mathbf{H}, \mathbf{H}^{(t-1)}) &= \sum_i \sum_j (x_{i,j} \ln x_{i,j} - x_{i,j}) + \\ &+ \sum_i \sum_j \sum_k \frac{z_{i,k} h_{k,j}^{(t-1)}}{\sum_l z_{i,l} h_{l,j}^{(t-1)}} (\ln(z_{i,k} h_{k,j}) - \ln \frac{z_{i,k} h_{k,j}^{(t-1)}}{\sum_l z_{i,l} h_{l,j}^{(t-1)}}) + \\ &+ \sum_i \sum_j \sum_k z_{i,k} h_{k,j} + \zeta\mathrm{tr}[\mathbf{B}_r] - \theta\mathrm{tr}[\mathbf{W}_r].\end{aligned} \tag{15}$$

It is straightforward to show that $\mathbf{G}_c(\mathbf{H}, \mathbf{H}) = Y_c(\mathbf{H})$. In order to prove that $\mathbf{G}_c(\mathbf{H}, \mathbf{H}^{(t-1)}) \geq Y_c(\mathbf{H})$ since, $\ln(\sum_k z_{i,k} h_{k,j})$ is convex, the following inequality holds:

$$-\ln(\sum_k z_{i,k} h_{k,j}) \leq -\sum_k a_k \ln \frac{z_{i,k} h_{k,j}}{a_k} \tag{16}$$

for all non-negative a_k that satisfy $\sum_k a_k = 1$. By letting $a_k = \frac{z_{i,k} h_{k,j}^{(t-1)}}{\sum_l z_{i,l} h_{l,j}^{(t-1)}}$ we obtain:

$$-\ln(\sum_k z_{i,k} h_{k,j}) \leq \sum_k \frac{z_{i,k} h_{k,j}^{(t-1)}}{\sum_l z_{i,l} h_{l,j}^{(t-1)}} (\ln(z_{i,k} h_{k,j}) - \ln \frac{z_{i,k} h_{k,j}^{(t-1)}}{\sum_l z_{i,l} h_{l,j}^{(t-1)}}). \quad (17)$$

From (17) it is straightforward to show that $\mathbf{G}_c(\mathbf{H}, \mathbf{H}^{(t-1)}) \geq Y_c(\mathbf{H})$. Thus, $\mathbf{G}_c(\mathbf{H}, \mathbf{H}^{(t-1)})$ is an auxiliary function of $Y_c(\mathbf{H})$.

In this decomposition we have two different update rules. One for the genuine class and one for the impostor class. For $l = 1, \ldots, N^G$ (genuine class) the update rules for the coefficients $h_{k,l}$ for the reference person r are given by letting $\frac{\partial G_c(\mathbf{H}, \mathbf{H}^{(t-1)})}{\partial h_{k,l}} = 0$. Then,

$$\frac{\partial G_c(\mathbf{H}, \mathbf{H}^{(t-1)})}{\partial h_{k,l}} = -\sum_i x_{i,l} \frac{z_{i,k} h_{k,l}^{(t-1)}}{\sum_n z_{i,n} h_{n,l}^{(t-1)}} \frac{1}{h_{k,l}} + \sum_i z_{i,k} + \\ +2\zeta(h_{k,l} - \mu_k^{(G)}) \frac{1}{N_G} - 2\theta(\mu_k^{(G)} - \mu_k^{(I)}) \frac{1}{N_G} = 0. \quad (18)$$

The quadratic equation (18) is expanded as:

$$-\sum_i x_{i,l} \frac{z_{i,k} h_{k,l}^{(t-1)}}{\sum_n z_{i,n} h_{n,l}^{(t-1)}} + (1 - (2\zeta + 2\theta) \frac{1}{N_G} (\frac{1}{N_G} \sum_{\lambda, \lambda \neq l} h_{k,\lambda}) + 2\theta \frac{1}{N_G} \mu_k^{(I)}) h_{k,l} + \\ + \frac{1}{N_G} (2\zeta - (2\zeta + 2\theta) \frac{1}{N_G}) h_{k,l}^2 = 0. \quad (19)$$

By solving the quadratic equation (19) the update rules for the $h_{k,l}$ of the genuine class are:

$$h_{k,l} = \frac{T + \sqrt{T^2 + 4 \frac{1}{N_G}(2\zeta - (2\zeta + 2\theta)\frac{1}{N_G}) h_{k,l}^{(t-1)} \sum_i z_{i,k}^{(t-1)} \frac{x_{i,j}}{\sum_n z_{i,n}^{(t-1)} h_{n,l}^{(t-1)}}}}{2\frac{1}{N_G}(2\zeta - (2\zeta + 2\theta)\frac{1}{N_G})} \quad (20)$$

where T is given by:

$$T = (2\zeta + 2\theta) \frac{1}{N_G} (\frac{1}{N_G} \sum_{\lambda, \lambda \neq l} h_{k,\lambda}) - 2\theta \frac{1}{N_G} \mu_k^{(I)} - 1. \quad (21)$$

The update rules for the coefficients $h_{k,l}$ for the impostor class of the reference person r are given by letting $\frac{\partial G_c(\mathbf{H}, \mathbf{H}^{(t-1)})}{\partial h_{k,l}} = 0$:

$$\frac{\partial G_c(\mathbf{H}, \mathbf{H}^{(t-1)})}{\partial h_{k,l}} = -\sum_i x_{i,l} \frac{z_{i,k} h_{k,l}^{(t-1)}}{\sum_n z_{i,n} h_{n,l}^{(t-1)}} \frac{1}{h_{k,l}} + \sum_i z_{i,k} - 2\frac{1}{N^I} \theta(h_{k,l} - \mu_k^{(G)}) = 0 \quad (22)$$

where $j = N_G + 1, \ldots, L$. By solving the quadratic equation (22) the update rules for the $h_{k,l}$ are given by:

$$h_{k,l} = \frac{2\theta \mu_k^{(G)} + N_I + \sqrt{(2\theta \mu_k^{(G)} + N_I)^2 - 8N_I \theta h_{k,l}^{(t-1)} \sum_i z_{i,k}^{(t-1)} \frac{x_{i,j}}{\sum_n z_{i,n}^{(t-1)} h_{n,l}^{(t-1)}}}}{4\theta}. \quad (23)$$

It can be easily proven that the update rules for the bases matrix $\mathbf{Z}_r = [z_{i,k}]$ for the reference person r are given by:

$$z_{i,k}^{(t)} = z_{i,k}^{(t-1)} \frac{\sum_j h_{k,j}^{(t)} \frac{x_{i,j}}{\sum_l z_{i,l}^{(t-1)} h_{l,j}^{(t)}}}{\sum_j h_{k,j}^{(t)}} \tag{24}$$

and

$$z_{i,k}^{(t)} = \frac{z_{i,k}^{(t)}}{\sum_l z_{l,k}^{(t)}}. \tag{25}$$

When someone claims that a test image $\mathbf{x}$ corresponds to a reference facial class r, then $\mathbf{x}$ is projected using the $\mathbf{Z}_r^\dagger$ matrix as $\acute{\mathbf{x}} = \mathbf{Z}_r^\dagger \mathbf{x}$.

6 Experimental Results

The experiments were conducted in the XM2VTS database using the protocol described in [16]. The images were aligned semi-automatically according to the eyes position of each facial image using the eye coordinates. The facial images were down-scaled to 64×64 resolution. Histogram equalization was used for normalizing the facial images. The XM2VTS database provides two experiment setups namely, Configuration I and Configuration II [16]. Each Configuration is divided in three different sets the training set, the evaluation set and the test set. The training set is used to create client and impostor models for each person. The evaluation set is used to learn the thresholds.

The training set of the Configuration I contains 200 persons with 3 images per person. The evaluation set contains 3 images per client for genuine claims and 25 evaluation impostors with 8 images per impostor. Thus, evaluation set gives a total of $3 \times 200 = 600$ client claims and $25 \times 8 \times 200 = 40.000$ impostor claims. The test set has 2 images per client and 70 impostors with 8 images per impostor and gives $2 \times 200 = 400$ client claims and $70 \times 8 \times 200 = 112.000$ impostor claims. In the training set the matrices of the basis images for NMF and LNMF decompositions are learned. These matrices are common for all persons. In case of CSNMF the training set is used for calculating for each reference person r a different set of bases for feature selection. For visual comparison a number of 25 images for the NMF, the LNMF and the proposed CSDNMF (for the first person in the training set) are given in Figure 1.

The facial images have been projected using these bases into a low dimensional feature space and the normalized correlation was used in order to define the similarity measure between two faces as:

$$D(\mathbf{x}_r, \mathbf{x}_t) = \frac{\acute{\mathbf{x}}_r^T \acute{\mathbf{x}}_t}{||\acute{\mathbf{x}}_r|| ||\acute{\mathbf{x}}_t||} \tag{26}$$

where $\mathbf{x}_r$ and $\mathbf{x}_t$ are the reference and the test facial image respectively, while $\acute{\mathbf{x}}_r$ and $\acute{\mathbf{x}}_t$ are their projections to one of the subspace.

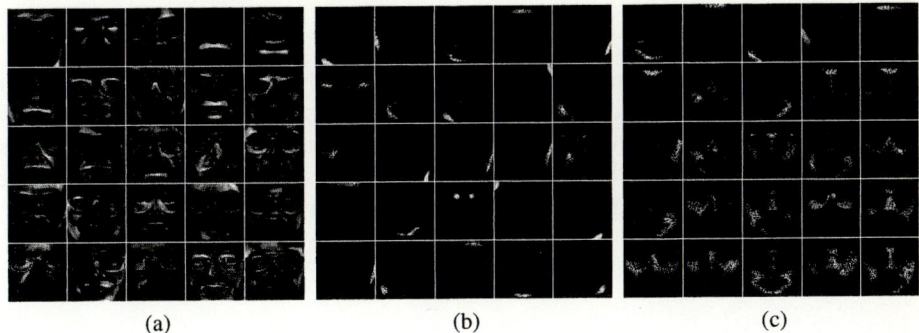

Fig. 1. A set of 25 bases images for (a) NMF, (b) LNMF and (c) CSDNMF

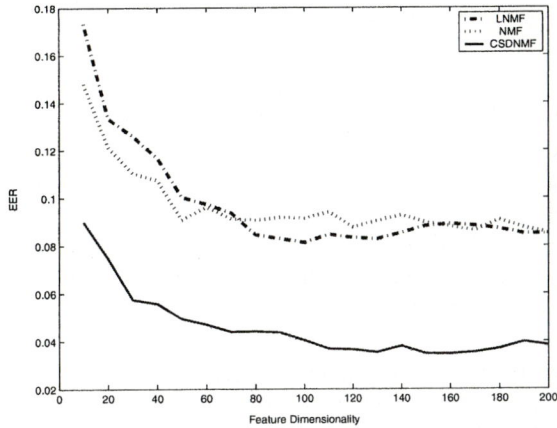

Fig. 2. EER as a function of feature dimension

The similarity measures for each person, calculated in both evaluation and training set form the distance vector $\mathbf{d}(r)$. The elements of the vector $\mathbf{d}(r)$ are sorted in descending order and are used for the person specific thresholds on the distance measure. Let $T_Q(r)$ denote the Q-th order statistic of the vector of distances, $\mathbf{d}(r)$. The threshold of the person r is chosen to be equal to $T_Q(r)$. Let $\mathbf{x}_r^1$, $\mathbf{x}_r^2$ and $\mathbf{x}_r^3$ be the 3 instances of the person r in the training set. A claim of a person (with a facial image $\mathbf{x}_t$) to the identity r is considered valid if $\max_j\{D(\mathbf{x}_r^j, \mathbf{x}_t)\} < T_Q(r)$. Obviously when varying Q, different pairs of *False Acceptance Rate* and *False Rejection Rate* can be created and that way a *Receiver Operating Characteristic* (ROC) curve is produced and the *Equal Error Rate* (EER) can be measured [11,16].

The performance of the NMF, LNMF and CSDNMF algorithms for various feature dimensions in the test set of Configuration I is illustrated in Figure 2. The best EER achieved for CSDNMF is 3.4% when more than 110 dimensions are kept. The best EER for NMF and LNMF is more than 8%. That is, a decrease of more than 4% in terms of EER has been achieved.

7 Conclusions

We incorporated discriminant constraints in the cost of NMF decomposition in order to extract class-specific discriminant non-negative decomposition. We solved the new optimization problem by developing update rules for both the weighting coefficients and the bases. We applied the new decomposition to frontal face verification where better performance than NMF and LNMF has been achieved.

Acknowledgment

This work is funded by the integrated project BioSec IST-2002-001766 (Biometric Security, http://www.biosec.org), under Information Society Technologies (IST) priority of the 6th Framework Programme of the European Community.

References

1. M. Kirby and L. Sirovich, "Application of the karhunen-loeve procedure for the characterization of human faces.," *IEEE Transactions Pattern Analysis and Machine Intelligence*, vol. 12, no. 1, pp. 103–108, Jan. 1990.
2. D.D. Lee and H.S. Seung, "Learning the parts of objects by non-negative matrix factorization," *Nature*, vol. 401, pp. 788–791, 1999.
3. S.Z. Li, X.W. Hou, and H.J. Zhang, "Learning spatially localized, parts-based representation," in *CVPR*, Kauai, HI, USA, December 8-14 2001, pp. 207–212.
4. P. N. Belhumeur, J. P. Hespanha, and D. J. Kriegman, "Eigenfaces vs. fisherfaces: Recognition using class specific linear projection.," *IEEE Transactions on Pattern Analysis and Machine Intelligence*, vol. 19, no. 7, pp. 711–720, July 1997.
5. D. Guillamet, J. Vitria, and B. Schiele, "Introducing a weighted non-negative matrix factorization for image classification," *Pattern Recognition Letters*, vol. 24, no. 14, pp. 2447 – 2454, 2003.
6. L. Weixiang and N. Zheng, "Non-negative matrix factorization based methods for object recognition," *Pattern Recognition Letters*, vol. 25, no. 9-10, pp. 893–897, 2004.
7. D. Guillamet and Vitria, "Evaluation of distance metrics for recognition based on non-negative matrix factorization," *Pattern Recognition Letters*, vol. 24, no. 9-10, pp. 1599 – 1605, 2003.
8. S. Wild, J. Curry, and A. Dougherty, "Improving non-negative matrix factorizations through structured initialization," *Pattern Recognition*, vol. 37, pp. 2217–2232, 2004.
9. D. Donoho and V. Stodden, "When does non-negative matrix factorization give a correct decomposition into parts ?," *Advances in Neural Information Processing Systems*, vol. 17, 2004.
10. A. Tefas, C. Kotropoulos, and I. Pitas, "Face verification using elastic graph matching based on morphological signal decomposition," *Signal Processing*, vol. 82, no. 6, pp. 833–851, 2002.
11. A. Tefas, C. Kotropoulos, and I. Pitas, "Using support vector machines to enhance the performance of elastic graph matching for frontal face authentication," *IEEE Transactions on Pattern Analysis and Machine Intelligence*, vol. 23, no. 7, pp. 735–746, 2001.
12. C. Kotropoulos, A. Tefas, and I. Pitas, "Frontal face authentication using discriminating grids with morphological feature vectors.," *IEEE Transactions on Multimedia*, vol. 2, no. 1, pp. 14–26, Mar. 2000.

13. C. Kotropoulos, A. Tefas, and I. Pitas, "Frontal face authentication using morphological elastic graph matching.," *IEEE Transactions on Image Processing*, vol. 9, no. 4, pp. 555–560, Apr. 2000.
14. D.D. Lee and H.S. Seung, "Algorithms for non-negative matrix factorization," in *NIPS*, 2000, pp. 556–562.
15. G.H. Golub and C.F. VanLoan, *Matrix Computations*, third ed. John Hopkins Univ. Press, 1996.
16. K. Messer, J. Matas, J.V. Kittler, J. Luettin, and G. Maitre, "Xm2vtsdb: The extended m2vts database," in *AVBPA'99*, 1999, pp. 72–77.

Partial Relevance in Interactive Facial Image Retrieval

Zhirong Yang and Jorma Laaksonen*

Laboratory of Computer and Information Science,
Helsinki University of Technology,
P.O. Box 5400, FI-02015 HUT, Espoo, Finland
{zhirong.yang, jorma.laaksonen}@hut.fi

Abstract. For databases of facial images, where each subject has only a few images, the query precision of interactive retrieval suffers from the problem of extremely small class sizes. A novel method is proposed to relieve this problem by applying partial relevance to the interactive retrieval. This work extends an existing content-based image retrieval system, PicSOM, by relaxing the relevance criterion in the early rounds of the retrieval. Moreover, we apply linear discriminant analysis as a preprocessing step before training the Self-Organizing Maps (SOMs) so that the resulting SOMs have stronger discriminative power. The results of simulated retrieval experiments suggest that for semantic classes such as "black persons" or "bearded persons" the first image which depicts the target subject can be obtained three to six times faster than by retrieval without the partial relevance.

1 Introduction

Most existing face recognition systems (e.g. [6]) require the user to provide a starting image, which is however not practical e.g. when searching for a criminal based on a witness' powers of recall. To address this problem, some interactive facial image retrieval systems such as [1,7] have been proposed, which are mainly based on learning the relevance feedback from the user. A query is performed in multiple rounds and usually aims at retrieving all *subject hits*, i.e. the images that depict a specific subject.

The early appearance of the first subject hit is critical for the success of the retrieval. Unlike content-based image retrieval (CBIR) systems based on general images, the query precision on facial images suffers from the problem of extremely small sizes of the *subject classes* [7]. If only images that depict the correct person are regarded as relevant, many pages of only non-relevant images would be displayed. Because the negative responses from the user in the early

---

* This work was supported by the Academy of Finland in the projects *Neural methods in information retrieval based on automatic content analysis and relevance feedback* and *New information processing principles*, a part of the Finnish Centre of Excellence Programme 2000–2005.

rounds provide little semantic information, the iteration progresses in a nearly random manner.

In practice, a human user seldom uses the subject classes as the sole relevant criterion in facial image retrieval. Instead, she may exploit some partial knowledge of the target subject, e.g. gender or race, to track down the first subject hit. The partial knowledge of an *aspect* probably divides the whole collection into several *semantic classes*, and the search target can be characterized by only one or an intersection of some such semantic classes. This provides a secondary level of relevance, which is helpful for reducing the number of displayed images in the retrieval.

In this paper we propose a novel method which adaptively learns partial relevance during the interactive retrieval. First, we extend our existing PicSOM CBIR system [7] by replacing the membership of a subject class with that of a semantic class as the new relevance criterion until the first subject hit appears. Second, we apply supervised learning as a preprocessing step before training the Self-Organizing Maps (SOMs) so that the resulting SOMs have stronger discriminative power. The empirical results show that the number of displayed images can be significantly reduced by employing these two strategies.

2 SOMs in Image Indexing and Retrieval

The PicSOM system [7] employs the Self-Organizing Map to learn the relevance feedback from the user. After training a SOM with low-level visual features extracted from the images, its map units are associated with the images of the database by locating the best-matching map unit (BMU) for each image. The SOM training preserves the topology in the original feature space, which in image retrieval means that mutually similar images are connected to topologically near map units.

In each round of the image query, the PicSOM system presents the user a set of facial images. The user marks images that she considers relevant, and the remaining ones are implicitly regarded as non-relevant. The SOM units are awarded a positive score for every relevant image mapped in them. These scores appear as attached positive impulses on the SOM surface. Likewise, associated non-relevant images result in negative scores and impulses. Let us denote the cumulative sets of relevant and non-relevant images up to query round r on mth SOM as $\mathcal{D}^+(r,m)$ and $\mathcal{D}^-(r,m)$, respectively. For the kth map unit, we obtain the following response:

$$x[k]_m^r = \frac{1}{|\mathcal{D}^+(r,m)|} \sum_{i \in \mathcal{D}^+(r,m)} \delta(c_m(i), k) - \frac{1}{|\mathcal{D}^-(r,m)|} \sum_{i \in \mathcal{D}^-(r,m)} \delta(c_m(i), k), \quad (1)$$

where $c_m(i)$ denotes the BMU of the image i on the mth SOM. This way, we obtain a zero-sum sparse value field on every SOM in use. Afterwards, the Pic-SOM system spreads the responses to the neighboring units and their associated images by applying a low-pass convolution over the SOM surface. Figure 1 illustrates how the positive and negative responses are first mapped on a 16×16-sized

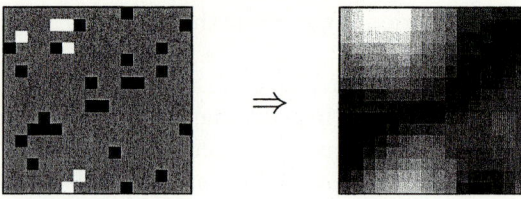

Fig. 1. An example of how a SOM surface is convolved with a window function. Left: the selected and rejected images are shown with white and black marks, respectively. Right: the convolution result, where relevance information is spread around the centers.

SOM to produce the sparse value field and how the responses are expanded in the convolution.

More than one feature can be involved simultaneously and the PicSOM system has a separate trained SOM for each. The convolutions provide implicit feature weighting because SOMs which match the user's expectations and impression of image similarity – and thus produce areas or clusters of high positive response – will produce larger score values than the others. The total scores for the candidate images are then obtained by simply summing up the mapwise values in their BMUs. Finally, a number of unseen images with the highest total scores are displayed to the user in the next round.

3 Partial Relevance for First Subject Hit

Most interactive facial image retrieval tasks aim at finding all images of a given subject. This procedure can be seen to consist of two stages. The goal of the first is retrieve the first subject image, and the remaining hits are obtained in the second stage. In this section we discuss two strategies for improving the query performance in the first stage, i.e. speeding up the appearance of the first subject hit.

3.1 Relevance Criterion in Two Stages

We identify two relevance criteria in interactive facial image retrieval: *subject relevance* for the membership in the precise target subject class and *partial relevance* for the membership in a wider semantic class. The first criterion represents the ultimate query goal while the second corresponds to a certain property of the target subject. The following query procedure illustrates how a user might look for an image of a specific Asian person:

1. The system displays a random set of images;
2. If one of the subject hits appears, the first stage terminates; otherwise goto step 3;
3. The user marks the images that depict Asian people as relevant, while leaving the others unmarked;
4. The system applies the retrieval algorithm described in Section 2, and displays the images with the highest scores; goto step 2.

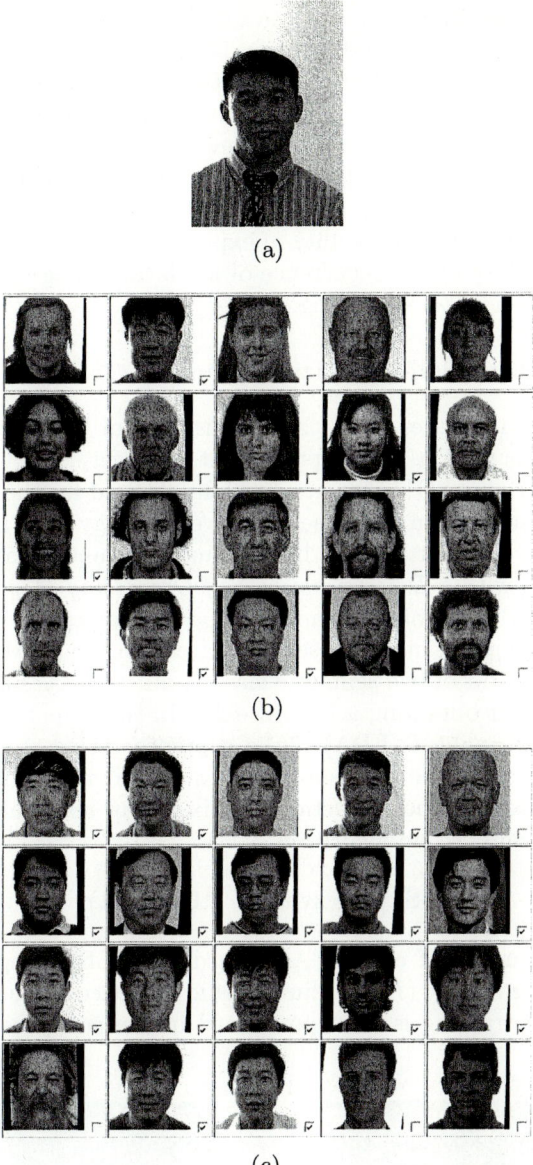

Fig. 2. A query example of looking for a specific Asian man: (a) the target subject; (b) the screen shot of the query in the first round, where the images are randomly selected from the database, and the user marks the images which are partially relevant as depicting Asian persons; (c) the third round, where more images of Asian people are shown and the first subject hit appears (1st row, 4rd column).

Figure 2 visualizes the above procedure for a specific subject. Notice that the example image of the target subject is not input to the system because that information only exists in the mind of the user. PicSOM learns the partial relevance of the displayed images and steers the query towards the target.

In the simulation experiments of the previous study [7], we used the subject relevance throughout the interactive retrieval, which led to only mediocre precision. We now replace the subject relevance with the partial relevance in the first stage. This simulates the user's ability of exploiting partial knowledge, which increases the probability of the occurrence of a relevant image and provides more information for the feedback learning.

3.2 Discriminative Self-organizing Maps

Some small semantic classes, such as the existence of beard, play a significant role in recognizing a person. The improvement, however, is only limited for these classes if the underlying SOMs are not specially devised for the partial relevance feedback. In this subsection we present a novel strategy that further speeds up the appearance of the first subject hit for small semantic classes by replacing the original SOMs with a *Discriminative Self-Organizing Map* (DSOM).

A DSOM is a Self-Organizing Map for a specific aspect in which the semantic classes are densely spread in nearly separate areas on the SOM. Figure 3 visualizes an example DSOM of two semantic classes, *mustache_yes* and *mustache_no*.

Different ways for obtaining a DSOM exist. In this paper, we apply Fisher's linear discriminant analysis (LDA) [2] as a preprocessing step before training the SOMs. Let $\mathbf{B}$ denote the between-class covariance matrix and $\mathbf{W}$ the within-class covariance matrix. The projection matrix $\mathbf{U}$ can be obtained by using the singular value decomposition algorithm

$$[\mathbf{U}, \mathbf{S}, \mathbf{V}] = \text{svds}(\mathbf{W}^{-1}\mathbf{B}, K - 1), \tag{2}$$

where K is the number of classes. Afterwards, the LDA-preprocessed feature vectors are projected to the $(K-1)$-dimensional subspace by multiplying with $\mathbf{U}$. The normal SOM training is then performed in the subspace to generate the

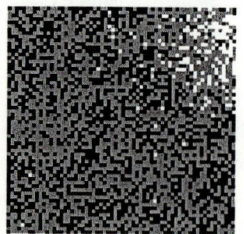

Fig. 3. A 64 × 64 DSOM example shown on the left. The white points represent the class members of *mustache_yes* and black points for *mustache_no*. The normal SOM without discriminative preprocessing is shown on the right for comparison.

DSOM. If more than one feature contributes to identifying the semantic class, the training samples are obtained by concatenating the LDA vectors from different features before input to the SOM training procedure.

Through the LDA preprocessing, the images of a semantic class are very likely connected to map units that situate nearby. If some images in the semantic class are displayed and marked as relevant, the relevance feedback learning algorithm on the DSOM will probably award higher scores to the other images of the same class, and then show these images to the user in the imminent rounds.

In the interactive retrieval, the user first needs to choose one of the offered aspects such as gender, race, etc, and the system loads the respective DSOM. The query procedure is the same as the one described in the previous section except that the relevance feedback learning algorithm operates on the DSOM instead of the original SOMs.

4 Experiments

4.1 Data

We have used the FERET database of facial images collected under the FERET program [4]. After face segmentation, 2409 frontal facial images (poses "fa" and "fb") of 867 subjects were stored in the database for the experiments. The number of images belonging to a subject varies from one to twenty, the statistics of which are shown in Table 1. We used the ground truth data of five aspects from the FERET collection for computing the LDA projection matrices. The statistics of the respective semantic classes are shown in Table 2.

In our experiments the coordinates of the facial parts (eyes, nose and mouth) were obtained from the ground truth data of the FERET collection, with which we calibrated the head rotation so that all faces are upright. Afterwards, all face boxes were normalized to the same size, with fixed locations for the left eye (31,24) and the right eye (16,24) in accordance to the MPEG-7 standard. The box sizes of the face and facial parts are shown in the second column of Table 3.

After extracting the raw features within the boxes mentioned above, we applied singular value decomposition to obtain the eigenfeatures of the face and facial parts [5]. The numbers of principle components preserved are shown in the third column of Table 3.

Table 1. Histogram of cardinality of subject classes

cardinality of subject class	number of subjects
1	2
2	632
3~4	164
5~6	42
7~20	27
average: 2.78	total: 867

Table 2. Statistics of the aspects and respective semantic classes

aspect	semantic classes(images/subjects)
race	white(1541/558) Asian(388/131) black(199/72) misc(371/106)
gender	male(1495/501) female(914/366)
glasses	yes(262/126) no(2147/741)
mustache	yes(256/81) no(2153/786)
beard	yes(144/51) no(2265/816)
whole database	2409/867

Table 3. Specification of the used facial features

feature name	normalized size	eigenfeature dimensions
face	46×56	48
left eye	24×16	10
right eye	24×16	10
nose	21×21	10
mouth	36×18	13

4.2 Discriminative Power Measurement of DSOM

First we analyzed the discriminative power of the Self-Organizing Maps without performing actual queries. We adopted the ρ measurement [3], which is based on the normalized *spatial entropy* of the class distribution on a SOM surface because it takes the map topology into account.

Let $X_s^\mathcal{C}$ denote the number of images of a given class $\mathcal{C}$ connected to the sth map unit of a SOM, and suppose the cardinality of $\mathcal{C}$ is $N^\mathcal{C}$. The probability histogram is then written as $P(s) = X_s^\mathcal{C}/N^\mathcal{C}$. The entropy of $\{P(s)\}_{s=0,...,M-1}$ can be given by

$$H = -\sum_{s=0}^{M-1} P(s) \log P(s) , \qquad (3)$$

where M is the size of the SOMs, $64 \times 64 = 4096$ in our experiments.

However, the topology of the map becomes more significant as the size of the SOM is increased. With larger SOMs, the measure is thus less informative as the number of images sharing a BMU becomes overly small. To overcome this drawback, spatial entropy takes the spatial properties of the distribution over a large SOM into account. Suppose G is the maximum value of $X_s^\mathcal{C}$ over s. The spatial entropy is then given by

$$H_{\text{sp}} = -\sum_m \sum_{i=0}^{G} P(i, I_s = m) \log P(i|I_s = m) , \qquad (4)$$

where $I_s = \sum_{t \in \mathcal{N}_s} X_t^\mathcal{C}$ is the number of images that have been mapped to a predefined neighborhood of s, denoted by $\mathcal{N}_s$. In our experiments $\mathcal{N}_s$ was the 9×9 rectangular region surrounding s. A normalized performance measure is then obtained by

Table 4. Resulting ρ values for different aspects using the DSOMs constructed by the various features

semantic classes	face	left eye	right eye	nose	mouth	concatenated
white	0.07 (0.02)	0.06 (0.02)	0.09 (0.05)	0.02 (0.03)	0.06 (0.04)	0.11
Asian	0.17 (0.06)	0.18 (0.12)	0.11 (0.14)	0.11 (0.09)	0.08 (0.08)	0.26
black	0.27 (0.17)	0.13 (0.12)	0.13 (0.11)	0.13 (0.09)	0.31 (0.23)	0.44
male	0.17 (0.12)	0.08 (0.04)	0.09 (0.05)	0.06 (0.03)	0.08 (0.03)	0.21
female	0.16 (0.12)	0.10 (0.08)	0.08 (0.09)	0.05 (0.04)	0.09 (0.07)	0.23
glasses_yes	0.20 (0.03)	0.19 (0.16)	0.20 (0.24)	0.22 (0.23)	—	0.32
glasses_no	0.06 (0.02)	0.10 (0.04)	0.06 (0.05)	0.09 (0.09)	—	0.10
mustache_yes	0.30 (0.08)	—	—	0.14 (0.14)	0.37 (0.31)	0.39
mustache_no	0.03 (0.02)	—	—	0.04 (0.04)	0.04 (0.04)	0.03
beard_yes	0.52 (0.08)	—	—	—	—	0.52
beard_no	0.04 (0.02)	—	—	—	—	0.04

$$\rho = 1 - \frac{H_{sp}}{H} . \quad (5)$$

The ρ measure is zero for a completely random distribution since the neighborhood does not provide any information about the number of data points mapped to a map unit. Conversely, ρ is near one for a highly localized distribution. Table 4 shows the resulting ρ values of the DSOMs. For comparison, we also show in parentheses the ρ values for the SOMs trained without the LDA preprocessing.

As expected, the LDA projection enhances the discriminative power for nearly all the resulting SOMs. This is especially significant for the face feature, probably because the classes in the high-dimensional representation are not well separated with the Euclidean metric. A further enhancement is obtained by concatenating the projected components of the individual features.

4.3 Retrieval Experiments

Suppose N and S are the number of all images and the cardinality of the target subject class, respectively. Let j denote the random variable for the position of the first subject hit when using random retrieval. It is not difficult to prove that the mean of j is $E\{j\} = (N-S)/(S+1)$. Thus the improvement compared with the random retrieval can be quantified by the following *first subject hit advantage* (FSHA) measurement:

$$\text{FSHA}(i; N, S) = \frac{E\{j\}}{i} = \frac{N-S}{i \cdot (S+1)}, \quad (6)$$

where $i \in \{0, 1, \ldots, N-S\}$ is the position of the first subject hit using the improved retrieval. FSHA equals one when the retrieval is done in a random manner and increases when the retrieval is able to return the first relevant image earlier. For example, it equals two when the first subject hit occurs in the position whose index is half of the expected index in the random retrieval.

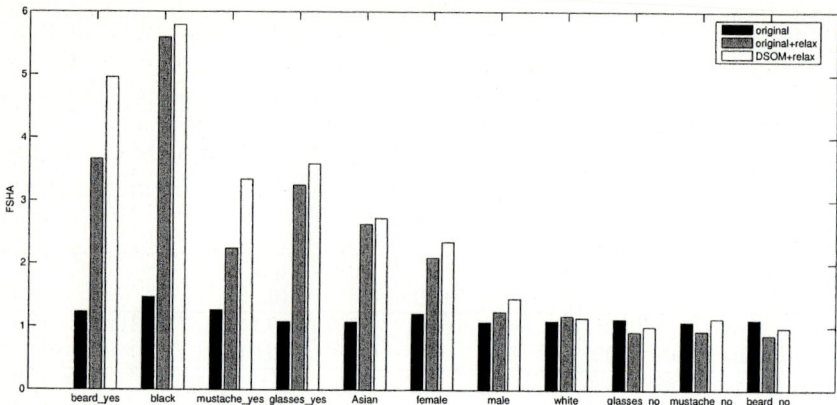

Fig. 4. The FSHAs of the retrieval experiments, where the semantic classes are ordered by their sizes. The results using the original retrieval algorithm are shown as the left bar (black) for comparison.

First, we conducted a set of experiments to test the query performance by only relaxing the relevance criterion. Each experiment iterates over every image $\mathcal{I}$ in a particular semantic class $\mathcal{C}$. In each loop the retrieval goal for the first stage is to search an image $\mathcal{I}'$ which depicts the same subject as $\mathcal{I}$ does, by using $\mathcal{C}$ as the relevance criterion. The position of the first subject hit was recorded and used to compute the FSHA. The median FSHAs for different semantic classes are shown as the middle bars (gray) of each group in Figure 4.

Second, we examined the improvement by using both DSOM and relaxing the relevance criterion. The FSHAs were estimated by a 20-fold cross-validation of the subjects. The median FSHA values are shown as the right bar (white) of each group in Figure 4.

It can be seen that all the FSHAs of the original query procedure without partial relevance are very close to unity. By only relaxing the relevance criterion, the FSHAs for the seven smallest semantic classes soars up, ranging from 2.1 to 5.6. Further improvement can be obtained by learning the partial relevance with the DSOM, especially for the classes beard_yes and mustache_yes. The highest FSHA, 5.8, is achieved for the semantic class black. In addition, the improvement for the smallest classes by using DSOM confirms the static results by the ρ measurement in Table 4. Significant increase of FSHAs can be achieved by using those DSOMs which have $\rho > 0.2$.

5 Conclusions and Future Work

We proposed an approach to speed up the appearance of the first subject hit in interactive facial image retrieval by exploiting partial relevance. The semantic information about the target subject is gradually learned during the user interaction procedure. Although SOM is not as good as some dedicated classification techniques, the proposed technique, DSOM, has the distinguished advantage that it softly uses the labeled data and can be readily integrated into the framework of interactive retrieval. The technique in this paper can easily be extended to the interactive CBIR on other types of image collections.

We employed LDA in this paper because it is simple and stable. LDA models each class with a single Gaussian distribution and all semantic classes of one aspect share a same within-class covariance matrix. In recent years many research findings have extended LDA to more complicated distributions. Some more advanced methods will be incorporated for further improvement. Moreover, we constructed a DSOM by applying supervised learning as a preprocessing step before the normal SOM training. An alternative approach would be to replace the Euclidean distance in SOM training with the Riemannian metric learned from the discriminative information. In addition, the current binary relevance feedback interface of PicSOM only supports the use of a single aspect, and in the future we shall extend the design to accommodate the parallel use of multiple aspects and DSOMs.

References

1. J. Ruiz del Solar and P. Navarrete. FACERET: An interactive face retrieval system based on Self-Organizing Maps. In *Proc. of Image and Video Retrieval : International Conference, CIVR 2002*, pages 157–164, London, UK, July 2002.
2. R. A. Fisher. The use of multiple measurements in taxonomic problems. *Annals of Eugenics*, 7, 1963.
3. Markus Koskela, Jorma Laaksonen, and Erkki Oja. Entropy-based measures for clustering and SOM topology preservation applied to content-based image indexing and retrieval. In *Proceedings of 17th International Conference on Pattern Recognition (ICPR 2004)*, volume 2, pages 1005–1008, Cambridge, UK, August 2004.
4. P. J. Phillips, H. Moon, S. A. Rizvi, and P. J. Rauss. The FERET evaluation methodology for face recognition algorithms. *IEEE Trans. Pattern Analysis and Machine Intelligence*, 22:1090–1104, October 2000.
5. M.A. Turk and A.P. Pentland. Face recognition using eigenfaces. In *Computer Vision and Pattern Recognition, proceedings of CVPR'91, IEEE Computer Society Conference on*, pages 586–591, Maui, HI USA, June 1991.
6. X. Wang and X. Tang. A unified framework for subspace face recognition. *IEEE Transactions on Pattern Analysis and Machine Intelligence*, 26(9):1222–1228, 2004.
7. Zhirong Yang and Jorma Laaksonen. Interactive retrieval in facial image database using Self-Organizing Maps. In *Proc. of IAPR Conference on Machine Vision Applications (MVA2005)*, pages 112–115, Tsukuba Science City, Japan, May 2005.

An Integration of Biometrics and Mobile Computing for Personal Identification

J. You[1], K.H. Cheung[1], Q. Li[1], and P. Bhattacharya[2]

[1] Department of Computing, The Hong Kong Polytechnic University
[2] Concordia Institute for Information Systems Engineering,
Concordia University, Canada

Abstract. This paper presents a new approach to efficient and effective personal identification for the security of network access by combining techniques in biometrics and mobile computing. To overcome the limitations of the existing password-based authentication services on the Internet, we propose a dynamic feature selection scheme to extract multiple personal features and integrate them in a hierarchical structure for fast and reliable identity authentication. To increase the speed and flexibility of the process, we use mobile agents as a navigational tool for parallel implementation in a distributed environment, which includes hierarchical biometric feature extraction, multiple feature integration, dynamic biometric data indexing and guided search.

Keywords: Biometrics computing, feature extraction and indexing, guided search, identity authentication and verification, mobile computing.

1 Introduction

It is very important to authenticate individuals in the various domains of today's automated, geographically mobile and increasingly electronically wired information society [1]. However, the traditional security measures such as passwords, PIN (Personal Identification Number) and ID cards can barely satisfy the strict security requirements because the use of passwords, PINs and ID cards is very insecure (*i.e.,* they can be lost, stolen, forged or forgotten). Biometric technology provides a totally new and yet an effective solution to authentication, which changes the conventional security and access control systems by recognising individuals based on their unique, reliable and stable biological or behavioral characteristics [2] [3]. To meet the challenge and immediate need for a high performance Internet authentication service, we apply biometrics computing technology to achieve fast and reliable personal identification. Considering the reliability and the convenience of biometric data collection from users, four biometric features (*i.e.,* fingerprints, palmprints, hand geometry and face) are used in our proposed system. We adopt a dynamic feature selection scheme for the application-oriented authentication tasks.

It is very important to access and retrieve an individual's biometrics information from large data collections that are distributed over large networks. However, it is difficult to have a uniform search engine that suits various needs. In this paper, we use mobile agents as a navigational tool for a flexible approach to index and search distributed biometrics databases, which can 1) simultaneously extract useful biometrics information from different data collection sources on the network, 2) categorize images by using an index-on-demand scheme that allows users to set up different index structures for fast search, and 3) support a flexible search scheme that allows users to choose effective methods to retrieve image samples.

Although biometrics databases are distributed, most of the current research on biometrics computing has been focused on a single-machine-based system. In order to effectively index and search for images with specific features among distributed image collections, it is essential to have a sort of "agent" that can be launched to create an index based on specific image feature or to search for specific images with a given content. In this paper, we use mobile agents as a tool to achieve network-transparent biometrics indexing and searching.

In addition, we introduce a new system structure for dynamic allocation of mobile agents using on-line task scheduling to address the limitations of the current approaches and to achieve greater flexibility. The proposed multi-agent system structure is enhanced by push-based technology [4].

2 Fundamentals of Biometrics Computing

2.1 Wavelet Based Multiple Feature Extraction

In contrast to the existing approaches which extract each biometric feature individually, we introduce a hierarchical approach for multiple biometrics feature representation and integration. We categorize the biometric features into three classes based on their nature (i.e., texture feature, shape feature and frequency feature). We then apply a wavelet-based scheme to combine the different feature classes based on their wavelet coefficients. The following highlights the extraction of texture and shape features.

Texture features can be represented by the related wavelet coefficients. If an image is decomposed into three wavelet layers, there will be ten sub-images. For each sub-image, the standard deviation of the wavelet coefficients is calculated to represent its texture feature component. Consequently, ten standard deviations, corresponding to ten sub-images, are used as the texture representation for the image.

Shape features can be represented in a hierarchical fashion by extending the conventional spline snake model and moments measurement. The original image is decomposed into a series of sub-band images via the wavelet transform. At each level, a B-spline curve, the so-called spline snake, is determined to link the image boundary feature points. In addition, we also apply a wavelet transform to decompose the original image into a collection of sub-bands ranging from low to high resolutions. The related first-, second- and third-normalized central moments for each sub-image are computed and the average values (within the same moment category) for all sub-bands are used as the individual shape feature components.

2.2 Dynamic Biometrics Feature Indexing

We propose a wavelet-based biometrics image hierarchy and a multiple feature integration scheme to facilitate the dynamic biometrics indexing. Our approach is characterized as follows. 1) To apply wavelet transforms to decompose a given biometric image into three layers of 10 sub-images. 2) To use the mean of the wavelet coefficients in three layers as the global feature measurements with respect to texture and shape, and then index them as tabular data in a global feature summary table. 3) To calculate the mean of the wavelet coefficients of the sub-band images (horizontal, vertical and diagonal) in different layers as local biometrics information, and then index them as tabular data in a local biometrics summary table. 4) To detect the interesting points of the objects in the original image and then store them in a table for fine match.

To achieve dynamic indexing and flexible similarity measurement, a statistically-based feature-selection scheme is adopted for multiple feature integration. Our algorithm extends the use of the Symmetrical Tau criterion [5] to guide the process of combining multiple biometrics features for retrieval. The combination process involves the normalization of feature components in each feature vector and the adjustment of weights for each component. Instead of using individual features to calculate the corresponding Tau as initially defined, we use the combined feature vector to obtain the relevant Tau. Such a process is iteratively repeated by dynamically adjusting the weights associated with each feature component: 1) Identify all of the individual features to be used for retrieval and obtain their feature vectors. For n features $\mathbf{f}_i$ ($i = 0, 1, ..., n-1$), there will be n individual feature vectors $\mathbf{V}_i$ ($i = 0, 1, ..., n-1$). 2) Apply Gaussian normalization to the above feature vectors. 3) Initialize a set of weights α_i ($i = 0, 1, ..., n-1$) and obtain its corresponding combined feature vector $\mathbf{V}_c = \sum_{i=0}^{n-1} \alpha_i \mathbf{V}_i$. 4) Calculate the corresponding Tau using the following formula:

$$Tau = \frac{\sum_{j=1}^{J}\sum_{i=1}^{I}\frac{P(ij)^2}{P(+j)} + \sum_{i=1}^{I}\sum_{j=1}^{J}\frac{P(ij)^2}{P(i+)} - SUM}{2 - SUM} \quad (1)$$

where the contingency table has I rows and J columns; $P(ij)$ is the probability that a variable belongs both to row category and to column category j; P(i+) and P(+j) are the marginal probabilities in row category i and column category j, respectively, and $SUM = \sum_{i=1}^{I} P(i+)^2 + \sum_{j=1}^{J} P(+j)^2$. 5) Adjust the set of weights, and obtain a new combined feature vector $\mathbf{V'}_c$ and calculate the corresponding Tau. 6) Repeat Step 5 for all of the given adjustment weight sets. 7) Find the maximum value of Tau from the sequences of Tau obtained in the previous stage. 8) Choose the combined feature with the maximum Tau value.

2.3 Guided Search

A key issue in biometrics-based verification and identification is feature matching, which is concerned with verifying and identifying the biometrics features that best match a query sample provided by a user. The conventional approaches often use fixed matching criteria to select the candidate images. By contrast, we propose using selective matching criteria that are associated with a user's query for more flexible search. Our system supports two types of queries: a) to pose a query by using a sample image, and b) to use a simple sketch as a query.

In the case of query by using a sample image, the search follows the process of multiple feature extraction and image similarity measurement that was described in the previous sections. Based on the nature of the query image, the user can add additional component weights during the process of combining image features for image similarity

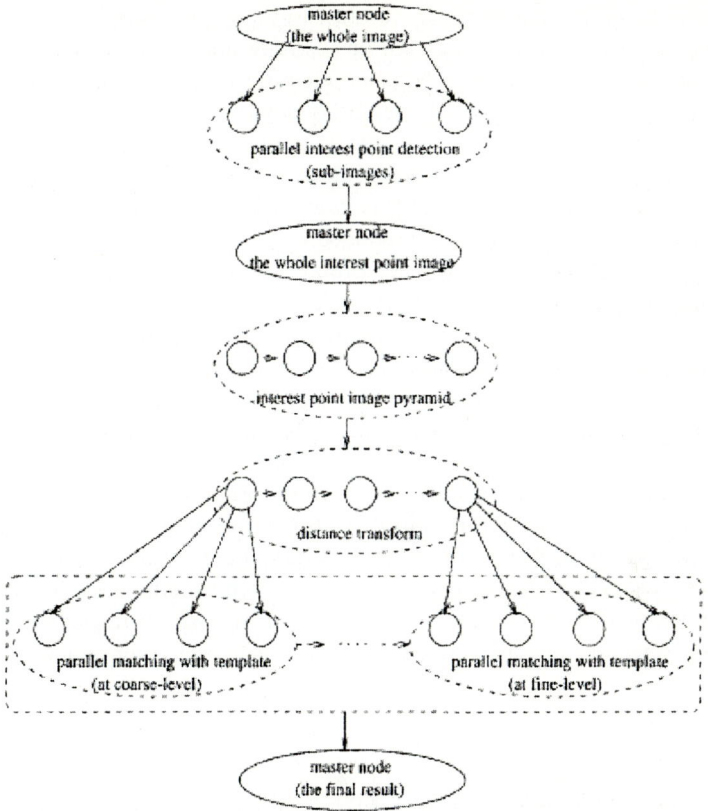

Fig. 1. Structure of hierarchical image matching

measurement. In the case of query by using a simple sketch provided a user, we apply a B-spline based curve matching scheme to identify the most suitable candidates from the image database. The goal here is to match and recognize the shape curves that were selected in the previous stage. These candidate curves are then modeled as B-splines and the matching is based on comparing their control points (such as the ordered corner points obtained from boundary tracing at the initial stage). Such a process involves the following steps: 1) projective-invariant curve models: uniform cubic B-splines, 2) iterative B-spline parameter estimation, and 3) invariant matching of the curves. In the case of a query by using a sample image, we use an image component code in terms of texture and shape to guide the search for the most appropriate candidates from a database at a coarse level, and then apply image matching at a fine level for the final output. Fig. 1 shows the structure of the proposed hierarchical matching.

3 Parallel Biometrics Computing Using Mobile Agents

Our wavelet-based hierarchical image matching scheme implemented using parallel virtual machine (PVM) is an original contribution[6]. That algorithm is extended using mobile agents in this work. In contrast to the conventional parallel implementation where either dedicated hardware or software are required, the parallel implementation of our biometrics-based personal identification algorithms is carried out by using mobile agents in a distributed computing environment. A mobile agent is an autonomous software entity which is capable of migrating autonomously from one host to another, making its requests to a server directly and performing tasks on behalf of its master. Some of the advantages of this model are better network bandwidth usage, more reliable network connection and reduced work in software application design [7]. To achieve flexibility and efficiency, we propose a multi-agent system with a hybrid agent computing paradigm. There are two classes of agents: global agents and local agents. The global agents handle inter-image coordination, query processing and reasoning. Each global agent may consist of a few sub-agents. The following list describes the five global agents and their associated sub-agents that are proposed in our system: 1) Coordinator Agent which coordinates other global agents and image agents, 2) Query Agent which processes users' complex queries using three sub-agents including query understanding, query reasoning and query feature formation. 3) Wavelet Agent which generates wavelet coefficients for multiple feature representation and integration using three sub-agents such as wavelet transform, feature representation and feature integration. 4) Verification/Identification Agent which performs hierarchical feature matching for identity verification and identification using two sub-agents responsible for matching criterion selection feature matching. 5) User Interface Agent which manages all

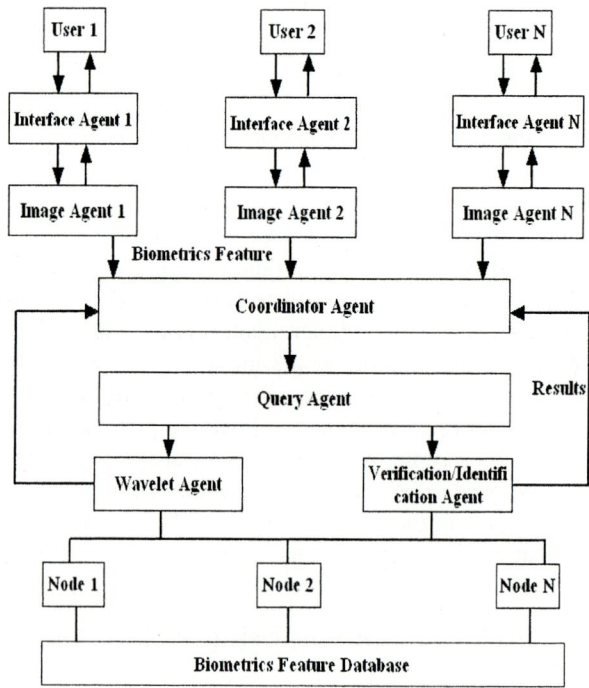

Fig. 2. Mobile Agent architecture model

user interactions. In addition, the local agents are referred to as *Image Agents*, which are responsible for performing relevant biometrics computing tasks on each individual image. This proposed agent architecture model is illustrated in Fig. 2. Together with Fig. 1, one can see that a parallel computing is naturally implemented.

4 Experimental Results

The biometrics image samples that were used for testing are of size 232×232 with a resolution of 125 dpi and 256 grayscales. Four types of biometrics features, namely hand geometries, fingers, palmprints and faces are considered. A total of 2,500 images from 500 individuals are stored in our database. These biometrics samples were collected from both female and male adults within the age range from 18 to 50. A series of experiments were carried out to verify the high performance of the proposed algorithms.

4.1 Dynamic Feature Selection and Multi-level Similarity Measures

The dynamic selection of image features is demonstrated by multi-level palmprint feature extraction for personal identification and verification. The experiment is carried out in two stages. In stage one, the global palmprint features are extracted at coarse level and candidate samples are selected for further processing. In stage two, the regional palmprint features are detected and a hierarchical image matching is performed for the final retrieval. Fig. 3 illustrates the multi-level extraction of palmprint features.

In our system, we consider multiple palmprint features and adopt different similarity measures in a hierarchical manner to facilitate a coarse-to-fine palmprint matching scheme for personal identification. Four palmprint features are extracted – Level-1

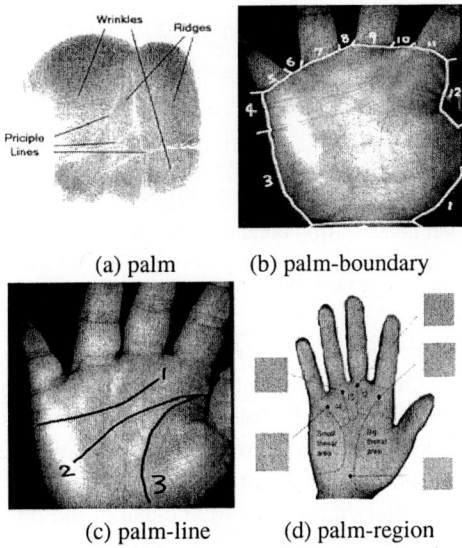

Fig. 3. Multi-level feature extraction

Table 1. The system performance of accuracy

	False Reject Rate	Correct Reject Rate
T_a	1.69%	92.47%
T_b	1.10%	86.62%
T_c	0.73%	79.27%

global geometry feature, Level-2 global texture energy, Level-3 local "interest lines, and Level-4 local texture feature vector. More specifically, the palm boundary segments are used as Level-1 global geometry feature. The 'tuned' mask based texture energy measurement is used for Level-2 global texture feature representation [8]. The dominant feature lines in palmprint are extracted as Level-3 local 'interest feature lines [9]. A 2D Gabor phase coding is used to form Level-4 local texture feature vector. We begin initial searching for the best similar palmprint matching group with Level-1 global geometry feature. The candidates with small distance differences will be considered for further coarse-level selection by global texture measurement. The selected candidates will be subjected to fine matching based on texture feature vector. The false rejection and correct rejection rates of the first three levels are given in Table 1.

4.2 Hierarchical Feature Matching Test

The performance of the proposed coarse-to-fine curve-matching approach is further demonstrated in the second test, which is face recognition for personal identification. At a coarse level, a fractional discrimination function is used to identify the region of interest in an individual's face. At a fine curve-matching level, the active contour tracing algorithm is applied to detect the boundaries of interest in the facial regions for the final matching. Fig. 4 illustrates the tracing of facial curves for face recognition.

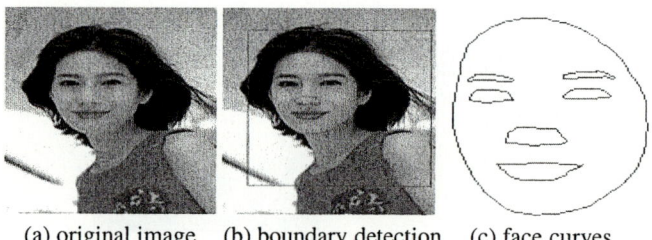

(a) original image   (b) boundary detection   (c) face curves

Fig. 4. Face curve extraction

To verify the effectiveness of our approach, a series of tests were carried out using a database of 200 facial images collected from different individuals under various conditions, such as uneven lighting, moderate facial tilting and partial occlusion.

Table 2 lists the correct recognition rate of the coarse-level detection.

To show the robustness of the proposed algorithm for face detection that is invariant to the perspective view, partial distortion and occlusion, the fine-level curve matching is applied to facial images with different orientations and expressions. Fig. 5 illustrates sample images of the same person from various perspective views and under different conditions. Table 3 and Table 4 summarizes the test results for 100 cases.

Table 2. Performance of face detection at coarse-level

Face Condition	Correct Detection Rate
unevenness of lighting	98%
multiple faces	95%
moderate tilt of faces	97%
partial sheltering	85%

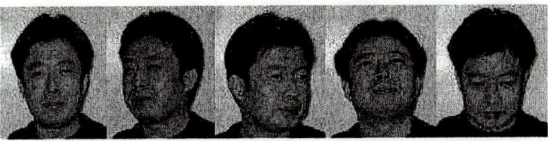

(a) The face samples at different orientations

The face samples of different conditions

Fig. 5. The face samples

Table 3. Performance of face recognition at different orientions

Viewing Perspective	Correct Classification Rate
-20^0 (vertical)	84%
-10^0 (vertical)	86%
$+10^0$ (vertical)	86%
$+20^0$ (vertical)	83%
-20^0 (horizontal)	85%
-10^0 (horizontal)	87%
$+10^0$ (horizontal)	87%
$+20^0$ (horizontal)	84%

Table 4. Performance of face classification with different conditions

Face Condition	Correct Classification Rate
partial occlusion	77%
various expressions	81%
wearing glasses	82%

4.3 Evaluation of System Efficiency

To test the increased efficiency of the proposed agent-based approach, a group of external assistant agents were employed. The central agent controller is responsible for dissectting the task and assembling the final result. The increased speed ratio of different patterns is illustrated in Fig. 6.

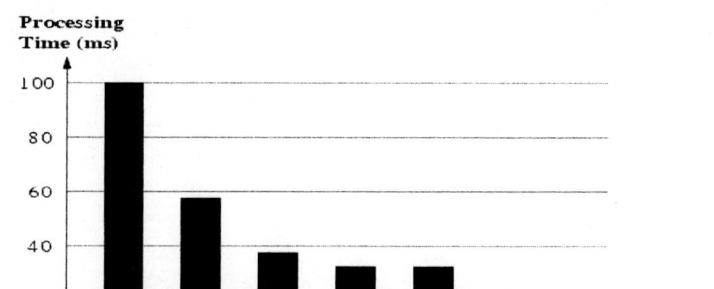

Fig. 6. The increased efficiency ratio of different patterns

Table 5. The evaluation of system efficiency – average RTT for 100 trials

Server Location	Execution Time (ms) Server 1	Execution Time (ms) Server 2
A. Client Machine		
user requirement		
query processing	210	285
B. Server Machine		
feature extraction	1020	1315
feature integration	360	430
C. Client Machine		
coarse-level matching	1320	1830
fine-level matching	2510	3280
TOTAL RTT	5420	7140

The system efficiency is further judged using the round trip time (RTT) test. Instead of calculating the difference between the arrival and departure time at the server, the RTT test uses the total round trip time for the agents involved. RTT is determined from all of the fragments of time that are spent on each of the various operations, starting with the collection of user requirements, continuing with biometrics feature extraction, similarity measurement, and searching for the best matching. Two servers are used in this test. Server 1 is located on the same local area network (LAN) as the client machine, whereas Server 2 is situated at a remote site within the campus. Table 5 shows the average execution time at different stage for 100 trials. It is noted that most of the execution time is spent on the fine-level matching. In practice, the network traffic should be considered for real applications.

5 Conclusion

This paper explores the integration of pattern recognition techniques, distributed computing methodology, and agent technology to provide an effective and efficient approach to identity authentication using personal features (biometrics). To overcome the limitations of the current security systems, which use fixed pre-selected features and have bottlenecks of slow performance and platform dependence, we develop a parallel biometrics based personal identification and verification system using mobile agents. To tackle the key issues such as biometrics feature extraction, indexing and search, we propose a hierarchical approach to fast content-based biometric image retrieval by dynamic indexing and guided search. The experimental results confirm that our approach is feasible for on-line identity authentication and verification and will be useful for many other security applications.

Acknowledgment

The authors from the Hong Kong Polytechnic University are most grateful for the support from the Hong Kong Polytechnic University. In addition, Prabir Bhattacharya would like to thank that the NSERC, Canada and the Canada Research Chair programme for his support.

References

[1] A. Jain, R. Bolle and S. Pankanti, *Biometrics: Personal Identification in Networked Society*, Kluwer Academic Publishers, 1999.
[2] B. Miller, "Vital signs of identity," *IEEE Spectrum*, vol. 32, pp. 22-30, 1994.
[3] W. Shen, M. Surette and R. Khanna, "Evaluation of automated biometrics-based identification and verification systems," *Proceedings of the IEEE*, vol. 85, no. 9, pp. 1464-1478, 1997.
[4] George V. Cybenko, B. Brewington, R. Gray, K. Moizumi, D. Kotz, and D. Rus, "Mobile Agents in Distributed Information Retrieval," In *Matthias Klusch, editor, Intelligent Information Agents*, Chap. 12. Springer-Verlag. ISBN 3-540-65112-8
[5] X. Zhou and T.S. Dillon, "A statistical-heuristic feature selection criterion for decision tree induction," *IEEE Trans. Patt. Anal. Machine Intell.*, vol. PAMI-13, no. 8, pp. 834-841, 1991.
[6] J. You and P. Bhattacharya, "A Wavelet-based coarse-to-fine image matching scheme in a parallel virtual machine environment," *IEEE Trans. Image Processing*, vol. 9, no. 9, pp. 1547-1559, 2000.
[7] P. Dasgupta, N. Narasimhan, L.E. Moser and P.M. Smith, "MAGNET: Mobile agents for networked electronic trading," *IEEE Trans. on Knowledge and Data Engineering*, vol. 11, no. 4, pp. 509-525, 1999.
[8] J. You, W.X. Li and D. Zhang, "Hierarchical palmprint identification via multiple feature extraction," *Pattern Recognition*, vol. 35, pp. 847-859, 2002.
[9] D. Zhang, W.K. Kong, J. You and M. Wong, "Low-resolution based on-line palmprint identification," *IEEE Trans. Pattern Analysis and Machine Intelligence (PAMI)*, vol. 25, no. 9, September, pp. 1041-1050, 2003.

Eyes Segmentation Applied to Gaze Direction and Vigilance Estimation

Zakia Hammal, Corentin Massot, Guillermo Bedoya, and Alice Caplier

Laboratoy of Images and Signals, Grenoble, 38031 Cedex, France
`zakia_hammal@yahoo.fr, firstname.name@lis.inpg.fr`

Abstract. An efficient algorithm to iris segmentation and its application to automatic and non-intrusive gaze tracking and vigilance estimation is presented and discussed. A luminance gradient technique is used to fit the irises from face images. A robust preprocessing which mimics the human retina is used in such a way that a robust system to luminance variations is obtained and contrast enhancement is achieved. The validation of the proposed algorithm is experimentally demonstrated by using three well-known test databases: the FERET database, the Yale database and the Cohn-Kanade database. Experimental results confirm the effectiveness and the robustness of the proposed approach to be applied successfully in gaze direction and vigilance estimation.

1 Introduction

During the past two decades a considerable scientific effort has been devoted to understand the human vision. Since early works on the visual process study ([1]), many promising applications have considered the eyes movements as well as the vigilance characteristics as behavioral information (see [2],[3], [4],[5]), in order to develop sophisticated human-machine interfaces. In recent years, the evolution of the user interfaces for computer systems have been producing a significant impact since they are oriented to the development of intelligent multi-modal interfaces. The key idea for those systems is to make the communication/interaction with machines more intuitive.

We can define the human-machine interaction improvement from two perspectives: at the communication level with the analysis of gaze direction, and at the interpretation level of the user state with the analysis of vigilance. In this paper, an efficient algorithm is proposed to achieve the automatic irises boundaries segmentation which is used for gaze direction and vigilance estimation. In order to evaluate the performances of the proposed system, the gaze direction estimator has been compared to other existing systems ([13]).

In spite of the fact that iris boundaries automatic segmentation is a well-known problem, we propose a new and efficient solution as an alternative to the usual methods. Provided that many approaches fail when luminance conditions are variable, a robust preprocessing filter which mimic the human retina is used, in such a way that a system tolerant to variable illumination conditions is obtained. A luminance gradient-based technique is used for iris segmentation, obtaining a robust fitting of the irises from face images. Additionally, the developed system requires only one single digital camera, contrary to most existing systems, which have to use more sophisticated and expensive equipments, such as infrared cameras, multiple digital cameras or optical zooming ([3],[4],[5]). Finally, our approach does not need any manual initialization nor any learning step, so that a fully automatic system is presented. The developed eyes segmentation algorithm has been intensively tested using three different test databases: the FERET database [9] (static images of faces), the YALE database [10] (static images of expressive faces) and the Cohn-Kanade database [11] (facial expressions sequences).

The paper is organized as follows: Section 2 introduces the robust filter preprocessing and the proposed segmentation approach. Some results are described and discussed. In Section 3, the use of the developed algorithm to gaze direction and vigilance estimation is presented. The interest of our approach to be used in real applications is also demonstrated.

2 Iris Segmentation

Many real-world applications require accurate and real time iris segmentation, and a lot of scientific effort has been dedicated to this field. In this work we are interested in iris segmentation in a frame acquired with a single digital camera. We start with the localization of the face in the first frame of a given sequence. Face extraction is under the scope of this paper and we use the MPISearch algorithm [6] based on the work of Viola and Jones [7]. This algorithm extracts a square bounding box around the face (Figure 2 left). Then it is automatically tracked by block matching for the rest of the sequence.

2.1 Retinal Prefiltering

The video sequences are acquired in non-constraint illumination conditions. In order to avoid problems with luminance variations, a pre-filtering stage is applied to each frame using a model of the retinal processing [8]. The variations of illumination are smoothed by a filter that uses a non-linear adaptation stage and a multi-stage combination of low and high spatial frequencies. This yields to an enhancement of the contour and at the same time to a local correction of luminance variations (Figure 1).

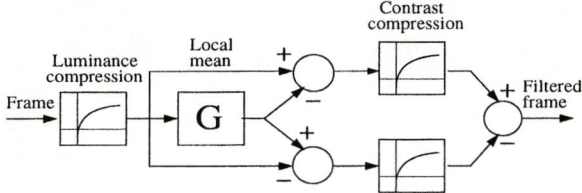

Fig. 1. Retinal preprocessing. A luminance compression is first applied on the frame. Then a Gaussian filter ($size = 15$ pixels, $\sigma = 2$ pixels) realizes a local averaging which is combined and compressed leading to a contrast enhancement. A final combination gives the pre-filtered frame.

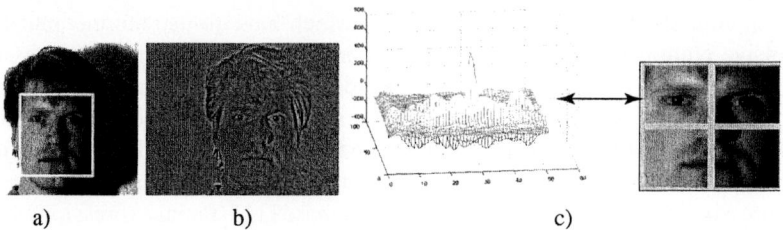

Fig. 2. a) image with a dissymetrical illumination (the lite comes from the right of the face) and example of face extraction; b) image filtered by the retinal filter; c) evolution of the NFLG during the scanning of the search area of the iris corresponding to the upper left square of the rectangle surrounding the face.

2.2 Iris Segmentation Algorithm

Iris contour is the frontier between the dark area of iris and the eye white. This contour is supposed to be a circle made of points of maximum of luminance gradient. Since the eyes could be slightly closed, the upper part of the iris could be occluded. Then, for each iris, we look for the lower part of the iris circle. Each iris semi-circle maximizes the normalized flow of luminance gradient ($NFLG_t$) defined at time t as:

$$NFLG_t = \frac{1}{length(C_{sc})} \sum_{p \in C_{sc}} \vec{\nabla} I_t(p) . \vec{n}(p) \qquad (1)$$

where $I_t(p)$ is the luminance at point p and at time t, $n(p)$ is the normal to the boundary at point p and C_{sc} is the boundary of the lower semi-circle. The $NFLG_t$ is normalized by the length of C_{sc}.

In order to select the semi-circle which maximizes the $NFLG_t$, several candidates scanning the search area of each iris are tested. The size of the iris is taken proportionnal to the head size given by the face detection algorithm ([6]). The search area for each iris is limited to the upper right or upper left part of the face bounding box (Figure 2 right). This division of the face has been determined after a study of 400 images of face

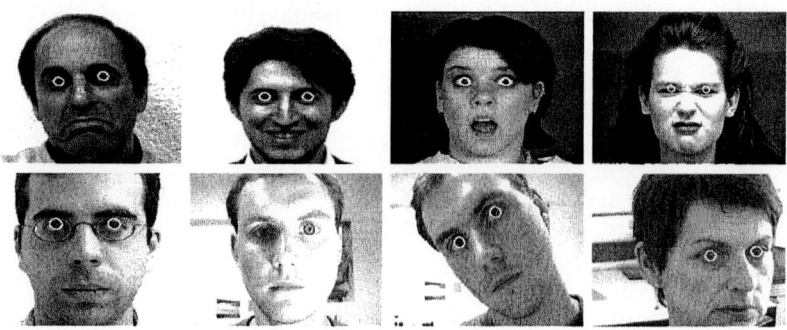

Fig. 3. Results of segmentation of the iris on the Yale database, the Cohn-Kanade database and from sequences acquired at our laboratory

(ORL database [12]). Even in the case of a rotated face, if the irises are both visible, the validity of the proportions is still true.

Figure 3 shows different iris segmentation results by using different test databases: the first row shows the robustness of our algorithm to different facial expressions, while the second row shows respectively the detection in case of spectacles, of bad illumination conditions, inclination of the face and vertical rotation.

3 Automatic System for Gaze Direction and Vigilance Estimation

3.1 Gaze Direction Estimation

We present an automatic approach to estimate the gaze direction estimation of the user in front of a computer screen. The proposed method shows an accurate detection of the position of the iris in the face. It emerges as one promising alternative to the existing systems ([13]), which usually require a device and/or impose acquisition and calibration constraints that are awkward to use. Some of the additional advantages of our method are that it uses a commercially available video acquisition system made of a single camera (e.g., a webcam) placed above or below the screen (Figure 4). Our system makes the assumption that the head is kept fixed, but this assumption can be removed using a head pose tracking system.

Geometrical Model and Approximation of the Projection Function. We have to define the projection function, which establishes the relationship between the position of the iris center in an image and its projection on the screen.

We define the following geometrical model (Figure 4 left). O is the center of the screen; (A, B) represents the height of the screen (a similar model can be done for the width); C is the center of the iris; H is the orthogonal projection of C and is the center of the reference screen plane; α is the angle between CH and CO and represents the position of the user relatively to the screen; x is the coordinate on AB of the point fixed by the user; the angles between CO and Cx is noted θ_x, between CO and CB is noted θ_1 and between CO and CA is noted θ_2. In order to find the analytical formulation of the projection function, we express the angles α and θ_x obtaining the following set of equations:

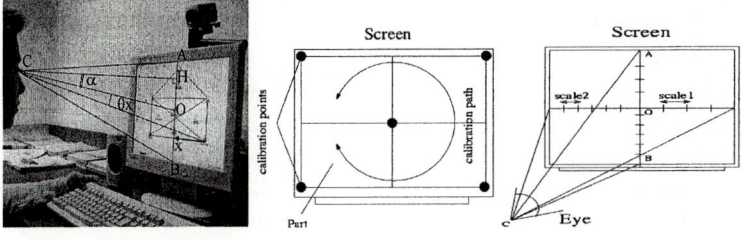

Fig. 4. Left: overview of the system and geometrical model; middle: calibration configuration; right: scale configuration.

$$AO = OB = AH + HO = 1 (convention)$$
$$cos(\alpha) = CH/CO$$
$$cos(\alpha + \theta_x) = CX/CH \qquad (2)$$
$$1 = CO^2 + CA^2 - 2cos(\theta 2)CO * CA$$
$$1 = CO^2 + CB^2 - 2cos(\theta 1)CO * CB$$
$$4 = CA^2 + CB^2 - 2cos(\theta 1 + \theta 2)CA * CB$$

The resolution of the set of equations (2) leads to:

$$HX = CH * tan(\alpha + \theta_x) \qquad (3)$$

Equation 3 shows that the estimation of gaze direction depends on the distance to the screen CH and on the angle α. Figure 5 left presents the variation of the distance Hx with a fixed α and different values of CH. The analysis of these curves points out the fact that for $CH >= CH_{min}$ the projection function tends to be linear. Figure 5 right presents the comparison between the projection function and its equivalent linear approximation. We estimate that taking $CH_{min} = 3.OA$, i.e., $\approx 30cm$ and $\alpha <= \alpha_{max} = 10°$, the projection function is linear. These values correspond to usual work conditions justifying the use of a linear approximation for the projection function (Figure 5 right).

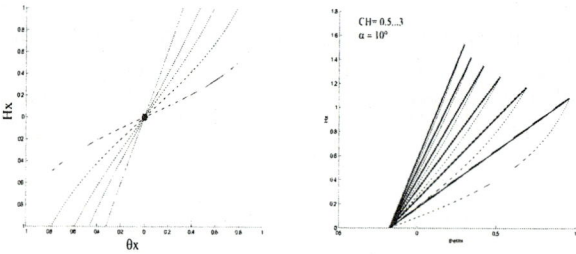

Fig. 5. Evolution of the projection function in relation to CH (left) and linear approximation (right)

Implementation. The screen is divided into four parts around the screen center O (Figure 4 middle). According to the position C of the user in front of the screen (CO is not necessary perpendicular to the screen, Figure 4 right), a better precision can be obtained, if we ensure differences on the scales of each part at each coordinate. A specific scale is thus associated to each part. The step scale corresponds to the distance covered on the screen for one unit of movement of the iris (e.g. $1unit = 1pixel$). For example, scale 1 of Figure 4 right has to be greater than scale 2. It is because a displacement of one pixel of the iris center in the image plane will be greater in the top right part of the screen than in the top left part.

Gaze Direction Estimation. We calculate the gaze direction using the projection of the iris centre position on the screen. The system just takes into account the spatial displacement of the iris in the face and not any velocity information. The process is divided into two steps : the calibration which automatically initializes the system and the detection itself.

a) **Calibration.** The calibration consists in automatically defining the x and y scales for each part of the screen. For this, five points are necessary : the center and the four corners of the screen (Figure 4 middle). In the calibration stage, the user has to be in front of the screen at a normal distance (50cm to 80cm), while a camera is located above or under the screen. When the calibration procedure begins, five points appear dynamically on the screen one by one beginning by the center and finishing at each corner. The user has only to follow them with his eyes. The major difficulty is that human cannot precisely fix a given position without any dispersion. In order to overcome this problem, each point of calibration appear on the screen during 1 second. The histogram of the positions is analyzed and four extreme positions (two according to the x coordinate and two, to the y coordinate) that have been fixed the most often are used for the calibration.

b) **Detection of Gaze Direction.** For each image, the right and the left iris center positions are extracted. Each center is related to one point of the screen by the projection process. To eliminate transitory positions (occurring during the movement of the eye towards its new position), we introduce the notion of fixation which is a region fixed during several frames (6 frames at 25 frames/second). At the end of the sequence we obtain what we call a "fixation map", which represents the whole set of fixations. The fixations can overlap, so we associate at each position a value corresponding to the number of times that this position has been fixed.

The gaze position of the user on the screen corresponds to the barycenter of the set of points that belong to the same fixation region obtained in the fixation map. In addition to the spatial position, the system automatically computes the chronological order of the fixations. The final result consists in recovering the whole set of barycenters of the regions of fixation and the order in which they appeared during the sequence (number associated) (Figure 6 right, Figure 7).

Precision Measures to Determine the System Performance. In order to evaluate the precision of our gaze direction estimation, an experimental setup, consisting in a grid of 18 black points plotted on the screen (Figure 6 left) is used to estimate the user gaze position during the fixation of these points. The camera is placed under the screen (1024x768), considering that the usual work conditions in front of a computer screen, vary in a range between 50cm to 80cm. The subject was asked to sequencially fix the black points and this experiment is carried out 10 times. We obtain a mean precision of $0.8°$ which means that the fixations are accurately detected. Figure 6 left presents the result of the estimation of the user gaze direction on the grid defined before. The white circles represent the estimated user mean fixation position for each fixed black point. These results are very satisfactory in the context of human-computer interaction.

One of the potential application is the study of the strategy of a document exploration, like in figure 6 right which presents the analysis of a geographical map. The system is able to detect the user attention during the exploration. Each point represents the position of the gaze position on the map and its temporal apparition.

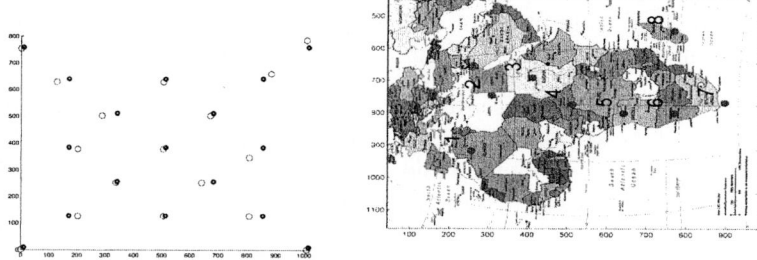

Fig. 6. Left: grid made of black points corresponding to the different positions used to estimate the precision (the size is 1024x768 pixels and corresponds to the whole screen); white circles represent the results of the user gaze detection on the grid; right: analysis of the exploration strategy of a geographical map; the points are situated on the really observed countries with their chronological order.

Comparison with a Commercial System. We present two kinds of comparison results: a fixation map and a trajectory map. In the fixation map, the user has to fix each icon presented in the image in a free order. On Figure 7 left, each point represents one fixation (barycenter of a region of fixation). The associated number indicates the order in which the different icons have been looked at by the user. The video sequences are acquired by a camera with a frame rate of 25 frames per second. They are acquired in usual work conditions in front of a computer screen with the head kept fixed.

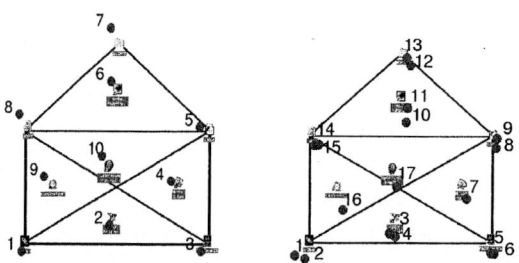

Fig. 7. Left: fixation map with our system; right: fixation map with Eye-Link.

In order to evaluate the performances of our detection system, we have made the same experiments as the infra-red detector Eye-Link system (a commercial eye tracker [13]) (Figure 7 right). The comparison of the detection obtained by both systems points out a similar quality of our results.

In Figure 8 we aim at rebuilding the ocular trajectory of a user. He has to follow the edges of a drawn house. Our results (Figure 8 left) have been compared with those obtained with the Eye-Link (Figure 8 right). Our trajectory is composed of the whole set of points corresponding to the gaze locations, contrary to the Eye-Link one which only connects some fixations points. This explains that the Eye-Link trajectory is more rectilinear.

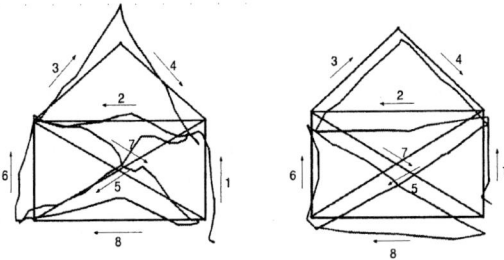

Fig. 8. Left: trajectory map with our system; right trajectory map with Eye-Link.

3.2 Vigilance Estimation

To analyze the vigilance, different sequences have been acquired in our laboratory. The video sequences are acquired by a standard camera at 25 frames per seconds and during 10 minutes. The subjects were asked to simulate three states: normal blinking, fast blinking and drowsiness respectively.

Blink Detection. A blink corresponds to the transition of the state of each eye from *open eye* to *closed eye*. The *open* or *closed* state of each eye is related to the presence or the absence of an iris. The automatic detection of the eye state is based on the analysis of the $NFLG_t$ and the study of the normalized quantity of luminance (NQL_t) which is defined by the relation:

$$NQL_t = \frac{\sum_{p \in S_{sc}} I_t(p)/nbr}{sup_{p \in S_{sc}} I_t(p)} \qquad (4)$$

where $I_t(p)$ is the luminance at pixel p at time t, S_{sc} is the surface of the candidate semi-circle and nbr the number of its points. Let $NFLG_m$ and NQL_m be the mean values of the $NFLG_t$ and the NQL_t for the open eyes. These values are computed on a temporal window with a width Δ_t and situated between $t - \Delta_t$ and t. Δ_t corresponds to the time needed for one blink at normal blinking frequency. The evaluation of $NFLG_m$ and NQL_m at different time t allows the system to re-adapt itself to varying conditions of acquisition (like change in conditions of illumination). At time t, the maximum of $NFLG_m$ and the minimum of NQL_m overall the already estimated values are computed. Indeed $NFLG_t$ depends on the degree of opening of the eye (Figure 9 right) and taking the maximum value ensures to consider the $NFLG_t$ of the highest opening of the eye. On the contrary, as the iris is a dark area NQL_t decreases with the opening of the eye (Figure 9 left) and taking the minimum value ensures to consider the NQL_t of the highest opening of the eye. At frame t, eyes are detected as open if the following relations are satisfied:

$$(NFLG_t \geq max(NFLG_m) * c_{NFLG} \qquad (5)$$
$$and(NQL_t \leq min(NQL_m) * c_{NQL}))$$

When the eyes start closing, the iris semi-circle is less and less visible so that $NFLG_t$ is decreasing. Once the eyes are closed, the value of $NFLG_t$ is inferior to the maximum of $NFLG_m$ multiplied by a coefficient c_{NFLG} (first condition for closed eyes). Sometimes the value $NFLG_t$ along the selected semi-circle when the eyes are closed does not check the first condition because of the lashes: the semi-circle coincides with the lashes which are made of points of maximum gradient of luminance (frontier between the skin and the lashes). As a result, the $NFLG_t$ along the selected semi-circle is superior or equal to the defined threshold. For this reason, we add the normalized mean value of luminance of the surface of the semi-circle. If the eyes are closed, NQL_t is higher or equal to the minimum of NQL_m multiplied by a coefficient c_{NQL} (second condition for closed eyes) because the surface of the selected semi-circle corresponds to a clear area (area of eyelids) in the case of closed eye, instead of a dark area (area of iris) in the case of open eye. The coefficients c_{NFLG} and c_{NQL} are taken, so that an eye is considered open if more than $\frac{1}{3}$ of the semi circle is visible (Figure 10 first row second column) and is considered closed otherwise. These coefficients are computed as the mean on ten subjects of the ratio between their maximum and minimum value of $NFLG_t$ and of NQL_t.

Figure 9 shows the temporal evolution of $NFLG_t$ and NQL_t and the results after thresholding. On these curves, there are two blinkings: the first one is very quick and the second one occurs during several frames (it might correspond to a short sleeping).

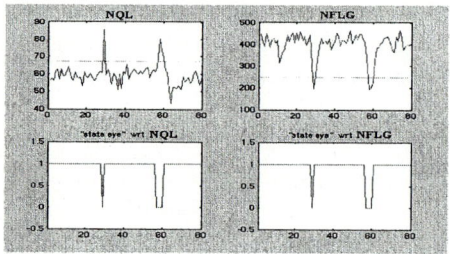

Fig. 9. Top left : temporal evolution of NQL_t and threshold (dashed line); top right, temporal evolution of $NFLG_t$ and threshold (dashed line); bottom left, eye state after NQL_t thresholding; bottom right, eye state after $NFLG_t$ thresholding (0 stands for closed eye and 1 stands for open eye).

Estimation of the Vigilance. We estimate the vigilance or interest level of a user by the evaluation of the frequency of blinking. In case of "normal" vigilance level, the blinking frequency evaluated on our sequences is in average 18 blinks per minute. These values are coherent with the values found in the medical literature (12 to 20 per minute). To estimate the level of vigilance, the blink frequency is computed at each time t inside a temporal window Δ_t analyzing the last 6 seconds (period of one blink at a normal blinking frequency). The detection of one or two blinks corresponds to a normal blinking frequency. If the frequency is higher, the ratio between the duration of the open eye states and the closed eye states indicates whether it is a case of fast blinking (eyes are found open two times longer) or a case of drowsiness (eyes are found closed two times longer). If the frequency is lower, then the same ratio indicates wether it is a case of normal blinking (the eyes are kept open during all the temporal window) or a case of drowsiness (the eyes are kept closed).

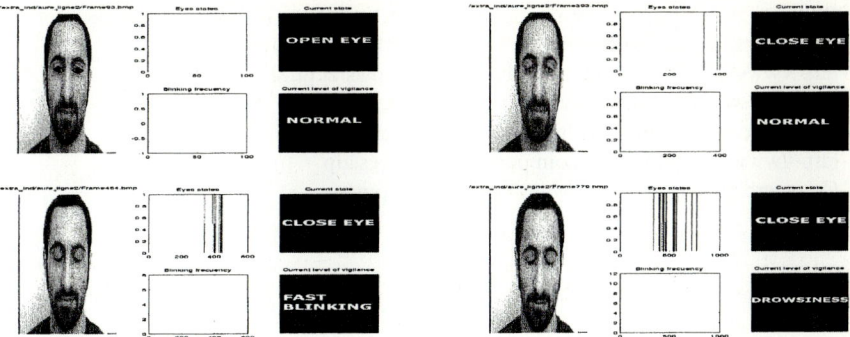

Fig. 10. Estimation of the vigilance. For each figure: left: current image; middle, top: past evolution of the eyes states, bottom: past evolution of the blinking frequency; right, top: current detected eye state, bottom: current vigilance level.

Figure 10 shows four frames taken from one of the sequences described below and examples of detection of the eyes state and of the vigilance level.

4 Conclusion

In this paper, we have presented an efficient algorithm for iris segmentation. The results are accurate and robust to luminance variations. We have presented two associated applications in human-machine interaction domain: an accurate and low constrained gaze direction estimation system working with a single commercially available video acquisition system. Secondly, we presented an analysis of the frequency of the blink, which can be used in the detection of the vigilance level of the user. Preliminary results and comparative experiments with existing systems show the interest and the robustness of the proposed approach.

References

1. Buswell, G.T.: How people look at pictures. University of Chicago Press (1920)
2. Zhu, Z., Qiang, Q.: Robust Real-Time Eye Detection and Tracking and Variable Lighting Conditions and Various Face Conditions. Computer Vision and Image Understanding. 98 (2005) 124–154
3. Hansen, D.W., Pece, A.E.C.: Eye Tracking in the Wild. Computer Vision and Image Understanding. 98 (2005) 236–274
4. Noureddin, B., Lawrence, P.D., Man, C.F.: A Non-Contact for Tracking gaze in a Human-Computer Interface. Computer Vision and Image Understanding. 98 (2005) 52–82
5. Wang, J., Sung, E., Venkateswarlu, R.: Estimating the eye gaze from one eye. Computer Vision and Image Understanding. 98 (2005) 83–103
6. MPIsearch algorithm for face detection http://mplab.ucsd.edu/grants/project1/free-software/MPTWebSite/introductionframe.html
7. Viola, P., Jones, M.: Robust real time face detection. International Journal of Computer Vision 57(2) (2004) 137–154

8. Beaudot, W.: The neural information in the vertebra retina : a melting pot of ideas for artificial vision. PhD thesis, tirf laboratory, Grenoble, France. (1994)
9. http://www.itl.nist.gov/iad/humanid/feret/feret_master.html
10. http://cvc.yale.edu/projects/yalefaces/yalefaces.html
11. http://vasc.ri.cmu.edu/idb/html/face/facial_expression/
12. http://www.uk.research.att.com:pub/data/att_faces.zip
13. Commercial website: http://www.eyelinkinfo.com/

Bilinear Discriminant Analysis for Face Recognition

Muriel Visani[1], Christophe Garcia[1], and Jean-Michel Jolion[2]

[1] France Telecom Research & Development,
4, rue du Clos Courtel, 35512 Cesson-Sevigne, France
{muriel.visani, christophe.garcia}@rd.francetelecom.com
[2] Laboratoire LIRIS, INSA Lyon, 20, Avenue Albert Einstein,
Villeurbanne, 69621 cedex, France
Jean-Michel.Jolion@insa-lyon.fr

Abstract. In this paper, we present a new statistical projection-based face recognition method, called Bilinear Discriminant Analysis (BDA). The proposed technique effectively combines two complementary versions of Two-Dimensional-Oriented Linear Discriminant Analysis (2DoLDA), namely Column-Oriented Linear Discriminant Analysis (CoLDA) and Row-Oriented Linear Discriminant Analysis (RoLDA). BDA relies on the maximization of a generalized bilinear projection-based Fisher criterion. A series of experiments was performed on various international face image databases in order to evaluate and compare the effectiveness of BDA to RoLDA and CoLDA. The experimental results indicate that BDA outperforms RoLDA, CoLDA and 2DPCA for face recognition, while leading to a significant dimensionality reduction.

1 Introduction

In the eigenfaces [1] (resp. fisherfaces [2]) method, the 2D face images of size $h \times w$ are first transformed into 1D image vectors of size $h \cdot w$, and then a Principal Component Analysis (PCA) (resp. Linear Discriminant Analysis (LDA)) is applied to this high-dimensional vector space, where statistical analysis is costly and may be unstable. To overcome these drawbacks, Yang et al. [3] proposed the Two Dimensional PCA (2DPCA) method, that aims at performing PCA directly using the face image matrices. It has been shown that 2D PCA is more effective [3] and robust [4] than the eigenfaces method when dealing with face segmentation inaccuracies, low-quality images and partial occlusions.

In [5], we proposed the Two-Dimensional-Oriented Linear Discriminant Analysis (2DoLDA) approach, that consists in applying LDA to image matrices. We have shown on various face databases that 2DoLDA provides better face recognition results than both 2DPCA and the Fisherfaces method, and that it is more robust to variations in lighting conditions, facial expressions and head pose.

In this paper, we propose a novel supervised projection method called Bilinear Discriminant Analysis (BDA) that outperforms 2DoLDA while substantially reducing the computational cost of the recognition step.

The remainder of the paper is organized as follows. In section 2, we remind the theory and algorithm of 2DoLDA. In section 3, we describe the principle and algorithm of the proposed BDA method, pointing out its advantages over previous methods. In section 4, a series of three experiments, on different international data sets, is presented to demonstrate the effectiveness and robustness of BDA and compare its performances with respect to RoLDA, CoLDA and 2DPCA. Finally, conclusions are drawn in section 5.

2 Two-Dimensional Oriented Linear Discriminant Analysis (2Do LDA)

In [5], we introduced a version of 2DoLDA that will further be called Row-Oriented Linear Discriminant Analysis (RoLDA). However, 2DoLDA may be implemented in two different ways: RoLDA and Column-oriented LDA (CoLDA). Let us first present RoLDA.

The model is constructed from a training set Ω containing n face images of C people, with multiple views per person. The set of images corresponding to one person is called a *class*. Let us denote Ω_c the set of n_c images belonging to class c. Each face image is stored as a $h \times w$ matrix X_i, labelled by its belonging class. Let us consider a $w \times k$ projection matrix P, and the following projection:

$$X_i^P = X_i \cdot P \qquad (1)$$

The matrix X_i^P, of size $h \times k$, is the signature of X_i using RoLDA. Our aim is to determine, for a fixed size $h \times k$, the optimal matrix P^* jointly maximizing separation between different classes and minimizing separation between signatures from the same class. Under the assumptions of multinormality and homoscedasticity of the image matrices rows, P^* maximizes the following *generalized Fisher criterion* [5]:

$$J(P) = \frac{|P^T S_b P|}{|P^T S_w P|} \qquad (2)$$

S_w and S_b being respectively the *generalized within-class* and *between-class covariance matrices* of the training set:

$$S_w = \sum_{c=1}^{C} \sum_{X_i \in \Omega_c} (X_i - \bar{X}_c)^T (X_i - \bar{X}_c) \text{ and } S_b = \sum_{c=1}^{C} n_c (\bar{X}_c - \bar{X})^T (\bar{X}_c - \bar{X}) \qquad (3)$$

with $\bar{X}_c$ and $\bar{X}$ being mean images, computed respectively from Ω_c and Ω. If S_w is non-singular (which is generally verified as $w << n$), the k columns of P^* are the eigenvectors of $S_w^{-1} S_b$ with largest eigenvalues. A numerically stable way to compute them is given in [6].

Analogously, CoLDA relies on the following projection: $X_i^Q = Q^T \cdot X_i$ (4) where Q is a $h \times k$ projection matrix, and the $k \times w$ matrix X_i^Q is the signature of X_i using CoLDA. Under the assumptions of multinormality and homoscedasticity of the image matrices columns, we can consider the following generalized Fisher criterion:

$$J(Q) = \frac{|Q^T \Sigma_b Q|}{|Q^T \Sigma_w Q|} \quad (5)$$

where Σ_w and Σ_b are respectively the within-class and between-class covariance matrices of the set $(X_i^T)_{i \in \{1...n\}}$:

$$\Sigma_w = \sum_{c=1}^{C} \sum_{X_i \in \Omega_c} (X_i - \bar{X}_c)(X_i - \bar{X}_c)^T \text{ and } \Sigma_b = \sum_{c=1}^{C} n_c (\bar{X}_c - \bar{X})(\bar{X}_c - \bar{X})^T (6)$$

Let us denote Q^* the optimal projection matrix of size $h \times k$, maximizing criterion (5). If Σ_w is non-singular, the columns of Q^* are the k eigenvectors of $\Sigma_w^{-1} \Sigma_b$ with largest eigenvalues.

For RoLDA and CoLDA, there are at most $C-1$ eigenvectors corresponding to non-zero eigenvalues; their number k can be selected using the Wilks Lambda criteria, which is also known as *stepwise discriminant analysis* [7]. This analysis shows that the number k of eigenvectors required by both methods is comparable and generally inferior to 15, even if the number of classes is large, as shown in Fig. 2.(a), reporting on an experiment performed on 107 classes.

Recognition is performed by using the Euclidean distance between the signatures of the face images, and the nearest neighbour rule.

3 Bilinear Discriminant Analysis (BDA)

3.1 Why Combine CoLDA and RoLDA?

We conducted four experiments highlighting the complementarity of RoLDA and CoLDA. In the following, all the face images are centered and cropped to a size of $h \times w = 75 \times 65$ pixels.

The first two experiments are performed on subsets of the Asian Face Database PF01 [8] containing 107 people. They illustrate the fact that, depending on the training and test data, RoLDA and CoLDA outperform each other. In the first experiment, the training and test sets, illustrated in Fig. 1.(a-b), contain respectively 5 near-frontal views per person (535 images) and 4 non-frontal views per person (428 images). These two sets differ in the head pose. Fig. 2. (a) shows

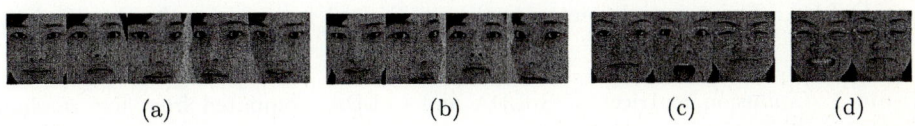

(a)   (b)   (c)   (d)

Fig. 1. Extracts of (a) the training set and (b) the test set used for the first experiment; Extracts of (c) the training set and (d) the test set used for the second experiment.

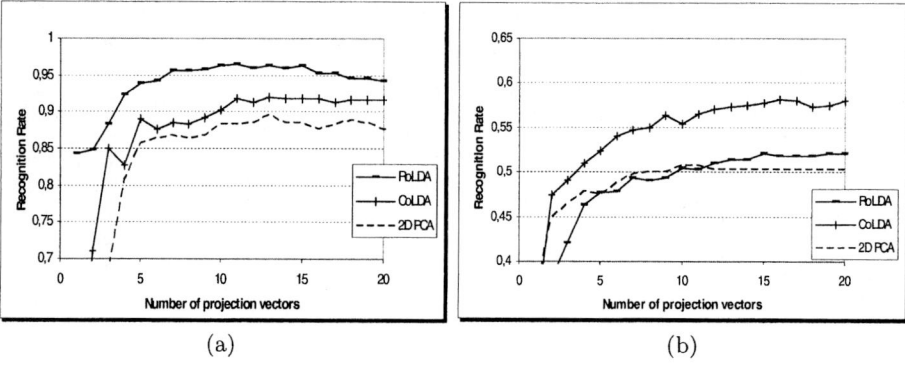

Fig. 2. Compared recognition rates of RoLDA, CoLDA and 2DPCA on a subset of the PF01 database showing (a) head pose changes and (b) facial expression changes, when varying the number k of projection vectors.

that both CoLDA and RoLDA are highly effective (recognition rates superior to 92 %), and outperform 2DPCA. However, RoLDA outperforms CoLDA, with a 4,5% improvement of the recognition rate between their respective maxima.

The second experiment is performed on a subset of the PF01 database containing 107 people, with five different facial expressions. This subset is randomly partitioned into a training set and a test set, illustrated in Fig. 1.(c-d). From Fig. 2.(b) we can see that, even if RoLDA and CoLDA are not highly performing (the recognition rates are inferior to 60%), both of them outperform 2DPCA. However, CoLDA is more effective than RoLDA, with a 5,6% improvement of the recognition rate between their respective maxima.

The third and fourth experiments provide further comparison of the performances of CoLDA and RoLDA. They are performed on the Yale Face Database [2], that contains 15 people and 11 views per person, with occlusions and variations in lighting conditions and facial expressions. In the third experiment, the Yale database is randomly partitioned into a training set containing four views per person, and a test set containing six views per person. To ensure homoscedasticity, the views of each set are consistent among the classes, e.g. all the "wink" views are included in the test set, and all the "neutral" in the training set. This operation is repeated five times. From each partition, we compute a confusion matrix with $k = C-1 = 14$ (see Table 1.) In each confusion matrix, the top left cell contains the number of faces correctly classified by both RoLDA and CoLDA. The top right entry is the number of faces correctly classified by

Table 1. Confusion matrices of RoLDA and CoLDA, computed from five random partitions of the Yale Face Database

53	10		71	11		72	8		55	5		63	2
11	16		5	3		4	6		14	16		7	18
(a)			(b)			(c)			(d)			(e)	

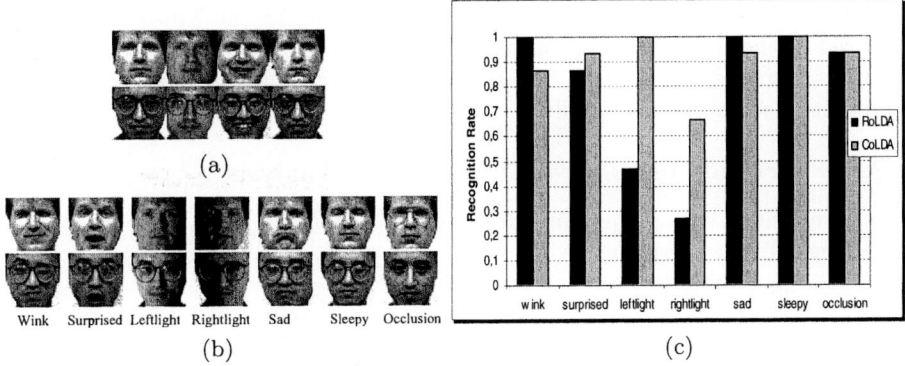

Fig. 3. Extracts (a) of the training set and (b) of the seven test sets, taken from Yale and used for the fourth experiment. Any subject not wearing eyeglasses in the training set wears eyeglasses in the "occlusion" set, and *vice-versa*. (c) Compared recognition rates of CoLDA and RoLDA, computed from the seven test sets illustrated in (b).

RoLDA, but misclassified by CoLDA. The bottom left cell contains the number of faces correctly classified by CoLDA, but misclassified by RoLDA. The bottom right entry is the number of faces misclassified by both methods. Table 1.(a) shows that, on the first random partition of the Yale database, the performances of RoLDA and CoLDA are comparable (the recognition rates are respectively $\frac{53+10}{53+10+11+16} = 70\%$ and 71,1%). However, classification results are very different: 21 samples (23,3% of the test set) are correctly classified by only one method. Moreover, 82,2% $\gg$ max(70%, 71, 1%) of the query faces are recognized by at least one of the two methods. Table 1.(b-c) illustrate the fact that RoLDA generally outperforms CoLDA. Table 1.(d-e) show that, in some configurations where the rate of misclassification by both methods is high -respectively $\frac{16}{90} = 17,8\%$ and 20% for partitions (d) and (e)-, CoLDA outperforms RoLDA.

The fourth experiment provides further qualitative analysis. The training set, illustrated in Fig. 3.(a), contains four views for each of the 15 subjects, with variations in lighting conditions and facial expressions. Then, seven test sets, illustrated in Fig. 3.(b) and corresponding to the remaining views, are built. Fig. 3.(c) illustrates the fact that, even if RoLDA is generally more effective than CoLDA, in some cases CoLDA drastically outperforms RoLDA, especially when the test set contains dissimetries of the image following the vertical axis ("leftlight" and "rightlight"). CoLDA can also slightly outperform RoLDA when the test set shows strong facial expression changes, e.g. "surprised". Choosing between CoLDA and RoLDA therefore requires a preliminary qualitative analysis of the training and test sets, which is a difficult task. As both RoLDA and CoLDA have high performances but give different recognition results, appropriately combining them can lead to a highly effective method.

In 2DoLDA, considering image matrices instead of vectors (as in the Fisherfaces method) when performing LDA leads to a reduced computational cost when building the model, and to a reduced storage cost [5]. But the size of the signatures is $h \times k$ for RoLDA and $k \times w$ for CoLDA, and may be large. As exposed in the following section, using BDA leads to a drastic reduction in the signatures size, and therefore reduces the computational cost during the recognition step, which is often online.

3.2 Description of Bilinear Discriminant Analysis

Let us consider two projection matrices $Q \in \mathbb{R}^{h \times k}$ and $P \in \mathbb{R}^{w \times k}$, and the following bilinear projection:

$$X_i^{Q,P} = Q^T X_i P \qquad (7)$$

where the $k \times k$ matrix $X_i^{Q,P}$ is the signature of X_i using BDA. For any fixed k, let us search for the optimal pair of matrices (Q^*, P^*), maximizing the following generalized Fisher criterion:

$$(Q^*, P^*) = \underset{(Q,P) \in \mathbb{R}^{h \times k} \times \mathbb{R}^{w \times k}}{\mathrm{Argmax}} \frac{|S_b^{Q,P}|}{|S_w^{Q,P}|} \qquad (8)$$

$$= \underset{(Q,P) \in \mathbb{R}^{h \times k} \times \mathbb{R}^{w \times k}}{\mathrm{Argmax}} \frac{|\sum_{c=1}^C n_c (\overline{X_c^{Q,P}} - \overline{X^{Q,P}})^T (\overline{X_c^{Q,P}} - \overline{X^{Q,P}})|}{|\sum_{c=1}^C \sum_{i \in \Omega_c} (X_i^{Q,P} - \overline{X_c^{Q,P}})^T (X_i^{Q,P} - \overline{X_c^{Q,P}})|} \qquad (9)$$

$S_w^{Q,P}$ and $S_b^{Q,P}$ being the within-class and between-class covariance matrices of the signatures set $(X_i^{Q,P})_{i \in \{1,...,n\}}$.

This objective function is biquadratic and has no analytical solution. We therefore propose an iterative procedure that we call *Bilinear Discriminant Analysis*. Let us expand the expression (9):

$$(Q^*, P^*) = \underset{(Q,P) \in \mathbb{R}^{h \times k} \times \mathbb{R}^{w \times k}}{\mathrm{Argmax}} \left[\frac{|\sum_{c=1}^C n_c (P^T(\overline{X_c} - \overline{X})^T QQ^T (\overline{X_c} - \overline{X}) P)|}{|\sum_{c=1}^C \sum_{i \in \Omega_c} (P^T(X_i - \overline{X_c})^T QQ^T(X_i - \overline{X_c})P)|} \right] \qquad (10)$$

For any fixed $Q \in \mathbb{R}^{h \times k}$, using equation (10), the objective function (9) can be rewritten:

$$P^* = \underset{P \in \mathbb{R}^{w \times k}}{\mathrm{Argmax}} \left[\frac{|P^T \left[\sum_{c=1}^C n_c (\overline{X_c^Q} - \overline{X^Q})^T (\overline{X_c^Q} - \overline{X^Q})\right] P|}{|P^T \left[\sum_{c=1}^C \sum_{i \in \Omega_c} (X_i^Q - \overline{X_c^Q})^T (X_i^Q - \overline{X_c^Q})\right] P|} \right] = \underset{P \in \mathbb{R}^{w \times k}}{\mathrm{Argmax}} \frac{|P^T S_b^Q P|}{|P^T S_w^Q P|} \qquad (11)$$

S_w^Q and S_b^Q being respectively the *generalized within-class covariance matrix* and the *generalized between-class covariance matrix* of the set $(X_i^Q)_{i \in \{1...n\}}$, each X_i^Q being computed using (4). Therefore the columns of the matrix P^* are the k eigenvectors of $S_w^{Q-1} S_b^Q$ with largest eigenvalues, obtained by applying RoLDA on the set of the projected samples X_i^Q. Let us denote $A = P^T(\overline{X_c} - \overline{X})^T Q$, matrix of size $k \times k$. Given that, for every square matrix A, $|A^T A| = |AA^T|$, the objective function (9) can be rewritten:

$$(Q^*, P^*) = \underset{(Q,P) \in \mathbb{R}^{h \times k} \times \mathbb{R}^{w \times k}}{\mathrm{Argmax}} \left[\frac{|\sum_{c=1}^C n_c (Q^T (\overline{X_c} - \overline{X}) PP^T (\overline{X_c} - \overline{X})^T Q)|}{[\sum_{c=1}^C \sum_{i \in \Omega_c} (Q^T (X_i - \overline{X_c}) PP^T (X_i - \overline{X_c})^T Q)|} \right] \qquad (12)$$

For any fixed $P \in \mathbb{R}^{w \times k}$, using equation (12) the objective function (9) can be rewritten $Q^* = \underset{Q \in \mathbb{R}^{h \times k}}{\text{Argmax}} \frac{|Q^T \Sigma_b^P Q|}{|Q^T \Sigma_w^P Q|}$, where Σ_w^P and Σ_b^P are respectively the generalized within-class and between-class covariance matrices of the set $((X_i^P)^T)_{i \in \{1...n\}}$, each X_i^P being computed using (1). Therefore, the columns of Q^* are the k eigenvectors of $(\Sigma_w^P)^{-1} \Sigma_b^P$ with largest eigenvalues, obtained by applying CoLDA on the set of the projected samples X_i^P.

3.3 Algorithm of the BDA Approach

Let us initialize $P_0 = I_w$, the identity matrix of $\mathbb{R}^{w \times w}$, and $k_0 = C-1$. The proposed algorithm for BDA is:

1. For $i \in \{1, \ldots, n\}$, compute $X_i^{P_t} = X_i P_t$;
2. Apply CoLDA to $(X_i^{P_t})_{i \in \{1,\ldots,n\}}$: compute $\Sigma_w^{P_t}$, $\Sigma_b^{P_t}$ and, from $(\Sigma_w^{P_t})^{-1} \cdot \Sigma_b^{P_t}$, compute Q_t, of size $h \times k_t$;
3. For $i \in \{1, \ldots, n\}$, compute $X_i^{Q_t} = (Q_t)^T X_i$;
4. Apply RoLDA to $(X_i^{Q_t})_{i \in \{1,\ldots,n\}}$: compute $S_w^{Q_t}$, $S_b^{Q_t}$ and, from $(S_w^{Q_t})^{-1} \cdot S_b^{Q_t}$, compute P_t, of size $w \times k_t$;
5. Compute $\alpha = -(n - \frac{w+C}{2} - 1) \ln \left[\prod_{j=k_t+1}^{C-1} \frac{1}{1+\lambda_j} \right]$;
6. <u>if</u> $\alpha < p\text{-}value[\chi^2((w-k_t)(C-k_t-1))]$, <u>then</u> $t \leftarrow t+1$, $k_t \leftarrow k_{t-1}-1$, and return to step 1;
7. <u>else</u> $k_t \leftarrow k_{t-1}$, $Q \leftarrow Q_{t-1}$ and $P \leftarrow P_{t-1}$.

The stopping criterion (steps 5.-7.) derives from the Wilks Lambda criterion, testing the discriminatory power of the $C-k_t-1$ eigenvectors of $(S_w^{Q_t})^{-1} \cdot S_b^{Q_t}$ removed at step 4., by keeping in P_t only the k_t eigenvectors with highest eigenvalues $(\lambda_j)_{j \in \{1...k_t\}}$. We consider the following test: H_0: at least one of the eigenvectors $k_t+1,\ldots,C-1$ is discriminative, and H_1: non H_0. Under H_0, it can be easily shown that $-(n - \frac{w+C}{2} - 1) \ln(\prod_{j=k_t+1}^{C-1} \frac{1}{1+\lambda_j})$ corresponds to a χ^2 distribution, with $(w-k_t)(C-k_t-1)$ degrees of freedom. The p-value can be chosen at a confidence level of 5%. If $\alpha < p\text{-}value$, the $C-k_t-1$ last eigenvectors can be removed and the stepwise analysis goes on. If $\alpha > p\text{-}value$, the eigenvector $k_t+1=k_{t-1}$ is discriminative and should be kept.

Recognition is performed in the BDA projection space, by using the Euclidean distance between face image signatures, and the nearest neighbour rule.

We can note that the computational cost of one comparison is $o(k^2)$ for BDA, versus $o(h \cdot k)$ for RoLDA and 2DPCA, and $o(w \cdot k)$ for CoLDA; therefore BDA drastically reduces the computational cost of the recognition step.

4 Experimental Results

Three experiments are performed on the Asian Face Database PF01 [8], the FERET [9] [1] face database, and the ORL Database [10], to assess the effectiveness of BDA and compare it with RoLDA, CoLDA and 2D-PCA.

---

[1] Portions of the research in this paper use the FERET database of facial images collected under the FERET program.

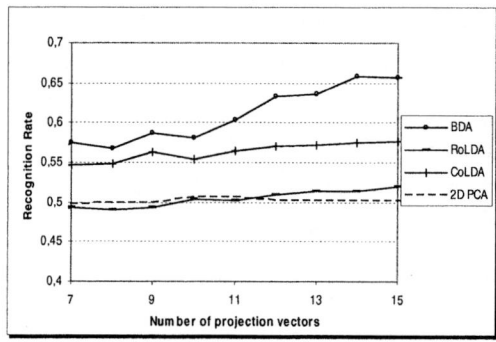

Fig. 4. Compared recognition rates of BDA, RoLDA, CoLDA and 2DPCA, on the subset of PF01 with expression variations, when varying the number k of eigenvectors.

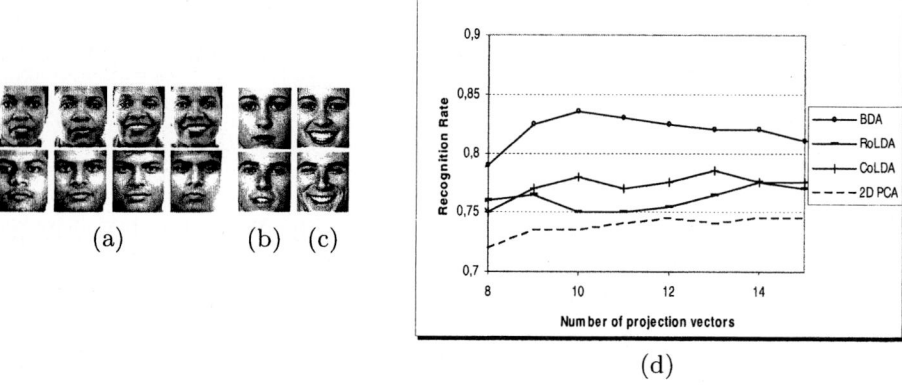

Fig. 5. Extracts (a) of the training set and (b-c) of the two test sets to be matched. (d) Compared recognition rates of BDA, RoLDA, CoLDA and 2DPCA, when matching the test sets (b) and (c).

The training and test sets used for the first experiment, differing in the facial expressions, were used for the second experiment reported in section 3.1 and are illustrated in Fig. 1.(c-d). From Fig. 4., we can see that BDA strongly outperforms RoLDA, CoLDA and 2DPCA.

The second experiment, performed on FERET, aims at evaluating the generalization power of BDA. Indeed, LDA-based methods are known to be more effective when comparing faces of known people, but provide worse generalization results than unsupervised methods. The training set, illustrated in Fig. 5.(a), contains 818 images of 152 people with at least four views per person, taken on different days and under different lighting conditions. Two test sets, each one containing 200 people with one view per person and illustrated in Fig. 5.(b-c), are compared. The test sets are taken from FERET, but none of the 200 people is registered in the training set. From one test set to the other, the facial expres-

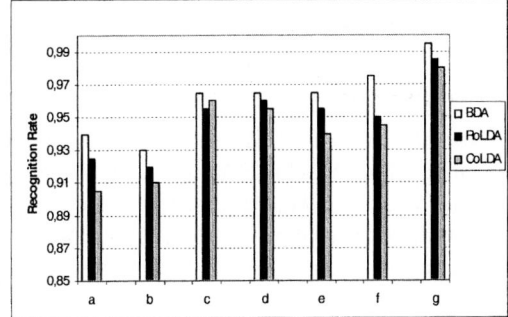

Fig. 6. Compared recognition rates of BDA, RoLDA and CoLDA on 7 random partitions of the ORL database

Table 2. Contingency table summed up over 7 random partitions of ORL

		∩ BDA
RoLDA ∩ CoLDA	1297	1292
RoLDA ∩ ⌐CoLDA	33	24
⌐RoLDA ∩ CoLDA	22	14
⌐RoLDA ∩ ⌐CoLDA	48	17
Total	1400	1347

sions vary. From Fig. 5.(d) we can conclude that, when the training set contains many classes with important variations inside the classes, BDA provides better generalization than the other methods.

For the third experiment, the ORL database is randomly partitioned into a training set containing five views, and a test set containing the five remaining views, for each of the 40 persons. This operation is repeated seven times and BDA, RoLDA and CoLDA are applied. Fig. 6. shows that BDA provides better recognition rates than RoLDA and CoLDA on all the random partitions, whenever RoLDA outperforms CoLDA (partitions (a-b) and (d-g)) or CoLDA outperforms RoLDA (partition (c)). The results are computed from the optimal number of projection vectors, which is $k = 14$ for the three methods. For further analysis, the contingency table summed up over partitions (a-g) is given in Table 2. The total number of query faces is $7 \cdot 200 = 1400$. The logical symbol "⌐" stands for "not", i.e. the entry in the second row and first column of the table is the number of faces recognized by RoLDA, but misclassified by CoLDA. The logical symbol "∩" stands for "and": the entry in the second row and second column is the number of samples correctly classified by RoLDA and BDA, but misclassified by CoLDA. From Table 2. we can see that BDA correctly classifies $\frac{1292}{1297} = 99,6\%$ of the samples that were recognized by both RoLDA and CoLDA. Moreover, it recognizes the major part of the samples that were recognized by only one of the two methods (72,7% for RoLDA and 63,6% for CoLDA). It also correctly classifies 35,4% of the samples that were misclassified by both methods, which shows the effectiveness of the BDA iterative algorithm. It should be noted that, as the face images have been cropped to a size of 75×65 pixels, the size of one sample signature is $75 \cdot 14 = 1050$ for RoLDA, $65 \cdot 14 = 910$ for CoLDA, and only $14^2 = 196$ for BDA.

5 Conclusion

In this paper, we have proposed a new supervised statistical projection based technique, named Bilinear Discriminant Analysis, that can be successfully applied to face recognition. This method effectively combines two complementary versions of 2DoLDA, through an iterative algorithm maximizing a generalized Fisher criterion relying on bilinear projections.

A series of experiments, performed on various international databases, have shown the complementarity of the two versions of 2DoLDA and highlighted that the proposed iterative algorithm outperforms 2DoLDA and 2DPCA; as a consequence it also outperforms the fisherfaces and eigenfaces methods. Moreover, BDA provides image signatures of reduced size compared to 2DoLDA and 2DPCA, which results in an important computational gain during the recognition step.

Acknowledgement. This research was supported by the European Commission under contract FP6-001765 aceMedia.

References

1. Turk, M.A., Pentland, A.D.: Eigenfaces for Recognition. Journal of Cognitive Neuroscience. **3**(1) (1991) 71–86.
2. Belhumeur, P.N., Hespanha, J.P., Kriegman, D.J.: Eigenfaces vs Fisherfaces : Recognition Using Class Specific Linear Projection. IEEE Trans. on Pattern Analysis and Machine Intelligence, Special Issue on Face Recognition. **19**(7) (1997) 711–720.
3. Yang, J., Zhang, D., Frangi, A.F., Yang, J.Y.: Two-Dimensional PCA: A New Approach to Appearance-Based Face Representation and Recognition. IEEE Trans. on Pattern Analysis and Machine Intelligence. **26**(1) (2004) 131–137.
4. Visani, M., Garcia, C., Laurent, C.: Comparing Robustness of Two-Dimensional PCA and Eigenfaces for Face Recognition. In Proc. of the International Conference on Image Analysis and Recognition (ICIAR 04). Springer Lecture Notes in Computer Science (LNCS 3211), A. Campilho, M. Kamel (eds) (Sept. 2004) 717–724.
5. Visani, M., Garcia, C., Jolion, J.M.: Two-Dimensional-Oriented Linear Discriminant Analysis for Face Recognition. In Proc. of the International Conference on Computer Vision and Graphics (ICCVG 2004). To appear in Computational Imaging and Vision series (Sept. 2004).
6. Swets, D.L., Weng, J.: Using Discriminant Eigenfeatures for Image Retrieval. IEEE Trans. on Pattern Analysis and Machine Intelligence. **18**(8) (1996) 831–836.
7. Jenrich, R.I.: Stepwise Discriminant Analysis. In A. Enslein, A. Ralston, and H. S. Wilf (eds.), Statistical Methods for Digital Computers. Wiley Interscience, New York, N.Y, (1977) 76–95.
8. Hwang, B.W., Roh, M.C., Lee, S.W.: Performance Evaluation of Face Recognition Algorithms on Asian Face Database. IEEE International Conference on Automatic Face and Gesture Recognition. Seoul, Korea, (May 2004) 278–283.
9. Phillips, P.J., Wechsler, H., Huang, J., Rauss, P.: The FERET Database and Evaluation Procedure for Face Recognition Algorithms. Image and Vision Computing. **16**(5) (1998) 295–306.
10. Samaria, F., Harter, A.: Parameterisation of a Stochastic Model for Human Face Identification. Proceedings of the IEEE Workshop on Applications of Computer Vision. Sarasota, Florida, (Dec. 1994).

Adaptive Object Recognition Using Context-Aware Genetic Algorithm Under Dynamic Environment

Mi Young Nam and Phill Kyu Rhee

Dept. of Computer Science & Engineering, Inha University,
253, Yong-Hyun Dong , Nam-Gu,
Incheon, South Korea
rera@im.inha.ac.kr, pkrhee@inha.ac.kr

Abstract. Adaptation to dynamically changing environment is very important since advanced applications become pervasive and ubiquitous. This paper addresses a novel method of adaptive object recognition using environmental context-awareness and genetic algorithm and t-test. The proposed method tries to distinguish the category of input environment and decides an optimal classifier combination structure accordingly by GA and t-test. It stores its experiences in terms of the data context categories and the evolved artificial chromosomes so that the evolutionary knowledge can be used later. The proposed method has been evaluated in the area of face recognition. Most previous face recognition schemes define their system structures at the design phases, and the structures are not adaptive during operation. Such approaches usually show vulnerability under varying illumination environment. The context-awareness, modeling and identification of input data as context categories, is carried out by Fuzzy ART. The face data context is described based on the image attributes of light direction and brightness. The superiority of the proposed system is shown using four data sets: Inha, FERET and Yale database.

1 Introduction

Genetic algorithm is an efficient search and adaptation method by simulating the natural evolution mechanism. Recently, adaptation under dynamically changing environment is very important since advanced applications become pervasive and ubiquitous, and need to adaptive to their changing contexts. Ubiquitous sensing and recognition of human activity under dynamic environment enforce visual sensor based information processing more adaptive to application environment. In this paper, we present a robust and adaptive object scheme suitable for ubiquitous and pervasive applications using the genetic algorithm with the capability of context-awareness, called context-aware genetic algorithm.

Recognizing objects under dynamic environments is one of the final goals in the area of computer vision. Robust and intelligent computer vision needs highly invariance with regard to those variations. Much research has been devoted on this problem. However, most object recognition methods today can only operate successfully only under strongly constrained images captured in controlled environments.

In this paper, we discuss about adaptive object recognition based on context-aware genetic algorithm that can behave in a robust manner under variations of application environments. The context-aware genetic algorithm is a genetic algorithm with the capability of context-awareness. The context knowledge of an individual context category and its associated chromosome is stored in the context knowledge base in order to preventing repetitive search. It determines a most effective structure of classifier combination for a current environment by employing the context-aware genetic algorithm. The context-awareness consists of context modeling and identification. Context modeling can is be performed by an unsupervised learning method such as FuzzyArt, etc.

The context-aware genetic algorithm explores a most effective classifier combination structure for each identified context category. Both online and offline adaptation are required for applying GA to real-time application [1].

The proposed method has been tested using four data sets and their virtual data sets: Inha, FERET and Yale database where face images are exposed to different lighting conditon. We achieve encouraging experimental results showing that the performance of the proposed method is superior to those of most popular methods.

The major contributions of this paper are: This paper is organized as follows. In the section 2, we present the overview of the proposed object recognition schema including illuminant identification using FART and in the section 3, we present the proposed architecture for context-aware evolutionary computation and the overview of the proposed face recognition scheme. Finally, we give the experimental results and the concluding remarks in the section 4 and 5, respectively.

2 Context-Aware Genetic Algorithm for Object Recognition

The outline of object recognition scheme using the context-aware genetic algorithm will be presented. The scheme operates in the evolutionary mode or the action mode. In the evolutionary mode, the scheme accumulates its knowledge during adapting its application environments. In the action mode, it performs its task of recognition using the adapted scheme structure. The evolutionary mode of the scheme is either online adaptation or offline adaptation. The online adaptation approach directly interacts and commits application environments by trial-and-error if an environment context can hardly be identified. If environment context can be analyzed and identified, the offline adaptation approach is effective. In the offline adaptation, application environment context is modeled (clustered) into several categories, and the most effective classifier combination structure is searched by the genetic algorithm. We adopt the context knowledge base to avoid a blind search whenever an application environment changes, the scheme accumulates and stores environmental context knowledge in terms of context category and its corresponding action. Environment context-awareness will be discussed first, and the object recognition scheme using context-aware genetic algorithm will be followed.

2.1 Environmental Context-Awareness

We adopt the FuzzyART which is a variant of the ART system derived from the first generation of the ART, namely the ART1. It is a synthesis of the ART algorithm and

Fuzzy operators. The ART1 can only accept binary input patterns, but the FuzzyART allows both binary and continuous input patterns [2, 3]. The image space of object instance with varying illuminations must be clustered properly so that the location error can be minimized. However, the classification of images under varying illumination is very subjective and ambiguous. Thus, we adopt the FuzzyART method which shows robustness in subjective and ambiguous applications in order to achieve optimal illumination context clustering. The performance of clustering is improved by observing previously clustered data repeatedly. The outline of the FuzzyART algorithm is described in the followings:

Step 1. The fuzzy ART algorithm begins with an initialization of the weight matrices. Associated with cluster node$_j$ (0. N) is a vector $w_j = (w_{j1} \ldots w_{jm})$ of adaptive weight.

$$W_{j1}(0) = W_{j2}(0) = \ldots = W_{jm}(0) \tag{1}$$

Step 2. Present an input pattern and cluster node to the network. Next, compute the input to layer2. The input node is structured as 100 dimension of size 10*10

Step 3. Winner cluster select method and winner cluster determination.

Step 4. Vigilance test (Vigilance test between the winner class' node and input pattern): If the pattern is matched to within a specified vigilance criterion, then resonance occurs.

$$\frac{|I \wedge W_{ji}|}{|I|} \geq \rho \tag{2}$$

where I is input pattern. The term ρ is called the vigilance parameter, and must fall in the range , $0 < \rho < 1$.

Step 5. Replace winner cluster's forward weight (T) by 0 and go to Step 4.
Step 6. Control input node for winner cluster's node and cluster's backward weight.
Step 7. If the learning is not completed for all patterns, go to Step 2, otherwise stop.

One cluster center is updated every time an input vector x is clustered at random from the input data set. The cluster nearest to x has its position updated using the following equation.

$$m_i(new) = m_i(old) + \alpha(x - m_i(old)) \tag{3}$$

The cluster centers moved closer to x values this equation minimizes the error vector. Each hidden unit calculates the Mahalanobis distance of the input vector from the corresponding Gaussian. In this paper, centers are obtained from unsupervised learning (clustering), Fuzzy ART algorithm. Clustering (Fuzzy ART algorithm) and LMS are iterative. This is the most commonly used procedure, and typically provides good results. After finding a suitable cluster using the clustering algorithm, do laying center on this. The winning node j is what Fuzzy ART is its best match for the input pattern. An example of training data for the FART is shown Fig.1.

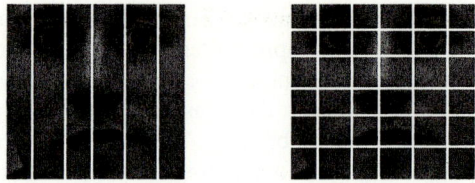

Fig. 1. Face data vectorization is 1x42 dimension

Fig. 2 shows images of three clusters various illuminant face dataset, we define 9 step environment.

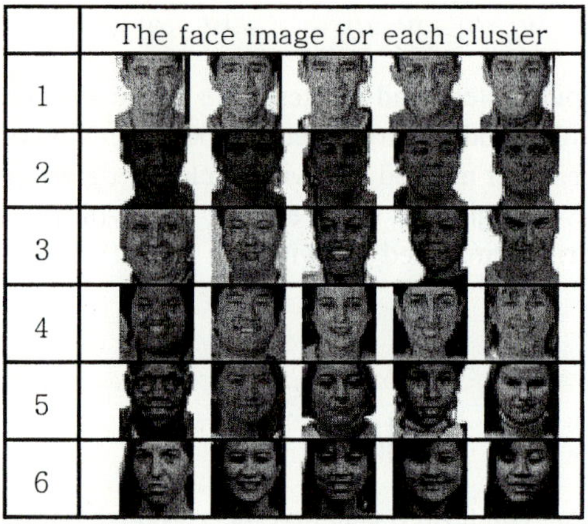

	The face image for each cluster
1	
2	
3	
4	
5	
6	

Fig. 2. Discriminant result for illumination conditions using FART

2.2 Robust Object Recognition Scheme Using Context-Aware Genetic Algorithm

The proposed object recognition scheme using context-aware genetic algorithm consists of the context identification module (CIM), the evolution module (EM), the Action module (AM), the evolutionary module (EM), and the context knowledge base (CKB) (see Fig. 4).

The CIM identifies a current context using context input data. Context can be various configurations, computing resource availability, dynamic task requirement, application condition, environmental condition, etc. Context describes a trigger of the scheme action using the previously accumulated knowledge of context-action relation in the CKB. The CKB over a period of time and/or the variation of a set of context informations of the system over a period of time. Context data is defined as any observable and relevant attributes, and its interaction with other entities and/or surrounding environment at an instance of time. Context data is denoted by attribute tuple as follows.

$$CD = < t, a1, a2, ..., as > \qquad (4)$$

where t is the time stamp and a1, a2, ..., as are the set of some attributes.

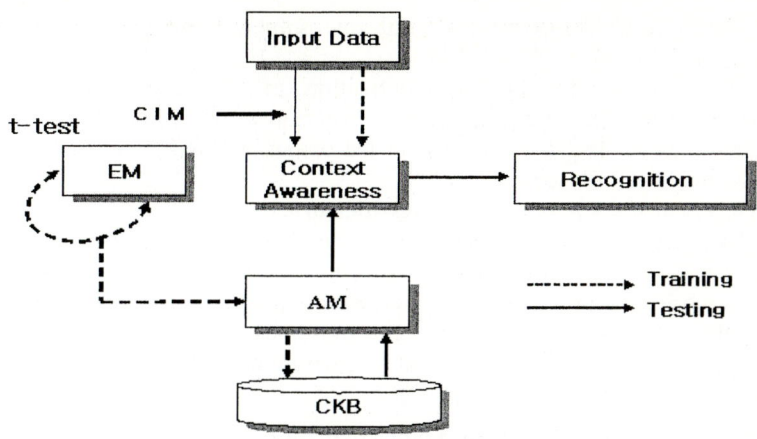

Fig. 3. The block diagram of the proposed ECC scheme

Derived context representation, processed context data, is generated from the context tuple, and represented as follows.

$$DC = <t, d1, d2, ..., dt> \quad (5)$$

where d_i is a processed attribute from a subset of context data. Context or context expression is denoted by the context elements as follows.

$$CE = <t, e1, e2, ..., eu> \quad (6)$$

where t is the time when the situation is identified and $e1, e2, ...,$ and eu are the set of context elements representing the context. They can be a module configuration, parameter values, thresholds, parameter types, threshold types, etc.

The AM consists of one or more action primitives. The action primitives can be heterogeneous, homogeneous, or hybrid operational entities. For example, the action primitives of a pattern classifier are divided into preprocessing, feature representation, class decision, post processing primitives. The EM searches for a best combining structure of action primitives for an identified context. The structures of optimal actions are stored in the CKB with the corresponding context expression.

Initially, the scheme accumulates the knowledge in the CKB that guarantees optimal performance for individual identified context. The CKB stores the expressions of identifiable contexts and their matched actions that will be performed by the AM. The matched action can be decided by either experimental trial-and-error or some automating procedures. In the operation time, the context expression is determined from the derived context representation, where the derived context is decided from the context data. The ECM searches the matched action in the CKB, and the AM performs the action.

Initially, adaptation knowledge is accumulated using offline adaptation method, and stored in the CKB in the evolution mode. The detail of the object recognition scheme constructing the CKB is given in the following:

Step 1. Cluster input images into several environment context categories using the Fuzzy ART(CIM).
Step 2. Start to search for an optimization of classifier structure for each environmental context category until a criterion is met, where the criterion is the fitness does not improve anymore or the predefined maximum trial limitation is encountered as follows.
   1) Generate initial population of classifier structures.
   2) Evaluate the fitness function of the scheme using the newly derived population of the classifier structures. If the criterion is met, Go to Step 3.
   3) Search for the population of the classifier structures that maximize the fitness function and keep those as the best chromosomes.
   4) Applying GA's genetic operators to generate new population from the current classifier structures. Go to Step 2.2).
Step 3. Update the CKB (Context Knowledge Base) for the identified illumination category and the derived classifier structure.

The adaptive object recognition task is carried out using the knowledge of the CKB evolved in the evolutionary mode as follows:

Step 1. Identify the illumination situation in the CAM
Step 2. Search for the chromosome from the CKB representing the optimal classifier structure corresponding to the identified illumination category.
Step 3. Perform the task of recognition using the restructured feature vector.
Step 4. If the system performance is measured to fall down below the predefined criterion, the system activates the evolution mode, and/or evolves the system periodically or when it is needed using either online or offline adaptation methods.

3 The Context-Aware Genetic Algorithm for Face Recognition

The proposed method has been tested in the area of object recognition. We deal with image objects the spacial boundaries of which can be well estimated in prior, called spacially well-defined object classes [2]. Face images are in the class of well-defined image objects, the spacial boundaries of which can be well estimated in prior.

3.1 Face Recognition Using the Context-Aware Genetic Algorithm

In general, it is almost impossible or very difficult to decide an optimal classifier or classifier structure at the design step considering all possible factors of run-time variations. We employ the strategy that the classifier structure, is allowed to evolve or adapt itself dynamically during operation in accordance with changing environment contexts. Changes in image capturing environment can include lighting direction, brightness, contrast, and spectral composition, etc. The architecture of face recognition using the context-aware genetic algorithm is given in Fig. 4.

We assume that sufficient dataset where face images are exposed to varying environments is available or has been captured. Initially, the CIM clusters face data images into several environmental context categories, and constructs the context model of face images as discussed in session 3. The CIM is implemented by FART[14].

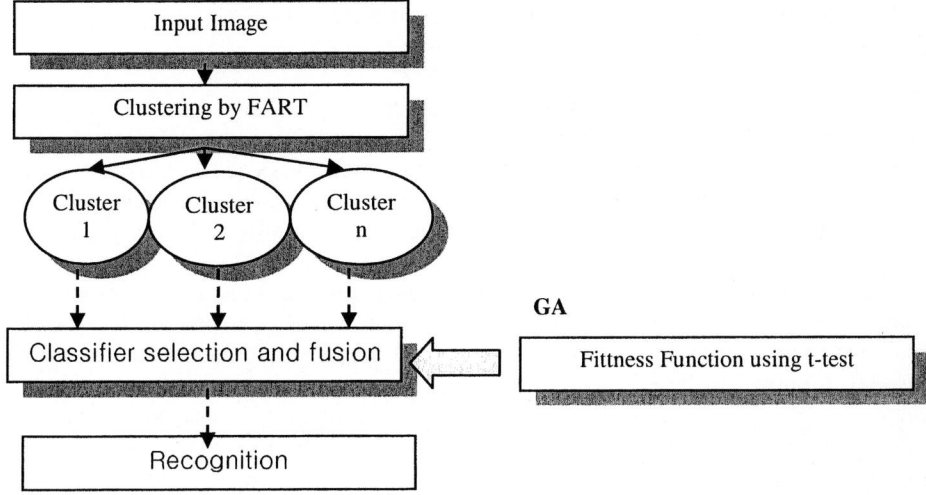

Fig. 4. The proposed situation-aware classifier fusion system

FART has the capability of unsupervised learning itself. It can distinguish environmental context in terms of brightness, contrast, spectral composition, and light direction. The evolutionary module EM is implemented by Genetic algorithm (GA). GA explores the structure of the AM adaptive to an operational environment. In the action mode, the system searches for a most effective classifier structure based on the identified category of the input image. The knowledge of effective classifier structure for an environment is described by the pair of context category and corresponding artificial chromosome. The detail of the EM is be discussed in the following.

The GA is employed to search among the different combinations of classifiers. The optimality of the chromosome is defined by classification accuracy and generalization capability. Fig. 6 shows a possible encoding of chromosome description.

As the GA searches the genospace, the GA makes its choices via genetic operators as a function of probability distribution driven by fitness function. The genetic operators used here are selection, crossover, and mutation [5. 12].

| FR1 | FR2 | ... | FRn | CLS1 | CLS2 | ... | CLSn |

Fig. 5. A possible chromosome description of the proposed schema FR: face representation, CLS: Classifier Selection.

3.2 The Face Recognition Scheme Using the Context-Aware Genetic Algorithm

The recognition system learns an optimal structure of multi-classifier and Gabor representation by restructuring its structure and parameters. Preprocessing is performed for providing nice quality images as much as possible using conventional image filtering techniques. The image filters employed here is the lighting compensation, histogram equalization, opening operation, boost-filtering [6]. We use

5 classifiers, Eigenface, Gabor3, Gabor13, Gabor 28, and Gabor30, for the AM. The details of classifiers are given in the followings.

Classifier Gabor3, Gabor13, Gabor 28, Gabor30

The Gabor wavelet transform guided by an evolutionary approach has been employed to adapt the system for variations in illumination. The proposed approach employs Gabor feature vector, which is generated from the Gabor wavelet transform. The kernels of the Gabor wavelets show biological relevance to 2-D receptive field profiles of mammalian cortical cells. Gabor wavelet is biologically motivated convolution kernels in the shape of plane waves restricted by gabor kernel. The receptive fields of the neurons in the primary visual cortex of mammals are oriented and have characteristic frequencies. This could be modeled 2-D gabor wavelet. Gabor wavelet is known to be efficient in reducing redundancy and noise in images. The gabor wavelet has shown to be particularly fit to image decomposition and representation. Gabor wavelet shows desirable characteristics in orientation selectivity and special locality. The face image representation transformed by gabor wavelet has the properties of scale, locality, and differentiation, which provide robust characteristics to image variation from illumination changes, facial expression, etc. Face gabor vector is generated as shown Fig. 6. The feature is extracted 11 feature points. We adopt 4 Gabor based classifiers: Gabor3, Gabor13, Gabor28, Gabor30. They are different only in the number of feature points.

Classifier Eigen Face based face classifier

The eigenface is constructed registration images of FERET, Yale, our Lab database. We made in covariance matrix of registration data. The eigenface is belong to global recognition. The registration data computed covariance matrix.

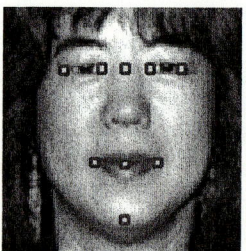

Fig. 6. An example of feature points for face recognition

4 Experimental Results

The feasibility of the proposed method has been tested in the area of face recognition using our lab, FERET[7], Yale [8]. The data set is our lab, FERRET, AR, and Yale where face images are exposed to various illumination conditions. Experiments have been carried out to compare the performance of the proposed evolvable classifier combination, that the best among individual classifiers. We used 1000 images of 100 persons from our lab data set, 330 images of 33 persons excluding 99 images of wearing sunglasses from AR face data set, 60 images of 15 persons from Yale Face DB, and 2418 images of 1209 persons from FERET data set. The above data sets are merged for training and testing the CAM(see session 3). The data context of the merged data is analyzed by the FART. Fig. 7 shows the examples of five category data context.

The first experiment is performed using the data set accumulated by our lab. The data set has 1000 face images from 100 people. We used 5 image for registration for each people. The remaining 500 images are used as the normal images. We used 99 registration images and 198 test images from the AR face image set excluding images wearing sunglasses. For the Yale data set, we used 15 registration face image and 45 test images, The FERET gallery images of 1196 people is used for registration and 1196 probe_fafb_expression images are used for test.

The proposed method has been compared with the t-test based classifier combination [9]. In the t-test based classifier combination, the decision whether to select the best classifier or fuse several classifiers is carried out by correlation rate between highest accuracy classifier and second highest classifier. Correlation table is fitness function.

Table 1. Performance evaluation of single classification for each cluster

	PCA	Gabor3	Gabor13	Gabor28	Gabor30	Number of Data
Cluster0	93% (295)	91.5% (290)	96.5% (306)	96.2% (305)	96.5% (306)	317
Cluster1	100% (61)	88.5% (54)	100% (61)	98.36% (60)	100% (61)	61
Cluster2	99.4% (157)	79.1% (125)	88.6% (140)	89.9% (142)	92.4% (146)	158
Cluster3	100% (148)	75% (111)	83.8% (124)	86.5% (128)	85.1% (126)	148
Cluster4	93.7% (194)	88.9% (184)	95.% (197)	97.6% (202)	97.1% (201)	207
Cluster5	100% (74)	91.9% (68)	94.6% (70)	94.6% (70)	95.9% (71)	74
Total Rate	96.3% (929)	86.3% (832)	93% (898)	94% (907)	94.4% (911)	965

Table 2. Face recognition rate using Single Classifier

	PCA	Gabor3	Gabor13	Gabor28	Gabor30
Ferret DB	60.35%	59.59%	64.96%	82.06%	82.06%
Yale DB	58.91%	68.99%	77.83%	80.46%	80.46%
Inha DB	94.2%	93.72%	94.44%	95.79%	95.79%

Table 3. Comparison of recognition accuracy between t-test based combination and the proposed method

Database	Classifier fusion (Using t-test table)	The proposed method (t-test and GA)
FERET DB	93.5%	95.4%
Yale DB	96%	98.5%
Inha DB	96%	99%

Table1, 2 and Table 3 show performance evaluation of single classification and recognition accuracy comparison between t-test based combination and the proposed method. Table 3 shows a recognition rate of proposed method and comparison with other methods. It is 99 % for our Lab DB, 98.5 % for Yale dataset and 95.4% for FERET dataset.

Table 4 shows comparison of rank1 correct acceptance among Eigenface, Eigenface by Bayesian, EP and the proposed method. From Table 4, it becomes apparent that the proposed method shows good recognition performance.

Table 4. Comparative Testing Performance: FERET database

Method	Rank1 correct acceptance
Eigenface[9]	83.4%
Eigenface by Bayesian[10]	94.8%
Evolutionary Pursuit[11]	92.14%
Proposed method	95.4%

The proposed method performs better than simplicity method of computation and back propagation neural network because those methods don't adapt a general filtering environment. In own experimental results, the proposed method shows recognition rate of over 95.4 % for FERET dataset, which exceeds the performance of the other popular methods.

5 Conclusion

In this paper, Evolvable Classifier Combination, a novel method of classifier combination using data context-awareness is proposed and applied to object recognition problem. The proposed method tries to distinguish its input data context and evolves the classifier combination structure accordingly by Genetic algorithm (GA). It stores its experiences in terms of the data context category and the evolved artificial chromosome so that the evolutionary knowledge can be used later. The proposed method has been evaluated in the area of face recognition. Data context-awareness, modeling and identification of input data as data context categories, is carried out using hybrid method of FART. The face data context can be decided based on the image attributes such as, light direction, contrast, brightness, spectral composition, etc. The proposed scheme can optimize itself to a given data in real-time by using the identified data context and previously derived chromosome. The proposed method is tested using three datasets: Inha, FERET, Yale database. There fore another important topic for classifier fusion.

References

1. N. Mori, et. al.,: Adaptation to a Dynamic Environment by Means of the ENvironment Identifying Genetic Algorithm. IECON (2000)
2. Issam Dagher, Michael Georgiopoulos, Gregory L. Heileman, George Bebis : An Ordering Algorithm for Pattern Presentation in Fuzzy ARTMAP That Tends to Improve Generalization Performance. IEEE Trans. Neural Network, vol.10, no.4. July (1999)
3. Ramuhalli, P., Polikar, R., Udpa L., Udpa S. : Fuzzy ARTMAP network with evolutionary learning.Proc. of IEEE 25th Int. Conf. On Acoustics, Speech and Signal Processing (ICASSP 2000), vol. 6, Istanbul, Turkey (2000) pp.3466-3469
4. D. Swets and J. Weng : Using discriminant eigenfeatures for image retrieval. IEE Trans. PAMI, vol. 18, no.8, (1996) pp. 831-836
5. D. Goldberg : Genetic Algorithm in Search, Optimization, and Machine Learning, Addison-Wesley. (1989)
6. R. C. Gonzalez, and R. E. Woods : Digital Image Processing, Addison-Wesley Publishing Company. (1993)
7. P.Phillips : The FERET database and evoluation procedure for face recognition algorithms. Image and Vision Computing, vol.16, no.5, (1999) pp.295-306
8. http://cvc.yale.edu/projects/yalefaces/yalefaces.html
9. M. Turk and A. Pentland : Eigenfaces for recognition. J. Cong. Neurosci. vol.13, no.1, (1991) pp. 71-86
10. B.Moghaddam, C.Nastar, and A,Pentland : A Bayesian similarity Measure for direct Image Matching. Proc. of Int. Conf. on Pattern Recognition, (1996)
11. Chengjun Liu and Harry Wechsler: Evolutionary Pursuit and Its Application to Face Recognition. IEEE Trans. on Pattern Analysis and Machine Intelligent, vol.22, no.6, (2000) pp.570-582
12. L. Kuncheva: Switching Between Selection and Fusion in Combining Classifiers. AnExperiment, IEEE Transaction on Systems, Man and Cybernetics—PARTB, vol.32, no.2, APRIL (2002) pp.146-156

A Multi-scale and Multi-pose Face Detection System

Mi-Young Nam and Phill-Kyu Rhee

Dept. of Computer Science & Engineering,
Inha University, Yong-Hyun Dong, Incheon, Korea
rera@im.inha.ac.kr, pkrhee@inha.ac.kr

Abstract. In this paper, the framework and implementation of a real time multi-scale face detection system using appearance-based learning method and multi-pose hybrid learning approach. Multiple scale and pose based object detection is attractive since it could accumulate the face models by autonomous learning process. Face image, however, can be approximated even though it is represented with many scales. A real time face detection determines the location and size of each human face(if any) in an input image. Detecting varying human face in video frames is an important task in many computer vision applications such as human-computer interface. The face detection proposed in this paper employs hybrid learning approach and statistical method. We employ FuzzyART and RBF Network and Mahalanobis distance. We achieve a very encouraging experimental results.

1 Intorduction

We carry a conceptual idea of real world objects in our thought as Socrates explained to homogeneous. The difficulties in visual detection are caused by the variations in viewpoint, viewing distance, illumination, etc. Detecting face under various viewpoints and lighting conditions is the final goal of computer vision. Robust face detection needs high invariance with regard to those variations. Much research has been done to solve this problem[1]. The face detection systems can be divided into three major categories[2]: model-based method, image invariant method, and appearance-based learning method. In the model-based method, an face model is defined, and this model is matched to the image. The second one, image invariant method is based on a matching set of image pattern relationships. The last one learns the features of face images of categorized object examples. Appearance-based approach has been employed successfully in the computer vision areas [3]. Face Detection determines the location and size of each human face(if any) in an input image. Detecting varying pose human face in video frames is an important task in many applications such as human-computer interface, and biometric security, etc. In this paper, FuzzyART(Fuzzy Adaptive Resonance Theory) and RBF are employed to simulate the capacity of the high level cell in the attentive process face detection system. Detection of multiple view faces should model the faces of multiple viewpoints and under various illumination conditions [1]. A simple linear model can hardly handle the multiple view problems. In a view-based approach, the viewpoints are quantized into a group, view subspace which defines the dominant possible appearance of the face images with the viewpoints. An alternative approach is the parametric method where labeled training data is sorted according to the view values, and construct a view distribution [3]. Multiple scale and view based face detection is attractive since it could accumulate the face models by autonomous learning process. One problem in this approach is the face images can only be approximated with many scales and views. A tradeoff must be considered between the size of multiple scale and view representation of the face and its accuracy. The feature space for face detection with multiple scale and viewpoints must be partitioned into subspaces properly so that the location error can be minimized. However, the partitioning of multiple scales and viewpoints is very subjective and ambiguous. Another problem is the accumulation of properly labeled training data. The pose invariant face detection system proposed in this paper employs combined supervised and unsupervised learning. We employ FuzzyART and RBFN for optimal pose estimation for an optimal face detecting architecture. We achieve very encouraging results in real timesystem. The outline of this paper is as follows. In section 2, we present the architecture of the proposed face detection system. The pose classification process is discussed in section 3. In section 3, we present the face recognition process. We give real time retrieval experimental results in section 5. Finally, we give concluding remarks.

2 The Proposed System Architecture

We propose a general scheme of face detector for multiple viewpoints and scales. The specific task we are discussing in this paper is a generic face detector which is invariant viewing angles and scales. The system consists of the multi-scale module, the object vector representation module, face detector. Initially, seed appearance models of an object is manually gathered and classified for training the detector module. The detector with prior classes is trained by the initial seed data set. The proposed system architecture is shown in Fig.1.

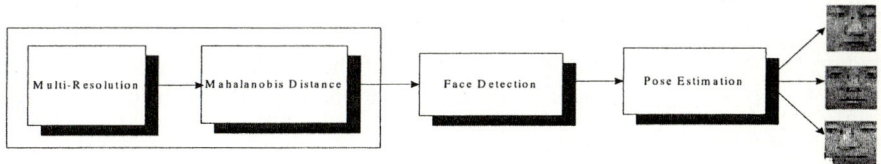

Fig. 1. Face detection architecture

2.1 Scale-Invariance by Pyramid

The problem is formulated as a classification problem - Face and NonFace. Initially, a training set of faces is gathered. Each training face image is scaled to 20x20 and normalized using max-min value normalization. According to vectorize way, affected much face detection performance. Searched for vectorization method that is optimized by an experiment, as a result, raised good performance. We vectorized facial image to

54 dimensions. Therefore, we could improve performance through efficient vectorization and dimension decrease. Training image contains 3000 grayscale face pictures of size 20 x 20. We have vectorized on each training image for each cell, we create a vector of 54 dimension that face image's multi Resolution and blocked area average value. Training data is vectorized that can display performance by maximum doing not lose face characteristic information. This vectorization have enhanced face detection rate. Face' feature don't reduce and face detection result is enhancement. Training data and vector of training shows Fig.2. Training Image transfer to grayscale image, green value is high weighted green.

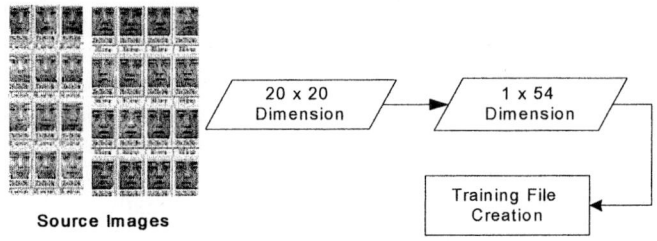

Fig. 2. Training face data and vectorization: mean value per each block

Squared Mahalanobis distance [4] is a useful method that measures free model course free pattern relationship similarity degree. The center of cluster is determined by the mean vector, and the shape of the cluster is determined by the covariance matrix Mahalanobis distance shows Eq. 1.

$$r^2 = (x - \mu_x)' \Sigma^{-1} (x - \mu_x) \quad (1)$$

where μ_x is average vector of face's vector, Σ is Covariance matrix of independent elements. Eigenvalues determine the length of these axes. In order to determine how a single boundary relates to the collection of boundaries in the learning set, a distance measure needs to be defined. In the active shape model literature, the evaluation of boundary feature values is performed in terms of the mahalanobis distance, i.e. the distance to the average normalized by the variation in each dimension. Following

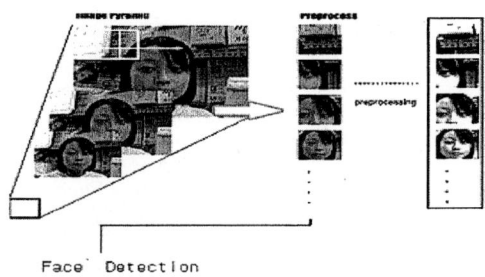

Fig. 3. Scale-Invariance by Pyramid

Cootes et al., we use a mahalanobis distance model to compute the distance of a feature function to the average of the learning set[4, 5, 6]. We divided only face image space into several probability clusters. The generation seen therefore forms model in 3,000 face images and computed mahalanobis distance, and the computed result decides face and non-face. Multi-resolution consists of nine steps by an experiment, and offset established by four pixels for face detection of various size. These models gathered and categorized manually are used to construct initial object detector with their possible pattern variations in a high-dimensional image vector space.

Fig.4 shows result that mahalanobis distance of face and non-face image by Eq1. The distance is normalized between 0 and 255. Mahalanobis distance of face has lower reaction value and distance of non-face have higher reaction value. When the system is given an image in which to find the faces, the image is rescaled to multi-resolution, it takes each sub-window of the image, rescales them to size of 20x20, applies the preprocessing, and computes the mahalanobis distance. The distance leading to a classification of each window(area) as a face or non-face. If the mahalanobis distance of sub-window is lower than threshold, is a face area. We estimate whether test image is face or not by.

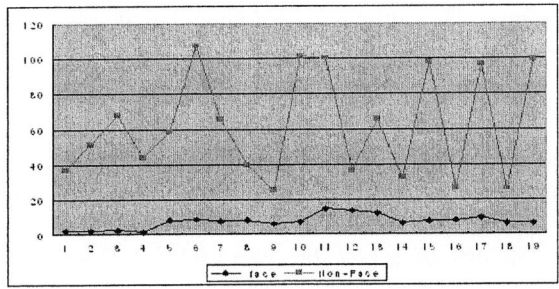

Fig. 4. The comparison of Mahalanobis distance of face and non-face image

The above experiment result mahalanobis distance is effective to face detection, but is sensitive in pose. Therefore, pose classification is important. In this paper, integrate FuzzyART and RBF for pose's classification.

2.2 Search Space Reduction Using Facial Color

Skin –color provides good information for extracting area of the. Several defferent Kinds of color space have been proposed, and Terrillon discussed which is fast for modeling a Gaussian skin color distribution. We can classify Skin area using example-based method. Skin Color's area is computed 1,200 face images of 20 x 20 size. We used YCrCb Color model. A conversion from RGB to YCrCb color model. We is represented CrCb color value for illumination. Figure 2 is a sample face images for a skin color histogram.

Input image is 320x240 size. We noticed that Skin color in the color space are in a multi region. We define skin color as colors when histogram value over a threshold because face images contain non-skin color. The threshold value is determined empirically.

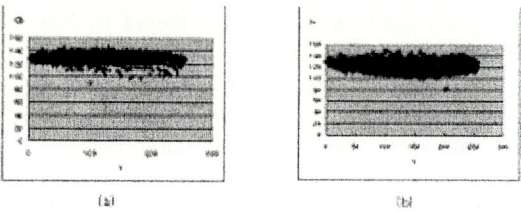

Fig. 5. Skin color distribution in face image of 20 x 20 size

3 Pose Analysis Using Hybrid Learning

In the proposed approach, pose classification is dealt with as local targets to be detected in an image. We formulate the face detector generator to learn to discriminate object patterns which can be measured formally, not intuitively as most previous approaches did. The pose estimator classifies a face pattern into one of the view (pose) set. The facial pose estimation can be used to verify the detection of multi-view faces. In this paper, we propose how combined supervised learning and unsupervised learning. The proposed learning based classifier generator has advantages over previous approaches.

3.1 Pose Estimation by FART+RBF

The RBF networks, just like MLP networks, can therefore be used in classification and/or function approximation problems. In the case of a RBF network, we usually prefer the hybrid approach, described below [7, 8, 9,10]. The RBFs, which have a similar architecture to that of MLPs, however, achieve this goal using a different strategy. One cluster center is updated every time an input vector x is chosen by FuzzyART from the input data set. The cluster nearest to x has its position updated using

$$W_{ji}(t+1) = \beta(I \wedge W_{ji}(t)) + (1-\beta)W_{ji}(t) \quad (2)$$

FuzzyART is a varient of ART system derived from the first generation of ART, namely ART1. It is a synthesis of ART algorithm and Fuzzy operator. ART1 can only accept binary input pattern, but FuzzyART allows both binary and continuous input patterns[3,10]. The feature space of object instance with multiple viewing angles must be clustered properly so that the location error can be minimized. However, the classification of multiple viewing points is very subjective and ambiguous. Thus, we adopt FuzzyART and RBF methods for achieving an optimal pose classification architecture. Executed step is as following to FuzzyART[11,12,13]. In this Paper, Clustering's performance improves by studying repeatedly about done data.

The cluster center is moved closer to x because this equation minimizes the error vector. Each hidden unit calculates the distance of the input vector from the corresponding Gaussian:

$$\phi_j(x) = \exp\{-\frac{\|x-\mu_j\|^2}{2\sigma_j^2}\} \quad (3)$$

In this paper, centers are obtained from unsupervised learning (clustering), FuzzyART algorithm. The weights between the hidden units and the output layer, denoted by w_{kj}, are regular multiplication weights (as in a MLP)

$$y_k(x) = \sum_{j=1}^{M} w_{kj} \phi_j(x) + w_{k0} \qquad (4)$$

where x is the input vector, m_j is the jth prototype vector, σ_j is the width of the Gaussian of that prototype or cluster centre.

There are various approaches for training RBF networks. In this paper, centers are obtained from unsupervised learning (clustering), FuzzyART algorithm. Clustering (FuzzyART algorithm) and LMS are iterative. This is the most commonly used procedure. Typically provides good results. After finding a suitable cluster using clustering algorithm, do laying center on this. The winning node μ_j is what FuzzyART is its best match for the input pattern. Hidden node's center determined by unsupervised learning, FART.

As showed Fig.6, the idea is to train the network in two separate stages in first stage, we perform an unsupervised training (FuzzyART) to determine the Gaussians' parameters (j, j). In the second stage, the multiplicative weights w_{kj} are trained using the regular supervised approach. Input pattern is vectorized for grayscale image size of 20x20 pixels, input node had mosaic of size of 10x10 pixels. The transformation from the input space to the hidden unit space is non-linear, whereas the transformation from the hidden-unit space to the output-space is linear. RBF classifier expand input vectors into a high dimensional space. RBF network has architecture that of the traditional three-layer back-propagation. In this paper, hidden units are trained using FuzzyART network and basis function used are Gaussians. Proposed network input consists of n normalized and rescaled size of 1/2 face images fed to the network as 1 dimension vector. And input unit has floating value [0,1] The vector value is normalized. In case learn by FuzzyART, performance is best in case used picture itself by input node vectorized.

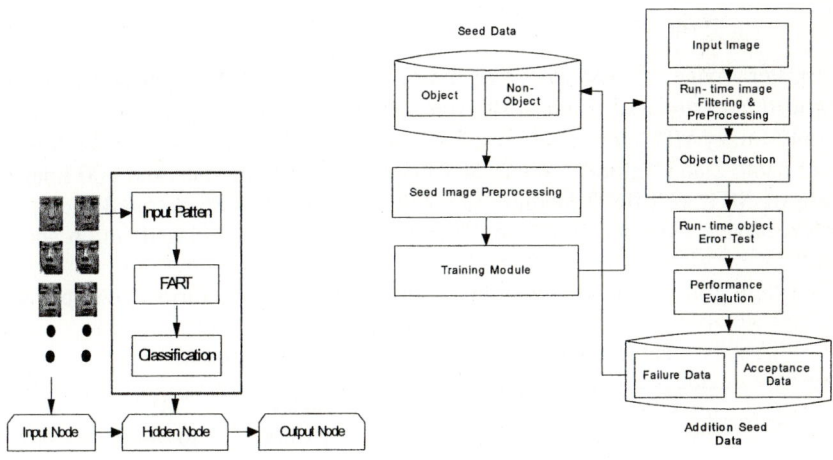

Fig. 6. Training System Architecture

4 Experiment

The experiment of the proposed method for the face detection has been performed with images captured in various environments 600 images are captured and considered in the experiments. The superiority of the proposed method is discussed in the following. We should note that to pose estimation, figure 4 shows face detection in real-time image by using multi-resolution.

Face detection result shows table1. As explained in frontal image and the test images have size of 320 x 240 pixels and encoded in 256 gray scale levels. We resized to various size using multi-resolution of 5 steps. Rescaled images is transferred Each face is normalized into a re-scaled size of 20x20 pixels and each data – training image and test images – is preprocessed by histogram equalization and max-min value normalization.

Fig.10 shows the face detection and tacking result in real time system and face recognition schema is shown Fig.10 The left image is recognized image ranking.

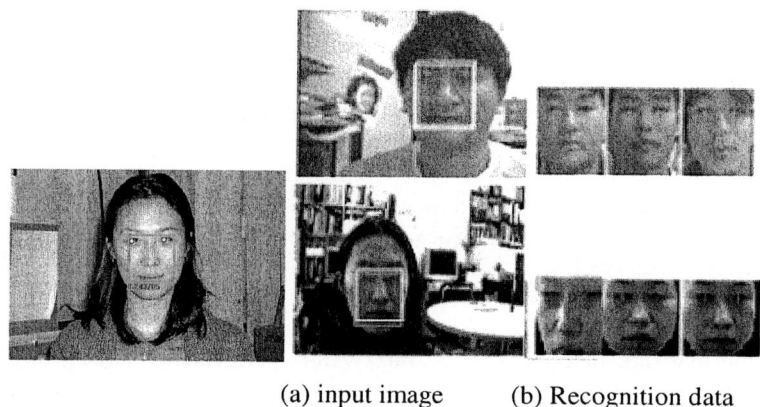

(a) input image   (b) Recognition data

Fig. 7. Real -Time Face Detection

A register image is generated five image that is left shift, right shift, up, down transformed experimental result is showed tables. The clustering results of face pose using only FuzzyART and integration FuzzyART and RBF is given in the following Table 1, Table 2 and Table 3. We used 1000 images by train data and 600 images by test data of MIT +UMIST database and ORL database. We separated face images through recursive learning of 4 times. Result about pose data classification shows in Table 2.

By we were going to do studying repeatedly, clustering's performance improved.

Table 1. Pose Estimation Result – Our Lab Dataset

Data	RBFN+FART	FART	BP
Front Image	597/600	591/600	497/600
Left Image	597/600	593/600	498/600
RightImage	600/600	599/600	485/600

Table 2. UMIST & MIT Database

Data	Accept	FAR
Front Image	292/300	8/300
Left Image	48/49	1/49
Right Image	298/300	2/300

Table 3. ORL Database: 40 Person * 9 Pose

Data	Accept	FAR
Front Image	40/40	1/40
Left Image (4 Pose)	120/120	1/120
Right Image(4 pose)	118/120	2/120

Table 4. FERET Database : fafb and fafc dataset

Dataset	Accept	FAR
Fafb dataset	98.07%	1.35%
Fafc dataset	92.78%	5.15%

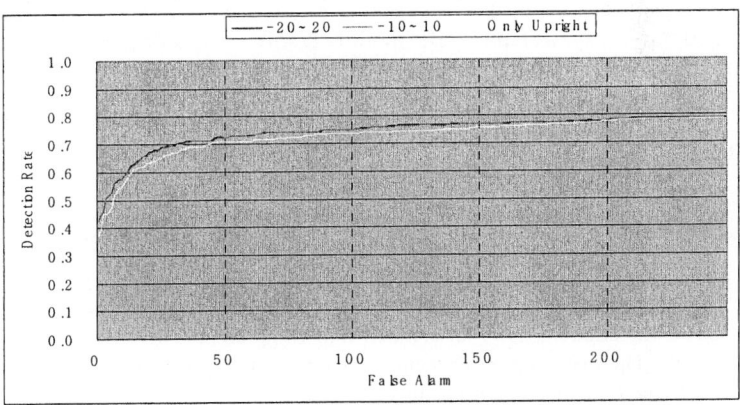

Fig. 8. Face detection rate in CMU database: Training data's size is 20~20 and 10 ~10

Fig. 9. Face detection example in CMU

We could improve pose classification's performance for face through recursive studying like experiment result. The combined effect of eye glasses is also investigated. In this experiment, the factor of glasses and illumination was considered and experimental images were classified by the factor of glasses and illumination. We classified bad illumination images into the image including a partially lighted face, good images into that including g a nearly uniformly lighted face.

5 Concluding Remarks

In this paper, we propose a novel generic appearance-based object detection, especially for variance in scale and viewing points in real-time system. Even though much research has been done for object detection, it still remains a difficult issue. The proposed system could accumulate the object models by autonomous learning process. In appearance-based approach, the object can only be approximated with many scales and views, where the partitioning of multiple scales and viewpoints is very subjective and ambiguous. A tradeoff representation of pose and its accuracy is treated with the FuzzyART and the RBF Network method. The feature space for object detection with multiple scale and viewpoints are partitioned into subspaces so that the location error can be minimized. mahalanobis distance computing module explores the subspaces of multiple viewpoints for an efficient face detecting structure, and integrated the FuzzyART and RBF module resolves the subjective and ambiguous problem of partitioning boundaries. The experiment shows very encouraging results.

References

1. Li, S.Z.; Zhenqiu Zhang.: FloatBoost learning and statistical face detection. Pattern Analysis and Machine Intelligence, IEEE Transactions on , Vol. 26. (2004) 1112 – 1123
2. A. Mohan, C. Papageorgiou, and T. Poggio, "Example-Based Object Detection in Images by Components, IEEE Trans. on PAMI, vol. 23, No. 4. (2001) pp.349-361
3. T.Kasuba : Simplefied Fuzzy ARTMAP. AI Expert, pp.18-25, November (1993)
4. B.K.L. Erik Hjelmas: Face Detection: A Survey. Computer Vision and Image Understanding, vol. 3. no.3. (2001) 236-274.
5. T.F. Cootes, G.J. Edwards, and C.J Taylor. Active appearance models. IEEE Trans. Pattern Analysis and Machine Intelligence, Vol.23, No.6, (2001) pp.681-685
6. T.F. Cootes, A. Hill, C.J. Taylor, and J. Haslam. Use of active shape models for locating structure in medical images. Image and Vision Computing, Vol. 12, No.6, (1994) 355-365
7. Shakunaga, T.: An Object Pose Estimation System Using A Single Camera. Proc. of IEEE international conference, Vol.2. (1992) pp.7~10
8. Paulino, A. Araujo, H. : Pose Estimation for central catadioptric system : an analytic Approach. Proc. Of Pattern recognition, (2002) pp. 969-699
9. Huang, J. Shao, X Wechsler, H.: Face Pose discrimination using support vector machanism(SVM). Proc. of Pattern Recognition, Vol.1. (1998) pp.154-156
10. M. H. Hassoun : Fundamentals of Artificial Neural Networks. MIT Press, 1995.
11. G.A. Carpenter et al : Fuzzy ARTMAP : A neural network architecture for inceremetal supervised learning of analog multidimensional maps. IEEE Trans. Neural Networks, Vol.3, No. 5 pp.698-712, . September 1992.

Conditionally Dependent Classifier Fusion Using AND Rule for Improved Biometric Verification

Krithika Venkataramani and B.V.K. Vijaya Kumar

Department of Electrical and Computer Engineering, CyLab,
Carnegie Mellon University, Pittsburgh PA 15213, USA
{krithika, kumar}@ece.cmu.edu

Abstract. Statistical dependence of classifiers has recently been shown to improve accuracy over statistically independent classifiers. In this paper, we focus on the verification application and theoretically analyze the AND fusion rule to find the favorable conditional dependence that improves the fusion accuracy over conditionally independent classifiers. Based on this analysis, we come with a method to design such classifiers by training the classifiers on different partitions of the training data. The AR face database is used for performance evaluation and the proposed method has a false rejection rate (FRR) of 2.4% and a false acceptance rate of 3.3% on AND fusion, which is better than an FRR of 3.8% and FAR of 4.3% when classifiers are designed without taking account the AND fusion rule.

1 Introduction

Biometric verification is being used to replace physical and virtual access techniques such as keys and passwords since biometrics cannot be lost or stolen. A classifier is built on enrollment of a person's biometric features to discriminate between the features of the person and features of other people, as well as to tolerate the distortions between different variations in the features of the person. During verification, the classifier produces an output score using the input test feature. Typically, by setting thresholds on the score, a decision is made whether the input feature is from an authentic, i.e. from the same person, or from an impostor, i.e. from some other person. In practical applications, there would be large variability present in the biometric features obtained. For example, in the face recognition vendor test (FRVT) 2002 [1], which involved 37,437 individuals and 121,589 images, the best-performing algorithm had a FRR of 10% at 1% FAR [1]. In such cases, multiple classifier fusion can improve accuracy.

Classifier fusion is a topic of much investigation and many methods of fusion have been proposed [2-8]. Some typical approaches to combining classifiers are: (i)a classifier ensemble combined using a fusion rule [2-4], (ii) dynamic classifier selection where the best classifier to use is chosen based on the test feature [5,6].

Typically classifier ensembles are fused in parallel by combining scores [2] (e.g. sum rule, product rule, etc.) or combining decisions [3] (e.g. majority rule). Kittler *et. al.* [2] formulate the sum, product, min, max, and median of classifier *a posteriori* probabilities as simplifications or bounds of the maximum *a posteriori* probability of the ensemble of classifiers when classifiers are conditionally independent. In practice, the classifier output scores are normalized as an estimate of the classifier *a posteriori* probabilities. Varshney [3] develops methods of finding the best decision fusion rule when the probability density functions of classifiers are given and the classifiers are conditionally independent. If the classifier outputs are interpreted as fuzzy membership values or belief values, Dempster-Shafer [4] techniques are used for combination.

Kleinberg [7] introduced the concept of stochastic discrimination (SD) for generation of multiple weak classifiers which are combined to form a strong classifier. These classifiers, as well as their combination, are over-training resistant under certain strong mathematical assumptions of indiscernibility between training and test sets with respect to the weak classifiers. This requirement would lead to a requirement for a large training set, which may not be available in practice.

Ho *et al* [5] introduced the concept of dynamic classifier selection (DCS) as an alternative to classifier ensemble combination where the most appropriate classifier is chosen to make the decision. Giacinto and Roli [6] proposed a DCS method based on the concept of choosing the best classifier based on the classifier's local accuracy (CLA) around the test feature. Shin and Sohn [8] proposed a combination of DCS and classifier ensemble method for fusion. Multiple decision trees are built, but two clusters of trees are chosen based on the local accuracy of the test sample, and these are combined through majority voting.

Usually, the classifiers are generated independent to the fusion method and various fusion methods are applied to these classifiers to find the best method. Some methods of generating classifiers are bootstrapping [9] and Boosting [9]. In bootstrapping [9], multiple classifiers are generated in an independent and parallel manner by training on random samples of the training set. In Boosting [9], classifiers are generated in a sequential manner by training more on misclassified samples by the current ensemble.

In this paper, we focus on decision fusion from classifier ensembles for biometric verification. Kuncheva *et al* [10] show that negatively dependent classifiers can improve MAJORITY voting rule performance over independent classifiers. For different fusion rules, the favorable dependence statistics vary. Here, we apply the idea to AND rule fusion. Theoretical analysis of the statistics of the classifiers for optimal fusion with the AND rule is done and the favorable conditional dependence of classifier decisions to improve AND fusion performance over conditional independence is found. The same principle can be applied for other fusion rules to find their favorable conditional dependence. Based on the theoretical analysis, we come up with a method of designing classifiers by partitioning the training set in a manner optimal to the fusion rule. We compare the performance of this design method to a method where classifiers are generated independent to the fusion rule and show the superiority of this design method. We evaluate the verification performance of the AND rule on the AR face database [11] using the Fisher Discriminant [12] as the base classifier. However, the design method can be applied to other base classifiers.

The rest of the paper is organized as follows. Section 2 is a theoretical analysis of the AND rule to find the favorable conditional dependence of classifiers for improved AND fusion. In Section 3, a design method to come up with such classifiers is provided along with results on the AR database. Conclusions are given in Section 4.

2 Analysis of Conditionally Dependent Classifiers for the AND Rule

In verification applications, we wish to differentiate between two classes, authentics and impostors. Let H_0 and H_1 be the two hypotheses denoting impostors and authentics, respectively. To provide clarity of analysis, we analyze the AND rule for two classifiers. We assume there are two classifiers, each providing a binary decision u_j. The AND rule provides a global decision u_0 based on the individual classifier decisions. If all classifiers declare authentic ($u_1 = u_2 = 1$), then the AND rule declares authentic ($u_0 = 1$) and otherwise declares impostor ($u_0 = 0$). The error probabilities of interest in verification are the probability of false acceptance P_{FA} and the probability of false rejection P_{FR}, which are defined as follows for the two-classifier AND rule.

$$P_{FA}^{AND(1,2)} = P(\mathbf{u} = \begin{bmatrix} 1 & 1 \end{bmatrix} | H_0), \quad \mathbf{u} = \begin{bmatrix} u_1 & u_2 \end{bmatrix} \tag{1}$$

$$P_{FR}^{AND(1,2)} = P(\mathbf{u} = \begin{bmatrix} 0 & 0 \end{bmatrix} | H_1) + P(\mathbf{u} = \begin{bmatrix} 1 & 0 \end{bmatrix} | H_1) + P(\mathbf{u} = \begin{bmatrix} 0 & 1 \end{bmatrix} | H_1) \tag{2}$$

When the classifier decisions are conditionally independent, we have

$$P(\mathbf{u} = \begin{bmatrix} i & j \end{bmatrix} | H_i) = P(u_1 = i | H_i) P(u_2 = j | H_i), \quad i = 0,1 \; j = 0,1 \tag{3}$$

In the paper, we may loosely mention conditional independence (dependence) or conditionally independent (dependent) classifiers for classifiers whose decisions are conditionally independent (dependent) but the meaning should be clear. For fixed individual classifier error probabilities, the P_{FA} and P_{FR} for or the two-classifier AND rule are fixed for conditionally independent classifiers and are given by

$$\text{independent } P_{FA}^{AND(1,2)} = P(u_1 = 1 | H_0) P(u_2 = 1 | H_0) = P_{FA}^1 P_{FA}^2 \tag{4}$$

$$\text{independent } P_{FR}^{AND(1,2)} = 1 - P(u_1 = 1 | H_1) P(u_2 = 1 | H_1) = P_{FR}^1 + P_{FR}^2 - P_{FR}^1 P_{FR}^2 \tag{5}$$

where the superscripts on P_{FA} and P_{FR} refer to the classifier. When the classifier decisions are conditionally dependent, the error probabilities may be larger or smaller than the expressions in Eq.(4) and Eq.(5) for conditionally independent classifier decisions. Our interest is to know the conditional dependence for which the error probabilities are smaller for the AND fusion rule when the *individual classifier error probabilities are fixed*. For making the error probability on H_i smaller than its corresponding value for conditionally independent classifiers, we need to consider only the joint probability of the classifier decisions conditioned on H_i. The favorable conditional dependence on H_i may be different from the favorable conditional dependence on H_j, $j \neq i$. This does not pose a problem but states the criteria on the classifier design in order to simultaneously satisfy both the conditions. Further, the conditional dependence favorable for one fusion rule may be different from the conditional dependence favorable for another fusion rule. Hence each fusion rule must be analyzed separately. However, the analysis will be similar for different fusion rules.

We first focus on finding the conditional dependence for which $P_{FA}^{AND(1,2)}$ is smaller than that of conditionally independent classifiers for the AND rule ($P_{FA}^1 P_{FA}^2$) (Eq.6), for fixed individual classifier false acceptance probabilities (Eq.(7), Eq.(8)).

$$P_{FA} = P(\mathbf{u} = [1\ \ 1] | H_0) < P_{FA}^1 P_{FA}^2 \tag{6}$$

$$P_{FA}^1 = P(\mathbf{u} = [1\ \ 0] | H_0) + P(\mathbf{u} = [1\ \ 1] | H_0) \tag{7}$$

$$P_{FA}^2 = P(\mathbf{u} = [0\ \ 1] | H_0) + P(\mathbf{u} = [1\ \ 1] | H_0) \tag{8}$$

We also have the constraint that the sum of all probabilities is equal to 1 (Eq.(9)).

$$P(\mathbf{u} = [0\ \ 0] | H_0) + P(\mathbf{u} = [0\ \ 1] | H_0) + P(\mathbf{u} = [1\ \ 0] | H_0) + P(\mathbf{u} = [1\ \ 1] | H_0) = 1 \tag{9}$$

We thus have three constraints (Eq.(7) to Eq.(9)) and one inequality (Eq.(6)) while there are four variables, one for each of the four combinations of decisions. This implies that each term of the joint conditional probability must satisfy the following inequalities.

$$P(\mathbf{u} = [0\ \ 0] | H_0) < (1 - P_{FA}^1)(1 - P_{FA}^2) \tag{10}$$

$$P(\mathbf{u} = [1\ \ 1] | H_0) < P_{FA}^1 P_{FA}^2 \tag{11}$$

$$P(\mathbf{u} = [0\ \ 1] | H_0) > P_{FA}^2 - P_{FA}^1 P_{FA}^2 \tag{12}$$

$$P(\mathbf{u} = [1\ \ 0] | H_0) > P_{FA}^1 - P_{FA}^1 P_{FA}^2 \tag{13}$$

subject to the constraint in Eq.(9). We note from the last two inequalities, Eqs.(12 and 13), the probability of $u_1 \neq u_2$ conditioned on H_0 is larger for the favorable conditionally

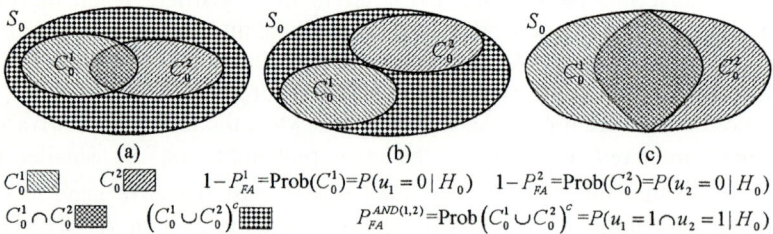

Fig. 1. (a) The general case of a pair of classifiers on impostors. (b) The best pair of conditionally dependent classifiers when $P_{FA}^1 + P_{FA}^2 \geq 1$. (c) The best pair of conditionally dependent classifiers when $P_{FA}^1 + P_{FA}^2 < 1$.

dependent case than the conditionally independent case. In other words, the two classifier decisions must disagree more than independent classifiers on the impostor data to make the false acceptance probability for the AND rule smaller than that of conditionally independent classifier decisions. This statement is always true but the converse is not true in general. For the general case of N classifiers, this solution is *one* of the many possible solutions.

Fig. 1a) illustrates the idea pictographically. The area of the sets C_0^i represents the probability of correct classification by the ith classifier. The union of the sets represents the correct classification of the AND rule. When the intersection of the sets is smaller than that of conditionally independent classifiers, the union of the sets is larger or $P_{FA}^{AND(1,2)}$ is smaller than that of conditionally independent classifiers.

The Q statistic [13] could be used as a measure of the conditional dependence. The Q statistic between a pair of classifiers j and k is defined as

$$Q_{jk} = \frac{N^{11}N^{00} - N^{01}N^{10}}{N^{11}N^{00} + N^{01}N^{10}} \tag{14}$$

where N^{ab} is the number of elements for which classifier j declares a and classifier k declares b. The Q statistic takes values between 1 and -1 and is zero when the classifiers are conditionally independent. For large number of observations, the frequencies can be approximated to probabilities. An indication to the sign of the Q statistic as a measure of the favorable conditional dependence for the AND rule could be obtained by considering the numerator of the Q statistic. From Eqs.(10 to 13), we have

$$\frac{N^{11}N^{00} - N^{01}N^{10}}{N^2} < \left(P_{FA}^1 P_{FA}^2\right) \cdot \left((1-P_{FA}^1)(1-P_{FA}^2)\right) - \left(P_{FA}^2(1-P_{FA}^1)\right) \cdot \left(P_{FA}^1(1-P_{FA}^2)\right) = 0 \tag{15}$$

This implies that the Q statistic of the conditionally dependent classifiers on the impostor data, Q^{H_0}, would need to be negative for making the false acceptance of the two-classifier AND rule smaller than that of conditionally independent classifiers.

From Fig. 1b) and 1c), we can see that the smallest $P_{FA}^{AND(1,2)}$ is obtained when the union of the sets is the largest and is given by

$$\text{smallest } P_{FA}^{AND(1,2)} = \begin{cases} P_{FA}^1 + P_{FA}^2 - 1, & P_{FA}^1 + P_{FA}^2 \geq 1 \\ 0, & P_{FA}^1 + P_{FA}^2 \leq 1 \end{cases} \tag{16}$$

For this special case, the joint probability of the classifier decisions are as follows.

$$P(\mathbf{u} = [0\ 0] | H_0) = \begin{cases} 0, & P_{FA}^1 + P_{FA}^2 \geq 1 \\ 1 - (P_{FA}^1 + P_{FA}^2), & P_{FA}^1 + P_{FA}^2 \leq 1, \end{cases} \tag{17}$$

$$P(\mathbf{u} = [1\ 1] | H_0) = \begin{cases} (P_{FA}^1 + P_{FA}^2) - 1, & P_{FA}^1 + P_{FA}^2 \geq 1 \\ 0, & P_{FA}^1 + P_{FA}^2 \leq 1, \end{cases} \tag{18}$$

$$P(\mathbf{u} = [0\ 1] | H_0) = \begin{cases} 1 - P_{FA}^1, & P_{FA}^1 + P_{FA}^2 \geq 1 \\ P_{FA}^2, & P_{FA}^1 + P_{FA}^2 \leq 1, \end{cases} \tag{19}$$

$$P(\mathbf{u}=[1\ 0]\mid H_0) = \begin{cases} 1 - P_{FA}^2, & P_{FA}^1 + P_{FA}^2 \geq 1 \\ P_{FA}^1, & P_{FA}^1 + P_{FA}^2 \leq 1, \end{cases} \quad (20)$$

In each case, Q^{H_0} at the smallest probability of false acceptance would be -1 since either of N^{11} or N^{00} (proportional to $P(\mathbf{u}=[1\ 1]\mid H_0)$ or $P(\mathbf{u}=[0\ 0]\mid H_0)$, respectively) is zero.

We now focus on finding the conditional dependence for which $P_{FR}^{AND(1,2)}$ is smaller than that of conditionally independent classifiers (Eq.(21)), for *fixed* individual classifier false rejection probabilities P_{FR}^1 and P_{FR}^2 (Eq.(22-23)).

$$P_{FR}^{AND(1,2)} = 1 - P(\mathbf{u}=[1\ 1]\mid H_1) < P_{FR}^1 + P_{FR}^2 - P_{FR}^1 P_{FR}^2 \quad (21)$$

$$P_{FR}^1 = P(\mathbf{u}=[0\ 0]\mid H_1) + P(\mathbf{u}=[0\ 1]\mid H_1) \quad (22)$$

$$P_{FR}^2 = P(\mathbf{u}=[0\ 0]\mid H_1) + P(\mathbf{u}=[1\ 0]\mid H_1) \quad (23)$$

The other constraint is due to the fact that all probabilities sum to 1 (Eq(24)).

$$P(\mathbf{u}=[0\ 0]\mid H_1) + P(\mathbf{u}=[0\ 1]\mid H_1) + P(\mathbf{u}=[1\ 0]\mid H_1) + P(\mathbf{u}=[1\ 1]\mid H_1) = 1 \quad (24)$$

This implies that each term of the joint conditional probability must satisfy the following inequalities.

$$P(\mathbf{u}=[0\ 0]\mid H_1) > P_{FR}^1 P_{FR}^2 \quad (25)$$

$$P(\mathbf{u}=[1\ 1]\mid H_1) > (1 - P_{FR}^1)(1 - P_{FR}^2) \quad (26)$$

$$P(\mathbf{u}=[0\ 1]\mid H_1) < P_{FR}^1 - P_{FR}^1 P_{FR}^2 \quad (27)$$

$$P(\mathbf{u}=[1\ 0]\mid H_1) < P_{FR}^2 - P_{FR}^1 P_{FR}^2 \quad (28)$$

subject to the constraint of Eq.(24). We note from the first two inequalities, Eqs.(25 and 26) that the classifier decisions must agree more on the authentic data to make the false rejection probability for the AND rule smaller than that of conditionally independent classifier decisions. From Eqs.(25 to 28), we have

$$\frac{N^{11}N^{00} - N^{01}N^{10}}{N^2} > (1 - P_{FR}^1)(1 - P_{FR}^2) \cdot P_{FR}^1 P_{FR}^2 - (1 - P_{FR}^2)P_{FR}^1 \cdot (1 - P_{FR}^1)P_{FR}^2 = 0 \quad (29)$$

Hence the Q statistic on authentics, Q^{H_1}, would be positive with favorable conditional dependence for the AND rule.

Fig. 2 illustrates the idea. The area of each of the sets C_1^i represents the probability of correct classification of the ith classifier on authentics. When the intersection of the sets is larger, $P_{FR}^{AND(1,2)}$ is smaller than that of conditionally independent classifiers. When the intersection is the largest, we have the smallest possible $P_{FR}^{AND(1,2)}$.

$$\text{smallest } P_{FR}^{AND(1,2)} = \max(P_{FR}^1, P_{FR}^2) \tag{30}$$

This happens when the joint probability of the classifier decisions is as follows.

$$P(\mathbf{u} = [0 \quad 0] | H_1) = \min(P_{FR}^1, P_{FR}^2) \tag{31}$$

$$P(\mathbf{u} = [1 \quad 1] | H_1) = \min(1 - P_{FR}^1, 1 - P_{FR}^2) \tag{32}$$

$$P(\mathbf{u} = [0 \quad 1] | H_1) = \begin{cases} P_{FR}^1 - P_{FR}^2, & P_{FR}^1 > P_{FR}^2 \\ 0, & P_{FR}^1 < P_{FR}^2 \end{cases} \tag{33}$$

$$P(\mathbf{u} = [1 \quad 0] | H_1) = \begin{cases} 0, & P_{FR}^1 > P_{FR}^2 \\ P_{FR}^2 - P_{FR}^1, & P_{FR}^1 < P_{FR}^2 \end{cases} \tag{34}$$

Q^{H_1} is +1 at the smallest possible $P_{FR}^{AND(1,2)}$ for the AND rule, since either of N^{10} or N^{01} (proportional to $P(\mathbf{u} = [1 \quad 0] | H_1)$ or $P(\mathbf{u} = [0 \quad 1] | H_1)$, respectively) is zero.

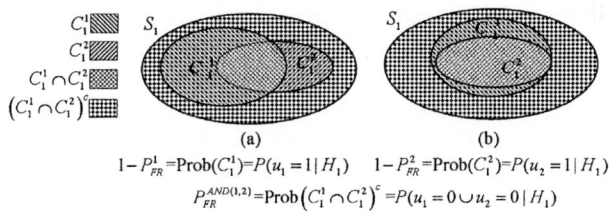

Fig. 2. (a) The general case of a pair of classifiers on authentics. (b) The best pair of conditionally dependent classifiers.

Due to lack of space in this paper, we are unable to show the favorable dependence statistics for the general case of AND fusion using N classifiers. However, the general idea can be explained. Similar to the analysis from Fig.1, it can be seen that when the union of the sets C_0^i, $i = 1, \ldots, N$ is larger, $P_{FA}^{AND(1,\ldots,N)}$ is smaller than for conditional independence. Although there are many solutions by which the union is larger, *one solution* is *all pairs of sets* have smaller intersection, i.e. Q^{H_0} between *all pairs of classifiers* is negative. And similar to the analysis from Fig. 2., $P_{FR}^{AND(1,\ldots,N)}$ is smaller when the intersection of all the sets C_1^i, $i = 1, \ldots, N$ is larger. While there are many solutions for the intersection of all sets to be larger, *one solution* is all pairs of sets have larger intersection, i.e. Q^{H_1} between *all pairs of classifiers* is positive. In the next section, we implement a method of finding two conditionally dependent classifiers favorable for the AND rule.

3 Design of Conditionally Dependent Classifiers for the AND Rule

The AR face database [11] is used here for performance evaluation. It contains color images of expression, illumination and occlusion variations taken at two sessions separated by two weeks. There is some slight pose variation also present in the images. Registered and cropped grayscale images (size 64×64 pixels) of 95 people are used for evaluation here because of missing data for some of the people. Performance on 20 images of expression, illumination and scarf occlusion per class is evaluated here since the registration of sunglass images is difficult. Fig. 3 shows sample images of one person in the AR database used here for evaluation.

The Fisher linear Discriminant [12] is chosen here as the base classifier because it has shown good performance in biometric verification and it uses both authentic and impostor data during training. While more details are given in [12], the Fisher Discriminant finds a projection direction where the distance between the two class means is maximized while the scatter of the two classes is minimized. When the number of training images is smaller than the dimension of the images, then the within class scatter matrix, used in finding the projection direction, is singular and the classical Linear Discriminant Analysis (LDA) fails. To avoid this, a Gram Schmidt (GS) Orthogonalization based approach for LDA proposed in [12] is used here. While details of the implementation can be found from [12], this method finds the projection direction that is in the null space of the within class scatter matrix and in the non-null space of the scatter matrix. The dimension of the projection vector is the same as the image dimension.

Three images from each person (images 1, 4 and 5 from the first row of Fig. 3) are used for training. By using training data from all 95 classes, i.e. 3 authentic images and 94*3 impostor images, a Fisher Discriminant classifier [12] is found for each class. This classifier is tested on all the 20 images of all classes. By setting thresholds on the projection values, decisions are made. When the false acceptance rate is equal to the false rejection rate, it is called the equal error rate (EER). The thresholds are tuned for each class and the average EER over all classes with a single classifier is 4.4%.

We desire to reduce this EER by designing two classifiers (from the same training set) and fusing them with the AND rule. If we did not use any knowledge of how the two classifiers should be for fusion with the AND rule, one way to design the two classifiers is to use bootstrapping [9]. A random subset of the authentic training data and a random subset of the impostor training data on which to train each classifier are generated here by random sampling with replacement of the training data. We compare this method to a more informed way of generating the two classifiers based on the knowledge obtained from Section 2.

From Fig.1 of Section 2, we can see that when the intersection of the sets C_0^i is smaller, then the union of the sets C_0^i is larger and hence P_{FA}^{AND} is smaller than the corresponding values for conditional independence. Since the sets stand for correct classification on impostors, we conjecture that when the intersection of the impostor training sets of the classifiers is small, the probability of correct classification of both classifiers will be small. Since the union of the sets should be large, the impostor training subsets of different classifiers should cover different regions of the impostor space and the union of all training subsets should cover the entire impostor space. From Fig. 2 of Section 2, we can see that when the intersection of the sets C_1^i is larger, P_{FR}^{AND} is smaller than the corresponding values for conditional independence. Since the intersection should be as large as possible for P_{FR}^{AND} to be small, we conjecture that the authentic training subsets of the classifiers should overlap completely and should cover the entire authentic space. Here, we partition the impostor training sets into two disjoint subsets, male impostors and female impostors, to train two classifiers. The entire authentic training set is used to train both classifiers. In future, better clustering methods of choosing the training subsets for the multiple classifiers will be investigated.

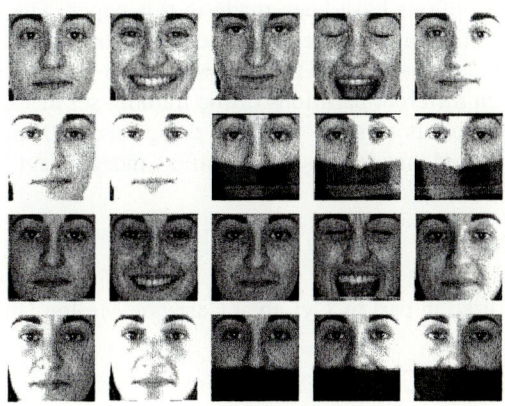

Fig. 3. Sample face images of one person in the AR database

Table 1. Results of fusion (95% confidence interval of the error rates) when classifiers are designed indepedent of the fusion rule and when they are designed by taking into account the fusion rule by our proposed method.

	EER^1(%)	EER^2(%)	$FAR^{AND(1,2)}$ (%) / $FAR^1 \cdot FAR^2$(%)	$FRR^{AND(1,2)}$ (%) / $1-(1-FRR^1)(1-FRR^2)$ (%)
Random subsets of training set	7.4±1.18	7.7±1.20	4.3±0.09 / 1.7±0.06	3.8±.86 / 6.0±1.07
Proposed method	5.5±1.03	8.9±1.28	3.3±0.08 / 2.0±0.07	2.4±0.68 / 3.7±0.83

Table 1 provides the results of both approaches to design classifiers. The thresholds on the Fisher projections for the two classifiers were chosen so that FAR is equal or close to FRR for the AND rule (thus equal to EER of the AND rule). This is done by varying the thresholds to compute the ROC curve and the point on the ROC curve where FAR is *equal or closest to* FRR corresponds to the pair of desired thresholds. As expected, the proposed method of designing classifiers has a lower FAR and FRR for the AND rule than the method where independent and random subsets of the training set are used to design classifiers. The proposed design method also has lower error rates than the single classifier which uses all training samples.

Table 1 also shows the theoretical values for the AND rule FAR and FRR *if the classifiers were independent*. These numbers are obtained in a purely theoretical manner and *do not* represent practically designed classifiers. These are simply used to check if the designed classifiers have the desired conditional dependence statistics as given in Section 2. It is seen that the designed classifiers have favorable conditional dependence on authentics. It may not be possible to obtain desired conditional dependence statistics between the classifiers, but the proposed design method is better than designing the classifiers without taking into account the applied fusion rule.

4 Conclusions

Three important contributions have been made in this paper. The first is a theoretical analysis to find the conditional dependence of the classifiers which are favorable for the AND fusion rule. The second is use this knowledge to come up with a method of designing classifiers on different partitions of the training set that take into account the AND fusion rule. The last is to show that this design method improves AND fusion performance over a method that designs the classifiers independent to the fusion rule.

Acknowledgment

The research is supported in part by CyLab at Carnegie Mellon University.

References

1. Phillips, P.J., *et al*: FRVT 2002: Evaluation Report. (2003)
2. J. Kittler, M. Hatef, R.P.W. Duin, J. Matas, "On Combining Classifiers," IEEE Transactions on Pattern Analysis and Machine Intelligence, Vol. 20, **3** (1998) 226 - 239
3. Varshney, P. K.: Distributed detection and data fusion. Springer-Verlag, New York (1997)
4. Xu, L., *et al*: Methods of combining multiple classifiers and their applications to handwriting recognition. IEEE Trans. Systems, Man & Cybernetics, Vol. 22, **3** (1992)
5. Ho, T. K., *et al*: Decision combination in multiple classifier systems. IEEE Trans. PAMI, Vol. 16, **1** (1994) 66 – 75
6. G. Giacinto, F. Roli, An approach to the automatic design of multiple classifier systems, Pattern recognition letters, Vol. 22, pp. 25-33, 2001.
7. Kleinberg, E. M.: An overtraining-resistant stochastic modeling method for pattern recognition. The annals of statistics, Vol. 24, **6** (1996) 2319-2349
8. Shin, H.W., Sohn, S.Y.: Selected tree classifier combination based on both accuracy and error diversity. Pattern recognition, Vol. 38 (2005) 191-197
9. Hastie, T.: The elements of statistical learning. Springer, New York (2001)
10. Kuncheva, L.I., Whitaker, C.J., Shipp, C.A., Duin, R. P.W.: Limits on the majority vote accuracy in classifier fusion. Pattern Analysis and Applications, Vol. 6 (2003) 22-31
11. Martinez, A.M., Benavente, R.: The AR Face Database. CVC Technical Report #24 (1998)
12. Zheng, W., Zou, C., Zhao, L.: Real-time face recognition using Gram-Schmidt orthogonalization for LDA. ICPR (2004) 403-406
13. Kuncheva L.I., Whitaker, C.J.: Measures of diversity in classifier ensembles. Machine Learning, Vol. 51 (2003) 181-207

Measurement of Face Recognizability for Visual Surveillance[*]

Hsi-Jian Lee[1] and Yu-Cheng Tsao[2]

[1] Department of Medical Informatics,
Tzu-Chi University, Hualien, Taiwan 970
[2] Department of Computer Science and Information Engineering,
National Chiao Tung University, Hsinchu, Taiwan 300

Abstract. In this paper, we propose a method to evaluate the possible recognition degree of a face, called face recognizability, before face recognition. If we can measure the recognizability, we can increase the system efficiency by avoiding recognizing the faces with poor recognizabilities. Based on the features of the orientation distribution on the face regions, we found the facial components. Then we collected lines on the face with major orientations. Last, we used the triangle formed by two eyes and mouth, the degree of the face shape symmetry and intensity symmetry to define the measurement of face recognizability. Experimental results show that recognizability can be used as a measurement to determine whether we need to perform face recognition or not.

1 Introduction

The security problem is an important issue with the increasing crime rate. The setup of a surveillance system becomes essential in many enterprises and organizations. To extract a suspect from recorded films, a safe guard has to check the films manually, which is a time-consuming task. The system also needs much storage for recording. Vision-based surveillance systems are brought to avoid these disadvantages.

A vision-based surveillance system generally contains modules like foreground segmentation, face extraction, and so on. The foreground segmentation module segments persons from recorded images. The face extraction module locates face regions from the segmented persons. These modules are helpful to reduce the workload of safe guards. However, the work of recognition is still ineffective. Not all detected faces have to be recognized, because recognition systems can only recognize well frontal faces. Faces with orientations or covers may be recognized incorrectly. Therefore, a method that can determine whether a face is appropriate for recognition is very helpful.

Background subtraction is a popular method for foreground segmentation, especially under a relatively stationary background. It attempts to detect moving

---

[*] Thanks to Ministry of Economic Affairs, R.O.C., for funding 93-EC-17-A-02-S1-032.

regions in an image by differencing between the current image and a reference background image in a pixel-by-pixel manner. Yang and Levine [1] proposed an algorithm to construct the background primal sketch by taking the median value of the pixel color over a series of images. Stauffer and Grimson [2] presented an adaptive background mixture model for real-time tracking.

Many research studies have been proposed for detecting faces in these applications. These methods can be roughly classified into four categories [3]: knowledge-based, feature-based, template matching and appearance-based. In the first category, most proposed methods encode human knowledge of a typical face. These methods are designed mainly for face location. Yang and Huang [3] proposed a hierarchical knowledge-based method to detect faces. In the second category, the proposed methods try to find invariant features for face detection. The commonly used facial features include eyebrows, eyes, nose, mouth, etc. Zhou et al. [4] presents a framework of orientation analysis for rotated human face detection. Sirohey [5] proposed a localization method which used an edge map and heuristic to remove and group edges. Yow and Cippola [6] proposed a feature-based method which utilize a large amount of image evidence. Augusteijn and Skufca [7] developed a method that infers the presence of a face through the identification of face-like textures. Jun et al. [8] proposed a fast search scheme of gravity-center template matching in an image for human face detection. Hsiun and Fan [9] proposed a system to detect multiple faces in complex backgrounds. In the third category, several standard patterns of a face are stored to describe the face as a whole or the facial features separately. The correlations between an input image and the stored patterns are computed for detection [10]. In the last category, the models are learned from a set of training images which should capture the representative variability of facial appearances [11].

In the paper, we assume that the surveillance environment is indoors. The light condition is stable and the digital camera is stationary. Input images are gray-scale and only a single person is in the processing image. We aim to measure the recognizable degree for the face, called recognizability. In general, a frontal view face has the best recognizability. When the face is tilt, swing and rotation, the recognizability of the face is low. Covers on faces, beard and hair will affect the recognizability.

2 Head and Facial Component Extraction

2.1 Head Extraction

Input images usually contain complex background. The foreground objects must first be segmented. We apply a background subtraction scheme to segment regions of moving objects in an image sequence by comparing each new frame to a model of the scene background.

To extract a head, one can find the neck from a human region since the neck is narrower than its upper and lower components such as the head and the shoulder. The neck location can be found according to the first valley in the horizontal projection profile. However, if a person bows his head, a portion of the head can be lower than the neck location. A part of head may be lost. The extraction method should be improved by adopting other procedures.

Because the shape of a head is approximately an ellipse, we adopt an ellipse to represent the head region. There are several methods to find an ellipse fitting a certain region, including gravity center-based ellipse finding methods and Hough transforms. The ellipse finding algorithm we propose consists of five steps. The details are described as follows:

1. Choose two horizontal lines (A, B) in the upper zone and lower zone. The upper zone for choosing line A is between $0.1*h$ and $0.3*h$; the lower zone for choosing line B is between $0.7*h$ and $0.9*h$, where h is the height of the segmented head in horizontal projection.
2. Since the head shape is not a perfect ellipse, we can take multiple lines in the two zones. In our experiments, we take two lines in regions A and B.
3. Compute the intersection point between the foreground contour and two lines. Connect the midpoints in these two lines by a straight line C.
4. Along the orthogonal direction on both sides of line C and get the distance to the contour. Choose the point (x_0, y_0) in line C, whose distances to both sides are equal and the longest. This point (x_0, y_0) is regarded as the center of an ellipse.
5. Find the major axis a and minor axis b.

This method can find several ellipses for the segmented head quickly. We select the largest ellipse as the head region.

2.2 Facial Component Identification

Next we will extract the facial components from the head. In a human face, the orientations of facial components are strong. For the upright and frontal face, the facial components can be roughly divided into two groups: horizontal (for most organs such as eyebrows, eyes and mouth) and vertical (for nose and cheek). The facial components will form darker lines in the face. If we can find the lines in the face, we will locate the facial components. Our facial component identification consists of the following stages: face extraction, orientation analysis, line detection, line filtering, and facial component identification

Stage1: Face Extraction
First, the system needs to segment the face component from the head. When the light condition is stable, the intensity range of skin should be located in a range, between 65 and 145, trained from 40 faces in our experiments. We can use the property to segment the face from the head and then find the face contour by a tracing algorithm.

Stage 2: Orientation Analysis
An orientation histogram is constructed by statistical analysis of the face images. We then compute the possible orientations of the facial components from the orientation histogram because of the strong orientations of the facial components. To compute the orientation histogram, we have to calculate the gradient and the strength for every

pixel. The face has several major peaks in the orientation distribution, which define the orientation characteristic for the analyzed region.

Stage 3: Line Detection
According to line orientations, we will detect the lines along these orientations. The procedure of the line detection is as follows:

1. Select k angles, $(t_1, t_2, ..., t_k)$ with respect to the major peaks from the orientation histogram.
2. For each angle t_i, $(i = 1, 2, ..., k)$

   i. Detect $point_1(x_1, y_1)$ with angle t_i from top to bottom and left to right.
   ii. Compute the coordinate $point_2(x_2, y_2)$ from $point_1$ and t_i. (d is 5 in our experiment)

$$\begin{bmatrix} x_2 \\ y_2 \end{bmatrix} = \begin{bmatrix} x_1 \\ y_1 \end{bmatrix} + \begin{bmatrix} d \\ d \tan t_1 \end{bmatrix} \qquad (1)$$

   iii. If the angle of $point_2$ is also t_i, then connect $point_1$ and $point_2$ as a line segment.
   iv. Let $point_2$ be $point_1$, and go back to Step 2 until the angle between $point_1$ and $point_2$ is different with t_i.

An example of line detection is shown in Figure 1(a).

Stage 4: Line Filtering
There are several false lines detected from previous processes, which may be formed by face contour, cheek and eyeglass frame. Since the lines formed by the shadow of the facial contour and the hair are near the head contour, we remove the lines near the face contour. Figure 1(b) shows an example of line filtering based on the face contour.

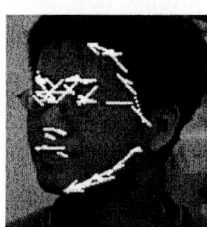 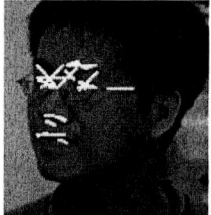

Fig. 1. (a) The result of line detection. (b) The result after contour filtering.

The vertical distribution value of line-centers formed by two eyes and mouth has higher values than that of cheek or glass frame. To remove these lines, we delete the lines whose centers belong to low distribution values in the vertical projection. The remainder lines should belong to the facial components.

Stage 5: Facial Component Identification
For the lines remained after filtering, we will find the lines that can represent facial components. For instance, the lines formed by eyes whose intensity values should be

darker and whose location is higher than other. The lines formed by the mouth whose intensity values should be darker than those around the mouth and the location is low.

We will use these properties to identify the lines corresponding to facial components. The procedure of the identification includes three steps:

1. Remove the lines with light intensity values.
2. Identify the lines with the appropriate properties of facial components.
3. Merge the lines with similar properties of the facial components.

Figure 2 shows an example of facial component identification.

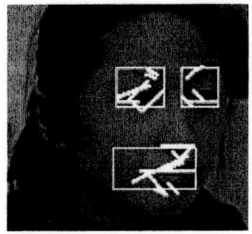 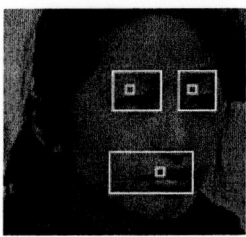

Fig. 2. (a) The result of identifying the lines with the appropriate properties of facial components. (b) The result of merging the lines in the same facial components.

3 Computation of Face Recognizability

There are several factors that will affect face recognition rates. The size of a detected face is related with its recognition accuracy. A frontal face can be recognized better than an oriented face. Before we recognize a human face using detected facial features, we use a simple measurement, called recognizability, to indicate the possibility of face recognition. If a lower measurement is obtained, the recognition rate may be poor and face recognition is not recommended.

To measure the face recognizability, we analyze facial features under various orientations. Faces can be classified into three classes: frontal faces, oriented faces, and side faces. The orientation distribution of a frontal face is symmetric along an axis. The triangle formed by the centers of eyes and mouth, called eyes-mouth triangle, will be an isosceles triangle in the center region of the head. For an oriented face, the intensity distribution of face regions should be asymmetric with respect to the symmetric axis. The eyes-mouth triangle may not be an isosceles triangle. For a side face, the eyes-mouth triangle may not be formed because several facial components cannot be detected. After analyzing face properties, each detected face will be classified according to the two measurements.

Measurement 1: Shape symmetry
The symmetric degree of a triangle is defined as follows:

$$S = \frac{Min(\overline{E_1M}, \overline{E_2M})}{0.5\overline{E_1E_2}} \quad (2)$$

where E_1 and E_2 are the centers of the two eyes and M is the intersection of the vertical projection on the line joining two eye centers from the mouth center. The value of S is between 0 and 1, which is near 1 when the triangle is close to an isosceles triangle and low when the triangle is deformed from an isosceles triangle.

Measurement 2: Intensity symmetry
A human face is strongly symmetric with respect to the line dividing the nose vertically. To measure the symmetry, we divide the face image into left and right regions. The symmetric axis can be found from the orthogonal orientation of the line formed by two eyes. To compute the face intensity symmetry, we define the following measurement along the symmetric axis.

$$P = \frac{2 * MatchedPixels(left, right)}{SumOfPixels(left, right)} \quad (3)$$

where *left* is the left region; *right* is the right region of the face; *MatchedPixels* is the number of pixels between the left and the right face that have the same intensity value; *SumOfPixels* is the sum of the left and the right face. In our experiments, if $P >= 0.90$, the region is symmetric and the face is frontal. Otherwise, the region is asymmetric and the face belongs to oriented.

The value of recognizability, *Recog*, is defined as $S * P * size$. Figure 3(a) shows two frontal faces and Fig. 3(b) two oriented faces. For side faces and the faces with covers, the eyes-mouth triangles cannot be found. The measurement S is non-computable and *Recog* is assigned as 0. Figure 3(c) shows five side faces.

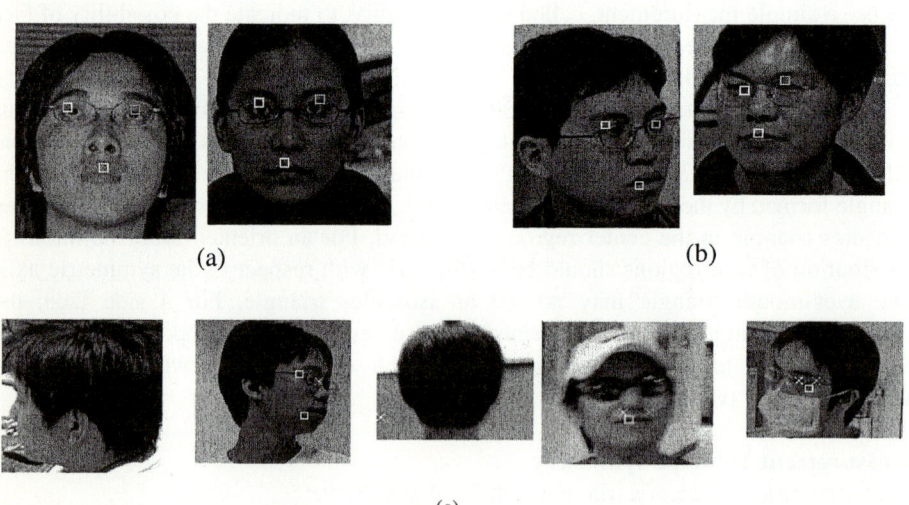

Fig. 3. Examples of face classification

4 Experimental Results and Discussion

The proposed approach has been implemented on a personal computer with Pentium IV 2GHz CPU. The input images are gray scales, ranging between 640 x 480 and 1024 x 768. The sizes of detected faces are between 46 x 56 and 152 x 170. There are 229 images from 15 people. The recognition system is developed in [12]. We take 75 images from 15 people as training samples, each person takes 5 images from different views. There are 30 frontal faces, 104 oriented faces and 20 side faces. The faces with different sizes will be tested in our experiments. The recognizability and the recognition rate with the relative sizes, 100%, 80% and 60% are listed in Tables 1-3.

From Tables 1-3, we can found that the recognition rate of the face with the same recognizability is lower when the size of the detected face is smaller. Class 1 faces have higher recognizability values than those of Classes 2 and 3. The recognizability is related to the recognition rate. There are some errors that cannot be handled properly, as shown in Fig. 4, a tilted head and a face with heavy shading.

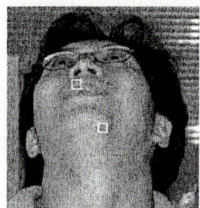

Fig. 4. A tilted head and a face with heavy shading

Table 1. The recognizability and the recognition rate with the size rate 100%

	Class 1	Class 2			Class 3
Recognizability	1	0.8 ~ 1	0.4 ~ 0.8	0 ~ 0.4	0
Recognition Rate	90% (28/31)	82% (34/41)	67% (25/37)	30% (8/26)	0% (0/19)

Table 2. The recognizability and the recognition rate with the size rate 80%

	Class 1	Class 2			Class 3
Recognizability	0.8	0.64 ~ 0.8	0.32 ~ 0.64	0 ~ 0.32	0
Recognition Rate	64% (22/34)	52% (20/38)	32% (12/37)	24% (6/25)	0% (0/20)

Table 3. The recognizability and the recognition rate with the size rate 60%

	Class 1	Class 2			Class 3
Recognizability	0.6	0.48 ~ 0.6	0.24 ~ 0.48	0 ~ 0.24	0
Recognition Rate	59% (19/36)	35% (14/39)	28% (11/38)	23% (7/30)	0% (0/20)

5 Conclusions and Future Work

In this paper, we have presented a system for measurement of face recognizability. Our system first segments the foreground objects from an input image. An ellipse finding algorithm method has been proposed to extract the human head. We have also proposed a method to extract facial components under various orientations by detecting the lines with the major peaks in the orientation histogram. We also used line-centers to represent the locations of facial components.

The recognizability was computed from the facial features such as the triangle formed by the facial components, the degree of shape symmetry and the degree of intensity symmetry. Experimental results have shown that face recognizability can supply a reliable measurement to the recognition system.

To improve the performance of our system, the foreground segmentation should be more efficient by adding other color information. The facial component identification can also be more accurate by adding color information. The recognizability measurement should be more reliable by adding more features.

References

[1] H. Yang, M.D. Levine, "The background primal sketch: an approach for tracking moving objects," *Machine Vision and applications*, Vol. 5, pp. 17-34, 1992.
[2] C. StauOer and W. Grimson, "Adaptive background mixture models for real-time tracking," *Proceedings of the IEEE CS Conference on Computer Vision and Pattern Recognition*, Vol. 2, pp. 246–252, 1999.
[3] G. Yang and T. S. Huang, "Human Face Detection in Complex Background," *Pattern Recognition*, vol. 27, no. 1, pp. 53-63, 1994.
[4] J. Zhou, X. Guang Lu, D. Zhang and C.Y. Wu, "Orientation analysis for rotated human face detection," *Image and Vision Computing*, Volume: 20, Issue: 4, pp. 257-264, April, 2002.
[5] S.A. Sirohey, "Human Face Segmentation and Identification," *Technical Report CS-TR-3176*, Univ. of Maryland, 1993.
[6] K.C. Yow and R. Cipolla, "Feature-Based Human Face Detection," *Image and Vision Computing*, vol. 15, no. 9, pp. 713-735, 1997.
[7] M.F. Augusteijn and T.L. Skujca, "Identification of Human Faces through Texture-Based Feature Recognition and Neural Network Technology," *Proc. IEEE Conf. Neural Networks*, pp. 392-398, 1993.
[8] M. Jun, Y. Baocai, W. Kongqiao, S. Lansun, and C. Xuecun, "A hierarchical multiscale and multiangle system for human face detection in a complex background using gravity-center template," *Pattern Recognition*, Volume: 32, Issue: 7, pp. 1237-1248, July, 1999.
[9] L.C. Hsiun and K.C. Fan, "Triangle-based approach to the detection of human face," *Pattern Recognition*, Volume: 34, Issue: 6, pp. 1271-1284, June, 2001.
[10] R. Bruneli and T. Poggio, "Face recognition: features versus templates," *IEEE Transactions, Pattern Analysis and Machine Intelligence*, vol. 15, no. 10, pp. 1042-1052, 1993.
[11] M. Turk and A. Pentland, "Eigenfaces for recognition," *Journal of Cognitive Neuroscience*, vol. 3, no. 1, pp. 71- 86, 1991.
[12] [Authors], "Face recognition using edge distance in sampling lines," 2005.
[13] L.L. Huang, A. Shimizu, Y. Hagihara and H. Kobatatke, "Gradient feature extraction for classification-based face detection," *Pattern Recognition*, pp. 2501-2511, 2003.

A Fingerprint Authentication Mobile Phone Based on Sweep Sensor[*]

Qi Su, Jie Tian[**], Xinjian Chen, and Xin Yang

Center for Biometric Research and Testing (CBRT),
Key Laboratory of Complex Systems and Intelligence Science, Institute of Automation,
Chinese Academy of Sciences, Graduate School of the Chinese Academy of Sciences,
P. O. Box 2728, Beijing 100080, China
tian@doctor.com
http://www.fingerpass.net

Abstract. With the advancement of mobile technology, mobile phones can store significant amount of sensitive and private information. The security issue of mobile phones becomes an important field to investigate. This paper proposes a prototype of fingerprint authentication mobile phone based on sweep sensor MBF310. The prototype is composed of the front-end fingerprint capture sub-system and the back-end fingerprint recognition system. A sweep fingerprint sensor MBF310 is used to fit the request of the mobile phone in the field of the size, cost, and power consumption. The performance of the proposed prototype is evaluated on the database built by the sweep fingerprint sensor. The EER is 4.23%, and the average match time of the prototype is about 4.5 seconds.

1 Introduction

With the advancement of mobile technology, mobile phones can run more powerful applications (e.g. camera, MP3, handwriting recognition) and store significant amount of sensitive and private information (e.g. address book, SMS, scheduler and even a bank account). Moreover, with the number of mobile phone user rapidly increasing, nowadays, the mobile phone has become a necessary part of our daily life.

Currently, many mobile phones come with a four-digit Personal Identification Number (PIN) and a numerical entry key as a tool for user authentication [1]. They can't satisfy the increasing need of effective protection of the mobile phone against unauthorized access. As the merits of convenient use, low cost and accuracy, fingerprint authentication is the best replacement or complement passwords among numerous biometrics authentication technologies.

---

[*] This paper is supported by the Project of National Science Fund for Distinguished Young Scholars of China under Grant No. 60225008, the Key Project of National Natural Science Foundation of China under Grant No. 60332010, the Project for Young Scientists' Fund of National Natural Science Foundation of China under Grant No.60303022.

[**] Corresponding author: Jie Tian; Telephone: 8610-62532105; Fax: 8610-62527995.

This paper proposes a fingerprint authentication mobile phone based on BIRD E868. The fingerprint mobile phone is composed of a fingerprint recognition sub-system and a fingerprint capture sub-system. The fingerprint recognition sub-system includes the enroll unit, match unit and system Application Program Interface (API). Integrated a MBF310 sweep sensor, the fingerprint capture sub-system is responsible for capturing the fingerprint image frames, reconstructing the image and sending it to the recognition sub-system.

In this paper, section 2 describes the structure of the fingerprint authentication mobile phone. Section 3 illustrates the software of fingerprint mobile phone. Section 4 shows the experimental results and the conclusion is in section 5.

2 The Fingerprint Authentication Mobile Phone

The fingerprint authentication mobile phone is composed of two parts. One is the front-end fingerprint capture sub-system and the other is back-end fingerprint recognition sub-system. The structure of the whole system is shown in Fig. 1.

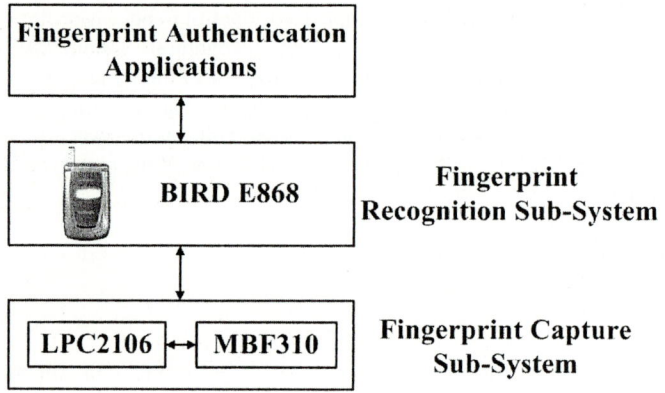

Fig. 1. The fingerprint authentication mobile phone block diagram

The hardware platform of the fingerprint authentication mobile phone includes the BIRD mobile phone E868 [2] and the fingerprint capture sub-system. The E868 mainly targets the high-end business market. The central process unit of the E868 is a 16-bit embedded processor S1C33 and its working frequency is 13 MHz.

The fingerprint capture sub-system is an external module. It is controlled by an ARM-Core processor LPC2106 [3] and uses a solid-state capacitive fingerprint sweep sensor MBF310 [4] for taking fingerprint image. The LPC2106 processor receives the commands from the mobile phone via Universal Asynchronous Receiver and Transmitter (UART) interface and controls fingerprint sensor MBF310 to capture the fingerprint image. Because of the limitation of the sweep sensor, the processor need reconstructs the original image frames to a full fingerprint image, and sends it to the mobile phone.

The MBF310 includes 218 columns and 8 rows of sensor plate which can provide a resolution of 500 dpi fingerprint image. A 2 Kbytes asynchronous FIFO is integrated in the sensor. It serves as a data buffer which can efficiently prevent the data from loss. With the technical advance of the smaller size, lower cost and low power consumption, the LPC2106 and MBF310 are suitable for mobile hand-held devices, such as E868 mobile phone.

3 System Software Descriptions

The prototype of fingerprint authentication mobile phone includes two main functions: enroll and match. The block diagram of the two functions is shown in Fig 2. Each function is composed of 4 process stages. The first three stages are the same. They are fingerprint image capture, fingerprint preprocess and feature extract. The last stage of enroll is to save the fingerprint features to the feature database, while the last one of the match is to search inquired features in the database and output the result.

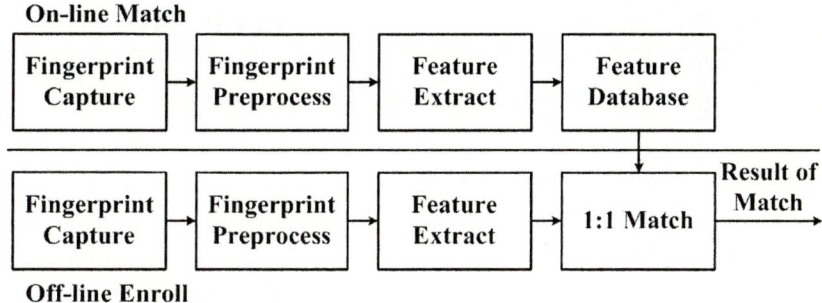

Fig. 2. Flowchart of enroll and match

3.1 Fingerprint Capture

The process of fingerprint acquisition is completed in the fingerprint capture subsystem (shown in Fig. 3). Because of the feature of the sweep sensor MBF310, the reconstruction algorithm is necessary to obtain a full fingerprint image. The acquisition process has two main parts:

1) When the finger sweeps vertically over the MBF310, the sensor will read the fingerprint image frames continuously. After an image frame is captured, the sensor can directly fill the FIFO and set the FIFO full flag to inform the LPC2106. Because of this virtue, the sensor can reduce the burden of the LPC2106 and can quicken the process of fingerprint acquisition.

2) When the LPC2106 receives the FIFO full flag, it will read the whole image frame from the FIFO at once. It saves the image frame in its inner RAM and reconstructs the fingerprint image by using the linear correlation algorithm which adopts the virtue of the registration algorithm proposed by Hassan Foroosh etc [5].

In fact, because of the limitation of the LPC2106's memory space, the part one and part two execute alternately. The LPC2106 will reconstruct the image when the sensor is capturing the next image frame. Because the speed of the finger swept over the sensor will influence the size of the image, we limit the format of the full fingerprint image to 200×200, 8-bit grey level. After finishing the process of fingerprint acquisition, the LPC2106 sends the fingerprint image to the mobile phone by UART interface.

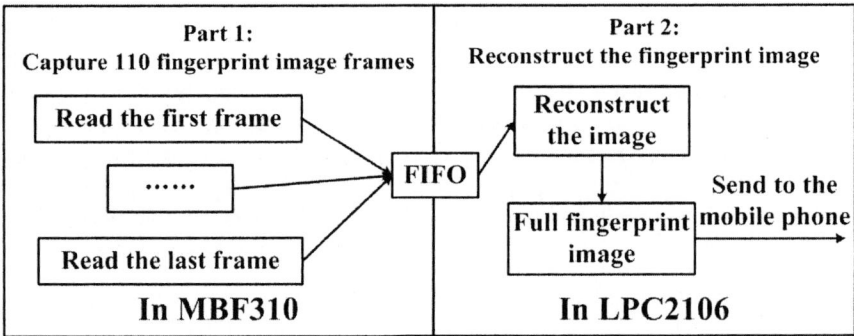

Fig. 3. The fingerprint capturing block diagram

3.2 Fingerprint Recognition Algorithm

In fingerprint preprocess stage, fingerprint enhancement algorithm based on filtering in frequency domain [6] is used. After the fingerprint image is converted from spatial domain to frequency domain by Fourier transforming, the image is enhanced by the proposed filter in frequency domain. Then we compute the average grey value in each of the 8 directions to estimate the orientation field (Fig. 4). The '*' donates the pixel in the image and the directions are limited from 0 degree to 180 degrees.

2	3	4	5	6
1				7
0		*		0
7				1
6	5	4	3	2

Fig. 4. Eight directions of a pixel

To reduce the influence of noise, we use the algorithm proposed by Yuliang He [7] to get the thinned ridge fingerprint map and to extract the minutiae. We use Cartesian coordinate system to represent each minutia saved in the fingerprint template.

$$m_i(p) = (x_i, y_i, \theta_i)^T \quad (1)$$

Where $m_i(p)$ denotes i^{th} minutia of the fingerprint image p, x_i, y_i, θ_i denote the x-coordinate, y-coordinate and direction of the ith minutia respectively.

Because of using sweep sensor MBF310, the non-linear deformations of the fingerprint image are more serious than those captured by an area sensor. The main idea of the match algorithm is using an affine transformation model T to relate the fingerprint template and the minutiae set of the inquired fingerprint. We use the Maximum-likelihood estimation to calculate the optimal deformation parameters [8]. To define a matching criterion, a probability density function (Equation 2) is used to measure the global similarity which consists of local minutia similarity.

$$p(d_i(\theta, t_x, t_y, s_x, s_y)) = (f(\Delta\beta_i) \times e^{-d_i(\theta, t_x, t_y, s_x, s_y)/2\sigma^2})/(2\pi\sigma^2) \qquad (2)$$

Five variables in the affine transformation model are used to describe the rotation, scale, translation deformations between the template and the inquired image, where t_x and t_y represent horizontal and vertical translation respectively, s_x and s_y correspond to horizontal and vertical scale respectively, θ denotes rotation. $f(x)$ is used to evaluate the type of a minutia. i represents the ith pair of the minutiae pick-up from two minutiae sets.

3.3 Energy Management

Because the E868 mobile phone is battery-powered, we propose a method that is suitable for the external module to balance the system performance and battery duration. The fingerprint capture sub-system works in the slave mode. It waits for the commands come from the application software running into the E868, and carries out the relevant operations. After finishing the operations, the LPC2106 and MBF310 will go into sleep mode waiting for the next commands. When the sub-system is in the sleep mode, the power consumption is less than 500 μA current.

In addition, the LPC2106 processor possesses a power management unit, which can turn off selected peripheral. So we can reduce the energy consumption of the sub-system in the normal operation through shutting down the unused peripherals.

4 Experimental Results

Fig. 5 shows the prototype of fingerprint authentication mobile phone. The prototype has achieved the functions of fingerprint enroll and match. Moreover, we develop an address book with the support of fingerprint authentication APIs. The address book can verify the true user by fingerprint authentication.

We use two different kinds of methods to test the performance of the prototype of fingerprint authentication mobile phone. One method is to test the EER (Equal Error Rate), FNMR (False Rejection Rate), FMR (False Match Rate) of the proposed algorithm on a PC, and the other method is to test other runtime performance, including the average match time and the maximum template size of the prototype by using the applications running on the mobile phone.

The fingerprint database on the PC totally includes 480 fingerprints. Thumb, forefinger and middle finger of both hands (six fingers total) of 20 volunteers were captured by the sweep fingerprint sensor MBF310. Four fingerprint images were taken per finger.

As the result of the tests, the value of EER of the proposed algorithm is 4.23%. The value of FNMR equals to 6.24% for FMR = 1%. The average match time is about 4.5 seconds and the maximum template size is smaller than 128 bytes.

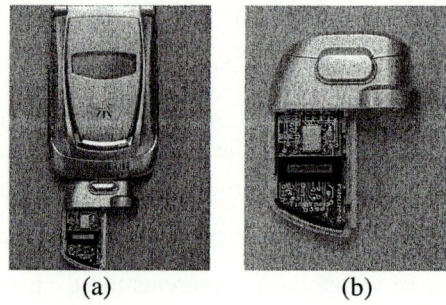

(a) (b)

Fig. 5. The appearance of the fingerprint recognition mobile phone (a) and fingerprint capture sub-system (b).

5 Conclusion

In this paper, we have designed a prototype of fingerprint authentication mobile phone based on sweep sensor MBF310. It consists of the front-end fingerprint capture sub-system and back-end fingerprint recognition sub-system. The hardware platform is composed of E868 mobile phone and the external fingerprint capture module based on MBF310. The system software includes enroll and match functions. The proposed algorithm is optimized prior being ported to the prototype. The performance of the proposed algorithm is evaluated on the 480 fingerprints database captured by the MBF310. The EER is 4.23%. The average match time of fingerprint authentication mobile phone is about 4.5 seconds. Further works will be focused on the system performance optimization and the security implementations of the fingerprint authentication mobile phone.

References

1. Wayne A. Jansen, Authenticating Users on Handheld Devices, Proceedings of the Canadian Information Technology Security Symposium, May 2003. http://csrc.nist.gov/mobile security/Publications
2. Ningbo Bird Mobile Communications Co. Ltd., BIRD DOEASY E868 Mobile Business Elite Introduce, http://doeasy.net.cn/index_2.htm
3. Philips Semiconductors Co. Ltd., LPC2106/2105/2104 USER MANUAL, http://www.semiconductors.philips.com

4. Fujitsu Microelectronics America, Inc., MBF310 Solid State Fingerprint Sweep Sensor Datasheet, Rev. V4.0, http://www.fma.fujitsu.com
5. Hassan Foroosh, Josiane Zerubia, and Marc Berthod, Extension of Phase Correlation to Sub-pixel Registration, IEEE Trans. on Image Processing, vol. 11, Mar. 2002, No.3, pp.188–200
6. Xinjian Chen, Jie Tian, Xin Yang, A Matching Algorithm Based on Local Topologic Structure, Proceedings of ICIAR2004, LNCS 3211, pp. 360-367
7. Yuliang He, Jie Tian, Xiping Luo, and etc., Image Enhancement and Minutia Matching in Fingerprint Verification, Pattern Recognition Letters, Vol.24, 2003, pp.1349-1360
8. Yuliang He, Jie Tian, Qun Ren, and etc.□Maximum-Likehood Deformation Analysis of Different-Sized Fingerprints, Proceedings of AVBPA2003, LNCS 2688, pp.421-42
9. Dario Maio, Davide Maltoni, Raffaele Cappelli, and etc., FVC2004: Third Fingerprint Verification Competition, Proceedings of ICBA 2004, LNCS 3072, pp.1-7

A Robust and Efficient Algorithm for Eye Detection on Gray Intensity Face

Kun Peng[1], Liming Chen[1], Su Ruan[2], and Georgy Kukharev[3]

[1] Laboratoire d'InfoRmatique en Images et Systems d'information (LIRIS),
Département MI, Ecole centrale de Lyon, BP 163, 36 avenue Guy de Collongue,
69131 Ecully Cedex, France
{Kun.Peng, Liming.Chen}@ec-lyon.fr

[2] Equipe Image, CReSTIC, Département GE&II, IUT de Troyes, 9 rue de Quebec,
10026 Troyes, France
s.ruan@iut-troyes.univ-reims.fr

[3] Faculty of Computer Science and Information Technology,
Technical University of Szczecin, Zolnierska 49,
71-210 Szczecin, Poland
pmasicz@wi.ps.pl

Abstract. This paper presents a robust and efficient eye detection algorithm for gray intensity images. The idea of our method is to combine the respective advantages of two existing techniques, feature based method and template based method, and to overcome their shortcomings. Firstly, after the location of face region is detected, a feature based method will be used to detect two rough regions of both eyes on the face. Then an accurate detection of iris centers will be continued by applying a template based method in these two rough regions. Results of experiments to the faces without spectacles show that the proposed approach is not only robust but also quite efficient.

1 Introduction

As one of the salient features of the human face, human eyes play an important role in face recognition. In fact, the eyes can be considered salient and relatively stable feature on the face in comparison with other facial features. Therefore, when we detect facial features, it is advantageous to detect eyes before the detection of other facial features. The position of other facial features can be estimated using the eye position [1]. In addition, the size, the location and the image-plane rotation of face in the image can be normalized by only the position of both eyes.

Eye detection is divided into eye position detection [1, 2] and eye contour detection [3, 15, 16]. (The second plays an important role in applications such as video conferencing and vision assisted user interface [2]. However, most algorithms for eye contour detection, which use the deformable template proposed by Yuille et al. [3], require the detection of eye positions to initialize eye templates. Thus, eye position detection is important not only for face recognition but also for eye contour detection. In this paper eye detection means eye position detection.

The existing work in eye position detection can be broadly classified into three categories: template based methods [3-6], appearance based methods [7-9] and feature based methods [10-14]. In the template based methods, a generic eye model, based on the eye shape, is designed firstly. Template matching is then used to search the image for the eyes. While these methods can detect eyes accurately, they are normally time-consuming. The appearance based methods [7-9] detect eyes based on their photometric appearance. These methods usually need to collect a large amount of training data, representing the eyes of different subjects, under different face orientations, and under different illumination conditions. These data are used to train a classifier such as a neural network or the support vector machine and detection is achieved via classification. Feature based methods explore the characteristics (such as edge and intensity of iris, the color distributions of the sclera and the flesh) of the eyes to identify some distinctive features around the eyes. Although these methods are usually efficient, they lack accuracy for the images which have not high contrast. For example, these techniques may mistake eyebrows for eyes. In summary, these approaches lack either efficiency or accuracy, and they are not ideal for some real applications.

In this paper, we propose a robust and efficient algorithm for eye detection on gray intensity face, based on combining the feature base methods and template based approaches. Combining the respective strengths of different complementary techniques and overcoming their shortcomings, the proposed method uses firstly the feature based method to find out broadly the two regions of eyes in a face, and the template based method is then used to locate the center of iris accurately.

The template based approaches are usually time-consuming. Its inefficiency comes from two main factors. Firstly, in order to improve the accuracy, these methods have to match the whole face with an eye template pixel by pixel. Secondly, as we don't know the size of eyes for an input face image, we need to repeat the matching process with eye templates of different sizes. That is to say, we have to perform the template matching several times. So the solution to improve the efficiency of this algorithm focuses on two points: reducing the area in the face image for template matching and cutting down the times of this type of matching. In fact, our method firstly detects the two rough regions of eyes in the face using a feature based method. Thus the following template matching will be performed only in these two regions which are much smaller than the whole face. In addition, we can evaluate the size of eye template according to the size of these two regions. In other words, profiting from possibility of evaluating the size of eyes, our algorithm performs the template matching just once. Altogether, the proposed method combines the accuracy of template based methods and the efficiency of feature based methods.

2 Proposed Method

2.1 Architecture

Currently, there are a lot of promising face detection methods [17-19]. This paper therefore assumes that (1) a rough face region has been located or the image consists of only one face, and (2) eyes in face image can be seen.

The architecture of the proposed approach is shown in Fig. 1. When a face image is presented to the system, face detection will be firstly performed to locate the rough face region. The second step, which uses an efficient feature based method, is to locate two rough regions of eyes in the face. In the same time, on the basis of these two regions, the sizes of two eyes will be evaluated, and the templates of eyes will be created according to the estimated sizes. Finally, the precise locations of the two centers of iris will be found out after template matching is applied in these two rough regions.

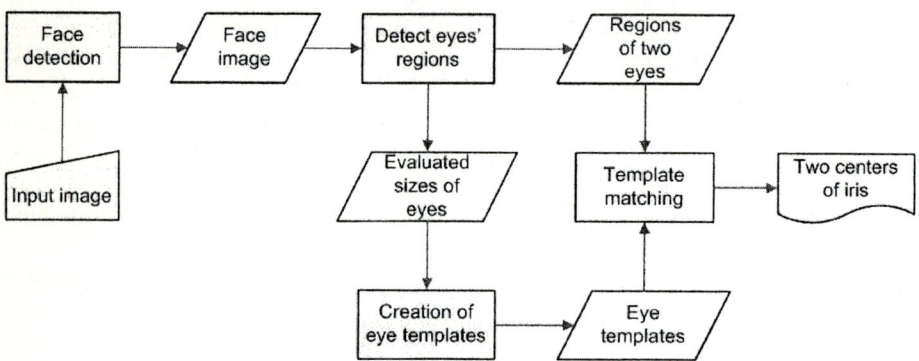

Fig. 1. Flowchart of proposed method

2.2 Detection of Eyes' Regions

When the rough face region is detected, as we have said, an efficient feature based method will be sequentially applied to locate the rough regions of both eyes which will be used to the following affining detection. Fig. 2 shows the processes of the proposed method:

The first step is to calculate the gradient image (b) of the rough face region image (a). Then we apply a horizontal projection to this gradient image. As we know that the eyes locate in the upper part of the face and that the pixels near the eyes are more changeful in value comparing with the other parts of face, it is obvious that the peak of this horizontal projection in the upper part can give us the horizontal position of eyes. According to this horizontal position and the total height of the face, we can easily line out a horizontal region (c) in which the eyes locate.

And then we perform a vertical projection to all pixels in this horizontal region of image (c), and a peak of this projection can be found near the vertical center of face image. In fact, the position of this vertical peak can be treated as the position of vertical center of face (d), because the area between both eyes is most bright in the horizontal region.

In the same time, a vertical projection will be done to the gradient image (b). There are two peaks of projection near the right and left boundary of face image which correspond to right and left limit of the face (e). In addition, from these two vertical limit lines, the width of face can be easily estimated.

Combining all results from (c), (d) and (e), we can get an image segmented like (f). Finally, based on the result of (f) and the estimated width of face, the regions of both eyes can be lined out (g).

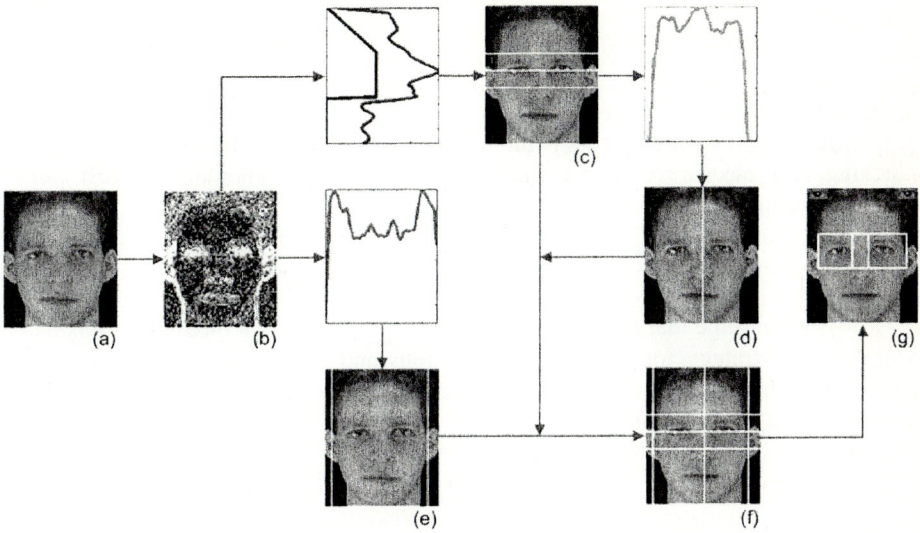

Fig. 2. Detection of eyes' regions

2.3 Creation of Eye Templates

After the two rough regions of eyes are detected, template matching will be used to locate the precise positions of iris centers in these regions. Because the matching region reduces from the whole face to the two rough regions, the efficiency of algorithm is well improved.

Obviously, the first obligatory step for a template matching is to create a template. It's easy to find out eye templates which can be obtained from a real face image. But the template can't be directly used for matching, because the size of the eye in the template is not same as that in the input image. A simple solution for this problem is to perform the process of matching several times, and each time we will use the template with different size. But this method is very ineffective.

Concerning our algorithm, in order to improve the efficiency, the size of the eyes will be estimated automatically. Thus the process of matching can be only performed just once. As we have said, the width of face is already estimated (see Fig. 2), and the size of eye template can be easily decided according to the width of face and the geometric structure of human face. The last image (g) in Fig. 2 shows two eye templates (at two top corners) created basing on the estimated eye sizes.

2.4 Localization of Iris Centers

Suppose that we have a template $g[i, j]$ and we wish to detect its instances in an image $f[i, j]$. An obvious thing to do is to place the template at a location in an image and to detect its presence at that point by comparing intensity values in the template with the corresponding values in the image. Since it is rare that intensity values will match exactly, we require a measure of dissimilarity between the intensity values of the template and the corresponding values of the image. Several measures may be defined:

$$\max_{[i,j]\in R}|f-g|, \quad \sum_{[i,j]\in R}|f-g| \quad \text{or} \quad \sum_{[i,j]\in R}(f-g)^2, \tag{1}$$

where R is the region of the template.

The sum of the squared errors is the most popular measure. In the case of template matching, this measure can be computed indirectly and computational cost can be reduced. We can simplify:

$$\sum_{[i,j]\in R}(f-g)^2 = \sum_{[i,j]\in R}f^2 + \sum_{[i,j]\in R}g^2 - 2\sum_{[i,j]\in R}fg. \tag{2}$$

Now if we assume that f and g are fixed, then $\sum fg$ gives a measure of mismatch. A reasonable strategy for obtaining all locations and instances of the template is to shift the template and use the match measure at every point in the image. Thus, for an $m \times n$ template, we compute:

$$M[i,j] = \sum_{k=1}^{m}\sum_{l=1}^{n}g[k,l]f[i+k,j+l], \tag{3}$$

where k and l are the displacements with respect to the template in the image. This operation is called the *cross-correlation* between f and g.

Our aim will be to find the locations that are local maxima or are above a certain threshold value. However, a minor problem in the above computation was introduced when we assumed that f and g are constant. When applying this computation to images, the template g is constant, but the value of f will be varying. The value of M will then depend on f and hence will not give a correct indication of the match at different locations. This problem can be solved by using normalized cross-correlation. The match measure M then can be computed using:

$$C_{fg}[i,j] = \sum_{k=1}^{m}\sum_{l=1}^{n}g[k,l]f[i+k,j+l]$$

$$M[i,j] = \frac{C_{fg}[i,j]}{\left\{\sum_{k=1}^{m}\sum_{l=1}^{n}f^2[i+k,j+l]\right\}^{1/2}}. \tag{4}$$

3 Experimental Results

In this section, we present the experimental results of our algorithms. We use the images in the ORL database, a well-known free database of faces, to do our experiments. In this database, there are completely photographs of 40 persons, of which each one has 10 various views. The 10 views of the same person include faces looking to the right, to the left, downward and upward (see the first line of Fig. 3). All faces in this database are presented by images in gray-level with the size of 92×112.

We made experiments using all faces without spectacles which concerns 227 face images and 29 persons. The success rate of proposed algorithm for all 227 faces is 95.2%.

Fig. 3 shows examples of the images for which the proposed algorithm could correctly detect the irises of both eyes. In the first line, there are five face views of the same person. And the images in the second line are faces of five different persons.

The execution time of the proposed algorithm is about 0.982 second on average by a PC whose CPU is Pentium IV, 1.8 GHz. It's remarkable that this execution time is reckoned for a program written in Matlab. Obviously, the execution time would be reduced a lot if the program is transplanted from Matlab to C or C++.

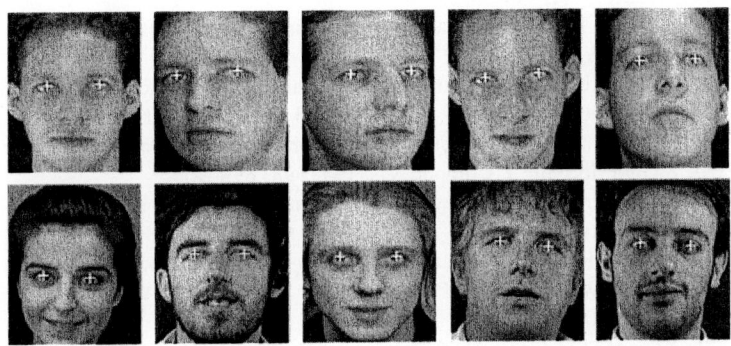

Fig. 3. Examples for faces without spectacles

4 Conclusion

A robust and efficient eye detection method for gray intensity faces is reported in this paper. The proposed algorithm combines two existing techniques: feature base method and template based method. The proposed algorithm firstly makes use of feature based methods to detect two rough regions of eye. The precise locations of iris centers are then detected by performing template matching in these two regions.

The proposed method has been tested by images from ORL face database. Experimental results show that this method works well with the faces without spectacles. For 227 faces without spectacles, the detection accuracy is 95.2%. In addition, the average execution time of proposed algorithm shows that this approach is also quite efficient.

References

1. F. R. Brunelli, T. Poggio, Face recognition: features versus templates, IEEE Trans. Pattern Anal. Mach. Intell. 15 (10) (1993) 1042–1052.
2. Y. Tian, T. Kanade, J.F. Cohn, Recognizing upper face action units for facial expression analysis, Proceedings of the IEEE Conference on Computer Vision and Pattern Recognition, Hilton Head Island, South Carolina, 2000, Vol. 1, pp. 294–301.
3. A.L. Yuille, P.W. Hallinan, D.S. Cohen, Feature extraction from faces using deformable templates, Int. J. Comput. Vision 8 (2) (1992) 99–111.

4. X. Xie, R. Sudhakar, H. Zhuang, On improving eye feature extraction using deformable templates, Pattern Recognit. 27 (1994) 791–799.
5. K.M. Lam, H. Yan, Locating and extracting the eye in human face images, Pattern Recognit. 29 (1996) 771–779.
6. M. Nixon, Eye spacing measurement for facial recognition, in: Proc. of the Society of Photo-Optical Instrument Engineers, 1985.
7. A. Pentland, B. Moghaddam, T. Starner, View-based and modular eigenspaces for face recognition, in: Proc. IEEE Conf. on Computer Vision and Pattern Recognition (CVPR'94), Seattle, WA, 1994.
8. W. min Huang and R. Mariani, Face detection and precise eyes location, in: Proc. Int. Conf. on Pattern Recognition (ICPR'00), 2000.
9. J. Huang, H. Wechsler, Eye detection using optimal wavelet packets and radial basis functions (rbfs), Int. J. Pattern Recognit. Artif. Intell. 13 (7) (1999) 1009–1025.
10. G.C. Feng, P.C. Yuen, Variance projection function and its application to eye detection for human face recognition, Int. J. Comput. Vis. 19 (1998) 899–906.
11. G.C. Feng, P.C. Yuen, Multi-cues eye detection on gray intensity image, Pattern Recognit. 34 (2001) 1033–1046.
12. S. Kawato, J. Ohya, Real-time detection of nodding and head-shaking by directly detecting and tracking the between-eyes, in: Proc. 4th IEEE Int. Conf. on Automatic Face and Gesture Recognition, 2000, pp. 40–45.
13. Y. Tian, T. Kanade, J.F. Cohn, Dual-state parametric eye tracking, in: Proc. 4th IEEE Int. Conf. On Automatic Face and Gesture Recognition, 2000.
14. S.A. Sirohey, A. Rosenfeld, Eye detection in a face image using linear and nonlinear filters, Pattern Recognit. 34 (2001) 1367–1391.
15. G. Chow, X. Li, Toward a system for automatic facial feature detection, Pattern Recognition 26 (1993) 1739–1755.
16. K.M. Lam, H. Yan, Locating and extracting the eye in human face images, Pattern Recognition 29 (5) (1996) 771–779.
17. H.A. Rowley, S. Baluja, T. Kanade, Neural network-based face detection, IEEE Trans. Pattern Anal. Mach. Intell. 20 (1) (1998) 23–38.
18. K.K. Sung, T. Poggio, Example-based learning for viewbase human face detection, IEEE Trans, Pattern Anal. Mach. Intell. 20 (1) (1998) 39–51.
19. P.C. Yuen, G.C. Feng, J.P. Zhou, A contour detection method: initialization and contour model, Pattern Recognition Lett. 20 (2) (1999) 141–148.

Silhouette Spatio-temporal Spectrum (SStS) for Gait-Based Human Recognition

Toby H.W. Lam, Tony W.H. Ao Ieong,
and Raymond S.T. Lee

Department of Computing,
The Hong Kong Polytechnic University,
Hung Hom, Kowloon, Hong Kong
{cshwlam, cswhai, csstlee}@comp.polyu.edu.hk

Abstract. Gait has received substantial attention from researchers. Different from other biometrics, gait can be captured in a distance and it is difficult to disguise. In this paper, we propose a feature template: Silhouette Spatio-temporal (SStS). It generates by concatenating silhouette projection vectors (SPV) which is formulated by projection of silhouette in vertical direction. We applied the Principle Component Analysis (PCA) for dimension reduction of the input feature space for recognition. The proposed algorithm has a promising performance, the identification rate is 95% in SOTON dataset and 90% CASIA dataset. Experiments showed that SStS has a high discriminative power and it is suitable for real-time gait recognition system.

1 Introduction

Today, Biometrics has received substantial attention from researchers. Biometrics is method of recognizing a human according to physiological or behavioral characteristic. Gait is one of the biometrics that different from the traditional biometrics. It is not required to stay closer enough to or touch the input device. In early medical research, Murray, Drought and Kory [1] had formed some rules of gait analysis. It showed that gait is unique and it is difficult to disguise. Different from other biometrics, gait can be captured in a distance. Besides, it is only necessary to capture the sequence of gait in low resolution.

In this paper, we propose a Spatio-temporal template, called Silhouette Spatio-temporal Spectrum (SStS), for gait recognition. SStS is formulated by concatenating a sequence of silhouette projection vector (SPV). SPV is the projection of the silhouette image in vertical direction. We use SStS as the feature template for recognition. We further apply Principal Component Analysis (PCA) on SPV for reducing the dimensionality of the input space and optimizing the class separability of different SPV. We use the SOTON dataset [2] and CASIA dataset [3] to demonstrate the efficacy of the proposed method. The rest of this paper is organized as follows. We show the related work about gait recognition in section 2. In section 3, we show the detail about Silhouette Spatio-temporal Spectrum (SStS) and the proposed recognition algorithm.

The experimental results and analysis are shown in section 4. Conclusion appears in section 5.

2 Related Work

Model-free recognition used motion information without any model reconstruction for recognition. Most of the current gait recognition algorithms are model-free recognition. Model-free approaches, or namely holistic approaches, usually use sequence of binary silhouettes. The silhouettes of moving object in video are extracted by using segmentation techniques like background subtraction.

Murase and Sakai [4] proposed a parametric eigenspace representation for moving object recognition. The extracted silhouette images projected to the eigenspace by using PCA. The sequence of movement forms a trajectory in the eigenspace, called parametric eigenspace representation. All the reference patterns are saved in a database. The input image sequence of movement is preprocessed to form a sequence of binary silhouette and these formed a trajectory in the eigenspace. The smallest distance between the input trajectory and the reference sequence would be the best match. Huang, Harris and Nixon [5] applied the similar technique for gait recognition. They used Linear Discriminating Analysis (LDA) or namely canonical analysis, for gait recognition. The advantage of using LDA is the best discrimination between different classes. Wang and Tan proposed a new transformation method for reducing the dimensionality of the input feature space [6]. The transformation is done by unwrapping human silhouette to generate a distance signal. The time-varying distance signals are applied to eigenspace transformation based on PCA. The recognition performance of our proposed algorithm is compared with Wang and Tan's algorithm and the detail of the experimental results are shown in section 4.

3 Recognition Algorithm

In this section, we talk about how to create SStS for recognition and the detail about the gait recognition algorithm by using SStS and PCA.

3.1 Silhouette Spatio-temporal Spectrum (SStS)

Silhouette Spatio-temporal Spectrum (SStS) is an image which embedded the spatial and temporal information of gait. SStS uses silhouettes as the basis of the feature. First, the silhouette image is extracted by simple background subtraction and thresholding [5]. The bounding box of the silhouette image in each frame is calculated. The silhouette image is extracted according to the size of the bounding box and resized to a standard size (128 pixels x 88 pixels).The normalized silhouette image is projected to vertical direction to generate a silhouette projection vector (SPV). The sequences of projection vector concatenate to form a Silhouette Spatio-temporal Spectrum (see Fig. 1). Experiments show that SStS has a higher discriminative power than unwrapping representation [6]. The detail of the experimental results is shown in section 4.

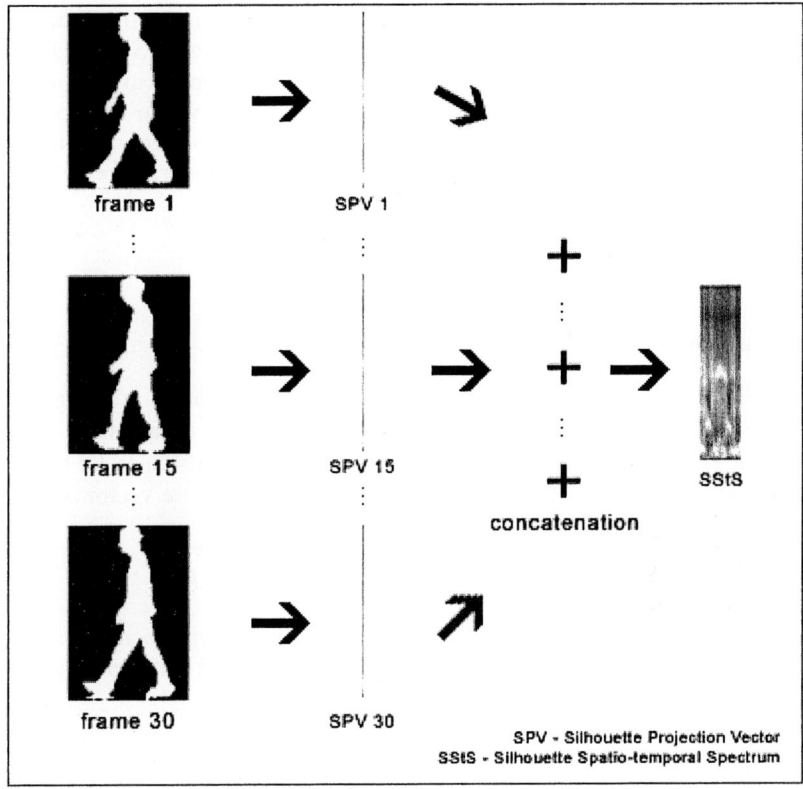

Fig. 1. Examples of Silhouette Spatio-temporal Spectrum

3.2 Principle Components Analysis (PCA)

The main objective of Principle Components Analysis (PCA) is to reduce the dimension of the feature space by maximize the variance of classes. The silhouette projection vectors (SPV) in silhouette Spatio-temporal Spectrum (SStS) are used for PCA training. Suppose there are C classes for training, each class $c \in C$ has N_c of silhouette Spatio-temporal Spectrum $SStS_{c,i}$ where i is the instance label. Each $SStS_{c,i}$ contains $Nframe_{c,i}$ frame of silhouette projection vector $SPV_{c,i,j}$ where j is the instance label. The total number of training samples is $N_{total} = Nframe_{1,1} + Nframe_{1,2} + \ldots + Nframe_{c,Nc}$. The mean of all samples SPV_{mean} and the covariance martrix of all samples SPV_{cov} define as follows:

$$SPV_{mean} = \frac{1}{N_{total}} \sum_{c \in C} \sum_{i=1}^{N_c} \sum_{j=1}^{Nframe_{c,i}} SPV_{c,i,j} \qquad (1)$$

$$SPV_{cov} = \frac{1}{N_{total}} \sum_{c \in C} \sum_{i=1}^{N_c} \sum_{j=1}^{Nframe_{c,i}} (SPV_{c,i,j} - SPV_{mean})(SPV_{c,i,j} - SPV_{mean})^T \qquad (2)$$

A transformation matrix $T_p = [t_1, t_2, ... t_p]$ is obtained for variance maximizeation. In T_{pca}, $t_1, t_2...t_p$ are the eigenvectors of the samples covariance matrix SPV_{cov} corresponding to p largest eigenvalues. These eigenvectors are orthonormal to each others and they span the eigenspace. The mean of silhouette projection vector SPV_i of the input silhouette Spatio-temporal Spectrum is calculated for PCA projection. The SPV_m is projected to points P_m in p-dimensional eigenspace by using the transformation matrix T_{pca}. (eqn. 3)

$$p_i = T_{pca}^T SPV_i = [t_1, t_2, ..., t_p]^T SPV_i \qquad (3)$$

3.3 Recognition

Suppose there is an input image sequences, $SStS_i$ is generated by using proposed algorithm which mentioned in section 3.1. The mean of SPV_i is calculated from $SStS_i$ and used for PCA projection to form p_i by (3). The Euclidean distance Ed between the projected testing feature vector and the projected training feature vector is calculated by (4).

$$Ed(p_r, p_i) = \sqrt{(p_r - p_i)^T (p_r - p_i)} \qquad (4)$$

where p_r is the projected feature vector of training silhouette projection vectors$_i$. The testing sample is classified as class c if the Euclidean distance Ed is minimum among other training samples.

4 Result and Analysis

We use SOTON and CASIS datasets for evaluation. CAISA contains 20 persons; each person contains 3 views (lateral view, frontal view and oblique view) and 4 sequences per view. There are total 240 walking sequences. In this paper, we only deal with the lateral view gait recognition problem. Therefore, we only use lateral view sequences (80 sequences) for our experiment. SOTON dataset contains 115 persons, total 2,128 walking sequences. The sequence can be divided into two categories: (a) walk from left to right and (b) walk from right to left. After background subtraction and image binarization, the silhouettes is extracted and normalized to 88 x 128 pixels. We adopted the scheme of FERET [7] for the evaluation and measure the identification rate and the verification rate by cumulative match score. We implemented Wang's unwrapping transformation algorithm [6]. The performance of our proposed algorithm is compared with the performance of the Wang's unwrapping algorithm. All experiments are implemented by Matlab and run in a PC computer with P4 2.26GHz and 512MB memory.

4.1 Direct Comparison

We used SOTON and CASIS datasets in this experiment. We use SOTON for three tests: (a) 50% of the image sequences in each class is used for training and other 50% is used for testing; (b) 75% of the image sequences in each class is use for training and other 15% is used for testing; (c) 90% of the image sequences in each class is used for training and other 10% is used for testing. We do not use PCA for dimension reduction, instead we calculated the Euclidean distance between the input feature vector and the reference vector directly (direct comparison). Nearest Neighbor classifier is adopted in this experiment. Table 1 shows the experiment results by using SStS and unwrapping methods for comparison. The average identification rate of SStS in three different tests is around 98% and it is higher than Wang's method by around 4%.

Table 1. Recognition rates by using SStS and unwrapping in SOTON database (direct comparison)

Method	SStS			Unwrapping		
Rank	Top 1	Top 5	Top 10	Top 1	Top 5	Top 10
a. 50% train 50% test	97.09%	98.41%	98.50%	93.25%	97.09%	98.22%
b. 75% train 25% test	98.57%	98.75%	98.75%	94.12%	97.33%	97.86%
c. 90% train 10% test	98.39%	99.20%	99.60%	95.58%	98.39%	98.39%

4.2 PCA

The experiment setup is the same as 4.1. However, we use PCA for dimension reduction before classification. 95% of the accumulated variance of eigenvalues is chosen in this experiment. Table 2 shows the experimental results of the recognition rate by SStS and Wang's unwrapping method. The recognition rate by using our proposed algorithm SStS and Wang's algorithm is nearly the same in SOTON dataset. The rank order statistic for three different tests is shown in Fig. 2.

Table 2. Recognition rates by using SStS and unwrapping in SOTON database (PCA)

Method	SStS			Unwrapping		
Rank	Top 1	Top 5	Top 10	Top 1	Top 5	Top 10
a. 50% train 50% test	92.22%	96.34%	96.91%	93.16%	97.56%	98.31%
b. 75% train 25% test	94.30%	97.15%	97.50%	94.47%	97.33%	98.04%
c. 90% train 10% test	94.78%	97.99%	98.80%	94.38%	97.59%	98.39%

We further apply our proposed recognition algorithm to CASIA dataset. As we mentioned before, we investiage the problem of gait recognition in lateral view. Therefore, we use the lateral view of CASIS dataset only. The lateral view of CASIA contains total 80 walking sequences, each class contains 4 sequences. We use CASIA for two tests (I) 50% of the image sequences in each class is used for training and other 50% is used for testing; (II) 75% of the image sequences in each class is use for training and other 15% is used for testing. The results are tabulated in Table 3. The identification by using SStS is 97.50% in (I) and 95.50% in (II). In [6], the identification rate is 70% in leave-one-out in lateral view of CAISA dataset. The result showed that the performance of our proposed algorithm is better than Wang's unwrapping algorithm.

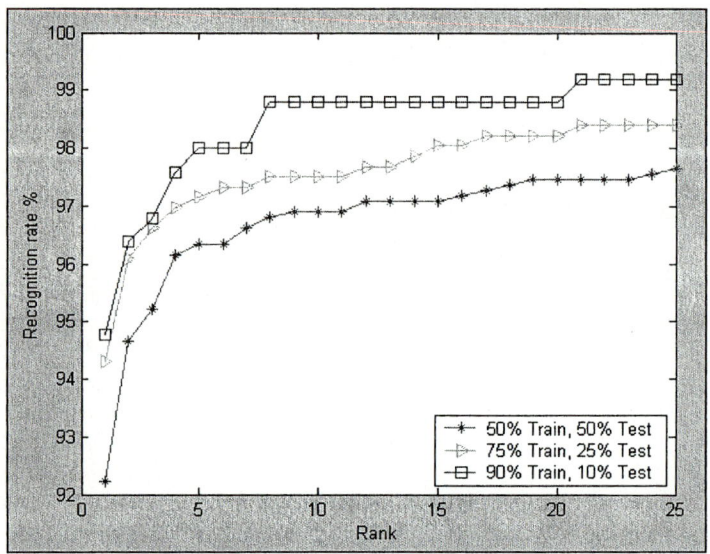

Fig. 2. Identification performance in terms of rank order statistics in SOTON database (SStS with PCA)

Table 3. Recognition rates by using SStS in CASIA database (PCA)

Rank	Top 1	Top 5	Top 10
I. 50% train 50% test	92.50%	100%	100%
II. 75% train 25% test	90.00%	100%	100%

5 Conclusion

In this paper, we used Silhouette Spatio-temporal Spectrum (SStS) as the feature template for the gait recognition. The recognition performance is quite promising in SOTON and CASIA dataset. Experiments showed that SStS has a higher discriminative power than unwrapping distance signal. During data preparation, we found that the processing time for feature extraction by unwrapping is much longer than our proposed method. The average processing time in unwrapping transformation is 250s in CASIA and the average processing time in SStS formation is 1s in CASIA. The reason that long processing time in unwrapping transformation is that it needs to unwrap the contour of the silhouette to form a distance signal in each frame. It is much time consuming processing. It showed that SStS is more suitable than unwrapping for real-time gait recognition application. Currently, we investigate and apply some kernel methods for the gait recognition by using SStS.

Acknowledgements

This work was partially supported by the CERG iMASS Project (B-Q569) and the CRG CORN Project (G-T850) from the Hong Kong Polytechnic University.

References

1. M.P. Murray, A.B. Drought and R.C. Kory, "Walking patterns of normal men," Journal of Bone and Joint Surgery, Vol. 46 – A, No. 2, pp. 335-60
2. J. D. Shutler, M. G. Grant, M. S. Nixon, and J. N. Carter "On a Large Sequence-Based Human Gait Database", The 4th International Conference on Recent Advances in Soft Computing, Nottingham (UK), pp 66-71, 2002
3. CASIA Gait Database, http://www.sinobiometrics.com
4. H. Murase, R. Sakai,"Moving object recognition in eigenspace representation: gait analysis and lip reading, " Pattern Recognition Letters, Vol. 17, pp. 155-62, 1996
5. P.S. Huang, C.J. Harris and M.S. Nixon, "Human Gait Recognition in Canonical Space Using Temporal Templates," IEE Proceedings - Vision, Image and Signal Processing, 146(2), pp. 93-100, 1999
6. L. Wang and T. Tan, "Silhouette Analysis-Based Gait Recognition for Human Identification," IEEE Trans on PAMI, Vol. 25 (12), 1505-1518, 2003
7. J. Phillips, H. Moon, S. Rizvi, and P. Rause, "The FERET Evaluation Methodology for Face Recognition Algorithms," IEEE Trans. PAMI, Vol. 22, No.8, pp. 1090-1104, Oct. 2000

Adaptive Estimation of Human Posture Using a Component-Based Model

Kyoung-Mi Lee

Department of Computer Science, Duksung Women's
University Seoul, Korea
kmlee@duksung.ac.kr

Abstract. To detect a human body and recognize its posture, a component-based approach is less susceptible to changes in posture and lighting conditions. This paper proposes a component-based human-body model that comprises ten components and their flexible links. Each component contains geometrical information, appearance information, and information on the links with other components. The proposed method in this paper uses hierarchical links between components of human body, so that it allows to make coarse-to-fine searches and makes human-body matching more time-efficient. To adaptively estimate the posture in change of posture and illumination, we update the component online every time a new human body is incoming.

1 Introduction

Determining the posture of the human-body has recently become an important issue in computer vision. To detect a human body and recognize its posture, a full-body approach is subject to a high degree of transformation because the method is affected significantly by changes in posture and lighting conditions. Therefore, a component-based approach has been widely adopted to consider each part of the human body a component and to subsequently use the relationships between the components to represent the entire human body. A pictorial structure is developed by using links that can acquire geometric arrangement between different parts [1]. In [2], the relationships between the locations of parts are represented in terms of variable configuration. The pairs of parts are connected with visual springs that are created on the basis of their relative positions.

In this paper, we estimate the posture of the human body by matching the human body configuration after finding the connection points and the respective parts of the human body in an image. Each part of the human body is represented as a component that includes shape, position, and connection, while each part is connected in a hierarchical manner. Coarse-to-fine searches are then utilized to make an efficient matching of the human-body. Additionally, whenever a new example arrives, each component is updated to adaptively estimate the human posture related to changes in posture and illumination.

2   Matching with a Component-Based Model

In this section, we introduce a human body model that connects body parts in hierarchical manner and a description to make the matching of the human body with this model. The human body model that consists of components classifies different parts into head, torso, arms, and legs through generic search, after which more detailed classification is used to make the human-body parts matching complete. Also, the components are updated online every time a new human body is incoming.

2.1   Component-Based Human-Body Model

In this section, we introduce a human-body model that consists of ten body parts as components, and subsequently connects the components in a hierarchical manner (Fig. 1). Each part contains geometrical information (position, relative size, and shape) and appearance information (average color and standard deviation). Additionally, each part includes information on its link with other parts, such as the connectible sides out of the four sides that represent each part, names of parts being connected, the connecting angles, and the connecting distances. A human-body model can be represented as follows:

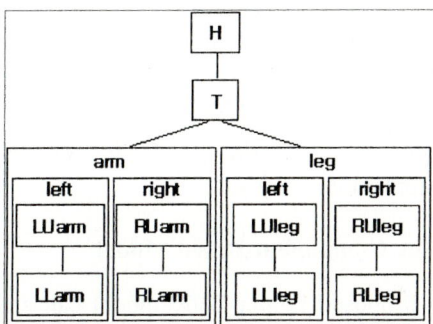

Fig. 1. A component-based hierarchical human model consists of head (H), body (T), left upper arm (LUarm), left lower arm (LLarm), right upper arm (RUarm), right lower arm (RLarm), left upper leg (LUleg), left lower leg (LLleg), right upper leg (RUleg), right lower leg (RLleg). Lines between components mean their hierarchical relations for matching.

$$Human_i = (g_i, a_i, R_i), \qquad i=1, ..., I \qquad (1)$$

where *Human* represents a human-body model that consists of I (=10) number of parts, while g_i and c_i refer to geometrical and appearance information on each part, respectively, and R_i represents information on the link between parts.

The proposed human-body model is made up of hierarchical relationships. Using such a hierarchical structure can improve efficiency in time-usage by restricting the search space for matching. Different from the star-like structures used in [2], however, the proposed component-based model has a standard tree structure. The human-body model first classifies the different parts into head, torso, arms, and legs through generic search, after which more detailed classification is used to make the matching of human-body parts complete.

2.2 Matching with a Hierarchical Search

Estimating postures with a component-based human-body model is a matching process which is used to configure a proper human-body model by combining the detected components. The human-body model (Eq. (1)) is matched to take the combination that has the least variance or the most matching probability,

$$d_i = \sum_i \min_j \|g_i - p_j\| + \sum_i \min_j \|a_i - q_j\| + \sum_i \min_j \|R_i - r_j\| \qquad (2)$$

$$HumanScore = \sum_{i=1}^{I} d_i$$

where (p_j, q_j, r_j) refer to geometrical information and appearance information regarding the j-th component and its relationships to other components.

In this paper, matching of coarse-to-fine searches is adopted. This method limits the relationship between components to tree structures in a top-down model, and restricts the matching sequence in a hierarchical way, so as to reduce the range of any search for different components [7]. For example, the left arm is matched prior to a detailed search for the upper/lower left arm, and the matching probability of the left arm, d_{Larm}, is considered to be the sum of the matching probability of the upper/lower left arm (d_{LUarm} / d_{LLarm}): $d_{Larm} = d_{LUarm} + d_{LLarm}$. To detect the other parts, such a hierarchical technique can be applied iteratively.

2.3 Online Update of the Component-Based Model

Each component of the proposed human-body model can change with posture and lighting environments, so it is necessary that the geometrical and appearance information to be updated. If a set of human examples is given, the model is simply updated by calculating averages, μ, and standard deviations, σ, of each component. However, such a batch update is not suitable for maintaining the model in an online environment. Therefore, instead of collecting all previous examples each time a new example is modeled, it is more useful to extend the human model with only the new example.

When an n-th example, h_n, is modeled, the averages and standard deviations of i-th component of the human model are updated as follows:

$$\mu_{i,n} = \frac{\mu_{i,n-1} + h_{i,n}}{n} \text{ and } \sigma_{i,n} = \sqrt{\frac{(n-1)u_{n-1} + (\mu_{i,n} - h_{i,n})^2}{n}}$$

where h_i is the geometrical, g_i, or appearance, a_i, information of the i-th component, $u_{n-1} = (\sigma_{i,n-1})^2 + (\mu_{i,n} - \mu_{i,n-1})^2$. It follows that Eq. (1) and (2) can be respectively modified as follows:

$$Human_i = \left[\left(\mu_i^g, \sigma_i^g\right), \left(\mu_i^a, \sigma_i^a\right), R_i\right] \quad \text{and}$$

$$d_i = \sum_i \min_j \left\|\frac{\mu_i^g - p_j}{\sigma_i^g}\right\| + \sum_i \min_j \left\|\frac{\mu_i^a - q_j}{\sigma_i^a}\right\| + \sum_i \min_j \left\|R_i - r_j\right\| \quad (3)$$

Thus, after training on *n* examples, each component represents the statistical information of the corresponding body part in the component space. This makes it possible to adaptively estimate human posture in case of posture and lighting changes.

3 Estimating Human-Body Posture

Estimating postures using component-based models is a process of creating a model that possesses different components allocated to each part of human body. In this section, we describe the method with which a human body is located in an image and human body parts are matched.

3.1 Detecting an Estimated Human-Body Area

In a given color image (Fig. 2(a)), the skin color is the most useful data which can be used to detect a person. People may wear different attire and accessories, so that, in reality, it is very difficult to estimate human-body posture according to skin color alone. In this paper, we assume that it is possible to detect at least a human face using

Fig. 2. Detection of an estimated human area. (a) Original image, (b) Skin color pixels, (c) Skin color regions, and (d) an estimated human area.

the color of the skin. Given a color image, we apply a Median smoothing filter, and then a skin-color filter [3], to make a semantically binary image consisting of skin color pixels and non-skin (black) color pixels (Fig. 2(b)).

Such a binary image is grouped according to connected skin pixels and is segmented into regions [4]. After grouping, we will come up with a list of connected skin areas, and remove the unnecessary areas that have low probability of being a part of the human-body. Fig. 2(c) shows the candidate areas that are found outside of the detected skin-colored areas.

The human body can be located only around the skin-color ranges; this makes the search more efficient if we search for only the relevant parts of the whole image. The range of the human-body search can be defined as α ($\alpha > 1.0$) times the area that contains all of the detected skin-colored areas (Fig. 2(d)).

3.2 Detecting Human-Body Parts with Generic Search

Before estimating accurate human body posture, we can combine components with connecting relations, which leads to the rough-cut detection of human-body parts. Such combination is measured by Eq. (3) to find the best combination. The human model (Fig. 1) detects the color data outside of the assumed test clothes in the estimated human body area if information on clothes is given. We then generate a list of areas that have the color of the clothes, and remove the unnecessary areas that do not meet the minimum conditions for area, size, and rectangularity (Fig. 3(a)).

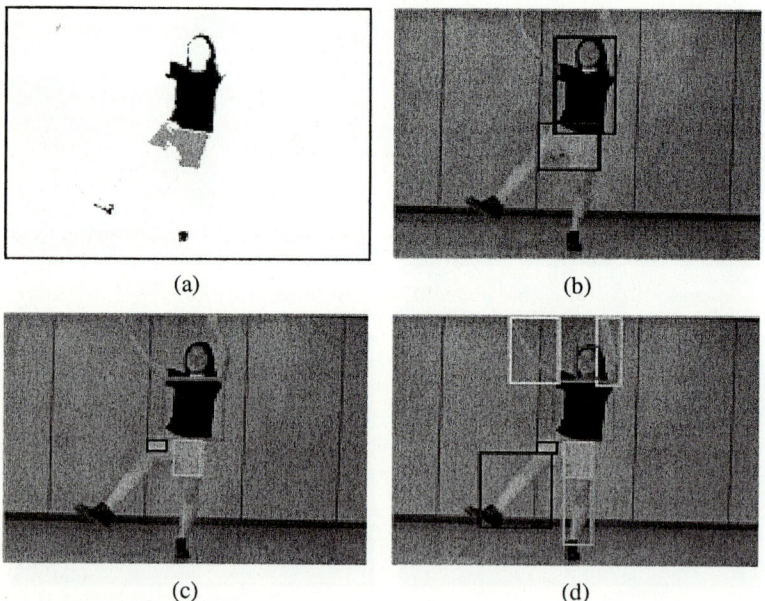

Fig. 3. Detection of human body parts using course search: (a) Clothes, (b) body and upper leg candidates, (c) estimated body and upper legs, and (d) coarse human model construction.

A head is located at the top of an image, does not reach beyond full length of an arm, and has the densest skin color compared to other body parts. In the image, two types of data – the shape data and the connection data that a head is located closest to the torso – are used to detect the head. After finding skin regions as head candidates located around the top area, we selected the most head-like region. The torso is then detected using the fact that it is located at the upper part of an image compared to the other candidate areas, while its area is larger than the given size condition. (Fig. 3(b)). Searching the list of the human body candidate areas, we can detect the limbs, which are connected to the torso. Combining the torso and the four limbs leads to the detection of both arms and both legs connected to the torso (Fig. 3(c)). Fig. 3(d) shows a human-body model that is detected with a generic search.

3.3 Estimating Precise Human-Body Posture

Based on the rough-cut human-body model (Sec. 3.2), we can make a more precise estimation of human body posture by combining other data, including the angles and lengths of the parts of the human body. In most cases, detailed search is required for the arms and legs. In this paper, we chose a more refined search for only the arms.

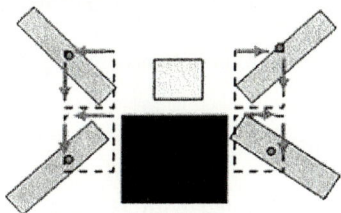

Fig. 4. Fine search for arms: detection of an elbow

By dividing the arm into upper and lower parts, we can estimate the arm posture after getting the arm angle and connection data. An arm consists of a shoulder, the tip of a hand, and an elbow that connects these two parts. Combining these three parts of an arm leads to an estimation of the posture of the upper and lower arms. The elbow is detected from the arm model constructed in Sec. 3.2, after defining the search area as the area that is a product of width × length from the point closest to the torso to the length of the upper arm (Fig. 4). The part that is closer to the torso is assumed to be the shoulder, whereas, the most distant part is considered as the tip of a hand. The elbow search is comprised of two steps: (i) a rough-cut boundary search that traces the skin-color areas, moving from the inside to the outside and from top to bottom; and (ii) the location of the central point of the boundary. For more accurate estimation of arm posture, we divide possible postures into five different cases, the first four being when each of the arms is individually raised or lowered, and the fifth, where a hand is placed on the waist. Fig. 4 shows the direction of elbow search in the four cases. Out of the four arm postures, we are estimating the posture of left arm as an example in this paper. The position for an arm signifies the four vertexes of the edges of an arm. The closest vertex to the torso is the shoulder while the farthest one is the tip of the hand. Given the connection with the torso, if one hand is placed on the waist on the side of the other hand, the upper left point of the torso is the left shoulder and the upper right point becomes the right shoulder.

We can also apply such fine searches for the legs. The leg angle is achieved by using the position data of a leg, that is, y coordinate value, and the external shape data, or compression rate (space of leg area / space of the smallest circumscribed rectangle). When a leg is lifted, the minimum y coordinated values of both legs, that do not differ when standing with both legs, will differ widely with the added effect that one leg gets longer in an oblique line, so that the compression rate of the leg drops lower than a certain rate. Fig. 5 shows an estimated human body posture.

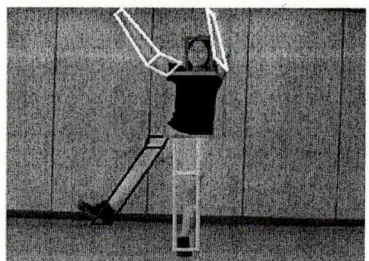

Fig. 5. Estimation of human posture using fine search

4 Results and Conclusions

The proposed algorithm is implemented with Java platform on Windows 2000 XP. The images used in this experiment are taken from the 108 images (420×316) that are acquired with Sony DSC-P10. These images contain a variety of postures (Fig. 7). The proposed method estimate of human body posture with a hierarchical search has been applied to a hundred and two images, with an average processing time of 0.615 seconds. Compared to the processing time in [5], 3-5 seconds, and that in [6], 10 seconds, the proposed method is 4.88-16.26 times more efficient.

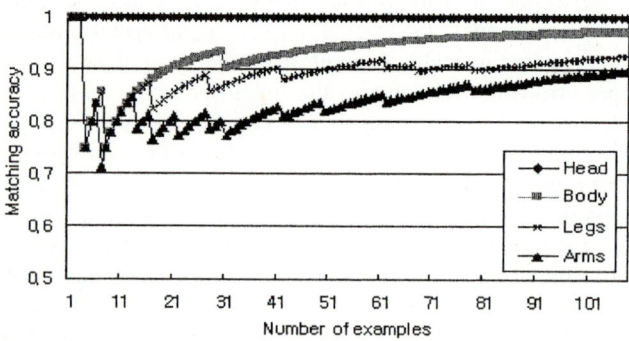

Fig. 6. Matching accuracy of each human body part for estimating postures

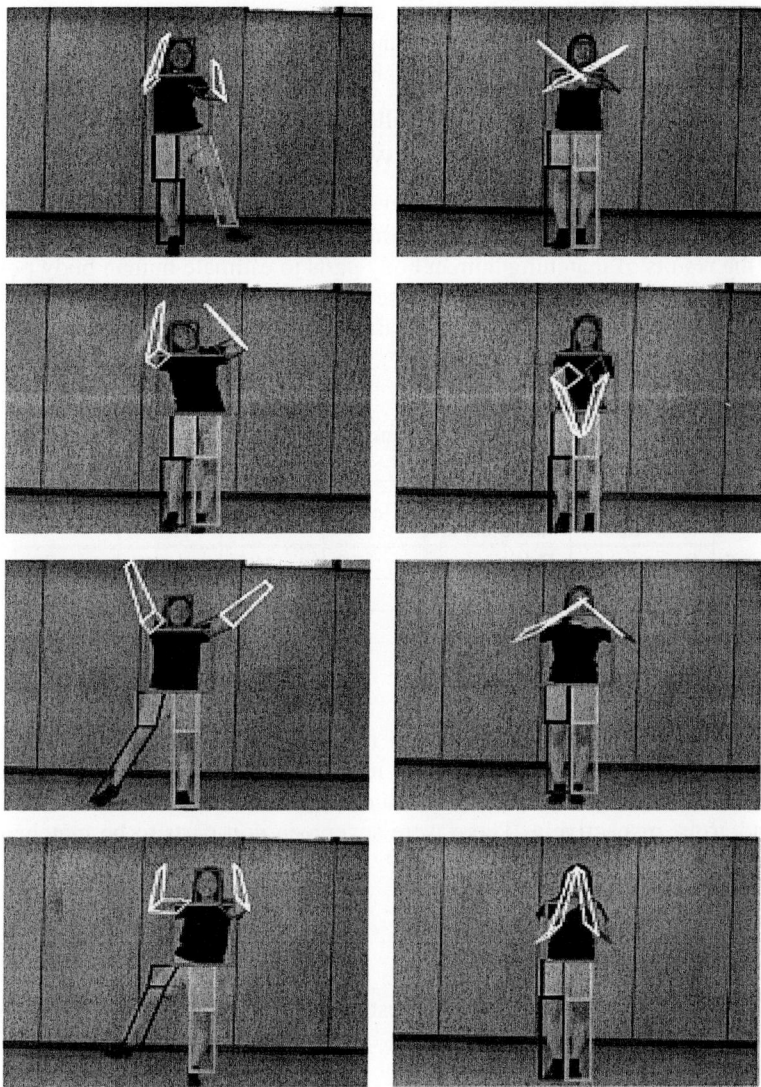

Fig. 7. Matching results

Fig. 6 shows the results of matching human-body parts to estimate human-body posture. The first target of our search shows 100% matches of head, followed by torso (body) with a high matching rate of 97.22%. Arms and legs that are matched by dividing the parts into upper and lower parts result in matching rate of 89.81% and 92.59%, respectively. The estimation rate for human-body posture is calculated on the assumption that it is good only when all the human-body parts are matched correctly.

Well(Human) = **Well**(Head) & **Well**(Body) & **Well**(Arm) & **Well**(Leg) where the function **Well**(A) means how well A is matched and the operator '&' represents an AND operation. The **Well**() function can be acquired according to the hierarchical structure. For instance, arm matching is determined as follows:

Well(Arm) = **Well**(LArm) & **Well**(RArm)

Well(LArm) = **Well**(LUArm) & **Well**(LLArm)

With this matching method, we get 87.96% estimation rate of human-body posture.

Matching accuracy was measured after the updating of every example. Fig. 6 shows the results of matching human body parts to estimate human body posture. Fig. 6 illustrates that as the system is processed on a greater number of examples, its ability to correctly match the human body part in images increases. After a few examples, the matching rate becomes stable.

Table I. Confusion matrix on 108 test images

Class		Head	Body	Arm	Leg
True	Predicted				
Positive	Positive	108	105	97	100
Positive	Negative			2	3
Negative	Positive		3	8	6
Negative	Negative				

Table I shows the matching counts for well-matched parts with the proposed matching algorithm. We achieved 108 match counts of head, 105 of body, 97 of arms, and 100 of legs. Two arms and three legs were detected, but mismatched to legs and arms, respectively. There were seventeen non-parts to be matched to body, arm, and leg.

5 Conclusion

In this paper, we propose a method to estimate postures of the human body through hierarchical relations of a component-based human-body model. The proposed method has the following advantages over the other methods proposed so far:

(i) A component-based method is useful for estimating an appropriate human body posture even when all of the components are not clearly detected due to partial distortion. The component-based human-body model proposed in this paper makes use of the external shape, including color and size of human-body components, the flexible connection data, and the hierarchical relationship data. Color data is used to detect a human-body part or a group of body parts, and external data and connection data are leveraged to combine these parts to estimate the posture.

(ii) Hierarchical structure data restricts the range of searches for possible combinations, which makes the estimation of human body posture more time-efficient.

(iii) Additionally, the proposed component-based method makes for a better estimation of the human body because it uses an adaptive model that has been developed using many examples and is less affected by different lighting conditions or postures than other methods.

The most difficult problem in estimating human-body posture is the fact that the colors and forms of human body fluctuates widely and that it is not easy to extract the relative position and connection data for body parts in an image. The future tasks of this project add learning and implement an adaptive system that can recognize the posture of people out of an image that contains different people with different postures against a more complicated background. Also, we can extend our work to detect the rear of a person.

Acknowledgements

This work was supported by Korea Research Foundation Grant No. R04-2003-000-10092-0 (2004).

References

1. Fischler, M.A. and Elschlager, R.A., The representation and matching of pictorial structures, IEEE tran. on Computers, 22(1) (1973) 67-92.
2. Felzenszwalb, P.F. and Huttenlocher, D.P., Efficient matching of pictorial structures, in Proc. of CVPR (2000) 66-73.
3. Garcia, C. and Tziritas, G., Face detection using quantized skin color regions merging and wavelet packet analysis, IEEE tran. on Multimedia, 1(3) (1999) 264-276.
4. Lee, K.-M., Component-based online learning and its application to face detection, in Proc. of CGIM (2004) 285-290.
5. Holstein, H. and Li, B., Low density feature point matching for articulated pose identification, in Proc. of BMVC (2002) 678-687.
6. Mittal, A., Zhao, L., and Davis, L.S., Human body pose estimation using silhouette shape analysis, in Proc. of International conference on advanced video and signal based surveillance (2003) 263-270.
7. Hogg, D. C., Model-based vision: A Program to see a walking person, Image and Vision Computing, 1(1) (1983) 5-20.

Fusion of Locally Linear Embedding and Principal Component Analysis for Face Recognition (FLLEPCA)

Eimad Eldin Abusham, David Ngo, and Andrew Teoh

Faculty of Information Science and Technology, Multimedia University,
75450 Bukit Beruang, Melaka, Malaysia
{eimad.eldin, david.ngo, bjteoh}@mmu.edu.my
http://fist.mmu.edu.my/

Abstract. We proposed a novel approach for face recognition to address the challenging task of recognition using a fusion of nonlinear dimensional reduction; Locally Linear Embedding (LLE) and Principal Component Analysis (PCA) .LLE computes a compact representation of high dimensional data combining the major advantages of linear methods, With the advantages of non-linear approaches which is flexible to learn a broad of class on nonlinear manifolds. The application of LLE, however, is limited due to its lack of a parametric mapping between the observation and the low-dimensional output. In addition, the revealed underlying manifold can only be observed subjectively. To overcome these limitations, we propose our method for recognition by fusion of LLE and Principal Component Analysis (FLLEPCA) and validate their efficiency. Experiments on CMU AMP Face EXpression Database and JAFFE databases show the advantages of our proposed novel approach.

1 Introduction

Face recognition system from images is of particular interest to researchers owing to its wide scope of potential applications such as identity authentication, access control and surveillance. It is quite a challenging task to develop a computational model for face recognition because faces are complex, multidimensional, and meaningful visual stimuli.

Much research on face recognition, both by computer vision scientists and psychologists, has been done over the last decade. From the aspect of computer vision, generally, face recognition can be distinguished into two categories: geometric feature-based approaches and template matching approaches.

In the first category, facial feature values depend on the detection of geometric facial features like eye corners and nostril. However, it is time-consuming and complex about modeling face. The second category assumes that an image as single or multiple arrays of pixel values. The virtue of template methods is that it is not necessary to create representations or models for objects.

Most recognition systems using linear method are bound to ignore subtleties of manifolds such as concavities and protrusions, and this is a bottleneck for achieving highly accurate recognition. This problem has to be solved before we can make a high performance recognition system. Generally speaking, faces are empirically thought to constitute of highly nonlinear manifold in the observation space [7].

We therefore assume that an effective face recognition system should be based on "face manifold", and the full variations in lighting condition, expression, orientation, etc. may be viewed as intrinsic variables which generate nonlinear face manifold in the observation space.

While there are many impressive results about how to mine the intrinsic invariants of face manifold, manifold learning on face recognition has fewer reports. A possible explanation is that the practical face data include a large number of intrinsic invariant and have high curvature both in the observation space and in the embedded space; meanwhile the effectiveness of current manifold learning methods strongly depend on the selection of neighbor parameters.

Of recent, manifold learning provides an interesting way to discover the intrinsic dimensionality of image manifold. However, most of manifold learning methods lack an effective way to model relationship from face manifold into low-dimensional space without dimensionality limitation and have fewer applications on face recognition. We therefore propose a fusion of LLE and PCA to model mapping relationship between low-dimensional embedded space and face manifolds in the observation space.

2 Problem Statement

For face images, classical dimensionality reduction methods include Eigenface [1], Independent Component Analysis (ICA) [2, 3], Linear Discriminate Analysis [4], and Local Feature Analysis (LFA) [5, 6], etc. The linear methods have their limitations. Firstly, they cannot reveal the intrinsic distribution of a given data set. Secondly, if there are changes in pose, facial expression and illumination, the projections may not be appropriate and the corresponding reconstruction error may be much higher. To overcome these problems, we propose a new algorithm combing the advantages of linear and nonlinear methods, which is the combination of locally linear embedding and principal component analysis. Locally Linear Embedding [7, 8], which is able to do nonlinear dimensionality reduction in an unsupervised way. A disadvantage of LLE algorithm is that mapping of test samples is difficult for computation cost of eigen-matrix. Thus our novel approach manages to overcome these problems.

3 Previous Work on Face Recognition

Earlier, face recognition systems were mainly based on geometric facial features and template matching [15, 16]. In those works, a face is characterized by a set of features such as mouth position; chin shape, nose width and length, which are potentially insensitive to illumination conditions. Brunelli et al. [15] compared this approach with a traditional template-matching scheme that produced higher recognition rates for the same face database (90% against 100%). Cox, Ghosn and Yianilos [17] proposed a mixture distance technique which achieved the best reported recognition rate among the Geometric feature approaches using the same database. Those results were obtained in an experiment where the features were extracted manually. The Principal

Component Analysis technique was first suggested for the characterization of human faces by Kirby and Sirovich [18] and later extended by Turk and Pentland [1]. Many refinements to the original idea were further introduced [19,20,21,22]. Several psychologists and neurophysiologists use PCA to model the way the human brain stores, retrieves and recognizes faces. The experiments of Turk and Pentland [1] achieved recognition rates around 96%, 85% and 64% respectively for lighting, orientation and scale variation. Recognition rate around 95% are reported by Pentland and Moghaddam (1994) [19] for a database consisting of 3000 accurate registered and aligned faces.

Junping Zhang, Stan Z. Li, and Jue Wang presented a new algorithm, which is Manifold Learning and Applications in Recognition [23]. Samaria & Harter presented an approach based on Hidden Markov Models that achieved a recognition rate of 95% for the ORL database at the expense of a high computational overhead. All those works, as well as this one, rely on a preprocessing to detect a face in a scene and to compensate for variation of lighting, position, rotation and scale.

The work reported here studies face recognition systems consisting of nonlinear manifold learning technique local linear embedding used for dimensionality reduction and a standard PCA, followed respectively by a Euclidean distance classifier. Roweis, S., originally proposed the LLE approach Saul, L [7]. In the first step, an n-pixel face image is projected onto embedding space, whose basis is given by the d (d < N) eigenvectors (d+1), which is embedding space. In the second step the PCA maps the projection of the input image on the face space onto discriminate features. Based on distance measures Euclidean distance used as classifier.

4 Locally Linear Embedding and Principal Component Analysis

4.1 Locally Linear Embedding

Locally Linear Embedding is a powerful method for nonlinear mapping. LLE establishes the mapping relation between the observed data and the corresponding low-dimensional one, the locally linear embedding algorithm is used to obtain the low-dimensional data Y $(Y \subset R^r)$ of the training set X $(X \subset R^N, N>>d)$, Y^* are optimal eigenvectors obtain by LLE from training data is define as follow:

$$Y^* = \arg\min_Y Y^T (I-W)^T (i-W) Y \qquad (1)$$

The details of LLE algorithm can be referred as to [7].

4.2 Principal Component Analysis

PCA generates a set of orthonormal basis vectors, known as principal components (PCs), which maximize the scatter of all the projected samples.

Let $X = [X_1, X_2, \ldots, X_n]$ be the sample set of the original images.

After normalizing a new image set $C = [C_1, C_2, \ldots, C_n]$ is derived. Each C_i represents a normalized image with dimensionality N, $C_i = (c_{i1}, c_{i2}, \ldots, c_{in})^t$, $(i = 1, 2, \ldots, n)$, the details of PCA algorithm can be referred as to [1].

5 The Proposed FLLEPCA Algorithm

In our proposed novel method data are first mapped into the intrinsic low-dimensional space base on LLE as in equation 1 and then mapped into the projection space based on PCA. We subtract the unknown samples x_i from entire embedding space obtain by LLE considering the neighbor of unknown samples, the weighted values among unknown data and training data are first calculated.

$$z_i = \| x_i - Y^* \|. \tag{2}$$

Then calculate the average face of the entire weighted values.

$$\Psi = \frac{1}{M} \sum_{i=1}^{M} z_i. \tag{3}$$

Having calculated the average, we set up a new group of images Φ, obtained from the difference between each image of the training set and the average features. Thus, each image Φ differs from the average image of the distribution. Each individual distance is calculated by subtracting them from the average image, which derives a new space of images in the following.

$$\Phi_i = z_i - \Psi (i=1,...,M). \tag{4}$$

Then, we calculate the eigenvectors of covariance matrix C. Since we know that only the eigenvectors with the larger eigenvalues are necessary for the face recognition, we used only ($M'<M$) eigenvectors. Every image from each class is projected into the "projection space" in the following way:

$$\Omega_i = U^T (z_i - \Psi), i=1,...,Nc. \tag{5}$$

Face recognition is performed by extracting the new image submitted for recognition compared with the images of the classes stored in the database, calculated in the same manner using the Euclidean distance. Thus, each image submitted for face recognition is projected in the projection space by obtaining the vector $\tilde{\Omega}$ in the following way:

$$\Omega = U^T (\Gamma - \Psi). \tag{6}$$

Hyphen is subject to a special rule. If the first word can stand alone, the second word should be capitalized. The font sizes are given in Table 1.

Here are some examples of headings: "Criteria to Disprove Context-Freeness of Collage Languages", "On Correcting the Intrusion of Tracing Non-deterministic Programs by Software", "A User-Friendly and Extendable Data Distribution System", "Multi-flip Networks: Parallelizing GenSAT", "Self-determinations of Man".

6 Experiment Results

Experiments were carried out to evaluate the face recognition of the proposed FLLEPCA in face recognition performance using two face databases, namely the CMU AMP Face EXpression Database [25] and JAFFE database [24]. The CMU AMP Face EXpression Database consists of 75 different images for 13 peoples with varied poses and expression. The JAFFE database consist of 213 images of 10 Japanese females, the head is almost frontal pose, in our experiments the databases is used for oriental face recognition. For CMU AMP Face EXpression Database, the 75 images of 13 persons are randomly partitioned into two sets; namely: 520 training images and 455 test images without overlapping, each one containing 64x64=4096 pixels. As for dimensionality reduction, the reduction dimensions of training set are set to be 100.The JAFFE database is partitioned into two sets; 18 images of the 10 persons are randomly extracted to make 180 training set and remaining images are as the test images. In our experiments, two parameters neighbors factors K' and d dimension of LLE algorithm need to be predefined first, we set K' to be 40 for CMU AMP Face EXpression Database and set d to 100. For JAFFE database 18 for K' and 100 for d. The result is tabulated in table 1 and illustrated in figure 1 show the performance of FLLEPCA It can be seen from the figure and table that FLLEPCA algorithm has good recognition result. From the experiments we have seen that the LLE works better when we set d to low dimensions that means less eigenvectors. And PCA works better if we have used more eigenvector (more dimension), that mean we have to select a proper dimension in order to achieve a good recognition rate. We found that the dimension d of LLE between 100 and 150 is stable; if it is more or less than that dimension, the recognition rate will decrease for CMU AMP Face EXpression Database. For JAFFE Database the good dimension is 70 as stated in table 1.

Table 1. Recognition Rate

LLE (Dimension)	JAFFE Database (%)	CMU AMP Face Expression DB (%)
40	81.8	84.08
50	87.88	90.33
60	81.8	84.08
70	93.93	90.33
80	87.88	90.33
100	90.9	90.33
150	87.88	90.33
170	69.7	63.7

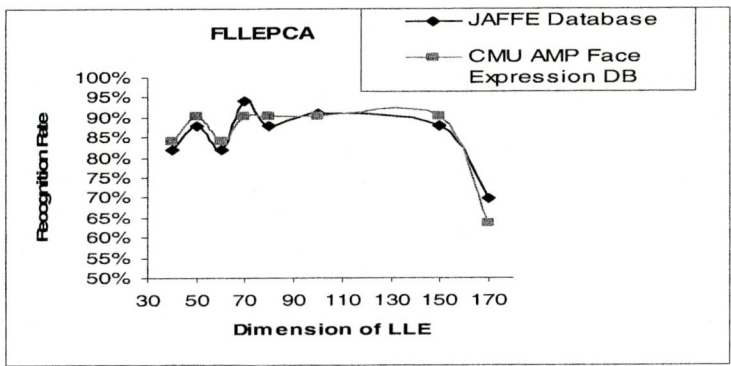

Fig. 1. Recognition Rate (%)

7 Discussions

The experiments have been systematically performed. These experiments reveal a number of interesting points:

In all the experiments, the recognition performance increases if the number of K' (LLE) increase till a certain number (which is the number of images per class) after which it declines.

Embedding space by LLE approach encodes more discriminating information in the low dimensional face subspace by preserving single local coordinate which is important for classification, an efficient and effective subspace representation of face images should be capable of charactering the nonlinear Manifold structure. By discovering the face manifold structure, our approach can identify the person with various poses and expressions. The LLE approach appears to be the best at simultaneously handling variation in pose and expression.

8 Conclusions and Future Works

Face recognition is introduced in this paper in order to detect the underlying nonlinear manifold structure in the manner of embedding space then use a classifier. To the best of our knowledge, this is the first devoted work on face recognition that uses this combination for face recognition. The Embedding is obtained by LLE that optimally preserves a single global coordinate system of lower dimensionality. Experimental results on the Face Expression database show the effectiveness of our method.

We are currently trying to implement the face recognition using Radial Basic Function in order to highly discriminate the classes.

Acknowledgement. This work is supported by the research Center of Multimedia University.

References

1. M.Turk, A. Pentland.: Eigenfaces for Recognition, Journal of Cognitive Neuroscience,(1991), Vol. 3. 71-86.
2. Marian Stewart Bartlett, Terrence J. Sejnowski: Independent components of face images: A Representation for face recognition, Proceedings of the 4th Annual Jount Symposium on Neural Computation, Pasadena, CA, (1997).
3. Marian Stewart Bartlett: Face image analysis by unsupervised learning and redundancy Reduction, Ph.D. Thesis at University of California, San Diego (1998)
4. P. N. Belhumeur, J. P. Hespanha and D. J. Kriegman: Eigenfaces vs. Fisherfaces: Recognition using class specific linear projection, IEEE Trans. on PAMI, Vol. 19, No.7, (1997) 711-720.
5. Penio S Penev, Joseph J Atick: Local Feature Analysis: A general statistical theory for object representation, Network: Computation in Neural Systems 7, Vol. 3. (1996) 477-500.
6. Penio S Penev, Local Feature Analysis: A statistical theory for information representation and transmission, Ph.D. Thesis at The Rockefeller University (1998)
7. Roweis, S., Saul, L.: Nonlinear dimensionality reduction by locally linear embedding. Science Vol. 290 (2000) 2323–2326.
8. Saul, L., Roweis, S.: Think globally, fit locally: unsupervised learning of nonlinear manifolds. Technical Report MS CIS-02-18, University of Pennsylvania (2002)
9. Steve Lawrence, C. Lee Giles: Face Recognition: A Convolution Neural Network Approach. IEEE Transactions on Neural Networks, Special Issue on Neural Networks and Pattern Recognition, Vol. 8. No 1 (1997) 98-113.
10. Wendy S. Yambor Bruce A. Draper J. Ross Beveridge: Analyzing PCA-based Face Recognition Algorithms: Eigenvector Selection and Distance Measures.
11. D. de Ridder and R.P.W. Duin: Locally linear embedding for classification. Technical Report PH-2002-01, Pattern Recognition Group, Dept. of Imaging Science & Technology, Delft University of Technology, Delft, The Netherlands, (2002).
12. Y. Weiss.: Segmentation using eigenvectors: a unifying view. In Proc. of the IEEE Int. Conf. on Computer Vision (ICVV'99), (1999) 975–982.
13. Joshua B. Tenenbaum, Vin de Silva, John C. Langford: A Global Geometric framework for Nonlinear Dimensionality Reduction, Science, Vol.290 No. 5500 (2000) 2319–2322.
14. M. Turk and Pentland: Face Recognition Using Eigenfaces, in Proc. IEEE International Conference on Computer Vision and Pattern Recognition, Maui, Hawaii, (1991).
15. R.Brunelli and T.Poggio: Face Recognition: Features versus Templates, IEEE Transactions On Pattern Analysis and Machine Intelligence, vol. 15, (1993) 1042-1052.
16. Samal and P.A. Iyengar: Automatic recognition and analysis of human faces and facial Expressions: A survey, Pattern Recognition, vol. 25 (1992) 65-77.
17. I.J. Cox, J. Ghosn and P.N Yianilos, Feature-Based Face Recognition Using Mixture Distance, IEEE Conference on Computer Vision and Pattern Recognition, (1996).
18. M. Kirby and L. Sirovich: Application of the Karhunen-Loeve procedure for the characterization of human faces, IEEE Trans. Pattern Analysis and Machine Intelligence, Vol. 12, No.1 (1990).
19. A. Pentland, B. Moghaddam, and T. Strainer: Viewbased and modular eigenspaces for face recognition, Proc. of IEEE Conference on Computer Vision and Pattern Recognition, (1994).
20. A. Pentland, et al.: Experiments with Eigenfaces, International Joint Conference on Artificial Intelligence, Chambery, France (1993).

21. B. Moghaddam and A. Pentland: Probabilistic Visual Learning for Object Detection, 5th Int. Conference on Computer Vision, (1995).
22. R. P. N. Rao, D. H. Ballard: Natural basis functions and topographic memory for the face Recognition, in International Joint Conference on Artificial Intelligence, Montreal, Canada, (1995) 10-17.
23. Junping Zhang, Stan Z. Li, and Jue Wang: Manifold Learning and Applications in Recognition. In Intelligent Multimedia Processing with Soft Computing., Springer-Verlag, Heidelberg, 2004.
24. http://www.irc.atr.jp/~mlyons/jaffe.html
25. Advance Multimedia Processing Lab. http://amp.ece.cmu.edu/Projects/FaceAuthentication/Download.htm

Proposal of Novel Histogram Features for Face Detection

Haijing Wang[1], Student Member (IEEE), Peihua Li[2], and Tianwen Zhang[1]

[1] Harbin Institute of Technology, School of Computer Science and Technology,
P.O.Box 1071, Harbin, Heilongjiang 150001, China
ninhaijing@yahoo.com
[2] Heilongjiang University, College of Computer Science and Technology, China
peihualj@hotmail.com

Abstract. This paper presents novel features for face detection in the paradigm of AdaBoost algorithm. Features are multi-dimensional histograms computed from a set of rectangles in the filtered images, and they represent marginal distributions of these rectangles. The filter banks consist of intensity, Laplacian of Gaussian (Difference of Gaussians), and Gabor filters, aiming at capturing spatial and frequency properties of human faces at different scales and different orientations. The best features selected by AdaBoost, pairs of filter and rectangle, can thus be interpreted as boosted marginal distributions of human faces. The result of preliminary experiments demonstrate that the selected features are much more powerful to describe the face pattern than the simple features of Viola and Jones and some variants which can only capture several moments of ONE dimensional histogram in intensity images.

1 Introduction

Face detection has extensively been studied [15] because of many interesting applications in fields such as security, multimedia retrieval, and human computer interaction. In recent years, Viola and Jones [13] present a seminal paper dealing with face detection surprisingly rapidly, whereas maintaining comparable performance with the state of art face detection algorithms. The success of their work depends on the proposal of redundant simple rectangle features computed by integral images, features selection with AdaBoost algorithm, and the cascade classifier architecture.

Many researchers present their work following the idea of Viola and Jones, mainly addressing two problems: 1) improving the convergence performance of the algorithm (training time on the order of weeks reported in [13]); and 2) pursuing more powerful features to represent example patterns. Li et al. [4] introduce new rectangle features to detect multi-view faces by FloatBoost. Wu et al. [14] present an algorithm based on the forward feature selection and produce cascades of similar quality with two orders of magnitude less computational time. Lienhart et al. [5] evaluate different boosting algorithms and different classifiers. From the view of feature selection, Murphy et al. [9] use a set of filters, including edge filters, corner detection filters, and a Laplacian filter, to convolve the image, and the second and the fourth moments are utilized to construct weak learners of one dimensional histogram from the special patch on the filtered images.

In this paper, we present novel features for face detection in the paradigm of AdaBoost algorithm. The features used are multi-dimensional histograms computed from a set of rectangles in the filtered images. Our filter bank is similar to that in [16], in which a set of filters are selected from the filter bank based on histogram characterizing distribution of texture according to Maximal Entropy. Our algorithm comprise four parts: filter selection, histogram statistics, fit normal distribution, and feature selection based on AdaBoost learning, as listed below.

- **Filter bank for face detection.** We convolve each image patch with three kinds of filters: intensity, Laplacian of Gaussian (Difference of Gaussians), and Gabor filters, to capture spatial (frequency) properties of human faces at different scales and different orientations.
- **Histogram statistics as feature.** We summarize the responses of the patch convolved with filters using histograms, which represent marginal distributions of these patches.
- **Fit Normal distribution as the proposal of weak learner.** We make a very simple assumption by fitting the normal distribution for each histogram feature only to positives (faces) in the sample set. Then for each weak learner we determine the best threshold to separate face and non-faces examples in accordance with this Gaussian.
- **Feature selection using AdaBoost learning.** To decide which features describe the face pattern best, features are selected by AdaBoost learning. The best features (pairs of filter and rectangle) can thus be interpreted as boosted marginal distributions of human faces.

This paper is arranged as follows. The bank of filters is described in Section 2. In Section 3, we present the histogram feature set. Weak learner based on Gaussian assumption is shown in Section 4. In Section 5, the AdaBoost training of our detector is described. Experiments and discussion are presented in Section 6. Finally, conclusions and directions for future research are given.

2 Filter Bank for Human Face Detection

Transform domain features can exhibit high "information packing" properties compared with the original input samples by filtering operation and capture spatial and frequency properties of human faces at different scales and different orientations. Our filter bank includes three kinds of filters: 1) the intensity filter $\delta(\cdot)$, which captures the DC component; 2) the isotropic center-surround filters, i.e., the Laplacian of Gaussian (LoG)/ Difference of Gaussians (DoG) filters; and 3) the Gabor filters [1] with both sine and cosine components.

2.1 Intensity Filter

The ideal impulse in the image plane is defined using Dirac distribution $\delta(\cdot)$, which captures the DC component. We may express the image function as a linear combination of Dirac pulses located at the points (a, b) that cover the whole image plane

$$\int_{-\infty}^{\infty} \int_{-\infty}^{\infty} f(a,b)\delta(a-x, b-y)dadb = f(x,y) \quad (1)$$

where samples are weighted by the image function $f(x, y)$.

2.2 Laplacian of Gaussian(LoG)/Difference of Gaussians(DoG)

Considering the Laplacian operator of an image smoothed by a 2D Gaussian smoothing, we get a convolution mask of a Laplacian of Gaussian (LoG) operator shown as Equ. (2):

$$\text{LoG}(x,y) = \frac{1}{\pi\sigma^4}\left(1 - \frac{x^2+y^2}{2\sigma^2}\right)e^{-\frac{x^2+y^2}{2\sigma^2}} \quad (2)$$

where the standard deviation σ is proportional to the size of the neighborhood on which the filter operates. It can be shown that LoG is the derivative with respect to $2\sigma^2$ of a Gaussian. In order to avoid the large computation of the LoG operator, the DoG operator (Difference of Gaussians) (see Equ.(3)) can be used as an approximation to the LoG by taking the difference of two Gaussians having different standard deviations.

$$\text{DoG}(x,y) = \frac{1}{2\pi\sigma_1^2}e^{-\frac{x^2+y^2}{2\pi\sigma_1^2}} - \frac{1}{2\pi\sigma_2^2}e^{-\frac{x^2+y^2}{2\pi\sigma_2^2}} \quad (3)$$

The ratio $\sigma_1/\sigma_2 = 1.6$ results in a good approximation of the LoG.

2.3 Gabor Filter

In the spatial domain, a Gabor wavelet [1] is a complex exponential modulated by a Gaussian function. Its kernels are similar to the 2D receptive field profiles of the mammalian cortical simple cells, exhibiting desirable characteristics of spatial locality and orientation selectivity.

The Gabor filters can be defined as follows, assuming that $\sigma_x = \sigma_y = \sigma$ [6]:

$$\psi_{\mu,\nu}(\boldsymbol{z}) = \frac{\|\boldsymbol{k}_{\mu,\nu}\|^2}{2\pi\sigma^2}e^{-\frac{\|\boldsymbol{k}_{\mu,\nu}\|^2\|\boldsymbol{z}\|^2}{2\sigma^2}}[e^{i\boldsymbol{z}\boldsymbol{k}_{\mu,\nu}} - e^{-\frac{\sigma^2}{2\|\boldsymbol{k}_{\mu,\nu}\|^2}}] \quad (4)$$

where μ and ν define the orientation and scale of the Gabor kernels, $\boldsymbol{z}=(x,y)$ is a given pixel, $\|\cdot\|$ denotes the norm operator, and the wave vector $\boldsymbol{k}_{\mu,\nu}$, restricted by a Gaussian envelope function, is defined as follows:

$$\boldsymbol{k}_{\mu,\nu} = k_\nu e^{i\phi_\mu} = \begin{pmatrix} k_\nu \cos\phi_\mu \\ k_\nu \sin\phi_\mu \end{pmatrix}, \quad k_\nu = a^{-\nu}f_{max}, \quad \phi_\mu = \mu\frac{2\pi}{n}, \quad \mu = \{0,\ldots,n-1\} \quad (5)$$

where k_ν is the ν-th frequency, and let $f_{max} = \pi/2$ be the highest frequency desired, and a is the frequency scaling factor ($a > 1$). Useful values for a include

$a = 2$ for octave spacing and $a = \sqrt{2}$ for half-octave spacing. The width σ/k_ν of the Gaussian is controlled by the parameter $\sigma = 2\pi$. ϕ_μ is the μth orientation and n is the number of orientations to be used. However, often the computation can be reduced to half since responses on angles $[\pi, 2\pi]$ are phase shifted from responses on $[0, \pi]$ in a case of a real valued input.

3 Feature Generation with Integral Histogram Image

Image filters remove information redundancies in the previous section. We assume that a set of reference patterns (templates) are available in this section. To seek statistical models that avoid making strong assumptions about distributional structure while still retaining good properties for estimation. The best compromise we found was histograms.

Take 64×64 image for example, it includes 892 different rectangle spatial templates. Fig.1 shows 59 reference patterns with the top left point $(0,0)$. Other rectangle templates are created in step of eight pixels. Each template includes 256 pixels at least. Both width and height of the template are no less than eight pixels.

Fig. 1. Example spatial templates with the top left point $(0,0)$ for 64×64 image. The orange rectangles are the masks used to calculate histogram feature.

Inspired by the work of Viola and Jones [13], our histogram features can be computed very rapidly using an intermediate representation for the image which is called the "integral histogram image". Given an $n \times m$ image, create $(n+1) \times (m+1)$ arrays of length L (the number of possible gray levels), noted as $H_{x,y}[p]$. Initialization $H_{x,0}[p] = 0$, $H_{0,y}[p] = 0$, and integral row histogram $h_{x,y}[p] = 0$, where $x = 0, \ldots, m$; $y = 0, \ldots, n$, and $p = 1, \ldots, L$. The integral histogram $H_{x,y}[p]$ at location (x, y) is according to the histogram of the image above and to the left of (x, y), inclusive:

$$H_{x,y}[p] = \sum_{x' \leq x, y' \leq y} \delta(x', y') \qquad (6)$$

where $\delta(x', y') = 1$ if the intensity of pixel (x, y) belongs to the p-th bin of histogram; otherwise $\delta(x', y') = 0$. Using the following pair of recurrences:

$$h_{x,y}[p] = h_{x,y-1}[p] + \delta(x,y), \quad H_{x,y}[p] = H_{x-1,y}[p] + h_{x,y}[p], \quad p = 1, \ldots, L \quad (7)$$

the integral histogram can be computed in one pass over the original image. Using the integral histogram any rectangular histogram can be computed in four array references.

4 Proposal of Weak Learner Under Gaussian Assumption

Building a model for the face detection task is challenging because of the difficulty in characterizing prototypical "non-face" images. Instead we make a very simple assumption by fitting the normal distribution for each histogram feature only to positives (faces) in the sample set. Then for each weak learner we determine the best threshold to separate face and non-faces examples in accordance with this Gaussian.

Assume now that the likelihood function of feature λ_i with respect to histogram feature of sample $\mathbf{x}$ in the d-dimensional feature space, which is according to the dimensions of the histogram, follow the general multivariate normal density $\mathcal{N}(\mu, \Sigma)$:

$$p(\mathbf{x}|\lambda_\mathbf{i}) = \frac{1}{(2\pi)^{d/2}|\Sigma_i|^{1/2}} \exp\left(-\frac{1}{2}(\mathbf{x} - \mu_i)^T \Sigma_i^{-1}(\mathbf{x} - \mu_i)\right), i = 1, \ldots, M \quad (8)$$

where M is the feature count, the d-component mean vector of the feature λ_i is described as

$$\mu_i = \mathcal{E}[\mathbf{x}] = [v_1, v_2, \ldots, v_d]^T \quad (9)$$

the $d \times d$ covariance matrix Σ_i is defined in Equ.(10), $|\Sigma_i|$ and Σ_i^{-1} are it determinant and inverse.

$$\Sigma_i = \mathcal{E}[(\mathbf{x} - \mu_i)(\mathbf{x} - \mu_i)^T] = [\sigma_{pq}]_{d \times d}, \quad p, q = 1, \ldots, d \quad (10)$$

where $(\mathbf{x} - \mu_i)^T$ is the transpose of $(\mathbf{x} - \mu_i)$.

Given histogram features $\mathbf{X} = (\mathbf{x_1}, \mathbf{x_2}, \ldots, \mathbf{x_n})$, $\mathbf{x_k} = [x_{1k}, x_{2k}, \ldots, x_{dk}]^T \in \mathbf{X}$, the j-th component of μ_i is described as $v_j = \sum_{k=1}^n x_{jk} \omega_k$, where ω_k is the weight of $\mathbf{x}_k$, and $\sum_{i=1}^m \omega_i = 1$. In Equ.(10), σ_{pq} is defined as $\sigma_{pq} = \sum_{k=1}^n \omega_k (x_{pk} - \nu_p)(x_{qk} - \nu_q)$. The feature value of all samples (both positives and negatives) can now be reached via Equ.(8). Next, features are selected by AdaBoost learning.

5 Learning Classification Functions by AdaBoost

Utilizing AdaBoost [2], each trained classifier produces a weak classification rule with one feature. The weight distribution is updated at each round of learning. The threshold of the final strong classifier is decided by the prescribed hit ratio of the strong classifier to the training example set. The construction of the final cascade detector depends on the ratio of false positives for the training set. Features used are the histogram feature described in the previous section. To speed up the process of detection, only intensity filter is adopted at the first few stages. Then Difference of Gaussians and Gabor filters are added to the feature set used for training.

6 Experiments and Discussion

In this section, we first introduce the training data set, filters, and feature set. Then preliminary learning results and detection results are described. Finally based on the results, we give a detailed discussion.

6.1 Preliminary Experiment Results

We crop 8,664 frontal face images as training samples from below sources: ORL[11], BioID[1], Caltech[2], PIE[12], FG-NET[3], IMM[4], JAFFE[7], AR[8], and YaleB[3] face set. The negative samples are collected by selecting random sub-windows from a set of 24,621 images which do not contain faces. For each layer, the maximum size of the negative set is 8,000. Each sample is scaled to 64 by 64 pixels. We take histogram equalization for both training samples and test samples to make each image with equally distributed brightness levels over the whole brightness scale.

To DoG filter, nine groups of (σ_1, σ_2) (see Equ.(3)) are taken into account. We choose two scales and five orientations $(0, \pi/8, 3\pi/8, 5\pi/8, 7\pi/8)$ for Gabor filter. Thus, our feature set includes 1,402 histogram features, which is far less than the size of Viola and Jones' feature set.

The final detector of Viola and Jones is a 38 layer cascade of classifiers which included a total of 6,060 features [13]. However, our cascade detector only includes 13 layers with 507 features. It is trained following two steps: "coarse" learning, which speeds up both training and detection and "fine" learning, which picks up more "meaningful" features. The coarse learning gets 332 intensity histogram features with eight layers. Fig.2 shows the first four selected features.

To demonstrate that our whole feature set is powerful to describe the face pattern, we continue to train the 9th and 10th layer by two ways. When the training features are only based on intensity filter, the detector holds 141 and 201 features for the 9th and 10th layer, respectively. However, when the whole feature set based on intensity, LoG/DoG, and Gabor filters is used, there are four features and nine features at the 9th and 10th layer achieving the same performance. Thus the whole feature set is used to "fine" learning. Finally, we get five layers hold 175 features by fine learning, which include 49 features based on the intensity filter, 55 features based on DoG filters, 71 features based on Gabor filters. Because our features contain rich information for face detection, our approach has potential to decrease the number of features, which is supported by the preliminary result.

We train a cascaded classifier containing six 20-feature classifiers according to what Viola and Jones do in the part of their experiment [13]. The first stage classifier in the cascade is trained using 5000 faces and 10000 non-face sub-windows randomly chosen from non-face images. The second stage classifier is trained on

---

[1] http://www.humanscan.de/support/downloads/facedb.php
[2] http://www.vision.caltech.edu/html-files/archive.html
[3] http://sting.cycollege.ac.cy/~ alanitis/fgnetaging/index.htm
[4] http://www.imm.dtu.dk/~aam

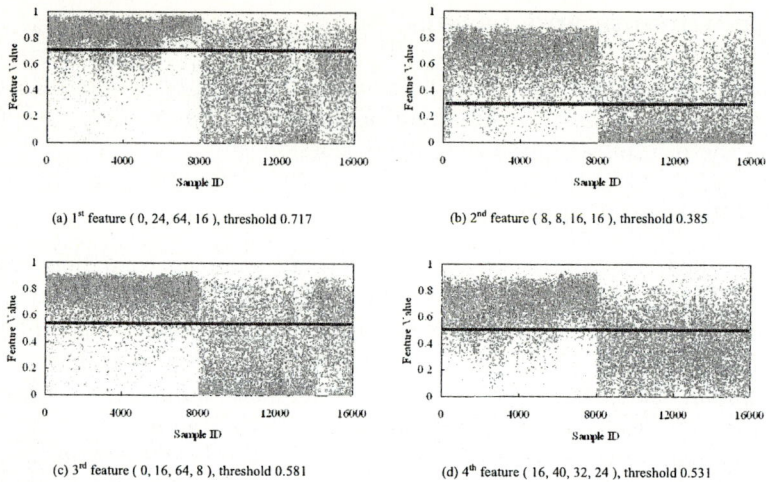

Fig. 2. The choice of first four features in the detector. X axis represents the sample ID. The first 8,000 samples are positives and the Id from 8,000 to 16,000 represents negatives. Y axis is the feature value. The threshold is represented by red line. For example, the first feature is located at $(0, 24)$ with 64 pixels width and 16 pixels height. And its threshold is 0.717.

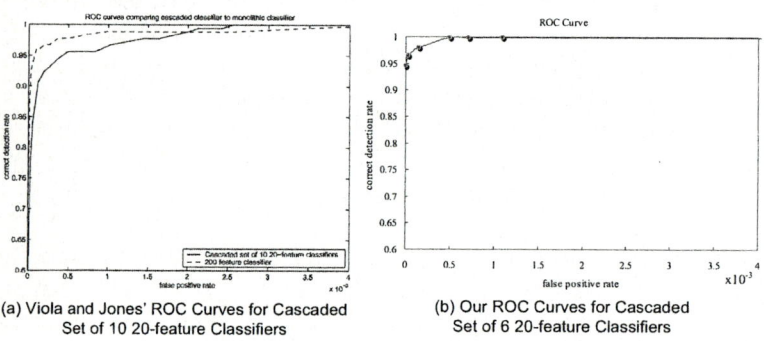

(a) Viola and Jones' ROC Curves for Cascaded Set of 10 20-feature Classifiers

(b) Our ROC Curves for Cascaded Set of 6 20-feature Classifiers

Fig. 3. ROC curves comparing a cascaded classifier containing ten 20-feature classifiers (by Viola and Jones) with our cascaded classifier containing six 20-feature classifiers.

the same 5000 faces plus 1094 false positives of the first classifier. This process continues so that subsequent stages are trained using the false positives of the previous stage. ROC curves comparing the performance of our detector and Viola and Jones' are given in Fig. 3. The experiment result proves that the features selected by our detector are more powerful than Viola and Jones' detector.

A prototype implementation of the discussed face detection framework is ongoing. In the following, we show the preliminary results of this ongoing work. This is an original unoptimized face detection system combining our novel feature set. The detector scans across the image at multiple scales and locations. Scaling

Fig. 4. Output of our face detector on a number of test images from the CMU new test set.

is achieved by scaling the image. And the test set is the CMU new frontal face test set without containing line drawn faces. The detection rate achieves 89% with 125 false detections. Figure 4 shows the output of our detector on some test images.

6.2 Discussion

Based on the above results, we can conclude the following.

- **Variation of training set.** By observing the performance of our face detector on the test set, we have noticed a few different failure modes. The face detector was trained with frontal, upright faces. It is possible that adding new tilted images to the training set will improve the performance of our detector. The size of our detector is 64 by 64. However, the test set includes more small size faces. We will train 48×48 or 32×32 detector in our future work.
- **Variation of lighting.** We also noticed that some failures are caused by harsh back lighting in which the faces are very dark while the background is relatively light. And our feature selection depends on the gray distribution greatly. The current preprocessing step, histogram equalization, makes each image with equally distributed brightness levels over the whole brightness scale. However, there are limits with no knowledge of the structure of faces. Rowley [10] presented the methods to use linear lighting models of faces to explicitly compensate for variations in lighting conditions before attempting to detect a face. Integrating the idea on intelligently correcting lighting variation to our framework will improve the detection performance of our detector.
- **Weak functions.** We derive the functional form of our detector using a Gaussian distribution to model variation in visual appearance. The problem is, we have no idea whether the Gaussian distribution used here are in the right place, because it is not tractable to analyze the joint statistics of large numbers of pixels. The initial face detection framework can be extended to choose other weak functions, such as the fisher linear discriminant.
- **Histogram features.** The current histogram range is divided equally to n units. One way to improve the expression of the features is to make the histogram boundary chosen adaptively.

7 Summary and Conclusions

This paper presents novel histogram features for face detection in the paradigm of AdaBoost learning. First, intensity, Laplacian of Gaussian (Difference of Gaussians), and Gabor filters are used to capture spatial and frequency properties of human faces at different scales and different orientations. Then, the responses of the patch convolved with filters are summarized with multi-dimensional histograms. For simplicity and efficiency, we fit normal distribution to histogram features only based on positives. Finally, the best features are selected with AdaBoost learning. The experiment result demonstrates that the selected features are powerful to describe the face pattern.

References

1. Daugman, J.G.: Uncertainty relation for resolution in space, spatial frequency, and orientation optimized by two-dimensional cortical filters. Journal Opt. Soc. Amer. **2** (1985) 1160–1169

2. Freund, Y., Schapire, R.E.: Experiments with a new boosting algorithm. Machine Learning: Proceedings of the Thirteenth International Conference. (1996) 148–156
3. Georghiades, A.S., Belhumeur, P.N., Kriegman, D.J.: From Few To Many: Generative Models For Recognition Under Variable Pose and Illumination. IEEE Int. Conf. on Automatic Face and Gesture Recognition. (2000) 277–284
4. Li, S.Z., Zhang, Z.: FloatBoost Learning and Statistical Face Detection. IEEE Trans. Pattern Anal. Mach. Intell. **26** (2004) 1112–1223
5. Lienhart, R., Kuranov, A., Pisarevsky, V.: Empirical Analysis of Detection Cascades of Boosted Classifiers for Rapid Object Detection. MRL Technical Report. Microprocessor Research Lab, Intel Labs. (2002)
6. Liu, C., Wechsler, H.: Gabor feature based classication using the enhanced fisher linear discriminant model for face recognition. IEEE Trans. Image Processing. **11** (2002) 467–476
7. Lyons, M.J., Akamatsu, S., Kamachi, M., Gyoba, J.: Coding facial expressions with gabor wavelets. Third IEEE Int. Conf. on Automatic Face and Gesture Recognition, Nara Japan (1998)
8. Martinez, A., Benavente, R.: The AR Face Database. Technical Report. Purdue Univ. (1998)
9. Murphy, K., Torralba, A., Freeman, W.T.: Using the forest to see the trees: a graphical model relating features, objects, and scenes. Advances in Neural Information Processing Systems 16 (NIPS). (2003)
10. Rowley, H.A.: Neural Network-Based Face Detection. PhD thesis, Carnegie Mellon Univ. (1999)
11. Samaria, F., Harter, A.: Parameterisation of a stochastic model for human face identification. Proceedings of the 2nd IEEE Workshop on Applications of Computer Vision. (1994)
12. Sim, T., Baker, S., Bsat, M.: The CMU pose, illumination, and expression (PIE) database. Proc. of the IEEE International Conference on Automatic Face and Gesture Recognition. (2002)
13. Viola, P., Jones, M.J.: Robust Real-Time Face Detection. International Journal of Computer Vision. **57** (2004) 137–154
14. Wu, J., Rehg, J.M., Mullin, M.D.: Learning a Rare Event Detection Cascade by Direct Feature Selection. Advances in Neural Information Processing Systems 16 (NIPS). (2004)
15. Yang, M.H., Kriegman, D.J., Ahuja, N.: Detecting Faces in Images: A Survey. IEEE Trans. Pattern Analysis and Machine Intelligence. **24** (2002) 34–58
16. Zhu, S.C., Wu, Y.N., Mumford, D.B.: Filters, Random Field and Maximum Entropy (FRAME): Towards a Unified Theory for Texture Modeling. International Journal of Computer Vision. **27** (1998) 107–126

Feature Selection Based on KPCA, SVM and GSFS for Face Recognition

Weihong Li, Weiguo Gong, Yixiong Liang, and Weiming Chen

Key Lab of Optoelectronic Technology & Systems of Education Ministry of China,
Chongqing University, Chongqing 400044, China
{weihongli, wggong, yxliang, wmchen}@cqu.edu.cn

Abstract. The feature selection is very important for improving classifier's accuracy and reducing classifier's running time. In this paper, a novel feature selection method based on KPCA, SVM and GSFS is proposed for face recognition. The proposed method can be described as follows, first KPCA is used for extracting initial face features, secondly, the extracted features are divided into some single feature sets, and then the single feature sets are trained separately by SVM to obtain the best feature set through GSFS. In this way, the dimensionality of the initial features can be reduced and also the best features can be obtained. Experimental results on ORL, IITL and UMIST face databases indicate the effectiveness of the proposed method.

1 Introduction

The feature selection problem is an old and difficult problem studied in pattern recognition, statistics and machine learning. Actually, the feature selection problem is to solve how to obtain the best features with the smallest classification error from the initial features and reduce running time. So the feature selection problem can be addressed to in the following two ways: (1) given a fixed $m \ll n$, find the m features that give the smallest expected generalization error; or (2) given a maximum allowable generalization error γ, find the smallest m or the feature subsets with smallest dimensionality. For different purposes feature selection methods are different [1], [2]. In the field of face recognition, principal component analysis (PCA) and kernel principal component analysis (KPCA) are two typical feature selection methods. PCA linearly transforms the original inputs into new uncorrelated features. KPCA is a nonlinear PCA developed by using the kernel method. Because KPCA firstly maps the original inputs into a high-dimensionality feature space using the kernel method and then calculates PCA in the high-dimensionality feature space. KPCA performs better than PCA in face feature selection [3]. Support Vector Machine (SVM) as a popular classification tool is well applied to pattern recognition [4]. A SVM is to find the hyperplane that separates the largest possible fraction of points of the same class on the same side, while maximizing the distance from the either class to the hyperplane [5]. Generalized Sequential Forward Selection (GSFS) is basically a SFS method but here r features are added to the current feature set at each stage of the algorithm.

In this paper, we present a novel face feature selection method based on KPCA, SVM and GSFS for face recognition. We use KPCA for extracting the initial face feature set. Because the dimensionality of the extracted initial face feature set still might be high it is necessary to reduce the dimensionality further. So we use SVM and GSFS for obtaining the best feature set to improve classification accuracy and to reduce the dimensionality. To verify the feasibility of the proposed method, experiments on ORL, IITL and UMIST face databases are executed separately. Experimental results show the effectiveness of the method.

The rest of this paper is organized as follows. Section 2 gives a brief review to KPCA, SVM. In Section 3, the feature selection method based on KPCA, SVM and GSFS is presented. Section 4 gives the experimental results, followed by the conclusions in the last section.

2 KPCA and SVM

2.1 KPCA

Principal component analysis (PCA) is a well-known method for feature extraction. By calculating the eigenvectors of the covariance matrix of the original inputs, PCA linearly transforms a high dimensionality input vector into a low-dimensionality one whose components are uncorrelated. Nonlinear PCA has also been developed through using different algorithms. Kernel principal component analysis (KPCA) is one type of nonlinear PCA developed by generalizing the kernel method into PCA [6]. KPCA firstly maps the original inputs into a high-dimensionality feature space using the kernel method and then calculates PCA in the high-dimensionality feature space. The functional form of the mapping $\Phi(x)$ does not need to be known since it is implicitly defined by the choice of kernel, $k(x_i, x_j) = (\Phi(x_i), \Phi(x_j))$, or inner product in feature space. With a suitable choice of kernel the data can become separable in feature space despite being non-separable in the original input space. Hence kernel substitution provides a route for obtaining non-linear algorithms from algorithms previously restricted to handling linearly separable data sets.

Three steps of KPCA algorithm are

- Step 1: Compute the dot product matrix K by using kernel function $K_{ij} = k(x_i, x_j)$;
- Step 2: Compute Eigenvectors of K and normalize them $\lambda_k(\alpha_k \cdot \alpha_k) = 1$;
- Step 3: Compute projections of a test point onto the Eigenvectors V^k using kernel function. $kPC_k(x) = (V^k \cdot \Phi(x)) = \sum_{i=1}^{m} \alpha_i^k k(x_i, x)$.

2.2 SVM

Support Vector Machine (SVM) is a state of the art classification algorithm that is known to be successful in a wide variety of applications [7]. High generalization ability of the method makes it particularly suited for high dimensionality data. The basic idea of SVM is to maximize the margin around the separating hyperplane between two classes, which can be formulated as the following convex quadratic programming problem:

$$\sum_{i=1}^{m} \alpha_i - \frac{1}{2} \sum_{i,j=1}^{m} \alpha_i \alpha_j y_i y_j x_i^T x_j ,$$

$$s.t. 0 \leq \alpha \leq C (i=1, \cdots, m), \sum_{i=1}^{m} \alpha_i y_i = 0 ,$$

where $\{x_1, \cdots, x_m\}$ is a training set in R^d space, $\{y_1, \cdots, y_m\}$ is class label data, and $\alpha_i (\geq 0)$ are Lagrange multipliers. C is a parameter that assigns penalty cost to misclassification of samples. By solving the above optimization problem, the form of decision function can be derived as

$$f(x) = w^T x + b,$$

where $w = \sum_{i=1}^{m} \alpha_i y_i x_i$ and b is a bias term. Only vectors corresponding to nonzero α_i contribute to decision function, and are called support vectors. High generalization ability of SVM is based on the idea of maximizing the margin. The margin is $M = 2/ \parallel w \parallel$.

3 Feature Selection Method Based on KPCA, SVM and GSFS

According to the characteristics of KPCA, SVM and GSFS we can construct an outline of the proposed method for feature selection as shown in figure 1.

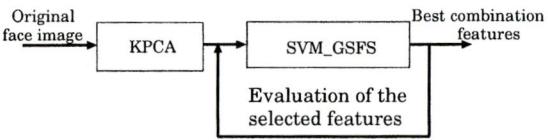

Fig. 1. The outline of the proposed method for feature selection

From figure 1 it can be seen that KPCA is used for extracting initial face features from original face image data as mentioned in Section 2.1. After done, the extracted initial face features may be divided into some signal feature sets. Thus active feature training set can be constructed by using the support vectors of SVM and the support vectors are used for replacing to the initial face feature set. Lastly, the best feature combination set can be obtained by GSFS. The procedure carried out by SVM_GSFS is as follows:

(1) Divide the extracted initial face features into some single feature sets $F_1^i = \{f_i\}$, $f_i \in F, i = 1, \cdots, n$;

(2) Calculate out the corresponding margin set M_1^i and support vector set $V_1^i = \{v_i\}$, $i = 1, \cdots, n$, through training F_1^i by SVM;

(3) According to $j = \arg\min_{i \in \{1,2,3,\cdots,n\}} M_1^i$, obtain the best single feature set $F_j = \{f_j\}$ and the active training feature set $V_j = \{v_j\}$;

(4) Add r new features into F_1 and update the active training feature set V_1. Then train V_1 once more by SVM;

(5) At step k, obtain the best combination feature set F_k and the active training feature set V_k;

(6) At step $k+1$, the combination feature set and the active combination training feature set are $F_{k+1}^i = F_k \cup \{f_i\} \cup \{f_{i+1}\} \cup \cdots \cup \{f_{i+r-1}\}$, $V_{k+1}^i = V_k \cup \{v_i\} \cup \{v_{i+1}\} \cdots \cup \{v_{i+r-1}\}$, $f_i, \cdots, f_{i+r-1} \in F_k^{av}$, $F_k^{av} = \{f_s \mid f_s \in F, f_s \notin F_k\}$;

(7) Training V_{k+1}^i once more by SVM, according to $j = \arg\min_{f_i,\cdots,f_{i+r}\in F_k^{av}} M_{k+1}^i$, obtain the best combination feature set $F_{k+1} = F_{k+1}^j$ and the active combination training feature set $V_{k+1} = V_{k+1}^j$;

(8) Repeat from step (4) to step (7), until no significant margin reduction is found or the desired number of features is obtained.

4 Experimental Results

In KPCA, polynomial kernel function $K(x_i, x_j) = (x_i \cdot x_j)^d$ is adopted for extracting initial face features. Then SVM and GSFS are used for obtaining the best feature combination set. Lastly, a linear SVM is designed for classification experiments.

4.1 Experiment 1: ORL Face Database

Experiment 1 was carried out on ORL face database. There are 10 different images of 40 distinct subjects in the ORL face database. For some of the subjects, the images were taken at different times, varying lighting, slightly rotation and facial expressions as shown in figure 2. Six images per subject were arbitrarily picked up as training samples and four images as testing samples. Table 1 shows the relationship between polynomial kernel parameter d and classification rate. From Table 1, we can see that when d changes from 0.4 to1.5 the classification rate is the best one. Table 2 shows the comparison between feature dimensionality and classification rate or running time in the ORL face database.

Fig. 2. A sample of ORL face database

Table 1. Relationship between polynomial kernel parameter d and classification rate

d	0.1-0.2	0.2-0.3	0.4-1.5	2.0	2.5-3.0	3.5	4.0
Classification rate(%)	96.88	97.50	**98.13**	97.50	96.88	97.50	96.88

Table 2. Comparison between feature dimensionality and classification rate or running time in the ORL face database

	Feature dimensionality	Classification rate(%)	Running time (s)
Originality features	10304	97.5	15.1020
KPCA	239	98.13 ($d = 0.8$)	0.2300
KPCA_SVM_GSFS	99	98.75	0.1200

4.2 Experiment 2: IITL Face Database

Experiment 2 was executed on IITL face database. The IITL face database was build by Intelligential Information Technology Lab of Chongqing University, China. The face database consists of 1456 images of 52 distinct subjects. Each subject covers different poses from profile to frontal views with different lightings, facial expressions, sexes and appearances. Figure 3 shows a sample of these subjects.

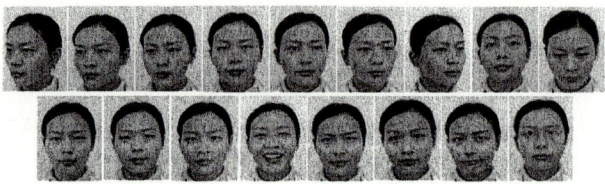

Fig. 3. A sample of IITL face database

Table 3. Relationship between polynomial kernel parameter d and classification rate

d	0.1-0.5	0.6-1.0	2.0	3.0	4.0
Classification Rate(%)	86.82	86.36	**90.45**	90.00	90.00

Table 4. Comparison between feature dimensionality and classification rate or running time in the IITL face database

	Feature dimensionality	Classification rate (%)	Running time (s)
Originality features	10304	86.36	14.456
KPCA	239	90.45(d = 2.0)	0.220
KPCA_SVM_GSFS	99	91.81	0.1813

In the same way of Experiment 1, six training samples and eleven testing samples are randomly taken out from 40 subjects in the IITL face database. Table 3 shows the relationship between polynomial kernel parameter d and classification rate. From Table 3, it can be seen that when d is 2.0 the best classification rate is obtained. Table 4 shows the comparison between feature dimensionality and classification rate or running time in the IITL face database.

4.3 Experiment 3: UMIST Face Database

Experiment 3 was carried out on UMIST face database [8]. The UMIST face database consists of 575 images of 20 distinct subjects. Each subject covers different poses from profile to frontal views with different races, sexes and appearances. Figure 4 shows a sample of these subjects. In the same way of Experiment 1, six training samples and

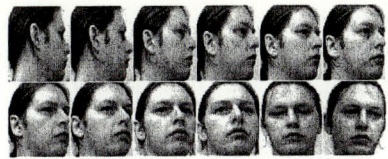

Fig. 4. A sample of UMIST face database

Table 5. Relationship between polynomial kernel parameter d and classification rate

d	0.1-0.5	0.6-1.5	2.0	2.5	3.0	4.0
Classification rate (%)	**91.92**	86.92	86.53	85.77	84.23	84.08

Table 6. Comparison between feature dimensionality and classification rate or running time in the UMIST face database

	Feature dimensionality	Classification rate (%)	Running time (s)
Originality features	10304	86.92	13.7190
KPCA	119	91.92 ($d = 0.4$)	0.2350
KPCA_SVM_GSFS	99	92.30	0.1950

thirteen testing samples are randomly taken out from the UMIST face database. Table 5 shows the relationship between polynomial kernel parameter d and classification rate. From Table 5, it can be seen that when d changes within 0.1 to 0.5 the classification rate is the best one. Table 6 shows the comparison between feature dimensionality and classification rate or running time in the UMIST face database.

4.4 Discussion on Selecting Feature Dimensionality

It should be noted that during the KPCA stage, all eigenvectors corresponding to non-zero eigenvalues are selected, thereby the selection of KPCA dimensionality is fulfilled automatically. After done, 239, 239 and 119 features are obtained separately.

If the KPCA_SVM_GSFS is used, according to the results in all experiments, in average meaning, 99 features selected from the initial 10304 ones are necessary for each experiment to obtain the optimal classification. So 99 features are retained from all features for experimental analysis.

5 Conclusions

According to the experimental results in three face databases, we can make the following conclusions:

(1) Although KPCA can not only reduce the feature dimensionality but also improve the classification accuracy the proposed method base on KPCA, SVM and GSFS is more efficient than KPCA.

(2) The polynomial kernel parameter d affects their classification rate for the each face database. For the ORL face database, the classification rate is best when d is around 1. It indicates that the images in the ORL face database include more linear components, and then ones of the other two face databases include more nonlinear components.
(3) For different face databases, the selection of training sample and testing sample numbers affect classifier performance. The reason caused the phenomena will be studied in our further work.

Acknowledgements

This work is supported by the Scientific Technology Key Project of Ministry of Education (02057) and Key Project of Chongqing Natural Science Foundation (CSTC2005BA2002, CSTC2005BB2181), China.

References

1. Grandvalet, Y., Canu, S.: Adaptive Scaling for Feature Selection in SVMs. In: Thrun, S., Becker, S., Obermayer, K. (eds.): Advances in Neural Information Processing Systems, Vol. 15. MIT Press, Cambridge (2003) 553–560
2. Weston, J., Mukherjee, S., Chapelle, O., Pontil, M., Poggio, T., Vapnik, V.: Feature Selection for SVMs. In: Advances in Neural Information Processing Systems, Vol. 13. MIT Press, Cambridge (2000) 668-674
3. Cao, L. J., Chua, K. S., Chong, W.K., Lee, H. P., Gu, Q. M.: A Comparison of PCA, KPCA and ICA for Dimensionality Reduction in Support Vector Machine. Neurocomputing. **55** (2003) 321–336
4. Guo, G. D., Li, S. Z., Chen, K. L.: Support Vector Machine for Face Recognition. Image and Vision computing. **19** (2001) 631–638
5. Burges, C.: Simplified Support Vector Decision Rules. Proceedings of the 13th International Conference on Machine Learning. (1996) 71–77
6. Scholkopf, B., Smola, A., Muller, K.R.: Nonlinear Component Analysis as a Kernel Eigenvalue Problem. Neural Computation. **10** (1998) 1299–1319
7. Burges, C.: A Tutorial on Support Vector Machines for Pattern Recognition. Data Mining Knowledge Discovery. **2** (1998) 121-167
8. Graham, D.B., Allinson, N. M.: Characterizing Virtual Eigensignatures for General Purpose Face Recognition. In: Wechsler, H., Phillips, P. J., Bruce, V., Soulie, F. F., Huang, T. S. (eds.): Face Recognition: From Theory to Application. NATO ASI Series F, Computer and Systems Sciences, Vol. 163. Springer-Verlag, Berlin Heidelberg New York (1998) 446-456

Eigen and Fisher-Fourier Spectra for Shift Invariant Pose-Tolerant Face Recognition

Ramamurthy Bhagavatula and Marios Savvides

Carnegie Mellon University, Department of Electrical and Computer Engineering,
5000 Forbes Avenue, Pittsburgh PA, 15213-3890
`{marioss, rbhagava}@andrew.cmu.edu`

Abstract. In this paper we propose a novel method for performing pose-tolerant face recognition. We propose to use Fourier Magnitude Spectra of face images as signatures and then perform principal component analysis (PCA) and Fisherfaces (LDA) leading to new representations that we call Eigen and Fisher-Fourier Magnitudes. We show that performing PCA and Fisherfaces on the Fourier magnitude spectra provides significant improvement over traditional PCA and Fisherfaces on original spatial-domain image data. Furthermore, we show analytically and experimentally that our proposed approach is shift-invariant, i.e., we obtain the same Fourier-Magnitude Spectra regardless of the shift of the input image. We report recognition results on the ORL face database showing the significant improvement of our method under many different experimental configurations including the presence of noise.

1 Introduction

Face recognition [1] has been an area of continuing and growing research due to its increasing application in fields such as biometrics and security. However, it is also a challenging area of research due to the variability in facial features due to pose and illumination variations. Two well-known methods for face recognition are Principal Component Analysis (PCA) [2], [3] and Fisherfaces [4]. Both are dimensionality reduction methods, however PCA seeks projections that best represent the data in the minimum squared error sense while Fisherfaces seeks projections that best separate the data classes based on maximizing the Fisher criterion [5].

In this paper we propose to compute the Fourier-Magnitude Spectra of the face images and then perform PCA and Fisherfaces on those to demonstrate that Fourier magnitudes of images are much more effective than spatial image representations for pose-tolerant face recognition. Along with demonstrating the pose tolerance of the methods, we will show that Fourier magnitudes additionally provide a shift-invariant model (i.e. even if the input image is shifted, the Fourier magnitude spectra remain the same).

2 Eigenfaces

Eigenfaces or PCA method introduced by Turk and Pentland [2] (also sometimes referred to as Karhunen Loeve transform or Hotelling Transform) is one of the most common methods applied in face recognition. PCA is applied to an ensemble of face images to compute the principal directions of variation in the high-dimensional face space. These resulting principal components are named Eigenfaces and a few of these Eigenfaces (corresponding to their largest eigenvalues) are then used to form a basis to represent the original data. PCA finds a linear subspace that represents the training data in the least mean squared error sense. The principal directions of variation are identified by diagonalizing the covariance matrix $\mathbf{C}$ of the training data, defined as

$$\mathbf{C} = \sum_{1}^{N} \{x_i - m\}\{x_i - m\}^T = \mathbf{XX}^T, \qquad (1)$$

where $\mathbf{X}$ is a matrix of size $M \times N$ where M is the number of pixels in each face image and N is the number of training images and $\mathbf{m}$ is the mean of the training images. Each column of $\mathbf{X}$ contains a training face image lexicographically reordered and placed along the column (note that these images are in the spatial domain). PCA involves solving the following eigenvalue problem:

$$\mathbf{XX}^T \mathbf{v} = \mathbf{Cv} = \lambda \mathbf{v}, \qquad (2)$$

where the covariance matrix $\mathbf{C}$ is symmetric and positive semi-definite. Thus the eigenvectors computed in Eq. (2) form an orthogonal basis that best represents the variance in the training data in the minimum mean squared error sense.

3   Eigen Fourier Magnitudes (FM-PCA)

In this paper, we propose to represent the face images by their Fourier-Magnitude Spectrums and model the intra-class variations of the magnitude spectra using PCA. We first compute the two-dimensional Fourier transforms of all the images, and then retain the magnitude spectra of these transforms and then perform eigen-analysis to find the principal directions of variations. We denote this method as Fourier-Magnitude PCA (FM-PCA). It has been shown in [6] that performing PCA using the complete Fourier transforms does not provide any advantage over performing PCA in the spatial domain. This is because the Fourier transform is a unitary transformation and in fact the eigenvectors obtained in the frequency domain are exactly the Fourier transforms of the eigenvectors obtained by performing PCA in the spatial domain data.

However, when we discard either the phase or the magnitude in the Fourier transform and then do PCA, this is completely different from doing spatial domain PCA. In fact Savvides [6] has shown that phase information is more tolerant to illumination variations, and here we show that the Fourier magnitude spectrums are more tolerant to pose variations, thus depending on type of variation at hand one can employ a different feature representation.

We also show that FM-PCA has other advantages over the PCA method, such as shift-invariance, i.e., even if the input image is shifted, the resulting Fourier magnitudes remain exactly the same and hence are invariant to shifts and more importantly are not prone to registration errors of the input image as is the case with traditional spatial-domain PCA.

4 Experimental Datasets

The face database used in our experiment is the Olivetti Research Laboratory (ORL) dataset. This dataset is comprised of 40 people each with 10 images yielding a total of 400 images. Each image is 112 × 92 pixel size with the face occupying most of the image, however there is considerable variation among the face imagery with respect to angle, expression, and size of the face (scale changes) as shown in Figure 1.

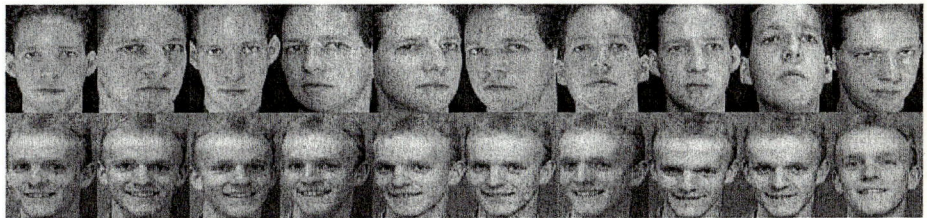

Fig. 1. Face images from Persons 1 and 5 from ORL database

There are also people with glasses who also take off their glasses during their captured 10 face images. An important aspect of this dataset is that within the face images of a single person there is significant intra-class pose variation as shown in Fig. 1.

4.1 Face Recognition Using FM-PCA

Following the methodology described above, we set out to determine if Fourier Magnitude PCA (FM-PCA) yields better results than spatial domain PCA in terms of recognition. By demonstrating this, we will show that FM-PCA is more tolerant to intra-class pose variation. In this particular dataset pose variation is significant. To determine which method yielded better performance we performed experiments involving different training sets, variable size training sets, varying image sizes, addition of additive white Gaussian noise (AWGN), and introduction of registration errors on the complete ORL dataset.

For each class or person we randomly select a pre-set number of images to train from. For each experiment, the number of images trained upon and the training list remains the same for each person. Using these training sets, we generate two different eigen-spaces for each class. One eigen-subspace is based on the raw spatial-domain face images. The second subspace is from the Fourier Magnitude spectra of the same training face images.

Each testing image is projected onto each person's eigenspace and reconstructed. From the reconstructed image, we measure the reconstruction error which indicates how well the test image is modeled by the eigenspace. This was repeated for traditional spatial-domain PCA and our proposed FM-PCA method. We ran experiments involving the previously mentioned variations (different training sets, variable size training sets, etc.) for both methods for each number of training images and computed the average recognition accuracy (Table 1). These results clearly show an increased recognition rate of our proposed FM-PCA over the traditional spatial-domain PCA, PCA variants [7], [8], and other classification methods [9], [10].

Table 1. Recognition accuracy with different numbers of training images with ORL dataset

Number of Training Images	3	4	5	6	7	8	9
FM-PCA	92.96%	96.30%	98.03%	98.6%	99.08%	99.49%	99.84%
PCA	89.28%	93.14%	95.38%	96.48%	97.18%	97.61%	98.28%

5 Fisherfaces (Fisher LDA)

Fisher linear discriminant analysis (FLDA) [5] is a popular tool for multi-class pattern recognition. FLDA finds the optimal projection vectors **w** such that the projected samples have a small within-class scatter (i.e., compact clusters), and large between-class scatter (separating the classes far apart). This is done by maximizing the ratio of determinant of the projected between-class scatter matrix $\mathbf{S_B}$ to the determinant of the within-class scatter matrix $\mathbf{S_W}$, shown below:

$$\mathbf{S_B} = \sum_{i=1}^{c}(\mathbf{m_i} - \mathbf{m})(\mathbf{m_i} - \mathbf{m})^T, \quad (3)$$

$$\mathbf{S_W} = \sum_{i=1}^{c}\sum_{k=1}^{N_i}(\mathbf{x_k^i} - \mathbf{m_i})(\mathbf{x_k^i} - \mathbf{m_i})^T, \quad (4)$$

where N_i is the number of training images in the ith class, **m** is the mean of the training images, and the superscript on **x** indicates its class. The Fisher ratio that must be maximized is as follows:

$$J(\mathbf{w}) = \frac{|\mathbf{w}^T \mathbf{S_B} \mathbf{w}|}{|\mathbf{w}^T \mathbf{S_W} \mathbf{w}|}. \quad (5)$$

However in most pattern recognition applications where the dimensionality of the data is larger than the number of samples (such as face identification), the within-class scatter matrix $\mathbf{S_W}$ is not full rank leading to zero determinant. This is also true for the between-class scatter matrix $\mathbf{S_B}$ which is of at most rank C-1 as defined in Eq. (3). Since there are at most N training images in total from all C classes, the rank of $\mathbf{S_W}$ is at most of rank N-C. To avoid a singular matrix $\mathbf{S_W}$, [4] proposed to first perform PCA on the data to reduce the dimensionality to N-C and then perform multi-class FLDA in the reduced-dimensional space. This cascade of transformations has been termed Fisherfaces. Maximizing the Fisher criterion in Eq. (5) leads to the following generalized eigenvalue problem:

$$\mathbf{S_B}\mathbf{w} = \lambda \mathbf{S_W}\mathbf{w}. \quad (6)$$

From Eq. (6), we observe that the number of non-zero eigenvalues is dominated by the scatter matrix with the smaller rank. In this case S_B has rank C-1 as there are C classes, therefore after performing LDA in the PCA space we obtain a maximum of C-1 optimal projection vectors **w**. Once LDA is performed, we can cascade the two projections into one transformation for convenience:

$$W_{\text{fisherface}} = W_{\text{PCA}} W_{\text{LDA}}. \tag{7}$$

For identification, all the training faces are projected into the Fisherface subspace in Eq. (7), and typically a simple nearest neighbor classifier is used to label the test face based on the residue.

5.1 Face Recognition Using Fisher-Fourier Magnitudes (Fisher-FM)

To compare Fisher-Fourier Magnitudes (Fisher-FM) to Normal-Fisher(faces), we performed experiments in which we compared the recognition rates of the two methods while varying image size. Training and testing image dimensions varied from their original 112×92 down to 64×64 and finally 32×32 pixels. By doing this we can measure the performance of our proposed method when presented with varying face resolutions. This is turn approximates the scenario of low-resolution cameras and non-uniform range to camera situations which result in scaling issues.

As stated above, Fisherfaces maximizes the ratio of between-class-scatter to within-class-scatter. Thus we expect that the projected data classes should be well and closely clustered to their projected class means. FM-Fisher accomplishes better class separation more effectively than traditional Fisherfaces.

FM-Fisher achieves a much smaller within-class-scatter and a much larger between-class-scatter than Normal-Fisher as demonstrated in Figure 2. This allows FM-Fisher to achieve a higher recognition rate than traditional-Fisherfaces in most cases as indicated in Table 2 (showing average of multiple experiments using a random set of different training images).

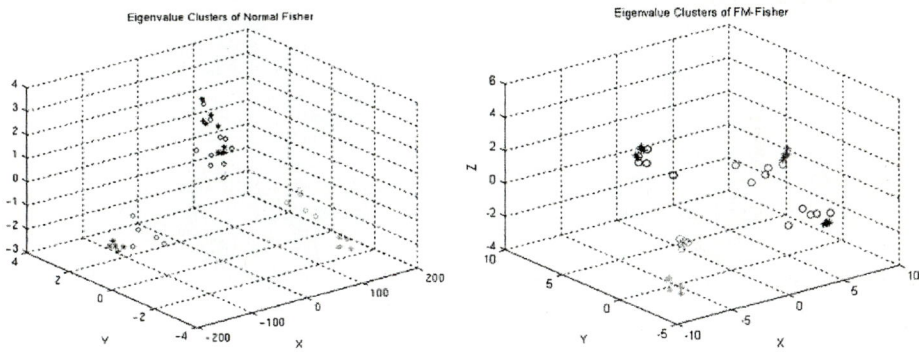

Fig. 2. 3-D plots of eigenvector clusters. (Left) Normal Fisher (Right) FM-Fisher. The * represent the eigenvector of the training imagery while the ° represent the eigenvector of the testing imagery. For these plots we only trained and tested on 4 people (i.e. 4 classes) which are each represented by a single color or cluster.

Table 2. Recognition accuracy with different image sizes

Image Size (pixels)	32×32	64×64	112×92	128×128
FM-Fisher	80.8%	83.25%	84.58%	84.39%
Normal Fisher	77.69%	79.50%	77.36%	74.00%

6 Effect of Registration Errors in Test Images

Registration errors occur when the input images are not correctly centered that typically arise from poor face segmentation. However, the classification algorithm is typically trained on images which are perfectly centered. These offsets in the test image can create significant errors in recognition as the image looks different due to shifts. Such shifts do not affect the Fourier-Magnitude spectra. This tolerance allows for FM-PCA and FM-Fisher to operate with high recognition rates even in the presence of such registration errors.

We verified the improved shift-tolerance of FM-PCA versus PCA by performing experiments on the complete dataset using 5 different random training images. The training images were zero-padded to fit in the center of an area twice the dimensions of the original image. FM-PCA and PCA were trained using this set of training images. Testing images was similarly padded, but positioned at different locations from the original centered images. These shifts ranged from -10 to 10 pixels in each direction.

The results of these experiments clearly show that FM-PCA is shift-tolerant while PCA is not. Even small registration errors caused significant decreases in recognition rates. Figure 2 demonstrates the average of the experiments. It is also clear that FM-PCA is not affected by registration errors due to the shift-invariance of the Fourier Magnitudes Spectra (FM).

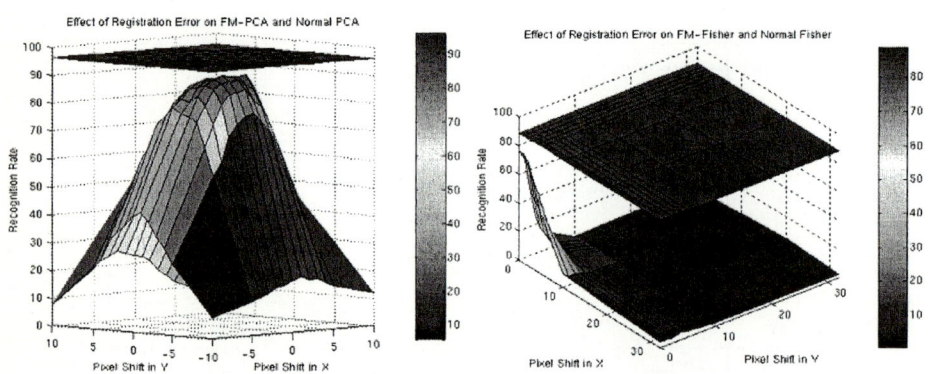

Fig. 3. (Left) Average recognition rates of traditional Spatial-FLDA (bottom surface) and Fisher-FM (top surface) as a function of pixel shift in the input image. (Right) Average recognition rates of traditional Spatial-PCA (bottom surface) and FM-PCA (top surface) as a function of registration error. The upper surface represents the accuracy of our frequency domain approach and the bottom surface represents traditional spatial domain approach which degrades rapidly with registration error.

Similarly, we performed experiments (with 5 random training images) using FM-Fisher and Normal-Fisher and computed the average recognition results. The complete dataset was tested using 5 training images. In these experiments, we zero-padded the images into areas twice their original dimensions. Training images were centered in this area, but the testing images were shifted in different amounts. In the Fisher experiments we used shift values ranging from 0 to 32 pixels in each direction. The effect of these shifts was dramatic as Fisher recognition rate degraded to below 50% with shifts of more than 8 pixels in any one direction. Figure 3 shows the averages of these experiments.

The results of both sets of experiments on Fisher and PCA clearly show that their FM counterparts are completely shift-invariant and thus are far more robust. Due to the high likelihood of registration errors in real word applications, FM-PCA and FM-Fisher will be far more applicable than their normal version.

7 Effect of Noise in Test Images

Another potential problem in real-world face recognition system, is the presence of noise in the images (e.g. due to camera thermal noise). To evaluate the tolerance of our proposed method to noise we added white Gaussian noise to the test images as shown in Figure 4. The level of noise introduced varied from 20 dB to 12 dB (SNR) at intervals of 0.5 dB. However, it is important to note that the subspaces were trained on noise-free images; it is only the test images that were corrupted with noise. We ran 50 experiments (using different set of random training images) for each noise level and the averaged results are shown below in Table 3. Our results clearly show that FM-PCA has a higher noise tolerance than traditional spatial PCA.

Table 3. Recognition accuracy with different levels of AWGN noise

Noise Level (dB)	PCA	FM-PCA	Noise Level (dB)	PCA	FM-PCA
12	88.00%	89.50%	16.5	88.00%	95.5%
12.5	88.00%	88.50%	17	88.00%	95.00%
13	88.00%	92.00%	17.5	88.00%	95.50%
13.5	88.50%	93.00%	18	88.50%	95.50%
14	88.50%	93.50%	18.5	88.00%	96.50%
14.5	88.00%	93.50%	19	88.00%	96.00%
15	88.50%	92.00%	19.5	88.00%	96.00%
15.5	88.00%	94.50%	20	88.00%	96.00%
16	88.50%	93.50%			

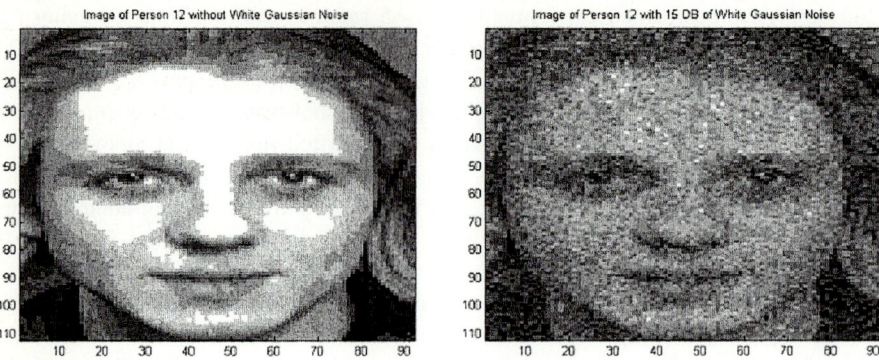

Fig. 4. Images of Person 12. (Left) Original image. (Right) Image with 15dB of Additive White Gaussian Noise (AWGN).

8 Conclusion

This paper shows a novel approach of representing facial images using the Fourier-Magnitude spectra. By performing PCA and Fisherfaces using the Fourier-Magnitude Spectra (Eigen and Fisher-Fourier Magnitudes), we can achieve significantly higher face recognition accuracy than using their traditional spatial counterparts. Furthermore we show both analytically and through experimentation that our approach is *shift-invariant*. This is in contrast to the traditional spatial approach in which any small registration errors of the test input images significantly degrade the performance. We also show that our approach is particularly good for handling pose variations and our results also indicate tolerance in the presence of significant noise levels. Future work includes extending the use of Fourier Magnitude Spectra to other classification methods including Kernel based PCA, LDA variants, and Support Vector Machines.

Acknowledgements

This research is sponsored in part by Carnegie Mellon University's CyLab.

References

1. R. Chellappa, C. L. Wilson, and S. Sirohey, "Human and machine recognition of faces: a survey," *Proceedings of the IEEE*, vol. 83, pp. 705-741, 1995.
2. M. A. Turk and A. P. Pentland, "Face recognition using eigenfaces," Computer Vision and Pattern Recognition, 1991.
3. T. Chen, Y. J. Hsu, X. Liu, and W. Zhang, "Principle component analysis and its variants for biometrics," presented at Image Processing. 2002. Proceedings. 2002 International Conference on, 2002.

4. P. N. Belhumeur, J. P. Hespanha, and D. J. Kriegman, "Eigenfaces vs. Fisherfaces: recognition using class specific linear projection," *IEEE Transactions on Pattern Analysis and Machine Intelligence,*, vol. 19, pp. 711-720, 1997.
5. P. E. Hart, R.O. Duda, and D.G. Stork, *Pattern Classification (2nd Edition)*.
6. Marios Savvides, B. V. K. Vijaya Kumar, P.K.Khosla, "Eigenphases vs. Eigenfaces," International Conference in Pattern Recognition(ICPR), Cambridge, U.K., 2004.
7. Jian Yang; Zhang, D.; Frangi, A.F.; Jing-yu Yang, "Two-dimensional PCA: a new approach to appearance-based face representation and recognition" Pattern Analysis and Machine Intelligence, IEEE Transactions on Volume 26, Issue 1, Jan 2004 Page(s):131 – 137
8. Phiasai, T.; Arunrungrusmi, S.; Chamnongthai, K., "Face recognition system with PCA and moment invariant method," Circuits and Systems, 2001. ISCAS 2001. The 2001 IEEE International Symposium on Volume 2, 6-9 May 2001 Page(s):165 - 168 vol. 2
9. Rizk, M.R.M.; Taha, A., "Analysis of neural networks for face recognition systems with feature extraction to develop an eye localization based method," Electronics, Circuits and Systems, 2002. 9th International Conference on Volume 3, 15-18 Sept. 2002 Page(s):847 - 850 vol.3
10. O. Ayinde and Y. Yang. "Face recognition approach based on rank correlation of gabor-filtered images." *Pattern Recognition*, 35(6):1275–1289, 2002.

Q-Gram Statistics Descriptor in 3D Shape Classification

Evgeny Ivanko and Denis Perevalov

Institute of Mathematics and Mechanics Ural Branch Russian Academy of Sciences,
16, S.Kovalevskaja street, 620219, Ekaterinburg GSP-384, Russia
ivanko@ural.ru, denis.perevalov@mail.ru
http://www.isg.uran.ru

Abstract. In this article we propose simple descriptor for the purposes of 3D objects recognition and classification. Princeton Shape Benchmark 2004 is used for testing the proposed descriptor. Small size (512b) of the proposed descriptor and short generation and comparison times combine with relatively high recognition abilities. Surprisingly, we found that despite its simplicity and the small size the proposed descriptor took the first place in "coarser" classification test, where all 3D models were divided into 6 large classes: buildings, household, plants, animals, furniture, vehicles and a miscellaneous class not included in averaged retrieval results.

1 Q-Gram Shape Descriptor

The development of information technologies and 3D shape scanning techniques leads to the growth of 3D object databases. Large volumes of various 3D data require advanced algorithms of the shape recognition and automated classification. In comparison with the image recognition, shape recognition is rather young and poorly known. A three dimensional object often does not allow applying of two dimensional approach due to a high time complexity and difficulties with a suitable 3D object description. Thus the construction of a small, but an informative shape descriptor is one of the basic tasks in many areas of the shape recognition and automated classification. In this paper we continue to investigate 3D descriptors, started in [5,6], and propose a simple descriptor for the automated classification of 3D shapes. Princeton Shape Benchmark 2004 [12] showed that in spite of the small size of the proposed descriptor and the small time needed to generate and compare the descriptors, the precision of the automated classification is relatively high.

There are two main approaches to the representation of 3D shapes: polygonal and voxel. The proposed shape descriptor and comparison procedure deal with binary voxel representation. So before constructing the descriptor we convert polygonal models to the binary voxel representation in the voxel lattice of fixed size $N \times N \times N$ (the lattice is called *voxel cube*).

The conversion process consists of 3 stages including normalization and filling the inner area. Firstly, the polygonal model is normalized for rotation by aligning its principal axes to the $x-$, $y-$, and $z-$axes. The ambiguity between positive and negative axes is resolved by choosing the direction of the axes so that the area of the model on the positive side of the $x-$, $y-$, and $z-$axes is greater than the area on the negative side [3]. Then, the model is normalized for the size by isotropically rescaling it to the maximum size, which fits $N \times N \times N$ voxel cube. The next step is the voxelization, which is similar to the rasterization of the vector pictures into the pixel lattice: every small cube of the lattice contains a voxel only if it is crossed by the polygons of normalized model. Finally we fill in all inner areas in the discrete voxel object using 6-neighbour topology on cubic lattice. Thus in the result we get the solid voxel object inside the voxel cube.

Once the voxel representation is obtained, 3D object descriptor may be constructed as follows. Let's consider binary three-dimensional 2-grams (small cubes $2 \times 2 \times 2$). There are $2^{2 \times 2 \times 2} = 256$ possible two-coloured 3D 2-grams. Let's number possible 2-grams from 1 to 256 and designate i-th 2-gram as Q_i. The descriptor of 3D shape is the vector V in 256-dimensional space, whose i-th coordinate is the number of Q_i 2-grams in the voxel representation of 3D shape. (descriptor V is called *2-GR* below)

In order to count 2-grams as described above we need to browse the obtained voxel object and read for each position (h, j, k) three dimensional 2-gram Q from cube $[h, h+1] \times [j, j+1] \times [k, k+1]$. Usually the most part of 2-grams in the voxel object is completely empty or completely filled. We found that distributions of these two 2-grams are low informative and may be omitted. Such omission often allows to decrease the size of the variables, where V coordinates are stored. So if Q is neither empty nor filled, we get such i that $Q = Q_i$ and increase $V[i]$ by 1.

Time complexity of the construction of the descriptor V from the voxel object is linear in the size of voxel cube $N \times N \times N$. In our experiments we used $N = 32$. Such a lattice contains $(32-1)^3 = 29791$ different positions (h, j, k). It allows to store each coordinate of vector V in 2-byte variable ($29791 < 256 \times 256 = 65536$). There are 256 coordinates. Thus the resulting size of the descriptor V is 512 bytes.

In order to measure the similarity between two 3D objects O_1 and O_2 we measure the similarity between corresponding vectors-descriptors V_{O_1} and V_{O_2}. There are many known measures of the similarity for vectors. In our experiments we used following simple measure:

$$d = \sum_{i=1}^{256} |V_{O_1}[i] - V_{O_2}[i]|. \tag{1}$$

2 Princeton Shape Benchmark 2004

Princeton Shape Benchmark (PSB) appeared in 2004 is one of the most exhaustive benchmarks for 3D shape automated recognition today. It contains a database of 1,814 classified 3D models collected from 293 different Web domains. All models are divided into training and test sets (907 models each). There are 4 main human classifications given to the objects in the database: "The base classification provides the grouping with finest granularity in this experiment.

It contains the 92 classes ... Most classes contain all the objects with a particular function (e.g., microscopes). Yet, there are also cases where objects with the same function are partitioned into different classes based on their forms (e.g., round tables versus rectangular tables). In the alternative classifications, we recursively merge classes to form coarser granularity groups. Specifically, the "Coarse" classification merges objects with similar overall function to form 44 classes, the "Coarser" classification merges groups further to form the 6 classes (buildings, household, plants, animals, furniture, vehicles), plus a miscellaneous class not included in averaged retrieval results. Finally, the "Coarsest" classification merges those classes until just two classes remain: one with man-made objects and the other with naturally occurring objects." [12]

Every studied measure of similarity is used for constructing the distance matrix, which represents the dissimilarity of all pairs of models in the training or test sets of the database. Distance matrix is used as input data for six PSB statistics tools: *"Nearest Neighbor:* the percentage of the closest matches that belong to the same class as the query. This statistic provides an indication of how well a nearest neighbor classifier would perform. Obviously, an ideal score is 100%, and higher scores represent better results [1,12]. *First-Tier and Second-Tier:* the percentage of models in the query's class that appear within the top K matches, where K depends on the size of the query's class. Specifically, for a class with $|C|$ members, $K = |C| - 1$ for the first tier, and $K = 2(|C| - 1)$ for the second tier. The first tier statistic indicates the recall for the smallest K that could possibly include 100% of the models in the query class, while the second tier is a little less stringent (i.e., K is twice as big). These statistics are similar to the "Bulls Eye Percentage Score" ($K = 2|C|$), which has been adopted by the MPEG-7 visual SDs [16]. In all cases, an ideal matching result gives a score of 100%, and higher values indicate better matches [12]. *E-Measure:* a composite measure of the precision and recall for a fixed number of retrieved results [13]. The intuition is that a user of a search engine is more interested in the first page of query results than in later pages. So, this measure considers only the first 32 retrieved models for every query and calculates the precision and recall over those results. The E-Measure is defined as [10,13]: $E = 2/(1/P + 1/R)$. The E-measure is equivalent to subtracting van Rijsbergen's definition of the E-measure from 1. The maximum score is 1.0, and higher values indicate better results. *Discounted Cumulative Gain (DCG):* a statistic that weights correct results near the front of the list more than correct results later in the ranked list under the assumption that a user is less likely to consider elements near the end of the list. Specifically, the ranked list R is converted to a list G, where element G_i has value 1 if element R_i is in the correct class and value 0 otherwise. Discounted cumulative gain is then defined as follows [7]:

$$DCG_1 = G_1; \qquad DCG_i = DCG_{i-1} + \frac{G_i}{lg_2(i)}, \quad if\ i > 1 \qquad (2)$$

This result is then divided by the maximum possible DCG (i.e., that would be achieved if the first C elements were in the correct class, where C is the size of the class) to give the final score:

$$DCG = \frac{DCG_k}{1 + \sum_{j=2}^{|C|} \frac{1}{lg_2(j)}} \qquad (3)$$

where k is the number of models in the database. The entire query result list is incorporated in an intuitive manner by the discounted cumulative gain [10], so we typically use it to summarize results when comparing algorithms." [12]

Given a classification and a distance matrix computed with any shape matching algorithm, a suite of PSB benchmark tools produces statistics and visualizations that facilitate evaluation of the match results. [12]

The 12 shape matching algorithms included in PSB-2004 are all similar in that they proceed in three steps: the first step normalizes the models for differences in scale and possibly translation and rotation; the second step generates a *descriptor* for each model; and the third step computes the distance between every pair of shape descriptors, using their L_2 difference unless otherwise is noted. The differences between the algorithms lie mainly in the details of their shape descriptors: "*D2 Shape Distribution:* a histogram of distances between pairs of points on the surface [11]. *Extended Gaussian Image (EGI):* a spherical function giving the distribution of surface normals [4]. *Complex Extended Gaussian Image (CEGI):* a complex-valued spherical function giving the distribution of normals and associated normal distances of points on the surface [8]. *Shape Histogram (SHELLS):* a histogram of distances from the center of mass to points on the surface [1]. *Shape Histogram (SECTORS):* a spherical function giving the distribution of model area as a function of spherical angle. *Shape Histogram (SECSHEL):* a collection of spherical functions that give the distribution of model area as a function of radius and spherical angle [1]. *Voxel:* a binary rasterization of the model boundary into a voxel grid which is represented by the 32 spherical descriptors representing the intersection of the voxel grid with concentric spherical shells [12]. *Spherical Extent Function (EXT):* a spherical function giving the maximal distance from center of mass as a function of spherical angle [13]. *Radialized Spherical Extent Function (REXT):* a collection of spherical functions giving the maximal distance from center of mass as a function of spherical angle and radius [15]. *Gaussian Euclidean Distance Transform (GEDT):* a 3D function whose value at each point is given by composition of a Gaussian with the Euclidean Distance Transform of the surface. *Spherical Harmonic Descriptor (SHD):* a rotation invariant representation of the GEDT obtained by computing the restriction of the function to concentric spheres and storing the norm of each (harmonic) frequency [9]; *Light Field Descriptor (LFD):* a representation of a model as a collection of images rendered from uniformly sampled positions on a view sphere. The distance between two descriptors is defined as the minimum L1 difference, taken over all rotations and all pairings of vertices on two dodecahedra [2]."

Every model was normalized for size by isotropically rescaling it so that the average distance from points on its surface to the center of mass is 0.5. Then, for all descriptors except D2 and EGI, the model was normalized for translation by moving its center of mass to the origin. Next, for all descriptors except D2, SHELLS, SHD, and LFD, the model was normalized for rotation by aligning its principal axes to the $x-$, $y-$, and $z-$axes. The ambiguity between positive and negative axes was resolved by choosing the direction of the axes so that the area of the model on the positive side of the $x-$, $y-$, and $z-$axes was greater than the area on the negative side [7]. Every spherical descriptor (EGI, CEGI, Sectors, etc.), was computed on a 64×64 spherical grid and then represented by its harmonic coefficient up to order 16. Similarly, every 3D descriptor (e.g., Voxel and GEDT) was computed on a $64 \times 64 \times 64$ axial grid, translated so that the origin is at the point $(32, 32, 32)$, scaled by a factor of 32, and then represented by 32 spherical descriptors representing the intersection of the voxel grid with concentric spherical shells. Values within each shell were scaled by the square-root of the corresponding area and represented by their spherical harmonic coefficients up to order 16. Histograms of distances (D2 and Shells) were stored with 64 bins representing distances in the range $[0, 2]$. All descriptors, except LFD, were scaled to have L_2-norm equal to 1. The LFD comprises 100 images encoded with 35, 8-bit, coefficients to describe Zernike moments and 10, 8-bit, coefficients to represent Fourier descriptors.

For more details about PSB-2004 refer [12].

3 Results

Shape descriptors from [12] and proposed vector descriptor V (called below 2-GR) were used for the construction of the distance matrix that reflects the dissimilarity of all pairs of the models in the training set. Five PSB statistics tools generate five numbers that show the accuracy of the automated classification in relation to one of the four human made classifications.

Table 1. Comparing 2-GR with 12 shape descriptors by PSB statistics utilities, using base classification

Descr. name	Size of descr. (bytes)	Gener. time (sec)	Comp. time (10^{-4} sec)	Nearest Neighbor	First Tier	Second Tier	E-Msr.	DCG
LFD	4700	3.25	13	0.657	0.380	0.487	0.280	0.643
REXT	17416	2.22	2.29	0.602	0.327	0.432	0.254	0.601
SHD	2184	1.69	0.27	0.556	0.309	0.411	0.241	0.584
GEDT	32776	1.69	4.5	0.603	0.313	0.407	0.237	0.584
2-GR	512	0.105	0.035	0.555	0.287	0.391	0.230	0.563
EXT	552	1.17	0.08	0.549	0.286	0.379	0.219	0.562
SECSH.	32776	1.38	4.51	0.546	0.267	0.350	0.209	0.545
VOXEL	32776	1.34	4.5	0.540	0.267	0.353	0.207	0.543
SECT.	552	0.90	0.14	0.504	0.249	0.334	0.198	0.529
CEGI	2056	0.37	0.27	0.420	0.211	0.287	0.170	0.479
EGI	1032	0.41	0.14	0.377	0.197	0.277	0.165	0.472
D2	136	1.12	0.02	0.311	0.158	0.235	0.139	0.434
SHELLS	136	0.66	0.02	0.227	0.111	0.173	0.102	0.386

Table 2. Comparing 2-GR with 12 shape descriptors by PSB statistics utilities, using "coarse" classification

Descriptor name	Nearest Neighbor	First Tier	Second Tier	E-Msr.	DCG
LFD	0.75	0.303	0.419	0.257	0.683
REXT	0.678	0.280	0.393	0.231	0.653
SHD	0.636	0.286	0.397	0.228	0.647
GEDT	0.68	0.265	0.373	0.215	0.641
EXT	0.625	0.24	0.351	0.203	0.624
2-GR	0.568	0.243	0.36	0.196	0.602
VOXEL	0.631	0.232	0.337	0.191	0.612
SECSHELL	0.623	0.228	0.33	0.187	0.61
CEGI	0.561	0.237	0.356	0.19	0.604
SECTORS	0.573	0.218	0.32	0.186	0.603
EGI	0.505	0.226	0.355	0.184	0.598
D2	0.388	0.177	0.281	0.139	0.548
SHELLS	0.303	0.141	0.238	0.108	0.515

Table 3. Comparing 2-GR with 12 shape descriptors by PSB statistics utilities, using "coarser" classification

Descriptor name	Nearest Neighbor	First Tier	Second Tier	E-Msr.	DCG
2-GR	0.723	0.324	0.490	0.15	0.759
LFD	0.781	0.285	0.483	0.147	0.758
REXT	0.724	0.285	0.482	0.14	0.75
GEDT	0.734	0.276	0.475	0.133	0.743
EXT	0.692	0.277	0.474	0.131	0.74
SHD	0.69	0.275	0.468	0.133	0.741
CEGI	0.617	0.301	0.502	0.128	0.739
EGI	0.583	0.297	0.511	0.125	0.737
SECSHELL	0.698	0.269	0.465	0.123	0.735
VOXEL	0.682	0.273	0.461	0.126	0.734
SECTORS	0.668	0.255	0.455	0.121	0.729
D2	0.497	0.248	0.45	0.104	0.71
SHELLS	0.413	0.244	0.445	0.094	0.702

The four tables below represent the results of the comparison of 2-GR with other 12 known shape descriptors. The results in Table 1 that concern the known shape descriptors were taken from [12]. In Tables 2-4 such results were kindly sent to us by Princeton Shape Retrieval and Analysis Group. 2-GR computations were performed on a Windows PC with a Pentium4 CPU running at 1.7 GHz, 1GB of memory and GeForce2 MX200 32Mb video card.

We want to note that 2-GR is a small descriptor (only D2 and SHELLS are the smaller). The generation time of 2-GR descriptor is more than three

Table 4. Comparing 2-GR with 12 shape descriptors by PSB statistics utilities, using "coarsest" classification

Descriptor name	Nearest Neighbor	First Tier	Second Tier	E-Msr.	DCG
EGI	0.892	0.657	0.939	0.101	0.929
CEGI	0.89	0.643	0.921	0.099	0.926
2-GR	0.884	0.595	0.969	0.097	0.912
LFD	0.901	0.581	0.902	0.088	0.905
REXT	0.885	0.577	0.903	0.088	0.904
GEDT	0.894	0.573	0.896	0.085	0.899
VOXEL	0.851	0.571	0.891	0.084	0.899
EXT	0.836	0.569	0.916	0.082	0.897
SECSHELL	0.864	0.572	0.886	0.083	0.899
SHD	0.827	0.579	0.893	0.083	0.897
SECTORS	0.842	0.573	0.899	0.082	0.896
D2	0.696	0.576	0.898	0.074	0.888
SHELLS	0.673	0.577	0.897	0.074	0.889

times less than the smallest generation time (CEGI). Time of comparison is a little bigger than the smallest time (D2, SHELLS). These benefits combine with the high classification accuracy showed in four tests with "base", "coarse", "coarser" and "coarsest" classifications. In all four classifications 2-GR descriptor was among the six descriptors that produced the best results. Surprisingly, we found that despite its simplicity and the small size 2-GR descriptor took the first place in "coarser" classification test, where all 3D models were divided into 6 large classes: buildings, household, plants, animals, furniture, vehicles and a miscellaneous class not included in averaged retrieval results. All the above allows considering 2-GR descriptor as a perspective feature for 3D shape recognition.

Acknowledgements. We want to thank Phil Shilane, the member of Princeton Shape Retrieval and Analysis Group, for his support with PSB-2004. We also want to thank Institute of Mathematics and Mechanics and especially Yurij I. Kuzyakin, Ural Branch, Russian Academy of Sciences for financial support.

References

1. M. Ankerst, G. Kastenmuller, H.-P. Kriegel, and T. Seidl. Nearest neighbor classification in 3D protein databases. In Proc. ISMB, 1999.
2. D.-Y. Chen, M. Ouhyoung, X.-P. Tian, and Y.-T. Shen. On visual similarity based 3D model retrieval. Computer Graphics Forum, pages 223-232, 2003.
3. M. Elad, A. Tal, and S. Ar. Content based retrieval of VRML objects - an iterative and interactive approach. In 6th Eurographics Workshop on Multimedia 2001, 2001
4. B. Horn. Extended Gaussian images. Proc. of the IEEE, 72(12):1671-1686, December 1984.
5. E. Ivanko, D. Perevalov, B. Wilson. Provisional Patent Application 60/585738, USA, 2004.

6. Ivanko E., Perevalov D. On Using Sign Method For 3D Images Recognition And Classification // International Conference on Computing, Communications and Control Technologies: CCCT'04, Austin, Texas USA. 2004. - Volume V, P.248-251
7. K. Jarvelin and J. Kekalainen. IR evaluation methods for retrieving highly relevant documents. In 23rd Annual International ACMSIGIR Conference on Research and Development in Information Retrieval, 2000.
8. S. Kang and K. Ikeuchi. Determining 3-D object pose using the complex extended Gaussian image. In CVPR, pages 580-585, June 1991.
9. M. Kazhdan, T. Funkhouser, and S. Rusinkiewicz. Rotation invariant spherical harmonic representation of 3D shape descriptors. In Symposium on Geometry Processing, June 2003.
10. G. Leifman, S. Katz, A. Tal, and R. Meir. Signatures of 3D models for retrieval. pages 159-163, February 2003.
11. R. Osada, T. Funkhouser, B. Chazelle, and D. Dobkin. Matching 3D models with shape distributions. Shape Modeling International, pages 154-166, May 2001.
12. Princeton Shape Benchmark (2004), http://shape.cs.princeton.edu/benchmark
13. C. K. van Rijsbergen. Information Retrieval. Butterworths, 1975.
14. D. Saupe and D. V. Vranic. 3D model retrieval with spherical harmonics and moments. In B. Radig and S. Florczyk, editors, DAGM 2001, pages 392-397, September 2001.
15. D. V. Vranic. An improvement of rotation invariant 3D shape descriptor based on functions on concentric spheres. In IEEE International Conference on Image Processing (ICIP 2003), volume 3, pages 757-760, September 2003.
16. T. Zaharia and F. Preteux. 3D shape-based retrieval within the MPEG-7 framework. In SPIE Conf. on Nonlinear Image Processing and Pattern Analysis XII, volume 4304, pages 133-145, January 2001.

A New Inpainting Method for Highlights Elimination by Colour Morphology

Francisco Ortiz and Fernando Torres

Automatics, Robotics and Computer Vision Group Dept. Physics,
Systems Engineering and Signal Theory. University of Alicante,
P.O. Box 99, 03080 Alicante, Spain
{fortiz, Fernando.torres}@ua.es

Abstract. In this paper, we present a new application of the mathematical morphology: a single-image approach for the automatic detection and elimination of highlights in colour images. We use a 2D-histogram that allows us to relate the achromatic and saturation signals of a colour image and to identify interior brightness. To eliminate the highlights detected, we use an image-inpainting method, by means of connected vectorial filters of the mathematical morphology. This new filter operates exclusively on bright zones, reducing the high cost of processing the connected filters and avoiding over-simplification. The new method proposed here achieves good results, which are similar to those obtained from other multimedia techniques, yet does not require either costly multiple-view systems or stereo images.

1 Introduction

In visual systems, images are acquired in work environments in which illumination plays an important role. Sometimes, a bad adjustment of the illumination can introduce highlights (brightness or specular reflectance) into the objects captured by the vision system. Highlights in images have long been disruptive to computer-vision algorithms. The presence of such brightness alters the pattern recognition process because the previous stage of detection of edges in the objects fails: in a morphological watershed, the highlights and specular reflectances are considered as different objects in the environment in which they are located and therefore it is not possible to perfectly detect the objects in the scene.

To effectively eliminate the highlights in captured scenes, we must first identify them. The dichromatic reflection model, proposed by Shafer [1], is one tool that has been used in many methods for detecting specularities. It supposes that the interaction between the light and any dielectric material produces different spectral distributions within the object (specular and diffuse reflectance). The specular reflectance has the same spectral makeup as the incident light, whereas, the diffused component is a product of illumination and surface pigments. Based on this model, Lin *et al* [2] have developed a system for eliminating specularities in image sequences by means of stereo correspondence. Bajcsy *et al* [3] use a chromatic space based on polar coordinates that allows the detection of specular and diffuse reflections by means of the previous knowledge of the captured scene. Klinker *et al* [4] employ a pixel-clustering algorithm that has been shown to work well in detecting brightness in images of plastic objects.

Wolff [5], for his part, removes highlights by taking advantage of differences in polarization between diffuse reflections and highlights. These above-mentioned approaches have produced good results but entail requirements that limit their applicability, such as the use of stereo or multiple-view systems, a long processing time, the previous knowledge of the scene, or the assumption of a homogeneous illumination. Furthermore, some techniques merely detect brightness without eliminating it.

In this paper, we explain a new application of the mathematical morphology, an automatic and single-image system for the detection and elimination of brightness in colour images. The organisation of this paper is as follows: In Section 2, we present the extension of the geodesic operations to colour images. Section 3 shows the algorithm used for detecting highlights. The elimination process and our experimental results are presented in Section 4. Finally, our conclusions are outlined in the final section.

2 Vector Connected Filters in HSV Colour Space

Morphological filters by reconstruction have the property of suppressing details while preserving the contours of the remaining objects [6,7]. The use of such filters in colour images requires an ordered relationship among the pixels of the image. For the vectorial morphological processing, the HSV colour space with a lexicographical ordering $o_{lex}=v{\rightarrow}s{\rightarrow}h$ [8], will be used.

Once the orders have been defined, the morphological operators for the reconstruction of colour images can be applied. Geodesic dilation is an elementary geodesic operation. Let g denote a marker colour image and f a mask colour image (if $o_{lex}(g) \leq o_{lex}(f)$, then $g \wedge_v f = g$). The vectorial geodesic dilation of size 1 of the marker image g with respect to the mask f can therefore be defined as:

$$\delta_{vf}^{(1)}(g) = \delta_v^{(1)}(g) \wedge_v f \qquad (1)$$

where $\delta_v^{(1)}(g)$ is the vectorial dilation of size 1 of the marker image g. This propagation is limited by the colour mask f. The vectorial geodesic dilation of size n of a marker colour image g with respect to a mask colour image f is obtained by performing n successive geodesic dilations of g with respect to f:

$$\delta_{vf}^{(n)}(g) = \delta_{vf}^{(1)}\left[\delta_{vf}^{(n-1)}(g)\right] \qquad (2)$$

with $\delta_{vf}^{(0)}(g) = f$.

Geodesic transformations of images always converge after a finite number of iterations. The propagation of the marker image is limited by the mask image. Morphological reconstruction of a mask image is based on this principle. The vectorial reconstruction by dilation of a mask colour image f from a marker colour image g, (both with $D_f = D_g$ and $o_{lex}(g) \leq o_{lex}(f)$) can be defined as:

$$R_{vf}(g) = \delta_{vf}^{(n)}(g) \tag{3}$$

where n is such that $\delta_{vf}^{(n)}(g) = \delta_{vf}^{(n+1)}(g)$.

3 Highlight Detection by HSV Colour Space

It is known that the specularities in the chromatic image have a high value (achromatic signal) and a low saturation in the HSV colour model. Androutsos *et al* in [9] make a division of the luminance-saturation space (HLS) and they conclude that if the saturation is greater than a 20% and the luminance is greater than a 75%, the pixels are chromatic, while if the saturation is lower than a 20% and the luminance is greater than 75%, the pixels are very luminous or highlights. Our criterion is similar and it is based, initially, on the division of the value-saturation space in different homogenous regions that segment the chromatic image.

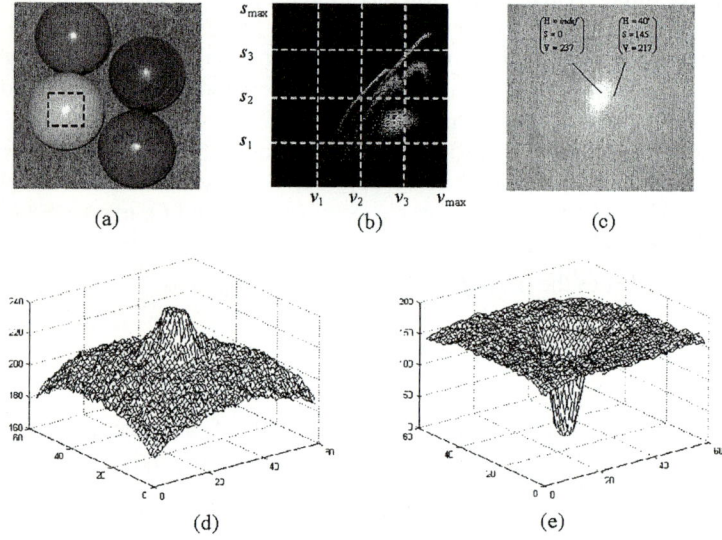

Fig. 1. Identification of highlights in colour image by co-ordinates of VS diagram. (a) Original colour image. (b) Grouping of co-ordinates in VS diagram, $s_1=(1/4)s_{max}$, $s_2=(1/2)s_{max}$, $s_3=(3/4)s_{max}$, $s_{max}=255$, $v_1=(1/4)v_{max}$, $v_2=(1/2)v_{max}$, $v_3=(3/4)v_{max}$, $v_{max}=255$, (c) Highlights in a zone of original colour image. (d) 3D map of value signal in highlighted area. (e) 3D map of saturation signal in highlighted area.

The hue signal is not used because it is very unstable. The co-ordinates [(v_3-v_{max}),(0-s_1)] of the VS diagram (Figure 1.b) define the exact limits of the region in which the highlights of a contrasted colour image (Fig.1.a) are present. Different co-ordinates within this region will identify from the highest or strong specular reflection (central sparkle of brightness) to even soft inter-reflections, which generally represent the transition from specular reflectance to diffuse reflectance. Figure 1.c shows a data transition (in HSV co-ordinates) for a bright area (yellow balloon) of the original image. The great v and smaller s of highlighted area can be seen in Figures 1.d and 1.e.

All the highlights will be located in [(v_3-v_{max}),(0-s_1)] region of the VS diagram, but not all of the co-ordinates in that area will correspond to specularities. The achromatic axes zone could be considered to be a highlight. This is partly true, as it only occurs in grey-scale images. In the HSV colour space, if value v decreases, the brightness has a similar surface colour (diffuse reflection) as the objects on which such highlight appears and the saturation s is increased.

Another important aspect to be taken into consideration is that not all of the images will have the same dynamic range and, therefore, the signals of value v and saturation s of highlights will not always correspond to the region [(v_3-v_{max}),(0-s_1)] of the VS diagram, previously presented. In addition, what happens in the case of colored light sources (incandescent lamps, A, C)? A new contrast enhancement is the solution.

3.1 Contrast Enhancement by Colour Morphology

The previous problems of highlights localization could be solved with a contrast enhancement by histogram equalisation. Nevertheless, the histogram equalisation of the original image is only feasible in the achromatic signal. Furthermore, this operation might well cause an excessive increase in value v, an over-saturation and a false detection of brightness.

The best solution is to apply a new vector-morphological contrast enhancement for luminous pixels, which operates in chromatic images by means of a previously established lexicographical order $o_{lex}=v \rightarrow s \rightarrow h$. Specifically, the vector top-hat operator is added to the original image to enhance bright objects [10]. We denote the colour-morphological contrast enhancement by:

$$f' = f + WTH_v(f) \tag{4}$$

where f is the new contrasted colour image and $WTH_v(f)$ is the vectorial top-hat by opening, which is made with a structuring element of size t. The top-hat is defined as follows:

$$WTH_v(f) = f - \gamma_v(f) \tag{5}$$

The contrast enhancement achieved with this new operator is visually very good. Furthermore, the operation expels the highlights to the limits of the RGB cube. In the HSV colour space, the specular reflectance is located in the co-ordinate v_{max} with minimum saturation. As such, all of the specularities are identified along this value, from $s=0$ to a threshold of s, which we shall denominate by s_{sp}, such that $s_{sp}<s_1$. In our investigation, after a process of morphological contrast enhancement, we have

observed that the v and s signals of the original image have been altered, approaching the axis v_{max}, with the movement flow shown in Figure 2. Such transitions depend on relationship between the sizes of the highlighted area (b) and the structuring element (t) employed in the vectorial operation of top-hat. When $b \leq t$, all of the highlights (strong or weak) are located in the v_{max} line for any kind of image. In all other cases ($b > t$), the weaker highlights will be located outside of this co-ordinate, as can be seen in the graph. In Figure 3 we show the difference between the contrast enhancement by histogram equalization and the new morphological contrast operator that does not excessively increase the intensity of the image and it is effective in the regions of mild specularities.

The detection of weak specularities stops in all of the images at a threshold of s, smaller than s_1, (concretely, $s=(1/4)s_1$). We can thus fix the specularities at $[v_{max}, (0-s_{sp})]$, where $v_{max}=255$ and $s_{sp}=(1/4)s_1$ or 16. This is similar to the success of detection of specularities presented in [11] with other polar colour space.

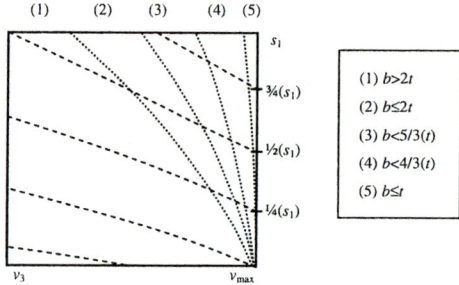

Fig. 2. Movement flow for value v and saturation s in the $[(v_3-v_{max}),(0-s_1)]$ area of the VS diagram after the new morphological contrast enhancement. All of the highlights are located in the v_{max} line $[v_{max}, 0]$ if highlighted area (b) is smaller than the structuring element (t).

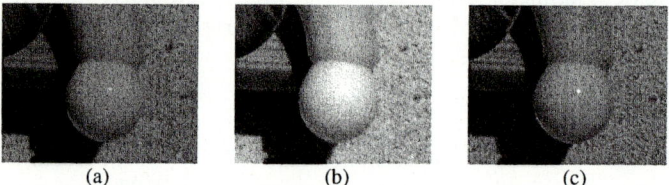

Fig. 3. Contrast enhancement of color image. (a) Chromatic real scene. (b) Contrast enhancement by histogram equalization. (c) Contrast enhancement by top-hat contrast operator.

4 Highlight Elimination by Inpainting Process

Digital inpainting, the technique of reconstructing small damaged portions of an image, has received considerable attention in recent years. This technique has a wide range of applications, including the removal of text, defects or scratches from images. Inpainting methods are based on different strategies. Bertalmio *et al* [12] pioneered a digital image-inpainting algorithm based on partial differential equations (PDEs). Tan et al [13] presented a new single-image highlight removal that incorporates illumination-based constraints into image inpainting. In this paper, we present an inpainting process that is based on colour mathematical morphology, as a traditional inpainting which propagates boundary values.

To eliminate the highlight that was previously detected with the VS diagram, we propose the use of geodesic filters of mathematical morphology. Specifically, a vectorial opening by reconstruction applied exclusively to the specular areas of the image and their surroundings. In this case, a new mask-image $h(x,y)$ represents the pixels of f with which we will be operating. The mask-image h is a dilation of size (e) of the mask of specularities (pixels with $(v,s) \in [v_{max}, (0-s_{sp})]$). Assuming that $D_h = D_f$, each pixel (x,y) has a value of $h(x,y) = \{0,1\}$, where $h(x,y)=1$ in the new areas of interest in the image. The size e of the structural element of the dilation will determine the success of the reconstruction and the final cost of the operations, since this size defines the area to be processed by the filters. In all the cases, the relation $b \leq t \leq e$ must to be satisfied.

In the geodesic filter, f is first eroded. The eroded sets are then used for a reconstruction of the original image. The new filter is then defined, taking into account the fact that, in this case, the operation will not affect all the pixels (x,y), but only those in which $h(x,y)=1$:

$$\gamma_{v\,f,h}^{(n')} = \left\{ \delta_{v\,f}^{(n')}(\varepsilon_v^{(e)}(f)) \mid \forall f(x,y) \Rightarrow h(x,y)=1 \right\} \quad (6)$$

where n' is such that $\delta_{v\,f}^{(n')}(\varepsilon_v^{(e)}(f)) = \delta_{v\,f}^{(n'+1)}(\varepsilon_v^{(e)}(f))$. The vectorial erosion of the opening by reconstruction is also done with a structural element of size e. This erosion replaces highlight pixels (high o_{lex}) by the surroundings chromatic pixels (low o_{lex}). The vectorial geodesic dilation (iterated until stability is achieved) then reconstructs the colour image without recovering the specularities, as it were demonstrated in [14]. This is the same approach successfully used for the attenuation of the colour objects in medical images [8], the gaussian noise reduction [15] or the filling the holes [16]

The study is carried out on a set of real chromatic images that are quite representative of countless common materials (i.e., plastic, ceramics, fruit, wood, etc.). In Figure 4 we present the results obtained from the application of our geodesic filter in a representative subset of different real scenes. With the new filter, we avoid some of the main inconveniences that arise in geodesic reconstruction: i.e., the high cost of processing due to multiple iterations of the reconstruction and the over-simplification of the image [17].

The size e of the structuring element for morphological operations in highlight elimination depends on: the sizes b and t of the first step of the algorithm, posterior applications and real-time requirements. A low e (1,2) is recommended for visual inspection and a high e (6,7…) is better for multimedia and image restoration. The new pixel codification of the original highlight is obtained by vectorial inpainting process with the use of our geodesic filter.

Fig. 4. Vectorial inpainting by geodesic filter for highlight removal in original colour images. Over-simplification is not present in the results. (a-b) "Balloons", (c-d) "Tomatoes", (e-f) "Vases", (g-h) "Umbrella".

The reduction of the value signal v and the recuperation of saturation s in a detailed area of specular reflectante of "Balloons" image (Figure 1.c) it is quite significant; the indefinite hue for strong highlight also disappears, as can be seen in Figure 5.

Our new method achieves a reduction in total time cost, for all of the images, of between 50% and 70%, with respect to a global filter. The cost of our inpainting is linear in relation to the size of the structuring element (e) and iterations (n') of the morphological operations.

In comparison to other non-morphological inpainting methods, and specifically the one presented by Bertalmio *et al* [12], our method achieves similar visual results in a

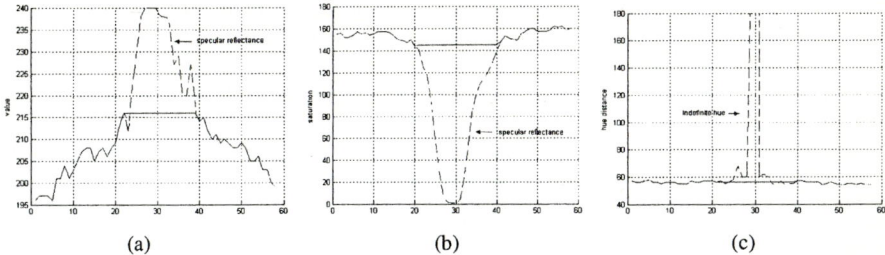

Fig. 5. 2D-maps of inpainting for removing the specular reflectance in highlight area of "Balloons", ($e=7$, $t=7$, $b=5$). Substitution of: value signal (a), saturation signal (b) and hue (c).

shorter CPU time (1 or 2 seconds versus a few minutes for a relatively small inpainting area). An illumination-constrained method presented by Tan *et al* [13] can lead a more accurate results in inpainting. In addition, the surface textures obscured by highlights are better recovered. Nevertheless, this method requires significant computation.

It should also be noted that our algorithm eliminates the highlight area, and it detects the highlight as well. As in the case of many inpainting methods, the only limitation to this technique is the reconstruction of highly textured areas.

5 Conclusions

In this paper, we have presented a new method for the elimination of highlights in colour images for different applications, such as visual inspection, multimedia or restoration.

The use of a new connected vectorial filter allows us to eliminate the specular reflectance previously detected by means an inpainting process. The inpainting is made by an extension of the geodesic transformations of the mathematical morphology to colour images in HSV colour space. The possibility of eliminating highlights in colour images without causing over-simplification has been demonstrated. In addition, the elimination of brightness has been achieved within a very short processing time with respect to a global geodesic reconstruction or other inpainting techniques.

Based on the success shown by these results, we are now working on an improvement of our method for eliminating specularities in real-time environments: we work in multi-processor configurations for colour geodesic operations in order to reduce the processing time required for these operations as much as possible.

References

1. Shafer, S.A.: Using color to separate reflection components. Color Research Appl. Vol. 10 (1985) 210-218
2. Lin, S. Li, Y., Kang, S., Tong, X., Shum, H.: Diffuse-Specular Separation and Depth Recovery from Image Sequences. Lecture Notes in Computer Science, Springer-Verlag. Vol. 2352 (2002)

3. Bajcsy, R., Lee, S., Leonardis, A.: Detection of diffuse and specular interface reflections and inter-reflections by color image segmentation. International Journal on Computer Vision. Vol. 17 (1996) 241-271
4. Klinker, G., Shafer, S.A., kanade, T.: Image segmentation and reflection analysis through color. In: Proc. SPIE. Vol. 937 (1988) 229-244
5. Wolff, L.: Using polarization to separate refelction components. In: Proc. IEEE Computer Vision and Pattern Recognition (1989) 363-369
6. Vicent, L.: Morphological Grayscale Reconstruction in Image Analysis: Applications and Efficient Algoritms. IEEE Transactions on Image Processing. Vol. 2. (1993) 176-201
7. Crespo, J. Serra, J., Schafer, R.: Theoretical aspects of morphological filters by reconstruction. Signal Processing. Vol. 47 (1995) 201-225
8. Ortiz, F., Torres, F., De Juan, E., Cuenca, N.: Colour mathematical morphology for neural image analysis. Journal of Real Time Imaging. Vol. 8, i.6 (2002) 455-465
9. Androutsos, D., Plataniotis, K., Venetsanopoulos, A.: A novel vector-based approach to color image retrieval using a vector angular-based distance measure. Computer Vision and Image Understanding, Vol. 75 (1999)
10. Soille, P. A note on morphological contrast enhancement. Technical Report RT-PS-001. École des Mines d'Alès-EERIE (1997)
11. Torres, F., Angulo, J., Ortiz, F.: Automatic detection of specular reflectance in colour images using the MS diagram. Lecture Notes in Computer Science, Springer-Verlag. Vol. 2756 (2003) 132-139
12. Bertalmio, M., Sapiro, G., Caselles V., Ballester, C.: Image Inpainting. In: International Conference on Computer Graphics and Interactive Techniques (2000) 417-424
13. Tan, P., Lin, S., Quon, L., Shum, H.Y.: Highlight removal by illumination-constrained inpainting. In: Proc. of IEEE International Conference on Computer Vision (2003)
14. Ortiz, F., Torres, F.: Vectorial morphological reconstruction for brightness elimination in colour images. Journal of Real Time Imaging. Vol. 8, i.6 (2004) 379-387
15. Ortiz F., Torres F., Gil P.: Gaussian noise elimination in colour images by vector-connected filters. In: Proc. IEEE 17th International Conference on Pattern Recognition. Vol. 4 (2004) 807-811
16. Soille, P., Gratin, C.: An efficient algorithm for drainage networks extraction on DEMs. In: Journal of Visual Communication and Image Representation. Vol. 5, i.2 (1994) 181-189
17. Ortiz, F.: Procesamiento morfológico de imágenes en color. Aplicación a la reconstrucción geodésica. PhD Thesis, University of Alicante (2002)

Clustering of Objects in 3D Electron Tomography Reconstructions of Protein Solutions Based on Shape Measurements

Magnus Gedda

Centre for Image Analysis, Uppsala University, Uppsala, Sweden
magnus.gedda@cb.uu.se

Abstract. This paper evaluates whether shape features can be used for clustering objects in Sidec™ Electron Tomography (SET) reconstructions. SET reconstructions contain a large number of objects, and only a few of them are of interest. It is desired to limit the analysis to contain as few uninteresting objects as possible. Unsupervised hierarchical clustering is used to group objects into classes. Experiments are done on one synthetic data set and two data sets from a SET reconstruction of a human growth hormone (1hwg) in solution. The experiments indicate that clustering of objects in SET reconstructions based on shape features is useful for finding structural classes.

1 Originality and Contribution

Volume images of protein solutions are produced by electron tomography reconstructions. These each contain a large number of objects where only a few are of interest. High resolution volume images of this kind are relatively unexplored and no automatic or semi-automatic classification techniques of the objects have previously been examined. The objective is to use clustering on the reconstructions to group all objects representing the protein of interest into one cluster. All clusters containing uninteresting objects can then be avoided and thereby speed up the analysis considerably. This paper is an initial evaluation of whether shape features can be used for clustering objects in this type of volume images.

2 Introduction

Sidec™ Technologies AB produce and analyse three dimensional (3D) images of proteins. They use electron microscopy and a refinement method called constrained maximum entropy tomography (COMET) [1] to create digital representations of density volumes, and their technique is called Sidec™ Electron Tomography (SET). The reconstructed density volumes are examined visually to gain structural information about the proteins of interest in the sample [2,3]. The samples examined at Sidec are proteins in solution [2] or in tissue [3]. In this paper only reconstructions of proteins in solution are considered. The reconstruction results are 3D visualisations of individual molecules of interest at

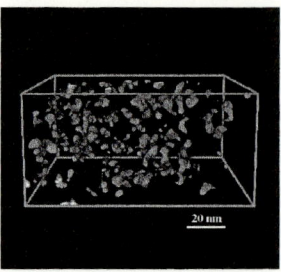 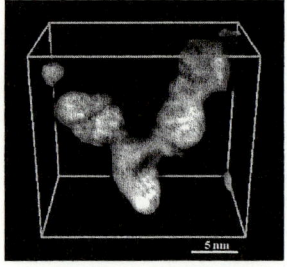

Fig. 1. Left: SET reconstruction. Right: Molecule extracted from SET reconstruction.

a resolution of approximately $2\,nm$ (see Fig. 1). Each reconstruction produces a large number of objects, of which only a few are of interest. The majority of objects are artefacts from the reconstruction method or uninteresting objects present in the solution. Since the procedure for examening each object includes several steps and is time consuming, much of the analysis work is wasted on uninteresting data. Hence, it is desirable to have as few uninteresting objects as possible in the analysis without loosing any of the interesting objects.

Three experiments were carried out to test whether hierarchical clustering [4] with shape features is a feasible method to distinguish the proteins of interest, or at least reduce the number of objects needing visual examination. The first experiment was made on volume images created from the Protein Data Bank (PDB) [5] to examine whether the features work on synthetic volume objects with sizes similar to objects of interest in SET reconstructions. The second experiment was made on large objects from a SET reconstruction to examine whether the features work on real data. The last experiment was made on objects from a SET reconstruction, where each volume corresponded to the volume of a rather small protein of interest.

3 Method

To classify the objects in SET volume reconstructions unsupervised hierarchical clustering was used. Unsupervised techniques are the only option in this case since we do not know which, or how many, classes exist in the volume. This means that all minimisation of criteria functions (direct loss minimisation), such as k-means [4], are ruled out. They need a hint for each class as a prerequisite, and we cannot create a hint for each class if we do not know how many classes are present in the volume. Using qualified guesses and estimating the validity of the result introduces informed interaction and is hence not a good option. Neural networks [4] are also ruled out since collecting and labelling a large set of sample patterns for training is too costly and would most likely perform poorly due to all the noise and randomness in a reconstruction. All statistical classifiers, such as maximum-likelihood [6], are also ruled out due to the shortage of a priori information. There is no information about the probability distributions involved, and there is no information about which, or how many, classes we can expect to find in the density volume. We cannot use any form of probability density estimation or parametric learning [6] since not even the distribution types of the classes involved are known. This only leaves the option to use a cluster analysis technique [4].

Hierarchical clustering groups the objects based on a similarity measure derived from a number of feature measures of the objects. Initially each object is registered to a separate class. In each step the two most similar classes are merged into one class, and the clustering is complete when all objects belong to the same class. Similarity is measured in distance defined by a specific distance metric. The most similar classes are then the classes closest to each other in feature space. In this paper the mean metric [4] was used when calculating the class to class distance,

$$d_{\text{mean}}(D_i, D_j) = ||\boldsymbol{\mu}_i - \boldsymbol{\mu}_j||, \qquad (1)$$

where D_i and D_j are cluster i and j, and $\boldsymbol{\mu}_i$ and $\boldsymbol{\mu}_j$ are their mean vectors respectively. A mean vector is obtained by adding up all the feature vectors of a cluster and dividing by the number of objects in the cluster. Hierarchical clustering can use a dendrogram to illustrate the result of the classification (see Fig. 2). With a dendrogram we can follow the classification with respect to the similarity measure. At each point on the similarity scale, the corresponding classification can be read from the diagram. A long distance without any change in the dendrogram implies a natural grouping, and this can be used to guess the number of classes. The dendrogram is also useful to reveal subclusters since these are the first to become merged.

Selecting the measurements on which to base each component of the feature vector has a profound influence on the eventual performance of the classification system [6]. The features used in this paper were easily extracted shape measurements (see Table 1) and the focus of this project was to examine whether clustering is feasible on objects from SET reconstructions. All features were normalised by subtracting the mean and dividing by the standard deviation. Features like volume can have a wide range of possible values and will affect the classification to a higher degree than other features that are limited to a very small range of values in comparison. By normalising the features we give all features an equal weight in the classification process.

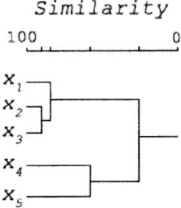

Fig. 2. A dendrogram illustrating hierarchical clustering

Table 1. Object features and dependencies

Feature	Dependence
Volume	Number of nonzero voxels.
Compactness	Number of surface voxels divided by volume.
Length	Extension along the first principal axis.
Width	Extension along the second principal axis.
Thickness	Extension along the third principal axis.
Flatness	Thickness divided by length.

4 Data and Experimental Design

For the first experiment, noise free synthetic protein molecules were created from the proteins' atom positions available in the PDB [5]. From a PDB entry, a volume image, where the grey-levels depict density, can be generated by placing a gauss kernel at each atom position and multiplying by the mass of that atom [7]. The total density in a voxel is then calculated by adding contributions from gauss kernels in the vicinity of the voxel. In these images we used a σ of 1 leading to a resolution of $2\,nm$. The aim of the first experiment was to examine whether it is possible to classify volume objects with shapes and sizes similar to objects segmented from SET reconstructions. 33 volume objects of similar volumes, but with different structures, were created from the PDB and used in the experiment.

In the two other experiments objects from one SET reconstruction containing a protein solution of human growth hormone (1hwg) was used. The reconstruction was segmented into separate objects by grey-level thresholding. The first experiment on the SET data used the 33 largest segmented objects, none of them being the protein of interest. The aim of this experiment was to examine the shape grouping capability of the classifier when working on volume objects from real SET reconstructions.

The second experiment on the SET data used 25 objects of sizes similar to the protein 1hwg. The protein has a molecular weight of approximately $75\,kDa$, and the molecular weights of the classified objects correspond to the interval $[50\,kDa, 100\,kDa]$. In the SET reconstructions we have roughly 9 voxels per kDa, hence, the sizes of the volume objects range approximately from 500 to 1000 voxels.

In all experiments, the clustering procedure was run until six classes remained. This number was chosen arbitrarily.

5 Results and Interpretation

The clusters resulting from experiment number one are shown in Fig. 3. We have a few natural shape characteristics represented, such as spheres, rods and hexagons. Upon visual inspection we see that the classifier has formed classes based on the shape characteristics of the proteins. We see that the clustering

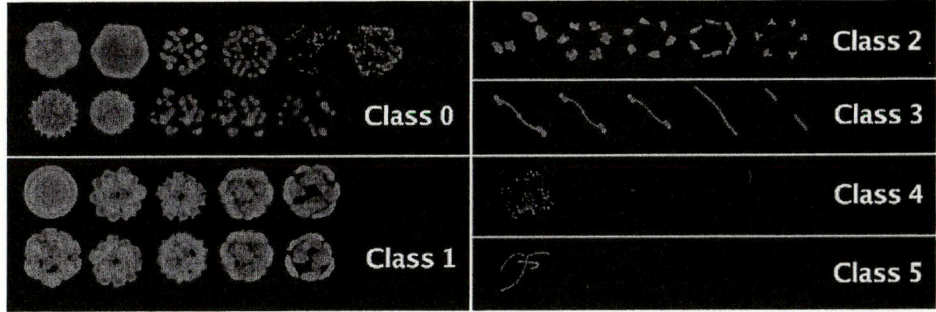

Fig. 3. Clustering result of volume objects reconstructed from the PDB

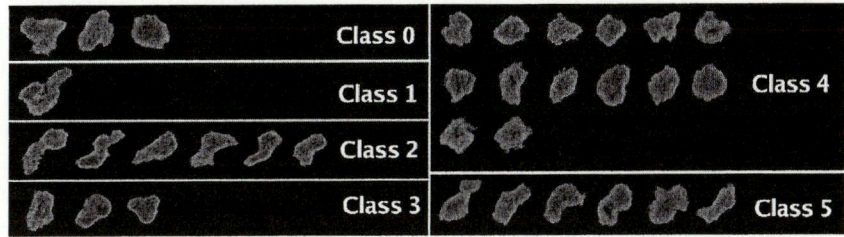

Fig. 4. Clustering result of large SET volumes

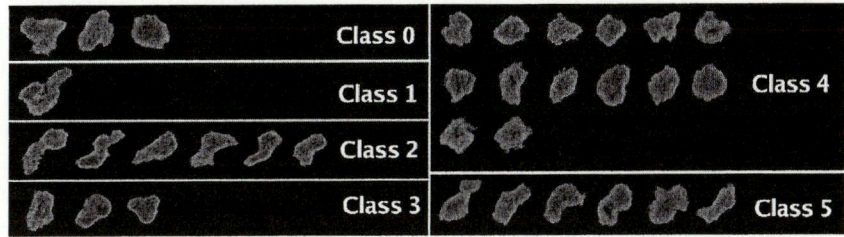

Fig. 5. Clustering result of SET volumes of similar size to 1hwg

works and, hence, that the shape features are sufficient to distinguish the structures in this experiment.

The clusters resulting from experiment number two (see Fig. 4) show that even though it is harder to find natural groupings of those objects than the objects in the first experiment, we still see that there is a similarity between the object structures in each class. Hence, the extracted features seems sufficient to distinguish the structures in this experiment.

In the clusters resulting from experiment number three (see Fig. 5), it is not as easy to distinguish the similarities among the objects in each class as in the previous experiments. According to a scientist working with SET reconstructions from the third experiment, class 1 and class 3 to 5 consist of uninteresting objects. After examining the most probable objects in 3D he concluded that one of the objects in class 0 could very well be a protein of the sought kind, and one object in class 2 most certainly was. From that simple visual evaluation we get an indication that the clustering has worked in the sense that it produced four clusters of uninteresting objects and two clusters containing objects of interest, and the extracted features seemed able to distinguish the structures in this case.

6 Conclusions

The experiments indicate that clustering of volume objects from SET reconstructions is definitely worth further investigation. This initial analysis gives an indication that simple clustering approaches can decrease the workload for those working with analysis of electron tomography reconstructions of protein solutions. This is an important first step towards improved SET reconstruction analysis techniques. The features used in these experiments only represent shape and do not use the density information in the objects. To improve the results more descriptive features, which take the density information into account, are needed. Future work consists of extracting object features from the medial grey-level based representation of proteins presented in [8] and decompositions [9] of objects, and use these along with other, more specialised features. Further investigations also include using the dendrogram to see if it is possible to guess how many classes the reconstructions contain. We also need a robust method for evaluating the experiments. A quantitative and/or statistical analysis is desirable. However, in biological applications it is often hard to define a method for quantitative analysis, and the validation is referred to subjective visual assessments. In this application domain, where we lack objective information, the validation problem becomes even more prominent. To achieve robust methods for evaluation we need SET reconstructions where more a priori information about the contents is available, preferably many reconstructions containing only a single type of protein as well as many reconstructions containing multiple types of proteins. More reconstructions would also enable us to measure the intraobserver variability, and more observers would be desirable for measuring the interobserver variability.

Acknowledgement

Thanks to Sidec^{TM} Technologies AB for providing a development environment and the SET reconstructions.

References

1. Skoglund, U., Öfverstedt, L., Burnett, R., Bricogne, G.: Maximum-entropy three-dimensional reconstruction with deconvolution of the contrast transfer function: a test application with adenovirus. Journal of Structural Biology **117** (1996) 173–188

2. Sandin, S., Öfverstedt, L., Wikström, A., Wrange, O., Skoglund, U.: Structure and flexibility of individual immunoglobulin g molecules in solution. Structure **12** (2004) 409–415
3. Banyay, M., Gilstring, F., Hauzenberger, E., Öfverstedt, L., Eriksson, A., Krupp, J., Larsson, O.: Three-dimensional imaging of in situ specimens with low-dose electron tomography to analyze protein conformation. ASSAY and Drug Development Technologies **2** (2004) 561–567
4. Duda, R.O., Hart, P.E., Stork, D.G.: Pattern Classification. John Wiley & Sons, New York, USA (2001)
5. Bergman, H., Westbrook, J., Feng, Z., Gilliland, G., Bhat, T., Weissig, H., Shindyalova, I., Bourne, P.: The protein data bank. Nucleic Acids Research **28** (2000) 235–242
6. Sonka, M., Hlavac, V., Boyle, R.: Image Processing, Analysis, and Machine Vision. Brooks/Cole Publishing Company, Pacific Grove, California, USA (1999)
7. Pittet, J., Henn, C., Engel, A., Heymann, J.: Visualizing 3D data obtained from microscopy on the internet. Journal of Structural Biology **125** (1999) 123–132
8. Sintorn, I.M., Gedda, M., Mata, S., Svensson, S.: Medial grey-level based representation for proteins in volume images. To appear in Proc. of Iberian Conference on Pattern Recognition and Image Analysis, Estoril, Portugal, Lecture Notes in Computer Science. (2005)
9. Sintorn, I.M., Mata, S.: Using grey-level and shape information for decomposing proteins in 3D images. In: Proceedings 2nd IEEE International Symposium Biomedical Imaging. (2004) 800–803

Improving Tracking by Handling Occlusions

Daniel Rowe, Ignasi Rius, Jordi Gonzàlez, and Juan J. Villanueva

Computer Vision Centre/Department of Computer Science,
Universitat Autònoma de Barcelona,
08193 Bellaterra, Barcelona, Spain
drowe@cvc.uab.es

Abstract. Keeping track of a target by successive detections may not be feasible, whereas it can be accomplished by using tracking techniques. Tracking can be addressed by means of particle filtering. We have developed a new algorithm which aims to deal with some particle-filter related problems while coping with expected difficulties. In this paper, we present a novel approach to handling complete occlusions. We focus also on the target-model update conditions, ensuring proper tracking. The proposal has been successfully tested in sequences involving multiple targets, whose dynamics are highly non-linear, moving over clutter.

1 Introduction

The increasing number of potential image-based applications is causing an important development in monitoring techniques. Many applications perform this task by successive detections, and associating segmented targets between frames. A detection involves scanning the whole image. However, a target cannot be segmented while it is being occluded by other targets, by static scene objects or if it is over clutter. Depending on the detection approach, other problems may also arise: *background subtraction* usually detects holes when an object is removed from its place. In addition, when the target is partially over clutter, the target is often split detected. It also necessitates keeping a background model, which may not be possible if the background is in motion or if the illumination changes suddenly. Other approaches, such as *optical flow*, may present problems in motion backgrounds. *Frame differencing* is very sensitive to noise and introduces holes inside homogeneous regions of the target.

On the other hand, tracking can cope with these issues. Usually, the target's state is predicted according to a learned target's dynamic model and, subsequently, it is corrected in accordance with new measures. However, predicting allows the consideration of other approaches when no evidence can be obtained from the image. In addition, different hypotheses can be considered simultaneously.

This paper focuses on tracking by means of particle filtering. This approach has been explored by several previous algorithms, including *Condensation* [5]. However, most of these algorithms cannot cope with multiple-target tracking and present several misbehaviours inherited from particle filtering, such as *sampling impoverishment* [6]. We have developed an algorithm which aims to deal with sampling impoverishment while tracking multiple targets, whose dynamics are highly non-linear, moving through an environment with complex clutter [9]. On the other hand, the main causes of catastrophic failures are erroneous updating of the appearance model and inappropriate handling of occlusions. In this paper, we present a novel approach to handling complete occlusions while we consider the target-model update conditions to ensure proper tracking despite noisy measures, estimate errors, partial or complete occlusions and changes in illumination conditions or the camera angle.

The remainder of this paper is organized as follows. Section 2 covers the probabilistic framework, reviews *Condensation* and exposes its misbehaviours. Section 3 describes our algorithm while section 4 develops appearance model updating and occlusion handling. Finally, section 5 shows the experimental results and section 6 concludes this paper.

2 Probabilistic Tracking Framework

Since tracking requires reasoning over time under uncertainty, a probabilistic framework is commonly used [10]. The computation of the belief state[1] $\mathbf{S}_t$ given all evidence to date $\mathbf{e}_{1:t}$ is called *filtering*. Under certain assumptions, the posterior pdf $P(\mathbf{S}_t \mid \mathbf{e}_{1:t})$ can be calculated through *recursive estimation*:

$$P(\mathbf{S}_t \mid \mathbf{e}_{1:t}) \propto \underbrace{\underbrace{P(\mathbf{e}_t \mid \mathbf{S}_t)}_{\text{likelihood}}}_{\text{updating}} \underbrace{\int \underbrace{P(\mathbf{S}_t \mid \mathbf{s}_{t-1})}_{\text{trans. model}} \underbrace{p(\mathbf{s}_{t-1} \mid \mathbf{e}_{1:t-1})}_{\text{previous post.}} d\mathbf{s}_{t-1}}_{\text{prediction}}. \tag{1}$$

The pdf is projected forward according to the transition model, making a prediction. Then, it is updated in agreement with the new evidence, $\mathbf{e}_t$. When no assumptions are made with respect to the distributions involved, this problem is overcome by simulating N i.i.d. random samples from the posterior pdf, $\{\mathbf{s}_t^i; i = 1 : N\}$. This approach leads to the so-called *particle filters* [4,1]. Such methods were first introduced in computer vision by Isard and Blake in the form of *Condensation* [5].

The method works as follows: the posterior pdf at time $t-1$ is represented by a weighted set of samples, $\{\hat{\mathbf{s}}_{t-1}^i, \overline{\pi}_{t-1}^i; i = 1 : N\}$. The temporal prior $\{\hat{\mathbf{s}}_t^i\}$ is obtained by applying the transition model $P(\mathbf{S}_t \mid \mathbf{s}_{t-1})$ to each sample. The likelihood $P(\mathbf{e}_t \mid \mathbf{S}_t)$ is represented by weights π_t^i. The set is re-sampled using normalized weights $\overline{\pi}_t^i$ as probabilities. This sample set represents the posterior at time t, $p(\mathbf{s}_t \mid \mathbf{e}_{1:t})$. Expectations can be approximated as:

---

[1] Notation: bold case denotes vectors and matrices whereas non-bold case denotes scalars. Matrices are in uppercase. In a probabilistic context, uppercase denotes probability density functions (pdf) and random variables; lowercase denotes probabilities and variable instances. $\mathbf{X}_{\tau_1:\tau_2}$ denotes a variable set from time $t = \tau_1$ to $t = \tau_2$.

$$\mathbb{E}_{P(\mathbf{S}_t|\mathbf{e}_{1:t})}(\mathbf{S}_t) \simeq \sum_{i=1}^{N} \pi_t^i \hat{\mathbf{s}}_t^i. \qquad (2)$$

Although particle filters have been widely used in recent years, they have important drawbacks [6]. *Sampling impoverishment* is one of the main ones: samples are spread around several *modes* pointing out hypotheses in the state space, but most of them may be spurious. Unfortunately, there is a non-negligible probability of losing modes, a low probability of recovering them and the remaining modes could be all spurious. Therefore, computed expectations in different runs may have high variance although computed expectations within the same algorithm run have low variance making the tracker look stable. In addition, *Condensation* was designed to keep multiple-hypotheses, but only for a single target.

This area being as challenging as it is, a great number of improvements have been introduced in recent years [12,11], but there is still much ground to cover. Different approaches have been taken in order to overcome these issues. Nummiaro et al. [8] use a particle filter based on colour histogram cues. Histograms may, in some cases, be robust to partial occlusions and rotations but no shape analysis is taken into account. Moreover, no multiple-target tracking is considered and complete occlusions are not handled. Comaniciu et al.'s [2] approach relies on gradient-based optimization and colour-based histograms. In this case, no dynamic model is used; therefore, no occlusion can be predicted. Deutscher et al. [3] present an interesting approach called *annealing particle filter* which aims to reduce the required number of samples, even though pruning hypotheses with lower likelihood could be inappropriate in a cluttered environment. They combine edge and intensity measures but they focused on motion analysis, and thus, no occlusion handling is explored. Some effort have been done in contour tracking [7] even though it may be inappropriate, if used as the only cue, in crowded scenarios because of multiple occlusions.

3 An Approach to Robust Tracking

We have proposed an algorithm based on particle filtering [9]. The motion of the central point of a bounding box is modelled using first-order dynamics in image coordinates. The l-labelled target's state is defined as $\mathbf{s}_t^l = \left(\mathbf{x}_t^l, \mathbf{u}_t^l, \mathbf{w}_t^l, \mathbf{A}_t^l\right)^T$, where components are position, speed, bounding-box size and pixel appearance matrix. A label l associates one specific appearance model to the corresponding samples, allowing multiple-target tracking. Evidence $\mathbf{e}_t$ is given by input images $\mathbf{I}_t$.

After the initialization, no sample will be generated using detection algorithms since it would mask tracking misbehaviours. Thus, we will test just tracking performances by means of propagating hypotheses and weighting them according to evidence. The scene is not explored looking for changes or movement and only the pixels within the bounding boxes will be evaluated. Of course, combining this algorithm with detection can do nothing but improve the general performance, providing the system with error-recovery capabilities.

3.1 Transition Model

The position, speed and size of each sample are predicted according to:

$$\hat{\mathbf{x}}_t^{i,l} = \mathbf{x}_{t-1}^{i,l} + \mathbf{u}_{t-1}^{i,l}\Delta_t + \xi_{\mathbf{x}}^i,$$
$$\hat{\mathbf{u}}_t^{i,l} = \mathbf{u}_{t-1}^l + \xi_{\mathbf{u}}^i,$$
$$\hat{\mathbf{w}}_t^{i,l} = \mathbf{w}_{t-1}^{i,l} + \xi_{\mathbf{w}}^i. \qquad (3)$$

The random vectors $\xi_{\mathbf{x}}^i, \xi_{\mathbf{u}}^i, \xi_{\mathbf{w}}^i$ provide the system with a diversity of hypotheses. Sample likelihoods depend on sample position and size, but they do not depend on their speeds. Thus, if speeds were propagated considering the previous speed, they would be in quasi open loop —although there is still a weak relation (since speeds are used to predict positions, and position errors can be measured), a considerable delay is introduced. Thus, their values could become completely different from the true one in a few frames. Targets could be tracked since we are in a multiple-hypothesis scenario, but an important proportion of samples would be wasted. In order to avoid this phenomenon, we feed-back the estimated target speed $\mathbf{u}_{t-1}^l$ at time $t-1$ into the prediction of $\hat{\mathbf{x}}_t^{i,l}$.

3.2 Likelihood Function

The likelihood function gives the pdf of image features given the state. The selected features are pixel-oriented. Thus, the appearance will be given by a matrix whose elements are the pixel intensity values. Given the predicted position $\hat{\mathbf{x}}_t^{i,l}$ and bounding-box size $\hat{\mathbf{w}}_t^{i,l}$, the corresponding image subregion is denoted by $\mathbf{I}_t^p$. The model appearance matrix must be scaled according to the sample size. Let $\mathbf{A}^s$ be the scaled matrix for the model. Considering a smooth process, we assume that the appearance is constant between frames. Assuming also *White Additive Gaussian Noise* (WAGN), the likelihood of every pixel of $\mathbf{I}_t^p$ according to the target's model can be expressed as:

$$\mathcal{N}\left(\mathbf{I}_t^p(a,b); \mathbf{A}_t^s(a,b), \sigma_n^2\right). \qquad (4)$$

We define the following similarity measure as the mean of pixel likelihoods:

$$\frac{1}{M}\sum_{a,b\in\mathbf{A}_t^s}\mathcal{N}\left(\mathbf{I}_t^p(a,b); \mathbf{A}_t^s(a,b), \sigma_n^2\right), \qquad (5)$$

and this value can be used as the sample likelihood:

$$\begin{aligned}P(\mathbf{I}_t\mid\mathbf{S}_t) &= P\left(\mathbf{I}_t\mid\mathbf{x}_t^{i,l},\mathbf{w}_t^{i,l},\mathbf{A}_t^l\right)\\ &= P(\mathbf{I}_t^p\mid\mathbf{A}_t^s)\\ &= \frac{1}{M}\sum_{a,b\in\mathbf{A}_t^s}\mathcal{N}\left(\mathbf{I}_t^p(a,b);\mathbf{A}_t^s(a,b),\sigma_n^2\right),\end{aligned} \qquad (6)$$

where M is the number of pixels of the appearance model, (a,b) defines a pixel in the appearance matrix $\mathbf{A}_t^s$ and σ_n^2 is the estimated camera noise variance. Thus, samples can be weighted according to:

$$\pi_t^{i,l} = p\left(\mathbf{I}_t\mid\hat{\mathbf{s}}_t^{i,l}\right). \qquad (7)$$

3.3 Weight Normalization

As has been stated, samples are spread around several modes, which point out different hypotheses of target states. Two kind of modes can be distinguished: samples can be clustered because they belong to different targets or because they are in the same state-space region. Thus, samples with different labels form different modes, and thereby several targets can be tracked simultaneously; secondly, samples with the same label could be spread around different modes, allowing us to keep several hypotheses for a single target which is over clutter.

Multiple-target tracking causes several problems including the fact that the target with higher likelihood may monopolise the sample set. Those targets whose samples exhibit lower likelihood have higher probability of being lost, since the probability of propagating one mode is proportional to the cumulative weights of its samples. In order to avoid single target modes absorbing other target samples, genetic drift [6] must be prevented. This fact happens due to the lack of *genetic memory*: a memory term, which takes into account the number of targets being tracked, is therefore included. Hence, weights are normalized according to:

$$\bar{\pi}_t^{i,l} = \frac{\pi_t^{i,l}}{\sum_{i=1,j=l}^{N} \pi_t^{i,j}} \frac{1}{L}, \tag{8}$$

where L is the number of targets being tracked. Each weight is normalised according to the total weight of the target's samples. Thus, all targets have the same probability of being propagated, since the addition of the weights of all samples for each target sums $\frac{1}{L}$. This approach allows multiple-target tracking using a single particle filter. All targets can be tracked despite the expected differences between their likelihoods and the genetic drift phenomenon.

3.4 State Estimation

The l-target position and speed are estimated according to:

$$\begin{aligned} \mathbf{x}_t^l &= \left(\mathbf{x}_{t-1}^l + \mathbf{u}_{t-1}^l \Delta_t\right)(1 - \alpha_{\mathbf{x}}) + \left(L \sum_{i=1}^{N} \bar{\pi}_t^{i,l} \hat{\mathbf{x}}_t^{i,l}\right) \alpha_{\mathbf{x}}, \\ \mathbf{u}_t^l &= \mathbf{u}_{t-1}^l (1 - \alpha_{\mathbf{u}}) + \frac{\mathbf{x}_t^l - \mathbf{x}_{t-1}^l}{\Delta_t} \alpha_{\mathbf{u}}, \end{aligned} \tag{9}$$

where $\alpha_{\mathbf{x}}, \alpha_{\mathbf{u}} \in [0,1]$ denote adaptation rates. Target speeds are not estimated according to sample speeds and their weights, since significant errors would be introduced: samples are chosen only because of sample weights, which do not directly depend on the current speed. This fact could imply a significant amount of jitter and many samples would be wasted. Therefore we compute targets' speeds from successive position estimates. Further, we enhance both position and speed estimates by regularising them according to their histories.

4   Main Causes of Catastrophic Failures

The target's size and appearance model must also be updated in order to cope with illumination changes, different points of view or changes in the shape of articulated targets. However, updating the appearance model is a sensitive task. Inaccurate adaptations surely lead to catastrophic failures. It must be ensured that no updating is done with noisy measures. Thus, during the initialization stage, the mean over time of the maximum sample likelihoods is computed. Models are then only updated when two conditions hold: (i) the target is not occluded and (ii) the likelihood of the estimated target's state is close to or higher than this mean. Every time an updating is carried out, the mean over time of the maximum sample likelihood is also updated:

$$Mean_k = Mean_{k-1} + \frac{1}{k}\left(MaxSampleLhood_k - Mean_{k-1}\right). \qquad (10)$$

The size of each target is estimated according to:

$$\mathbf{w}_t^l = \mathbf{w}_{t-1}^l (1 - \alpha_\mathbf{w}) + \left(L \sum_{i=1}^{N} \overline{\pi}_t^{i,l} \mathbf{w}_t^{i,l} \right) \alpha_\mathbf{w}, \qquad (11)$$

where $\alpha_\mathbf{w} \in [0,1]$ denotes the adaptation rate. Subsequently, the resized appearance models are updated following an adaptive approach:

$$\mathbf{A}_t^l = \mathbf{A}_{t-1}^{l,s} (1 - \alpha_\mathbf{A}) + \mathbf{I}_t^{l,p} \alpha_\mathbf{A}, \qquad (12)$$

where $\alpha_\mathbf{A} \in [0,1]$ is the learning rate.

Occlusions are also a main cause of catastrophic failures. Partial occlusions may cause inaccurate position and size updating. Thus, the target's estimated position would be shifted and its size adapted up to the area that can be seen. Moreover, the appearance model may be updated with completely erroneous values which would cause target loss in few frames. The situation during complete occlusion could be even worse: since the likelihood of the occluded target would be meaningless, the re-sampling phase would propagate random samples, quickly losing the target. Hence, a proper handling of occlusions is crucial.

Firstly, occlusions are predicted according to the dynamic models. When the predicted occlusion exceeds a certain percentage, the situation is pointed out. Subsequently, by exploring the maximum sample likelihoods and comparing them with recent historical values, we can conclude which target is being occluded. Once an occlusion is detected, the target state turns into Occluded and its historical likelihood until then is stored. This status involves several changes in the normal development of the process. First of all, the adaptation rates $\alpha_\mathbf{x}, \alpha_\mathbf{u}$ are set to zero: the target estimated speed is kept constant and the position is updated only according to its speed. In addition, no size or appearance adaptation is performed. Finally, those samples belonging to the occluded target are not re-sampled according to their weights —since they are meaningless— but are just propagated. As a result, samples spread around the target because of the uncertainty predictions terms. The other target's samples are normally re-sampled, but they cannot be assigned to the occluded target since otherwise this one would monopolise the whole sample set.

When the occlusion is no longer predicted or a sample likelihood exceeds the value previous to the occlusion, the target's status turns into NOTOCCLUDED, which immediately implies sample re-sampling, thereby pruning those samples with lower weights. In addition, position and speed are again updated.

5 Experimental Results

The performance of the algorithm has been tested using two sequences involving humans. Two targets are tracked simultaneously, despite their being articulated and elastic objects whose dynamics are highly non-linear, and that move through an environment with complex clutter.

(a) Frame 4: tracking   (b) Frame 24: updating

(c) Frame 80: occluded   (d) Frame 140: recovery

Fig. 1. Experiment involving an opposite translation and merging. Image notation: each target's estimated position is denoted by a bounding box and tagged accordingly; the target's estimated trajectory is drawn and milestones are placed every 20 frames; each predicted sample is drawn using a dark circle, whereas a re-sampled particle is drawn in a light one.

(a) Frame 12: updating   (b) Frame 38: tracking

(b) Frame 50: occluded   (c) Frame 102: recovery & exiting

Fig. 2. Experiment involving an overtaking

The first sequence involves an opposite translation and merging. Both targets start moving from opposite positions and meet near the second actor's initial position. The first target's speed decreases unevenly from five pixels per frame and the second one from two pixels per frame to nearly zero during the first part of the sequence. The first target is almost completely still from frames 70 to 130, occluding the second target. The latter crosses at a very low speed while performing a rotation. Thus, significant speed, size and appearance changes can be observed. The background intensity levels are so similar to the target ones that constitute a source of clutter.

The tracker performance is shown in Fig. 1. Both targets' appearance models are updated when reliable measures are obtained, see Fig. 1.(b). Occlusion is correctly detected avoiding re-sampling of samples of the occluded target and erroneous dynamic and appearance models updating, see Fig. 1.(c). The tracker successfully recovers from occlusion, see Fig. 1.(d).

The second sequence involves an overtaking. The second target moves faster than the first one, overtaking her. An almost complete occlusion can be observed from frame 40 to 60. The street-lamps constitute a source of clutter and cause partial occlusions to both targets. Fig. 2 shows the target performance.

6 Conclusions

We have extended the novel approach to particle filtering presented in [9]. One of *Condensation*'s great misbehaviours —sampling impoverishment, critical in a multiple-tracking scenario— is overcome by redefining weight normalisation. Dynamics updating is set by feed-backing the estimated speed into the prediction stage. The target's speed is estimated from successive position estimates. Both position and speed estimates are now regularised. Thus, sample wastage is significantly reduced and trajectory jitter is considerably attenuated. Both contributions reduce the required number of samples to perform tracking of multiple targets. Size changes are explored and appearance is adaptively updated, ensuring proper tracking. Occlusions are properly handled by means of prediction and likelihood measures.

The tracker deals with multiple-target tracking whose dynamics are highly non-linear, despite using a constant speed approach. They move through an environment with complex clutter, which mimics the target appearances, and strong noise. Moreover, their trajectories intersect causing a complete occlusion of one of the targets. It copes with heavy appearance and shape changes.

The tracker has been successfully tested in experiments despite the fact that no detection is ever used after initialization. Future research will be focused on colour-based likelihoods in order to enhance the disambiguation of targets from clutter.

Acknowledgments. This work has been supported by the Spanish CICYT TIC 2003-08865 and the Generalitat de Catalunya Research Department (DURSI).

References

1. S. Arulampalam, S. Maskell, N. Gordon, and T. Clapp. A tutorial on particle filters for on-line non-linear/non-gaussian bayesian tracking. *Tran. on Signal Processing*, 50(2):174–188, 2002.
2. D. Comaniciu, V. Ramesh, and P. Meer. Kernel-based object tracking. *IEEE Trans. on Pattern Analysis and Machine Intelligence*, 25(5):564 – 577, 2003.
3. J. Deutscher and I. Reid. Articulated body motion capture by stochastic search. *International Journal of Computer Vision*, 61(2):185 – 205, 2005.
4. A. Doucet. On sequential simulation-based methods for bayesian filtering. Technical Report TR310, Cambridge University, 1998.
5. M. Isard and A. Blake. Condensation – conditional density propagation for visual tracking. *International Journal of Computer Vision*, 29(1):5–28, 1998.
6. O. King and D. A. Forsyth. How does CONDENSATION behave with a finite number of samples? In *6th ECCV, Dublin, Ireland*, volume 1, pages 695–709, 2000.
7. J. MacCormick and A. Blake. A probabilistic exclusion principle for tracking multiple objects. In *ICCV*, pages 572–578, 1999.
8. K. Nummiaro, E. B. Koller-Meier, and L. Van Gool. An adaptive color-based particle filter. *Image and Vision Computing*, 21(1):99–110, 2003.

9. D. Rowe, I. Rius, J. Gonzàlez, X. Roca, and J.J. Villanueva. Probabilistic Image-based Tracking: Improving Particle Filtering. In *2nd IbPRIA, Estoril, Portugal*, 2005.
10. R. Russell and P. Norvig. *Artificial Intelligence, a Modern Approach*, chapter 13-15. Prentice Hall, second edition, 2003.
11. R. van der Merwe, N. de Freitas, A. Doucet, and E. Wan. The Unscented Particle Filter. Technical Report TR380, Cambridge University, 2000.
12. X. Varona, J. Gonzàlez, X. Roca, and J.J. Villanueva. iTrack: Image-based Probabilistic Tracking of People. In *15th ICPR, Barcelona, Spain*, volume 3, pages 1110–1113, 2000.

Image Reconstruction with Polar Zernike Moments

Yongqing Xin[1,*], Miroslaw Pawlak[1], and Simon Liao[2]

[1] Department of Electrical and Computer Engineering, University of Manitoba
{yxin, pawlak}@ee.umanitoba.ca
[2] Department of Applied Computer Science, University of Winnipeg
s.liao@uwinnipeg.ca

Abstract. As an orthogonal moment, Zernike moment (ZM) is an attractive image feature in a number of application scenarios due to its distinguishing properties. However, we find that for digital images, the commonly used Cartesian method for ZM computation has compromised the advantages of ZMs because of their non-ideal accuracy stemming from two inherent sources of errors, i.e., the geometric error and the integral error. There exists considerable errors in image reconstruction using ZMs calculated with the Cartesian method. In this paper, we propose a polar coordinate based algorithm for the computation of ZMs, which avoids the two kinds of errors and greatly improves the accuracy of ZM computation. We present solutions to the key issues in ZM computation under polar coordinate system, including the derivation of computation formulas, the polar pixel arrangement scheme, and the interpolation-based image conversion etc. As a result, ZM-based image reconstruction can be performed much more accurately.

1 Introduction

Zernike moment, first introduced for image analysis by Teague [1], is an orthogonal moment based on Zernike polynomials. The Zernike basis is a set of complete and orthogonal functions on the unit disk $\mathbb{D}$, defined as [2,3]:

$$V_{nm}(x,y) = R_{nm}(\rho)e^{jm\theta}, \quad (1)$$

where $\rho = \sqrt{x^2 + y^2}$, $\theta = \tan^{-1}(y/x)$. Here n is a non-negative integer and m is an integer such that $n - |m|$ is even and non-negative. $R_{nm}(\rho)$ is the radial polynomial:

$$R_{nm}(\rho) = \sum_{s=0}^{(n-|m|)/2} \frac{(-1)^s (n-s)! \rho^{n-2s}}{s!(\frac{n+|m|}{2}-s)!(\frac{n-|m|}{2}-s)!}. \quad (2)$$

Based on Zernike polynomials, the Zernike moment with order n and repetition m of a continuous function $f(x,y)$ is defined as

---

* This research is supported by NSERC and TRLabs.

$$A_{nm} = \frac{n+1}{\pi} \int \int_\mathbb{D} f(x,y) V_{nm}^*(x,y) dx dy, \quad (3)$$

where * denotes complex conjugate.

Image reconstruction from a finite number of moments, L, can be performed with the following formula:

$$\hat{f}(x,y) = \sum_{i=1}^{L} [\hat{A}_{n_i m_i} V_{n_i m_i}(x,y) + \mathbf{I}(m_i \neq 0) \hat{A}_{n_i,-m_i} V_{n_i,-m_i}(x,y)], \quad (4)$$

where $\mathbf{I}(\cdot)$ is the indicator function.

Due to its distinguishing characteristics such as the magnitude invariance to image rotation and high efficiency of image representation, Zernike moment is an attractive image feature playing an important role in various areas. It has been demonstrated that Zernike moment and pseudo-Zernike moment have the best overall performance among the commonly used moments [4]. In recent years, significant efforts and progress have been made in the research of Zernike moment to explore its properties, computation and applications [2,5,6,7,8,3,9,10,11,12].

However, in practice we find that based on the conventional method for ZM computation, the superior properties of Zernike moment are not ideal. In particular, considerable errors exist in image analysis and reconstruction via Zernike moments, and ZM magnitude invariance to image rotation is not satisfactory. This issue stems from the inaccuracies in the conventional computation of ZMs [13,6,7]. In this paper, we take a different approach to the computation of Zernike moments. We show that if Zernike moments are calculated in polar coordinate system, the geometric error can be eliminated and numerical error can be reduced greatly. With the proposed approach, the accuracy of Zernike moments is significantly improved. As a result, image analysis and reconstruction can be performed accurately and effectively via Zernike moments with very high orders.

2 Conventional Approach to the Computation of Zernike Moment

For a digital image, $f(i,j), i = 1, ..., N, j = 1, ..., N$, its ZMs cannot be computed by (3) directly, but rather, the following formula is commonly used to compute ZMs approximately:

$$\hat{A}_{nm} = \frac{n+1}{\pi} \sum \sum f(i,j) h_{nm}(x_i, y_j), \quad (5)$$

where $x_i = (2i - N - 1)/N$, $y_j = (2j - N - 1)/N$, and the double summation is performed over all (i,j) pairs that satisfy $(x_i, y_j) \in \mathbb{D}$. The factor

$$h_{nm}(x_i, y_j) = \int \int_{\text{pixel }(i,j)} V_{nm}^*(x,y) dx dy \quad (6)$$

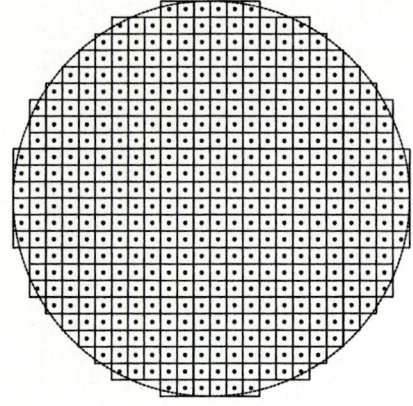 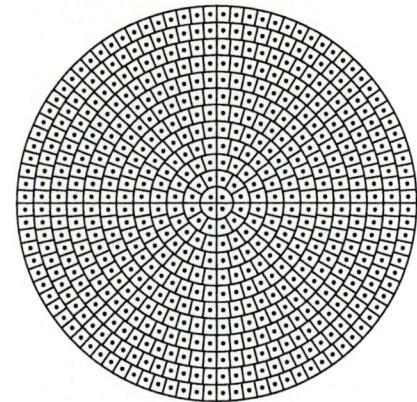

Fig. 1. Illustration of the conventional Cartesian pixel grid for ZM computation

Fig. 2. Illustration of the proposed polar pixel grid for ZM computation

is usually approximated by

$$h_{nm}(i,j) \approx 4N^{-2}V_{nm}^*(x_i, y_j). \tag{7}$$

However, as pointed out in [6], the accuracy of Zernike moments computed via (5) suffers from two sources of errors, namely the geometric approximation error and the integral approximation error. The former is due to the fact that the total area covered by all the square pixels involved in the computation of Zernike moments via (5) is not exactly the unit disk, as illustrated by the ragged border in Fig. 1. The latter results from the numerical integration via an approximation formula like (7). Although some techniques can be deployed [6] to alleviate the inherent accuracy problems, the two kinds of errors can never be eradicated as long as the computation of Zernike moments is performed under Cartesian coordinate system.

To see the negative effect of these two kinds of errors on image reconstruction, let us look at an example. We use (5) and (7) to calculate the ZMs of a 128 × 128 image Lena up to the order of 200. Afterwards these ZMs are used to reconstruct the image via (4), up to the orders 20, 50, 80, 120, 150, 180 and 200 respectively. The original image and reconstructed images are shown in Fig. 3. It is evident that the image reconstruction error due to the inaccuracy of ZMs becomes larger as the moment order increases, especially along the border of the unit disk.

3 Computing Zernike Moments in Polar Coordinate System

3.1 Principles

To remove the geometric error and integral error in ZM computation, we need to take a different approach from the existing Cartesian method. It is intuitive that

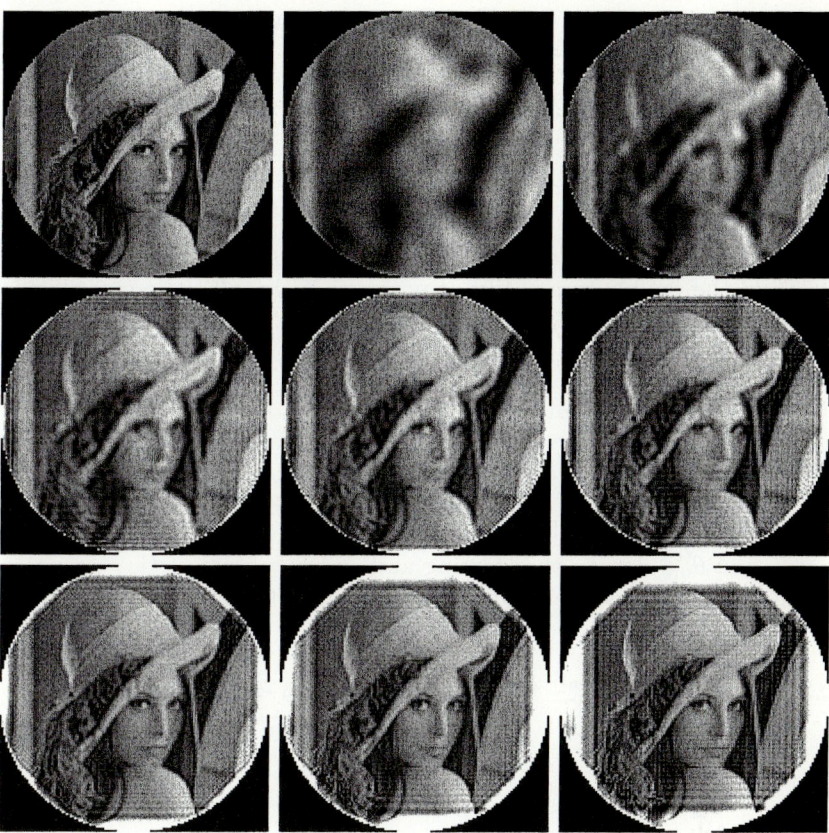

Fig. 3. Image reconstruction via conventional Cartesian ZMs. From upper-left to lower-right: original Lena, reconstructed Lena with ZMs up to orders 20, 50, 80, 100, 120, 150, 180, and 200 respectively.

geometric error might be avoided by an appropriate design of non-square pixels, whose areas add up to that of the unit disk (π). On the other hand, we use analytical method instead of numerical approximation for the pixelwise integration of basis polynomials, which is accurate and efficient in moment computation [14]. Equation (1) reveals that Zernike polynomials are immediate functions of polar coordinates ρ and θ, rather than Cartesian coordinates x and y. This prompts us that adoption of polar coordinates could facilitate the computation of Zernike moments. For this purpose, we rewrite (3) in its equivalent form based on polar coordinates

$$A_{nm} = \frac{n+1}{\pi} \int_0^{2\pi} \int_0^1 f(\rho,\theta) R_{nm}(\rho) e^{-jm\theta} \rho d\rho d\theta. \qquad (8)$$

If a digital image is approximated as a piece-wise constant function composed of constant-intensity sectors, denoted by $\Omega_{u,v}$, which are concentric about the origin and satisfy

$$\bigcup_{\text{All }(u,v)} \Omega_{u,v} = \mathbb{D} \text{ and } \Omega_{u,v} \cap \Omega_{u',v'} = \emptyset, \forall (u,v) \neq (u',v'), \tag{9}$$

we can get an approximate version of (8) as

$$\hat{A}_{nm} = \frac{n+1}{\pi} \sum_u \sum_v \hat{f}(\rho_u, \theta_v) h_{nm}(\rho_u, \theta_v), \tag{10}$$

where $\hat{f}(\rho_u, \theta_v)$ is the estimated image intensity of sector (u,v), centered at (ρ_u, θ_v), and the double summation is performed over all the sectors inside the unit disk. The factor $h_{nm}(\rho_u, \theta_v)$ is an integral over $\Omega_{u,v}$:

$$h_{nm}(\rho_u, \theta_v) = \int\int_{\Omega_{u,v}} R_{nm}(\rho) e^{-jm\theta} \rho d\rho d\theta = \int_{\rho_{u,v}^{(s)}}^{\rho_{u,v}^{(e)}} R_{nm}(\rho) \rho d\rho \int_{\theta_{u,v}^{(s)}}^{\theta_{u,v}^{(e)}} e^{-jm\theta} d\theta, \tag{11}$$

where $\rho_{u,v}^{(s)}$ and $\rho_{u,v}^{(e)}$ denote the starting and ending radials of $\Omega_{u,v}$ respectively, while $\theta_{u,v}^{(s)}$ and $\theta_{u,v}^{(e)}$ denote the starting and ending angles of $\Omega_{u,v}$ respectively. (11) is the product of two definitive integrals, whose exact value can be obtained analytically as follows.

$$\int_{\rho_{u,v}^{(s)}}^{\rho_{u,v}^{(e)}} R_{nm}(\rho) \rho d\rho = \sum_{s=0}^{(n-|m|)/2} \frac{(-1)^s (n-s)! [(\rho_{u,v}^{(e)})^{n-2s+2} - (\rho_{u,v}^{(s)})^{n-2s+2}]}{(n-2s+2) s! (\frac{n+|m|}{2} - s)! (\frac{n-|m|}{2} - s)!}. \tag{12}$$

$$\int_{\theta_{u,v}^{(s)}}^{\theta_{u,v}^{(e)}} e^{-jm\theta} d\theta = \begin{cases} \frac{j}{m} \left[e^{-jm\theta_{u,v}^{(e)}} - e^{-jm\theta_{u,v}^{(s)}} \right], & m \neq 0 \\ \theta_{u,v}^{(e)} - \theta_{u,v}^{(s)}, & m = 0 \end{cases}. \tag{13}$$

Combining (10), (11), (12) and (13), we obtain precisely the Zernike moment of the function $\hat{f}(\cdot, \cdot)$, without introducing any geometric error or integral error in the process.

3.2 A Polar Pixel Structure for ZM Computation

In theory there are numerous schemes satisfying the conditions (9), but a good design should meet some requirements. Firstly, the sizes of all the sectors (pixels) should be as close as possible, because the given Cartesian image function has a uniform pixel size everywhere. Secondly, the number of polar pixels inside the unit circle should not be smaller than that of the Cartesian pixels inside the unit circle, so that the necessary image resolution could be maintained without loss of information contents. Thirdly, the polar pixel structure should be as simple and regular as possible, in order to facilitate the storage and computation processes.

Following these guidelines, we propose a pixel arrangement scheme illustrated by Fig. (2). In this structure, the unit disk is uniformly divided along the radial direction into U sections, with the separating circles located at $\{\frac{k}{U}, k = 1, ..., U\}$; the kth ring-shape section is equally divided into $V(2k-1)$ sectors by rays starting from the origin, with angles $\{(i-1)\frac{2\pi}{V(2k-1)}, i = 1, ..., V(2k-1)\}$. V is the number of sectors contained in the innermost section.

A bigger U or V results in more sectors and thus more accurate image representation, but at the cost of more computation workload and more computer memory for storage. In practice, we recommend setting $V = 4$ and $N/2 \leq U \leq N$ for an $N \times N$ image.

With this polar pixel arrangement scheme, the formula for ZM computation (10) can be further rewritten as

$$\hat{A}_{nm} = \frac{n+1}{\pi} \sum_{u=1}^{U} \sum_{v=1}^{V(2u-1)} \hat{f}(\rho_u, \theta_v) \int\int_{\Omega_{u,v}} R_{nm}(\rho) e^{-jm\theta} \rho d\rho d\theta. \quad (14)$$

3.3 Generation of the Polar Image

To use the polar method for ZM computation, we need to convert a given Cartesian image into a polar image with a pixel grid like Fig. 2. This issue can be addressed by image interpolation. There are a number of existing interpolation techniques [15] we can use to determine polar pixels, such as nearest neighbor method, bilinear method and bicubic method. Although nearest neighbor and bilinear methods are easy to implement, they produce considerable interpolation errors. Here we adopt bicubic interpolation [15] to generate the polar image. The value of a polar pixel is determined by the 16 neighboring Cartesian pixels. The 1-D kernel function is a cubic spline:

$$h(x) = \begin{cases} 1 - \frac{5}{2}|x|^2 + \frac{3}{2}|x|^3, & |x| \leq 1 \\ 2 - 4|x| + \frac{5}{2}|x|^2 - \frac{1}{2}|x|^3, & 1 < |x| \leq 2 \\ 0, & \text{otherwise.} \end{cases} \quad (15)$$

Suppose (ρ_u, θ_v) is the central point of Sector (u, v). Then the value of Sector (u, v) can be estimated via convolution of the given Cartesian image function $f(x_i, y_j)$ with the above kernel function $h(x)$

$$\hat{f}(\rho_u, \theta_v) = \sum_{i=m-1}^{m+2} \sum_{j=n-1}^{n+2} f(x_i, y_j) h\left(\frac{\rho_u \cos \theta_v - x_i}{\Delta}\right) h\left(\frac{\rho_u \sin \theta_v - y_j}{\Delta}\right), \quad (16)$$

where $m = \lfloor \frac{\rho_u \cos \theta_v}{\Delta} \rfloor$ and $n = \lfloor \frac{\rho_u \sin \theta_v}{\Delta} \rfloor$, and $\Delta = x_i - x_{i-1} = y_j - y_{j-1}$ is the pixel width of the image $f(x_i, y_j)$.

As a result, a very smooth and accurate polar image can be generated from the given Cartesian image.

4 Simulation Results

To verify the effectiveness of the proposed polar approach for image reconstruction, we first repeat the experiments described in Section 2, but with the introduced polar method for the computation of ZMs. We still calculate the ZMs

Fig. 4. Image reconstruction via proposed polar ZMs. From upper-left to lower-right: original Lena, reconstructed Lena with ZMs up to orders 20, 50, 80, 100, 120, 150, 180, and 200 respectively.

of the 128 × 128 image Lena up to the order of 200, and subsequently these ZMs are used to reconstruct the image via (4), up to the orders 20, 50, 80, 120, 150, 180 and 200 respectively. The original image and reconstructed images are shown in Fig. 4. Comparing Fig. 3 and Fig. 4, one can see that the rather obtrusive reconstruction error resulting from the conventional Cartesian ZM based approach does not exist in the proposed polar ZM based reconstruction.

To compare more objectively the performances of the two approaches in terms of image reconstruction, we experimented on more different numbers of ZMs for image recovery. To be specific, ZMs up to order $\{n = 2i\}_{i=0}^{100}$ were used to reconstruct the image respectively. The quality of each reconstructed image is measured by peek signal-to-noise ratio (PSNR), which is define as

$$\mathrm{PSNR}(f, \hat{f}) = 10 \log_{10} \frac{f_{\max}^2}{\sigma_e^2}, \quad \sigma_e^2 = \frac{1}{N^2} \sum_{i=1}^{N} \sum_{j=1}^{N} [\hat{f}(x_i, y_j) - f(x_i, y_j)]^2, \quad (17)$$

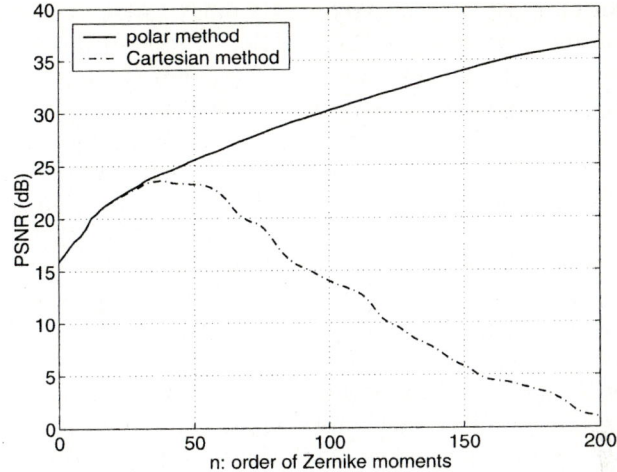

Fig. 5. The quality of reconstructed image in terms of PSNR as a function of the order of Zernike moments, for a comparison of Cartesian and polar moments.

where f is the original image and $\hat{f}$ is the reconstructed image, both with dimensions $N \times N$, $f_{\max}$ is the maximum pixel value of image f, and $sigma_e^2$ is the mean square error. The test results are shown in Fig. 5, in which two important conclusions can be drawn. First, for small orders of ZMs, approximately $n < 20$, the quality of the reconstructed images via polar ZMs is similar to that of the reconstructed images via Cartesian ZMs. But as n becomes larger, the former gets better and better than the latter. Second, the quality of polar ZM-reconstructed images increases monotonically with n. However, in the Cartesian case, as n increases to a certain point, approximately 40, the image quality reaches its maximum value, and then as L increases further, the image quality gets worse and worse. This is because the reconstruction error incurred by geometric error and numerical error increase with n, and at some point it outweighs the quality gain from the population increase of ZMs [6].

5 Discussion

Some issues related to the proposed algorithm are worth discussing here.

- **Accuracy of ZM Computation.** Although the proposed polar algorithm has avoided the geometric error and integral error inherent in the conventional Cartesian method, the accuracy of Zernike moments is still not perfect. The image resampling process incurs a slight inaccuracy of ZMs. However, this inaccuracy is much more smaller than that existing in the Cartesian algorithm, which can be seen clearly from experimental results.

- **Algorithm Complexity.** Comparing to its Cartesian counterpart, the proposed polar algorithm for ZM computation is more complex, because it involves necessarily the process of image interpolation. However, this increase of complexity is insignificant when the number of moments to be calculated is large, because image interpolation needs to be performed only once before ZM computation. For example, on a Pentium 4 1.8GHz computer, the interpolation takes 0.09 seconds for a 128×128 input image and an output polar image with $U = 64, V = 4$ (equivalently, 16384 pixels), while the computation of ZMs up to order 50 takes 7.13 seconds with the proposed polar algorithm. Therefore we can see that the bottleneck of computation does not lie in the process of image interpolation.
- **Algorithm Implementation.** Although the implementation of the proposed algorithm is not the focus of this paper, we did employ some techniques in our experiments for its fast implementation. The measures fall into two categories. First, we find and compute the common factors in the computation and store their values in memory, and later use them directly. for example, the item $e^{-j2\theta}$ is repeatedly used in the calculation of $A_{2,2}, A_{4,2}, A_{6,2}, ...$, and thus its value can be stored to save repeated calculation. Second, the factorials in (12) are time-consuming, and direct computation should be avoided. They can be implemented efficiently via recursive formulas. The details of some fast algorithms can be found in literature [8, 3, 16].
- **Significance of the Algorithm.** The ZM accuracy improvement benefitted from the proposed algorithm brings a number of advantages in applications. As mentioned above, image reconstruction based on Cartesian ZMs yields errors along the border of the unit circle, especially when high order moments are used. A zero-zone around the circle border was used [13] to circumvent the problem. Nevertheless there are some applications, like image watermarking [10, 11], where a zero-zone is not allowed. The proposed algorithm provides a solution to the problem. On the other hand, the errors of traditional Cartesian ZMs compromise the useful property of rotational invariance, but now the proposed polar algorithm makes the property close to ideal [11, 12], which is significant in such applications as invariant watermarking and pattern recognition.

6 Conclusion

We have proposed a novel approach to accurate ZM computation in polar coordinate system, in an effort to improve the performance of image reconstruction via Zernike moments. In particular, we gave a polar pixel arrangement scheme, under which the formula for ZM computation was derived. Image conversion from Cartesian grid to the proposed polar grid is addressed through bicubic interpolation. It was shown that with this polar algorithm, the two kinds of errors from which the Cartesian method suffers do not exist anymore. The effectiveness of the proposed polar method was verified by the simulation results.

References

1. M. R. Teague, "Image analysis via the general theory of moments," *J. Optical Soc. Am.*, vol. 70, pp. 920–930, 1980.
2. A. Khotanzad and Y. H. Hong, "Invariant image recognition by Zernike moments," *IEEE Trans. Pattern Anal. Mach. Intell.*, vol. 12, no. 5, pp. 489–497, 1990.
3. R. Mukundan and K. Ramakrishnan, *Moment Functions in Image Analysis: Theory and Applications*, World Scientific, 1998.
4. C. Teh and R. T. Chin, "On image analysis by the methods of moments," *IEEE Trans. Pattern Analysis and Machine Intelligence*, vol. 10, no. 4, pp. 496–513, 1988.
5. O. D. Trier, A. K. Jain, and T. Taxt, "Feature extraction methods for character recognition–a survey," *Pattern Recognition*, vol. 29, no. 4, pp. 641–662, 1996.
6. S. X. Liao and M. Pawlak, "On the accuracy of Zernike moments for image analysis," *IEEE Trans. Pattern Analysis and Machine Intelligence*, vol. 20, no. 12, pp. 1358–1364, 1998.
7. M. Pawlak and S. X. Liao, "On the recovery of a function on a circular domain," *IEEE Transactions on Information Theory*, vol. 48, no. 10, pp. 2736–2753, 2002.
8. R. Mukundan and K. Ramakrishnan, "Fast computation of Legendre and Zernike moments," *Pattern Recognition*, vol. 28, no. 9, pp. 1433–1442, 1995.
9. H. S. Ginis, S. Plainis, and A. Pallikaris, "Variability of wavefront aberration measurements in small pupil sizes using a clinical shack-hartman aberrometer," *BMC Ophthalmology*, vol. 4, no. 1, 2004.
10. Y. Xin, S. Liao, and M. Pawlak, "A multibit geometrically robust image watermark based on Zernike moments," in *International Conference on Pattern Recognition (ICPR) 2004*, 2004, vol. IV, pp. 861–864.
11. Y. Xin, S. Liao, and M. Pawlak, "Robust date hiding with image invariants," in *IEEE Canadian Conference on Electrical and Computer Engineering (CCECE) 2005*, Saskatoon, Canada, 1–4 May 2005.
12. Y. Xin, S. Liao, and M. Pawlak, "On the improvement of rotational invariance of zernike moments," in *International Conference on Image Processing (ICIP) 2005*, Genova, Italy, 11–14 Sept. 2005.
13. S. X. Liao, *Image Analysis by Moments*, Ph.D. Thesis, University of Manitoba, 1993.
14. J. Flusser, "Refined moment calculation using image block representation," *IEEE Transactions on Image Processing*, vol. 9, no. 11, pp. 1977–1978, 2000.
15. R. G. Keys, "Cubic convolution interpolation for digital image processing," *IEEE Trans. ASSP*, vol. 29, no. 6, pp. 1153–1160, 1981.
16. X. Y. Jiang and H. Bunke, "Simple and fast computation of moments," *Pattern Recognition*, vol. 24, no. 8, pp. 801–806, 1991.

Texture Exemplars for Defect Detection on Random Textures

Xianghua Xie and Majid Mirmehdi

Department of Computer Science,
University of Bristol, Bristol BS8 1UB, England
{xie, majid}@cs.bris.ac.uk

Abstract. We present a new approach to detecting defects in random textures which requires only very few defect free samples for unsupervised training. Each product image is divided into overlapping patches of various sizes. Then, density mixture models are applied to reduce groupings of patches to a number of textural exemplars, referred to here as texems, characterising the means and covariances of whole sets of image patches. The texems can be viewed as implicit representations of textural primitives. A multiscale approach is used to save computational costs. Finally, we perform novelty detection by applying the lower bound of normal samples likelihoods on the multiscale defect map of an image to localise defects.

1 Introduction

Visual inspection has been one of the major applications of computer vision since the early 1980s. Numerous works have reported on detecting imperfections on a variety of surfaces [1,2,3], such as textile, ceramics, and wood. Some of the materials display complex patterns but appear visually regular on a larger scale, e.g. textile. Some others, such as printed ceramic tiles, may display very complex patterns that are random in appearance. Detecting subtle local defects on such surfaces turns out to be rather difficult [3].

A variety of statistical techniques have been investigated for defect detection, such as graylevel co-occurrence matrices. For those materials that exhibit a high degree of regularity and periodicity, e.g. textiles, template-based methods and Fourier-domain analysis have also proved useful for defect detection. Amongst other filtering-based techniques, Gabor filters have been applied, as shown in [2], due to their ability to analyse texture by achieving optimal joint localisation in the spatial and frequency domains. Randen and Husøy [4] present a thorough comparative review of texture analysis using filtering techniques.

However, the supremacy of filter bank based methods have been challenged by several authors. For instance, in [5], Varma and Zisserman argued that a large variety of signals (e.g. textures) can be analysed by just looking at small neighbourhoods. They used 7×7 patches to generate a texton based representation and achieved better performance than the filtering based methods they compared against when classifying material images from the Columbia-Utrecht

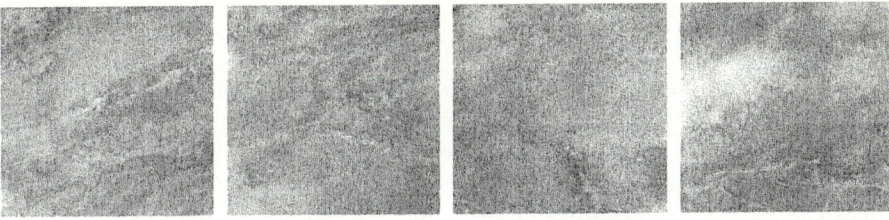

Fig. 1. Example marble tiles from the same family whose patterns are different but visually consistent

database. The results demonstrated that textures with global structures can be discriminated by examining the distribution of local measurements. This is a key factor in our approach in this paper. In [6], the authors also advocated the use of local pixel neighbourhood processing in the shape of local binary patterns as texture descriptors. Other works based on local pixel neighbourhoods are those that apply Markov Random Field (MRF) models, e.g. [1,7], where the inspection process was treated as a hypothesis testing problem on the statistics derived Recently in [8], Jojic et al. defined the epitome as a miniature, condensed version of an image containing the constitutive elements of its shape and textural properties needed to reconstruct the image. The epitome also relies on *raw* pixel values to characterise textural and colour properties rather than popular filtering responses. An image is defined by its epitome and a smooth, *hidden* mapping from the epitome to image pixels.

Inspired by the success of non-filtering local neighbourhood approaches, in this paper we propose a new approach to detecting and localising defects on random (or regular) textured surfaces. In a random texture application such as ceramic tile production, the images may appear different in textural pattern from one to another. However, the visual impression of the same product line remains consistent, e.g. see Figure 1. There exist textural primitives that impose consistency within the product line. Instead of recovering all the variations amongst images from a relatively large number of samples in a supervised manner for a traditional classification approach [9], we learn, in unsupervised fashion, textural primitive information from a very small number of training samples. We name these representations *texture exemplars* or *texems*.

Recently, the authors in [10] proposed novelty detection for classification of tiles using eigenfilters, but were not able to localise defects, essential when it is necessary to understand the nature and formation of the defects. Novelty detection is important from a practical viewpoint, not only because it is difficult to collect a wide range of defective samples for training for a more traditional classification based approach, such as neural networks, but also because some defects are usually unpredictable and occur only during production. To ensure computational efficiency we also extend the overall method into a multiscale framework.

In section 2, the proposed method is presented, including learning the texems, the multiscale approach, and the novelty detection stage. Experimental results are given in section 3. Section 4 concludes the paper.

2 Proposed Method

We consider that each product image is produced by putting together a certain number of subimage patches of various sizes, possibly overlapped. As the images of the same product contain the same textural elements, one product image can be generated from the patches extracted from other images. Thus, for a few given samples we can easily obtain a large number of patches of various sizes (which can in turn generate a large set of new images with the same visual impression). However, it is computationally prohibitive to perform defect detection based on such a large number of patches. Also, the patches themselves contain lots of redundant information. We can reduce the number of patches by learning a relatively small number of primitive representatives, i.e. texems.

The proposed method is related to the texton model in the sense that both try to characterise textural images by using micro-structures. Textons were first introduced by Julesz [11] as the atoms of pre-attentive human visual perception. An image is considered as a superposition of a number of image bases selected from an over-complete dictionary. The image bases are generated by a smaller number of texton elements, selected from a dictionary of textons [12]. Textons have attracted much attention in vision applications, including image classification and motion modelling. Recently, in [12], Zhu et al. presented generative models for learning the fundamental image structures from textural images. However, the proposed method is significantly different from the texton model in that it relies directly on the subimages instead of using base functions. The texems are implicit representations of textural primitives, which makes them more flexible as they come at different sizes, while textons are explicit representations. For example, if the texem size reduces to a single pixel, it becomes histogram analysis. If the texems are the same size as the input images, then the problem turns into image template analysis. Each texem indeed becomes a template. In general our texems contain multiple textural primitives which as a whole describe a family of textures. This implicit representation at various sizes avoids the difficulties of explicitly finding the best primitive representation, e.g. the optimum window size as in the case of textons (for example see [5]).

In brief, we break down a defect free image into overlapping paches of various sizes, and group similar sized patches into a multidimensional space, dependent on the patch size, and describe the clusters found using a Gaussian mixture model. The representative texture exemplars are then learned through an EM algorithm applied on the mixture density parameters. Then, as we are interested in localising the defective regions, we extract a small patch at each pixel position of the testing image and classify it using the set of texems obtained at the training stage.

2.1 Learning Textural Exemplars (Texems)

The texture exemplars, referred to as *texems*, are image representations at various sizes that encapsulate the texture or visual primitives of a given image. For instance, in the case of an example random texture, the textural primitives are consistent from one image to another, hence texems can characterise a family of images of the random texture. Each texem, denoted as $\mathbf{m}$, is defined by a mean, $\boldsymbol{\mu}$, and a corresponding covariance matrix, $\boldsymbol{\omega}$, i.e. $\mathbf{m} = \{\boldsymbol{\mu}, \boldsymbol{\omega}\}$.

The original image $\mathbf{I}$ is broken down into a set of P patches $\mathbf{Z} = \{\mathbf{Z}_i\}_{i=1}^{P}$, each containing pixels from a subset of image coordinates. The shape of the patches can be arbitrary, but in this study we used square patches of size $d = N \times N$. The patches may overlap and can be of various sizes, e.g. as small as 5×5 to as large as required (here 20×20). We assume that there exist K texems, $\mathcal{M} = \{\mathbf{m}_k\}_{k=1}^{K}$, $K \ll P$, for image $\mathbf{I}$ such that each patch in $\mathbf{Z}$ can be generated from a texem with certain added variations. In other words, the original image $\mathbf{I}$ can be reconstructed by the texems with a certain reconstruction error.

To learn these texems the P patches are projected into a set of higher dimensional spaces. The number of these spaces is determined by the number of different patch sizes and their dimensions are defined by the corresponding value of d. Each pixel position contributes one coordinate of a space. Each point in a space corresponds to a patch in $\mathbf{Z}$. Then each texem and its covariance matrix represent a class of patches in the corresponding space. We assume that each class is a multivariate Gaussian distribution with mean $\boldsymbol{\mu}_k$ and covariance matrix $\boldsymbol{\omega}_k$, which corresponds to $\mathbf{m}_k$ in the spatial domain. Thus, the probability density function for a particular patch $\mathbf{Z}_i$ given that it belongs to the kth texem $\mathbf{m}_k$, is:

$$p(\mathbf{Z}_i|\mathbf{m}_k, \theta) = \frac{1}{\sqrt{(2\pi)^d |\boldsymbol{\omega}_k|}} \exp\{-\frac{1}{2}(\mathbf{Z}_i - \boldsymbol{\mu}_k)^T \boldsymbol{\omega}_k^{-1}(\mathbf{Z}_i - \boldsymbol{\mu}_k)\}, \qquad (1)$$

where $\theta = \{\boldsymbol{\alpha}_k, \boldsymbol{\mu}_k, \boldsymbol{\omega}_k\}_{k=1}^{K}$ is the parameter set containing $\boldsymbol{\alpha}_k$, which is the *prior* probability of kth texem constrained by $\sum_{k=1}^{K} \boldsymbol{\alpha}_k = 1$, the mean $\boldsymbol{\mu}_k$, the covariance $\boldsymbol{\omega}_k$. Since all the texems $\mathbf{m}_k$ are unknown, the parameter set θ can be determined first by marginalizing the joint distribution by summing across the texems, $p(\mathbf{Z}_i|\theta)$, and then optimising the data log-likelihood expression of the entire set $\mathbf{Z}$, given by

$$\log p(\mathbf{Z}|K, \theta) = \Sigma_{i=1}^{P} \log p(\mathbf{Z}_i|\theta) = \Sigma_{i=1}^{P} \log(\Sigma_{k=1}^{K} p(\mathbf{Z}_i|\mathbf{m}_k, \theta)\boldsymbol{\alpha}_k). \qquad (2)$$

Hence, the objective is to estimate the parameter θ for a given number of texems. The *Expectation Maximization* (EM) technique can be used to find the maximum likelihood estimate of our mixture density parameters from the given data set $\mathbf{Z}$. That is to find $\hat{\theta}$ where

$$\hat{\theta} = \arg\max \log(\mathcal{L}(\theta|\mathbf{Z})) = \arg\max \log p(\mathbf{Z}|K, \theta). \qquad (3)$$

Then the two steps of the EM stage are as follows. The E-step involves a soft-assignment of each patch $\mathbf{Z}_i$ to texems, $\mathcal{M}$, with an initial guess of the true parameters, θ. We denote the intermediate parameters as $\theta^{(t)}$. The probability that patch $\mathbf{Z}_i$ belongs to the kth texem may then be computed using Bayes rule:

$$p(\mathbf{m}_k|\mathbf{Z}_i, \theta^{(t)}) = \frac{p(\mathbf{Z}_i|\mathbf{m}_k, \theta^{(t)})\boldsymbol{\alpha}_k}{\Sigma_{k=1}^{K} p(\mathbf{Z}_i|\mathbf{m}_k, \theta^{(t)})\boldsymbol{\alpha}_k}. \qquad (4)$$

The M-step then updates the parameters by maximizing the log-likelihood, resulting in new estimates:

$$\hat{\alpha}_k = \frac{1}{P}\Sigma_{i=1}^{P}p(\mathbf{m}_k|\mathbf{Z}_i,\theta^{(t)}), \quad (5)$$

$$\hat{\mu}_k = \frac{\Sigma_{i=1}^{P}\mathbf{Z}_i p(\mathbf{m}_k|\mathbf{Z}_i,\theta^{(t)})}{\Sigma_{i=1}^{P}p(\mathbf{m}_k|\mathbf{Z}_i,\theta^{(t)})},$$

$$\hat{\omega}_k = \frac{\Sigma_{i=1}^{P}(\mathbf{Z}_i-\hat{\mu}_k)(\mathbf{Z}_i-\hat{\mu}_k)^T p(\mathbf{m}_k|\mathbf{Z}_i,\theta^{(t)})}{\Sigma_{i=1}^{P}p(\mathbf{m}_k|\mathbf{Z}_i,\theta^{(t)})}.$$

The E-step and M-step are iterated until the estimations are stabilises. Then, the texems can be easily obtained by projecting the parameters back to the spatial domain. Various sizes of texems can be used and they can overlap to ensure they capture sufficient textural characteristics.

2.2 A Simple Multiscale Approach

In order to capture sufficient textural properties, texems can be from as small as 3×3 to larger sizes such as 20×20. However, the dimension of the space we transform patches $\mathbf{Z}$ into will increase dramatically as the dimension of the patch size d increases. This means that a very large number of samples and high computational costs are needed in order to accurately estimate the pdf in very high dimensional spaces, forcing the procurement of a large number of training samples. Therefore, instead of generating variable-size texems, we learn fixed size texems in a multiscale. This will result in (multiscale) texems with a very small size, e.g. 5×5. A simple multiscale approach by using a Gaussian pyramid is sufficient.

Let us denote $\mathbf{I}^{(n)}$ as the nth level image of the pyramid, $\mathbf{Z}^{(n)}$ as all the image patches extracted from $\mathbf{I}^{(n)}$, l as the total number of levels, and $S^{\downarrow}$ as the downsampling operator. We then have $\mathbf{I}^{(n+1)} = S^{\downarrow}G_{\sigma}(\mathbf{I}^{(n)})$, $\forall n, n = 1, 2, ..., l-1$, where G_{σ} denotes the Gaussian convolution. The finest scale layer is the original image, $\mathbf{I}^{(1)} = \mathbf{I}$. We then extract multiscale texems from the image pyramid using the method presented in the previous section. Similarly, let $\mathbf{m}^{(n)}$ denote the nth level of multiscale texems and $\theta^{(n)}$ the parameters associated at the same level, which will then be used for novelty detection at the corresponding level of the pyramid. During the EM process, the stabilised estimation of a coarser level is used as the initial estimation for the finer level, i.e. $\hat{\theta}^{(n,t=0)} = \theta^{(n+1)}$, which helps speed up the convergence and achieve a more accurate estimation.

2.3 Novelty Detection

Once the texems are obtained from a single training image, we then can work out the minimum bound of normal samples in each resolution level in order to perform novelty detection. A small set of defect free samples (e.g. 4 or 5 only) are arranged within a multiscale framework, and patches with the same texem size are extracted. The probability of a patch $\mathbf{Z}_i^{(n)}$ belonging to texems in the corresponding nth scale is $p(\mathbf{Z}_i^{(n)}|\theta^{(n)}) = \Sigma_{k=1}^K p(\mathbf{Z}_i^{(n)}|\mathbf{m}_k^{(n)},\theta^{(n)})\alpha_k^{(n)}$. The minimum probability of a patch $\mathbf{Z}_i^{(n)}$ at level n across the training images is treated as the lower bound of the data likelihood, denoted as $\Lambda^{(n)}$:

$$\Lambda^{(n)} = \min(p(\mathbf{Z}_i^{(n)}|\theta^{(n)})), \quad \forall\, \mathbf{Z}_i^{(n)} \in \mathbf{Z}^{(n)}. \tag{6}$$

This completes the training stage in which with only a very few non-defective images, we determine the texems and an automatic threshold for marking new image patches as good or defective.

In the testing stage, the image under inspection is again layered into a multiscale framework and patches at each pixel position (x,y) at each level n are examined against the learned texems. The probability for each patch is then calculated, $p(\mathbf{Z}_i^{(n)}|\theta^{(n)})$, and compared to the minimum data likelihood, $\Lambda^{(n)}$, at the corresponding level. Let $Q^{(n)}(x,y)$ be the probability map at the nth resolution level. Then, the potential defect map, $\mathcal{D}^{(n)}(x,y)$, at level n is:

$$\mathcal{D}^{(n)}(x,y) = \begin{cases} 0 & \text{if } Q^{(n)}(x,y) \geq \Lambda^{(n)} \\ \Lambda^{(n)} - Q^{(n)}(x,y) & \text{otherwise.} \end{cases} \tag{7}$$

We then need to combine the information coming from all the resolution levels to build the certainty of the defect at position (x,y). We follow a method described in [2] which combines information from different levels of a multiscale pyramid and reduces false alarms. It assumes that a defect must appear in at least two adjacent resolution levels for it to be certified as such. Using a logical AND, implemented through the geometric mean, of every pair of adjacent levels, we initially obtain a set of combined maps as:

$$\mathcal{D}^{(n,n+1)}(x,y) = [\mathcal{D}^{(n)}(x,y)\mathcal{D}^{(n+1)}(x,y)]^{1/2}. \tag{8}$$

Please note that each $\mathcal{D}^{(n+1)}(x,y)$ is scaled up to be the same size as $\mathcal{D}^{(n)}(x,y)$. This operation reduces false alarms and yet preserves most of the defective areas. Next, the resulting $\mathcal{D}^{(1,2)}(x,y)$, $\mathcal{D}^{(2,3)}(x,y)$, ..., $\mathcal{D}^{(l-1,l)}(x,y)$ are combined in a logical OR, as the arithmetic mean, to provide a final map for the defects detected across all the scales:

$$\mathcal{D}(x,y) = \frac{1}{l-1}\sum_{n=1}^{l-1}\mathcal{D}^{(n,n+1)}(x,y), \tag{9}$$

where $\mathcal{D}(x,y)$ contains the joint contribution of all the resolution scales and marks the defects.

3 Experimental Results

We applied the proposed method to a variety of tile data sets with different types of defects including physical damage, pin holes, textural imperfections, pattern mis-registrations, and many more. The test samples, at 512×512 pixels,

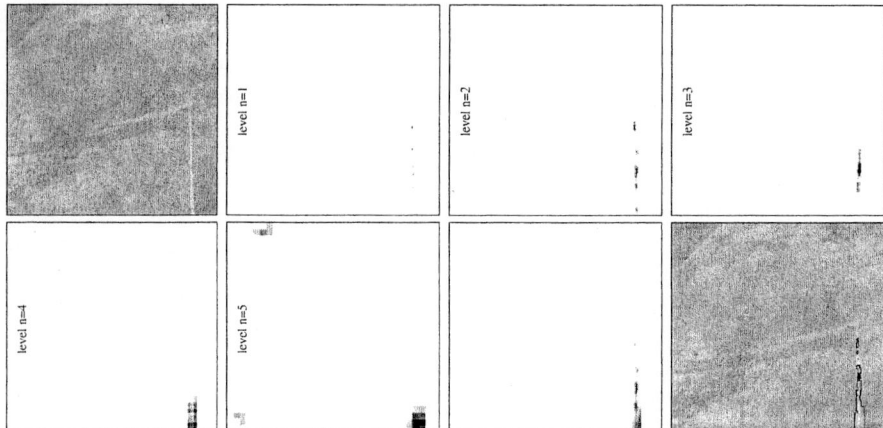

Fig. 2. Localising textural defects - from top left to bottom right: original defective tile image, detected defective regions at different levels $n = 1, 2, ..., 5$, the joint contribution of all resolution levels, and the final defective regions superimposed on the original image.

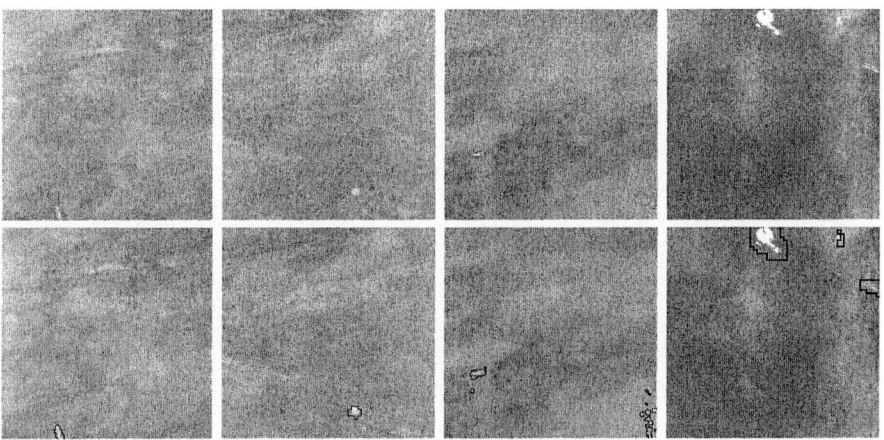

Fig. 3. Defect detection - first row: original images, second row: superimposed defective regions from left - surface defect, small bump, surface defect and a cluster of pin holes, and missing print.

were appropriately pre-processed to assure homogeneous luminance, spatially and temporally. In our experiments, only one defect free sample was used to extract the texems, and only five to generate the lower bound data likelihoods $\Lambda^{(n)}$. The number of texems at each level were empirically set to 12, and the size of each texem was set to 5×5 pixels. The number of multiscale levels was $l = 5$. These parameters were fixed throughout our experiments on a variety of random texture tile prints.

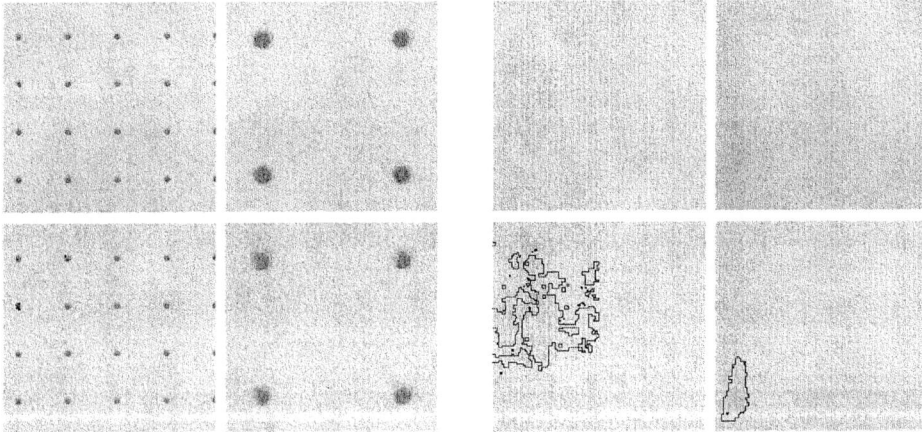

Fig. 4. Detecting defects in regular patterns - first column: original defective image and superimposed defective regions; second column: closeup views of normal and abnormal dot patterns from the previous image; third and fourth columns: two defective samples of a different regular texture with pattern irregularities and superimposed defective areas.

Figure 2 shows a random texture example, from the same family as in Figure 1, with a defect in the lower right region introduced by a printing problem. The detected potential defective regions at each resolution level n, $n = 1, 2, ..., 5$ are marked on the corresponding images in Figure 2. It can be seen that the texems show good sensitivity to the defective region at different scales. As the resolution progresses from coarse to fine, additional evidence for the defective region is gathered. This evidence is then combined, shown in the bottom-right of Figure 2, to produce the defect map $\mathcal{D}$. The final image shows the superimposed defects on the original image. As mentioned earlier, the defect fusion process can eliminate false alarms, e.g. see the extraneous false defect regions in level $n = 5$ which disappear after the operations in (8) and (9).

More examples of different textures are shown in Figure 3. In each family of patterns, the textures are varying but of the same visual impression. In each case the proposed method could find from very small surface defects to large variable shaped defects such as the missing print as shown in the last example.

The proposed method can also detect defects in regular patterns. For example, the first two images of Figure 4 show three incompletely printed dots at the top-left corner of the regular pattern. Each dot is composed of one larger, lighter dot as background and one smaller, darker dot positioned in the centre (see the closeup view in the second column of the Figure 4). In other two examples in Figure 4, printing error and smudge defects damaging the local pattern regularity in a grid-like pattern were correctly detected.

Next, we compare our results with those obtained by using the epitome [8]. Two example cases are shown in Figure 5. We apply the epitome for texture segmentation (with software provided by the authors of [8]), however, we

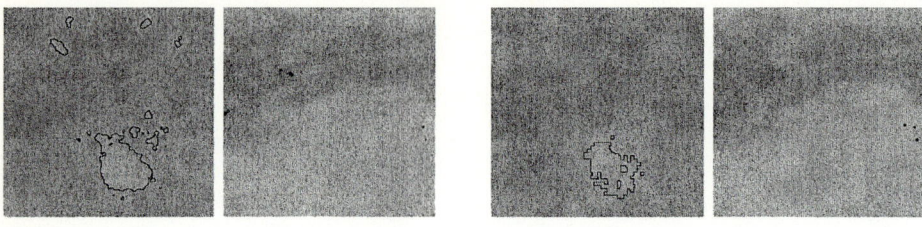

Fig. 5. Leftmost two images: examples of novelty detection using epitomes which produced many false positives or failed to locate the true defects. Rightmost two: novelty detection results using texems which successfully detected all the true defects (a print defect and three pin holes).

extend it into a similar framework as the proposed method for better comparative analysis. Hence, we generate the multiscale version of an image and at each scale, we learn an appearance epitome using 5×5 image patches at each scale, resulting in epitomes varying from 7×7 to 24×24. Using these multiscale epitomes, we perform novelty detection, similar to the method described in Section 2.3. It involves finding a match in the epitome for an image patch under inspection. As the epitome is still larger than the patch itself and there are numerous comparisons across the image, the detection procedure is computationally very expensive. The results show that our method is less sensitive to false alarms.

As patches are extracted from each pixel position at each resolution level, a typical *training stage* involves examining over 0.25 million patches (for a 512×512 image) to learn the texems in multiscale. This takes around 25 minutes on an AMD Athlon XP Processor (1.4GHz) to obtain the texems and to determine the thresholds for novelty detection. The testing stage is much faster, requiring about one minute to inspect one tile image. However, it will cost the epitome based method several hours to perform training or testing. The computation time of our method can be greatly reduced by examining every other pixel (or fewer).

The examples show the ability of texems ability in localising small or large defects on highly textured surfaces. We evaluated our defect detection rate across 1512 tiles from eight different families of textures and obtained very good results with 95.87% sensitivity, 89.47% specificity, and 92.67% overall accuracy.

4 Conclusions

We presented an automatic defect detection and localisation algorithm for random textures. The proposed method only trained on a very small number of defect free samples with the aid of novel texems that are implicit representations of primitive textural information. The texems are at present only applicable to graylevel images and we intend to extend them to colour analysis. This can be achieved by modifying the inference procedure that derives them. The computational needs of the method are somewhat demanding for a real-time inspection.

We shall investigate various avenues to achieve a rate of around 2-4 surfaces per second which is an acceptable tile industry norm. While we present this work with respect to ceramic tiles, the proposed method should be suitable to other flat textured surfaces, such as textiles and wood.

Acknowledgments

This work is funded by EC project `G1RD-CT-2002-00783 MONOTONE`, and X. Xie is partly funded by the ORSAS, Universities UK.

References

1. Cohen, F., Fan, Z., Attali, S.: Automated inspection of textile fabrics using textural models. IEEE T-PAMI **13** (1991) 803–809
2. Escofet, J., Navarro, R., Millán, M., Pladellorens, J.: Detection of local defects in textile webs using Gabor filters. Opt. Eng. **37** (1998) 2297–2307
3. Kittler, J., Marik, R., Mirmehdi, M., Petrou, M., Song, J.: Detection of defects in colour texture surfaces. In: IAPR MVA. (1994) 558–567
4. Randen, T., Husøy, J.: Filtering for texture classification: a comparative study. T-PAMI **21** (1999) 291–310
5. Varma, M., Zisserman, A.: Texture classification: Are filter banks necessary? In: CVPR. (2003) 691–698
6. Ojala, T., Pietikäinen, M., Mäenpää, T.: Multiresolution gray-scale and rotation invariant texture classification with local binary patterns. IEEE T-PAMI **24** (2002) 971–987
7. Özdemir, S., Baykut, A., Meylani, R., Ercil, A., Ertüzün, A.: Comparative evaluation of texture analysis algorithms for defect inspection of textile products. In: CVPR. (1998) 1738–1740
8. Jojic, N., Frey, B., Kannan, A.: Epitomic analysis of appearance and shape. In: ICCV. (2003) 34–42
9. Kumar, A.: Neural network based detection of local textile defects. PR **36** (2003) 1645–1659
10. Monadjemi, A., Mirmehdi, M., Thomas, B.: Restructured eigenfilter matching for novelty detection in random textures. In: BMVC. (2004) 637–646
11. Julesz, B.: Textons, the element of texture perception and their interactions. Nature **290** (1981) 91–97
12. Zhu, S., Guo, C., Wang, Y., Xu, Z.: What are textons? IJCV **62** (2005) 121–143

Semantic-Based Cross-Media Image Retrieval

Ahmed Id Oumohmed, Max Mignotte, and Jian-Yun Nie

DIRO, University of Montreal, Canada
{idoumoha, mignotte, nie}@iro.umontreal.ca

Abstract. In this paper, we propose a novel method for cross-media semantic-based information retrieval, which combines classical text-based and content-based image retrieval techniques. This semantic-based approach aims at determining the strong relationships between keywords (in the caption) and types of visual features associated with its typical images. These relationships are then used to retrieve images from a textual query. In particular, the association *keyword/visual feature* may allow us to retrieve non-annotated but similar images to those retrieved by a classical textual query. It can also be used for automatic images annotation. Our experiments on two different databases show that this approach is promising for cross-media retrieval.

1 Introduction

In general, a content-based image retrieval (CBIR) system tries to determine the most similar images to a given query image by using one or a combination of several low-level visual feature(s) such as color, texture or shape. Depending on the content of each image, it's highly difficult to choose the appropriate feature(s) to use and eventually the manner to combine them. While users are mostly interested by the high-level (i.e., abstract) concepts presents within an image query, the most similar images to this latter according to some low-level visual features can be non-relevant in the sens of semantics. This is known as the semantic gap. Usually, an annotated-based image retrieval (ABIR) system is based on a certain model representation of the concepts (words) associated to each image (document). Given a textual query, a such system scores and ranks images according to the importance of each word of text query to images. In this case, the search result is more limited to images that are really annotated by at least one of the words that form the textual query. In this work, we attempt to reach the same objective by finding non-annotated, but similar, images to those retrieved by a classical textual query. To this end, and based on a training set of several images annotated by the same single word, we propose an unsupervised learning procedure which determine the most representative visual feature (visual semantic) of this word. Given an image query and the words of its caption, the user can choose the characterization of a certain word as a new search criterion.

1.1 Related Work

Organizing a set of images into clusters was used by Chen, Wang and Krovetz [1] in their CBIR system (*CLUE*). Instead of sorting images by feature similarities with respect to a query image, the system retrieves image clusters. Especially, the user can navigate between queries according to each defined cluster (semantic *clue*). After the resemblance between the query image and target images are evaluated and sorted, a collection of target images that are "close" to the query image are selected as the neighborhood of the query image. The set of descriptor vectors of this collection is clustered into a dynamically-defined number of regions. This approach offers a different manner to present and visualize the most similar images to a given query image with an interesting interaction with the user.

Among the semantic-based approach, but only image content-based, different kinds of methods have already been investigated. We can cite, for example, the approach used in [2] which consists in grouping images into semantically meaningful categories. This system was applied on 6931 vacation photographs to obtain a classification such indoor/outdoor, city/landscape, etc. This classification is performed by a Bayesian classifier under the constraint that the test image does belong to one of the classes beforehand established by human subjects. We can also cite the approach used in [3] which clusters the image regions into 10 clusters (cloud, grass, etc.) and uses a probabilistic approach to define a semantic codebook of every cluster. Nevertheless, some recent studies [4] have tried to automatically create associations between visual features and keywords. The basic idea is to use a set of annotated images as a set of learning examples, and to extract strong associations between annotation keywords and the visual features of the images. In particular, a segmentation algorithm, such Blobword [5] or Normalized-cuts [6] is used to produce segmented regions, then for each region, feature information (color, texture, position and shape) is computed. The set of computed features are clustered into regions which are called "blobs" which define the vocabulary for the set of images. Finally images are annotated by the means of a cross-media relevance model.

Among the semantic-based approach trying to model the relationships between image features and associated text, we can cite the interesting work of Barnard et al. [7]. Their approach searches to provide a statistical joint distribution for associated words and features of each region of an image (image segments). After a training step which consists in estimating the parameters of a mixture of (Gaussian) distributions, a query search consists in computing the probability of each candidate image of emitting the query items. This method remains nevertheless highly dependent of the segmentation results and parameters associated to the segmentation (number of classes). Besides it is also highly dependent of the assumption that the cluster-conditional distribution of *index terms* (words or image segments) (i.e., the likelihood of this model) is unimodal and Gaussian. We can also cite the work of Wang et al. in [8] which try to address the challenging and -closely related problem- of automatic linguistic indexing of pictures. Association between an image and textual description of a concept is modeled via a likelihood given by a two-dimensional multi-resolution hidden markov model (HMM) whose parameters is learned in a training step. Once again, a query search consists in computing the likelihood of each candidate image for each pre-learned concept. As in applications, where this strategy is commonly used (e.g., handwritten text and speech recognition), this method remains highly dependent of the parameter estimation step of the HMM which is then used for the recognition step. In the case of 2D signal (i.e., image) this estimation may not to efficiently model all the diversity of the different concepts and classes of images.

1.2 Our Approach

Instead of using pre-segmented image regions, described by multiple features (color, texture, shape, etc.), our approach uses the whole image content and tries to find out the most representative visual feature(s). Compared to [4], our approach has the advantage of not being dependent of a specific segmentation and can take into account relationships between regions (e.g., airplane-sky, animal-grass,boat-sea, etc.). Besides, some (key)words are best represented by one feature than by considering several features (e.g., sea with texture and cathe-

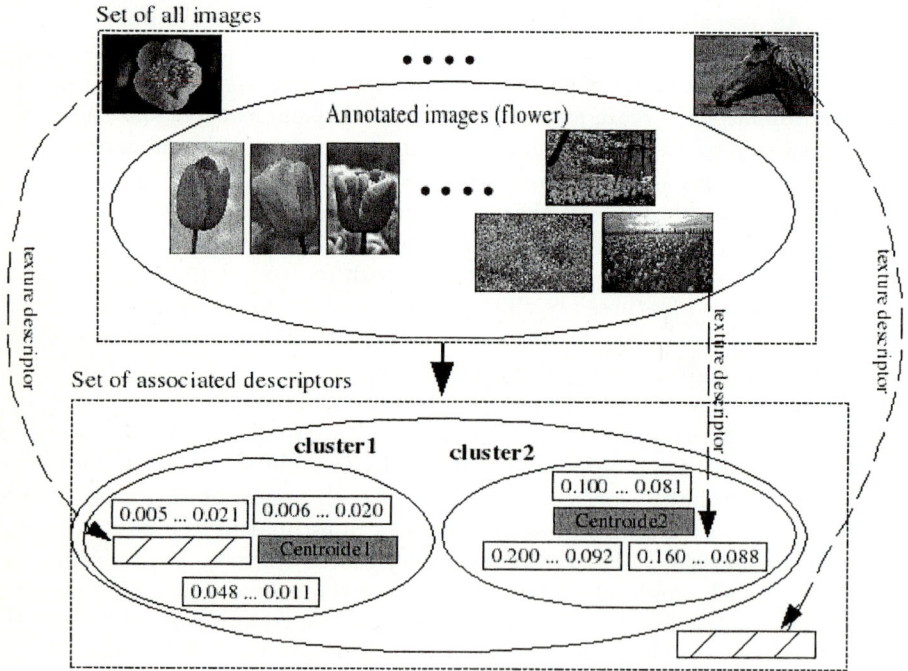

Fig. 1. For each word, the training data is the set of corresponding annotated images which yield to three sets of descriptors (vectors) according to each high-level visual feature. Each set of descriptors is clustered in several regions. The figure shows an example of clustering in 2 regions for the set associated to the texture feature.

dral with contours) which can introduce noise in the automatic retrieval model if they are not relevant. Our approach tries to identify such strong associations between words and visual features.

Our training data for each word is the set of images annotated by this word. This dataset is exploited to obtain several sets of descriptor vectors according to the high-level visual features which will later be associated with the aforementioned (key)word. Each set of descriptors is then clustered by using several number of partitions (cf. Fig. 1 showing an example of clustering associated to a feature with respect to 2 partitions). This clustering allows our system to automatically estimate or capture the optimal number of partitions associated to the number of classes of images in the sens of their visual content (e.g., four types of mountains, six types of cars, etc.). Each cluster is then described by some statistical and spatial characterizations. We also describe the quality and the performance of a query based on the centroid feature (i.e., a model associated to a virtual image) of each clusters. According to some criteria on these descriptions, the key-word is associated with its most representative high-level visual feature, the number of regions used in the clustering and the corresponding cluster centroid.

This unsupervised learning process also allows to propose a new image retrieval method by prompting the user to submit both a query image and a query key-word. To this end, the centroid of the cluster which contains the descriptor of the query image (and which can be viewed as the learned semantic concept of the key-word) can be exploited as a virtual image to perform the query. In particular, this visual semantic allows to retrieve similar images to the image query in the sens of the visual semantic of the given key-word.

1.3 Outline of the Paper

The reminder of the paper is organized as follows: In section 2, we will present the image processing techniques developed for this retrieval system; i.e., the considered visual features (texture, contours and shape/color) as well as their corresponding similarity measures. In section 3, we will describe the way that relationships between keywords and visual features are extracted by the means of a learning procedure. In section 4, we will present some experimental results on the annotated *'St Andrews University Library Photographic Collection'* and *Corel©* databases and we conclude.

2 Image Processing Retrieval Techniques

Edge, texture and shape (including color) informations are important cues for pattern recognition and retrieval purposes in large image database. In our approach, we have considered these cues as the three fundamental classes of visual characteristics, which we will call features in this paper. For each of the features, we consider a descriptor and an associated discriminant measure of similarity $S_{feature}$.

Edge Descriptor: Wavelet-based measures have often been used in content-based image retrieval (CBIR) systems because of their appealing ability to describe the local texture and the distribution of the edges of a given image at multiple scales. We use the Harr wavelet transform on the gray-level component of the image. The procedure of image decomposition into wavelets involves recursive numeric filtering. It is applied to the set of pixels of the digital image which is decomposed with a family of orthogonal basis functions obtained through translation and dilatation of a special function called *mother* wavelet. Three scales of transformation are considered here. For decomposition of each scale, we compute the mean and the standard deviation (μ_n and σ_n) of the energy distribution in each (of the $n = 10$) sub-band. This leads to an edge descriptor $\{\mu_{n=1}, \sigma_{n=1}, \ldots, \mu_{n=10}, \sigma_{n=10}\}$ of 20 components. For this descriptor, the similarity measure (S_{edge}) we use is the weighted-mean-variance distance.

Texture Descriptor: Tamura *et al.* [9] have proposed to characterize image texture along the dimensions of contrast, directionality, coarseness, line-likeness, regularity and roughness. Coarseness refers to the average of the best representative sizes of the *textons* (i.e., texture resolution representation). To describe the texture feature, we use the coarseness and directionality histograms. We make two adjustments to the well known coarseness algorithm [9]. First, we set some predefined texture resolutions $\{2, 8, 14, 20, 26, 32, 38\}$ instead of $2^k \times 2^k$ with $k = 0, 1, \ldots, 6$, then, we deal with homogeneous regions bigger than the maximum of texture resolutions taken in account. After thresholding, the oriented edges are quantized into an 8-bin histogram. The similarity measure ($S_{texture}$) used is the Jeffrey divergence [10].

Shape and Color Descriptor: Extraction of shapes contained in an image remains a difficult task. Following [11], we first estimate a segmented image from which we extract the contours of different regions. The segmented image defines a set of connected pixels belonging to a same class. In this procedure, the noise is taken into consideration, edges are always connected, and the only parameter adjustment is the number of regions used in the segmentation procedure. Then, for each edge pixel, we define a direction (horizontal, vertical, first or second diagonal) depending on the disposition of its neighboring edge pixels and compute a 4-bin histogram. We complete this information by computing a 32-bin color histogram by using the HSV color space. The similarity measure S_{shape} used for this 36-bin histogram is the weighted-mean-variance distance.

3 Associating Words with Representative Images and Features

Given a set of training images with caption, we try to automatically determine one or several clusters of images representative for each word, together with the most discriminative feature(s), i.e. *texture, edge* and *shape-color*. The principle is as follows: for each word, we try to group the images associated with it into several clusters (at different scales) according to each feature. Using one cluster as a visual query, if we can find many images annotated with the word among the most similar images according to the associated feature, then the cluster and the feature are considered to be characteristic for the word. In this way, each word can be associated with zero, one or several clusters and features.

More precisely, let us define some notations: let $\mathbf{I}$ and $\mathbf{I}_w$ be respectively the set of all images in the training dataset and the set of all images that are annotated with the keyword w. $|.|$ will designate the cardinal or the number of elements of a considered set: by applying the three visual features characterizations to $\mathbf{I}_w$, we obtain three sets of descriptors $\mathbf{D}_{I_w}^{texture}$, $\mathbf{D}_{I_w}^{edge}$ and $\mathbf{D}_{I_w}^{Shape}$. We will use the notation $\mathbf{D}_{I_w}^{feature}$ to refer to each of these descriptors.

For a fixed number of regions (we consider 1, 2,..., 5 regions in our case), we use the Generalized Loyd [12] algorithm to cluster each set $\mathbf{D}_{I_w}^{feature}$ in R partitions, thus, we obtain several $_c^R\mathbf{D}_{I_w}^{feature}$ clusters, where R denote the number of partitions used in the clustering and c the cth cluster in this R-clustering. The error-distance used in the clustering of $\mathbf{D}_{I_w}^{feature}$ is the similarity measure of the feature $S_{feature}$. For each value of R, this clustering allows us to approximate the distribution of the set of samples $\mathbf{D}_{I_w}^{feature}$ by R spherical distributions with identical radius. The centers (centroids) of these approximated spherical distributions are then considered as prototype vectors and are denoted by $_c^R P_{I_w}^{feature}$. Several values of R are used to take in account the fact that a given word may be associated to many images classes. For example, the word BOAT may be associated with images with small shape of boat in sea, or with a closer view of boat, and so on. For each cluster $_c^R\mathbf{D}_{I_w}^{feature}$, its associated centroid is used as a descriptor vector of a virtual image representative of the word. The virtual image will be used to query the whole training database $\mathbf{I}$ to get the closest descriptors (or images) according to the similarity measure associated to the feature $feature$. The training process is as follows:

- First, in order to associate each (key-)word w with the most discriminant class of visual characteristic $Feature$, we use the following strategy: for each considered cluster $_c^R\mathbf{D}_{I_w}^{feature}$, we count the number of images annotated by the word w that are retrieved among the first X ($X = 20$ in our case) retrieved images for each $Feature$. Let $topX^{feature}$ be this number. We count the sum of the $topX^{feature}$ resulting from the query by all corresponding prototype vectors. We then consider the class of visual feature for which this sum is maximal.

- Second, in order to define a set of prototype vectors associated to the pre-estimated class of visual feature, we adopt the following strategy: we characterize a given cluster $_c^R\mathbf{D}_{I_w}^{feature}$ by three measures: its proportion ρ within $\mathbf{I}_w$ (simply, $\rho = |_c^R\mathbf{D}_{I_w}^{feature}|/|\mathbf{I}_w|$), its standard deviation σ (computed according to the similarity measure of $feature$), and an empirical measure P which represents the number of images, not annotated by the word w, for which the distance between its descriptor vector and the prototype vector $_c^R P_{I_w}^{feature}$ is less than the pre-estimated standard deviation σ, namely

$$P = |\{I \notin \mathbf{I}_w \mid S_{feature}(_c^R\mathbf{D}_{I_w}^{feature}, {_c^R}P_{I_w}^{feature}) < \sigma\}|/|I|$$

Once one feature or several weighted features are fixed, we choose representative prototype vectors regarding to P, their proportion and their standard deviation as follows: we use a first criterion to exclude prototype vectors for which $P > 0.05$ and $\rho < 0.05$. If there is no remaining prototype vector, then we ignore this criterion. The second criterion is to retain prototype vectors for which ρ/σ is greater than a threshold. The result of the training process is that a word may be associated with zero, one or several clusters of representative images, together with an associated feature to each cluster (i.e., vectors associated with high peak spherical distribution).

4 Experimental Results and Conclusion

The experimental results are based on the historical image database *'St Andrews University Library Photographic Collection'* provided by *ImageCLEF 2004* [13]. This database contains 28133 images with caption. The caption text associated to each image contains around tens of (key)words. Our goal was to improve textual and multi-words queries by extending words to their associated visual features but our experiments in this context are extremely difficult due to the poor quality of the images of this database and also due to the presence of some (key)words used in the request with an abstract concept. ("Scotland", "north", "tournament", etc.). For our experiments, we have also considered a set of 20000 images extracted from the Corel© database where each image is annotated by a few concrete and significant keywords. To test the relevance of our approach, we remove each word from the caption of 50% of associated images. We use these images as references and we try to see how our approach is able to retrieve these images with a query made of the removed word. We will emphasis on two aspects of our results: the retrieved reference images and the non-annotated images retrieved but also related to the word in consideration.

Figure 2 shows some words with the estimated weights for each class of visual feature. Most associations have a significant meaning: animal is associated to shape and texture features, ocean is most described by shape (probably due to the presence of boats or due to the color component included with shape descriptor), tiger is described by texture and contours, zebra is associated to texture, etc. However, some words have almost the same weights for the three features, for example water, sky, garden and tree. This may be due to the high number of learning vectors. The word texture is strangely associated with shapes and contours. By choosing clusters with high value of P, we can guess to obtain more images that are not annotated by the word, but which are related to this word. In other hand, low values of this measure may yield to more images that are really annotated by the word; this may be useful in the case of queries with multiple words, so to eventually improve the text retrieval result. Figure 4 shows three semantic query results for the words flower, canal and grass: the algorithm described in 3 was used to produce these results. It shows also a query for word grass according to its second relevant feature. Even if the reference images were not retrieved successfully, we can see that most of images are related to the query word.

database	word	selected feature			Number of training vectors
		Feature 1	Feature 2	Feature 3	
C O R E L	water	contours (74)	shape (65)	texture (61)	2550
	sky	contours (66)	texture (65)	shape (60)	2323
	tree	texture (85)	contours (79)	shape (72)	2242
	people	contours (76)	texture (60)	shape (51)	1908
	grass	contours (35)	shape (28)	texture (27)	1061
	flower	shape (61)	contours (51)	texture (16)	934
	wild	contours (17)	texture (15)	shape (15)	707
	bird	texture (24)	contours (12)	shape (9)	595
	plant	contours (13)	shape (10)	texture (8)	439
	garden	texture (14)	contours (14)	shape (14)	301
	sunset	shape (19)	contours (15)	texture (8)	260
	ice	contours (8)	texture (6)	shape (5)	240
	ocean	shape (44)	contours (26)	texture (15)	231
	animal	shape (11)	texture (7)	contours (3)	204
	ski	contours (4)	shape (1)	texture (0)	153
	texture	shape (17)	contours (10)	texture (8)	126
	rural	contours (7)	texture (3)	shape (3)	124
	insect	contours (10)	shape (7)	texture (1)	123
	tiger	texture (14)	contours (10)	shape (9)	73
	zebra	texture (13)	contours (9)	shape (8)	26
St-AND-REW	street	contours (119)	shape (101)	texture (96)	2348
	church	contours (57)	texture (48)	shape (48)	2721
	boat	texture (61)	shape (40)	contours (37)	1740
	golfer	texture (18)	shape (14)	contours (10)	309
	canal	texture (3)	shape (3)	contours (2)	178
	swing	texture (8)	contours (1)	shape (1)	94

Fig. 2. A list of concepts with their discriminative features ranked by the sum of $top20^{feature}$ over all the clusters of the feature (criterion used to choose the most discriminative feature or eventually to combine several features)

Corel word	top10	top20	top50	top100	ref10	ref20	ref50	ref100	vis20	vis40	vis60
flower (shape)	2	2	3	7	2	3	5	8	9	17	28
animal (shape)	1	1	2	3	0	0	0	0	6	9	16
birds (texture)	1	1	4	5	1	1	3	5	3	7	9
ice (contours)	0	0	0	1	0	0	0	1	0	0	0
grass (contours)	0	0	0	5	0	1	1	4	9	15	26

St-Andrew word	top10	top20	top50	top100	vis20	vis40	vis60
canal (texture)	0	1	1	2	10	17	29
street (contours)	1	4	14	26	12	26	37
boat (texture)	1	4	8	10	4	9	12

Fig. 3. Some statistics about the top retrieved images for some words. topX is the number of images annotated by the word among the first X retrieved images. Identically, refX and visX are related respectively to reference images and visually accepted images (a subjective judgment).

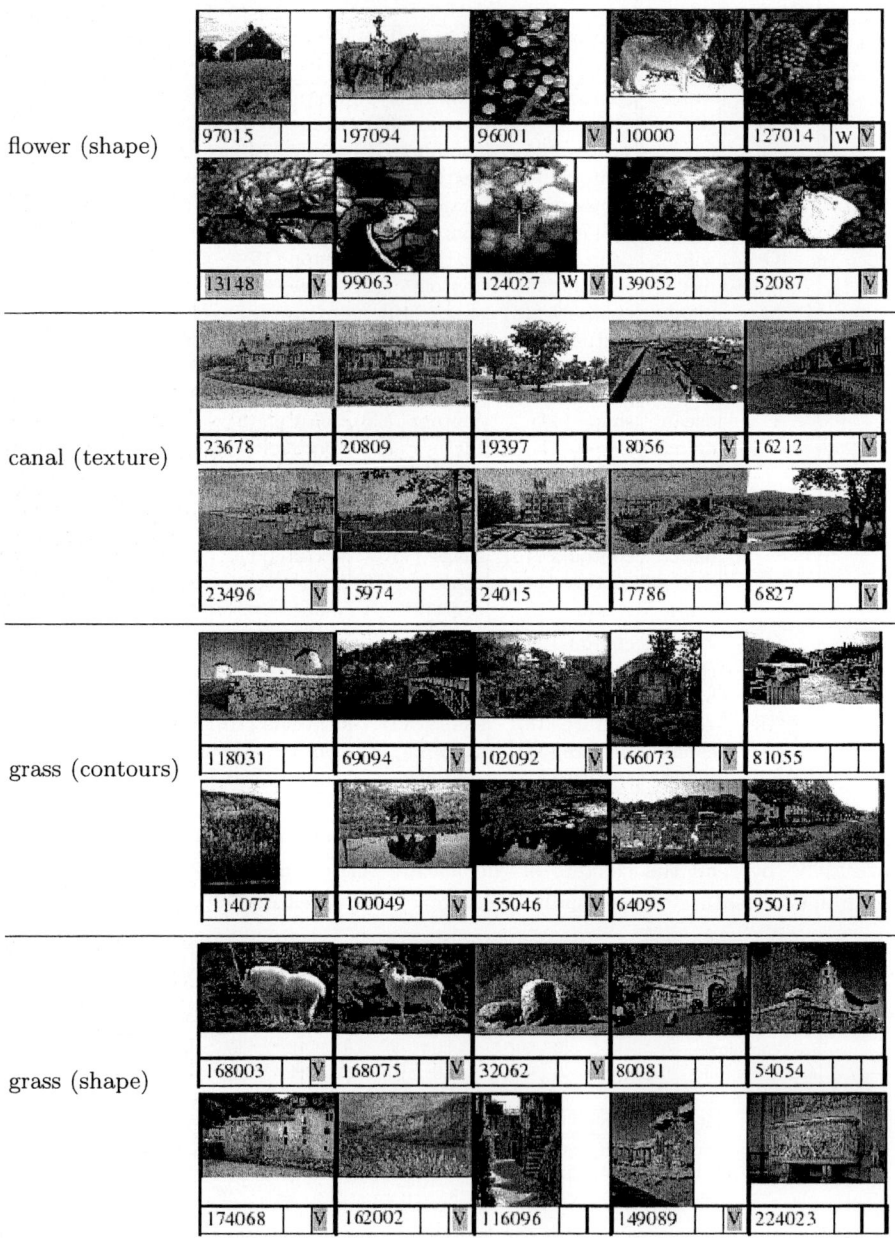

Fig. 4. Semantic query results for concepts flower (shape), canal (texture) and grass (contours). The last query is made according to the best cluster of feature shape. The identification number is shown above each image. Annotated images are marked by a W box. Visually related images to the concept are marked by V box. Reference images have their identification number in a gray box.

References

1. Yixin Chen, James Z. Wang, and Robert Krovetz. Content-based image retrieval by clustering. In *MIR '03: Proceedings of the 5th ACM SIGMM international workshop on Multimedia information retrieval*, pages 193–200, New York, NY, USA, 2003. ACM Press.
2. Aditya Vailaya, A. T. Figueiredo, Anil K. Jain, and Hong-Jiang Zhang. Image classification for content-based indexing. *IEEE Transactions on Image Processing*, 10:117–130, 2001.
3. W. Wang, Y. Song, and A. Zhang. Semantic-based image retrieval by region saliency. In *Int'l Conf. on Image and Video Retrieval*, July 2002.
4. J. Jeon, V. Lavrenko, and R. Manmatha. Automatic image annotation and retrieval using cross-media relevance models. In *ACM SIGIR*, 2003.
5. Chad Carson, Megan Thomas, Serge Belongie, Joseph M. Hellerstein, and Jitendra Malik. Blobworld: A system for region-based image indexing and retrieval. In *Third International Conference on Visual Information Systems*, pages 509–516. Springer, 1999.
6. J. Shi and J. Malik. Normalized cuts and image segmentation. *IEEE Transactions on Pattern Analysis and Machine Intelligence*, 22:888–905, 2000.
7. K. Barnard, P. Duygulu, and D. Forsyth. Modeling the statistics of image features and associated text, 2002.
8. Jia Li and James Z. Wang. Automatic linguistic indexing of pictures by a statistical modeling approach. *IEEE Trans. Pattern Anal. Mach. Intell.*, 25(9):1075–1088, 2003.
9. H. Tamura, S. Mori, and T. Yamawaki. Texture features corresponding to visual perception. *IEEE Transactions on Systems, Man, and Cybernetics*, 8:460–473, 1978.
10. J. Puzicha, Y. Rubner, C. Tomasi, and J. Buhmann and. Empirical evaluation of dissimilarity measures for color and texture. In *International Conference on Computer Vision*, volume 2, pages 1165–1173, September 1999.
11. M. Goldberg, P. Boucher, and S. Shlien. Image compression using adaptative vector quantization. *Communications, IEEE Transactions on [legacy, pre - 1988]*, 34:180–187, 1986.
12. Y. Linde, A. Buzo, and R.M. Gray. An algorithm for vector quantizer design. *IEEE Transactions on Communications*, COM-28:84–95, 1980.
13. Carmen Alvarez, Ahmed Id Oumohmed, Max Mignotte, and Jian-Yun Nie. Toward cross-language and cross-media image retrieval. In *Working Notes for the CLEF 2004 Workshop*, volume 1, pages 525–534, September 2004.

Texture Image Retrieval: A Feature-Based Correspondence Method in Fourier Spectrum*

Celia A. Zorzo Barcelos[1,2], Márcio J.R. Ferreira[2], and Mylene L. Rodrigues[2]

[1] Federal University of Goiás, Catalão-GO, Brazil
[2] Federal University of Uberlândia,
Caixa Postal 593, CEP 38.400-902 Uberlândia-MG, Brazil
celiazb@ufu.br
{marcio, mylene}@pos.facom.ufu.br

Abstract. This paper presents an effective texture descriptor invariant to translation, scaling, and rotation for texture-based image retrieval applications. The proposed texture descriptor is built taking the Fourier space of the image. In order to find the best texture descriptor, a quantization scheme based on Lloyd's technique is proposed. As frequency descriptors are not invariant to all geometrical transformations as scaling and rotation, the modal analysis is applied to overcome these problems. Our image database is extracted from Brodatz album as well other sources. The proposed method is also compared with other content-based techniques and their performance is evaluated through several experiments. The effectiveness of both methods is measured by the commonly used retrieval performance measurement - Precision and Recall.

1 Introduction

Analysis, classification and texture retrieval have been, over the last few years, the target of intense research in Computational Vision and Digital Image Processing. Such methods are used in different areas as medical image analysis, geo-processing, military applications, security and personal identification, etc.

Texture retrieval passes through the difficult step of texture representation or description. What is seen as a relatively easy task to the human observer, becomes a difficult challenge when the analysis is made by a computational algorithm. How can we copy the human brain in its capability to analyze, classify and recognize textures? Putting aside these questions about human brain workings, and focusing mainly on the necessity of how to describe a texture from its content, different approaches and models have been proposed.

Some content-based algorithms (color, texture, spacial information, shape, etc, [1], [2], [3]), play a crucial role in image retrieval. Texture is widely used for image classification and retrieval. Because of this, a great amount of texture analysis methods have been developed and different approaches have been explored. The most common approaches are statistical and structural. When

---

* This work is partially supported by CAPES, FUNAPE and CNPq.

dealing with statistics, texture is described using statistic measurements, like direction, contrast and coarseness, where probability and inferences are applied [1,4]. Image statistics methods compute primitive image features and their functions, such as color histograms [5], shape [6,7] and texture measurements [4] and use them for indexing, matching and segmenting images. Structural models use a certain amount of the local characteristics derived from the local frequency domain [8].

Therefore, not different from the employed approach, all models have as their objective to obtain a canonic texture representation, or, a texture representation that is invariant to rotation, scale, translation, zoom, brightness and robust in the presence of noise and other irregularities throughout the texture [9,10].

Shapiro and Brady proposed in [11] a point-feature correspondence model using a modal analysis of the shapes. As the first step, m image feature-points are chosen to represent each image. Then, a $m \times m$ square proximity matrix H is created. That matrix has the aim of recording feature distances.

For the final step of the method, the matching of two image patterns is analyzed by an association matrix Z, which records the Euclidean distance between the modal matrices.

Following the ideas of Shapiro and Brady [11], Carcassoni et al. [12] proposed a texture retrieval model based on spectral points, using homogeneous texture as fabric and wrapping papers. In such a method, for all database images, the Fourier transform is used to pass from the spatial to the frequency domain, then the power spectrum is computed with the aim of choosing the N highest peaks, which will be used to represent the whole texture. For each, query or database image, as in [13] and [14], a proximity relationship of the peaks is calculated.

As the next step, the modal analysis is applied with the goal of making the image robust to some transformations, such as rotation. The clusterization [15] is calculated and once again the proximity relationship and the modal analysis are applied. Image similarity is measured by comparing the modal matrix that represents the query image with all the other modal matrices that represent each database image.

Considering that there may exist two or more different textures having the N highest power spectrum peaks with the same magnitude, leading to an erroneous matching, we propose a model where a quantization scheme based on Lloyd's technique [16] is used to represent the whole texture.

2 The Feature-Based Correspondence

The modal correspondence method of Shapiro and Brady [11] has the aim of matching patterns correspondences between two images I_1 and I_2 using feature-points correspondence and they also explored the modal approach of an image based on the spatial distribution of its features by comparing the eigenvectors of a feature proximity matrix.

According to the authors, the modal representation allows rotations and translations maintaining the same recognition achieved by the original image.

The idea of the method is to match points by analyzing their distances between images. For each image, a number m of feature-points is chosen, with x_i, $(i = 1, ..., m)$, representing each pattern-feature. A relationship between these points is constructed by a square proximity matrix H, which records feature distances within the image, as follow:

$$H_{ij} = e^{-r_{ij}^2/2\sigma_x^2}. \tag{1}$$

where $r_{ij}^2 = ||x_i - x_j||^2$ which is a Gaussian function that aims to model the probability of adjacency among features. This function is not a good choice to control distortion effects because its is fragile when dealing with structural differences. The interaction among image features in the same image is controlled by σ_x, i.e., it controls whether the feature will have global or local knowledge of its surrounding.

The proximity matrix H is symmetric and its principal diagonal has value 1. After this H matrix is computed, the modal analysis will be applied, creating the orthogonal modal matrix V, which has the eigenvectors as its columns $V = (E_1|, ..., |E_m)$, where E_i are the eigenvectors of the proximity matrix H and each row of V is called as a feature vector F_i.

The association matrix Z is computed by the Euclidian distance between feature vectors:

$$Z_{ij} = ||F_{i1} - F_{j2}||^2. \tag{2}$$

The matching is given by those elements in Z which have the lowest values in their row and column. A perfect match is given by the 0 value and no match is indicated for values equal or greater than 2.

3 The Eigenvector Method for Texture Retrieval

The eigenvectors can be used for recognition purposes. Based on this idea, Carcassoni, Ribeiro and Hancock in [12] present a retrieval method that uses modal analysis of spectral peaks for retrieval textures in an image database.

They commence by summarizing the structure of the power spectrum using the N highest peaks frequency vectors, denoting the frequency vector of the ith peak of an image I^α by $U_i^\alpha = (u_i, v_i)$, and concatenating these frequency vectors according to their order of energy from high to low. Next, as in [13] the Sigmoidal Weighting Function is used to compute the proximity matrix of the N first highest peaks:

$$H_\alpha(i,j) \frac{2}{\pi |U_i^\alpha - U_j^\alpha|} \log \cosh[\frac{\pi}{s}|U_i^\alpha - U_j^\alpha|]. \tag{3}$$

The modal structure of this domain peak proximity matrix ϕ is calculated. The eigenvectors are computed and sorted according to their eigenvalues order of magnitude, i.e., $|\lambda_1^\alpha| > |\lambda_2^\alpha| > ... > |\lambda_N^\alpha|$, to build the modal matrix $N \times N$, $\phi^\alpha = (\phi_1^\alpha|\phi_2^\alpha|...|\phi_N^\alpha)$.

The cluster centers are calculated by

$$C_n^\alpha = \frac{\sum_{i=1}^{N} |\phi^\alpha(i,n)| U_i^\alpha}{\sum_{i=1}^{N} |\phi^\alpha(i,n)|}. \qquad (4)$$

The cluster centers are used to compute a cluster center proximity matrix given by (3), and repeating the procedure above, the modal structure of the cluster center proximity matrix is calculated and used to gauge similarity ([17,18]) of different power spectra and perform texture matching.

The similarity between the query texture and the textured images in the database is measured by the following equation:

$$w_q = max_\alpha \{w^\alpha\}.$$

where:

$$w_q = \sum_{l=1}^{M} \sum_{m=1}^{M} exp[-k \sum_{n=1}^{M} (\psi^q(l,n) - \psi^\alpha(m,n))^2]. \qquad (5)$$

where k is a constant and $M \leq N$.

It is worth noting that when the modal matrix elements are very different, there are no significant contributions, made by those elements, to the final result and when the lines of the matrices are very close, the value of the above sum will be greater.

4 The Proposed Method

Following the ideas presented in [12] and considering that two different textures can have the N first power spectrum peaks with almost the same magnitude, and to avoid the retrieval error caused by ambiguity between textures having similar power spectra, we propose the use of quantized points to represent the power spectrum. These points were chosen using a variation of Lloyd's technique [16].

4.1 The Spectrum Representation

The power spectrum of an image $I^\alpha = I(x,y)$ is defined by the Fourier transform of its autocorrelation. Details on two-dimensional spectral estimation can be found in [19] and [20].

For the purpose of recognition, in this paper, a quantity of S values will be taken from each image in order to represent its spectrum. Here, the representative elements q_i, $i = 1, ..., S$, will be chosen using a modified Lloyd's technique [21] for quantization.

A quantization scheme consists of a set $Q = \{Q_1, Q_2, ..., Q_S\}$ and a set of levels called quanta $q = \{q_1, q_2, ..., q_S\}$. Q is defined in such a way so that two sets $\{Q_i\}$ and $\{Q_j\}$ have an empty intersection and the union of all Q_j covers the entire spectrum of the image I. Also, a set $\{t_k\}$, $k = 1, ..., S+1$, denominated separators, should be chosen in such a way as to satisfy the condition: $t_1 < q_1 <$

$t_2 < q_2 < \cdots < q_S < t_{S+1}$, where S is the number of levels (quanta) that will be used to represent an image.

In order to construct the quanta and the separator sets, we start by sorting the peaks into a non-decreasing order according to their magnitude.

Let S_1 be an integer number, defined by the user, as the number of quanta that will be used for grouping the image frequency values. The first step of the algorithm will create a set of quanta $\{q_k\}$ and a set $\{t_k\}$ of separators following Lloyd's technique [16].

After that, the separators t_j are defined as: $t_j = t_{j-1} + A$, with $j = 2, 3, ..., S_1$, where the quantity A is

$$A = \frac{\int_\Omega dF(s)}{S_1}, \tag{6}$$

the image domain is represented by Ω and $F(s)$ is a probability distribution associated with the image I^α: $F(s) = P\{|I(x,y)| < s\}$.

The end points t_1 and t_{S+1} are defined a priori, as the lower and upper limit, respectively, of the values that represent the frequency domain of an image I^α. We will take here, q_j values as integer numbers between $m = min\{|U_i|, i = 1, ..., N \times N\}$ and $M = max\{|U_i|, i = 1, ..., N \times N\}$.

The goal of the second step is to create a new set of separators $\{\bar{t}_i\}$, such that

$$\bar{t}_i = t_1 + \frac{i(T-t_1)}{S_2}, \tag{7}$$

$i = 2, ..., S_2 - 1$, where $T = t_{S_1+1}$ and S_2 is an integer constant defined by the user.

The third step starts with the union of the separators $\{t_i\}$, $i = 1, ..., S_1$, obtained in the first step, with the separators $\{\bar{t}_j\}$, $j = 1, ..., S_2$, obtained in the second step. A new ordered and renamed separator set $\{t_k\}$, $k = 1, ..., S$; $S \leq S_1 + S_2 + 1$ is created.

After that, the calculus of each quantum q_j as the center of mass of the corresponding Q_i is performed:

$$q_j = \frac{\int_{Q_j} s dF(s)}{\int_{Q_j} dF(s)}. \tag{8}$$

The next step is to establish some correspondence (relationship) among these values and analyze proximities between images through the proximity between these correspondence among the frequency values (q_j's).

4.2 Relationship Building Among the Representative Points of an Image

Texture retrieval, in this work, is performed through modal analysis of the frequency vectors which were chosen to approach the power spectrum space. To measure the proximity among the points set of an image, the Sigmoidal Weighting Proximity matrix (3) is used, with q_i^α representing the image pattern points, computed as shown in section 4.1.

The proximity matrix establishes a relationship among the representative points of an image I^α [13], and the modal matrix $N \times N$, ϕ^α is obtained in the same way as described in Section 3, in (3). The eigenvectors are of unit length and are mutually orthogonal, and hence form an orthonormal basis, making the method robust to some transformations, as rotation, for example.

4.3 The Matching

Similarity between images is measured by the comparison of the ϕ^q matrix query with all the other ϕ_i^α matrices in the database.

For retrieval purposes we use the w_q values, defined in (5), in decreasing order to perform recognition.

5 Experimental Results

The size of the images under study is 256×256 pixels in 256 gray-level. Our image database is composed of 800 images. Among them there are homogeneous and non-homogenous textures. We work with both, synthetic and real images like flowers, landscape, clouds, trees, tissues, architectures, floors, vegetation, etc, as well as images extracted from the Brodatz digital album [22] and Outex database [23].

We divided our experiments into two distinct groups. In the first one, our image database is composed of only regular images as those used by the authors in [12]. From this database several experiments were performed using both methods and their effectiveness was measured by the use of the precision and recall curves, as shown in section 6. The second group of experiments were performed using all the images in the database, which means, the homogeneous and non-homogeneous ones but, using only the proposed method. This procedure was adopted with the aim of avoiding erroneous conclusions about Carcassoni's method [12].

To build our regular image database, we extracted from [23], 100 images in their original size of 746×538 pixels and we divided each of them into 5 overlapping subimages, thus creating a database with 500 images. In this case, the images that should be retrieved by submitting a query, are composed of these subimages without the need of human evaluation or judgment for choosing the most similar images to a given query. More details about relevant sets can be found in section 6.

We use $N = 6$ as the number of the point patterns and $k = 1.2$ as the number of the constant in (5).

In figure 1, we present three experiments using regular textures as query images: a soil, a plastic and a tissue image. In the three experiments, all the ranking retrieved by the proposed method is composed of subimages of the query image, while in Carcassoni's method [12] this proportion is 66%. One realizes that the quantization scheme of the proposed method is more robust for choosing the image representatives, once it reaches better results. The textures are labeled: (a) for the query image, (b-d) and (e-g) present the most similar images among the five top ranked images using the proposed method and Carcassoni's, respectively.

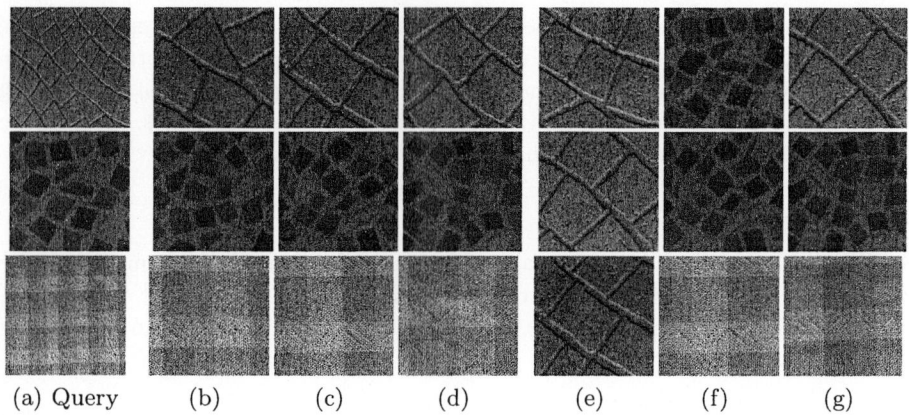

(a) Query   (b)   (c)   (d)   (e)   (f)   (g)

Fig. 1. Ranking achieved by the proposed method (b-d) in contrast with the one formed by Carcassoni's (e-g). Here, each line presents an experiment.

The following experiments show some of the reached results for the second group of experiments, where we used all the images present in the database and submitted the queries only in the proposed method. The textures are labeled: (a) for the query image and (b-d) for the most similar images among the five top ranked images.

The first experiment, shown in figure 2, the query image represents a landscape texture with the sun in its background. The proposed method was able to capture this kind of pattern in the retrieved textures 2(b) and (c) while in texture 2(d) we have an image which belongs to the same class of the query image. Such a result can be considered very satisfactory and sometimes desirable for

(a) Query   (b)   (c)   (d)

Fig. 2. In the first experiment (the four images of the top), one realizes that there exists the presence of a sun shape in the two first images of the ranking.

any retrieval system, where the algorithm is able to explore not only the main pattern of the texture but also some of its components.

In the third experiment in figure 2, a noisy landscape image with 0db Gaussian noise was used as the query image. Here one can clearly see that the proposed method is robust in the presence of noise, even though a high noise level, besides retrieving the noiseless version of the query image, it also retrieved images that are very similar to the query image.

It is worth registering that in the second group of experiments, the Carcassoni's technique was not able to reach the same good results as the proposed method.

6 Effectiveness Measurements

The most common measurement technique for retrieval purposes, Precision and Recall curves [24], was used to evaluate both methods presented in this paper. The curves compare the effectiveness when dealing with the image database composed by only homogeneous textures. To apply such a curve we have to consider the image collection, a set of ranking images (A) retrieved by the system and also a set of relevant images (R) for each query. As relevant images we understand, images that we wish to be retrieved for a given query.

Recall is the fraction of the relevant images which have been retrieved: $recall = |R \cap A|/|R|$ and Precision is the fraction of the retrieved images which are relevant: $precision = |R \cap A|/|A|$.

In this framework, the relevant answer set of each query is given by its subimages as described in section 5.

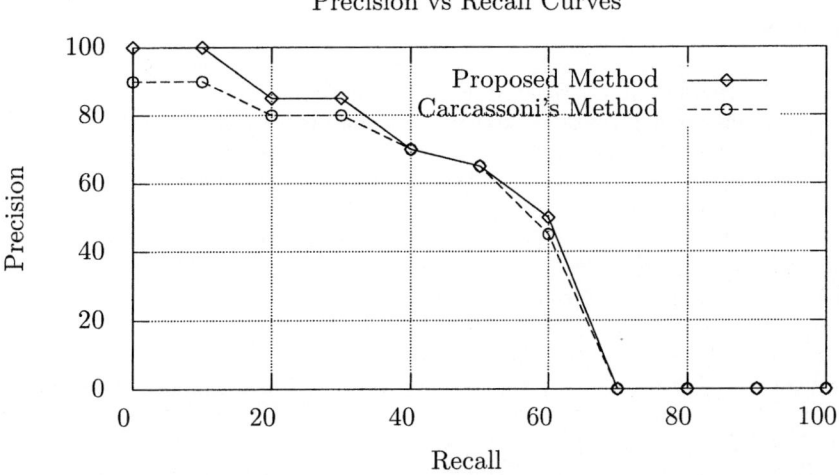

Fig. 4. Precision vs Recall for both methods using an homogenous database

The effectiveness was measured taking into consideration the results obtained at the submission of 20 distinct queries for both methods. As we know, the main goal of any retrieval system is to obtain the highest recall and precision values (%) as possible.

The graph plotted in figure 4, shows the performance evaluation comparing the two techniques here presented. Analyzing the graph, one can see that the performance of the proposed method is better than the Carcassoni's, despite the small difference between the curves. The superiority of the proposed method can be confirmed along all the curves in the highest precision region, where the recall $\leq$ 20 %.

7 Conclusion and Future Directions

In this paper we propose a new technique, inspired on Carcassoni et al. work [12], to retrieve textures in an image database. The retrieval is achieved by analyzing the similarity between the relationship among representative points from the power spectrum of the query image and the database images. A variant of the Lloyd's technique [16] is used to obtain the most representative points in the power spectrum to represent itself.

The experiments proved that the proposed technique has shown itself robust. This can clearly be seen at the Precision and Recall curve (figure 4). The proposed technique can be considered an improvement of the Carcassoni's technique, as it reached better results even for non-homogeneous textures.

Although better results have been gauged, an investigation about how the clusterization could offer better texture retrieval in large database, has been carried out. Another subject under consideration, is the number N of points used to represent an image, and how this number may affect the retrieval performance.

References

1. Pentland, A., Piccard, R.W., Sclaroff, S.: Photobook: Content-based manipulation of image databases. International Journal of Computer Vision **3** (1996) 233–254
2. Zachary, J., Iyengar, S.S., Barhen, J.: Content based image retrieval and information theory: A general approach. JASIST - Journal of the American Society for Information Science and Technology **52** (2001) 840–852
3. Hirata, K., Kato, T.: Query by visual example - content based image retrieval. In: EDBT '92: Proceedings of the 3rd International Conference on Extending Database Technology, London, UK, Springer-Verlag (1992) 56–71
4. Rao, A.R.: A taxonomy for texture description and identification. Springer-Verlag New York, Inc., New York, NY, USA (1990)
5. Androutsas, D., Plataniotis, K., Venetsanopoulos, A.: Image retrieval using directional detail histograms. Image and Video Databases VI, Proccedings of SPIE **99** (1998) 129–137
6. Kato, T.: Database architecture for content-based image retrieval in image storage and retrieval systems. Proccedings of SPIE **3846** (1992) 112–123
7. Manjunath, B.S., Ma, W.Y.: Texture features for browsing and retrieval of large image data. IEEE Transactions on Pattern Analysis and Machine Intelligence **8** (1996) 837–842

8. Gimel'farb, G., Jain, A.: On retrieving textured images from an image database. Pattern Recognition (1996) 1461–1483
9. Cohen, S., Guibas, L.: Shape-based indexing and retrieval: some first steps. In: ARPA 1996 Proceedings of Image Understanding Workshop. Volume 2. (1996) 1209–1212
10. Guidava, V., Raghavan, V.: Design and evaluation of algorithms for image retrieval by spatial similarity. Information Systems **13** (1995) 115–144
11. Shapiro, L., Brady, J.: Feature-based correspondence - an eigenvector approach. Image and Vision Computing **10** (1992) 283–288
12. Carcassoni, M., Ribeiro, E., Hancock, E.: Eigenvector method for texture recognition. International Conference on Image Processing **3** (2002) 321–324
13. Carcassoni, M., Hancock, E.R.: Correspondence matching using spectral clusters. In: 12th Scandinavian Conference on Image Analysis - SCIA01. (2001) 243–249
14. Carcassoni, M., Hancock, E.R.: Correspondence matching with modal clusters. PAMI **25** (2003) 1609–1615
15. Carcassoni, M., Hancock, E.: Point pattern matching with robust spectral correspondence. IEEE Computer Society Vision and Pattern Recognition **1** (2000) 649–655
16. Lloyd, S.: Least squares quantization in pcm. IEEE Transactions on information theory **2** (1982) 129–137
17. Ravela, S., Manmatha, R.: On computing global similarity in images. In: WACV '98: Proceedings of the 4th IEEE Workshop on Applications of Computer Vision (WACV'98), IEEE Computer Society (1998) 82–87
18. Zachary, J., Iyengar, S.S.: Information theoretic similarity measures for content based image retrieval. JASIST - Journal of the American Society for Information Science and Technology **52** (2001) 856–867
19. Horn, B.: Robot Vision. The MIT Eletrical Engering and Computer Science Series, McGrall Hill, NJ (1986)
20. Kay, S.: Modern Spectral Estimation. Prentice-Hall Signal Processing Series, Englewood Cliffs, NJ (1988)
21. Souza, A.M.R., Barcelos, C.A.Z.: Sobre eliminação de ruídos e quantização no processo de restauração de imagens. Revista Horizonte Científico (2002) 1–16
22. Brodatz, P.: A Photographic Album for Artists and Designers. Dover, New York (1966)
23. Ojala, T., Menp, T., M., M.P., J., J.V., Kyllnen, J., Huovinen, S.: Outex - new framework for empirical evaluation of texture analysis algorithms. 16th International Conference on Pattern Recognition **1** (2002) 701–706
24. Yates, R.B., Neto, B.R.: Modern Information Retrieval. Addison Wesley (1999)

Surface Reconstruction from Stereo Data Using Three-Dimensional Markov Random Field Model

Hotaka Takizawa[1] and Shinji Yamamoto[2]

[1] University of Tsukuba, 305-8573, Japan
takizawa@cs.tsukuba.ac.jp
http://www.pr.cs.tsukuba.ac.jp/~takizawa
[2] Chukyo University, 470-0393, Japan

Abstract. In this paper, we propose a method for reconstructing the surfaces of objects from stereo data. The proposed method quantitatively defines not only the fitness of the stereo data to surfaces but also the connectivity and smoothness of the surfaces in the framework of a three-dimensional (3-D) Markov Random Field (MRF) model. The surface reconstruction is accomplished by searching for the most possible MRF's state. Experimental results are shown for artificial and actual stereo data.

Keywords: Stereo vision, Surface reconstruction, 3-D MRF model, fitness, connectivity and smoothness.

1 Introduction

Surface reconstruction from depth data is one of the most important issues in computer vision[1]. It can provide effective clues for solving the problems of recognizing objects in higher-level recognition processes such as object recognition, scene description[2], and scene interpretation[3]. Hence, extensive works have been dedicated to surface reconstruction from depth data.

In works[4][5][6], surface models were generated from depth data obtained from laser scanners. On the other hand, several research groups have focused on the use of stereo vision. Although the stereo vision is a natural way to obtain depth data, the data is often noisy and sparse. Therefore, surface reconstruction obtained by methods[7][8][9] that simply interpolate points in stereo data, are easily disturbed by noises. For effective surface reconstruction, we have to consider a belief in surface reconstruction itself as well as the fitness of stereo data to surfaces.

In this paper, we propose a method for reconstructing the surfaces of objects from stereo data. The proposed method quantitatively defines not only the fitness of stereo data to surfaces but also the connectivity and smoothness of the surfaces in the framework of a 3-D MRF model. The surface reconstruction is employed by searching for the most possible MRF's state.

Fig. 1 illustrates the outline of our method. First, a stereo camera system observes a target object (objects) to be recognized such as a box in the illustration, and the 3-D positions of *edges*, which correspond to feature points on the object surfaces, are calculated by applying an edge-based stereo matching method to stereo images taken by the stereo camera system. Next, the method sets a rectangular solid, namely volume of interest (VOI), that includes all the edges, and then divides the VOI into $M_x \times M_y \times M_z$ rectangular solids that are enough smaller than the target object. The smaller rectangular solids are called *cells* in this method. In each cell, three types of object models are generated: *solid*, *hollow* and *surface* (the details are described in Sec.2). The method makes a combination of these object models, and defines a MRF's posterior energy function which represents the possibility of the appearance of the object model combination. By changing the parameters of the object models (such as the positions and directions of the surface models), the method searches for the most possible models' state that min-

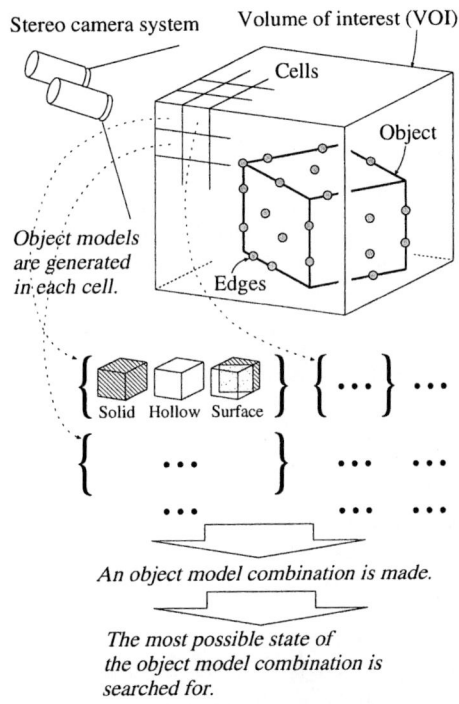

Fig. 1. The overview of our method

imizes the energy function. The optimal state determines the surfaces that are not only well fitted to the edges, but also connected smoothly with one another.

2 Object Models

The following three types of object models are used:

Solid: A solid model represents that the cell is completely included in space occupied by a target object.
Hollow: A hollow model represents that the cell is completely excluded from the object.
Surface: A surface model represents that the cell crosses the surface of the object. The proposed method assumes that each cell has, at most, one surface inside, and that the surface can be approximated by a single flat plane patch. These assumptions would be reasonable because cells are enough smaller than target objects. Fig. 2 illustrates an example of a surface model. One side of the surface model corresponds to the inside of the target object, and the other side corresponds to the outside of it.

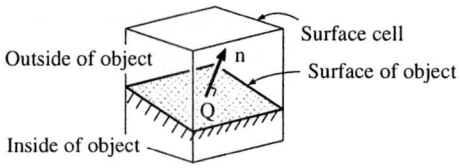

Fig. 2. Surface model

Let L_s denote a cell at a site s. A surface model in L_s is represented by a control point on the surface, $Q_s = (x_s, y_s, z_s)$, and its normal vector $\boldsymbol{n}_s$. The normal vector is set from inside to outside, and is represented by two angles as follows:

$$\boldsymbol{n}_s = \boldsymbol{n}_s(\phi_s, \psi_s), \qquad (1)$$

where ϕ_s and ψ_s are the azimuthal and zenith angles in the world coordinate system, respectively.

Let $P_s(SL)$, $P_s(HL)$ and $P_s(SF)$ denote the probabilities of appearance of solid, hollow and surface models in L_s, respectively. They satisfy the following equation:

$$\sum_{o \in \{SL, HL, SF\}} P_s(o) = 1. \qquad (2)$$

3 Evaluation of Interrelationships Between Adjoining Object Models

Objects – especially artificial objects – often have smooth (or flat) surfaces. To reconstruct such objects from stereo data as accurately as possible, the connectivity and smoothness of surfaces should be considered. In our method, they are evaluated using interrelationships between object models that adjoin each other in a 26 neighborhood system. This neighborhood system provides the six types of pairs of adjoining object models as shown in Table 1. Some of them are consistent, but the others not. In this section, the consistency of the interrelationships are defined individually.

Table 1. Six types of pairs of adjoining object models

	Solid	Hollow	Surface
Solid	1	3	4
Hollow	3	2	5
Surface	4	5	6

Let $L_{t \in N(s)}$ denote an adjoining cell of L_s in the 26 neighborhood system N, and $h(o_s, o_t)$ the consistency of two adjoining object models: $o_s \in \{SL, HL, SF\}$

in a cell L_s and $o_t \in \{SL, HL, SF\}$ in its adjoining cell $L_{t \in N(s)}$. $h(o_s, o_t)$ is defined to vary in the following range: $OK \leq h(o_s, o_t) \leq NG$, where OK and NG represent that the pair is consistent and inconsistent with each other, respectively.

3.1 Solid and Solid

This pair is consistent because it means that both the cells are within objects. Therefore, $h(SL, SL) = OK$.

3.2 Hollow and Hollow

This pair is also consistent. $h(HL, HL) = OK$.

3.3 Solid and Hollow

This pair is not consistent because the inside of an object attaches to its outside without any boundaries (i.e. surfaces). $h(SL, HL) = NG$.

3.4 Surface and Solid

The consistency of this pair varies depending on the parameters of the surface model. Fig. 3 shows an example of an inconsistent pair. In this method, the surface in the surface cell is straightly extended to the solid cell, generating the dotted region as shown in the figure. The interpolation of the dotted region by each object model is inconsistent. The consistency of the pair is defined using the volume of such an inconsistent region as follows:

$$h(SF, SL) = (1 - r^{inc}) \cdot OK + r^{inc} \cdot NG, \qquad (3)$$

where r^{inc} is the ratio of the volume of the inconsistent region to that of the whole solid cell.

3.5 Surface and Hollow

The consistency of this pair is defined in the same way as Sec. 3.4.

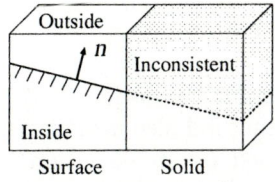

Fig. 3. A pair of adjoining surface and solid models. The interpretation of the dotted region is inconsistent with each other.

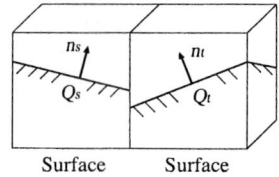

Fig. 4. A pair of adjoining surface models

3.6 Surface and Surface

Two adjoining surfaces would prefer to smoothly connect to each other. To evaluate the connectivity and smoothness of adjoining surfaces, the following two preliminary evaluation values are introduced (see Fig.4):

$$h_1^{pre} = \left\{\theta(\boldsymbol{n}_s, \boldsymbol{q}_{st}) - \frac{\pi}{2}\right\}^2 + \left\{\theta(\boldsymbol{n}_t, \boldsymbol{q}_{st}) - \frac{\pi}{2}\right\}^2, \tag{4}$$

$$h_2^{pre} = \{\theta(\boldsymbol{n}_s \times \boldsymbol{q}_{st}, \boldsymbol{n}_t \times \boldsymbol{q}_{st})\}^2, \tag{5}$$

where $\boldsymbol{q}_{st}$ is a vector from Q_s to Q_t, and $\theta(\boldsymbol{n}_1, \boldsymbol{n}_2)$ is an angle between $\boldsymbol{n}_1$ and $\boldsymbol{n}_2$. The operator '×' generates an outer product of two vectors.

These values vary in the following ranges:

$$0 \le h_1^{pre} \le \frac{\pi^2}{2}, \tag{6}$$

$$0 \le h_2^{pre} \le \pi^2. \tag{7}$$

The more smoothly the surface models connect to each other, the closer these preliminary values are to zero.

Using the preliminary evaluation values, the consistency of the pair is defined as follows:

$$h(SF, SF) = (1 - r^{hh}) \cdot OK + r^{hh} \cdot NG, \tag{8}$$

where

$$r^{hh} = \frac{\alpha \cdot h_1^{pre} + \beta \cdot h_2^{pre}}{\alpha \cdot \frac{\pi^2}{2} + \beta \cdot \pi^2}, \tag{9}$$

α and β are weighting coefficients for the preliminary evaluation values.

4 Observation Model

The degree of the fitness of a point to a surface is often measured by an Euclidean distance between them. Our method also uses an Euclidean distance to evaluate the fitness of an edge obtained by stereo vision to a surface model. For the obtained edges $e^{(i)}$ $(i = 1, 2, ..., I)$, the following fitness function is used:

$$f(e^{(i)}, SF) = \{d(e^{(i)}, SF)\}^2, \tag{10}$$

where $d(e, SF)$ is an Euclidean distance from the edge to the surface model.

In addition, the method should also define the fitness of an edge to solid and hollow models. An edge might fall into solid and hollow cells when the determination of the edge position is disturbed by noises. The fitness functions for edges in solid and hollow cells are simply defined as follow:

$$f(e^{(i)}, SL) = D_{long}^2, \tag{11}$$

$$f(e^{(i)}, HL) = D_{long}^2, \tag{12}$$

where D_{long} is a constant value, and

$$d(e^{(i)}, SF) < D_{long}. \tag{13}$$

In this method, all the edges are supposed to be independent of one another and to be dependent only on the cells in which the edges exist.

5 Formulation of Possibility of Object Model Combination Using 3-D MRF Model

The MRF models[10] are used to represent the probability distribution of the values of a set of random variables. Each MRF value depends only on the values of neighboring random variables. The MRF models are successfully applied to image segmentation[11], object recognition[4], dynamic image processing[12], or medical image processing[13], etc. Our method uses the MRF model to compute the optimal state of the object models in the $M_x \times M_y \times M_z$ cells.

Let w_s be a vector that is composed of the eight parameters of the three object models in L_s as follows:

$$w_s = \Big(P_s(SL), P_s(HL), P_s(SF), x_s, y_s, z_s, \phi_s, \psi_s\Big), \tag{14}$$

and W_s a random variable for w_s. w and W are used to denote the sets of w_s and W_s, respectively.

Given a set of the independent edges $e = \{e^{(1)}, e^{(2)}, ...\}$, the most possible parameters w^* can be obtained by minimizing the following posterior energy function:

$$U(w \in W|e) = \sum_{c \in C} V_c(w) - \lambda \cdot L(e|w), \tag{15}$$

where C is a set of cliques of adjoining variables in the MRF, and $V_c(w)$ measures the potential (energy) of clique c under parameters w, $L(e|w)$ is a likelihood which evaluates the possibility that the edges e come from the object models of the parameters w, and λ is a constant weighting coefficient. w^* is the *maximum a posteriori* (MAP) estimate of w. To search for w^*, the gradient decent method is used with several initial conditions. For example, the cells facing to the cameras are supposed to be hollow.

The definitions of clique potentials and edge likelihood are described below.

5.1 Clique Potential

For efficiency concerns, our method only considers 1-cliques and 2-cliques which are composed of a single MRF variable and two adjoining MRF variables, respectively (in other words, $V_c(\boldsymbol{w}) = 0$, $c > 2$).

A 1-clique consists of a single MRF variable(i.e. $c = \{o_s\}$), and its potential is defined as follows:

$$V_1(w_s) = - \sum_{o_s \in \{SL, HL, SF\}} P_s(o_s) \log P_s(o_s). \tag{16}$$

A 2-clique consists of two adjoining MRF variables (i.e. $c = \{o_s, o_{t \in N(s)}\}$), and its potential is defined as follows:

$$V_2(w_s, w_{t \in N(s)}) = \sum_{o_s, o_t \in \{SL, HL, SF\}} P_s(o_s) \cdot P_t(o_t) \cdot h(o_s, o_t). \tag{17}$$

5.2 Edge Likelihood

Let $e_s^{(i)}$ denote an edge existing in $L_{s(i)}$. The likelihood of the edge is defined using the fitness function (described in Sec.4) as follows:

$$L(e|w) = -\frac{1}{I} \sum_i \sum_{o_{s(i)} \in \{SL, HL, SF\}} P_s(o_{s(i)}) \cdot f(e_s^{(i)}, o_{s(i)}). \tag{18}$$

6 Experimental Results

Three experiments are performed in this paper. One is carried out with artificial depth data that are generated for quantitatively evaluation of the quality of reconstructed surfaces. The others are done with range data obtained from actual scenes.

6.1 Experiment 1

One hundred edges are artificially generated as follows:

$$(x_m, y_n, z) = (10m, 10n, 75 + N(\sigma)), \tag{19}$$

where $m = 0, 1, ..., 9$, $n = 0, 1, ..., 9$, and $N(\sigma)$ is a gaussian random value with mean 0.0 and standard deviation σ. If $\sigma = 0$, the edges are on a single plane. $2 \times 2 \times 2$ cells are used for the edges.

Fig.5(a) and (b) show the results of surface reconstruction. The edges are generated with $\sigma = 5$. The circle marks indicate the edges, and plane patches indicate the reconstructed surfaces. In Fig.5(b), the surfaces are well fitted to the edges even though the edges are widely distributed.

Fig.5(c) shows relationship between σ and the mean fitting errors, $\bar{e}$, of the edges to the reconstructed surfaces. These errors can be mostly kept under the corresponding σs.

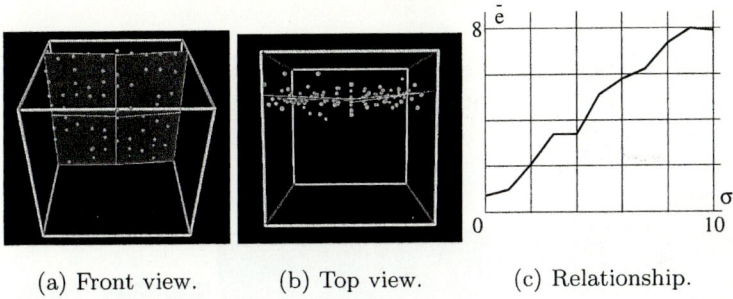

(a) Front view. (b) Top view. (c) Relationship.

Fig. 5. The results of surface reconstruction for artificial range data, and relationship between noises in the range data (σ) and the fitting errors ($\bar{e}$).

6.2 Experiment 2

Fig. 6(a) and (b) show a pair of stereo images of an actual scene including a box, and Fig. 6(c) shows depth data obtained from the stereo images. $9 \times 7 \times 7$ cells are used for the scene.

Fig. 6(d), (e) and (f) show the results of surface reconstruction. They are the front, right and top view of the reconstructed box, respectively. Fig 6(f) confirms that the two front surfaces of the box are reconstructed by the surface models. In addition, all the solid and hollow cells are recognized correctly.

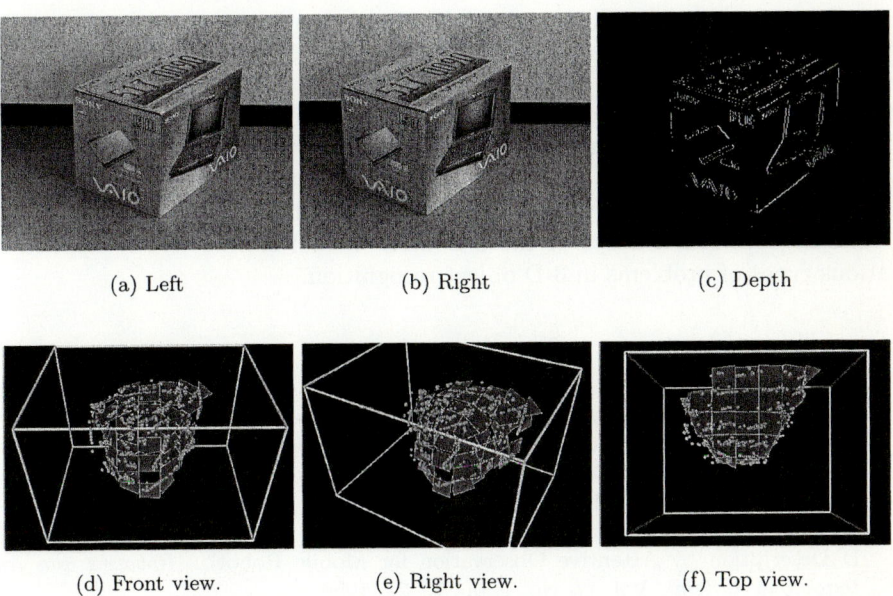

(a) Left (b) Right (c) Depth

(d) Front view. (e) Right view. (f) Top view.

Fig. 6. A pair of stereo images, their depth data(the depth is coded in gray values), and the results of surface reconstruction.

6.3 Experiment 3

Fig. 7(a) shows a (left) image of another scene that consists of a desk and wall. Fig. 7(b) and (c) show the front and side view of reconstructed surfaces. Fig 7(c) confirms that the surfaces of the desk and wall are reconstructed faithfully.

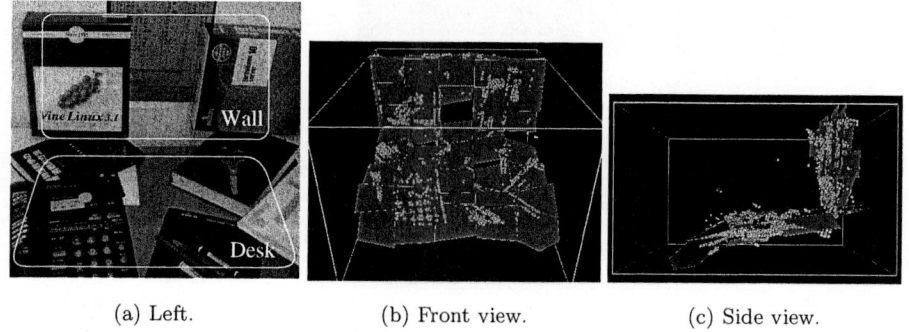

(a) Left. (b) Front view. (c) Side view.

Fig. 7. A (left) image of another scene, and the results of reconstruction.

7 Conclusion

This paper has described a novel method for reconstructing the surfaces of objects from stereo data. The connectivity and smoothness of surfaces and the fitness of edges to the surfaces are formulated in the framework of the 3-D MRF model, and the surface reconstruction is employed by searching for the most possible MRF's state. Three experimental results are shown.

The applicability of the 3-D MRF model is not limited to surface reconstruction that is exemplified in this paper. We have also used the 3-D MRF model for recognizing lung cancers in CT images that are volume data of human bodies[14][15]. The concept of the 3-D MRF model can be widely applied to various types of problems in 3-D object recognition.

References

1. Yoshiaki Shirai. *"Three-Dimensional Computer Vision"*. Springer-Verlag, 1987.
2. Akira Okamoto, Yoshiaki Shirai, and Minoru Asada. "Integration of Color and Range Data for Three-Dimensional Scene Description". *IEICE Trans. on Information and Systems*, Vol. E76-D, No. 4, pp. 501–506, 1993.
3. Hotaka Takizawa, Yoshiaki Shirai, and Jun Miura. "Selective Refinement of 3-D Description by Attentive Observation for Mobile Robot". *Robotics and Autonomous Systems*, Vol. 17, No. 1, pp. 15–23, 1996.
4. Mark D. Wheeler and Katsushi Ikeuchi. "Sensor Modeling, Probabilistic Hypothesis Generation, and Robust Localization for Object Recognition". *IEEE Trans. on Pattern Analysis and Machine Intelligence(PAMI)*, Vol. 17, No. 3, pp. 252–265, 1995.

5. Haris Baltzakis, Antonis Argyros, and Panos Trahanias. "Fusion of range and visual data for the extraction of scene structure information". In *International Conference on Pattern Recognition*, 2002.
6. Andrew Willis, Jasper Speicher, and David Cooper. "Surface Sculpting with Stochastic Deformable 3D Surfaces". In *International Conference on Pattern Recognition*, 2004.
7. O.D.Faugeras, E.Le Bras-Mehlman, and J.D.Boissonnat. "Representing Stereo Data with the Delaunay Triangulation". *Artificial Intelligence*, Vol. 44, pp. 41–87, 1990.
8. W.E.L. Grimson. *"From Images to Surfaces, A Computational Study of the Human Early Visual System"*. MIT Press, 1981.
9. De Floriani L. and Puppo E. "Constrained Delaunay Triangulation for Multiresolution Surface Description". In *Proc. International Conference on Pattern Recognition'88*, 1988.
10. Stuart Geman and Donald Geman. "Stochastic Relaxation, Gibbs Distribution, and the Bayesian Restoration of Images". *IEEE Trans. on Pattern Analysis and Machine Intelligence(PAMI)*, Vol. PAMI-6, No. 6, pp. 721–742, 1984.
11. Paul B. Chou and Christopher M. Brown. "The Theory and Practice of Baysian Image Labeling". *International Journal of Computer Vision*, Vol. 4, pp. 185–210, 1990.
12. S. Kamijo, Y.Matsushita, K.Ikeuchi, and M.Sakauchi. "Occlusion Robust Tracking Utilizing Spatio-Temporal Markov Random Field Model". *International Conference on Pattern Recognition (ICPR'00)*, Vol. 1, p. 1140, 2000.
13. Jose L. Marroquin, Edgar Arce Santana, and Salvador Botello. "Hidden Markov Measure Field Models for Image Segmentation". *IEEE Trans. on Pattern Analysis and Machine Intelligence(PAMI)*, Vol. 25, No. 11, pp. 1380–1387, 2003.
14. Hotaka Takizawa, Shinji Yamamoto, Tohru Matsumoto, Yukio Tateno, Takeshi Iinuma, and Mitsuomi Matsumoto. "Recognition of Lung Nodules from X-ray CT Images Using 3D Markov Random Field Models". In *Proc. of the 16th International Conference on Pattern Recognition(ICPR2002)*, Vol. 1, pp. 10099–10102, 2002.
15. Hotaka Takizawa, Shinji Yamamoto, Tohru Nakagawa, Tohru Matsumoto, Yukio Tateno, Takeshi Iinuma, and Mitsuomi Matsumoto. "Recognition of Lung Nodule Shadows from Chest X-ray CT Images Using 3D Markov Random Field Models". *Systems and Computers in Japan*, Vol. 35, No. 8, pp. 1401–1412, 2004.

Unsupervised Markovian Segmentation on Graphics Hardware

Pierre-Marc Jodoin, Jean-François St-Amour, and Max Mignotte

Université de Montréal,
Département d'Informatique et de Recherche Opérationnelle (DIRO),
P.O. Box 6128, Studio Centre-Ville, Montréal, Québec, H3C 3J7
{jodoinp, stamourj, mignotte}@iro.umontreal.ca

Abstract. This contribution shows how unsupervised Markovian segmentation techniques can be accelerated when implemented on graphics hardware equipped with a Graphics Processing Unit (GPU). Our strategy exploits the intrinsic properties of local interactions between sites of a Markov Random Field model with the parallel computation ability of a GPU. This paper explains how classical iterative site-wise-update algorithms commonly used to optimize global Markovian cost functions can be efficiently implemented in parallel by *fragment shaders* driven by a *fragment processor*. This parallel programming strategy significantly accelerates optimization algorithms such as ICM and simulated annealing. Good acceleration are also achieved for parameter estimation procedures such as K-means and ICE. The experiments reported in this paper have been obtained with a mid-end, affordable graphics card available on the market.

1 Introduction

Image segmentation is generally understood as a mean of dividing an image into a set of uniform regions. Here, the concept of *uniformity* makes reference to image features such as color or lightness intensity. Among the existing classification approaches proposed in the literature, segmentation models can roughly be divided between *feature-space based* and *image-space based* families [1]. Because image-space based techniques incorporate information from the image to be segmented and the segmentation map, the results they produce are generally more precise, although at the cost of heavier computational loads.

Among the *image-space based* techniques are the Markovian algorithms [2,3] which incorporate both image and spatial characteristics by using Markov Random Fields (MRF) as *a priori* models. The first contribution in that field came from Geman *et al.* [2] who proposed the concept of *Maximum a Posteriori* (MAP) as *image-space* criteria. While some authors proposed *ad-hoc* MAP energy-based functions, others used probabilistic functions to model the way the desired (hidden) label field is distributed. The shape of these probabilistic functions depends on parameters that are either supposed to be known (or manually adjusted) or estimated in a first step of processing. In the latter case, estimation algorithms such as Expectation Maximization (EM) or its stochastic Markovian extension called Iterative Conditional Estimation (ICE) [4,5] have demonstrated their efficiency.

Markovian models are known to be flexible and precise. However, they are also known to be slow, especially when implemented along with a stochastic optimizer such as simulated annealing (SA) [6] and/or with a parameter estimation step. Although some deterministic optimization algorithms such as ICM [3] or HFC [7] dramatically reduce computation times, Markovian algorithms are still far from being real-time. In this contribution, we show how processing times of classical unsupervised Markovian segmentation algorithms can be significantly reduced when implemented on mid-end programmable graphics hardware equipped with a Graphical Processor Unit (GPU). Although such graphics hardware is built to process vertices, lights and textures in the context of image synthesis, many applications beyond traditional graphics have been demonstrated to run on GPUs [8,9,10]. Recently, some computer vision tasks, such as anisotropic diffusion, segmentation by level-set and motion estimation were successfully implemented on a GPU [10]. Parallel implementations of Markovian algorithms applied to motion detection [11] and picture restoration [12] have been already proposed in the past. Unfortunately, these methods were build upon dedicated, expensive and sometimes obsolete architectures.

The rest of the paper is organized as follows. In Section 2, a review of the Markovian segmentation theory is proposed while Section 3 and 4 present estimation and optimization algorithms. Section 5 gives a look to the graphics hardware architecture and presents how a Markovian segmentation algorithm can be implemented on such hardware. Finally, Section 6 and 7 show some experimental results and conclude.

2 Unsupervised Markovian Segmentation

Let X and Y be respectively the *label field* (the segmentation map to be estimated) and the *observation field* (the input image to be segmented). Each field is defined on a rectangular lattice of size $\mathcal{N} \times \mathcal{M}$, represented by $S = \{s \,|\, 0 \leq s < \mathcal{N} \times \mathcal{M}\}$ where s is a site located at the Cartesian position (i,j). It is common to represent a *realization* of a field with a low-case variable such as x or y. For each site $s \in S$, x_s takes a value in $\Delta = \{e_1, e_2, ..., e_N\}$ and y_s takes a value in $\Gamma = \{\epsilon_1, \epsilon_2, ..., \epsilon_\zeta\}$ ($\epsilon_1 = 0$ and $\epsilon_\zeta = 255$ for grayscale images and ϵ_i is a 3D vector with a value contained between $(0,0,0)$ and $(255, 255, 255)$ for color images).

In the context of the *MAP* [2], the objective of a segmentation algorithm is to estimate *the best* label field x given y or equivalently the *optimal* solution $\hat{x}_{\text{MAP}}$ which maximizes the *posterior* probability function $P(X = x | Y = x)$ (written $P(x|y)$ to simplify notation). In accordance with Bayes theorem, the optimal label field is obtained when

$$\hat{x}_{\text{MAP}} = \arg\max_{x} \frac{P(y|x)P(x)}{P(y)} \qquad (1)$$

where $P(y|x)$ is the likelihood, $P(x)$ the prior and $P(y)$ the evidence. Since $P(y)$ isn't related to x, without lost of generality, this equation can be simplified to $\hat{x}_{\text{MAP}} = \arg\max_x P(y|x)P(x)$.

If X and Y are MRFs, according to the Hammersley-Clifford theorem, the likelihood and prior probability functions have a Gibbsian shape, respectively, $P(y|x) \propto \exp\{-W(x,y)\}$ and $P(x) \propto \exp\{-V(x)\}$, where $W(x,y)$ and $V(x)$ are *energy* functions. Incorporating these two Equations to the MAP framework leads to the optimization formulation $\hat{x}_{\text{MAP}} = \arg\min_x \{W(x,y) + V(x)\}$. Assuming that the noise in the observed image y is uncorrelated, since X and Y are MRFs, the global energy functions $W(x,y)$ and $V(x)$ can be represented by a sum of *local* energy functions

$$\hat{x}_{\text{MAP}} = \arg\min_x \sum_{s \in S} \{W_s(x_s, y_s) + V_{\eta_s}(x_s)\} \qquad (2)$$

where η_s stands for the neighborhood around site s (in this contribution, we use a second-order neighborhood). V_{η_s} is a sum of potential functions of the form $V_{\eta_s} = \sum_{c \in C_s} V_c(x_s)$, where C_s is the set of binary cliques linking s to sites $r \in \eta_s$. Here, the Potts model was used to represent V_{η_s}.

In the case of a *probabilistic* segmentation, input data y_s is related to a class x_s according to a distribution $P(y_s|x_s)$. Consequently, the energy function $W_s(x_s, y_s)$ has to be designed according to that distribution, namely $W_s(x_s, y_s) \propto -\ln P(y_s|x_s)$. A very popular function used to model $P(y_s|x_s)$ is the multidimensional Gaussian distribution

$$P(y_s|x_s) = \frac{1}{\sqrt{(2\pi)^d |\Sigma_{x_s}|}} \exp\left\{-\frac{1}{2}(y_s - \mu_{x_s})\Sigma_{x_s}^{-1}(y_s - \mu_{x_s})^T\right\}$$

where d is the dimensionality of y_s ($d = 3$ for color images and $d = 1$ for grayscale images) and $(\mu_{x_s}, \Sigma_{x_s})$ are the mean and variance-covariance of class x_s. Thus, the energy function of Eq. (2) can be written as

$$\sum_{s \in S} \{\underbrace{\frac{1}{2}(\ln|\Sigma_{x_s}| + (y_s - \mu_{x_s})\Sigma_{x_s}^{-1}(y_s - \mu_{x_s})^T)}_{W_s(x_s, y_s)} + V_{\eta_s}(x_s)\}.$$

In the case of *unsupervised* segmentation, the Gaussian parameters $\Phi = \{(\mu_i, \sigma_i) | 1 \leq i < N\}$ has to be estimated conjointly with x or preliminary to the segmentation step. Many parameter estimation algorithms are available among which EM, K-means and ICE [5] are the most popular.

3 Parameter Estimation

The two parameter estimation algorithms we have implemented are K-means and ICE [5]. K-means is an iterative clustering method [4] that assumes input data $\{y_s\}$ are distributed within K spherical clusters of equal volume. At each iteration, every site s are assigned to the nearest cluster before a second

Table 1. K-means and ICE algorithms. Here $n, m \in [1, d]$

1	$\mu_i \leftarrow$ random initialization, $\forall \mu_i \in \Phi_\mu$
2	For each site $s \in S$
2a*	$x_s \leftarrow \arg\min_{e_i \in \Gamma} \|y_s - \mu_{e_i}\|^2$
3	$\mu_i \leftarrow \frac{1}{N_i} \sum_{x_s = e_i} y_s$, $\forall \mu_i \in \Phi_\mu$
4	Repeat steps 2-3 until each mean μ_i no longer moves
5	$\Sigma_i^{nm} \leftarrow \frac{1}{N_i} \sum_{x_s = e_i} (y_s^n - \mu_{e_i}^n)(y_s^m - \mu_{e_i}^m) \forall \Sigma_i \in \Phi_\Sigma$

1	$\Phi \leftarrow K$-means
2	For each site $s \in S$
2a*	$P(e_i\|y_s) = \frac{1}{Z_s} \exp\{(W(e_i, y_s) + V_{\eta_s}(e_i))\} \forall e_i \in \Gamma$
2b*	$x_s \leftarrow$ according to $P(x_s\|y_s)$, randomly select $e_i \in \Gamma$
3a	$\mu_i \leftarrow \frac{1}{N_i} \sum_{x_s = e_i} y_s \ \forall \mu_i \in \Phi_\mu$
3b	$\Sigma_i^{nm} \leftarrow \frac{1}{N_i} \sum_{x_s = e_i} (y_s^n - \mu_{e_i}^n)(y_s^m - \mu_{e_i}^m) \forall \Sigma_i \in \Phi_\Sigma$
5	Repeat steps 2-3 until Φ no longer changes

step re-estimates the center of mass of every cluster. The resulting K-means clustering minimizes the sum-of-square error function $\sum_{i=1}^{N} \sum_{x_s = e_i} \|y_s - \mu_i\|^2$ [4]. The variance-covariance of each cluster is estimated once the algorithm has converged.

Because K-means is a deterministic algorithm, it is sensitive to noise and is likely to converge toward local minima. Furthermore, its assumption that all clusters are spherical with equal volume is simplistic an often unsuited to some observed images. Thus, many authors suggest to refine Φ with a more realistic model, less sensitive to noise and local minima such as the stochastic ICE estimation algorithm. Details of this algorithm are presented in [5] while Table 1 presents a version adapted to this paper.

4 Optimization Procedures

Because Eq. (2) has no analytical solution, it has to be solved with an optimization algorithm such as simulated annealing (SA) [2] or ICM [3]. SA is a stochastic algorithm built upon a temperature variable that slowly decreases toward zero with time. If the cooling rate is small enough, this annealing schedule theoretically guarantees the convergence to the global MAP. The ICM algorithm is a hill climbing deterministic algorithm that isn't guaranteed to converge toward global minima. However, it is drastically faster than SA and generates fairly good results when properly initialized. As Besag mentioned [3], it can be understood as an instantaneous freezing in SA. Both algorithms are presented in Table 2.

5 Graphics Hardware Architecture

Graphics hardware is highly optimized to solve traditional computer graphics problems. Nowadays, graphics hardware is most of the time embedded on a graphics card which can receive/send data from/to the CPU or the main memory via the system bus, be it PCI, AGP or PCIe. Most graphics hardware are

Table 2. Simulated annealing and ICM algorithms

1	$T \leftarrow T_{\text{MAX}}$
2	For each site $s \in S$
2a*	$P(e_i\|y_s) = \frac{1}{Z_s}\exp\left\{\frac{1}{T}\left(W(e_i, y_s) + V_{\eta_s}(e_i)\right)\right\}, \forall e_i \in \Gamma$
2b*	$x_s \leftarrow$ according to $P(x_s\|y_s)$, randomly select $e_i \in \Gamma$
3	$T \leftarrow T*\text{coolingRate}$
5	Repeat steps 2-3 until $T \leq T_{\text{MIN}}$

1	Initialize x (with ICE and/or K-means)
2	For each site $s \in S$
2a*	$x_s = \arg\min_{e_i \in \Gamma}(W(e_i, y_s) + V_{\eta_s}(e_i))$
3	Repeat steps 2 until x stabilizes

designed to fit the so-called *graphics processing pipeline* [13,14]. This pipeline is made of various stages which sequentially transform images and geometric input data into an output image stored in a section of graphics memory called the *framebuffer*. Part of the framebuffer (the front buffer) is meant to be visible on the display device.

During the past few years, the major breakthrough came when the vertex processing and fragment processing stages have been made *programmable*. These two stages can now be programmed using C-like languages to process vertex and fragments in parallel. Let us mention that a fragment is a per-pixel data structure created at the rasterization stage and containing data such as color, texture coordinates and depth. A fragment is meant to update a unique location in the framebuffer. Because the GPU is a *streaming processor* (i.e. a processor with inherent parallel processing abilities) mapping general computation problems to its unique architecture becomes very interesting [10].

A fragment processor is designed to load and execute in parallel a program (also called a *shader*) on each fragment generated during the rasterization stage [13,15]. Thus, a fragment shader is executed whenever a graphics primitive such as a polygon or a line is rendered. To be effective though, the shader must be initially loaded, compiled and linked on the GPU. This is illustrated by the two C/C++ programs of Table 3[1]. The first algorithm represents an ICM program whereas the second one represents a K-means program. The first section of these programs (line 1 to 7 and line 1 to 10) is written in C/C++ and runs on the CPU. This section essentially compiles, links and loads the shader, renders a graphics primitive and manipulates texture memory. Its crucial to understand that the shader (as opposed to traditional CPU programs) is loaded, compiled, linked and executed *during the runtime* execution of the C/C++ program. The shader (second section of Table 3) is launched on every fragment when the primitive –here a rectangle polygon– is rendered (line 4 and 5). After the primitive has been rendered, the results returned by the shaders is located in the framebuffer. This buffer can be copied in another section of the graphics memory (line 6 of the ICM code) or transfered back into central memory (line 7 of ICM code and

---

[1] Although other CPU programming languages such as JAVA could be used, C and C++ are by far the most widely utilized at the moment.

Table 3. High level representation of ICM and K-means hardware programs. The upper sections (line 1 to 7 and 1 to 10) are C/C++ CPU programs used to load the shader, render the scene and manage textures. The lower sections (line 1-2) are the fragment shaders launched on every fragment (pixel) when the scene is rendered (line 4 and 5).

1 Copy the input image y into texture memory.
2 Compile, link and load the ICM shader on the GPU.
3 Specify shader parameters ($N, \mathcal{N}, \mathcal{M}, \Phi$ for example).
4   Render a rectangle covering a window of size $\mathcal{N} \times \mathcal{M}$
5   Copy the framebuffer into texture memory
6 Repeat steps 4 and 5 until convergence
7 Copy the framebuffer into a C/C++ array if needed

1 $\hat{x}_s \leftarrow \arg\min_{e_i \in \Gamma} W(e_i, y_s) + V_{\eta_s}(e_i)$
2 framebuffer$_s \leftarrow \hat{x}_s$

1 Copy the input image y into texture memory.
2 Compile, link and load the K-means shader on the GPU.
3 $\Phi \leftarrow$ Init Gaussian parameters.
4   Specify shader parameters ($N, \mathcal{N}, \mathcal{M}$ and Φ_μ).
5   Render a rectangle covering a window of size $\mathcal{N} \times \mathcal{M}$
6    $E \leftarrow$ Copy the framebuffer into a C/C++ array.
7    $\mu_i \leftarrow \frac{1}{N_i}\sum_{E_s=e_i} y_s, \quad \forall \mu_i \in \Phi_\mu$
8 Repeat steps 4 to 7 until convergence.
9 $\Sigma_i^{nm} \leftarrow \sum_{E_s=e_i}(y_s^n - \mu_{e_i}^n)(y_s^m - \mu_{e_i}^m), \quad \forall \Sigma_i \in \Phi_\Sigma$
10 Copy the framebuffer into a C/C++ array if needed

1 $x_s \leftarrow \arg\min_{e_i \in \Gamma} \|y_s - \mu_{e_i}\|^2$
2 framebuffer$_s \leftarrow x_s$

lines 6 and 10 of K-means code). This last operation involves data traffic on the system bus and thus induces significant latency.

5.1 General-Purpose Computation on the GPU

The fragment processor is better suited for image processing problems than the vertex processor, simply because it is the only part of the graphics pipeline that has access to both input memory (texture memory) and output memory (the framebuffer). Although fragment shaders can be written in C-like languages [13,15], they have some specificities as compared to ordinary C/C++ programs. The most important ones are the following:

1. a fragment shader is made to process every fragment in parallel;
2. the only memory in which a fragment shader can write into is the write-only *framebuffer* and *depthbuffer*;
3. the only data a fragment shader can read is contained in the texture memory, in built-in variables or in user-defined variables. As such, it cannot read the content of the framebuffer or the depthbuffer;

4. since fragments are processed in parallel, fragment shaders cannot exchange information. GPUs do not provide its shaders with access to general-purpose memory.

With such specificities, minimizing a global Markovian energy function such as Eq. (2) can be tricky. In fact, three main problems have to be overcome. The first problem is to make sure the rasterization stage generates one fragment for each pixel of the input image y. Such one-to-one mapping from the input pixels to the output buffer is achieved by rendering a screen-aligned rectangle covering a *window* with exactly the same size than the input image (see line 4 and 5 of Table 3). In this way, the rasterization stage generates $\mathcal{N} \times \mathcal{M}$ fragments, one for each input pixel y_s.

The second problem comes from the fourth limitation. Since GPUs provide no general-purpose memory, one might wonder how can the prior energy function V_{η_s} have access to the labels x_t contained in the (write-only) framebuffer. This situation is handled by coping the framebuffer (i.e. the section of texture memory containing the label field x computed after an iteration) into texture memory (line 5 of ICM, Table 3). In this way, at the next iteration, the texture memory (which can be read by the fragment shader) will contain the label field x computed during the previous iteration. Thus, V_{η_s} is computed with labels iteratively updated and not sequentially updated as it is generally the case. Such strategy was already proposed by Besag [3]. As observed by some authors [11], the difference between these two updating schemes is very narrow, although the former might infer some small energy oscillations.

The last problem with shaders comes with their inability to generate random numbers such as needed by the stochastic algorithms SA and ICE. As a workaround, we generate an image containing random values at the beginning of the CPU application. This random image is then copied in texture memory where the shader can access it. Although this strategy isn't as efficient as a good random number generator, the results generated are very close to the ones obtained with standard CPU programs.

5.2 ICM and SA on Graphics Hardware

As shown in Table 3, y is first copied into texture memory. A fragment program is then launched on every pixel in order to solve Eq. (2) (line 4 of ICM, Table 3). The output labels are then copied in the framebuffer. Because the next ICM iteration needs the newly computed label field to proceed, the framebuffer content is copied back to the texture containing the label field information. This operation is extremely efficient because no data needs to be transmitted between the GPU and the CPU. The SA method is implemented in a manner very similar to the ICM algorithm, the only difference being that it requires a random function inside the fragment program. This situation is handled with the workaround presented in the previous Section. Notice that because fragment programs can only write in the framebuffer during a rendering pass, multiple rendering passes are used to simulate ICM/SA iterations.

5.3 K-Means and ICE on Graphics Hardware

Unlike the optimization methods, K-means and ICE are not perfectly suited to a mapping to the GPU. While the first step of these algorithms (assigning *the best* label x_s to each image pixel, line 2a and 2a, 2b of Table 1) is perfectly implementable in parallel, the second step (Gaussian parameters computation, line 3 and 3a, 3b of Table 1) is not. As such, we have to take a simple hybrid approach: execute line 2 on the GPU (parallel processing) and line 3 on the CPU (sequential processing).

To do so, the input image y is first copied in texture memory so it is accessible by the fragment processor. A fragment program is then activated for each pixel that determines in parallel the *best* class e_i for that pixel. The result is then outputted in the framebuffer. Once every pixel have been assigned a label (line 2), the Gaussian parameters for every class now need to be recomputed (line 3). Because this operation can't be parallelized, the framebuffer image containing the current class of each pixel is read back to CPU memory, where the computation takes place. Once the parameters are re-estimated, they are passed back to the GPU after which a new iteration can begin. This hybrid approach is illustrated by the K-means algorithm of Table 3.

6 Experimental Results

We first implemented the four algorithms presented in Section 3 and 4 in C++. Then, we adapted these programs to the graphics hardware architecture by replacing with Cg code[2] the instructions identified with a star ($*$) in Table 1 and 2. We used OpenGL to render the polygon and manage texture memory, and used the Cg Runtime Library [15] to load, compile and link the fragment shader. The software and hardware version of these programs run in the same C++ environment and thus, can be fairly compared.

The performances of each implementation was evaluated by varying the number of segmentation classes and the size of the images to be segmented. Processing times have been obtained by averaging results obtained after segmenting several grayscale and color images. The acceleration factor between the software and hardware version of the programs is presented in Fig. 1. In the leftmost graphics, the programs were launch over images of size ranging from 64×64 to 1024×1024 with a number of classes set to 4. In the other graphics, results were obtained after segmenting images of size 256×256 with different number of classes.

The SA parameters T_{MAX}, T_{MIN} and the cooling rate were respectively set to 10.0, 0.05 and 0.99. This setting corresponds to a total of 500 iterations as opposed to 10 iterations for K-means, ICE, and ICM. Let us note that the number of iterations for the software and hardware implementations is exactly the same. The results were obtained on a computer equipped with AMD Athlon 64 Processor 3200+ and an NVIDIA GeForce 6800 GT graphics card.

---

[2] Cg is a C-like hardware language program developed by NVIDIA.

Notice that the speedup factor between hardware and software version of ICM and SA (between 20 and 120) is more important than the one for K-means and ICE (between 2 and 8). This can be explained by the fact that both K-means and ICE algorithms have to exchange information (for the Gaussian parameter estimation) with the CPU which is major bottleneck for such hardware programs. Also, the speedup factor for K-means is larger than for ICE because ICE has to estimate and invert the variance-covariance matrix which isn't required for K-means. This extra load on the CPU makes ICE less efficient than K-means. Similarly, the speedup factor for SA and ICM is more important on color images than on grayscale images. This is explained by the fact that the global energy function of Eq. (2) is more expensive to compute for color images than for grayscale images. Thus, parallelizing this costly CPU operation leads to a more important acceleration factor. Notice that the acceleration factor is larger when segmenting large images and/or segmenting images with many classes.

With our actual hardware implementation, a color image of size 128×128 is segmented in 4 classes at a rate of 76 fps for ICM, 1.4 fps for SA, 2.5 fps for ICE and 14 fps for K-means. These frame rates do not however include the time needed to load, compile and link the shaders which vary between 0.1 second and 5 seconds. Although this might seem prohibitive, the initialization step is done only once at the beginning of the program. In this way, when segmenting more than one image (or segmenting an image of size larger than 128×128), this initialization time soon gets negligible as compared to the acceleration factor.

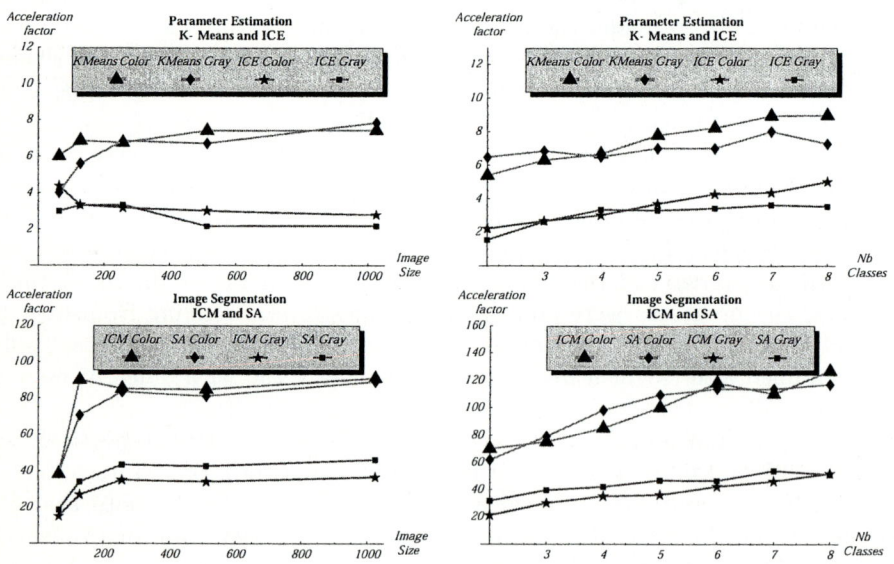

Fig. 1. Acceleration factor for K-means, ICE, SA and ICM obtained on grayscale and color images.

7 Conclusion

This paper exposed how Markovian algorithms devoted to image segmentation can be significantly accelerated when implemented on programmable graphics hardware. Even if GPUs were built to process traditional graphics primitives, we demonstrated how fragment programs can be adapted to the context of Markovian estimation and optimization algorithms such as K-means, ICE, ICM and SA. The acceleration factor between software and hardware implementation was more impressive for the optimization algorithms (between 20 and 120) than the estimation ones (between 2 and 8). Results have shown that remarkably fast optimization was achievable, especially over large images and/or with a large number of classes.

As future work, we plan to implement on graphics hardware energy-based computer vision tasks such as motion estimation, motion segmentation and stereovision. Because these tasks can be defined on a Markovian framework similar to the one presented in this paper, we have good reasons to believe that the hardware version of these algorithms will be more efficient that its software counterpart. We also look forward to implement and compare the most popular optical flow techniques on graphics hardware (Horn and Schunck, Lucas Kanade, Anandan, etc.[16]).

References

1. Lucchese L. and Mitra S.: Color Image Segmentation: A State-of-the-Art Survey. Proc. of INSA-A (2003)
2. Geman S. and Geman D.: Stochastic Relaxation, Gibbs Distributions, and the Bayesian Restoration of Images. J. IEEE Trans. Pattern Anal. Machine Intell. 6,6 (1984) 721–741
3. Besag J.: On the Statistical Analysis of Dirty Pictures. J. Roy. Stat. Soc. 48,3 (1986) 259–302
4. Bishop C.: Neural Networks for Pattern Recognition. Oxford University Press, ISBN:0-19-853849-9 (1996)
5. Pieczynski W.: Statistical Image Segmentation. J. Machine Graphics and Vision, 1,1 (1992) 261–268
6. Kirkpatrick S., Gelatt C. and Vecchi M.: Optimization by Simulated Annealing. J. Science, 220,4598 (1983) 671–680
7. Chou P. and Brown C.: The Theory and Practice of Bayesian Image labeling. in Proc. of ICCV. 185–210 (1990)
8. Kruger J. and Westermann R.: Linear algebra operators for GPU implementation of numerical algorithms. J. ACM Trans. Graph. 22,3 (2003) 908–916
9. Moreland K. and Angel E.: The FFT on a GPU. In proc. of Workshop on Graphics Hardware (2003) 112–119
10. http://www.gpgpu.org/
11. Dumontier C., Luthon F. and Charras J-P.: Real-Time DSP Implementation for MFR-Based Video Motion Detection. J. IEEE Trans. on Img. Proc. 8,10 (1999) 1341–1347

12. Murray D., Kashko A. and Buxton H.: A Parallel Approach to the Picture Restoration Algorithm of Geman and Geman on a SIMD Machine. J. Image and Vision Computing 4 (1986) 141–152
13. Rost R.: OpenGL Shading Language. 1st Ed.,Addison-Wesley (2004)
14. Akenine-Moller T. and Haines E.: Real-time Rendering 2e Edition, AK Peters (2002)
15. Fernando R. and Kilgard M.: The Cg Tutorial: The Definitive Guide to Programmable Real-Time Graphics. Addison-Wesley, (2003)
16. Barron J., Fleet D. and Beauchemin S.: Performance of optical flow techniques. J. Int. J. Comput. Vis. 12,1 (1994) 43–77

Texture Detection for Image Analysis

Sébastien Chabrier, Bruno Emile, and Christophe Rosenberger

Laboratoire Vision et Robotique - UPRES EA 2078,
ENSI de Bourges - Université d'Orléans,
10 boulevard Lahitolle,
18020 Bourges, France

Abstract. Many applications such as image compression, pre-processing or segmentation require some information from the regions composing an image. The main objective of this paper is to define a methodology to extract some local information from an image. Each region is characterized in terms of homogeneity (region composed with the same grey-level or a single texture) and its type (textured or uniform). The decision criterion is based on the use of classical texture attributes (cooccurrence matrix and grey-levels moments) and a support vector machine in order to realize the fusion of the different attributes. We then characterize each region considering its type by appropriate features.

1 Introduction

Many images such as outdoor scenes or satellite images contain textured regions. In many domains of image processing (adaptive compression, identification of the blur degradation or adaptive segmentation), the knowledge of the global nature of an image, the localization and the characterization of the regions (textured or uniform) can contribute to the development of some adaptive processing methods [11].

Many methods have been proposed to detect textured and uniform regions in an image [15]. This is usually achieved by considering the standard deviation of the grey levels. This approach has the major drawback of not taking into account the grey level distribution of the image and for this reason some errors might occur. Many texture attributes can participate in the characterization of the textured areas of an image [14], [2], [6], [16], such as for example statistical moments, local histograms [9] and grey level cooccurrence parameters [4]. An evaluation of texture measures was made in [1] for ground cover identification and logical operators could be used for texture classification [8], [13].

In order to extract some *a posteriori* information (homogeneous or inhomogeneous region) and to adapt some image processing algorithms, we propose an approach for the localization and characterization of textured and uniform areas in an image. Each region is described in terms of homogeneity and type of primitive. The fusion of different texture attributes improves the characterization of a region. This paper offers the possibility to obtain a complete image or region characterization. This paper is organized as follows. Section 2 presents the local characterization method. Section 3 gives some experimental results on a large image database. Finally, some conclusions about this work are given in section 4.

2 Developed Method

The determination of the type of a region in an image is a very important step for image analysis. A region is then described using appropriate features (see Figure 1).

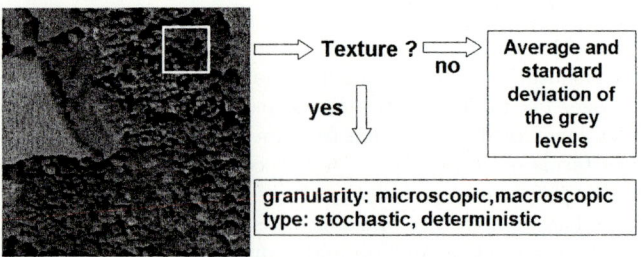

Fig. 1. Local image analysis

2.1 Image Database

We used two image databases. The first one was composed of 1.950 homogeneous images of size 128×128 pixels containing one region (with stationary statistics) : 100 textures with low and high contrast [3] , 50 textures at different orientations [3], 500 textures extracted from Oulu's University texture database[1], 100 textures extracted from the MeasTex's database [2], 100 uniform images with grey level between 0 and 255, 100 uniform images with impulse noise between 0 and 100%, 500 uniform images with white Gaussian additive noise with different values of the standard deviation $\{5, 10, 20, 30, 40, 50, 60, 70, 80, 90\}$, 500 uniform images with white Gaussian multiplicative noise with different values of the standard deviation $\{5, 10, 20, 30, 40, 50, 60, 70, 80, 90\}$. The second database contained 300 inhomogeneous images with 2 to 5 regions of different types: textured [3] and uniform with Gaussian noise.

2.2 Texture Attributes

We use different classical texture attributes from the literature. Two kinds of features were tested, 15 derived from the cooccurrence matrix [7] and 4 grey level moments [10] (see Table 1).

---

[1] http://www.outex.oulu.fi/
[2] http://www.cssip.uq.edu.au/meastex/www/for_images.html

Table 1. Texture attributes

A1	Angular Second Moment	A11	Difference Entropy
A2	Contrast	A12	Information Measures of Correlation 1
A3	Correlation	A13	Information Measures of Correlation 2
A4	Sum of Squares : Variance	A14	Information homogeneity
A5	Inverse Difference Moment	U	Trace of the cooccurrence matrix
A6	Sum Average	M1	Average grey level
A7	Sum Variance	M2	Standard deviation
A8	Sum Entropy	M3	Dissimilarity
A9	Entropy	M4	Kurtosis
A10	Difference Variance		

In order to identify the ability of these texture attributes to define the type of a region, we studied the evolution of these attributes on each image database. First of all, we tried to answer the following question: can we distinguish a texture from a uniform region? In this case, we worked on the first image database composed of homogeneous images. The second question was as follows: can we quantify how much texture an in-homogeneous image has?

2.3 Case 1: Homogeneous Image

The homogeneous image database was composed of 1950 images. A few examples of this database are given in figure 2. The goal of this study is to determine the type of each image namely textured or uniform. For each attribute, we compute the correlation factor with a ground truth which contained the value 0 in the case of a uniform image and the value 1 in the case of a texture. The closer the absolute value of the correlation factor is to 1, the more relevant is the attribute for texture detection. Some results are presented in table 2.

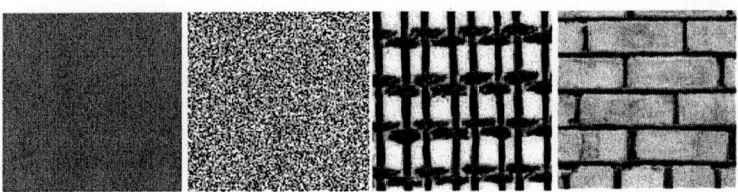

Fig. 2. Examples of homogeneous images

Table 2 highlights the correct behavior of an attribute to detect texture : A03 and A13 (the A13 attribute uses the computation of A03). The A03 attribute corresponds to the computation of the grey-levels correlation in the image. Figure 3 shows the values of the A03 attribute on the homogeneous image database. First 750 images are textured and the following ones are uniform or noisy. As we can see in this case, noisy uniform and textured images can be easily distinguished by a threshold for example of 0.1.

Table 2. Correlation factor of the various texture attributes compared to a ground truth in the homogeneous case

A01	A02	A03	A04	A05	A06	A07	A08	A09	A10
-0,2329	-0,2016	**0,9649**	0,0954	-0,0556	0,3436	0,2798	0,3719	0,2139	-0,1776
A11	A12	A13	A14	U	M1	M2	M3	M4	
-0,0138	-0,8265	**0,8981**	-0,1594	-0,1594	0,0126	-0,1057	0,0047	-0,1472	

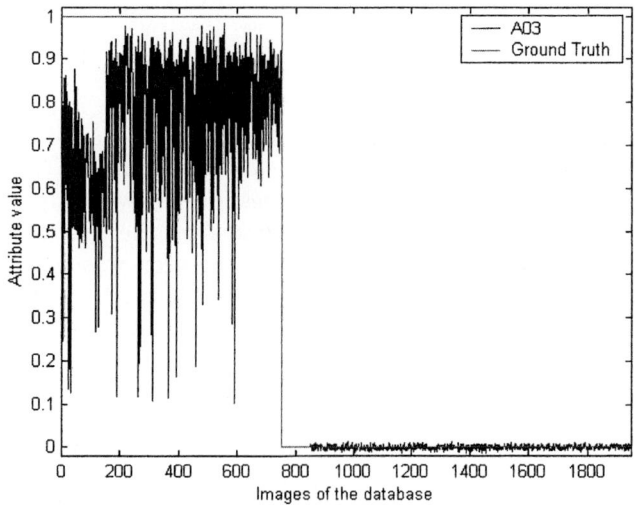

Fig. 3. Value of the A03 attribute on the homogeneous image database

2.4 Case 2: Inhomogeneous Image

The inhomogeneous image database (composed of 2 or more regions) was made up of 4 sets of 300 images from 2 to 5 regions. Each of these sets contained three images subsets: 100 images with uniform noisy regions only, 100 images with textured and uniform noisy regions, 100 images with textured regions only. A few examples of this image database are given in figure 4. The tested attributes are the same as in the previous section (A0 to A14, U and M1 to M4). The comparison was also carried out by the correlation factor compared to a ground truth which contained the value 0 in the case of uniform images, 1 in the case of mixed images and 2 in the case of textured images.

Table 3 highlights the correct behavior of two criteria to recognize the nature of an image : A05 and U. The A05 attribute corresponds to a calculation of the transition of the grey levels and U is the percentage of transitions of the same grey levels.

Figure 5 shows the values of the attributes A05 and U for the inhomogeneous image database. The 2-region images are presented from 1 to 300, the 3-region images from 301 to 600, the 4-region images from 601 to 900 and the 5-region

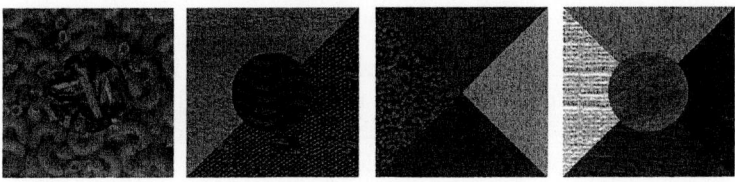

Fig. 4. Examples of inhomogeneous images

Table 3. Correlation factor of the various attributes compared to a ground truth in the inhomogeneous case

A01	A02	A03	A04	A05	A06	A07	A08	A09	A10
0.1929	-0.1150	0.2032	0.1438	**0.5457**	-0.1528	0.1534	0.2933	-0.0209	0.0726
A11	A12	A13	A14	U	M1	M2	M3	M4	
-0.2773	-0.3840	0.4307	**0.5390**	**0.5390**	-0.4341	-0.0478	0.1748	0.0114	

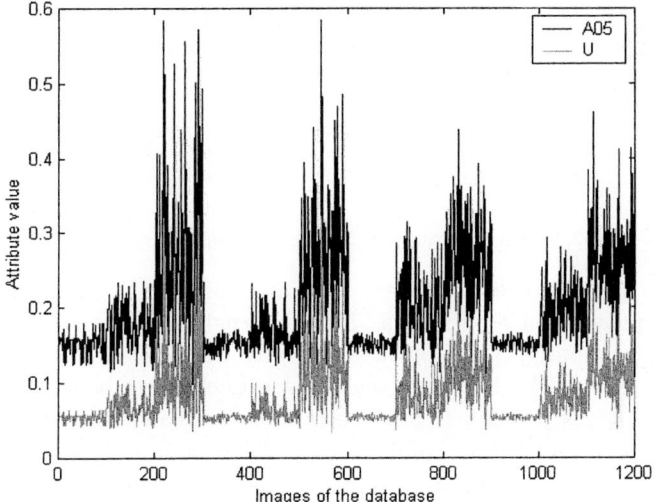

Fig. 5. Value of the A05 and U attributes on the inhomogeneous image database

images from 901 to 1200. The first 100 images of each database correspond to uniform images, the next 100 correspond to mixed images, and the last 100 correspond to textured images.

As we can see in Figure 5, these data are nearly separated, but it seems difficult to have a 100% correct separation for this image database. In order to achieve this goal, we suggest using a support vector machine for the recognition of the different types of images.

2.5 Recognition by a Support Vector Machine

Let us suppose we have a training set $\{\mathbf{x}_i, \mathbf{y}_i\}$ where $\mathbf{x}_i$ is the texture attributes vector describing a region or an image represented by its type $\mathbf{y}_i$ in the learning database. The goal of supervised classification is to identify the type of a local image area. For two classes problems, $y_i \in \{-1, 1\}$, the Support Vector Machines implements the following algorithm. First of all, the training points $\{\mathbf{x}_i\}$, are projected in a space $\mathcal{H}$ (of possibly infinite dimension) by means of a function $\Phi(\cdot)$. Then, the goal is to find an optimal decision hyperplane in this space, in the sense of a criterion that we will define shortly. Note that for the same training set, different transformations $\Phi(\cdot)$ lead to different decision functions. A transformation is achieved in an implicit manner using a kernel $K(\cdot, \cdot)$. Consequently, the decision function can be defined as :

$$f(\mathbf{x}) = \langle w, \Phi(\mathbf{x}) \rangle + b = \sum_{i=1}^{\ell} \alpha_i^* y_i K(\mathbf{x}_i, \mathbf{x}) + b \qquad (1)$$

with $\alpha_i^* \in \mathbb{R}$. The values w and b are the parameters that define the linear decision hyperplane. In the proposed system, we used a polynomial kernel of order 2. In SVMs, the optimality criterion to maximize is the margin, that is the distance between the hyperplane and the nearest point $\Phi(\mathbf{x}_i)$ of the training set. The α_i^* allowing to optimize this criterion can be defined by solving the following problem:

$$\begin{cases} \max_{\alpha_i} \sum_{i=1}^{\ell} \alpha_i - \frac{1}{2} \sum_{i,j=1}^{\ell} \alpha_i \alpha_j y_i K(\mathbf{x}_i, \mathbf{x}_j y_j) \\ \text{with constraints,} \\ 0 \leq \alpha_i \leq C, \\ \sum_{i=1}^{\ell} \alpha_i y_i = 0. \end{cases} \qquad (2)$$

where C is a penalization coefficient for data points located in or beyond the margin and provides a compromise between their numbers and the width of the margin. Originally, SVMs have essentially been developed for two classes problems ($y_i \in \{-1, 1\}$). However, several approaches can be used for extending SVMs to multiclass problems. The method we used in this communication, is called *one against one*. Instead of learning N decision functions, each class is discriminated here from another one. Thus, $\frac{N(N-1)}{2}$ decision functions are learned and each of them makes a vote for the affectation of a new point $\mathbf{x}$. The class of this point $\mathbf{x}$ becomes then the majority class after the vote.

3 Experimental Results

In order to be able to classify an area according to its characteristics, the 19 attributes (previously defined) were calculated on a database of 3.450 images. To evaluate the performances of characterization of an image, 5 classes of images were first defined: homogeneous uniform, homogeneous textured, inhomogeneous uniform, inhomogeneous textured and inhomogeneous with uniform and textured regions. The global image database has been cut out in a training database and

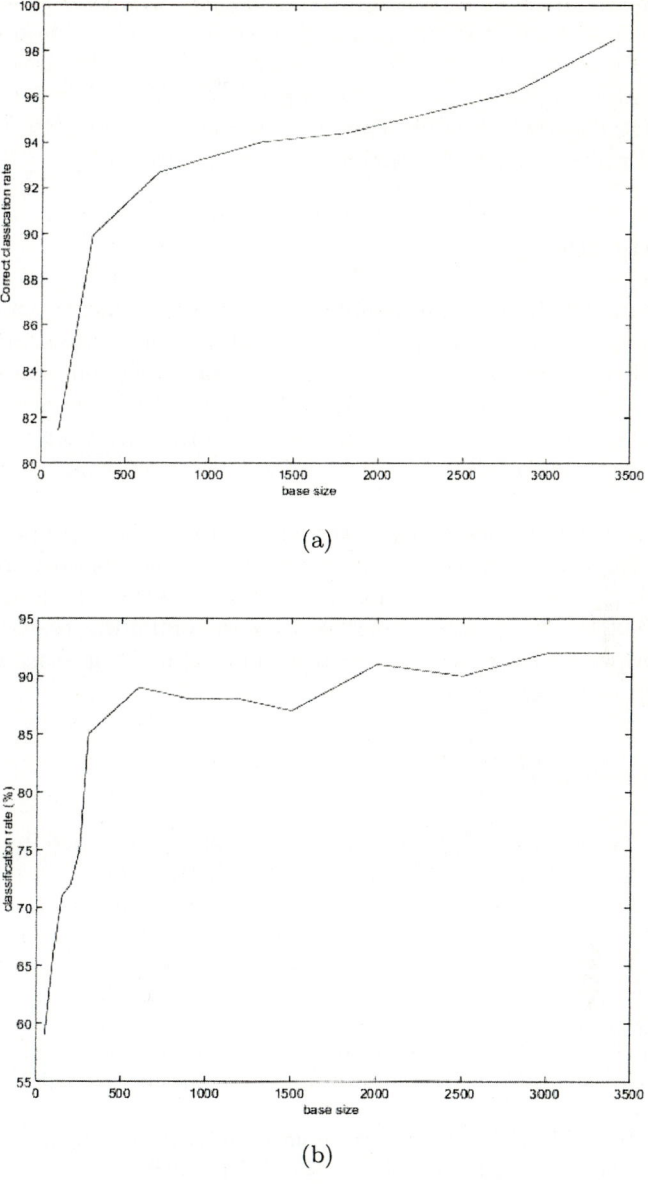

Fig. 6. Correct classification rate for a (a) coarse and (b) precise image characterization

a test one. The images of the training database were selected randomly among the 3.450 images and the remainder made up the test database. We present in Figure 6 (a) the correct classification rate according to the size of the training database. In this case, with a training database composed of only 300 images, we obtained a correct classification rate of 90%. If we now consider a more precise characterization, we use 14 classes instead of 5. In this case an image with 2 regions is distinguished from an image with 3 regions. The obtained results are presented in Figure 6 (b). Figure 6 shows, with a training database of 300 images, we already have a correct classification rate equal to 85%. If we increase the size of the training database, the efficiency is about 90% to end with a 94% correct classification rate if we use the complete training database.

4 Conclusions

We propose in this paper a methodology for image characterization. We combined the classical texture attributes and a support vector machine to identify the type of a region or an image. The experimental results on a large and significant image database show good results. We have a 100% correct classification rate to detect texture in a homogeneous image. In the case of an inhomogeneous image, we have a 94 to 98% correct classification rate depending on the desired precision.

Prospects for this work concern the application of the proposed approach to adaptive segmentation and compression. When the region is recognized as uniform or noisy, we would compute the average and the standard deviation of the grey levels. As for textured regions, we can compute a texture model [12] for the description of the type of texture (deterministic or stochastic) and its granularity (macroscopic or microscopic).

Acknowledgments

The authors would like to thank financial support provided by the Conseil Régional du Centre and the European union(FSE).

References

1. M.F. Augusteijn, L.E. Clemens and K.A. Shaw, "Performance evaluation of textre measures for ground cover identification in satellite images by means of a neural network classifier", IEEE Transactions on Geoscience and Remote Sensing, 33(3), 616-626, (1995).
2. V. Ballarin, E. Moler, M. Brun, "Scale invariant texture classification with mathematical morphology", EUSIPCO (4), 2533-2536 (1998).
3. P. Brodatz, Textures "A photographic album for artists and designers", Dover, New York, (1966).
4. J.M. Cartensen, "Cooccurence feature performance in texture classification", Proc. of the Scandinavian Conference on Image Analysis, (1), 831-838 (1993).
5. S. Chabrier, C. Rosenberger, H. Laurent, B. Emile and P. Marche, "Evaluating the segmentation result of a grey-level image", EUSIPCO, 2004.
6. T. Hofmann, J. Puzicha, J. M. Buhmann, "Unsupervised Texture Segmentation in a Deterministic Annealing Framework", IEEE Transactions on Pattern Analysis and Machine Intelligence 20(8), 803-818 (1998).

7. R.M. Haralick, K. Shanmungan, I. Dinstein, "Textural features for image classification", IEEE Transactions on Systems Man and Cybernetics, 6(3), (1979).
8. V. Manian, R. Vasquez and P. Katiyar, "Texture classification using logical operators", IEEE Transactions on image processing, 9(10, 1693-1703, (2000).
9. J. Puzicha, T. Hofmann, J. M. Buhmann, "Histogram Clustering for Unsupervised Segmentation and Image retrieval", Pattern Recognition Letters 20(9), 899-909 (1999).
10. A. Rosenfeld and E. Troy, "Visual Texture Analysis", Tech. Report, 70-116, 1970.
11. C. Rosenberger, "Implementation of an Adaptive Image Segmentation System", Phd thesis Université de Rennes I, (1999).
12. C. Rosenberger and K. Chehdi, "Towards a complete adaptive analysis of an image", International Journal of Electronic Imaging, 12(2), 292-298, (2003).
13. Maneesha Singh and Sameer Singh, "Texture algoithms: performance variability across data sets", 34(1), Taylor and Francis, Cybernetics and Systems (2003).
14. K. Valkealahti, E. Oja, "Reduced Multidimensional Cooccurrence Histograms in Texture Classification", IEEE Transactions on Pattern Analysis and Machine Intelligence, 20(1), (1998).
15. C. S. Won, Y. Choe, "Image block classification using stochastic image segmentation", Electronics Letters 32(16), 1462-1463 (1996).
16. S. C. Zhu, X. W. Liu, Y. N. Wu, "Exploring Texture Ensembles by Efficient Markov Chain Monte Carlo. Toward a trichromacy theory of texture " IEEE Transactions on Pattern Analysis and Machine Intelligence 22(6), 554-569, (2000).

Evaluation of the Quality of Ultrasound Image Compression by Fusion of Criteria with a Genetic Algorithm

C. Delgorge, C. Rosenberger, G. Poisson, and P. Vieyres

Laboratoire Vision et Robotique, UPRES EA 2078,
IUT de Bourges - Bâtiment Recherche,
63 av. de Lattre de Tassigny, 18020 Bourges Cedex, France
Cecile.Delgorge@bourges.univ-orleans.fr

Abstract. The goal of this work is to propose a criterion for the evaluation of ultrasound image compression. We want to measure the image quality as easily as with a statistical criterion, and with the same reliability as the medical assessment. An initial psychovisual experiment is proposed to medical experts, and represents our reference value for the comparison of the evaluation criteria. Several statistical criteria are selected from the literature. We define a cumulative absolute similarity measure as a distance between the criterion to evaluate and the reference value. A fusion method by a genetic algorithm is proposed to improve the results obtained by each criterion separately. We show the benefit of fusion through some experimental results.

1 Introduction

The European project OTELO (mObile Tele-Echography using an ultra-Light rObot) allows an ultrasound expert to perform an echography examination on a remotely located patient with a teleoperated probe-holder robot. For such an emergency telemedicine application, a low bandwidth and real time examination are the main technical constraints of the system. Due to the reduced available bandwidth of some communication links, an image compression is needed to deliver, from the patient's station to the expert's station, ultrasound images of 'acceptable' quality and in real time. In the framework of a robotized tele-echography, ultrasound images are compressed at the patient station and sent to the specialist. These received images are the only feedback information available to the medical expert to remotely control the distant robotized system [1]. The diagnosis made by the specialist strongly depends on the quality of these images. This work has been realized in the framework of the European project OTELO where we had to choose an image compression technique and an evaluation method of the global performances of this compression technique.

There are several methods to evaluate the quality of an image. In the image processing literature, the most frequently used measures are the mean square error (MSE) and the peak signal to noise ratio (PSNR)[2]. They are part of the pixel difference-based distortion measures set, and they are very popular due to their mathematical facility. Others criteria can also be found such as statistical measures: Linfoot, based on the power spectral density [3] or the Moran-I statistics [4]. The important drawback of this kind of criterion is the fact that it does not always correspond to the human visual system (HVS), which corresponds to an observer's visual perception.

Image quality, especially in medical specialty, is traditionally evaluated with a visual test where experts examine a large set of images and score each one on its quality (contrast, details) and its distortion. The most common psychovisual study is the Receiver Operating Characteristics Curves method (ROC method) [5] [6]. Such tests are time and human consuming and they need a large database of images to test. These qualitative and subjective evaluations may depend on the medical speciality. Psychovisual tests require a strict protocol which is very difficult to implement.

If the mathematical criteria can easily offer a tool to evaluate the quality of a compressed image with respect to the original ultrasound image, the evaluation of a medical image echography diagnosis remains dependent on the specialist's ability to detect potential pathologies in one given image. This subjective element in the clinical diagnosis has led us to define a psychovisual test whose results are our absolute reference. The goal of this work is to study the behavior of several statistical criteria compared to a clinical evaluation. Statistical measures are easy to use but are not always as reliable as the expert's judgement. The idea is to determine if a combination of these criteria allows an improvement of the evaluation quality.

Section 2 presents the evaluation of compressed ultrasound images firstly by a psychovisual test. In section 3, we analyse the ability of 21 statistical criteria to reproduce the expert's judgment. Section 4 shows the definition of a new criterion by combining the best criteria in order to improve the evaluation quality. The conclusion is discussed in section 5.

2 The Psychovisual Evaluation: The Expert Reference

We performed a study to evaluate the quality of ultrasound image compression according to psychovisual measures. The survey was performed on 15 ultrasound images, each one was compressed with 5 different techniques. We then have a database composed of 75 compression results. The goal of this work is not to compare the performance of these compression methods, but to quantify the specialist's perception of the image quality.

The test was held following a rigorous protocol regarding the lighting conditions around the examinee:

- the intensity of light falling on the video monitor and on the examinee's face is measured using an incident type exposure meter and set to $8.5 +/- 0.5$ and $10 +/- 0.5$, respectively.
- we use a single monitor for all the examinees, its contrast is fixed, its resolution is set to 1024x768 at 32 bits/pixel.

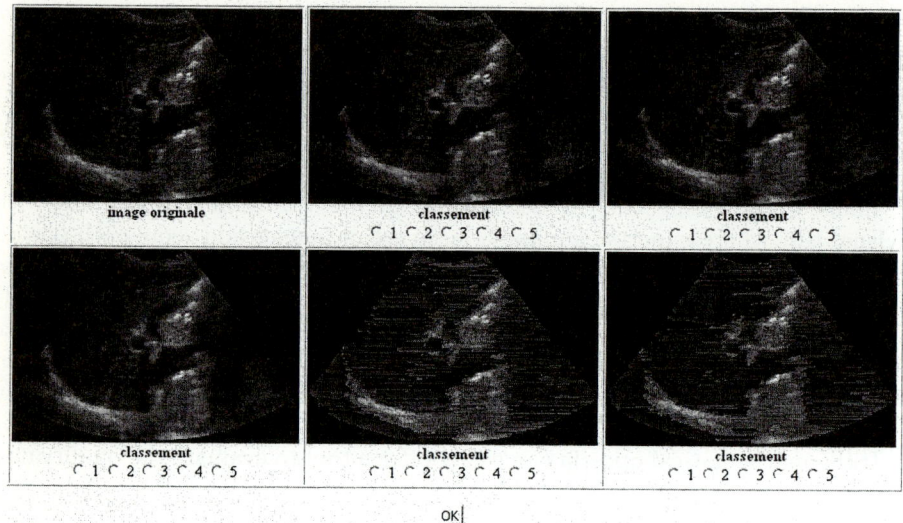

Fig. 1. Test interface presented to the medical expert

The whole test is composed of a sequence of 15 different screens. Each screen presents, for one particular image, the original image and 5 compression results. An illustration of such a screen is presented in figure 1.

The experts have to compare and sort from worst to best the compressed ultrasound images with respect to the original one. A score ranging from 1 to 5 is given from worst to best quality, respectively. The test campaign was held in October 2004 and involved 13 medical experts (10 practiced the complete test), all specialized in ultrasonography. For each compression result, we measured the score average value given by the experts. We also analysed for the whole data 15 sorting results, which is a permutation of $\{1, 2, 3, 4, 5\}$. The standard deviation of the expert's scores for one compression result is a value between 0 (case when all the experts give the same score) and 2 (case when 5 experts select rank 1 and the 5 others score 5). The average standard deviation measured on these results is equal to 0.67. The 0.67 value shows that most of the experts agreed on the quality of a given image; their answers were homogeneous and the results were consistent.

3 Statistical Quality Criteria

The advantage of a psychovisual method, such as the one developed in the previous section, is that the results are closely related to the medical expertise. However, this is a very time and manpower consuming approach. We studied some statistical criteria and compared them with respect to the results of the previous psychovisual test. We selected different types of criteria: distance measures, denoted D_x ; correlation measures C_x ; spectral measures S_x ; PSNR

Table 1. Statistical criteria chosen for the study

D1	Minkowsky - Mean absolute error	S3	Block spectral magnitude error
D2	Minkowsky - Mean square error	S4	Block spectral phase error
D3	Minkowsky - Modified infinity norm	S5	Block spectral phase-magnitude error
D4	Neighborhood error - 8 neighbours	S6	Block spectral error
D5	Neighborhood error - 24 neighbours	P1	Peak signal to noise ratio
D6	Multiresolution error	T1	Contrast measure
C1	Normalized cross correlation	H1	Absolute norm Human Visual System
C2	Image fidelity	H2	$L2$ norm Human Visual System
C3	Czekonowski correlation	H3	similarity
S1	Spectral phase error	H4	DCTune error
S2	Spectral phase-magnitude error		

measure P_1 ; contrast measure T_1 ; human visual system based measures H_x. These criteria are real valued and have different ranges [7] (see table 1).

As we have relative measures, we can compare the quality of different compression results. The criteria are sorted according to their own variation (e.g. the PSNR values are ranked from their highest to their lowest values, the Minkowski errors are ranked from their lowest to their highest values). For each screen of the psychovisual study, the 5 compression results are sorted according to the average score given by the medical experts. Given this sorting, we can extract 10 comparisons results for each pair of compression results given by the medical experts and by using an evaluation criterion.

In order to define the similarity between each criterion and our reference given by the experts' scores, an absolute difference is measured between the criterion comparison and the expert's one. We define the cumulative similarity of correct comparison (SCC):

$$SCC = \sum_{k=1}^{15}\sum_{i=1}^{10} |A(i,k) - B(i,k)| \qquad (1)$$

where $A(i,k)$ and $B(i,k)$ are respectively the expert and the criterion results for the ith comparison of page k. A comparison result is a value in $\{-1,1\}$. If a compression result is better than another one, the comparison value is set to 1 otherwise it equals -1. In order to more easily compare this error measure, we also define the similarity rate of correct comparison (SRCC), which represents the absolute similarity of comparison referenced to the maximal value :

$$SRCC = (1 - \frac{SCC}{SCC_{max}}) * 100 \qquad (2)$$

where SCC_{max} corresponds to the biggest difference of the 150 comparison results. In our case, $SCC_{max} = 150 * 2 = 300$.

Figure 2 presents the value of $SRCC$ for each evaluation criterion. We can distinguish that the four best criteria are D5, T1, S2 and S1. We can reach in this case a maximal value of 65.3%. That means that this criterion is able to

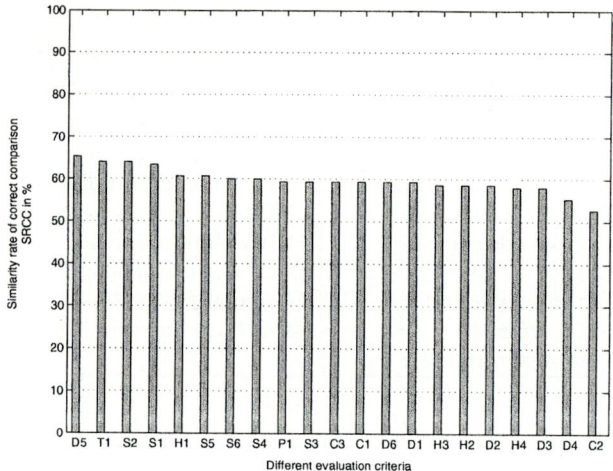

Fig. 2. Efficiency of each evaluation criterion to reproduce the expert's judgment

reproduce the ability of a medical expert to compare two compression results in 65.3% cases. One can notice that the $PSNR$ criterion that is very often used for the comparison of compression results is only ranked at the 9th place.

We will now try to fuse different criteria in order to improve these results.

4 Fusion of Criteria

A possible method consists in combining linearly the best criteria. When combining N criteria, the goal is then to determine the optimal values $(a_i, i = 1..N)$ of a linear combination of the criteria values giving the closest behavior to the medical assessment. The new criterion Cr is defined as:

$$Cr = \sum_{i=1}^{N} a_i.Cr_i \qquad (3)$$

where Cr_i is the ith criterion defined in the previous section. We propose here to use again the similarity rate of correct comparison computed on the 75 compression results. The optimization method we use is a genetic algorithm.

Genetic algorithms determine solutions of functions by simulating the evolution of a population until the survival of the best fitted individuals [8]. The survivors are individuals obtained by crossing-over, mutation and selection of individuals from the previous generation. A genetic algorithm is defined by considering five essential data:

1. *Genotype*: a set of characteristics of an individual such as its size. A vector of linear coefficients (a, b, c, d) is considered as an individual (in the case of four criteria to fuse).
2. *Initial population*: a set of individuals characterized by their genotypes. It is composed of a set of random values of parameters.

3. *Fitness function*: this function quantifies the fitness of an individual to the environment by considering its genotype. We take a similarity rate of correct comparison (SRCC) with the expert's evaluation on the 75 compression results.
4. *Operators on genotypes*: they define alterations on genotypes in order to evaluate the population during generations. There are three types of operators:

   – Selection of an individual: individuals that are not adapted to the environment do not outlive to the next generation. We used the normalized geometric ranking selection method which defines a probability P_i for each individual i to be selected:

   $$P_i = \frac{q(1-q)r - 1}{1 - (1-q)^n} \quad (4)$$

   where
   $$\begin{array}{l} q : \text{the selection probability of the best individual} \\ r : \text{the rank of the individual, where 1 is the best} \\ n : \text{the population size} \end{array} \quad (5)$$

   – Individual mutation: the genes of an individual are modified in order to better adapt to the environment. We use the Non-Uniform mutation process which randomly selects one chromosome j, and sets it equal to a non-uniform random number:

   $$x'_i = \begin{cases} x_i + (b_i - x_i)f(G) & \text{if } r_1 < 0.5 \\ x_i - (x_i + a_i)f(G) & \text{if } r_1 \geq 0.5 \end{cases} \quad (6)$$

   where
   $$\begin{array}{l} f(G) = (r_2(1 - \frac{G}{G_{max}}))^b \\ r_1, r_2 : \text{uniform random numbers in}[0, 1] \\ a_i, b_i : \text{minimal and maximal values of the chromosome } x_i \\ G : \text{the current generation} \\ G_{max} : \text{the maximum number of generations} \\ b : \text{a shape parameter} \end{array} \quad (7)$$

   – Crossing-over: two individuals can reproduce by combining their genes. We use the arithmetic crossover which produces two complementary linear combinations of the parents:

   $$\begin{array}{l} X' = rX + (1-r)Y \\ Y' = (1-r)X + rY \end{array} \quad (8)$$

   where
   $$\begin{array}{l} X, Y : \text{genotype of the parents} \\ r : \text{a uniform random number in}[0, 1] \\ X', Y' : \text{genotype of the linear combination of the parents.} \end{array} \quad (9)$$

   The crossing-over is tested during x tries. If after x tries, none child is better if considering the fitness function, the parents X and Y stay to

the next generation. Otherwise, the crossing-over creates two children X' and Y' and the parents do not survive. The number of individuals in the population is still constant.
5. *Stopping criterion* : this criterion allows to stop the evolution of the population. We choose to consider the stability of the standard deviation of the evaluation criterion of the population.

Given these five information, the execution of the genetic algorithm is realized in four steps:

1. definition of the initial population and computation of the fitness function of each individual,
2. selection and crossing-over of individuals of the population,
3. evaluation of individuals in the population,
4. back to step 2 if the stopping criterion is not satisfied.

5 Experimental Results

We used a population of size 20.000 and 1000 iterations. The mutation probability is set to 0.05 (that is to say that 5% of the 20.000 individuals will mute at each generation), the selection probability is set to 0.08 (8% of the individuals are selected to survive at the next generation) and the crossing-over is tested during 20 tries.

Figure 3 (a) presents the evolution of the similarity rate of comparison by merging different criteria. Given a number N of criteria to fusion, we take the N best criteria derived from the previous analysis. For example, by merging the three best criteria , we obtain a similarity rate of comparison equal to 72%. The envelop curve corresponds to a minimum value we should have obtained. It is built, for each number of criteria merged, as the maximum obtained with the current criteria and with all the last ones. Indeed, the evolution of the similarity rate should necessarily increase. If we have defined the optimal value with N criteria, the optimal value with $N + 1$ criteria should be as high as with N criteria because we can take for the $N + 1$ linear coefficient criteria the value 0. We can explain this difference with the expected behavior by the fact that we did not use enough individuals in the population or iterations. In this case, the global optimal value is not reached.

Figure 3 (b) shows the results of the fusion when using the criterion selection. In this case, instead of only determining the N linear coefficients, we also determine the best criteria to use. For N criteria to fusion, we have to determine $2.N$ values by using the previous genetic algorithm. In this case, we obtain a higher value of the similarity rate of correct comparison (75.3%).

We used the toolbox GAOT [8] in ©Matlab as implementation of the genetic algorithm. The determination of the linear coefficients and the criteria given a number of criteria takes about 4 minutes (training phase) on a PC ©Pentium 4 (2 Ghz).

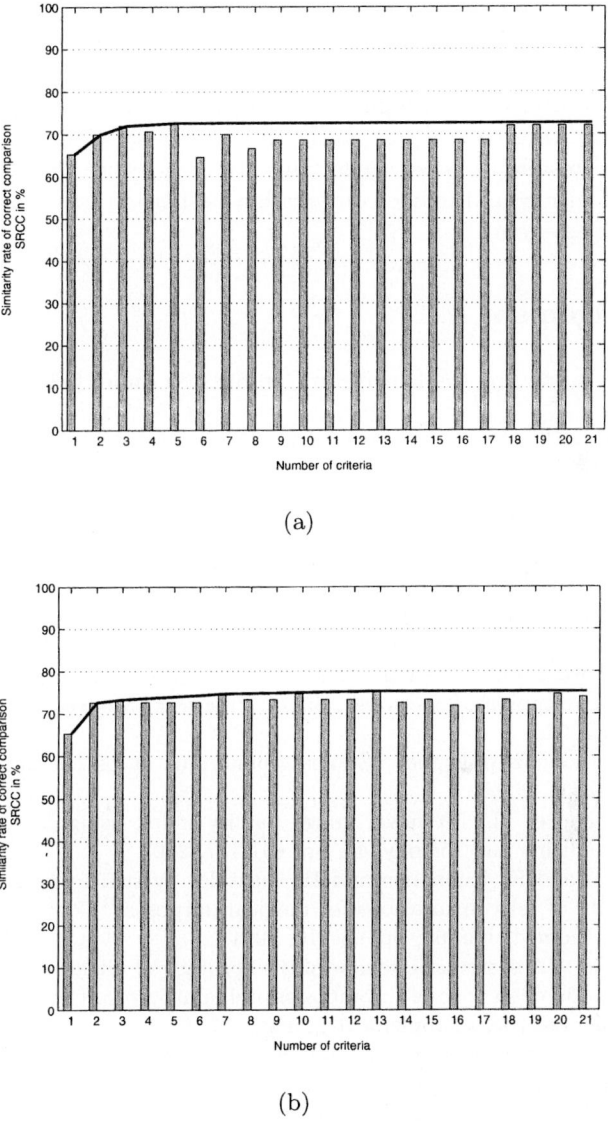

Fig. 3. Fusion results: (a) without criterion selection, (b) with criterion selection

6 Conclusions

We expose in this paper a comparison of some evaluation criteria to quantify the quality of image compression. We implemented a psychovisual study involving 10 medical experts to identify the statistical criteria having the best behavior compared to the medical assessment. This study allows us to select three criteria among the 21 tested ones : neighborhood error (24 neighbors), contrast measure and spectral phase-magnitude error. The best similarity rate obtained with a single criterion is 65.3%. A genetic algorithm performs the criteria fusion in order to improve, with a significant effect, the evaluation efficiency. The proposed criterion provides a higher value of the similarity rate of correct comparison (75.3%) improving significantly the possibility to evaluate the quality of compression results. A prospect for this study is to use this criterion for the comparison of ultrasound image compression best fitted for a mobile robotized tele-echography system.

Acknowledgement

This work was funded by the European Commission under OTELO project (IST 2001-32516).

References

1. Delgorge C., Courreges F., Bassit L. Al , Novales C., Rosenberger C., Smith-Guerin N., Bru C., Gilabert R., Vannoni M., Poisson G., Vieyres P., "A tele-operated mobile ultrasound scanner using a light weight robot", IEEE Transactions on Information Technology in BioMedicine, special issue mHealth, (9) 1, pp. 50-58, 2005.
2. Deepak S. Turaga and Yingwei Chen and Jorge Caviedes, "No reference PSNR estimation for compressed pictures", Signal Processing Image Communication, 19, pp. 173-184, 2004.
3. Christine Fernandez-Maloigne, "Couleur numerique et psychometrie", Computer Art Journal, 1(1), 2004.
4. Tzong-Jer Chen et al., "A novel image quality index using Moran I statistics", Physics in Medicine and Biology, 48, pp. 131-137, 2003.
5. H. Lamminen and K. Ruohonen and H. Uusitalo, "Visual tests for measuring the picture quality of teleconsultations for medical purposes", Computer Methods and Programs in Biomedicine, 65, pp. 95-110, 2001.
6. B. Kassai et al., "A systematic review of the accuracy of ultrasound in the diagnosis of asymptomatic deep venous thrombosis: preliminary results", Journal of Thrombosis and Haemostasis, I-supplement 1, n P1443, 2003.
7. Ismail Avcibas and Bulent Sankur and Khalid Sayood, "Statistical evaluation of image quality measures", Journal of Electronic imaging, 11(2), pp. 206-223, 2002.
8. P. Wall, "A Genetic Algorithm for Resource-Constrained Scheduling", PhD Thesis, MIT, 1996.

3D Model Retrieval Based on Adaptive Views Clustering

Tarik Filali Ansary[1], Mohamed Daoudi[2], and Jean-Phillipe Vandeborre[1]

[1] MIIRE Research Group,
(GET / INT / LIFL UMR USTL/CNRS 8022)
{filali, vandeborre}@enic.fr
[2] Université François-Rabelais,
Laboratoire d'Informatique de Tours (EA 2101)
mohamed.daoudi@univ-tours.fr
http://www-rech.enic.fr/miire

Abstract. In this paper, we propose a method for 3D model indexing based on 2D views, named AVC (Adaptive Views Clustering). The goal of this method is to provide an optimal selection of 2D views from a 3D model, and a probabilistic Bayesian method for 3D model retrieval from these views. The characteristic views selection algorithm is based on an adaptive clustering algorithm and using statistical model distribution scores to select the optimal number of views. Starting from the fact that all views do not contain the same amount of information, we also introduce a novel Bayesian approach to improve the retrieval. We finally present our results and compare our method to some state of the art 3D retrieval descriptors on the *Princeton 3D Shape Benchmark* database.

1 Introduction

The use of three-dimensional image and model databases throughout the Internet is growing both in number and size. The development of modeling tools, 3D scanners, 3D graphic accelerated hardware, Web3D and so on, is enabling access to three-dimensional materials of high quality. In recent years, many systems have been proposed for efficient information retrieval from digital collections of images and videos. However, the solutions proposed so far to support retrieval of such data are not always effective in application contexts where the information is intrinsically three-dimensional. A similarity metric has to be defined to compute a visual similarity between two 3D models, given their descriptions.

For example, Kazhdan et al. [1] describe a general approach based on spherical harmonics. From the collection of spherical functions calculated on the voxel grid of the 3D object, they compute a rotation invariant descriptor by decomposing the function into its spherical harmonics and summing the harmonics within each frequency. Then, they compute the L_2-norm for each component. The result is a 2D histogram indexed by radius and frequency.

In 3D retrieval using 2D views, the main idea is that two 3D models are similar, if they look similar from all viewing angles. Funkhouser et al. [2] apply view based similarity to implement a 2D sketch query interface. In the preprocessing stage, a descriptor of 3D model is obtained by 13 thumbnail images of boundary contour as seen from 13 view directions. Using aspect graphs, Cyr and Kimia [3] specify a query by a view of 3D objects. A descriptor of 3D model consists in a number of views of the 3D models. The number of views is kept small by clustering views and by representing each cluster with one view, which is represented by a shock graph. Schiffenbauer [4] presents a complete survey of aspect graphs methods. Using shock matching, Macrine et al. [5] apply indexing using topological signatures vectors to implement view based similarity matching more efficiently. Recently, Chen et al. [6] defend the intuitive idea that two 3D models are similar if they also look similar from different angles. Therefore they use 100 orthogonal projections of an object and encode them by Zernike moments and Fourier descriptors. They also point out that they obtain better results than other well-known descriptors. Tangelder and Veltkamp [7] present a complete survey on 3D shape retrieval.

In this paper, we propose a method for 3D model indexing based on 2D views, named AVC (Adaptive Views Clustering). The goal of this method is to provide an optimal selection of 2D views from a 3D model, and a probabilistic Bayesian method for 3D models indexing from these views. This paper is organised in the following way. In section 2, we present the main principles of our method for characteristic views selection. In section 3, we present the Bayesian Information Criteria (BIC). In section 4, our probabilistic 3D models indexing is presented. Finally, the results obtained from a collection of 3D models are presented showing the performances of our method. We compare our method to some state of the art 3D retrieval descriptors on the *Princeton 3D Shape Benchmark* database.

2 Selection of Characteristic Views

Let $D_b = \{M_1, M_2, \ldots, M_N\}$ be a collection of N three-dimensional models. We wish to represent each 3D model M_i by a set of 2D views that best represent it. To achieve this goal, we first generate an initial set of views from the 3D model, then we reduce it to the only views that best characterise the 3D model. This idea comes from the fact that all the views of 3D model do not have equal importance: there are views that contain more information than others.

In this paragraph, we present our algorithm for characteristic views selection from a three-dimensional model.

2.1 Generating the Initial Set of Views

To generate the initial set of views for a model M_i of the collection, we create 2D views (projections) from multiple viewpoints. These viewpoints are equally spaced on the unit sphere. In our current implementation, there are 320 views. The views are silhouettes only, which enhance the efficiency and the robustness of image metric. Orthogonal projection is applied in order to speed up the retrieval process and reduce the size of the used features. To represent each of these 2D views, we use 49 coefficients of Zernike moment descriptor [8]. Consequently to the use of Zernike moments, the approach is robust against translation, rotation and scaling.

2.2 Characteristic Views Selection

As every 2D view is represented by 49 Zernike moment coefficients, choosing a set of characteristic views that best caraterise the 3D models (320 views), is equivalent to choose a subset of points that represent a set of 320 points in 49 dimensions space. The problem of choosing X characteristic views that best represent a set of $N = 320$ views, is well known as *clustering problem*.

Data clustering is a well known problem in the Mathematical and Computer-Science communities. The literature in this domain is huge. One of the widely used method is K-means [9]. Its attractiveness lies in its simplicity and in its local-minimum convergence properties. However, it has one main shortcomming: the number of clusters K has to be supplied by the user.

As we want from our method to adapt the number of characteristic views to the geometrical complexity of the 3D model, using K-means is not suited. To avoid this problem, we use a method derivative from K-means. Instead of a fixed number of clusters, we propose to use a range in which we will choose the best number of clusters. In our case the range will be $[1, \ldots, 40]$. In this paper, we assume that the maximum number of characteristic views is 40. This number of views is a good compromise between speed, descriptor size and representation.

We proceed now to demonstrate how to select the characteristic views set and also how to select the best K within the given range. In essence, the algorithm starts with K equal to 1 and continue to add characteristic views where they are needed until the upper bound is reached. During this process, for each K, we save the characteristic views set.

To add new characteristic views we used the idea presented in X-means clustering method by Dan Pelleg [10]. In a first step, in every cluster of views represented by a characteristic view, we select two views that have the maximum distance in this cluster. Next, in each cluster of views, we run a local K-means (with $K = 2$) for each pair of selected views. By local we mean that only the views that are in the cluster are used in this local clustering.

At this point, a question arises: "are the two new views giving more information on the region than the original characteristic view?". To answer this question, we use Bayesian Information Criteria (BIC) [11], that scores how likely the representation model (using one or two characteristic views) is fitting the data. Other criteria like Akaike Information Criteria (AIC) [12] could also be used. It appears to be some debate on the relative merits of AIC versus BIC, but this discussion is far behind the scope of this paper. Estimating the BIC score will be discussed in the next section.

According to the outcome of the test, the model with the higher score is selected. These clusters of the views which are not represented well by the current centroids will receive more attention by increasing the number of centroids in them.

We continue alternating between global K-means and K-means on clusters owned by characteristic views until the upper bound for characteristic views number is attained. Then we compare the BIC score of each characteristic views set. Finally, the best characteristic views set will be the one that gets the highest BIC score on all the views. Algorithm 1 gives an overview of the characteristic views selection algorithm.

Algorithm 1. Characteristic views selection algorithm

Number of characteristic views = 1
while Number of characteristic views < Maximum number characteristic views **do**
  Make global K-means on all the views (The start centers are the characteristic views).
  Save the characteristic views set and it's BIC Score.
  for all cluster of views **do**
    Make K-means (with K=2) on the cluster.
    Choose the representation with the higher BIC score. The original characteristic view or the two new characteristic views
    Update the number of characteristic views.
  end for
end while
Select the K and the characteristic view set with the higher BIC score.

---

3 Bayesian Information Criteria

To calculate the BIC score for a *representation model* Mod_j having the cluster of views V, we use the formula introduced by Schwarz [11]:

$$BIC(Mod_j) = \hat{l}_j(V) - \frac{P_j}{2} \log N . \quad (1)$$

With P_j the number of parameters in Mod_j. This is also know as the Schwarz criterion [11]. $\hat{l}_j(V)$ is the log-likehood of the data according to the j-th model and taken at the maximum likelihood point. N is the number of views in the cluster $N = |V|$. In our case the models are all spherical Gaussians which is the type assumed by K-means. The Maximum Likehood Estimate (MLE) for variance is:

$$\hat{\theta}^2 = \frac{1}{N-K} \sum_i (Dist(V_i, Vc_i)^2) . \quad (2)$$

With $Dist(V_i, Vc_i)$ the Euclidean distance between the Zernike moments of the respective views V_i and Vc_i, the characteristic view associated with the view V_i. The log-likehood of the data is:

$$\hat{l}_j(V) = \sum_i \left(\frac{1}{\sqrt{2\pi}\hat{\theta}^{49}} - \frac{1}{2\hat{\theta}^2} \parallel Dist(V_i, Vc_i) \parallel^2 + \log \frac{N_{(i)}}{N} \right) . \quad (3)$$

Figure 1 shows the evolution of the BIC score with the number of views. Theses curves show that an optimal number of views exists where the BIC score

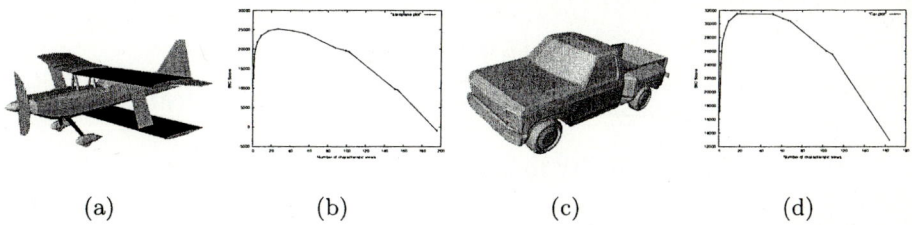

(a) (b) (c) (d)

Fig. 1. Two models from the database and their corresponding BIC Score curves

is maximised. For the aeroplane model in figure 1(a), the number of optimal views is 29. For the car model in figure 1(c), only 17 views are needed as the 3D model is less complex then the first one. This is comming from the fact that the more the 3D model is geometrically complex, the more its 2D views are different. This leads to a higher number of views to best represent it.

4 Probabilistic Approach for 3D Indexing

Each model of the collection D_b is represented by a set of characteristic views $V = \{V_1, V_2, \ldots, V_C\}$, with C the number of characteristic views. To each characteristic view corresponds a set of represented views called V_r. Considering a 3D request model Q, we wish to find the model $M_i \in D_b$ which is the closest to the request model Q. This model is the one that has the highest probability $P(M_i/Q)$. Knowing that each model is represented by its characteristic views, $P(M_i/Q)$ can be written:

$$P(M_i|Q) = \sum_{k=1}^{C} P(M_i|V_Q^k)P(V_Q^k|Q) \ . \tag{4}$$

With C the number of characteristic views of the model Q. Let H be the set of all the possible hypotheses of correspondence between the request view V_Q^k and a model M_i, $H = \{h_1^k \vee h_2^k \vee \ldots \vee h_N^k\}$. A hypothesis h_p^k means that the view p of the model is the view request V_Q^k. The sign $\vee$ represents *logic or operator*. Let us note that if an hypothesis h_p^k is true, all the other hypotheses are false. $P(M_i|V_Q^k)$ can be expressed by $P(M_i|H^k)$. We have:

$$P(M_i|H^k) = \sum_{j=1}^{N} P(M_i, V_{M_i}^j|h_j^k) \ . \tag{5}$$

The sum $\sum_{j=1}^{N} P(M_i, V_{M_i}^j|h_j^k)$ can be reduced to the only true hypothesis $P(M_i, Vc_{M_i}^j|H_j^k)$. In fact, a characteristic view from the request model Q can match only one characteristic view from the model M_i. We choose the characteristic view with the maximum probability.

$$P(M_i|Q) = \sum_{k=1}^{K} Max_j(P(M_i, V_{M_i}^j|h_j^k))P(V_Q^k|Q) \ . \tag{6}$$

Using the Bayes theorem we obtain:

$$P(M_i|Q) = \sum_{k=1}^{K} Max_j \left(\frac{P(h_j^k|V_{M_i}^j, M_i)P(V_{M_i}^j|M_i)P(M_i)}{\sum_{i=1}^{N}\sum_{k=1}^{K} P(h_j^k|V_{M_i}^j, M_i)P(V_{M_i}^j|M_i)P(M_i)} \right) P(V_Q^k|Q) . \tag{7}$$

With $P(M)$ the probability to observe the model M.

$$P(M_i) = \alpha e^{(-\alpha.|M_i|)/\sum_{i=N}^{i=1}|M_i|} . \tag{8}$$

Where $|M_i|$ is the number of characteristic views of the model M_i. α is a parameter to hold the effect of the probability $P(M_i)$. The algorithm conception makes that, the more complex is the geometry of the 3D model, the greater is the number of its characteristic views. Indeed, simple object (e.g. a cube) are more frequent and got more probability of appearance then complex ones. This kind of object can be at the root of more complex objects.

On the other hand:

$$P(V_{M_i}^j|M_i) = 1 - \beta e^{(-\beta.N(Vr_{M_i}^j)/320)} . \tag{9}$$

Where $N(Vr_{M_i}^j)$ is the number of views represented by the characteristic view j of the model M. The greater is the number of represented views $N(Vr_{M_i}^j)$, the more the characteristic view $V_{M_i}^j$ is important and the best it represents the three-dimensional model. The β coefficient is introduced to reduce the effect of the view probability. We use the values $\alpha = \beta = 1/100$ which give the best results during our experiments.

The value $P(h_j^k|V_{M_i}^j, M_i)$ is the probability that, knowing that we observe the characteristic view j of the model M_i, this view is the k view of the 3D query model Q:

$$P(h_j^k|V_{M_i}^j, M_i) = 1 - D_{(Q^k, h_{V_{M_i}^j})} . \tag{10}$$

With $D_{h_q, h_{V_{M_i}^j}}$ the Euclidean distance between the 2D Zernike descriptors of the view k of the request model Q and $V_{M_i}^j$ the characteristic view j of the three-dimensional model M_i.

In this section, we have presented our Bayesian retrieval framework, which takes into account the number of characteristic views of the model and the importance (amount of information) of its views. In the following section we present the results of experiments made by our method on *Princeton 3D Shape Benchmark* database [13].

5 Experiments and Results

We implemented the algorithms, described in the previous sections, using C++ and the TGS OpenInventor libraries. The system consists in an off-line characteristic views extraction and an on-line retrieval process. In the off-line process, the characteristic views selection takes about 18 seconds per model on PC with a Pentium IV 2.4 GHZ CPU. In the on-line process, the comparison takes less then 1 second for 1814 3D models. To measure the performance, we used a standard benchmark database: the *Princeton 3D Shape Benchmark* [13]. The database contain 1814 models manually classified into 161 classes. Figure 2 shows a

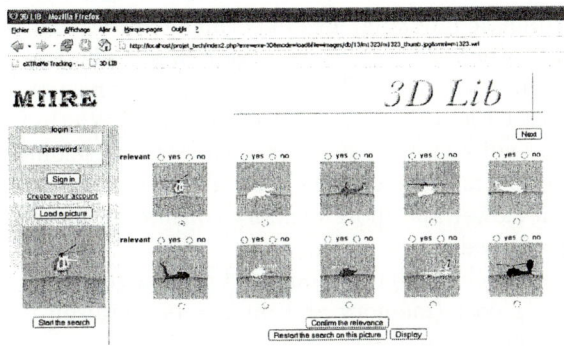

Fig. 2. Screenshot of the 3D models retrieval system

request using our 3D retrieval system. On the left side, the request 3D model is presented. The right side shows the 3D models which have the higher probabilities of matching the 3D request model. We use several different performance measures to objectively evaluate our method: the First Tier (FT), Second Tier (ST), Nearest Neighbour (NN), E-Measure, Discounted Cumulative Gain (DCG) and Normalised Discounted Cumulative Gain (N-DCG) match percentages, as well as the recall-precision plot [13]. As mentioned in the introduction, we compared our method to state of the art descriptors, Spherical Harmonics [1], Radialized Spherical Extent Function(REXT) [14], Gaussian Euclidean Distance Transform (GEDT) [1] and Light Field Descriptor (LFD) [6].

In our experiment, we use each of the five shape matching algorithms to compute distances between all pairs of models in the test and analyse them with the *Princeton 3D Shape Benchmark* evaluation tools to quantify the matching performance with respect to the classification.

Every model was normalised for size by isotropically rescaling it so that the average distance from points on its surface to the center of mass is 0.5. Then, all the models was normalised for translation by moving its center of mass to the origin.

Figure 3 shows the recall precision plots for our method AVC and the other shape descriptors. Table 1 shows micro averages storage requierement (for our method, we used 23 views that is the average number of views for all the database models) and retrieval statistics for each algorithm. Storage size is given in bytes. We found that micro and macro-average results gave consistent results, and we decided to present micro-averaged statistics.

We find that the shape descriptors based on 2D views (LFD and our method) provides the best retrieval precision in this experiment. We might expect shape descriptors that capture 3D geometric relationships would be more discriminating than the ones based solely on 2D projections, the opposite is true. However, our method and the LFD takes more time to compare than the other descriptors, since it requires searching over multiple possible image correspondances.

We can notice that our method provides more accurate results with the use of Bayesian probabilistic indexing. The experiment shows that our method gives better performances then 3D harmonics, Radialized Spherical Extent Function and Gaussian Euclidean Distance Transform on the *Princeton 3D Shape Benchmark* database. Light Field Descriptor gives better results than our method but uses 100 views, does not adapt the number of views to the geometrical complexity and uses two descriptors for each view (Zernike moments and Fourier descriptor), which make it slower and more memory consuming descriptor compared to the method we presented.

Overall, we can conclude that our method gives a good compromise between quality (relevance) / cost (memory and online comparaison time) between the shape descriptors we compared to.

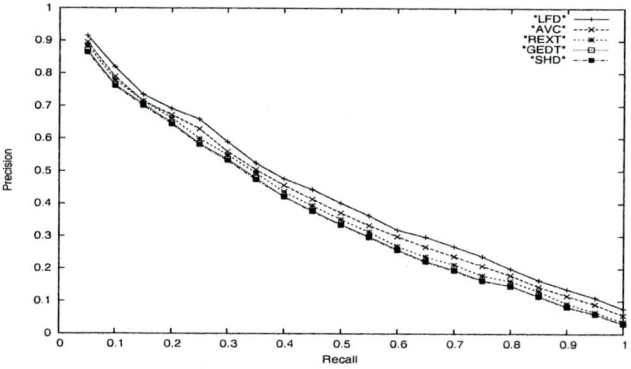

Fig. 3. Recall Precision on *Princeton 3D Shape Benchmark* database

In order to assess the robustness of our method, we apply the following transformations for all classified 3D models. Each transformed 3D model is then used to query the test database.

The average recall and precision of all the 1814 classified models are used for the evaluation (figure 5). The robustness is evaluated by the following transformation:

1. noise: each vertex of 3D model is applied three random number to x-, y- and z-axis translation (±15% times of the length of the model's bounding box). Figure 4(b) shows a typical example of the noise effect;
2. decimation: for each 3D model, randomly select 20% polygons to be deleted. Figure 4(c) shows a typical example of the effect.

Table 1. Retrieval performances

Methods	Storage size	Discrimination					
		NN	FT	ST	E-Measure	DCG	N-DCG
LFD	4,700	65.7%	38.0%	48.7%	28.0%	64.3%	21.3%
AVC with proba	**1,113**	**60.6%**	**33.2%**	**44.3%**	**25.5%**	**60.2%**	**13.48%**
REXT	17,416	60.2%	32.7%	43.2%	25.4%	60.1%	13.3%
GEDT	32,776	60.3%	31.3%	40.7%	23.7%	58.4%	10.2%
AVC without proba	**1,113**	**58.2%**	**31.1%**	**42.7%**	**25.1%**	**59.9%**	**11,8%**
Spherical Harmonics	2,184	55.6%	30.9%	41.1%	24.1%	58.4%	10.2%

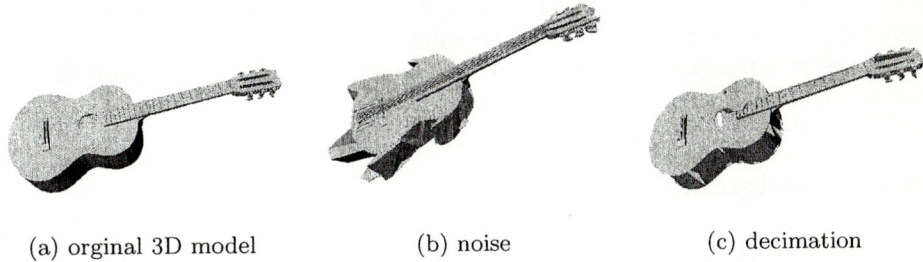

(a) orginal 3D model   (b) noise   (c) decimation

Fig. 4. Robustness evaluation of noise and decimation from a 3D model

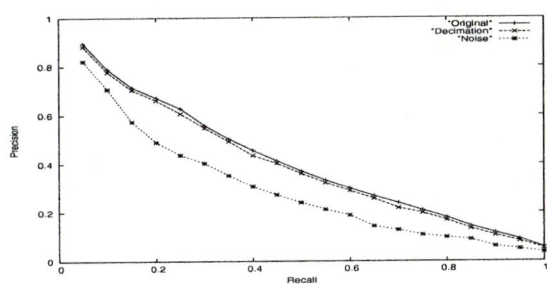

Fig. 5. Recall Precision on *Princeton 3D Shape Benchmark* database

Experimental results of the robustness evaluation is shown in Figure 5. These experimental results prove that our approach is robust against noise and decimation.

6 Conclusion

In this paper, we propose a 3D model retrieval system based on characteristic views similarity called AVC (Adaptive Views Clustering). Starting from the fact that the more the 3D model is geometrically complex, the more its 2D views are different, we propose a characteristic views selection algorithm that corresponds the number of views to its geometrical complexity. Our approach is based on alternating global k-means and adding new characteristic views where needed. The characteristic views set with the higher BIC score is choosed to represent the 3D model. The number of views varies from 1 to 40. We also propose a new probabilistic retrieval approach that takes into account that not all the views of 3D models have the same importance, and also the fact that geometrically simple models have more probability to be relevant than more complex ones. Based on some standard measures, experiments and comparaison to some state of the art methods on *Princeton 3D Shape Benchmark* database, show the accurate results of our approach. The AVC method we proposed gives a good quality/cost compromise compared to other well-known methods. Our method is robust against noise and model degeneracy. It can be suitable against topologically ill-defined 3D models. A practical 3D models retrieval system based on our approach will be soon available on the web for on-line tests.

Acknowledgments

This work is supported by the French Research Ministry and the RNRT (Réseau National de Recherche en Télécommunications) within the framework of the SEMANTIC-3D National Project (http://www.semantic-3d.net). We would like to thank Professor Dan Pelleg from Carnegie Mellon University for the help he provided on X-means, Julien Tierny and the reviewers for their help to make this paper more complete.

References

1. Kazhdan, M., Funkhouser, T., Rusinkiewicz, S.: Rotation invariant spherical harmonic representation of 3d shape descriptors. In: Symposium on Geometric Processing. (2003)
2. Funkhouser, T., Min, P., Kazhdan, M., Haderman, A., Dobkin, D., Jacobs, D.: A search engine for 3D models. ACM Transactions on Graphics **22** (2003) 83–105
3. Cyr, C., B.Kimia: 3D object recognition using shape similarity-based aspect graph. In: ICCV01. (2001) 254–261
4. Schiffenbauer, R.: A survey of aspect graphs. Technical Report TR-CIS-2001-01, CIS (2001)
5. Macrini, D., Shokoufandeh, A., Dickenson, S., Siddiqi, K., S.Zucker: View based 3-D object recognition using shock graphs. In: ICPR. Volume 3. (2002) 24–28
6. Chen, D., Tian, X., Shen, Y., Ouhyoung, M.: On visual similarity based 3D model retrieval. In: Eurographics. Volume 22. (2003) 223–232
7. Tangelder, J., Veltkamp, R.: A survey of content based 3D shape retrieval methods. In: Shape Modeling International. (2004) 145–156
8. Khotanzad, A., Hong, Y.: Invariant image recognition by Zernike moments. IEEE Transactions on Pattern Analysis and Machine Intelligence **12** (90) 489 – 497
9. Duda, R., Hart, P.: Pattern classification and scene analysis. John Wiley and Sons (1973)

10. Pelleg, D., Moore, A.: X-means: Extending k-means with efficient estimation of the number of clusters. In: International Conference on Machine Learning. (2000) 727–734
11. Schwarz, G.: Estimating the dimension of a model. The Annals of Statistics **6** (1978) 461–464
12. Akaike, H.: Information theory and extention of the maximum likehood principle. In: International symposium on information theory. (1973) 267–281
13. Shilane, P., Min, P., Kazhdan, M., Funkhouser, T.: The princeton shape benchmark. In: Shape Modeling International. (2004)
14. Varnic, D.: An improvement of rotation invariant 3d shape descriptor based on functions on concentric spheres. In: ICIP. (2003) 757–760

Colour Texture Segmentation Using Modelling Approach

Michal Haindl and Stanislav Mikeš

Institute of Information Theory and Automation,
Academy of Sciences CR, 182 08 Prague, Czech Republic
{haindl, xaos}@utia.cas.cz

Abstract. A fast and robust type of unsupervised multispectral texture segmentation method with unknown number of classes is presented. Single decorrelated monospectral texture factors are represented by four local autoregressive random field models recursively evaluated for each pixel and for each spectral band. The segmentation algorithm is based on the underlying Gaussian mixture model and starts with an over segmented initial estimation which is adaptively modified until the optimal number of homogeneous texture segments is reached. The performance of the presented method is extensively tested on the Prague segmentation benchmark using nineteen most frequented segmentation criteria.

1 Introduction

Segmentation is a fundamental process affecting the overall performance of an automated image analysis system. Image regions, homogeneous with respect to some usually textural measure, which result from a segmentation algorithm are analysed in subsequent interpretation steps. Texture-based image segmentation is area of intense research activity in recent years and many algorithms were published in consequence of all this effort. These methods are usually categorized [1] as region-based, boundary-based, or as a hybrid of the two. Different published methods are difficult to compare because of lack of a comprehensive analysis together with accessible experimental data, however available results indicate that the texture segmentation problem is still far from being solved. Spatial interaction models and especially Markov random fields-based models are increasingly popular for texture representation [2], [1], [3], etc. Several researchers dealt with the difficult problem of unsupervised segmentation using these models see for example [4], [5], [6], [7] or [8], which is also addressed in this paper.

2 Texture Representation

Static smooth multispectral textures require three dimensional models for adequate representation. However if we slightly compromise spatial-spectral correlations description these textures can be represented by a set of simpler 2D data models with fewer parameters per model. Natural texture data space can be decorrelated only approximately thus the independent spectral component representation suffers with some loss of image information. Because the segmentation is less demanding application than texture synthesis, it is sufficient if such a representation maintains discriminative power of the full model even if its visual modelling strength is imperceptibly compromised.

Spectral factorization using the Karhunen-Loeve expansion transforms the original centered data space θ indexed on the rectangular $M \times N$ finite lattice I into a new data space with K-L coordinate axes $\tilde{Y}$. This new basis vectors are the eigenvectors of the second-order statistical moments matrix

$$\Phi = E\{\tilde{Y}_r \tilde{Y}_r^T\}$$

where the multiindex r has two components $r = [r_1, r_2]$, the first component is row and the second one column index, respectively. Components of the transformed vector $\tilde{Y}_r$ are mutually uncorrelated. If we assume further on Gaussian distribution of vectors $\tilde{Y}_r$ then they are also independent, i.e.,

$$p(\tilde{Y}_r) = \prod_{k=1}^{n} p(\tilde{Y}_{r,k})$$

and single monospectral random fields can be represented independently.

2.1 Texture Factor Model

We assume that single monospectral texture factors $(Y_r = \tilde{Y}_{r,k})$ can be modelled using a causal autoregressive random field model (CAR). The 2D CAR model can be expressed as a stationary causal uncorrelated noise driven 2D autoregressive process [9]:

$$Y_r = \gamma X_r + e_r , \qquad (1)$$

where $\gamma = [a_1, \ldots, a_\eta]$ is the parameter vector, I_r^c is a causal neighborhood index set with $\eta = card(I_r^c)$ and e_r is a white Gaussian noise with zero mean and a constant but unknown variance σ^2, X_r is a corresponding vector of the contextual neighbours Y_{r-s} and $r, r-1, \ldots$ is a chosen direction of movement on the image index lattice I.

The selection of an appropriate CAR model support (I_r^c) is important to obtain good texture representation. An optimal neighbourhood can be found analytically using the Bayesian approach ([9]). The Bayesian parameters estimation of a CAR model can be found analytically also under few additional and acceptable assumptions. The recursive Bayesian parameter estimation of the causal AR model with the normal-gamma parameter prior which maximize the posterior density is [9]:

$$\hat{\gamma}_{r-1}^T = \hat{\gamma}_{r-2}^T + \frac{V_{x(r-2)}^{-1} X_{r-1} (Y_{r-1} - \hat{\gamma}_{r-2} X_{r-1})^T}{(1 + X_{r-1}^T V_{x(r-2)}^{-1} X_{r-1})} , \qquad (2)$$

where
$$V_{x(r-1)} = \sum_{k=1}^{r-1} X_k X_k^T + V_{x(0)} .$$

Local texture for each pixel is represented by four parametric vectors per spectral band ($r_3 = 1, 2, \ldots, n$, for colour textures $n = 3$). Each parameter vector contains local estimations of CAR model parameters. These models have identical contextual neighbourhood I_r^c but they differ in their major movement direction (top-down, bottom-up, rightward, leftward), i.e.,

$$\tilde{\gamma}_{r,r_3}^T = \{\tilde{\gamma}_{r,r_3}^t, \tilde{\gamma}_{r,r_3}^b, \tilde{\gamma}_{r,r_3}^r, \tilde{\gamma}_{r,r_3}^l\}^T .$$

The parametric space $\tilde{\Theta}$ is subsequently smooth out and its dimensionality is reduced using the Karhunen-Loeve feature extraction (analogously to the spectral space decorrelation). Finally we add the average local spectral values $\zeta_{r,i}$ to the resulting feature vector (Θ_r).

3 Mixture Model Based Segmentation

Multi-spectral texture segmentation is done by clustering in the CAR parameter space Θ defined on the lattice I where

$$\Theta_r = [\gamma_{r,1}, \zeta_{r,1}, \gamma_{r,2}, \zeta_{r,2}, \ldots \gamma_{r,n}, \zeta_{r,n}]^T .$$

$\gamma_{r,i}$ is the parameter vector (2) computed for the i-th transformed spectral band for the lattice location r. We assume that this parametric space can be represented using the Gaussian mixture model (GM) with diagonal covariance matrices due to the CAR parametric space decorrelation. The Gaussian mixture model for CAR parametric representation is as follows:

$$p(\Theta_r) = \sum_{i=1}^{K} p_i\, p(\Theta_r \,|\, \nu_i, \Sigma_i) , \tag{3}$$

$$p(\Theta_r \,|\, \nu_i, \Sigma_i) = \frac{|\Sigma_i|^{-\frac{1}{2}}}{(2\pi)^{\frac{d}{2}}} e^{-\frac{(\Theta_r - \nu_i)^T \Sigma_i^{-1} (\Theta_r - \nu_i)}{2}} . \tag{4}$$

The mixture model equations (3),(4) are solved using a modified EM algorithm. The algorithm is initialized using ν_i, Σ_i statistics estimated from the corresponding rectangular subimages obtained by regular division of the input texture mosaic. An alternative initialization can be random choice of these statistics. For each possible couple of rectangles the Kullback Leibler divergence

$$D\left(p(\Theta_r \,|\, \nu_i, \Sigma_i) \,\|\, p(\Theta_r \,|\, \nu_j, \Sigma_j)\right) = \int_\Omega p(\Theta_r \,|\, \nu_i, \Sigma_i) \log\left(\frac{p(\Theta_r \,|\, \nu_i, \Sigma_i)}{p(\Theta_r \,|\, \nu_j, \Sigma_j)}\right) d\Theta_r \tag{5}$$

is evaluated and the most similar rectangles, i.e.,

$$\{i,j\} = \arg\min_{k,l} D\left(p(\Theta_r \mid \nu_l, \Sigma_l) \,\|\, p(\Theta_r \mid \nu_k, \Sigma_k)\right)$$

are merged together in each step. This initialization results in K_{ini} subimages and recomputed statistics ν_i, Σ_i. $K_{ini} > K$ where K is the optimal number of textured segments to be found by the algorithm. Two steps of the EM algorithm are repeating after initialization. The components with smaller weights than a fixed threshold $(p_j < \frac{0.1}{K_{ini}})$ are eliminated. For every pair of components we estimate their Kullback Leibler divergence (5). From the most similar couple, the component with the weight smaller than the threshold is merged to its stronger partner and all statistics are actualized using the EM algorithm. The algorithm stops when either the likelihood function has negligible increase $(\mathcal{L}_t - \mathcal{L}_{t-1} < 0.05)$ or the maximum iteration number threshold is reached.

The parametric vectors representing texture mosaic pixels are assigned to the clusters according to the highest component probabilities, i.e., Y_r is assigned to the cluster ω_j if

$$\pi_{r,j} = max_j \sum_{s \in I_r} w_s \, p(\Theta_{r-s} \mid \nu_j, \Sigma_j) \;,$$

where w_s are fixed distance-based weights, I_r is a rectangular neighbourhood and $\pi_{r,j} > \pi_{thre}$ (otherwise the pixel is unclassified). The area of single cluster blobs is evaluated in the post-processing thematic map filtration step. Thematic map blobs with area smaller than a given threshold are attached to its neighbour with the highest similarity value. If there is no similar neighbour the blob is eliminated.

4 Experimental Results

The algorithm was tested on natural colour textures mosaics from the Prague Texture Segmentation Data-Generator and Benchmark [10]. The benchmark test mosaics layouts and each cell texture membership are randomly generated and filled with colour textures from our large (more than 1000 high resolution colour textures) colour texture database. The benchmark ranks segmentation algorithms according to a chosen criterion. We have implemented three groups of criteria – region-based [11], pixel-wise [12], [13] and consistency measures [14]. The region-based [11] performance criteria mutually compare ground truth (GT) image regions with the corresponding machine segmented regions (MS). They are the correct, oversegmentation, undersegmentation, missed and noise criteria, i.e., *correct* > 75% GT (ground truth) region pixels are correctly assigned, *oversegmentation* > 75% GT pixels are assigned to a union of regions, *undersegmentation* > 75% pixels from a classified region belong to a union of GT regions, missed (GT in none of the previous categories) and noise (MS in none of the previous categories). Our pixel-wise criteria group contains the most frequented classification criteria such as the omission and commision errors, class accuracy,

Table 1. Benchmark criteria: CS = correct segmentation; OS = over-segmentation; US = under-segmentation; ME = missed error; NE = noise error; O = omission error; C = commision error; CA = class accuracy; CO = recall – correct assignment; CC = precision – object accuracy; I. = type I error; II. = type II error; EA = mean class accuracy estimate; OA = overall accuracy; MS = mapping score; RM = root mean square proportion estimation error; CI = comparison index; GCE = Global Consistency Error; LCE = Local Consistency Error.

	Prague Segmentation Benchmark – Colour			
	presented method	GMRF method [8]	Blobworld [15]	EDISON [16]
CS	46.24	32.43	15.73	12.68
OS	76.21	50.76	1.16	86.93
US	3.81	14.23	10.25	0.00
ME	7.66	13.19	67.95	2.48
NE	9.59	16.19	71.58	4.65
O	7.03	8.76	9.36	14.83
C	0.83	3.22	7.03	0.17
CA	27.04	23.87	21.10	16.05
CO	68.54	62.23	54.00	31.55
CC	96.05	87.47	70.64	98.09
I.	31.46	37.77	46.00	68.44
II.	1.11	4.38	9.69	0.24
EA	76.10	66.10	56.29	41.29
OA	68.54	62.23	54.00	31.55
MS	66.07	54.91	35.37	31.13
RM	3.56	5.45	8.17	3.21
CI	78.83	69.64	59.00	50.29
GCE	8.52	16.56	38.29	3.54
LCE	5.55	8.69	27.28	3.43

recall, precision, etc. Finally the last criteria set incorporates the global and local consistency errors [14].

Tab. 1 compares the overall benchmark performance of the proposed algorithm (segmentaton time 11 min/img on the Athlon 2GHz processor) with the Blobworld [15] (30 min/img), Edison [16] (10 s/img) and our previously published method [8] (55 min/img), respectively. These results demonstrate very good pixel-wise, correct region segmentation and low undersegmentation properties of our method while the oversegmentation results are only average. For all the pixel-wise criteria or the consistency measures our method is either the best one or the next best with marginal difference from the best one.

Fig. 1 shows four selected 512×512 experimental benchmark mosaics created from five to eleven natural colour textures. The last three columns demonstrate comparative results from three alternative algorithms. Hard natural textures were chosen rather than synthesized (for example using Markov random field models) ones because they are expected to be more difficult for the underlying segmentation model. The second column demonstrates robust behaviour of our algorithm but also infrequent algorithm failures producing an oversegmented thematic map for some textures. Such failures can be corrected by more elaborate postprocessing step. The Blobworld [15] and Edison [16] algorithms on these data performed steadily worse as can be seen in the last two columns of Fig. 1, some areas are undersegmented while other parts of the mosaics are oversegmented. Resulting segmentation results are promising however comparison with other algorithms is difficult because of lack of sound experimental evaluation results in the field of texture segmentation algorithms. The overall accuracy of pixelwise correct segmentation for this example is 69%. This result can be further improved by an appropriate postprocessing.

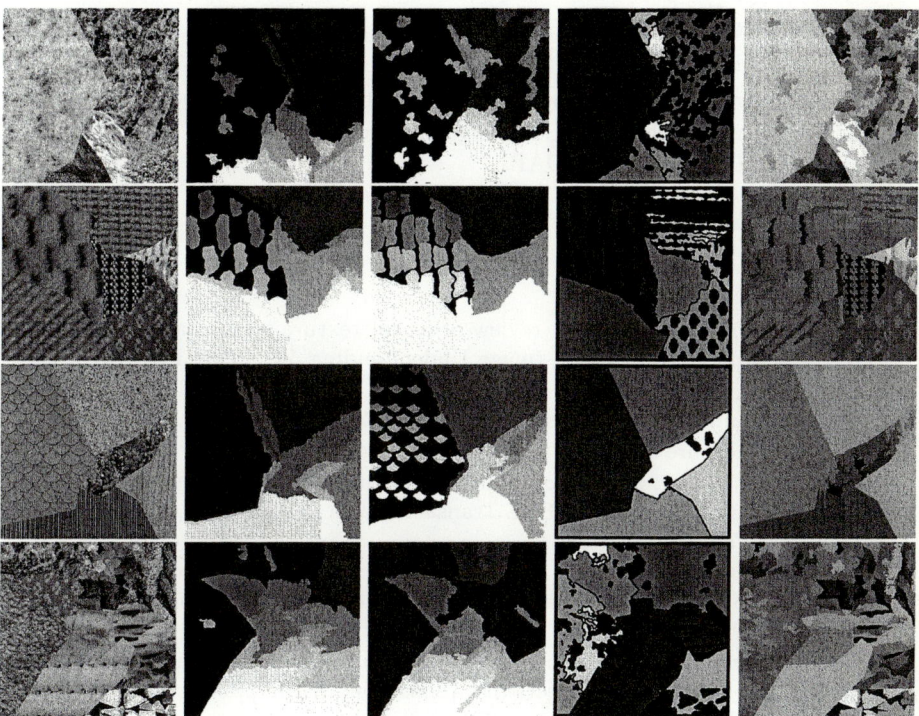

Fig. 1. Selected experimental texture mosaics from the benchmark, our segmentation results (2. column), GMRF method [8] (3.column), Blobworld [15] (4. column), and Edison [16] segmentation results (rightmost column), respectively.

5 Conclusions

We proposed novel efficient and robust method for unsupervised texture segmentation with unknown number of classes based on the underlying CAR and GM texture models. Although the algorithm uses the random field type model it is extremely fast because it uses efficient recursive parameter estimation of the model and therefore is much faster than the usual Markov chain Monte Carlo estimation approach. Usual handicap of segmentation methods is their lot of application dependent parameters to be experimentally estimated. Our method requires only a contextual neighbourhood selection and two additional thresholds. The algorithm's performance is demonstrated on the extensive benchmark tests on natural texture mosaics. It performs favorably compared with three alternative segmentation algorithms and it is faster than our previously published GMRF method. These test results are encouraging and we proceed with more elaborate postprocessing and some alternative texture representation models such as an alternative 3D CAR random field model.

Acknowledgements

This research was supported by the EC projects no. IST-2001-34744, FP6-507752, and partially by the GAAV grants no. A2075302, T400750407 and MŠMT project 1M6798555601 DAR.

References

1. Reed, T.R., du Buf, J.M.H.: A review of recent texture segmentation and feature extraction techniques. CVGIP–Image Understanding **57** (1993) 359–372
2. Kashyap, R.: Image models. In T.Y. Young, K.F., ed.: Handbook of Pattern Recognition and Image Processing. Academic Press, New York (1986)
3. Haindl, M.: Texture synthesis. CWI Quarterly **4** (1991) 305–331
4. Panjwani, D., Healey, G.: Markov random field models for unsupervised segmentation of textured color images. IEEE Transactions on Pattern Analysis and Machine Intelligence **17** (1995) 939–954
5. Manjunath, B., Chellapa, R.: Unsupervised texture segmentation using markov random field models. IEEE Transactions on Pattern Analysis and Machine Intelligence **13** (1991) 478–482
6. Andrey, P., Tarroux, P.: Unsupervised segmentation of markov random field modeled textured images using selectionist relaxation. IEEE Transactions on Pattern Analysis and Machine Intelligence **20** (1998) 252–262
7. Haindl, M.: Texture segmentation using recursive markov random field parameter estimation. In Bjarne, K., Peter, J., eds.: Proceedings of the 11th Scandinavian Conference on Image Analysis, Lyngby, Denmark, Pattern Recognition Society of Denmark (1999) 771–776
8. Haindl, M., Mikeš, S.: Model-based texture segmentation. In Campilho, A., Kamel, M., eds.: Image Analysis and Recognition. Lecture Notes in Computer Science 3212, Berlin, Springer-Verlag (2004) 306 – 313
9. Haindl, M., Šimberová, S.: A Multispectral Image Line Reconstruction Method. In: Theory & Applications of Image Analysis. World Scientific Publishing Co., Singapore (1992) 306–315
10. : Prague texture segmentation data-generator and benchmark. http://mosaic.utia.cas.cz (2004)

11. Hoover, A., Jean-Baptiste, G., Jiang, X., Flynn, P.J., Bunke, H., Goldgof, D.B., Bowyer, K., Eggert, D.W., Fitzgibbon, A., Fisher, R.B.: An experimental comparison of range image segmentation algorithms. IEEE Transaction on Pattern Analysis and Machine Intelligence **18** (1996) 673–689
12. Rosenfield, G.: Analysis of thematic map classification error matrices. Photogrammetric Engineering and Remote Sensing **52** (1986) 681–686
13. Martin, D., Fowlkes, C., Malik, J.: Learning to detect natural image bounderies using brightness and texture. IEEE Transactions on Pattern Analysis and Machine Intelligence **26** (2004) 1–19
14. Martin, D., Fowlkes, C., Tal, D., Malik, J.: A database of human segmented natural images and its application to evaluating segmentation algorithms and measuring ecological statistics. In: Proc. 8th Int'l Conf. Computer Vision. Volume 2. (2001) 416–423
15. Carson, C., Thomas, M., Belongie, S., Hellerstein, J.M., Malik, J.: Blobworld: A system for region-based image indexing and retrieval. In: Third International Conference on Visual Information Systems, Springer (1999)
16. Christoudias, C., Georgescu, B., Meer, P.: Synergism in low level vision. In Kasturi, R., Laurendeau, D., Suen, C., eds.: Proceedings of the 16th International Conference on Pattern Recognition. Volume 4., Los Alamitos, IEEE Computer Society (2002) 150–155

Human-Centered Object-Based Image Retrieval

Egon L. van den Broek[1,4], Eva M. van Rikxoort[2,4], and Theo E. Schouten[3]

[1] Department of Artificial Intelligence, Vrije Universiteit Amsterdam,
De Boelelaan 1081a, 1081 HV Amsterdam, The Netherlands
egon@few.vu.nl
http://www.few.vu.nl/~egon/
[2] Image Sciences Institute, University Medical Center Utrecht,
Heidelberglaan 100, 3584 CX Utrecht, The Netherlands
eva@isi.uu.nl
http://www.isi.uu.nl/
[3] Institute for Computing and Information Science, Radboud University Nijmegen,
P.O. Box 9010, 6500 GL Nijmegen, The Netherlands
T.Schouten@cs.ru.nl
http://www.cs.ru.nl/~ths/
[4] Nijmegen Institute for Cognition and Information, Radboud University Nijmegen,
P.O. Box 9104, 6500 HE Nijmegen, The Netherlands

Abstract. A new object-based image retrieval (OBIR) scheme is introduced. The images are analyzed using the recently developed, human-based 11 colors quantization scheme and the color correlogram. Their output served as input for the image segmentation algorithm: agglomerative merging, which is extended to color images. From the resulting coarse segments, boundaries are extracted by pixelwise classification, which are smoothed by erosion and dilation operators. The resulting features of the extracted shapes, completed the data for a <color, texture, shape>-vector. Combined with the intersection distance measure, this vector is used for OBIR, as are its components. Although shape matching by itself provides good results, the complete vector outperforms its components, with up to 80% precision. Hence, a unique, excellently performing, fast, on human perception based, OBIR scheme is achieved.

1 Introduction

More and more, the world wide web (www), databases, and private collections are searched for audio, video, and image material. Subsequently, As a consequence, there is a pressing need for efficient, user-friendly, multimedia retrieval and indexing techniques. However, where speech and handwriting recognition algorithms are generally applicable, image and video retrieval systems are only successful in a closed domain. These techniques have in common they are computational expensive and their results are judged as non-intuitive by its users.

In this paper, these drawbacks are tackled, for the field to content-based image retrieval (CBIR). An object-based approach on CBIR is employed: object-based image retrieval (OBIR), inspired by the findings of Schomaker, Vuurpijl, and De Leau [1], who showed that 72% of the people are interested in objects when searching images.

Moreover, a human-centered approach is chosen, based on the 11 color categories used by humans in color processing, as described in Section 2. These 11 color categories are also utilized for texture analysis, as discussed in Section 2.1, and for image segmentation, done by agglomerative merging (see Section 3.1). From the resulting, coarse image segments, the shape of the object is derived using pixelwise classification (Section 3.2). Next, erosion and dilation operations are applied on the boundary in order to smooth it, as described in Section 3.3. Section 3 introduces the shape matching algorithm. OBIR is conducted using four query schemes (see Section 5): two of them are based on color and texture, one on the object boundaries, and one on their combination. The results are presented in Section 6 followed by a discussion in Section 7.

2 Color and Texture in 11 Categories

As mentioned by Forsyth and Ponse [2]: "It is surprisingly difficult to predict what colors a human will see in a complex scene." However, it is known that humans use 11 color categories (red, green, blue, yellow, orange, brown, pink, purple, black, white, and gray) when processing color. These 11 color categories are considered universal and optimal [3,4]. These categories should, therefore, be: (i) generic, (ii) computationally cheap, and (iii) can be expected to yield results that are intuitive for users. Then these advantages support the aim of tackling the computational burden of CBIR (cf. QBIC uses a scheme with 4096 colors [5]) and to provide intuitive results for the users [6]. Therefore, we adopted the 11 color quantization scheme [7]: a unique color space segmentation, based on data gathered through experiments in which subjects categorized colors into the 11 color categories. So, the color distribution of images is characterized by a color vector with 11 color values.

Besides color, texture is an important feature for the human visual system [8]. Texture analysis can be done based on intensity differences, but nevertheless, color is important in texture recognition of color image material. With respect to color representation, Fujii, Sugo, and Ando [8] stated that "considering the effective computational strategy in our visual system, it is quite possible that not all the information carried out by the high-dimensional sensory representation is preserved for rapid judgments of natural textures." Taken this into account, the 11 color category quantization scheme should perfectly fit the job, and is, therefore, applied to color-based texture analysis.

For the analysis of texture, various methods are available, such as: statistical methods (e.g., co-occurrence matrices and autocorrelation features), geometrical methods (e.g., Voronoi tessellation features and structural methods), model based methods (e.g., random field models and fractals), and signal processing methods (e.g., spatial domain filters, Fourier domain filtering, Gabor models, and Wavelet models). Originally, they were developed for gray-value images but some of them have recently been adapted to fit texture analysis on color images.

2.1 The Color Correlogram

For the current research, one of the most intuitive texture analysis methods is applied: the color correlogram, as suggested by Huang, Kumar, Mitra, Zhu, and Zabih [9], which is constructed from an image by estimating the pairwise statistics of pixel color. In order to (i) provide perceptual intuitive results and (ii) reduce the computational cost, the 11 color scheme for quantization of color is chosen.

The color correlogram $C_{\bar{d}}(i,j)$ counts the co-occurrence of pixels with colors i and j at a given distance $\bar{d}$. The distance $\bar{d}$ is defined in polar coordinates (d, α), with discrete length and orientation. In practice, α takes the values 0°, 45°, 90°, 135°, 180°, 225°, 270°, and 315°. The color correlogram $C_{\bar{d}}(i,j)$ can now be defined as follows:

$$C_{\bar{d}}(i,j) = \Pr(\mathrm{I}(p_1) = i \wedge \mathrm{I}(p_2) = j \mid |p_1 - p_2| = \bar{d}), \qquad (1)$$

where Pr is probability and p_1 and p_2 are positions in the color image I. Let N be the number of colors in the image, then the dimension of the color correlogram $C_{\bar{d}}(i,j)$ will be $N \times N$, which is in our scheme 11×11. This algorithm yields a symmetric matrix. Hence, only angles up to 180° need to be considered. A direction insensitive color correlogram can be defined for each distance (d) by averaging the four color correlograms of the different angles (i.e., 0°, 45°, 90°, and 135°).

From the color correlogram, a large number of textural features can be derived, such as: energy, entropy, correlation, inverse difference moment, inertia, Haralick's correlation, cluster shade, and cluster prominence, which characterize the content of the image. Based on previous research [10], the combination of entropy, inverse difference moment, cluster prominence, and Haralick's correlation, with distance $d = 1$ is used, resulting in a vector of four texture features.

3 Shape Extraction

The shape extraction phase is divided in three stages: (i) coarse image segmentation, (ii) pixelwise classification, and (iii) smoothing. The coarse image segmentation uses only texture information to segment the image in texture regions. In the pixelwise classification phase, only color information is used because the regions are too small for our texture descriptor to be informative. The complete process of shape extraction is illustrated in Figure 1.

3.1 Segmentation by Agglomerative Merging

Segmentation is applied by agglomerative merging, as described by Ojala and Pietikäinen [11]. Their algorithm was introduced for gray-scale images but is extended to color images, using a color texture descriptor. The algorithm is applied using the color correlogram as texture descriptor based on the 11 color quantization scheme.

At the initial state of the agglomerative merging algorithm, the images are divided in sub blocks of size 16×16 pixels. At each stage of the merging phase, the pair of blocks with the lowest merger importance (MI) is merged. This merger importance is defined by the distance measure MI [9]. For two images I and I', the MI distance measure is defined as follows:

$$MI = |I - I'| = \sum_{i,j=0}^{m-1} |C_{\bar{d}}(i,j) - C'_{\bar{d}}(i,j)|, \qquad (2)$$

where m is the number of bins used and $C_{\bar{d}}(i,j)$ and $C_{\bar{d}}(i,j)$ are the average color correlograms of images I and I' (see Equation 1), and $\bar{d}$ is set to 1 (see Section 2.1).

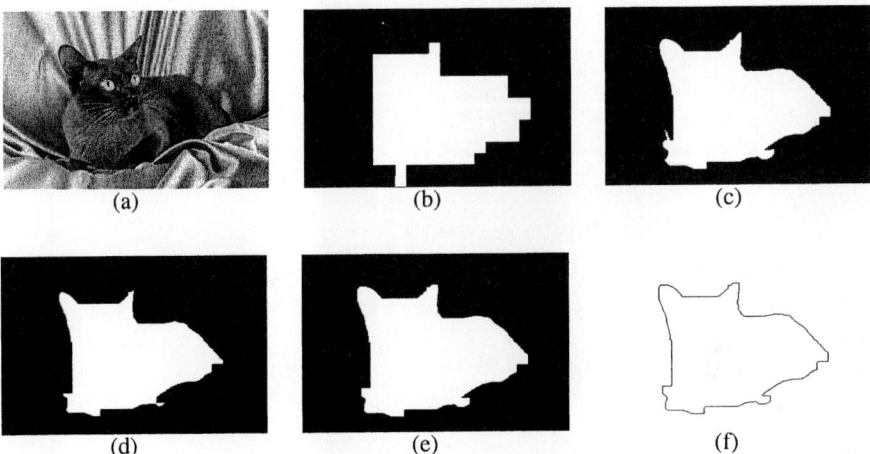

Fig. 1. (a) The original image (b) The coarse segmentation (c) The object after pixelwise classification (d) The object after erosion (e) The object after dilation (f) The final shape.

The closer MI is to zero, the more similar the texture regions are. When two regions are merged, the MI-values between this region and all adjacent regions are computed. The agglomerative merging phase continues until the experimentally determined stopping criterion (Y), given in Equation 3 is met:

$$MI_{stop} = \frac{MI_{cur}}{MI_{max}} < Y, \qquad (3)$$

where MI_{cur} is the merger importance for the current best merge, MI_{max} is the largest merger importance of all preceding merges. For the current dataset, Y is determined to be 0.700. When the coarse segmentation phase is complete, the center segment of the image is selected to be the object of interest for OBIR.

3.2 Pixelwise Classification Based on the 11 Colors

After the center object has been identified in the coarse segmentation phase, pixelwise classification [11] is applied to improve localization of the boundaries of the object. In pixelwise classification, each pixel on the boundary of the center object is examined. A disk with radius r is placed over the pixel and the 11 color histogram is calculated for this disk and all adjacent segments. Next, the distance between the disk and the adjacent segments is calculated, using the intersection distance measure [7] based on the 11 color histogram. The pixel is relabeled if the label of the nearest segment is different from the current label of the pixel. This process is repeated as long as there are pixels that are being relabeled.

The radius r of the disk determines how smooth the resulting boundaries are: a small radius will produce ragged regions, a larger radius will produce smoother boundaries but may fail in locating the boundaries accurately. In order to tackle these problems we used a two-step approach: In the first iterations, a relatively small radius of 5 is used,

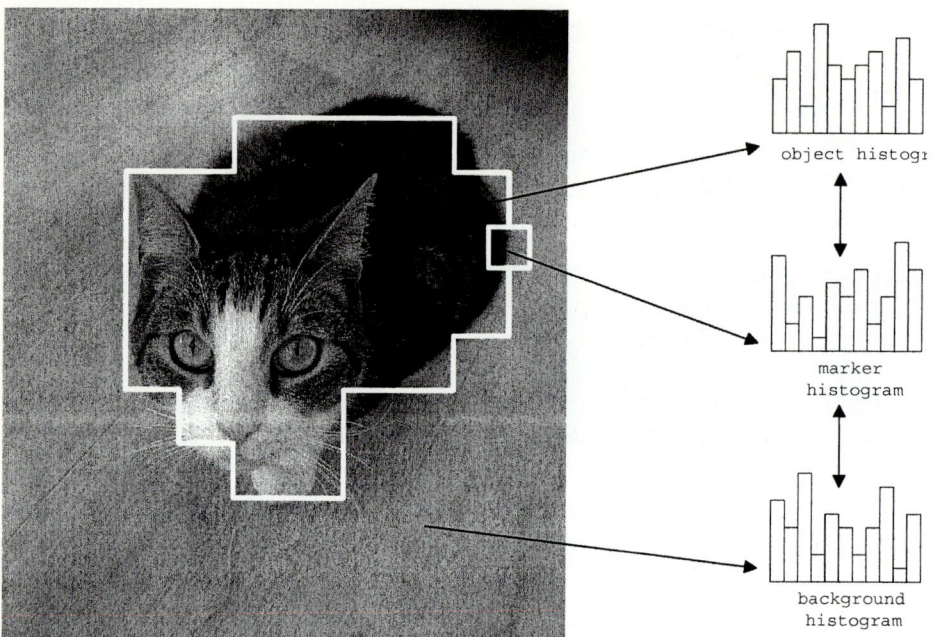

Fig. 2. The process of pixelwise classification illustrated. A pixel at the boundary is selected and a marker is placed over it. Next, the color histogram over this marker is calculated as well as the histograms of the center segment and the background. The histogram over the marker is compared to the other histograms and the pixel is assigned to the area with the most similar histogram (of the background or the object).

in order to locate the boundaries correctly. Secondly, a radius of 11 is used to produce more stable segments.

3.3 Smoothing

Although the pixelwise classification phase produces correct object boundaries, the shapes are smoothed to optimize for the shape matching phase. Smoothing is done using two fundamental operations: dilation and erosion.

Given two sets A and B in $\mathbb{Z}^2$, the dilation of A by B is defined as:

$$A \oplus B = \{x \,|\, (B)_x \cap A \neq \emptyset\}, \tag{4}$$

where $(B)_x$ denotes the translation of B by $x = (x_1, x_2)$ defined as:

$$(B)_x = \{c \,|\, c = b + x, \text{for some } b \in B\} \tag{5}$$

Thus, $A \oplus B$ expands A if the origin is contained in B, as is usually the case.

The erosion of A by B, denoted $A \ominus B$, is the set of all x such that B translated by x, is completely contained in A, defined as

$$A \ominus B = \{x \,|\, (B)_x \subseteq A\} \tag{6}$$

Thus, $A \ominus B$ decreases A.

The smoothing starts with two iterations of erosion with a square erosion marker (B) of size 3×3 pixels. Next, two iterations of dilation are applied with the same marker.

4 Shape Matching

Shape matching has been approached in various ways. A few of the frequently applied techniques are: tree pruning, the generalized Hough transform, geometric hashing, the alignment method, various statistics, deformable templates, relaxation labeling, Fourier and wavelet transforms, curvature scale space, and classifiers such as neural networks [12].

Recently, Andreou and Sgouros [12] discussed their: "turning function difference", as a part of their G Computer Vision library. It is an efficient and effective shape matching method. However, Schomaker et al. [1] introcuded a similar approach five years before. In the current research, the latter, original approach is adopted. This "outline pattern recognition", as the authors call it, is based on three feature vectors containing: (i) x and y coordinates, normalized using the center of gravity of the shape and the standard deviation of all radii, (ii) the running angle (θ) along the edge of the segment ($cos(\theta), sin(\theta)$), which contains more information on the local changes of direction, and (iii) the histogram of angles in the shape: the probability distribution $p(\theta)$ [1].

The algorithm proved to be translation, scale, and rotation invariant. Based on this algorithm, the outline-based image retrieval system Vind(X) was developed and has been used successfully since then. Vind(X) relies on outline-outline matching: the user draws an outline, which is the query. This outline is matched against the outlines of objects on images, present in its database. Subsequently, the images containing the best matching outlines are retrieved and shown to the user.

The Vind(X) system provides excellent retrieval results. However, in order to make its techniques generally applicable, automatic shape extraction techniques had to be developed. Moreover, these techniques had to be computationally cheap in order to preserve its fast retrieval, as much as possible. The latter was already achieved by the techniques as described in the previous sections. In combination with the matching algorithm of Vind(X), unsupervised OBIR was applied.

5 Method

In Sections 2 and 3, color, texture, and shape features are defined. They are combined and used in four distinct query schemes for object matching, using four vectors:

1. color and texture, for object versus complete images
2. color and texture
3. shape
4. color, texture, and shape combined

Feature-based and shape-based image retrieval was employed by two separate retrieval engines, connected to the same database, both using the intersection distance

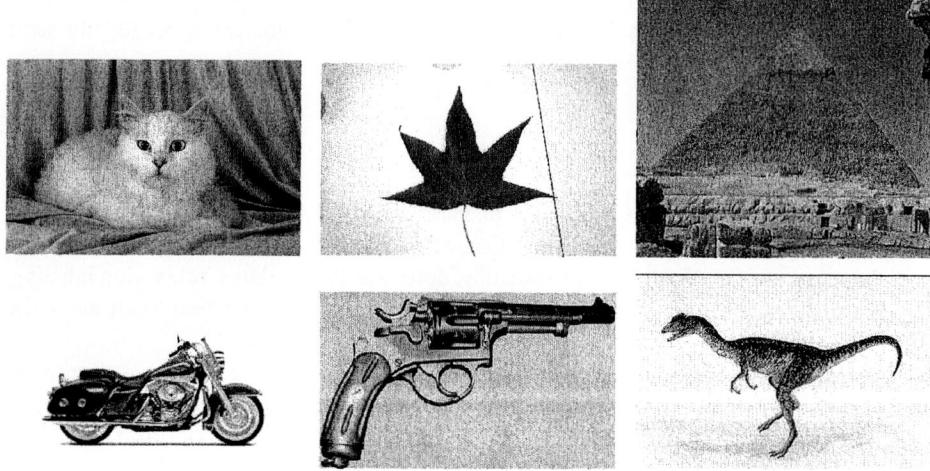

Fig. 3. Sample images from the database used

measure for ranking their results. For both engines, the number of retrieved images (n) could be chosen by the user. All query schemes performed an object - object comparison, except scheme 1 for which object features are matched with the features of the complete images in the database. For query scheme 4, for each image its ranks on both engines are summed and divided by two.

In total, the database used, consists of 1000 images gathered from the Corel image database, a reference database for CBIR applications, and from the collection of Fei-Fei [13]. Since we are interested in objects, the six categories chosen represent objects: cats, leaves, revolvers, motorbikes, pyramids, and dinosaurs.

Adopted from the field of Information Retrieval, the performance of CBIR systems can be determined by the measures recall and precision. Recall signifies the proportion of relevant images retrieved from the database in response to the query. Precision is the proportion of retrieved images that is relevant to the query.

6 Retrieval Results

Recall and precision are calculated for each of the four different query schemes, as defined in Section 5, using a variable number of images retrieved. The precision of the retrieval results for the four schemes are plotted in Figure 4(a), for 5–25 images retrieved. The recall of the retrieval results for the four schemes are plotted in Figure 4(b), for the complete dataset.

All four schemes performed well, as shown in Figure 4(a) and 4(b). However, note that with the combined approach, four of the top five images are relevant; i.e., an average precision of 80% was achieved. Moreover, the recall achieved with the combined approach converges much faster to 100% than with the other approaches.

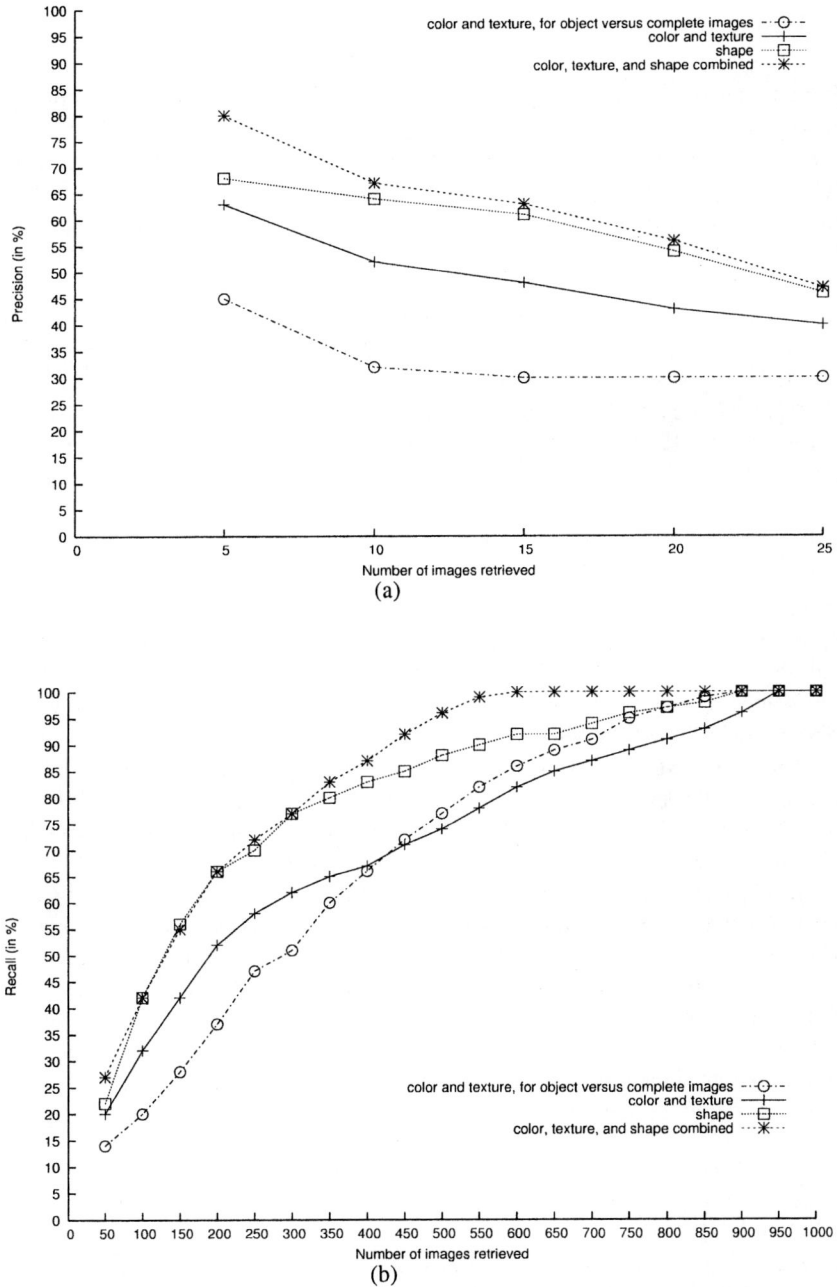

Fig. 4. Average precision (a) and recall (b) of retrieval, with global and local color&texture features, outline of extracted objects from images, and their combination.

7 Discussion

The rationale of the CBIR approach presented in this paper is that it be human centered. This is founded on two principles: (i) CBIR should be object-based and (ii) it should utilize the 11 color categories, as used by humans in color processing [7]. Both principles contribute to efficient CBIR, providing intuitive results for users. It was shown that the 11 color categories work well for describing color distributions, for the extraction of texture descriptors [10], and for object segmentation, as illustrated by the recall and precision of the retrieval results.

The success of matching the 2D shapes of segmented objects with each other is striking. This can, at least partly, be explained by the fact that "photographers generate a limited number of 'canonical views' on objects, according to perceptual and artistic rules" [1]. Moreover, even in the most recent research still (computationally expensive) gray-scale techniques are applied [14]. In contrast, we are able to extract shapes from color images. This is very important, since most of the image material available on the www and in databases is color.

In contrast with the reality on the www, the images in our database all contain images of objects against a rather uniform background, as illustrated in Figure 3. With our database, a first step is made toward processing real world images, where in comparable, recent work [15], object images are used that lack a background.

Despite the success of the current approach on real world images, it also has some drawbacks. First, it should be noted that the number of categories and its members were limited and follow-up research should be conducted with a larger database, incorporating a large number of categories. Second, in further developing the engine, the segmentation parameter should be set dynamically; i.e., setting the parameter to a minimum value and resetting it dynamically during the merging phase, based on the texture differences between the remaining blocks. This would obviate the current dependency on a good pre-defined parameter setting. Third, the ultimate goal would be to identify all objects in an image, instead of one, as is currently the case. Fourth, we expect that the use of artificial classifiers can improve the results, compared to the distance measures, used in the current research. When these drawbacks have been overcome, the resulting CBIR engine can be applied to real-world images instead of only to object-classes.

In this paper, a highly efficient scheme for the extraction of color, texture, and shape features is introduced. Combined with the intersection distance measure, it forms the basis of a unique, excellently performing, fast object-based CBIR (OBIR) engine, which provides results intuitive for its users.

Acknowledgments

Lambert R.B. Schomaker, Louis G. Vuurpijl, and Edward L. de Leau are honored, for their work on the initial version of the Vind(X) system. Without their effort, the NWO ToKeN project Eidetic (project-number: 634.000.001), which funded this research, would not have been undertaken. In addition, the authors are grateful to the anonymous reviewers and to Eduard Hoenkamp for their valuable comments.

References

1. Schomaker, L., Vuurpijl, L., Leau, E. de: New use for the pen: outline-based image queries. In: Proceedings of the 5th IEEE International Conference on Document Analysis, Piscataway (NJ), USA (1999) 293–296
2. Forsyth, D.A., Ponse, J.: Computer Vision: A modern approach. Pearson Education, Inc., Upper Saddle River, New Jerssey, U.S.A. (2002)
3. Berlin, B., Kay, P.: Basic color terms: Their universals and evolution. Berkeley: University of California Press (1969)
4. Derefeldt, G., Swartling, T., Berggrund, U., Bodrogi, P.: Cognitive color. Color Research & Application **29** (2004) 7–19
5. Hafner, J.L., Sawhney, H.S., Equitz, W., Flickner, M., Niblack, W.: Efficient color histogram indexing for quadratic form distance functions. IEEE Transactions on Pattern Analysis and Machine Intelligence **17** (1995) 729–736
6. Smeulders, A.W.M., Worring, M., Santini, S., Gupta, A., Jain, R.: Content-based image retrieval at the end of the early years. IEEE Transactions on Pattern Analysis and Machine Intelligence **22** (2000) 1349–1380
7. Broek, E.L. van den, Kisters, P.M.F., Vuurpijl, L.G.: Content-based image retrieval benchmarking: Utilizing color categories and color distributions. Journal of Imaging Science and Technology **49** (2005) [in press]
8. Fujii, K., Sugi, S., Ando, Y.: Textural properties corresponding to visual perception based on the correlation mechanism in the visual system. Psychological Research **67** (2003) 197–208
9. Huang, J., Kumar, S.R., Mitra, M., Zhu, W.J., Zabih, R.: Image indexing using color correlograms. In Medioni, G., Nevatia, R., Huttenlocher, D., Ponce, J., eds.: Proceedings of the IEEE Conference on Computer Vision and Pattern Recognition. (1997) 762–768
10. Broek, E.L. van den, Rikxoort, E.M. van: Parallel-sequential texture analysis. In Singh, S., Perner, P., Apte, C., eds.: Proceedings of the 3rd International Conference on Advances in Pattern Recognition (ICAPR2005). (2005) [conditionally accepted]
11. Ojala, T., Pietikäinen, M.: Unsupervised texture segmentation using feature distribution. Pattern Recognition **32** (1999) 477–486
12. Andreou, I., Sgouros, N.M.: Computing, explaining and visualizing shape similarity in content-based image retrieval. Information Processing & Management **41** (2005) 1121–1139
13. Fei-Fei, L., Fergus, R., Perona, P.: Learning generative visual models from few training examples: An incremental bayesian approach tested on 101 object categories. In Pece, A.E.C., ed.: Proceedings of the 2004 Conference on Computer Vision and Pattern Recognition Workshop, Washington, D.C., USA (2004)
14. Shih, M.Y., Tseng, D.C.: A wavelet-based multiresolution edge detection and tracking. Image and Vision Computing **23** (2005) 441–451
15. Gevers, T., Stokman, H.M.G.: Robust histogram construction from color invariants for object recognition. IEEE Transactions on Pattern Analysis and Machine Intelligence **26** (2004) 113–118

Multi-scale Midline Extraction Using Creaseness

Kai Rothaus and Xiaoyi Jiang

Department of Computer Science, University of Münster,
Einsteinstrasse 62, D-48149 Münster, Germany
{rothaus,xjiang}@math.uni-muenster.de

Abstract. Applying the divergence operator on the gradient vector field is known as a robust method for computing the local creaseness, defined as the level set extrinsic curvature. Based on this measure, we present a multi-scale method to extract continuous midlines of elongated objects of various widths simultaneously. The scale-space is not built on the input image, but on the gradient vector field. During the iterative construction of the scale-space the current solution keeps thin objects even when they are located near more dominant structures. The representation of the midlines is realised as curves in the image plane, consisting of equidistant sample points. At each sample point the tangential direction of the curve is computed directly with the smoothed gradient vector field.

1 Introduction

In this paper we address the problem of extracting a continuous midline of elongated objects of various widths. There are various applications of midline extraction in the field of image analysis, for instance vessel detection (see Figure 1), analysis of heart fibres (see Section 3), description of characters, plant root detection [1], analysis of aerial images [8] and finger print analysis. The constraint on the objects of interest is a relatively homogeneous color and an elongated shape. In all these applications, the midlines give us a natural representation of the underlying structures.

Our method is based on a scale-space analysis. Such a multi-scale approach offers the advantage to process images or other objects with various parameter adjustments simultaneously. This leads to different results, which have to be finally combined to a single solution. Therefore, the most challenging task of multi-scale approaches is a consistent combination scheme. Compared to other approaches, the proposed operator minimises the effect of erasing the inferior structure at crossings, bifurcations and neighbouring objects. Furthermore, we directly provide the tangential direction of the midline at the sample points.

In the literature, several definitions of valley and ridge-lines can be found. The theoretical framework of our method is based on differential geometry [3]. Considering the graph G of an d dimensional grey-scale image function $L(\xi)$ (with $\xi = (\xi_1, \ldots \xi_d)$) as a hyper-surface (in an $(d+1)$-dimensional space), one can define ridge and valley points using local characteristics of this hyper-surface. More precisely, we analyse the image gradient ∇L on the boundary of a small

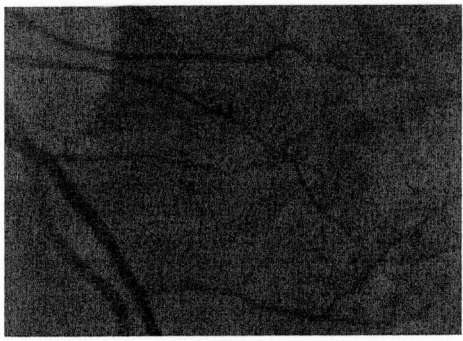

Fig. 1. Retinal angiography

neighbourhood in G surrounding the point $(\xi, L(\xi))$. This can be done by choosing the eigenvectors of the Hessian matrix of L as the local coordinate system. Maintz et. al. [6] formulate a class of ridge measure based on the isophote curvature, which are the curves on G featuring the same level of grey-scale. Since these measures show a poor performance at saddle zones in discrete domains [5], López et. al. have developed a different discretisation, namely $\kappa = -\text{div}\,(\nabla L/\|\nabla L\|)$. Their measure is the fundament of our method, extended by a scheme to combine single solutions.

We have found other works on multi-scale operators for midline extraction [2], [4], [8]. The commonness of these approaches is the design of the scale-spaces, which is built directly on the input image L. Typically, these approaches result in fragmentary midlines, due to the fact that we have a loss of spatial precision, when smoothing in the image space. In contrast, we are smoothing the gradient tensor field $\nabla L \cdot \nabla L^t$ component-wise using different Gaussians convolution kernels. This offers the advantage of a more robust localization of the midlines due to the fact that even for thin objects, the gradients at the borders are present in large scales. In the case of applying large Gaussian masks directly on L, thin objects are razed. Furthermore, combining midlines of different image scales could lead to points of discontinuity, when there is an erratic change in the width of the object.

2 Scale-Space Approach

Our approach can be divided into the subtasks: computation of the structural tensor (Section 2.1), iterative construction of the scale-space (Section 2.2), application of the divergence operator on the combined vector field (Section 2.3) and finally the extraction of the midlines (Section 2.4). At the end of this section we discuss the choice of the parameters (Section 2.5). Since we use second order derivation to compute κ, we need an idealised gradient vector field. The cross-profile of the elongated structures, which we want to analyse, are frequently bar-like. Since the gradients of such an object could be very small or even vanish near the midline, we wish to propagate the meaningful gradients at the edges towards the midline. Smoothing the image has known side-effects, which we want to avoid.

The main idea is to construct the scale-space not on the image, but on the image gradient $\nabla L(x,y)$. We present a method for smoothing the vector field such that the meaningful gradients at the edges are propagated towards the midlines. The computation of the image gradient in a specific scale is realised by an analysis of a component-wise smoothed structured tensor, which is computed as $\nabla L \cdot \nabla L^t$. For each image location we compute the local structure tensor and convolve the components of this matrices along the image plane. During the iteration we keep up the vector field, which contains the currently best gradient vectors.

2.1 Structural Tensor

Initially, we compute the image gradient vector field at the pixel grid with the Sobel operator. The used Gaussian mask should be chosen relatively small, since edges introduced by noise are automatically erased in the further process. The edge magnitude is normalised into the interval $[0,1]$. To compensate local differences in contrast we boost the edge magnitude s by the function $b_{t_{\mathrm{infl}}}(s) = 1 - \exp\left(-\frac{s^2}{2 \cdot t_{\mathrm{infl}}^2}\right)$. Let t_{conf} denotes the value of $b_{t_{\mathrm{infl}}}$ at its inflection point t_{infl}, which is an external parameter. Gradients holding a magnitude of greater than t_{conf} are considered as confident and will be treated more carefully.

Following the approach of López et. al. [5] we apply the component-wise smoothing of the structured tensor and compute the gradient at each image position as the eigenvector to the greatest eigenvector of the smoothed structured tensor field. The motivation of this approach is, that the structured tensor is a symmetrical matrix of the form:

$$ST(x,y) = \begin{pmatrix} L_x(x,y)^2 & L_x(x,y) \cdot L_y(x,y) \\ L_x(x,y) \cdot L_y(x,y) & L_y(x,y)^2 \end{pmatrix},$$

with the eigenvector ∇L to the eigenvalue

$$\lambda = s^2 = L_x^2 + L_y^2. \tag{1}$$

We utilise this property to compute the gradient magnitudes of the different scales.

2.2 Forming the Scale-Space

After computing $ST(x,y)$ for each grid position we construct the scale-space on this structural tensor. For each scale we compute the gradient vector field, which consists of the eigenvector $g_k(x,y)$ to the greatest eigenvector $\lambda_k(x,y)$ of the component-wise smoothed version of $ST(x,y)$. Depending on λ_k we compute the new gradient magnitude. Since the sign of $g_k(x,y)$ is not clear, we have to reconstruct it by some additional considerations.

During the iterative construction of the scale-space we keep $v_{\text{opt}}(x, y)$, the optimal gradient vector field computed so far, with $s_{\text{opt}} := \|v_{\text{opt}}\|$ denoting its magnitude. The scale-space is built by component-wise convolution of the structural tensor repeatedly with the same Gaussian mask G_σ with standard deviation σ. Due to the fact, that the family of Gaussian distributions build a half-group under the convolution operator $\star$, the standard deviation during the k-th iteration is $\sigma_k = \sigma\sqrt{k}$, i.e. $(G_\sigma)^{\star k} = G_{\sigma_k}$.

In the following we explain one iteration step k at a fix grid point (x_0, y_0). Smoothing the structural tensor $ST(x, y)$ results in a matrix of the form

$$\begin{pmatrix} m_{xx} & m_{xy} \\ m_{xy} & m_{yy} \end{pmatrix} := \left((G_\sigma)^{\star k} \star \begin{pmatrix} L_x^2 & L_x L_y \\ L_x L_y & L_y^2 \end{pmatrix} \right)(x_0, y_0)$$

with greatest eigenvalue $\lambda_k = 0.5 \cdot (s_k^2 + p_k)$, where $s_k^2 = m_{xx} + m_{yy}$ is equal to the square of smoothed vector magnitudes and $p_k = \sqrt{(m_{xx} - m_{yy})^2 + 4\, m_{xy}^2}$ can be viewed as a measure of parallelism. If the considered neighbourhood surround (x_0, y_0) consists of parallel gradients, p_k takes the maximum value s_k^2. On the other hand $p_k = 0$ at locations where two orthogonal gradient directions occur (equally weighted). As mentioned above, the gradient vector v_k is computed as the eigenvector to the eigenvalue λ_k. The new magnitude is determined by taking two numbers into account, namely λ_k and the quotient $\frac{p_k}{s_k^2} \in [0, 1]$. Taking the eigenvalue as magnitude is a consistent extension of the property (1). On the other hand the term $\frac{p_k}{s_k^2}$ is a measure of parallelism and furthermore independent of the edge magnitudes in the neighbourhood. We choose the geometrical mean of these values as the new squared edge magnitude

$$s_{\text{new}}^2 = \sqrt{0.5 \cdot (s_k^2 + p_k) \cdot \frac{p_k}{s_k^2}}. \quad (2)$$

In image regions with no preferred gradient orientations the magnitude are pruned by this combination, due to the fact that p_k is low. On the other hand the gradients are boosted in image regions with a clear major orientation even when there is a low base level of gradient magnitudes.

If $s_{\text{new}} > s_{\text{opt}}$ we further process in updating the actual vector v_{opt}, otherwise we leave v_{opt} unchanged. An open problem not discussed yet is the unknown sign of the eigenvector v_k. López et. al. [5] propose an alignment into the half-space to which the original gradient points. This could lead to opposed islands of gradients at regions with relative homogeneous grey values. Another side effect is a possible erasement of the gradients introduced by small objects lying in the neighbourhood of dominant structures. Due to this unwanted behaviour we make a consensus decision based on the image gradient g_k introduced by the smoothed version of the original image $G_{\sigma\sqrt{k}} \star L$ and the actual vector v_{opt}. With respect to the iterative smoothing process and equation (2) we compute two thresholds (in case of $k > 1$):

$$t_{\text{low}} := \sigma_k^{-1} \cdot \sqrt{0.5 \cdot t_{\text{conf}}} \quad \text{and} \quad t_{\text{high}} := \sqrt{0.5 \cdot t_{\text{conf}}}$$

Let cos_{grad} denote the cosine of the angle between v_k and g_k, cos_k denote the cosine of the angle between v_k and v_{opt}. The decision rule for the sign of v_k is based on

$$sgn := \begin{cases} cos_{\text{grad}} & \text{if } \lambda_k < t_{\text{low}} \text{ or } s_{\text{opt}} < t_{\text{low}} \text{ or } k = 1 \\ cos_k & \text{if } \lambda_k \geq t_{\text{high}} \text{ and } s_{\text{opt}} \geq t_{\text{low}} \\ (\lambda_k - t_{\text{low}}) \cdot cos_{\text{grad}} & \\ + (t_{\text{high}} - \lambda_k) \cdot cos_k & \text{otherwise.} \end{cases}$$

If sgn is negative the orientation of v_k is reversed by multiplying v_k with -1. This case differentiation is motivated by the consideration that we want to keep informations of consistent gradients. For small values of s_{opt} or λ_k the orientation of g_{opt} is possibly uncertain (first case), so that the decision on the sign should only depend on the smoothed gradient g_k. On the other side, when λ_k and s_{opt} are sufficiently great, we take only the orientation of the currently optimal gradient g_{opt} into account (second case). The third case is a fuzzy-like compromise between the exclusive decisions. Finally, we replace v_{opt} by v_k with the magnitude s_{new}.

2.3 Computing the Creaseness Measure κ

Since the combination of the different scales could introduce boundary effects, we apply the same smoothing procedure on the resulted gradient vector field, but only with a single iteration. The divergence operator computes κ under the constraint that the norm of each vector is 0 or 1. A normalisation of all gradient vectors, which have a positive norm, causes unwanted effects at homogeneous image regions, since the vectors at the propagation hold no confident orientation. To avoid this problem we apply the boosting function $b_{0.33}$ on the vector magnitudes instead of the normalisation.

The divergence operator is based on deviations. Since the vector field has been smoothed already, we implement deviations by the mean of finite forward difference and finite backwards difference with an increment of one pixel. The result is a scalar field, which holds the values $-\kappa(x, y)$.

An additional smoothing of the scalar field κ leads to the extraction of less erratic midlines, but could cause misbehaviour in regions with undefined gradient vectors. In that case we produce vectors, which have no direction, but a positive norm. Due to this problem the smoothing of κ should be used with care. We choose triangular convolution kernels of size three in both image dimensions. This kernel reduces the occurrence of unwanted side-effects, but achieves continuous midlines. The remaining vectors are denoted as the idealised gradient vectors.

2.4 Extraction of the Midlines

In the following we explain the extraction process for dark elongated structures. Firstly we apply a non maximum suppression (non minimum suppression for light objects). This results in a set of potential midline points, denoted as candidates.

Each candidate features an orientation, which is computed as the perpendicular to the idealised gradient vector at this location.

Afterwards we link the candidates together forming midline segments. Thereby two neighboured candidates are only linked, if several conditions are valid. Segments with less than three points are selected.

Finally, the segments are resampled by equidistant sample points, since on a diagonal oriented segment one can obtain more candidate points than on horizontal or vertical segments. The resampling of a segment seg is done by traversing it from its starting point and keeping the distance, which is covered so far. We compute the tangential direction of seg for all locations with an integral distance to the starting point. This can be done by a linear interpolation of the orthogonal vectors on the smoothed gradient direction at the nearest pixel locations on the segment.

2.5 Parameter Adjustment

The presented method can be adjusted by four numerical parameters, namely σ_{Sobel}, t_{infl}, σ_{iter} and n_{iter}. The influence of the standard deviation σ_{Sobel} of the Gaussian mask for the construction of the gradient vector field has been discussed in various works. The parameter t_{infl} offers the possibility to control the inflection point of the boosting function $b(s)$. A low value results in the consideration of low contrast edges of the input image. The choice of the standard deviation σ_{iter} defines the smallest structures which are preserved during the iteration. Since the Gaussian of the iteration k has a standard deviation $\sigma_{iter}\sqrt{k}$, the decreasing of σ_{iter} causes more iterations to achieve the same blurring effect. Obviously, this correlation behaves quadratically. The parameter n_{iter} defines the maximal width of the elongated objects, for which the midlines are correctly computed. The increase of n_{iter} has primarily effects on regions with an actual

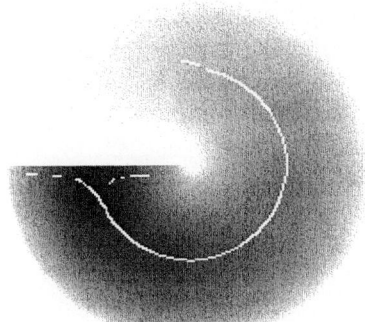
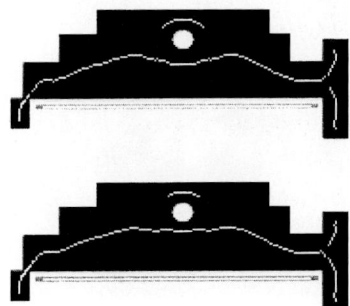

Fig. 2. Result on helix function of Maintz et. al. [6] ($\sigma_{Sobel} = 0.0$, $t_{infl} = 0.05$, $\sigma_{iter} = 1.5$, $n_{iter} = 100$)

Fig. 3. Top row: Result on primitive objects ($\sigma_{Sobel} = 1.0$, $t_{infl} = 0.1$, $\sigma_{iter} = 1.5$, $n_{iter} = 50$); Bottom row: $n_{iter} = 100$

low response, but there could occur unwanted side-effects. It is not possible to avoid these side-effects generally, due to semantical ambiguity. For example, the dominant structure of a horizontal line, which is an arrangement of vertical dark bars, depends on the context. This gap cannot be closed by a multi-scale approach. Experiments have shown, that $\sigma_{\text{Sobel}} = 1.5$, $t_{\text{infl}} = 0.2$, $\sigma_{\text{iter}} = 1.5$ and $n_{\text{iter}} = 5$ are suitable default values. The manual adjustment of these parameter is easy and mainly depends on the particular application (for instance the range of object widths and the quality of the image). In addition to these numerical parameters we offer the possibility to exclude the additional smoothing before and after the application of the divergence operator, due to the discussed problems.

3 Results

We have tested our method on artifical data and on real applications. In the following we discuss the results on some problematic situations. The figures show the extracted midlines overlayed on the original image. A vertical direction is coloured with red and a horizontal with turquoise.

Maintz et.al. [6] present the function $f(r,\varphi) = \alpha r (1 - r) \phi$ as an example, where their ridge seeking approach fails. Figure 2 depicts that our approach does a fine job for this smooth function. We choose the parameter settings $\sigma_{\text{Sobel}} = 0.0$, $t_{\text{infl}} = 0.05$, $\sigma_{\text{iter}} = 1.5$ and $n_{\text{iter}} = 100$ to achieve this result. Decreasing the number of iterations results in a less complete extraction at the lighter regions. The extreme poor contrast in this regions leads to some gaps of 1 pixel in the extracted midlines, which could be closed easily by an additional post-processing step. The misbehaviour at the darkest regions is caused by the dominant horizontal edge. This effect cannot be avoided, since this edge holds

 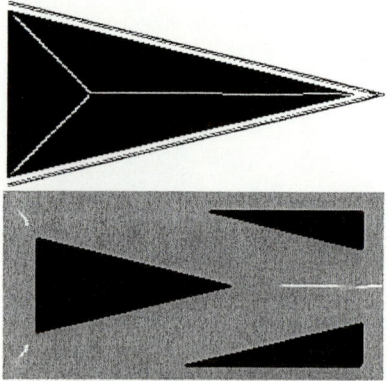

Fig. 4. Result on test function of López et. al. [5] ($\sigma_{\text{Sobel}} = 1.0$, $t_{\text{infl}} = 0.2$, $\sigma_{\text{iter}} = 1.5$ and $n_{\text{iter}} = 5$)

Fig. 5. Top row: Result on triangle ($\sigma_{\text{Sobel}} = 1.5$, $t_{\text{infl}} = 0.2$, $\sigma_{\text{iter}} = 1.5$, $n_{\text{iter}} = 50$); Bottom row: CLSEC approach [5] on triangle

the clearest contrast. Our method yields an exact placements of the midline at the pixels with distance 1/2 to the center.

In contrast to the smooth function $f(r,\varphi)$, the second example image holds a collection of very simple objects. This arrangement aims to test our method in situations where the width and the orientation of the dark objects changes rapidly. The result, which is presented in Figure 3, shows a continuous midline as far as the object branches at the right ending. The produced gaps are fairly small and should be closeable by a post-processing step. The small white circle at the top of the object pushes the midline downwards. Increasing the number of iterations reduce this effect (bottom image $n_{\text{iter}=100}$), so that the midlines course in the middle of the dominant dark object. In fact it is hard to define where the correct midline should course in such situations. It is remarkable that the thin, light grey line under the dominant structure is recognised correctly.

The third example image is presented by López et. al. [5] as an example that the divergence operator causes the extraction of continuous midlines. Due to the fact, that our method also utilises the divergence operator as a creaseness measure, the result (see Figure 4) is comparable with the performance reached by López et. al. with their method (denoted by CLSEC), which is not a multiscale approach.

Figure 5 depicts the advantage of our scale-space approach in contrast to CLSEC [5]. While our operator completely extracts the midlines of the triangle and of the small lines, CLSEC is not adjustable to extract both structures.

Additional to this visual inspections, we have tested the robustness of our method with respect to the computed tangential direction. We have produced a gradient vector field of an idealised torus with inner radius of 160 pixels and outer radius of 220 pixels. The ground truth is given, since we know the correct locations and local directions of the midline. The local displacement is of subpixel level and the maximal recognised deviation of the tangential direction is about 0.001°.

We have applied our method on two types of real images. Figure 6 depicts the result on a retinal angiography for the purpose of vessel extraction. In Figure 8 the extraction of myocyte strings in a slices (see Figure 7) of heart fibres is

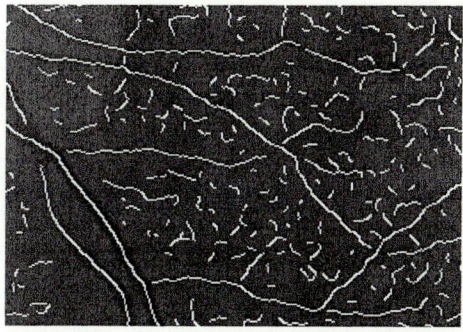

Fig. 6. Result on a retinal angiography for vessel extraction

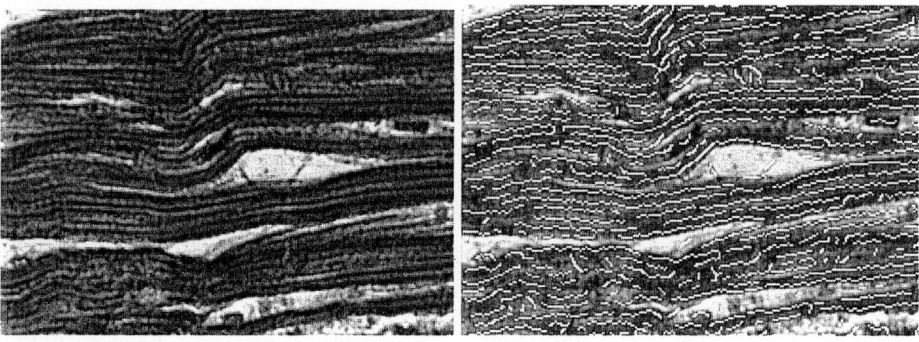

Fig. 7. Slice of heart fibres

Fig. 8. Result on a slice showing heart fibre

shown. The task of this application is the analysis of the myocyte orientation and the architecture of the heart [7]. Medical experts have reviewed the quality of the extraction results as positive and consistent. Furthermore, we analyse the distribution of the myocyte orientations utilising a statistical model. The result is the major orientation of the myocytes and its variance [7].

4 Discussion

In this paper we have proposed a method for midline extraction of elongated objects. All earlier multi-scale approaches to extracting ridges and valleys smooth the input image directly. To our knowledge the current work is the first one based on smoothing the gradient vector field. The advantage of this approach are the extraction of continuous midlines and the preservation of thin structures. Additionally we compute the tangential direction of the midlines in a unified framework together with the localisation of the midlines. Our test results on both artifical and real data have demonstrated the robustness and broad applicability of our method.

References

1. Erz G. and Posch S. A region based seed detection for root detection in minirhizotron images. In *DAGM-Symposium*, pages 482–489, 2003.
2. J.M. Gauch and S.M. Pizer. Multiresolution analysis of ridges and valleys in greyscale images. *IEEE Trans. on PAMI*, 15(6):636–646, June 1993.
3. S. Kalitzin, J. Staal, B.M. ter Haar Romeny, and M.A. Viergever. A computational method for segmenting topological point-sets and application to image analysis. *IEEE Trans. on PAMI*, 23(5):447–459, May 2001.
4. T.M. Koller, G. Gerig, G. Szekely, and D. Dettwiler. Multiscale detection of curvilinear structures in 2-d and 3-d image data. In *Proc. of the 5th ICCV*, pages 864–869, June 1995.

5. A.M. López, F. Lumbreras, and J. Serrat. Creaseness from level set extrinsic curvature. In H. Burkhardt and B. Neumann, editors, *Proc. of the 5th ECCV*, pages 156–169, 1998.
6. J.B.A Maintz, P.A. van den Elsen, and M.A. Viergever. Evaluation of ridge seeking operators for multimodality medical image matching. *IEEE Trans. on PAMI*, 18(4):353–365, April 1996.
7. Lunkenheimer P.P., Redmann K., Kling N., Rothaus K., Jiang X., Cryer C.W., Wübbeling F., Niederer P., Ho S.Y., and Anderson R.H. The three-dimensional architecture of the left ventricular myocardium. *submitted for publication*, 2005.
8. C. Steger. An unbiased detector of curvilinear structures. *IEEE Trans. on PAMI*, 20(2):113–125, February 1998.

Automatic Indexing of News Videos Through Text Classification Techniques

G. Percannella, D. Sorrentino, and M. Vento

Dipartimento di Ingegneria dell'Informazione e Ingegneria Elettrica,
Università di Salerno Via Ponte don Melillo,
1 – Fisciano (SA), I-84084 – Italy
{pergen, dsorrentino, mvento}@unisa.it

Abstract. In this paper we discuss about the applicability of text classification techniques for automatic content recognition of the scenes from news videos. In particular, the news scenes are classified according to a predefined set of six categories (National Politics, National News, World, Finance, Society & Culture and Sports) by applying text classification techniques on the transcription of the anchorman speech. The transcription is obtained using a commercial tool for speech to text. The application of text classification techniques for the automatic indexing of news videos is not new in the scientific literature, but, to the best of our knowledge, no paper reports a detailed experimentation. In our experimentations we considered different issues concerning the application of text categorization and speech recognition for news story classification: in fact, we calculated the overall performance obtained by using text categorization on the ideal transcription, as it could be obtained by employing a perfect speech recognition engine, and the transcription provided by a commercial speech recognition tool; furthermore, in our experimentation we were also interested to characterize the performance in terms of the portion of the news story by which the transcription is obtained. The experimentations have been carried out on a database of Italian news videos. This experimental validation represents the main contribution of this paper.

1 Introduction

Among all the different sources of video material nowadays available, news videos received great attention by the scientific community. This is mainly due to the fact that broadcasters are interested in building large digital databases of their resources, so to allow reuse, after a suitable indexing procedure, of the archived material for other TV programs.

In the recent past, research efforts have been concentrated mostly on the problem of the news video segmentation in stories by using video information [1], [2] or by combining audio and video information [3]. An important step towards an effective indexing of the news videos is the classification of the detected news stories within a certain set of categories (national politics, national news, world news, sports, weather, advertising, etc…).

In the scientific literature, only few authors have faced the problem of the classification of the news stories [4], [5]. In particular in [4], the authors propose to employ a two-level multi-modal framework that firstly classifies shots according to a wide set of categories (intro, single anchor, two anchors, advertising, weather, sport, ... shot); then, the detection and classification of the stories is obtained through an HMM approach according to a very simple and fixed taxonomy (generic news, sport, ...). In [5], the authors propose to employ a multi-level probabilistic framework based on the Hidden Markov Models and the Bayesian Networks paradigms for the news stories segmentation and the classification, respectively. The classification is performed applying a Text Classification technique [6] on the ideal transcription of the audio track. The classification of the text is done through a two levels Bayesian Network, where the nodes of the first level are related to the outputs of a set of sensors that process the transcription of the audio track. These sensors extract semantic information on the news story on the basis of the presence of some specific keywords.

Text Classification is a quite mature research topic; today, Text Classification techniques are widely used for automating several processes in the field of Information Retrieval, web filtering, textual document indexing. Even if the application of the text classification to the video indexing is not new, at the moment there is no paper reporting a detailed experimental validation of this idea.

The use of text classification techniques for the automatic indexing of news videos is very promising. For this reason in this paper we investigate about the effectiveness of text classification applied on the transcription of the audio track for news stories topic recognition. For our experimentations we built-up a news video database consisting of about eight hours with 143 news stories from the main Italian public network (namely, RAI 1) and the main Italian private network (namely, CANALE 5). In our experimentations we considered different issues concerning the application of text categorization and speech recognition for news story classification: in fact, we calculated the overall performance obtained by using text categorization on the ideal transcription, as it could be obtained by employing a perfect speech recognition engine, and the transcription provided by a commercial speech recognition tool; furthermore, in our experimentation we were also interested to characterize the performance in terms of the portion of the news story by which the transcription is obtained. This experimental validation represents the main contribution of this paper.

The organization of the paper is the following: in section 2, it is described the method for news story classification based on the use of text classification and speech recognition. In section 3, the database used is reported together with the tests carried out in order to assess the performance of the method. Finally, in section 4, some conclusions are drawn.

2 The Method for News Story Classification

Most news videos are constituted by three parts, as depicted in Figure 1: the *opening titles*, a sequence of N *news stories* and, finally, the *Closing titles*. Each news story is composed by two parts: a first shot with the anchorman that introduces the news, followed by the news report, i.e. a sequence of i shots ($i \geq 0$) where the news is commented in details by a reporter. In order to classify the news stories, firstly, it is necessary to segment the video in news stories [1], [2], [3], [4], [5]. Then, the classification of the news stories can be performed by a text categorization algorithm applied on the transcription of the speech. The latter can be obtained using a "speech to text" tool.

Fig. 1. The typical structure of a news video: the *opening titles*, a sequence of N *news stories* and the *closing titles*.

The system architecture of the news story classification method proposed and tested in this paper is constituted by two modules: the *speech to text* and the *text classification* modules, as depicted in Figure 2.

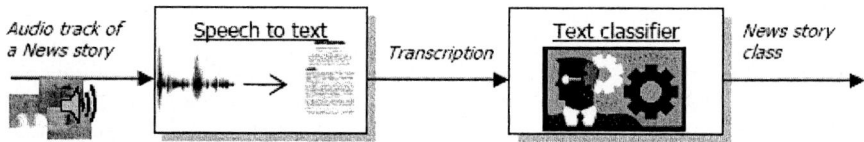

Fig. 2. System architecture of the news story classification method tested in this paper

The problem of text classification is a widely debated issue in the scientific literature. Text categorization can be formulated as the problem of assigning a text document d_j to a class $c_i \in \{c_1, c_2, \ldots, c_n\}$ by using some features extracted from d_j. There are different methods for features extraction from textual documents. The typical solution, adopted also in this paper, finds the most discriminant features on the basis of a statistical approach: to each term t_k is assigned a weight w_k related to the occurrences of the term t_k in the document. One of the most commonly used methods for calculating w_k consists in computing the function *tfidf* (Term Frequency-Inverse Document Frequency) [7], defined as:

$$tfidf(t_k, d_j) = \#(t_k, d_j) \cdot \log \frac{|Tr|}{\#Tr(t_k)} \quad (1)$$

where $\#(t_k, d_j)$ represents the occurrences of t_k within d_j, $\#Tr(t_k)$ is the *document frequency* of the term t_k, i.e. the number of documents of the training set Tr where the term t_k occurs.

Since the length can vary significantly among different documents, the weight associated to the term t_k is usually calculated by normalizing the *tfidf*:

$$w_{kj} = \frac{tfidf(t_k, d_j)}{\sqrt{\sum_{s=1}^{|T|} tfidf(t_k, d_j)^2}} \qquad (2)$$

Generally, some preprocessing is carried out before features extraction, as the removal of the tags (for instance the HTML tags) and of the *stop words* (i.e. pronouns, prepositions, ...), the *stemming* operation that allows to reduce the dimension of the representation space of the document by grouping under the same term the words sharing the same morphological radix (for instance the words walk, walker, walked, walking, ...).

Finally, in the scientific literature several classification techniques have been proposed for text classification as bayesian classifiers, support vector machines, Rocchio algorithm, classifiers based on tree representation. For our experimentations we implemented the Naïve Bayes classifier that is used by most probabilistic methods of text classification [8], [9], [10], [11]. In fact, the Naïve Bayes classifier is characterized by an optimal value of the recognition rate/computational complexity ratio and can be trained very easily.

3 Experimental Results

In the recent past some efforts have been spent by other researchers in building video databases for benchmarking purposes [12, 13]. Unfortunately, these data can not be used for our experimentations since in most cases they are not publicly available [12], while in other cases they are not adequate for our aims [13]. Hence, in order to assess the performance of the proposed system we had to build a new video database. In particular, the test database used in this paper (about eight hours) is composed by eight news videos from the main Italian public network (namely, RAI 1) and eight videos from the main Italian private network (namely, CANALE 5). Then, the tests were carried out on the two TV-networks, separately. All the news videos of our dataset are presented by a single speaker; moreover, all the eight videos of RAI 1 (CANALE5) are presented by the same anchorman (anchorwoman). We built a larger dataset for training the text classification module. This dataset was realized by collecting the flash news from the ANSA website (http://www.ansa.it - ANSA is the main Italian agency for the collection, publication and distribution of journalistic information).

In order to define the ground truth, all the news of the training and of the test datasets were categorized according to the following six classes: National Politics, National News, World, Finance, Society & Culture and Sports. The composition of the dataset of the two TV-networks and of the ANSA dataset are reported in Table 1 and 2, respectively. In particular, the true class of the ANSA news were already available on the website, while the RAI1 and CANALE5 dataset were manually labeled.

The proposed system was implemented and tested by using the MALLET [14], an open source tool for text classification, and the Dragon Naturally Speaking [15], a commercial speech to text module.

Table 1. Composition of the video dataset used for testing the text classification algorithm

	NATIONAL POLITICS	NATIONAL NEWS	WORLD	FINANCE	SOCIETY and CULTURE	SPORT	TOTAL
RAI 1	9	21	14	8	9	5	**66**
CANALE5	5	29	12	12	16	3	**77**

As already stated in the introduction, in this paper we are interested to quantitatively evaluate the applicability of text classification and speech recognition techniques for automatic content recognition of the scenes from news videos. For the sake of readability the overall experimental procedure is sketched in Figure 3. In particular, in our experimentations we considered different issues concerning the application of text categorization and speech recognition for news story classification: in fact, we calculated the overall performance obtained by using text categorization on the ideal transcription, as it could be obtained by employing a perfect speech recognition engine, and the transcription provided by a commercial speech recognition tool; furthermore, in our experimentation we were also interested to characterize the performance in terms of the portion of the news story by which the transcription is obtained.

3.1 Experimentation: 1st Phase

As a first step of our experimentation we tested the text classification technique described in the previous section on the ANSA dataset. In particular, we performed a ten fold cross validation. This method was used to obtain a more realistic estimate of the performance of the method. Therefore, we divided the database in ten subsets. Then, we performed ten tests: in each one, nine subsets were used as training set and the remaining for testing (leave one out validation). Finally, the overall performance was obtained as the average performance on the ten folds. The recognition rate was 88,8%.

Table 2. Composition of the ANSA dataset used for training the text classification algorithm

	NATIONAL POLITICS	NATIONAL NEWS	WORLD	FINANCE	SOCIETY and CULTURE	SPORT	TOTAL
ANSA	196	279	439	396	486	404	**2200**

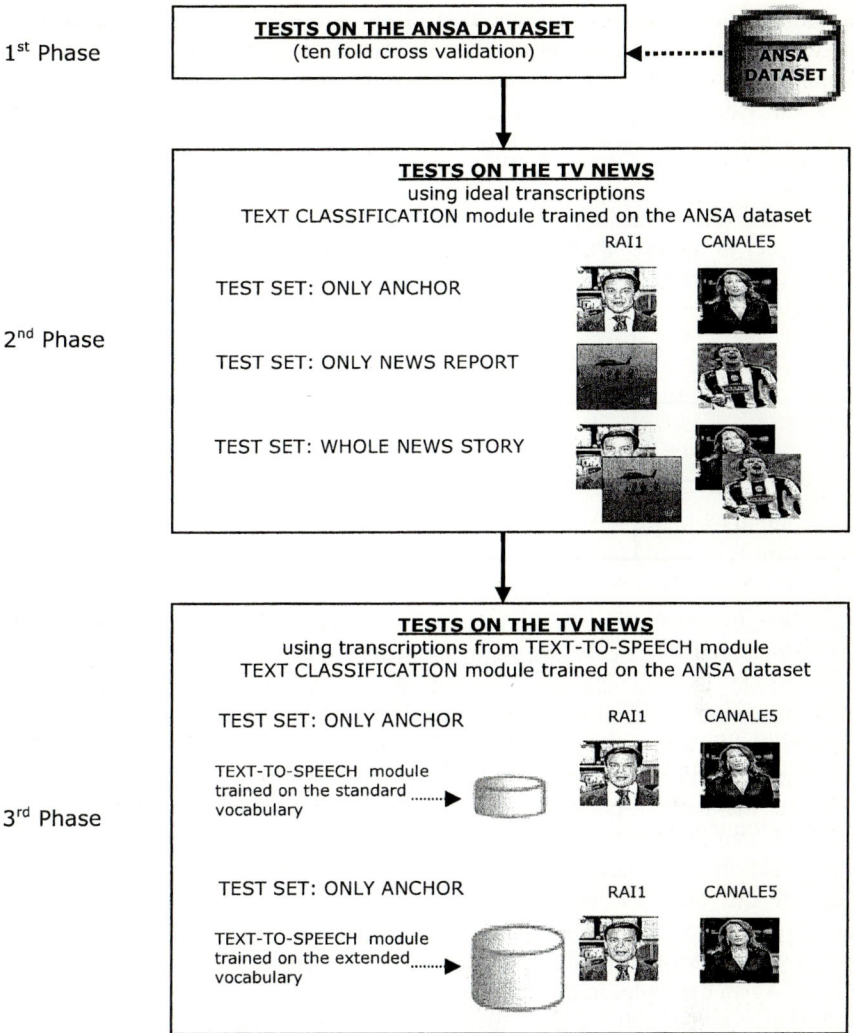

Fig. 3. Experimental procedure employed in this paper to test the system

3.2 Experimentation: 2nd Phase

The second step of our experimentation was aimed at assessing the performance of the text classification algorithm on the video news without considering the errors due to the speech recognition module. In order to carry out this test, the ideal transcriptions were manually obtained. Furthermore, in our experimentation we were also interested to characterize the performance of the text classification algorithm in terms of the used portion of the news story. In fact, as described in the previous section, a news story is typically constituted by two parts: the anchor shot and the sequence of news report shots. For this reason, for each TV network we carried out three different tests using the ideal transcription of 1) the whole news story, 2) only the anchor part of the news story, 3) only the news report part of the news story. In particular, we are interested to evaluate the contribute provided by each part of a news story. In Table 3 there are reported the performance on the three test sets; the performance is expressed in terms of the recognition rate.

Table 3. Recognition rate of the text classification algorithm applied on the ideal transcription with respect to the two TV networks. Performance accounts for the case of transcriptions extracted on the whole news story, on the anchor shot only, on the news report shot only.

	ONLY ANCHOR	ONLY NEWS REPORT	WHOLE NEWS STORY
RAI1	92,4%	92,4%	95,5%
CANALE5	74,4%	84,3%	87,0%

The results reported in Table 3 demonstrate that the transcription of the speech of part or of the whole news story can be effectively used to classify the news story according to the six classes reported above. As it could be expected, higher performance are obtained when the transcription of the whole news story is used. This is particularly evident on the news videos of CANALE5. In fact, in this case most information is in the news report portion of the news story, while on the news videos of RAI1, the news report and the anchor sections provide the same results. Our opinion is that the different performance obtained on the two datasets, when only the anchor section of the news stories is used, depends on the different style of the news video of the two TV networks. In fact, the RAI1 anchorman introduces and summarize in a certain detail the news; differently, the anchorman of CANALE5 just provides few information about the news that is analyzed in dept in the news report section. As an example, in the Table 4 we report two cases of news introduced by the CANALE5 anchorman with only few words, which give rise to erroneous classifications.

Table 4. Recognition rate of the text classification algorithm applied on the ideal

Real transcription (in italian)	Transcription translated in English	Classification results	
"Nel calcio è scoppiato il caso Adriano"	"The Adriano case has exploded within the football world"	Society and Culture *Sports* Other	50.0% 44.7% 0.3%
"Vicino a Torino si è consumata una terribile tragedia familiare"	"Close to Torino there has been a terrible family tragedy"	Sports World Society and Culture *National News*	43.7% 30.0% 15.0% 4.9%

For a more detailed analysis, in Figures 4.a and 4.b there are reported the performance of the text classification algorithm on the ideal transcriptions with respect to the six categories of news stories. The performance are expressed in terms of recall (ρ) e precision (π), which are defined as follows:

$$\rho = \frac{TP_i}{TP_i + FN_i} \qquad (3)$$

$$\pi = \frac{TP_i}{TP_i + FP_i} \qquad (4)$$

where TP = true positive, FP = false positive and FN = false negative (missed).

On the RAI1 dataset the performance is reasonably good and stable across all the categories. The lowest values resulted on the *Finance* and the *Society and Culture* classes. Contrarily, on the CANALE5 dataset the best results are obtained on the *Finance* class, while the performance on *Society and Culture* class is low again. It is very interesting to note the different behavior of the system with respect to the *Finance* class on the two datasets; this can be explained by considering that the videos of CANALE5 always present a news from the Stock Exchange with a very standardized structure. Hence, terms like Wall Street, NASDAQ, MIBtel occur very often, simplifying the correct classification. Differently, RAI1 presents news from the Stock Exchange in a specific economical news video after the main edition of the television news.

3.3 Experimentation: 3rd Phase

The final step of our experimentations consisted in the use of the text categorization algorithm on the transcription obtained using the speech recognition module. However, we observed that speech recognition can be reliably used only on the anchor portion of the news story. In fact, the audio track of the anchor portion is noiseless, the speech is fluent, but not fast and the words are pronounced sharp. On the other side, the speech of the news report part is often noisy due to environmental sounds. Moreover, it is possible to train the speech recognition module for each anchorman of a TV network: in fact, the number of anchormen is usually less than ten for all the editions of each TV network. On the contrary a specifically trained speech recognition module cannot be used on the news report audio track, due to its theoretically infinite number of speakers. This aspect contributes to further lower the performance on the news report part of the news story.

Following the above considerations, in our experimentations we considered only the transcription provided by the speech recognition engine on the anchor portion of the news story. In particular, we carried out two experiments applying the text classification algorithm on the transcription provided by the speech recognition module trained in the first case on the standard vocabulary provided with the tool, while in the second case it was used an extended vocabulary including some non-italian words, names of some important cities and persons. In Table 5, there are reported the performance obtained in the two experiments.

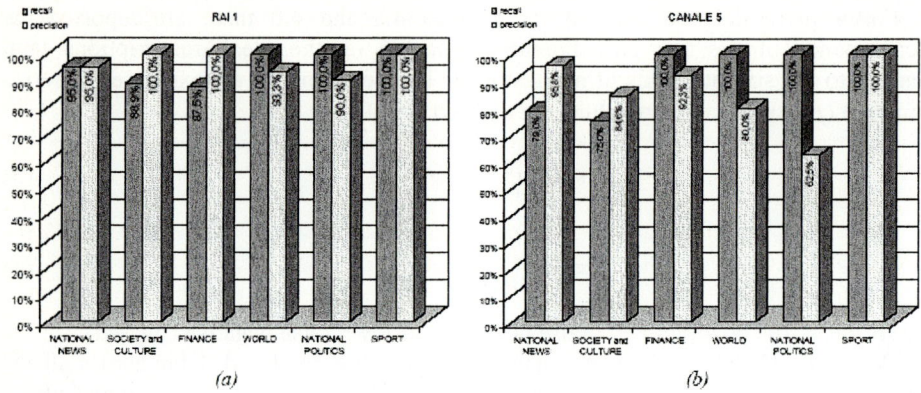

Fig. 4. Performance of the text classification algorithm on the ideal transcriptions with respect to the six news stories categories on the (*a*) RAI1 and the (*b*) CANALE5 datasets.

From the results in Table 5, it is possible to note that in both cases the use of the speech recognition module trained on the standard vocabulary produces a degradation of the recognition rate of about 6-7%. In particular, the use of an extended vocabulary allows to significantly improve the performance in case of CANALE5, while on the RAI1 dataset the use of the extended vocabulary is completely irrelevant. The different contribution given by the use of an extended vocabulary on the two datasets can be explained by considering the different style of the two TV networks. In fact, the anchor part of the CANALE5 news videos is very concise: hence, the name of important cities and persons, as those added to the extended vocabulary, are very useful to classify the news story. Differently, the RAI1 anchor part is much more detailed, so that the words added to the vocabulary do not contribute to improve performance.

Table 5. Performance of the text classification algorithm applied on the real transcriptions provided by the speech recognition module trained on the standard and on the extended vocabulary. For the sake of completeness it is reported also the performance obtained on the ideal transcription of the anchor shot only.

	STANDARD VOCABULARY (real transcriptions)	EXTENDED VOCABULARY (real transcriptions)	SHOT ANCHOR (ideal transcriptions)
RAI 1	86,0%	86,0%	92,4%
CANALE 5	66,9%	72,2%	74,0%

4 Conclusions

In this paper we faced the problem of news story classification according to a set of six categories by applying an algorithm of text classification on the transcription of the audio track. This experimental validation represents the main contribution of this paper to the state of the art. In fact, to the best of our knowledge, in the scientific literature no paper reports a detailed experimentation performed on real data. The tests have been carried out on eight hours of news videos from the main Italian public network (namely, RAI 1) and the main Italian private network (namely, CANALE 5). These preliminary experimental results demonstrates the possibility of classifying news stories using the transcription obtained by using a speech to text module to the anchor portion of the news story.

Future work will be devoted to the experimentation of the method on a much larger dataset in order to obtain a more reliable experimental validation.

References

1. M. De Santo, G. Percannella, C. Sansone, M. Vento, "Combining experts for anchorperson shot detection in news videos", Pattern Analysis and Applications, 7(4), Springer, Berlin, 2004
2. X. Gao, X. Tang, "Unsupervised Video-Shot Segmentation and Model-Free Anchorperson Detection for News Video Story Parsing", IEEE Transactions on Circuits and Systems for Video Technology, 12(9), 765-776, 2002.
3. M. De Santo, G. Percannella, C. Sansone, M. Vento, "Combining Audio-based and Video-based Shot Classification Systems for News Videos Segmentation", accepted for publication on Int. Workshop on Multiple Classifier Systems, 2005.
4. L. Chaisorn, T.S. Chua, C.H. Lee, "A Multimodal Approach to Story Segmentation for News Video", World Wide Web, 6(2), 187-208, 2003.
5. F. Colace, P. Foggia, G. Percannella, "A Probabilistic Framework for TV-News Stories Detection and Classification", accepted for publication on IEEE Proc. of International Conference on Multimedia and Expo, 2005.
6. W. Cohen, Y. Singer, "Context Sensitive Learning Methods for Text Categorization", ACM Transactions on Information Systems, 17(2), 141–173, 1999.
7. G. Salton, C. Buckley, "Term Weighting Approaches in Automatic Text Retrieval", Inform. Process. Man., 24(5), 513–523, 1988.
8. Y. Kim, S. Hahn, and B. Zhang, "Text Filtering by Boosting Naïve Bayes Classifiers", Proc. Int. ACM SIGIR Conf. on Research and Development in Information Retrieval, 168-175, 2000.
9. P. Domingos, M. Pazzani, "On the Optimality of the Simple Bayesian Classifier under Zero-One Loss", Machine Learning, 29, 103-130, 1997.
10. N. Friedman, D. Geiger, M. Goldszmidt, "Bayesian Network Classifiers", Machine Learning, 29(2-3), 131-163, 1997.
11. M. Sahami, "Learning Limited Dependence Bayesian Classifiers", Proc. of Int. Conf. on Knowledge Discovery and Data Mining, AAAI Press, 335-338, 1996.
12. http://www-nlpir.nist.gov/projects/trecvid/trecvid.data.html
13. ISO/IEC JTC1/SC29/WG11/N2467, Description of MPEG-7 Content Set.
14. MALLET, Advanced Machine Learning for Language, http://mallet.cs.umass.edu.
15. Dragon Naturally Speaking 8, ScanSoft Inc., http://www.scansoft.com.

Weighted Adaptive Neighborhood Hypergraph Partitioning for Image Segmentation

Soufiane Rital[1], Hocine Cherifi[2], and Serge Miguet[1]

[1] LIRIS CNRS, Lyon II University, Lyon, France
{Soufiane.Rital, Serge.Miguet}@liris.cnrs.fr
[2] LIRSIA, University of Bourgogne, Dijon, France
Hocine.Cherifi@u-bourgogne.fr

Abstract. The aim of this paper is to present an improvement of a previously published algorithm. The proposed approach is performed in two steps. In the first step, we generate the Weighted Adaptive Neighborhood Hypergraph (WAINH) of the given gray-scale image. In the second step, we partition the WAINH using a multilevel hypergraph partitioning technique. To evaluate the algorithm performances, experiments were carried out on medical and natural images. The results show that the proposed segmentation approach is more accurate than the graph based segmentation algorithm using normalized cut criteria.

Keywords: hypergraph, neighborhood hypergraph, hypergraph partitioning, image segmentation, edge detection and adaptive thresholding.

1 Introduction

Image segmentation is an important step in computer vision. Several algorithms have been introduced to tackle this problem. Among them are approaches based on graph partitioning [1,2,3,4,5,6].

The graph approaches carry the appeal of a strong theoretical basis and the advantage of being applicable not only to the segmentation of images, but also to other low, mid, and high level vision tasks. For grouping pixels into regions with a graph-theoretic approach, a graph is usually defined as $G(X, e)$, where the nodes X represent the pixels (one node per pixel) and the edges e represent the weights $w(i, j)$ that connect pairs of nodes.

One of the most frequently used techniques to partition a graph is by means of the cut cost function. The goal of the cut algorithm is to find two sub-graphs A and B of G that minimize the value of : $cut\{A, B\} = \sum_{i \in A, j \in B} w(i, j)$ and with the obvious constraints $A \cup B = X$, $A \cap B = \emptyset$, and $A \neq \emptyset$, $B \neq \emptyset$.

Several alternatives to the above criterion have been proposed to date [4,1,3]. Of particular note is the normalized cut criterion (Ncut) of Shi and Malik [1], which attempts to rectify the tendency of the cut algorithm to favor isolated nodes of the graph.

A hypergraph is an extension of a graph in which edges are allowed to connect arbitrary, non-empty sets of vertices (as shown in Fig. 1). Similarly to graphs,

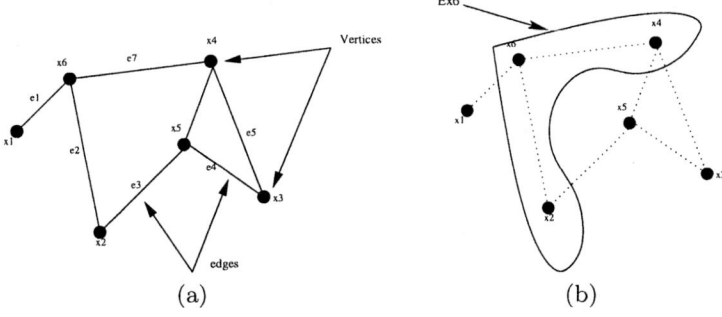

Fig. 1. An example graph and a hypergraph

hypergraphs can be used to represent the structure of many applications, such as data dependencies in distributed databases, component connectivity in VLSI circuits and image analysis [7,8,9,10]. Also, like graphs, hypergraphs may be partitioned such that a cut metric is minimized. However, hypergraph cut metrics provide a more accurate model than graph partitioning in many cases of practical interest. For example, in the row-wise decomposition of a sparse matrix for parallel matrix-vector multiplication, a hypergraph model provides an exact measure of communication cost, whereas a graph model can only provide an upper bound [11,12]. It has been shown that, in general, there does not exist a graph model that correctly represents the cut properties of the corresponding hypergraph [13]. Recently, several serial and parallel hypergraph partitioning techniques have been extensively studied [14,15,12] and tools support exists (e.g. hMETIS [16], PaToH [11] and Parkway [17]). These partitioning techniques showed a very great efficiency in distributed databases and VLSI circuits fields.

In this paper, we present a new hypergraph-based image segmentation algorithm using hypergraph partitioning techniques. The basic idea of this algorithm can be described as follows. It first builds a weighted hypergraph of the given gray-scale image. Then the algorithm partitions this representation into a set of vertices, representing homogeneous regions. The hypergraph partitioning is done by a fast multilevel programming algorithm. Our contribution consists in presenting an Adaptive Image Neighborhood Hypergraph representation (WAINH). The WAINH is the most significant step in the segmentation algorithm, because it makes it possible to connect the given gray-scale image and the existing hypergraph partitioning techniques.

The adaptive representation captures the local properties of the gray-scale image and the whole key information for the segmentation purpose. This leads to a new hypergraph-based technique which is more relevant to image segmentation than our previous work [9].

The remainder of this paper is organized as follows: in section 2, we introduce the weighted adaptive image neighborhood hypergraph. The hypergraph partitioning for image segmentation is introduced in section 3. In section 4, we illustrate the performances of the proposed approach. The paper ends with a conclusions and perspectives in section 5.

2 Adaptive Image Neighborhood Hypergraph (AINH)

A hypergraph is a pair $H = (X, E)$, where $X = x_1, x_2, \ldots x_n$ is the set of vertices (or nodes) and $E = E_1, E_2, \ldots, E_m$, with $E_i \subseteq X$ for $i = 1, \ldots, m$, is the set of hyperedges.

Let us note $G(X; e)$ a graph and $H(X, E)$ a hypergraph. The hypergraph having the vertices of G as vertices and the neighborhood of these vertices as hyperedges (including these vertices) is called the *neighborhood hypergraph* of graph G. To each graph G we can associate a neighborhood hypergraph (figure 1):

$$H_G = (X, (E_x = \{x\} \cup \Gamma(x))) \quad where \quad \Gamma(x) = \{y \in X, (x,y) \in e\} \quad (1)$$

In this paper, the image will be represented by the following mapping:

$$I : X \subseteq \mathbb{Z}^2 \longrightarrow C \subseteq \mathbb{Z}^n$$

Vertices of X are called pixels, elements of C are called colors. A distance d on X defines a grid (a connected, regular graph, without both loop and multi-edge). Let d' be a distance on C, we have a neighborhood relation on an image defined by:

$$\Gamma_{\lambda,\beta}(x) = \{x' \in X, |d'(I(x), I(x'))| \leq \lambda \quad and \quad d(x, x') \leq \beta\}. \quad (2)$$

The neighborhood of x on the grid will be denoted by $\Gamma_{\lambda,\beta}(x)$. To each image I, we can associate a hypergraph called *Image Neighborhood Hypergraph*(INH) [8]:

$$H_{\Gamma_{\lambda,\beta}}(I) = (X, (\{x\} \cup \Gamma_{\lambda,\beta}(x))_{x \in X}) \quad (3)$$

The figure 2 illustrates an example of image neighborhood hypergraph representation.

On a grid Γ_β, to each pixel x we can associate a neighborhood $\Gamma_{\lambda,\beta}(x)$, according to a predicate λ. The threshold λ can be carried out in two ways. In the first way, the λ is given for all the pixels of the image. In the second way, the λ is generated locally and applied in an adaptive way to the image I.

In this paper, the attribute λ is computed in an adaptive way depending on the local properties of the image. The value of λ will be estimated by:

$$\lambda = Median\ \{I(y) - Median(F(x))\}_{\forall y \in F} \quad (4)$$

F is the window centered in x with the size $[2\beta + 1 \times 2\beta + 1]$.

This $H_{\Gamma_{\lambda,\beta}}(I)$ combinatorial representation is more relevant than the previous one introduced in [9], because it takes into account both the local and global aspects of the image. Hence $H_{\Gamma_{\lambda,\beta}}(I)$ offers new facilities for handling the topology and the geometry of the image. Consequently, it gives more information about the nature of the image to analyze.

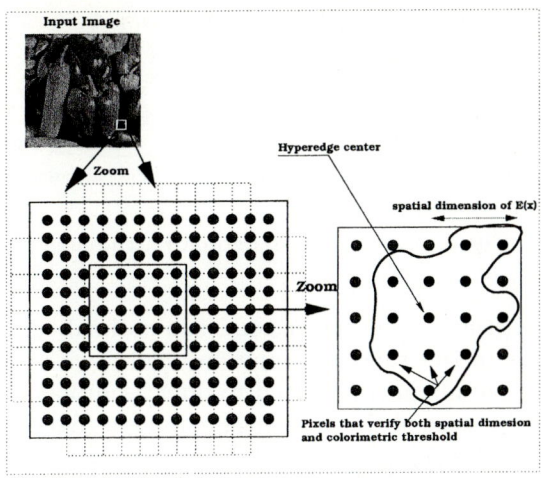

Fig. 2. An example of INH representation

3 Multilevel WAINH Partitioning

From $H_{\Gamma_{\lambda,\beta}}(I)$, we define a Weighted Adaptive Image Neighborhood Hypergraph (WAINH) according to the two maps functions f_{w_v} and f_{w_h}. The first map f_{w_v} associates an integer weight w_{xi} with every vertex $x_i \in X$. The weight is defined by the intensity in each pixel. The map function f_{w_h} associates to each hyperedge a weight w_{hi} defined by the mean intensity in this hyperedge. The WAINH is defined by:

$$H_{\lambda,\beta} = (X, E_{\lambda,\beta}, w_x, w_h), \forall x \in X, \quad f_{w_x}(x) = I(x)$$

$$\forall E(x) \in E_{\lambda,\beta}, \quad f_{w_h}(E(x)) = \frac{1}{|E(x)|} \sum_{i=1}^{|E(x)|} I(x_i)_{x_i \in E(x)}$$

The formal definition of the k-way hypergraph partitioning technique is as follows : find k disjoint subsets X_i, $(i = 0, \ldots, k-1)$ of the vertex set X with part (region) weights W_i $(i = 0, \ldots, k-1)$(given by the sum of the constituent vertex weights), such that, given a prescribed balance criterion $0 < \epsilon < 1$, $W_i < (1 + \epsilon)W_{avg}$ holds $\forall i = 0, \ldots, k-1$ and an objective function over the hyperedges is minimized. The W_{avg} denotes the average part weight.

If the objective function is the hyperedge cut metric, then the partition cost (or cut-size) is given by the sum of the costs of hyperedges that span more than one part. Alternatively, when the objective function is the $(k-1)$ metric, the partition cost is given by : $P_{cost} = \sum_{i=0}^{|E|-1}(\gamma_i - 1)w_{hi}$

Computing the optimal bisection of a hypergraph under the hyperedge cut metric (and hence the $(k-1)$ metric since $k = 2$ for a bisection) is known to be NP-complete [18]. Thus, researches have focused on developing polynomial

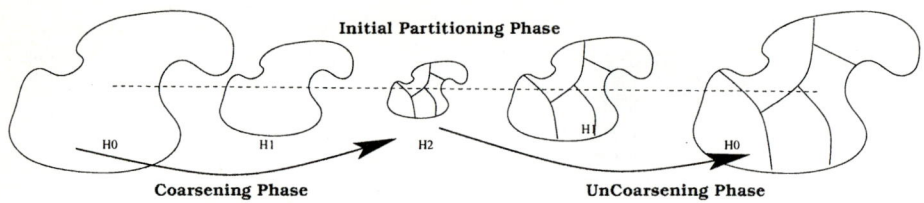

Fig. 3. Multilevel Hypergraph Partitioning

time heuristic algorithms resulting in good sub-optimal solutions. Because it scales well in terms of run time and solution quality with increasing problem size, the multilevel paradigm is preferred to direct solution approaches. Below, we describe the main steps of the multilevel paradigm (figure. 3).

i. Coarsening phase: $H_{\lambda,\beta}$ is approximated via a succession of smaller hypergraphs that maintain its structure as accurately as possible. A single coarsening step is performed by merging the vertices of the original hypergraph together to form vertices of the coarse hypergraph, denoted by a map $f_{merge}: X \rightarrow X_{coarse}$, where

$$\frac{|X|}{|X_{coarse}|} = r, \quad r > 1, \qquad (5)$$

and r is the prescribed reduction ratio. The map f_{merge} is used to transform the hyperedges of the original hypergraph $H_{\lambda,\beta}$ to the hyperedges of the coarse hypergraph. Single vertex hyperedges in the coarse hypergraph are discarded as they cannot contribute to the cut-size of a partition of the coarse hypergraph. Several f_{merge} maps functions have been proposed [19] (figure 4): edge coarsening, hyperedge coarsening and modified hyperedge coarsening.

ii. Initial partitioning phase: During the initial partitioning phase, a partitioning of the coarsest hypergraph $H_{\lambda,\beta}{}^{coarse}$ is computed, such that it minimizes

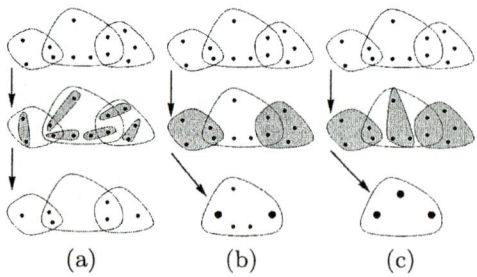

Fig. 4. Coarsening phase : (a) Edge coarsening : connected pairs of vertices are matched together. (b) Hyperedge coarsening : all the vertices belonging to a hyperedge are matched together. (c)Modified hyperedge coarsening : we match together all the vertices in a hyperedge as well as all the groups of vertices belonging to a hyperedge.

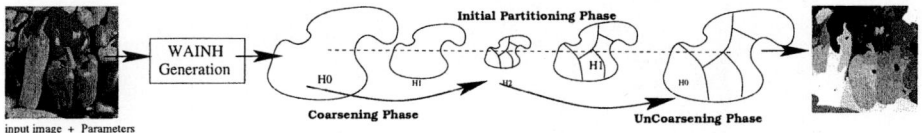

Fig. 5. The two steps of the proposed segmentation algorithm. The input parameters are: intensity threshold λ, spatial threshold β and the number of desired regions k.

the cut. Since this hypergraph has a very small number of vertices, the time to find a partitioning using any of the heuristic algorithms tends to be small.

iii. Uncoarsening phase: During the uncoarsening phase, a partitioning of the coarser hypergraph is successively projected to the next level finer hypergraph, and a partitioning refinement algorithm is used to reduce the cut-set (and thus to improve the quality of the partitioning). Since the next level finer hypergraph has more degrees of freedom, such refinement algorithms tend to improve the solution quality.

Figure 5 illustrates the proposed algorithm. It starts with a WAINH generation followed by a multilevel hypergraph partitioning.

4 Experimental Results

A set of gray-scale images with different homogeneous areas was chosen in order to demonstrate the performances of our algorithm. The simulations are grouped in two parts. Firstly, the evaluation of the algorithm according to the WAINH representation, then the evaluation of the proposed algorithm compared to the existing methods.

We will first describe the various stages of implementation of the proposed algorithm.

1. For WAINH generation, we use an adaptive threshold λ. It is estimated using Equation (4) while the parameters value (β,k) are adjusted in experiments.
2. For WAINH partitioning, and in the coarsening phase, we use the hyperedge coarsening approach. In the initial partitioning phase, we compute the k-way partitioning of the coarsest hypergraph using the multilevel hypergraph bisection algorithm [15]. In the uncoarsening phase, we use the F.M. refinement algorithm [14].

For the coarsening, initial partitioning and uncoarsening phases we use the Hmetis package [16].

We will now show the effect of the weighted hypergraph generation on the quality of the image segmentation results. For this study, we implement two weighted neighborhood hypergraph representations : the WAINH representation defined in section 3, and the WINH representation used in our previous work [9].

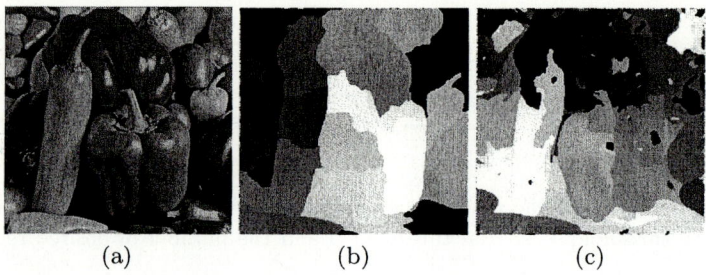

(a) (b) (c)

Fig. 6. WAINH and WINH comparison. (a) Peppers image. (b,c) Outputs of the proposed algorithm using WINH ($\lambda = 20$, $\beta = 1$ and $k = 51$) and WAINH ($\beta = 1$ and $k = 51$) representations respectively.

The WINH representation uses a global threshold λ. This means that all the hyperedges $E_{\lambda,\beta}(x)$ are generated with the same threshold λ.

Figure 6 shows the segmentation results of Peppers image obtained, using WAINH and WINH representations. From this figure, we note that the proposed algorithm using WINH representation tends to divide large constant areas into multiple segments. The reader might see that we could improve the results by using WAINH representation. Indeed, the use of WAINH representation in the proposed algorithm involves the detection of more significant regions with high precision. Consequently, weighted hypergraph representation influences segmentation quality. The improvement of this representation leads to an improvement of the segmentation quality. These remarks can be observed on each image of the set.

We will now evaluate the WAINH representation according to the mapping function f_{w_v} and f_{w_h}. Independently of these two functions, we can generate three representations. (1) Using weighted vertices only, (2) using weighted hyperedges only and (3) using both weighted vertices and weighted hyperedges.

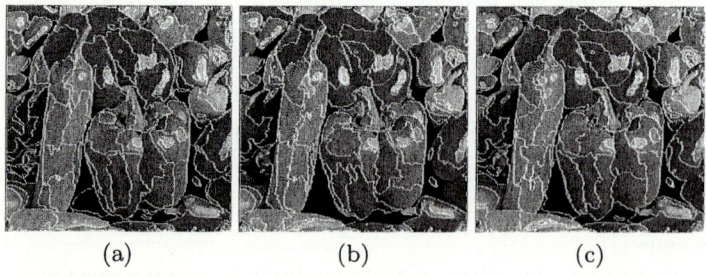

(a) (b) (c)

Fig. 7. The output of the proposed algorithm with WAINH (a) using weighted vertices only, (b) using weighted hyperedge only, (c) using both weighted vertices and weighted hyperedges. The parameters of the algorithm: $\beta = 1$ and $\mu = 51$.

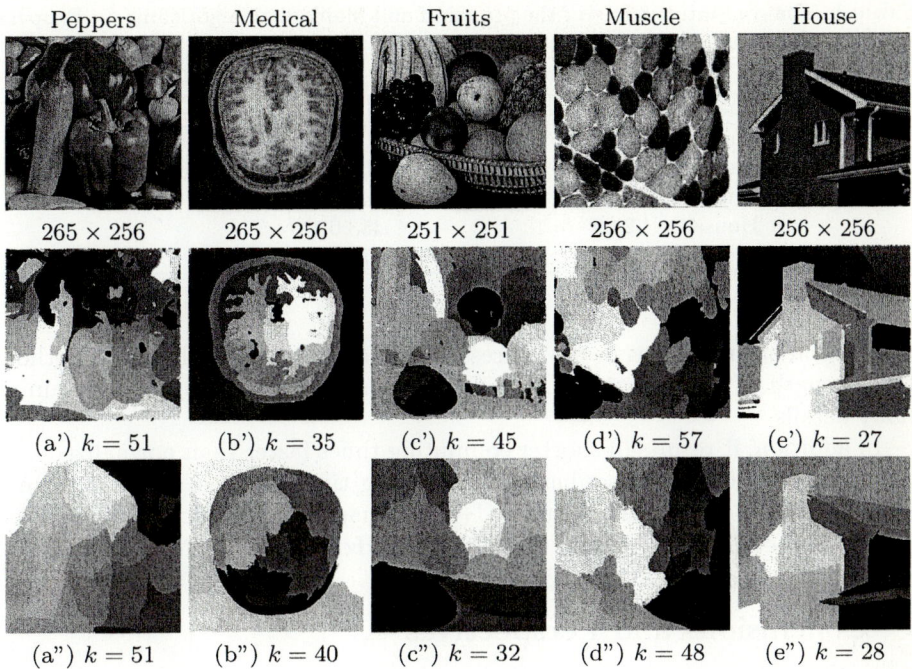

Fig. 8. A comparison between proposed and normalized cut algorithms. (a',b',c',d',e') The outputs of the proposed algorithm with $\beta = 1$. (a",b",c",d",e") The output of normalized cut algorithm.

The goal of this study is to evaluate the proposed algorithm according to these three representations and more particularly to the quantity of information contained in these representations.

Figure 7 shows the results of the proposed algorithm using these three WAINH representations. From this figure, we note that the algorithm with these three representations gives comparable results. But, in some areas containing more details and more useful information, we can see that the last representation WAINH (using both weighted vertices and weighted hyperedges) gives significant results. Indeed, the third WAINH gives more key information about the image used in multilevel neighborhood hypergraph partitioning technique for the segmentation purpose.

To evaluate the WAINH representation used in our segmentation approach, the discussion so far used only one Peppers image. In this study, we show several additional results on different types of images. These additional results are compared to the results of Shi and Malik segmentation algorithm [1] (Normalized Cuts detection Ncut). This algorithm use the same parameters for all images, namely, the optimal parameters given by the authors.

Figure 8 shows a comparison between the proposed and Ncut algorithms on Peppers, Medical, Fruits, Muscle and House images. According to the segmentation results on these images, we note that our algorithm make a better

Table 1. The computing times of the proposed and Malik et al. algorithms for Peppers, Medical, Fruits, Muscle and House images

Image	proposed (in second)	Ncut (in second)
Peppers	3.22	402.75
Medical	2.90	463.64
Fruits	3.25	447.78
House	2.69	453.62
Muscle	3.78	477.28

localization of the regions in the processed image compared to the Ncut method. The strength of this algorithm is that it better detects the regions containing many details.

In addition, it results in shorter computing times faster than normalized cuts algorithm. The table 1 describes the computing times of these two algorithms. They have been implemented using C++ language in a notebook with the following characteristics: Pentium Centrino, 1,5GHz, 512 Mo RAM.

5 Conclusions and Perspectives

We have presented a weighted adaptive image neighborhood hypergraph partitioning for image segmentation. The segmentation is accomplished in two stages. In the first stage, a weighted adaptive image neighborhood hypergraph is generated. In the second stage, a hypergraph partitioning is computed using a multilevel technique is computed. Experimental results demonstrate that our approach using the weighted adaptive neighborhood hypergraph performs better than the same algorithm using a global representation and the normalized cut algorithm. Currently, we work on the extension of the proposed algorithm on color images.

References

1. Shi, J., Malik, J.: Normalized cuts and image segmentation. IEEE Transactions on Pattern Analysis and Machine Intellignece **22** (2000)
2. Soundararajan, P., Sarkar, S.: An in-depth study of graph partitioning measures for perceptual organization. IEEE Trans. Pattern Anal. Mach. Intell. **25** (2003) 642–660
3. Martinez, A.M., Mittrapiyanuruk, P., Kak, A.C.: On combining graph-partitioning with non-parametric clustering for image segmentation. Computer Vision and Image Understanding **95** (2004) 72–85
4. Wang, S., Siskind, J.M.: Image segmentation with ratio cut - supplemental material. IEEE Trans. Pattern Anal. Mach. Intell. **25** (2003)
5. Soundararajan, P., Sarkar, S.: Analysis of mincut, average cut, and normalized cut measures. Proc. Third Workshop Perceptual Organization in Computer Vision (2001)

6. Timothee Cour, Florence Benezit, J.S.: Spectral segmentation with multiscale graph decomposition. IEEE International Conference on Computer Vision and Pattern Recognition (to appear) (2005)
7. Rital, S., Bretto, A., Aboutajdine, D., Cherifi, H.: Application of adaptive hypergraph model to impulsive noise detection. Lecture Notes in Computer Science **2124** (2001) 555–562
8. Rital, S., Cherifi, H.: A combinatorial color edge detector. Lecture Notes in Computer Science **3212** (2004) 289–297
9. Rital, S., Cherifi, H., Miguet, S.: Neighborhood hypergraph partitioning for image segmentation. First International Conference on Pattern Recognition and Machine Intelligence (18-22, 2005)
10. Bretto, A., J.Azema, Cherifi, H., Laget, B.: Combinatorics and image processing. Graphical Models and Image Processing **5** (1997) 265–372
11. Catalyurek, U., Aykanat, C.: Hypergraph-partitioning-based decomposition for parallel sparse-matrix vector multiplication. IEEE Trans. Parallel Distrib. Syst. **10** (1999) 673–693
12. Trifunovic, A., Knottenbelt, W.: A parallel algorithm for multilevel k-way hypergraph partitioning. In: Proceedings of 3rd International Symposium on Parallel and Distributed Computing. (2004)
13. Ihler, E., Wagner, D., Wagner, F.: Modeling hypergraphs by graphs with the same mincut properties. Inf. Process. Lett. **45** (1993) 171–175
14. Sanchis, L.A.: Multiple-way network partitioning. IEEE Transactions on Computers (1989) 6281
15. Karypis, G., Aggarwal, R., Kumar, V., Shekhar, S.: Multilevel hypergraph partitioning: applications in vlsi domain. IEEE Trans. Very Large Scale Integr. Syst. **7** (1999) 69–79
16. Karypis, G., Kumar, V.: hmetis 1.5: A hypergraph partitioning package. Technical report, University of Minnesota, Available on http://www.cs.umn.edu/hmetis (1998)
17. Trifunovic, A., Knottenbelt, W.: Parkway 2.0: A parallel multilevel hypergraph partitioning tool. In: Proceedings of 19th International Symposium on Computer and Information Sciences (ISCIS 2004). Volume 3280. (2004) 789–800
18. Garey, M., Johnson, D.: Computers and Intractability: A Guide to the Theory of NP-Completeness. W.H. Freeman and Co. (1979)
19. Karypis, G.: Multilevel hypergraph partitioning. Technical report #02-25, University of Minnesota (2002)

Parallel-Sequential Texture Analysis

Egon L. van den Broek[1,3] and Eva M. van Rikxoort[2,3]

[1] Department of Artificial Intelligence, Vrije Universiteit Amsterdam,
De Boelelaan 1081a, 1081 HV Amsterdam, The Netherlands
egon@few.vu.nl, http://www.few.vu.nl/~egon/
[2] Image Sciences Institute, University Medical Center Utrecht,
Heidelberglaan 100, 3584 CX Utrecht, The Netherlands
eva@isi.uu.nl, http://www.isi.uu.nl/
[3] Nijmegen Institute for Cognition and Information,
Radboud University Nijmegen,
P.O. Box 9104, 6500 HE Nijmegen, The Netherlands

Abstract. Color induced texture analysis is explored, using two texture analysis techniques: the co-occurrence matrix and the color correlogram as well as color histograms. Several quantization schemes for six color spaces and the human-based 11 color quantization scheme have been applied. The VisTex texture database was used as test bed. A new color induced texture analysis approach is introduced: the parallel-sequential approach; i.e., the color correlogram combined with the color histogram. This new approach was found to be highly successful (up to 96% correct classification). Moreover, the 11 color quantization scheme performed excellent (94% correct classification) and should, therefore, be incorporated for real-time image analysis. In general, the results emphasize the importance of the use of color for texture analysis and of color as global image feature. Moreover, it illustrates the complementary character of both features.

1 Introduction

The origin of the color name *lilac* lies in the Sanskrit *nilla 'dark blue'*, of which the Persian made *nIlak 'bluish'*, from *nIl 'blue'*. In the Arabic, the meaning evolved to a description of a plant with flowers of this color: the *Sering*. In 1560, the *Sering* was brought to Vienna, by an Austrian ambassador. From there, the plant reached France and the word's meaning evolved to *"a variable color averaging a moderate purple"*[1].

The latter example illustrates that there is more with colors than one would think at first glance. The influence of color in our everyday life and the ease with which humans use color are in stark contrast with the complexity of the phenomenon color, a topic of research in numerous fields of science (e.g., physics, biology, psychology, and computer science). Despite their distinct views on color, scientists in these fields agree that color is of the utmost importance in image processing, both by humans and by computers. However, the use of color analysis increases the computational cost for image analysis algorithms, since instead of one dimension, three dimensions are present. Therefore, color images are often converted to gray-scale images, when texture analysis has to be performed (e.g., see Figure 1). Not surprisingly, with this conversion texture information is lost; e.g., using a standard conversion, red, green, and blue can result in the same gray-scale. Nevertheless, as Palm [2] already denoted: "The integration of color and texture is still exceptional". However, in the literature three distinct approaches to combine color and texture can be found: parallel, sequential, and integrative [2]. In the parallel approach, color and texture are evaluated separately, as shown in Figure 1. Sequential approaches use color analysis as a first step of the process chain: After the color space is quantized, gray-scale texture methods are applied, as shown in Figure 2. The integrative method uses the different color channels of an image and performs the texture analysis methods on each channel separately.

Palm [2] used an integrative method to test classification results on color textures and found that the use of color improved classification performance significantly. Drimbarean and Whelan [3] used three texture analysis methods on five different color spaces, with one (coarse) color quantization scheme in an integrative method to test classification results. The use of color improved performance, but no single color space outperformed the others. Mäenpää and Pietikäinen [4] used five different color spaces and two texture analysis techniques to determine whether color and texture should be used in parallel or sequential. They concluded that combining color and texture gave only minimal performance improvement, and that, when combining color and texture, the sequential approach should be preferred.

However, no reports are available that combine studies toward the influence of varying the color space, the quantization scheme, and the way color and texture are combined, for either the parallel approach, the sequential approach, or a combined approach. In this paper, each of these variations is applied. Moreover, the new parallel-sequential approach is introduced: the color correlogram combined with the color histogram.

In the next two sections, we discuss the color spaces and the quantization schemes applied on them and the texture analysis technique used. In Section 4, the texture processing schemes, the texture database, and the classifiers used are briefly described. As baselines, the co-occurrence matrix, the color histogram, and the color correlogram are applied, in Section 5. In Section 6, the new parallel-sequential approach is introduced and directly compared with the parallel approach. We end this paper with a conclusion.

2 Color

A color space specifies colors as tuples of (typically three) numbers, conform to certain specifications. For image processing purposes, color spaces are often quantized. The color space in which this is done determines the perceptual intuitivity of the quantization up to a high extend. Moreover, the axes of the color space can be quantized, using a different scheme for each axis. Again, this depends on the color space of choice.

A color space is perceptually intuitive if distances between points in that space (i.e., 'colors') have a relation to perceived closeness of these 'colors' by human observers. If that relation is constant one can even speak of perceptual uniformity. In this section, we describe the color spaces used and the quantization schemes applied on them. The quantization of color images transformed into gray-scale images will not be described for every color space since it is the same for every color space: the gray-scale axis is divided in the number of bins needed for the specific quantization scheme.

A quantization scheme, either applied to gray-scale or to color images, provides the means to determine an intensity or color histogram. Such a histogram can be determined for parts of the image as well as for the image as a whole. The latter application of the intensity or color histogram is applied in the current research. It describes the global color characteristics of an image.

The RGB (Red, Green, and Blue) color space is the most used color space for computer graphics and is not perceptually uniform. Each color-axis (R, G, and B) is equally important and is quantized with the same precision. The conversion from a RGB image to a gray value image simply takes the sum of the R, G, and B values and divides the result by three.

The HSV (Hue, Saturation, and Value) color space is more closely related to human color perception than the RGB color space [5] and is perceptually intuitive but not perceptually uniform. Hue is the color component of the HSV color space. When Saturation is set to 0, Hue is undefined and the Value-axis represents the gray-scale image. The most common quantization of HSV is in 162 ($18 \times 3 \times 3$) bins.

The YUV and YIQ color spaces have been developed for television broadcasting. The YIQ color space is the same as the YUV color space, where the I-Q plane is a $33°$ rotation of the U-V plane. The Y signal represents the luminance of a pixel and is the only channel used in black and white television. The U and V for YUV and I and Q for YIQ are the chromatic components. The Y channel is defined by the weighted values of R(0.299), G(0.587), and B(0.144), where the weights resemble the intensity values of the R, G, and B components. The YUV and YIQ color spaces are not perceptually uniform. When the YUV and YIQ color spaces are quantized, each axis is quantized with the same precision. In addition, to optimize color appearance, the YUV color space is often sampled. The samplings we used to construct the color correlogram are: 4:4:4, 4:2:2, and 4:1:1, where the numbers denote the relative amount of respectively Y on each row, U and V on each even-numbered row, and U and V on each odd-numbered row in the image.

The first color space developed by the Commission Internationale de l'Eclairage (CIE) is the XYZ color space. The Y component is the luminance component defined by the weighted sums of R(0.212671), G(0.715160), and B(0.072169). The X and Z are the chromatic components. The XYZ color space is not a perceptually uniform color space. In quantizing the XYZ space, each axis is quantized with the same precision.

The CIE LUV color space is a projective transformation of the XYZ color space that is perceptually uniform. The L-channel of the LUV color space is the luminance of the color. The U and V channels are the chromatic components. So, when U and V are set to 0, the L-channel represents a gray-scale image. In quantizing the LUV space, each axis is quantized with the same precision.

Another view on color representation is the concept of 11 color categories (i.e., black, white, red, green, yellow, blue, brown, purple, pink, orange, and gray), as introduced by Berlin and Kay [6]. Since then, several researchers discussed the topic; see Derefeldt et al. [7] for an overview. Van den Broek et al. [8] developed a method to describe the complete HSI color space, based on a limited set of experimentally determined, categorized colors. This method provided a unique color space segmentation, which can be applied as an 11 color categories, quantization scheme.

3 Texture

Before texture can be analyzed, either a simple color to gray-scale conversion followed by a gray-scale quantization or a color quantization scheme has to be applied, as discussed in the previous section. Next, several texture analysis techniques can be applied, both for general and for specific purposes. We have chosen for one of the more intuitive texture descriptors: the co-occurrence matrix [9], which was developed for intensity based texture analysis. However, it can also be applied for color induced texture analysis; then it is denoted as the color correlogram [10], a sequential color-based texture analysis method: first color is quantized and second texture is analyzed.

3.1 The Co-occurrence Matrix / The Color Correlogram

The co-occurrence matrix $C_{\bar{d}}(i, j)$ counts the co-occurrence of pixels with gray values i and j at a given distance $\bar{d}$. The distance $\bar{d}$ is defined in polar coordinates (d, α), with discrete length and orientation. In practice, α takes the values $0°, 45°, 90°, 135°, 180°, 225°, 270°,$ and $315°$. The co-occurrence matrix $C_{\bar{d}}(i, j)$ can now be defined as:

$$C_{\bar{d}}(i,j) = \Pr(\mathrm{I}(p_1) = i \wedge \mathrm{I}(p_2) = j \mid |p_1 - p_2| = \bar{d}), \tag{1}$$

where Pr is probability, and p_1 and p_2 are positions in the gray-scale image I.

The algorithm yields a symmetric matrix; hence, only angles up to $180°$ need to be considered. A single co-occurrence matrix can be defined for each distance d by averaging four co-occurrence matrices of different angles (i.e., $0°, 45°, 90°,$ and $135°$).

The color correlogram is the color-based equivalent of the co-occurrence matrix. So, for the color correlogram, not the intensity is quantized, but a color space is quantized. In Equation 1, i and j denote two gray-values. Subsequently, the color correlogram can be defined by Equation 1, with i and j being two color values.

Because of the high dimensionality of the matrix, the individual elements of the co-occurrence matrix are rarely used directly for texture analysis. Instead, textural features can be derived from the matrix. In previous research [11], we determined which feature-distance combinations, derived from the co-occurrence matrix or color correlogram, perform best. The best classification was found using a combination of four features: entropy, inverse difference moment, cluster prominence, and Haralick's correlation, with $d = 1$. Consequently, this configuration was chosen for this research.

4 Method

For the co-occurrence matrix, the color histogram, and the color correlogram, for each color space, five quantization schemes were applied. A complete overview of the schemes applied is presented in Table 1. In total, 170 different configurations were applied: 30 for the co-occurrence matrix, 20 for the color histogram, 45 for the color correlogram, and 75 for the combined approaches.

The VisTex texture database [12], which consists of 19 labeled classes, was used as test bed both for the baselines (see Section 5) and for the comparison between the parallel and parallel-sequential approach for texture analysis (see Section 6). The classes

Table 1. The quantization schemes applied on the six color spaces and on the 11 color categories, for each texture descriptor. Note that YUV* is sampled for the color correlogram (see Section 2).

Color space	Co-occurrence matrix	Color histogram / Color correlogram
RGB	8, 16, 32, 64, 128	8, 64, 216, 512, 4096
HSV	8, 16, 32, 64, 128	27, 54, 108, 162, 324
YIQ, YUV*, XYZ, LUV	8, 16, 32, 64, 128	8, 27, 64, 125, 216
11 colors		11, 27, 36, 70, 225

Table 2. The *best* classification results (%) of the color histogram, the co-occurrence matrix, and the color correlogram, for several color space - quantization scheme (#bins) combination.

Color space	Co-occurrence matrix		Color histogram		Color correlogram	
	#bins	%	#bins	%	#bins	%
RGB	8	56%	4096	87%	8	68%
HSV	32	58%	27	88%	162	74%
YIQ	8	54%			125	53%
YUV 4:4:4	8	54%			27	52%
XYZ	64	56%			27	71%
LUV	8	58%	64	84%	27	66%
11 colors			11	84%	27	72%

with less than 10 images were not used in this experiment. This resulted in four classes: bark (13 images), food (12 images), fabric (20 images), and leaves (17 images). In order to generate more data for the classifiers, we adapted the approach of Palm [2] and Mäenpää and Pietikäinen [4]: the original images were split into four sub-images, resulting in a database of 248 textures.

For all research described in this paper, a combination of three classifiers was used: a linear discriminant classifier, a 1-nearest neighbor classifier, and a probabilistic neural network, taken from the MATLAB® library using their default parameters. The output of this classifier combination was determined using the technique of majority voting [13]: when at least two of the three classifiers agree on the class label of a sample image, this label is given else the label false is given. The training and test set for the classifiers were composed using random picking, with the prerequisite that each class had an equal amount of training data.

5 Three Baselines

As a first baseline, the co-occurrence matrix as standard, intensity-based texture analysis is used. The results are presented in Table 2. The complete results are available online [14]. The CIE LUV quantized in 8 bins and the HSV color space quantized in 32 bins performed best with a classification performance of 58%. Overall, the performances among different color spaces were about the same. Hence, for intensity-based texture analysis, the choice of color space is not essential. The quantization scheme chosen is important, usually a lower number of bins performs better: In no instance, the largest number of bins gave the best results.

Next to texture, the global color distribution within an image is frequently used as feature for image classification and image retrieval. Therefore, as a second baseline, we conducted an image classification experiment, using color solely by calculating the color histograms. In Table 2, the best four classification results are presented. The complete results are available online [14]. Classification by use of quantizations of the RGB color space results in a low performance (i.e., ranging from 19–48%), except for the 4096 bin quantization scheme (as used in QBIC [15]). However, the latter suffers from an unacceptable computational load, especially for real-time image analysis applications (e.g., content-based image retrieval). Therefore, the RGB color space is not suitable for color-based image classification. The classification using the coarsest LUV quantization (8 bins) did have a poor performance. All other quantizations, using the LUV color space, resulted in high classification performance. The color-based texture classification, using the coarse 11 color quantization scheme, performed well (84%) (see Table 2), especially when considering its low computational complexity. The 27 and 162 bins quantizations of the HSV color space performed best with 88% and 89%.

As the third baseline, sequential texture analysis is performed (see Figure 2), with the color correlogram using six different color spaces. The results are presented in Table 2. In addition, the 11 color categories scheme was applied using several quantization schemes (see Section 4). The HSV color space performed best in combination with the color correlogram (see Table 2). This can be explained by the relatively high precision in color (Hue) quantization of the HSV 162 bins scheme. However, the color correlogram founded on the 11 color categories also performed good with 72% precision.

An interesting result is the fact that using more bins usually does not improve performance. In no instance, the largest number of bins gave the best results. This result emphasizes the importance of using a coarse color quantization scheme such as that of the 11 color categories in which one can represent colors [7].

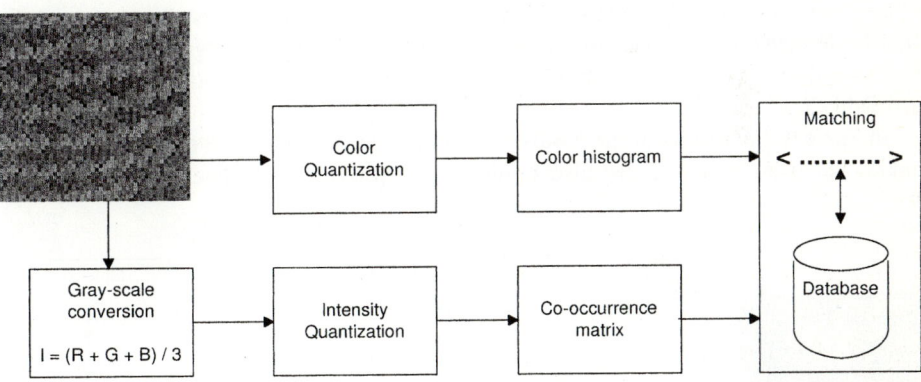

Fig. 1. The parallel approach for texture analysis, using global color features and local intensity differences. In parallel, the color histogram is determined, after the quantization of color, and the co-occurrence matrix is calculated, after the conversion to gray-scale and the quantization of gray values.

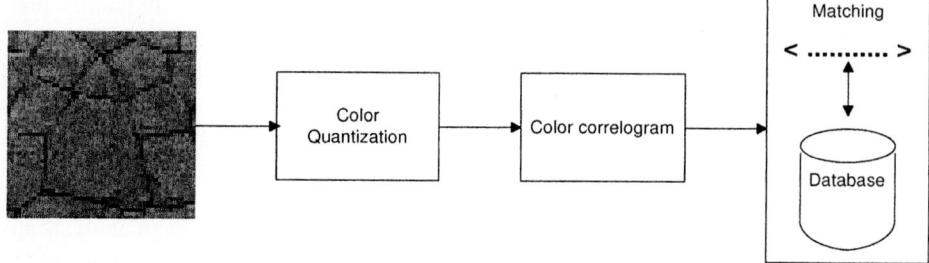

Fig. 2. The sequential approach for texture analysis: after color quantization the color correlogram is utilized.

6 Parallel-Sequential Texture Analysis: Color Histogram and Color Correlogram

In the previous sections, we have discussed the classification of the VisTex images, using intensity-based texture features (i.e., the co-occurrence matrix), color histograms, and a sequential of color and texture: the color correlogram. However, better classification results may be achieved when these methods are combined.

In the current section, a new color induced texture analysis approach is introduced: the parallel-sequential approach, which combines the color correlogram and the color histogram, as is visualized in Figure 3. This new approach is compared with the parallel texture analysis approach: the co-occurrence matrix combined with the color histogram, as is visualized in Figure 1.

First, the color histogram data and texture features were concatenated. The six best color histograms were used in combination with both the two best quantization schemes of each color space (for the color correlogram) and the best intensity quantization scheme (for the co-occurrence matrix). The RGB color histogram was excluded since it only performs well with a quantization that is computationally too expensive (see Table 2).

In Table 3, the results of the parallel approach (i.e., combination of color histogram and co-occurrence matrix, see also Figure 1) are provided. In general, the color his-

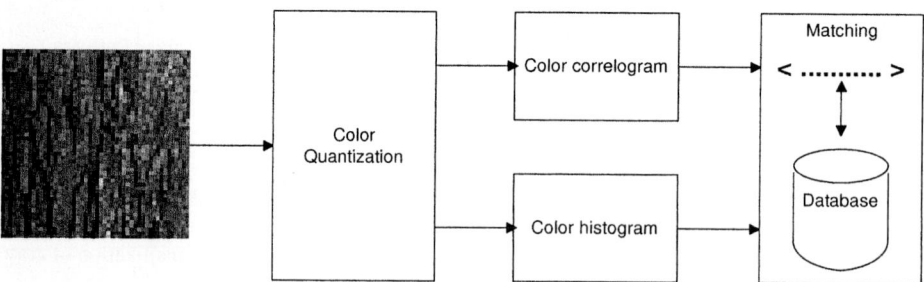

Fig. 3. The new parallel-sequential approach for texture analysis which yields in parallel: global color analysis, using the color histogram, and color induced texture analysis, using the color correlogram.

Table 3. The classification results of *the best combinations* of color histograms with co-occurrence matrices (the parallel approach, see also Figure 1) and with color correlograms (the parallel-sequential approach, see also Figure 3), using several quantizations of color spaces.

		Color histogram				
		11 colors	HSV-27	HSV-162	LUV-64	LUV-125
Co-occurrence matrix	HSV-32	88%	90%	92%	82%	90%
	LUV-8	84%	89%	92%	82%	88%
	RGB-8	84%	89%	92%	82%	88%
	XYZ-64	87%	84%	91%	79%	90%
	YUV/YIQ-8	83%	87%	92%	81%	89%
Color correlogram	11 colors-27	**94%**	92%	**96%**	92%	89%
	HSV-27	93%	87%	92%	92%	91%
	LUV-27	90%	89%	91%	88%	89%
	RGB-8	92%	91%	93%	86%	87%
	XYZ-27	87%	89%	92%	84%	**94%**

togram based on the HSV 162 bins quantization scheme performed best (91 − 92%). However, the computationally much cheaper 11 color quantization scheme did also have a high performance (88%), when combined with the on HSV 32 bins based co-occurrence matrix (see Table 3). Therefore, the latter combination should be taken into account for real-time systems, using color and texture analysis.

The new parallel-sequential approach has a correct classification ranging from 84% to 96% (see Table 3). So, the combination color histogram with color correlogram improved the classification performance significantly, compared to each of them separately (cf. Table 2 and 3).

The configurations using coarse color quantizations for the definition of the color correlogram, outperformed the more precise color quantizations for all color spaces. The 11 color categories color quantization using 27 bins for the color correlogram, performed best on average (92.6%), followed by the HSV-27 bins configuration (91.0%). Concerning the color histogram configurations, the highest average correct classification was provided by the HSV-162 bins color histogram (92.8%), followed by the 11 color categories color histogram with 91.2%.

The best color correlogram - color histogram combinations were: the 11 colors, 27 bins correlogram & 11 colors histogram, the 11 colors, 27 bins correlogram & HSV-162 color histogram, and the XYZ, 27 bins correlogram & LUV-125 color histogram (the percentages are denoted bold in Table 3). When considering the computational complexity of these combinations, the first combination should be preferred, with its feature-vector of size 15: 11 colors + 4 features derived from the 11 colors 27 bins color correlogram, as described in Section 4.

7 Conclusion

Determining the optimal configuration for color-based texture analysis is very important since the success of image classification and image retrieval systems depends on this configuration. Therefore, in this paper, a series of experiments was presented exploring a variety of aspects concerning color-based texture analysis. The color histogram, the co-occurrence matrix, the color correlogram, and their combinations (i.e., the parallel and sequential approach) were compared with one another, using several color spaces and quantization schemes. A new texture analysis method: the parallel-sequential approach, was introduced.

The worst classification results were obtained when only intensity-based texture analysis (i.e., the co-occurrence matrix) was used, the best classification performance in this setting was 58% for the HSV and CIE LUV color spaces. Including color sequentially, using the color correlogram, gave better results (74%). The parallel approach (i.e., color histogram combined with the co-occurrence matrix improved the performance substantially (see Table 3). However, by far the best classification results were obtained using the new parallel-sequential approach (i.e., color histogram and color correlogram combined, a performance of 96% correct classification was obtained, using the HSV 162 bins color histogram in combination with the color correlogram for the 11 color categories with 27 bins. These results indicate that the use of color for image analysis is very important, as classification performance was improved by 38%, compared with the most widely used, intensity-based, co-occurence matrix. Moreover, in general, coarse color quantization schemes perform excellent and should be preferred to more precise schemes.

The success of the parallel-sequential approach emphasizes the importance of both the global color distribution in images, as identified by the color histogram, and the importance of the utilization of color with the analysis of texture. As was shown, ignoring color in either texture analysis or as a global feature impairs the classification of image material substantially. Moreover, the complementary character of global color and color induced texture analysis is illustrated.

Follow-up research should challenge the parallel-sequential approach, by exploring and comparing different texture analysis methods with the parallel-sequential approach introduced in this paper. Moreover, the use of combining texture analysis methods should be investigated since it might provide the means to increase classification results [16]. Preferably, this research should be conducted using a much larger database of textures.

Regardless of texture analysis methods, note that the computationally inexpensive and well performing 11 color categories are human-based. In further work, we will investigate whether the texture analysis techniques discussed in the current paper can mimic human texture classification. This is of the utmost importance as it is the human who will use and judge the systems in which texture analysis techniques are incorporated [8,15].

Acknowledgments

The Dutch organization for scientific research (NWO) is gratefully acknowledged for funding the ToKeN Eidetic project (nr. 634.000.001), in which this research was conducted. We would like to thank Merijn van Erp, Peter M.F. Kisters, and Theo E. Schouten for reviewing previous versions of the manuscript. Further, we thank Eduard Hoenkamp for proof reading the final manuscript. Last, we would like to thank the reviewers for their constructive criticism.

References

1. Genootschap Onze Taal: Onze Taal Taalkalender. Den Haag: SDU (2003)
2. Palm, C.: Color texture classification by integrative co-occurrence matrices. Pattern Recognition **37** (2004) 965–976
3. Drimbarean, A., Whelan, P.F.: Experiments in colour texture analysis. Pattern Recognition Letters **22** (2001) 1161–1167
4. Mäenpää, T., Pietikäinen, M.: Classification with color and texture: jointly or separately? Pattern Recognition **37** (2004) 1629–1640
5. Lin, T., Zhang, H.: Automatic video scene extraction by shot grouping. In: Proceedings of the 15th IEEE International Conference on Pattern Recognition. Volume 4., Barcelona, Spain (2000) 39–42
6. Berlin, B., Kay, P.: Basic color terms: Their universals and evolution. Berkeley: University of California Press (1969)
7. Derefeldt, G., Swartling, T., Berggrund, U., Bodrogi, P.: Cognitive color. Color Research & Application **29** (2004) 7–19
8. Broek, E.L. van den, Schouten, Th.E., Kisters, P.M.F.: Efficient color space segmentation based on human perception. [submitted]
9. Haralick, R.M., Shanmugam, K., Dinstein, I.: Textural features for image classification. Transactions on Systems, Man and Cybernetics **3** (1973) 610–621
10. Huang, J., Kumar, S.R., Mitra, M., Zhu, W.J., Zabih, R.: Image indexing using color correlograms. In Medioni, G., Nevatia, R., Huttenlocher, D., Ponce, J., eds.: Proceedings of the IEEE Conference on Computer Vision and Pattern Recognition. (1997) 762–768
11. Broek, E.L. van den, Rikxoort, E.M. van: Evaluation of color representation for texture analysis. In Verbrugge, R., Taatgen, N., Schomaker, L.R.B., eds.: Proceedings of the 16th Belgium-Netherlands Artificial Intelligence Conference, Groningen - The Netherlands (2004) 35–42
12. Massachusetts Institute of Technology: Vision Texture. URL: http://vismod.media.mit.edu/vismod/imagery/VisionTexture/vistex.html [Last accessed on May 20, 2005]
13. Kittler, J., Hatef, M., Duin, R.P.W., Matas, J.: On combining classifiers. IEEE Transactions on Pattern Analysis and Machine Intelligence **20** (1998) 226–239
14. Broek, E.L. van den, Rikxoort, E.M. van: Supplement: Complete results of the ICAPR2005 texture baselines. URL: http://www.few.vu.nl/~egon/publications/pdf/ICAPR2005-Supplement.pdf (2005)
15. Smeulders, A.W.M., Worring, M., Santini, S., Gupta, A., Jain, R.: Content-based image retrieval at the end of the early years. IEEE Transactions on Pattern Analysis and Machine Intelligence **22** (2000) 1349–1380
16. Sharma, M., Singh, S.: Evaluation of texture methods for image analysis. In Linggard, R., ed.: Proceedings of the 7th Australian and New Zealand Intelligent Information Systems Conference, Perth, Western Australia, ARCME (2001) 117–121

Region Growing with Automatic Seeding for Semantic Video Object Segmentation

Yue Feng, Hui Fang, and Jianmin Jiang

EIMC, University of Bradford, UK
{yfeng1, hfang, jjiang1}@Bradford.ac.uk

Abstract. As content-based multimedia applications become increasingly important, demand for technologies on semantic video object segmentation is growing, where the segmented objects are expected to be in line with human visual perception. Existing research is limited to semi-automatic approach, in which human intervene is often required. These include manual selection of seeds for region growing or manual classification of background edges etc. In this paper, we propose an automatic region growing algorithm for video object segmentation, which features in automatic selection of seeds and thus the entire segmentation does not require any action from human users. Experimental results show that the proposed algorithm performs well in terms of the effectiveness in video object segmentation.

1 Originality and Contribution

Although research on image segmentation remains intensive for the past decades, most of the algorithms developed are limited to region segmentation, where segmented regions maintain high level of texture consistency but fail to address the issue of human content understanding [9]. In this paper, we report our recent efforts in developing segmentation algorithms towards semantic object segmentation, where objects segmented are consistent with human content understanding rather than texture consistent regions. The originality of our work lies in the fact that we propose to use a two-stage approach to carry out the segmentation. While the first stage identifies a number of texture-consistent regions by following the low-level routes, the second stage ensures that seeds are selected across the boundaries of different texture consistent regions, and thus making the proposed segmentation close to semantic objects.

Another contribution in this paper is that we proposed a novel method for region growing with automatic seeding, which explores the possibility of developing a video object segmentation algorithm based on the concept of seeded region growing. Compared with the latest reported region growing method [15], the proposed algorithm features in: (i) the initial seeds for region growing can be automatically selected; (ii) a correction procedure is built into the system to improve the boundary of segmented object, and (iii) the segmented objects deliver semantic information.

2 Introduction to the Problem

Existing research on video object segmentation can be roughly summarized into two approaches [5], temporal-to-spatial [13, 15] and spatial-to-temporal [3, 4]. The temporal-to-spatial approach sequentially extracts objects by iteratively determining the successive dominant motion parameters, and those regions or sets of pixels which conform to the dominant motion parameters are taken to construct an object. The remaining regions or pixels are regarded as undetermined. The process continues to estimate the dominant motion parameters for those undetermined regions until all objects are extracted [14]. In the spatial-to-temporal approach [13], an over-segmented image is first obtained by extracting spatial features from regions, and then a region-merging procedure is adopted to identify meaningful objects by using temporal information such as motion parameters. As these two approaches basically involve no action from human users, the segmented objects are often not consistent with human visual perception. Consequently, practical application of these algorithms is normally limited to region segmentation rather than video object segmentation.

To improve the accuracy and effectiveness, people tend to revisit those region-based image segmentation [3, 4, 11, 15~18] techniques, in which regions are segmented by grouping together pixels with similar intensity and smooth texture. The idea of region growing is one of the most fundamental concepts used in image segmentation techniques [1, 2], in which the regions with connected pixels of similar values could provide important cues for extracting semantic objects.

The first step to start region growing procedure is to select seeds [7, 12, 15, 16, 18], which often determines the final segmentation results by subsequent region grow. Such operations are normally referred to as seeded region growing (SRG) [15], which is one of the efficient algorithms for image segmentation. The problem here is that as the selection of seeds influences the accuracy of final segmentation, seeded region growing expects human users' intervention by selecting initial seeds manually, which would become a major drawback for video object segmentation. To explore the possibility of developing a new video object segmentation algorithm based on the concept of seeded region growing, we try to design a scheme, where initial seeds can be automatically selected. As a result, the proposed video object segmentation algorithm can be clearly seen to have two elements, automatic seeding and region growing.

3 Design of the Proposed Algorithm

The printing area is 122 mm × 193 mm. The text should be justified to occupy the full line width, so that the right margin is not ragged, with words hyphenated as appropriate. Please fill pages so that the length of the text is no less than 180 mm.

To automatically select the seeds for region growing, we use a competitive learning neural network to do the initial segmentation [8]. In this way, the initial segmentation will provide a space with secured boundaries for seed selection. Considering most of digital videos are already in compressed format at the source, such as MPEG videos, we follow the MPEG compression scheme to design the initial segmentation. Given N blocks of 64 DCT coefficients inside each video frame, we construct a feature vector by extracting DC coefficients only and feed the DC coefficients into a competitive learning neural network to see if the DC should be taken as an object DC or a background DC. Prior to the segmentation, the competitive learning neural network is trained by a set of video frames, where video object DC coefficients and background DC coefficients are manually selected to enable the neural network to learn their differences. As this process is essentially carried out in compressed domain and only one DC coefficient out of each block is required, the operation cost is expected to be very small and the processing speed is high. In other words, if the video frame size is M×N, the proposed initial segmentation is carried out for a reduced DC image with only M/8×N/8 DC coefficients. This is because MPEG compresses videos in terms of such blocks. By examining the DCT properties, it can be seen that the DC image extracted essentially consists of average pixels, where each DC coefficient is the average value of all 64 pixels inside the block. Therefore, each DC coefficient can be calculated in pixel domain as follows:

$$DC(m,n) = \frac{1}{8}\sum_{i=0}^{7}\sum_{j=0}^{7} f(m+i, n+j) \qquad (1)$$

where (m, n) represent the location of the top-left pixel inside each block.

To ensure that the training stage is adaptive to the content of input videos, we take the first five video frames as the training sequence to prepare for the initial segmentation. As the accuracy of the NN classification can not be 100% guaranteed, we do not use the training results directly but as guidelines for initial seed selection. This is done by constructing a skeleton of the roughly segmented regions delivered by NN to select the initial seeds. Since the skeleton is located at the heart of those roughly segmented regions, the outcome for seeds is not domain dependent.

Figure-1 illustrates an example of such initially segmented results, where part (a~f) show the original video frames out of five video clips, and part (g~i) the initially segmented objects.

In the segmented illustration (part (g~i) of Figure-1), the object region is represented as the non-black area and the black part is regarded as the background region. As we only use the DC coefficients not pixels, the results shown are not very accurate and their boundaries are blocking. This is the direct result of our proposed algorithm, where segmentation is done in terms of blocks rather than pixels. However, as we are using the segmentation for the purpose of selecting initial seeds, the blocking effect can be ignored and such initial segmentation is sufficient for this purpose.

After the coarse segmented regions are obtained, the next step is to choose the initial seeds for region growing. Considering the fact that selection of initial seeds has great influence upon the final segmentation accuracy, we propose a narrowing-down approach to ensure that each seed selected is indeed located inside the initially segmented region. To this end, we firstly generate a skeleton of the roughly segmented region by characterizing the luminance feature of those object pixels. Among all the segmented object pixels, we remove those non-reliable pixels on the boundaries of the object region, and keep those pixels located in the middle of the object region between two boundaries. As a result, the process generates a skeleton for each object region. Similarly, for background regions, we also remove those pixels on its boundaries and only keep those reliable pixels (located in the middle of background region between two ends of the boundaries). This operation enables us to generate another skeleton to characterize the background region. For the 46th frame of 'mother and daughter' given in part (a) of Figure-1, we illustrate the skeletons generated in Figure-2, where part (a) illustrates the object skeleton and part (b) the background skeleton.

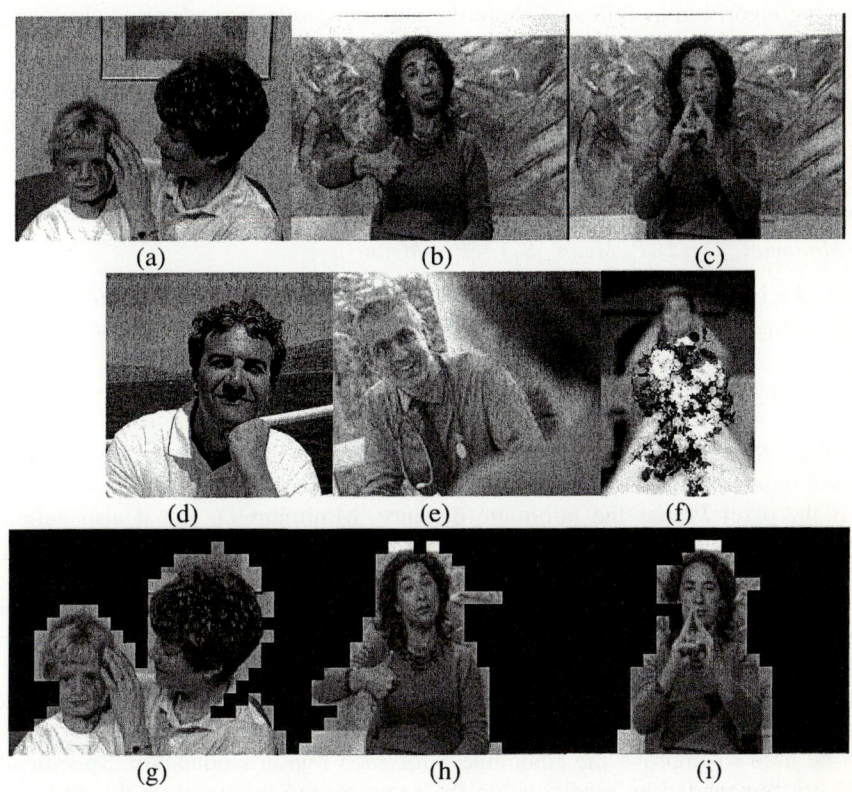

Fig. 1. (a~i) Original Frame of 'Mother and daughter' No.46, 'Silent' No.60 'Silent' No.229, 'Seaman' No. 39, 'Talking' No 25, and 'Wedding' No. 23, respectively; (g, h, i) Segmented results of (a), (b), and (c), respectively.

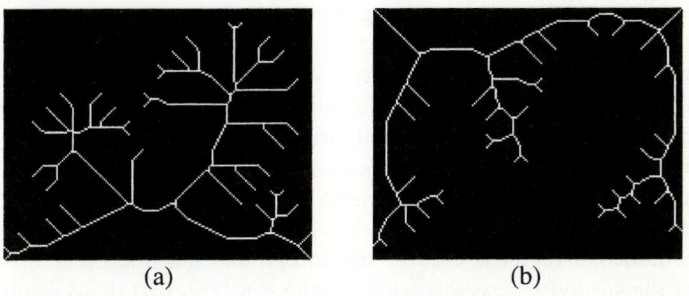

Fig. 2. (a) The skeleton of the object region; (b) And background region.

Correspondingly, the pixels on the object skeleton can be selected as the seeds for object region growing, and the pixels on the background skeleton are selected as the seeds for background region growing.

Based on the existing work on region growing [15, 18], we design our region growing algorithm as follows, where the automatic selection of initial seeds is taken into consideration.

1: We set the skeletons of foreground and background as the seeded regions for object and background, respectively (*So*: the seeds of object region, and *Sb*: the seeds of background region);

2: Given each seed pixel Si, (*Si*∈ *So* or *Sb*), examine its 8 connected neighbouring pixels via:

$$Minimum\_D = D(P_k, Mean\_S_f) = |P_k - Mean\_S_f| \quad (2)$$

where *Pk* is the *kth* neighbouring pixel of the seed ($k \in [0,7]$), and *Mean_ Sf* is the mean value of all the pixels (*Si*) inside the seeded region (So or Sb).

$$Mean\_S_f = \frac{1}{n}\sum_{i=1}^{n} S_i \quad (3)$$

Where Si the ith pixel in the seeded region and n is the number of pixels inside the seeded region.

If the pixel *Pk* has the minimum distance, Minimum_D, and it also neighbours with *Si*, we grow the pixel into *Si*, and updates the mean value of *Si*, Otherwise, we label the pixel *Pk* with the seed for later processing.

3: Process all the labelled pixels. At this stage, each labelled pixel is grown into its labelling seed if this pixel neighbours with the seed or if majority of its neighbours belong to the labelling seed.

4: To ensure that each pixel examined is grown into the right region, a correction procedure is further added to process those remaining labelled pixels. This procedure can be used to improve the smoothness for each region's boundary. Specifically, if they are surrounded by pixels within the same seeded region, they should be grown into this region no matter what seed they are labelled by their distance calculation.

4 Experiments and Conclusions

The proposed automatic seeded region growing algorithm is implemented by software in Matlab and tested by using five test videos (Mother and daughter, Silent, Seaman, Talking and Wedding), which are publicly available. The test sequences are in YUV format and their frame size is 144×176. Figure-3 illustrates the experimental results achieved by the proposed region-grow algorithm.

In order to compare the performance of our proposed algorithm with the existing research in relevant areas, we implemented the semi-automatic region growing algorithm reported in [15] as our benchmark. For specific implementation, we manually selected two seeded regions: one for the foreground and the other for background. The size of the seeded region is a window of 8×8. The first three results of [15] are shown in Figure-4.

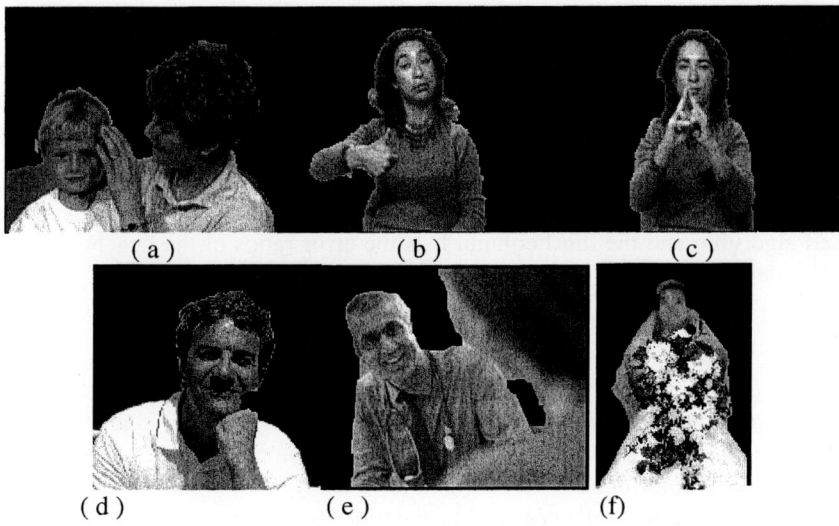

Fig. 3. Results of our proposed algorithm. (a) "Mother and daughter" frame 80. (b) "Silent" frame 60. (c) "Silent" frame 229. (d) 'Seaman' No. 39, 'Talking' No 25, and 'Wedding' No. 23.

In both Fig.3 and Fig.4, the segmented object area is represented as the non-black and the black area is treated as the background region. Compared with the results of the existing seeded region growing, which involves manual selection of initial seeds, as shown in Fig 4, the accuracy of the object area in the proposed algorithm shown in Fig 3 is seen to be improved, and the object boundary is also smoothed, although there still exist some parts of the pixels, which are either over-segmented or under-segmented.

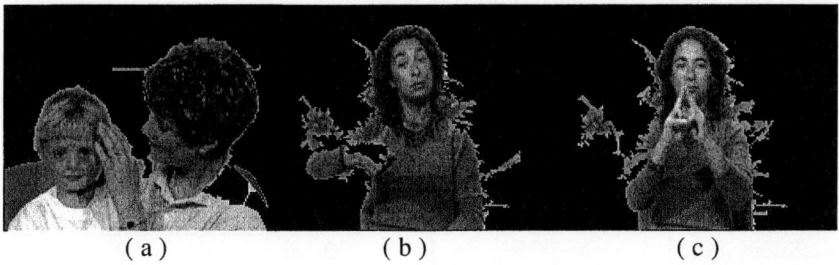

Fig. 4. The results of SRG. (a) "mother and daughter" frame 80. (b) "silent" frame 60. (c) "silent" frame 229.

In addition, we also applied a simple pixel-based quality measurement algorithm [19] to compare our results with that achieved by benchmark [15]. The quality measurement uses the spatial distortion of an estimated binary video object mask to get the error ratio. The smaller the ratio, the better the results achieved. The measurement is defined as follows:

$$d(O_n^{est}, O_n^{ref}) = \frac{\sum_{(x,y)} O_n^{est}(x,y) \oplus O_n^{ref}(x,y)}{\sum_{(x,y)} O_n^{ref}(x,y)} \quad (4)$$

Where $O_n^{est}(x,y)$ and $O_n^{ref}(x,y)$ represents the estimated and reference binary object masks at frame n, and $\oplus$ means binary 'XOR' operation. The comparative results are listed in Table 1, where the second column lists the error ratios of our proposed algorithm and the third column lists the error ratios of the benchmark reported in [15] and [6].

5 Conclusions

In this paper, we proposed an automatic seeded region growing algorithm to extract video objects from MPEG compressed videos. In comparison with existing research in this area, our contribution can be highlighted as: (i) we introduced a neural network to carry out an initial segmentation in compressed domain (block-based segmentation). This technique enables the proposed algorithm to select seeds for region-grow at locations where texture consistency is guaranteed; (ii) via the initial block-based segmentation, we propose an automatic seeded region growing for semantic object segmentation. On one hand, existing region-grow is often semi-automatic, on the other, the initial segmentation enables the proposed algorithm to select seeds across the boundaries of different regions, and thus achieve certain level of bridging the gap between low-level segmentation and high-level object segmentation. Experiments benchmarked by the representative existing research support that our proposed algorithm is effective towards semantic video object segmentation, and achieves some improvement upon the existing research. From the details of the algorithm design, it can be seen that the proposed algorithm is rapid, robust, self-contained, and easy-to-use without involving any intervention from users.

Table 1. Error ratio evaluation of the proposed algorithm compared with the benchmark reported in [15] and [6]

	Our proposed algorithm	Algorithm in [15]	Algorithm in [6]
Silent_80	1.79	2.58	2.15
Silent_229	2.03	3.11	2.03
Mother and daughter	1.52	2.76	2.33
Talking	3.53	5.65	3.05
seaman	3.21	3.21	3.15
Wedding	2.29	2.29	2.16

References

1. Cheng, S. C, 'Region-growing approach to colour segmentation using 3D clustering and relaxation labeling'; Vision, Image and Signal Processing, IEE Pro. 150(4) 270- 276
2. Y. L. Chang, X. B. Li; 'Adaptive image region-growing'; IEEE transactions on image processing. Vol. 3. No 6. Nov.
3. S. Chien, Y. Huang, L. Chen; Predictive watershed: a fast watershed algorithm for video segmentation; IEEE trans. on circuits and systems for video technology, 13(5). May 2003
4. Moscheni. F, Bhattacharjee, S., Kunt, M. "Spatiotemporal segmentation based on region merging". IEEE Trans. Pattern Anal. Mach. Intell. 20, 89-915.
5. C. M. Kuo, C. H. Hsieh, and Y. R. Huang, "Automatic extraction of moving objects for head-shoulder video sequence", J. Vision. Communication. Image R.xxx (2004) xxx-xxx
6. C. Kim, J. Hwang; 'Fast and automatic video object segmentation and tracking for content-based applications', IEEE trans on circuits and systems for video technology, 12(2) Feb. 2oo2.
7. Salgado, L.; Garcia, N.; Menendez, J.M.; Rendon, E.; Efficient image segmentation for region-based motion estimation and compensation, Circuits and Systems for Video Technology, IEEE Transactions on , Vol 10(7), Oct. 2000, 1029 – 1039
8. H. Liu; Yun, D. Y. Y.;' Segmentation-based vector quantization of images by a competitive learning neural network', Singapore ICCS/ISITA '92. 'Communications on the Move', 16-20 Nov. 1992 vol.1 350 – 354.
9. Haralick R. M. and Shapiro L.G., Computer and Robot Vision, Reading, 1992, 525-540.
10. W. Y. Ma, B. S. Manjunath; 'Edge Flow: A technique for boundary detection and image segmentation'; IEEE transactions on image processing, VOL. 9, NO.8, August 2000.
11. A. Mehnert, P. Jackway; 'An improved seeded region growing algorithm'; Pattern Recognition Letters 18(1997) 1065-1071.
12. M. D. G. Montoya, C. Gil, I.Garcia; 'The load unbalancing problem for region growing image segmentation algorithms'; J. Parallel Distrib. Computer. 63(2003) 387-395.
13. Hotter, M; 'Object-oriented analysis-synthesis coding based on moving two-dimensional object'; Signal Process: Image Commun. 2, 409–428.
14. Diehl, N. "Object-oriented motion estimation and segmentation in image sequences". Signal Process: Image Commun. 3, 23–56.
15. Adams R. and Bischof L; "Seeded region growing", IEEE Trans. Pattern Anal. Machine Intell, vol.16, no.6, 1994, 641-647.
16. C. Revol, M. Jourlin; 'A new minimum variance region growing algorithm for image segmentation'; Pattern Recognition Letters 18(1997) 249-258.
17. E. Sifakis; I. Grinials; G. Tziritas; 'Video Segmentation Using Fast Marching and Region Growing Algorithms'; EURASIP journal on applied signal processing 2002: 4, 379-388.
18. S. W. ZUCKER, "Region growing: childhood and adolescence," Computer Graph. Image process, vol. 5, pp.382-399, 1976.
19. C. Kim and J.-N. Hwang, "Fast and robust moving object segmentation in video sequences," in Proc. Int. Conf. Image Processing (ICIP'99), vol. 2, Kobe, Japan, Oct. 1999, pp. 131–134.

Object Coding for Real Time Image Processing Applications

Asif Masood and Shaiq A. Haq

Department of Computer Science and Engineering, University of Engineering and Technology, Lahore, Pakistan
asif_phd@hotmail.com, sh@shaiq.com

Abstract. This paper presents an object coding scheme based on varying Bezier polynomials between cubics, quadratics and linears. Extracted data points, without any other overhead, are the end product of this scheme which form set of Bezier control points. Corner detection as a preprocessing phase simplifies subsequent coding operation and properties of Bezier splines are exploited to extract final data points. The proposed method results in high data reduction without any compromise to the quality of reconstructed shapes. The coding scheme is suitable for real time image processing applications due to its high compression ratio, efficient and accurate representation of given shapes.

1 Introduction

Computers are the efficient and error free solution to many problems. Demand for computer based applications/processing has immensely increased in last two decades. Computers play an important role in image processing as well. Due to heavy image sizes, real time processing of images and videos had always been a difficult task. An efficient coding/representation of images is one solution to this problem and it has become an important area of research today. Object-based description of images especially for processing videos is quite natural where an actor is filmed in front of a blue screen and then moved in front of any desired background. Different objects in an image can be represented by its boundary [1-2] or by the interior of shape [3-4]. In boundary representation texture of an object is eliminated. This representation is more efficient and still preserves the complete shape of an object. Shape boundaries are not efficient enough to be used for real time applications and need some coding.

Researchers have proposed various coding schemes for an efficient representation of boundaries. One of the first coding was chain coding [5]. Chain codes describe an object by a sequence of unit-size line segments with a given orientation. It has attracted considerable attention over last 30 years [6-9]. There have been many extensions to this basic scheme such as generalized chain codes [6], where the coding efficiency has been improved with the use of links of different length and different angular resolution. Linear approximation or polygonal approximation [10-13] is another coding method, in which the data points (also called dominant points) considerably reduce, at the cost of some approximation error or distortion. Recently proposed algorithms [12-13] may represent the object by about $1/5^{th}$ of the total boundary points depending upon the shape of an object. For circular shapes the number of dominant points and associated distortion may considerably increase.

Boundaries can be represented more efficiently with various spline curves. This involves finding the location of control points by minimizing approximation error. Researchers have introduced various curve approximation techniques using different spline models like B-splines [14], Hermite interpolation [15] and rational cubic interpolation [16]. This is very efficient representation but may cause extra smoothing of boundary, especially at its corner positions [17]. In this paper we present a coding scheme with Bezier splines which is an improvement to the existing methods and it causes high reduction of data points while preserving the original shape of object.

Rest of the paper is organized as follow. Section 2 describes the proposed framework in which the original contributions are highlighted. The coding scheme is applied in two phases namely object segmentation and data point extraction which are explained in section 3 and 4 respectively. Results are demonstrated in section 5 and section 6 concludes this presentation.

2 Proposed Framework

The proposed algorithm is designed to code real objects which can be of varying shapes and design. A simple curve approximation technique may not be able to preserve the original shape accurately. Therefore, our coding scheme consists of two phases. In phase 1, initial characteristic points are detected using some corner detection algorithm [19-22]. Corners are the robust features that provide important information of objects. Precise detection of corner points plays an important role for accurate and efficient coding of objects. After corner detection objects are decomposed into segments at those corner points. Each segment is then processed by phase 2 of proposed coding scheme.

In phase 2, suitable data points for each segment are extracted. Processing of these segments is completely independent from each other, thus parallel processing can speed up the process. We use curve approximation with Bezier curve to find the ultimate data points which form control points of approximating piecewise Bezier spline. Most of the proposed curve approximation techniques are based on finding interpolating data points along the original curve [24-28]. Such algorithms are easy to implement but high reduction in data points can result if the data points are allowed to deviate away from the target curve [29]. This technique is presented in this paper. We have gone even one step ahead in proposed coding scheme where the polynomial of approximating curve is adjusted according to given segments, in which first, second and third order polynomial can be used i;e., approximation with straight lines, quadratics and cubics. During the process any segment can be decomposed into subsegments and different Bezier polynomial can be applied on each subsegment. The proposed scheme results in high data reduction (upto $1/25^{th}$ of object boundary) without compromising to the quality of resultant shape. Approximating curve segments through these data points are stitched together to attain the ultimate shape of object. The coding scheme is presented in next two sections.

3 Object Segmentation

Object coding can be very expensive operation and lack in accuracy if applied directly to the complete shape. Corner detection process can avoid extra smoothing of objects and preserve the original shape especially at its sharp corner. Objects are decomposed into segments from their natural break points (corners) as a preprocessing step. Corner detectors can efficiently mark these break points in an object.

Authors have presented various corner detection algorithms [19-22] and we use SAM04 algorithm [19] for detection of corner points. This is an efficient algorithm which can accurately mark corners of an object. The algorithm is briefly described here. Readers are referred to [19] for details. It works in two passes. In first pass, perpendicular distance of all contour points between P_i and P_k are calculated from the straight line joining these contour points. For any contour point P_i, $1 \leq i \leq n$ where n is the number of points in a closed loop, P_k is calculated as:

```
If      (i+L) ≤ n
Then    P_k = P_{i+L}
Else    P_k = P_{(i+L)-n}
```

L is a length parameter which takes care of object scaling and resolution. Default value of L is 14. Point P_j is the point with maximum perpendicular distance. P_j is selected as a candidate corner point if its perpendicular distance (d_j) is greater than parameter D and the distance d_j is assigned to P_j. Distance parameter D checks the local sharpness and opening angle of corners. It also controls the wrong selection of corners due to noise and other irregularities. Default value of D is 2.6. The perpendicular distance d_j from point $P_j(x,y)$ to the straight line joining the point $P_i(x,y)$ and $P_k(x,y)$ can be calculated as:

```
If       m_x = 0
Then     d_j = |P_{j,x} - P_{i,x}|

Else     m = m_y / m_x = (P_{k,y} - P_{i,y}) / (P_{k,x} - P_{i,x})

Where    m = m_y / m_x = (P_{k,y} - P_{i,y}) / (P_{k,x} - P_{i,x})
```

Next candidate corner point is detected for a new straight line by incrementing both i and k. The process continues for $i=1$ to n. Higher value of d_j is assigned to P_j if more than one straight line may respond to same corner P_j. Superfluous corners are discarded in second pass. The candidate corner is superfluous if any other candidate with higher value of d_j is in the range R. For any candidate corner point to live, it must be the strongest corner (highest value of d_j) among the R number of points on its both sides. Default value of R is equal to L but it must be given lower value to enable detection of closely located corners.

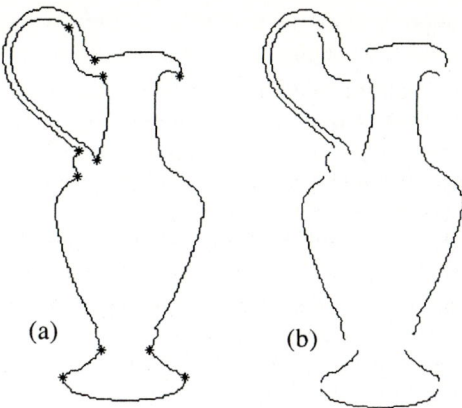

Fig. 1. Object segmentation. (a) An object (Shape of jug) marked with corner points. (b) After segmentation from detected corner points.

Corner points are detected from an object and it is then broken into segments from those corner points. The object is processed segment-wise in next phase of shape coding. Fig 1 shows the result of object segmentation using SAM04 [19] algorithm. Fig 1a is the object marked with detected corner points and fig 1b is the object after segmentation. Processing for data point extraction on each segment is independent of other segments therefore parallel processing can speed-up the remaining process.

4 Data Points Extraction

In this phase of object coding, data points are extracted for a given segment of an object using Bezier splines [18]. Bezier splines are the approximating curves and have number of properties like simple, easy and efficient implementation, which make them highly useful and convenient for object coding. In general, a Bezier curve section can be fitted to any number of control points, which determine the degree of its polynomial. For $n+1$ control points represented with $p_k = (x_k, y_k)$, with k varying from 0 to n, the position vector $P(u)$ along the Bezier curve describes the path between p_0 and p_n, which can be given as:

$$P(u) = \sum_{k=0}^{n} p_k BEZ_{k,n}(u), \quad 0 \leq u \leq 1 \tag{1}$$

The Bezier blending functions $BEZ_{k,n}(u)$ are the bernstein polynomials [23]:

$$BEZ_{k,n}(u) = C(n,k) u^k (1-u)^{n-k} \tag{2}$$

where $C(n,k)$ are the binomial coefficients:

$$C(n,k) = \frac{n!}{k!(n-k)!} \tag{3}$$

The above implementation is used to calculate an approximating Bezier curve through given control points. For segment coding, we need to perform a reverse operation i;e., to find Bezier control points for a given segment such that a Bezier curve through them is a replica of given segment. These control points would form the data points of that curve.

Control points from a given segment can be evaluated by exploiting the properties of Bezier curves. The extracted data points would be the control points of approximating cubic, quadratic or linear Bezier curves. For cubics, Bezier curve would require four control points (p_0, p_1, p_2, p_3). Among them two control points (p_0, p_3) are the segment endpoints and other two (p_1, p_2) are to be searched, which lies along the tangents (T_1 & T_2) of a segments at its endpoints. To optimize the search algorithm, it is implemented in two phases. Phase 1 is very efficient but determines an approximate location of control points. Positions of these control points are refined in phase 2 which is relatively slow but accurate.

Search for the control points P_1 & P_2 starts from the control points P_0 & P_3 respectively. These control points are searched along the tangent lines T_1 & T_2. Control points P_1 & P_2 are moved, along their respective tangents, one after another and approximation error (AE) is minimized. Each control point can move in any direction, along its tangent, if it causes reduction in overall approximation error (AE). The process continues till P_1 or P_2 stop moving. At this point AE will minimize. The algorithm for search of control points (P_1 & P_2) is given as:

```
1. P₁ = P₀
2. P₂ = P₃
3. Calculate M₁ and M₂
4. Calculate AE
5. Do   P₁ = P₁ ± M₁    While(AE reduces)
6. Do   P₂ = P₂ ± M₂    While(AE reduces)
7. Repeat step 5 and 6 till P₁ or P₂ stop changing
```

In above algorithm M_1 & M_2 represents one step movement for control points P_1 & P_2 respectively. The same algorithm in run in both phase 1 and phase 2 of control points search, the difference lies only in the computation of AE, M_1 and M_2. Approximation error (AE) is the distance between two curves i;e., original and computed curve. Computed curve is the cubic Bezier curve computed with current position of control points. In phase 1, AE is the accumulated distance between two curves at five equally separated points along the curve. In phase 2, AE is the total area between two curves i;e., accumulated distance of all the points. One step movement for phase 1 and phase 2 can be computed as :

$$M_1 = C_w - C_0$$
$$M_2 = C_{n-w} - C_n$$

Where C_0 and C_n is the first and last point of the given curve and w is the window size. Value of w is 1 for smooth curves but it must be given higher value for non-smooth or irregular curves (object outlines). The algorithm is separated in two phases to optimize the control point search. Phase 1 is computationally very efficient but looks for an approximate location of control points P_1 and P_2. Fig 2a shows approximating curve after phase 1. Phase 2 is an expensive operation but require slight adjust of control points. Fig 2b shows approximating curve after phase 2. It can be observed that approximating curve get close to given segment in phase 1 and covers the target segment very accurately after phase 2.

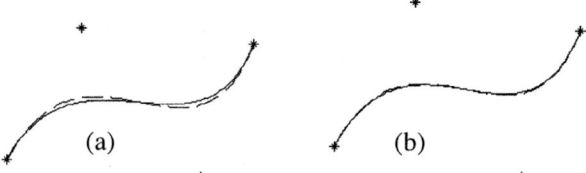

Fig. 2. Extracted data point (cubic Bezier control points) their respective curve drawn over a given segment (dashed line). (a) After Phase 1. (b) After Phase 2.

The approximating Bezier curve will introduce some AE. If this max value of AE at any point along the curve is beyond specified threshold error limits (default limit is 2 pixels) then the segment is recursively decomposed into subsegments at maximum error point. Each subsegment is then processed for data point extraction again. This process will continue till all segments are within threshold error limit. Fig. 3 shows segment before and after segment subdivision.

Fig. 3. Segment subdivision. (a) Before segment subdivision. (b) After Segment Subdivision.

Segments, which are already under threshold error limits, are also tested for lower polynomial approximations (quadratic and linear). Data points with lowest possible polynomial, without causing any further decomposition of segments, are finally assigned to the segment. Calculation of quadratic Bezier control points (p_0, p_1, p_2) is a simple procedure. Among them (p_0, p_2) are the segment endpoints and p_1 lies at the intersection point of segment tangents (T_1 & T_2). Similarly a linear Bezier would be the straight line between two endpoints which are Bezier control points (p_0 & p_1).

5 Result Demonstration

Data points are the end product of this coding scheme, which are actually the control points of piecewise Bezier splines. These data points completely represent the actual object which can be reconstructed any time through a piecewise Bezier spline approximating these data points. Any operation (like transformation, scaling, rotation and shearing etc) on these data points results in transformation of complete shape.

The proposed coding scheme results in high data reduction without making any significant compromise to the quality of reconstructed shape. Authors have introduced various quantitative parameters (like integral square error or maximum error) to estimate the accuracy of reconstructed shape. These quantitative parameters generally ignore difference of shapes at high curvature points and other critical areas of an object. Therefore human judgment, of reconstructed shapes, by visual appearance is always rated very high. Results of two shapes are demonstrated in fig 4&5.

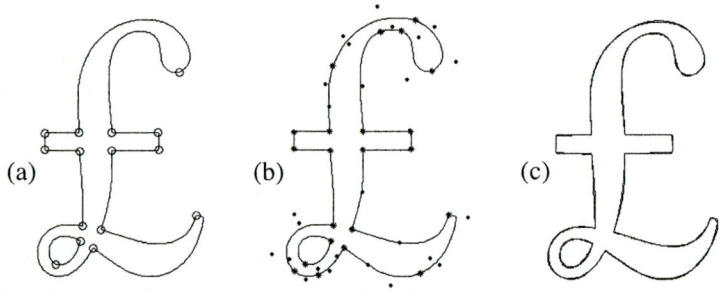

Fig. 4. Results of object coding. (a) Original shape marked with corner points. (b) Original shape marked with complete set of data points. (c) Reconstructed shape drawn over original.

Coding results for an object (£) are demonstrated in fig 4. Original shape marked with detected corner points, using SAM04 [19], are shown on fig 4a. Complete set of detected data points are shown in fig 4b. Segment endpoints are shown with asterisks (*) and their intermediate control points are marked with dots (·). Each segment is represented by either two, three or four data points, depending upon the Bezier polynomial suited for that segment. Table 1 lists the number of linear, quadratic and cubic data segments finalized for this shape. The original shape was distributed into 23 segments at the detected corner and subdivision points. Distribution of segments were 12, 4 & 7 cubics, quadratics and linears respectively. The complete shape is represented with just 50 data points.

The coding of object (£) achieve compression ratio (CR) of 24.94, where CR is ratio between total number of boundary points to the number of data points. Generally, the CR value of polynomial approximation algorithms [12-13] ranges from 4 to 6 depending upon shape. Representation of object boundaries, with spline curves, normally involves various overheads in the form of control parameters. That's why inspite of low quality representation and lower CR value, polynomial approximation is sometimes preferred over curve approximation. In presented technique, no overhead or control parameters are involved. Therefore, a simple Bezier curve through detected data points can very accurately reconstruct the object boundary. For the shape of character pound (£) computed boundary is drawn over original for an easy comparison in fig 4c. One can hardly find it deviating away from original shape.

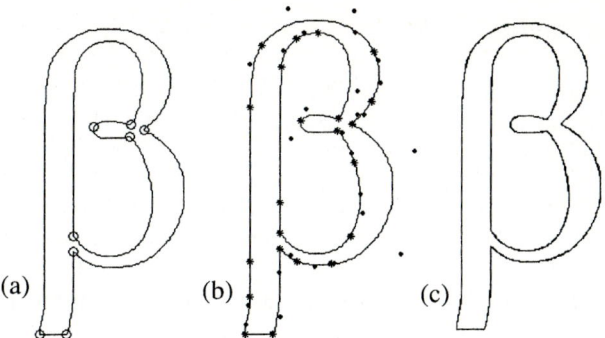

Fig. 5. Results of object coding. (a) Original shape marked with corner points. (b) Original shape marked with complete set of data points. (c) Reconstructed shape drawn over original.

Result for another shape (β) is demonstrated in fig 5. Boundary marked with corner points is shown in fig 5a. The detected data points are shown in fig 5b. Accuracy of this shape is also similar to fig 4. Outcome of its coding, results in 53 data points. Among 23 segments of this shape just 4 are the linear due to the type of shape. Note that CR for this shape is even higher than previous one. Reconstructed shape in fig 5c also covers the original boundary very accurately.

Table 1. Quantitative details of reconstructed shapes of fig 4 & 5

Shape	Segments				D Pts	B Pts	CR
	Linear	Quad	Cubic	Total			
£	7	4	12	23	50	1247	24.9
β	4	7	12	23	53	1536	29

6 Conclusion

An object coding scheme based on Bezier curves is presented in this paper. Corner detection, as a preprocessing phase, simplifies the coding process and plays major role in preserving the original shape of an object. The proposed scheme has obvious advantages over previously presented similar techniques which are as follow. Data points are the approximation points rather than simple interpolants and approximation points highly reduce the set of data points. Bezier curve with varying polynomials causes even further reduction of these data points. Detected data points, without any overhead, can represent the shape completely. Therefore a traditional Bezier curve through these data points can very accurately reconstruct the boundary of an object. Authors feel that compression ratio in this technique can further improve by introducing some intelligence to the recursive subdivision method of section 4.

Acknowledgements

First author acknowledges the Higher Education Commission (HEC) of Pakistan for providing funds and University of Engineering and Technology (UET) Lahore for facilitating this research work.

References

1. Kartikeyan B., Sarkar A.: Shape description by time series. IEEE trans. on PAMI, 11 (1989) 977-984.
2. Kashyap R., Dhellapa R.: Stochastic models for closed boundary analysis: Representation and reconstruction. IEEE trans. on information theory, 27 (1981) 627-637.
3. Blum H.: A transformation for extracting new descriptors of the shape. In Whaten-Dunn, editor, Models of the Perception of Speech and Visual Forms, MIT Press (1967) 362-380.
4. Koenderink J.J., van Doorn A.J.: The internal representation of solid shape with respect to vision. Biol. Cyber, 32 (1979) 211-216.
5. Freeman H.: On the Encoding of Arbitrary Geometric Configurations. IEEE Transactions on Elec. Computer, 10 (1961) 260-268.
6. Saghri J., Freeman H.: Analysis of the precision of generalized chain codes for the representation of planar curves. IEEE Trans.PAMI, 3 (1981) 533-539.
7. Koplowitz J.: On the performance of chain codes for quantization of the line drawings. IEEE Trans. On PAMI, 3 (1981) 180-185.
8. Neuhoff D., Castor K.: A rate and distortion analysis of chain codes for line drawings. IEEE Trans on info. theory, 31 (1985) 53-68.
9. Kaneko T., Okudaira M.: Encoding of arbitrary curves based on the chain code representation. IEEE Trans on Comm, 33 (1985) 697-707.
10. Cronin T.M.: A boundary concavity code to support dominant points detection. Pattern Recognition Lett. 20 (1999) 617-634.
11. Ray B.K., Ray K.S.: Detection of significant points and polygonal approximation of digital curves. Pattern Recognition Lett. 13 (1992) 443-452.
12. Marji M., Siy P.: A new algorithm for dominant points detection and polygonization of digital curves. Pattern Recognition 36 (2003) 2239-2251.
13. Sarfraz M., Asim M.R., Masood A.: Piecewise polygonal approximation of digital curves. Proc. of 8th IEEE International Conference on Information Visualisation, IEEE Computer Society Press, USA, (2004) 991 – 996.
14. Hölzle G.E.: Knot placement for piecewise polynomial approximation of curves. Computer Aided Design, 15(5) (1983) 295-296.
15. Sarfraz M., Razzak M.F.A.: An algorithm for automatic capturing of font outlines. Journal of Computers & Graphics, Elsevier Science, 26(5) (2002) 795-804.
16. Sarfraz M., Khan M.: Towards automation of capturing outlines of Arabic fonts. Proc. of the Third KFUPM Workshop on Information and Computer Science: Software Development for the New Millennium, Saudi Arabia, (2000) 83-98.
17. Sarfraz M.: Some algorithms for curve design and automatic outline capturing of images. Int. J. Image Graphics 4(2) (2004) 301-324.
18. Bezier P.: Mathematical and practical possibilities of UNISURF in Barnhill. Computer Aided Geometric Design. Academic Press, New York, (1974).
19. Sarfraz M., Masood A., Asim M.R.: A new approach to corner detection. Proc. of International Conference on Computer Vision and Graphics (2004).

20. Chetverikov D, Szabo Z.: A simple and efficient algorithm for detection of high curvature points in planner curves. Proc. 23rd workshop of Australian Pattern Recognition Group, Steyr, (1999) 175-184.
21. Beus H.L., Tiu S.S.H.: An improved corner detection algorithm based on chain coded plane curves. Pattern Recognition, 20 (1987) 291-296.
22. Rosenfeld A., Weszka J.S.: An improved method of angle detection on digital curves. IEEE Trans. Computer, 24 (1975) 940-941.
23. Hearn D., Baker M.P.: Computer Graphics, Prentice Hall publication (1997).
24. Saux, E., Daniel M.: Data reduction of polynomial curves using B-splines. Computer-Aided Design, 31,8 (1999), 507-515.
25. Lyche T., Morken K.: A Data-reduction strategy for splines with applications to the approximation of functions and data. IMA Journal of Numerical Analysis. 8 (1988), 185-208.
26. Hamann B., Chen J.L.: Data point selection for piecewise linear curve approximation. Computer-Aided Design 25,11 (1993), 699-710.
27. Razdan A.: Knot placement for B-spline curve approximation. Technical Report, Arizona State University, (1999).
28. Lu F., Milios E.: Optimal spline fitting to planar shape. Signal Process 37 (1994) 129-140.
29. Masood A., Sarfraz M.: Cubic Bezier approximation for capturing outlines of 2D objects. accepted for publication in the Proc. of 1st International Conference on Geometric Modeling, Visualization & Graphics in conjunction with 8th Joint Conference on Information Sciences, USA (2005).

Designing a Fast Convolution Under the LIP Paradigm Applied to Edge Detection

José M. Palomares[1], Jesús González[2], and Eduardo Ros[2]

[1] Department of Electrotechnics and Electronics,
Escuela Politécnica Superior, University of Cordoba,
E.14071, Cordoba, Spain
[2] Department of Computer Architecture and Computer Technology,
E.T.S. Ingeniería Informática, University of Granada
E.18071, Granada, Spain

Abstract. The *Logarithmic Image Processing* model (LIP) is a robust mathematical framework for the processing of transmitted and reflected images. It follows many visual, physical and psychophysical laws. This works presents a new formulation of a 2D–convolution of separable kernels using the LIP paradigm. A previously stated LIP–Sobel edge detector is redefined with the new proposed formulation, and the performance of the edge detectors programmed following the two formulations (the previous one and the new one proposed) is compared. Another operator, Laplacian of Gaussian, is also stated under the LIP paradigm. The experiments show that both methods obtain same results although our proposed method is much faster than the previous one.

1 Introduction

Many image processing methods involve linear operations between two or more images, producing a resulting new image. These operations can be simple ones, such as, addition, subtraction, multiplication, etc., or much more complex ones. Some problems may arise, for example, in the addition of two images. Within the real world, this operation produces a new image which is also visible to the human eye; however, due to the limited bit–depth in conventional representation standards, the addition of two images can produce "out–of–range" problems, because when two images are digitally added, it is possible to obtain a value above the maximum value allowed (for example, with 8 bits of bit–depth, maximum value would be 255).

The *Logarithmic Image Processing* (usually called LIP) is a technique initially stated by Pinoli and Jourlin [1, 2] in late 1980's to deal with transmitted images obtained from microscopy and later, further developed by Deng et al. [3]. This framework follows many laws of the human vision system, both physical and psychophysical (i.e. *Fechner's law*, *Weber's law*, etc.). LIP is considered to be a good choice, better than other models [4], because it is at the same time mathematically well–justified, physically consistent, psychophysically coherent with higher primates visual system, and computationally affordable. Furthermore, any technique is suitable to be adapted to work under this methodology, usually obtaining better results. Deng and Pinoli [5] showed the effectiveness and applicability of LIP to the edge detection field. They used LIP to state an operator called *LIP–Sobel*. Although they did not describe explicitly the procedure to create any generic filter, it is easy to abstract a generic methodology to be able to design filters under the LIP paradigm.

In this contribution, we focus on the convolution, which is a mathematical tool used to compute the response of a given signal to a given impulse. New images are obtained taking into account context (causal) information. This operation is computationally expensive and, in many cases, it becomes a bottleneck that limits the system performance. Our aim is to provide a formulation of a convolution under the LIP model for image processing. We will focus specifically in the 2D–convolutions which make use of separable kernels, because this kind of operators is one of the most common in the image processing field.

2 Brief Outline of LIP

There are two possible ways to apply LIP philosophy to any image processing technique: to use the "original" images with some special operators, or to work with "transformed" images applying the usual operators. The first option is produced by means of an algebraic vectorial space defined by a set of image values (usually named, *grey tone functions* or simply *grey tone*) which are the "usual" images with an inversion of the scale. We will notate *grey tone* of f as $\widehat{f} = M - f$, where f is the original image and M the (unreachable) maximum value allowed. In this framework, a special sum operator ($\triangle$), a new scalar multiplication operator ($\triangle$), and a new subtraction ($\triangle$) are also defined. Based on these, further operators have been proposed, for example, a LIP–Summatory has been defined as:

$$\bigtriangleup_{i=1}^{n} \widehat{f_i} = \widehat{f_1} \triangle \widehat{f_2} \triangle \ldots \triangle \widehat{f_n}, \tag{1}$$

where $\widehat{f_i}$ $(i = 1 \ldots n)$ are n different *grey tone functions*.

The second option is to transform the image, afterwards, to work using the "usual" operators, and finally, to restore the resulting image to the original space by the inverse of the transforming function. The transformation is done using a function called *isomorphic transformation* defined by:

$$\widetilde{f} = \varphi(\widehat{f}) = -M \cdot \ln\left(1 - \frac{\widehat{f}}{M}\right), \tag{2}$$

The transformed *grey tone functions* will be notated $\widetilde{f}$. The inverse of the transforming function (called *inverse isomorphic transformation*) is:

$$\widehat{f} = \varphi^{-1}(\widetilde{f}) = M \cdot \left(1 - e^{-\frac{\widetilde{f}}{M}}\right), \tag{3}$$

3 LIP 2D-Convolution with Separable Kernels

In this section, a mathematical description of a 2D convolution will be introduced. We will focus on a convolution with a separable kernel, that is, given a 2D filter, F, which is separable, where $F = \mathbf{a}^T \times \mathbf{b}$. Let $\mathbf{a}$ and $\mathbf{b}$ be two row vectors, then:

$$\operatorname{conv2D}(I, F) = \operatorname{conv1D}(\operatorname{conv1D}(I, \mathbf{a}^T), \mathbf{b}) = \sum_{i=0}^{n-1} \left(\mathbf{b}(n{-}i) \cdot \left(\sum_{j=0}^{m-1} \mathbf{a}(m{-}j) \cdot I_{(i+1, j+1)} \right) \right) \quad (4)$$

We are willing to compute the LIP version of the 2D-convolution of Eq. 4:

$$\operatorname{conv2D}_{\mathrm{LIP}}(\widehat{I}, F) = \mathop{\triangle}\limits_{i=0}^{n-1} \mathbf{b}(n{-}i) \,\triangle\, \left(\mathop{\triangle}\limits_{j=0}^{m-1} \mathbf{a}(m{-}j) \,\triangle\, \widehat{I}_{(i+1, j+1)} \right)$$

which could be computed using the isomorphic transformation shown in Eq. 2:

$$\varphi\!\left(\operatorname{conv2D}_{\mathrm{LIP}}(\widehat{I}, F)\right) = \sum_{i=0}^{n-1} \mathbf{b}(n{-}i) \cdot \left(\sum_{j=0}^{m-1} \mathbf{a}(m{-}j) \cdot \varphi\!\left(\widehat{I}_{(i+1, j+1)}\right) \right) =$$

$$= \sum_{i=0}^{n-1} \mathbf{b}(n{-}i) \cdot \left(\sum_{j=0}^{m-1} \mathbf{a}(m{-}j) \cdot \left(-M \cdot \ln\!\left(\frac{M - \widehat{I}_{(i+1, j+1)}}{M} \right) \right) \right) \quad (5)$$

If we rename $\left(M - \widehat{I}_{(i+1, j+1)}\right)$ as $I_{(i+1, j+1)}$, and let us make $K = \ln(M) \cdot \sum_{j=0}^{m-1} \mathbf{a}(m{-}j) \cdot \sum_{i=0}^{n-1} \mathbf{b}(n{-}i)$, we further simplify Eq. 5:

$$\varphi\!\left(\operatorname{conv2D}_{\mathrm{LIP}}(\widehat{I}, F)\right) = -M \cdot \left[\sum_{i=0}^{n-1} \mathbf{b}(n{-}i) \left(\sum_{j=0}^{m-1} \mathbf{a}(m{-}j) \cdot \ln(I_{(i+1, j+1)}) \right) - K \right] =$$

$$= M \cdot \left(K - \operatorname{conv1D}\!\left(\operatorname{conv1D}(\ln I, \mathbf{a}^T), \mathbf{b}\right) \right) \quad (6)$$

Finally, applying the inverse isomorphic transformation (Eq. 3) to the Eq. 6:

$$\operatorname{conv2D}_{\mathrm{LIP}}(\widehat{I}, F) = \varphi^{-1}\!\left(\varphi\!\left(\operatorname{conv2D}_{\mathrm{LIP}}(\widehat{I}, F)\right) \right)$$

$$= M \cdot \left(1 - e^{\operatorname{conv1D}\left(\operatorname{conv1D}(\ln I, \mathbf{a}^T), \mathbf{b}\right) - K} \right). \quad (7)$$

4 Application of the *LIP-Convolution*

After having stated a new formulation of the convolution under LIP paradigm, we will show its effectiveness in a pair of particular image processing applications. The *Sobel* and the *Laplacian of Gaussian* edge detectors will be redefined under the LIP paradigm and some experiments will be applied to images of two sizes: 512×512 and 256×256 pixels.

4.1 LIP–Sobel

Deng and Pinoli proposed [5] a reformulation of the well–known *Sobel* method using the LIP paradigm. In that case, since they were concerned with a particular filter with concrete values, they could develop an adapted formula, which however, was not general, but specific to that very task. This new method detected edges either in well or poorly lit areas of intensity images, making the detectors more robust and almost illumination invariant.

Authors stated the *LIP–Sobel grey tone **vector***, $\boldsymbol{g} = (g_x, g_y)$, given by:

$$g_x = \left(\widehat{f_1} \triangle \left(2 \triangle \widehat{f_4}\right) \triangle \widehat{f_7}\right) \triangle \left(\widehat{f_3} \triangle \left(2 \triangle \widehat{f_6}\right) \triangle \widehat{f_9}\right) \tag{8}$$

$$g_y = \left(\widehat{f_1} \triangle \left(2 \triangle \widehat{f_2}\right) \triangle \widehat{f_3}\right) \triangle \left(\widehat{f_7} \triangle \left(2 \triangle \widehat{f_8}\right) \triangle \widehat{f_9}\right) \tag{9}$$

Deng and Pinoli [5] define the *LIP–Sobel* by just translating the positive and negative values of the original Sobel filter into $\triangle$ or $\triangle$, respectively. Using the LIP isomorphism $\varphi(\cdot)$ from Eq. 2, we obtain,

$$g_x = M - M\left(\frac{f_3 f_6^2 f_9}{f_1 f_4^2 f_7}\right), \quad g_y = M - M\left(\frac{f_1 f_2^2 f_3}{f_7 f_8^2 f_9}\right) \tag{10}$$

where $f_i = M - \widehat{f_i}$, $i = 1, \ldots, 9$ (Proof in [5]).

To evaluate the LIP–Sobel method, the well–known "peppers" image (shown in Fig. 1.a) has been used. The original image has been darkened progressively from right to left (shown in Fig. 1.b).

LIP–Sobel by Deng & Pinoli's Method. The standard Sobel is applied on the darkened image and the magnitude of the gradient is shown in Fig. 1.c. The LIP–Sobel method as proposed by Deng and Pinoli, stated in Eq. 10, is applied on Fig. 1.b and the resulting magnitude of the gradient of the image is shown in Fig. 1.d. It is to be noted that the edges in the dark regions are not clearly detected in Fig. 1.c, however, in Fig. 1.d the edges in the dark regions are more homogenously detected. This behaviour is a beneficial collateral fact.

LIP–Sobel by the *LIP–Convolution*. The standard Sobel filter is built up by separable filters, obtained by two vectors, $\boldsymbol{a} = [-1, 0, 1]$ and $\boldsymbol{b} = [1, 2, 1]$. In order to obtain the LIP–Sobel using the *LIP–Convolution*, we applied Eq. 7, using $\boldsymbol{a}$ and $\boldsymbol{b}$ as stated previously, to the darkened image (Fig. 1.b). The edges detected by this method are the same as those computed by the method proposed by Deng and Pinoli (See Fig. 1.d); the Mean Squared Error (MSE) is $3.6 \cdot 10^{-13} \pm 4.7 \cdot 10^{-13}$. This is caused by the limited computational precision using floating point variables of simple precision. With those negligible differences, we can state that both methods reach the same result.

4.2 LIP–LoG

In this section, we will show that the LIP–convolution is a general option, and another experiment with a different filter size is applied to a different image.

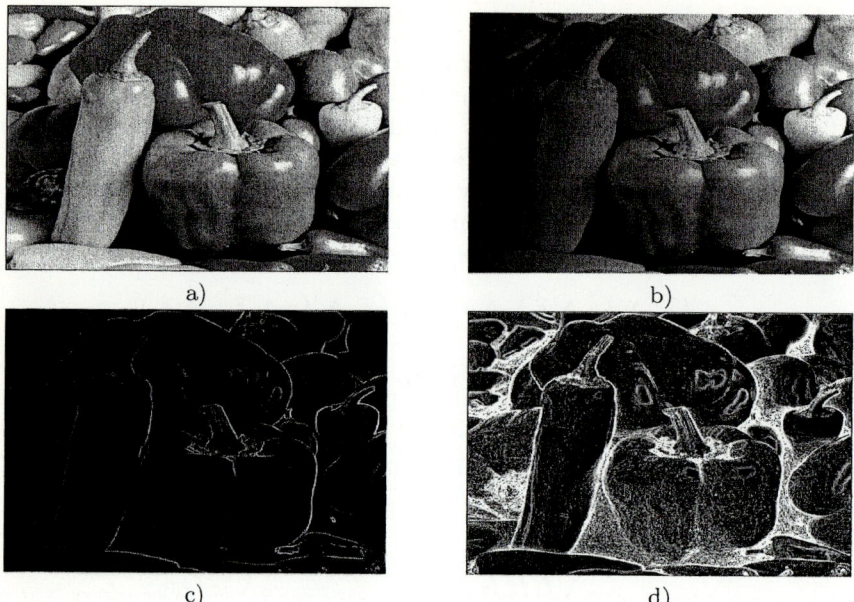

Fig. 1. a) Original 'peppers' image. b) Darkened 'peppers' image. c) Standard Sobel applied on Darkened 'peppers' image. (Magnitude of the gradient). d) LIP–Sobel applied on Darkened 'peppers' image. (Magnitude of the gradient).

Another edge detection filter is the Laplacian of Gaussian, known as LoG. The Laplacian operator is the sum of the second–order unmixed partial derivatives of the image, which, in this case have been previously blurred with a Gaussian mask. The 2D LoG operator is a convolution of a given image with a 2D LoG filter, shown in Eq. 11.

$$LoG(I, \sigma) = \nabla^2 \left\{ \text{conv2D}\left(I, G_\sigma(x, y)\right) \right\} = \text{conv2D}\left(I, \left(\nabla^2 G_\sigma(x, y)\right)\right), \quad (11)$$

where $G_\sigma(x, y)$ stands for the 2D Gaussian function stated in Eq. 15 and $\nabla^2 G(x, y)$ is the sum of the second–order unmixed partial derivatives of $G(x, y)$ shown in Eq. 12.

$$H(x, y) = \nabla^2 G(x, y) = \frac{\partial^2 G(x, y)}{\partial x^2} + \frac{\partial^2 G(x, y)}{\partial y^2} = \frac{x^2 + y^2 - 2\sigma^2}{\sigma^4} e^{-\frac{x^2+y^2}{2\sigma^2}} \quad (12)$$

The Laplacian of Gaussian edge detector is usually implemented using a 2D filter, as it has been stated above, however, the LoG filter has been demonstrated to be separable (see [6] for the demonstration of separability) and that approximation is the one used in this framework, either for the original LoG or for the LIP–LoG by the *Convolution method*. In the implementation of the LIP–LoG using the Deng and Pinoli's methodology, we could not make use of the separable kernels, but of the 2D Laplacian of Gaussian kernel stated in Eq. 12.

The separable formulation of the LoG is shown in Eq. 13:

$$LoG(I,\sigma) = \nabla^2\left\{\text{conv2D}\left(I,G_\sigma\right)\right\} = \text{conv1D}\left(\text{conv1D}\left(I,a_\sigma(x)\right),g_\sigma(y)\right) + $$
$$+ \text{conv1D}\left(\text{conv1D}\left(I,a_\sigma(y)\right),g_\sigma(x)\right) \quad (13)$$

where $G_\sigma(x,y)$ stands for the 2D Gaussian function, $g_\sigma(t)$ stands for the 1D Gaussian function, and $a_\sigma(t)$ is the second–order derivative of a 1D Gaussian function, respectively defined by:

$$G_\sigma(x,y) = \frac{1}{2\pi\sigma^2} e^{-\frac{x^2+y^2}{2\sigma^2}} \quad (14)$$

$$g_\sigma(t) = \frac{1}{\sqrt{2\pi}\sigma} e^{-\frac{t^2}{2\sigma^2}} \quad (15)$$

$$a_\sigma(t) = \frac{\partial^2 G_\sigma(t)}{\partial t^2} \quad (16)$$

In order to use a different filter size than Sobel (which is 3×3), we will use a different size for the LoG filter, i.e. we will take a 7×7 filter. Thus, there exists 49 elements, each one with a different value obtained from the LoG formula in 15. This refers to the size of the Gaussian filter and obviously, of the second–order partial derivatives of it.

Although Deng and Pinoli did not state explicitly a LIP–LoG filter, it is easy to extend the mechanism they used in the LIP–Sobel to deal with this new task. The LIP–LoG formula is given by:

$$LoG_\triangle^{7\times 7}(\widehat{f}) = \bigtriangleup_{i=1}^{7}\bigtriangleup_{j=1}^{7}\left(H(i,j)\triangle\widehat{f}(i,j)\right) \quad (17)$$

which is translated into the formula:

$$LoG_\triangle^{7\times 7}(\widehat{f}) = \prod_{i=1}^{7}\prod_{j=1}^{7}\left(f(i,j)^{H(i,j)}\right), \quad (18)$$

where $H(i,j)$ is the 2D LoG filter defined in Eq. 12 and $f(i,j)$ are each of the 49 different grey tone functions in the image involved in every convolution.

We tested these operators in a new experiment using a different image. The famous "Lenna" image (see Fig. 2.a) has been darkened by means of a horizontal darkening stripe over her eyes (see Fig. 2.b). The standard LoG (with $\sigma = 1.0$) is obtained applying Eq. 11 on the darkened "Lenna" image (see Fig. 2.c).

LIP–Average by Deng & Pinoli's Method. The result image of applying the Eq. 18 with $\sigma = 1.0$ on the darkened image is shown in Fig. 2.d. For both Fig. 2.c and Fig. 2.d, a thresholded zero crossing detector has been applied. The threshold was selected to be the same value in order to compare the accuracy of the detection, but as the intention of this contribution is not the precise selection

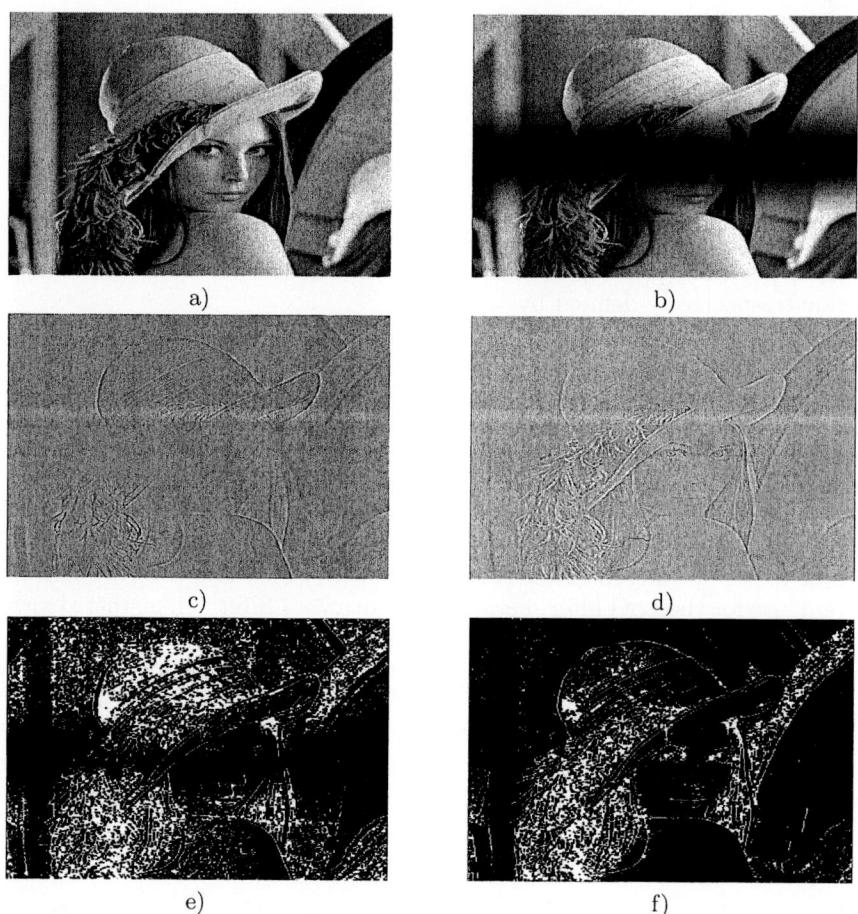

Fig. 2. a) Original 'Lenna' image. b) Darkened 'Lenna' image. c) Standard LoG applied on darkened image. d) LIP–LoG applied on darkened image. e) Thresholded standard LoG applied on darkened image (*threshold=10*). f) Thresholded LIP–LoG applied on darkened image (*threshold=10*).

of the threshold value for each case, it should be taken as an example. In any case, it is easy to observe that the zero crossing slopes in the darkened zone (for example, the eyes) of the image are clearly visible in Fig. 2.f, on the contrary, the borders in Fig. 2.c in the darkened zone of the image are very dull, and thus, in Fig. 2.e all those zero crossings are eliminated because there are very small differences in the slopes.

LIP–LoG by the *LIP–Convolution*. The LoG filter has a size of 7×7 but for the LIP–LoG operator by the *LIP–Convolution* method, we used a separable kernel composed of a pair of 7–element vectors. The first vector, g_σ, holds the values of a 1D Gaussian function with $\sigma = 1.0$ generated by Eq. 16 with $t = [-3, -2, -1, 0, 1, 2, 3]$, the second vector, $\boldsymbol{a_\sigma}$, contains the values obtained from Eq. 16 with the same interval t stated above. Assuming $\sigma = 1.0$ and applying Eq. 13 with $\boldsymbol{a}$ and $\boldsymbol{g}$ vectors defined in Eq. 19 and 20, respectively, the image shown in Fig. 2.d is obtained, exactly the same result as with the LIP–LoG by Deng and Pinoli's method.

$$\boldsymbol{a_\sigma} = [0.0355, 0.1620, 0, -0.3989, 0, 0.1620, 0.0355] \tag{19}$$

$$\boldsymbol{g_\sigma} = [0.0044, 0.0540, 0.2420, 0.3989, 0.2420, 0.0540, 0.0044] \tag{20}$$

4.3 Speedup Analysis

In this Section, we will focus on the computation time spent by each method and experiment. For this task, we have programmed the algorithms and tested them on a set of two experiments with two different sizes for the images for which time consumption and speedup were calculated. We considered the results of the experiments using the Deng and Pinoli's method as the base reference time, and we computed the gain of speed, or "speedup", of each method for every experiment compared to that base reference time. If the speedup value is above one, it means that the new system is faster than the reference one. In order to facilitate the comparison of the performance of the different methods, another alternative speedup is also computed, taking the time for the *LIP–Convolution* experiments as the base reference time.

From the obtained results, shown in Tab. 1 for the Sobel edge detector experiment and in Tab. 2 for the Laplacian of Gaussian experiment, we can infer that the *LIP–Convolution* is much faster than the original Deng and Pinoli's method. One of the reasons for this speedup is due to the use of separable kernels that this new formulation allows, in opposition to the Deng and Pinoli's method, in which there does not exist a technique to make use of the separability of the filters. Another reason for the speedup is that the *LIP–Convolution* makes use of additions and multiplications, opposed to the Deng and Pinoli's method, which is based on multiplications or divisions and exponentiations, much slower and computationally more expensive than the first ones. On the other hand, the standard algorithms are faster, however, the standard operators do not behave invariantly against illumination changes.

A special note must be done on the processing time of the LIP–LoG by the Deng and Pinoli's method with respect of the others. Taking into account the philosophy expounded by Deng and Pinoli in [5], in which only 2D masks were considered, we have implemented the LIP–LoG by the Deng and Pinoli's method using a 2D LoG mask, obtained from Eq. 12, which is much slower than two consecutive 1D convolutions. Besides, the final implementation does not make use of convolutions (sums of multiplications, as stated above) but makes use of multiplications of exponentiations, which are much slower. And, finally, we cannot take a common exponentiation for all the values, and thus, many exponentiations have to be computed. As the LoG is symmetrical, we made

Table 1. Computation time and speedup comparison (time in seconds) of the Sobel and LIP–Sobel experiment

Size	Method	Time	Speedup	Alt. Speedup
512 × 512	Standard Sobel	0.1978	4.34	1.60
	Deng & Pinoli	0.8577	1.00	0.37
	LIP–Convolution	0.3165	2.71	1.00
256 × 256	Standard Sobel	0.0541	3.63	1.53
	Deng & Pinoli	0.1963	1.00	0.42
	LIP–Convolution	0.0826	2.38	1.00

Table 2. Computation time and speedup comparison (time in seconds) of the LoG and LIP–LoG experiment

Size	Method	Time	Speedup	Alt. Speedup
512 × 512	Standard LoG	0.1357	57.71	1.59
	Deng & Pinoli	7.8312	1.00	0.03
	LIP–Convolution	0.2163	36.20	1.00
256 × 256	Standard LoG	0.0390	30.88	1.63
	Deng & Pinoli	1.2042	1.00	0.05
	LIP–Convolution	0.0636	18.93	1.00

common exponentiations for all the values which are the same in the LoG filter, this way, the exponentiations were reduced to a 25% of the original amount.

5 Conclusions

Taking into account that convolution is a very useful and widely employed tool in the fields of image and video processing, and that LIP is a very robust mathematical framework, we have combined in this work these two techniques into a general formulation of the convolution under the *LIP* paradigm, *LIP–Convolution*. This formulation has been designed generically: any 2D separable kernel of any size can be applied.

Two versions of LIP–Sobel were programmed, the original method (called here Deng and Pinoli's method) and the proposed method (called *LIP–Convolution*). After several executions of the LIP–Sobel, the results obtained show that both methods are equivalent in terms of accuracy. Nevertheless, the computation time shows that the *LIP–Convolution*, proposed in this work, is a very advantageous alternative. It is more than two times faster than the Deng and Pinoli's method. These results are due to the use of separable kernels and the use of multiplications and additions instead of multiplications/divisions and exponentiations, which are computationally much slower. Another experiment has been exposed, the Laplacian of Gaussian, using a different image. In this experiment, it is also shown that the *LIP–Convolution* method is the fastest one and obtains a very large speedup, maintaining the same results.

As a final remark, we have stated a new generic operator which will allow logarithmic image processing, with the same benefits that the LIP paradigm provides but much more general than any previously stated one (any separable filter of any size is suitable) and with significant speedups. Furthermore, we expect to achieve larger speedups using parallel computing primitives available in conventional platforms (such as the SSE instruction set in the Intel x86).

Acknowledgments

We want to thank specially the referees and the Program Chair for their valuable suggestions.

This work has been partially supported by the Spanish Ministry of Science and Technology under project DEPROVI (DPI2004–07032).

References

1. Jourlin, M., Pinoli, J.C.: Logarithmic Image Processing. Acta Stereologica **6** (1987) 651–656
2. Jourlin, M., Pinoli, J.C.: A Model for Logarithmic Image–Processing. Journal of Microscopy **149** (1988) 21–35
3. Deng, G., Cahill, L.W., Tobin, G.R.: The Study of Logarithmic Image–Processing Model and Its Application to Image–Enhancement. IEEE Transactions on Image Processing **4** (1995) 506–512
4. Pinoli, J.C.: A General Comparative Study of the Multiplicative Homomorphic, Log–Ratio and Logarithmic Image Processing Approaches. Signal Processing **58** (1997) 11–45
5. Deng, G., Pinoli, J.C.: Differentiation–Based Edge Detection using the Logarithmic Image Processing Model. Journal of Mathematical Imaging and Vision **8** (1998) 161–180
6. Vernon, D.: Machine Vision — Automated Visual Inspection and Robot Vision. Prentice Hall (1991)

Local Feature Saliency for Texture Representation

M.K. Bashar, N. Ohnishi, and K. Agusa

Graduate School of Information Science, Nagoya University,
Furo-cho, Chikusa-ku, Nagoya 464-8603, Japan
khayrul@agusa.i.is.nagoya.ac.jp
http://www.ohnishi.i.is.nagoya-u.ac.jp/ khayrul/

Abstract. Towards the goal of object/region recognition in images, texture characterization is a very important and challenging task. In this study, we propose a salient point based texture representation scheme. It is a two-phase analysis in the multiresolution framework of discrete wavelet transform. In the first phase, each wavelet sub-band (LH or HL or HH) is used to compute multiple texture features, which represents various aspects of texture. These features are converted into binary images, called salient point images (SPIs), via an automatic threshold technique that maximizes inter-block pattern deviation (IBPD) metric. Such operation may facilitate combining multiple features for better segmentation. In the final phase, we have proposed a set of new texture features, namely non-salient point density (NSPD), salient point residual (SPR), saliency and non-saliency product (SNP). These features characterize various aspects of image texture like fineness/coarseness, primitive distribution, internal structures etc. K-means algorithm is used to cluster the generated features for unsupervised segmentation. Experimental results with the standard texture (Brodatz) and natural images demonstrate the robustness of the proposed features compared to the wavelet energy (WE) and local extrema density feature (LED).

Keywords: Texture, wavelet transform, feature saliency, binary domain texture features, segmentation.

1 Introduction

Among various analysis techniques, signal processing based multiresolution approaches have drawn a lot of attention in the recent years for texture segmentation [1],[6], [8], [9], [10] and/or texture-based indexing and retrieval [3], [5], [7]. Recently, some researchers [5], [7] introduced the concept of interest or salient points that guides to extract conventional texture features (Gabor statistics) with computational efficacy. K. Karu et al. [4] introduced a scheme for texture coarseness measure attributed by local extrema density, which identifies the level of texture in images. However, their coarseness measure is found unsuitable for texture segmentation.

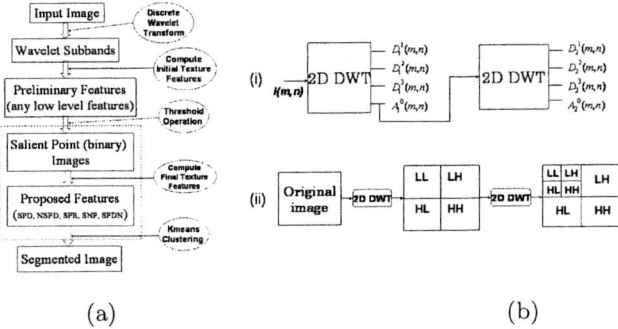

Fig. 1. System representation and wavelet decomposition. (a) A simple block diagram of the proposed approach, (b) wavelet decomposition (i) Functional decomposition (2-levels); (ii) Block diagram for 2 -level decomposition.

In a recent study [10], wavelet intermittency based texture features (salient point density, SPD and salient point distribution non-uniformity, SPDN), were proposed. However, a single criterion may not represent multiple aspects of texture alone. One possible solution is to include more texture features of diverse nature for binary space formation. Such an approach may also facilitate combining multiple texture features in the binary domain. We then propose three texture features, namely NSPD, SPR, and SNP, which are found effective for texture segmentation. Typical texture features like norm-1 energy, norm-2 energy, standard deviation, average residual, entropy, and coefficient intermittency indices are attempted for binary space formation. A simple methodology of our approach is shown in Fig. 1(a).

The rest of the paper is organized as follows. Section 2 describes the proposed scheme in details including an automatic threshold algorithm. In section 3, the proposed features are validated through experimental details and comparison. Finally, the contribution is discussed and concluded through section 4.

2 Proposed Scheme

The proposed scheme is based on the concept of feature saliency in the multiresolution framework to be detailed in the following sub-sections.

2.1 Motivation

In image analysis, the word "feature saliency" may refer to its distinctness or rarity in representing image objects. In our study, it refers to relatively high feature values, which have a correspondence with high level concepts. Since image texture is a generalized concept with perceptual and structural components that form image objects. Hence, feature saliency should represent all kinds of variability (including interest points) that are responsible for real surface formation.

Analyzing such a critical concept has already proved fruitful in the multiresolution domain. We thus represent salient points in the discrete wavelet transform domain [11] as locations of reasonably high values for various low level features. However, to represents reliable surface property in each resolution level, a fixed number of salient points is mandatory. We thus define feature saliency loosely by a threshold based technique, which may include more characteristic points than just corners or edges.

2.2 Salient Point Representation

We represent salient points in the multiresolution framework of wavelet transform using Daubechies' D4 wavelets (decomposition is shown in Fig. 1(b)). We assume that various textures are independent in their inherent structures, which may be approximated by feature saliency.

Over the past years, many texture features have been proposed. Some are in the image domain, while the others in the transform domain. However, finding appropriate features for combination is quite challenging. We thus investigate the potentiality of individual feature in our current study. Selection strategy of multiple features and their combination techniques will be explored in future. Some of the texture features are norm2 energy, norm1 energy, standard deviation, average residual, entropy, and intermittency index. If the detail sub-bands of wavelet transform are represented by $D_j^i(m,n)$, we can specify various texture features by

$$F_{ij}^1(m_0, n_0) = \frac{1}{N_W^2} \sum_{m=0}^{N_W-1} \sum_{n=0}^{N_W-1} |D_j^i(m,n)|^2 \tag{1}$$

$$F_{ij}^2(m_0, n_0) = \mu_{ij}$$

$$= \frac{1}{N_W^2} \sum_{m=0}^{N_W-1} \sum_{n=0}^{N_W-1} |D_j^i(m,n)| \tag{2}$$

$$F_{ij}^3(m_0, n_0) = -\frac{1}{N_W^2} \sum_{m=0}^{N_W-1} \sum_{n=0}^{N_W-1} |D_j^i(m,n)|^2 \log |D_j^i(m,n)|^2 \tag{3}$$

$$F_{ij}^4(m_0, n_0) = \frac{1}{N_W^2} \sum_{m=0}^{N_W-1} \sum_{n=0}^{N_W-1} |D_j^i(m,n) - \mu_{ij}| \tag{4}$$

$$F_{ij}^5(m_0, n_0) = \sqrt{\frac{1}{N_W^2} \sum_{m=0}^{N_W-1} \sum_{n=0}^{N_W-1} (D_j^i(m,n) - \mu_{ij})^2} \tag{5}$$

$$F_{ij}^6(m_0, n_0) = N^2 \frac{(D_j^i(m_0, n_0))^2}{\sum_{m=1}^{N} \sum_{n=1}^{N} (D_j^i(m_0, n_0))^2} \tag{6}$$

Here preliminary feature images are represented by $F_{ij}^f(m_0, n_0)$, where (m_0, n_0) is the center of the neighborhood kernel of size ($N_W \times N_W$). Note that we used (5 × 5) kernel to obtain preliminary features except $F_{ij}^6(m,n)$.

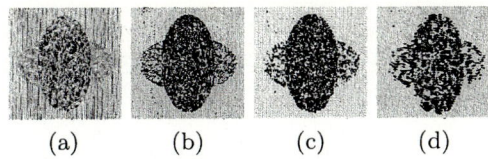

(a)   (b)   (c)   (d)

Fig. 2. Salient point (black pixels) images for the bb35 image at the level-1, level-2, and level-3 of wavelet decomposition. (a) Original bb35 image; Salient point images at threshold 0.75: (b) SPI11 (LH), (c) SPI21 (LH), and (d) SPI31 (LH).

By adopting a simple threshold technique on the low level features $F_{ij}^f(m,n)$, we can obtain a salient point (binary) image:

$$SPI_{ij}^f(m,n) = \begin{cases} 1 & \text{if } F_{ij}^f(m,n) \geq F_{th}, \\ 0 & \text{Otherwise.} \end{cases} \qquad (7)$$

Here F_{th} is the threshold value for individual low level feature. Fig. 2 shows three salient point images for the LH sub-band of mos32 images corresponding to level-1, level-2, and level-3 wavelet decomposition, respectively. Having obtained the binary images corresponding to all sub-bands, we can compute the following texture features.

2.3 Proposed Texture Features

We define the proposed texture features in the salient point or binary space as explained above. Binary representation provides us with many advantages (like feature selection and combining to be explored in future) including computational efficacy.

i) NSPD Feature. Since non-salient points may play roles for representing smooth texture surfaces, we may define non-salient point density (NSPD) by

$$NSPD_{ij}^f(m_0, n_0) = 1.0 - SPD_{ij}^f(m_0, n_0), \qquad (8)$$

where

$$SPD_{ij}^f(m_0, n_0) = \frac{1}{w^2} \sum_{(m,n) \in W_{ij}} SPI_{ij}^f(m,n). \qquad (9)$$

Here w^2 is the size of feature window W_{ij}. Since the sum of the SPD and NSPD is equal to 1.0, NSPD characterizes symmetrically opposite nature to SPD.

ii) SPR Feature. It is logical to think that there is a certain difference between the concentrations of salient and non-salient points for each texture. This may also contribute to image texture. We thus define another feature regarded as salient point residual (SPR):

$$SPR_{ij}^f(m,n) = |SPD_{ij}^f(m,n) - NSPD_{ij}^f(m,n)| \qquad (10)$$

This feature indicates the proportional effects of the high and low activity points in texture regions.

iii) SNP Feature. Another way to analyze the overall structural property of texture is to combine salient and non-salient points locally. We thus obtain a feature named as saliency and non-saliency product (SNP):

$$SNP_{ij}^f(m,n) = \begin{cases} 1.0 - PROD_{ij}^f(m,n) & \text{if } SPD_{ij}^f(m,n) \geq NSPD_{ij}^f(m,n), \\ 0.25 + PROD_{ij}^f(m,n) & \text{Otherwise.} \end{cases} \tag{11}$$

Here

$$PROD_{ij}^f(m,n) = SPD_{ij}(m,n) \times NSPD_{ij}^f(m,n). \tag{12}$$

Such representation describes whether salient or non-salient points are dominant in a sample texture region. This feature can be modeled by using different translations (Eq. 10), which produce non-overlapping feature values for the saliency and non-saliency dominance. In stead of translation, different weights can also be used for obtaining uncorrelated features. For the given test data, a weight of 100 and 50 can be used for SPD and NSPD dominance, respectively. Note that all of the mentioned features are computed at every location of binarized sub-band, where $m, n = 0, 1, ..., N - 1$.

2.4 Effect of Changing the Size of Feature Window

The size of the feature window plays an important role during segmentation. If we assume each texture to have a fixed average frequency, the required window size should be equal to or greater than the period of the lowest average frequency texture. We can approximate minimum and maximum frequency in a texture image by Fourier analysis. Integrating this frequency information with wavelet analysis, approximate window size per sub-band can be fixed. However, an experiment shows that overall classification accuracy (as analyzed by the confusion matrices obtained from segmented image) for a given image-set remains more or less constant after a window size of 16 × 16 (an example is shown in Fig. 3(a) and (b)).

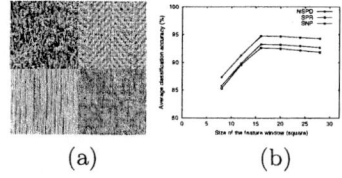

(a)   (b)

Fig. 3. Effect on classification accuracy (mos41 image) for varying window-size. (a)Original mos41 image (b)Accuracy vs. window size (8, 12, 20, 24, 28) for NSPD, SPR, and SNP.

2.5 Automatic Feature Threshold

Selecting suitable threshold value for initial features is a challenging task. An ideal solution is to compute segmentation accuracy for various threshold values and to choose the one which maximizes accuracy. However, this process is computationally expensive because it has to go through the steps of binarization, feature extraction, and segmentation for each threshold. Since we compute the texture features in the binary domain, we can develop an alternate solution, which maximizes inter-block pattern (1-count, 01Change count) deviation (IBPD) per sub-band. The idea is form an appropriate binary array that ensure maximal separation among various texture regions or objects. A simplified algorithm is given below:

1. Take a wavelet sub-band (LH, HL, or HH).
2. Compute initial texture features $F_{ij}^f(m,n)$ at every pixel of sub-bands.
3. For each feature, calculate minimum (min_F) and maximum (max_F) feature values. Compute N_{th} (currently, we use 50) number of threshold values within the feature range by $th_F(i) = min_F + i * step$, where $i = 0, 1, ..., N_{th}$ and $step = (max_F - min_F)/N_{th}$.
4. For each threshold, generate a binary image, SPI_{ij}^f, per wavelet sub-band.
5. Divide each binary image into non-overlapping blocks (currently, we use 16×16 block) and compute a set of pattern measures (currently, we use two measures, i.e., average number of 1-count and polarity-count (0 to 1 as "+", 1 to 0 as "-")) for all sub-blocks.
6. Compute a performance index called "inter-block pattern deviation (IBPD)", which is the standard deviation of the pattern measures mentioned above.
7. Take a new threshold and repeat steps 4-6 above to obtain a set of IBPD per pattern measure.
8. Compute thresholds corresponding to maximum IBPD for all measures. Take an average to obtain the final threshold F_{th}.
9. Repeat above steps for all sub-bands and for all initial features.

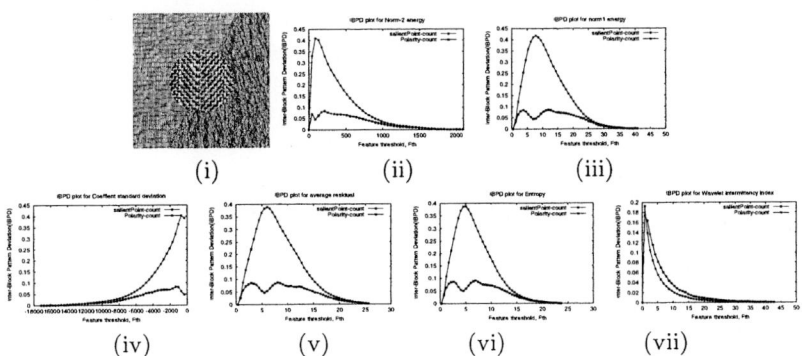

Fig. 4. Inter-Block Pattern Deviation(IBPD) plots for mos31 image. (i) Original mos31 image; IBPD plots for(ii) F_{ij}^1 (iii) F_{ij}^2, (iv) F_{ij}^3, (v) F_{ij}^4, (vi) F_{ij}^5 and F_{ij}^6 features (only for LH sub-band).

Fig. 4 shows IBPD plots for all initial features against feature threshold values for mos31 image (only LH sub-band). The two curves in each plot correspond to IBPD values for 1-count and polarity-count pattern measures, respectively. Expected threshold value is obtained by averaging threshold values corresponding to IBPD peaks in the above plots.

3 Segmentation Experiment

We have performed experiments over 20 mosaic texture (Brodatz album) and 10 natural texture images (digital camera). All are gray level images of size 256 × 256). In all experiments, we used three levels of wavelet decomposition, which produces 9 detail sub-bands.

To investigate threshold based binary approach, we have performed an experiment using mos31 and mos41 images. Six mentioned features $F_{ij}^f(m,n)$ per wavelet sub-band are computed through local neighborhood operation using 5×5 window. Respective binary arrays are obtained by manual thresholding, where $F_{th} = factor \times max(F_{ij}^f)$. Segmentation results (Fig. 5) for NSPD features shows our binary approach is applicable for various texture features.

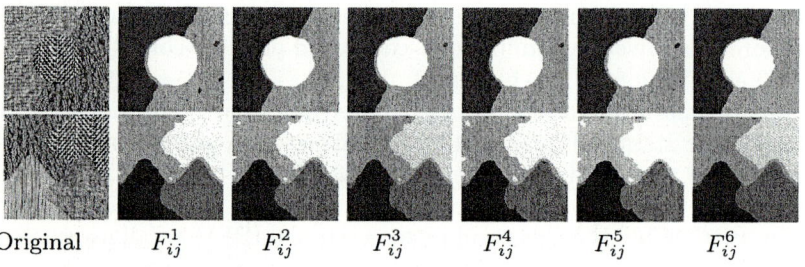

Fig. 5. Segmentation results of mos31 and mos41 images (256 × 256) using manual threshold values. Only NSPD for all initial features ($F_{ij}^f : f = 1, 2, ..., 6$) is used. Values for parameter "factor" in (row1) are 0.1, 0.2, 0.05, 0.25, 0.25, and 0.75, while the same for (row2) are 0.03, 0.14, 0.02, 0.11, 0.1, and 0.25. Feature window is 16 × 16.

3.1 Results

Results for the proposed features (NSPD, SPR, SNP) are shown in Fig. 6 using manual thresholding. For mosaic images, we used a fixed threshold (0.75), while various thresholds(in the range from 0.6 to 1.5) are used for the natural images. Clearly, the proposed features produce nice segmentation results for textures with diverse complexities. Results for SPD, SPDN, WE, and LED are also shown for comparison.

Observation shows that LED segments all expected classes with noisy results. On the other hand, WE produces relatively noise-free segmentation than LED. But due to the rigid nature, WE sometimes fails to capture all relevant classes

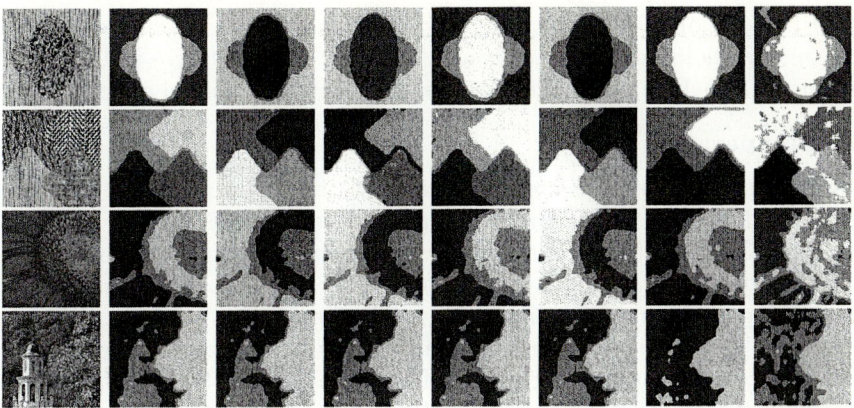

(i)Original (ii)SPD (iii) NSPD (iv) SPR (v) SNP (vi) SPDN (vii)WE (viii) LED

Fig. 6. Segmentation Results of mos32, mos41, ns31, and ns32 images. (i) Original images; Results obtained for F_{ij}^6 initial feature using (ii) SPD, (iii) NSPD, (iv) SPR, (v) SNP, (vi) SPDN, (vii) WE, and (viii) LED features. Feature window size is 16×16 for all features except SPDN, which requires a size of 20×20.

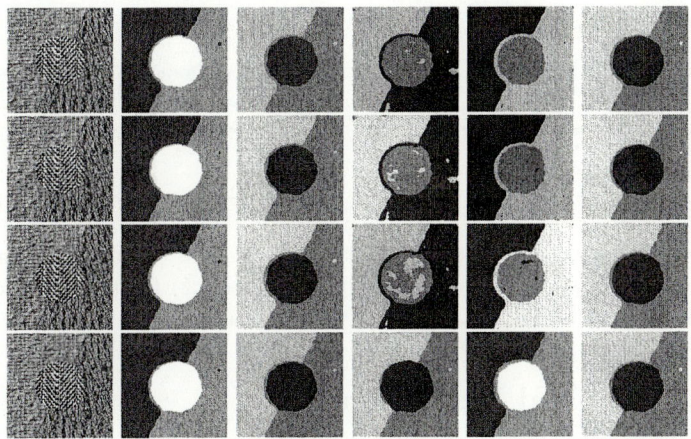

(i) mos31 (ii)SPD (iii) NSPD (iv) SPR (v) SNP (vi) SPDN

Fig. 7. Segmentation results of mos31(256 256) using automatic thresholding for various initial features ($F_{ij}^1, F_{ij}^2, F_{ij}^4, and F_{ij}^6$; top to bottom). Results for all features are not shown for space limitation.

(see results for mos41 and ns32 images in Fig.6). However, we always obtain faithful segmentation results by our proposed features. Among the proposed features, the results are comparable except minor variations in accuracy (see subsection 3.2).

Automatic threshold selection (see section 2.5) can also produce nice segmentation as shown in Fig. 7. However, SPR and SNP results are a bit inferior to NSPD, SPD or SPDN in automatic case. This reveals the necessity of more accurate threshold value by automatic method. One tentative solution to this problem is to include more pattern measures during threshold selection.

3.2 Comparative Study

We have also performed a comparative study between our proposed features (NSPD, SPR, SNP) with some existing features like WE [3], [6], [8], LED[4], and SPD, SPDN [10]. The rate of misclassification is computed for 20 mosaic (Brodatz) images as shown in Fig. 8(a), where x-axis represents image indices of increasing number of texture classes. The bar-diagram in Fig. 8(b) shows the average misclassification rate against various features. This confirms the achievement of the lowest misclassification (varies from 5.48 % to 6.2 %) by the proposed features. An approximate performance order of the proposed features (for manual thresholds) is (i) SPR, (ii) NSPD, and (iii) SNP, while the same for automatic threshold is (i) NSPD, (ii) SNP, and (iii) SPR, respectively.

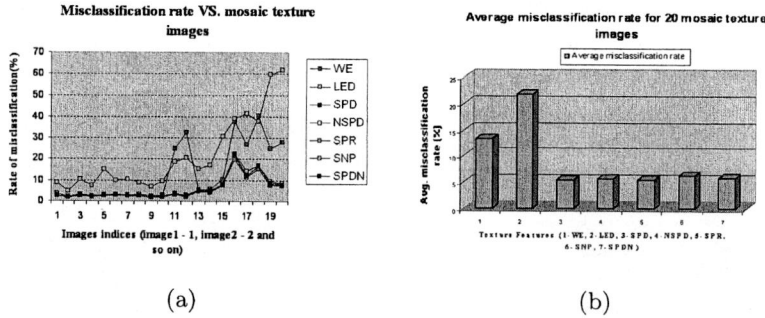

Fig. 8. Misclassification analysis; (a) Misclassification rate (%) across images and (b) average (over 20 mosaic images) misclassification rate (%) for the proposed (NSPD, SPR, SNP) and existing (WE, LED, SPD, SPDN) features.

4 Conclusion and Discussion

We have proposed a set of new texture features (NSPD, SPR, and SNP) in the multiresolution framework. An interesting fact is that all of these features are extracted in the binary domain. Experimental results on the mosaic (Brodatz) and natural images demonstrate the superior performance of the proposed features compared to the conventional WE or LED features. We also proposed an automatic threshold selection technique that maximizes property (1-count, polarity-count) deviation among regional binary patterns. Note also that the binary domain may facilitate developing strategies for multiple feature selection and combination. A single binary array for multiple features may be obtained by logical OR operation, while repeatability of salient points can be used for feature selection. These issues along with the external noise sensitivity analysis will be explored in future.

Acknowledgements

We would like to thank my laboratory friends for their suggestions. Thank also goes to IMI-COE for financial support.

References

1. Dunn, D., Higgins W.E.: Optimal Gabor filters for Texture Segmentation. IEEE Trans. Image Process. **4(7)** (1995) 947-963
2. Addison, Paul S.: The Illustrated Wavelet Transform Handbook. IOP, Bristol UK (2002)
3. Manjunath, B. S., Ma, W. Y.: Texture feature for browsing and retrieval of large image data. IEEE Trans. Pattern Anal. Machine Intell. **18(8)**, (1996) 837-842
4. Karu, K., Jain, A. K., Bolle, R. M.: Is there any texture in the image? Pattern Recognition. **29** (1996) 1437-1446
5. Tian, Q., Sebe, N., Lew, M. S., Loupias, E., Huang, T. S.: Image retrieval using wavelet-based salient points. J. Electronic Imaging, **10(4)**, (2001) 835-849
6. Lee, K. L., Chen, L. H.: Unsupervised Texture segmentation by determining the interior of texture regions based on wavelet transform. Int'l. J. Pattern Recognition Artificial Intell., **15(8)** (2001) 1231-1250
7. Bres, S., Jolion, J. M.: Detection of Interest Points for image indexation. Proc. 3rd Intl. Conf. on Visual Info. Syst. June 2-4 Amsterdam, Netherlands(2002) 427-434
8. Jain, A. K., Farrokhnia, F.: Unsupervised texture segmentation using Gabor filters. Pattern Recognition. **24(12)** (1991) 1167-1186
9. Bashar, M. K., Matsumoto, T., Ohnishi, N.: Wavelet transform-based locally orderless images for texture segmentation. Pattern Recognition Letters. **25(15)** (2003) 2633-2650
10. Bashar, M. K., Ohnishi, N.: Wavelet-based Salient Energy Points for Unsupervised Texture Segmentation. Int'l. J. Pattern Recognition and Artificial Intelligence. Article in Press (to appear May-June 2005)
11. Mallat, S.: The theory for multiresolution signal decomposition: the wavelet representation. IEEE Trans. Pattern Anal. Mach. Intell. **11(7)** (1989) 654-693

A Segmentation Algorithm for Rock Fracture Detection

Weixing Wang[1,2] and Eva Hakami [2]

[1] Department of Computer Science & Technology, Chongqing University of Posts & Telecommunications, Post code: 400065, China
[2] ITASCA Geomekanik AB at Stockholm, Sweden
znn525d@yahoo.com, wangwx@cqupt.edu.cn

Abstract. Recognition of rock fractures is crucial in many rock engineering applications. In order to successfully applying automatic image processing techniques for the problem of rock fracture detection and description, the key (and hardest task) is the robust image segmentation of rock fractures. A one-pass valley-edge detection algorithm ("valley" or ("ridge") means here finding locally dark (or bright) line-like or curve-like features) was studied. The image segmentation algorithm is for delineating rock fractures based on multiple scale and valley-edge detection techniques. Results indicate that this approach is useful in this domain of images.

1 Introduction

In rock engineering, the measurement of failure, fault, crack, fracture and different textures on material surface is very important. Exposed rock faces provide a window to characterize discontinuities hidden inside a rock mass, and having an efficient method for mapping exposed rock faces is important for good understanding of discontinuities which in turn significantly influence the strength, stability, deformation and hydraulic properties of rock masses. The techniques of image processing and computer vision can be applied as a powerful tool for obtaining more detailed information and analysis.

The advantages of image analysis and computer vision measurement methods, compared to the other methods, are (1) high speed, e.g. in a few seconds, thousands of objects can be measured; (2) high accuracy, because of the digitization technology, measurement accuracy can be reached by changing camera lens, however, the object size limitation of measurement process only depends on image acquisition systems; (3) non-touching measurement, it can measure the objects which are difficult to reach by a man (i.e. micro-fracture net etc.); and (4) multiple and detailed measurements, e.g. measuring fracture space, aperture, orientation and surface characteristics of multiple fractures.

Lemy and Hadjigeorgiou [1] extracted fractures from the enhanced images using edge and line detection algorithms. The nature of these features is identified using artificial neural networks, and the discontinuity network is characterized using geotechnical criteria. Maerz [2], Reid and Harrison [3] traced fractures based on thresholding algorithms converting gray-level images into binary images. Johansson [4] presented three different fracture tracing algorithms for single rock fracture or crack.

The similar work has been done by Kemeny and Randy [5], Lee and Kim [6], Wang and Pavlidis [7], Harrison [8], Sun [9], Hu [10], and Whittaker [11].

As the above literature review, the previous research work mainly concentrated on the two aspects: (1) the algorithms for fractures image binarization based on grey level information, and (2) the algorithms for tracing single rock fracture based on the properties of discontinuities. The algorithms were mainly used for either the images of single rock fracture or the images of well-oriented rock fractures. For the images multiple and randomly oriented rock fractures, there is no standard algorithm studied. Therefore, this paper proposes a new algorithm for auto-tracing multiple and randomly oriented rock fractures based on multiresolution and valley-edge detection techniques.

In the following sections: first, a brief description of visual properties of rock fracture and basic consideration of image segmentation are outlined; then a one-pass valley edge detection algorithm is described based on sample images; thirdly the thin and randomly oriented rock fracture tracing algorithm is depicted based on the one-pass valley edge detection algorithm; fourthly, it states how to add multiresolution technique into the above fracture tracing algorithm for thick and randomly oriented rock fractures; and finally, the discussions and conclusions are given.

2 Fracture Properties and Image Segmentation Consideration

In most cases, rock surface is rough, except for the variations of colors and gray-scales, three dimensional surface roughness is the another property comparing to other applications. For image processing and analysis, fractures or cracks belong to linear curved objects; the length of an object is much longer than width. Inside the object, it may be empty or filled by different materials. The filling materials are with different colors. Since the large fracture width and rock surface color variation, it is usual that there are many gaps on one object. Another property is that some fault object appears on an image due to rough and noised surface. Random and multiple fractures may form a complicated network where fractures cross each other. All the properties make image processing and segmentation harder than other applications. The followings are reprehensive examples for different types of fractures or cracks (Fig. 1).

We here use gray-scale information (a color band) to trace the fracture curves. To develop the algorithm, several aspects must, generally speaking, be considered: (a) gray flatness or smoothness; (b) curvature variation; (c) magnitude strength; (d) computational searching costs; and (e) distance linking etc.

On the surface of rock mass, the objects of fracture often appear as step edges or ridge edges. The aim of image processing and image segmentation is to auto-tracing rock fractures, which is one of the most difficult tasks in image processing and image segmentation, due to the complicated properties on the rock surface.

Segmentation algorithms for monochrome images are generally based on one of two basic properties of gray-level values: discontinuity and similarity. In the first category, the approach is to partition an image based on abrupt changes in gray level.

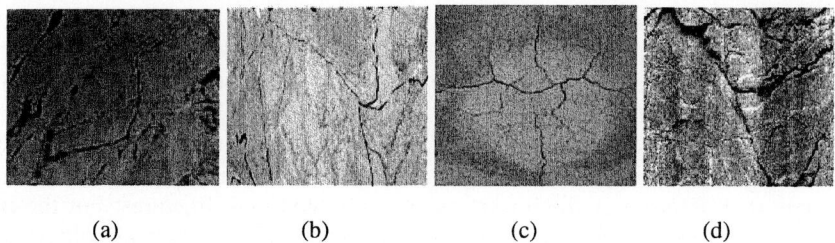

Fig. 1. Four different types of rock fracture images. (a) fractures are oriented in the similar direction, but the aperture vary much; (b) fractures have different gray-scales, (c) fractures form a network, and (d) very rough surface with 3D structures.

An edge, in the image analysis literature, is a jump in intensity. The cross section of a so-called ideal edge has the shape of a ramp: infinite slope and flat portions on either side of the discontinuity. In smoother versions of the ideal edges, the first derivative (in appropriate direction) assumes a local maximum at a so-called edge point or edge pixel. A well-known edge detector of this type is the Canny edge detector, locating local maxima in gradient magnitude (=steepest slope). However, in our case we are more interested in another class of detectors, for example, those known as *ridge detectors* in the image analysis literature. A ridge can be simply thought of as a double edge (a bar edge). Between the step parts there is a narrow plateau or peak. Sometimes, ridge detectors are expressed as follows: a bright (dark) ridge point is defined a point for which the intensity assumes a local maximum in the main principal curvature direction.

Based on the above consideration, we developed a special valley edge detection algorithm for thin rock fracture tracing, presented as the follows.

3 One-Pass Valley Edge Detection for Thin Fracture Tracing

A valley-edge detector tries to detect the lowest valley point in a certain direction. If it is, the pixel is used as the valley-edge candidate, and its direction and location are marked, for further processing to form a valley-edge, by thinning and tracing procedures.

In Fig. 2a-b, when examining a pixel p, check the four different directions shown in the figure, to determine whether p is the valley-edge point or not. As an example, a small kernel valley-edge detection function runs as follows:

In the 90° direction:

If $f(x, y) < f(x-1, y)$, then $F_1^0 = f(x-1, y) - f(x, y)$,

If $f(x, y) < f(x+1, y)$, then $F_2^0 = f(x+1, y) - f(x, y)$,

If $f(x-1, y) < \alpha f(x-2, y-1) + \beta f(x-2, y) + \gamma f(x-2, y+1)$, then

$$F_3^0 = \alpha f(x-2, y-1) + \beta f(x-2, y) + \gamma f(x-2, y+1) - f(x-1, y);$$

If $f(x+1, y) < \alpha f(x+2, y-1) + \beta f(x+2, y) + \gamma f(x+2, y+1)$ then

$$F_4^0 = \alpha f(x+2, y-1) + \beta f(x+2, y) + \gamma f(x+2, y+1) - f(x+1, y)$$

where, we just use 4x4 kernel as illustration example, so,

$\alpha + \beta + \gamma = 1; \alpha = \gamma = 0.3; \beta = 0.4,$

if increase the kernel size, the more parameters are needed in the similar way.

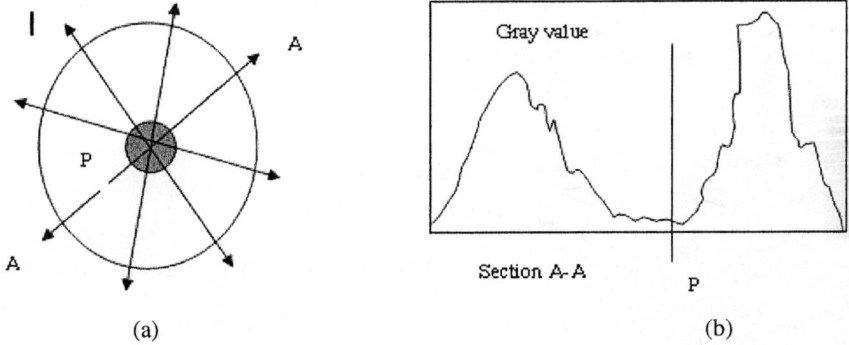

(a)   (b)

Fig. 2. The diagram for valley-edge detection algorithm

And similar expressions in the 0^0, 45^0 and 135^0 directions. In the direction θ, calculate the following sum:

$$T_\vartheta = w_1 F_1^\vartheta + w_2 F_2^\vartheta + w_3 F_3^\vartheta + w_4 F_4^\vartheta$$

$\theta = 0^0$, 45^0, 90^0 or 135^0; w_i (i=1,2,3,4) are weights, e.g. $w_1 = w_2 = 1.2$, $w_3 = w_4 = 0.8$. The weights are decided according to the distance (L) between the testing pixel and its neighborhoods. The distance L is pre-determined based on image resolution and quality and smoothing is done prior to valley-edge detection.

T_{max} =max(T_0, T_{45}, T_{90}, T_{135}). If T_{max} is greater than a threshold T (here we set T as 11 in the following rock fracture images), the detected point will be marked as a valley-edge candidate. Here we merely stress that for each direction two values are calculated, and two values are obtained, f1 and f2 (=two 2nd differences at two scales). A weighted sum of these (in e.g. the 135 degree direction) is: after valley-edge detection, a post-processing subroutine must be added. In the post-processing subroutine, several functions are used, such as thinning, bridging of small gaps, and removal of short curves or lines (refer to Figs. 3-4).

The algorithm is robust for the images which involve thin fractures and less noise, but if an image consists of much noise or the fractures are thick, the noise remove procedure is a hard task, and the detection result may show too many details for thick fractures. Instead of smoothing out the noise and alleviating unnecessary details in thick fractures, we suggested using multiresolusion technique. The next section will present how to use the technique before and during fracture tracing.

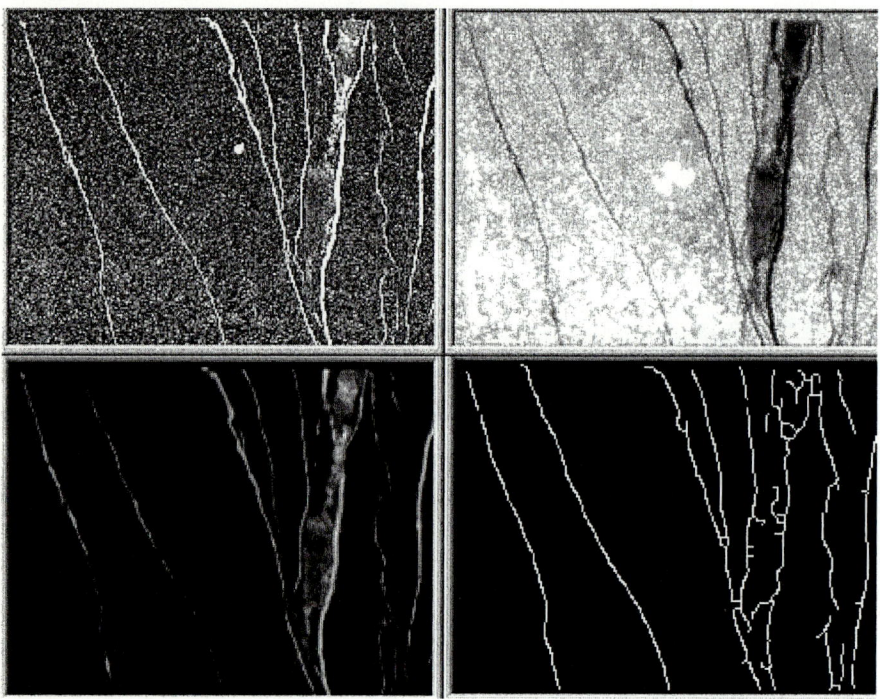

Fig. 3. Example 1 of thin fracture tracing by the new algorithm. The top-left image is original image, the top-right image is inverted and enhanced image, the bottom-left image is a magnitude image by Robert edge detector, and the bottom-right image is the result image.

Fig. 4. Example 2 of thin fracture tracing by the new algorithm. The left image is original image, the middle image is a magnitude image, and the right image is the result image.

4 Tracing Algorithm for Thick Fracture and Noise Images

Multi-scale representations are more or less related to scale-space theory, notably the theories of pyramids, wavelets and multi-grid methods [12]. For the complicated rock fracture images, the methodology of Multi-scale representations is very useful as we tested. If most fractures on an image are very thin, the fine-detailed information on the image is very important for fracture tracing, and the image preprocessing algorithm must avoid to destroying the details. On the contrary, if fractures are thick, it is necessary to remove the detailed information on the rock surface, because the detailed information may produce a lot of fault fractures. In general, the multiple scale technique makes image structures at coarse scales corresponding to simplifications of corresponding structures at fine scales.

By using the knowledge of multiple scales, we combine the valley edge detection results of different scale images, and have a promising fracture tracing result which is difficult to be obtained by using other methods. A gray scale fracture image of 734x596 pixels is presented in Fig. 5(a); its fracture tracing result is in Fig. 5(b), where mainly including three steps: setup the image into four resolution levels; do ridge edge detection for each image; and fracture gap link. In Fig. 5(a), the noise edges randomly distributed on the whole image surface, and thick fracture cannot be detected properly by using just valley edge detection. The fracture mapping result is processed based on the combination of multiple scales, valley edge detection and fracture tracing methods. The question is how to scale the image into different scale levels here, in the following; we will give a brief description of the question.

The image scale is reduced. Let

$x = 1,...,n$, $y = 1,...,m$, and $f(x, y)$ is the original image. Then

$f(x_k, y_k)$, $x_k = 1,...,n/2^k$, $y_k = 1,...,m/2^k$, $k = 1,2,3,...$

where, $k \leq K$, $m \geq 2^K$, $n \geq 2^K$.

To obtain valuable scaled $f(x_k, y_k)$, we tried several image shrink methods (e.g. used Gaussian, average, medium, adaptive, maximum and minimum etc. filters). The figure 6 is one of the examples to show the differences among the rock fracture image shrink methods.

In figure 6, since fractures in Fig. 5(a) have low gray values, Maximum filter (in original image, choose maximum gray value pixel, of four neighboring pixels, as a new pixel in the shrink image) eras thin fractures, on the contrast, Minimum filter make fractures sharpen, but the noise are sharp too. In our case, we use Minimum filter to shrink image for three times, then smooth the scaled image by a Gaussian filter.

One of typical examples is shown in Fig. 7. The original image has a rough surface with thick fractures, if the developed ridge detection and fracture tracing algorithms are directly used without image scale operations, the detection result will include a lot of fault fractures. When we shrink the original image one time, the detection result will be better. The best detection result is in Fig. 7(d), where, we shrink the image for three times before ridge detection and fracture tracing.

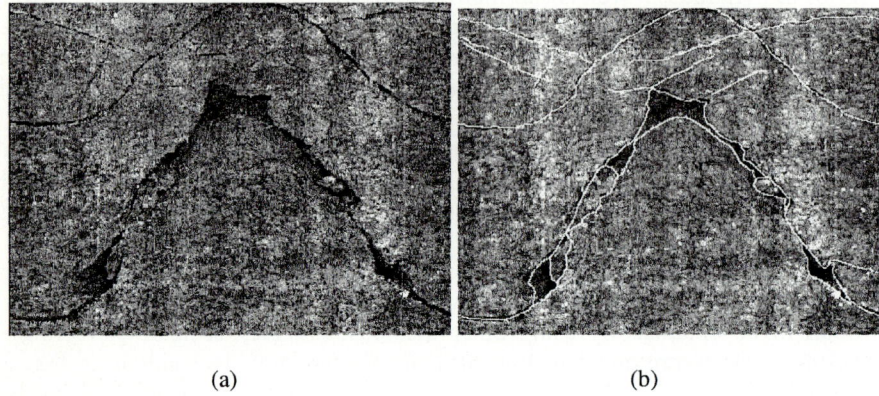

(a)   (b)

Fig. 5. One example of rock fracture images: (a) Original image of resolution 734x596; and (b) Fracture tracing result.

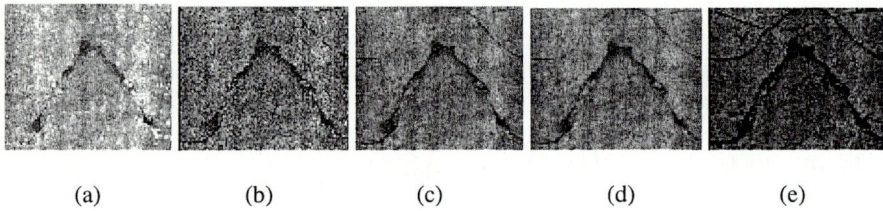

(a)   (b)   (c)   (d)   (e)

Fig. 6. Shrink image three times on the image in Fig. 5(a): (a) Maximum filter; (b) Odd lines; (c) Average filter; (d) Middle filter; and (e) Minimum filter

In order to trace the fractures, we need to link the gaps between valley edges. This task requires the extraction of information about attributes of endpoints, in particular orientation and neighborhood relationships. As usual, after image enhancement and valley-edge detection for each resolution image, the valley edges are thinned into a width of one pixel, but some gaps in the valley edges prevail and noise is still present in the image. To close the gaps, it is necessary to trace valley edges. To do this, the new algorithm first detects significant endpoints of curves (or lines). Then, it estimates the directions for each endpoint based on local directions of valley-edge pixels. Finally, it traces fractures according to the information of directions of each new detected pixel (new endpoint) and an intensity cost function. The valley-edge tracing starts from the detected endpoints to see which neighborhood has the highest gray value, and when a new pixel is found as valley-edge point, it is used as new endpoint. If the end point cannot be found, the various threshold values are changed until a new endpoint is determined.

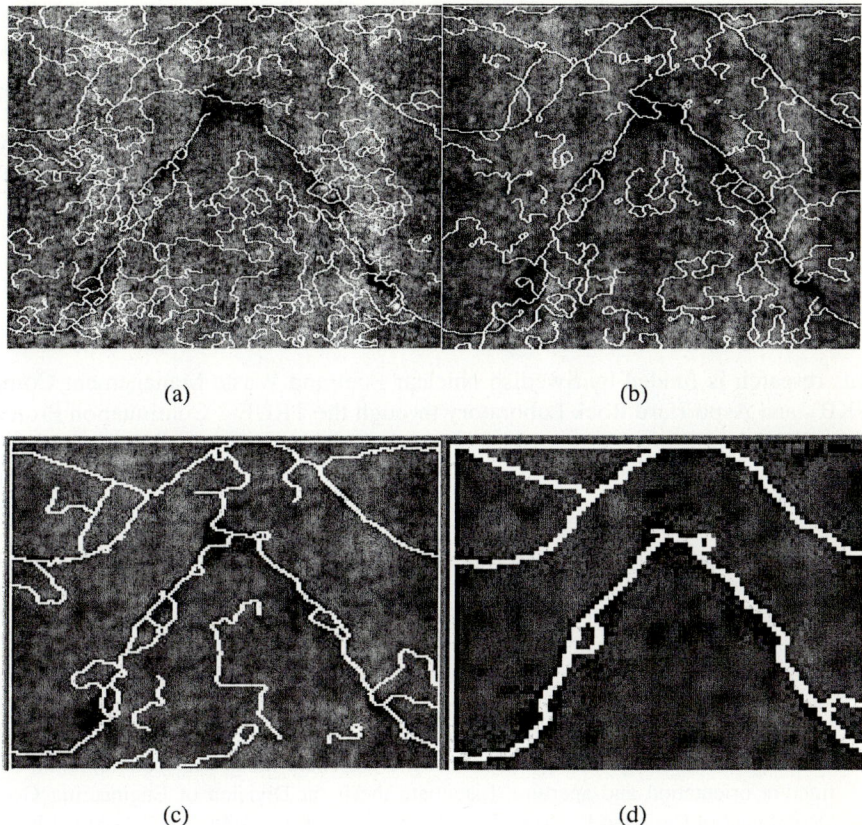

Fig. 7. Valley edge detection result: (a) Image of resolution 734x596; (b) Image of resolution 367x298; (c) Image of resolution 183x149; and (d) Image of resolution 91x74.

Before it starts to trace from another detected endpoint, the tracing procedure continues until a fracture is fully traced. When there is no detected endpoint for continuous tracing, the valley-edge tracing procedure stops. For each resolution image, special tracing thresholds have been setup. The basic idea of image segmentation is to use multiple scale concepts to find maximum information about each fracture and trace the boundaries of the fractures.

5 Conclusion

For this study, the presented fracture tracing algorithm is based on mutiresolution, ridge edge detection and fracture gap tracing methods, and it is the robust for noise fracture tracing, especially for the rough rock surface with thick cracks or fractures. By using multiresolution technology can alleviate producing noise fractures, the new ridge edge detection can directly produce a binary image without the step for threholding gradient magnitude image, and the gap link procedure consists of a number of procedures (or sub-algorithms) for fracture thinning, curvature detection, and gap link. The developed algorithms have been coded into a program, and a number of fracture images have been tested. The testing results show that the developed algorithm is much better that ordinary thresholding algorithms or simple line or curve detection algorithms. The next step of work is to use neural network to classify images into different classes, then use pyramid methods to divide original image into several scale levels, to use the tracing algorithm with different parameters for rock fracture network detection.

Acknowledgement

This research is funded by Swedish Nuclear Fuel and Waste Management Company (SKB), and Äspö Hard Rock Laboratory through the TRUE-1 Continuation Project.

References

1. Lemy F., Hadjigeorgiou J.: Discontinuity trace map construction using photographs of rock exposures□International Journal of Rock Mechanics and Mining Sciences □Volume 40, Issue 6 , September 2003, Pages 903-917.
2. Maerz N.: Photoanalysis of rock fabric. PhD thesis, University of Waterloo, Canada, 1990.
3. Reid TR, Harrison JP, A semi-automated methodology for discontinuity trace detection in digital images of rock mass exposures. Int J Rock Mech Min Sci 2000; 37:1073–89. Trevor.
4. Maria Johansson, Digital image processing of borehole images for determination of rock fracture orientation and aperture, Licentiate thesis, at Division of Engineering Geology, Department of Civil and Environmental Engineering, KTH, 1999, TRITA-AMI LIC 2041.
5. Kemeny, J., Randy Post: Estimating three-dimensional rock discontinuity orientation from digital images of fracture traces, Computer & Geosciences, v. 29 n. 1, p.65-77 February, 2003.
6. Lee SW, Kim YJ.: Direct extraction of topographic features for gray scale character recognition. IEEE Trans Pattern Anal. Machine Intell; 17(7): 724-729, 1995.
7. Wang L, Pavlidis T.: Direct gray-scale extraction of features for character recognition. IEEE Trans Pattern Anal Machine Intell; 15(10): 1053-67, 1993.
8. Harrison JP., Improved analysis of rock mass geometry using mathematical and photogrammetric methods. Ph.D. thesis, Imperial College, London, UK (1993).
9. Sun G. X., Reddish D. J., Whittaker B. N.: Image analysis technique for rock fracture pattern studies around longwall excavations, Trans. Instr Min. Metall, Sect. A: Min. industry, v. 101, A127-204, London (1992).
10. Hu J, Sakoda B, Pavlidis T.: Interactive road finding for aerial images, IEEE Workshop on Applications of Computer Vision (1992).
11. Whittaker RN, Singh RN, Sun G.: Rock fracture mechanics, principles, design and applications. Amsterdam: Elsevier (1992).
12. Lindeberg, T., Scale-space theory: A basic tool for analysing structures at different scales, of Applied Statistics, 21(2), pp. 224--270, 1994. (Supplement on Advances in Applied Statistics: Statistics and Images: 2).

ELIS: An Efficient Leaf Image Retrieval System

Yunyoung Nam[1], Eenjun Hwang[2,*], and Kwangjun Byeon[1]

[1] Graduate School of Information and Communication,
Ajou University, Suwon, Korea
{youngman, byeon}@ajou.ac.kr
[2] Department of Electronics and Computer Engineering,
Korea University, Seoul, Korea
ehwang04@korea.ac.kr

Abstract. In this paper, we present an effective and robust shape-based leaf image retrieval system that supports two novel features: improved MPP algorithm and revised dynamic matching method. The improved MPP algorithm reduces the number of points for the shape representation considerably. Moreover, the new dynamic matching method, which is a revised Nearest Neighbor search, reduces the matching time. We implemented a prototype system based on these features and performed several experiments to show its effectiveness. We compare its performance with other known methods and report some of the results.

1 Introduction

So far, many researchers have proposed techniques for content-based image retrieval using image features such as image color, shape, texture, and spatial relationship. In particular, shape-based image retrieval has received efficient and interesting approach. Specifically, shape recognition methods have been proposed and implemented into face recognition, iris recognition, and fingerprint recognition. Nevertheless, if images contain similar color or texture, shape-based image retrieval is more effective than other approaches using color or texture. For instance, leaves of most plants are green or brown; but the leaf shapes are distinctive and thus can be used for identification.

Like typical content-based image retrieval, shape-based image retrieval is composed of three steps. The first step is to detect edge points. Among the existing edge detection methods [1] [2], we use Canny Edge Detection method [3]. The next step is to represent shapes in such a way that it is invariant to translation, rotation, scale, and viewing angle changes. The last step is shape matching that determines how similar shapes are to a given query image.

In general, shape representations are classified into two categories: boundary-based and region-based. The former describes a region of interest using its external characteristics [4] while the latter represents a region of interest using its internal characteristics [1]. We choose the external representation since our primary concern is shape characteristics such as length of boundary, orientation of straight line, the extreme points to join, or number of concaves. For the shape representation, we can use MPP

---

[*] Corresponding author. Tel.:+82-2-3290-3256.

(Minimum Perimeter Polygons) algorithm [5-7]. MPP is a polygonal approximation method to identify curvature descriptions [8] [9], but it only uses outside boundary of the strip of cells. Nevertheless, it takes long time to retrieve images due to the consideration of many unnecessary points. In order to relieve this problem, we propose an improved MPP algorithm for the shape representation.

Another important issue of shape-based image retrieval is the shape matching method on which the retrieval performance heavily depends. There are several approaches to the shape-matching problem. In this paper, we develop a new dynamic shape-matching algorithm with the intention to reduce matching time.

The rest of this paper is organized as follows. Section 2 describes shape representation methods. Section 3 presents how to perform image matching and retrieval. In section 4, some of the experimental results are presented and finally the last section concludes the paper and discusses some future work.

2 Shape Representation Methods

Shape-based image retrieval includes edge detection, shape representation and shape matching. There exist many shape representation methods: chain codes [10], Fourier transform [11], and MPP. Chain codes are used to represent a boundary by a connected sequence of straight-line segments of specified length and direction. The Fourier transform converts the function from space domain to frequency domain with the derived sine wave coefficients describing a given 1-D function.

A boundary can be approximated with arbitrary accuracy by a polygon. In case of closed curve, the approximation is exact when the number of segments in the polygon is equal to the number of points in the boundary, so that each pair of adjacent points defines a segment in the polygon. MPP is a method for defining curvatures when a change of the slope occurs with the control points approximately uniformly spaced along the curvatures. Algorithm 1 shows the steps for finding the MPP of a region and Fig. 1 shows examples of image representation using MPP.

However, when an image contains plenty of the straight lines along the boundary, segmentation result using MPP may include many useless points and show poor performance for shape matching. In order to relieve this problem, we merge points along boundary if their angle exceeds some threshold. Algorithm 2 shows the details of the point merging algorithm.

Algorithm 1. MPP algorithm

```
1.  Obtain the cellular complex.
2.  Obtain the region internal to the cellular complex.
3.  Use function boundaries to obtain the boundary of the re-
    gion in step 2 as a 4-connected, clockwise sequence of
    coordinates.
4.  Obtain the Freeman chain code of this 4-contected se-
    quence using function fchcode.
5.  Obtain the convex and concave vertices form the chain
    code.
6.  Form an initial polygon using the vertices, and delete
    from further analysis any white dots that are outside
    this polygon.
```

7. Form a polygon with the remaining concave an convex points
8. Delete all black dots that are concave vertices
9. Repeat steps 7 and 8 until all changes cease, at which time all vertices with angles of 180 are deleted. The remaining dots are the vertices of the MPP

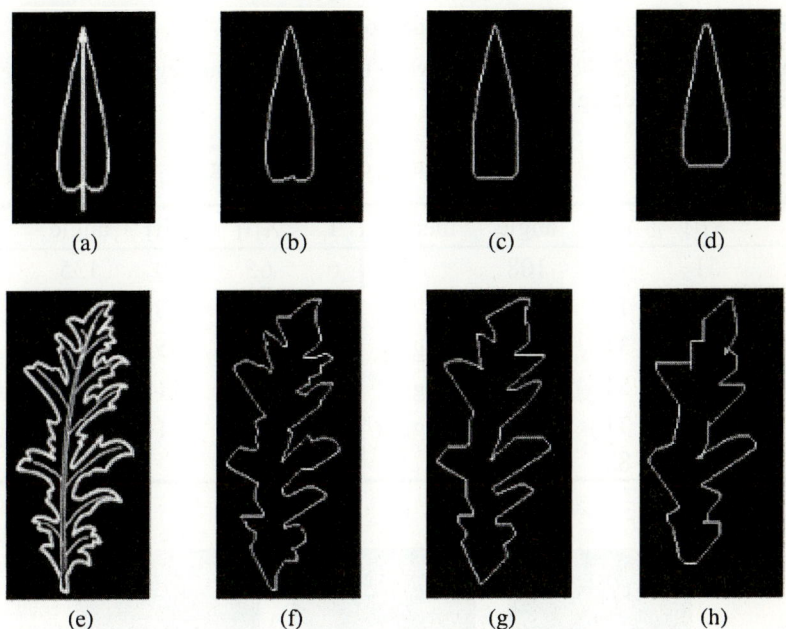

Fig. 1. Examples of image segmentation using MPP. (a) and (e) are original images, (b) and (f), (c) and (g), (d) and (h) are results, respectively, when the cell size is 2, 3, 5.

Algorithm 2. Point merging

```
Input:    point : (X, Y) coordinates;
          N : the number of points;
          threshold : specific angle value;
find_sequence(point, N, threshold){
  for ( i=0; i<N; i++){
    a=get_distance(point[i-1], point[i+1]);
    b=get_distance(point[i], point[i-1]);
    c=get_distance(point[i], point[i+1]);
    angle=acos((b^2+c^2-a^2)/(2*b*c));
    if(angle < threshold)
       add_point(result, point[i]);
  }
  return result;
}
```

In this algorithm, a, b, and c are the sides of a triangle. Let the angle opposite the side c be A. Then, we can define cosine A as follows:

$$\cos A = \frac{b^2 + c^2 - a^2}{2bc} \qquad (1)$$

$$a = \sqrt{(x_j - x_i)^2 + (y_j - y_i)^2} \qquad (2)$$

where (x_i, x_j) and (y_i, y_j) are coordinates of two points.

Table 1 and Fig. 2 show the result when the points of the segment are merged with the threshold 160 degree.

Table 1. Example of point merging

I	X[i]	Y[i]	angle	merge	I	X[i]	Y[i]	angle	merge
0	51	16	108		6	65	90	135	
1	55	16	108		7	41	90	135	
2	60	31	176	merging	8	36	85	135	
3	65	51	180	merging	9	36	71	166	merging
4	70	71	166	merging	10	41	51	180	merging
5	70	85	135						

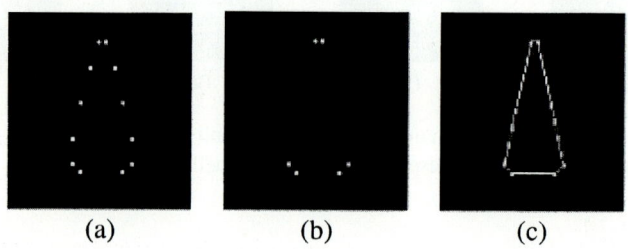

(a)   (b)   (c)

Fig. 2. Image segmentation using point merging

For the invariance, we adjust angles with respect to the longest distance between two points, and then detect left, right, top, bottom points for scale invariance as shown in Algorithm 3. Fig. 3 shows the steps to adjust the original image.

Algorithm 3. Adjustment algorithm

```
Input: crt_1, crt_2 : two points of Criterion

Rotating_point (point, N, crt_1, crt_2){
    cos=(crt_2[X]-crt_1[X])/get_distance(crt_1, crt_2);
    sin =sqrt(1- cos^2);
    for (i=0; i<N; i++){
        point[i][X]= cos*(point[i][X]-crt_1[X])+sin*
            (crt_1[Y]- point[i][Y])-crt_1[X];
        point[i][Y]= sin*(point[i][X]-crt_1[X])-cos*
```

```
            (crt_1[Y]-point[i][Y])- crt_1[X];
        if(crt_1[Y]<=point[i][Y])
            add_point(result,point[i])
    }
    return result;
}
```

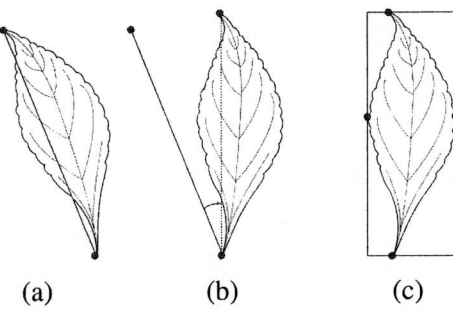

Fig. 3. Image Adjustment based on viewing angle and scale (a) Original image (b) Rotational adjustment (c) 4 edge points detection for scale invariance.

3 Image Matching and Retrieval

The final step of image retrieval is image matching and browsing. In this section, we present an efficient dynamic matching method for obtaining ranks of all database images in an approximate order of similarity to the query image. Typically, a similarity query is defined as finding the most similar data object. In the case of image databases, a similarity query is to find out the most similar images to a given image with respect to the given features.

3.1 Similarity Measure

After extracting points of interest from images, we perform shape matching to measure the similarity between images. Generally, similarity between two objects is measured by simply evaluating the Euclidean distance [12] between objects' corresponding points, and accordingly the distance between two images are calculated by the following equation.

$$D(U,V) = \sqrt{\sum_{i=1}^{k}(u_i - v_i)^2} \qquad (3)$$

where U and V are the query and database image, respectively, and u_i and v_i are their i_{th} features, respectively, and k is dimension of the feature space.

According to the Euclidean distance, we can also evaluate similarity between query and database image using the following equation.

$$S(U,V) = \frac{1}{|u|}\sum_{i=1}^{|u|}\min(D_i(u,v)) \qquad (4)$$

where $|u|$ is the number of points of interest extracted from the query image and $\min(D_i(u,v))$ is the minimum distance between u_i and v_i.

If we use the brute-force algorithm, the time complexity T is $O(|u| \| v|) = O(n^2)$ to search the shortest path between u_i and v_i. For the linear time complexity, we use $\varepsilon-nearest\ neighbor(\varepsilon-NN)$ search algorithm where the time complexity is $O(D\text{polylog}(N))$ [13].

3.2 Dynamic Matching Algorithm

Even though the time complexity of $\varepsilon-nearest\ neighbor(\varepsilon-NN)$ searching algorithm is linear, it may take long time to match images for large database. In order to reduce the matching time, we developed a dynamic matching algorithm. Typical leaf shape has roughly symmetric distribution. Symmetry can occur in any orientation as long as the image is the same on either side of the central axis. The axis of symmetry is vertical and this makes a good model for symmetry in visual information. Using this property, the matching scope on the shape can be reduced by $1/2 \times 1/2 = 1/4$ times with respect to full matching. Moreover, the matching process may stop when the accumulated similarity value is beyond the threshold.

Even the improved MPP algorithm can produce many points of interest for complicated images. To solve this problem, we created a function called *SMP* based on the sampling methodology. Let $|u|$ and $|v|$ be the number of points of interest extracted from the query image and database image, respectively. If $|u|$ is less than $|v|$, the number of interest points can be reduced by $|v|/|u|$ when we use $SMP(v)$ function. Algorithm 4 below describes the dynamic matching algorithm.

Algorithm 4. Dynamic matching algorithm

```
Dynamic_matching(input_image, db_image, N, threshold){
  input_point=condensing_point(input_image);
  db_point=condensing_point(db_image);
  if(sizeof(input_point) < sizeof(db_point))
    SMP(db_point);
  for (i=0; i<N/2; i++){
    NN_point=NN_search(input_point[i], db_point);
    Sim = S(input_point[i], NN_point, N/2);
    if(Sim > threshold) { Sim = -1; break; }
  } return result;
}
```

4 Experimental Results

We have implemented a prototype shape-based leaf image retrieval system as part of a nationwide project that aims to develop an information bank for all domestic native plants. In the experiments, we used as hardware platform PCs with Dual 2.8 GHz Xeon Processors and 1GB of RAM and Microsoft SQL Server 2000 as underlying DBMS.

In order to show the effectiveness of our proposed algorithm, we compare it with other methods including Fourier Descriptor and Moment Invariants. In addition, we considered a hybrid-search scheme that uses not only leaf shape, but also leaf arrangement for better performance. Fig. 4 shows a variety of leaf arrangements, which can be classified into (a) alternate, (b) opposite, and (c) verticillate. While the alternate arrangement has one leaf per node, the opposite arrangement has two leaves per node and the verticillate has three or more per node.

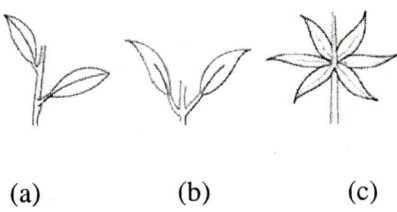

(a)   (b)   (c)

Fig. 4. Leaf arrangement

The leaf arrangement of user-sketched image is identified by leaf base and the number of leaves per node. The leaf base indicates the shape of the leaf base where it attaches to the stem.

In order to evaluate its performance, we collected 1032 leaf images from "*The Korea Plant Picture Book*" [14]. The representation must be invariant to viewing angle change. For this reason, we adjust the viewing angle using Algorithm 2 above.

Fig. 6 shows the recalls and precisions of our improved MPP, MPP, Fourier Descriptor, and Moment Invariants. Precision is the fraction of retrieved images that is relevant to a query. In contrast, recall measures the fraction of the relevant images that have been retrieved. Recall is a non-decreasing function of rank, while precision can be regarded as a function of recall rather than rank. In general, the curve closest to the top of the chart indicates the best performance.

In this figure, for example, our proposed algorithm achieves approximately 1.25 times better precision and recall than MPP. In addition, it achieves approximately 2.11 times better precision and recall than Fourier Descriptor.

Table 2 illustrates the average response time of the NN-search and Dynamic matching with different cell sizes. From the table, we can observe that regardless of matching method used, the response time decreases as the cell size increases. Overall, our proposed method achieved approximately 2.2 times faster response time than the NN-search.

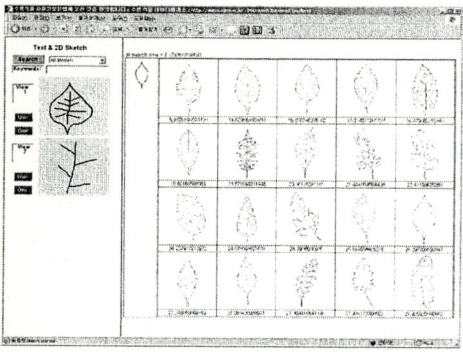
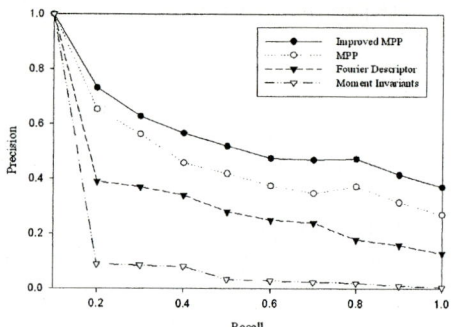

Fig. 5. User Interface   **Fig. 6.** Precision and recall curve

Table 2. Average retrieval response time in seconds

Cell size	Response Time		A / B
	NN-search (A)	Dynamic matching (B)	
5	29.57	13.57	2.18
7	16.58	7.26	2.28
9	12.45	5.80	2.15

5 Conclusions and Future Work

In this paper, we have presented a shape-based leaf image retrieval system. To improve the efficiency of leaf representation, we revised the MPP algorithm to reduce the number of points of interest. For the matching, we proposed a dynamic matching algorithm that reduces the matching time. In addition, by using hybrid-search scheme that considers leaf shape as well as leaf arrangement, we further improved the overall system performance. To evaluate its effectiveness, we have implemented a prototype system and compared our proposed scheme with Fourier Descriptor and Moment Invariants. Experimental results show that the proposed algorithm is more efficient than other methods. In the future, we will improve the shape representation algorithm such that it can consider not only a contour but also a leaf vein.

Acknowledgments

This research was supported by University IT Research Center Project and a grant (no. BDM0100211) to JRL from the Strategic National R&D Program through the Genetic Resources and Information Network Center funded by the Korean Ministry of Science and Technology.

References

1. Gonzalez, Rafel C., Woods, Richard C.: Digital Image Processing. Addison-Wesley. (1992)
2. Lin, H. J., Kao, Y. T.: A prompt contour detection method. the Distributed Multimedia Systems (2001)
3. Michael Heath, et al.: A Robust Visual Method for Assessing the Relative Performance of Edge Detection Algorithms. IEEE Transactions on Pattern Analysis and Machine Intelligence, Vol.19. No.12. (1997) 1338-1359,.
4. Sundar, H., Silver, D., Gagvani, N., Dickinson, S.: Skeleton based shape matching and retrieval. Shape Modeling International. (2003) 130
5. Kurozumi Y., Davis W.A.: Polygonal approximation by the minimax method. Computer Vision, Graphics and Image Processing. (1982) 248-264
6. Sklansky, Chazin et al.: Minimum perimeter polygons of digitized silhouetts. (1972)
7. Sklansky J.: Finding the Convex Hull of a Simple Polygon. Pattern Recognition Letters, Vol.1 No.2. (1982) 79-84
8. Nishida, H.: Structural feature indexing for retrieval of partially visible shapes. Pattern Recognition, Vol.35. No.1. (2002) 55-67
9. Loncaeic, S.: A survey of shape analysis techniques. Pattern Recognition, Vol.31. No.8. (1998) 983-1001
10. Freeman, H., Saghri, J.: Comparative Analysis of Line Drawing Modelling Schemes. Computer Graphics and Image Processing, Vol. 12. (1980)
11. Chang, C., Wenyin, L. and Zhang, H.: Image Retrieval Based on Region Shape Similarity. Electronic Imaging Storage and Retrieval for Image and Video Databases (2001)
12. Veltkamp, R.: Shape matching: similarity measures and algorithms. Technical Report UU-CS-2001-03, Netherlands (2001)
13. Indyk, P., Motwani, R.: Approximate nearest neighbors: towards removing the curse of dimensionality. The 30 annual ACM symposium on Theory of computing, (1998) 604-613
14. Lee, C.B.: The Korea Plant Picture Book. ISBN-8971871954, Hang-moon-sa, (1982).

Mosaicing and Restoration from Blurred Image Sequence Taken with Moving Camera

Midori Onogi and Hideo Saito

Keio University, Department of Information and Computer Science,
Yokohama, Japan
{midori, saito}@ozawa.ics.keio.ac.jp
http://www.ozawa.ics.keio.ac.jp/Saito/

Abstract. A wide-area image can be synthesized from an image sequence taken with a moving camera by using image mosaicing techniques. However, motion blur caused by the motion of the camera may significantly degrade the quality of the synthesized image. In this paper, we propose a new method for generating a deblurred mosaic from an image sequence that is degraded by motion blur under the condition that we do not have any information about the intrinsic and extrinsic parameters of the moving camera during input acquisition. In this method, we assume the objects in the scene can be classified into two regions in order to handle depth. In this paper, the displacement vectors of the features, which are computed using the KLT feature tracker on the consecutive frames, are classified into two regions. Here, the classified vectors provide a Point Spread Function (PSF) of the blurred image, and a homography between two consecutive frames for segmentation and mosaicing. Experimental results show that the Signal to Noise Ratio of the generated images can be significantly improved by our proposed method.

1 Introduction

In general, the resolution and the field of view of a digital image are limited by the camera. Image mosaicing techniques [3, 9] have been used to synthesize a wide-area image from a number of images, which are taken from different camera pose and/or positions. Mosaicing in more general cases of camera motion can be performed by projecting thin strips from the images onto manifolds which are adapted to the motion[11]. These 2D image alignment methods for image mosaicing can be applied successfully when the scene can be approximated by one plane such as in aerial photography, where the scene can be considered flat because the camera is far from the scene. However, these methods fail when the scene is 3D which includes different depths. In order to handle 3D parallax, a depth invariant mosaicing method by computing the camera motion using space-time volume has been developed[14]. Zhigang Zhu et. al. proposed a method for generating stereoscopic mosaics from images captured by a video camera mounted on an airborne platform with GPS/INS measurements using a parallel-perspective representation [13].

Since such image sequences are sometimes captured using a moving camera, the motion makes the captured images blurred. As motion blur due to camera motion may significantly degrade the image quality, a considerable amount of research has been dedicated to restore these images. Blurred images can be deblurred by using image deconvolution [5]. A general motion blur PSF can be recovered from various devices [1]. Motion blur correction from multiple images has recently been tried as well. Rav-Acha et.al. proposed a method for image deblurring from two images having motion blur in different direction[7]. Synthesizing a super-resolved image from multiple images is also an active research topic [3, 8, 10]. Motion deblurring has also been addressed in the context of temporal super-resolution [2].

In most of the research on image restoration, motion blur is considered shift invariant. However, in practice, the motion blur is shift variant because a 3D scene has multiple depths, so the applicability is limited when the scene can not be considered flat. In addition, as many image mosaicing approaches do not consider motion blur, the quality of the mosaic synthesized from a blurred sequence is degraded.

In this paper, we propose a new method for generating a deblurred mosaic from a blurred image sequence captured by a moving camera, in which the intrinsic and motion parameters are unknown. In our proposed method, we combine methods for motion image deblurring and image mosaicing so that we can synthesize mosaic images without motion blur from image sequences taken with a moving camera.

The proposed method is achieved by deblurring each frame of the input sequence and generating a mosaic image from the deblurred frames. The proposed method also takes into account multiple regions with different depth and blur by segmenting each frame based on displacement differences of tracked points, and the estimation of the homography[1] and PSF for each region.

The proposed method first tracks a number of feature points over the input image sequences using the KLT feature tracker. By assuming that the object scene can be represented by two layers of planar regions, the displacement vectors of the features on the consecutive frames are classified into foreground points and background points. For each region, the displacement vectors are averaged for estimating the PSF of the motion blur. By applying the Wiener filter [5] with the estimated PSF for each region, the input image sequence can be deblurred. Our method then merges all the images in the input image sequence by image mosaicing techniques. For the image mosaicing, the homography of each region between the consecutive frames is estimated from the displacement vectors within the region. After the image mosaicing, we can finally synthesize a deblurred wide-area image from the input image sequence. We also have conducted experiments with various scenes consisting of a foreground object and

---

[1] The homography maps the projected point from one plane in a 3D scene to another plane.

a background object. Experimental results demonstrate that our method can generate higher quality mosaics than images without motion blur restoration.

2 Proposed Method

2.1 Corresponding Points

The moving camera provides a sequence of images. By computing corresponding points between consecutive frames, we can obtain the homographies between the consecutive frames for each region and the parameters of the PSF representing motion blur caused by camera motion. We compute corresponding points using the KLT feature tracker [6].

2.2 Classifying Corresponding Points

In order to make a mosaic of a scene that can be approximated by two layers, we need to classify the corresponding points into foreground points and background points.

Let $p_k^i = (x_k^i, y_k^i)$ denote the position of the ith feature point in the kth frame ($0 < k < m$, $0 < i < n$. m indicates the number of the images and n denotes the number of tracked feature points). First, we compute the displacement d_k^i between the consecutive frames of every corresponding point as

$$d_k^i = \sqrt{(x_{k+1}^i - x_k^i)^2 + (y_{k+1}^i - y_k^i)^2}. \qquad (1)$$

We assume that the displacements of the points in the foreground region are sufficiently larger than those in the background region for the classification as shown in Fig. 1. Then, we classify the points into foreground points and background points using the Discriminant Analysis Method in which the threshold is determined by maximizing $F(t)$, the ratio between inner-class and inter-class variance. $F(t)$ is represented as follows:

$$F(t) = \frac{\sigma_B^2}{\sigma_I^2}, \qquad (2)$$

where t is the threshold, σ_B^2 is inter-class variance and σ_I^2 is inner-class variance.

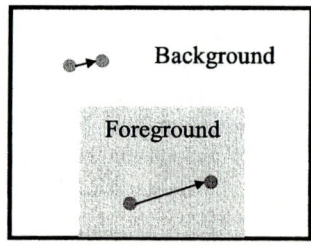

Fig. 1. Displacements of the corresponding points

2.3 Deblurring Images

As the distance from the camera to the foreground is different from the distance to the background region, the motion blur should be restored independently for each region. Since we assume that the translational component of motion of the camera is almost dominant, we can approximate the PSF as follows:

$$h(x,y) = \begin{cases} \frac{1}{w}, & x\cos\theta + y\sin\theta \leq \frac{2}{w} \\ 0, & x\cos\theta + y\sin\theta > \frac{2}{w} \end{cases}, \qquad (3)$$

where w and θ are the width and the angle of motion blur, respectively. Since we also assume that the motion vector between two consecutive frames is almost constant in each region, we can compute w and θ by an average vector of the displacement vectors of the corresponding points in each region. We can deblur each region of each frame using the PSF for the foreground region, $h_k^f(x,y)$, or the PSF for the background region, $h_k^b(x,y)$. Given the estimated PSF, we can deblur each frame using existing deconvolution algorithms. We deblur the images by a Wiener filter [5] in the frequency domain.

As the background regions of the frames are rarely blurred, these do not need to be deblurred in most of the cases. Artifacts from excessively enhancing the edges degrade the quality of images if the backgrounds are strongly deblurred.

2.4 Segmentation and Mosaicing

Given the deblurred frames, we generate a wide-area mosaic. When the scene can be considered flat such as in aerial photography, image mosaicing generally needs homographies between a base frame, which is selected as the standard image plane for merging, and every other frame. However, we consider our scene in 3D therefore a single plane is not enough. We generate mosaics for the foreground region and the background region separately by using a separate homography for each region rather than a single homography for the whole frame. It is necessary to segment the scene to handle this case.

Segmentation of the scene is done by splitting the scene into two layers of planer regions. First, we select a base frame, which is not necessarily the start frame, from the input frames. From the base frame, we manually select the vertices $\boldsymbol{v}_{base}^j$ ($0 < j < l$, l indicates the number of the vertices) on the border of the foreground region which approximates a polygon. The corresponding vertices in the kth frame $\boldsymbol{v}_k^j$ can be computed with

$$\boldsymbol{v}_k^j = \mathbf{H}_{base,k}^f \boldsymbol{v}_{base}^j, \qquad (4)$$

where $\mathbf{H}_{base,k}^f$ is the homography of the foreground region. This is shown in Fig. 2. However, to obtain $\boldsymbol{v}_k^j$, we must compute the foreground homography $\mathbf{H}_{base,k}^f$. We can obtain $\mathbf{H}_{base,k}^f$ by the product of the homographies of consecutive frames up to the kth frame.

$$\mathbf{H}_{base,k}^f = \mathbf{H}_{base,base-1}^f \mathbf{H}_{base-1,base-2}^f \cdots \mathbf{H}_{k+1,k}^f. \qquad (5)$$

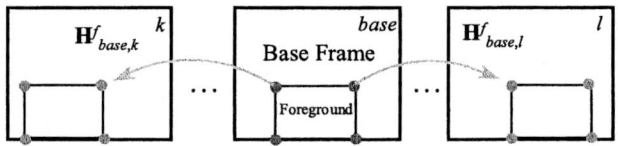

Fig. 2. Segmentation

The consecutive frame homographies can be obtained from the SVD of the foreground points that were obtained from corresponding point classification in section 2.2.

Each pixel in the foreground regions of the deblurred frames is transformed into a base frame by $\mathbf{H}^f_{base,k}$. The color values of the pixels in the same place are averaged, and then the foreground regions are merged into a foreground mosaic $I^f(x,y)$, while the background regions are also merged into a background mosaic $I^b(x,y)$ by the background homography $\mathbf{H}^b_{base,k}$ as shown in Fig. 3. $\mathbf{H}^b_{base,k}$ can also be computed in the same way as the foreground homography $\mathbf{H}^f_{base,k}$. Although each frame is deblurred as described in section 2.3, the artifacts from enhancing the edges remain in each image. By the averaging of the image mosaicing process, the effect of the artifacts can be decreased.

Given both foreground and background mosaics $I^f(x,y)$ and $I^b(x,y)$, we can finally generate the output image $O(x,y)$ as:

$$O(x,y) = I^f(x,y) \cdot M^f + I^b(x,y) \cdot \bar{M}^f, \qquad (6)$$

where M^f is a segmentation mask for the shape of the foreground region obtained from the vertices of the polygon in the base frame.

2.5 Removing mistracked corresponding points

The tracked corresponding feature points sometimes may include some wrongly tracked feature points. When there are such mistracked points, the accuracy in estimating the PSF and the homography between consecutive frames is reduced. Because the accuracy of the homography is very important for segmentation and image mosaicing, it is important to improve the accuracy. We remove the as many as possible of the mistracked feature points during the segmentation process with the following technique.

For All Frames
1. Compute Homography $\mathbf{H}^f_{base,k}$, and vertices v^j_k as in section 2.4.
2. *For All corresponding points*
If Foreground point
If Inside polygon   Keep point
Else   Delete point
If Background point
If Inside polygon   Delete point
Else   Keep point

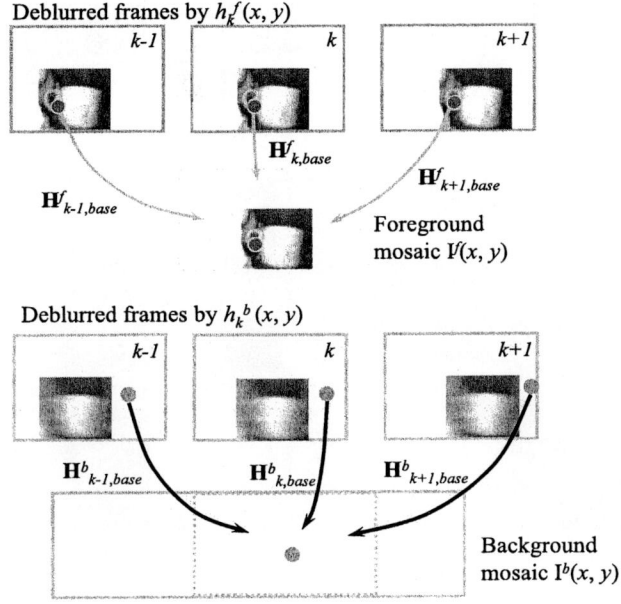

Fig. 3. Image mosaicing

3. **If** No deleted points Stop processing
Else Go to step4
4. Reclassify remaining points as in section 2.2. Go to step1.

With the new corresponding points, the input frames are deblurred as described in section 2.3. After deblurring images, we then segment the captured frames again, and merge the foreground and background images using the new points of each region.

3 Experimental results

We recorded a video sequence of a number of scenes, whereby a planar foreground object is in front of the background scene.

3.1 Blur removal

In Figs. 4a and 5a, we show examples taken from input image sequence that is blurred due to camera motion. Figs. 4b and 5b show individual frames deblurred by $h_k^f(x,y)$ using a Wiener filter. However, artifacts still remain in the deblurred frames. Figs. 4c and 5c show the output images generated by the proposed method. Figs 4d, e, and f show a close-up of the raw input image, a deblurred only output image, and a deblurred+mosaiced output image respectively. As can be seen from the figures, our method produces the clearest text.

(a) Raw input image sequence   (b) Deblurred foreground region input image sequence

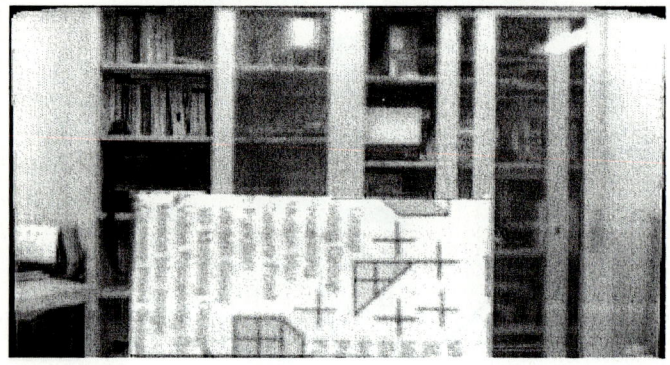

(c) Deblurred mosaic

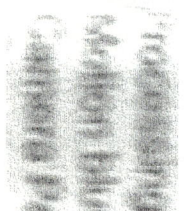 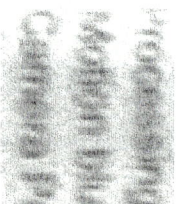 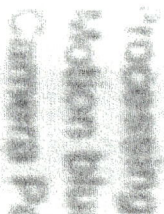

(d)Input image zoom-in (e)Deblurred only zoom-in (f)Deblurred mosaicing zoom-in

Fig. 4. A planar document is captured as the foreground region in the scene

3.2 Mistracked corresponding points removal

In Fig. 6, we show the input sequence in Fig. 4 including the mistracked corresponding points in the background region. These mistracked corresponding points are removed by image segmentation. We show a result when the mistracked corresponding points are not removed in Fig. 7. Since the accuracy of the homography computed from the points which include all the mistracked corresponding points is degraded, the input images are wrongly aligned. Consequently, the text in the foreground region can hardly be read. The width of the result image is also narrower than the image shown in Fig. 4c because of the poor accuracy of the homography.

3.3 S/N ratio

In order to validate the accuracy of the output image, we compute the Signal to Noise Ratio (S/N ratio) of the foreground regions of the images. S/N ratio SNR is expressed as:

(a) Raw input image sequence　　(b) Deblurred foreground region input image sequence

(c) Deblurred mosaic

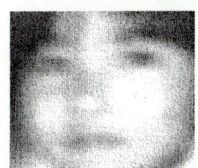 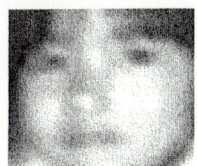 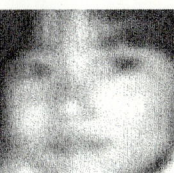

(d)Input image zoom-in　(e)Deblurred only zoom-in　(f)Deblurred mosaicing zoom-in

Fig. 5. A planar photo is captured as the foreground region in the scene

(a)Images before removing mistracked corresponding points　　(b)Images after removing mistracked corresponding points

Red dots represent corresponding points between two consecutive frames.

Fig. 6. Examples taken from image sequence including mistracked corresponding points

$$RSME = \sqrt{\frac{\sum [f(i,j) - F(i,j)]^2}{N}} \quad (7)$$

$$SNR = 20 \log_{10}\left(\frac{255}{RSME}\right), \quad (8)$$

where $f(i,j)$ represents evaluated image, and $F(i,j)$ represents the ground truth image captured without motion blur by using a tripod. N is the number of the

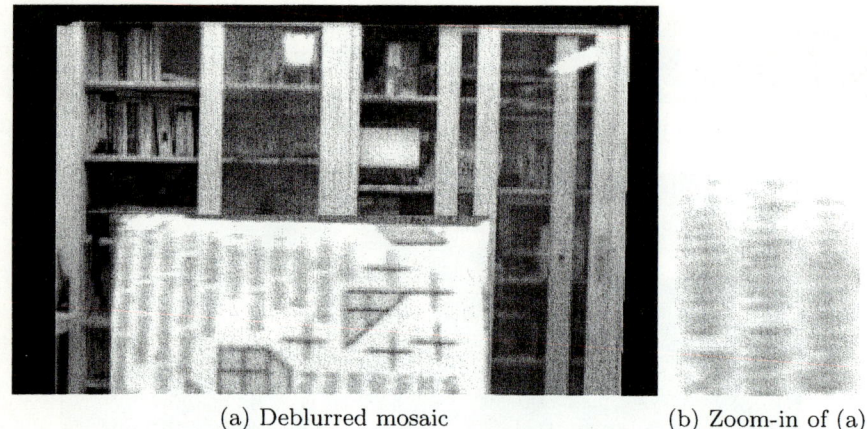

(a) Deblurred mosaic (b) Zoom-in of (a)

Fig. 7. A result without removing the mistracked corresponding points

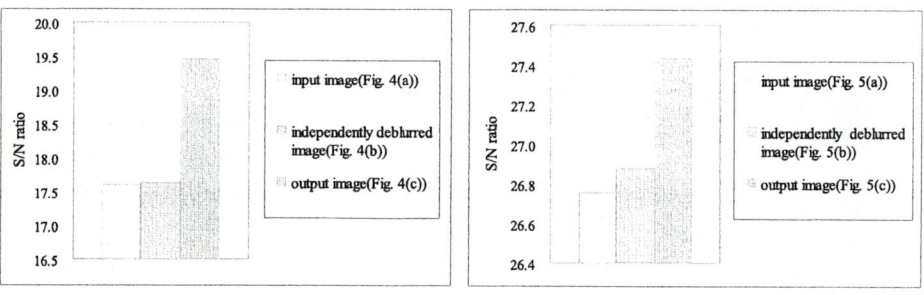

(a) S/N ratio of the images shown in Fig4 (b) S/N ratio of the images shown in Fig5

Fig. 8. S/N ratio

pixels in the foreground region. $RSME$ is the root square mean error. In Fig. 8, we see that S/N ratio of the images generated by the proposed method exceeds that of the images deblurred at each frame independently. The results show that our method is effective in restoration of motion blur, and in decreasing artifacts by deconvolution of the PSF.

4 Conclusion

In this paper, we have presented a method for generating a deblurred mosaic image from motion images captured by a handy moving camera, under the condition that the scene consists of the layers with different depth. By deblurring each frame and mosaicing them, we generate the deblurred image with a high S/N ratio. The experimental results demonstrate the validity of the proposed method.

Our proposed method has several possible applications. It could be applied to image mosaicing from blurred sequences captured from moving cars or trains out of the city in which a building stands in front of the background. Our approach could also be useful for mosaicing a group photo when the people stand in front of a planar background.

References

1. Moshe Ben-Ezra and Shree K. Nayar: Motion-Based Motion Deblurring. IEEE Trans. on PAMI, June 2004, Volume 26, Issue 6.
2. E. Shechtman, Y. Caspi, and M. Irani: Increasing Space-Time Resolution in Video. In Proc.ECCV, pp. 753-768, 2002.
3. D. Capel: Image Mosaicing and Super-Resolution (Book). Springer, 2004.
4. B. Bascle, A. Blake, and A. Zisserman: Motion deblurring and super-resolution from an image sequence. In Proc.ECCV, pp. 312-320, 1996.
5. A.K. Katsaggelos: Digital Image Restoration (Book). SpringerBerlin, 1991.
6. Bruce D. Lucas and Takeo Kanade: An Iterative Image Registration Technique with an Application to Stereo Vision. International Joint Conference on Artificial Intelligence, pp. 674-679, 1981.
7. A. Rav-Acha, S. Peleg: Two motion-blurred images are better than one. Pattern Recognition Letters, Vol 26, pp. 311-317, 2005.
8. S. Sei, H. Saito: Super-Resolved Image Synthesis from Uncalibrated Camera with Unknown Motion. IAPR Workshop on Machine Vision Applications (MVA02), pp. 420-423, Dec.2002
9. R. Szeliski: Video Mosaics for Virtual Environments. IEEE Computer Graphics and Applications, Vol. 16, No. 2, pp. 22-30, 1996.
10. I. Zakharov, D. Dovnar, Y. Lebedinsky: Super-resolution image restoration from several blurred images formed in various conditions. Prpc. International Conference on Image Processing 2003, pp. II-315-318,2003.
11. S. Peleg, B. Rousso, A. Rav-Acha, and A. Zomet: Mosaicing on Adaptive Manifolds. IEEE Trans. on PAMI, Oct. 2000, pp. 1144-1154
12. A. Zomet, S. Peleg, and C. Arora: Rectified Mosaicing: Mosaics without the Curl. CVPR'00, June 2000, Vol. II, pp. 459-465
13. Zhigang Zhu, Allen R. Hanson, and Edward M. Riseman: Generalized Parallel-Perspective Stereo Mosaics from Airborne Video. IEEE Trans on PAMI, February 2004, Volume 26, Issue 2
14. Alex Rav-Acha, Yael Shor, and Shmuel Peleg: Mosaicing with Parallax using Time Warping. Second IEEE Workshop on Image and Video Registration (IVR'04), Washington, DC, July 2004

Finding People in Video Streams by Statistical Modeling

S. Harasse, L. Bonnaud, and M. Desvignes

LIS-ENSIEG, 961 rue de la Houille Blanche BP 46 38402,
St. Martin d'Heres cedex, France
{harasse, bonnaud, desvignes}@lis.inpg.fr

Abstract. The aim of our project is to design an algorithm for counting people in public transport vehicles such as buses by processing images from surveillance cameras' video streams. This article presents a method of detection and tracking of multiple faces in a video by using a model of first and second order local moments. The three essential steps of our system are skin color modeling, probabilistic shape modeling and bayesian detection and tracking. An iterative process is used to estimate the position and shape of multiple faces in images, and to track them in video streams.

1 Introduction and Previous Works

Estimating the number of people in a noisy environment is a central task in surveillance. A real time count can be used to enforce the occupancy limit in a building, to manage transport traffic in real time, to actively manage city services and allocate resources for public events. Our project is to add a counting system for moving platforms such as buses, to an existing on-board digital video recorder, without requiring specific sensors or other equipment. Images are captured using a video camera placed in front of the vehicle entrance and are analyzed to determine the number of people stepping into and out of the bus. Acquisition rate is about 6 frames per second, and the recorder delivers JPEG images with a high compression rate (quality 50). The context of our application and the viewpoint of the camera are so that the scene background is dynamic. Indeed, outdoor scene as seen through windows is different at every bus stop, and there can be moving objects such as cars or other people that we should not count. Then the bus starts again and the background starts moving. The scene also vary much in lighting conditions, according to time of day and vehicle location.

Figure 1 shows a sequence from inside a vehicle. People can be viewed from the front and from the side.

Finding people in images is a difficult task [1] due to the high variability in the appearance of people. For human detection and tracking for surveillance, various approaches have been proposed in the past years [2,3].

Background subtraction [5] is often a first step to find objects of interest such as faces. Unfortunately, this approach needs a stationary background, whereas the background often changes in our application. Interframe motion based approaches [6] do not apply easily for the same reason.

Fig. 1. Original sequence

Classical template matching methods require the learning of several face patterns [8]. Recent works [9] on template matching deal with variation in scale, pose, or shape, in the context of pedestrian detection. In their acquisition conditions, the great variability of human is dramatically reduced which is not true for our application.

Feature based approaches extract invariant structural features from one or more images, and then classify extracted objects with statistical classifiers such as support vector machines [11], neural networks [12], probabilistic approaches [13], or cascades of filters [14]. Features are designed to be invariant to some changes in illumination and pose. Several works use Harr wavelets [14], DCT [15] or local descriptors [16]. However, the most widely adopted feature is skin color [2,3] since it forms a relatively tight cluster in color spaces, even when considering darker and brighter skins. Color is low level information, which permits fast processing and is robust to changes in pose and illumination.

This motivates our approach, which is to count people by finding and tracking faces, using skin color as the main information source.

The main problem of methods based on skin color is the determination of a threshold to be used on each pixel for deciding which pixels correspond to skin: this segmentation step gives a binary mask for further processing like clustering. This can lead to information loss if the skin color model is not accurate enough. Our method solves this problem by taking a Bayesian approach and deciding for skin or non-skin at an upper stage of processing, combining skin probabilities information with spatial and temporal information. A similar strategy has been used by [18] for single face tracking.

This article presents the main steps of our multiple faces tracking method. The next section deals with how skin probability maps are obtained from the images and skin model. Then the shape model is presented, as well as how it is integrated into a Bayesian framework. Our iterative method to estimate the faces positions and shapes is detailed. Finally some results of face detection and tracking are discussed.

2 Skin Model

A skin color model is needed in order to detect skin colored pixel in images. Skin chrominance is very specific, as opposed to its luminance. Thus our model is defined in a chrominance color space so that skin pixels can be easily recognized from non-skin pixels. The two-dimensional normalized-rg color space is efficient for this task. It is defined from the original RGB space by:

$$r = \frac{R}{R+G+B}, \quad g = \frac{G}{R+G+B}$$

In this color space, skin color can be accurately modeled by a single bidimensionnal gaussian probability distribution, whose parameters are learned from about 160 million skin pixels from the FERET faces database [19], by computing the mean vector and variance-covariance matrix of the sample set. The resulting gaussian probability density function is named g_{skin}, and is applied to each pixel of an image I to obtain a skin probability map S_I:

$$S_I(i,j) = g_{skin}(I(i,j))$$

where (i,j) is a position in the image I and $I(i,j)$ is the color of I at this position, in normalized-rg coordinates.

3 Face Shape Model and Bayesian Framework

3.1 Statistical Modeling

Our face detector is based on a statistical representation of the problem: a face is a skin region, parameterized by its position, shape and orientation. Our tracking application does not need an accurate representation of face shape. A elliptical shape is convenient since it does not require many parameters and is general enough to approximate most face shapes.

Let x be a 5-dimensional random variable modeling the position and shape of a skin object, by its first and second order moments:

$$x = (\mu_x, \sigma_x) \text{ with } \mu_x = (\mu_{x1}, \mu_{x2}), \sigma_x = \begin{bmatrix} \sigma_{x11} & \sigma_{x12} \\ \sigma_{x12} & \sigma_{x22} \end{bmatrix}$$

Our face model can be seen as an ellipse centered in μ_x with axes defined by covariance matrix σ_x. This model has been introduced in [18] for one single face tracking using color, whereas our algorithm is designed to track multiple faces.

And let z be a random variable representing each observed image. That is to say, the realizations for z are the images where faces are to be detected. The face detection problem then involves computing the probablity density $p(x/z)$, from which we can decide where faces are likely to be in the image.

Considering a bayesian framework, the a posteriori probability density $p(x/z)$ is proportional to the product of the observation density $p(z/x)$ by the prior density $p(x)$: $p(x/z) \propto p(z/x).p(x)$.

$p(x)$ describes all a priori information on expected faces, such as possible faces positions and sizes. This helps the algorithm to avoid detecting arms and legs that are also skin colored.

3.2 Observation Density

The observation probability density $p(z/x)$ must now be defined. It represents the probability to observe the image z, knowing that a skin object parameterized by x is present. The number of skin objects in the image is not known, and $p(z/x)$ should allow the estimation of the number of objects and their parameters. Since random variable x is defined as the parameters of only one object, it is 5-dimensional, which is reasonable, but it does not directly allow the estimation of many objects. Thus $p(z/x)$ is defined so that there is a local maximum for each x corresponding to a skin object in the image.

The function chosen for the observation probability is the correlation function between the skin map S_z of image z and the bidimensional gaussian g_x parameterized by x :

$$p(z/x) \propto \int S_z(t).g_x(t)dt$$

where t is a bidimensional variable.

$p(z/x)$ has local maxima for each skin object in z, with the hypothesis that objects are well separated from each other.

3.3 Skin Objects Detection

From this point, there are several ways to detect the objects in our image, including the exhaustive search of local maxima in the 5-dimensional function $x \mapsto p(z/x)$, or sampling algorithms like Condensation [17]. We propose a method that doesn't require the computation of $p(z/x)$ for all values.

The random variable x can be seen as two random variables μ_x and σ_x which represent the first and second order moments of the object respectively. The method proposed here estimates μ_x by using a priori information about σ_x, then estimates σ_x for each detected object, using an iterative process.

3.4 First Order Moment Estimation

The detection of the first order moments μ_x of objects in the image involves an a priori estimation of σ_x. σ_m is defined as the average covariance matrix representing a face. With this assumption, the observation density becomes:

$$p(z/\mu_x, \sigma_x = \sigma_m) \propto \int S_z(t).g_{\mu_x,\sigma_m}(t)dt$$

$$\propto \int S_z(t).g_{0,\sigma_m}(\mu_x - t)dt$$

The observation density with fixed $\sigma_x = \sigma_m$ is proportianal to the 2-dimensional convolution product of S_z by a gaussian function with covariance matrix σ_m, which is an inexpensive computation. Objects' first order moments are detected by finding the local maxima of the function.

3.5 Iterative Second Order Moment Estimation

Suppose that an object x_0 is present in the image, with first order moment μ_{x_0}. Its second order moment σ_{x_0} must be estimated so that $p(z/x_0)$ is a local maxima. If there is only one skin object in the image, the problem is simply resolved by computing the second order moment of the whole skin map:

$$\sigma_{x_0}^2 = \int (t - \mu_{x_0})^2 . S_z(t) dt$$

where t is a bidimensional variable. Since the number of objects in the image is unknown, our method is to estimate σ_{x_0} by using local moments iteratively. Let W be a 2-dimensional window defined in the same space as S_z, with $\int W(t) dt = 1$. The second order local moment of S_z centered in μ_{x_0} is defined as:

$$\sigma_{S_z,W}^2 = \int (t - \mu_{x_0})^2 . S_z(t) W(t) dt \qquad (1)$$

A sequence of local moments is defined as:

$$\begin{cases} \sigma_0 = 1 \\ \sigma_{n+1}^2 = \sigma_{S_z, g(\mu_{x_0}, \alpha.\sigma_n)}^2 \end{cases} \qquad (2)$$

where $g(\mu_{x_0}, \alpha.\sigma_n)$ is the bidimensional gaussian window of first and second order moments μ_{x_0} and $\alpha.\sigma_n$ respectively, with α chosen experimentally for convergence.

As expected, this sequence converges to the second order moment of the skin object. By using local moments, the computation of σ_{x_0} is not disturbed by the other objects in the image. The detection of multiple skin objects in the image can then be achieved. Figure 2 shows the results obtained with this method.

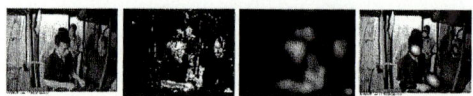

Fig. 2. (a) original image, (b) skin map, (c) local maxima (d) detected objects

4 Tracking

Our method for temporal tracking of detected skin objects is tighly related to the recursive method used for the second order local moment estimation. The tracking is composed of a prediction step followed by an observation step for each object.

Prediction Step. During the tracking of a skin object in the video stream, the past estimated positions and shapes are stored and used to predict the next state of the object. Any kind of prediction can be used here. For our application, a constant speed prediction gives good results since people enter the bus with a continuous motion:

$$\hat{x}_{t+1} = x_t + (x_t - x_{t-1})$$

Observation Step. The observation step corrects the predicted position and shape of the object with respect to the observed image. The gaussian function parameterized with the predicted state defines the window in which the first and second order local moments of the object are computed. This step is iterated by using the previously computed local moments as the parameters of the gaussian window:

$$\begin{cases} \mu_0 = \mu_{predicted} \\ \sigma_0 = \sigma_{predicted} \\ \mu_{n+1} = \mu_{S_z, g(\mu_n, \alpha.\sigma_n)} \\ \sigma^2_{n+1} = \sigma^2_{S_z, g(\mu_n, \alpha.\sigma_n)} \end{cases} \quad (3)$$

with $\mu_{S_z, g(\mu_n, \alpha.\sigma_n)}$ the first order local moment of S_z in the window $g(\mu_n, \alpha.\sigma_n)$, defined by:

$$\mu_{S_z, g(\mu_n, \alpha.\sigma_n)} = \int t.S_z(t).g(\mu_n, \alpha.\sigma_n) dt$$

In this sequence, the σ update step is the same as in equations 1 and 2. This sequence converges to the first and second order moments of each face for the current image.

5 Results

5.1 Faces Detection Results

The skin model and face detection algorithm have been validated on the *Caltech* image database, containing 873 images of faces from a total of 9352 images. 95% of the faces were successfully detected, while the false detection rate was 15%. These rates are similar to those (74% to 98%) of other efficient face detectors [2].

Figure 3 presents some results. Images (a) to (d) shows successful results obtained on face images. The color model is robust to lighting intensity variations as seen in Image (d). Image (e) is an example of detection failure, where observed skin color does not match the skin model. Image (f) presents a case of false detection when non-face objects have a color very similar to skin. Finally, images (g) to (i) are example of images in which there were no face, and no false detection occurred.

5.2 Face Tracking Results

Our tracking method has been tested under real conditions, on video streams from a transport vehicle. We used 3 hours of video and 3 cameras. The acquisition rate was 6 frame per second for each camera. The front camera was the most useful for our people counting application, whereas the other cameras were only used to validate the tracking method with a different scene. Several bus stops were simulated, with about 15 people getting in the vehicle each time. The total time for all bus stops sequences is about 10 minutes.

Experiments in an indoor office under controlled illumination conditions have also been made. 72 persons passed by the camera during 5 minutes, with many people crossings and turn-backs. The acquisition frame rate is 30fps in this sequence.

Fig. 3. Face detection examples

Figure 4 shows an example of tracking of several faces inside a transport vehicle during a stop. Four people were present in this sequence, and were all tracked successfully. Image (b) includes a false detection of a face, caused by pixels whose color is very similar to skin. Since those pixels are static, this false detection has no effect on the results of a people counting application.

Figure 5 shows an example of two people crossing during the office video sequence. The two faces have been tracked successfully. In the middle image, the two faces are very close from each other, but the constant speed prediction step manages to keep track of each face. The middle images also presents an example of false detection: an arm is detected as a face. This can be easily avoided with an appropriate prior probability map describing possible face positions and shapes.

It is difficult to describe quantitatively the performance of a face tracker. In the bus video sequences, each person entering the vehicle was present for about 30 images. During these 30 images, the face starts being tracked when it gets close enough to the camera (because small objects are intentionnally discarded

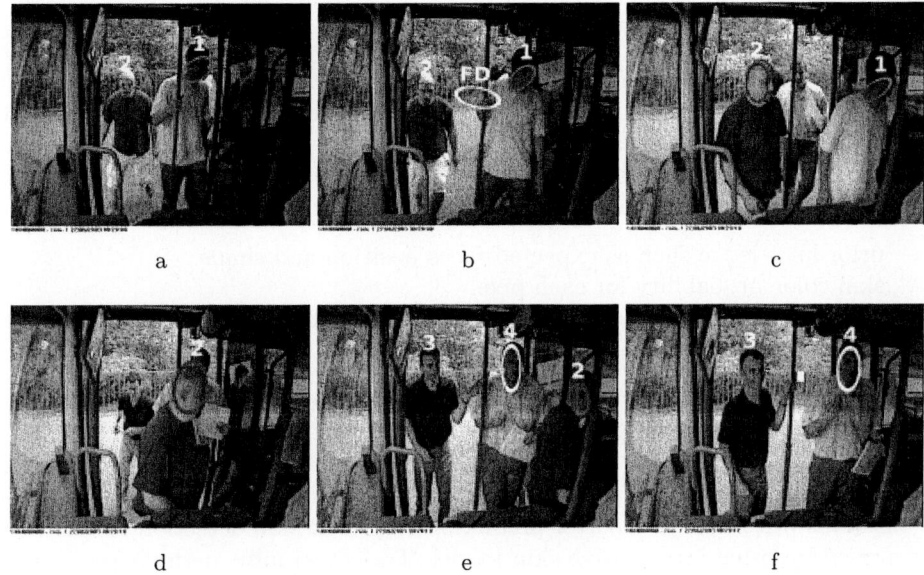

Fig. 4. Tracking example

Fig. 5. Office sequence crossing example

by the tracker), and the person is tracked successfully most of the time. Cases were people cross each other are the main difficulty we encountered since it happens that the tracker jumps from a face to the other. This happens when the two faces are very close from each other. The prediction step could be improved to help the tracker avoiding these tracking failures.

In a simple counting system, counting rate has an accuracy of 85% on office video, and 90% on video transport. These results have been obtained by counting tracked faces crossing a segment defined manually in image space. Most non-detections were caused by faces passing under the segment or people walking behind another person. False detections were caused by some arms being counted. The office video results are not as good as the vehicle results because there were more people crossing each other.

The processing rate is about 2 images/second with unoptimized C code, which is a third of the required rate for real time. This gap could be bridged by deferred processing of images between two bus stops for the counting application.

6 Conclusion and Perspectives

The main features of our method are the statistical modeling for detection and tracking and the iterative estimation of shape parameters. Only one parameter is needed: the minimum face size σ_m used for first order moment estimation. The statistical model is convenient since it helps to avoid thresholding during skin detection, and integrates efficiently several information sources:

- prior knowledge such as expected faces position and shape
- skin color probability for each pixel
- shape probability, modeled by a gaussian function whose parameters are estimated iteratively.

Other information sources can be easily added to our framework, as soon as they can be expressed as probability maps. The next step is to improve tracking robustness by learning the trajectories of tracked faces, in order to compute automatically a probability map for frequently appearing face shapes and positions. This will result in a better prediction step. The skin detection can also be improved by using an adaptive skin model. Trajectography methods could also be included for a more robust tracking in crossing situations.

References

1. S. Ioffe, D. A. Forsyth, "Probabilistic Methods for Finding People". IJCV 43(1), pp 45-68, 2001.
2. M.H. Yang, D. Kriegman, and N. Ahuja. "Detecting face in images: a survey", IEEE PAMI, 24(1), pp 34-58, 2002.
3. Erik Hjelmas "Face Detection: A Survey", Computer Vision and Image Understanding, 83(3), pp. 236-274, 2001.
4. C. Wren, A. Azarbayejani, T. Darell, A. Pentland, "Pfinder: Real-time tracking of human body", IEEE PAMI, 19(7), pp. 780-785, 1997.
5. I. Haritaoglu, D. Harwood, and L. Davis, "W4: A real-time system for detection and tracking of people and monitoring their activities", IEEE PAMI, 22(8), pp. 809-830, 2000.
6. Collins, Lipton, Kanade, Fujiyoshi, Duggins, Tsin, Tolliver, Enomoto, and Hasegawa, "A System for Video Surveillance and Monitoring: VSAM Final Report," CMU-RI-TR-00-12, Carnegie Mellon University, May, 2000.
7. G. Yang, T.S. Huang, "Human face detection in complex background", Pattern recognition,27(1):53, 1994.
8. Y.H. Kwon and N. da Vitoria Lobo, "Face Detection Using Templates", International Conference on Pattern Recognition, pp. 764-767, 1994.
9. H. Nanda and L. Davis, "Probabilistic template based pedestrian detection in infrared videos". IEEE Intelligent Vehicles, 2002, Versailles, France, pp 15-20, 2002,
10. C. Stauffer and E. Grimson, "Similarity templates for detection and recognition", Computer Vision and Pattern Recognition, pp. 221-228, Kauai, HI,. 2001.
11. F. Xu, X. Liu, and K. Fujimura, "Pedestrian Detection and Tracking with Night Vision", IEEE Transactions on Intelligent Transportation Systems, 5(4), 2004
12. H. Rowley, S. Baluja, T. Kanade, "Neural Network-Based Face Detection," IEEE Trans. Pattern Analysis and Machine Intelligence,20(1), pp.23-38, 1998.

13. H. Schneiderman and T. Kanade, "Probabilistic Modeling of Local Appearance and Spatial Relationships for Object Recognition", IEEE CVPR, pp. 45-51, 1998.
14. P. Viola, M. J. Jones, "Robust Real-Time Face Detection", International Journal Computer Vision, 57(2), pp. 137-154, 2004.
15. Z. M. Hafed, M. Levine, "Face Recognition Using the Discrete Cosine Transform", International Journal of Computer Vision, 43 (3): pp 167-188, 2001
16. V. Vogelhuber and C. Schmid, "Face Detection based on Generic Local Descriptors and Spatial Constraints", ICPR, Vol. 1, pp 1084-1087, 2000.
17. M. Isard and A. Blake, "Condensation – conditional density propagation for visual tracking", International Journal of Computer Vision 29(1), pp. 5–28, 1998.
18. K. Schwerdt and J. L. Crowley, "Robust face tracking using color", 4th Intl Conf on Automatic Face and Gesture Recognition, Grenoble, France, 2000, pp. 90–95.
19. P. J. Phillips, H. Moon, P. J. Rauss, and S. Rizvi, "The FERET evaluation methodology for face recognition algorithms", IEEE Transactions on Pattern Analysis and Machine Intelligence, Vol. 22, No. 10, October 2000.

Camera Motion Estimation by Image Feature Analysis

Thitiporn Lertrusdachakul, Terumasa Aoki, and Hiroshi Yasuda

The University of Tokyo,
153-8904 Tokyo, Japan
{pom, aoki, yasuda}@mpeg.rcast.u-tokyo.ac.jp

Abstract. In this paper, we propose an algorithm to characterize camera motion in video sequences based on image feature analysis. The approach predicts camera motion using spatio-temporal information obtained from tracking selected feature points throughout an image sequence. The spatio-temporal information provides the advantage of rich visual characteristic along a larger temporal scale over the traditional approaches, which tend to formulate computational methodologies on a few adjacent frames. The algorithm detects five basic camera motions of stationary, panning, tilting, zooming, and the combination of panning and tilting. We conduct the experiments to verify the proposed approach using real compressed video sequences. The experimental results have demonstrated the performance of proposed approach in determining camera motion.

1 Introduction

Recent advances in data compression and communication technologies have made digital video increasingly available and more pervasive. MPEG-7 provides a rich set of standardized tools to describe multimedia content. The meaning and manipulation of the content have become more accessible to the users and enable the generation of new unique applications. Search and browsing performances become more effective since the detail of content that can be described using MPEG-7 is quite comprehensive. In a video sequence, motion features provide the easiest access to the temporal dimension and are hence of key significance in video indexing. When used in combination with other features such as color or texture, they significantly improve the performance of similarity-based video-retrieval systems. They also enable motion-based queries, which are useful in contexts in which motion has a rich meaning such as sport or surveillance [1]. Camera motion is one aspect to help infer higher-level semantic content and query information in video retrieval. Nevertheless, the efficient methodology for annotating the visual information of camera motion is still inapplicable. Several approaches have been developed to estimate camera motion based on the analysis of optical flow computed between consecutive images [2]-[4]. However, the estimation of optical flow, which is usually based on gradient methods or block matching methods, is computationally expensive [5]. Some approaches directly manipulate MPEG-compressed video to extract camera motion using the motion vectors as an alternative to optical flow [6]-[9]. However, the accuracy in detecting camera zoom operation is difficult to achieve because of noise in motion vectors due to independent object motion in the frame or the MPEG encoding process, such as quantization errors, and other artifacts. Moreover, the MPEG encoder delivers numerous wrong motion vectors on the background when formed by large uniform regions. In this paper, we propose an approach to characterize camera motion based on the image feature analysis. The motion trajectories of image features are calculated and used to determine the global motion of a shot in video sequences.

2   Spatio-temporal Characteristic of Image Features

Image features are local, meaningful, and detectable parts of an image, which can be classified into two categories: a global property of an image (global feature), and a part of the image with some special properties (local feature) [10]. Edges and corners are basic features for image recognition and motion analysis. Edges are the most salient and useful features in images, since solid objects, surfaces, and shadows all produce edges. Corners are another type of image features. They are stable across image sequences and are very useful in image matching for stereo and object tracking for motion [11]. The motion is unambiguous at a corner while it is ambiguous at an edge. Therefore, we select corner as the image feature for camera motion analysis. Harris corner detector is used since it is relatively simple, efficient and reliable. By observing the motion trajectories of image features along a shot, we envisage the possibilities of accomplishing the spatio-temporal characteristic of camera motion in video sequences. Figure 1 shows examples of spatio-temporal characteristic of various camera motions. Given a video consists of image sequence with (x, y) image dimension and t temporal dimension. The camera motion can be inferred directly from the spatio-temporal information of the feature points. For instance, motion trajectories of horizontal lines in both (t, x) and (t, y) dimensions as shown in Fig. 1(a) depict static camera motion. Motion trajectories of slanted lines with negative slope in (t, x) dimension and horizontal lines in (t, y) dimension indicate pan right while tilt up has the horizontal trajectories in (t, x) dimension and slanted lines with positive slope in (t, y) dimension. For zoom out, the motion trajectories are expanded in for both (t, x) and (t, y) dimensions. The combination between pan left and tilt up has the motion trajectories of slanted lines with positive slope in both (t, x) and (t, y) dimensions.

3   Camera Motion Characterization

In our approach, camera motion is estimated by analyzing the motion trajectories of image features. The spatio-temporal characteristic of image features is determined into two steps. The first step is to extract the image features and track those feature points along a shot. We define the region to represent the whole image as the shaded area shown in Fig. 2. The corners are entirely detected in this specific area. Because the edge pixels have some noise, we omit those pixels for feature detection and tracking (i.e., five pixels in our case). The width of shaded area is equal to 20 percent of the total length. In the case that a number of detected image features or the distribution of feature points is too small, the whole pixels will be used for feature detection. Ten image features that have the longest tracking duration are selected as the good feature points for camera motion analysis. Then the algorithm computes slope, y-intercept and standard deviation for each motion trajectory.

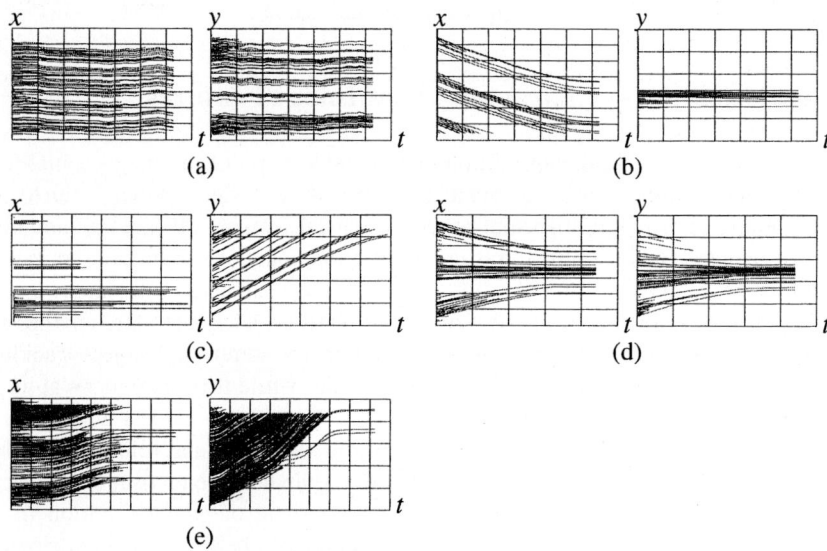

Fig. 1. Spatio-temporal characteristic of various camera motions, *(a) stationary, (b) pan right, (c) tilt up, (d) zoom out, and (e) pan left-tilt up.*

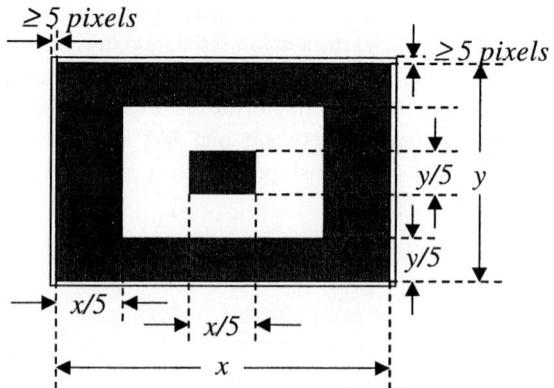

Fig. 2. Feature detection area

The second step is to classify a frame into camera motion. We consider five motion classes; stationary (stationary camera and little scene motion), panning, tilting (camera rotation around its horizontal/vertical axis), zooming (focal length change of the lens of a stationary camera), and the combination of panning and tilting. The camera motion is estimated from spatio-temporal characteristic of the good feature points using the process described in Fig. 3. The algorithm first determines the easiest cases, which are stationary, panning, and tilting without object motion. Then zooming operation is examined. This can reduce the computational process when a shot consists of no object motion. Next, the algorithm repeats detection of the first block diagram with including object motion before going to the last process of panning-tilting detection. The concept of stationary, panning, and tilting detection is described in Fig. 4. Motion trajectories of horizontal lines (i.e. small standard deviation) in both (t, x) and (t, y) dimensions indicate static camera motion. Motion trajectories of slanted lines in (t, x) dimension with positive slope indicate pan left and negative slope indicate pan right. For (t, y) dimension, positive slope indicates tilt up and negative slope indicates tilt down. When the object motion is concerned, we consider a dominant motion class as the camera motion of a shot. The algorithm to classify zooming motion is described in Fig. 5. In zooming operation, the motion trajectories are either expanded in or out for both (t, x) and (t, y) dimensions. The algorithm determines whether they are expanded in or out by comparing the y–intercept of positive and negative slope. If the y-intercept of negative slope is greater, it is expanded in which refers to zooming out operation. Otherwise, it will be zooming in. If the characteristic of motion trajectories does not fall into any motion classes, the camera motion is unknown.

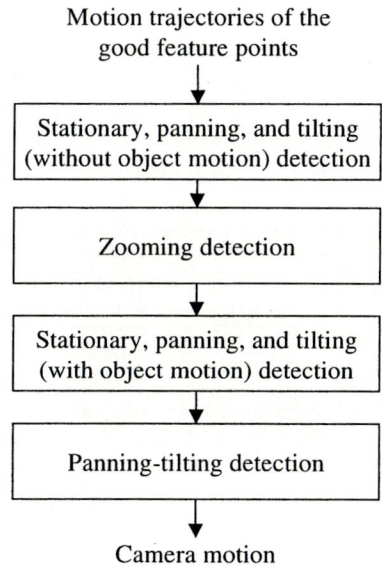

Fig. 3. Block diagram of camera motion characterization

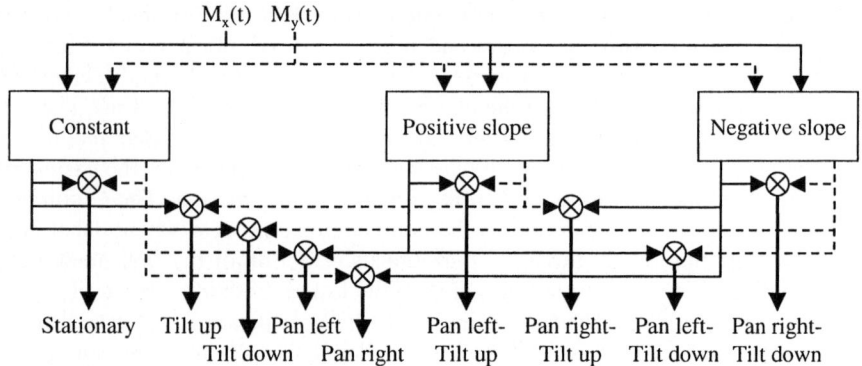

Fig. 4. The concept of stationary, panning, and tilting detection, $M_x(t)$ and $M_y(t)$ are the motion trajectories in (t,x) and (t,y) dimensions, respectively.

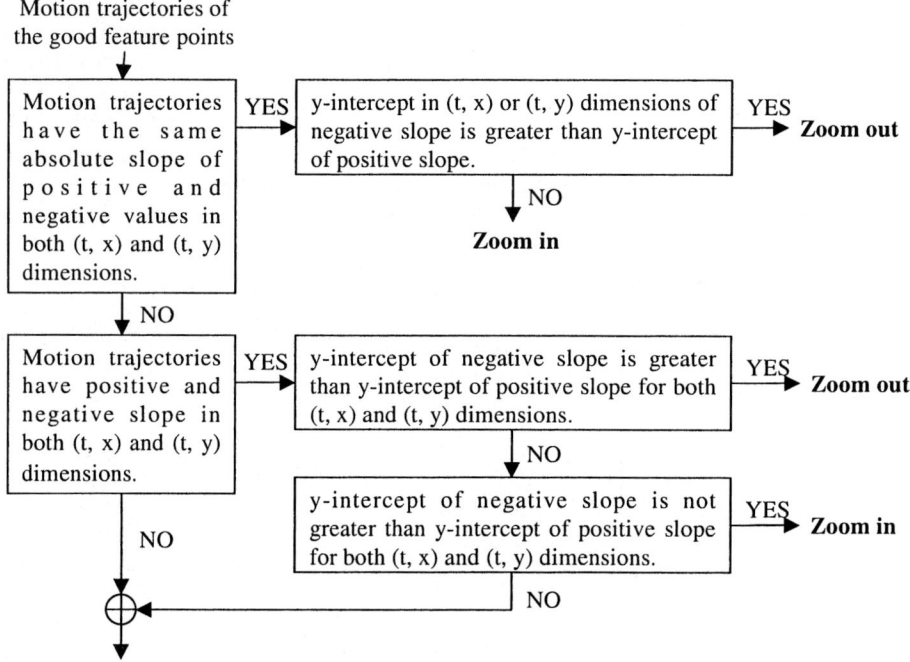

Fig. 5. Block diagram of zooming detection

4 Experimental Results

We conduct the experiments using the proposed approach to estimate camera motion of a variety of shots in video sequences. Totally 50 shots are examined. The examples of shots used in experiments and their feature points are shown in Fig. 6. The corresponding motion trajectories can be seen in Fig. 1. Table 1 summarizes the performance of the proposed approach comparing with manual annotation. The effectiveness of camera motion characterization is evaluated into two aspects; precision and recall. From the experimental results, the camera motions of combining between panning-tilting and zooming cannot be detected. They were passed through the last process and were detected as the unknown motion. However, the overall results have demonstrated the performance of proposed approach to determine camera motion.

Fig. 6. Examples of shots used in experiments and their feature points, *(a) stationary, (b) pan right, (c) tilt up, (d) zoom out,* and *(e) pan left-tilt up.*

5 Conclusions

In this paper, we proposed the camera motion characterization based on image feature analysis. The motion trajectories of selected feature points are used to determine global motion and dominant motion class of a shot in video sequences. The camera motion can be inferred directly from spatio-temporal characteristic of the image features. The method can reduce the computational process because it does not use the whole pixels in frames. The algorithm is evaluated using real compressed video sequences. The proposed approach works well in detecting the well-known basic camera motions (i.e., stationary, panning, tilting, zooming, and the combination of panning and tilting). We believe that our approach can be further extended to detect more complicated motions in the future.

Table 1. The performance of camera motion characterization

Motion	Correctly detected	Missed	Falsely detected	Recall	Precision
Static	12	0	0	1.0	1.0
Panning	10	0	0	1.0	1.0
Tilting	8	0	0	1.0	1.0
Zooming	8	2	0	0.8	1.0
Panning-tilting	8	2	0	0.8	1.0

References

1. Iain, E. G. R.: H.264 and MPEG-4 Video Compression: Video Coding for Next-generation Multimedia. Wiley (2003)
2. Jinzenji, K., Ishibashi, S., Kotera, H.: Algorithm for Automatically Producing Layered Sprites by Detecting Camera Movement. International Conference on Image Processing, Vol. 1. (1997) 767-770
3. Denzler, J., Schless, V., Paulus, D., Niemann, H.: Statistical Approach to Classification of Flow Patterns for Motion Detection. International Conference on Image Processing, Vol. 1. (1996) 517-520
4. Bouthemy, P., Gelgon, M., Ganansia, F.: A Unified Approach to Shot Change Detection and Camera Motion Characterization. IEEE Trans. Circuits Syst. Video Technology, Vol. 9. (1999) 1030-1044
5. Jin, R., Qi, Y., Hauptmann, A.: A Probabilistic Model for Camera Zoom Motion Detection. The Sixteenth Conference of the International Association for Pattern Recognition. (2002)
6. Wang, R., Huang, T.: Fast camera motion analysis in MPEG domain. International Conference on Image Processing, Vol. 3. (1999) 691-694
7. Jong-Il, P., Inoue, S., Iwadate, Y.: Estimating Camera Parameters From Motion Vectors of Digital Video. IEEE Workshop Multimedia Signal Processing. (1998) 105-110
8. Ardizzone, E., La, Cascia, M., Avanzato, A., Bruna, A.: Video Indexing Using MPEG Motion Compensation Vectors. IEEE International Conference on Multimedia Computing and Systems, Vol. 2. (1999) 725-729

9. Jae-Gon, K., Hyun, S. C., Jinwoong, K., Hyung-Myung, K.: Efficient Camera Motion Characterization for MPEG Video Indexing. IEEE International Conference on Multimedia and Expo, Vol. 2. (2000) 1171-1174
10. Trucco, E., Verri, A.: Introductory Techniques for 3-D Computer Vision. Prentice Hall, Englewood Cliffs, NJ (1998)
11. Feature Detection. http://www.mdh.se/iel/kurser/lr2240/Feature- Detection.html

Shape Retrieval by Principal Components Descriptor

Binhai Wang, Andrew J. Bangham, and Yanong Zhu

School of Computing Sciences, University of East Anglia,
Norwich, NR4 7TJ, UK
bw@cmp.uea.ac.uk

Abstract. Shape information is an important distribution to Content-Base Image Retrieval (CBIR) systems. There are two major types of shape descriptors, namely region-based and contour-based. In this paper we present a shape retrieval method that makes use of a contour-based descriptor, Principal Components Descriptor (PCD). In PCD, shapes are aligned on principal axes and described by a combination of the mean shape and weighted eigenvectors. The retrieval is achieved by comparing the weights of the eigenvectors. The developed approach is applied to Sharvit's Silhouettes database and the results are compared with MPEG-7 standard contour-based descriptor, Curvature Scale Space (CSS). The comparison indicates that PCD shows higher accuracy than CSS.

1 Introduction

Great efforts have been made to find efficient and robust content-based methods for image retrieval, as a result of the dramatically increasing amount of digital images and image data in various databases. Popularly used low level image features in Content-Base Image Retrieval (CBIR) include shape, texture and colour. It is believed that shape is one of the most basic features because humans can easily recognize objects only using the contours of objects. Contour-based descriptors have two major advantages. It is easy to obtain the object boundaries from actual images by segmentation, and the contour-based analysis is computationally low cost.

A number of contour-based description methods have been previously proposed. Autoregressive (AR) [1] and High-Resolution Pursuit (HRP) [2] regress shapes by a linear combination of bases with corresponding weights. Each basis contains useful features, which are used to retrieve shapes. Nevertheless, the extraction of such features is a complicated process and the regression of complex contours with a small number of bases might not be accurate enough. Fourier Descriptor (FD) [3] maps shapes from the spatial domain to the frequency domain. The low frequency part presents the fundamental shape and the high frequency part represents the shape details. Shape analysis in the frequency domain is rotation and dilation invariant, insensitive to noise, and able to extract global features. However, FD is sensitive to the variant phases of frequency components. Since wavelet transform and multi-resolution decomposition has been developed in recent two decades, wavelet is also used to describe shapes [4]. Wavelet Descriptor (WD) transforms shapes in the spatial domain to the spacial-frequency domain and compare shapes along the spacial axis in a certain sub-band. WD can easily remove noise-like details and extract fundamental shapes. However, one of its disadvantages is that it is sensitive to the starting point and it needs to be overcome in the matching procedure. Curvature Scale Space (CSS) [5] [6] uses maxima of curvature zero-crossing points in scale space as feature vector to represent and index shapes by comparing the positions of these maxima. Although CSS makes use of curvature, a very important feature of planar curves, it is difficult and complicated for matching due to the various numbers of maxima in different shapes.

Principal Components Analysis (PCA) is an efficient method for shape analysis. By applying PCA, a shape can be represented by the mean shape plus weighted principal components. Principal Components Descriptor (PCD) extracts features from the weights of principal components and indexes shapes by measuring the Euclidian distance of the weights on first several principal components. The second section of the paper describes the details of the developed method. The third section presents the experiment results, evaluations and a comparison of PCD and the MPEG-7 standard descriptor, CSS. Conclusions are given in the final section.

2 Method

2.1 Pre-processing

Several preprocessing procedures need to be undertaken before applying PCD to shapes. These include segmentation, boundary extraction and shape normalisation. Segmentation for images can be well performed by several existing methods, such as morphological scale space filtering [7] and Expectation-Maximization [8]. The segmented object, however, could be either with some noise on the edge or seriously distorted, if the segmentation is not perfect. For the former situation, the proposed approach can remove the effect of noise on the edge by ignoring minor components in the shape description. Nevertheless, the latter situation would seriously effect the further processing because the the serious distortion makes the shape meaningless. Since the paper focuses only on the shape retrieval and the experiments are all based on the shape database in which segmentation has already been done perfectly, we assume that the segmentations is efficiently performed in pre-processing. After segmentation, a contour-based shape is obtained by recording the positions of the pixels on the edge in the order of clockwise (or anti-clockwise) direction, which means that the contents of an object are always on the right-hand (or left-hand) side of the edge curve. This step is quite similar with getting 8-connectivity chain code. The points on an edge are represented as $\mathbf{p}_k = [x_k, y_k]^T$, where k is the index of the edge points. Therefore a shape containing n points on its edge can be repressed as $\mathbf{S} = [\mathbf{p}_1, \mathbf{p}_2, \ldots, \mathbf{p}_n]$. And then, a normalisation process is performed so that the points with same index on edges are corresponding. One of the commonly used normalisation methods is *Procrustes*, which uses an iterative process to minimize the distance from the shapes to their mean. However, Procrustes is not suitable for retrieval because it suffers from the variant start sampling points and it globally normalises all shapes in a database to the mean shape. If the query shape is from outside of the database, a normalisation of all shapes in the database and the query shape needs to be performed again. Therefore, a local normalisation method is developed for the retrieval case, which is named Principal Axes Method (PAM). It contains four basic steps: translation, rotation, dilation and re-sampling.

Translation. All shapes are first translated so that their centroid is at the origin. The translated shape is

$$\mathbf{V} = [\mathbf{p}_1 - \mathbf{p}_c, \mathbf{p}_2 - \mathbf{p}_c, \ldots, \mathbf{p}_n - \mathbf{p}_c] \tag{1}$$

where $\mathbf{p}_c = \frac{1}{n}\sum_{k=1}^n \mathbf{p}_k$ is the centroid and n is the number of sampling points on each shape.

Rotation. $\mathbf{V}$ in Eq.(1) is also the matrix of variance corresponding to the origin. Thus the covariance matrix of all translated points is

$$\mathbf{C} = \frac{1}{n}\mathbf{V} \cdot \mathbf{V}^T \tag{2}$$

Since this is a 2-dimension system, there are two eigenvalues, λ_1 and λ_2 ($\lambda_1 > \lambda_2$), and two corresponding mutually orthogonal eigenvectors, $\mathbf{e}_1$ and $\mathbf{e}_2$. Since $\mathbf{e}_1$ and $\mathbf{e}_2$ provide the principal axes of a shape, given the rotation matrix $\mathbf{R} = [\mathbf{e}_1, \mathbf{e}_2]^{-1}$, the shape can be rotated to a normalised space by

$$\mathbf{B} = \mathbf{R} \cdot \mathbf{V} \tag{3}$$

An example of orientation normalisation of a fish shape using the principal axes is given in Fig. 1.

Dilation. All shapes need to be scaled in order to normalise their sizes and make all points on edges be corresponding. After translation and rotation, the centroid and principal axes of a shape are coincided with the origin and coordinates. The dilation is performed by scaling the bounding box of all shapes to the same width, while preserving their width/height ratio. Let w and h be the width and height of the boundary box, the dilation matrix is

$$\mathbf{D} = \begin{bmatrix} 1/w & 0 \\ 0 & 1/w \end{bmatrix} \tag{4}$$

Thus final normalised shape after dilation is

$$\mathbf{S}' = \mathbf{D} \cdot \mathbf{B}. \tag{5}$$

Re-sampling. After translation, rotation and dilation, N points are evenly sampled along the shape contour, starting from the farthest intersection point of the contour and the x-axis. An example of the re-sampling is given in Fig. 1(e).

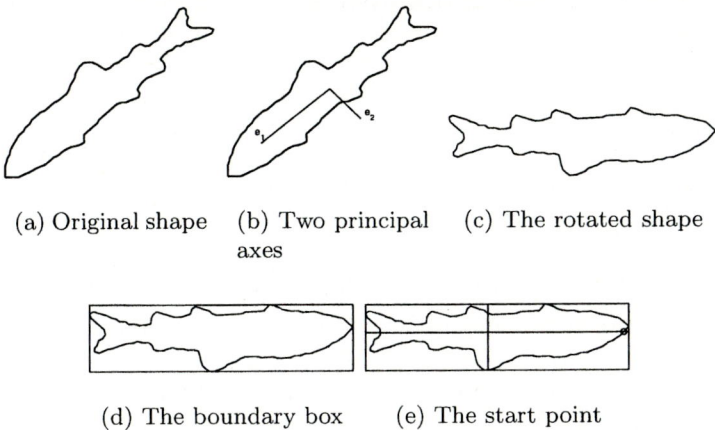

Fig. 1. Shape normalisation: (a) is the original shape, (b) shows two principal axes of the shape, (c) is the shape after rotating, (d) is the shape with boundary box and the circle in (e) is the start point of resampling.

2.2 Principal Components Descriptor

After the pre-processing, all the shapes are in a normalised space. By applying PCA to these shapes, we can obtain a parameterised shape model and reduce the dimensionality of the feature vector. We rearrange the representation of a shape to a $2 \times N$ dimensional vector $\mathbf{s} = [x_1, \ldots, x_N, y_1, \ldots, y_N]^T$, where (x_i, y_i) is the position of the ith sampling points. Thus, the mean shape of a database containing M shapes is

$$\bar{\mathbf{s}} = \frac{1}{M} \sum_{i=1}^{M} \mathbf{s}^i, \tag{6}$$

and the covariance matrix is

$$\mathbf{C} = \frac{1}{M} \sum_{i=1}^{M} (\mathbf{s}^i - \bar{\mathbf{s}})(\mathbf{s}^i - \bar{\mathbf{s}})^T. \tag{7}$$

The eigenvalues $[\lambda_1, \ldots, \lambda_M]$ of the covariance matrix are sorted so that $\lambda_i \geq \lambda_{i+1}$). A shape $\mathbf{s}^i$ in the database can be represented by

$$\mathbf{s}^i = \bar{\mathbf{s}} + \mathbf{P}\mathbf{b}^i + \varepsilon \tag{8}$$

Where, $\mathbf{P} = [\mathbf{p}_1, \ldots, \mathbf{p}_t]$ is the matrix of the eigenvectors corresponding to the first t largest eigenvalues, $\mathbf{b}^i = [b_1^i, \ldots, b_t^i]^T$ is the vector of their weights and ε is the error. The error decreases when the number of eigenvectors increases. The eigenvectors with the largest eigenvalues are the more significant axes to represent the covariance [9]. In practice, a small number of eigenvectors with large value eigenvalues are sufficient for describing shapes and the eigenvectors with small value eigenvalues describe the noise-like details on shapes, which should be avoided in feature extraction.

2.3 Feature Extraction and Matching

Given the shapes in a database, the mean shape and the eigenvectors are invariant. Since a shape can be approximately described by the mean shape and a number of eigenvectors with associated weights, the vector of weights can be used as feature vector. Since all eigenvectors are orthogonal, the feature vector can be calculated by projecting the error between a shape and the mean shape to the orthogonal eigenvector space, if the error in Eq. (8) is ignored, i.e.

$$\mathbf{b}^i = \mathbf{P}^T(\mathbf{s}^i - \bar{\mathbf{s}}). \tag{9}$$

The distance between two shapes is defined by the Euclidian distance of their feature vectors

$$Dis(\mathbf{s}^i, \mathbf{s}^j) = (\mathbf{b}^i - \mathbf{b}^j)^T(\mathbf{b}^i - \mathbf{b}^j). \tag{10}$$

The distance between a given query shape to each of the shapes in the database is calculated using Eq.(10) and all the shapes are sorted with respect to the distance to the query shape.

2.4 Summary

Given a shape database(it is assumed that the segmentation and boundary extraction have been done perfectly), a summary of the procedure of the feature extraction and retrieval is following:

1. Normalise all shapes in the database following the procedure of translation, rotation, dilation and re-sampling described in Sec. 2.1. The normalisation makes all shapes relevant and removes the effects of variant scales, rotations and starting points.
2. Calculate the mean shape and covariance matrix using Eq. (6) and Eq. (7), respectively. Find the eigenvalues and eigenvectors of the covariance matrix and sort them according to the eigenvalues. Create the eigenmatrix using the first t eigenvectors, $\mathbf{P} = [\mathbf{p}_1, \ldots, \mathbf{p}_t]$.
3. Compute the feature vectors of all shapes in the database by Eq. (9).
4. Given a query shape, normalise it using same method in step 1.
5. Compute the feature vector of the query shape by Eq. (9) and the distances between the query shape and the shapes in the database using Eq. (10). Index the shapes according the values of distances.

3 Experiments and Evaluations

3.1 Experiments

The presented approach is tested using Sharvit's Silhouettes database [10], which contains 1070 binary images including airplanes, folks, animals, cartons, etc. The shapes in the database have variant orientations, sizes and translations. The object boundaries are first extracted from these images. All shapes are then normalised by the method described in Sec. 2.1. In feature extraction, the number of eigenvectors, t, is experimentally selected as 20. Then, 10 shapes are randomly select from the database as the query shapes. The first 7 retrieval results using both PCD and CSS are shown in Fig. 2. In order to compare it with CSS, the retrieval results using CSS are listed in Fig. 2 as well.

The results show that the proposed method can correctly identify similar shapes in the database provided a query shape. Despite different starting position, orientation and size of shapes, the retrieval is successful in almost all cases, which implies that the PCD approach is highly robust to orientation and size of shapes. In result 4, 7, 8 and 10, the similar shapes with extremely different orientation are retrieved, which means that it is invariant to shape rotation. In result 7, 8, and 9, the similar shapes with different scales are listed, which implies that the method can eliminate the effect of dilation. Comparing the retrieval re-

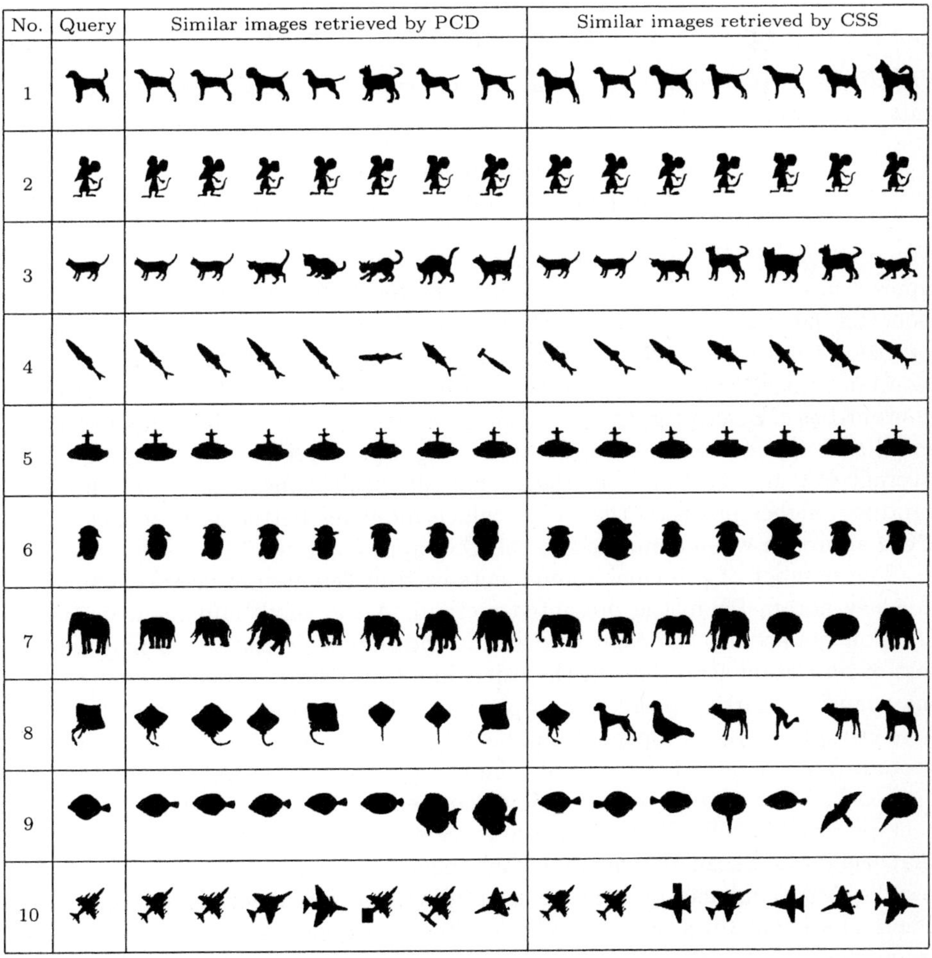

Fig. 2. The results of experiments using PCD and CSS

sults using PCD and the ones using CSS, we can find that for some complicated shapes, especially for query shape 6, 7, 8 and 9, the PCD can find similar shapes more efficiently. A more detailed statistical evaluation and comparison is given in the next section.

3.2 Evaluations

One of most efficient evaluation methods for image retrieval is *Precision versus recall graph* (PR graph), which is a standard evaluation method and popularly used by CBIR community [11] because PR graphs present abundant information of retrieval result and can be easily understood. In the PR graph,

Precision is the percentage of similar images retrieved with respect to the total number of images retrieved.

$$P = \frac{\text{No. of similar images retrieved}}{\text{Total No. of images retrieved}} \qquad (11)$$

Recall is the percentage of similar images retrieved with respect to the total number of similar images in database.

$$R = \frac{\text{No. of similar images retrieved}}{\text{Total No. of similar images in database}} \qquad (12)$$

We use average PR graphs to evaluate the overall performance of the PCD approach. Leave-one-shape-out experiments are performed on the Sharvit's Silhouettes database using manually built ground-truth of the database. The recall-precision values are calculated for each shape and the average recall and precision are achieved in the end. To perform an objective evaluation, the MPEG-7 contour-based descriptor, CSS, is implemented following the algorithm described in [6] and applied to the same database. Fig. 3(a) presents a comparison of the average PR graph of both methods. For all recall values, the PCD approach produces higher precision than CSS, which indicates better performance of the PCD approach when compared to the CSS approach.

The number of principal components used in the feature vectors, namely t, is a key parameter in the presented method. A too small number of principal components are not sufficient to describe the shapes precisely and may lead to loss of important features. On the other hand, too many principal components may cause overfitting problem and produce inferior retrieval results. Therefore, it is crucial to find an optimal number of principal components in the feature vectors. To evaluate the effects of different t values on the performance of our approach, The average precision is calculated for different t values when the average recall is 20%. The results are presented in Fig. 3(b). It can be observed that using more than 10 principal components is sufficient to provide satisfying results. A maxima can be seen when around 20 principal components are used. There is a slight drop when more than 20 components are used, as a result of including noise-like details represented by minor components. Overall, from 15 to 20 is a reasonable range for the choice of component numbers.

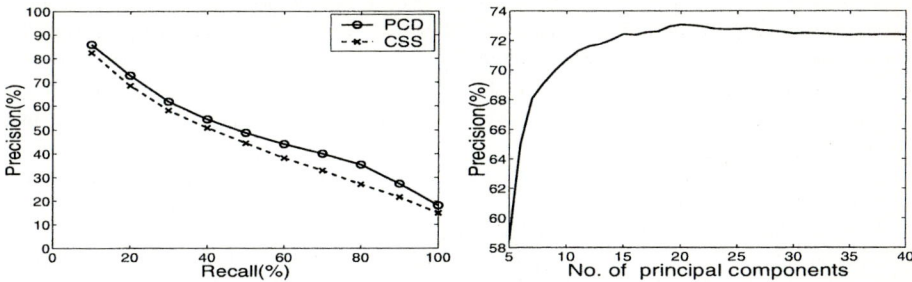

(a) Precision versus recall graphs of PCD and CSS

(b) Precision versus the no. of principal components in the feature vector

Fig. 3. Evaluation results

The experiments and evaluations have proven that the proposed approach is more efficient in shape retrieval. However, it is found that the proposed method is less efficient when applied to certain shapes where too many points distribute on the less important parts, for example the tail of a ray. It would make PAM find two meaningless axes in stead of the real ones of an object. Thus, the normalisation may fail and the re-sampled points on the shape would not be corresponding to the other shapes in the database. This would make the retrieval difficult and may lead to inferior retrieval results.

4 Conclusions

We have presented a novel approach to contour-based shape retrieval based on PCD and evaluated the proposed approach using a public database. The experiment results reveal that the PCD approach is highly robust to orientation and size of the shapes and able to identify shapes with largely different poses. To perform a precise evaluation, the proposed approach is compared with the MPEG-7 CSS algorithm. The comparison shows that the proposed approach outperforms the CSS approach.

References

1. Kauppinen, H., Seppannen, T., Pietikainen, M.: An experimental comparison of autoregressive and fourier-based descriptors in 2d shape classification. In: IEEE Trans. on Pattern Analysis and Machine Intelligence. Volume 17. (1995) 201–207
2. Jaggi, S., Karl, W., Mallat, S., Willsky, A.: Silhouette recognition using high-resolution pursuit. In: Pattern Recognition. Volume 32. (1999) 753–771
3. Zahn, C., Roskies, R.: Fourier descriptor for plane closed curves. In: IEEE Trans. on Computers. Volume 21. (1972) 269–281
4. Chuang, G.H., Kuo, C.C.: Wavelet descriptor of planar curves: theory and application. In: IEEE Trans. on Image Processing. Volume 5. (1996) 56–70

5. Mokhtarian, F., Mackworth, A.: A theory of multiscale, curvature-baes shape representation for planar curves. In: IEEE Trans. on Pattern Analysis and Machine Intelligence. Volume 14. (1992) 789–805
6. Mokhtarian, F., Abbasi, S., Kittler, J.: Robust and efficient shape indexing through curvature scale space. In: Proceedings of the British Machine Vision Conference, Edinburgh,UK, BMVA (1996)
7. Bangham, J.A., Hidalgo, J.R., Harvey, R., Cawley, G.: The segmentation of images via scale-space trees. In Carter, J.N., Nixon, M.S., eds.: BMVC, Southampton, British Machine Vision Association (1998) 33–43
8. Carson, C., Belongie, S., Greenspan, H., Malik, J.: Blobworld: Image segmentation using expectation-maximization and its application to image querying. In: IEEE Transactions on Pattern Analysis and Machine Intelligence. Volume 24. (2002) 1026–1038
9. Cootes, T., Taylor, C., Cooper, D., Graham, J.: Active shape models - their training and application. In: Computer Vision and Image Understanding. Volume 61. (1995) 38–59
10. Sharvit, D., Chen, J., Tek, H., Kimia, B.: Symmetry-based indexing of image database. In: Journal of Vissual Communication and Image Representation. Volume 9. (1998) 366–380
11. Müller, H., Müller, W., Squire, D., Marchand-Maillet, S., Pun, T.: Performance evaluation in content-based image retrieval: overview and proposals. In: Pattern Recognition Letters. Volume 22., Elsevier (2001) 593–601

Automatic Monitoring of Forbidden Areas to Prevent Illegal Accesses

M. Leo, T. D'Orazio, A. Caroppo, T. Martiriggiano, and P. Spagnolo

CNR- ISSIA via Amendoda 122/D-I,
70126 Bari, Italy
{leo, dorazio, caroppo, martiggiano, spagnolo}@issia.ba.cnr.it

Abstract. Surveillance systems that automatically detect illegal behaviors performed by unaware people have a wide range of applications: security, healthcare, conservation of cultural heritage and so on. In particular monitoring public areas such as museums and archaeological sites is a challenging problem that has to be solved in order to avoid irreparable damages to historical heritage. In this paper a system able to check by common digital RGB cameras unexpected accesses to forbidden areas in a public museum is presented. The reliability of the proposed framework is shown by large experimental tests performed in the Messapic Museum of Egnathia (Italy).

1 Introduction

Archaeological sites and museums, scattered across the world, keep physical remains of past human activity and they testify thousands of years of endeavors to develop culture, science and civilization.

Unfortunately archaeological finds are fragile and non-renewable therefore it is very important to plan adequate precautionary measures to avoid irreparable damages to the cultural heritage caused by visitors.

In general the preservation of the archaeological heritage is insured by a lot of strict rules that visitors have to observe. The monitoring of visitor behaviors is either performed by watchman or by traditional surveillance systems consisting of cameras, storage devices, video monitors and security personnel.

Both solutions are tedious as security staff or watchman need to identify specific and unusual events from a large number of very common and repetitive events. A solution of these problems might be a visual system able to automatically detect illegal behaviors performed by visitor in archaeological site or museums.

Automatic recognition of human behaviors is one of the most exciting and challenging problem in the computer vision research field.

Open literature proposes different methods for understanding human actions and good review can be found in [1,2,3]. Basically, works in recognition of behaviors of unaware humans can be classified into three categories. The first one consists of methods that perform recognition of human behaviors by detecting and tracking the hands and/or eventually some other major body components like arms, head or legs [4,5]. These algorithms, besides, being very complex and time consuming, require a very narrow field of view and a considerable amount of prior knowledge that generally is impossible to get in unaware human context as surveillance.

The second category consists of methods that perform recognition of human behaviors by using space-temporal information of the human body configuration (posture analysis) [6,7,8,9,10]. These algorithms, generally, are not view invariant and are based on the assumption that human activities can be deduced just from human body posture; the reliability of these approaches has been proved only for a limited number of human activities, very often in contrived scenarios.

Finally, the third category of algorithms for the recognition of human behaviours, to witch our work belongs, uses the analysis of the spatial and temporal properties of human motion (position in the scene, moving velocity and so on) [11,12,13,14].

In this paper we address the problem of automatically detect in real time violations of forbidden areas. In some cases this problem can be solved using a simple window in the image and monitoring the optical flow to detect access violations. Nevertheless, this kind of approaches gives good results only when the camera observes the scene in a proper direction and avoid the problems of the perspective projection. But in many real contexts such as the surveillance of large areas, the simple motion detection is not significant unless it is combined with a position information on the ground plane. Besides the presence of shadows can alter the moving blob shape and gives rise to false alarms. For this reason we propose a three steps algorithm: at first the RGB digital images acquired by non-professional cameras are used to detect moving objects; then shadow regions are removed by temporal photometric gain analysis and finally, for each detected moving object, the approximate 3D localization is obtained by homographic transformations. Whenever the 3D position of a moving object falls in a forbidden area the system automatically detects the event and provides an alarm signal.

The rest of the paper is organized as follow: an overview of the proposed system is provided in section 2 where motion detection, shadow removing and 3D localization algorithms will be detailed; section 3 presents, instead, the experimental results obtained on the real image sequences acquired by IEEE 1394 cameras in the Messapic Civic Museum of Egnathia (Brindisi, Italy).

2 System Overview

The proposed system works on the RGB images acquired by common digital cameras. The acquired images are firstly processed by a motion detection algorithm performed through background subtraction. In this phase the background is automatically built and updated by temporal statistical analysis. After motion detection a shadow removing procedure is performed on each image in order to discard shadow regions that, generally, alter the shape of the moving objects. After shadow removing, moving points are merged in regions on the basis of their spatial relationship. Finally the centre of the bounding box of each moving region is considered and the corresponding coordinates on the ground plane are extracted by homographic projection.

The following subsections explain the details of each step involved.

2.1 Motion Detection

The motion detection step has been achieved by implementing a novel background subtraction algorithm. It is essentially a variation of [15] with the advantages of allowing the background modeling also in cases of motion in the initial image sequences, and also of being more robust in cases of multiple reflections in indoor contexts. The proposed motion detection approach is composed by three distinct phases: firstly, a model of the background needs to be created; then a background subtraction procedure is used to distinguish moving objects from static ones. Finally, an updating algorithm adapts the background to any variation in light conditions.

The background modeling algorithm implemented is very reliable because it does not require any assumption about the presence of moving objects in the scene.

It uses a sliding window (of N frames) whose first frame is assumed as first coarse background model, even if there are moving objects. Then, each frame of this window is compared with the coarse background: if a pixel value is similar (in all the three color channels) to the correspondent in the model image, mean value and standard deviation are evaluated for that point.

Practically, for each pixel, 6 parameters are considered: $\mu_R, \mu_G, \mu_B, \sigma_R, \sigma_G, \sigma_B$ where μ_n e σ_n represent respectively the mean value and the standard deviation in the n-th color band.

After checking all frames of the examined window, the statistical parameters are maintained only for those pixels with intensity values similar to the model for almost 90% of the whole considered window.

After this, a new sliding window is examined using as referring model the statistical parameters where maintained and the intensity values of the first image for those points in which the statistical parameters were rejected in the previous window.

This procedure is iterated until mean and standard deviation values have been maintained for all the pixels.

After the model construction, the system is able to automatically detect the presence of moving objects. For this purpose, a simple subtraction algorithm has been implemented. It is based on the evaluation of the difference between current image and the model; this difference is calculated for each color band. A pixel will be considered as a moving point if it differs more than two times from the relative variance at least in one color band. Formally, denoting with I_{OUT} the output binary image:

$$I_{OUT}(x,y) = \begin{cases} 1 & \text{if} \quad \begin{aligned} &|I_R(x,y)-\mu_R(x,y)|>2*\sigma_R(x,y) \vee \\ &|I_G(x,y)-\mu_G(x,y)|>2*\sigma_G(x,y) \vee \\ &|I_B(x,y)-\mu_B(x,y)|>2*\sigma_B(x,y) \end{aligned} \\ 0 & \text{otherwise} \end{cases}$$

In order to make the system substantially insensible to variations in light conditions, an updating module has been implemented. The characteristics of the applicative context requires some specific constraints: in particular, objects that differ from the background image have always to be detected, that is they will be never included in the background model in order to maintain information about the presence of object removed from the scene until anomalous conditions will be restored.

So, the updating procedure starts from the output of the last algorithm, and only the pixels corresponding to static points ($I_{OUT}(x,y)=0$) will be updated. In detail, for each point, a weighted mean between the historic value and current value is carried out.

The parameter α used for the updating can vary in [0,1] and smoothes the relative relevance of the current image instead of the background one.

$$\mu_R^{t+1} = \begin{cases} \alpha * \mu_R^t + (1-\alpha) * I_R^t & \text{if } I_{OUT} = 0 \\ \mu_R^t & \text{if } I_{OUT} = 1 \end{cases}$$

2.2 Shadow Removing

After the background subtraction, in the resulting binary image many small clusters of pixels are still observable: a one-step filter removes blobs whose size is lower than a certain threshold. Finally, an image with only foreground objects is generated, where each object contains also its own shadows. The presence of shadows is a great problem for a motion detection system, because they alter real size and dimension of the objects and they make very difficult any following automatic scene interpretation attempt. This problem is mostly remarked in indoor contexts, where shadows are emphasized by the presence of many reflective objects; in addition shadows can be detected in every direction, on the floor, on the walls but also on the ceiling, so typical shadow removing algorithms, that assume shadows in a plane orthogonal with the human plane, cannot be used.

To prevent all these problems, correct shapes of the objects must be extracted: the system needs the implementation of a shadow removing algorithm.

The shadow removing approach here described starts from the assumption that a shadow is a uniform decreasing of the illumination of a part of an image due to the interposition of an opaque object with respect to a bright point-like illumination source. From this assumption, we can note that shadows move with their own objects but also that they have not a fixed texture, as real objects: they are half-transparent regions which retain the representation of the underlying background surface pattern. Therefore, our aim is to examine the parts of the image that have been detected as moving regions from the previous segmentation step but with a texture substantially unchanged with respect to the corresponding background. The algorithm looks for moving points whose attenuation values, at each color band, are similar; differently, moving points belonging to true foreground regions will have different attenuation values. In addition, these attenuation value will be lower than 1, because of the minor light that illuminates the shadow regions. Formally, we evaluate, for each moving point (x,y) the attenuation values S at each color band:

$$S_R(x,y) = \frac{I_R(x,y)}{B_R(x,y)} \quad S_G(x,y) = \frac{I_G(x,y)}{B_G(x,y)} \quad S_B(x,y) = \frac{I_B(x,y)}{B_B(x,y)}$$

where $I_n(x,y)$ and $B_n(x,y)$ are respectively the intensity value in the n-th color band of the pixels (x,y) in the current image and in the background image.

After this, pixels with an uniform attenuation will be removed:

$$I_{OUT}(x,y) = \begin{cases} 0 & \text{if } S_R(x,y) \cong S_G(x,y) \cong S_B(x,y) \wedge S_R(x,y), S_G(x,y), S_B(x,y) < 1 \\ 1 & \text{otherwise} \end{cases}$$

The output of this phase provides a motion image with the real shape of the moving objects, without any artifacts due to noise or shadows.

2.3 Localization of the Moving Objects in the Scene

After Motion Detection and Shadow Removing each pixel in the acquired image is labeled as belonging to the background or to some moving object. To perform the localization of the moving object in the 3D scene is, at this point, important to analyze the spatial relationship between moving pixels and aggregate them in uniform regions (connectivity analysis). The proposed system makes use of the 8 connectivity criterion: two pixels are part of the same object, regardless of whether they are connected along the horizontal, vertical, or diagonal direction. Each object is now localized in the 2D image plane but, due to the perspective distortion, it is not possible to determine its position in the 3D scene. To localize them in the 3D scene a further step must be introduced. For each detected moving region a point p is considered: it is obtained as the intersection of the vertical line passing through the center of the bounding box of the considered region and the lower side of the same bounding box.

To localize the point p in the 3D scene an homographic relationship between the image plane and the ground plane is introduced.

The relation between the generic point $P(kx_i, ky_i, kz_i, k)$ belonging to the ground plane and its corresponding point $p(u_i, v_i, 1)$ in the image plane is:

$$\mathbf{P} = \mathbf{M}\mathbf{p} \rightarrow \begin{bmatrix} kx_i \\ ky_i \\ kz_i \\ k \end{bmatrix} = \begin{bmatrix} m_{11} & m_{12} & m_{13} \\ m_{21} & m_{22} & m_{23} \\ m_{31} & m_{32} & m_{33} \\ m_{41} & m_{42} & m_{43} \end{bmatrix} \begin{bmatrix} u_i \\ v_i \\ 1 \end{bmatrix} \quad (1)$$

To get the position in the scene of the moving object detected in the image plane the 11 unknown items of the matrix M have to be computed (m_{43} can be set to 1 considering that this is an homogenous linear system). The m_{ij} elements can be discovered considering 4 couples of points for which the coordinates both in the ground planes and in the image plane are a priori known.

3 Experimental Results

The experiments were performed in the Messapic Civic Museum of Eganthia (Brindisi, Italy). This museum have a lot of rooms containing important evidence of the past: the smallest archeological finds are kept under lock in proper showcases but the largest ones are exposed without protection. The areas next to the unprotected finds are forbidden to the visitors and a cord separates forbidden from allowed areas.

Sometime visitors step over the cord in order to touch the finds or to see them in more detail. In our experiment a IEEE 1394 camera was placed in the main room of the museum in order to monitor the behaviors of the visitors in the area where were placed some of the most important messapic archaeological finds.

The acquired images were sent to a laptop (Pentium III, 1200 Mhz, RAM 512, HD 30 Gb) where run the algorithms described in the previous section.

In figure 1A it is possible to see a frame acquired by the camera where the 4 red markers indicate the point of the ground plane chosen to discover the parameters of the homographic projection. The matrix M obtained by solving the homogeneous liner system (1) for the aforesaid 4 point is:

$$M = \begin{pmatrix} 0.0599709 & -0.0300762 & 9.030553 \\ -0.0493247 & -0.0313738 & 43.0326 \\ 0 & 0 & 0 \\ 0.000152512 & 0.0313815 & 1 \end{pmatrix}.$$

In figure 1B the plan of the acquired area is reported: the green color indicates allowed areas whereas pink color indicates forbidden areas. The red points correspond to the red reference points in figure 1A.

The room was monitored for about 1 hour (10 frame/sec). During the experiment several visitors came to the room but nobody of them went inside the forbidden areas. Some illegal accesses were performed by some actors.

In the figures 1A and 1B are furthermore pointed out the reference coordinate systems for both the image plane and the ground plane; onto the image plane the measure unit is the "pixel coordinate" whereas onto the ground plane is the "meter".

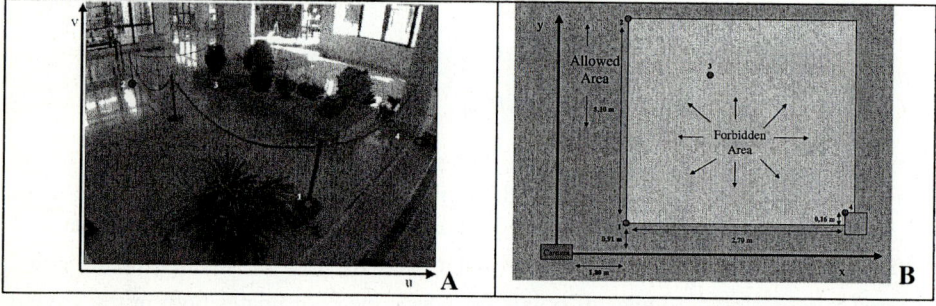

Fig. 1. A) A frame acquired by the camera where the 4 red markers indicate the point of the ground plane chosen to discover the parameters of the homographic projection. **B)** the plan of the acquired area: the green color indicates allowed areas whereas pink color indicates forbidden areas. Red point correspond to the red point in figure 1A. Each figure reports also the reference coordinate systems used in the experiment.

In figure 2 the column A shows some frames extracted meanwhile a person steps over the cord and access to the forbidden area, whereas the column B shows the relative images containing the moving points detected before the shadow removing step and finally the column C shows the results obtained after shadow removing. The relative position of the moving person onto the image plane and onto the ground plane are respectively reported in columns A and C. By comparing the position of the moving person onto the ground plane with the boundary lines of the forbidden area the system detected that in the third and fourth rows the person is performing an illegal access and it sent an alarm to avoid dangerous interaction of the transgressor with the finds.

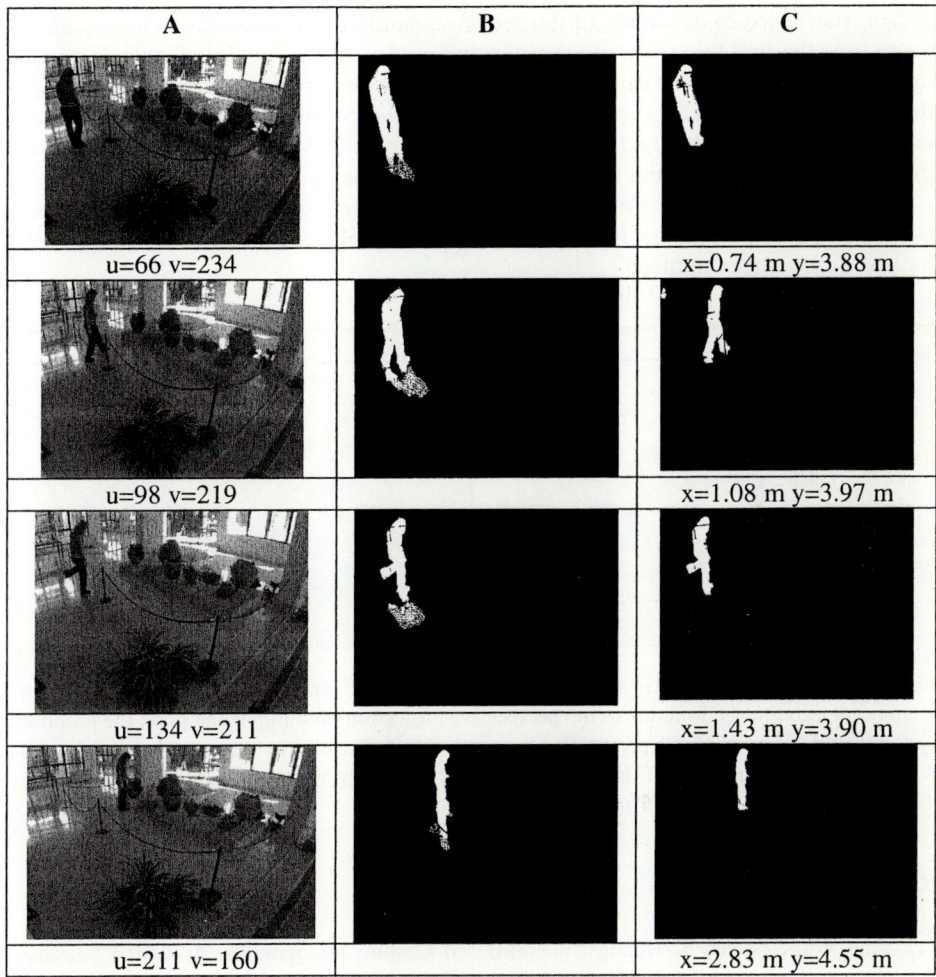

Fig. 2. The column **A** (on the left) shows some frames extracted meanwhile an actor performed the step over the cord; the column **B** shows the corresponding people segmentation results before shadow removing step and finally, the column **C** shows the relative images containing only the moving objects (after shadow removing step).

In figure 3 the benefits of using the proposed approach is evident: the figure A on the left shows a visitor that stays behind the limit of the forbidden area but he seems very close to the find due to the perspective projection onto the image plan. In this case every approach based only on motion detection could wrongly detect an access violation and send a false alarm. The proposed approach instead detects the real position of the visitor and it is able to label this situation as normal. In the figure B on the right the visitor is inside the limit of the forbidden area. In this case the position estimation indicates the access violation and an alarm could be provided.

The proposed algorithm was tested on a large number of normal activities and on 15 forbidden situations that have been recorded during the 1 hour monitoring. The system succeeded in detecting all the access violations. Of course the systems can fail every time the first two steps of the algorithm produce a not precise people segmentation. In fact the position evaluation, as explained in the previous section, depends on the exact estimation of the people shape: for instance the presence of shadows can modify the point p, obtained as intersection between the vertical line passing through the bounding box center and the lower side of the same bounding box.

Future work will be addressed to monitoring different activities such as the people trajectories evaluation, the interaction between people, the number of people who look at a each museum piece.

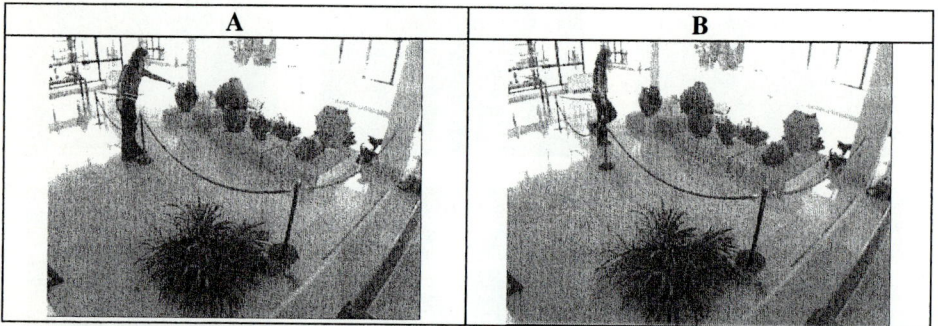

Fig. 3. Two critical situations: **A)** a visitor stays behind the limit of the forbidden area but he seems very close to the find due to the perspective projection onto the image plan; the proposed system avoid the error of the perspective perception and classifies as normal this behaviors. **B)** A visitor is inside the limit of the forbidden area. In this case the position estimation indicates the access violation and an alarm can be provided.

References

1. Ying Wu, Thomas S. Huang "Vision-Based Gesture Recognition: A Review" *Lecture Notes in Computer Science* 1739, 1999, pp.103-114
2. C. Cedras, M. Shah "Motion based recognition: a survey", *Image and Vision Computing*, vol.13, n.2, pp. 129-155, 1995
3. D.M. Gravila "The visual analysis of human movement: a survey" *Computer Vision Image Understanding*, vol.73, n.1, pp.82-98, 1999
4. Jezekiel Ben-Arie, Zhiqian Wang, Purvin Pandit, Shyamsundar Rajaram "Human Activity Recognition Using Multidimensional Indexing", *IEEE Transactions on Pattern Analysis and Machine Intelligence,* Volume 24, Issue 8 (August 2002) pp. 1091 – 1104
5. H. Ren, G. Xu "Human Action Recognition in a Smart Classroom" *Fifth IEEE International Conference on Automatic Face and Gesture Recognition, 2002*
6. A. Galata, N. Johnson, D. Hogg, "Learning Variable-Length Markov Models of Behavior", *Computer Vision and Image Understanding*, 81, pp. 398-413 (2001)
7. A. Elgammal, V. Shet, Y. Yacoob, and L. S. Davis "Learning Dynamics for Exemplar-based Gesture Recognition" *in the proc. of the IEEE Conference on Computer Vision and Pattern Recognition (CVPR03)*, Madison, Wisconsin, June 16-22, 2003

8. R.T. Collins, A.J. Lipton, T. Kanade, H. Fujiyoshi, D. Duggins, Y. Tsin, D. Tolliver, N. Enomoto, O. Hasegawa, "A System for Video Surveillance and Monitoring", *Technical Report CMU-RI-TR-00-12*, Carnagie Mellon University, 2000.
9. C. Wren, A. Azarbayejani, T. Darrell, and A. Pentland "Pfinder: Real-time tracking of the human body" *IEEE Transactions on PAMI*, 19(7):780–785, 1997.
10. B. Boulay and F. Bremond and M. Thonnat, "Human Posture Recognition in Video Sequence" *In the Proc. Joint IEEE International Workshop on VS-PETS, Visual Surveillance and Performance Evaluation of Tracking and Surveillance*, 2003, pp. 23-29
11. P. Remagnino and G.A. Jones, "Classifying Surveillance Events from Attributes and Behavior" *in the Proceeding of the BMVC*, Sept. 10-13, Manchester, pp. 685-694, 2001.
12. C. Stauffer and W.E.L. Grimson, "Learning Patterns of Activity Using Real-Time Tracking" *IEEE transactions on PAMI*, vol. 22, n.8, pp. 747-757, August 2000.
13. D. Ayers, M. Shah, "Monitoring human behavior from video taken in an office environment", *Image and Vision Computing* 19 (2001) pp.833-846
14. Nair, V. and Clark, J.J., "Automated Visual Surveillance Using Hidden Markov Models", *in the proc. of the 15th Vision Interface Conf.*, Calgary, pp 88-92, May 2002
15. T. Horprasert, D. Harwood, and L.S. Davis, "A Statistical Approach for Real-time Robust Background Subtraction and Shadow Detection" *Proc. IEEE ICCV'99 FRAME-RATE Workshop*, Kerkyra, Greece, September 1999

Dynamic Time Warping of Cyclic Strings for Shape Matching

Andrés Marzal and Vicente Palazón*

Dept. Llenguatges i Sistemes Informàtics,
Universitat Jaume I de Castelló, Spain
{amarzal, palazon}@lsi.uji.es

Abstract. Cyclic strings are strings with no starting or ending point, such as those describing a closed contour. We present a new algorithm to compute a similarity measure between two cyclic sequences based on Dynamic Time Warping. The algorithm computes the optimal alignment between both sequences and is based on the cyclic edit distance algorithm proposed by Maes. The algorithm runs in $O(mn \lg m)$ time, where m and n are the lengths of the compared strings. Experiments on a shape classification and shape retrieval with a public database are presented.

1 Introduction

Contour matching is an important problem in shape classification and retrieval. Contours are *cyclic strings*: strings with no beginning or end. A cyclic string can be viewed as the set of strings obtained by cyclically shifting a representative string. Fig. 1 (a) shows the contour of two shapes whose representative strings start at arbitrarily chosen points.

Dynamic Time Warping (DTW) defines a dissimilarity measure based on an optimal alignment of two (non-cyclic) strings and has been successfully applied to speech recognition, on-line handwritten text recognition, time series alignment, etc. Some approaches to shape matching represent contours with global features such as Fourier descriptors or invariant moments [2]. Recently, DTW has been applied to the comparison of Fourier descriptors [6]. Global features comparison may detect a high similarity in shapes which are perceptually very different, since no local information is taken into account. The Curvature Scale-Space (CSS) description is a shape signature based on peaks detection in a space of curvature inflection points that depends on gaussian smoothings of the contour [9]. The CSS captures some local properties, such as the distribution of "relevant" curvature points along the contour, but is difficult to code as a string when some detail is needed.

Other approaches directly represent contours with cyclic strings (chaincodes, sequences of edges and/or angles in polygons, the curvature along the contour,

---

* This work has been supported by the Spanish *Ministerio de Ciencia y Tecnología* and FEDER under grant TIC2002-02684.

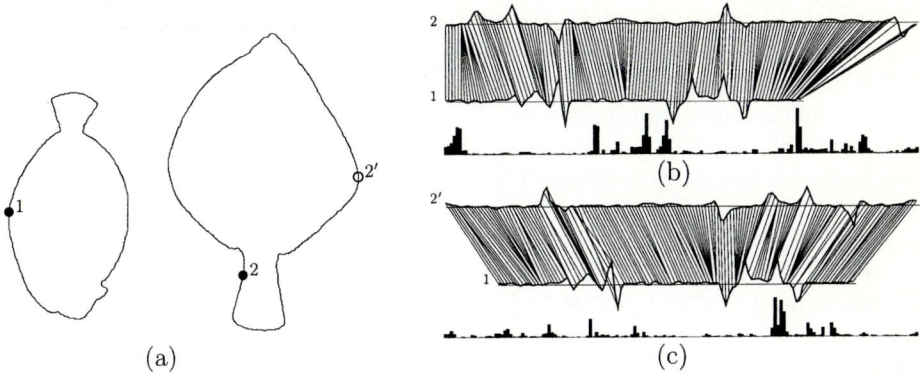

Fig. 1. (a) Two fish shapes. The black dots indicate starting points in their (clockwise) contour coding as strings of curvature values. (b) Optimal alignment of the curvatures starting at black dots. The absolute value of the distance between aligned points is shown under the alignment. The DTW dissimilarity is the sum of these values. (c) A more significant alignment is possible if the curvature string of the second shape starts at $2'$.

etc). These strings can be compared with the *cyclic edit distance* (CED) [7,8], which is defined in terms of the *edit distance* [11], a well-known metric between (non-cyclic) strings. Maes presented an $O(mn \lg m)$ algorithm to obtain the CED by computing some non-crossing shortest paths in an "extended edit graph". In [1,4], Marzal *et al.* improved the running time of this algorithm by proposing a Branch and Bound exploration of its search space. In [5], Bunke and Bühler obtained an *approximate* value for the CED in $O(mn)$ time. Mollineda *et al.* proposed in [10] other heuristics to approximate the value of the CED.

In [8], Maes applied the (exact) cyclic edit distance computation to the recognition of shapes described with polygons. As Maes pointed out, the edit distance has some drawbacks when applied to this problem: it is sensitive to segmentation inconsistencies in the polygons. Each primitive (edge or angle) of one polygon is either aligned with one and only one primitive of the other polygon (a substitution), or deleted/inserted. This makes difficult to properly align similar regions of polygons represented by a different number of edges. A DTW dissimilarity measure seems more natural for optimally aligning contours. DTW aligns each vertex of the contour with one or more points in the other contour: there is no need to introduce insertion/deletion operations and, therefore, elastic deformations of the shapes are not penalized. There have been attempts to present a DTW dissimilarity measure for cyclic strings: an approximate method has been presented, for instance, in [3]. In this paper we introduce the Cyclic DTW dissimilarity and show that it cannot be computed by just replacing edit operation with alignments in the CED algorithm. An exact computation algorithm that runs in $O(mn \lg m)$ time is presented and used in a silhouettes classification and shape retrieval task on a publicly available database.

2 Edit Distance and Dynamic Time Warping

Let $A = a_1 a_2 \ldots a_m$ and $B = b_1 b_2 \ldots b_n$ be two strings in Σ^*, where Σ^* is the closure under concatenation of a set Σ, and let λ denote the empty string, i.e., a sequence of length 0. For any string A, let $A_{1:i}$ be the substring $a_1 a_2 \ldots a_i$. An *edit operation* is a pair of strings of length less than or equal to 1, $(x, y) \neq (\lambda, \lambda)$, denoted by $x \to y$. Edit operations are classified as *insertions* $(x \to \lambda)$, *deletions* $(\lambda \to y)$, and *substitutions* $(x \to y)$, where $x, y \in \Sigma$. A string B results from another string A via the edit operation $x \to y$ if there are two strings C and D such that $A = CxD$ and $B = CyD$. An *edit sequence* is a sequence of edit operations, $e = e_1 e_2 \ldots e_k$, and it transforms A into B if B can be obtained from A by successive application of the edit operations. Edit operations can be weighted by means of a function $\gamma : (\Sigma \cup \{\lambda\}) \times (\Sigma \cup \{\lambda\}) \to \mathbb{R}^{\geq 0}$ satisfying $\gamma(x \to y) + \gamma(y \to z) \geq \gamma(x \to z)$. The *weight of an edit sequence* $e = e_1 e_2 \ldots e_k$ is defined as $\gamma(e) = \sum_{1 \leq i \leq k} \gamma(e_i)$. An optimal edit sequence from A to B is an edit sequence of minimum weight that transforms A into B. The (weighted) *edit distance* (ED) between A and B will be denoted with $d(A, B)$ and is defined as the weight of an optimal edit sequence from A to B. Wagner and Fischer presented this recursive equation [11]:

$$d(A_{1:m}, B_{1:n}) = \begin{cases} 0, & \text{if } n = m = 0; \\ d(A_{1:m-1}, B_{1:n}) + \gamma(a_m \to \lambda), & \text{if } m > 0 \text{ and } n = 0; \\ d(A_{1:m}, B_{1:n-1}) + \gamma(\lambda \to b_n), & \text{if } m = 0 \text{ and } n > 0; \\ \min \begin{cases} d(A_{1:m-1}, B_{1:n-1}) + \gamma(a_m \to b_n), \\ d(A_{1:m-1}, B_{1:n}) + \gamma(a_m \to \lambda), \\ d(A_{1:m}, B_{1:n-1}) + \gamma(\lambda \to b_n) \end{cases} & \text{if } m > 0 \text{ and } n > 0. \end{cases}$$
(1)

This equation formulates the $d(A, B)$ computation problem as a shortest path problem in the so-called *edit-graph*. This graph is an array of nodes (i, j), where $0 \leq i \leq m$ and $0 \leq j \leq n$, connected by horizontal, vertical and diagonal arcs, as can be seen in Fig. 2 (a). The horizontal arc arriving to node (i, j) represents $a_i \to \lambda$, the vertical arc represents $\lambda \to b_j$, and the diagonal arc represents $a_i \to b_j$. Each path from $(0, 0)$ to (m, n) is an *edit path* and its weight is the weight of its associated edit sequence. The value of $d(A, B)$ can be computed in $O(mn)$ time [11].

An *alignment* between two sequences A and B is a sequence of pairs (i_0, j_0), $(i_1, j_1), \ldots, (i_{k-1}, j_{k-1})$ such that (a) $1 \leq i_\ell \leq m$ and $1 \leq j_\ell \leq n$; (b) $0 \leq i_{\ell+1} - i_\ell \leq 1$ and $0 \leq j_{\ell+1} - j_\ell \leq 1$; and (c) $(i_\ell, j_\ell) \neq (i_{\ell+1}, j_{\ell+1})$. The pair (i_ℓ, j_ℓ) is said to *align* a_{i_ℓ} with b_{j_ℓ}. The weight of an alignment is $\sum_{0 \leq \ell < k} \gamma(a_{i_\ell}, b_{j_\ell})$. An alignment between A and B is optimal if its weight is minimum. The *Dynamic Time Warping* (DTW) *dissimilarity* measure of A and B will be denoted with $D(A, B)$ and is defined as the weight of the optimal alignment between both sequences. The DTW dissimilarity computation is a restricted linear assignment problem and can be solved with this recurrence:

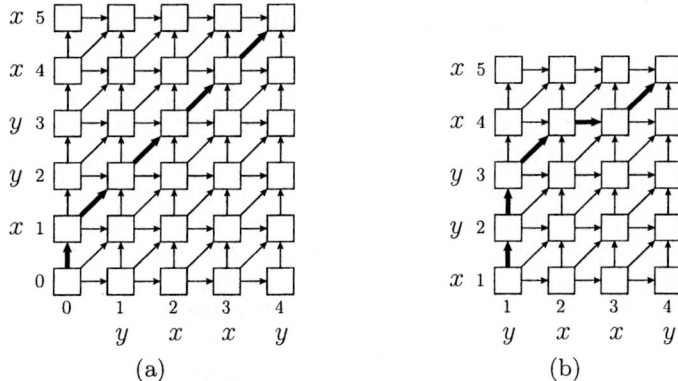

Fig. 2. (a) Edit graph for $A = xxyy$ and $B = xxyy$. Thick arrows are on the optimal edit path. (b) Warping graph for A and B and its optimal warping path (alignment).

$$D(A_{1:m}, B_{1:n}) = \begin{cases} \gamma(a_1, b_1), & \text{if } n = m = 1; \\ D(A_{1:m-1}, B_{1:n}) + \gamma(a_m, b_1), & \text{if } m > 1 \text{ and } n = 1; \\ D(A_{1:m}, B_{1:n-1}) + \gamma(a_1, b_n), & \text{if } m = 1 \text{ and } n > 1; \\ \min \begin{Bmatrix} D(A_{1:m-1}, B_{1:n-1}), \\ D(A_{1:m-1}, B_{1:n}), \\ D(A_{1:m}, B_{1:n-1}) \end{Bmatrix} + \gamma(a_m, b_n), & \text{if } m > 1 \text{ and } n > 1. \end{cases}$$
(2)

This recurrence is similar to (1) and solving it is equivalent to solving a shortest path problem on a graph similar to the edit graph: the *warping graph*, which is depicted in Fig. 2 (b). Arcs ending at node (i, j) are weighted with the same value, $\gamma(a_i, b_j)$. Warping paths start at node $(1, 1)$ and end at node (m, n). $D(A, B)$ can be computed in $O(mn)$ time.

Alignments of pairs of symbols in DTW can be assimilated to substitutions in edit distances, but DTW allows for one-to-many correspondences. This makes DTW appropriate to model "elastic distortions" of strings describing shapes or time series. On the other hand, DTW alignments have no insertions or deletions and seem preferable to edit distances when these operations do not naturally arise. There are alternative definitions of the DTW (different arcs in the warping graph or weighting functions that affect differently diagonal arcs). For the sake of clarity, we will consider only DTW similarity as defined in (2).

3 Cyclic Edit Distance

A cyclic shift σ of a string $A = a_1 a_2 \ldots a_m$ is a mapping $\sigma : \Sigma^* \to \Sigma^*$ defined as $\sigma(a_1 a_2 \ldots a_m) = a_2 \ldots a_m a_1$. Let σ^k denote the composition of k cyclic shifts and let σ^0 denote the identity. Two strings A and A' are cyclically equivalent if $A = \sigma^k(A')$, for some k. The equivalence class of A is $[A] = \{\sigma^k(A) : 0 \le k < m\}$ and it is called a *cyclic string*. The *cyclic edit distance* (CED) between $[A]$ and

[B] is defined as $d([A],[B]) = \min_{0 \leq k < m}(\min_{0 \leq \ell < n} d(\sigma^k(A), \sigma^\ell(B)))$. Maes [7] showed:

Lemma 1 (Maes). $d([A],[B]) = d([A], B) = \min_{0 \leq k < m} d(\sigma^k(A), B)$. □

Therefore, the value of $d([A],[B])$ can be obtained by computing m edit distances in $O(m^2n)$ time. Maes proposed a more efficient procedure that computes m shortest paths in an *extended edit graph* (see Fig. 3 (a)). Let $P(k)$ be a shortest path between nodes $(k,0)$ and $(k+m,n)$ in the extended edit graph. The edit distance $d(\sigma^k(A), B)$ is the weight of $P(k)$. When computing $d(\sigma^k(A), B)$, one can take advantage of the "non-crossing" property of edit paths [7] (see Fig. 3 (b)): "Let j, k, and l be three integers such that $0 \leq j < k < l \leq m$, and let $P(j)$ and $P(l)$ be two non-crossing minimum weighted paths in the extended edit graph. There is a shortest path $P(k)$ from $(k,0)$ to $(k+m,n)$ that lies between $P(j)$ and $P(l)$." This property leads to a Divide and Conquer, recursive procedure: when $P(j)$ and $P(l)$ are known, $P((j+l)/2)$ is computed by only taking into account those nodes of the extended edit graph lying between $P(j)$ and $P(l)$; then, optimal paths bounded by $P(j)$ and $P((j+l)/2)$ and optimal paths bounded by $P((j+l)/2)$ and $P(l)$ can be recursively computed. The recursive procedure starts after computing $P(0)$ (by means of the standard edit distance) and $P(m)$, which is $P(0)$ shifted m positions to the right. Each recursive call generates up to two more recursive calls and all the calls at the same recursion depth amount to $O(mn)$ time. Total computation time is, therefore, $O(mn \lg m)$.

The suboptimal algorithm proposed by Bunke and Bühler in [5] to approximate the CED finds the minimum cost path between any start node and any terminal node in the extended edit graph. This edit path transforms a substring of AA into B and can be computed in $O(mn)$ time.

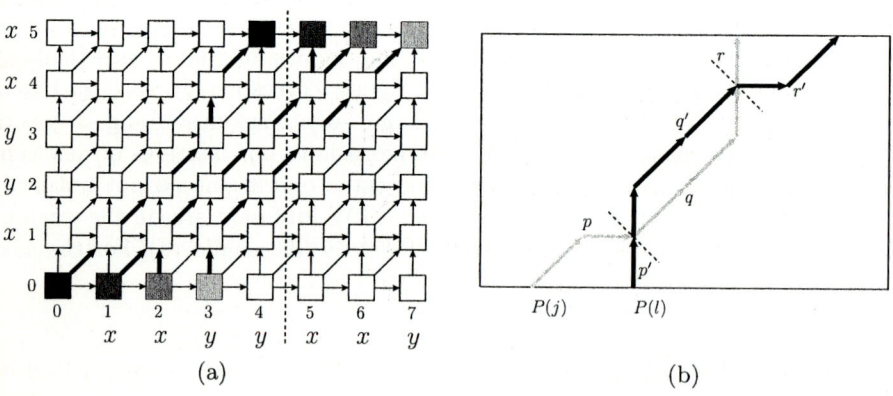

Fig. 3. (a) Extended edit graph for A and B. The optimal path for the cyclic edit of A and B is the optimal path starting and ending at nodes with the same colour. (b) $P(j)$ is the optimal edit path for $\sigma^j(A)$ and B, and $P(l)$ is the optimal path for $\sigma^l(A)$ and B. Crossing paths can be avoided: if the weight of q is greater than the weight of q', $P(j)$ can be improved by taking q' instead of q.

4 Cyclic Dynamic Time Warping

A *cyclic alignment* between A and B is a sequence of pairs $(i_0, j_0), (i_1, j_1), \ldots, (i_{k-1}, j_{k-1})$ such that, for $0 \leq \ell < k$, (a) $1 \leq i_\ell \leq m$ and $1 \leq j_\ell \leq n$; (b) $0 \leq i_{(\ell+1) \bmod m} - i_\ell \leq 1$ and $0 \leq j_{(\ell+1) \bmod n} - j_\ell \leq 1$; and (c) $(i_\ell, j_\ell) \neq (i_{(\ell+1) \bmod m}, j_{(\ell+1) \bmod n})$. The *weight of a cyclic alignment* $(i_0, j_0), (i_1, j_1), \ldots, (i_{k-1}, j_{k-1})$ is defined as $\sum_{0 \leq \ell < k} \gamma(a_{i_\ell}, b_{j_\ell})$. An optimal cyclic alignment is a cyclic alignment of minimum weight.

Lemma 2. *If $m > 1$, $n > 1$, and $(i_0, j_0), (i_1, j_1), \ldots, (i_{k-1}, j_{k-1})$ is an optimal alignment between A and B, there is at least one ℓ such that $i_\ell \neq i_{(\ell+1) \bmod m}$ and $j_\ell \neq j_{(\ell+1) \bmod n}$.*

Proof: Any alignment including (i_ℓ, j_ℓ), $(i_\ell + 1, j_\ell)$, and $(i_\ell + 1, j_\ell + 1)$ can be "improved" by removing $(i_\ell + 1, j_\ell)$, since $\gamma(a_{i_\ell+1}, b_{j_\ell}) \geq 0$. Analogously, any alignment including (i_ℓ, j_ℓ), $(i_\ell, j_\ell + 1)$, and $(i_\ell + 1, j_\ell + 1)$ can be "improved" by removing $(i_\ell, j_\ell + 1)$. □

Lemma 3. *The Cyclic DTW dissimilarity between $[A]$ and $[B]$, $D([A],[B])$, can be computed as $D([A],[B]) = \min_{0 \leq k < m} \left(\min_{0 \leq l < n} D(\sigma^k(A), \sigma^l(B)) \right)$.*

Proof: The demonstration is trivial when $m = 1$ or $n = 1$. Let us consider that $m > 1$ and $n > 1$ and let $(i_0, j_0), (i_1, j_1), \ldots, (i_{k-1}, j_{k-1})$ be an optimal alignment between A and B. Let ℓ be an index such that $i_\ell \neq i_{(\ell+1) \bmod m}$ and $j_\ell \neq j_{(\ell+1) \bmod n}$ (Lemma 2). This cyclic alignment weight is

$$D(\sigma^{(i_\ell+1) \bmod m}(A), \sigma^{(j_\ell+1) \bmod n}(B)),$$

which is considered by the double minimisation. □

In general, it is not true that the Cyclic DTW distance $D([A],[B])$ equals $\min_{0 \leq k < m} D(\sigma^k(A), B)$ orexm $\min_{0 \leq k < n} D(A, \sigma^k(B))$, as the following counter-example shows: let $\Sigma = \{x, y\}$ and let $\gamma(\cdot, \cdot)$ be 0 if both arguments are equal, and 1 in other case; the distance $D([xyx], [yxy])$ is 0, since $D(xxy, xyy) = 0$, but $D(xyx, yxy) = 3$, $D(yxx, yxy) = 1$, $D(xxy, yxy) = 1$ $D(xyx, xyy) = 1$, and $D(xyx, yyx) = 1$. Therefore, an equivalent of Lemma 1 does not hold for Cyclic DTW dissimilarities and Maes algorithm cannot be directly applied.

Theorem 1. *The Cyclic DTW between strings A and B, $D([A],[B])$, is*

$$\min_{0 \leq k < m} \left(\min(D(\sigma^k(A), B), D(\sigma^k(A)a_{k+1}, B)) \right).$$

Proof (sketch): Each alignment induces a segmentation on A and a segmentation on B. All the symbols in a segment are aligned with the same symbol of the other cyclic sequence. There is a problem when $b_{n-p}b_{n-p+1} \ldots b_n$ and $b_1 b_2 \ldots b_{1+q}$, for some $p, q \geq 0$, belong to the same segment of B. In that case, the optimal path cannot be obtained by simply shifting A, since b_n must be aligned with the last symbol of $\sigma^k(A)$ and b_1 must be aligned with its first symbol, i.e., they never fall in the same segment. The string $\sigma^k(A)a_{k+1}$, formed by appending to $\sigma^k(A)$

its first symbol, permits to align $b_{n-p}b_{n-p+1}\ldots b_n$ and $b_1b_2\ldots b_q$ with the first symbol of $\sigma^k(A)$, since a_{k+1} also appears at the end of $\sigma^k(A)a_{k+1}$. □

For each value of k, $D(\sigma^k(A), B)$ can be obtained as a subproduct of the computation of $D(\sigma^k(A)a_{k+1}, B)$. The value of $D(\sigma^k(A)a_{k+1}, B)$, for each k, can be obtained by computing a shortest path in an *extended warping path* similar to the extended edit graph. Since the non-crossing property of edit paths also holds for warping paths, the Divide and Conquer approach proposed by Maes can be applied to Cyclic DTW. It should be taken into account that, differently from Maes algorithm, the optimal path for $P(k)$ can finish at node $(k+m, n)$ o $(k+m+1, n)$.

The running time of the algorithm is $O(mn \lg n)$: the recursion divides the search space in two balanced halfs and all recursive operations at the same recursion require total $O(mn)$ time.

Bunke and Bühler approach to approximate the Cyclic Edit Distance can be trivially extended to approximate the Cyclic DTW in $O(mn)$ time. Hereafter, this modified algorithm will be called Bunke and Bühler DTW.

5 Experiments

In order to assess the Cyclic DTW performance in classification and shape retrieval tasks, we have used the database publicly available at the web page www.lems.brown.edu/vision/software/ [12]. It contains 1070 silhouettes. The shapes belong to 41 categories representing animals, tools, bones, hands, etc. Some categories contain only one image and others contain up to 60[1]. The eight directions chaincode of each contour was computed and the shape was represented as a series of coordinates $(X(t), Y(t))$. The starting point of the chaincode was chosen arbitrarily. In order to avoid discretisation errors, the contours were smoothed with a gaussian kernel, which depends on the standard deviation (stdev). Then, the curvature of each smoothed contour was computed at each point t as $\kappa(t) = (\dot{X}(t)\ddot{Y}(t) - \ddot{X}(t)\dot{Y}(t))/(X(t)^2 + Y(t)^2)^{3/2}$. The curvature is invariant with respect to translation and rotation. The γ function is defined as $\gamma(\kappa_A(t), \kappa_B(t')) = \sqrt{|\kappa_A(t) - \kappa_B(t')|}$.

In order to compare the DTW, the Bunke and Bühler DTW and the Cyclic DTW dissimilarities, we performed nearest neighbour classification with each dissimilarity measure and for different gaussian smoothings. Table 1 shows the error rate for different gaussian smoothings of the curve. The Cyclic DTW always outperformed the other comparison techniques. The best results were obtained for stdev=10: a 5.52% error rate with the Cyclic DTW. Some classification errors with the Cyclic DTW are shown in Fig. 4. It can be seen that most of them can be explained in terms of actual shapes similarity.

We also performed a shape retrieval experiment and computed the precision P (percentage of relevant shapes among the retrieved shapes) and the recall R

---

[1] The "donkey" category contains only one image and has been joined to the "cattle" category.

Table 1. Classification error rate for DTW, Bunke and Bühler DTW (BB), and Cyclic DTW (CDTW) and different gaussian smoothings.

stdev	DTW	BB	CDTW
3	33.40%	32.55%	10.01%
5	23.39%	20.77%	6.55%
10	18.86%	16.46%	5.52%
15	21.05%	18.33%	5.89%
20	23.01%	22.36%	12.54%
30	29.28%	27.03%	13.47%

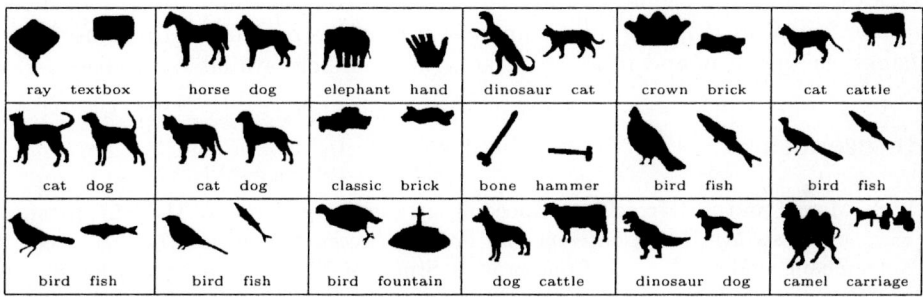

Fig. 4. Some classification errors. The left shape of each pair was misclassified and its corresponding right shape is its nearest neighbour according to the curvatures CDTW dissimilarity measure. Most classification errors are due to actual similarities between shapes of different classes.

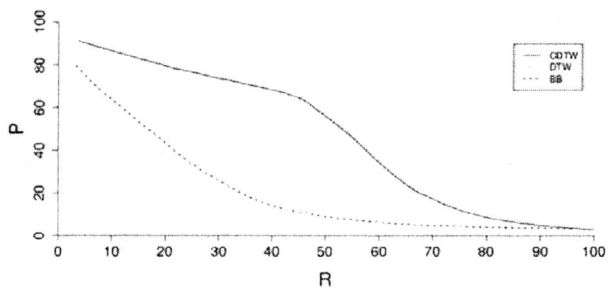

Fig. 5. Precision P (number of relevant shapes among the retrieved ones, in %) as a function of recall R (% of relevant shapes recovered w.r.t. all relevant shapes in the database) for stdev=10. DTW corresponds to the (non-cyclic) Dynamic Time Warping dissimilarity, BB to Bunke and Bühler's approximate algorithm, and CDTW to the Cyclic Dynamic Time Warping distance.

(percentage of relevant shapes retrieved w.r.t. the relevant shapes in the database) for queries with k retrieved documents, where k ranges from 1 to 1070. The results for stdev=10 are shown in Fig. 5. It can be seen that the precision is high for up to a 50% recall.

6 Conclusions

We have defined the Cyclic Dynamic Time Warping dissimilarity and defined to compute it in $O(mn \lg m)$. The method is based on the cyclic edit distance algorithm proposed by Maes. We have shown that Maes algorithm cannot be directly applied to cyclic DTW dissimilarities computation by just replacing the edit operations by alignments of symbols: two conventional DTW dissimilarities must be computed for each cyclic shift of one string. Fortunately, one of these dissimilarities can be obtained as a subproduct of the other.

The cyclic DTW dissimilarity has been applied to shape classification/retrieval and can be useful in other tasks, such as comparison of cyclic sequences in bioinformatics [13]. The new comparison measure has shown to be useful in shapes classification and retrieval tasks with a publicly available database.

References

1. A. Marzal and S. Barrachina. Speeding up the computation of the edit distance for cyclic strings. *Int. Conference on Pattern Recognition*, pages 271–280, 2000.
2. D. Zhang and G. Lu. A Comparative Study of Fourier Descriptors for Shape Representation and Retrieval. In *5th Asian Conf. on Computer Vision*, Jan 2002.
3. E. Milios, E.G.M. Petrakis. Shape Retrieval Based on Dynamic Programming. *IEEE Transaction on Image Processing*, 1(1):141–147, 2000.
4. G. Peris and A. Marzal. Fast Cyclic Edit Distance Computation with Weighted Edit Costs in Classification. *Proc. Int. Conf. on Pattern Recognition*, 4, 2002.
5. H. Bunke and H. Bühler. Applications of Approximate String Matching to 2D Shape Recognition. *Pattern Recognition*, 26(12):1797–1812, 1993.
6. I. Bartolini and P. Ciaccia. WARP: Accurate Retrieval of Shapes Using Phase of Fourier Descriptors and Time Warping Distance. *IEEE Transactions on Pattern Analysis and Machine Intelligence*, 27(1):142–147, 2005.
7. M. Maes. On a Cyclic String-to-String Correction Problem. *Information Processing Letters*, 35:73–78, 1990.
8. M. Maes. Polygonal Shape Recognition using String Matching Techniques. *Pattern Recognition*, 24(5):433–440, 1991.
9. F. Mokhtarian. Silhouette-Based Isolated Object Recognition through Curvatute Scale Space. *IEEE Transaction on Pattern Analysis and Machine Intelligence*, 17(5):539–544, 1995.
10. R. A. Mollineda, E. Vidal, and F. Casacuberta. *Efficient Techniques for a very Accurate Measurement of Dissimilarities between Cyclic Patterns*, volume 1876, pages 121–126. Springer, 2000.
11. R.A. Wagner and M.J. Fischer. The String-to-String Correction Problem. *Journal of ACM*, 21(1):168–173, 1974.
12. D. Sharvit, J. Chan, H. Tek, and B.B. Kimia. Symmetry-based Indexing of Image Databases. In *CBAIVL98*, pages 56–62, 1998.
13. S. Uliel, A. Fliess, and R. Unger. Naturally occurring circular permutations in proteins. *Protein Engineering*, 14(8):533–542, 2001.

Meeting the Application Requirements of Intelligent Video Surveillance Systems in Moving Object Detection

Donatello Conte[1], Pasquale Foggia[2], Michele Petretta[1], Francesco Tufano[1], and Mario Vento[1]

[1] Dipartimento di Ingegneria dell'Informazione ed Ingegneria Elettrica,
Università di Salerno Via P.te Don Melillo 1 I-84084 Fisciano (SA), Italy
{dconte, mpetretta, ftufano, mvento}@unisa.it
[2] Dipartimento di Informatica e Sistemistica, Università di Napoli "Federico II",
Via Claudio 21 I-80125 Napoli, Italy
foggiapa@unina.it

Abstract. In a video surveillance system, moving object detection is the most challenging problem especially if the system is applied to complex environments with variable lighting, dynamic and articulate scenes, etc. Furthermore, a video surveillance system is a real-time application, so discouraging the use of good, but computationally expensive, solutions. This paper presents a set of improvements of a basic background subtraction algorithm that are suitable for video surveillance applications. Besides we present a new performance evaluation scheme never used in the context of moving object detection algorithms.

1 Introduction

Video surveillance applications need to work in the absence of detailed a priori knowledge about the objects of interest, and this reason makes preferable the use of segmentation algorithms working without models. These algorithms, usually, try to segment the frame of the video into two regions: foreground (pixels belonging to the objects of interest) and background. In a second phase the foreground pixels are grouped to determine the blobs representing the objects. In video surveillance systems, background subtraction is the most used approach for the object detection step. Frequently in literature background and reference image are synonymous. The basic idea is to obtain the foreground region comparing the current image to a reference image. The background pixels can be either represented by a single color value [9] or by a probabilistic distribution. In [6] the authors use a uniform distribution; this choice is effective only if the background model is always perfectly synchronized with scene changes. Alternatively, in order to reduce the sensitivity to the variation of the light conditions or to mitigate waving tree problems (they occurs when part of the background of the scene is detected as object of interest because it is performing little movements), a simple statistical model is used introducing a Gaussian description of the background pixels [15]. Although this solution mitigates errors due to a not perfectly synchronized reference image, on the other side it produces a system less sensitive in the regions where a great variance of colors has been calculated (also for the detection of the objects of interest). To avoid this loss of sensitivity, a more complicated statistical model for pixel representation, Mixture of Gaussian (MOG) has been proposed [12, 4,]. Friedman and Russell [4] introduced, for a traffic monitoring system, the possibility of classifying pixels according to a Gaussian representation for each class (vehicle, shadow or road), Stauffer and Grimson [12], instead, used multiple Gaussians for representing different background illumination conditions.

For outdoor scenes, illumination conditions, usually, change significantly during the day because of sun position or meteorological events; some false positives (objects detected by the system that do not truly exist) derive by these circumstances: this is the *light of day* problem [13]. In fact, if the background is not accurate or consistent with current scene condition, the detection cannot result reliable. The background model, essentially, may be updated using two different ways: non recursive [13, 8] and recursive techniques [6, 15, 7]. The first ones process, for each frame, a sliding window of N past frames and calculate the median value [8] or a linear prediction [13] of the background parameters. The recursive techniques update the background model using current frame and previous background information; it is used as input of a Wiener filter in the Pfinder system [15]. In [7], instead, the reference image is updated using an Infinite Impulse Response filter. Although these algorithms reduce the errors due to slow illumination changes, they don't result able to solve sudden illumination changes or structural background changes. In fact the recursive techniques, as well as the non recursive ones, have to find a compromise for the choice of the update rate: a too fast update rate may cause motionless object to be incorporated in the background, whereas a slow update rate causes the background to be not consistent with illumination changes. Others algorithms, similarly to our approach divide the frame into two or more regions in order to apply different policies for the background updating. In particular [6, 5, 1] apply fast update rate only for the pixels belonging to instantaneous background region, while the regions belonging to the detected object are not updated. The drawback of these approaches is that errors in the objects detection may produce an erroneous reference image compromising the detection performance of the successive frames. A different approach was presented in [10]: the authors proposed a preprocessing step using the illumination eigenspace in order to make the frames to analyze independent from the lighting condition.

Nowadays all the techniques of object detection supply good results under particular circumstances, where the environment is completely controlled with respect to key factors such ad the lighting or the position of the camera. For video surveillance applications these conditions can not be assumed in the general case because the environment in which the system has to work is typically characterized by variable lighting, dynamic and articulated scenes that affect the detection performance. In this paper we present an algorithm suitable for real time applications and robust enough for outdoor scenes. In real time applications more performance constraints have to be considered than in the case of post-processing applications. For these reasons an improvement of the algorithm of background maintenance has been developed and a set of heuristics have been added to the plain background based approach. Furthermore, the results of an extensive experimentation process (described in detail), are shown, in order to validate the effectiveness of the heuristics within real applications. The effectiveness of our approach is validated by means of a new evaluation scheme (Section 3). The experimentations are performed on the standard PETS database [3] which is recognized to be a benchmark for object detection.

2 Heuristics for Improving Detection

A video analysis system for video surveillance application is generally composed of different functional blocks: object detection, object tracking and behavior analysis. The first block locates the objects of interest and describes them by means of their bounding box. The latter is evaluated as the smallest rectangle, whose sides are parallel to the edges of the frame in which the object is inscribed. In the following the bounding boxes will simply called boxes. Then the object tracking block preserves the identity of objects across the frames assigning them unique IDs. In this way we obtain the trajectories of every object and, after a perspective correction, a classification of the objects behavior can be done. If some behaviors are classified as interesting events, the system reacts appropriately on the basis of the application context.

The object detection is divided into three steps (Fig. 1): the pixel segmentation processes the input frames producing a foreground pixel mask, that is obtained thresholding the absolute difference between the current image frame and the reference image; then, a morphological dilatation filter is applied to the foreground pixel mask; finally, by a connected components labelling algorithm the blob segmentation step identifies semantically separated objects and localizes them.

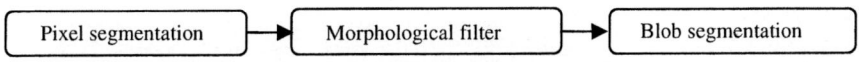

Fig. 1. Object Detection Phases

In order to make the system robust also in outdoor conditions, in the following we will propose a set of improvements for an adaptive background based algorithm: adaptive threshold, noise filtering, shadow filtering, broken object recovery. In the presented algorithm the reference image pixels are represented by their RGB values. The values of the parameters, required by each heuristic were chosen on the basis of a training phase.

2.1 Adaptive Threshold and Noise Filtering

In the simplest algorithms for the object detection [9] the threshold for the pixel segmentation is chosen statically depending on the scene. As regards the definition of the threshold, we have chosen an algorithm that differs from the basic approach for the introduction of a dynamic strategy to update the threshold in order to adapt it to the reference image changes. The main idea is to increase or decrease the threshold on the basis of the brightness changes of the scene. A similar strategy is shown in Gupte et al. [5]. But, whereas in [5] the authors change the threshold on the basis of the static distribution of intensity levels in the current frame, we adapt the threshold on the basis of the variation of the intensity during the image sequence. The threshold is updated according to the following formula:

$$Th = \begin{cases} Th \cdot (1-\Delta_L) & \text{if } \dfrac{|I'|-E^{I-n}[I]}{E^{I-n}[I]} < \chi \\ Th \cdot (1+\Delta_H) & \text{if } \dfrac{|I'|-E^{I-n}[I]}{E^{I-n}[I]} > \chi \end{cases} \quad (1)$$

Where Th is the current threshold; It is the average of the pixels intensity; Et-n[I] is the moving average of I calculated by the last n frames; χ is a percentage (we have chosen a value of 25%); ΔL and ΔH are the rate respectively of the decrement and increment of the threshold (we have chosen for both a value of 0.3). The value of the threshold has an upper and a lower bound.

In the pixel analysis, often, some conditions cause little isolated background areas to be detected as foreground pixels. We have added a noise filter that operates at blob level to remove the spurious objects according to their dimensions and density respect to the bounding box area.

2.2 Shadow Filtering

In the pixel analysis, often, some conditions cause little isolated background areas to be detected as foreground pixels. We have added a noise filter that operates at blob level to remove the spurious objects according to their dimensions.

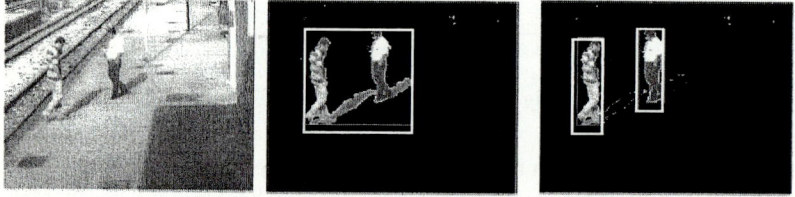

Fig. 2. Foreground mask before (left) and after (right) shadow filtering

The *shadows* problem is very hard to solve at pixel level. In [1] the authors try to detect the shadows considering the properties of the HSV color space. A very interesting approach [11] considers three properties for the detection of the shadows: the presence of a uniform dark region, the luminance changes with respect to the previous frame and the shadow's edges. We propose a technique for the shadow suppression that results very little time consuming but which performances are comparable to [1, 11] for the proposed application. For each object, bounded by its box, we define its *histogram* as the function that associate for a box abscissa *x*, the number of foreground pixels over that column; this histogram is normalized by the relative box height. A foreground pixel is recognized as shadow pixel if:

$$H(x) < T_h \wedge B(x,y) - I(x,y) > T_i \quad (2)$$

Where $H(x)$ is the histogram value at x abscissa, T_h is the histogram threshold (equal to 0.4), $B(x,y)$ and $I(x,y)$ are the image reference and current frame intensity, and finally T_i (equal to 35) is the intensity threshold. So the recognized shadow pixels are eliminated from the foreground mask. When a foreground mask depurated from shadows pixels has been obtained, the connected component labelling is executed again on the regions interested by shadow removal. In Fig. 2 wan example of the results of our algorithm.

2.3 Background Maintenance Algorithm

As regard the image reference updating strategy we use the algorithm proposed by Gupte et al. [5] with some improvements. After pixel segmentation, we have the binary object mask to distinguish the moving pixels from the others. We call instantaneous background those locations where the mask is 0 and detected objects region that location where the mask is 1. The basic updating formula (IIR filter) used as a starting point is:

$$B_{n+1}(x, y) = (1-\alpha) * B_n(x, y) + \alpha * I(x, y). \qquad (3)$$

Where $B_n(x,y)$ is a reference image pixel at time n and α is a coefficient representing the update speed. The first difference in comparison with the author of the work [5] is that we use two different updating speeds depending on the region: for the instantaneous background pixels, the new values are updated very quickly using $\alpha=0.5$. Instead for the detected objects region a very slow update policy is needed. The optimal α value depends on the application, in our experiments, we chose it equal to 0.0001. Even so a problem afflicts this approach: it is represented by the condition in which during a quick illumination change, such as the transit of a cloud in front of the sun, a slowly moving or stopped object is present in the scene. In this case the scene area under the stopped object is not updated. This inconsistency causes the creation of a wrong foreground blob when the above-mentioned object leaves its position. In [5] this problem is not solved, so we have introduced a new processing step, to improve the technique. Specifically, for each object, it is calculated, for the pixels adjacent to its bounding box, the average variation (Δ) between the reference image at frame n and n+1. On the basis of this variation we update the background pixels behind the identified object according to the following formula:

$$B_{n+1}(x, y) = B_n(x, y) + \Delta. \qquad (4)$$

2.4 Broken Object Recovery

It is worth to notice that in a real context the problem of object camouflage is very frequent. In fact for a wrong detection it is not needed that the whole object camouflages itself with the scene. If only a part of it is similar to the background, it may be broken, after foreground detection, into two or more blobs. This causes a serious loss of precision for the detector and it may affect successive tracking and classification steps. The problem cannot be solved by any pixel level algorithm and only a little number of works faces this problem at higher levels. Marcenaro et al. [9] deal with this problem merging regions that are partially overlapped or near; the main drawback of this approach is that it can merge different objects in an unique blob. We present a slight improvement that try to solve this drawback. The base hypothesis is that, if the video frame rate is higher than 6-7 fps, object dimensions cannot change suddenly.

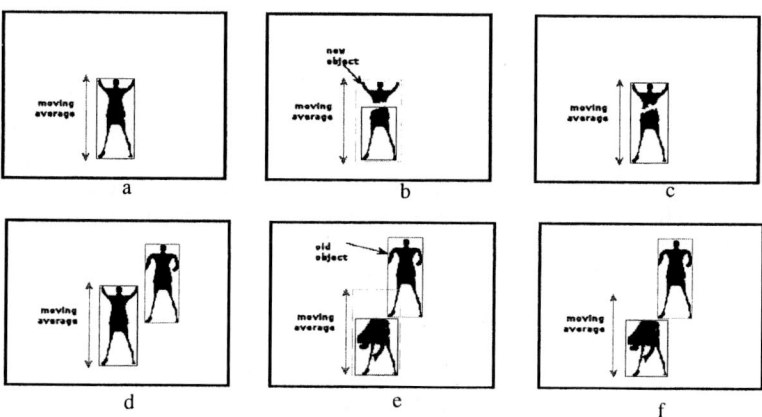

Fig. 3. Broken object heuristics: a, b, c) An example with object adjustment – a) Frame t-1 – b) Frame t – c) Frame t after application of the heuristics; d, e, f) An example without object adjustment – d) Frame t-1 – b) Frame t – c) Frame t after application of the heuristics.

If the current object height results lower by a fixed percentage than the average height, the system checks whether there is a new object (an object that is appeared in the current frame) within the bounding box of the object modified according to the calculated average height. If this check succeeds, the new object is removed and the old one is extended to enclose the corresponding region. In Fig. 3 there is an example of the described approach.

3 Experimental Results

Whereas there are several approaches to evaluate the performances of the tracking algorithms, it has not been made much effort (besides some exceptions [13, 2]) to evaluate the performances of the moving object detection step. One reason is the huge effort needed to produce the ground truth. In fact a detailed ground truth requires the evaluation of each pixel of each frame. Furthermore, an evaluation at pixel level, i.e. counting misdetected pixels (as in [13]), provides a measure that is not so meaningful. Here we use a quantitative method, widely used in other contexts, but never in the evaluation of this kind of algorithms. The method is described in the following. The ground truth is defined, for each frame, as the box coordinates representing the real moving objects present in the frame. We used an evaluation scheme (presented in [14] in the context of text detection in video sequences) which exploits geometrical information (overlap) in the precision and recall measures. The goal of a detection evaluation scheme is to take a list of ground truth boxes $G_i = 1..|G|$ and a list of detected boxes $D_j = 1..|D|$ and to measure the quality of the match between the two lists. From the two lists G and D of detected boxes and ground truth boxes, two overlap matrices σ and τ are created. The rows $i = 1..|G|$ of the matrices correspond to the ground truth boxes and the columns $j = 1..|D|$ correspond to the detected boxes. The values are calculated as follows:

$$\sigma_{ij} = \frac{Area(G_i \cap D_j)}{Area(G_i)} \qquad \tau_{ij} = \frac{Area(G_i \cap D_j)}{Area(D_j)} \qquad (5)$$

The matrices can be analyzed in order to determine the correspondences between the two lists:

one-to-one matches: G_i matches against D_j if row i of both matrices contains only one non-zero element at column j and column j of both matrices contains only one non-zero element at row i. The overlap area needs to have a certain size compared to the rectangle in order to be considered successful ($\sigma_{ij} \geq e_1$ and $\tau_{ij} \geq e_2$).

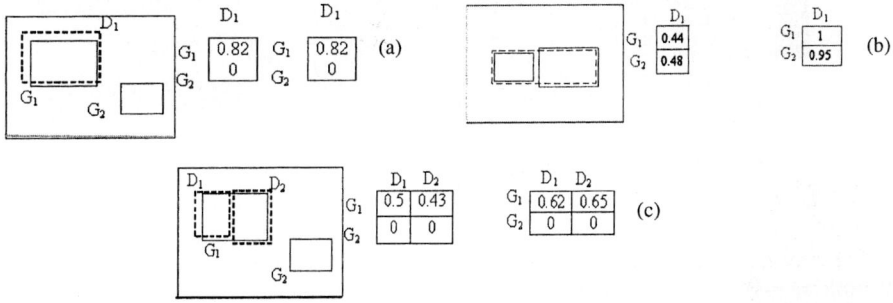

Fig. 4. a) One-to-one matching; b) One-to-many matches with one detected box; c) One-to-many matches with one ground truth box.

one-to-many matches with one ground truth box: G_i matches against several detected boxes if row i of the matrices contains only one non-zero element at column j. The two additional constraints of $\Sigma_j \sigma_{ij} \geq e_3$ and $\forall j : \tau_{ij} \geq e_4$ ensure respectively that the single ground truth rectangle is sufficiently detected and that each of detected rectangles is precisely enough.

one-to-many matches with one detected box: D_j matches against several ground truth boxes if column j of the matrices contains only one non-zero element at row i. Also here we add the constraints of $\Sigma_i \tau_{ij} \geq e_5$ and $\forall i : \sigma_{ij} \geq e_6$.

Based on this matching strategy, the recall and precision measures are given as follows:

$$recall = \frac{\sum_i Match_G(G_i)}{N}, \qquad precision = \frac{\sum_j Match_D(D_j)}{M} \qquad (6)$$

$$Match_G(G_i) = \begin{cases} 1 & \text{if } G_i \text{ matches against a single detected box} \\ 0 & \text{if } G_i \text{ does not match against any detected box} \\ \tau & \text{if } G_i \text{ matches against several detected box} \end{cases} \qquad (7)$$

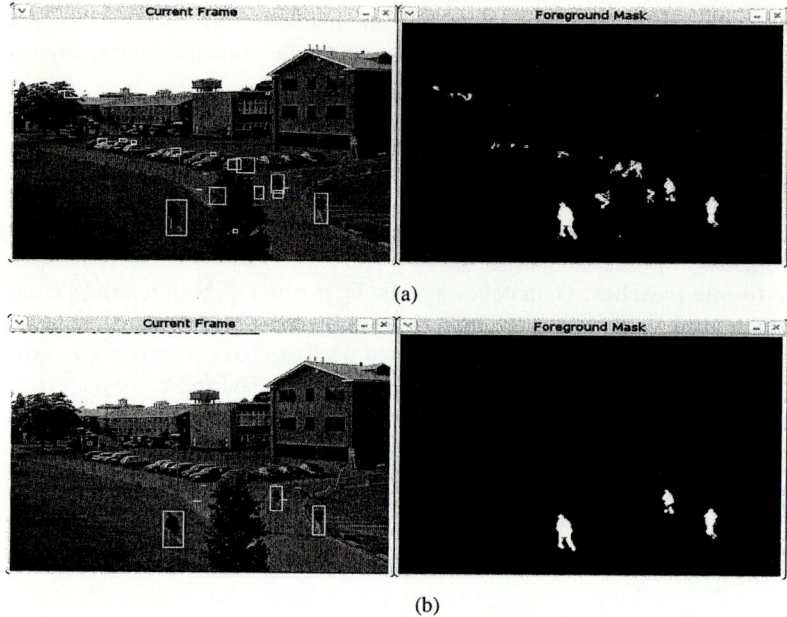

Fig. 5. Results on PETS dataset: a) Standard Algorithm; b) Improved Algorithm.

The τ value was chosen equal to 0,8 considering that for 80% of the condition of multiple matching the tracking step does not result damaged. The function $Match_D(D_j)$ is defined accordingly. This evaluation takes into account one-to-many matches, but "punishes" them slightly. These measures provide an intuitive figure of how many boxes have been detected correctly and how many false alarms have been produced.

Two sequences from PETS2001 dataset [3] have been chosen as testing set. Some other sequences from the same database have been used to tune our algorithm parameters. The two test sequences are: the "testing" sequence – dataset 2 – camera 1 from 80 to 1487 and the "testing" sequence – dataset 4 – camera 1 from 1 to 1082.

In Fig. 5 one example showing the foreground mask and the moving objects detected by the basic and the improved algorithms on PETS dataset, is provided. In Fig. 6 the results of the basic algorithm and the algorithm with the novel heuristics, added step by step, are shown.

First of all we want to remark that the absolute values cannot be taken into account in a comparison with other algorithms because of the different evaluation schema used. You can notice that the original algorithm has performances surely improvable, especially for the precision index. Adding the improvement on the threshold the indexes increase a lot. This proves the effectiveness of the novel improvement. The noise filter raises enormously the precision index because of the reduction of numerous false positive. The drawback is a slight reduction of the recall index.

Finally, with the other heuristics (shadow filtering and broken object resolution) the precision index continue to increase. Here we want to underline that in a video surveillance system we are interested to recognize the events occurring in the scene avoiding false alarms (i.e. inexistent events). Therefore the effort to try new solution for the last two problems has been justified by the most favorable precision index obtained.

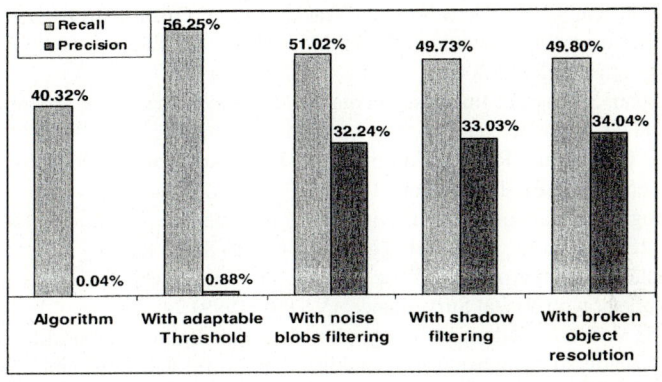

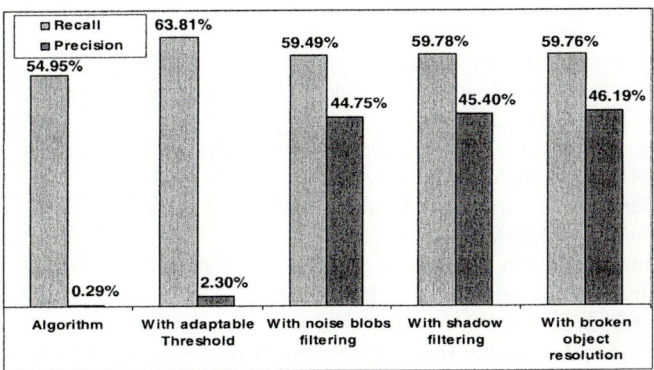

Fig. 6. Results on PETS 2001: a) Dataset 2 Camera 1; b) Dataset 4 Camera 1.

4 Conclusions

In this paper we discussed some improvements of a classical background subtraction algorithm. Furthermore we have shown the application of an evaluation scheme never used in moving object detection algorithms. The results, within the video surveillance framework, are promising. In the future we want to assess the performances of our approach carrying out a comparison with other algorithms using the presented evaluation scheme. Moreover we want to evaluate the sensitivity of the algorithm varying the heuristics parameters on a large number of sequences.

References

1. R. Cucchiara, C. Grana, M. Piccardi, A. Prati, Detecting Moving Objects, Ghosts, and Shadows in Video Streams. IEEE Trans. PAMI. Vol. 25-10 (2003) 1337-1342.
2. T. Ellis, M. Xu, Object Detection and Tracking in an Open and Dynamic World. Workshop on Performance Evaluation of Tracking Systems (PETS2001) (2001).
3. ftp://pets.rdg.ac.uk/PETS2001/.
4. N. Friedman, S. Russell, Image segmentation in video sequences: a probabilistic approach. 13th Annual Conference on Uncertainty in Artificial Intelligence (1997).
5. S. Gupte, O. Masoud, R. F. K. Martin, N. P. Papanikolopoulos, Detection and Classification of Vehicles. IEEE Transac. on ITS. Vol. 3-1 (2002) 37-47.
6. I. Haritaoglu, D. Harwood, L.S. Davis. "W4: real-time surveillance of people and their activities". IEEE Transac. on PAMI. Vol. 22 - 8 (2000) 809 – 830.
7. J. Heikkilä, O. Silvén, A Real-Time System for Monitoring of Cyclists and Pedestrians. IEEE Workshop on Visual Surveillance, (VS'99) (1999) 74 - 81.
8. B. Lo, S. Velastin, Automatic congestion detection system for underground platforms. 2001 International symposium on intelligent multimedia, video, and speech processing (2001) 158 - 161.
9. L. Marcenaro, M. Ferrari, L. Marchesotti, C.S. Regazzoni. Multiple object tracking under heavy occlusions by using Kalman filters based on shape matching, IEEE International Conference on Image Processing. Vol. 3 (2002) 341 – 344.
10. Y. Matsushita, K. Nishino, K. Ikeuchi, and M. Sakauchi, Illumination Normalization with Time-Dependent Intrinsic Image for Video Surveillance IEEE Trans. on PAMI. Vol. 26 – 10 (2004) 1336 - 1347
11. J. Stauder, R. Mech, J. Ostermann, Detection of moving cast shadows for object segmentation. IEEE Transac. on Multimedia. Vol. 1 – 1 (1999) 65 - 76.
12. C. Stauffer, W.E.L. Grimson. "Learning patterns of activity using real-time tracking". IEEE Trans. on PAMI. Vol. 22 – 8 (2000) 747 – 757.
13. K. Toyama, J. Krumm, B. Brumitt, B. Meyers, Wallflower: Principles and Practice of Background Maintenance. Seventh IEEE International Conference on Computer Vision. Vol. 1 (1999) 255 - 261.
14. C. Wolf, "Text Detection in Images taken from Videos Sequences for Semantic Indexing", Ph.D. Thesis at INSA de Lyon, 20, rue Albert Einstein, 69621 Villeurbanne Cedex, France (2003).
15. C. R. Wren, A. Azarbayejani, T. Darrel, A. P. Pentland, Pfinder: Real-Time Tracking of the Human Body. IEEE Trans. PAMI. Vol. 19-7, (1997) 780-785.

Classification Using Scale and Rotation Tolerant Shape Signatures from Convex Hulls

Muhammad Zaheer Aziz[1], Baerbel Mertsching[1], and Asim Munir[2]

[1] GET Lab, Paderborn University,
Paderborn, Germany
{aziz, mertsching}@upb.de
[2] Dept of CS, International Islamic University,
Islamabad, Pakistan
asim_munir@yahoo.com

Abstract. A novel real-time approach for classification or identification of objects is presented here that is suitable for visual attention system of mobile robots. The proposed method constructs convex hulls for regions found in an image using a new external scanning technique. Then a cleaning step produces refined polygons that are in turn used for extracting shape signatures for the regions. In the training phase, shape signatures are collected from test data to find a mean signature for a particular object. A small database is created for all objects related to a specific context in which classification is to be performed. In classifying phase, signatures obtained from objects found in a given image are compared with those present in the database for identification. Nearest signature from the database to a given one is taken as identity of the later. Results have proved efficiency and accuracy of this method.

1 Introduction

Classification and recognition of objects present in static or dynamic scenes are central issues in computer vision. Techniques usually start with a segmentation process and then analysis of the obtained regions is performed. Different approaches have been applied to deal with shape analysis of regions. These techniques can be divided into two major categories. The first one involves all pixels of the region while the other processes only the boundary pixels. The later is computationally efficient as less number of pixels is involved.

The research presented in this paper in one of the milestones towards a broader goal of real-time visual attention model for mobile robots. Visual attention aims to mimic the ability of natural vision systems to select just the relevant aspects from an image [5]. In this context, quick and approximate classification of regions extracted from images is required in the early stages of processing. For this purpose, amount of data to be processed has to be minimized in order to achieve real-time output. On the other hand, involved objects can appear in different orientations and scales during movement of camera(s) installed on a robot. Hence the method of classification has to be tolerant to scale and orientation of attended objects.

2 Problem Definition

Visual attention starts with computation of saliencies in an image due to different features such as eccentricity, color contrast, orientation, and symmetry [16] etc. An array of saliency maps is constructed for these features that are finally combined into a master map. Salient regions of the image appear prominently after this process. The shape of highlighted regions does not essentially match with that of the actual ones. Figure – 1 demonstrates some feature maps and the master map. The said problem can be observed in the master map shown in Fig.1 – e.

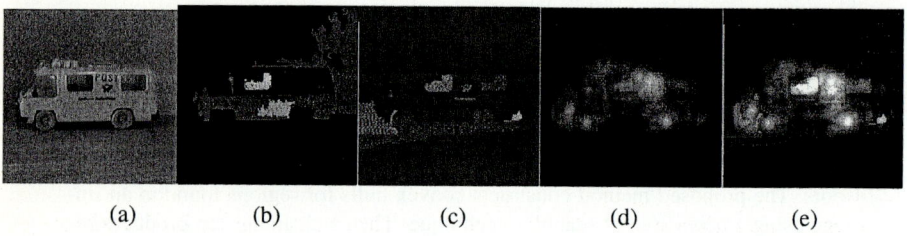

(a)   (b)   (c)   (d)   (e)

Fig. 1. Some of the steps in process of visual attention (a) Input Image (b) Eccentricity (c) Colour contrast (d) Symmetry (e) Master map.

In the next step of visual attention process, a mechanism for inhibition of return (IOR) explores through the salient portions of image as a biological vision system would do. For this purpose an attention window moves inside the image to attend one area at a time. It is responsibility of the IOR process to provide equal opportunity to all objects and not to keep attending a single object while ignoring others. Hence an object once attended has to be identified so that its priority is inhibited in the next cycle of attention. As most of the object shape is distorted in master saliency maps of currently available attention models hence shape based object identification is difficult at this stage.

Our approach of attention is to compute saliency maps and master map according to the shape of actual regions and include a shape-based object identification mechanism for implementation of IOR. The set of objects to be classified will be constrained to occurrences of objects in a sequence of video frames from camera head of a robot. The second aspect of the problem is that the hardware installed on mobile robots has limited computational resources and sometimes algorithms need to be hardwired. This paper addresses the problem of object identification at IOR stage of artificial visual attention.

We require a shape matching technique that may not necessarily be an accurate classifier for a large set of arbitrary objects but should be fast and practically suitable to recognize instances of objects in a sequence of frames. Secondly, in order to maintain low complexity and cost of hardware, the solution has to be simple and small preferably involving straightforward mathematical computations with minimum iterations through the image.

We choose mechanism of identification using shape signatures from convex hulls of regions for solution of the problem in hand. So the following sections will give a brief overview of the literature related to this area and then present a method tailored to meet the requirements of above mentioned problem domain. The developed method is experimented on software test-bed to find its feasibility for actual hardware platform.

3 Related Work

The concept of convex hulls has been a problem of computational geometry and many methods have been developed for building convex hulls for finite clusters of points. There has been significant amount of work to make the algorithms as efficient as possible. In general the Convex Hull, for a finite set of points P, is defined as the smallest convex set that contains P [18]. The resulting subset can be imagined as a group of points that would lie on a stretched rubber band around the given set of points. Shape of the rubber band will be convex and will enclose all the points.

Convex hulls have been used in some machine vision based applications such as computation of convexity feature [26] in objects or finding concavities in order to separate two overlapping regions [22] and pattern recognition in pixelized images [2].Its use has been avoided in real time applications due to the requirement of heavy computational resources even by the quickest of the available methods.

Several methods were devised over the period of time to improve the processing speed. Graham's scan [12] tries to eliminate processing of unnecessary points in determining whether the points lie inside some triangle. It finds extreme points in linear time by performing a lexicographic sorting step first. The method of Jarvis [17], called Jarvis' march, is based on the objective to identify hull edges instead of isolating the extreme points. The method declares the lexicographically lowest point p_1 as a hull vertex. The next vertex p_2 of the edge will be the one that has the least polar angle with respect to p_1. The algorithm marches around the hull finding extreme points on the hull in order, one at a time. The techniques influenced by the basic idea of Quick Sort are popular with the group name of Quick Hull techniques. These techniques partition the cluster of points into two subsets. Each of these subsets will contain one of the two polygonal chains that will be concatenated to form the convex hull polygon. This idea has been utilized in techniques presented in [8] and [6] etc.

The group of techniques using the divide and conquer rule divide the computational problem into sub problems of nearly equal size. The main feature is to apply the principle of balancing [1]. If the original set of points is divided into two sets S_1 and S_2, the convex hull (CH) of original set will be given as

$$CH(S_1 \cup S_2) = CH(CH(S_1) \cup CH(S_2))$$

The work on convex hull construction with pixelized images includes solutions such as [2]. More work is also available in effort to improve time and memory efficiency for example [3] and [19]. Some of the recent works on the convex hull include [14] where an algorithm is presented with $O(|C^q| \ log \ \delta(C))$. Here C is supposed to be a significantly round object, $|C^q|$ is the number of vertices in discrete hull C^q, and $\delta(C)$ is diameter of given object. The method proposed by Franck Nielsen et al [21] is based on marriage-before-conquest paradigm. Another method by Helmut Ratschek et al [23] is based upon a version of Graham's scan. An algorithm by Wei Chen et al [7] constructs a convex superhull for unsorted points. A more recent algorithm was presented in [4] where convex hull of polygonal line is computed in linear time of $O(\log n)$.

For the purpose of object identification through convex hulls, methods such as those given in [11] and [25] use affine invariants of convex hulls for shape matching. Feature extraction from convex shapes for similarity measure have been proposed in [15] using Minkowski addition. The features mentioned in it are useful in our work but their method goes through heavy mathematical procedures hence we will derive some of these features algorithmatically to reduce requirements of computational resources.

It is difficult to select a single algorithm of convex hull construction from above mentioned methods, which is appropriate for the constrained situation described in section – 2. Classical solutions are obviously far too heavy for the limited hardware resources of a mobile robot. The faster algorithms also have drawbacks accompanied with their advantages. Some require input of polygonal line, already convex region, or online feeding of points. Others involve heavy mathematical calculations before they decide that a point is part of convex hull or not. Similarly recursive procedure calls can easily overflow system stack for a reasonably sized input image. Involvement of heavy mathematical operations and/or recursive calls can increase cost and complexity of hardware. Hence we propose a simplified approach towards the problem that can be implemented practically on the prescribed resources.

4 Proposed Method

The proposed method begins with segmentation of the given image using a constrained region growing algorithm. The constraints that control the production of regions are threshold of color range (to accept a pixel as part of a region), minimum acceptable size of region, and maximum size of region. Convex hulls are constructed for the obtained regions and then a cleaning step is performed. A transformation tolerant shape signature is extracted from cleaned convex hulls for identification of objects. Figure 2 shows this architecture diagrammatically.

4.1 Convex Hull Construction

The central concept in convex hull construction is to scan the region externally by scan lines emitting from hull points and wrapping around the region circularly. A bounding rectangle will be considered around the region that will provide the other ends for the scan lines. A scan line will emit from a hull point and stop at a point on the bounding rectangle. If no region pixel is found on its way, then the next consecutive point from the rectangle will be selected and scan will start from the same hull point to the new target on the rectangle edge. Any pixel, belonging to the region, intercepting the scan line could be a candidate for being a convex hull vertex. The pixel nearest to the rectangle will be kept as the hull-point while others on the same line will be rejected. On finding the successive hull point, the scan lines will be originated from the newly found hull point towards the un-used points of the rectangle.

The initial step includes finding the minimum and maximum extents of the region in horizontal and vertical directions, locating the first (topmost) hull point, and finding dimensions of the bounding rectangle. This process starts with scanning through points of the region and finding the topmost point (x_t, y_t), rightmost point (x_r, y_r), bottommost point (x_b, y_b), and leftmost point (x_l, y_l) where

$$y_t = \text{Min}(y_i),\ x_l = \text{Min}(x_i),\ y_b = \text{Max}(y_i),\ x_r = \text{Max}(x_i)\ \forall\ (x_i, y_i) \in \text{Region}$$

Minimum and maximum values for y-coordinates are according to the default top to bottom growth of Y-coordinates in computer display systems. The topmost point (x_t, y_t) of the region is obviously also the topmost point of the convex hull. Hence the first hull point (x^h_i, y^h_i) is (x_t, y_t) where i is set to 1 in this initialization step.

The left, right, top and bottom extents of the bounding rectangle X_l, X_r, Y_t, and Y_b respectively are calculated as

$$X_l = x_l - k,\ X_r = x_r + k,\ Y_t = y_t - k,\ Y_b = y_b + k$$

The constant increment k is made at each side of the rectangle in order to provide necessary room for the scan lines to wrap around, especially at the extreme points of the region. Figure 3 shows the extents of a region and the extended bounding rectangle.

The algorithm generates scan-lines in four parts. In the first part, scan lines emit from the first point (x^h_1, y^h_1) towards left side of the bounding rectangle. A simple method that produces discrete coordinates of points on a scan line is the parametric equation of line

$$P = (B - A)\,t + A$$

In this form of line equation, a point P on the line between two given points A and B is a t times displacement from the point A along the vector $B - A$. An interval of 0 to 1 for t produces points on the segment from A to B.

Process of scan line generation is done in four parts. The first scan lines emit from (x^h_1, y^h_1) and their other ends are taken as (X_l, y) where y iterates from Y_t to Y_b. Each point on the scan line is examined whether it is part of the given region or not. When a region point intercepts a scan line then it is saved as hull point (x^h_i, y^h_i) and after incrementing the value of i. If more region points occur on the same scan line then only the last one towards the side of rectangle is kept. As soon as a hull point is found, it is set as origin for further scan lines. Figure 4 shows this process for detection of two hull points.

In the second part, scan lines will emit from (x^h_i, y^h_i) with current value of i towards points (x, Y_b) where x iterates from X_l to X_r. In the third part, same process will be repeated with scan lines emitting towards (X_r, y) where y iterates from Y_b to Y_t. Finally, similar scanning is done from latest hull point to (x, Y_t) where x iterates from X_r to X_l.

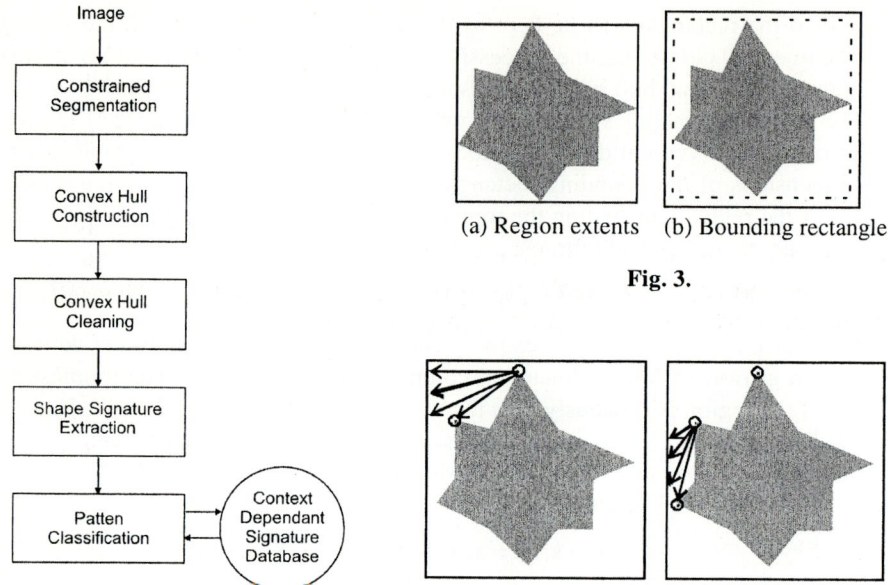

Fig. 2. Architecture of proposed method

Fig. 3.

(a) Region extents (b) Bounding rectangle

Fig. 4. Scan lines detecting hull points

4.2 Convex Hull Cleaning

The regions extracted from real-life images have lots of distortions. When convex hull is constructed for such regions, many unwanted hull vertices can emerge. Similarly stair-case effect in digital images causes production of some erroneous hull points, especially in case of zoomed images. These vertices do not contribute much in the shape of the hull but can cause significant disruptions in quantities of feature vectors that are computed using them. Hence a cleaning algorithm is necessary to remove such vertices with the objective to obtain similar hulls for different occurrences of the same region.

The cleaning algorithm performs two types of cleaning. Firstly it deletes vertices that are intersection of such edges that are incident on each other with an angle close to 180°. Hence for hull points (x^h_i, y^h_i), i iterates from 2 to n where n is the number of hull vertices. Let ϕ be the angle between the line joining (x^h_{i-1}, y^h_{i-1}) and (x^h_i, y^h_i) and the line joining (x^h_i, y^h_i) and (x^h_{i+1}, y^h_{i+1}). If $|\phi - 180|$ is less than a threshold then delete (x^h_i, y^h_i). For $i = n$, the first hull point (x^h_1, y^h_1) is used in place of (x^h_{i+1}, y^h_{i+1}).

In second phase of cleaning, those vertices are deleted that have very small distance from the line joining the vertices before and after it. Let D be the distance between the hull vertex (x^h_i, y^h_i) and the line joining the neighboring vertices (x^h_{i-1}, y^h_{i-1}) and (x^h_{i+1}, y^h_{i+1}) then the vertex (x^h_i, y^h_i) will be deleted if D is less than a threshold. Figure 4 shows some input segments to the algorithm and the resultant convex hulls along with cleaned convex hulls.

4.3 Computation of Shape Signature

Before we describe the shape signature, we define the features that formulate it. Let D_{maj} denote the length of major axis of convex hull and D_{min} be the length of minor axis. Let n is the number of vertices in the convex polygon. If we divide the vertices of convex hull using its minor axis then some of the vertices will be at one side of the line and the rest at the other side. We find distance of each vertex at one side of minor axis to the line of minor axis and then take maximum of these distances as d_1. Similarly the maximum of distances for vertices lying on the other side of minor axis will be d_2. Likewise, d_3 and d_4 are the two maximum distances from the major axis. Now the proposed shape signature can be defined as follows:

$$V_f = [\eta, \rho, r_d, R_d]$$

where $\eta = 1/n$, $\rho = D_{maj}/D_{min}$, $r_d = d_1/d_2$, and $R_d = d_3/d_4$

This vector is composed of ratios that are independent of locations of polygon vertices hence it remains tolerant to orientation and scale of input regions.

4.4 Object Classification

Shape signatures are extracted for a number of samples of a particular object. Mean of these signatures are stored as object identity in a small context related database. For classification of a given object, distance between its signature and those in the database is computed. Minimum of these distances decides the class / identity of the given object.

5 Experiments

The proposed method was implemented in a C++ program on Linux platform running on a Pentium-IV machine. Images having different objects, belonging to two different contexts, in different sizes and orientations were used as input for the program. In order to evaluate effectiveness of the method, artificial images were used so that shades and shadows may not create unwanted regions to degrade the testing. Shape signatures for these objects were collected and mean signature was obtained for each. Figure – 5 shows the steps performed for one sample for each context. The left column shows the input and the second one shows the produced convex hulls. Cleaned convex hulls can be seen in the third column, and the last column displays shape signatures for each object.

In the second part of experimentation, a different set of images was presented to the system in order to classify the objects in them. Each image contained occurrences of these objects in varying orientations and sizes. Figure – 6 show results of this classification for two sets of images belonging to above mentioned contexts. For the sake of summarization, classification of two objects per context is shown. The system picked the identified objects from the given images and marked them by circles. Each column of figure – 6 demonstrates selection (identification) of a specific object from various images. Computation time for processing of these images was also recorded. Figure 7 shows the average time consumed against number of objects present in a given image.

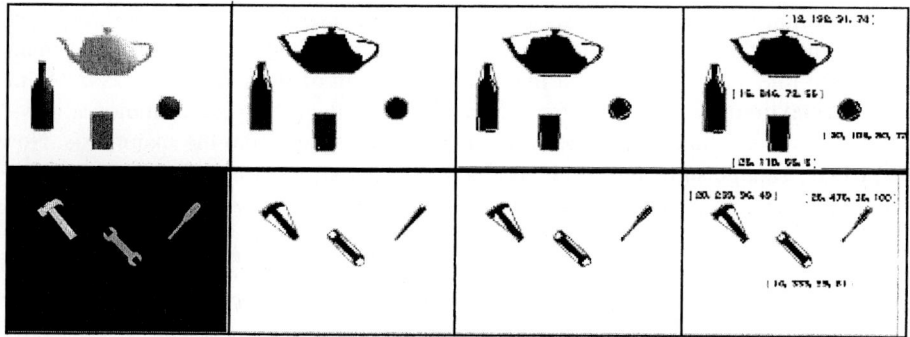

Fig. 5. (Left to Right) Input Images, Normal Convex Hulls, Cleaned Convex Hulls, and Shape Signatures of objects

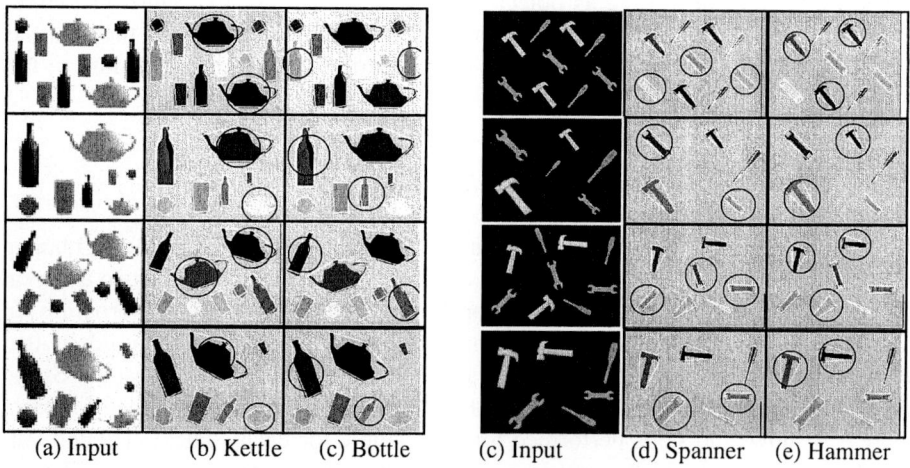

(a) Input   (b) Kettle   (c) Bottle   (c) Input   (d) Spanner   (e) Hammer

Fig. 6. Classification in two different contexts of objects

6 Discussion

One of the exceptions that may arise for this algorithm is the input of objects with convex curved boundaries. The resulting convex hull for such objects will have many vertices but, from those, non-useful ones will be automatically removed in the cleaning step described in section 4.2. Hence the final product will be reasonable for further processing. This effect can be observed on convex hull of ball in figure – 5. This cleaning step is also useful in creating similar polygons from different variants of the same shape as minor deviances in shape are removed before proceeding further. Another advantage that supports success of the proposed method in this problem is the theme in which it is applied (see section – 2). Occurrences of the same set of objects in different frames of a video sequence do not have much fluctuations of shape. Due to this restriction on input data, this method remains suitable for the problem in hand even when it does not guarantee a high discrimination power.

7 Conclusion

It has been successfully shown that convex hulls can lead to useful feature vectors that are able to classify objects on basis of shape. An innovative convex hull construction method was introduced that can process a complete image in real-time. Figure – 7 shows that an image, containing a moderate number of objects, can be processed (including the segmentation step) in 9 to 16 milliseconds. The proposed shape signatures from cleaned convex hulls have shown accuracy of classification in the given context. Figure – 8 shows the average deviation of different occurrences of objects from the mean vector. It is obvious that this deviation is higher when objects are greatly transformed, but it still stays under a certain level so that objects remain distinguishable, using a threshold on vector distance, as demonstrated in figure – 6. The approach has been experimented successfully on the software test-bed and now it can be utilized as a building block for object identification in inhibition of return stage of artificial visual attention.

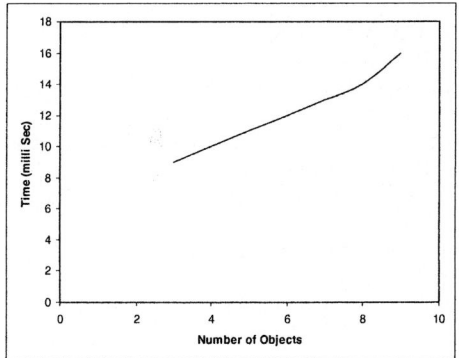 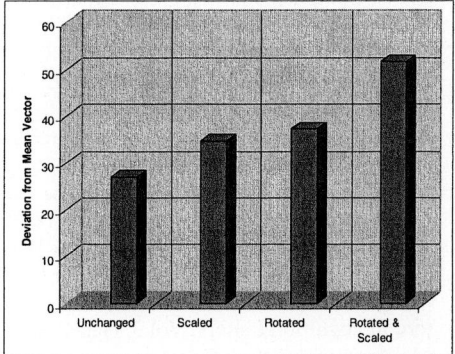

Fig. 7. Processing time　　　　　　**Fig. 8.** Average deviation of shape signatures

References

1. Aho A.V., Hopcroft J. E., Ullman J. D.: The Design and Analysis of Computer Algorithms, Addison – Wesley. (1974).
2. Akl S. G., Toussaint G. T.: Efficient convex hull algorithms for pattern recognition applications. Proceedings of the Fourth International Joint Conference on Pattern Recognition, Kyoto, Japan. (Nov. 1978) 483 – 488.

3. Bhattacharya Binay, Toussaint G. T.: Time-and-storage-efficient implementation of an optimal planar convex hull algorithm. Image and Vision Computing Vol. 1, No. 3, (Aug 1983) 140 – 144.
4. Bronnimann H., Chan T. M.: Space-Efficient Algorithms for Computing the Convex Hull of a Simple Polygonal Line in Linear Time. Lecture Notes in Computer Science. Springer-Verlag (2004) 161-171.
5. Backer G., Mertsching B., Bollmann M.: Data- and Model-Driven Gaze Control for an Active-Vision System. Pattern Analysis and Machine Intelligence, Vol. 23, Issue 12 , IEEE Transactions (Dec. 2001) 1415 – 1429.
6. Bykat A.: Convex Hull of Finite Set of Points in Two Dimensions. Information Processing Letters (1978) 296-298
7. Chen W., Deng X., Wada K., Kawaguchi K.: Constructing a Strongly Convex Superhull of Points. International Journal of Computational Geometry and Applications, Vol. 11, No. 5, (2001) 487-502.
8. Brunner H. E.: Algorithms in Combinatorial Geometry. Monographs on Theoretical Computer Science. Springer-Verlag, Germany (1987).
9. Eddy W.: A New Convex Hull Algorithm for Planar Sets. ACM Transactions on Mathematical Software (1977) 209 – 227.
10. Fernandez-Caballero A., Lopez M. T., Fernandez M. A., Mira J., Delgado A. E., Lopez-Valles J. M.: Accumulative Computation Method for Motion Features Extraction in Dynamic Selective Visual Attention. WAPCV (2004).
11. Flusser J.: Affine Invariants of Convex Polygons. IEEE Transactions on Image Processing, Vol. 11, No. 9, (Sept 2002) 1117 – 1118.
12. Graham R. L.: An Efficient Algorithm for Determining the Convex Hull of a Finite Planar Set. Information Processing Letters (1972) 132 - 133.
13. Green P. J., Silverman B. W.: Constructing the Convex Hull of a Set of Points in the Plane. Computer Journal, Oxford Journals (1979).
14. Har-Peled S.: An output sensitive algorithm for discrete convex hull. Computational Geometry, Vol. 10, Issue 2. Elsevier (1998) 125-138.
15. Heijmans H. J. A. M., Tuzikov A. V.: Similarity and Symmetry Measures for Convex Shapes Using Minkowski Addition.
16. Itti L., Koch C.: A saliency based search mechanism for overt and covert shifts of visual attention. Vision Research Vol. 10, No. 6, (2000) 1489 – 1506.
17. Jarvis R. A.: On the Identification of the Convex Hull of a Finite Set of Points in the Plane. Information Processing Letters (1973) 18 - 21.
18. McMullen P., Shephard G. C.: Convex Polytopes and the Upper Bound Conjecture. Cambridge University Press, Cambridge, England (1971).
19. McQueen M. M., Toussaint G. T.: On the ultimate convex hull algorithm in practice. Pattern Recognition Letters, Vol.3, (Jan 1985) 29 – 34.
20. Melkman A.: Online Construction of the Convex Hull of a simple Polygon. Information Processing Letters (1987) 11-12.
21. Nielsen F., Yvinec M.: An Output Sensitive Convex Hull Algorithm for Planar Objects. International Journal of Computational Geometry and App., Vol. 8, No. 1 (1998) 39-65.
22. Parker J. R.: Practical Computer Vision using C. John Wiley & Sons, USA (1994).
23. Ratscheck H., Rokne J.: Exact and Optimal Convex Hulls in 2D. International Journal of Computational Geometry and Applications, Vol. 8, No. 1 (1998) 39-65.
24. Rosenfeld A.: Picture Processing by Computers, Academic Press, New York (1969).
25. Yang Z., Cohen F. S.: Image Registration and Object Recognition Using Affine Invariant and Convex Hulls. IEEE Trans. on Image Processing, Vol. 8, No. 7, (1999) 934 – 946.
26. Zunic J., Rosin P. L.: A new convexity measure for Polygons. Pattern Analysis and Machine Intelligence. IEEE Transactions, Vol. 26, No. 7 (July 2004) 923 – 934.

On the Filter Combination for Efficient Image Preprocessing Under Uneven Illumination

Mi Young Nam and Phill Kyu Rhee

Dept.of Computer Science & Engineering, Inha University,
253, Yong-Hyun Dong, Nam-Gu,
Incheon, South Korea
`rera@im.inha.ac.kr, pkrhee@inha.ac.kr`

Abstract. In this paper, we investigate how to preprocess bad input face images for robust face recognition, under uneven illumination environments. Proposed filter combination shows nice performance under varying illumination, however, it can not provide the highest performance under normal illumination. We found that the performance of each preprocessing method for compensating illumination is highly affected by working illumination environment. Changing illumination poses a most challenging problem in face recognition. A previous research for illumination compensation has been investigated. This paper proposes a filter block for efficient face recognition. Since no priori knowledge of system working environment can be assumed. The proposed method can decide an optimal configuration of filter block by exploring the filter combination and the associated parameters to unknown illumination conditions. The illumination filter includes Retinex filter, end-in contrast stretching and histogram equalization filter. The proposed method has been tested to robust face recognition in varying illumination conditions (Inha DB, FERET DB). We made in illumination cluster using combined FART. Extensive experiment shows that the proposed system can achieve very encouraging performance in varying illumination environments. We furthermore show how this algorithm can be extended towards face recognition across illumination.

1 Introduction

Face recognition becomes an important task in computer vision and one of the most successful application areas recently. Face recognition technologies have been motivated from the application area of physical access, face image surveillance, people activity awareness, visual interaction for human computer interaction, and humanized vision. Even though many algorithms and techniques are invented, the task of face recognition still remains a difficult problem yet, and existing technologies are not sufficiently reliable. Dynamically changing illumination in a real world application poses one of the most challenging problem in face recognition systems.

The most crucial problem in a face recognition is to eliminate or bypass the effect of changing illumination [1]. As shown in Fig.1, the same person looks very much different with varying illumination environments. Recently, several researchers have tried to attack this problem. Liu and Wechsler have introduced EP (Evolutionary

Persuit) for face image encoding, and have shown its successful application. However, EP needs too large search space to be employed in real world applications.

The illumination cone approach has proposed a generative model that can be used to render face images under novel illumination conditions. The illumination cone for sample pose space is approximated by a linear subspace. The illumination cone approach, however, assumes the pose of face images is fixed. In practical situation, face location may not be accurate enough, and the illumination cone approach leads to dramatic corruption of its performance due to the landmark mismatches.

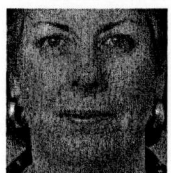 

Fig. 1. The face images which shows the variances in varying illumination(FERET DB)

In this paper, the filter fusion guided by an evolutionary approach has been employed to adapt the system for variations in illumination. The proposed approach employs filter fusion, which is generated from the retinex algorithm. Even though the Gabor wavelet provides the nice properties for face recognition as discussed above, they cannot provide sufficiently reliable solution in changing environments such as variations in illumination. The proposed recognition system adopts the adaptive strategy. The illumination filter fusion adapts itself by reorganizing its structure and parameters. The proposed system has been tested using face images which exposed to different illumination environments. The feasibility and effectiveness of the proposed face recognition system are investigated. We achieved very encouraging experimental results. The outline of this paper is as follows. In section 2, we present the previous problems of preprocessing under uneven illumination environment. In section 3, we present the proposed Face Recognition using Selective Preprocessing and Adaptive Gabor Feature Space. We give experimental results in section 4. Finally, we give concluding remarks.

2 Problems of Preprocessing Under Uneven Illumination Environment

Recently, Retnix filtering method shows high performance in handling bad illuminant images. However, it cannot provide an optimal image preprocessing normal illuminant images. We will examine the above dilemma in solving.

2.1 Histogram Equalization Filter

To improve contrast of image, histogram equalization is used. If the distribution of gray level was biased to one direction or scaled value was not uniformly distributed, histogram equalization is a good solution for image enhancement. The result of histogram equalization is achieved by following three steps [5].

    1) Count the number of occurrence for each gray scale levels and draw histogram.
    2) Find the normalized cumulative histogram.
    3) Find the new contrast value by mapping normalized cumulative histogram to gray scale.

2.2 Ends-in Contrast Stretching

The contrast stretching of the image is distribution of light and dark pixels and applied to an image to stretch a histogram to fill the full dynamic range of the image [5].

$$output(x) = \begin{vmatrix} 0 & \text{for } x < low \\ 255 \times (x - low)/(high - low) & \text{for } low \leq x \leq high \\ 255 & \text{for } high < x \end{vmatrix} \quad (1)$$

2.3 Retinex

Color constancy is excellent for all forms of the retinex but color rendition was elusive as a result of the gray world assumption implicit to the retinex computation. A color restoration was developed and applied after the multi scale retinex in order to overcome this color loss but with a modest dilution in color constancy.

The single-scale retinex is given by [4,5,6,7].

$$R_i(x, y) = \log I\ (x, y) - \log[F(x, y) \times I_i(x, y)] \quad (2)$$

Where,

    $I_i(x, y)$: Image distribution,

    i_{th} : Color band,

    $F(x, y)$: The normalized surround function.

2.4 The Recognition Results by Preprocessing

Facial landmarks are encoded with sets of complex Gabor wavelet coefficients called jets.

Table 1 and 2 show examples from the database before and after processing with our proposed method. We find that normal images show a best performance Retinex algorithm and histogram equalization. A bad illuminant images (fafc dataset) show best performance in Retinex preprocessing system.

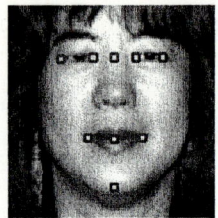

Fig. 2. The nine features selection for face recognition

Table 1. Face recognition for 9 feature points each person

Database	No filter	H.E.	Retinex
Inha Database	1200 / 1259 (95.31%)	1220 / 1259 (96.9%)	1142/ 1259 (90.07%)
FERET fafb	876 / 1195 (73.3%)	900 / 1195 (75.31%)	231 / 1195 (19.33%)
FERET fafc	5 / 194 (2.5%)	27 / 194 (13.91%)	162 /194 (83.50%)

Table 2. Face recognition ratio using multiple preprocessing methods

Dataset\Methods	Retinex + H.E	H.E + Retinex	Contrast stretching
FERET fafc dataset (bad illumination)	20.00%	72.68%	28.35%
Our lab dataset	97.30%	92%	97.06%
FERET fafb (normal illumination)	80%	78.03%	78%

3 Face Recognition Using Selective Preprocessing and Adaptive Gabor Feature Space

3.1 Proposed Method for Face Image Preprocessing

The proposed method has been tested to adapt the system for image processing in varying illumination condition. The system learns the changing environment, and adapts by restructuring its structure and parameters. Illumination condition is generated using genetic algorithm. Filter fusion is gain enhanced face recognition ratio.

FuzzyART is a variant of ART system derived from the first generation of ART, namely ART1 [14]. The feature space of object instance with multiple viewing angles must be clustered properly so that the location error can be minimized. In this paper, clustering's performance improves by studying repeatedly about done data. Fig. 4 shows the clustering result by FART.

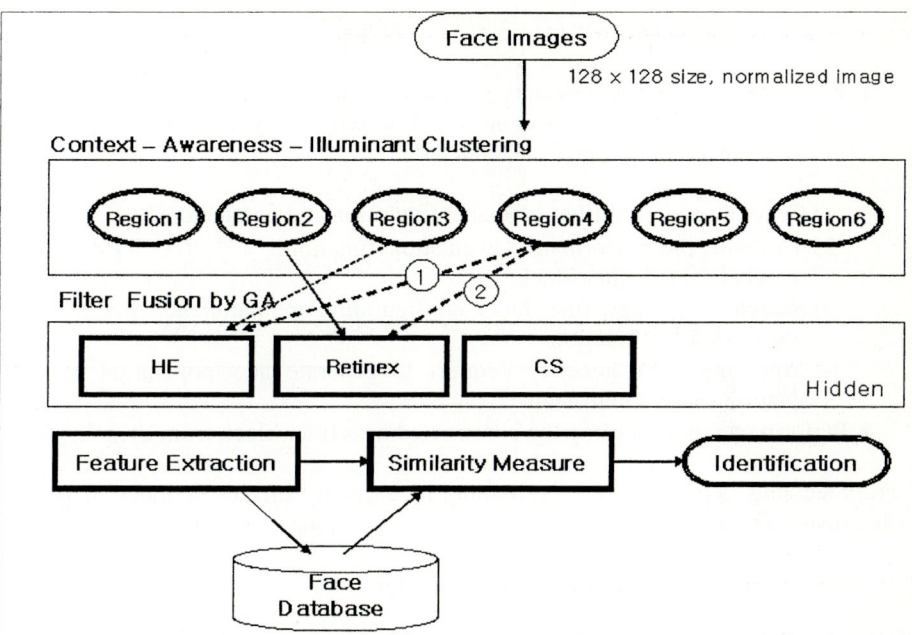

Fig. 3. Filter fusion based face recognition architecture

Cluster	Image number	Examples
Region 0	228	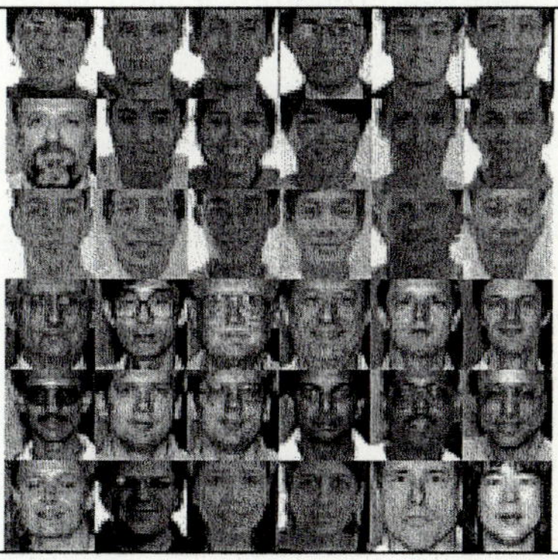
Region 1	157	
Region 2	131	
Region 3	148	
Region 4	157	
Region 5	217	

Fig. 4. Face illumination clustering by proposed method

As shown Fig.4, the details of face recognition process using the proposed adaptive filter fusion is given in the following:

1. Perform filtering, and derives Gabor representation $F(x_j)$ for each fiducial point, and normalized it.
2. Concatenate the Gabor representations for fiducial points to generate total Gabor vector.

$$V = (F^{(\ell)}(\vec{x_1})\ F^{(\ell)}(\vec{x_2})\ldots F^{(\ell)}(\vec{x_n})) \quad (3)$$

3. Begin the classifier architecture optimization until a criterion is met, where the criterion is the performance does not improve anymore or the predefined maximum trial limitation is encountered.

    1) Generate an initial filter block configuration and parameters.
    2) Evaluate the performance evaluation function, $\pi(V) = \lambda_1 \eta_s(V) + \lambda_2 \eta_g(V)$ for the newly adapted filter block.
    3) Search for the new filter block configuration and parameters that maximize the evaluation function.
    4) Applying GA's genetic operators to generate new population of Gabor feature space. Go to Step 3.

4. Perform recognition using the constructed new filter block from Step 3.

Preprocessing is performed for providing nice quality images as much as possible using image filtering techniques discussed in the previous session [11].

3.2 Feature Description Using Gabor Wavelet

Feature space is represented by Gabor wavelet. Gabor wavelet efficiently extracts orientation selectivity, spatial frequency, and spatial localization. It is a simulation or approximation to the experimental filter response profiles in visual neurons [8]. Gabor wavelet is used for image recognition due to its biological relevance and computational properties. Gabor wavelet is one of the successful models that simulate biologically motivated receptive fields. A receptive function can be defined for different classes of visual neurons. The receptive fields of the neurons in the primary visual cortex of mammals are oriented and have characteristic frequencies. These could be modeled 2-D Gabor filter. The Gabor filter is known to be efficient in reducing redundancy and noise in images [9]. Gabor wavelet is biologically motivated convolution kernels in the shape of plane waves restricted by Gabor kernel. The Gabor wavelet has shown to be particularly fit to image decomposition and representation. The convolution coefficients for kernels of different frequencies and orientations starting at a particular fiducial point are calculated. The Gabor kernels for a fiducial point are defined as follows:

$$\phi_{\mu,\nu}(\vec{x}) = \frac{\|\vec{k}_{\mu,\nu}\|^2}{\sigma^2} \exp\left(-\frac{\|\vec{k}_{\mu,\nu}\|^2 \|\vec{x}\|^2}{2\sigma^2}\right) \left[\exp(i \vec{k}_{\mu,\nu} \cdot \vec{x}) - \exp\left(-\frac{\sigma^2}{2}\right)\right] \quad (4)$$

where μ and ν denote the orientation and dilation of the gabor kernels, $(\vec{x}) = (x,y)$, $\|\cdot\|$ denotes the norm operator, and the wave vector $(\vec{k})_{\mu,\nu}$ is defined as follows:

$$(\vec{k})_{\mu,\nu} = (k_\nu \cos\phi_\mu, k_\nu \sin\phi_\mu)^t \quad (5)$$

where $k_\nu = 2^{-\nu+2}$ and $\phi_\mu = \pi\mu/8$.

The family of Gabor kernels is similar each other since they are generated from one mother wavelet by dilation and rotation using the wave vector $\overrightarrow{(k)}_{\mu,\nu}$. Each kernel is a product of a Gaussian envelope and a plane wave. The first term in the brackets in Eq. (5) determines frequency part of the kernel and the second term compensates for the DC value, which makes the kernels DC-free. The effect of the DC term vanishes when the parameter σ has sufficiently high values, where σ determines the ratio of the Gaussian window width to wavelength.

Gabor wavelet is usually used at five different frequencies, $\nu = 0, \ldots, 4$, and eight orientations, $\mu = 0, \ldots, 7$ [10]. The kernels show desirable characteristics of spatial locality and orientation selectivity, a suitable choice for face image feature extraction for classification.

4 Experimental Results

In this paper, image which we use where face images are exposed to lighting variant fafc dataset of FERET DB [12] as show to Fig.10. Fig.10 gives an example of images under varying illuminant.

(a) DataSet1 : FERET fafc dataseet

(b) DataSet2 : (128 x 128) Gray scale

Fig. 5. Experimental dataset

The dataset1 is the fafc dataset of FERET database is gray scale facial image and dataset2 is our lab dataset where face images are exposed to illumination variation and noise. As shown in Fig.7, we extracted 9 feature points. Therefore, size of the feature vector is 9× 40. We change two dimensions to one dimension of 1×360 size. Table 3 shows face recognition using filter fusion each cluster by discrimination FART.

As shown Table 3 and 4, proposed method shows good performance in bad illumination and filter fusion is good performance other illumination. This paper could correct recognition rate of occasion that handle Retinex and histogram equalization paratactically was high each different dataset under varying illumination, that Retinex algorithm is effective in performance in image for illumination. The experimental result of proposed method shows the recognition rate of 83% in fafc dataset and 97.3% in Inha database.

Table 3. Face recognition ratio for each 5 cluster (as shown Fig.4)

Cluster	Filter fusion	Voting Performance
Region 0	95.2	93.5%
Region 1	93	93.5%
Region 2	97.3	93.5%
Region 3	95.6	94%
Region 4	98.2	94%
Region 5	97	90%

Table 4. Face recognition ratio using proposed method

Dataset\Methods	Propose preprocessing method
FERET fafc dataset (bad illumination)	83.5%
Inha dataset	97.3%
FERET fafb (normal illumination)	80.48%

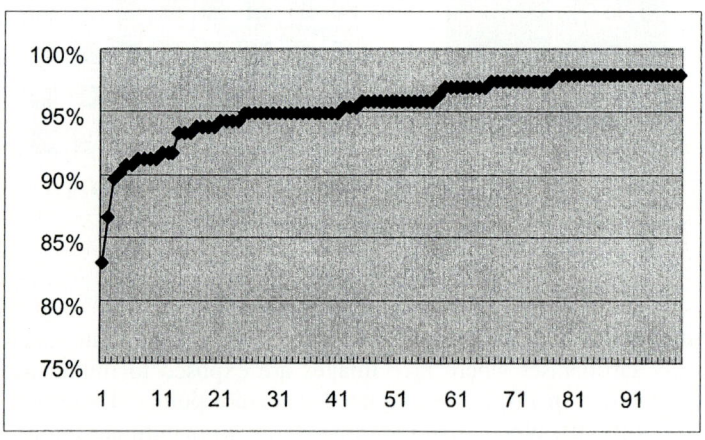

Fig. 6. Bad illumination FERET fafc database CMC curve

Different algorithm or sequence that compare with experiment result in system is as following [15]. From Tables, it becomes apparent that selected image filter method shows good recognition performance while general illuminant filter single filter do. This can interpret use existence and nonexistence and parameter of each image filter using genetic algorithm, because general filtering may appear result that flow image filter unconditionally, and drops preferably quality of original above zero because suitable parameter control is impossible.

Table 5. Performance of the proposed system comparing with other approaches

Algorithm	FERET fafc
arl_cor	0.052
arl_ef	0.186
ef_hist_dev_ang	0.072
ef_hist_dev_anm	0.237
ef_hist_dev_l1	0.258
ef_hist_dev_l2	0.041
ef_hist_dev_md	0.232
ef_hist_dev_ml1	0.392
ef_hist_dev_ml2	0.309
Excalibur	0.216
mit_mar_95	0.155
mit_sep_96	0.32
umd_mar_97	0.588
usc_mar_97	0.82
Proposed method	**0.835**

5 Concluding Remarks

In this paper, we address an efficient processing filter for efficient face recognition under varying illumination. Changing illumination poses a most challenging problem in face recognition. Most existing image processing technologies for robust face recognition are not sufficiently reliable under changing illumination. The proposed method image preprocessing performs well especially in changing illumination environments since it can adapt itself to external environment. The proposed method can decide an optimal configuration of filter fusion by exploring the filter combination and the associated parameters to unknown illumination conditions. Extensive experiment shows that the proposed system can achieve very encouraging performance in varying illumination environments.

References

1. Seung Yonng Lee: Illumination Direction and Scale Robust Face Recognition using Log-polar and Background Illumination Modeling. Thesis, Inha University, Korea, (2002)
2. H. Liu et. al., : Illumination Compensation and Feedback of Illumination Feature in Face Detection. Proc. International Conferences on Information-technology and Information-net, Beijing, vol. 3, (2001) pp.444-449
3. Rafael C. Gonzalez and Richard E. Woods, Digital Image Processing, Addison-Wesley, (1992)
4. Andrew Moore : Real-time Neural System for Color Constancy. IEEE Transactions on Neural Networks, vol. 2, no.2, (1991)

5. Funt, B.V., Ciurea, F., and McCann, J.: Retinex in Matlab. In *Proc. of IS&T/SID Eighth Color Imaging Conference*, (2000) pp. 112–121
6. Daniel J. Jobson, Zia-ur Rahman, Glenn A. Woodell : The Spatial Aspect of Color and Scientific Implications of Retinex Image Processing. SPIE, vol. 4388, (2001) pp117-128
7. Brian Funt, Kobus Barnard : Luminance-Based Multi-Scale Retinex. rmalize proceedings AIC Colour 97 8th Congress of the International Colour Association, (1997)
8. Bossmaier, T.R.J, "Efficient image representation by Gabor functions - an information theory approach," in J.J. Kulikowsji, C.M. Dicknson, and I.J. Murray(Eds.), Pergamon Press, Oxford, U.K. pp. 698 -704
9. Marios Savvides , B.V.K. Vijaya Kumar, P.K. Khosla, "Robust, Shift-Invariance Biometric Identification from Partial Face Images," presented at Proc of SPIE, Biometric Technologies for Human Identifications (OR51), Orlando, FL, (2004)
10. Marios Savvides, B.V.K. Vijaya Kumar, "Quad Phase Minimum Average Correlation Energy Filters for Reduced Memory Illumination Tolerant Face Authentication," *Lecture Notes in Computer Science, Springer-Verlag*, vol. 2688, (2003) pp.19-26
11. A. S. Georghiades, P. N. Belhumeur, and D. J. Kriegman, "From Few to Many: Illumination One Models for face recognition under Variable Lighting and Pose", IEEE Trans. on PAMI, vol.23, no.6, June (2001) pp.643-660
12. P.Phillips, "The FERET database and evaluation procedure for face recognition algorithms," Image and Vision Computing, vol.16, no.5, (1999) pp.295-306
13. D.M. Blackburn, J.M. Bone, and P.J. Phillips: FRVT 2000 Evaluation Report. February (2001)
14. Ramuhalli, P., Polikar, R., Udpa L., Udpa S.: Fuzzy ARTMAP network with evolutionary learning. Proc. of IEEE 25th Int. Conf. On Acoustics, Speech and Signal Processing, vol. 6. Istanbul, Turkey, (2000) pp.3466-3469

Image Merging Based on Perceptual Information

Mohd. Shahid and Sumana Gupta

Indian Institute of Technology, Kanpur, U.P
mshahid1@rediffmail.com

Abstract. Fusion is basically extraction of best of inputs and conveying it to the output. In this paper, we present an image fusion technique using the concept of perceptual information across the bands. This algorithm is relevant to visual sensitivity and tested by merging multisensor, multispectral and defocused images. Fusion is achieved through the formation of one fused pyramid using the DWT coefficients from the decomposed pyramids of the source images. The fused image is obtained through conventional discrete wavelet transform (DWT) reconstruction process. Results obtained using the proposed method show a significant reduction of distortion artifacts and a large preservation of spectral information.

1 Introduction

Image fusion has become important due to increasing number of sensors in remote sensing, photogrammetry and computer vision with complementary information. Images with high spatial information (Panchromatic) are required to be merged with high spectral information (Landsat) images. Fused image contains spatial and spectral information optimally. The goal of image fusion is to integrate complementary information from multisensor data such that the new image is more suitable for the purpose of human perception and computer processing tasks such as segmentation, feature extraction and object recognition. An obvious application of multisensor data fusion is to provide better target detection and identification than a single wide band sensor. An important step in image fusion is image registration. Image registration ensures that the information from each sensor is referring to the same physical structures in the environment[16]. Comprehensive research of the image registration problem can be found in [2,7] and some work on feature based image registration schemes have been presented [11,12,13]. In this paper, we assume that the images to be combined are already perfectly registered. Multisensor data often represents, complementary information about the region surveyed; thus image fusion provides an effective method to enable comparison and analysis of such data. One disadvantage with multisensors is the difficulty faced in registering the. Various methodologies adapted for fusion are Averaging, Multiresolution, Kalman Filtering[8], Fuzzy Logic[18] and Kalman-Fuzzy[9] based. Multiresolution based approach is widely used in literature. It has an advantage that edges which are hard to be seen at one level are easy to be seen at other level. In defense applications, sometimes images which are hard to be seen in visual (due to low contrast) are well seen in IR and vice versa. In concealed weapon detection (CWD) arms are easy to be seen in millimeter wave image than in CCD image [6]. In certain critical applications, where signals are required to be analyzed in real time, fusion plays an important role. Current definition of sensor fusion is very broad and the fusion can take place in at the signal, pixel, feature and symbol level[14,5,24]. Signal level fusion basically refers to a signal with more reliability. Pixel level requires that the fusion has to be done without extracting any information about the objects . Feature levels requires that features have to be extracted from the input images and then fused. Area based approaches are also adapted. Essential problem in fusion is to find the important information from the input images without discarding any of them. This information has to be transferred to the output image. Simple methods (e.g., cutting and pasting) cause edge artifacts. Zhang and Blum [25] presented a thorough investigation into several multiresolution fusion methodologies for a digital camera application. Simple image fusion requires averaging of information from inputs but generally it leaves us with loss of contrast. Multisensor image fusion using the wavelet transform [14] as introduced by Mitra has provided great utility. Mitra has adapted select max approach for coefficient selection. Petrovic [19] has provided gradient based image fusion. In this information is fused at the gradient domain itself before decomposition. Burt [3] has provided image fusion based on similarity measure.Fusion schemes are categorized according to their basic multiresolution/pyramid image representation approach and mechanisms for pyramid coefficient fusion. Multiresolution signal level image fusion, initially proposed by Toet[22,23] is based on the Ratio of Low Pass (RoLP), or contrast pyramid representation. A contrast pyramid is formed by dividing each level of the Gaussian low-pass pyramid[4] with the expanded version of the next coarser level. The Laplacian pyramid representation has been used by Akerman[1] and Liu and Yang[15]. This pyramid is formed by the difference between corresponding pyramid with their expanded low pass approximations.

This paper presents an image fusion technique based on perceptual information across the bands using the wavelet transform domain. Coefficients are appropriately combined, as explained later. In this paper different scenarios of images are considered like multisensor, multispectral and defocused images. Performance is quantitatively evaluated using objective measures proposed by Petrovic[20], universal quality measure proposed by Bovic[26], alongwith Root mean square (RMS) error of the fused image with respect to original spectral image.

2 Fusion Schemes

Multiresolution structure as used in conventional DWT based on Quadrature mirror filter (QMF) decomposition bank has been successfully employed in signal level image fusion[17]. Image is decomposed in four bands at each level. Lower band contains approximation (LL band) while the other bands contain detail information (LH, HL and HH bands). LL band is constructed by Low pass filtering row wise followed by low pass filtering column wise on original images.

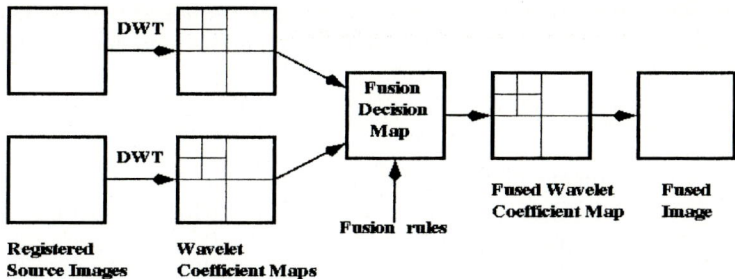

Fig. 1. Schematic diagram for wavelet based basic image fusion

Similarly, LH (Vertical band) band is constructed by High pass filtering row wise followed by Low pass filtering column wise. HL (Horizontal band) band consists of Low pass filtering row wise followed by High pass filtering column wise. HH (Diagonal band) band consists of High pass filtering row wise followed by high pass filtering column wise. Schematic diagram of wavelet based basic image fusion is shown in Fig. 1.

Fusion of information is preferred in high frequency domain. This is based upon the perception that human visual system is more sensitive to local luminance contrast. Number of decomposition level depends upon the resolution demanded.

The Fusion Procedure Contains the Following Steps:

1. Decomposition: Decompose the multisensor/multispectral input images using Mallat decomposition [17] and find approximation (LL) and detail (LH, HL and HH) bands. Repeat the same process for other input image.
2. Pyramid formation: Decomposition is further applied over the approximation. This creates sequence of different resolution pyramids.
3. Baseband Fusion: Baseband consists of low frequency information. Most of the energy in an image is concentrated in the low frequency region. Typically, an image is supposed to have an spectrum that decays with increasing frequency. Various base band fusion techniques are as follows.

I. Simple Approach: In this approach pyramids are averaged. Consider A and B as the input images and F the fused image. F_{LL}^k represents low level information of kth decomposition of fused image.

$$F_{LL}^k = \frac{A_{LL}^k + B_{LL}^k}{2}$$

It gives poor results for multisensor images but reasonably good results for multispectral and defocused images.
II. Spectral Replacement: This is based on the theory that IR camera preserves more low pass information as compared to visual (CCD) camera. Assume A is the IR image.

$$F_{LL}^k = A_{LL}^k$$

This method gives better results for multisensor images.

III. Offset Zero Mean Adding: This method is proposed by Petrovic [19], it provides optimal results for both multisensor as well as defocused images.

$$F_{LL}^k(i,j) = A_{LL}^k(i,j) + B_{LL}^k(i,j) - \frac{\mu_A(i,j) + \mu_A(i,j)}{2}$$

μ_A and μ_B are the mean values of the two input base band images. (i,j) represents a spatial location in the image. Like other arithmetic fusion, the fusion defined above is susceptible to destructive superposition, especially when base bands have opposing illumination levels. If the amount of zero mean information is low this causes only limited degradation in the fused image.

IV. Correlation Based: This approach is proposed by Burt [3]. Here, correlation among image pyramids is used as selection criteria. If correlation among image pyramids is more than certain threshold, they are averaged out. Otherwise based on energy proportion a weighted combination is used. This technique is more effective for defocused images.

4. Detail Band Fusion

It consists of High pass information of the image. Performance of fusion methods mainly depends on how well the high pass information is transferred to the fused image. This is because the human visual system is more sensitive to edge information. Various approaches for detail band fusion are described below:

I. Simple Approach: In this apporach detail pyramids are averaged as follows

$$F_{LH} = \frac{(A_{LH} + B_{LH})}{2}$$

$$F_{HL} = \frac{(A_{HL} + B_{HL})}{2}$$

$$F_{HH} = \frac{(A_{HH} + B_{HH})}{2}$$

It gives poor visual quality of fused image, because edges get blurred.

II. Select Max Approach: This method is proposed by Mitra [14]. In this method the coefficient absolute value is considered as an indication of saliency. Preference is given to a pixel with more saliency.

$$F_{LH}^k(i,j) = \begin{cases} A_{LH}^k(i,j), & \text{If } |A_{LH}(i,j)| > |B_{LH}(i,j)| \\ B_{LH}^k(i,j), & \text{otherwise} \end{cases}$$

$$F_{HL}^k(i,j) = \begin{cases} A_{HL}^k(i,j), & \text{If } |A_{HL}(i,j)| > |B_{HL}(i,j)| \\ B_{HL}^k(i,j), & \text{otherwise} \end{cases}$$

$$F_{HH}^k(i,j) = \begin{cases} A_{HH}^k(i,j), & \text{If } |A_{HH}(i,j)| > |B_{HH}(i,j)| \\ B_{HH}^k(i,j), & \text{otherwise} \end{cases}$$

The coefficients having maximum absolute value is transferred to the fused image. Mitra[14] has also proposed an area based saliency measure followed by Consistency verification.

III. Cross Band Fusion: This method is proposed by Petrovic [21]. Sum of absolute value across the bands is considered as a selection criteria.

$$F_{LH}^k(i,j) = \begin{cases} A_{LH}^k(i,j), \text{ If } |A_{LH}(i,j)| + |A_{HL}(i,j)| + |A_{HH}(i,j)| \\ \qquad\qquad > |B_{LH}(i,j)| + |B_{HL}(I,j)| + |B_{HH}(I,j)| \\ B_{LH}^k(i,j), \text{ otherwise} \end{cases}$$

He has proposed horizontal and vertical direction band fusion.

IV. Proposed Method: We have exploited the fact that image has a spectrum which decays with increasing the frequency.

Suppose that we have n level of decomposition. Then level one would represent the highest frequency sub band and would be finest level of resolution. The nth level would correspond to the lowest frequency sub band and would be at coarsest resolution. So, as we move from highest to lowest resolution level there is a decrease in energy content. These levels are related by father child relationship. As we move to higher decomposition levels, the magnitude of DWT coefficient at the same spatial position reduces. This rate of reduction in magnitude of coefficient with respect to the child is the basis of our selection criteria. Absolute value of coefficient is considered as the importance associated with that coefficient. A child becomes significant, if it's father is also significant. So, actual significance depends upon child's importance with respect to father's importance.

Consider two sets of images. For a particular band the coefficient chosen from the pyramids of both input images is the one, which shows higher rate of change of coefficient ratio with respect to it's father. Following steps are involved for the formation of fused image pyramid at k^{th} level. Suppose $F_{HL}^k(i,j)$ coefficient has to be selected among $A_{HL}^k(i,j)$ and $B_{HL}^k(i,j)$ coefficients.

1. Determine the $(k+1)^{th}$ level pyramid, and find the suitable parent for coefficients $A_{HL}^k(i,j)$ and $B_{HL}^k(i,j)$.
2. Take the ratio of the difference between absolute values of $(k)^{th}$ level and $(k+1)^{th}$ level to the $(k)^{th}$ level coefficient for both images.
3. Choose coefficient for which this ratio is more.

Repeat the same process for other bands.

$$F_{HL}^k(i,j) = \begin{cases} A_{HL}^k(i,j), \text{ If } \frac{|A_{HL}^k(i,j)|-|A_{HL}^{k+1}(i,j)|}{|A_{HL}^k(i,j)|} \\ \qquad\qquad > \frac{|B_{HL}^k(i,j)|-|B_{HL}^{k+1}(i,j)|}{|B_{HL}^k(i,j)|} \\ B_{HL}^k(i,j), \text{ otherwise} \end{cases}$$

$$F_{LH}^k(i,j) = \begin{cases} A_{LH}^k(i,j), \text{ If } \frac{|A_{LH}^k(i,j)|-|A_{LH}^{k+1}(i,j)|}{|A_{LH}^k(i,j)|} \\ \qquad\qquad > \frac{|B_{LH}^k(i,j)|-|B_{LH}^{k+1}(i,j)|}{|B_{LH}^k(i,j)|} \\ B_{LH}^k(i,j), \text{ otherwise} \end{cases}$$

$$F_{HH}^k(i,j) = \begin{cases} A_{HH}^k(i,j), \text{ If } \frac{|A_{HH}^k(i,j)|-|A_{HH}^{k+1}(i,j)|}{|A_{HH}^k(i,j)|} \\ \qquad\qquad > \frac{|B_{HH}^k(i,j)|-|B_{HH}^{k+1}(i,j)|}{|B_{HH}^k(i,j)|} \\ B_{HH}^k(i,j), \text{ otherwise} \end{cases}$$

This method basically emphasizes importance of particular coefficient across the bands in vertical direction. The level of decomposition is decided by the desired resolution. Fused image is reconstructed using standard DWT pyramid method.

3 Performance Measure

Measuring the quality of fused image is a very difficult task. It can be termed as application dependent. In literature, a few quantitative and qualitative measures are available. Petrovic [20] has suggested a quality measure based on emphasis to high frequency information in the image. Bovic [26] has provided an Universal approach to image quality measure. Petrovic quality measure is based upon edge preservation property. Universal quality measure works upon first and second order statistic of input and fused image. Both of the methods measure amount of information transferred from input images to the fused image. Quality measure close to 1 indicate ideally fused image whereas close to 0 indicate poor fused image. Spatial relation between input image with fused image is another measure. RMS error is used as a measure of spatial relation between fused image and spectral image. RMS error close to zero indicate best preservation of spectral information in fused image. Fused image obtained using Proposed method is compared with the fused image obtained using Select max approach. The performance of proposed technique is further tested and compared with respect to Mitra[14] select max with consistency verification technique using wavelet decomposition.

Additional quantitative measures are Mutual information based objective measure[10] and spatial or spectral correlation. MI measure exploits Kull-back criteria. Spatial correlation indicate how well CCD image is transferred to fused image whereas spectral correlation says how well spectral image is transferred to output fused image. Bar chart in Figure 4 shows Fusion quality improvement using proposed method compared to select max method[14]. Visual representation of input images(CCD and IR) with fused image using proposed across band and select max method[14] are given in figure 5.

4 Results and Discussion

The performance of proposed technique is tested and compared with respect to more conventional select max approach using wavelet decomposition [14]. Table I shows the results. The input image pairs are chosen from widest possible range of fusion applications like multisensor, multispectral and defocused images. Root mean square (RMS) error is taken as a criteria to measure how well input spectral information is transferred to the fused image. RMS error of select max is taken as a reference and set to unity. Reduction in RMS error using proposed method clearly indicates improved performance over select max approach. In table I, Set 1 consists of Multisensor images of AMB (CCD and IR). Fused image is shown in Figure 2. Set 2 consists Multisensor images of AMB (CCD and MMW). Set 3 consists of Multi Spectral Satellite image fusion performance.

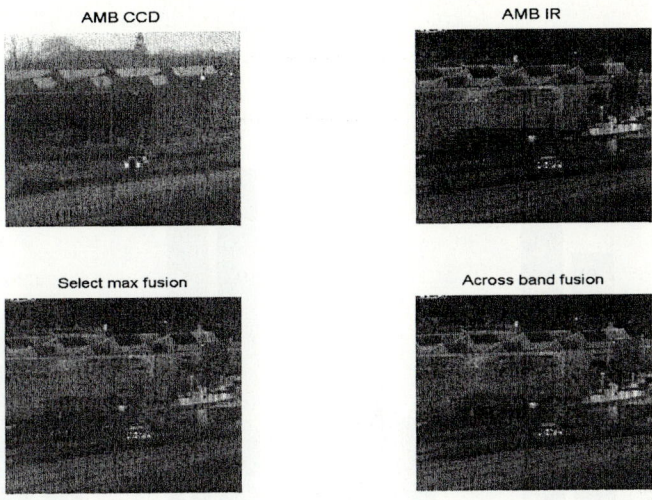

Fig. 2. Multisensor CCD (Left top) and IR (Right top) Image, Fused image using Selectmax(Left bottom) and fused image using Proposed Across band(Right bottom)

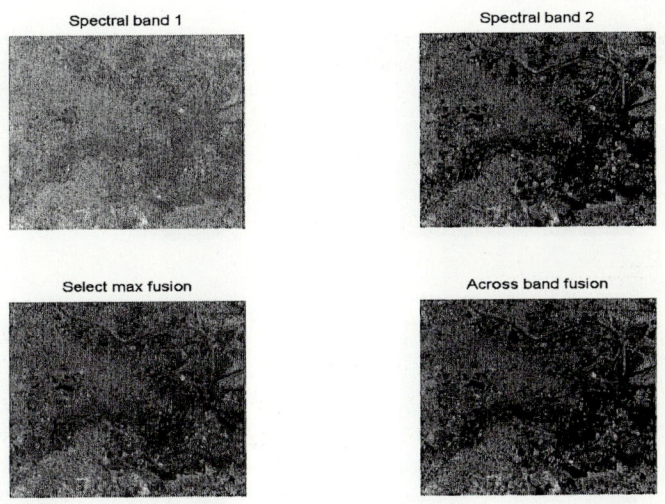

Fig. 3. Multispectral Band 1 (Left top) and Band 2 (Right top) Image, Fused image using Select max(Left bottom) and fused image using Proposed Across band(Right bottom)

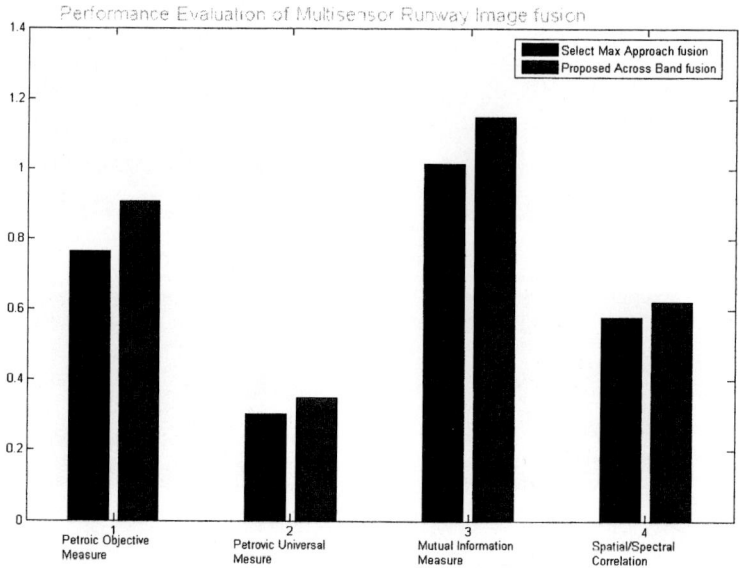

Fig. 4. Multisensor Runway image fusion Performance evaluation using Petrovic, Bovic, Mutual information and Spatial/spectral correlation measures

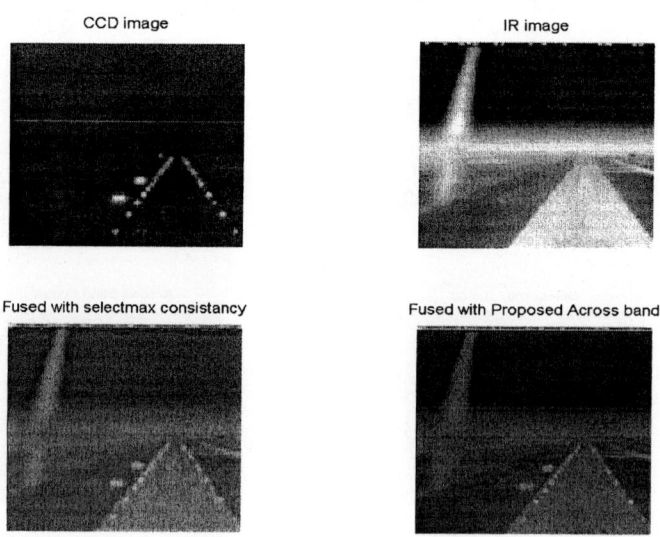

Fig. 5. Multisensor Runway CCD (Left top) and MW (Right top) Image, Fused image using Selectmax(Left bottom) and fused image using Proposed Across band(Right bottom)

Fused image is shown in Figure 3. Set 4 consists of defocused images of same sensor. RMS error has significantly reduced for this set.

Proposed method is compuationally more efficient compared to select max approach introduced by Mitra[14]. Select max method[14], requires consistency verification on decision map, which implies filtering with a majority filter. Consistency verified decision map is used for selecting coefficients from input image pyramids. In contrast to Select max[14], proposed across band fusion does not require consistency verification. In the proposed method consistency verification is inherent due to parent child relationship. Thus proposed method is clearly computationally inexpensive as compared to Select max approach [14]. It has drawback that for k^{th} level of resolution there is a need of an additional $(k+1)^{th}$ level pyramid decomposition.

Table 1. Performance measurement

Images	Approach	Bovic	Petrovic	RMS error
1. AMB	Select max	0.36	0.49	1
(CCD IR)	Proposed	**0.41**	**0.5**	**0.98**
2. AMB	Select max	0.42	0.52	1
(CCD MMW)	Proposed	**0.44**	0.52	**0.97**
3. Spectral	Select max	0.82	0.88	1
	Proposed	**0.84**	0.88	**0.94**
4. Defocused	Select max	0.80	0.8	1
	Proposed	**0.83**	0.8	**0.818**

5 Conclusion

Proposed method provides definite reduction in RMS error with an improved Bovic and/or Petrovic quality measures. In addition, we are able to preserve more spectral information in the fused image. Proposed method is based upon assumption that images are fully registered but in practical scenario they may be unregistered. So, registering multisensor images is another research area.

References

1. Akerman A., "Pyramid techniques for multisensor fusion," Proc. SPIE, vol. 1828, pp. 124-131, 1992.
2. Brown L., A survey of image grgistration techniques, ACM Computing Survey, 24, 1992, 325-376.
3. Burt P. and Kolczynski R., "Enhanced image capture through fusion," in Proc. 4th Int. Conf. Computer Vision, Berlin, Germany, 1993, pp. 173-182.
4. Burt P., "The pyramid as structure for efficient computation," in Multiresolution Image Processing and Analysis. New York: Springer- Verlag, 1984, pp. 6-35.
5. Chipman L., Orr T., Graham L., "Wavelets and image fusion", Proc. of SPIE, Vol. 2569 (1995), pp. 208-219.

6. Chen H.M., Seungsin lee, Raghuveer M.Rao, Slamani and P.K. Varshney, " Imaging for Concealed Weapon Detection", IEEE Signal Processing Magazine March 2005 pp- 52-61.
7. Elsen E., Pol E. and Viergever E., Medical image matching - A review with classification, IEEE Eng. Med. Biol. Mar. 1993, 26-39.
8. Escamilla P.J. and Mort N., Hybrid Kalman Filtr-Fuzzy Logic Adaptive Multisensor Data Fusion Architectures, Proceedings of the 42nd IEEE Conference on Dicision and Contral,pp.- 5215-5220, December 2003.
9. Escamilla P.J. and Mort N., A hybrid Kalman filter-Fuzzy logic architecture for multisensor data fusion, Proceedings of the 2001 IEEE International Symposium on Intelligent contral,pp. 364-369, Sep. 5-7, 2001
10. Guihong,"Information measure for performance of image fusion," Electronic letters pp - 313-315 March 2002.
11. Li H., Munjanath B. and Mitra S.K., Contour based multisensor image registration, in Proceedings 26th Asilomar Conference on Signal, Systems and Computers, Pacific Grove, CA, Nov. 1992, pp. 182-186.
12. Li H., Munjanath B. and Mitra S.K., A contour based approach to multisensor image registration, IEEE Trans. Image Processing, Vol. 4 No. 3, March 1995, pp. 320-334.
13. Li H., Munjanath B. and Mitra S.K., Registration of 3-D brain images by curve mathcing, in Proceedings IEEE medical imaging Conference, San Francisco, CA, Nov. 1993, pp. 1744-1748.
14. Li H., Munjanath B. and Mitra S.K., "Multisensor image fusion using the wavelet transform," Graph. Models Image Process., vol. 57, no. 3, pp. 235-245, Mar. 1995.
15. Liu X. and Yang W., "Enhanced visualization of images through fusion," Proc. SPIE, vol. 4231, pp. 340-345, Oct. 2000
16. Luo R. and Kay M., Data fusion and sensor intergration: state of the art in 1990s, in Data Fusion in Robotics and Machine Intelligence(M.Abidi and R.Gonzalez, Eds,) pp. 7-136, Academic Press, San Diego, 1992.
17. Mallat S., "A theory for multiresolution signal decomposition: The wavelet representation," IEEE Trans. Pattern Anal. Machine Intell., vol. 11, pp. 674-693, July 1989.
18. Mort M. and Prajitno P.J., A Multisensor Data fusion -based target tracking system, IEEE ICIT-2002, pp.- 427-432, Thiland
19. Petrovic V. and Xydeas C.,"Gradient based Multiresolution Image Fusion" IEEE Transaction on Image Processing, Vol. -13, No.-2, Feb 2004.
20. Petrovic V. and Xydeas C." Objective Pixel-level Image fusion Performance Measure", Proceedings of SPIE, vol - 4051 (2000) pp - 89-98.
21. Petrovic V. and Xydeas C., "Multiresolution image fusion using cross band feature selection," Proc. SPIE , vol. 3719, pp. 319-326, Apr. 1999.
22. Toet A., Ruyven L. V., and Velaton J., "Merging thermal and visual images by a contrast pyramid," Opt. Eng., vol. 28, no. 7, pp. 789-792, July 1989.
23. Toet A., "Hierarchical image fusion," Mach. Vis. Appl., vol. 3, pp. 3-11, 1990.
24. Uner M.K., Ramac L., Varshney P., Alford M., "Concealed Weapon Detection: An image fusion approach", Proc. of SPIE, Vol. 2942, 1997, pp. 123-132
25. Zhang Z. and Blum R., "A categorization of multiscale-decomposition based image fusion schemes with a performance study of a digital camera application," Proc. IEEE, vol. 87 pp. 1315-1326, Aug. 1999.
26. Zhou Wang and Alan Bovik C.,"An Universal image quality index", IEEE Signal Processing Letters, vol.-9, no. - 3, March 2002.

An Automated Video Annotation System

Wei Ren[1] and Sameer Singh[2]

[1] ATR Laboratory, University of Exeter, Exeter, UK
W.Ren@ex.ac.uk
[2] ATR Laboratory, University of Loughborough
s.singh@lboro.ac.uk

Abstract. Manually labeling video data is not only a labor intensive and time-consuming task, but also subject to human errors. In this paper, we present an automatic video annotation system. The system uses spatial attributions such as color, texture, shape, motion, and temporal hierarchical attributes among video objects. The system includes a new method of automatic video segmentation, object recognition and object-tracking scheme, and hierarchical object-based video representation model.

1 Introduction

Recent initiatives in digital video technology have significant applications in many areas, including digital libraries, video surveillance, law enforcement, automatic target recognition, traffic management, command and control etc. Large amounts of video data is being captured, produced and stored. However, without appropriate techniques that can make the video content more accessible, such data is becoming more and more difficult to manage. Video annotation (labeling of objects in frames) is important for spatio-temporal modeling that plays an important role in its semantic understanding and retrieval (Chauhan et al., 2004). An entirely manual annotation of video data (labeling of objects in each frame) is not possible with the rapidly increasing volume of video data, since it is not only a labor intensive and time-consuming task, but also subject to human errors. To manipulate a large video database, effective video annotation and object tracking are required by their content. In this paper, we describe an automatic video annotation system based on active learning and multi-objects tracking to automatically recognize and label video objects.

In this paper, we make four major contributions. Firstly, we propose a novel texture feature based on colour co-occurrence, which extends the concept of co-occurrence texture features (Haralick et al 1973). Secondly, automatic region grouping is an open problem in computer vision. In this paper, we propose a new approach by identifying sub-regions by supervised learning and then merge these neighbors with the same label sub-regions into video object. Thirdly, we present an extension of traditional point feature tracking mechanism, called "region tracking". Since all point tracking mechanisms always fail due to ambiguities in the visual data, fast motion, illumination and occlusion problems, we introduce model knowledge in the form of constraints on spatial neighborhood and temporal inheritance to groups of feature points. We also propose the use of color image Bezier enhancement to improve these images.

The remainder of the paper is organized as follows: In the next section, we briefly detail related work and in section 3 we outline how our system works. Section 4 shows our experimental results. Finally, conclusions follow in section 5.

2 Related Work

Extensive research efforts have been made with regard to the retrieval and annotation of video data. The simplest way to do that is by using free text based manual annotation. An example is the 'stratification' approach (Smith and Davenport, 1994), with a few extensions such as video algebra operations (Weiss et al., 1992) with examples including OVID (Oomata and Tanaka, 1994) and CVOT (Li et al., 1997). The goal of our research is to address the problem of manual video data labeling by developing automated labeling methods within an active learning and tracking framework based on spatio-temporal relationships among video objects. The concept of a video object can be associated to the frame region that conveys useful information, while the relationships among these objects changes during whole sequences can be defined as events. Modeling of these high-level concepts (objects and events) makes it possible to describe and capture objects in space and time and capture movements of objects, to allow high-level video retrieval (such as shape and semantic object level retrieval).

Similar attempts include NeTra-V (Deng and Manjunath 1998]) and VideoQ (Chang et al. 1998). NeTra-V deals with sub-region level video representation rather than object level. Tracking with NeTra-V gives low accuracy and fails on fast motion, illumination variation, etc. VideoQ simply matches the trajectory of an object by binary image similarity comparison. This kind of temporal interpretation fails with variation in time intervals. If the same action is played at different speeds it cannot be correctly interpreted. Oren et al. (1999) track pedestrians using wavelet templates which define the shape of an object in terms of a subset of the wavelet coefficients of the image. However, such techniques only work if the object shape is fully presented. It would be fail on cluttered scenes with object occlusion. Comaniciu and Meer (2003) proposed kernel-based (mean-shift) object tracking using a feature histogram-based target representation. This approach is used to track specific objects by comparing their data density.

3 Video Automatic Annotation System

We propose the following algorithm for automated annotation of objects in video sequences.

1. Video V is first segmented to identify key frames $(KF_1,...,KF_M)$ (section 3.1).
2. Segment key-frame KF_i into regions (section 3.2).
3. Label each sub-region in frame KF_i using a classifier trained on discriminatory color and texture features (section 3.2).
4. Merge the adjoining sub-regions with the same object label in frame KF_i. Spatially merge small adjacent isolated regions with $area < \delta$, where δ is threshold for maximum area to merge.

5. Check the mean intensity level and contrast of the frame after the key frame (KF_i+1) to decide whether enhancement is required (section 3.3.1).
6. Select good feature points (section 3.3.2) such as $A_i(x, y)$ in region A to track them to the next frame (KF_i+1) as point $A_{i+1}(x+v_x, y+v_y)$ within shot (Figure 1). $\overline{v} = [v_x \ v_y]^T$ is the displacement vector. Pyramidal tracking is performed to simultaneously track multiple objects (section 3.3).
7. If the region to which tracking point $A_{i+1}(x+v_x, y+v_y)$ belongs has the same color and texture property as the region to which $A_i(x, y)$ belongs (say object X), then the region to which $A_{i+1}(x+v_x, y+v_y)$ belongs will be labeled as X (section 3.3.3).
8. Repeat the above steps for tracking all frames within shot (between key frames KF_i and (KF_i+1).

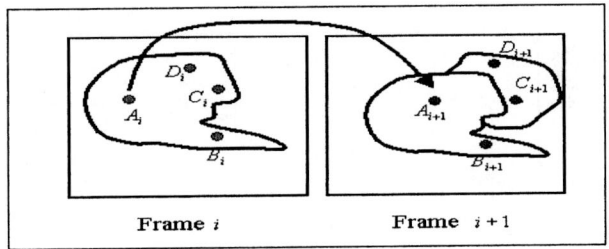

Fig. 1. Region tracking between successive frames, feature point A_i in frame F_i becomes point A_{i+1} in frame F_{i+1}.

The different stages of the above algorithm are described in more detail below.

3.1 Automatic Video Segmentation and Key Frame Selection

For efficient video indexing and retrieval, video segmentation is the crucial first step towards a concise and comprehensive content based video representation for browsing and retrieval purpose. In video segmentation, video is divided into a number of shots. A shot represents a physically temporal interval by camera movement. We automatically detect video transitions such as "cuts" to find key frames for annotation. The frames that lie between the key frames are then automatically annotated using this information as detailed later.

We use a total of 24 features through comparison difference of frame pair for color, shape, texture, motion and statistical characteristics after feature selection. Machine learning techniques such as neural network and *knn* (Nearest Neighbour) are used to automatically detect transition between video scenes, such as {*cut, fade-in, fade-out, dissolve*}. At the same time, camera movements such as panning-left, panning-right, tilting-up, and tilting-down are detected. We achieved an overall recognition rate of 98.1% with neural networks and 95.8% with *knn(k=5)*.

3.2 Automatic Object Identification by Supervised Learning

After video segmentation and detection of key frames, key frames are batch segmented as sub-regions using fuzzy c-means clustering algorithm. Color, texture, and shape features are extracted from these regions to be fed into a trained machine learning system to automatically predict these object labels. In our system, we extract a total of 60 features: 23 color features from different color space, 5 texture features from color co-occurrence matrix, and 27 LLT features and 5 color moment features (Mindru et al., 1999). We extend Haralick's co-occurrence matrix algorithm (Haralick et al., 1973) to work on color images and extract five color texture features, i.e. color co-occurrence matrix features.

3.3 Multi-object Tracking

Since automatic segmentation and region grouping is a difficult process for every frame, we use object tracking for annotating frames in between key frames (Figure 2).

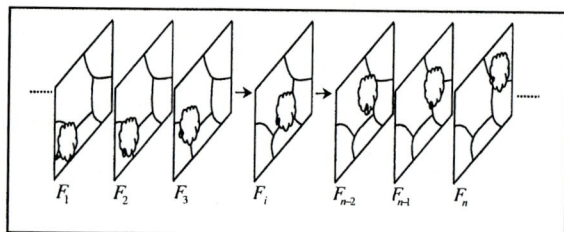

Fig. 2. Tracking an object across multiple frames

Object tracking takes full advantage of the temporal and logical structure of the video and temporal hierarchical relationships between video objects. For instance, an object may move in or out of a scene and its feature based classification will be uncertain due to the variable number of pixels of this object in different frames (the number of pixels may not be enough to extract unique features). However, object tracking is much more reliable and computationally cheaper task as classification of objects need not be performed in every frame. It is certainly not a straightforward task to track objects reliably and simple process that directly projects region contours to next frames (O'Connor et al., 2003). The main challenge in visual tracking is to robustly determine the image position of a target region (or features) of an object as it moves through a camera's field of view. What makes tracking difficult is the extreme variability often present in the images of an object over time.

3.3.1 Image Enhancement

A number of point tracking mechanisms fail due to ambiguities in the visual data, fast motion, illumination, and occlusion. We find that tracking points can be better retained if the images have good contrast quality. In our system, we first adopted a Bézier curve enhancement approach to enhance the total intensity level and improve texture representation by increasing the intensity variation. As the result, the tracking error and lost feature points are greatly reduced.

3.3.2 Target Points Selection and Target Localization

Once the objects have been identified in the key frames, they are next tracked using landmark points. Good target points selected are high frequency textured points, corner or texture edge points.

Let I and J be two successive images in a video sequence. We define the image windows displacement $\vec{d}$ as being the vector. To find the location corresponding to the target feature point in the current frame, the following residual function ε should be minimized:

$$\varepsilon(d) = \iint_W \left[J\left(x + \frac{d}{2}\right) - I\left(x - \frac{d}{2}\right) \right]^2 w(x) dx$$

where $w(x)$ is the weighting function and W is integration window size.

Efficient tracking is performed using a pyramid image representation where multiple image representations are used at different resolutions. An image at pyramidal level K is given as:

$$I^K(x,y) = \frac{1}{4} I^{K-1}(2x, 2y) +$$
$$\frac{1}{8}\left(I^{K-1}(2x-1,2y) + I^{K-1}(2x+1,2y) + I^{K-1}(2x,2y-1) + I^{K-1}(2x,2y+1)\right) +$$
$$\frac{1}{16}\left(I^{K-1}(2x-1,2y-1) + I^{K-1}(2x+1,2y-1) + I^{K-1}(2x-1,2y+1) + I^{K-1}(2x+1,2y+1)\right)$$

This is a recursive function. Compute I^1 from I^0, then compute I^2 from I^1, and so on. Let $K = 1, 2, ..., i, ..., N$ be a generic pyramidal level and let I^i be the image at level i.

We employ a pyramidal implementation of the classical Lucas-Kanade algorithm and extend Shi and Tomasi (1994) point feature tracking algorithm to region tracking as described below. Pyramidal tracking is performed as follows. First, optic flow is computed at the deepest pyramid level K. Then, the result of that computation is propagated to the higher level $K-1$ in a form of an initial guess for the pixel displacement (at level $K-1$). Given that initial guess, the refined optical flow is computed at level $K-1$, and the result is propagated to level $K-2$ and so on until level 0 (the original image). After computing the optic flow at level K, we find the residual pixel displacement vector $d^K = \left[d_x^K, d_y^K \right]$ and minimize the new image match error function $\varepsilon(d)$. In practice the values of K is chosen to be 2, 3, or 4.

3.3.3 Target Region Characterization

Let $(x_i)_{i=1...n}$ be an arbitrary set of n points in the d-dimensional space of color and texture features. Target region is characterized by multivariate kernel density estimate (Comaniciu and Meer 2002):

$$\hat{f}(x) = \frac{1}{nh^d} \sum_{i=1}^{n} K\left(\frac{x - x_i}{h}\right)$$

We use Epanechnikov kernel (Scott 1992):

$$K_E(x) = \begin{cases} \frac{1}{2} c_d^{-1}(d+2)(1 - x^T x) & x^T x < 1 \\ 0 & \text{otherwise} \end{cases}$$

We compare the similarity between two regions using Mahalanobis distance between density functions of two regions which is thresholded to match regions.

4 Experimental Result

We use a total of 59 video clips for testing our automated annotation system. Each video clip has about 1000~5000 frames and includes 4~6 scenes (shots). The camera transitions between scenes include cut, fade-in, fade-out, and dissolve. Temporal video transition and camera movement prediction uses leave-one-out strategy, where one video is for test and another video is for validation purpose. The remaining videos are used for training. In each trial, ten neural networks were trained and optimized for architecture. The validation video was used for deciding on the best network to make final decisions on test data.

In the key-frames labeling stage, training data for region labeling of key frames are still images. 30 videos are used for testing and the remaining 29 are used for training. We obtained 82.0% recognition rate using neural networks. In the tracking stage, object labels are propagated from key-frames of successive frames within each shot. Figure 3 shows the accuracy in tracking pixels correctly for our proposed system (each pixel's predicted object label in the successive frame is compared with manual ground-truth information for that pixel and error is calculated). The proportion of pixels correctly tracked is shown for the first 10 videos. It can be clearly seen that more than 97% of pixels are correctly tracked and labeled.

Figure 4 shows the comparison between our proposed method and a machine learning approach to labeling each frame without tracking. The computational cost with the neural network based system is up to 10 to 15 times more compared to our proposed system. In addition, the time taken by our tracking based approach is less variable across the ten videos tested.

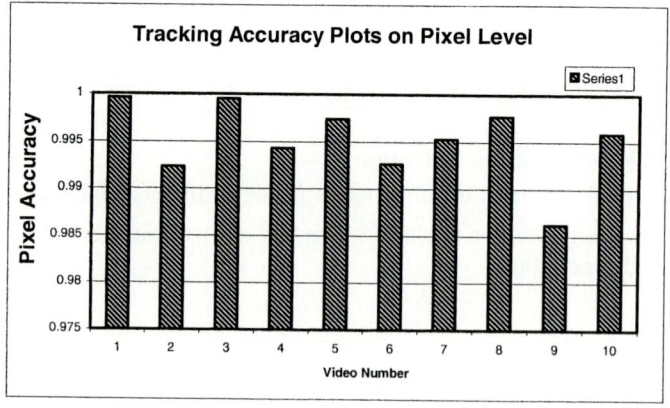

Fig. 3. Plots of tracking process accuracy evaluation on pixel level for first ten videos

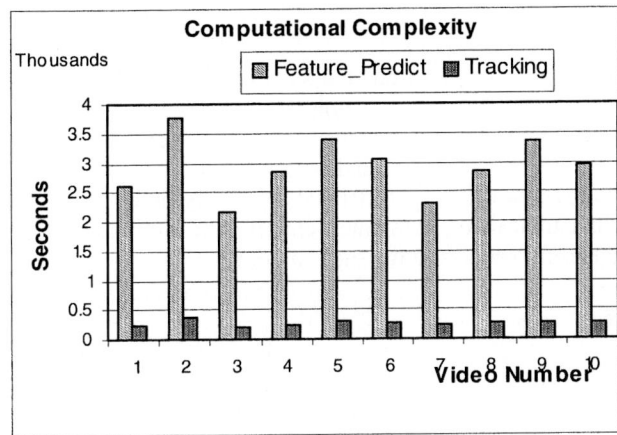

Fig. 4. The time taken in seconds for the ten videos for our proposed system (tracking) vs. neural network based classification of pixels in each frame (predict)

Fig. 5. Example results of automated annotation

5 Conclusion

In this paper we proposed an automated system for video annotation that accurately annotates videos for object labels (example results are shown in Figure 5). This information is very important for content-based video retrieval. Our system is much-faster than the traditional approach and uses a range of color and texture features for object classification and tracking. It depends critically on how well the key frames are labeled and rather than using automated classification for key frames, manual labels can also be tracked for objects in the same manner.

References

1. S-F. Chang, W. Chen, H. Meng, H. Sundaram, and D. Zhong, "A fully automated content based video search engine supporting spatio-temporal queries", IEEE Transaction on Circuits and Systems for Video Technology, Vol. 8, No. 5, pp. 602-615, Sept., 1998.
2. A. Chauhan, S. Singh and D. Grosvenor, "Episode detection in videos captured using a head mounted camera", Pattern Analysis and Applications, vol. 7, pp. 176-189, 2004.
3. D. Comaniciu and P. Meer, "Kernel-based object tracking", IEEE Trans. Pattern Analysis and Machine Intelligence, Vol. 25, No.5,, pp. 564-576, 2003.
4. D. Comaniciu and P. Meer, "Mean Shift: A robust approach toward feature space analysis", IEEE Trans. Pattern Analysis and Machine Intelligence, Vol. 24, pp. 1-18, 2002.
5. Y. Deng and B.S. Manjunath, ", "NeTra-V: towards an object-based video representation", IEEE Transactions on Circuits and Systems for Video Technology, Vol.8, No.5, pp.616-627, 1998.
6. R. M. Haralick, K. Shanmugam and I. Dinstein, "Texture features for image classification", IEEE Transactions on Systems, Man and Cybernetics, vol. 3, pp.610-621, 1973.
7. J. Z. Li, M.T. Zsu, D. Szafron. "Modeling video temporal relationships in an object database management system", Proc. SPIE Multimedia Computing and Networking (MMCN97), pp. 80-91, 1997.
8. F. Mindru, T. Moons and L. Van Gool, "Recognizing color patterns irrespective of viewpoint and illumination", Proc. CVPR'99, pp. 368-373, Fort Collins, Colorado, 1999.
9. N. O'Connor, S. Sav, T. Adamek, V. Mezaris, I. Kompatsiaris, T. Y. Lui, E. Izquierdo, C. F. Bennstrom, J.R. Casas., "Region and Object Segmentation Algorithms in the QIMERA Segmentation Platform", CBMI 2003 International Workshop on Content-Based Multimedia Indexing, Rennes, France , pp.22-24, September 2003.
10. E. Oomoto and K.Tanaka," Ovid: Design and implementation of video-object database system", IEEE Trans. On Knowledge and Data Engineering, 5(4), pp.629-643, 1994.
11. M. Oren, C. Papageorgiou,, P. Sinha, E. Osuna, and T. Poggio, *"Pedestrian detection using wavelet templates"*, Computer Vision and Pattern Recognition, pp. 193-199, 1999.
12. J. Shi and C. Tomasi, "Good features to track", In CVPR, pp. 593-600, 1994.
13. D.W. Scott, Multivariate Density Estimation, Wiley, 1992.
14. T.G.A. Smith, G. Davenport, "The stratification system: a design environment for random access video", Workshop on Network and operating system, La Jolla, CA, 1992.
15. R. Weiss, A. Duda, D. K. Gifford, "Content-based access to algebraic video", In Proc. IEEE First International Conference on Multimedia Computing and Systems, pp.140-151,May 1994.

Tracking by Cluster Analysis of Feature Points and Multiple Particle Filters

Wei Du and Justus Piater

University of Liège, Department of Electrical Engineering and Computer Science,
Institut Montefiore, B28, Sart Tilman Campus, B-4000 Liège, Belgium
`weidu@montefiore.ulg.ac.be, justus.piater@ulg.ac.be`

Abstract. A moving target produces a coherent cluster of feature points in the image plane. This motivates our novel method of tracking multiple targets by cluster analysis of feature points and multiple particle filters. First, feature points are detected by a Harris corner detector and tracked by a Lucas-Kanade tracker. Clusters of moving targets are then initialized by grouping spatially co-located points with similar motion using the EM algorithm. Due to the non-Gaussian distribution of the points in a cluster and the multi-modality resulting from multiple targets, multiple particle filters are applied to track all the clusters simultaneously: one particle filter is started for one cluster. The proposed method is well suited for the typical video surveillance configuration where the cameras are still and targets of interest appear relatively small in the image. We demonstrate the effectiveness of our method on different PETS datasets.

1 Introduction

Tracking of moving targets is an elementary task in many computer vision applications such as video surveillance, sports analysis, human computer interaction, etc. Many different types of features have been used for tracking including points, edges, color, and templates. In this paper, we explore point features as they are ubiquitous and can be easily detected by e.g. the popular Harris corner detector [1].

Most previous work on point tracking focused on reconstructing individual point trajectories as long as possible. For instance, the Kanade-Lucas-Tomasi (KLT) algorithm [2] matches points by minimizing the sum of squared intensity differences. As minimization is sensitive to local extrema, KLT fails easily in case of occlusions and target deformation. In Arnaud *et al* [3], a stochastic filtering framework that blends a dynamic prior model and measurements provided by a matching technique was introduced and proved capable of dealing with abrupt motion changes and partial occlusions. In Shafique *et al* [4], optimal matching was adopted to exploit similarity information of feature points in multiple frames so that tracking is done by means of k-frame point correspondence using graph theory. However, the key problem remains: when a target is occluded or deforms, feature points become less stable - corners disappear during occlusion or turn to edges during deformation - making tracking or matching individual points difficult.

In this paper, a novel method that attacks the instability problem with a different methodology is presented. The ultimate goal for most trackers is to detect and track moving targets, and the tracking of points is the means to achieve this goal. By observing that a moving target produces a coherent cluster of feature points in the image plane, tracking is converted to cluster analysis of feature points. First, feature points are detected by a Harris corner detector and tracked by a KLT tracker. Clusters of moving targets are then initialized by grouping spatially co-located points with similar motion using the EM algorithm [5]. Due to the non-Gaussian distribution of the points in a cluster and the multi-modality resulting from multiple targets, multiple particle filters [6] are applied to track the clusters in the following sequences. Therefore, instead of tracking individual points, we capture the stochastic properties of the clusters of feature points during tracking so that missing or unstable feature points don't affect the tracking results very much. Our method is well suited for the typical video surveillance configuration where the cameras are still and targets of interest appear relatively small in the image, thus feature points on them show strong coherence in space and motion. We demonstrate the effectiveness of our method on different PETS datasets [7].

The idea of tracking by cluster analysis was introduced by Pece [8] and borrowed into this work. Our contributions are, first, to apply it to points instead of regions, thus avoiding background modeling which is sensitive to illumination changes; second, to take motion coherence into account when computing measurements of clusters, which improves the robustness of cluster analysis; third, to integrate cluster analysis in the framework of particle filtering, which stabilizes the estimation of the cluster parameters significantly.

Section 2 describes the overview of our method and states the problem. Automatic initialization by EM based cluster analysis is given in Section 3. Section 4 introduces multiple target tracking using multiple particle filters. Results on sequences from PETS 2001 are illustrated in Section 5.

2 Overview

The motivation of this work is to develop a multitarget tracker for video surveillance applications. By detecting Harris corners and applying KLT in each frame, all the feature points with their associated velocities in the sequence are obtained, as shown in Figure 1. Points on moving targets exhibit large displacements, whereas points on the static background are characterized by very little motion.

An intuitive solution of tracking targets via feature points is to cluster coherent points using the EM algorithm [9]. However, the problems of using EM directly are, first, the number of points in a cluster varies from target to target and over time, depending on the size and appearance of the target. Sometimes few points in a cluster are detected due to the lack of texture information. Then, the spatial distribution of points in a cluster is not well represented by a Gaussian model; a finite uniform distribution is more appropriate. In contrast, the motion distribution of a cluster is well approximated by a Gaussian.

We apply multiple particle filters to solve these problems, as particle filters are well known for their ability to handle clutter and non-Gaussianity [10]. The main idea behind it is simple: Since feature points in a cluster are too sparse to model its distribution, a set of particles are sampled in a cluster. Each particle is evaluated according to some distance function so that it receives a weight reflecting the likelihood that the particle originates from the cluster. The cluster parameters are then updated from the weighted particles. Based on a prior motion model, the cluster distribution is propagated in the sequence so that the target is tracked. Multiple particle filters are applied to track multiple targets simultaneously. New filters are started when a large number of feature points exist that are not associated with any existing filters. Their parameters are initialized by clustering points using the EM algorithm. Existing filters are terminated when the total weights of their particles drop below a threshold. This happens in case of occlusions and targets leaving the scene.

Fig. 1. Result of the Harris corner detection and the KLT tracking. In the left panel, point distributions of clusters are shown in the image plane. All the corners in the sequence are displayed in the spatio-temporal space in the right panel. After removing background points, the structure of the trajectories of moving targets can be clearly seen.

2.1 Problem Statement

A feature point x_j is represented by its image coordinates u_j and its velocity s_j. A cluster of a target O_i is represented by a set of coherent feature points $\{x_j = (u_j, s_j), j = 1...n_i\}$, and is parameterized by a Gaussian $(o_i, \Sigma_i^o, v_i, \Sigma_i^v)$, where o_i is the spatial center, Σ_i^o is the spatial covariance, v_i is the average velocity, and Σ_i^v is the velocity covariance. The spatial and motion distributions of the points in a cluster are assumed independent.

Therefore, the problem of tracking is stated as: given the parameters of clusters in the previous frame, detect how many clusters are present in the current frame and assign each feature point to a cluster. In the following sections, we show how it is solved by initializing with EM based cluster analysis and tracking with multiple particle filters.

3 EM Based Cluster Analysis

Automatic initialization is crucial to the success of a video surveillance system. Targets should be located when they first appear. An EM based cluster analysis algorithm is applied when a large number of feature points exist that are not associated with any existing clusters. Note that new targets may not only occur at the borders but anywhere within the image.

Deciding the number of clusters in the data is usually the hardest problem in cluster analysis. A voting technique was devised to solve this problem. Intuitively, each point spreads a weight to its neighbors based on the distance between them. After voting, each point computes its weight by collecting all the votes received. Points near the center of a cluster tend to have a larger weight. This method is incidentally the first phase ("sparse voting") of tensor voting [11]. By looking for local maxima, the number of new clusters and their centers are detected.

Using these results for initialization, an EM algorithm is applied to estimate the cluster parameters. The probability that a feature point i originates from a cluster j can be estimated from its location and the velocity, defined as $f_j(i) \propto \exp(-\text{dist}(x_i, O_j)))$, where the distance between a point and a cluster is

$$\text{dist}(x_i, O_j) = \left(\begin{bmatrix} u_i \\ s_i \end{bmatrix} - \begin{bmatrix} o_j \\ v_j \end{bmatrix} \right)^T \begin{bmatrix} \Sigma_j^o & 0 \\ 0 & \Sigma_j^v \end{bmatrix}^{-1} \left(\begin{bmatrix} u_i \\ s_i \end{bmatrix} - \begin{bmatrix} o_j \\ v_j \end{bmatrix} \right). \tag{1}$$

According to Bayes' theorem, the posterior probability that point i is generated by one of the clusters j is $p_j(i) = \dfrac{w_j f_j(i)}{\sum w_j f_j(i)}$, where w_j is the prior probability of cluster j defined as the fraction of image pixels generated from cluster j. Points are associated with the cluster that maximizes the posterior probability. Once all the points are assigned, the parameters of each cluster are re-estimated by summing the evidence over all its points. This is iterated until EM converges to a local maximum of the likelihood of the observed data. A phase of K-Means clustering is inserted to obtain a better initialization so that the EM algorithm converges with fewer iterations. In fact, in cases where the targets are well separated, EM does not change the output of K-Means at all. Results are shown in Figure 2.

4 Multiple Particle Filters

Multiple particle filters are a simplified implementation of the mixture particle filter which is capable of maintaining the multi-modality of the posterior distribution and of tracking multiple targets simultaneously [6, 12, 13]. With a similar idea, we model each cluster with an individual particle filter, start a filter when a cluster is detected and terminate it when the cluster disappears.

Fig. 2. Results of initialization of clusters in the first frame. Feature points detected by the Harris corner detector and tracked by KLT are grouped into clusters representing targets.

4.1 Initialization of a Particle Filter

Given the initial parameters of a cluster obtained from the cluster analysis step, a particle filter is started. Two sets of particles are sampled in each filter: one from the initial distribution of the cluster and the other around each feature point in the cluster, shown in Figure 3.

Fig. 3. Results of initialization of multiple particle filters. The green dots are sampled particles.

Let $x_{m,t}^k = (u_{m,t}^k, s_{m,t}^k)$ be the m-th particle in the k-th filter (corresponding to the k-th cluster) at time t, so

$$x_{m,0}^k = \text{sample}(O_k) \text{ or } x_{m,0}^k = x_i + \begin{bmatrix} \varepsilon_u \\ \varepsilon_s \end{bmatrix}, \tag{2}$$

where $x_i \in O_k$, ε_u and ε_s are random variables modeling respectively the changes in space and motion.

The reason of sampling 2 sets of particles is because of the non-Gaussianity of the feature points in a cluster. In this way, the particles are scattered in the cluster and the distribution is fully and well approximated. In all experiments, 100 particles are sampled around a feature point, and the number of particles sampled from the cluster distribution is proportional to the size of the cluster.

4.2 Tracking by Multiple Particle Filters

A particle in filter k is propagated in the sequence based on the constant velocity assumption,

$$x^k_{m,t+1} = \begin{bmatrix} 1 & 1 \\ 0 & 1 \end{bmatrix} x^k_{m,t} + \begin{bmatrix} \varepsilon_u \\ \varepsilon_s \end{bmatrix}, \quad (3)$$

and weighted by a function of the distances between the particle and the feature points around it, defined as

$$w^k_{m,t+1} = \sum_i \exp(-\text{dist}(x^k_{m,t+1}, x_{i,t+1})), \quad (4)$$

where the distance is

$$\text{dist}(x^k_{m,t+1}, x_{i,t+1}) = (x^k_{m,t+1} - x_{i,t+1})^T \begin{bmatrix} \Sigma_u & 0 \\ 0 & \Sigma_s \end{bmatrix}^{-1} (x^k_{m,t+1} - x_{i,t+1}). \quad (5)$$

Σ_u and Σ_s are set to balance the influence of the distance in space and in velocity. The parameters of cluster k are then estimated from the weighted particles.

The computed parameters are not good enough because of the possible target deformation and the unstable feature point detection. For instance, the way that the weight is computed in Equation 4 tends to attract particles to the closest feature point. As a result, when new feature points appear in a frame, there may be few particles of large weights near them (especially when these new feature points are near the border of the cluster) so that their contributions to the estimation of the cluster parameters are unfortunately ignored.

To solve this problem, a one-step clustering is inserted to assign all the feature points to one of the clusters using their current parameters based on the distance defined by Equation 1. New particles are sampled around each feature point. The new sampled particles plus all the existing particles in a cluster are then reweighted by a function that averages the previously computed weight and the distances between particles and their clusters, defined as

$$w^k_{m,t+1} = \alpha \sum_i \exp(-\text{dist}(x^k_{m,t+1}, x_{i,t+1})) + (1-\alpha)\exp(-\text{dist}(x^k_{m,t+1}, O_{k,t+1})). \quad (6)$$

The first term of the above equation describes the similarity measurement of the particle with its neighboring feature points, while the second term penalizes how coherent the particle is with the cluster. Finally, the parameters of the cluster are refined from its reweighted particle set.

The final step of a particle filter is to resample particles based on their weights so that particles with small weights are likely to be discarded and those with large weights are duplicated. Note that a fixed number of particles in a filter are resampled during tracking.

In summary, the tracker consists of the following steps: (1) Prediction: particles are propagated using Equation 3. (2) Weighting: their importance weights are computed using Equation 4. (3) Clustering: assign feature points in the current frame to a cluster; new particles are sampled around each feature point. (4) Reweighting: particles are reweighted using Equation 6, and the parameters of the clusters are refined. (5) Resampling: resample particles using the Monte Carlo Sampling technique. These steps are iterated to propagate the distributions of the clusters in the sequence.

At the Clustering step, if a large number of feature points exist that are not associated with any existing filters, a new particle filter will be started and initialized by the EM based cluster analysis, as is stated in Section 3. At the Weighting step, if the total weight of all the particles in a filter drops below a threshold, the filter will be terminated. This happens when the target is occluded or leaves the scene.

5 Results

The proposed method is evaluated on different sequences from PETS2001. Figure 4 shows the result of tracking a subsequence of 300 frames in the sequence of Camera 1 of Dataset 1. Note that two crossing targets in the sequence are tracked separately during the occlusion, shown in the right panel of Figure 4, since they exhibit different motion.

Four challenging subsequences from the noisy sequence of Camera 1 of Dataset 3 are selected to evaluate the robustness of the method, as is demonstrated in Figure 5. They contain substantial and rapid illumination changes, shadows, severe occlusions and groups of people entering and leaving. The algorithm proves robust to substantial changes in illumination since the Harris corner detector is relatively insensitive to lighting changes. As shadows move along with the targets that cast them, they are tracked as a part of the targets and introduce only small jitter in the trajectories. The algorithm has problems maintaining a stable number of clusters in case of severe occlusions, because shadows connect distinct clusters and people move from one cluster to another. We are currently studying complementary methods for tracking individual targets using model-based approaches.

Figure 6 and 7 illustrate the results of the comparison of our method with direct KLT tracking and our previous background-subtraction method [14]. The first comparison shows that KLT tracker fails during target deformation and occlusions, because when corners turn to edges, the tracks of points slide along edges, and when occluded, points drift from one target to another; meanwhile, our method is able to capture the stochastic properties of targets and is not affected by unstable feature points. The second comparison shows that background models are difficult to maintain in the presence of rapid lighting changes and fail in such situations (consult Piater *et al* [14] for more details), whereas our method is less sensitive and continues to track. The only problem is that shadows show up or disappear when illumination changes rapidly, which affects the parameters of clusters.

Nevertheless, a practical drawback of our method is that tracks of targets tend to be lost if they move slowly or possess little texture. Another drawback is that the method is only capable of dealing with partial occlusions. In case of complete occlusion, new targets are detected and are not linked to their correspondences before occlusion due to the lack of other information such as the appearance of the targets. However, an advantage of our method is that the errors will not be propagated in the sequence so that interactive reinitialization is unnecessary.

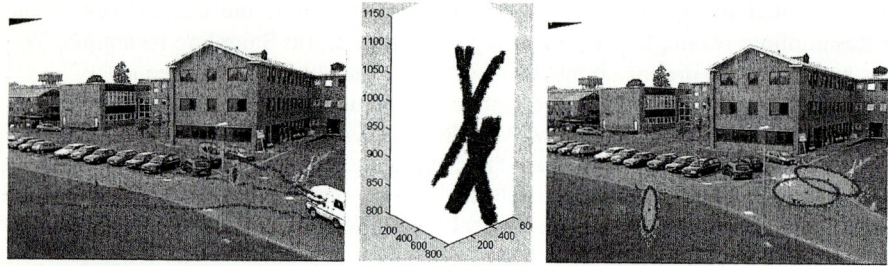

Fig. 4. Results of tracking. All the particles in the sequence are displayed in the spatio-temporal space in the middle panel.

Fig. 5. Results of tracking four noisy sequences to evaluate the robustness of our method. Note that only long trajectories with large certainties are displayed.

Fig. 6. Comparison of the method with direct KLT tracking. 3 KLT tracks are displayed in the middle panel. Note that the red one drifts from the group of people to the vehicle during occlusion (the first row of the right panel), and the blue one jumps from one leg of a pedestrian to another during deformation (the second row of the right panel). As our method captures the stochastic properties of the clusters of feature points, these unstable feature points don't affect the tracking results very much, shown in the left panel.

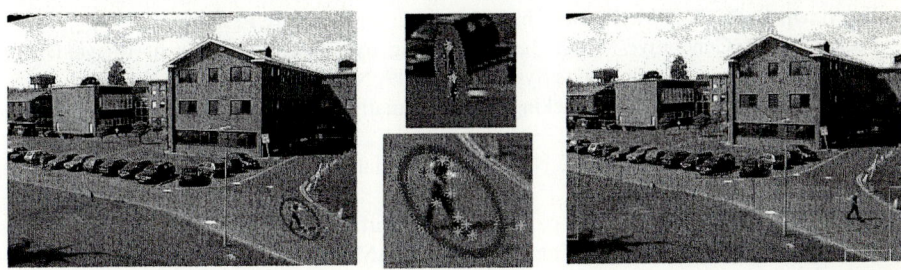

Fig. 7. Comparison of the method with our previous work which integrates background subtraction and motion history detection in the framework of a Kalman filter [14]. As expected, the track of the pedestrian is lost during the rapid illumination changes, shown in the right panel, whereas our new method succeeds in tracking in such situations, shown in the left panel. In the middle panel, two subimages of the same pedestrian at different time are displayed to show how the parameters of the cluster are affected by the shadow.

6 Conclusions and Future Work

This paper presents a novel method of tracking moving targets via feature points. The method is suitable for the video surveillance configuration where the cameras are still and targets are relatively small in the image so that feature points on a target form coherent spatio-temporal clusters. The EM algorithm and multiple particle filters are applied to cluster feature points and to track all the targets simultaneously. As demonstrated, the method is robust and capable of dealing with partial occlusions, shadows and illumination changes. We are currently focusing on tracking in difficult situations such as severe occlusions. Complementary methods for tracking individual targets over long sequences are being developed using model-based approaches and probabilistic data association. An extension of the current work to moving cameras is also ongoing and will broaden its application to e.g. sports analysis.

References

1. Harris, C., Stephens, M.: A Combined Corner and Edge Detector, Fourth Alvey Vision Conference, pp. 147-151, 1988.
2. Lucas, D.B., Kanade, T.: An Iterative Image Registration Technique with an Application to Stereo Vision, International Joint Conference on Artificial Intelligence, pp. 674-679, 1981.
3. Arnaud, E., Memin, E., Cernuschi-Frias, B.: A Robust Stochastic Filter for Point Tracking in Image Sequences, Asian Conference on Computer Vision, Korea, 2004.
4. Shafique, K., Shah, M.: A Noniterative Greedy Algorithm for Multiframe Point Correspondence, IEEE Transactions on PAMI, Vol. 27, No. 1, pp. 51-65, January 2005.
5. Dempster, A.P., Laird, N.M., Rubin, D.B.: Maximum Likelihood from Incomplete Data via the EM Algorithm, Journal of the Royal Statistical Society, Vol. 39, No. 1, pp. 1-38, 1977.
6. Lookingbill, A., Lieb, D., Stavens, D., Thrun, S.: Learning Activity-based Ground Models from a Moving Helicopter Platform, ICRA, Spain, 2005.
7. Ferryman, J.: PETS 2001 Datasets, http://visualsurveillance.org/PETS2001.
8. Pece, A.E.C.: Generative-Model-Based Tracking by Cluster Analysis of Image Differences, Robotics and Autonomous Systems, Vol. 49, No. 3, pp. 181-194, 2002.
9. Du, W., Piater, J., Verly, J.: Tracking by Perceptually Grouping Feature Points into Clusters, submitted.
10. Doucet, A., Freitas, N., Godor, N., eds: Sequential Monte Carlo Methods in Practice, Springer Verlag, 2000.
11. Medioni, G., Tang, C.K.: Inference of Integrated Surface, Curve and Junction Descriptions from Sparse 3-D Data, IEEE Transactions on PAMI, Vol. 20, No. 11, pp. 1206-1223, 1998.
12. Vermaak, J., Doucet, A., Perez, P.: Maintaining Multi-Modality through Mixture Tracking, International Conference on Computer Vision, Nice, France, 2003.
13. Okuma, K., Taleghani, A., Freitas, N.D., Little, J.J., Lowe, D.G.: A Boosted Particle Filter: Multitarget Detection and Tracking, ECCV, Vol. 1, pp. 28-39, 2004.
14. Piater, J., Crowley, J.: Multi-Modal Tracking of Interacting Targets Using Gaussian Approximations. Proceedings of the Second IEEE International Workshop on Performance Evaluation of Tracking and Surveillance, Hawaii, USA, 2001.

A Benchmark for Indoor/Outdoor Scene Classification

Andrew Payne and Sameer Singh

Research School of Infomatics,
Holywell Park,
University of Loughborough,
LE11 3TU
{a.m.payne, s.singh}@lboro.ac.uk

Abstract. Image scene classification is an integral part of many aspects of image processing. Indoor and Outdoor classification is a fundamental part of scene processing as it is the starting point of many semantic scene evaluation approaches. Many novel techniques have been developed to tackle this problem, but each technique relies on its own database of images thus reducing the confidence in the success of each method. We attempt here to look at the current field of indoor / outdoor scene classification and develop a benchmark model for evaluating current methods.

1 Introduction

Semantic image scene classification is a fundamental part of many areas of image processing such as Content-Based Indexing[1] and Image Retrieval [2], Digital Libraries[3], Vision-based Robotics Applications[4] and Digital Photography [5,6]. Indoor and outdoor scene classification is the basis for further image grouping, such as cityscape versus landscape classification[7,8]. The comparison of these methods is made difficult by the lack of a unified database of images for this purpose. A lot of the work in this area uses either images collected from other databases (e.g. the Kodak stock image database[9]), images collected for the specific algorithm from the Internet, or personal photographs[10]. For each method, the amount of data is highly variable. In this paper, we present a benchmark for image scene classification and evaluate some methods of indoor / outdoor classification on this data.

2 Background

The task of scene classification is a difficult problem because the high-level entities taken as typical of one type of scene may be a part of another type. For example, in indoor / outdoor classification, similar objects such as plants can exist in either class. Several methods for automatic classification have been proposed with varying degrees of success and most rely on low-level colour space and texture features. Very few rely on any single type of feature as they are typically not strong enough to separate the two classes and need to be boosted with high-level semantic features[9,11,12].

Once a set of features is determined, there is still a question of how to integrate the features into a classifier. Szummer and Picard[9] and Serrano et al.[13] use two pass systems in which the image is broken into several equal image sub-blocks. In the first pass, each block is labelled as indoor or outdoor based on the low-level colour and texture features separately. The second pass combines the results of the first pass to make a final image classification. Generally, this type of classification system produces the best results over this type of problem as colour and texture features are more likely to be uniform over smaller regions of the image. It might be noted that an image of too small a resolution will not be well broken into smaller image sub-blocks.

Colour features are used throughout the literature as an initial low-level feature. Szummer and Picard [9] and Serrano et al. [11,13] use colour space histograms based on the Ohta and LST colour spaces respectively. The intersection distance in their experiments showed better results than the Euclidean distance. Likewise, Miene et al. [14] use first order statistical features of distributions based on colour and greyscale histograms. Qiu et al.[3] conducted an extensive comparison of the different colour histogram features including opponent colour histogram, colour correlogram, MPEG-7 colour structure descriptor, colour pattern appearance histogram, and layered colour indexing. They found that there was no single feature set that works on all types of images, but that significant amounts of redundancy in histograms can be removed.

Texture features are also often used. Wavelet texture features determined using a two-level decomposition have been used by Serrano et al. [11,13] and they have shown these features to perform better than other texture features. The first feature is determined by filtering low-frequency coefficients with a Laplacian filter. The other features are found using the sub-band energy for all wavelet coefficients. Guerin-Dugue and Olivia[2] use local dominant orientation (LDO) distributions representing the entire image. This is based on the power spectrum of the image from which features are extracted to classify indoor from outdoor. In the indoor images there is a more balanced 0° to 90° orientation than the outdoor images which have a greater horizontal anisotropy. Fitzpatrick[15] proposes that in indoor images, the degree of vertical change in brightness is low whereas the degree of vertical orientation is high. In outdoor images, the degree of vertical change in brightness is high, where the degree of vertical orientation is low. Traherne and Singh[5] and Payne and Singh[6] rely on shape description of the texture of edges proposing that indoor (synthetic) images have a higher content of straighter edges than in outdoor (organic) images.

The role of semantic information is also well established and applied in this context. Some studies have combined the low-level colour and texture features with semantic information (such as the a priori knowledge that sky appears at the top of an outdoor image) in order to boost classification results. The basic idea is that by using the mid-level semantic information through a Bayesian network, the performance of a system will be improved [11,12]. Semantic information can also be gathered based on perceptual grouping, for example, on edge features such as straight line segments, longer linear lines, coterminations, "L" and "U" junctions, parallel lines, parallel groups and polygons. Iqbal and Aggarwal[16] demonstrate this concept for the detection of man-made objects in images. The use of text-based descriptions of scenes has also been used as a semantic cue about the class of an image[17].

3 Benchmark

Though other image databases exist with consumer photographs scenes (e.g. the Kodak and Corel databases), they are hard to acquire, had too few photographs or do not have any ground truth information. Considering the scene classification problem, we define the following constraints on a benchmark for this purpose:

1. The image data should be well categorised. Classification systems can only be well verified if the ground truth data is well placed into categories. Data should be collected to fill these groupings.
2. The categories should represent real-world types of images without retouching and preprocessing of a professional photographic nature. The images captured for each category should be taken of real scenes of a diverse nature.
3. There should be a sufficient number of images in each category. This point is considerably difficult to ascertain as each method suggests a different baseline number of images set by the specifics of the task at hand. Some methods report as few as 500 images in total, whereas others report thousands of image in their data set. We believe that 500 images in each category is a representative portion suitable for laboratory evaluation of novel classification techniques.
4. The dimensions of the images should be suitable for most image processing techniques with consideration taken for storage size. Images smaller than 640x480 pixels tend to loose the quality in detail that is required by higher-level semantic analysis.
5. The images should be stored in a suitable format. That is, the images should not be over-compressed thus introducing artifacts into the scene that might be interpreted as a part of the scene.

Our benchmark comprises 1000 images categorised into 500 indoor images and 500 outdoor images. The outdoor images are broken into the sub-categories of landscape images and city scenes and the landscape images are further broken down into mountains, beach, snow, and general outdoor scenes. Each image is 640x480 pixels and stored in a low compression JPEG format compatible with that used on-board in commercial digital cameras. Examples of the benchmark images can be seen in Figure 1.

Fig. 1. Example images from the benchmark. Images 1-8 represent the indoor images. Images 9-16 represent outdoor images.

4 Validation

In [6], we proposed a method of indoor / outdoor scene classification based on contour tracking and straightness through a 2-pass classification system. For completeness, we have used this method and other comparative methods to determine how well they would perform on our proposed benchmark. Four methods are compared on the benchmark set: contour straightness, Ohta colour histogram distance[9], sub-band energy of wavelet coefficients and LST colour histogram with wavelet coefficients[13]. The results in Table 1 have been achieved from these methods.

Table 1. Results for methods on the benchmark set. It is interesting to note that the Serrano et al. second method (combining wavelet texture features and colour) has a lower overall classification rate, but a more consistent rate between the two classes.

method	indoor	outdoor	combined
Payne/Singh	88.30%	87.36%	87.70%
Szummer/Picard	60.65%	60.61%	60.33%
Serrano et al. 1	93.45%	58.26%	72.78%
Serrano et al. 2	70.11%	60.43%	64.41%

In our experiments, we used the Ohta colour space, the axes of which are the 3 largest eigenvectors of the RGB space. It is defined in [9] as:

$$I1 = R + G + B$$

$$I2 = R - B$$

$$I3 = R - 2G + B$$

Moreover, the histogram distance, rather than being calculated with the Euclidean norm, is calculated using the histogram intersection norm:

$$dist(h^1, h^2) = \sum_{i=1}^{N} [h_i^1 - min(h_i^1, h_i^2)]$$

where h^1 and h^2 are the two histograms. The result is a measure of the amount of overlap between the two histograms.

In [13], a two-level wavelet decomposition is used to obtain texture features of an image. The features, the sub-band energies of the decomposition, are defined by:

$$e_k = \frac{1}{MN} \sum_{i=1}^{M} \sum_{j=1}^{N} | c_k(i,j) |^2$$

where M and N are the image dimensions of the coefficient c_k. The coefficient number k ranges from 2 to $4K$, where K is the number of decomposition levels.

When compared to the MSAR features originally used in [9], the wavelet decomposition out-performed them as well as being half the dimensionality. The LST colour space described in this work is similar to the Ohta colour space except for scaling factors.

$$L = \frac{k}{\sqrt{3}} I1$$

$$S = \frac{k}{\sqrt{2}} I2$$

$$T = \frac{k}{\sqrt{6}} I3$$

where $k = 255/max(R, G, B)$. The colour and textures features are combined using a two stage classification system where the colour and texture are independently used to determine region classification and the results are combined in the second stage by a 3rd classifier.

Misclassification between the two classes occurs on images where it is difficult to differentiate the overall structure of the image contents. For example, an indoor image with clutter or a large amount of organic material can be confused with an outdoor image. Similarly, an outdoor image with a large amount of synthetic elements will be misclassified by the tested approaches as an indoor image. Figure 2 demonstrates examples of this.

Fig. 2. Misclassified indoor and outdoor images. The first two images show cluttered indoor scenes misclassified as an outdoor scene. The second image pair shows outdoor scenes misclassified as indoor scenes.

5 Conclusion

In this paper we have presented a framework benchmark for indoor / outdoor scene classification. Through our validation experiment we have shown that not only is it possible to classify the images in the database, but it is also a challenging exercise for novel methods. The intention is that it will provide a testbed for the comparison of different scene classification techniques. We would encourage the use of this benchmark by the academic community and report their results with it. Details of how to download the benchmark are found at http://www.paaonline.net/benchmarks/minerva

References

1. A. Vailaya, M. Figueiredo, A. Jain and H. J. Zhang, "Image Classification for Content-Based Indexing", IEEE Transactions on Image Processing, Vol. 10, No. 1, pp 117-130, 2001.
2. A. Guerin-Dugue, A. Olivia, "Classification of Scene Photographs from Local Orientation Features", Pattern Recognition Letters, Vol. 21, pp. 1135, 2000.
3. G. Qiu, X. Feng, J. Fang, "Compressing Histogram Representations for Automatic Colour Photo Characterisation", Pattern Recognition, 2004.
4. S.Srinivasan, L. Kanal, "Qualitative Landmark Recognition Using Visual Cues", Pattern Recognition Letters, Vol. 18, pp 1405-1414, 1997.
5. M. Traherne, S. Singh, "An Integrated Approach to Automatic Indoor-Outdoor Scene Classification in Digital Images", Proc. 5th International Conference on Intelligent Data Engineering and Automated Learning, Exeter, UK, 2004.
6. A. Payne, S. Singh, "Indoor Vs. Outdoor Scene Classification In Digital Photographs", Pattern Recognition, in press, 2005.
7. A. Vailaya, A. K. Jain, H. J. Zhang, "On Image Classification: City Images vs. Landscapes", Pattern Recognition, Vol. 31, pp 1921-1936, 1998.
8. A. Vailaya, M. Figueiredo, A. Jain, H. J. Zhang, "Bayesian Framework for Hierarchical Semantic Classification of Vacation Images", IEEE International Conference on Multimedia Computing and Systems, Vol. 1, pp 518-523, 1999.
9. M. Szummer, R. Picard, "Indoor-Outdoor Image Classification", IEEE International Workshop on Content-Based Access of Image and Video Databases, ICCV '98, 1998.
10. L. Lu, K. Toyama, G. Hagar, "A Two Level Approach for Scene Recognition", IEEE Computer Society Conference on Computer Vision and Pattern Recognition, June 2005.
11. N. Serrano, A. Savakis, J. Luo, "Improved Scene Classification Using Efficient Low-Level and Semantic Cues", Pattern Recognition, 2004.
12. J. Luo, A. Savakis, "Indoor vs. Outdoor Classification of Consumer Photographs Using Low-Level and Semantic Features", Proceedings of the International Conference of Image Processing, Greece, 2001.
13. N. Serrano, A. Savakis, J. Luo, "A Computationally Efficient Approach to Indoor/Outdoor Scene Classification", IEEE International Conference on Pattern Recognition, 2003.
14. A. Meine, Th. Hermes, G. Ioannidis, R. Fathi, O, Herzog, "Automatic Shot Boundary Detection and Classification of Indoor and Outdoor Scenes", Information Technology: The 11th Text Retrieval Conference, 2003.

15. P. Fitzpatrick, "Indoor/Outdoor Scene Classification Project", http://www.mit.edu/people/paulfitz/pub/indoor-outdoor.pdf .
16. Q. Iqbal, J. K. Aggarwal, "Retieval by Classification of Images Containing Large Man-Made Objects Using Perceptual Grouping", Pattern Recognition, Vol. 35, pp 1462-1479, 2002.
17. S. Paek, C. L. Sable, V. Hatzivassiloglou, A. Jaimes, B. H. Schiffman, S. F. Chang, K. R. Mackeown, "Integration of Visual and Text Based Approaches for the Content Labelling and Classification of Photographs", ACM SIGIR'99 Workshop on Multimedia Indexing Retrieval, Berkeley, 1999.

Spinal Deformity Detection Employing Back Propagation on Neural Network

Hyoungseop Kim[1], Joo kooi Tan[1], Seiji Ishikawa[1], Marzuki Khalid[2], Max Viergever[3], Yoshinori Otsuka[4], and Takashi Shinomiya[5]

[1] Kyushu Institute of Technology, 1-1, Sensui-cho, Tobata, Kitakyushu
804-8550, Japan
kim@cntl.kyutech.ac.jp
[2] Center for AI and Robotics, Universiti Teknologi, Malaysia
[3] Image Science Institute, University Hospital Utrecht, The Netherlands
[4] National Sanatorium Chiba Higashi Hospital, Japan
[5] Nikon Co., LTD., Japan

Abstract. We propose a new technique for automatic spinal deformity detection from moire topographic images. Normally the moire stripes of a human body show a symmetric pattern. According to the progress of the deformity of a spine, asymmetry becomes larger. Numerical representation of the degree of asymmetry is therefore useful in evaluating the deformity. Displacement of local centroids and difference of gray value are calculated between the left-hand side and the right-hand side regions of the moire images with respect to the extracted middle line. Extracted 4 feature vectors (mean value and standard deviation from the each displacement) from the left-hand side and right-hand side rectangle areas apply to train a neural network. An experiment was performed employing 1,200 real moire images and 90.3% of the images were classified correctly.

1 Introduction

Spinal deformity is a disease mainly suffered by teenagers during their growth stage. There are many causes of spinal deformity, but all of them are unknown. The most common type is termed "idiopathic" that show 80% of the spinal deformity. There are two basic types of spinal deformity, which called structural and nonstructural spinal deformity (also called functional). To detect the deformity syndrome of the spine, moire method (*i.e.* moire images) has been applied in the mass screening in Japan. In the image screening, approximately 370000 moire images are obtained every year. Two doctors inspect about 200 to 300 moire images as per one hour in the visual screening. It is very tough work in practice and may lead them to misjudgment in these processes.

Normally human spine forms a straight line when viewed in the anterior or posterior. But, if one has spinal deformity, his spine is crooked and the ribs may stick out more on one side than the other side. When one afflicted with spinal deformity, spine often deforms in the shape of letter 'S' or 'C'. To checking the spinal deformity, moire method [1-3] has been proposed which takes moire topographic images of human backs. It checks symmetry/asymmetry of the moire patterns in a two-dimensional (2-D) way.

Automating judgment of spinal deformity by computer has been reported [4-9] employing moire images of human backs. To evaluate spatial distortion of human back, Idesawa et al. [4], Batoushe [5] and Ishikawa et al. [9] reconstructed 3-D shape of a human back from the moire images. Kim et al. [12] propose a technique for automatic spinal deformity detection based on evaluation of middle line's displacement. By the experiment employing only 120 real moire image, they achieve the classification rate of 83.2% by the linear discriminant function. Despite these efforts, their approaches did not succeed, because of the difficulty of image processing in extracting the moire stripes exactly. Thus they did not reach to the stage of classification experiments employing real data and yet there is no report concerning automatic detection or diagnosis of spinal deformity. In this paper, to classify the moire image into two categories i.e., normal or abnormal cases, we propose a new method employing neural network.

2 Geometric Index Representing the Degree of Asymmetry

Normally the moire stripes show symmetric patterns on the human body. But when one becomes spinal deformity, human spine has asymmetric moire pattern. Numerical representation of the degree of asymmetry may therefore be useful in the evaluating the spinal deformity. In order to analyze such shapes with approximate symmetry, some techniques are proposed [10]. Ishikawa et al. [11] proposed a technique for detecting symmetry axes on an approximately symmetric shape and applied it to extracting the middle line of a human back from its moire image.

2.1 Extraction of the ROI

To evaluate the asymmetric degree, we extract the middle line on the given moire image employing the approximate symmetry analysis [10]. The middle line is extracted in the following way.

We assume an original image is $f(x,y)$ where x and y are bounded positive integers, and its reflected image is represented by $f^r(x,y)$, $(x,y) \in R^r$. The $(p+q)$-th order moment of $f(x,y)$ is defined by

$$m_{pq} = \sum \sum_{(x,y) \in R} x^p y^q f(x,y) \qquad (1)$$

where R is a specified region. From the eq.(1), the centroid denoted by (x_c, y_c) is calculated.

The $f^r(x,y)$ is superposed onto the $f(x,y)$ by parallel translation $c \equiv (c_x, c_y)$ and rotation θ to find the best match. Note that the following geometrical restriction is taken into account with respect to c_x, c_y and θ ;

$$c_y = c_x \tan\frac{\theta}{2}. \tag{2}$$

In this paper, we assume the $\theta=0$, because the moire images are captured normally straight using position-supporter so that their middle lines keep vertical.

In the next stage, we extract the region of interest (ROI) from a given moire image. The ROI is extracted in the following way.

Let us denote a moire image of a human back by $I(x,y)$. The origin O of the xy-coordinate system is located at the lower left corner of the image. The ranges of the coordinates are $0 \leq x \leq x_e$ and $0 \leq x \leq y_e$. The middle line is defined in the first place on $I(x,y)$. Since the moire pattern of a human back usually exhibits asymmetry, an approximate symmetry axis is extracted from $I(x,y)$ and the axis is regarded as the middle line of the back. The middle line is located at $x=m$.

The ROI denoted by R is defined on $I(x,y)$ in the following way. Image $I(x,y)$ is binarized and histogram of the binarized pixels onto x-axis is calculated. The locations having the minimum frequency on the histogram are searched within $0 \leq x \leq m$ and $m \leq x \leq x_e$, and two such locations, $x=x_0$ and $x=x_1$, that are the nearest to the middle line are chosen from the respective ranges. The area R excludes arms of the subject and takes subject's physical dimensions into account. The ROI are automatically selected by this processing.

2.2 Degree of Asymmetry

Within the region R and at a certain position $y=i$, two rectangle areas are defined, at symmetric locations with respect to the middle line $x=m$. The width a of the rectangle area is defined by

$$a = \min\{m-l, r-m\}. \tag{3}$$

Here m is extracted middle line, l is minimum frequency of the left-hand side and r is minimum frequency of the right-hand side on the histogram. On the other hand, height of the area is defined empirically. The degree of asymmetry is calculated by following way.

Let us denote the rectangle areas of the left-hand side and right-hand side at $y=i$ by A_i^l and A_i^r, respectively. Here $i=1,2,…,N$. The centroids of A_i^l and A_i^r are denoted by $G_l(x_l,y_l)$ and $G_r(x_r,y_r)$, respectively. The centroid $G_l(x_l,y_l)$ is reflected with respect to the middle line $x=m$ into the region A_i^r and denoted by $G_l^*(x_l^*,y_l^*)$. The distance G between $G_l^*(x_l^*,y_l^*)$ and $G_r(x_r,y_r)$ is calculated by

$$G = \sqrt{(x_l^* - x_r)^2 + (y_l^* - y_r)^2}. \tag{4}$$

The mean μ_g and the standard deviation σ_g of the values G ($i=1,2,…,N$) are employed as the features representing the degree of asymmetry of the moire image in R. They are obtained from

$$\left.\begin{array}{l} \mu_g = \dfrac{1}{N}\sum_{i=1}^{N} G \\[2mm] \sigma_g = \sqrt{\dfrac{1}{N}\sum_{i=1}^{N}(G-\mu_1)^2} \end{array}\right\}. \tag{5}$$

Furthermore, in the same rectangle area difference of gray value D is calculated by

$$D = |D_l - D_r|. \tag{6}$$

Here D_l, D_r are mean vale of left-hand side and right-hand side rectangle area in the ROI. From the eq.(6) mean and standard deviation of the values D ($i=1,2,…,N$) are employed as the features representing the degree asymmetry of the moire image in R (See eq.(7)).

$$\left.\begin{array}{l} \mu_d = \dfrac{1}{N}\sum_{i=1}^{N} D \\[2mm] \sigma_d = \sqrt{\dfrac{1}{N}\sum_{i=1}^{N}(D-\mu_d)^2} \end{array}\right. \tag{7}$$

3 Classification Method

Neural networks have been proven in many researches as having a good discriminant property, which means excellent for pattern classification. Neural networks accept numerical inputs and provide classification based on these inputs by segregating the inputs. This application to automatic spinal deformity can provide the necessary inputs, which are numerical in nature to the neural network. The implementation is very easy, as we only need to train the neural network based on past data or even current data. In this case we find that the back propagation algorithm which is a supervised learning neural network to be very appropriate to solve this classification application of automatic spinal deformity detection.

A direct application would be to take the 4 feature vectors from the left-hand side and right-hand side rectangle areas (μ_g, μ_d, σ_g, σ_d in eq.(5) and eq.(7)) and apply them to train a NN employing back propagation algorithm for automatic spinal deformity detection.

Employed NN is consists of 3 layers, which included four input layers, five hidden layers and one output layers for training. Finally, unknown moire images are discriminated as normal or abnormal case automatically.

4 Experimental Results

According to the above-mentioned procedure, experiment was done employing 1200 real moire images. The employed moire images are separated into two groups such as training and test data sets. As a training data for this study, we selected randomly 800 (400 normal cases and 400 abnormal cases) moire images in the neural networks.

Remaining 400 moire images are used for classification. 200 out of 400 images are normal cases, whereas 200 are abnormal cases. The leave out method is employed in the classification to exclude biased data sampling. Classification rate $r[\%]$ is defined as follows:

$$r = \frac{k}{n} \times 100. \qquad (8)$$

Here k is the number of the data which classified correctly, n is number of the employed data. The image size is 256X256 pixels with 256 gray levels. Figure 1 illustrates experimental results. In Figure 1, (a) shows a normal moire image and (b) shows an abnormal moire image. Table 1 shows obtained classification rates. In average, classification rate of 90.3% was achieved. The processing time of a singe moire image is 3.4 second in average on a Pentium III (1GHz) personal computer running FreeBSD.

5 Discussions and Conclusion

In this paper, we developed a system to analyze a moire image of a human back in a 2-D way in order to automate the primary screening of spinal deformity detection based on neural network. This approach seems promising compared with existent other attempts which analyze moire images in a 3-D way. In fact, the present technique achieved the classification rate of 90.3% in the experiment employing 1200 real moire images, whereas other techniques based on 3-D analysis have not even performed such experiments. The present technique offers simpler 2-D image processing. This also can be reduces computation time. In more details, 87.5% (175 cases out of 200) of normal cases were recognized correctly and 93% (186 cases out of 200) of abnormal cases were recognized correctly in leave out method.

From this database, the results were a sensitivity of 0.93 at a specificity of 0.88. Furthermore, false positive fraction (FP) of the 0.13 and false negative fraction (FN) of the 0.07, positive predictive values (PPV) of 0.88, negative predictive value (NPV) of 0.93 were achieved under the receiver operating characteristic (ROC) analysis.

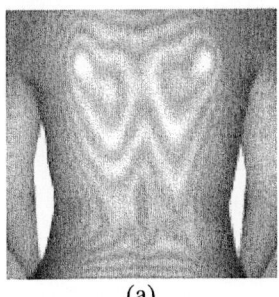
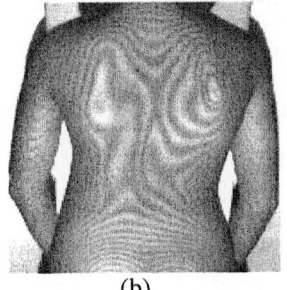

(a)   (b)

Fig. 1. Experimental results: (a) A normal case; (b) An abnormal case.

Figure 2 illustrates examples of misclassification. In Figure 2(a), a normal case is classified into abnormal, whereas an abnormal case is classified into normal in (b). In

Figure 2(a), gray values subtly differ in the vicinity of an edge particularly on the shoulder part. Some misclassified cases are found asymmetry of moire patterns. This is because gray values distribution in the rectangle regions unfortunately affected symmetrically when the local centroids and difference gray value were calculated. To escape from this difficulty, some other asymmetry features independent to local centroids displacement might be taken into account in conjunction with it. To obtain higher classification rates, the issue remains for further study.

Table 1. Obtained classification rates (%)

Training data set	Test data set	%
D1	D2UD3	89
D2	D1UD3	89.3
D3	D1UD2	92.5
	Average	90.3

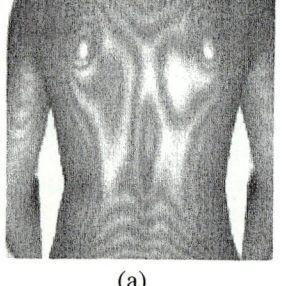 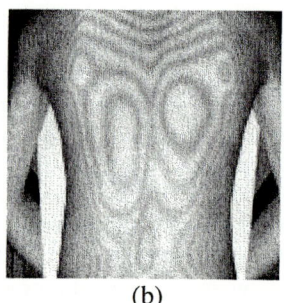

(a) (b)

Fig. 2. Examples of misclassification: (a) A normal case classified into abnormal; (b) An abnormal case classified into normal.

References

1. Ohtsuka, Y., Shinoto, A., Inoue, S.: "Mass school screening for early detection of scoliosis by use of moire topography camera and low dose X-ray imaging", *Clinical Orthopaedic Surgery*, **14**, 10, 973-984 (1979). (in Japanese)
2. Takasaki, H.: "Moire topography from its birth to practical application", *Optics and Lasers in Engineering*, **3**, 3-14(1982).
3. Takasaki, H.: "Moire topography", *Applied Optics*, **9(6)**, 1467-1472(1970).
4. Idesawa, M., Yatagai, T., Soma, T.: "Scanning moire method and automatic measurement of 3-D shapes", *Applied Optics*, **16**, 2152-2162 (1977).
5. Batouche, M.: "A knowledge based system for diagnosing spinal deformations: Moire pattern analysis and interpretation", *Proc. 11 Int. Conf. Pattern Recogn.*, 591-594 (1992).
6. Adair, I.V., Wijk, M.C., Armstrong, G.W.D.: "Moire topography in scoliosis screening", *Clin. Orthop.*, **129**, 165(1977).
7. Wilner, S.: "Moire topography for the diagnosis and documentation of scoliosis", *Acta Orthop. Scand.*, **50**, 295(1979).

8. Roger, R.E., Stokes, I.E., et al.: "Monitoring adolescent idiopathic scoliosis with moire fringe photography", *Engineering in Medicine*, **8**, 119(1979).
9. Ishikawa, S., Takagami, S., Kato, K., Ohtsuka, Y.: "Analyzing deformity of human backs based on the 3-D topographic reconstruction from moire images", *Proc. '95 Korea Automat. Control Conf.*, 244-247 (1995).
10. Minovic, P., Ishikawa, S., Kato, K.: "Symmetry identification of a 3-D object represented by octree", *IEEE Trans. Patt. Anal. Machine Intell.*, **PAMI-15**, 5, 507-514 (1993).
11. Ishikawa, S., Kosaka, H., Kato, K., Ohtsuka, Y.: "A method of analyzing a shape with potential symmetry and its application to detecting spinal deformity", *Comput. Vision, Virtual Reality, Robotics in Med.*, 465-470, Springer (1995).
12. Kim, Ishikawa, Otsuka et al.: "Spinal deformity detection based on the evaluation of middle line's displacement on a moire image of a human back", Proceedings of the International conference on control, automation and systems, 818-821(2001).

Bone Segmentation in Metacarpophalangeal MR Data

Olga Kubassova[1], Roger D. Boyle[1], and Mike Pyatnizkiy[2]

[1] School of Computing, University of Leeds, LS1 9JT Leeds, UK
{olga, roger}@comp.leeds.ac.uk
www.comp.leeds.ac.uk\{olga,roger}
[2] Biophysics, Russian State University,
168875 Moscow, Russia
mike@mcce.ru

Abstract. A robust, efficient segmentation algorithm for automatic segmentation of MR images of the metacarpophalangeal joint is presented. A preliminary segmentation detects bones in MR scans and uses histogram analysis, morphological operations and knowledge based rules to classify various tissues in the joint. The second part of the algorithm improves the segmentation mask and refines boundaries of bones using minimization of a sum of square deviations, automatic signal segmentation into an optimum number of segments, graph theory, and statistical analysis. The algorithm has been tested on 9 MR patient studies and detects 97% of all existing bones correctly with an average exceeding 80% mutual overlap between ground truth and detected regions

1 Introduction

Segmentation of various tissues in Magnetic Resonance (MR) Imaging is very valuable in further image analyses and has a wide range of applications, including data compression, visualization, and image registration. Successful segmentation is a critical pre-processing step towards high-level image analysis. In analyzing MR data, one needs to consider complications due to the inherent noise in the imaging process, partial volume effects (where more than one tissue is inside a pixel volume) as well as the wide range of imaging control parameters which affect the imaged tissue intensities. There is a significant inter-patient variance of these signal intensities for the same tissue. This makes it necessary to design adaptive signal processing algorithms which are robust for this wide range of variance in the data.

Image segmentation in general is a very difficult problem to automate. There is a variety of interactive methods [1, 2] which provide good results, but such solutions are not feasible for analyzing large amounts of data, and results are difficult to reproduce due to the subjective nature of human experts. Apart from being independent, automatic segmentation algorithms should provide reliable and robust segmentation, and be efficient in terms of usage of computational time and storage space.

This paper presents an efficient algorithm which combines heuristics about the general anatomy of the metacarpophalangeal (MCP) joint with image processing tools and pattern recognition techniques. The algorithm is designed to automatically detect rigid boundaries in MR slices of the joint.

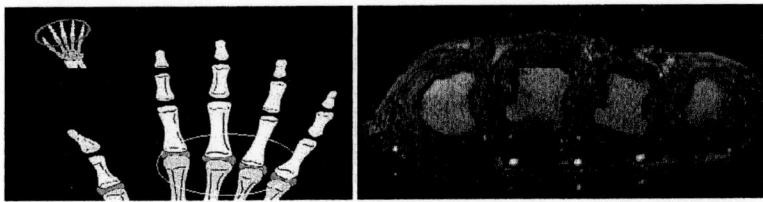

Fig. 1a. Location of the MCP joint; **Fig. 1b.** One of the MR scans of the joint. Brightareas in the scan represent fat and water inside the bone.

2   Terminology and Data Set

The images are used in the procedure to monitor development of rheumatoid arthritis. A typical MR scan (Fig. 1b) represents an MCP joint with 4 brighter regions, which is fat and water inside the bone. The boundaries of these regions are rigid, being the bone interior; hereafter, we refer to these regions as "bone". Each bone is surrounded by darker areas, which represent cartilage.

The work described here is to support a procedure in which 20 6-scan MR images are taken of the joints over a period of approximately 7 seconds.

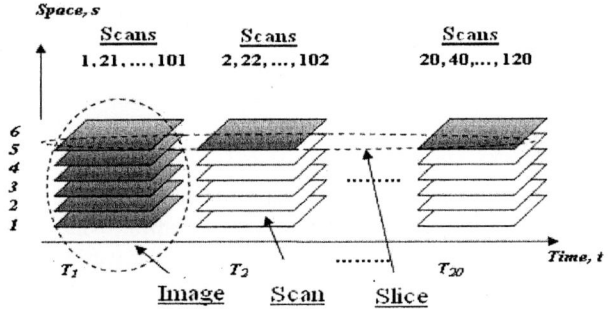

Fig. 2a. Structure of the 4D MR images dataset

About the 7th time instant, gadolinium is introduced with the effect of enhancing the intensity of parts of the image: in particular, the blood vessels and arthritically diseased areas neighbouring the joints. Analysis of dynamic contrast enhanced MR data sets involves calculation of signal intensity against time curve for each pixel in the image, because the shape of such curves carries information about the tissue. In such analysis it is assumed that each pixel represents the same area of tissue throughout the acquisition, and so if there is patient motion there will be errors in the calculated curves. To avoid such errors, each image in the temporal sequence should be registered to the first slice acquired. Characteristics of changes in enhancement are of interest, but their extraction can be complicated by slight movements of the patient during data capture, necessitating registration of scans with that captured in the first instant.

In this paper, the first stage in performing such a registration is described. This involves the segmentation of the bone structures, which will be used as features for rigid registration.

Bones may not be visible in every scan due to the poor resolution of the image, or the physical location of the scan. The phalanges of the joint are organized as shown in Fig. 3a. A scan can be taken between them, and some bones could be detected partially or missed as in Fig. 3b. The thumb is not included in this study, thus each scan shows 4 or fewer joints, which will be labelled 2-5, with 2 being the index finger and 5 being the little finger.

Fig. 3a. 6 Scans of 4 phalanges of the joint. A coronal plan of the phalanges; **Fig. 3b.** An axial MR section. Scan 5: 3 only bones are detected; **Fig. 3c.** Structure of the joint: Trabecular Bone, Cortical Shell, Articular Cartilage, Synovial Fluid, and Joint Cavity.

It is assumed that if a bone is visible in one scan in the time series for a slice, then it should be visible throughout the time series.

3 Segmentation

The algorithm consists of two main stages: a preliminary segmentation, which derives a mask for a bone boundary; and an adaptive segmentation, which improves the quality of the mask by extending or shrinking its boundaries towards the actual boundary. The preliminary segmentation uses a simple, robust, and efficient algorithm [8], which consists of a sequence of adaptive histogram analysis, thresholding, morphological operations and knowledge based rules for classifying bones from other tissues. Adaptive segmentation involves the minimization of a sum of square deviations about a mean (MLS) [4] in order to analyse the signal obtained; automatic signal segmentation into an optimum number of segments, using the L-method [12]; graph theory, and statistical analysis [6]; and median smoothing within a sliding window [10].

3.1 Preliminary Segmentation

Scans are pre-processed using a low-pass adaptive noise removal Wiener2 filter [9]. Each 2D scan is composed of light foreground and dark background, in such a way that regions of interest and background pixels have intensity levels grouped into two modes. An obvious way to extract the regions of interest from the background is to select a threshold value that separates these modes – this has been done using a simple algorithm [11]. Results can be seen in Fig. 4b.

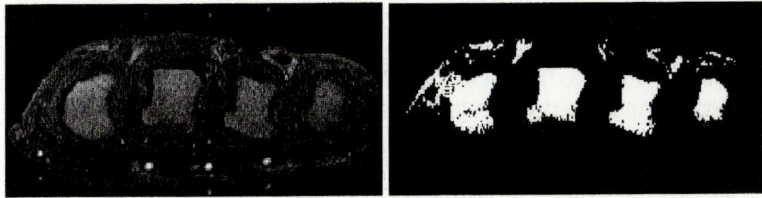

Fig. 4a. Original MR scan (one of the scans from the input slice); **Fig. 4b.** Results of the global thresholding on the scan in Fig. 4a.

Outlier regions have been removed using morphological opening [13] and a location classifier. The classifier has been trained using more than 1000 regions in a normalized coordinate system in order to define for each bone a coordinate interval in which it is presumed to appear.

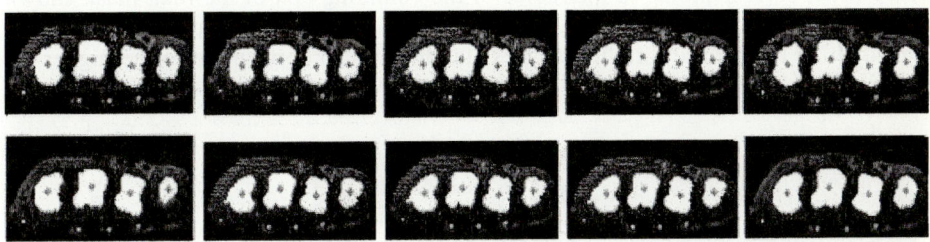

Fig. 5a. Results of local thresholding on the first 10 scans from one of the slices; regions representation bones are shown in white.

This initial segmentation is clearly usually inaccurate. We re-threshold locally to the regions and apply simple shape classification to reject regions of unlikely convexity, shape, etc. The classification is based on the assumption that the bones in scans can be approximated by ellipses and do not contain holes. Blood vessels, which also satisfy this assumption, are much smaller and normally appear closer to the sides of the joint, making their removal straightforward.

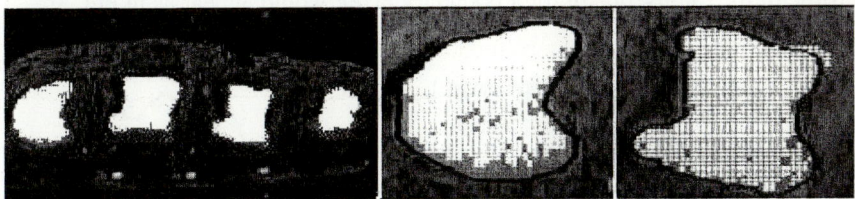

Fig. 6a. Final mask for one of the slices; **Fig. 6b.** Magnified final mask of the first bone in white. The black boundary is the actual boundary of the bone; **Fig. 6c.** Magnified final mask of the third bone in white. The black boundary is the actual boundary of the bone.

The procedure can cause different parts of the same bone to have different locations and intensities within one slice, and therefore differently detected in different scans. A union of all detected regions provides a 'segmentation mask' that is a superset of information about the bone. Such a mask derived from 20 scans of one of the slices is shown in Fig. 6a. The actual boundaries of the first and the third bones are shown in Fig. 6b and Fig. 6c in black. It is, of course, unlikely that the final mask boundary will coincide precisely with the actual boundary of the bone.

3.2 Adaptive Segmentation

The purpose of the adaptive segmentation is to detect a boundary of each bone within the whole slice as accurately as. As shown in Fig. 6b and Fig. 6c the preliminary regions can overlap the actual bones, but the boundaries of these regions do not coincide precisely. The adaptive segmentation starts by locating the centroid of the mask, and determining the diagonal length of the its bounding box. Half this diagonal is used as a 'radius', which is rotated in a [0, 2] interval. While rotating the radius, the corresponding image pixels' intensity profile along each radius has been considered. The profile, corresponding to the radius of the bounding box of the final mask shown in Fig. 7a, is shown in Fig. 7c. Darker tissues of the joint correspond to the lower intensities in the profile; brighter tissues (fat and water) correspond to the higher intensities.

Fig. 7a. MR scan with the final mask of the fourth bone. The white rectangle is a bounding box of the mask; **Fig. 7b.** Magnified final mask of the fourth bone; **Fig. 7c.** Signal profile of the 'radius' shown in black in Fig. 7a.

Thus, the problem of 2D image segmentation can be substituted by the problem of efficient 1D signal segmentation. The underlying model here assumes that the boundary pixel should separate a bright inner area (bone) from a darker outer area. Ideally, the profile of the radius, drawn for a boundary pixel, would appear as in Fig. 8b.

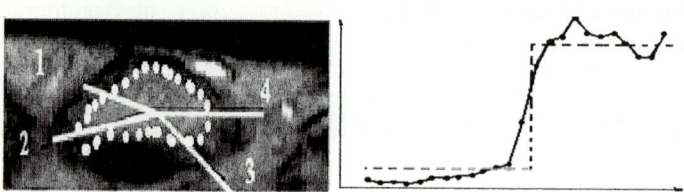

Fig. 8a. A bone with 4 radii in different directions. A boundary of the segmentation mask is shown by the dotted curve; **Fig. 8b.** The 'ideal' signal profile, corresponding to the radius (1) in Fig. 8a, and its approximation.

Boundaries of bones are fuzzy and sometimes discontinuous. Several different types of signal profiles have been observed; the most typical ones are shown in Fig. 9a, Fig. 9b and Fig. 9c.

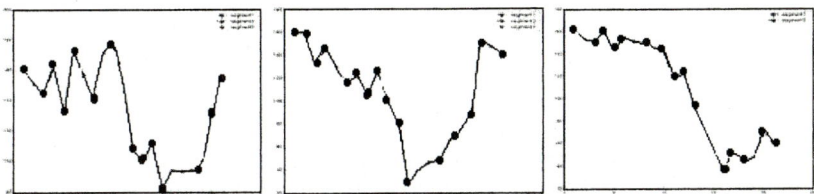

Fig. 9a. A signal profile corresponding to the radius (2) in Fig. 8a; **Fig. 9b.** A signal profile corresponding to the radius (3) in Fig. 8a; **Fig. 9c.** A signal profile corresponding to the radius (4) in Fig. 8a.

Each signal has been modelled as a sequence of segments formed by pixels of equal intensity. A sharp change between bright and dark areas is the optimum boundary pixel. If a current boundary pixel does not coincide with the optimum boundary pixel, the boundary along the radius is moved towards the optimum boundary pixel.

A minimization of least squares (MLS) algorithm [4], which minimizes the sum of squared deviations of the signal segments, has been chosen to analyze the signal. The MLS is calculated for various numbers of segments, and an optimum number selected via the L-method [12].

Signal profiles along each radius are analyzed and the optimal segment breakpoints located, allowing a suitable shift in the estimate for the "best" boundary pixel. This procedure is not perfect, and we remove outliers by applying median filtering with a sliding window, which analyzes the connectivity between neighbours. The result of signal segmentation before and after median filtering has been applied is shown in Fig. 10a and Fig. 10b, respectively.

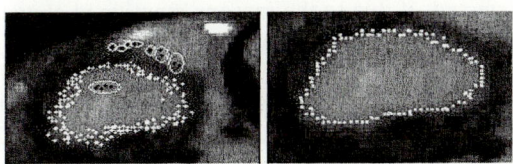

Fig. 10a. The results of adaptive segmentation, after each of the signal profiles has been segmented, before median filtering has been applied. Outliers are highlighted by white circles; **Fig. 10b.** The boundary after median filtering has been applied.

Median filtering is not sensitive to outliers; it accepts only those pixels which have the desired level of connectivity. Since the radius has been rotated in [0, 2] with a very small angle of rotation, the density of pixels near the actual boundary is high, the outliers instead appear sparsely.

The most challenging images with a lot of noise caused by the patient's movements and high contrast have been chosen in order to demonstrate the adaptive segmentation process. The proposed adaptive segmentation does not require a bone being smooth or of uniform intensity, since it operates along each radius independently; and it does not put any constraints on the shape or location of the region obtained as a result of the preliminary segmentation.

4 Experimental Results

4.1 Overview

We have presented an algorithm which locates region in slices which we expect to correspond to the rigid interior of bones with the aim of locating the boundaries as precisely as possible. Recalling that in some slices not all four bones will be observable, there are two separate evaluations to be performed;

- Determining with what reliability we can judge whether or not a bone is present. Clinical judgement has provided ground truth which is in most cases a "yes/no" judgement (that is, each of bones 2-5 is or is not observable). In a small number of cases, the expert is unsure. We are able to compare our results with this clinical judgement.
- Determining the quality of boundaries the segmentation delivers. We have manually determined best possible boundaries in 167 slices drawn randomly from the data set, and compare our results to what we will assume is the "correct" solution. Following most established practice [3] we present this judgement as the quality of region overlap, normalised by the region area. In fact, this metric can produce misleading results as they might mask the quality of the location of boundaries, which is the property that we seek to optimise for the subsequent registration tasks. Evaluation with a different, more suitable, edge-based metric is work in hand.

4.2 Presence / Absence of Bone Regions

The algorithm has been tested on 9 MRI datasets; and bones in each of 54 scans (6 per dataset) have been detected. If due to the reasons mentioned above a bone is missing, the algorithm is not expected to detect anything in this location. The results of the preliminary segmentation for 9 MR patient studies are shown in Table 1. In just a few cases the algorithm recognized cartilage as a bone. Cartilage and bone have a subtle difference in intensity and similar shape and location, making it difficult to distinguish between them. We detect the presence of 97% of all bones correctly.

Table 1. Results of the preliminary segmentation part of the algorithm. P1,...,P9 indicate the 9 patients; the slices are numbered 1-6. In each cell, A/B indicate the number of bones detected by an expert [A] and the number indicated by our algorithm [B].

N	P1	P2	P3	P4	P5	P6	P7	P8	P9
1	4/4	4/4	4/4	4/4	4/4	4/4	4/4	3/3	4/4
2	3/3	3/3	3/3	4/4	4/4	3/3	3/3	3/3	3/3
3	4/4	4/4	2/2	2/2	2/3	3/3	4/4	2/2	2/2
4	2/2	2/2	3/3	3/3	3/3	2/2	2/2	2/2	2/2
5	3/3	3/3	3/3	2/2	2/2	3/2	3/3	3/3	3/3
6	4/4	4/4	4/4	4/4	4/4	4/4	4/4	3/3	4/4

4.3 Quality of Segmented Regions

We have also conducted experiments with other popular segmentation techniques such as snakes [7] and region growing [5]. These other techniques have in most cases generated disappointing results, usually due to their sensitivity to parameter selection (for example, the internal/external force ratio for snakes and growth criterion for region growing). The approach we have developed is largely free of this parameter selection problem. Fig. 11a, Fig. 11b, Fig. 11c and Fig. 11d show examples of these techniques' performance.

As a measure of adaptive segmentation performance the percentage of the mutual overlap between the finally obtained and ground truth regions has been used [3]. With predefined initial boundaries we see good performance on all regions. In the example of Fig. 11d, the percent of mutual overlap with the detected and ground truth regions is more than 90%. This example is taken from the first time step; as the procedure progresses, the contrast within scans changes and makes segmentation more challenging; results earlier in the sequence are usually better.

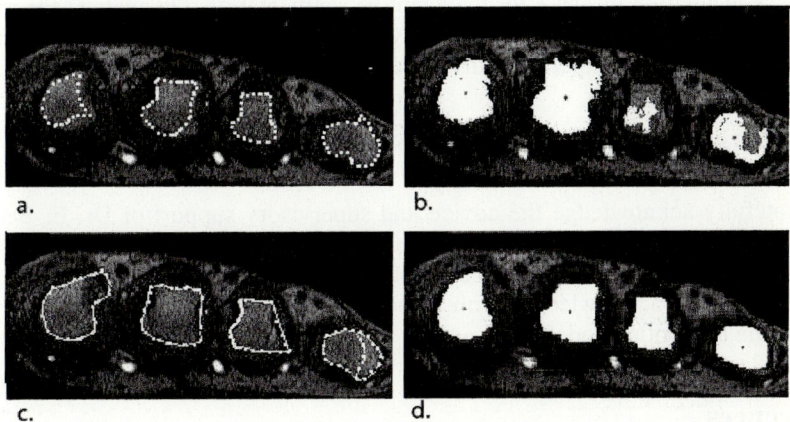

Fig. 11a. Results of the preliminary segmentation. Boundaries of the bones are shown in white; **Fig. 11b.** Example performance of a region growing technique on an MR scan; **Fig. 11c.** Example performance of snakes on an MR scan; **Fig. 11d.** Example performance of the adaptive segmentation technique on an MR scan.

The average performance of the adaptive segmentation measured over regions from all time steps for each study is shown in Table 2.

Table 2. Average mutual overlap percentage between ground truth and detected regions for 9 MR patient studies (P1,..., P9)

Patient	P1	P2	P3	P4	P5	P6	P7	P8	P9
% overlap	79	77	80	86	83	81	74	81	82

In our experiments less than 18% percent of all regions exhibit less than 70% mutual overlap, and less than 1% of regions have less than 60% mutual overlap, while about 16% of regions have more than 90% mutual overlap.

5 Conclusions

In this paper we have proposed an automatic algorithm for accurate segmentation of bone regions from MR data of the MCP joint. The algorithm is a two-step procedure, which brings together statistical and morphological image analysis, the MLS, signal processing methods and dynamic programming. Firstly, the algorithm detects the regions of the metacarpophalangeal joint which represent bones; 97% of all existing bones evident in images have been detected correctly. Secondly, the algorithm refines the boundaries of the regions using an adaptive segmentation technique. Refined boundaries of the bones will be used in the further analysis of the MR scans such as registration.

The mutual overlap between ground truth and detected regions is used as the performance evaluation measure for the adaptive segmentation. On average the resulting regions show more than 80% of mutual overlap with ground truth regions. Perceptual evaluation by medical experts confirms the approach generates results of value.

Acknowledgements

We gratefully acknowledge the advice and supervisory support of Dr. E. Berry and Dr. S. F. Tanner [Medical Physics, University of Leeds]. Dr. Tanner is further thanked for providing medical data and evaluation thereof.

O. Kubassova acknowledges with thanks the UK Research Councils for financial support via a Dorothy Hodgkin Award.

References

1. American College of Rheumatology of Osteoarthritis Guideline. Recommendations for the Medical Management of Osteoarthritis of the Hip and Knee. J. of Arthritis and Rheumatism, 43(2000) 1905-1915
2. ANALYZE Software System: http://www.hoise.com/vmw/articles/LV-VM-04-98-10.html (last access 26.05.05) and www. mayo.edu/bir (last access 26.05.05)
3. Bowyer, K.W.: Validation of Medical Image Analysis Techniques. In Sonka, M., Fitzpatrick, J. M. (eds): Handbook of Medical Imaging, SPIE Press, Bellingham, WA, (2000) 567–607
4. Golub, G. H., van Loan, C. F.: An Analysis of the Total Least Squares Problem SIAM. J. Numer. Anal., 17 (1979) 883–893
5. Gonzalez, R. C., Woods, R. E., Eddins, S. L.: Digital Image Processing. Prentice Hall, (2004) 407 – 410
6. Hogg, R. V., Allen, T. C.: Introduction to Mathematical Statistics. Prentice Hall Publ. (1994)

7. Kass, M., Witkin, A., Terzopoulos D.: Snakes: Active Contour Models. Int. J. of Computer Vision. 4(1987) 321 – 331
8. Kubassova, O., Boyle, R. D.: Segmentation of 4D Natural MR Images Based upon Morphological Image Analysis and Image Geometry. In Proc. PREP'05 Conference, Lancaster, UK, 3(2005) 186 - 188
9. Lim, K., Jae, S.: Two-Dimensional Signal and Image Processing, Englewood Cliffs, NJ. Prentice Hall, (1990) 536 – 540
10. MatLab Image Processing User Guide Online: http://www.mathworks.com/access/helpdesk/help/toolbox/images/images.shtml (last access 26.05.05)
11. Ridler, T. W., Calvard, S.: Picture Thresholding Using an Iterative Selection Method., In IEEE Trans. on Systems, Man and Cybernetics, 8(1978) 630 – 632
12. Salvador, S. Chan, P.: Determining the Number of Clusters/Segments in Hierarchical Clustering/Segmentation Algorithms. In Proc. 16th IEEE Intl. Conf. on Tools with AI, 6(2004) 576 – 584
13. Sonka M., Hlavac V., Boyle R. D.: Image Processing Analysis, and Machine Vision. PWS, (1999) 559 – 596

Lung Field Segmentation in Digital Postero-Anterior Chest Radiographs*

Paola Campadelli and Elena Casiraghi

Università degli Studi di Milano,
Computer Science Department, LAIV Laboratory
{Campadelli, Casiraghi}@dsi.unimi.it
http://homes.dsi.unimi.it/~campadell/LAIV

Abstract. This paper describes a lung field segmentation method, working on digital Postero-Anterior chest radiographs. The lung border is detected by integrating the results obtained by two simple and classical edge detectors, thus exploiting their complementary advantages. The method makes no assumption regarding the chest position, size and orientation; it has been tested on a non-trivial set of real life cases, composed of 412 radiographs belonging to two different databases. The obtained results and the comparison with more complicate techniques presented in the literature, prove the robustness of the algorithm and demonstrate that rather simple and general methods, properly combined to fit the requirements of a specific application, can provide better results.

1 Introduction

At the present time, chest radiography is the most common type of screening procedure for the initial detection of every type of abnormal pulmonary condition, due to its ability of revealing some unsuspected pathologic alterations, its non-invasivity characteristics, radiation dose and economic considerations. Nevertheless this is the most difficult radiograph to produce technically and to interpret diagnostically, as discussed in [1]. The first and mandatory step of an automatic system aimed at any type of computerized analysis on chest radiographs, is the lung field segmentation. At the state of the art, several lung segmentation methods based on classical techniques have been presented (e.g. [2], [3], [4], [5], [6], [7] [8], [9], [10]), and reviewed in [11]. Their weakness is due to the fact that they are based on assumptions regarding the chest position, size and orientation, and often violated in real life situations. Other methods have been proposed (e.g. [12], [13]), which get better results without making these strong assumptions, but by simply including some necessary knowledge about the generic chest shape.

Considering that the loss of (even small) parts of the lung area may cause the loss of some nodules, precision is a strong requirement when the segmentation mask defines the processing area of an automatic system aimed at the detection of subtle pathologies such as lung tumors. None of the known methods obtain

---

* Work partially financed by CIMAINA and PRIN 2004: "Novel clustering techniques in biomedical image segmentation".

precise results; moreover all of them detect the most visible parts of the left and right lung (*visible lung areas*), excluding those hidden behind the diaphragm, the heart and the spinal column (*hidden lung areas*), where tumors could be found.

All these reasons motivate the development of the segmentation method described in this paper, which is the first step of a lung nodules detection system. The algorithm avoids all the assumptions regarding the chest position, size and orientation, and it includes in the segmentation mask also the *hidden lung areas*. A precise contour is obtained by properly combining the results of two simple image segmentation techniques (sec. 2). Their appropriate integration takes into account the generic chest shape and can therefore recognize and repair their complementary errors, by exploiting the good characteristics of their individual results. For the same reason, the following step (sec. 3) separates the *hidden* from the *visible lung areas* by combining the results of simple derivative filters and those of a gray level clustering method.

The method has been developed and tested on 247 radiographs (154 of patients with lung nodules) in the standard *JSRT* database [14], which is the only known standard database publicly available. The images have been digitized with a 0.165 mm pixel size, a matrix size of 2048 × 2048, and 4096 gray levels. Before processing, they have been down-sampled to a dimension of 256 × 256 pixels (and will be referred as the *Images*): this experimental choice reduces the computational costs of the algorithm without worsening its performance. The algorithm has been also tested on 165 radiographs acquired from the *Niguarda Hospital* in Milan. They have a 0.160 mm pixel size, and a not fixed squared size. The comparison with the segmentation results obtained by the method described in [12], and applied to the *JSRT* database, proves that this is a better initialization step for a lung nodule detection system.

2 Segmentation of the Full Lung Area

In this section we will present the technique used for determining the external lung contour and the segmentation mask. The method that detects the external lung contour is based on the integration of the results obtained by two different algorithms. The first one detects the *most visible lung edges*, by means of steerable first derivative of Gaussian filters (sec. 2.1). These edges are also used to find the vertical lung axis and to initialize the second algorithm, which needs a starting point to track the lung edges and to detect a *continuous contour* along the external lung border (sec. 2.2). In order to define the segmentation mask, the obtained results are integrated, and other simple techniques are employed to define the bottom borders and those nearby the spine (sec. 2.3). A schematic diagram with the main steps of the method is shown in the top row of fig. 1.

2.1 Edge Detection by Derivatives of Gaussian Filters

The most visible lung edges are obtained by filtering the *Image* with first derivatives of Gaussian filters [15] at scale $\sigma = 1$, oriented along four directions $(0, \pi/4, \pi/2, 3\pi/4)$; for each direction, the top 10% of the output pixels are selected to

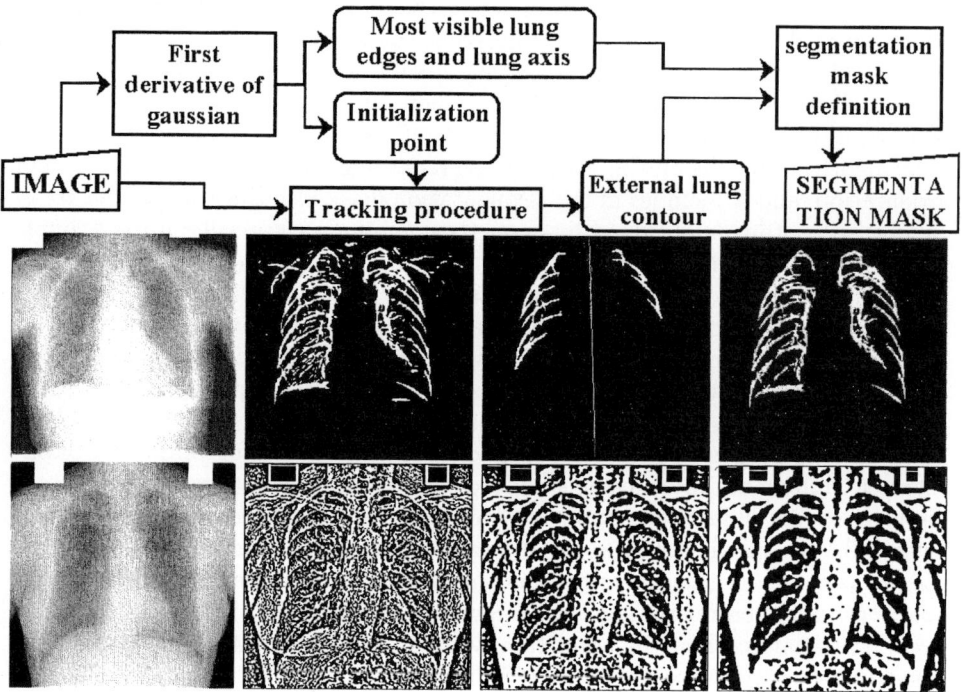

Fig. 1. Top row: Schematic diagram of the method; Middle row: *Image, Initial Edge image* and *Partial Edge image, Edge image*; Bottom row: the binary images $L_\sigma(\sigma = 1, 2, 3)$, capturing different levels of detail of the original image.

get four different *Binary images*, B_i. Their union (*Initial Edge image*) contains all the detected edges, while the union of $B_{\pi/2}$, $B_{\pi/4}$ and $B_{3\pi/4}$ (*Partial Edge image*) contains the main external rib cage borders and it is then used to find the vertical lung axis. To this aim each one of its rows is scanned to find the pixel at the center of the segment connecting the leftmost and rightmost pixels. A polynomial fitting method, that minimizes the $\chi - square$ error statistic, is used to fit all the found points with a line that defines the axis of the lung field (fig. 1, middle row). The axis is approximately located at the center of the spine, and it is therefore used to recognize and delete those edge regions, in the *Initial Edge image*, which belong to the dorsal column: they are the connected regions located in a "band" around the axis whose width is equal to 1/30 of the maximum width of the chest (this estimate is given by the maximum distance between the leftmost and rightmost pixels found in each row of the *Partial Edge image*, and used to find the axis). Other spurious details in the *Initial Edge image* correspond to little regions external to the lung; they are discarded by eliminating all the connected regions whose area is less than 0.05% of the total image area. The *Edge image* thus obtained contains a discontinuous outline of the lung borders (fig. 1, rightmost in the middle row); to get a continuous contour a second edge detection method is presented in the next section and the two results are then integrated (sec. 2.3).

2.2 External Contour Creation by Edge Tracking

In this section we describe a multi-scale method to get a continuous border of the lung field. As noted in [16], "an inherent property of objects in the world is that they only exist as meaningful entities over certain ranges of scale". In the case of lung borders their analysis at a small scale provides their more accurate representation, but the segmentation could be mislead by other fine details belonging to different structures. Alternatively a large scale guarantees smoothness and continuity of the contour. For this reason we choose to process the image at different scales, and finally combine the results; the combining procedure exploits the precision of the results obtained at the smallest scale, but at the same time produces reliable results thanks to the information obtained at larger scales. Our method works on three binary images L_σ ($\sigma = 1, 2, 3$) each capturing different levels of detail of the lung borders (fig. 1, bottom row); each L_σ is created by applying to the *Image* the Laplacian of Gaussian operator at scales $\sigma = 1, 2, 3$ experimentally set, and by selecting the output pixels with positive values. An edge tracking algorithm is applied to each L_σ image, in order to detect a continuous path describing the lung border at that scale; afterwards the different paths are fused to produce a robust external lung contour. The method works separately on the left and right lung; in the following we will describe it, for the generic image L_σ, and just for the left lung[1].

The starting point, P_S^B, for the edge tracking procedure must belong to the external border of the left lung, and it is therefore selected from the *Partial edge image*; P_S^B is the topmost point between those at the minimum distance from a line oriented at $3\pi/4$, and passing trough the origin of the coordinate system. This simple method finds a point located approximately on the top of the lateral part of the lung boundaries, where the lung border curvature changes greatly, since the edge orientation changes from horizontal (on the top border) to vertical (on the lateral border). If the pixel in position P_S^B is not set to 1 in the L_σ image[2], it is replaced by another point; the new P_S^B is the first point set to 1, and found by scanning a *search area* in the L_σ (fig. 2, left of top row), which is a parallelogram located below the old P_S^B, and on its left side. If no point is found, the algorithm reaches the end without creating any contour.

The edge tracking procedure creates two continuous contours along the external border of the considered lung: the **Bpath** is a contour starting from P_S^B and running towards the bottom of the chest, meanwhile the **Tpath** goes from P_S^B towards the top.

---

[1] The coordinate system has the origin in the top left corner of the image, the positive Y axis corresponding to the height and the positive X axis to the width. The lungs are distinguished by the axis found, w.r.t. their position in the image.
[2] Note that this point was chosen from the *Partial Edge image*.

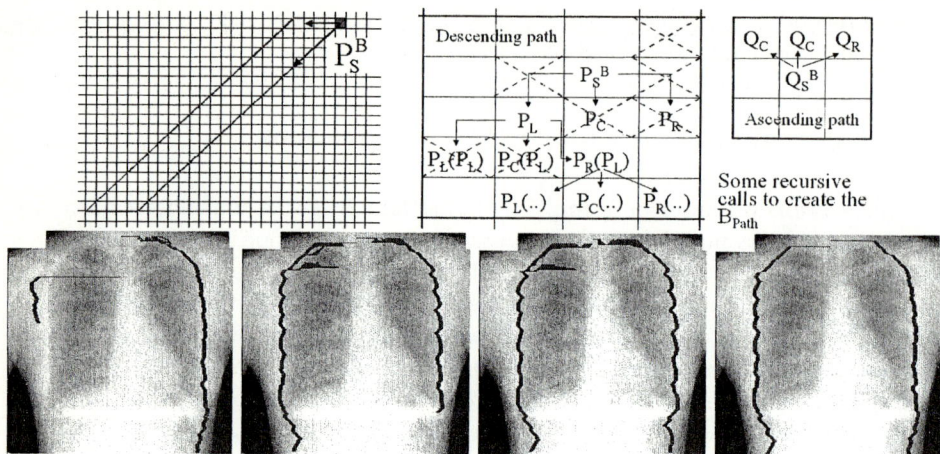

Fig. 2. top row: search area for the left path going to the bottom; Steps for the creation of the $DSet_B(P_S^B)$: the pixels with the cross are not inserted since set to 0; neighbors checked to created the $ASet_B(Q_S^U)$; bottom row: paths created on the images L_σ ($\sigma = 1, 2, 3$) and *Border Paths* created by combining the three paths.

The **Bpath** is created by first defining a set of pixels, $DSet_B(P_S^B)$, that may belong do the "descending" path. To this aim P_S^B is inserted in the set and its three $8-neighbors$, in the row below (P_L, P_C and P_R, see fig. 2), are considered. Those that are set to 1, are inserted in the set $DSet_B(P_S^B)$, and their three neighbors (in the row below) are recursively checked for insertion; this process goes on until at least one point is inserted in the $DSet_B(P_S^B)$. To have a more precise contour definition, this algorithm is also run in a bottom-up direction, using as starting point, Q_S^U, the bottommost pixel in the $DSet_B(P_S^B)$. Note that the neighborhood to be considered must be opportunely reversed (it is shown in fig. 2, rightmost on the top row). Once the "ascending" set $ASet_B(Q_S^U)$ is created, a unique chain of pixels (the *Bpath*) is created by taking, for each row, the rightmost pixel of the intersection of the $DSet_B(P_S^B)$ and the $ASet_B(Q_S^U)$.

The procedure used to create the **Tpath** starts from the point P_S^B and applies a similar recursive algorithm, just in ascending order, to the input image; as before, its output is a set of points $TSet_T(P_S^B)$. For each point considered, and already included in the set, the algorithm considers the pixel located above it and on its right side[3]. Both these neighbors are inserted in the $TSet_T(P_S^B)$ if they are set to 1, and the algorithm is recursively launched using them as starting points. The *Tpath* is created by taking, for each row, the rightmost among the pixels in the $TSet_T(P_S^B)$. The topmost pixel in the *Tpath* delineated is often above the *apex point* (i.e. the real lung top). Since the apex point is located where the lung border is horizontal, this point is found in the *Tpath* by computing its derivative; it is the first point, t_σ, whose derivative value is less than a threshold,

---

[3] These directions are chosen according to the shape of the lung top borders.

experimentally set to 0.05. The *Bpath* and *Tpath* form a final contour running from the top till the bottom of the chest.

The contours created on each image L_σ are shown in fig. 2. On the left, one example of a too short path is shown. Note that this is not a problem since a final contour can always be recovered by integrating the available paths. Indeed at least two paths have always been found for the 412 test images.

Since the top points $t_\sigma = (x_{t_\sigma}, y_{t_\sigma})$ ($\sigma = 1, 2, 3$) of the three paths may not be located at the same vertical position, the vertical coordinate of the topmost point, Y_{Top}, in the final border, is set to be the median of the y_{t_σ}. The left contour (*Left border path*) is then created starting from the row indexed by Y_{Top}, by selecting for each row the leftmost among all the pixels belonging to the different paths available at that row.

2.3 Definition of the Segmentation Mask

As noticed in sec. 2.1, even if the borders in the *Edge image* contain lots of edge pixels that are precisely adhering to the real lung borders, they are not continuous, the edges nearby the costophrenic angles could be missing and some edge pixels could be present that do not belong to the external borders of the lung field. On the other hand the contour obtained with the edge tracking algorithm, even though less precise, is always continuous and runs from a vertical position, that is a good approximation of the apex point of the lung, to the bottom of the image[4]. Therefore we developed a method that composes the correct information given by the two techniques, and defines a continuous *Lateral contour*; in this section we describe it for the left lung.

The integration procedure starts from the topmost point in the *Edge image*, and below Y_{Top}, and follows its external border to search for a continuous edge; when a hole is found, it is filled in by taking the pixels in the *Left border path*, whose advantage is to be always continuous. When the bottommost point, L_{angle}, in the *Edge image* is reached, the procedure ends after having included into the *Left Lateral contour* the part of *Left border path* below L_{angle}. To define a bottom boundary for the lung field, the positions of the costophrenic angles must be defined. These points are located at the intersection of the lateral contours and the bottom edges of the lung, due to the presence of the diaphragm. These are selected from the *Edge image* by searching for the region, on the right side of the pixel in the position of L_{angle}, whose bottommost point is the nearest to L_{angle} itself. The 5 leftmost and bottommost points of this region, are fitted with the method used in sec. 2.1, to find a line l interpolating them. The intersection between l (green colored in fig. 3) and the *Lateral contour* detected defines the point where the costophrenic angle is located. Repeating the same procedure for the right side the right costophrenic angle is found. A segment connecting the two costophrenic points closes the contour at the bottom. Nearby the spine, a

---

[4] Observe that the points characterizing the costophrenic angles are still uncertain since the contour, built by the edge tracking algorithm often runs till the bottom margin of the image, meanwhile the bottommost points in the left side of the *Edge image* may not correspond to the location of the costophrenic angle.

line parallel to the lung axis is created for each lung; it passes through the point in the *Edge image* that is the nearest to the axis.

3 Segmentation of the Visible Lung Area

In this section we describe the steps that detect the contours of the spine, the diaphragm and the heart, to separate the *visible* from the *hidden areas*. Since those two areas differ mainly for their pixels gray level, the separation is performed by a contour following procedure whose result is integrated with the one produced by a gray level clustering method [17]. This separation step has been helpful to detect and correct some errors of the previously described segmentation algorithm; furthermore it has been used to better characterize the *candidate regions* extracted by our computerized lung nodules detection system [18].

3.1 Edges Detected with Derivative Filters

To detect the **vertical edges** of the spine we filter the *Image*, on the left and right lung separately, with the horizontal Sobel filter, and apply a contour following procedure to the results. For each lung the starting point is selected between the 5% of the points with the highest value of the derivative and it is the nearest to the axis of the lung. The contour following procedure runs in descending and ascending direction separately. It proceeds by checking, for each row, the derivative value of the 3 points which are the 8-neighbors of the one selected at the line before, to find the one with the maximum value. It stops when the last point found is located on the border of the mask.

To detect the **horizontal edges** of the diaphragm, the *Image* is filtered, in the left and right lung separately, with a vertical Sobel filter and a similar contour following procedure is applied to the result; in the following we will describe the procedure just for the left lung. To select the starting point for the contour following procedure we consider the regions corresponding to the 5% of the pixels with the highest derivative value. Those edge regions always contain the bottom borders of the *visible lung area*, but may also contain some unwanted edges, belonging to the intestinal gases or other external structures. These undesired regions can be easily recognized for their shape; thus, we proceed discarding the connected regions with a convex shape, and the ones with a *rectangularity*[5] bigger then 0.33. The left bottom edge of the *left visible lung area* is then selected, for each lung, by taking the bottommost region located at the leftmost position. The starting point for the contour following procedure is selected from the bottom edge region; it is the point with the maximum value of the derivative. The procedure runs separately towards the right till it reaches the axis; running towards the left it reaches the lateral border and eventually defines a new costophrenic angle point; this allows to correct some errors due to extra parts wrongly included by the method described in sec. 2.

---

[5] The rectangularity is calculated as the fraction of the area of the region itself and the area of the maximum bounding box including it.

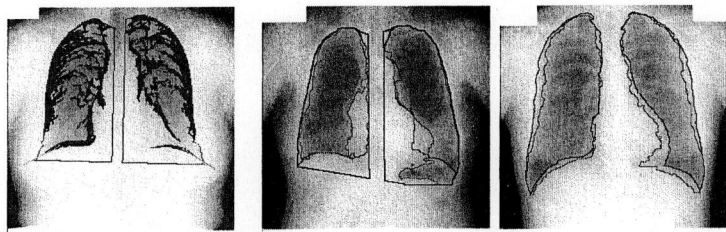

Fig. 3. Segments used to define the costophrenic angles; masks of the *visible areas* to be integrated.

3.2 Clustering Method

The second method used to define the *visible areas* is a clustering algorithm, which searches for three clusters in the *Image*. Each pixel is assigned to a certain cluster according to a distance measure based on the gray level of the pixel itself. The regions formed by the pixels belonging to the cluster whose representative has the highest gray value are then selected to give a rough definition of the *hidden areas*; fig. 3 shows the regions thus detected (red colored), together with the ones obtained by the derivative filters (blue colored). Note that the clustering wrongly excludes from the *visible areas* some regions attached to the external borders of the mask. They are ignored since we consider as external borders those created by the segmentation algorithm described in sec. 2. The two border lines that must be considered are the ones going from the top till the bottom of each lung and near to the axis; they are integrated by choosing for each row, the edge point which is the furthest from the axis.

4 Results

We tested our segmentation method on a rather substantial, relevant and nontrivial database of real life cases composed of the 247 images, in the *JSRT* database, and the 165 images, in the *Niguarda* database. To judge the obtained results, we compared the *segmentation masks*, created by our algorithm, with the *true lung masks* (the *ground truth*), manually defined by a human observer who traced the lung field borders. In this way we could detect the pixels wrongly included or excluded by each segmentation mask (the wrong pixels), and we defined as "error measure" the ratio between the number of the wrong pixels and the number of pixels in the *true lung mask*. This measure takes into account the big variations between the size of the chest of different patients. We detected errors when the error measure is bigger than 0.003.

According to this performance evaluation method, all the images in the *JSRT* database have been correctly segmented; meanwhile in the *Niguarda* database an error is detected in 6 images, shown in fig. 4 (i.e. the 4% of the total number of images in this database). Table 1 lists, for the 6 images, the

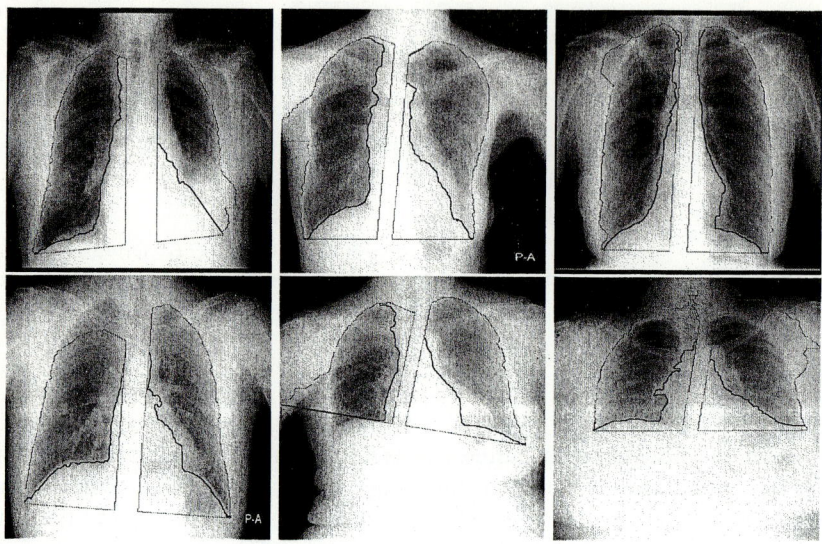

Fig. 4. results on the *Niguarda* (more critical) database: Top row - Image1, Image2, Image3, Bottom row - Image4, Image5, Image6.

Table 1. The errors in the six images

	Image1	*Image2*	*Image3*	*Image4*	*Image5*	*Image6*
# of the wrong pixels	368	897	2289	5818	3902	4100
True lung mask area	25672	28558	31074	30107	18407	17544
Error measure	0.01	0.03	0.07	0.19	0.21	0.23

number of wrong pixels, the pixel area of the *true lung mask* and the error measure. Notice that this is a good performance especially because the images in the *Niguarda* database are of low quality: they are noisy and often characterized by low contrast. Beside, lots of them contain chests with structural abnormalities, the patients are often tilted or rotated, the position of the chest in the radiograph is not always at the center and there is a lot of variation in the size of the thoraxes. Regarding the separation between the *visible* and the *hidden areas*, it is always precise.

To have a further proof of the efficacy of our method with respect to the existing strategies, we compared it to the lung segmentation method that has been reported as one of the best performing [12], and it has been applied to the *JSRT* database. Since its segmentation masks do not include the hidden areas they have been extended nearby the spine and at the bottom, as described in sec. 2.3. We used the same quantitative criteria to judge those results and we found 50 images with errors, their mean error measure is 0.1, and almost all of them are due to missing parts. Note that, if we should use this method to initialize a lung nodule detection system working on the *JSRT* database, 13 nodules would be lost; on the contrary, none of them are lost by our segmentation masks, confirming that this is a good initialization step for a lung nodule detection system.

References

1. Cj Vyborny, "The aapm/rsna physics tutorial for residents: Image quality and the clinical radiographic examination.," *Radiographics*, vol. 17, pp. 479–498, 1997.
2. A.Hasegawa *et al*, "Convolution neural network based detection of lung structure," *Proc. SPIE 2167*, pp. 654–662, 1994.
3. J.Duryea and J.M.Boone, "A fully automatic algorithm for the segmentation of lung fields in digital chest radiographic images," *Med. Phys.*, vol. 22, 1995.
4. X.W.Xu and K.Doi, "Image feature anlysis for computer aided diagnosis: accurate determination of ribcage boundaries chest radiographs," *Med. Phys.*, vol. 22, 1995.
5. M.F. McNitt-Gray, H.K. Huang, and J.W. Sayre, "Feature selection in the pattern classification problem of digital chest radiographs segmentation," *IEEE Trans. on Med. Imaging*, vol. 14, 1995.
6. S.G.Armato *et al.*, "Automated lung segmentation in digitized posteroanterior chest radiographs," *Academic radiology*, vol. 5, 1998.
7. M.S. Brown, L.S. Wilson, B.D. Doust, R.W. Gill, and C.Sun, "Knowledge-based method for segmentation and analysis of lung boundaries in chest x-rays images," *Computerized Medical Imaging and Graphics*, vol. 22, pp. 463–477, 1998.
8. F.M.Carrascal *et al.*, "Automatic calculation of total lung capacity from automatically traced lung boundaries in postero-anterior and lateral digital chest radiographs," *Medical Physics*, vol. 25, pp. 1118–1131, 1998.
9. O. Tsuji *et al.*, "Automated segmentation of anatomic regions in chest radiographs using an adaptive-sized hybrid neural network," *Med. Phys.*, vol. 25, 1998.
10. N.F. Vittitoe, R. Vargas-Voracek, and C.E. Floyd Jr., "Markov random field modeling in posteroanterior chest radiograph segmentation," *Med. Phys.*, vol. 26, 1999.
11. B. van Ginneken, B.M.ter H. Romeny, and M. Viergever, "Computer-aided diagnosis in chest radiography: A survey," *IEEE Trans. On Med. Imag.*, vol. 20, pp. 1228–1241, 2001.
12. B.van Ginneken and B.M.ter H. Romeny, "Automatic segmentation of lung fields in chest radiographs," *Medical Physics*, vol. 27, 2000.
13. B.van Ginneken, "Computer-aided diagnosis in chest radiographs," *P.h.D. dissertation, Utrecht Univ., Utrecht, The Nederlands*, 2001.
14. Shiraishi et al, "Development of a digital image database for chest radiographs with and without a lung nodule," *AJR*, vol. 174, 2000.
15. W.T.Freeman and E.H.Adelson, "The design and use of steerable filters," *IEEE Trans. on Pattern Analysis and Machine Intelligence*, vol. 13, 1991.
16. T. Lindeberg, "Scale-space: A framework for handling image structures at multiple scales," *Proceedings of CERN, School of Computing*, vol. The Nederlands, 1996.
17. T.Uchiyama and M.Arbib, "Color image segmentation using competitive learning," *IEEE Trans. on Pattern An. and Machine Int.*, vol. 16, 1994.
18. P.Campadelli, E.Casiraghi, and G.Valentini, "Support vector machines for candidate nodules classification," *Neurocomputing (Elsevier), In Press*, 2005.

Relationship Between the Stroma Edge and Skin-Air Boundary for Generating a Dependency Approach to Skin-Line Estimation in Screening Mammograms

Yajie Sun[1], Jasjit Suri, Rangaraj Rangayyan[2], and Roman Janer[1]

[1] Fischer Imaging Corporation, Denver, CO, USA 80241,
{ysun, rjaner}@fischerimaging.com
[2] Department of Electrical and Computer Engineering,
University of Calgary,
Calgary, Alberta, Canada T2N 1N4
{ranga}@calgary.ca

Abstract. Breast area segmentation or skin-line extraction in mammograms is very important in many aspects. Prior segmentation can reduce the effects of background noise and artifacts on the analysis of mammograms. In this paper, we investigate a novel method to estimate the breast skin-line in mammograms. Adaptive thresholding [1] yields a nearly perfect skin-line at the center of the image and around the nipple area with images from the MIAS database [2], but the upper and lower portions of the extracted boundary have been observed to be erroneous due to noise and artifacts. Because the distance from the edge of the stroma to the actual skin-line is usually uniform, we propose a method to estimate the skin-line from the edge of the stroma, with the information provided by the center portion around the nipple from adaptive thresholding. The results are compared with the ground-truth boundaries drawn by a radiologist [3] using polyline distance measure and shape smoothness measure. The results on 83 mammograms from the MIAS database are demonstrated. The proposed methods led to a decrease in a shape smoothness measure based upon curvature, on the average, from 65.6 to 20.0 over the 83 mammograms tested, resulting in an improvement of 69.5%.

1 Introduction

Accurate skin-line extraction is an important prerequisite for the enhancement and display of mammographic features, and for computer-aided diagnosis (CAD) of breast cancers. There has been considerable work on the development of skin-line extraction algorithms in the past decade [1, 3-7]. Bick et al. [4] used localized analysis based on modified histogram analysis, which consisted of global thresholding, region growing and morphological filtering. Abdel-Mottaleb et al. [5] used multiple thresholding to get different breast masks in order to locate the final skin-line. Ojala et al. [1] developed a robust thresholding method based on an analysis of image histogram that consisted of histogram thresholding, morphological filtering, and contour fitting.

Mcloughlin and Bones [6] used a greedy snake algorithm to locate the skin-line after initial segmentation. Wirth and Stapinski [7] developed a breast region segmentation method using active contours. A given mammogram was initially segmented using the threshold determined by Rosin's method, and the initial boundary was extracted. A modified greedy active contour algorithm was then used to locate the final smooth boundary on the original mammogram. The algorithm achieved acceptable results on 25 mammograms from the MIAS database [2]. Ferrari et al. [3] implemented a modified active contour model to obtain the skin-line. The initial segmentation was obtained using a threshold determined by the Lloyd-Max quantizer. The final breast skin-line was obtained using an adaptive active deformable contour model. The method was tested on 84 medio-lateral oblique (MLO) mammograms from the MIAS database with acceptable results.

We present a novel skin-line estimation method in this paper. The novelty of the proposed method is that we utilize the anatomical information to extract the breast skin-line, in comparison with other approaches only utilizes image intensities. The method is designed for robust extraction of the breast skin-line in mammograms with strong background noise, which may fail some other approaches. First, we use adaptive thresholding [1] to extract a nearly perfect skin-line around the nipple. The stroma edge (or the edge of the parenchyma) is not susceptible to noise due to its high contrast and brightness. The stroma edge is then extracted using Otsu's method [8]. A dependency is built between the stroma edge and the central portion of the skin-line using a distance measure based on the observation that the distances between the edge of the stroma and the actual skin-line in screening mammograms are usually uniform.

The paper is organized as follows: Section 2 presents the overall system. Section 3 provides a description of adaptive thresholding. In Section 4, the methods for the extraction of the edge of the stroma and spline fitting are presented. We have implemented several performance evaluation techniques, as described in Section 5, including the Constant Distance Curve (CDC), the shape smoothness measure from curvature, and the Polyline Distance Measure (PDM). The results of our analysis are shown in Section 6. We conclude the paper in Section 7.

2 Overall System

The overall design of our study is presented in Figure 1. We develop a method to obtain the final skin-line from the dependency between the edges of the stroma and the breast skin-lines. The edge of the stroma is extracted using Otsu's thresholding method [8], and then smoothed by spline fitting. We use an adaptive thresholding based on the work by Ojala et al. [1] to extract the initial boundary. Then, the central portion of the boundary near the nipple is used as the control segment to obtain the final skin-line from the edge of the stroma. Ground-truth breast skin-lines of the mammograms were traced by a radiologist [3]. A CDC computed from each ground-truth boundary is used for evaluation of the performance.

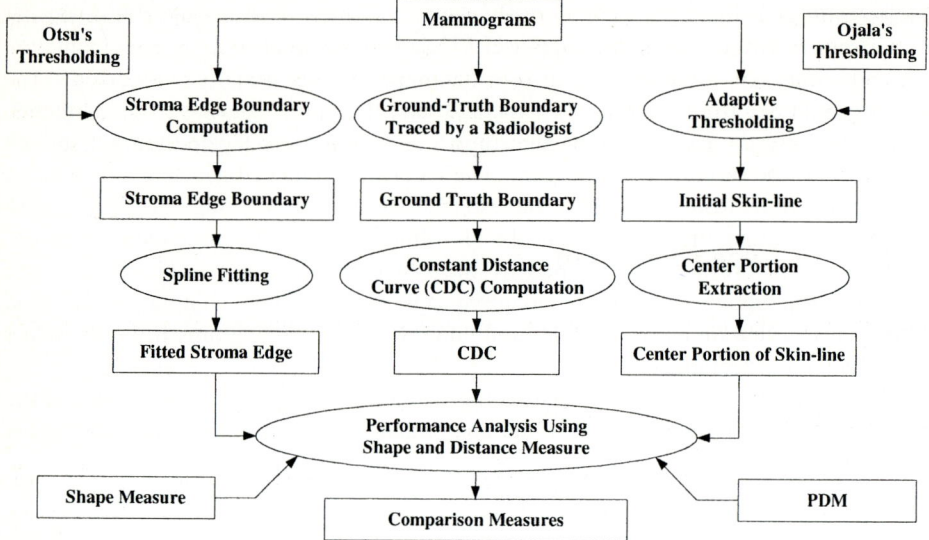

Fig. 1. The block diagram of our system

3 Adaptive Thresholding and Initial Skin-Line Extraction

In this section, we describe the extraction of initial skin-line boundary use adaptive thresholding.

3.1 Adaptive Thresholding

The selection of the threshold is based on an analysis of the histogram [1]. The calculation of the automatic threshold t_0 is based on the assumption that there is a "discontinuity" of histogram values between the breast mode P_{br} and the background mode P_{bg} [1]. The mammogram is thus thresholded using t_0.

3.2 Morphological Filtering

Due to uneven contrast along the breast boundary and noise near the boundary, the morphological *closing* and *opening* operators are used to clean thresholded binary image. The binary image is first processed by the closing operation with a disk-shaped structure element (SE) of diameter d_1. Then, the binary image is processed by an opening operation with a disk-shaped SE of diameter d_2. The parameters d_1 and d_2 are determined experimentally [2]. We used $d_1 = 5$ pixels and $d_2 = 21$ pixels.

3.3 Connected Component Analysis and Boundary Extraction

The connected component analysis method [9] is used to find the largest binary region, which corresponds to the breast region, from the morphologically filtered image. Connected component analysis works by scanning, pixel by pixel, from the top to the bottom to find the connected pixel region in an 8-connectivity system.

The breast skin-line is extracted from the breast region using 8-connectivity. The image is scanned from the bottom row upward to find the first non-zero pixel, which is the beginning of the breast boundary. The scanning procedure proceeds in the anti-clockwise direction to extract the next skin-line point.

4 Stroma Edge Extraction

The edge of the stroma is extracted by using Otsu's thresholding [8] and then smoothed by using spline fitting.

4.1 Stroma Edge by Otsu's Method

As described in Figure 1, the stroma edge is computed as a dependency. Otsu [8] developed an automatic method to segment an image into two regions based upon a bimodal histogram. Because the fatty peripheral area has low intensity near background intensities, and the stroma has a bright edge, we can use Otsu's method to obtain stroma segmentation and extract the edge. After obtaining the initial thresholded binary image using Otsu's thresholding method, morphological filtering, connected component analysis, and chain code boundary extraction are used to obtain the edge of the stroma.

4.2 Spline Fitting

Because the edge of the stroma is not usually smooth, a smoothing/fitting step is needed to establish a uniform dependency between the edge of the stroma and the skin-line. A spline fitting procedure is used to obtain the smoothed stroma edge. Splines are piecewise polynomials with pieces smoothly connected together [10]. In the present work, we used cubic spline fitting to obtain smoothed edge of the stroma. Figure 2 shows an example of spline fitting to the edge of stroma. Two zoomed views show the comparison before and after spline fitting.

5 Performance Evaluation

5.1 Constant Distance Curve (CDC)

A CDC is obtained by shifting the ground-truth (GT) boundary toward the fitted stroma edge with a certain distance. The distance is computed as the Euclidean distance from the center of the GT to the stroma edge. In the study, we compare the stroma edge and its spline-fitted boundary with the CDC, instead of the GT boundary. The CDC is closer to the stroma edge and its spline-fitted boundary, which makes the comparison more meaningful.

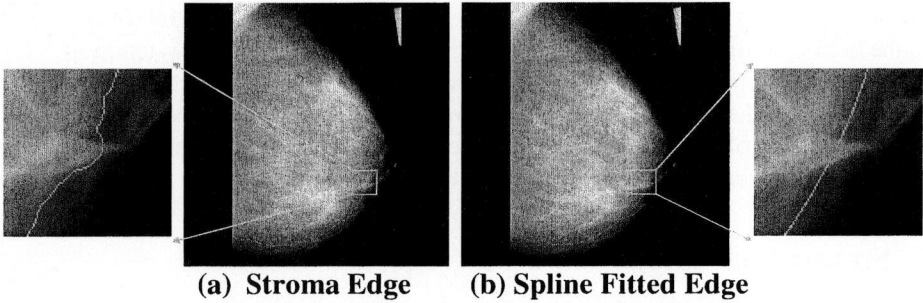

(a) Stroma Edge (b) Spline Fitted Edge

Fig. 2. Stroma edge extraction and fitting: (a) extracted stroma edge, (b) fitted stroma edge.

5.2 Shape Smoothness Measure

In order to compare the breast stroma edge and its spline-fitted edge, a measure of shape smoothness defined from the curvature is investigated. For a plane curve C, the curvature at a given point P has a magnitude equal to the reciprocal of the radius of an osculating circle [11]. The result is that where a curve is "nearly straight", the curvature will be close to zero, and where the curve undergoes a tight turn, the curvature will be large in magnitude. For a plane curve written in the form $y=f(x)$, the curvature κ is defined as:

$$\kappa = \frac{\frac{d^2y}{dx^2}}{\left[1+\left(\frac{dy}{dx}\right)^2\right]^{3/2}}$$

The shape smoothness measure (ς) of a plane curve C is then defined as the integration of the magnitude of the curvature over the length of the curve:

$$\varsigma = \int_0^L |\kappa| ds$$

where L is the length of the plane curve C and s is the arc length. We expect that the value of ς of a spline-fitted edge to be much smaller than that of the stroma edge.

5.3 Polyline Distance Measure (PDM)

In order to compare two boundaries, a quantitative error measure based on the average polyline distance of each boundary point was developed by Suri *et al.* [12]. Let B_1 be the first boundary, and B_2 be the second boundary. Let A be a point on B_1, and B, C be consecutive points on B_2. The polyline distance $d(A, BC)$ is defined as the minimum distance from A to line interval BC.

A quantitative error measure between the ideal boundary and the computer-estimated boundary can then be defined as the average polyline distance of all boundary points of the estimated and ideal boundaries. We will denote the measure as d_{poly}^{Error}, which is derived as follows:

$$d_b(A, B_2) = \min_{S \in sides B_2} d(A, S)$$

$$d_{vb}(B_1, B_2) = \sum_{v \in verticesB_1} d_b(A, B_2) \quad d_{poly}^{Error} = \frac{d_{vb}(B_1, B_2) + d_{vb}(B_2, B_1)}{\#vertices \in B_1 + \#vertices \in B_2}$$

Figure 3 shows an example of the PDM. The PDM between the two boundaries is $d_{poly}^{Error} = 0.963 \approx 1$ pixel.

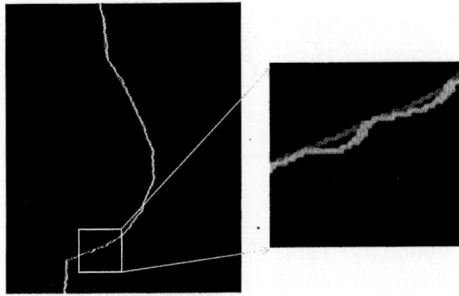

Fig. 3. The PDM between an ideal boundary (RED) and its estimated boundary (GREEN) is 0.963 pixel

6 Results

We tested the proposed method with a dataset of 83 mammograms from the MIAS database [2]. The ground-truth skin-lines were traced by a radiologist [3]. Figure 4 shows the clusters of thresholds automatically selected by the methods of Otsu (for

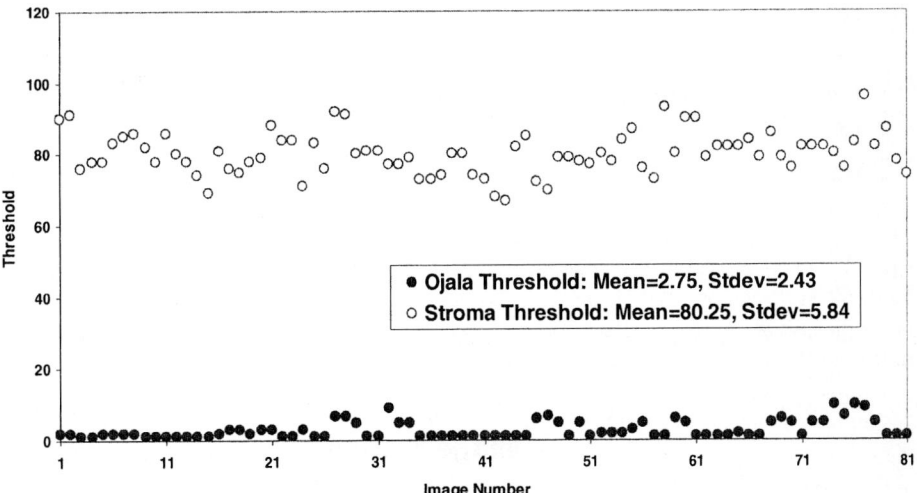

Fig. 4. The clusters of thresholds automatically selected by the methods of Otsu and of Ojala et al.. The mean value of Ojala threshold is 2.75, and mean value of Otsu threshold is 80.25.

stroma edge) and of Ojala et al. (for the initial skin-line). Table 1 shows the average PDM and standard deviation measures of the stroma edge and its spline-fitted edge in comparison to CDC. The standard deviation of the fitted edges is much lower. Hence, the fitted edge is much smoother.

Table 1. Average PDM and standard deviation on 83 Images

	Stroma vs. CDC	Fitted vs. CDC	Change
Average PDM (Pixels)	24.37	24.22	0.61%
Standard Deviation (Pixels)	9.63	9.36	2.82%

Shape smoothness can be measured from the curvature of the edge of the stroma and the fitted stroma boundary. Table 2 shows a comparison of the average and standard deviation of the shape smoothness measure ç over 83 images. With spline fitting, smoothness is improved 69.5% (ç drops from 65.6 to 20.0). Figure 5 shows shape smoothness of the edge of the stroma and its spline-fitted boundary on 83 images.

Table 2. Average Shape Smoothness from Curvature and Standard Deviation Over 83 Images

	Stroma Edge	Spline-Fitted Edge
Average Smoothness	65.6	20.0
Standard Deviation	19.52	5.33

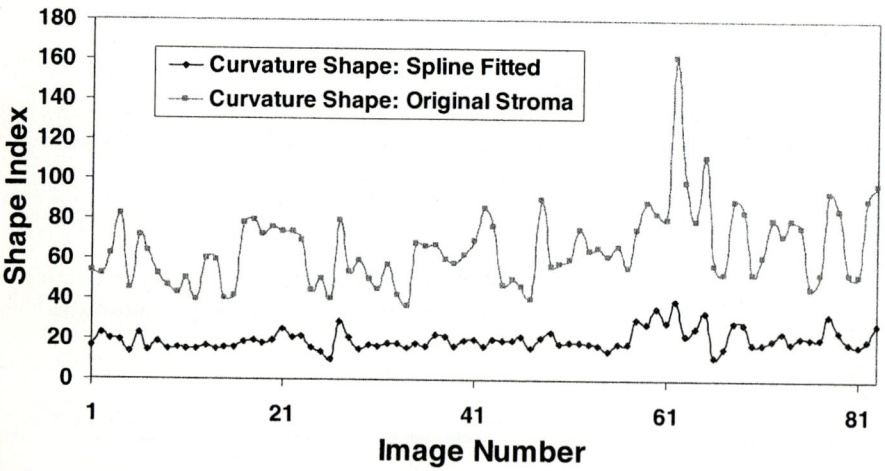

Fig. 5. Comparison of curvature-shape analysis on the original stroma edge and its spline-fitted edge

7 Conclusions

In the paper, we have proposed a novel approach for the estimation of the breast skin-line estimation based on the dependency relationship between the edge of the stroma of the breast on the given mammogram and the result of adaptive thresholding. The approach is based on the observation that the distance between the edge of the stroma and the skin-line is relatively uniform. It is an on-going research to obtain final skin-line in mammograms.

We have presented an automatic method for the extraction of the edge of the stroma based on Otsu's thresholding technique. A dependency relationship between an initial result based on adaptive thresholding and a spline-fitted stroma edge was analyzed using a constant distance curve, a polyline distance measure and a measure of the shape smoothness. The results were used for an on-going research to obtain an improved estimation of the skin-line in mammograms with strong background noise near skin-air boundary.

Accurate estimation of the breast skin-line is important in computer-aided analysis of mammograms. Further developments in this application could be expected from this initial investigation.

References

1. Ojala, T., Nappi, J., Nevalainen, O.: Accurate segmentation of the breast region from digitized mammograms. Computerized Medical Imaging and Graphics, 25 (2001) 47-59
2. Suckling, J., Parker, J., Dance, D. R., Astley, S., Hutt, I.: The Mammographic Image Analysis Society digital mammogram database. 2nd International Workshop on Digital Mammography, York, England, (1994) 375-378
3. Ferrari, R. J., Rangayyan, R. M., Frere, A. F., Desautels, J. E. L., Borges, R. A.: Identification of the breast boundary in mammograms using active contour models. Med. Biol. Engr. Comput. 42 (2004) 201-208
4. Bick, U., Giger, M., Schmidt, R. A., Nishikawa, R., Doi, K.: Automated segmentation of digitized mammograms. Acad. Radiol. 2 (1995) 1-9
5. Abdel-Mottaleb, M., Carman, C. S., Hill, C. R., Vafai, S.: Locating the boundary between the breast skin edge and the background in digitized mammograms. 3rd International Workshop on Digital Mammography, Chicago, IL. (1996) 467-470
6. McLoughlin, K. J., Bones, P. J.: Segmentation of the breast-air boundary for a digital mammogram image. Proc. Image Vision Computing New Zealand, Hamilton. (2000) 228-233
7. Wirth, M. A., Stapinski, A.: Segmentation of the breast region in mammograms using active contours. Proceedings of SPIE: Visual Communications and Image Processing, Vol. . (2003) 1995-2006
8. Otsu, N.: A threshold selection method from gray-level histograms. IEEE Trans. Systems, Man and Cybernetcs. 9 (1979) 62-66
9. Suri, J., Wilson, D., Laximinarayan, S.: Handbook of Medical Image Analysis: Advanced Segmentation and Registration Models. Springler Verlag (2005)
10. Unser, M.: Splines: A perfect fit for signal and image processing. IEEE Signal Processing Magazine. 16 (1999) 22-38
11. Casey, J.: Exploring Curvature. Wiesbaden, Germany: Vieweg (1996)
12. Suri, J., Haralick, R. M., Sheehan, F. H.: Greedy algorithm for error reduction in automatically produced boundaries from low contrast ventriculograms. International Journal of Pattern Analysis and Applications. 3 (2000) 39-60

Segmentation of Erythema from Skin Photographs for Assisted Diagnosis in Allergology

Elodie Roullot[1], Jean-Eric Autegarden[2], Patrick Devriendt[1], and Francisque Leynadier[2]

[1] ESME Sudria, Department Signal & Telecoms, 38 rue Molière, 94200 IVRY-SUR-SEINE, France
roullot@esme.fr
[2] Hôpital Tenon, Service d'allergologie, 4 rue de la Chine, 75020 Paris, France

Abstract. More than 2 people out of 10 suffer from allergies, which can take various forms, from eczema to anaphylactic reactions with possible lethal consequences. Diagnosis is achieved through so-called "prick-tests" or IDR (intra-dermo-reaction): the injection of a small quantity of substances suspected to cause the allergic manifestation induces an erythema, the size of which is a useful indicator for the diagnosis. The manual surface measurement is time-consuming and inaccurate. This article presents a method for the semi-automatic measurement of the erythema from a photograph of the skin, taken in such conditions that lighting problems are minimized. The method is based on region growing and takes advantage of the most significant color spaces; the Lab space appears to be the best suited. It was tested on nearly 100 images, taken by various operators, on patients with various skin pigmentations; it gave promising results and proved to be robust.

1 Introduction

Allergies are classified as the fourth most important public health problem in the world. Numerous epidemiologic studies show that 20 to 25% of people suffer from allergic troubles. Allergic manifestations take various forms, among which eczema, rhinitis, asthma, or even Quincke oedema or anaphylactic reaction, with possible lethal consequences.

In order to prevent from the most severe anaphylactic manifestations, it is necessary to have an acute knowledge of the substances that are responsible for the allergic reaction, called the "allergens". This diagnosis is achieved by the allergologist through cutaneous tests: "prick-tests" or IDR (intra dermo reaction). In prick-tests, a drop of solution containing the allergen to be tested is dropped on the forearm of the patient, which is then punctured in order to make the allergen penetrate into the skin; in IDR's, the allergen is injected into the skin with a syringe.

An allergic reaction locally induces a dilatation of blood vessels and the release of chemical substances due to the "axon reflex" [1], leading after 15 to 20 minutes to the apparition of an erythema, characterized by a local reddening of the skin and an increase in its temperature; at the center of the erythema a papula is formed, looking like a mosquito bite. The surface of the erythema is an indicator for the severity of the allergy.

The mean diameter of each erythema is measured with a scale; each value, corresponding to a given allergen, is compared to 2 reference values: the positive and negative standards. The positive standard indicates the standard degree of reaction of the patient and is achieved by the injection of codein phosphate which involves for everybody a positive reaction. The negative standard is achieved by the injection of physiological serum which never involves a positive reaction (only the puncture is involved in an eventual change in the skin appearance). The reaction induced by a given allergen is considered to be positive if it is equivalent to or larger than the positive standard; if it is comparable to the negative standard, the reaction is considered to be negative.

This technique appears very fastidious especially due to the huge number of allergens to be tested (up to 20); moreover, the measures are corrupted by errors due to the inter- and intra-operators variability, thus making a follow-up of the patients more difficult. Moreover, the diameter of the erythema does not give a good estimation of the surface, the measure of which would be preferred by the allergologists.

All these reasons make an automatic measure of the surface very challenging; the expected improvements are: less time spent for measuring, less intra- and inter-operators variations in the measurement, more accuracy thanks to the surface measurement instead of the diameter measurement, and the storage possibility, making a follow-up of the patients easier. However, the clinical motivation of this work is not to provide a fully automated diagnosis system, but rather to provide assistance to the allergologist to make his diagnosis. Thus, it should be focused on the segmentation problem but it should not be dealt with an automatic diagnosis whether the patient is allergic or not.

Several research works emerged during the last years, dealing with the automation of erythema detection. They make use either of spectroscopy, or of echography, or of visible imaging. Several teams including Kopola et al. [2], Dawson et al. [3], Ferguson-Pell et al. [4], Hajizadeh-Saffar [5] or Diffey [6] suggest calculating an "erythema index" from reflectance measures in different carefully chosen spectral bands, by means of a spectroscope. Several methods among these were evaluated by Riordan et al. [7]. Some of them allow detecting erythemas even in highly pigmented skins; however, all of them only provide an index (generally an erythema index and a melanin index) that characterizes the global change in color, whereas routinely the allergologist is interested in the size of the erythema.

Seidenari [8] et al., for their part, use echography to quantify erythemas induced by patch-tests; once again, this provides values representing the intensity of the reaction whereas the allergologist is interested in the surface.

The surface can only be obtained automatically from images of the skin; although the problem of segmentation is dealt with very often in the context of melanoma detection for example, this problem has been addressed very rarely in the context of erythema detection. Unfortunately, the methods used for segmenting melanomas can not be transposed easily for erythema detection, since melanoma images are much more contrasted than erythema images. Nischik et al. addressed the problem of erythema segmentation from visible light images and proposed a method for segmenting the erythema, based on the CIELab color space and on the comparison between two images acquired before and after prick-testing [1]. This method presents a major drawback: it implies a motion analysis in order to suppress artifacts due to the unavoidable motion between both images, since the reaction can be read 15 to 20 minutes after prick-testing.

We therefore propose an original approach to segment the erythema and provide a surface measurement of it, using only one image taken after reaction.
In Section 2 we briefly describe the image capture system and the image database; then we address in Section 3 a colorimetric study in order to extract the best color space to use. In Section 4 we describe the method, and the results are presented and discussed in Section 5.

2 Image Database

As said before, the detection is performed from digital photographs of the arm and forearm. These digital photographs are taken using a standard color CCD camera with a spatial resolution of 752 x 582 pixels. The camera is connected to a personal computer via a digitalization card (Ellips Riowin) allowing real-time visualization of the acquired image and eventual tuning of some acquisition parameters, as well as saving a color image in bitmap format (BMP).

The illumination system is composed of two neon tubes placed behind unpolished and translucent Plexiglas plates, in order to provide an homogeneous illumination and thus to avoid reflection artifacts.

90 images of the arm or forearm were acquired at *'anonymous'* hospital (*'town'*, *'country'*) from January 2003 to June 2004 on both male and female adult patients who agreed to take part in these tests. Most patients had lightly pigmented skins (Caucasian for most of them, and Metis or Mongoloid), and only one patient had a very dark skin (Negroid). Ten randomly chosen images formed the learning database and the others were used for evaluation purposes.

3 Colorimetric Study

A first examination of the learning database revealed that the classical RGB (red, green, blue) color space is not the best suited for the segmentation of erythemas. In this section, we study several color spaces to extract the best suited for discriminating the reddened skin from the "normal" skin. The CMY color space is the complementary color space to the RGB one: it is based on subtractive synthesis (as in printers) while the RGB space is based on additive synthesis (as in monitors). HSV (hue, saturation, value) and HSL (hue, saturation, luminance) systems correspond to a psychovisual description of color, based on the human eye function. The LMS color space is also based on the human eye: each stimulus L (long), M (middle) and S (short) represents the spectral sensitivity of the photoreceptive cells of the eye. The CIELab color space is derived from the XYZ standard color space, defined by the CIE in 1931 by a homographic transformation of the RGB space. L represents the luminance whereas a and b respectively represent the red-green chrominance and the blue chrominance.

All these values (R, G, B; C, M, Y; H, S, V; H, S, L; L, M, S; X, Y, Z; L, a, b) were computed for each image of the learning database. An SNR study revealed that the chrominance "a" provides the best discrimination of erythematous skin versus normal skin. These results confirm those obtained by Fullerton et al. [9] and Weatherall et al. [10]; they recommend the use of the Lab color space, which takes into account the non linearity of color perception by the human eye.

4 Color-Based Segmentation

4.1 Choice of the Method

As said before, the segmentation of erythema is a difficult task, because of the colorimetric heterogeneity of the skin (both the normal and the reddened skin present a marmor aspect), as well as because of the low contrast between erythema and normal skin. This problem belongs to the family of problems dealing with the segmentation of low SNR images. For such images, classical segmentation methods such as contour detection approaches are not well suited, that is why we concentrate our attention on constrained region segmentation approaches. Among these methods, structural ones are well suited to the problem since they allow constraining more or less the pattern of the extracted region [11].

Moreover, each image acquired represents the full arm or forearm, and can thus contain several erythemas corresponding to different allergens. It does not appear judicious to develop a system that would be able to recognize automatically to each kind of allergen each area of the arm corresponds, since it will induce many technical constraints for the operators performing the test, whereas it is not very constraining for him/her to have a minimum level of interaction with the system. On the contrary, the medical specialists generally prefer keeping a given degree of control on the automatic diagnosis process rather than obtaining results from a fully automatic system in which they have low confidence. Thus, it appears as a reasonable compromise to require the allergologist to click on the corresponding erythema when prompted with the name of an allergen, for example, as follows:
- launch image acquisition
- for each allergen:
    - if an erythema is present:
        - mouse click within the reaction area
        - detection is thus performed automatically from the given seed
        - view, validate and store the results, both quantitative (image) and qualitative (surface)
    - else, store the result (absence of reaction) and skip to next allergen.

Taking into account both the considerations about the segmentation problem and the integration of the algorithm within a future computer-aided diagnosis software, a method based on region growing with manual input of the seeds appears consistent. In the next subsection we describe our algorithm based on pixel aggregation, with a strong constraint on the connectivity of the region and a weak constraint on its pattern.

4.2 Segmentation Algorithm

The algorithm is based on region growing [11,12] where the initial regions have a unitary size and are chosen manually by mouse clicking. Aggregation of new pixels is iterative and depends on two criteria: adjacency and colorimetric similarity. Each iteration begins with the constitution of a candidate set, based on adjacency; all candidates satisfying the colorimetric criteria are aggregated, and the new region is then used for the following iteration. The algorithm stops when no more candidates are eligible for aggregation.

The different steps of the algorithm are detailed below:

- Initialization: manual choice of N seeds chosen within the erythema, forming the N initial regions R_i.
- For each region i:
    - selection of the candidate set C_i, i.e. the set of pixels adjacent to the current region, obtained with a morphological dilatation:

$$C_i = (R_i \oplus E_S) - R_i \tag{1}$$

where $\oplus$ represents the morphological dilatation with a 3x3 square structural element E_s.

- among the candidates c_i^k, selection of those satisfying the colorimetric similarity criterion:

$$a(c_i^k) > T\ (a(R_i)) \tag{2}$$

where a represents the chrominance "a" in the Lab color space, T is an automatic threshold computed from statistics in the region R_i.

- if no candidate was selected at the previous step, algorithm ends.
- else, creation of the new region R_{i+1} as the union of region R_i and selected pixels c_i^k.

4.3 Automatic Threshold Tuning

A statistical study of the chrominance "a" was performed on the 10 images of the learning database: a coarse thresholding helped select the arm and suppress the background, and then the histogram of the chrominance "a" was computed. This study revealed that the mean and variance of the chrominance varied sensibly from an image to another. Therefore the threshold was chosen as a function of the mean and variance of the chrominance "a". For the 10 images of the learning database, the erythema surface was computed for various thresholds and compared to the reference surface (which is described further in Section 5). The threshold T varies as follows:

$$T = \bar{a}(I) + \lambda \sigma_a(I) \tag{3}$$

where $\bar{a}$ is the mean chrominance over the image I, σ_a is the variance of "a" over the image I, and the parameter λ varies from 0.6 to 1.4. The value of λ giving the exact diameter is interpolated; over the learning database, the mean λ equals 0.97 meaning that the best threshold is $\bar{a}(I) + 0.97 \sigma_a(I)$.

The robustness of the parameter λ can also be evaluated from these tests: a variation of 10% of the standard deviation in the threshold induces a variation of about 5% in the diameter. We can therefore affirm that the threshold is quite robust.

5 Results and Discussion

5.1 Qualitative Study

The algorithm was tested on the 90 erythema images of the database. Among the 90 images, 89 concern patients with lightly pigmented skins (Caucasian, Mongoloid, Metis) and one patient has a highly pigmented skin (Negroid). Some results are shown on Figure 1 for the clear skins and on Figure 2 for the dark skin. On these images, blue pencil marks can be noticed, corresponding to the marks used by the physician; note that these marks do not appear in the "a" chrominance image and therefore do not disturb the algorithm (this would not be the case if a red pencil was used, as it was the case for some images that were therefore useless). When the system will be used instead of the manual measurement, these marks will not be needed anymore and will thus disappear. At this step of development, they are useful to compare the contour provided by the algorithm with the diameter estimated by the physician.

On Figure 1, it can be noticed that the lighting conditions differ considerably from one image to another; this does not seem to affect the algorithm, and confirms its robustness. Concerning the dark skin on Figure 2, the erythema of the unique negroid patient taking part in the tests could be detected in a satisfactory way.

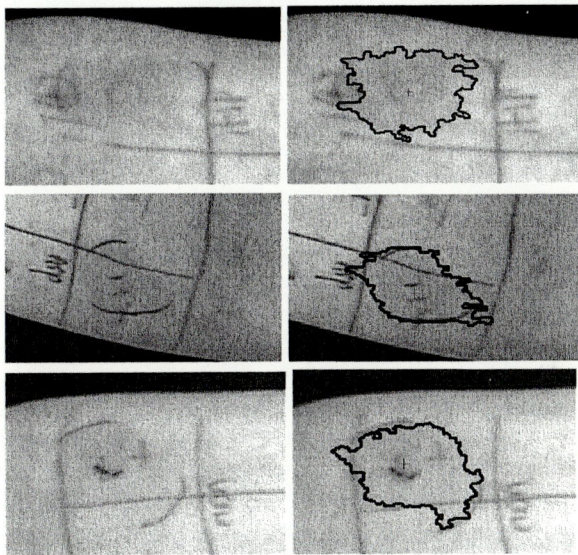

Fig. 1. Examples of results obtained on various skin types among Caucasian, Mongoloid, and Métis patients. Left, the regions of interest in the original images; Right, the results superimposed on the original regions of interest. Blue pencil marks can be noted, which correspond to the separations between the allergens being tested, and to the limits used by the physician for the diameter measurement.

In 5 images, the algorithm was not able to detect any contour. Possible reasons for these failures are: the low contrast of the image, due either to the image capture or to the skin reactivity of the patient; artifacts on the patient skin; defaults in the lighting systems providing an image with reflection artifacts that disturb the segmentation process.

The detection of an erythema lasts a few seconds, so that for one patient tested for 10 allergens, the total time including the mouse clicking, the automatic detection and storage of the results amounts to far less than one minute: less than the time for the patient to get dressed after the measurements. Routinely, the operators needs to draw the limits of the erythema before measuring (when measuring the diameter, the operator has to flatten the skin, which makes the skin reddening disappear), then measure, and finally report the value in a paper or electronic report; all these steps require several minutes and are much more time-consuming than the mouse-clicking and detection. Moreover, as said before, the measures are corrupted by an important variability between different operators and even between different measures taken by the same operators. The automatic detection provides a reproducible measure and proved to be nearly independent of the manual input of the seed (if the seed is chosen within the erythema and not on the border).

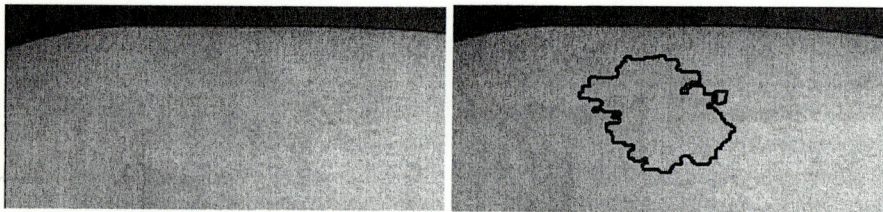

Fig. 2. Example of result obtained on a skin of type Negroid. On this unique example it seems that the algorithm does not encounter any particular problem detecting the contour of the erythema, although the erythema is hardly visible with the naked eye.

5.2 Quantitative Evaluation

Two options can be considered for evaluating the algorithm; the first one consists in comparing the results to the clinical measurements performed manually, and the second one consists in comparing to a ground-truth surface that remains to be defined.

Actually, the measurements conducted routinely are diameter measurements performed by the nurses with a scale. These measurements suffer from a very important intra- and inter-operators variability, mainly due to two reasons. Firstly, the use of the scale implies a deformation of the natural curve of the arm and pushing on the skin implies color changes that can affect the measurement. Secondly, the erythema contour is not necessarily a circle; the nurses take as "diameter" measurement the biggest distance between the erythema borders. This is not so easy to appreciate with the human eye and is another factor for the variability of the measurement. Therefore, a quantitative evaluation based on these measurements does not appear to be judicious, and it appears necessary to perform evaluation by comparing to a "ground-truth" value.

To this end, for each image of the database an expert was asked to draw the erythema contour as precisely as possible; actually he pointed as many points on the contour as he needed and the corresponding polygon (with many vertices) was considered to be the ground-truth boundary. A "goodness" measure was defined as the ratio between the provided surface and the ground-truth surface. Figure 3 shows the histogram of this ratio computed over the database.

Figure 4-(a) presents a "good" result of evaluation with the polygon and the detection result superimposed on the image. On this example, the evaluation metric (the surface ratio) is 95%; the area of the polygon is 6411 pixels² and that of the automatic contour is 6139 pixels². A fictive diameter was computed as $2\sqrt{area/\pi}$, giving 90 pixels for the ground-truth, 88 pixels for the automatic detection. These values can be compared to the diameter measured manually (corresponding to the pencil parks) to 111 pixels. The error of 2 pixels is very low compared to the 21 pixels difference between the manual measure and the ground-truth. The difference between the manual measurement and the ground-truth provides a surface ratio of 152%, which corresponds to the worst cases of the automatic detection, as shown on Figure 3 (left).

Figure 4-(b) and 4-(c) shows two of the worse results obtained with the automatic detection. For the left image, the surface ratio is 76%; for the right image, the surface ratio is 155%. When comparing the results of Figure 4, it can be noticed that even in the worse cases, the contour is not so bad and is anyway at least as good as the one that could have been drawn manually. This illustrates the fact that surface ratios of 80% or 150% for example are considered as acceptable by the experts, and also contribute to the improvement of the measurements when compared to the manual ones.

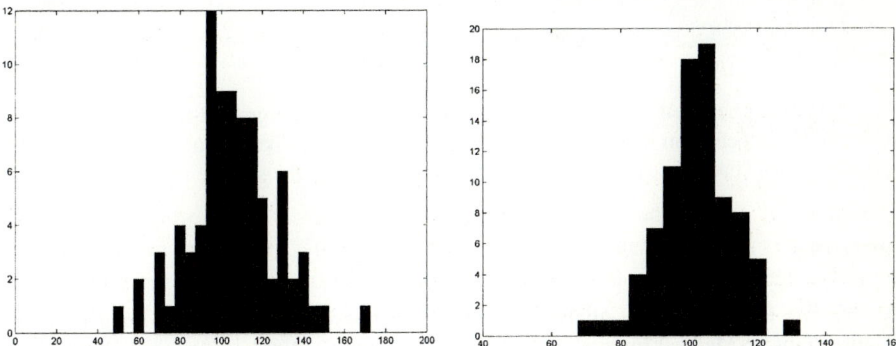

Fig. 3. Left: Histogram of the ratio between the surface provided by the algorithm and the ground-truth surface. This surface comparison leads to ratios that go very fast far away from the ideal ratio of 100%; this is due to the fact that the variation of surface is quadratic. Right: the same histogram after correction of the quadratic effect due to the surface measurement. As a consequence the ratios are homogeneous with diameter ratios and are thus easier to understand intuitively.

6 Conclusion

In this article, we addressed the problem of the automatic detection and quantification of reactions to allergic tests. This original problem was not addressed often in the literature, although it derives from an actual query from the allergologists.

In this study we focused on the segmentation problem; the automatic decision process was not addressed. Indeed the segmentation problem is the most difficult to solve because of the low contrast of erythema images and of the heterogeneity of the skin color. To this end a method was developed that combines color image analysis with a region growing algorithm; it provides a robust and reproducible contour detection from the manual input of a seed point within the erythema.

The method was applied on a database of nearly 100 images acquired during the consultations of allergologists at *'anonymous'* hospital. A rigorous evaluation allowed proving that the method has a satisfying detection rate and is quite robust. The physicians judged the software potentially helpful and very promising. In the future, it will be necessary to perform more tests especially on dark skins, since they were not well represented in the present database.

It is also planed to work on the acquisition and lighting systems: the system described in Section 2 is a provisory one and work is already being performed on a best suited system, such as those used by some dermatologists consisting of a digital camera together with a ring light.

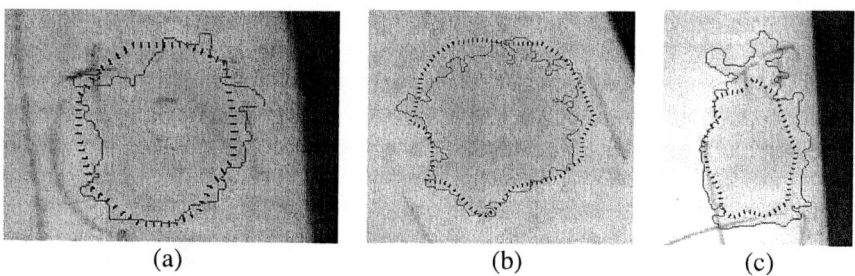

Fig. 4. Comparison between the automatic contour (solid line), the ground-truth (dashed line) and the manual diameter (on image (a): dark pencil marks looking like parenthesis) in a "good" case (a) and in two "bad" cases ((b): the surface ratio is 76%; (c): the surface ratio is 155%).

References

1. M. Nischik and C. Forster. Analysis of Skin Erythema Using True-Color Images. IEEE Transactions on Medical Imaging, 16(6):711-716, December 1997.
2. H. Kopola, A. Lahti, R. Myllyla, M. Hannuksela. Two-channel fiber optic skin erythema meter. Optical Engineering, 32:222-226, 1993.
3. J. B. Dawson, D. J. barker et al. A theoretical and experimental study of light absorption and scattering by in-vivo skin. Phys Med Biol 25(4):695-709, 1980.
4. M. Ferguson-Pell and S. Hagisawa. An empirical technique to compensate for melanin when monitoring skin microcirculation using reflectance spectrophotometry. Med Eng Physics 17(2):104-110, 1995.

5. M. Hajizadeh-Saffar, J. W. Feather and J. B. Dawson. An investigation of factors affecting the accuracy of in vivo measurement of skin pigments by reflectance spectrophotometry. Phys Med Biol 35(9):1301-1315, 1990.
6. B. L. Diffey and P. M. Farr. Quantitative aspects of ultraviolet erythema. Clin Phys Physiol Meas 12(4):311-325, 1991.
7. B. Riordan, S. Sprigle and M. Linden. Testing the validity of erythema detection algorithms. Journal of Rehabilitation Research and Development, 38(1), January/February 2001.
8. S. Seidenari and B. Belletti. The Quantification of Patch Test Responses: A Comparison Between Echographic and Colorimetric Methods. Acta Derm Venerol 78:364-366, 1998.
9. A. Fullerton, T. Fischer et al. Guidelines for the Measurement of Skin Color and Erythema. Contact Dermatitis 35:1-10, 1996.
10. I. L. Weatherall and B. D. Coombs. Skin Color Measurements in Terms of CIELAB Color Space Values. Journal of Investigative Dermatology 99:468-473, 1992.
11. J.-P. Cocquerez and S. Philipp. Analyse d'images : filtrage et segmentation. Masson, 1995.
12. H. Maître. Le traitement des images. Lavoisier, 2003.

Learning Histopathological Microscopy

James Shuttleworth[1], Alison Todman[1],
Mark Norrish[1], and Mark Bennett[2]

[1] Coventry University, Coventry, UK
j.shuttleworth@coventry.ac.uk
[2] The Royal Victoria Infirmary, Newcastle upon-Tyne, UK

Abstract. Histopathological tissue analysis by microscopy is a process that is subjective, prone to inter- and intra-observer variation. This, along with the problems associated with verbalising visual elements of the diagnostic process, make learning the skill quite difficult. Training is long and largely relies on an "apprentice" model, where trainees learn the skill by witnessing an expert at work. Here we present the first findings of a longitudinal study of a group of histopathology trainees. By monitoring the progress of the trainees, we hope to be able to provide information that will improve training and assessment. In this paper we discuss the results of early data collection and analysis, from a web-based study of trainee classification accuracy and classification time.

1 Introduction

Trainees entering the Histopathology SHO training programme in the UK are required to develop their skills in various areas over several years. With 20% of consultant histopathologist posts unfilled [1], an increase in trainees will be necessary to supply the required professionals to meet future demand.

Entry into the SHO schools is by open competition for medical staff who enrol with varying degrees of experience. During the programme, they are informally reviewed at 3 and 6 months with a more formal assessment at 9 months. During the programme, training is given in many areas, including macroscopic tissue examination, histopathological microscopy, cytology and autopsy.

The subjective nature [2] of histopathalogical microscopy and high levels of inter- [3] and intra-observer variation [4] makes difficult the process of acquiring proficiency in this area. This makes extensive use of supervised specimen analysis, in which an experienced histopathologist analyses routine biopsy specimens, while one or more trainees examines the tissue through the ancillary eye-pieces of multiheaded microscope while listening to the expert's verbalisation of the process and the result. The hands-on nature of the training requires significant commitment of time and effort on behalf of the trainee and trainer alike.

Training to make a diagnosis is based on correlating the given clinical information with the observed histological features. The SHO will review the microscope slide before bringing it to the consultant. Then each case is reviewed in the knowledge of the clinical information and the consultant will listen to the

SHO's observation and point out the other details which make up the diagnosis. The theoretical knowledge is assumed to be minimal - undergraduate level only. Half of one day per week is given over to the review of histopathological material and the theoretical basis of pathology. This is run at the same time as the "apprenticeship", the practical side of the training.

It has been observed by trainers that some trainees quickly develop an aptitude for tissue analysis, while others take longer or occasionally never develop the skill to an acceptable level.

Our hypothesis is that the decision-making process is different between experts and novices, and that expert decisions are based upon automatic pattern recognition rather than cognitive reasoning [5]. Not all trainees will develop an aptitude for pattern recognition in tissue analysis, and the training programme seeks to guide these individuals in other directions. Evaluation of trainees' performance is carried out after one year, when the skills of a trainee are reasonably well developed [6].

This paper presents a study of data collected from trainees recently joining the program. By analysing the decision-making performance of trainees through the first year of their training, we hope to determine the possibility of identifying trainees who are likely to develop an aptitude for tissue analysis early in the program, perhaps even before training begins.

Previous work [7,8] has investigated image features that correlate with classification, and identified a number of useful texture features for automated classification, such as correlation, angular second moment and entropy, that combined can be used to classify image regions with less than 2% error. It is hoped that the work presented here will lead to a better understanding of these image features. Also, by combining the results of this study with statistical analysis of the image data, we hope also to provide insight into the learning and decision-making process based on image features, which will help us to develop better tools to assist in the training process.

The aim of the current line of research is to gain a better understanding of *how* clinicians are *learning* to analyse the images. The second part of the study, currently underway, investigates further, and seeks to determine how trainees' mental organisation and clustering changes with experience and how it differs from that of experts.

2 Experimental Method

2.1 The Images

In total a set of 20 images, shown in Figure 1, were used, each measuring 256×256 pixels. The images were classified by a qualified, experienced gastrointestinal pathologist into one of three classes: normal, dysplasia, cancer. All images were taken from routine past cases and stained with H&E. Digitisation was carried out from $5 \mu m$ slices using a Leitz microscope and a digital camera and all image data has been anonymised, with respect to the factors discussed in [9].

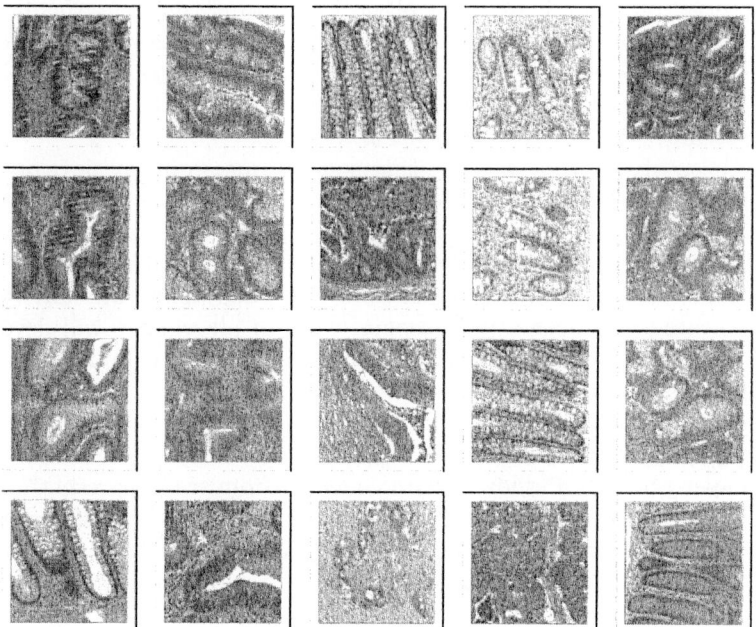

Fig. 1. The image set

2.2 Subjects and Data Collection

The subjects were 8 students who had just commenced training within one of the NHS training schools. The experiments were carried out within a purpose-built web-based experimental framework that allows individual subjects to view and classify images, and records the classification assigned to each image and the time taken to reach a decision in each case. The images shown in Figure 1 were displayed in a random order and the subjects were asked to classify each one into one of three classes: normal, dysplasia or cancer.

All data was anonymised by using randomly generated usernames, assigned to the trainees by their instructor. to comply with data protection guidelines.

Each user's data was recorded in a separate file, along with the date and time of completion.

3 Results

Table 1 shows the data collected from the trainees. Each column contains data for a single trainee. For each image, the trainee's decision and length of decision-making time was recorded. Decisions are shown as A for normal, B for dysplastic and C for cancer. All times are in seconds.

Table 1. Recorded data for each trainee showing classification for each image and time, in seconds

User ⇒ Image ⇓	138-0	260-1	121-0	172-0	260-0	129-0	136-0	115-0	193-0
i1	A,5.7	A,7.1	A,1.4	B,12.5	A,4.3	A,4.9	A,6.9	A,6.4	A,11.7
i10	B,6.6	A,5.3	A,5.6	B,11.1	A,1.9	A,7.1	A,46.3	B,8.4	B,18.8
i11	B,5.6	B,5.9	B,1.3	B,9.9	A,8.2	B,13.6	B,5.7	B,3.0	B,13.2
i12	B,10.1	B,9.2	B,2.5	B,11.7	B,2.1	C,3.4	B,8.1	B,3.7	B,6.9
i13	B,60.9	B,3.7	B,2.1	B,12.8	B,6.1	B,15.6	B,15.9	B,3.1	B,7.0
i14	B,6.9	B,10.9	B,9.5	B,8.6	A,8.4	B,6.6	B,10.0	B,6.1	B,11.7
i15	B,10.7	B,20.9	A,2.9	B,16.1	A,14.9	A,11.1	B,15.5	B,9.1	B,15.4
i16	B,9.7	A,4.8	A,8.3	B,25.7	A,2.6	B,12.9	A,35.9	A,14.6	B,12.9
i17	C,7.6	C,6.9	C,2.4	C,9.3	C,7.7	C,6.1	C,5.9	C,8.8	C,6.8
i18	B,12.5	B,5.8	B,3.1	C,10.3	A,24.3	C,7.7	C,8.2	C,11.1	C,11.6
i19	B,15.1	C,9.1	C,6.0	C,9.4	B,5.8	C,2.6	B,14.1	C,7.7	C,13.3
i2	A,6.7	A,4.6	A,6.0	A,9.2	A,5.1	A,54.2	A,14.2	A,5.3	A,38.1
i20	B,32.8	C,7.1	C,5.3	C,7.8	C,4.3	C,2.6	C,4.0	C,5.0	C,9.9
i3	A,8.0	A,14.0	A,3.7	A,20.9	A,2.8	A,5.2	A,10.4	A,2.6	A,12.6
i4	A,5.3	A,25.4	A,2.2	A,10.0	A,8.9	A,3.3	A,9.7	A,4.9	A,9.5
i5	A,7.1	A,6.6	A,1.3	A,14.5	A,2.7	A,8.9	A,46.0	A,2.8	A,67.5
i6	A,6.2	A,5.3	A,5.1	A,45.6	A,4.2	A,11.0	A,5.9	A,5.5	A,9.5
i7	A,61.1	A,9.1	A,2.6	A,19.6	A,2.5	A,4.5	A,8.2	B,10.5	A,10.7
i8	B,7.1	A,11.7	A,10.7	A,34.2	A,5.4	A,13.5	A,15.2	A,9.5	A,36.0
i9	B,7.5	B,16.5	B,8.6	B,8.3	A,18.6	C,4.1	B,8.3	B,6.2	B,18.1

4 Analysis

4.1 Accuracy and Speed

The most obvious relationship to look for is that between time taken to make a diagnosis and accuracy. Defining accuracy simply as the percentage of correct classifications, this can be plotted against average time. Figure 2 shows the nine collected records on these axes. There appears to be a correlation between average time and accuracy, with longer average times seeming to indicate a greater number of correct classifications. The correlation between these two fields is $r = 0.5$, giving a probability $p = 0.085$ that the correlation is spurious, or an effect of the limited sample size. While this is a low probability, it does not fall below the 0.05 threshold for significance. There are two outliers in the plot: one record has a score of just 50%, while another has a score of 90%, but a low average time. The low scoring record is the first attempt by trainee 260-0, who entered a second record the following day. This second attempt scored 75%, and probably indicates that the trainee initially misunderstood the instructions. It is possible that the high scoring trainee that made decisions quickly has more experience or aptitude than the others. Removing these outliers would give $r = 0.83, p = 0.01$. This indicates that the relationship is potentially very useful, but requires a larger data set to be certain.

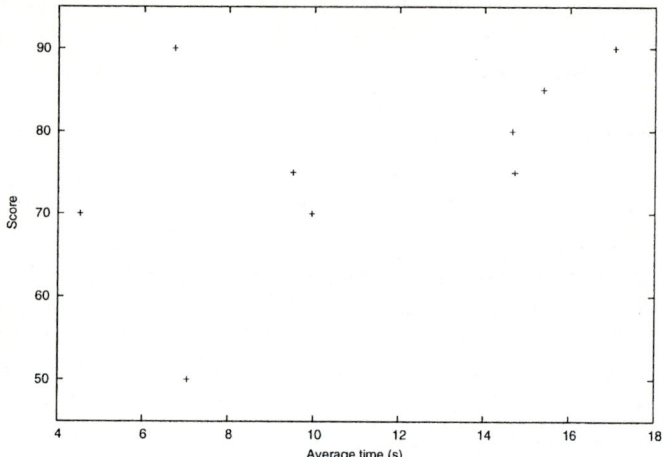

Fig. 2. Relationship between accuracy and average time

4.2 Time Deviation and Correctness

After examining the data along one axis, above, the next logical step is to change axes and examine the data on a per-image basis. Converting each trainees timing data into Z-scores, which are based on deviation from the mean, allows us to remove differences in the means, leaving information only on the relative times taken per image. The average Z-score per image then gives an indication of the time, relative to the mean, that the average trainee takes for each image. Plotting this against the number of trainees that correctly classified an image gives Figure 3.

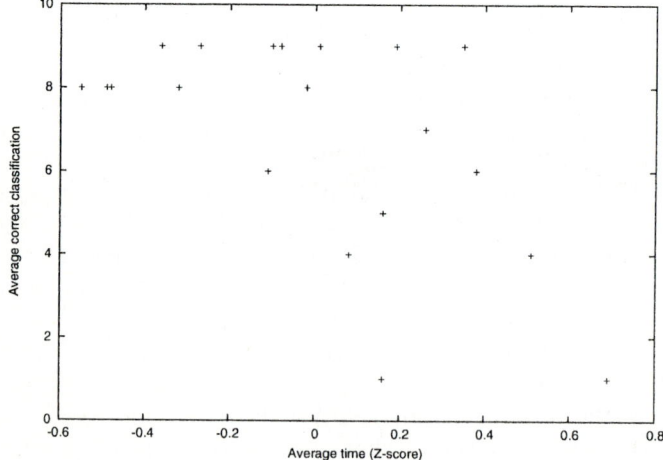

Fig. 3. Relationship between average Z-score and correct classifications

Interestingly, the relationship between correct classifications and average Z-score is negative: $r = -0.58$. Unlike the correlation between a trainee's mean time and score, this correlation is very significant ($p = 0.004$).

4.3 Visualisation

As well as statistical analyses of student data, we have produced prototype visualisation models for use by instructors. One particularly useful visualisation is shown in Figure 4.

The leftmost column shows the trainee username and run index. User 138, run 0 is first, for example. The rightmost column shows the percentage of correct classifications. The remaining 5 columns show the number of classifications and misclassifications as a coloured circle and, in the left corner of each cell, numerically. Column -2 gives the number of misclassifications such that the trainee's answer was two classes too low (normal when the correct answer was cancer). Column 2 shows the number of misclassifications where the trainee answered two classes too high. Columns -1 and 1 are misclassifications by one class and column 0 shows correct classifications.

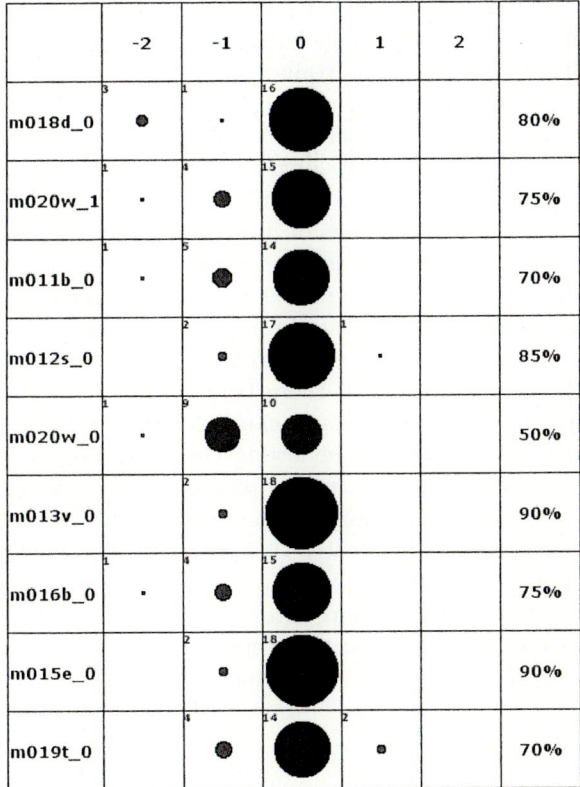

Fig. 4. Visualisation of group performance

The purpose of the visualisation is to give instant and intuitive feedback on the accuracy of the group, and the kind and number of misclassifications.

Interestingly, the majority of misclassifications are lenient. We expect this to change over time in two ways. Firstly, we expect there to be fewer misclassifications as the trainees' skills develop. Also we expect the bias to shift such that either there is no significant difference between the number of under and over classifications, or that the bias moves so that misclassifications are mostly assigning a higher grade to an image. The consequence of this kind of misclassification is simply further investigation, while a lenient misclassification may mean that the disease is diagnosed much later.

5 Discussion

The correlation between deviation from average mean time and case performance (as described in 4.2) gives some indication of the process trainees use to make classification decisions at this point in their training. Regardless of their average time, spending longer than average on an image doesn't appear to increase the likelihood of a correct classification. In fact, the cases that were most correctly classified were done in less than average time. This seems to indicate a more automatic decision making process that requires less cognitive resources. Taking longer than normal on a difficult image (suggesting more analysis) would appear to provide no benefit to the average trainee.

Although the correlation between mean time and performance (section 4.1) was not strong enough to be significant on this small data set, it is reasonable to assume that the hypothesis that longer average times are associated with higher classification accuracy will be shown to be significant with a larger data set. Assuming, then, for the purposes of discussion, that the correlation is not spurious, we can reason that at this stage in training, trainees that take a longer average time to make a diagnosis are more likely to make a correct classification. However, correlation does not necessarily imply causation. The factor causing a trainee to examine images for longer could also be responsible for a high classification accuracy. For example, these trainees might be, by nature, more careful and thorough: traits that would cause them to have spent more time and effort learning, practising and reviewing cases, leading to a higher score. These same traits would cause the trainee to spend longer on each case in the experiment. The previous correlation, showing a relationship between deviation from mean time and accuracy, indicates that correctly classified cases generally take less than average time.

If this does indicate that more a more automatic decision making process is a key factor in classification, we would expect the relationship between average time and accuracy to become progressively less pronounced as the subjects gain experience.

6 Conclusion

The results presented in this paper are the first findings of our investigation of the process of learning histopathological microscopy.

We have shown that a simple measurement of the time taken for a trainee to analyse images could possibly inform us of the level of skill of the trainee. Such information could be used to improve training and assessment.

Ongoing and planned work will seek to strengthen and build on these findings. We are currently examining more complex processes, using a pair comparison method after [10], to help build a model of subjects' mental organisation of the images, to investigate how this changes with training and time and to study how this compares to the mental map of the images used by experts. A better understanding of the process of learning histopathological microscopy will allow trainers to identify areas that students find difficult, and focus training accordingly.

As well as analysing trainee performance, we intend to seek relationships to statistical image features. Previous research [7] has shown a strong correlation between textural image features and classification, and it is reasonable to assume that these same features could be used to improve training by predicting which images trainees will find most difficult to classify or determining which features trainees and experts use to make diagnostic decisions.

This study will also continue, with testing of trainees carried out after further training and experience, to determine how the trainees improve, how to identify which trainees will develop the necessary skills and those that need more training as early as possible, and hopefully identify *why* some trainees are better at analysing tissue.

References

1. Cross, S.S., Stone, J.L.: Proactive management of histopathology workloads: analysis of the UK Royal College of Pathologists' recommendations on specimens of limited or no clinical value on the workload of a teaching hospital gastrointestinal pathology service. J Clin Pathol **55** (2002) 850–852
2. Bosman, P.F.T.: Dysplasia classification: Pathology in disgrace? Journal of Pathology **194** (2001) 143–144
3. Eaden, J., Abrams, K., McKay, H., Denley, H., Mayberry, J.: Inter-observer variation between general and specialist gastrointestinal pathologists when grading dysplasia in ulcerative colitis. Journal of Pathology **194** (2001) 152–157
4. Coppola, D., Karl, R.C.: Barrett's esophagus and barrett's-associated neoplasia: Etiology and pathologic features. Cancer Control, Journal of the Moffit Cancer Center **6** (1999)
5. Elstein, A.S., Schwarz, A.: Evidence base of clinical diagnosis: Clinical problem solving and diagnostic decision making: selective review of the cognitive literature. BMJ **324** (2002) 729–732
6. : Core training program in histopathology and related specialties. The Royal College of Pathologists (2001)
7. Shuttleworth, J.K., Todman, A.G., Naguib, R.N.G., Newman, B.M., Bennett, M.K.: Multiresolution colour texture analysis for classifying colon cancer images. In: Proceedings of the joint 4th Annual International Conference of the EMBS and Annual Fall Meeting of the BMES, Houston, USA (2002) 1118–1119

8. Todman, A.G., Naguib, R.N.G., Bennett, M.K.: Visual characterisation of colon images. In: Proceedings of Medical Image Understanding and Analysis (MIUA), Birmingham, UK (2001) 16–17
9. Tranberg, H.A., Rous, B.A., Rashbass, J.: Legal and ethical issues in the use of anonymous images in pathology teaching and research. Histopathology **42** (2003) 104–109
10. Mojsilović, A., Kovačević, J., Kall, D., Safranck, R., Ganapathy, S.K.: The vocabulary and grammar of color patterns. IEEE Transactions on Image Processing **9** (2000) 417–431

An Adaptive Rule Based Automatic Lung Nodule Detection System

Maciej Dajnowiec[1], Javad Alirezaie[1,2], and Paul Babyn[3,4]

[1] Department of Electrical and Computer Engineering, Ryerson University, Toronto, ON M5B 2K3
{mdajnowi, javad}@ee.ryerson.ca
[2] Department of Systems Design Engineering, University of Waterloo, Waterloo, ON N2L 3G1
[3] Department of Diagnostic Imaging, The Hospital for Sick Children, Toronto, ON M5G 1X8
Paul.Babyn@sickkids.ca
[4] Department of Medical Imaging, University of Toronto, Toronto, ON, M5S 3E2

Abstract. Automated lung nodule detection through computed tomography (CT) image acquisition is a new and exciting research area of medical image processing. Lung nodules are potentially cancerous growths in the lungs that often appear in CT images as distinct, high intensity spherical objects. We have developed a nodule detection system. The first stage of the nodule detection technique automatically segments the lung regions using a unique 3D region growing approach. The next stage identifies regions of interests (ROIs) by using adaptive multi-level thresholding (MLT) based on the cumulative density function (CDF) of the lung volume. The last stage reduces false positives (FPs) by using unique features such as vessel and lung wall connectivity, a modified bounding box and 3D compaction to compensate for partial volume artifacts due to thick CT slices. We obtain a sensitivity of 80% with approximately 3.05 FPs per slice.

1 Introduction

There is now significant research interest in identifying lung nodules in CT images using intelligent computer methods. CT has replaced chest radiography as the imaging modality of choice for diagnosis of lung nodules offering significant advantage in detection of small lung nodules with its good tomographic and spatial resolution. With its increase in accuracy, however, comes a significant increase in information to process. Analysis of chest radiographs involved review of only a couple of images whereas CT scans can produce in excess of several hundred images to inspect [5]. With the multiplicity of scans now performed daily this can be an overwhelming amount of data for a radiologist to review [1]. Computer aided techniques can be used as a tool to help radiologists identify lung nodules while reducing the burden of processing such large sets of information.

In particular, small lung nodules may be overlooked during diagnosis by errors in perception and the volume of information radiologists must analyze [3], [7], [8]. However detection of small nodules is important because they may represent the earliest stage of lung cancer. Lung cancer is now the most common form of cancer in both men and women [2]. It kills more people than the next three most common forms of cancer combined [8]. This emphasizes the need for finding ways to improve the diagnosis of lung cancer so it can be caught as early as possible. Early detection is the best way of increasing survival rates for lung cancer patients. The average five year survival rate of lung cancer patients is 14%, while for patients whose cancer is detected early it is 49% [8].

Segmentation techniques have already produced optimistic results in testing which indicates they can improve lung nodule detection in a clinical setting [6]. Our segmentation technique uses a MLT algorithm combined with a sequential rule based approach to reduce false positives (FPs). We focus on 5 mm thick CT slices since these are the most commonly used in general screenings. We look for nodules as small as 2.1 mm in diameter. We also use an advanced region growing technique with redundancy to include as much of the lung area in our search as possible. Our ROI approach of MLT specifically performs well in producing properly filled nodule candidates within the ROI set. In the FP reduction stage we are using a sequential rule based approach. We examine features such as contrast, lung wall and vessel connectivity, size, shape and depth in a sequential rule based approach.

2 Methods

Automatic segmentation of the lung regions from a series of CT images is the first step in developing a nodule detection technique. A threshold value is found that is based upon the complete CT data set [4]. All values above this threshold are considered to be body pixels while all the values below are considered to be non-body pixels. The lung mostly falls in the non-body category except for vessels and nodules which will exceed the threshold value. After thresholding, images from the beginning of the series are sequentially checked until two objects whose sizes exceed 1 percent of the total pixels in the image are found. This slide represents the first image where both lungs are present in the image, and are of substantial size. This slide forms the base mask from which the region growing technique extracts the remainder of the lungs. The next two slides are also obtained using the same thresholding technique and used as separate region growing masks. The reason for this being that the thresholding technique might not produce an optimum initial mask in case a vessel traverses a portion of the lung. This scenario can cut off a small piece of the lung. The exact same region growing technique is applied for all three slides independently producing three complete results. These data sets are then ORed together to produce the final result. This final result is then multiplied with the original CT series, effectively extracting the lung portion of each slide.

The region growing technique is applied using a mask image. The mask image is initially taken as the thresholded result. The lung region is filled to eliminate any holes in the lung regions (regions are defined as 8 connected in 2-D). This is done by only retaining regions that are connected to the background which exceed the threshold value. We then apply morphological operations to eliminate holes and to smooth the borders of the lungs.

The next step involves identifying the ROIs. For this we use an adaptive MLT algorithm that is applied to the original CT slices after lung segmentation. Aside from the lung segmentation no processing is done to the slices in order to prepare them for the ROI and FP reduction stages. The values in the lung are converted from their Hounsfield Unit (HU) values to gray level values.

$$gray\ level = HU + 1024 \tag{1}$$

The MLT technique uses a set of 30 thresholds. All objects above each threshold are considered to be separate ROIs. The thresholds are chosen using specific cumulative density function (CDF) values. By using the CDF our technique is adaptive making it robust to lung regions that have varied intensity distributions. We use three CDF values in order to choose our thresholds. Our top threshold is the 97.5% CDF gray level value. The middle threshold is the 92.5% CDF gray level value and the bottom threshold is the 65% CDF gray level value. The 65% CDF value is checked against an absolute bottom value of 300 which was selected as objectively the smallest gray level value which can have enough contrast with a black background to represent a feint nodule. If the 65% CDF value is larger than 300 than threshold levels in increments of 20 are used between the 65% CDF value and the 300 gray level value inclusively. Using steps of 20 is consistent with larger steps that can exist between the 92.5% and 65% CDF values. The region defined by the top and middle values produces 10 evenly spaced thresholds and the region defined by the middle and bottom values produces 20 evenly spaced thresholds. The top region defines very high intensity values producing well defined solid structures and is referred to as the vessel range. We try to identify well defined horizontal vessels and large groupings of vessels using the vessel range in addition to detecting nodule candidates. In the range between the 92.5% and 65% CDF thresholds, referred to as the nodule range, we are focusing only on nodule candidates. The vessel range ensures that only well defined, distinct high intensity structures could be considered as vessels rather than small structures joined by diffusions because only very high values thresholds are used as determined by the CDF of the lung volume. In addition, as a last stage of ROI extraction a binary image is determined by accepting pixels in the nodule range in an attempt to detect nodules that are connected to higher intensity structures and thus would not be segmented properly by traditional thresholding.

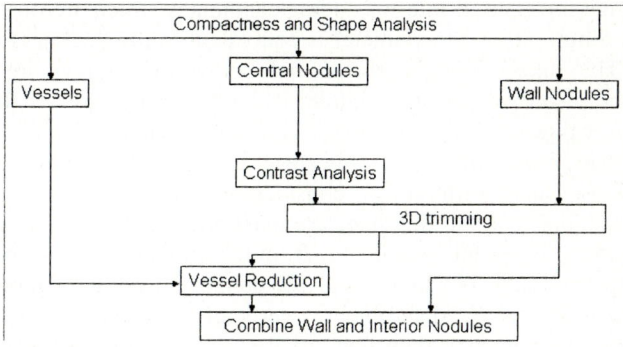

Fig. 1. An overview of the FP reduction process

The first stage of analyzing the ROIs includes obtaining a modified 2D bounding box and compactness from each nodule candidate. The modified bounding box is obtained by rotating the object based on its orientation using bi-cubic interpolation. From these modified bounding boxes the *axis ratio* and *compactness* are obtained. The *area* of the object is also obtained and is used in the FP reduction process. In our CT data sets the smallest nodule that could be detected had an area equivalent to a disk with a diameter of 2.1 mm. This represents the second time a thick slice nodule detection system has ever been able to detect nodules smaller than a 3 mm circle [3].

$$axis\ ratio = \frac{max(X\ length, Y\ length)}{min(X\ length, Y\ length)} \quad (2)$$

$$compactness = \frac{Area\ of\ Object}{Area\ of\ Bounding\ Box} \quad (3)$$

ROIs are considered potential interior nodules if their axis ratio is *below* 2, their *compactness* is greater than 0.6 and they have practically no contact with the lung wall. These values were obtained through analysis of nodule candidates in our experiments and show that interior nodules are generally compact and may exhibit some elliptical properties. At this stage we also identify vessels and vessel grouping candidates. Vessels candidates have an *axis ratio* of above 2.5 and they must be larger than a 5 mm circle ensuring only relatively large and well defined vessels are identified. By using a modified bounding box we help to identify diagonally oriented nodules and vessels by increasing their *compactness* and *axis ratio*. We also identify large groupings of vessels by finding objects which are larger than a 30 mm circle and have no more than 65% of their perimeter pixels contacting the lung walls. By using the angular orientation of the nodule candidate we are able to more accurately obtain the true *compactness* and *axis ratio* of all nodule candidates where in a normal bounding box only horizontally and vertically oriented nodules could be accurately analyzed.

We identify wall nodule candidates as those objects that have any contact with the lung walls and exceed the lung nodule minimum size criteria. Wall nodules do have to exceed a *compactness* value of 0.3; this is very lenient in order to only eliminate long curved objects that can appear along the lung wall contours.

The next stage looks at all interior nodule candidates which are one slice thick and smaller than a 5 mm circle, the diameter is equivalent to the thickness of the CT slice in the scan. The pixels directly above and below the nodule are averaged and compared to the mean value of the nodule. If the contrast is greater than 15% of the nodule's mean value or 100, whichever is smaller, than the nodule candidate is retained, otherwise it is eliminated. This stage targets small, isolated interior nodule candidates, whose main criteria for consideration is that they not be vertically connected. Candidates that fail this stage are most often vertically oriented vessels.

We now process the nodule candidates from the previous stage to better define the 3D shape of the nodules. We look at all 3D connected nodule candidates using 26 point connectivity. If any 2D slice object is vertically connected to an object which is larger than four times its size than that smaller object is eliminated. This condition attempts to better define the volumes of large nodules by pruning off small vessels, vascular objects and feint projections in adjacent slices. Once small objects are pruned the nodule candidates are once again processed, this time by keeping only those 2D slices of a nodule candidate whose areas are within 50% of the largest 2D slice of the 3D nodule candidate. This process is used to more compactly define the 3D space of a nodule, which is a particular issue when using 5 mm thick CT slices because of partial projections in slices. After this processing we have well defined 3D nodule candidates.

The next stage involves using the vessel data that we collected from the first stage. Any 3D interior nodule candidate that has a slice that is 3D connected to any of the vessels by more than half of the nodule at the connecting slice is considered to be part of the vessel and is eliminated. If the nodule candidate is only slightly connected to the vessel than this is interpreted as a weak connection and does not guarantee the nodule candidate is part of the vessel; rather, this more likely signals a vessel feeding the nodule or just one that passes near the nodule.

The next stage of the process looks at the vertical length of an interior nodule candidate and produces the nodule's *vertical ratio*.

$$vertical\ ratio = \frac{(slices-1) \times slice\ thickness}{max(X\ lengths, Y\ lengths)} \quad (4)$$

If any vertical ratio is greater than 3 then the interior nodule candidate is eliminated. The X and Y lengths are groups of values from each 2D slice of the nodule. The *vertical ratio* has a higher tolerance than the *axis ratio* because the vertical axis has larger units than the horizontal ones and thus projections in these units require a higher tolerance. In our CT slices the slice thickness is 5mm compared to approximately 0.7 mm for the X and Y dimensions of the image pixels in most cases.

The final step involves combining the wall and interior nodule candidates to provide a final set that represents the suspected nodules as defined by our system. Wall nodules are treated less strictly in the FP reduction process because they are inherently more suspicious than interior nodule candidates.

3 Results

Our results are presented through an example of the kind of nodules our system was able to detect. We then present sensitivity results along with FP statistics.

In Fig. 2 (b), our system detected three distinct types of nodules. It detected a relatively well formed nodule in the lower left portion, a tightly packed diffusion connected cluster in the bottom right and a group of spread out nodules in a diffusion in the top portion of the image. The tight cluster was actually grouped as one nodule that included the diffusion because the grouping was very compact. The nodules in the top grouping were identified individually because they were larger and more distinct than the tighter grouping.

In Fig. 3 a significantly different CT data set can be seen. The background of the image does not have the same contrast as in Fig. 2 and in the 2 slices presented there are a large number of nodules in diverse contexts. Fig. 3 (a) shows two nodules that are detected even when there is significant interference from the diaphragm. On the left side of Fig. 3 (a) the nodule is poorly formed and irregular but the system was still able to detect it, specifically because the system treats wall nodules differently from interior ones. There are many different nodules that were detected in Fig. 3 (b) such as the large wall nodule at the top left of the image. This nodule takes on the contour of the lung in this image and so makes it very elliptical. The *axis ratio* exceeds the threshold of 2 for interior nodules, but it meets the criteria of a wall nodule since for a strongly connected nodule there is no axis ratio limit. There are also opaque areas at the bottom of Fig. 3 (b) that contain nodules but with poor background contrast as compared to the slice in Fig. 2. The system was able to detect these nodules even given the challenges of an irregular background and significant interference from other vascular objects presented due to various connections to the nodules. Fig. 3 (b) also gives two examples of small wall nodules that are detected, one that is well formed and one above it that is relatively irregular and actually blends into the background the further it extends from the lung wall.

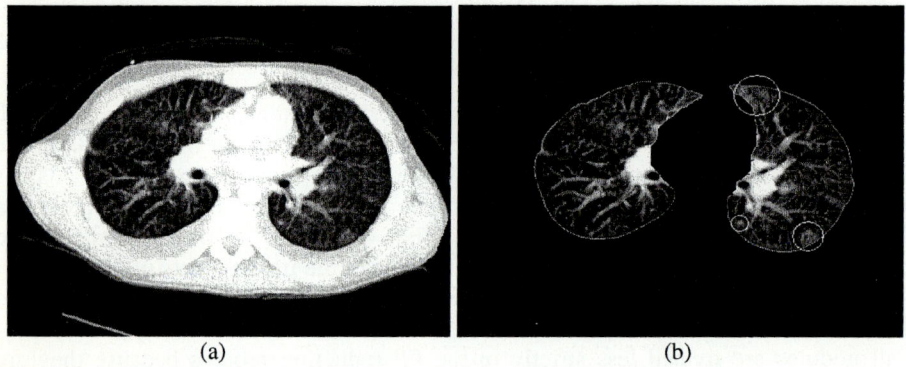

(a) (b)

Fig. 2. A sample CT slice. (a) Original CT slice. (b) Slice from (a) with lungs segmented and detection results highlighted.

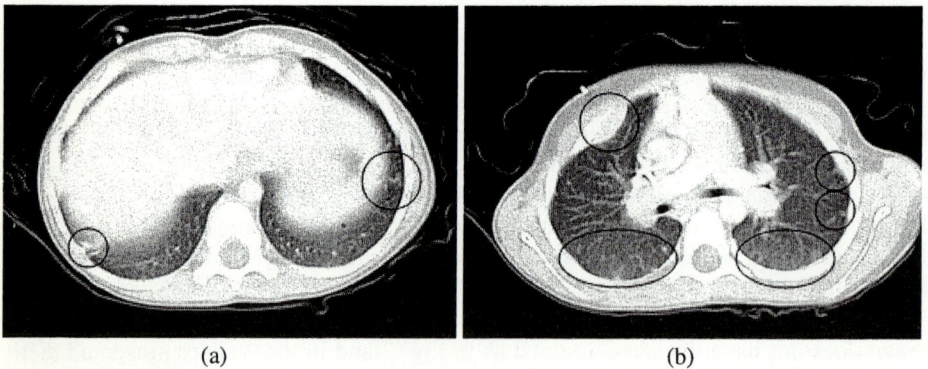

(a) (b)

Fig. 3. A pair of CT slices with a significant number of detection results highlighted

A comparison of the system to some other popular techniques is presented in table 1. At first glance our system may not appear to be among the top performers in the list but an analysis of the CT data will yield significant insight. There is only one other technique that tries to detect nodules that are smaller than a 3 mm circle using thick slice CT scans and that is the one developed by *Gurcan et al.* [3]. However, their own data set consists of only 63 nodules, 15 of which are smaller than a 4 mm circle. Our data set consists of 239 nodules, with 41 nodules being smaller than a 4 mm circle. Of these 41 nodules, 28 fell below our own minimum size criteria. This is a significantly larger and more challenging data set than the one used by *Gurcan et al.* [3] based on the number of nodules used and the number of small nodules present. In fact any of the 41 small nodules in our CT data set would not be detected by the system developed by *Kanazawa et al.* listed in table 1 as they all only target nodules larger than a 4 mm circle [5]. That means, even with perfect sensitivity performance on the nodules they could detect, based on size they could do no better than a sensitivity of 83%. Of the different techniques mentioned, the system developed by *Armato et al* actually had the most similar data set as they used 17 CT scans with a total of 187 nodules, compared with our own data that consists of 19 CT scans and 239 total nodules. Our system's performance when compared to that technique is actually very promising.

Table 1. A comparison of different reported lung nodule CAD systems [1], [3], [5], [8]

CT study	Sensitivity	FPs
Armato et al.	70%	3.0/slice
Gurcan et al.	84%	1.74/slice
Kanazawa et al.	90%	8.6/case
Zhao et al.	84.2%	5.0/case
Our approach	80%	3.0/slice

A look at table 2 shows a detailed, case by case, analysis of our system's performance. The sensitivity performance is shown to be approximately 80% with 3.05 FPs per slice (2891/947). The FP performance ranges significantly with a minimum of 1.46 and a maximum of 6.55. This shows how dependant the FP performance is on the actual CT data set. There is some correlation between the number of nodules and the number of FPs but there are also clear exceptions to the attempt at linking more nodules with higher FPs per slice. In fact, case ID58F had only one nodule but there were 4.89 FPs per slice, where case FB3F had 34 nodules, the third highest among cases, but only 1.98 FPs per slice. The variety between cases is significant as they range between 0 and 103 nodules. On a case by case basis the performance of the system ranged between 67% and 90%, which is a significantly smaller variance than the FP performance. The use of our tight bounding box helped to reduce FPs by an average of 10% when compared to a traditional bounding box approach. In addition the diversity and size of our data set reflects the importance we have placed in a robust data set to produce meaningful experimental result. Other systems have been shown to practically fail using a different data set, where initial testing showed excellent sensitivity and FP performance [3].

Table 2. A detailed presentation of the nodule detection system's performance on a case by case basis

Case	# of nodules	# detected	Sensitivity	FPs / slice
FB1F	1	0	0.00%	2.23
FB2F	0	0	N/A	1.46
FB3F	34	25	73.53%	1.98
FB4F	1	1	100.00%	1.80
FB5F	1	0	0.00%	2.07
FB6F	13	9	69.23%	3.33
FB7F	0	0	N/A	4.11
FB8F	1	1	100.00%	3.09
FB9F	8	6	75.00%	2.25
FB10F	1	0	0.00%	3.77
ID101F	58	52	89.66%	5.68
ID51F	0	0	N/A	4.06
ID52F	103	85	82.52%	6.55
ID53F	13	10	76.92%	3.20
ID54F	1	0	0.00%	3.76
ID55F	0	0	N/A	1.84
ID56F	0	0	N/A	2.07
ID57F	3	2	66.67%	2.18
ID58F	1	0	0.00%	4.89
Total	239	191	79.92%	3.05

4 Discussion and Conclusions

Our lung segmentation technique evolved from our analysis of a paper that was focused on lung segmentation [4]. Automatic lung segmentation is a crucial first stage in the nodule identification process because the segmentation needs to present a good representation of the lungs. The results of our technique are encouraging and it addresses the issue of including the top and bottom of the lungs as their volume decreases. This issue is resolved by using 3-D region growing to include connected components. Our technique also successfully retains disconnected components of the lung by using a combination of region growing and redundancy in the mask image used for region growing.

We are very encouraged by the performance of our ROI detection algorithm. The algorithm is more thorough and unique compared to those found in past techniques through its use of non-linear adaptive thresholding [2]. Through our experience, this approach does a good job of providing very full representations of nodules. This is important for the rule set because we have a good idea of what 2-D slices of nodules will look like coming out of the ROI stage. In addition the technique allows us to detect vessels by identifying a subset of thresholds where vessels are likely to be present. One of the major shortfalls of the MLT approach is that nodules connected to higher intensity objects can not be properly segmented from them. This is an issue that is important in future development of the system. As a precursor to this development our system also includes a single thresholding stage that identifies pixels within the nodule range rather than using a binary threshold limit to get an intensity mapping of ROIs. This approach can be expanded upon and an ROI extraction process that uses ranges rather than single value thresholds can be developed and evaluated. ROI extraction is a crucial step as accurate representations of lung volume objects is crucial to having good nodule detection results.

For FP reduction we have introduced the idea of identifying vessels in order to use their connectivity with nodule candidates to reduce FPs. We have also produced a modified bounding box which does a better job of characterizing lung nodules which have a non-trivial angular orientation. Our system is only the second system that can detect nodules smaller than a 3 mm circle using thick slice CT scans and between us we have had the opportunity to use a significantly larger data set for testing. One of the major challenges for our system is to reduce the number of FPs. Our sensitivity performance is very good, given the context of our data set, and so the focus of future development will be on improving FP reduction. Other techniques [1],[3] have successfully used linear discriminant analysis (LDA) to improve FP performance and exploring this technique is of immediate interest in our development of the system. In addition, more features for the nodule candidates will be examined with a focus on providing contextual information for the FP reduction system. Improving the contextual understanding of nodule candidates is the single most important area we need to improve upon in order to advance the FP reduction system.

The potential of our nodule detection technique is looking very promising as an aid for radiologists in detecting lung nodules. Our technique offers many innovative new stages that can be built upon and used by others in existing techniques to improve lung nodule detection. In addition there are many promising avenues of research to pursue in an attempt to improve the system.

References

1. S. G. Armato III, M. L. Giger, C. J. Morgan, J. T. Blackburn, K.Doi, and H. MacMahon, "Computerized Detection of Pulmonary Nodules on CT Scans", *Imaging and Therapeutic Technology*, RSNA, pp. 1303-1311, 1999
2. M. S. Brown, M. F. McNitt-Gray, J. G. Goldin, R. D. Suh, J. W. Sayre, and D. R. Aberle, "Patient-Specific Models for Lung Nodule Detection and Surveillance in CT Images", *IEEE Transactions on Medical Imaging*, Vol. 20, No. 12, pp. 1242-1250, December, 2001
3. M. N. Gurcan, B. Sahiner, N. Petrick, H. Chan, E. A. Kazerooni, P. N. Cascade, and L. Hadjiiski, "Lung Nodule Detection on Thoracic Computed Tomography Images: Preliminary Evaluation of a Computer-Aided Diagnosis System", *Medical Physics*, Vol. 29, No. 11, pp. 2552-2558, November 2002
4. S. Hu, E. A. Hoffman, and J. M. Reinhardt, "Automatic Lung Segmentation of Accurate Quantitation of Volumetric X-Ray CT Images", *IEEE Transactions on Medical Imaging*, Vol. 20, No. 6, pp. 490-498, June 2001

5. K. Kanazawa, Y. Kawata, N. Niki, H. Satoh, H. Ohmatsu, and R. Kakinuma, "Computer-aided Diagnosis for Pulmonary Nodules Based on Helical CT Images", *Proceedings* of the *International Conference on Pattern Recognition*, Vol. 2, pp. 1683-1685, Aug. 1998
6. D.T. Lin, C.R. Yan, and Lung Nodules, "Lung Nodules Identification Rules Extraction with Neural Fuzzy Network", *Proceedings of the International Conference on Neural Information Processing*, Vol. 4, pp. 2049-2053, Nov. 2002
7. W.A.H. Mousa, and M.A.U. Khan, "Lung Nodule Classification utilizing Support Vector Machines", *Proceedings* of the *International Conference on Image Processing*, Vol. 3, pp. 153-156, June 2002
8. B. Zhao, G. Gamsu, M. S. Ginsberg, L. Jiang, and L. H. Schwartz, "Automatic Detection of Small Lung Nodules on CT Utilizing a Local Density Maximum Algorithm", *Journal of Applied Clinical Medical Physics*, Vol. 4, No. 3, pp. 248-260, Summer 2003

Experiments with SVM and Stratified Sampling with an Imbalanced Problem: Detection of Intestinal Contractions

Fernando Vilariño, Panagiota Spyridonos, Jordi Vitrià, and Petia Radeva

Computer Vision Center. Universitat Autònoma de Barcelona,
Bellaterra 08193, Spain
fernando@cvc.uab.es
http://www.cvc.uab.es/~fernando

Abstract. In this paper we show some preliminary results of our research in the fieldwork of classification of imbalanced datasets with SVM and stratified sampling. Our main goal is to deal with the clinical problem of automatic intestinal contractions detection in endoscopic video images. The prevalence of contractions is very low, and this yields to highly skewed training sets. Stratified sampling together with SVM have been reported in the literature to behave well in this kind of problems. We applied both the SMOTE algorithm developed by Chawla et al. and under-sampling, in a cascade system implementation to deal with the skewed training sets in the final SVM classifier. We show comparative results for both sampling techniques using precision-recall curves, which appear to be useful tools for performance testing.

1 Introduction

Automatic detection of intestinal contractions is one paradigmatic example of classification with imbalanced datasets. Its prevalence is very low, and the data analysis requires high amounts of expert time.

Both the number of intestinal contractions, and their temporal distribution along the intestinal tract, characterize small bowel motility patterns that are indicative of the presence of different malfunctions. Different techniques have been applied for intestinal motility analysis in several medical imaging modalities. A good review about this issue can be found in [1].

The novelty of our research in this fieldwork relies on the use of Wireless Capsule Video Endoscopy images (WCVE) [2,3,4]. In this clinical domain, the specialist has to analyze a video, and manually label each frame where a contraction event happens. Usually, each video analysis may last one or two hours, and among a typical quantity of 20,000 frames, only 700 contractions are reported.

We focused our efforts on the automatic detection of intestinal contractions using video as data source. We have trained a SVM system with contraction and non-contractions frames from several videos, previously labelled by hand by the experts. The choice of SVM [5] is underpinned by the fact that empirical results show a good behavior of this technique with moderate skewed datasets. Recently, several methods have been developed to improve the performance of SVM classifiers on imbalanced problems [6,7]. Stratified sampling is based on re-sampling the original datasets in different ways: under-sampling the majority class or over-sampling the minority class. In this work, we show the preliminary results of a comparative study of under-sampling vs. SMOTE over-sampling technique [8]. Both techniques SVM and other popular single classifiers have been applied. With the purpose of reducing the imbalanced character of the datasets, we use a 2-steps cascade methodology that prunes false positives without loosing sensitivity.

In order to assess the performance of the different methods implemented, precision-recall curves are proposed. The main advantage of these plots is that they show both the sensitivity of the system and the noise introduced. A detailed explanation of the utility of these plots for imbalanced dataset is also developed.

The rest of the paper is organized as follows: Section 2 introduces the methodology used: the data description and the feature set, and describes the classification system. Section 3 shows the comparative results for several single classifiers and SVM, using different sampling methodologies. Finally, Section 4 is devoted to the discussion of results and suggestions for further research.

2 Methodology

2.1 Intestinal Contractions

Intestinal contractions are a dynamic event. The expert labels a frame in a video as a contraction if it corresponds to a temporal pattern that spans 9 frames as an average -corresponding to 5 seconds in real time-. The frame labelled as contraction is, therefore, the central frame of a sequence of 9 frames. Several examples of intestinal contractions can be found in Fig. 1.

With the aim of automatically detecting intestinal contractions, for each frame, 6 features were calculated based on well known intensity and texture descriptors: normalized intensity, contrast, hole detection based on a Laplacian filtering and 3 values from concurrence matrices. We build up a feature vector of

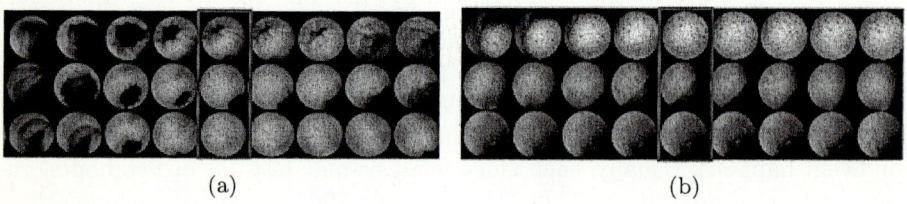

(a) (b)

Fig. 1. Video sequences obtained from wireless capsule endoscopy: typical patterns of contractions (a) and non-contractions (b) for 3 sequences of 9 frames. The central frame of these sequences is presented bounded by a rectangle.

6x9 features, associating with each frame the dynamic information of the whole sequence. All the chosen features are popular standard descriptors exhaustively used and referenced in the image analysis and computer vision literature [9,10]. As far as we know, no previous works have been published to describe the kind of intestinal events we are dealing with in this sort of image acquisition technology. We are developing our project in a continuous contact with the clinical experts, and on each research step, new information is added from the expert's knowledge about different typologies of contraction events. So, our aim is to get the most general and flexible feature set, so as to be adaptable to this dynamic scenario. We reached this optimal set through an exhaustive heuristic search achieved through the repetition of several experiments, and the analysis of the relevance of each feature for classification.

2.2 Classification System

Each video typically has 20,000 frames, among which only around 500 contractions are to be found. Since the system should classify all these 20,000 frames as contractions or as non-contractions, a highly skewed problem is presented. We adopted a pre-classification step with the aim of eliminating as many false positives as possible from the original video, without loosing many true contractions. This first stage was implemented in the following way: we consider each one of the features as single values that can be used to divide video frames into contractions and non-contractions using a single threshold. When a threshold is applied, all the video frames are divided into two separated sets: the positives, that will pass to the next step of the system, and the negatives that will be definitely rejected. We expect that most of the contractions of our video will lay in the positive set, and that many of the non-contractions will fall on the negative set. In order to guarantee this, we looked for the threshold value of every feature that kept the 99% of contractions in the positive set. Next, among all thresholds, we selected the one less non-contractions in the positive set. With this simple method, a ratio of 1:5 in the proportion between contractions and non-contractions was achieved. This strategy helps us to bound the knowledge that the classifier acquires from the video frames, in an attempt to reduce the variability of the samples in the decision space.

The second stage of the classification system was the SVM, trained only with the frames that passed the first stage. We used a radial basis function kernel (RBF) with g=0.01. Most classifiers tend to classify everything as the majority class -negative- as the imbalanced character is accented, so this is the optimal solution in terms of global error. For this kind of imbalanced problems, the performance of the SVM is less sensitive, as the classification strategy is based only on some samples -the support vectors- and the rest of the samples have no influence. However, several studies seem to show that stratified sampling is a useful tool for improving the final decision border in SVM [11,6]. We tested two different strategies of sampling: under-sampling the majority class and over-sampling with the SMOTE technique.

3 Experimental Results

For our experiments, 8 videos of 1-2 hours of length were used. These videos were labelled by the experts, identifying the frames where the contractions were present. An average of 500 contractions were labelled by the expert in each video. We applied the leave-one-out method: each run, one video was used for testing and the rest for training, in a resulting number of 8 runs. On each run, the threshold for the first step was calculated, and the SVM was trained exclusively with the frames that passed the first stage. We also trained a set of popular single classifiers for comparison purposes: linear, logistic, and 1,5,and 10 nearest neighbor (1-NN, 5-NN, 10-NN) [12].

Two sampling methods were tested: under-sampling and SMOTE. For under-sampling, we trained the classifiers choosing randomly from the training set a number of non-contractions equal to that of contractions, so the final training set for each leave-one-out run was build up with 500x7 contractions and the same number of non-contractions -around 7,000 training samples. For SMOTE, we replicated the positive samples up to the number of non-contractions. Since around 2,500 frames typically pass the first stage, this yields to a training set of around 35,000 samples. The discussion section analyzes this point, which deserves special attention.

We carried out our experiments in order to answer two main questions: 1) In what measure the sampling technique used affects the performance of the classifiers tested, and 2) In what measure SVM outperforms the rest of classifiers for our dataset. With the aim of illustrating both questions, we use the precision-recall curves *pr-curve*, that is a standard evaluation technique in the information retrieval community [13]. *Precision* is a measure in the interval [0,1] defined as the ratio of true positives detected over all the system output. It will be one when the system detects only positives, and zero when the system detects only negatives. In this way, a low precision value is associated with a high number of false positives, and it can be viewed as a measure of noise at the output stage. *Recall* -also known as *sensitivity*- is a measure in the interval [0,1] defined as the ratio of true positives detected over the total number of positives. It will be 1 when the system detects all the existing positives, and zero when no positive is detected. For imbalanced problems, both measures together give more information than ROC curves. In ROC curves [14,15], precision is substituted by 1-specificity, or false positive ratio, and so the proportion between positives and negatives is not taken into account.

In order to give response to question 1, comparative plots are presented in Fig. 2. We can see that no substantial improvement is achieved by any of both sampling techniques, neither for single classifiers nor for the SVM, and the classifiers performance seems to be quite invariant to the sample method. Regarding the performance of SVM with respect to the rest of the classifiers, both for under-sampling and SMOTE, SVM outperforms their competitors. Fig. 3 shows that only for low levels of recall -when almost no positive is detected- NN classifiers appear to be competitive. A quantitative approach can be analyzed by means of the area under the PR curve (AUPRC). The AUPRC gives us a metric

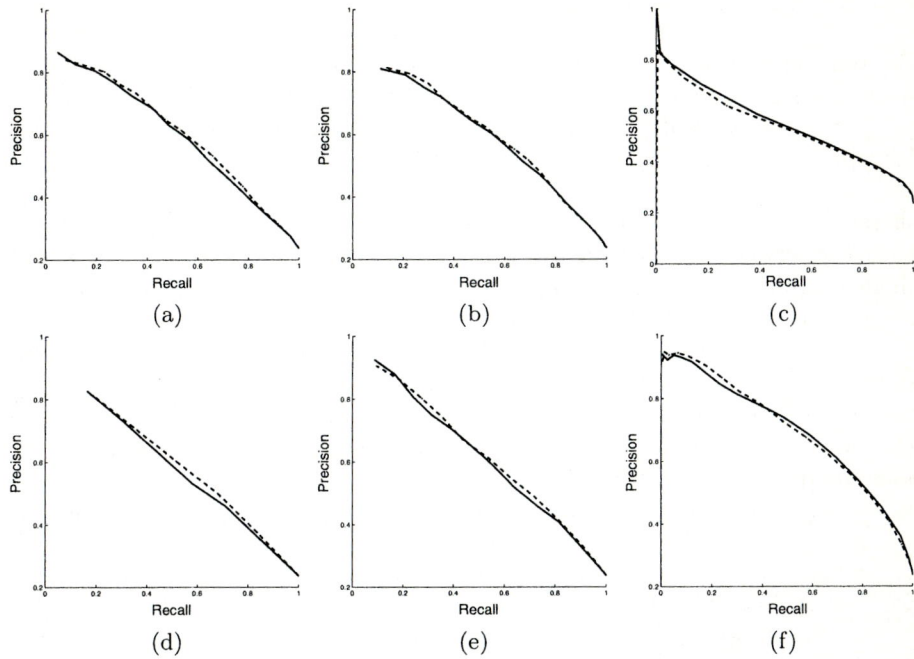

Fig. 2. Under-sampling (dashed) vs. SMOTE over-sampling (solid) for detection of intestinal contractions with several classifiers. (a) linear, (b) logistic, (c) 1-NN, (d) 5-NN, (e) 10-NN, (f) SVM.

for assessing the classifier performance. We calculated it using the polygonal rule, in the same way as it is done for the calculus of the area under a ROC curve [16]. Table 1 shows the AUPRC related to the graphs in Fig. 3.

Several important conclusions can be inferred from these results, which deserve special attention so next section is devoted to their analysis.

4 Discussion

We presented some preliminary results of our research in the automatic detection of intestinal contractions in video endoscopy, a highly imbalanced problem due to the low prevalence of contractions in video. In order to implement a classification system, a set of classical image descriptors based on luminance, contrast and texture was associated to each frame. The dynamic behavior was taken into account building up feature vectors containing all these basic descriptors for each one of the frames in a $+/-4$ frame neighborhood.

One of the main characteristics of our system is the cascade implementation. In a first step, we make an exhaustive search of a single threshold in the feature space that keeps the 99% of contractions and rejects the majority of the non-contractions. The video frames passing this threshold are sent to the second step,

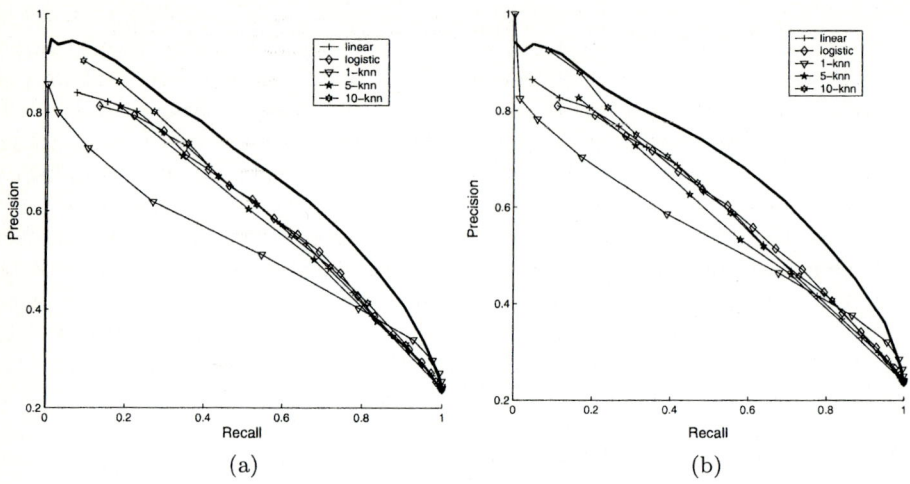

Fig. 3. Single classifiers vs. SVM (solid line) for (a) under-sampling and (b) SMOTE

Table 1. AUPRC for under-sampling and SMOTE experiments of Fig. 3. SVM outperforms all the rest in both cases.

Classifier	AUPRC Under-samp.	AUPRC SMOTE
Linear	0.6100	0.6021
Logistic	0.6067	0.6006
1-NN	0.5324	0.5485
5-NN	0.5946	0.5849
10-NN	0.6282	0.6216
SVM	**0.6934**	**0.6946**

consisting of a SVM classifier. It can be affirmed that this way of operating with imbalanced problems constitutes a rapid and efficient way of reducing the total number of false positives, i.e., reducing the ratio of the imbalanced datasets.

The plots of section 3 show a comparative study between two different methods of sampling: under-sampling the majority class and over-sampling the minority class, both for single classifiers and SVM. The choice of these single classifiers is due to two important reasons: 1) On the one hand, linear and logistic classifiers are simple and fast; K-NN is a non-parametric technique that makes no assumption over the probability density function; we aimed at finding out if there was the same difference in behavior with these classifiers in order to infer conclusion for the SVM. 2) On the other hand, for the SMOTE implementation the training set typically has around 35,000 samples in a 54 feature space. In this situation, most of the software implementations -PRTools were used [17]- did not present the possibility of testing some common classifiers such as Parzen or decision trees owing to this huge amount of data.

In this point, recent works have tested SMOTE with several classifiers in common public databases, such as UCI [8,6], showing improvement with respect to under-sampling in some experiments. The results seem to show that for our problem, not a hard assessment can be done in order to affirm that SMOTE outperforms under-sampling -maybe, slightly in the best of cases-. It must be pointed out that the aim of SMOTE is to provide a sufficient quantity of minority class samples to equilibrate the number of samples for the negative class. But this is not the only important issue: special attention must be paid to the fact that when we have very few samples for the minority class, they may not be enough to reconstruct the probability density function underlying them, which is basically the role of SMOTE. We suggest that this is the case of our data set, as well as of other examples presented in the papers mentioned above. Our efforts are focused on the research of this point and the theoretical and empirical confirmation of this hypothesis.

The final results of our SVM classifier outperform all the remaining classifiers. This fact has been illustrated by means of the precision-recall curves that are presented as a useful tool for the assessment of imbalanced problems. In terms of operating points, the plot in Fig. 3(b) shows that with an 80% of detection of all the existent contractions in the video, a 40% of detections is found in the system output. This appears to be a promising result that motivates us to follow this line of research improving the system, testing new classifiers and sampling methodologies.

The aim of this paper is twofold: 1) On the one hand to present our preliminary results showing that SVM outperforms the best of single classifiers used for this particular imbalanced problem of intestinal contractions. 2) On the other hand, to show that both sampling techniques used in this work yield to similar results for SVM. We cannot avoid deepening in the analysis of the consequences associated with our results. In fact, if the different sampling techniques used appear to have no effect in the final performance of the system, it is due to some relevant characteristics of our specific problem, closely related to the statistical properties underlying our datasets. Moreover, the sampling techniques we use, which seem to work for other studies -some of them already referenced in this paper-, appear to give no performance improvement for our problem. This is a very challenging and interesting line of work, in which our group is completely involved.

We could re-formulate last paragraph into the next question: "Why is performance improving using one sampling method problem-dependent in SVM with imbalanced datasets?". In this sense, the next experiment is to be of high interest and can help us to shed light in this scenario: Let us consider that we have two imbalanced datasets with samples N1 for the minority class -positives, contractions-, and N2 for the majority class -negatives, non-contractions- and, consequently N1≪N2 (this is the typical scenario of an imbalance problem). Now, keep N1 fixed and under-sample from N2 several times, to generate a smaller number of samples for training the classifier. Our purpose focuses on seeing the extent to which SVM is better as the skew or imbalance gets worse. The same experiment can be repeated over-sampling N1. This analysis is extremely important to draw any firm conclusions about classification performance. Nevertheless, the inference that can be obtained from it is not so straightforward, and it is worthy of special and subtle attention. In this point, and in order to understand why a specific classification performance is achieved, two main questions should be stated: how the data distribution *around the decision border* is for *both* datasets, and how *descriptive* the positive samples are for the probability density function (PDF) of its class. Why? The first question is strictly related to the decision of the margins for the SVM, the second one is strictly related to the way in which over-sampling will perform. This analytical study is of high relevance, but it also holds intrinsic difficulties related to the statistical description and the geometrical analysis necessary to understand how the real distribution of the whole data in the n-feature space is, an how well the distribution provided by the samples we use for training fits the real PDF of the minority class. Finally an equally interesting question is open: how the choice of the sigma parameter in the SVM may affect the final performance of the classification in this scenario. We are preparing a more extended work with all these points of study, including the proposed experiment for a further piece of research.

Finally, one of the main objectives of our future work aims at addressing the feature extraction problem, in order to achieve better descriptors for the intestinal contraction events, as well as deepening into the achievement of the optimal set of features that we need in order to properly describe an intestinal contraction -i.e., the feature selection problem-. We expect that our collaboration with the clinical experts will help us to advance in this challenging fieldwork, which is of vital importance for an optimal result.

References

1. Hansen, M.B. Small Intestinal Manometry. Physiological Research. 2002. 51, pp: 541-556.
2. Schulmann, S.K., Hollerbach M.D., et al. Feasibility and diagnostic of video capsule endoscopy for small bowel polyps. American Journal of Gastroenterollogy. 2005.
3. Brodsky, L. M. Wireless capsule endoscopy. Issues in Emerging Health Technologies. CCOHTA. 53. 2003.
4. Eliakim, R. Wireless capsule video endoscopy: Three years of experience. World journal of Gastroenterology. 2004. 10, pp: 1238-1239.
5. Vapnik, V. The nature of Statistical Learning Theory. Springer-Verlag, Ny. USA. 1995.
6. Akbani, R. Kwek, S., Japkowicz, N. Applying Support Vector Machines to Imbalanced Datasets. European Conference on Machine Learning. 2004. pp: 39–50.
7. Brank, J. Grobelnik, M. et al. Training text classifiers with SVM on very few positive examples. 2003. Technical Report MSR-TR-2003-34.
8. Chawla, N., Hall, L., Kegelmeyer, W. SMOTE: Synthetic Minority Over-sampling Technique. Journal of Artificial Intelligence Research. 2002. 16, pp: 341-378.
9. Gonzalez, R.C., Woods, R.E. Digital Image Processing. Prentice Hall. 2nd ed. 2002.
10. Russ, J., C. The Image Processing Handbook. IEEE Press. 2nd ed. 1994.

11. Crone, S. F., Lessmann, S., Stahlbock, R. Empirical Comparison and Evaluation of Classifier Performance for Data Mining in Customer Relationship Management. 3rd International Conference on KDDM. 1997.
12. Duda, R., O., Hart, P., E., Stork, D., G. Pattern Classification. Willey Inter-Science. Willey & Sons, Inc. 2001.
13. Van Rijsbergen, C. Information Retrieval. Dept. of Computer Science, University of Glasgow. 1979.
14. Metz, C. Basic Principles of ROC Analysis. Seminars on Nuclear Medicine. 1978. 8, pp: 283-298.
15. Swets, J., Pickett, R. Evaluation of Diagnostic Systems: Methods for Signal Detection Theory. New York. Academic Press. 1982.
16. Bradley, A. The Use of the Area Under the ROC Curve in the Evaluation of Machine Learning Algorithms. Pattern Recognition. 1997. 30, pp: 1145-1159.
17. Duin, R.P.W., Juszczak, P., Paclik, P., Pekalska, E., Ridder, D.M.J. Tax, PRTools4, A Matlab toolbox for pattern recognition, Delft University of Technology. 2004.

Multiple Particle Tracking for Live Cell Imaging with Green Fluorescent Protein (GFP) Tagged Videos

Sameer Singh[1], Harish Bhaskar[1], Jeremy Tavare[2], and Gavin Welsh[2]

[1] ATR Labs, Research School of Informatics, Loughborough University, UK
[2] Dept. of Biochemistry, School of Medical Sciences, University of Bristol, UK

Abstract. Particle tracking is important for understanding the mobile behaviour of objects of varying sizes in a range of physical and biological science applications. In this paper we present a new algorithm for tracking cellular particles imaged using a confocal microscope. The algorithm performs adaptive image segmentation to identify objects for tracking and uses intelligent estimates of neighbourhood search, spatial relationship, velocity, direction estimates, and shape/size estimates to perform robust tracking. Our tracker is tested on three videos for vesicle tracking in GFP tagged videos. The results are compared to the popular Harvard tracker and we show that our tracking scheme offers better performance and flexibility for tracking.

Keywords: Particle tracker, Vesicles, Insulin, Diabetes, Confocal Microscopy, Image Analysis.

1 A Novel Multiple Particle Tracker

Particle tracking has been used recently in a number of contexts. These include, but are not limited to: (a) Tracking and analyzing bacterial motion (Soni et al., 2003); (b) Analysis of nonhomogeneous spatial distribution of cytoskeletal polymers such as F-actin, microtubules, and intermediate filament and their auxiliary proteins by tracking microspheres (Tseng et al., 2002); (c) Protein or lipid tracking (Vrljic et al.); (d) Tracking single chromaffin granules beneath the plasma membrane in three dimensions (Qian, 2000); (e) Determining the relation between the degree of spatial heterogeneity and the mechanical properties of cross-linked actin filament networks (Tseng and Wirtz, 2001); (e) Tracking the sub-micron motion of individual organelles, microspheres, and molecules under microscopic observation (Cheezum et al., 2001); and (f) Tracking animal or insect colonies (Khan et al., 2003); (g) Genetic material tracking (Babcock et al. , 2004).

In this study we propose a novel particle tracker. The algorithm is capable of tracking multiple particles simultaneously and improves upon the image processing component of traditional trackers. The proposed tracker performs better quality image segmentation to ensure that all particles are properly identified. The tracking process uses a range of intelligent criteria to ensure that particles are not lost especially if they are travelling at multiple speeds and randomly accelerate. We first present the algorithm of our tracking procedure and then highlight its major strengths in comparison with Harvard tracker developed by researchers at Harvard University,Berg(2000)http://webmac.rowland.org/labs/bacteria/index_software.html.

A detailed comparison with Harvard tracker on experimental results follows in section IV.

Algorithm: Intelligent Particle Tracker

1) Take input from the user on their choice to track either all particles in the video or a selected number of particles through mouse input. The user also enters the name of a text file that contains the inputs to the system. The contents of the file includes: Input file name, Output file name, Thresholding cut-off, Starting frame number, End frame number, Frame rate, Scale of the video, Search radius, Velocity threshold and Velocity Thresholding state. The text file can either contain a single video clip of all the frames or a collection of small clips involving a subset of frames

2) Input Processing Module: This module accepts all user-defined parameters and integrates calls to other sub modules of the system. This procedure is looped across different clips as mentioned in the input text file. The various function calls include: Video Pre-processing module, Particle tracking module, Output display module and Statistics computation module.

3) Video Pre-processing Module: This module pre-processes the video clip to required specifications of the system. Pre-processing steps include:

    a) Generation of information from the original video such as number of frames, height and width of the video frames, etc.

    b) Repeat across all frames of the video and
        i. Perform adaptive thresholding (conversion into a binary image) of individual frames (Yasuda et al., 1980). Let us denote these N particles in the first frame of a video as $(p_1,..., p_N)$.
        ii. Also discard objects of size less than 2pixels.
        iii. Label all objects in the image with a unique address that remains the same as the object is tracked.
        iv. Generate region properties of the objects in the image such as area, shape, histogram information, etc.

4) Particle Tracking Module: This module is central to the tracking mechanism involved in the system. The module accepts the information on particles that need to be tracked from the previous step. This requires the following sub-processes.

a): Store the values of the coordinates of all objects in all frames into x and y variables.

b): If the particles are denoted as $(p_1,..., p_N)$, that can be represented as $(p_1^t,..., p_N^t)$ at time t, then track these as follows:

    i. For all particles p_i^t, if their position in frame t (x_i^t, y_i^t) is given by coordinates (x_i^t, y_i^t), then consider a search radius of size R with (x_i^t, y_i^t) as the centroid in frame $t+1$.

ii. Find the number of particles in this search radius. A total of M particles within this search radius can be represented as $(q_1,...q_j...,q_M)$, for $M \geq 0$. If $M = 0$, then follow step 4(e) of this algorithm. Otherwise, compute a vector of similarity between p_i^t and $(q_1,...,q_M)$. The similarity between each particle pairing is computed based on area, distance, shape, and histogram similarity using purity estimate of histogram (Singh and Singh, 2004). If these estimates for particle p_i^t are given as $p_i^t(A)$, $p_i^t(d)$, $p_i^t(S)$ and $p_i^t(H)$, and similarly for particle q_j^t are given as $q_i^t(A)$, $q_i^t(d)$, $q_i^t(S)$ and $q_i^t(H)$, and if these estimates are within [0,1] range, then the overall similarity is given by:

$$S = \sqrt{w_1(p_i^t(A)-q_i^t(A))^2 + w_2(p_i^t(d)-q_i^t(d))^2 + w_3(p_i^t(S)-q_i^t(S))^2 + w_4(p_i^t(H)-q_i^t(H))^2}.$$

The area estimates are normalised to be between [0,1] range, whereas shape and histogram purity measures are normally defined to lie within this range automatically. The weights are normally set to be the same for all similarity estimates except for distance matching that has higher weight.

iii. Link particle p_i^t to particle q_j^t for which S is the least.

e): If no matching particle is found within the search radius, i.e. either there is no particle within the search radius or those found can be better linked with other particles, then use directionality estimates to search for the best suited particle. For this purpose, do the following:

i. Calculate the direction of movement as the slope of the trajectory between particle p_i^t position in frame t and the previous frame $t-1$. If the angle of movement is angle θ between the line and the horizontal axis, then search for available orphans within en envelope of $(\theta - 45°, \theta + 45°)$ (see Figure 1(b)). This is based on the observation that particles do not move outside this envelope; the size of the envelope can also be increased if needed.

ii. An orphan O_k^t at time t is defined as a particle that has no linked path to previous frame. These orphans are not linked to a trajectory since they might have been lost in the tracking process or these might be new particles entering the image. The similarity metric S defined in step 4(d) is now performed for matching the particle to all orphans within the search envelope.

5) Output Display Module: The output display module is responsible for displaying and recording the output of the tracking process as made in the previous stage. The output of this module is a set of trajectory plots.

6) Statistics Computation Module: The purpose of the module is to derive various critical statistics from the tracking process on the video. The current set of statistics that the module has been trained to derive include: average speed of particles, standard deviation of the speed of particles, total number of objects in the video,

number of objects considered moving in the video, percentage of objects moving, directionality of objects in angles, displacement vector of objects in each frame, area, centroid, Convex Hull, Euler Number, Convex Image, Extrema, Bounding Box, Convex Area, Equiv Diameter, SubarrayIdx, Image, Solidity, Major Axis Length, Pixel List, Extent, Minor Axis Length, Pixel Idx List, Filled Image, Orientation, Filled Area and Eccentricity, Shape measure, of objects in each frame of the video.

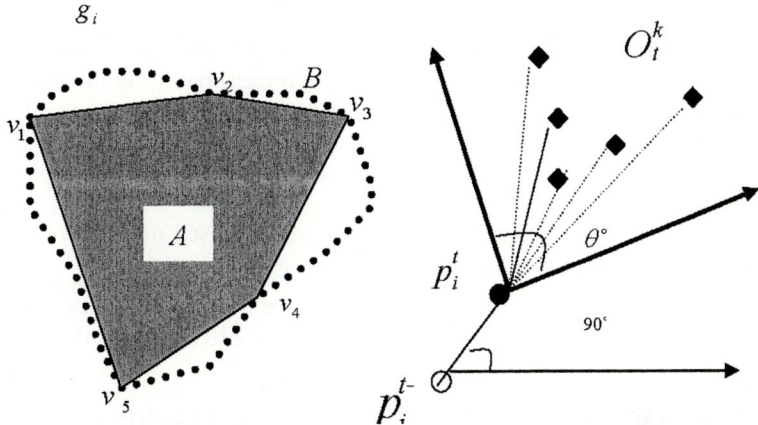

Fig. 1. The computation of the shape measure (a), and tracking objects outside search radius (b)

In this paper we propose a new measure of shape that is used in our particle tracking system. Each object is first segmented and edge traced to find its boundary. If the N boundary pixels on the object of interest B are given as $(g_1,...,g_N)$, then their curvature at each pixel is calculated as $(c_1,...,c_N)$. Starting with the first five pixels with the highest curvature, these pixels are joined together to form a closed polygon A (see Figure 1(b)). When a total of i pixels are joined together to form this polygon, which has area a_i for the closed polygon, and area b for the object of interest, and their overlap (common) area equals h_i, then an estimate of the amount of overlap can be calculated as $s_i = 2(h_i)/(a_i + b)$. As $i \rightarrow N$, $s_i \rightarrow 1$. If i is scaled to lie between [0,1], and since s_i already lies between [0,1] range, the area under the curve S that plots s_i on the vertical axis, and i on the horizontal axis, is an effective shape measure. It is unique for different shapes. Shapes that have too many high curvature points need more complex polygons to fit them (high value of $i \rightarrow N$ before s_i approaches unity), and will have a smaller value of S compared to shapes will less number of high curvature points on the boundary. Furthermore, the values of s_i can be weighted if needed to give more weight to high or low curvature points as needed.

Our model has several important differences compared to the popular Harvard tracker which is also based on the concept of nearest neighbour based particle tracking. These include:

1) Our software accepts mouse inputs from users to track specific objects of interest. This will be important for biologists in tracking their objects of interest.

2) We use adaptive thresholding (Yasuda et al., 1980) as opposed to fixed thresholding to select particles for tracking after the frames are enhanced using Gaussian sharpening.

3) The pairing of particles across frames is completely different in the two models. The Harvard model uses the nearest neighbour approach based on drawing a search radius and linking the centroid of a particle to the nearest other centroid. Our algorithm uses a set of if-then conditions (as discussed in the algorithm) to perform this process which is based on comparing a number of particle features based on directionality, shape, size, and data distribution.

4) Quality of tracking is much superior with our proposed model. We are able to track more particles for longer, and with higher accuracy.

We next discuss the problem of vesicle tracking for understanding the behaviour of insulin in diabetic cells, and how our model can be used effectively in this context.

2 Tracking Vesicles in GFP Tagged Videos of Living Cells

The regulation of cargo trafficking between intracellular compartments is central to the control of many cellular processes and as such has been an important area of study in the cell biology field. A major breakthrough in this field came through the cloning of green fluorescent protein (GFP) from the jellyfish Aequoria Victoria. GFP is a 27kDa protein which possesses intrinsic fluorescent properties which allows it to be expressed in a fluorescent form in a whole range of organisms and cell types from bacteria to man (Tsien, 1998). The localization and trafficking of any cloned protein can be monitored in a living cell by laser scanning microscopy by fusing GFP to one or other end of the protein.

In this paper we use multiple particle tracking to study the dynamics of GLUT4 vesicles in single living cells. Rapid sub-second imaging showed that GFP-GLUT4 vesicles exhibited two types of movement, firstly rapid vibrations around a point and secondly linear movements that were demonstrated to be along microtubules (Fletcher et al., 2000). It is known that insulin both increases the rate of movement of GLUT4 to the cell surface and decreases the rate by which GLUT4 can re-enter the cell. Thus to gain further insights into the molecular basis underlying these movements, and understand how insulin causes translocation to the cell surface, it is essential to develop methods by which we can accurately track and measure the speed and directionality of vesicles, and their fluorescent intensity, under a variety of conditions. However since the GLUT4 vesicles rapidly change direction, can coalesce or bud off from other vesicles, tubulate and can change shape, it has been very hard to develop vesicle trafficking software that can accurately and faithfully follow movement of a single vesicle between frames. Success in achieving these aims will allow dynamic tracking of multiple different types of intracellular organelles including peroxisomes, endosomes, lysosomes, and mitochondria in a quantitative manner.

3 Results

All of our experiments are performed on a total of three videos obtained in line with the work of Tavare et al. (2001). These videos were captured at different resolutions at 15 frames per second (video 1 at 196x 160 pixels, video 2 at 224 x 216 pixels and video 3 at 192 x 192 pixels). The resolution is increased in Matlab to 720 x 480 pixels for further analysis. The original video compression MSVC is changed to Indeo5. The image type is "indexed" and "true colour". Video 1 contains a total of 73 frames, video 2 162 frames and video 2 contains 92 frames. All analysis was performed on a AMD Athalon 2.16 GHz processor under windows environment using Matlab 6.5. The experiments are conducted to analyse: (a) The quality of adaptive thresholding (Yasuda et al., 1980) compared to fixed thresholding for detecting particles to track; (b) The computation of various statistics on the movement of particles in terms of their displacements, velocity, direction of movement and analysis of trajectories; (c) The ability to track fast accelerating particles that are outside the search windows of a defined radius; and (d) To interpret the results in a biological context. These experiments are discussed below.

A. Adaptive Image Segmentation

Particle trackers often use fixed image thresholding for finding the particles to track. This is not recommended for low-resolution images where the particles appear with varying image intensities. In our analysis we use adaptive thresholding. A 7x7 pixel window is used to split the image into local neighbourhoods that are independently thresholded. The thresholding is based on calculating the median of the window and then using it to label pixels as belonging to the particle or the background. The segmented image is then counted for the number of disjoint regions each of which is tracked. Our proposed method of particle detection is compared with the Harvard tracker and the results are shown in Figure 2 (a,b, and c for the results on the three videos). The first subplot shows the number of objects tracked by both models. Our model is capable of tracking roughly 4 to 5 times more objects than the Harvard tracker. The second subplot shows the proportions of "orphans" in each of the frames. Those frames are labelled as "orphans" that do not have a track associated with them, i.e. they are objects that now need to be tracked from start. Our algorithm shows a stable number of orphans (low variance) compared to large changes with the Harvard tracker.

B. Velocity of particles

Figure 3 shows the comparison of the two models when they calculate the velocity of the particles. A velocity distribution is plotted that shows the number of particles within each velocity range. Our method is more sensitive to particles moving at high speed. The plot shows that a lot more particles with higher velocity are better tracked with our method. The Harvard tracker can cope reliably with particle centroids moving with speeds up to 4 pixels per frame but method tracks velocity up to 8 pixels per frame. Furthermore, our tracker also computes velocity for a much larger number of particles as shown.

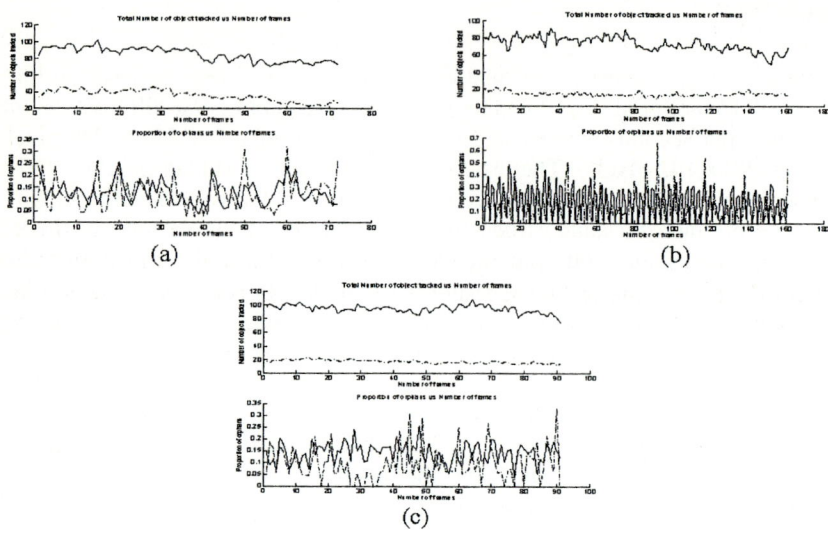

Fig. 2. A comparison of proposed tracking algorithm with Harvard tracker on (a) Video V_1 (b) V_2, and (c) V_3. The first graph shows the number of objects tracked by each model. The second graph shows the proportion of orphans (objects that could not be tracked) at each frame by both models.

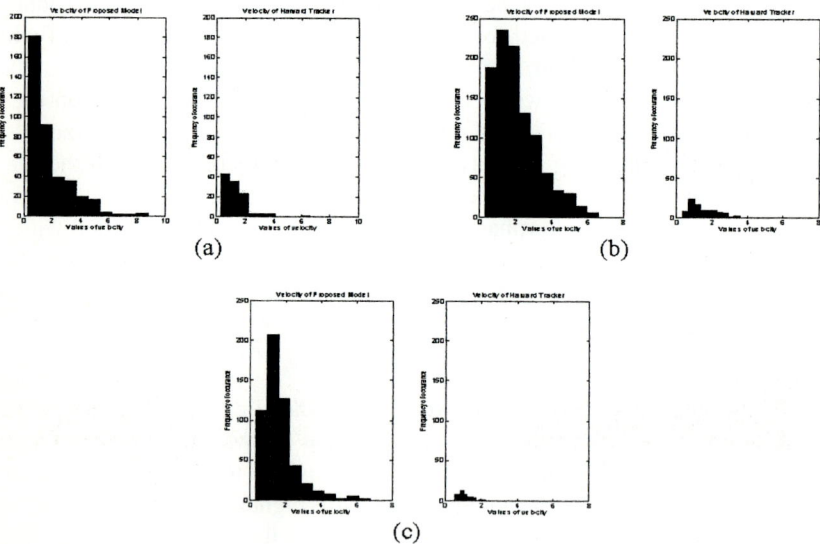

Fig. 3. A comparison of proposed tracking algorithm with Harvard tracker on (a) Video V_1 (b) V_2, and (c) V_3. The first histogram shows the numbers of particles tracked (frequency) within an average velocity range on the x- axis using the Harvard tracker. The second histogram is generated with our method.

C. Displacement of particles

The displacement of particles is important to measure (Sharma et al, 2004). Diffusion processes are special cases of Markov processes with continuous sample function, which serve as probabilistic models of physical diffusion phenomenon. Brownian motion is the category of motion for which the variance in time is linear and whose slope is diffusion constant. Other variations are classified as Non-Brownian motion. In small times, as transients are involved, most of the movements are nonlinear, hence, motion will be always non-Brownian. Figures 4(a,b,c) show the overall distance summed across all frames. Figures 4(d,e,f) show the direct line distance between the start and the end positions of the particles. In both cases, the performance of our model (marked with open circles) is superior to the Harvard tracker (marked with asterisks) as it can track longer distances and especially those particles that move the most.

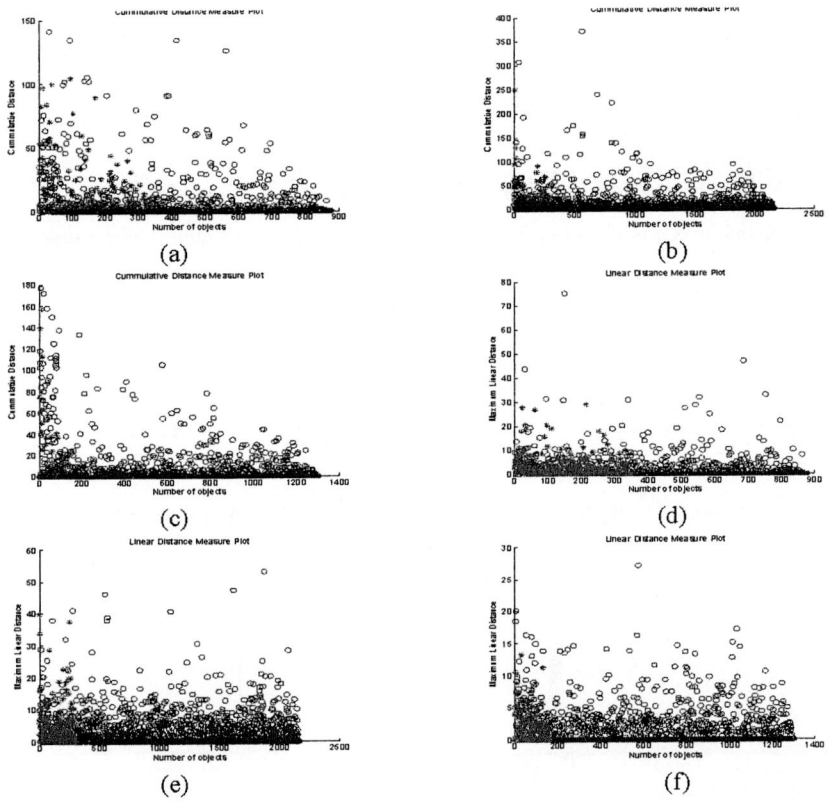

Fig. 4. (a,b,c) The overall distance (in pixels) travelled by the particles tracked using our proposed model and the Harvard tracker for videos V_1, V_2 and V_3; and Figures 4(d,e,f). The straight-line distance between the start and end positions of each particle tracked using our proposed model and the Harvard tracker videos V_1, V_2 and V_3.

We improve upon the basic idea of plotting mean square displacements against the time lag and then finding the slope of the line. Instead, we find the line of best fit (regression) that has the least square distance from all other points. The residuals from this line are calculated and plotted for each model. A high magnitude of residuals shows that the motion is Non-Brownian. Figure 5 shows these results (residuals) for the mean square displacements and Figure 6 the mean square change in direction.

In both figures, our model results are available for more number of objects. In general, our model results show higher residuals. Our tracker suggests that there is large variability in the motion of particles both in terms of displacement and directionality. The particles with high residuals cannot be easily predicted and require sophisticated tracking mechanism. It is evident that for displacement residual of greater than 4, the Harvard model is incapable of tracking objects.

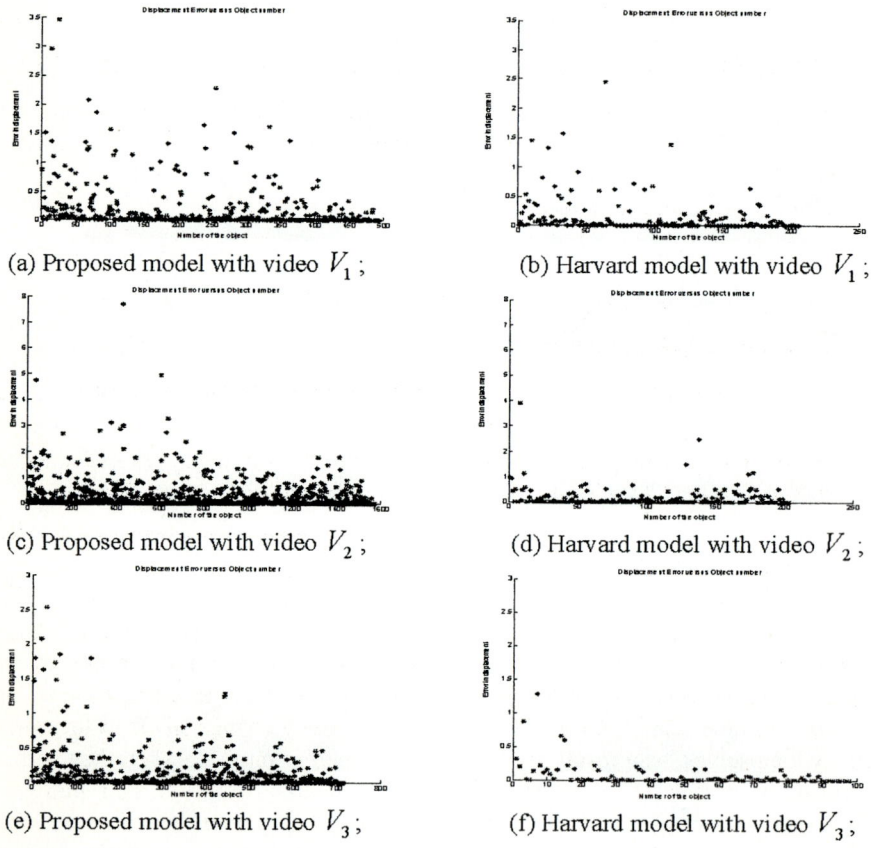

(a) Proposed model with video V_1;   (b) Harvard model with video V_1;

(c) Proposed model with video V_2;   (d) Harvard model with video V_2;

(e) Proposed model with video V_3;   (f) Harvard model with video V_3;

Fig. 5. The residuals calculated between the regression line that estimates the function plotting the variance in mean displacement of particles plotted as a function of time lag.

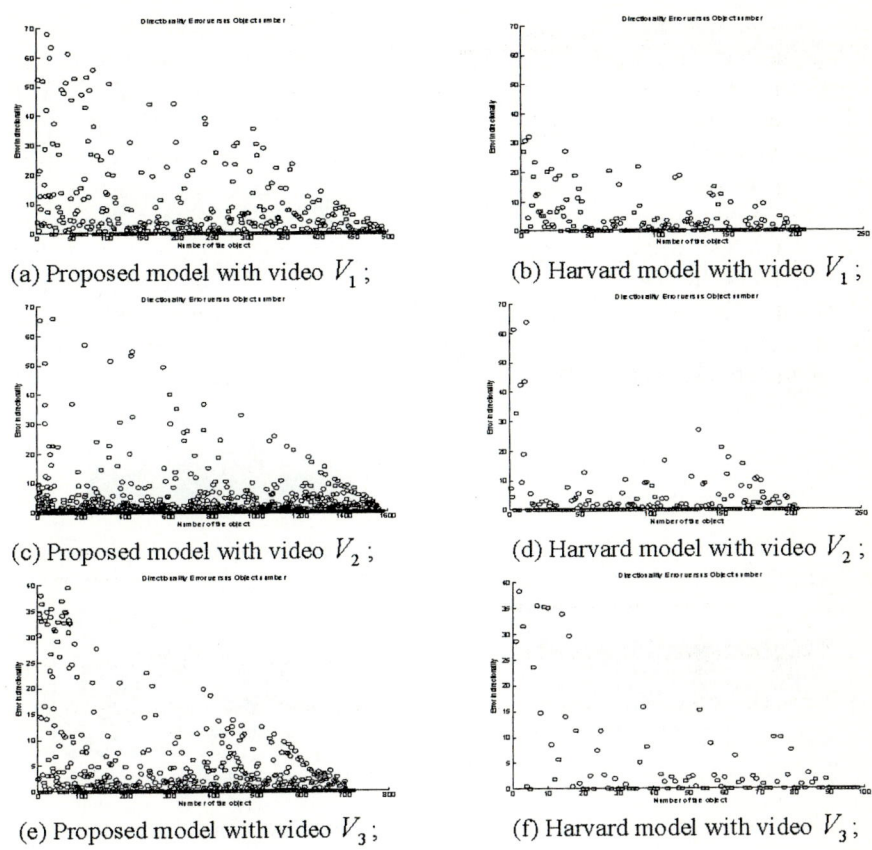

Fig. 6. The residuals calculated between the regression line that estimates the function plotting the variance in mean directionality of particles plotted as a function of time lag.

D. Analysis of Particle Shape

Figure 7 shows the mean and standard deviation of shape numbers S plotted for the tracked particles in the three videos. The output shows that there is considerable variability in the shapes of the particles tracked. The majority of the particles tracked are oval or round. Shape provides an important cue for tracking when no matching pair is found in the search radius. The particle can slowly change shape as they travel either by themselves, as a result of collision with another particle, when they split, or as a result of changes in segmentation quality (which is affected by illumination changes in particle appearance). Since the change is gradual, reasonable shape matching can be performed. Furthermore, shape is important to characterize not only for image analysis but also from a biological perspective. At present we are investigating this in our further research to evaluate the nature of some biologically important particles.

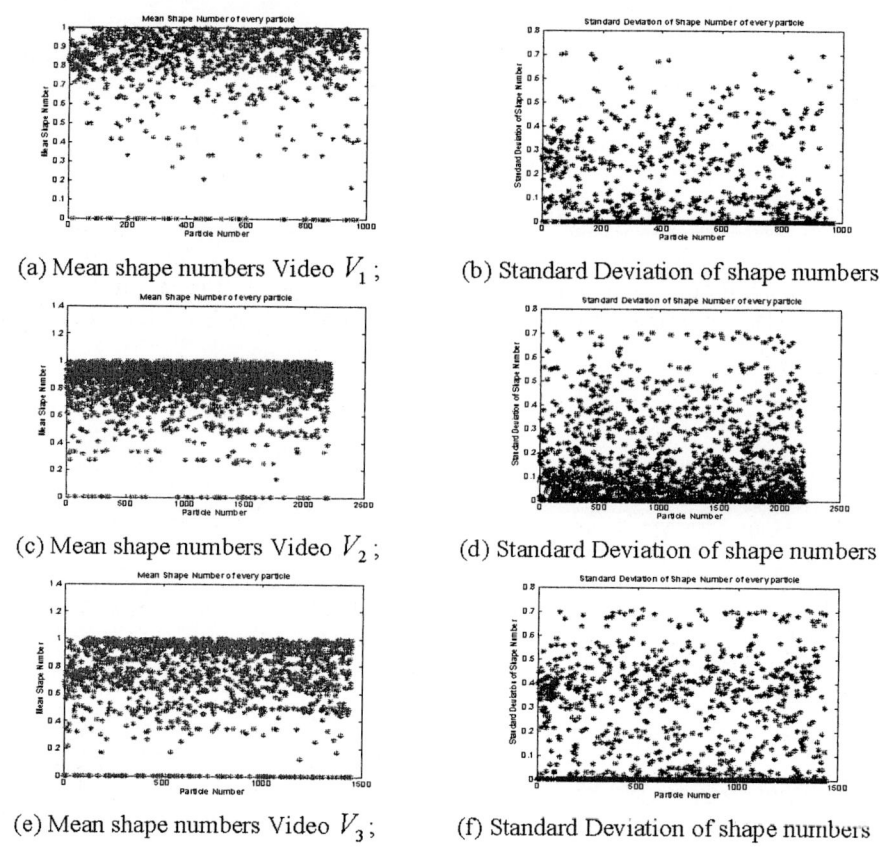

Fig. 7. Shape number statistics for the particles tracked in the three videos

4 Discussion and Conclusions

In this paper we proposed a novel particle tracking algorithm. We showed that this tracker is capable of tracking sub-cellular traffic with high accuracy and much better than the Harvard Tracker. Our future work will address this scheme for 3D tracking.

References

[1] H.P. Babcock, C. Chen and X. Zhuang, "Using single-particle tracking to study nuclear traficking of viral Genes", Biophysical Journal, vol. 87, pp. 2749 –2758, October 2004.

[2] H.C. Berg, "Motile behaviour of bacteria", Physics Today, vol. 53, issue 1, pp. 24-29, 2000.

[3] M.K. Cheezum, W.F. Walker, and W.H. Guilford, "Quantitative comparison of algorithms for tracking single fluorescent particles', Biophysical Journal, vol. 81, pp. 2378–2388, 2001.

[4] L.M. Fletcher, G.I. Welsh, P.B. Oatey, J.M. Tavare, "Role for the microtubule cytoskeleton in the regulation of insulin-stimulated glucose uptake and GLUT4 trafficking", Biochem J vol. 352, pp. 267-276, 2000.

[5] Z. Khan, T. Balch, and F. Dellaert, "An MCMC-based particle filter for tracking multiple interacting targets', Technical Report number GIT-GVU-03-35, October 2003.

[6] H. Qian, "Single-particle tracking: Brownian dynamics of visco-elastic materials", Biophysical Journal, vol. 79, pp:137–143, 2000.

[7] N. N. Sharma, M. Ganesh, and R. K. Mittal, "Non-brownian motion of nano-particles: an impact process model", IEEE Transactions on Nanotechnology, vol. 3, issue 1, 2004.

[8] G.V. Soni, B.M.J. Ali, Y. Hatwalney and G.V. Shivashankar, "Single particle tracking of correlated bacterial dynamics", Biophysical Journal, vol. 84, pp. 2634 –2637, April 2003.

[9] J.M. Tavare, L.M. Fletcher, G.I. Welsh, "Using green fluorescent protein to study intracellular signaling", J.Endocrinol. vol. 170, pp. 297-306.

[10] Y. Tseng and D. Wirtz, "Mechanics and multiple-particle tracking micro-heterogeneity of a-actinin-cross-linked actin filament networks', Biophysical Journal, vol. 81, pp. 1643–1656, 2001.

[11] R.Y. Tsien, "The green fluorescent protein", Ann Rev Biochem, vol. 67, pp. 509-544, 1998.

[12] M. Vrljic, S.Y. Nishinura, S. Brasselet, W.E. Moerner and H.M. McConnell. "Translational Diffusion of Individual Class II MHC Membrane Proteins in Cells", Biophysical Journal., vol. 83, pp. 2681-2692, 2002

[13] Y. Yasuda, M. Dubois, T.S. Huang, "Data compression for check processing machines", Proceedings of IEEE, vol. 68, pp. 874-885, 1980.

Author Index

Abusham, Eimad Eldin II-326
Agusa, K. II-570
Aksela, Matti I-71
Alcaim, Abraham I-522, I-514
Alexandre, Luís A. I-127
Alirezaie, Javad II-773
Almpanidis, George I-278
Alonso-Montes, C. II-165
Altınçay, Hakan I-146
Andreu, Gabriela I-636
Ansary, Tarik Filali II-473
Aoki, Terumasa II-618
Arbelaitz, Olatz I-99, I-381
Atienza, Vicente I-636
Autegarden, Jean-Eric II-754
Aziz, Muhammad Zaheer II-663

Babyn, Paul II-773
Badr, Ghada I-1
Bailly, Gérard I-390
Bangham, Andrew J. II-626
Barro, Senén I-89
Bashar, M.K. II-570
Bedoya, Guillermo II-236
Belaïd, Abdel I-619, I-646
Bennett, Mark II-764
Berar, Maxime I-390
Bhagavatula, Ramamurthy II-351
Bhaskar, Harish II-792
Bhattacharya, Bhargab B. I-257
Bhattacharya, Prabir I-315, II-226
Bhowmick, Partha I-257
Bigun, Josef I-436
Blostein, Dorothea I-209
Bonnaud, L. II-608
Boto, Fernando I-601
Boucher, A. I-627
Bouguila, Nizar I-172
Boyle, Roger D. II-726
Bres, Stéphane I-664
Brockwell, Anthony II-174
Buciu, Ioan II-206
Byeon, Kwangjun II-589

Campadelli, Paola II-736
Caplier, Alice II-183, II-236
Caroppo, A. II-635
Cartwright, Alexander N. II-20
Casey, M.C. I-297
Casiraghi, Elena II-736
Cecotti, Hubert I-619, I-646
Chabrier, Sébastien I-426, II-455
Chen, Guang I-560
Chen, Xinjian II-295
Chen, Kefei I-248
Chen, Liming II-302
Chen, Weiming II-344
Cherifi, Hocine II-522
Cheung, K.H. II-226
Chikkerur, Sharat II-20
Choi, Jaehun I-400
Coelho, R. I-514
Conte, Donatello II-653
Cordella, L.P. II-94
Cordy, James R. I-209, I-590
Cortes, Andoni I-601
Cox, Siân I-35
Cronin, Mark T.D. I-410

Dai, Huaping I-164
Dajnowiec, Maciej II-773
Danatsas, Dimitrios I-609
Daoudi, Mohamed II-473
Delac, Kresimir II-136
de Alencar, Vladimir Fabregas Surigué I-522
Del Buono, Nicoletta I-45
Delgorge, C. II-464
Desai, Bipin C. I-315
de Saint-Pern, Yves II-48
Desvignes, Michel I-390, II-608
Devriendt, Patrick II-754
Dönnes, Pierre I-446
D'Orazio, T. II-635
Du, A-Ning I-363
Du, Wei II-701
Duan, Fuqing I-529

Author Index

Eckmiller, Rolf   I-469, II-74
Eglin, Véronique   I-580, I-664
Emile, Bruno   II-455

Fang, Bin-Xing   I-363
Fang, Hui   II-542
Farooq, Faisal   II-30
Feng, Yue   II-542
Ferreira, Márcio J.R.   II-424
Finizio, I.   II-94
Foggia, Pasquale   II-653
Folino, Gianluigi   I-54

Gallardo-Caballero, Ramón   I-488
Garcia, Christophe   II-247
García-Orellana, Carlos J.   I-488
García Puntonet, Carlos   I-505
Gatos, Basilios   I-609
Gedda, Magnus   II-377
Girdziušas, Ramūnas   I-219
Girolami, Mark   I-183
Giugno, R.   I-63
Gobet, Fernand   I-108
Goerke, Nils   I-469, II-74
Gong, Weiguo   II-192, II-199, II-344
González, Jesús   II-560
González, Jordi   II-146, II-384
González de-la-Rosa, Juan-José   I-505
González-Velasco, Horacio   I-488
Gori, Marco   I-81
Górriz, Juan Manuel   I-505
Gotou, Naoto   I-538
Govindaraju, Venu   II-20, II-30
Grafulla-González, Beatriz   II-48
Grgic, Mislav   II-136
Grgic, Sonja   II-136
Guessoum, Abderrezak   I-654
Guo, Gongde   I-410
Guo, Jun   I-497, I-560
Gupta, Sumana   II-683
Gurrutxaga, Ibai   I-99, I-381

Haindl, Michal   II-484
Hakami, Eva   II-580
Hammal, Zakia   II-183, II-236
Haq, Shaiq A.   II-550
Harasse, S.   II-608
Harvey, Andrew R.   II-48
Haworth, Christopher D.   II-48

Hayashi, Akira   I-538
He, XiaoFu   II-120
Heneghan, C.   II-155
Heng, Pheng-Ann   I-268
Heo, Jingu   II-66
Hi, Yuliang   II-127
Higgins, Colin   I-569
Hoare, Zoë   I-28
Hotta, Kazuhiro   II-103
Hoyle, David C.   I-454
Hsu, Ching-Sheng   II-39
Hsu, Ping-Yu   I-371
Htwe, Swe Myo   I-569
Hwang, Doosung   I-400
Hwang, Eenjun   II-589

Ieong, Tony W.H. Ao   II-309
Iglesias, Roberto   I-89
Iivarinen, Jukka   I-192
Ishikawa, Seiji   II-719
Ivanko, Evgeny   II-360

Janer, Roman   II-746
Jiang, Jianmin   II-542
Jiang, Xiaoyi   II-502
Jin, Zhong   I-268
Jodoin, Pierre-Marc   II-444
Jolion, Jean-Michel   I-674, II-247
Journet, Nicholas   I-580

Kamel, Mohamed S.   I-335
Kang, Hee-Joong   I-478
Kawashima, Hiroaki   I-229
Khalid, Marzuki   II-719
Khurana, Udayan   I-325
Kim, Hyoungseop   II-719
Kim, Ungmo   I-400
Kintzler, Florian   I-469
Kiyavitskaya, Nadzeya   I-590
Kohlbacher, Oliver   I-446
Kotropoulos, Constantine   I-278
Koul, Anirudh   I-325
Krebs, Ronald   I-183
Kubassova, Olga   II-726
Kukharev, Georgy   II-302

Laaksonen, Jorma   I-71, I-219, II-216
Lam, Toby H.W.   II-309
Landais, Rémi   I-674
Lane, Peter C.R.   I-108

Author Index

Laurent, Hélène I-426
Le, Duy-Dinh I-461
Lebart, Katia I-305, II-48
Lee, Hsi-Jian II-287
Lee, Kyoung-Mi I-355, II-316
Lee, Raymond S.T. II-309
Leedham, Graham I-569, II-58
Leo, M. II-635
Lertrusdachakul, Thitiporn II-618
Leynadier, Francisque II-754
Li, Bin I-363
Li, Liang II-127
Li, Peihua II-334
Li, Q. II-226
Li, Weihong II-192, II-199, II-344
Liang, Yixiong II-192, II-199, II-344
Liao, Simon II-394
Lindsay, David I-35
Liu, Gang I-497
Liu, Yongguo I-248
Liu, Yu-Chin I-371
Lloret Galiana, Isidro I-505
Lu, Naijiang I-544
Lux, A. I-627

Macías-Macías, Miguel I-488
Maggini, Marco I-81
Martín, José I. I-99, I-381
Martiriggiano, T. II-635
Marques de Sá, J. I-127
Marzal, Andrés II-644
Masood, Asif II-550
Massot, Corentin II-236
Matsuyama, Takashi I-229
Mazzariello, C. II-94
Mertsching, Baerbel II-663
Meyrueis, Patrick I-654
Mich, Luisa I-590
Mignotte, Max II-414, II-444
Miguet, Serge II-522
Mikeš, Stanislav II-484
Mirmehdi, Majid II-404
Mischak, Harald I-183
Mitra, Sinjini II-174
Moreno, David L. I-89
Muguerza, Javier I-99, I-381
Mullot, Rémy I-580
Munir, Asim II-663
Mylopoulos, John I-590

Nam, Mi-Young II-257, II-268, II-673
Nam, Yunyoung II-589
Namane, Abderrahmane I-654
Neagu, Daniel I-410
Ngo, David II-326
Nguyen T, H.L. I-627
Nie, Jian-Yun II-414
Norrish, Mark II-764

Ohnishi, N. II-570
Onogi, Midori II-598
Oommen, B. John I-1
Ortiz, Francisco I-118, II-368
Otsuka, Yoshinori II-719
Oumohmed, Ahmed Id II-414

Pakkanen, Jussi I-192
Palazón, Vicente II-644
Palomares, José M. II-560
Pan, Yingjun II-192, II-199
Park, Jeho I-400
Partridge, Derek II-11
Pawlak, Miroslaw II-394
Payan, Yohan I-390
Payne, Andrew II-711
Penedo, M.G. II-165
Peng, Kun II-302
Perantonis, Stavros J. I-609
Percannella, G. II-512
Perevalov, Denis II-360
Pérez, Alberto I-636
Pérez, Jesús M. I-99, I-381
Persson, Martin I-436
Petillot, Yvan R. II-48
Petretta, Michele II-653
Pham, Tuan D. I-239
Piater, Justus II-701
Pitas, Ioannis II-206
Pizzuti, Clara I-54
Poisson, G. II-464
Politi, Tiziano I-45
Pratikakis, Ioannis I-609
Puente, S. I-118
Pulvirenti, A. I-63
Pyatnizkiy, Mike II-726

Radeva, Petia II-783
Rahman, Md. Mahmudur I-315
Rakotomamonjy, Alain I-426
Ramel, Jean-Yves I-580
Rangayyan, Rangaraj II-746

Raudys, Sarunas   I-136, I-154
Redmond, S.   II-155
Redpath, D.B.   I-305
Reforgiato Recupero, D.   I-63
Regueiro, Carlos V.   I-89
Ren, Wei   II-693
Rhee, Phill-Kyu   II-257, II-268, II-673
Rital, Soufiane   II-522
Rius, Ignasi   II-146, II-384
Rivero, Carlos   I-664
Roca, F. Xavier   II-146
Rodas, Ángel   I-636
Rodrigues, Mylene L.   II-424
Rodriguez, Clemente   I-601
Rogers, Simon   I-183
Romaniuk, Barbara   I-390
Rombaut, M.   II-183
Ros, Eduardo   II-560
Rosenberger, Christophe   I-426, II-455, II-464
Rothaus, Kai   II-502
Roullot, Elodie   II-754
Rowe, Daniel   II-146, II-384
Ruan, Su   II-302

Saito, Hideo   II-598
Sansone, C.   II-94
Sant'Ana, R.   I-514
Sarti, Lorenzo   I-81
Satoh, Shin'ichi   I-461
Savvides, Marios   II-66, II-174, II-351
Schatten, Rolf   II-74
Schouten, Theo E.   II-492
Shahid, Mohd.   II-683
Shinomiya, Takashi   II-719
Shi, PengFei   II-120
Shuttleworth, James   II-764
Silva, Luís M.   I-127
Singh, Maneesha   II-1, II-11
Singh, Sameer   II-1, II-11, II-84, II-693, II-711, II-792
Sorrentino, D.   II-512
Spagnolo, P.   II-635
Spalding, J. Dylan   I-454
Spezzano, Giandomenico   I-54
Spyridonos, Panagiota   II-783
St-Amour, Jean-François   II-444
Stentiford, Fred   II-112
Su, Qi   II-295
Suematu, Nobuo   I-538

Sun, Quan-Sen   I-268
Sun, Yajie   II-746
Sun, Yanmin   I-335
Sun, Youxian   I-164
Supper, Jochen   I-446
Suri, Jasjit   II-746

Takasu, Atsuhiro   I-199
Takizawa, Hotaka   II-434
Tan, Joo kooi   II-719
Taskaya-Temizel, T.   I-297
Tavare, Jeremy   II-792
Tefas, Anastasios   II-206
Teoh, Andrew   II-326
Tian, Jie   II-127
Todman, Alison   II-764
Tomsin, Mathilde   II-48
Torres, Fernando   I-118, II-368
Toussaint, Godfried   I-18
Tran, H.   I-627
Trucco, Emanuele   II-48
Tsao, Yu-Cheng   II-287
Tu, Shu-Fen   II-39
Tufano, Francesco   II-653
Tulyakov, Sergey   II-30
Tüzel, Ali   I-146

Vajda, Szilárd   I-619
Vandeborre, Jean-Phillipe   II-473
van den Broek, Egon L.   II-492, II-532
van Rikxoort, Eva M.   II-492, II-532
Venkataramani, Krithika   II-277
Vento, Mario   II-512, II-653
Viergever, Max   II-719
Vieyres, P.   II-464
Vijayakumar, B.V.K.   II-66, II-277
Vilariño, D.L.   II-165
Vilariño, Fernando   II-783
Villanueva, Juan J.   II-384
Vinet, Laurent   I-674
Visani, Muriel   II-247
Vitrià, Jordi   II-783

Wang, Binhai   II-626
Wang, Fei   I-345
Wang, Haijing   II-334
Wang, Jessica JunLin   II-84
Wang, Libin   I-248
Wang, Lingyu   II-58
Wang, Qingdong   I-164

Wang, Sheng-De   I-288
Wang, Weixing   II-580
Welsh, Gavin   II-792
Wong, Andrew K.C.   I-335
Wu, Fuchao   I-529
Wu, Kuo-Ping   I-288

Xia, De-Shen   I-268
Xie, Xianghua   II-404
Xin, Yongqing   II-394
Xu, Yunpeng   I-420, I-544, I-553

Yamamoto, Shinji   II-434
Yan, Long   I-497
Yang, Jing   I-553
Yang, Ma   I-569
Yang, Xin   II-127, II-295

Yang, Zhirong   II-216
Yasuda, Hiroshi   II-618
Yi, Xing   I-420
Yoo, Janghee   I-400
You, J.   II-226

Zafeiriou, Stefanos   II-206
Zanibbi, Richard   I-209
Zeni, Nicola   I-590
Zhang, Changshui   I-345, I-420, I-544
Zhang, Hong-Gang   I-560
Zhang, Tianwen   II-334
Zhu, Yanong   II-626
Ziou, Djemel   I-172
Zliobaite, Indre   I-154
Zorzo Barcelos, Celia A.   II-424
Zou, Hongxing   I-553

Lecture Notes in Computer Science

For information about Vols. 1–3560

please contact your bookseller or Springer

Vol. 3687: S. Singh, M. Singh, C. Apte, P. Perner (Eds.), Pattern Recognition and Image Analysis, Part II. XXV, 809 pages. 2005.

Vol. 3686: S. Singh, M. Singh, C. Apte, P. Perner (Eds.), Pattern Recognition and Data Mining, Part I. XXVI, 689 pages. 2005.

Vol. 3672: C. Hankin, I. Siveroni (Eds.), Static Analysis. X, 369 pages. 2005.

Vol. 3671: S. Bressan, S. Ceri, E. Hunt, Z.G. Ives, Z. Bellahsène, M. Rys, R. Unland (Eds.), Database and XML Technologies. X, 239 pages. 2005.

Vol. 3664: C. Türker, M. Agosti, H.-J. Schek (Eds.), Peer-to-Peer, Grid, and Service-Orientation in Digital Library Architectures. X, 261 pages. 2005.

Vol. 3663: W. Kropatsch, R. Sablatnig, A. Hanbury (Eds.), Pattern Recognition. XIV, 512 pages. 2005.

Vol. 3662: C. Baral, G. Greco, N. Leone, G. Terracina (Eds.), Logic Programming and Nonmonotonic Reasoning. XIII, 454 pages. 2005. (Subseries LNAI).

Vol. 3660: (Ed.), UbiComp 2005: Ubiquitous Computing. XVII, 394 pages. 2005.

Vol. 3659: J.R. Rao, B. Sunar (Eds.), Cryptographic Hardware and Embedded Systems – CHES 2005. XIV, 458 pages. 2005.

Vol. 3654: S. Jajodia, D. Wijesekera (Eds.), Data and Applications Security XIX. X, 353 pages. 2005.

Vol. 3653: M. Abadi, L.d. Alfaro (Eds.), CONCUR 2005 – Concurrency Theory. XIV, 578 pages. 2005.

Vol. 3649: W.M.P. van der Aalst, B. Benatallah, F. Casati, F. Curbera (Eds.), Business Process Management. XII, 472 pages. 2005.

Vol. 3648: J.C. Cunha, P.D. Medeiros (Eds.), Euro-Par 2005 Parallel Processing. XXXVI, 1299 pages. 2005.

Vol. 3645: D.-S. Huang, X.-P. Zhang, G.-B. Huang (Eds.), Advances in Intelligent Computing, Part II. XIII, 1010 pages. 2005.

Vol. 3644: D.-S. Huang, X.-P. Zhang, G.-B. Huang (Eds.), Advances in Intelligent Computing, Part I. XXVII, 1101 pages. 2005.

Vol. 3642: D. Ślezak, J. Yao, J.F. Peters, W. Ziarko, X. Hu (Eds.), Rough Sets, Fuzzy Sets, Data Mining, and Granular Computing, Part II. XXIV, 738 pages. 2005. (Subseries LNAI).

Vol. 3641: D. Ślezak, G. Wang, M.S. Szczuka, I. Düntsch, Y. Yao (Eds.), Rough Sets, Fuzzy Sets, Data Mining, and Granular Computing, Part I. XXIV, 742 pages. 2005. (Subseries LNAI).

Vol. 3639: P. Godefroid (Ed.), Model Checking Software. XI, 289 pages. 2005.

Vol. 3638: A. Butz, B. Fisher, A. Krüger, P. Olivier (Eds.), Smart Graphics. XI, 269 pages. 2005.

Vol. 3637: J. M. Moreno, J. Madrenas, J. Cosp (Eds.), Evolvable Systems: From Biology to Hardware. XI, 227 pages. 2005.

Vol. 3636: M.J. Blesa, C. Blum, A. Roli, M. Sampels (Eds.), Hybrid Metaheuristics. XII, 155 pages. 2005.

Vol. 3634: L. Ong (Ed.), Computer Science Logic. XI, 567 pages. 2005.

Vol. 3633: C. Bauzer Medeiros, M. Egenhofer, E. Bertino (Eds.), Advances in Spatial and Temporal Databases. XIII, 433 pages. 2005.

Vol. 3632: R. Nieuwenhuis (Ed.), Automated Deduction – CADE-20. XIII, 459 pages. 2005. (Subseries LNAI).

Vol. 3629: J.L. Fiadeiro, N. Harman, M. Roggenbach, J. Rutten (Eds.), Algebra and Coalgebra in Computer Science. XI, 457 pages. 2005.

Vol. 3628: T. Gschwind, U. Aßmann, O. Nierstrasz (Eds.), Software Composition. X, 199 pages. 2005.

Vol. 3627: C. Jacob, M.L. Pilat, P.J. Bentley, J. Timmis (Eds.), Artificial Immune Systems. XII, 500 pages. 2005.

Vol. 3626: B. Ganter, G. Stumme, R. Wille (Eds.), Formal Concept Analysis. X, 349 pages. 2005. (Subseries LNAI).

Vol. 3625: S. Kramer, B. Pfahringer (Eds.), Inductive Logic Programming. XIII, 427 pages. 2005. (Subseries LNAI).

Vol. 3624: C. Chekuri, K. Jansen, J.D.P. Rolim, L. Trevisan (Eds.), Approximation, Randomization and Combinatorial Optimization. XI, 495 pages. 2005.

Vol. 3623: M. Liśkiewicz, R. Reischuk (Eds.), Fundamentals of Computation Theory. XV, 576 pages. 2005.

Vol. 3621: V. Shoup (Ed.), Advances in Cryptology – CRYPTO 2005. XI, 568 pages. 2005.

Vol. 3620: H. Muñoz-Avila, F. Ricci (Eds.), Case-Based Reasoning Research and Development. XV, 654 pages. 2005. (Subseries LNAI).

Vol. 3619: X. Lu, W. Zhao (Eds.), Networking and Mobile Computing. XXIV, 1299 pages. 2005.

Vol. 3615: B. Ludäscher, L. Raschid (Eds.), Data Integration in the Life Sciences. XII, 344 pages. 2005. (Subseries LNBI).

Vol. 3614: L. Wang, Y. Jin (Eds.), Fuzzy Systems and Knowledge Discovery, Part II. XLI, 1314 pages. 2005. (Subseries LNAI).

Vol. 3613: L. Wang, Y. Jin (Eds.), Fuzzy Systems and Knowledge Discovery, Part I. XLI, 1334 pages. 2005. (Subseries LNAI).

Vol. 3612: L. Wang, K. Chen, Y. S. Ong (Eds.), Advances in Natural Computation, Part III. LXI, 1326 pages. 2005.

Vol. 3611: L. Wang, K. Chen, Y. S. Ong (Eds.), Advances in Natural Computation, Part II. LXI, 1292 pages. 2005.

Vol. 3610: L. Wang, K. Chen, Y. S. Ong (Eds.), Advances in Natural Computation, Part I. LXI, 1302 pages. 2005.

Vol. 3608: F. Dehne, A. López-Ortiz, J.-R. Sack (Eds.), Algorithms and Data Structures. XIV, 446 pages. 2005.

Vol. 3607: J.-D. Zucker, L. Saitta (Eds.), Abstraction, Reformulation and Approximation. XII, 376 pages. 2005. (Subseries LNAI).

Vol. 3606: V. Malyshkin (Ed.), Parallel Computing Technologies. XII, 470 pages. 2005.

Vol. 3604: R. Martin, H. Bez, M. Sabin (Eds.), Mathematics of Surfaces XI. IX, 473 pages. 2005.

Vol. 3603: J. Hurd, T. Melham (Eds.), Theorem Proving in Higher Order Logics. IX, 409 pages. 2005.

Vol. 3602: R. Eigenmann, Z. Li, S.P. Midkiff (Eds.), Languages and Compilers for High Performance Computing. IX, 486 pages. 2005.

Vol. 3599: U. Aßmann, M. Aksit, A. Rensink (Eds.), Model Driven Architecture. X, 235 pages. 2005.

Vol. 3598: H. Murakami, H. Nakashima, H. Tokuda, M. Yasumura, Ubiquitous Computing Systems. XIII, 275 pages. 2005.

Vol. 3597: S. Shimojo, S. Ichii, T.W. Ling, K.-H. Song (Eds.), Web and Communication Technologies and Internet-Related Social Issues - HSI 2005. XIX, 368 pages. 2005.

Vol. 3596: F. Dau, M.-L. Mugnier, G. Stumme (Eds.), Conceptual Structures: Common Semantics for Sharing Knowledge. XI, 467 pages. 2005. (Subseries LNAI).

Vol. 3595: L. Wang (Ed.), Computing and Combinatorics. XVI, 995 pages. 2005.

Vol. 3594: J.C. Setubal, S. Verjovski-Almeida (Eds.), Advances in Bioinformatics and Computational Biology. XIV, 258 pages. 2005. (Subseries LNBI).

Vol. 3593: V. Mařík, R. W. Brennan, M. Pěchouček (Eds.), Holonic and Multi-Agent Systems for Manufacturing. XI, 269 pages. 2005. (Subseries LNAI).

Vol. 3592: S. Katsikas, J. Lopez, G. Pernul (Eds.), Trust, Privacy and Security in Digital Business. XII, 332 pages. 2005.

Vol. 3591: M.A. Wimmer, R. Traunmüller, Å. Grönlund, K.V. Andersen (Eds.), Electronic Government. XIII, 317 pages. 2005.

Vol. 3590: K. Bauknecht, B. Pröll, H. Werthner (Eds.), E-Commerce and Web Technologies. XIV, 380 pages. 2005.

Vol. 3589: A M. Tjoa, J. Trujillo (Eds.), Data Warehousing and Knowledge Discovery. XVI, 538 pages. 2005.

Vol. 3588: K.V. Andersen, J. Debenham, R. Wagner (Eds.), Database and Expert Systems Applications. XX, 955 pages. 2005.

Vol. 3587: P. Perner, A. Imiya (Eds.), Machine Learning and Data Mining in Pattern Recognition. XVII, 695 pages. 2005. (Subseries LNAI).

Vol. 3586: A.P. Black (Ed.), ECOOP 2005 - Object-riented Programming. XVII, 631 pages. 2005.

3584: X. Li, S. Wang, Z.Y. Dong (Eds.), Advanced Mining and Applications. XIX, 835 pages. 2005. es LNAI).

Vol. 3583: R.W. H. Lau, Q. Li, R. Cheung, W. Liu (Eds.), Advances in Web-Based Learning – ICWL 2005. XIV, 420 pages. 2005.

Vol. 3582: J. Fitzgerald, I.J. Hayes, A. Tarlecki (Eds.), FM 2005: Formal Methods. XIV, 558 pages. 2005.

Vol. 3581: S. Miksch, J. Hunter, E. Keravnou (Eds.), Artificial Intelligence in Medicine. XVII, 547 pages. 2005. (Subseries LNAI).

Vol. 3580: L. Caires, G.F. Italiano, L. Monteiro, C. Palamidessi, M. Yung (Eds.), Automata, Languages and Programming. XXV, 1477 pages. 2005.

Vol. 3579: D. Lowe, M. Gaedke (Eds.), Web Engineering. XXII, 633 pages. 2005.

Vol. 3578: M. Gallagher, J. Hogan, F. Maire (Eds.), Intelligent Data Engineering and Automated Learning - IDEAL 2005. XVI, 599 pages. 2005.

Vol. 3577: R. Falcone, S. Barber, J. Sabater-Mir, M.P. Singh (Eds.), Trusting Agents for Trusting Electronic Societies. VIII, 235 pages. 2005. (Subseries LNAI).

Vol. 3576: K. Etessami, S.K. Rajamani (Eds.), Computer Aided Verification. XV, 564 pages. 2005.

Vol. 3575: S. Wermter, G. Palm, M. Elshaw (Eds.), Biomimetic Neural Learning for Intelligent Robots. IX, 383 pages. 2005. (Subseries LNAI).

Vol. 3574: C. Boyd, J.M. González Nieto (Eds.), Information Security and Privacy. XIII, 586 pages. 2005.

Vol. 3573: S. Etalle (Ed.), Logic Based Program Synthesis and Transformation. VIII, 279 pages. 2005.

Vol. 3572: C. De Felice, A. Restivo (Eds.), Developments in Language Theory. XI, 409 pages. 2005.

Vol. 3571: L. Godo (Ed.), Symbolic and Quantitative Approaches to Reasoning with Uncertainty. XVI, 1028 pages. 2005. (Subseries LNAI).

Vol. 3570: A. S. Patrick, M. Yung (Eds.), Financial Cryptography and Data Security. XII, 376 pages. 2005.

Vol. 3569: F. Bacchus, T. Walsh (Eds.), Theory and Applications of Satisfiability Testing. XII, 492 pages. 2005.

Vol. 3568: W.-K. Leow, M.S. Lew, T.-S. Chua, W.-Y. Ma, L. Chaisorn, E.M. Bakker (Eds.), Image and Video Retrieval. XVII, 672 pages. 2005.

Vol. 3567: M. Jackson, D. Nelson, S. Stirk (Eds.), Database: Enterprise, Skills and Innovation. XII, 185 pages. 2005.

Vol. 3566: J.-P. Banâtre, P. Fradet, J.-L. Giavitto, O. Michel (Eds.), Unconventional Programming Paradigms. XI, 367 pages. 2005.

Vol. 3565: G.E. Christensen, M. Sonka (Eds.), Information Processing in Medical Imaging. XXI, 777 pages. 2005.

Vol. 3564: N. Eisinger, J. Małuszyński (Eds.), Reasoning Web. IX, 319 pages. 2005.

Vol. 3562: J. Mira, J.R. Álvarez (Eds.), Artificial Intelligence and Knowledge Engineering Applications: A Bioinspired Approach, Part II. XXIV, 636 pages. 2005.

Vol. 3561: J. Mira, J.R. Álvarez (Eds.), Mechanisms, Symbols, and Models Underlying Cognition, Part I. XXIV, 532 pages. 2005.